BUREAU OF INTERNATIONAL RESEARCH
HARVARD UNIVERSITY AND RADCLIFFE COLLEGE

§

THE BRITISH COMMONWEALTH
AT WAR

THE

British Commonwealth

AT WAR

EDITORS

William Yandell Elliott & H. Duncan Hall

CONTRIBUTORS

WILLIAM YANDELL ELLIOTT	ERIC ROLL
H. DUNCAN HALL	GWENDOLEN M. CARTER
HEINRICH BRÜNING	B. S. KEIRSTEAD
CLAIRE NIX	FRED ALEXANDER
WILLIAM S. McCAULEY	F. L. W. WOOD

LUCRETIA ILSLEY

NEW YORK · ALFRED · A · KNOPF

1943

This book has been produced
in full compliance with all government regulations for the
conservation of paper, metal, and other essential materials.

Preface

This book was planned by Professor William Yandell Elliott before the outbreak of the war, and a grant made available for it by the Bureau of International Research of Harvard University and Radcliffe College, shortly after the war began. Some of the chapters were in first draft by 1941, while difficulties of communication especially delayed others and compelled changes of outline. As Professor Elliott undertook heavy responsibilities in connection with the war in the Office of Production Management, the bulk of the editorial work from early in 1941 fell to Mr. H. Duncan Hall. In their present form all the chapters have been revised to include events through the spring of 1942, and there are some references to later events.

The book makes no pretence at covering the whole of the vast canvas indicated by its title. Though it presents a fairly detailed picture of the British Commonwealth of Nations, fully organized for total war and nearing the peak of its great strength at the moment when the United States came finally into the war, whole sections of the story have been perforce omitted. There is no military history in the book — only passing references here and there to the great episodes. There is no chapter on the diplomatic, political, and psychological war waged by the British Commonwealth. In order to reduce the bulk of the volume the material prepared on the colonial Empire has had to be omitted. This the editors particularly regret, because a book on *The British Commonwealth at War* is obviously incomplete without details of the great contributions of the colonial Empire in man power, money, and vital resources or the strategical importance of certain key points like Colombo, Gibraltar, Aden, and Malta. Dictates of space, and the neutrality of Eire, have also resulted in the omission of a long chapter on Ireland's constitutional, political, and economic situation.

There is some disproportion in the space allotted to the different parts of the Commonwealth. The emphasis put upon the English system of war administration and the more elaborate treatment of such problems as labor and finance in Great Britain are due to the much greater importance of the organization of the United Kingdom, not only to the war effort, but in so far as it illustrates the organization of a highly industrialized country for war. It therefore offers a useful basis of comparison not only with our problems in the United States but also with the methods by which similar problems have been handled in the other countries of the Commonwealth.

The central emphasis of the book is twofold: first, how the British Commonwealth, as a whole, worked as a political instrument and a mutual security system under the impact of the war, and the effect of the war on its political, psychological, and constitutional structure; and second, how the British democracies and India adapted or transformed their political, administrative, and economic systems to fight a total war. The book is a study of democracy in action not merely on a national but also an international scale, since it deals with a unique international democratic organization of states.

The preparation of the book has been beset by difficulties inseparable from any attempt to make an objective and authoritative study of so vast and complex an organization as the British Commonwealth under the stress of the war. Information has not always been easy to obtain. But the thanks of the editors are due to a number of people in official positions in various parts of the Empire, particularly in the British Embassy in Washington, the British Library of Information in New York, the legations of the British Dominions in Washington, the offices of the British and of the Dominion High Commissioners in Ottawa, and the official representatives of India in New York and Washington, for freely giving their time and supplying valuable information without which the book could not easily have been completed. War conditions increased the difficulties of preparing and publishing a book contributed to by collaborators dispersed throughout the English-speaking world. The embarrassing promptness of some of the collaborators in delivering their manuscripts, for which the editors were grateful, nevertheless, confronted them with the difficulty, which they have failed in some cases to overcome, of keeping the prompt chapters up to date while waiting for the late comers. Some material went astray for reasons unknown — enemy action, or "friendly" censor, or merely perhaps loss in the mails.

The editors have done their best to coordinate the different chapters, but, apart from some unavoidable cutting, the authors remain responsible for their contributions. The chapter on India has been left anonymous because, apart from the editors, a number of people supplied material for it. We are indebted to Miss Claire Nix and Miss Edith Haley for the great pains to which they have been put to hold the book together through various stages and for their efforts to see it into print.

W. Y. E.

H. D. H.

CONTENTS

∽

THE BRITISH COMMONWEALTH
AT WAR

CHAPTER I

Introduction

by William Yandell Elliott

At the critical turning point in the war marked by the landing of Allied forces in Algeria and Morocco, after a cumulative series of disasters to the arms of the United Nations had shaken the faith of many as to its ultimate outcome, it is more than ever necessary to take stock of the war effort of the British Commonwealth of Nations.

Prompted by the shortages of tin and rubber that have already shown their effects, the dullest mind can have no doubt of the importance of the British Empire to the safety and defense of the United States. As shortages appear in many other essential war materials, this lesson will be driven home in unmistakable terms. The isolationists who asked, what interest had we in the fate of Britain's armies and Britain's Empire, who inquired why we should do battle for Singapore and the Dutch East Indies, why indeed we should not retire to our own shores and prepare ourselves against all comers, are now finding a brutal answer. Our own shores are not safe from attack; our continent is not self-sufficient for war.

The answer first was made plain in the shock of Pearl Harbor and the disaster to American arms by the sudden onslaught of Japan. It was brought home by the efforts of German submarines to blockade not only our own coasts but the Caribbean. Supplies from abroad that were essential to our war effort were suddenly threatened, and the very movement of gasoline and oil necessary to our whole economy in coastwise shipping has been tragically endangered.

Not only the manganese, chromite, tungsten, antimony, cobalt, and other minerals on which the war effort depends, but the supplies of the vital fibers, of many fats and oils, almost equally essential, are being seriously cut down by the loss of sea control in some vital areas of the war.

The civilian population has already begun to feel the pinch, not only in depleted supplies of sugar, coffee, and possibly other things that it has not been necessary or possible to ration, but in the inability to produce enough wool adequately to maintain civilian supplies of clothing. Bananas and cocoa have followed not far behind, with many other diminished imports that will cause dislocation and want.

These facts form an object lesson to all those who asked in the past, "Why defend American beyond its own shores?" Many of them who were prepared to defend South America as a duty to our own security in supply are learning with alarm that South America is not enough, and that its defense simply adds an insupportable burden if we are not to carry the war to the enemy; or if we were forced to fight alone on two ocean fronts, to say nothing of safeguarding the sea lanes in the far areas of the world from which some of the most necessary of our war supplies come.

Viewed in the simplest terms, the situation which has been critical and well-nigh desperate with the British fleet still in the picture would have been next to hopeless if the British Commonwealth had not been kept fighting. Our sheer self-interest in the preservation of England as the main front base of our own defense against Hitler has long been apparent to all who think at all. Even if England and her Empire were to go down today, we should have had those precious months, even years, of preparation without which we should have faced the fleets of Germany and her satellites, probably including Vichy, on the one flank and, who knows, perhaps the fleet of a Vichified England as well, and on the other the full weight of the Japanese onslaught.

The only answer that those who still criticize aid to Britain, Russia, China, the Dutch, and Australia can make to this analysis is that Japan would have been satisfied without attempting to smash us, and that Hitler would have permitted us to remain unarmed masters of the Western Hemisphere. It passes belief that men of good faith, now fully aware of the nature both of Hitler's and of Japan's ambitions, can ask to sacrifice the Allies who gave us precious time to arm, and who, if we can only ourselves support them adequately, can make victory possible. Are they of good faith who suggest this course?

Presumably, some of the revelations of the investigation into Mr. Viereck's activities in franking out German propaganda through both senators and representatives in our own Congress, *with their full knowledge* of the source of the material and of its objects, should teach us as a nation something of what we must do to protect our own sources of information, even official sources.

It is worth while commenting on some of the popular misconceptions fostered by those who did not need Mr. Viereck to prompt them after their line was taken, and they were committed to it. They seized on Churchill's remark, made in a mood of generous concession to the American Congress, that Pearl Harbor might not have been such a disaster had we not sacrificed planes to Britain and Russia. The plain fact, and it has been adequately attested by the report of the Roberts Commission, is that we had planes and ships entirely adequate to defend Pearl Harbor. The humiliating thing is that some of those planes and many of those ships were knocked out by a surprise that should never have been permitted, and that could not have been avoided by not sending planes to Britain or Russia. Indeed, it was the assumption, sedulously planted by isolationists, that we could not be attacked which led to the carelessness of the divided command at Hawaii. It was a state of mind which this country threw off with great reluctance. Mr. Churchill, in his broadcast made in the nadir of the depression that followed the loss of Singapore, said of the entry of the United States into the war, " That is what I have dreamed of, aimed at and worked for, and now it has come to pass." His language was of course seized upon by those who felt that our entry into the war was engineered by Great Britain. There is no question that Britain had desperately to depend on our full support and must have worked in exactly the way that Mr. Churchill described. On the other hand, the event that brought us into the war was not a further attack on Thailand or the Malay Peninsula or an overflow of Japanese forces towards Rangoon, but a carefully conceived blow at our own naval power. The war overflowed on us, as it was bound to do unless we conceded Japan control of the entire Pacific.

Japan, at least since the days of the Tanaka Memorial in 1927, and probably from the generation that followed the war with Russia, has understood the simple strategy of mastery. She could not accomplish her ends in the Pacific, and after that in South America and elsewhere, without crippling the United States. The Tanaka Memorial itself stated that Japan could not crush China without first crushing the United States. We had been given ample warning of her intention. Its realization was simply made more possible by the necessity we were under of meeting attack in the Atlantic as well.

The complexity of the strategy of a true world war, totally unlike the simple operations of the first so-called World War, staggers the minds of simple persons unused even to maps and totally free of any conception of the real struggle for world mastery that Germany and Japan have planned. Had we been more powerful, we might have driven a bargain with them, as Colonel Lindbergh and others suggested, and helped to divide the world with them, even joining in attacks on the weakened Empire of Britain and assisting in the destruction of Russia. But without the overwhelming strength that would have made such a bargain possible, regardless of its hideous moral implications, we had little to offer as an ally beyond the consent of impotence.

At this time the preservation of the British Empire in its main outlines and the restoration of a world in which the principles of the British Commonwealth can be extended to India more really than the governing class of England have previously been willing to consider become prime objectives in our war aims as well as our peace aims. It is not only that this great reserve of wealth and man power, if turned over to our enemies, would upset the future balance of the world so that our children's children would have to redress it if we were to be a free nation. The raw materials on which our industrial salvation desperately depends come in the main from areas that we must protect through the ability to protect not only South America, but South Africa and the Indian Ocean.

That is what makes the war effort of Australia and the war effort of South Africa, the war effort of New Zealand, the war effort of Canada, the dogged holding of the United Kingdom through slow starvation and imminent peril of invasion, essential to any American safety at the present time, and more than essential to any ultimate victory. In dark periods ahead, when disappointment may shake the stoutest hearts, it is essential never to forget that the will to victory must be fanned by our efforts and our help in those hearts that can aid us to victory. To maintain South Africa against wavering, to strengthen Australia as a future base to retake the Pacific, to join Canada in a mighty continental effort as one great North American war machine, these things are essential.

We must, it is clear, be able to maintain the supplies to ourselves on which the supplies to all others depend. Those ships that are carrying aid to the defense of others and to support offensives also bring back our supplies. Manganese for our steel mills, chromite, on which our whole war effort depends, mica, without which no plane flies, graphite, without which crucibles are at best reduced to a very low efficiency and must in many cases be completely altered, these depend upon control of the Indian Ocean. This is to say nothing of rubber and tin, the loss of which we are already beginning to count in terms of economic dislocation and the possible stagnation of our own domestic transportation system. The fibers for the ropes of our whole naval program, the fats and oils on which we depend for glycerine for explosives, as well as the molasses and other ingredients of ethyl alcohol for the same program, the nitrates and the copper of Chile as well as Bolivian tin, all these depend upon sea control. Japan could interdict us from South America and the Pacific with far greater success than Germany has had on our Atlantic coast if we did not make that move impossible by retaining bases past which Japan does not dare proceed and by denying her those bases without which her fleet cannot operate successfully in these waters.

It is of little use to bemoan the strategy that did not keep three hundred planes at Singapore as a minimum reserve, with the possibility of adding other hundreds within weeks rather than months. The planes that were then concentrated for American defense, had they been usable at Singapore, could have turned the whole tide of that operation, and could have provided the umbrella for the Prince of Wales and the Repulse, the loss of which so grievously upset the whole balance of naval power. Judgment has been entered on that chapter of omission. It was a tragic judgment, but its lesson was plain. We had to defend more adequately, and the British had to defend more adequately, the central areas of sea control. That is what the American people must understand in terms of the essential strategy of this war. To defend ourselves is to carry the war to the enemy and to prevent him from overrunning those island chains that give him the control which we have for long taken for granted. Freedom of the seas for war has not had really to be fought for by our nation since 1812.

Freedom of the seas, in short, means not a legal conception of ability to trade with neutrals or to enjoy without effort the large blessings of naval control; it means a desperate struggle now and henceforth to preserve that naval control against an alien balance of power brought to bear on our antiquated fleets, whittled down by years of pacifism and of isolationism.

Freedom of the seas, for that reason, means the maintenance of the British Commonwealth of Nations as our own front line. It means preserving, no matter what goes down, the essential areas, Australia, South Africa, if possible India, and at all cost the United Kingdom itself. The string of islands across the Indian Ocean, the Mauritius, Amirantes, and Seychelles Islands, the Maldive, and the Laccadive Islands would screen the Indian Ocean if we controlled Ceylon and Madagascar, even if the Indian frontier and the Andaman Islands should have gone down. To hold them is as essential as to hold Australia and New Zealand.

To whom shall we look for the protection of these areas? Not to ourselves alone; it is clear that we are unequal to the whole task. It is equally clear that the British and their dominions alone are unequal to the task. That was what Churchill's words in his Singapore speech really meant. Without the preservation of the huge man power of China and of Russia in the picture, we and the British together might not be equal to the task.

That is why an honest assessment of the war effort of the British Commonwealth, in order that we may judge our own responsibilities and what lies ahead of us to secure victory, is essential in the formulation of American strategy. That Empire as a world empire holds the key to world control. A study of its resources, of its politics, of the strategy of its defense, of its war production, is a vital element to every calculation we now must make to assure our own victory.

More than that, an understanding of this war effort and what it means will do more than any other single thing to allay the real anger and anguish that we as a people felt in seeing Singapore go down and in judging the British at fault.

In any unexpected reverse, the greatest problem is to keep Allies pulling together. The very human tendency is for each to blame the other. Both are to blame, but blame is of small use except as a spring board to profit by the lessons of defeat and turn them into victory. It is essential to maintain in the American people the courage that carried Washington through the darkest hours of the Revolution because of his unwavering faith in his cause. It is essential to call on the same courage that carried Lincoln through the Civil War. The backing that leadership will get will depend of course on the leadership itself. It is also essential in these times to provide those who must back the leader with the knowledge of what democracies elsewhere have been able to do and what we may expect of them. That is the object of this book.

It is a book hastily put together, partly out of date as it was being written, bound to be out of date before it is in print. It does not show as it might the failures of a complacent old Empire or of a smug ruling class that nurtured up its own destroyers. It does not analyze either the dry rot of easy habits of rule, or the courage that won the Battle of Britain. But it does give an idea of the scope of Britain's effort, of her weaknesses as well as her strength, of the administrative and political problems of the dominions as well as Britain, of her man power and her machine power.

It is interesting for an American to contrast Mr. Duncan Hall's emphasis on psychological factors and traditional institutions with Dr. Brüning's more analytical treatment of administrative problems. The book seems to me the more valuable for the contrast and the representation of different points of view. In this way it may stand a chance of being more than a tract for the times, such as books written under the compulsion of war emotions tend to be. At least it stands, by the contribution of it of the former German Chancellor, as a sign of hope for the international community of scholarship.

CHAPTER II

The British Commonwealth of Nations in War and Peace

by H. Duncan Hall

1. The Opening of the War Books

The closely guarded British War Book, wherein is set out in detail the whole complex procedure for the change-over from peace to war in Great Britain and the Empire, was taken from its safe and opened in Whitehall just before Munich, in September 1938. The similar War Books were opened at the same time in Ottawa, Canberra, Wellington, Pretoria, and Delhi. The " precautionary stage " telegram required by the War Book was dispatched to all parts of the British Empire warning them that war was likely to break out, thus enabling them to take their preliminary dispositions — such as ordering their naval vessels to their prearranged stations, manning coastal batteries, securing the safety of their shipping, looking after enemy shipping, controlling exchange. The actual " war telegram," announcing that war had broken out, was not sent then because of the postponement made possible by the Munich Conference.[1] But the War Books remained open. In some parts of the Empire they

---

[1] For the procedure in 1914 see Ernest Scott, *Australia during the War: Official History of Australia in the War of 1914–1918*, Vol. XI, p. 6 f.

were given a thorough revision in the light of the experience thus gained. When, twelve months later, the " war telegram " was finally dispatched from Whitehall to the dominions and to India and the colonies, the whole vast, international system of the British Empire and Commonwealth, composed of some sixty separate administrations, intermeshed as a single war machine.

To describe the legal and administrative processes involved in this act of " going to war " would require a large volume. The mere texts of the Orders-in-Council issued from London through the Colonial Office, and extending to all colonial dependencies the Emergency Powers (Defense) Act of August 1939, and the Local Defense Regulations issued in each colonial territory, covering the field of economic warfare as well as other essential measures of civil and military defense, would fill another. And the similar legislation, statutory orders, and regulations issued in the self-governing dominions and India would fill at least another stout volume. A study of these laws, orders, and regulations — issued everywhere in the scores of separate administrative capitals in the name of the common Crown — and of the actual carrying into effect of this legislation in the various countries and territories, would convey a better understanding of the real meaning of the British Empire than any study of mere constitutional theory. If the machinery, especially on the side of economic warfare, worked more smoothly and with greater speed than in 1914, it was due to several reasons: first, because the lessons learned and the precedents established in the First World War had not been forgotten; second, because of the experience gained in applying limited economic sanctions against Italy in 1935; and third, because of the chance to overhaul the machinery afforded by the false start of Munich.

But though the machinery geared in smoothly enough, was unity real or illusory? The answer is clear. When at the outset of the war Mr. Menzies, the Australian Prime Minister, spoke of this unity and of the spirit behind it, his words were typical of hundreds of declarations coming from all parts of the Empire except Eire: " We know," he said, " that the British nations throughout the world are at one. There is unity in the Empire ranks — one King, one flag, one cause. We stand with Britain." The dominions, it may be said, were free and adult nations; but what of the dependent colonies? As the Under-Secretary of State for the Colonies said in the House of Commons on November 20, 1940, " The outbreak of hostilities was the signal for a unanimous outburst of loyalty and support from all parts of the colonial Empire." [2] The free gifts given by every conceivable body in all of the colonies had reached in the first year of the war " the wonderful total " of £17,000,000. And, in addition, many millions had been expended by the various small communities on local defense. They gave the enemy no aid or comfort in Britain's darkest hours. Some were to fall because of weak links in the defenses of the oceanic Empire; but none by defection.

However it is looked at, this spontaneous solidarity stands out as a unique and remarkable fact. In 1917 General Smuts in a famous speech in London referred to the British Commonwealth of Nations as " the only League of Nations that has ever existed." The League of Nations born of the First World War did not survive twenty summers. But the British league weathered the tempest that destroyed the new League. When the League of Nations collapsed there fell with it a vast complex of still-born treaties, multilateral pacts, nonaggression treaties, and alliances built up by a generation of lawyers and statesmen at Geneva. But something else more fatal had happened: the very lifeblood of mutual trust and loyalty had frozen in the veins of international society.

War in the past has played a far greater part in moulding and reshaping the British Empire than is usually realized. The way in which this Second World War is reshaping the Empire-Commonwealth, how its political, constitutional, and technical machinery has stood the test, how the Commonwealth has actually functioned during the War, the real nature of its inner cohesion — this is the subject to be explored in the following pages.

The terms " Empire " and " Commonwealth " are used here more or less synonymously in accordance with the usage of official documents. Historically the term " Empire " was first applied to England, to denote not domination but rather the independence and equal sovereignty of England; that is, its complete freedom from any external control like that of the Holy Roman Empire. This is its essential meaning in the famous Statute 24 of Henry VIII — before Britain had colonies — which declared, " This realme of England is an Empire." The term " Commonwealth " came to be used to denote the possession of internal liberty. It was because of the growth inside the old historical Empire of a group of autonomous self-governing states, " freely associated " with the Mother Country and each other, that the term " British Commonwealth " began to be current about the time of the First World War.

---

[2] *Journal of the Parliaments of the Empire*, Vol. XXI, p. 32.

The term "The British Commonwealth of Nations" was first used in an official document in the Anglo-Irish Treaty of December 6, 1921, and in the Irish Free State Constitution Act of the Imperial Parliament, 1922.

The relation of the British Empire and the British Commonwealth is most authoritatively indicated in the Report of the Inter-Imperial Relations Committee of the Imperial Conference of 1926.[3] The Committee's report deals with "one most important element" in the Empire which had now "reached its full development — we refer to the group of self-governing communities composed of Great Britain and the Dominions. . . . *They are autonomous Communities within the British Empire, equal in status, in no way subordinate one to another in any aspect of their domestic or external affairs, though united by a common allegiance to the Crown, and freely associated as members of the British Commonwealth of Nations."*

To Nazi leaders, watching restlessly for signs of weakness in an opponent, this whole process of constitutional development which had turned an Empire into a Commonwealth of Nations, each member of which, in the words of the Balfour Report, "is now master of its destiny," was a clear sign of disintegration. When their own rearmament, their militarization of the Rhineland, and the taking over of Austria and the Sudetenland were met by appeasement, their judgment was confirmed. There is little doubt that Hitler invaded Poland in 1939 believing that neither England nor France would fight.

It is important to note that the policy of appeasement was not merely the policy of the Government of Neville Chamberlain. It was a policy shared in varying degrees by all the dominion cabinets and persisted in until the fall of Prague in March 1939. It was as near to being a common foreign policy of the whole British Commonwealth as any policy since 1919.

To those who desired the fall of the British Empire the signs seemed therefore propitious. It was not strange that in Berlin, Rome, and Tokyo, from 1937 onwards, there was incessant talk, some in the open and more underground, of the vast changes that were about to come in the frontiers, of the world and in the distribution of power as a result of the fall of the British Empire — changes more vast than those which followed upon the decline and fall of the Roman Empire.

---

[3] Cmd. 2768, 1926.

2. *The Commonwealth and the League*

Looked at from the outside nothing could have seemed more striking than the contrast between the British Commonwealth and the League of Nations. The former was gradually shedding its constitutional ties while the League was feverishly building a more and more intricate spider-web of contractual relations between its members. On one side stood the members of the Commonwealth busy removing all outworn bonds that might suggest any inequality of status and emphasizing the *freedom* of their association. This " freedom " included the absence of clearly defined commitments to come to each other's assistance or to submit disputes between themselves to any form of court or arbitral tribunal. On the other side stood the members of the League busy trying to strengthen their association by weaving between themselves an increasingly intricate pattern of treaties of mutual assistance and nonaggression. But the appearance was in fact very different from the reality. The British democracies, in shedding some of the legal structure of the old Empire, were clearing the decks for more effective action as a Commonwealth of " freely associated " nations; whilst at Geneva the growing mountain of paper was a sure sign of the malaise and weakness of the League. It was a modern instance of the endless weaving of legal formulae that went on in primitive intertribal assemblies, as in the Althing of mediaeval Iceland.[4] It was magic-thinking of the kind indulged in by primitive societies which sought, by the creation of magical formulae, to buttress up from the outside, as it were, their own lack of inner strength and cohesion.

The period in which the emphasis was laid by the British Dominions upon status, rather than upon their common interests and their obligations as members of the British Commonwealth, lasted for little more than fifteen years; it ended roughly in 1935, when the world began to be once more manifestly unsafe for small powers. The dominions which placed the most emphasis upon status were Canada, the most secure of all the dominions, and Eire and South Africa which, because some of their population had recently been at war with Britain, were under a deep psychological necessity to assert their independence. Australia and New Zealand, the most exposed to danger from war, the most British in the composition of their populations, the most free from memories of past friction with Britain, placed far less emphasis upon status and far

---

[4] See, for example, *The Burnt Njal Saga.*

more upon the sharing of mutual obligations with the other members of the Commonwealth and the making of contributions to the common defense. Neither Australia nor New Zealand had even taken the trouble to adopt the Statute of Westminster, so that legally the British Parliament could still pass laws extending to them — although, as the Statute itself states in its preamble, it would not be in accordance with " the established constitutional position " if the Parliament of the United Kingdom were to attempt to do so " otherwise than at the request and with the consent " of their governments.[4a]

Yet the continued existence of the legal power of the Imperial Parliament, unchanged by the Statute of Westminster, to legislate for any member state of the British Commonwealth, if it so requests, serves as a reminder of the underlying unity of the Empire.

Looked at from the inside, before the war, the Empire gave little of the appearance of imminent dissolution that seemed so clear to its enemies when they looked from the outside through veils of misunderstanding and wishful thinking. The pulling down of an old and out-of-date façade helped rather to reveal the solid lines of the structure. More was done in these years to rebuild what had been pulled down than was commonly realized. It was true that the rebuilding did not take the form of new contractual bonds. It consisted rather of the typically British expedients of conventions or understandings and new methods of consultation and cooperation.

There was considerable rebuilding of this sort in two directions after 1919. First, new and more effective machinery for the handling of foreign affairs was set up in the dominions, each of which created Departments of External Affairs.[5] In the second place, there was a great development in the free and rapid communication of information on foreign affairs between the parts of the Commonwealth, the setting up of an intra-Empire diplomatic system, and of closer liaison between the various defense departments. The danger of divergence in foreign policies was met in part by agreement upon new constitutional conventions of a positive character imposing the duty of consulting with one an-

[4a] In October 1942 the Government of Australia decided, because of practical difficulties in the drafting of legislation, to introduce a bill for the ratification of the statute.

[5] The first Department of External Affairs in any dominion was set up in Australia in 1901. It was dispersed in 1916 but reconstituted and attached to the Prime Minister's department in 1921. As is the practice in the other dominions, the Prime Minister usually held also the Portfolio of External Affairs. From 1934 the portfolio was held separately, and in 1935 a separate department was set up with two divisions, the Political Section and the International Cooperation Section. See *Annual Report of the Department of External Affairs*, Canberra, 1936. Appendix A.

other before taking action in foreign affairs and defense.[6]

The smooth functioning of the British Commonwealth on the eve of the war was due in no small measure to the fact that its statesmen had been for many years in frequent personal contact with each other at London, in Geneva, and elsewhere; that its leading officials in the departments dealing with foreign affairs and defense and economic matters had frequent personal contact with their opposite numbers. It was due also in a measure to the ceaseless work of the Empire Parliamentary Association, through its branches in all the Parliaments of the Empire, in bringing into close personal contact through conferences and by other means, a large number of the members of the Parliaments of the Empire. Because men knew one another, because they realized they had certain vital ideas and interests in common and acted upon the same unspoken fundamental assumptions, they were able to work together with a minimum of friction.[6a]

An explanation of the character of the British Commonwealth will not be found in any legal formulae or constitutional documents. The peoples of the Commonwealth are bound together by a multiplicity of institutional ties; but these are not gathered together in any logical or uniform system. Even a general concept like that of " equality of status " covers the utmost diversity of constitutional relationships. Each dominion with " dominion status " has its own peculiar relationship to Great Britain determined by many different factors drawn from its past history and present condition. One has adopted the Statute of Westminster, and another has not. One has special agreements regulating the utilization by the British navy of naval bases, another not — because it takes such use completely for granted. South Africa and Eire have their own Great Seal; Canada, Australia, and New Zealand use the Great Seal of the United Kingdom when they want to have issued by the King full powers to plenipotentiaries to negotiate and sign treaties. The governors of the Australian states are still able to act as agents of the British Government. The Governor-General on the other hand is no longer an agent or representative of the British Government, but (in the words of

---

[6] E.g., the decisions taken by the Imperial Conferences of 1923 and 1926 regarding prior notification or consultation in all negotiations affecting foreign relations. " Thus, no sooner had equality of status been recognized, and the right of each Dominion to formulate its own foreign policy been extended, by inference, indefinitely, than a convention was established to limit the exercise of that right in the interests of Commonwealth solidarity." *The British Empire*, Royal Institute of International Affairs, London, 1937, p. 218.

[6a] See *The Community of the Parliaments of the British Commonwealth* by H. Duncan Hall in the *American Political Science Review*, December 1942.

the Imperial Conference of 1926) the "representative of the Crown," acting in the role of a constitutional monarch.

With all this great diversity goes also a remarkable fluidity. There is fluidity in procedure and the working of institutions. The dominions in some capitals have their own diplomatic agents, but all of them including Eire use in many parts of the world the services of British diplomats and consular officials. It was even possible in November 1939 for a new member of the Australian Cabinet (who happened to be in Ottawa when selected) to be sworn in as an Australian Minister of the Crown by Lord Tweedsmuir, Governor-General of Canada, acting by request of Lord Gowrie, Governor-General of Australia. An Australian Prime Minister, Mr. Menzies, addressed the Canadian House of Commons from the floor of the House. The King on a visit to Canada in 1939 acted as King of Canada. "In person," he said on his return, "I presided over the Canadian Parliament at Ottawa, and assented to legislation; in person I received the credentials of the new Minister of Canada's great and friendly neighbor, the United States; in person I signed the Trade Treaty between the two countries."

There is the same fluidity in the matter of personnel. A Canadian becomes prime minister of Great Britain, and an ex-prime minister of Canada becomes a British peer. The Australian Minister in Washington, Mr. R. G. Casey, is suddenly appointed a member of the British War Cabinet and charged as Minister of State with the coordination of the Empire war effort in the Near and Middle East. Englishmen, Scotsmen, Welshmen, and Irishmen become prime ministers of the dominions. The late Prime Minister of New Zealand (Mr. Savage) was an Australian; the present Prime Minister (Mr. Fraser) was a Scotsman; and the Deputy Prime Minister (Mr. Nash) was an Englishman. Australians become British diplomats and command ships of the Royal Navy, and British naval officers serve in the Royal Australian Navy. In this diversity and fluidity — or as Winston Churchill put it "the glorious resilience and flexibility of our ancient institutions" — lies part of the secret of the strength of the Empire and its capacity to absorb shocks.

3. The Effect of the Failure of the League on Commonwealth Foreign Policy

At the last Imperial Conference to be held before the war, that of 1937, a cold wind was already blowing from Germany and there was less talk of status and autonomy than at any Imperial Conference held since 1918. Eire was absent. Prime ministers from the dominions were eager to point out that the great constitutional changes had not impaired the inner cohesion of the Commonwealth. The Australian Prime Minister, Mr. Lyons, said, " Despite the forebodings of some who saw in this development a threat to Imperial unity, never has the Empire been more united." And the British Prime Minister, Mr. Chamberlain, in his final speech, emphasized the " profoundly impressive " " solidarity of opinion " " on all big issues," despite the great diversity of the Empire.[7]

It was in this spirit that the whole range of foreign affairs was examined. Statements were made by each of the prime ministers of " the views of their respective governments." But " no attempt was made to formulate commitments which in any event could not be made effective until approved and confirmed by the respective Parliaments."

In this connection it is of interest to note that in 1937 for the first time in the history of the constitutional relations of the Empire, a Conference of Parliaments was held alongside and linked organically with the Conference of Governments. The conference of representatives of all parties in the Parliaments of the Empire was held shortly before the Imperial Conference of Governments. This interlinking was achieved by the arrangement made by the Empire Parliamentary Association, in calling the Parliamentary Conference, that the head of each parliamentary delegation should be a cabinet minister who was also a member of the subsequent Imperial Conference. It was thus possible to estimate in the Empire Parliamentary Conference the measure of unity likely to be attained by members of all parties in the various parliaments on any given question. If this expedient could have been adopted earlier in the postwar period, it might have enabled the prime ministers gathered in the Imperial conferences to coordinate more easily the foreign policies of their countries, and to agree upon a joint policy with the reasonable assurance that they would have their parliaments behind them.

But there was one great difficulty in coming to agreement on more than general principles in such Empire conferences. The common unifying principle on which the policies of each government and the general policy of the group, had been based — namely, the League of Nations — had been deliberately attacked by Japan, Italy, and Germany. As the Australian Prime Minister put it in 1937, " Of recent years the declared policy of the British Nations has been based on the League's

---

[7] *Summary of Proceedings*, Cmd. 5482, 1937, p. 53.

concept of permanent peace insured by the principles of conciliation, arbitration, and collective action. These principles constituted a focal point for a common Empire policy." It had not always been thus. Because of the use of the League made by Eire and South Africa to consolidate their independence, the League had seemed to many up to about 1930 to be an instrument of division rather than a unifying principle. But the great aggressions from 1931–37 made the League and its principles a rallying point for the Empire.

It was on the basis of these principles that the Empire had pursued a common policy in imposing sanctions upon Italy after the invasion of Abyssinia in 1935. Now that this basis had been shot away, through the failure of the nations to collaborate effectively by means of the League machinery to check Italy and to prevent the German remilitarization of the Rhineland, on what principles could the British Commonwealth fall back?

The Imperial Conference of 1937 gave no outward sign that it had discovered any. All that it could do was to state its "close agreement upon a number of general propositions," which amounted to a restatement of several of the general political and moral principles on which the Covenant of the League itself was founded. But in the discussions on defense, there was given the real answer to the attempt of the Axis powers to disintegrate the Empire by diplomatic and psychological war. The members of the British Commonwealth had their own inner mutual security system. The *outer rampart* of general collective security having been breached, the members of the British Commonwealth fell back upon the *middle rampart* — the mutual security system of the Commonwealth itself — and they began at the same time to strengthen the *inner ramparts* of national defense.

4. The Impact of the War upon the Commonwealth

I · HOW THE EMPIRE WENT TO WAR

The differing procedures adopted by the Dominions in entering the war throw some light on the nature of the British Commonwealth. Above all they illustrate the diversity which underlies such phrases as "dominion status." The procedures ran all the way from the separate and formal declaration of war on behalf of Canada, made by the King on the advice of his Canadian ministers, through the less formal procedures of Australia and New Zealand, to the extreme of complete neutrality in Eire. The Canadian procedure implied the doctrine of the divisibility of the Crown. The procedures of Australia and New Zealand were based on the conception of the unity of the Crown, and embodied the doctrine, " When the King is at war we are at war." In Canada and South Africa the procedure was adopted of securing a decision by Parliament; and only when Parliament had decided was the formal declaration of war issued.[8] In Australia and New Zealand, Parliament later approved unanimously the action already taken by the Government in declaring the existence of a state of war immediately upon the notification of Great Britain that she was at war with Germany.

It was not until September 10, 1939, seven days after Britain was at war with Germany, that a proclamation was issued in Ottawa declaring that " a state of war with the German Reich exists and has existed in our Dominion of Canada as from the tenth day of September, 1939." The procedure, as the Prime Minister outlined it to the House on the 11th, was intricate. Following the acceptance of an address from the Throne by the House on the 9th, the Cabinet had met and had decided, on the advice of the King's Privy Council of Canada, to forward a petition to the King with a view to the authorization by him of the issue of a proclamation declaring a state of war. The series of steps taken were: concurrence by the Privy Council; approval by the Governor-General; cabling of instructions to the High Commissioner in London; the submission of a petition to the King in London; his assent at 11:15 a.m. on September 10; and finally the publishing of the proclamation in Ottawa, an hour and ten minutes later, in a special edition of *The Canada Gazette*. There are many other details in the Canadian procedure which have to be taken into account in drawing any deductions from it in support of constitutional theories regarding the divisibility of the Crown or Dominion neutrality. Reference is made to some of these points in the discussion below regarding neutrality.

In Australia and New Zealand no separate proclamation of a state of war was issued by the King on behalf of these dominions. A few minutes after the British Prime Minister's broadcast announcement from London on September 3, 8 p.m. Australian time, that Britain was at war, the Australian ministers met in Melbourne, and approved a proclamation to be issued by the Executive Council declaring a state of war. Then the Australian Prime Minister at 9:15 p.m. broadcast to the Australian people a statement announcing that " Great Britain has declared war, and,

8 See Chapter X, on the South African declaration.

as a result, Australia is also at war." The proclamation appeared immediately afterwards in a special issue of the *Commonwealth Gazette,* No. 63, of September 3, 1939, and began with these words:

EXISTENCE OF WAR
PROCLAMATION

. . . I, the Governor General . . . acting with the advice of the Federal Executive Council, do hereby proclaim the existence of war.

This was, however, in the nature of an internal notification required under the Australian Defense Act, 1903–39. So far as New Zealand and Australia were concerned, the declaration of a state of war from an international point of view was an action taken at their request and on their behalf, by Great Britain as the leading state in the British Commonwealth of Nations. (Incidentally Great Britain had diplomatic representation in Berlin, which Australia and New Zealand had not.) The nature of this part of the procedure is shown by the telegram from the Government of New Zealand received in London on September 3.[9] The telegram refers to " the intimation just received that a state of war exists between the United Kingdom and Germany." It went on to associate His Majesty's Government in New Zealand with the British action with which they " entirely concur ":

The existence of a state of war with Germany has accordingly been proclaimed in New Zealand and H. M. New Zealand Government would be grateful if H. M. Government in the United Kingdom would take any steps that may be necessary to indicate to the German Government that H. M. Government in New Zealand associate themselves in this matter with the action taken by H. M. Government in the United Kingdom.

There was nothing doubtful about this procedure; it was clear-cut. It was based explicitly on the constitutional principle held firmly by most Australian and New Zealand statesmen and constitutional lawyers that " when the Empire (or the King) is at war, we are at war." Some at least of the leading statesmen and constitutional lawyers of Canada and South Africa have always adhered to the same constitutional principle. If there is division of opinion as to whether the " dominion status " of Canada and South Africa is actually in accordance with this constitu-

[9] *The Times,* London, September 4, 1939.

tional principle, there is no such division in Australia and New Zealand.[10]

Australia's declarations of war against Japan, Finland, Rumania, and Hungary were an important departure from former procedure. In these cases war was declared by the Governor-General under power specially assigned to him by the King to declare war against these four specifically mentioned countries. This power was issued by the King on the exclusive advice of the Australian Government.[11]

The case of South Africa is again different. Under the Status of the Union Act, 1934, the Governor-General of South Africa, acting on the advice of his South African ministers, is empowered to exercise the external prerogatives of the Crown, which include the proclamation of neutrality. The view held by some statesmen and lawyers in South Africa, especially General Hertzog, that this Act (together with the Royal Executive Functions and Seals Act, 1934,[12] the Statute of Westminster, 1931, and the Balfour Report, 1926) implied a right of secession and of neutrality, and gave a legal basis for the theory of the divisibility of the Crown, is not accepted by some other leading statesmen and lawyers, including some Afrikaners as well as British. For example, neither General Smuts, the present Prime Minister, nor Mr. Hofmeyer, Minister of Finance, has accepted these interpretations of the meaning of dominion status in South Africa. Mr. Hofmeyer in the debate on entry into the war declared that " he had, as a matter of constitutional theory, con-

---

[10] For this reason such statements as " The legal divisibility of the Crown even on the issue of peace or war may now be taken as established," go too far. H. V. Hodson, " The British Empire," *Pamphlets on World Affairs,* No. 2, New York, 1939.

[11] The Minister of External Affairs, Dr. H. V. Evatt, explained the procedure to Parliament on December 16 as follows: " As to the procedure adopted, there are three comments which should be made. First, it was important to avoid any legal controversy as to the power of the Governor-General to declare a state of war without specific authorization by His Majesty. . . . We therefore decided to make it abundantly clear that there was an unbroken chain of prerogative authority extending from the King himself to the Governor-General. For that purpose we prepared a special instrument, the terms of which were graciously accepted by His Majesty. . . . His Majesty assigned to His Excellency, the Governor-General, the power of declaring a state of war, first with Finland, Rumania, and Hungary, and second, a state of war with Japan. . . .

" Secondly, the procedure adopted was in accordance with the practice that, in all matters affecting Australia, both the King and his representative will act exclusively upon the advice of the Commonwealth Executive Council. The instrument will, in due course, be countersigned by the Prime Minister of the Commonwealth. United Kingdom Ministers took no part in the arrangements which were made directly with the palace authorities by our High Commissioner in London. Similarly, the actual proclamation of a state of war was made by his Excellency the Governor-General on the advice of his Executive Council.

" Thirdly, the history of the transactions illustrates the fact that separate action by the King's Governments in the United Kingdom and the selfgoverning Dominions is perfectly consistent with close cooperation in all matters affecting their common interests."

[12] See Chapter X.

sistently taken the line that when any part of the British Commonwealth was at war, the rest of the Commonwealth was also automatically at war." [13] General Smuts has upheld the view that the Commonwealth is *de jure* a unit in war, though on August 25, 1938, just before Munich, he declared that South Africa would not automatically be at war as in 1914, though she could not stand aside in case of war. Apart from all constitutional theories, it was the policy of immediate participation in the war, as proposed by General Smuts, which the South African Parliament supported, and which it has continued to support more strongly as the war develops. On September 6, 1939, three days after the information was received from London that Great Britain was at war with Germany, the Governor-General of South Africa issued a proclamation of war between South Africa and Germany.

But, whatever these differences in constitutional theory, there was solidarity in action. Anyone who went from Ottawa to Pretoria and from Pretoria to Canberra and Wellington in the first fortnight of September 1939 and who studied the legislative and administrative steps being taken in connection with the war, would not have found in them, and certainly not in the executive action being taken by the King-in-Council or on the King's behalf by the Governor-General-in-Council, or in the legislation by the King-in-Parliament, much ground for suspecting that there were important differences in constitutional theory in different parts of the Empire.

II · THE MYTH OF DOMINION NEUTRALITY

The difficulty of theorizing about the constitutional relations between the members of the British Commonwealth is vividly illustrated when we look at the much discussed problem of dominion neutrality and the effect of the war upon it. In discussing this problem, Eire must be regarded as a special case from which valid inference cannot safely be drawn regarding the constitutional relations of the members of the British Commonwealth. The time has gone when Eire set the pace and provided the precedents for constitutional development in the Commonwealth. By her own action in the present war she has placed herself in a position which, from a legal point of view, she claims to be one of merely " external association " with the Commonwealth. She has placed herself in the position Arthur Griffith warned against in the Dail on December 19, 1921, of being " half in the Empire and half out." By her action in

---

[13] *J. P. E.*, Vol. XX, p. 980.

proclaiming neutrality when the existence of the whole Commonwealth and the freedom of each of its members is at stake, she has adopted a policy which, so long as it lasts, makes her membership of a different kind from that of any other member.

When the new Irish Constitution came into effect in 1937 Britain and the dominions let it be known that they did not regard the new Constitution as putting Eire outside the Commonwealth.[14] Eire began in this war with neutrality; we do not know where she will end. A war still in midstream which has witnessed strange transformations might yet have in store another less startling change — a declaration of war by the King on behalf of Eire. De Valera, indeed, may have envisaged such a possibility when, in accordance with what appeared to be the will of the people, he chose the part of neutrality in 1939 after discussing the matter with the British Government. He let it be understood at that time in London that "external association" meant that if Eire were at any time to go to war, it would do so through the King, the agent of Eire in formal relations with foreign powers, the "King of Ireland" as the new Coronation Oath of 1937 declared him to be — with no sign of opposition from de Valera. The character of the war and the part being played in it by the millions of Irishmen abroad — especially in Australia and the United States — may have its influence on the mother country of Eire in deciding her final policy. The Irish abroad, like many individuals in Eire itself, take their full share in waging the common war.

The question of dominion neutrality must be looked at against the general background of neutrality in international relations as affected by the present war. It is in relation to this new international climate that the problem of neutrality in the British Commonwealth and the meaning of the events of September 1939 must be discussed.[15]

"Neutrality," according to Oppenheim, "may be defined as *the attitude of impartiality adopted by third States towards belligerents and recognized by belligerents, such attitude creating rights and duties be-*

---

[14] The statement issued by His Majesty's Government in the United Kingdom on December 30, 1937, read that "they were prepared to treat the new constitution as *not* effecting a fundamental alteration in the position of the Irish Free State, in future to be described under the new constitution as Eire or Ireland, as a member of the British Commonwealth of Nations. H. M. Government in the United Kingdom have ascertained that H. M. Governments in Canada, the Commonwealth of Australia, the Dominion of New Zealand and the Union of South Africa are also so prepared to treat the new constitution."

[15] In this light it is meaningless to say, as a recent writer said, "The result of the procedure followed in September 1939 may be regarded as settling for all time the question of Dominion neutrality." H. McD. Clokie, "The British Dominions and Neutrality," *American Political Science Review*, August 1940.

tween the impartial States and the belligerents." [16] By any such definition neither Canada, South Africa, Australia, nor New Zealand were in
any sense, at any time, neutral.[17]

There remains the narrow question whether the procedure adopted
in Canada and South Africa, in entering the war, established for these
two countries a theoretical right of neutrality in relation to fellow members of the Commonwealth. A case can be made out for this theory; but
the procedure has received no authoritative interpretation in this sense
by any member of any Government or in any Parliament or Court in
the British Commonwealth. On the contrary, since 1938 the weight of
authoritative opinion has been thrown heavily against views of the kind
that were current in the earlier years after the last war. And as far as we
can look into the future of the British Commonwealth, it is improbable that support will exist after this war for the idea that in theory or practice members of the British Commonwealth can be neutral in respect of
one another. For if the British Commonwealth is not an organization for
mutual security, if its members are not able to count on each other, at
least in time of dire crisis, what meaning and purpose can it have? It is
noteworthy that even in the one quarter where such an idea did receive
serious and powerful support — namely, from General Hertzog and the
five members of the South African Cabinet and sixty-seven members of
Parliament who supported him in the vote of September 5, 1939 — there
was a fundamental ambivalence. The resolution they supported simply
conjured away the war by a magic formula.[18] It was neither neutrality
nor anything else.

---

[16] Oppenheim, *International Law,* 1926, Vol. II, p. 475.

[17] The amendment moved by General Smuts on September 4, 1939, and approved by the
Union House, was that South Africa " should refuse to adopt an attitude of neutrality in this
conflict." On September 3 the Canadian Prime Minister sent a message to London pledging
whole-hearted support of Great Britain and caused a statement to be issued saying, " In the
event of the United Kingdom becoming engaged in war in the effort to resist aggression the
Government have unanimously decided, as soon as Parliament meets (September 7), to seek its
authority for effective cooperation by Canada at the side of Britain." *Bulletin of International
News,* September 9, 1939, p. 54.

[18] The full text reads as follows: " The existing relations between the Union of South
Africa and the various belligerent countries will, in so far as the Union is concerned, persist
unchanged as if no war is being waged. Upon the understanding, however, that the existing relations and obligations between the Union and Great Britain or any other member of the British
Commonwealth of Nations, in so far as such relations or obligations resulting from contractual
obligations relating to the naval base at Simonstown, or its membership in the League of Nations,
or in so far as such relations or obligations would result impliedly from the free association of the
Union with other members of the British Commonwealth of Nations, shall continue unimpaired
and shall be maintained by the Union, and no one shall be permitted to use Union territory for
the purpose of doing anything which may in any way impair the said relations or obligations."
J. P. E., Vol. XX, p. 969.

The discussions in the Canadian Parliament, in the debate of September 9 and in previous months of the same year, were especially noteworthy for declarations of policy, by Government and Opposition leaders in both Houses, which were more strongly against the theory and practice of neutrality, so far as Canada was concerned, than at any previous time since the First World War. On January 16, 1939, the Prime Minister, while reiterating the policy — to which he had for many years pledged himself — of consulting Parliament before Canada went to war, proceeded to quote the famous statement of Sir Wilfred Laurier, in the Canadian House of Commons in 1910: " If England is at war, we are at war and liable to attack. . . ." " This," Mr. Mackenzie King went on, " was a statement of Liberal policy then, . . . a statement of Liberal policy today, and as it will continue to be under the present Liberal administration." [19] The leaders of the Opposition at various times in both Houses were even more emphatic in the same sense. But perhaps the most noteworthy of the pronouncements on the subject were those made, in almost identical terms, on March 31 and September 9, 1939, by Mr. Lapointe, the French-Canadian jurist, Minister of Justice, and second in command in the Canadian Cabinet. The purpose of his statements on both occasions was to show the " insurmountable difficulties in the way of Canada being neutral from a practical point of view, and the almost insurmountable difficulties from a legal point of view." [20] On March 31 he had said that " the Statute of Westminster never purported to dissolve the bond between the nations of the Commonwealth. Indeed, it was intended to strengthen and maintain that bond, which is the principle of unity." [21] On September 9, Mr. Lapointe said: " It is impossible, practically, for Canada to be neutral in a big war in which England is engaged . . . we are using the diplomatic and consular functions of Great Britain throughout the world. Some of the most important sections of our criminal code are predicated on the absence of neutrality in the relations between Canada and Great Britain . . . our shipping legislation is predicated on our alliance with Great Britain. . . . If we had neutrality all Canadian ports would be closed to all armed vessels of Britain. . . . We would have to prevent enlistment on Canadian soil for the army or navy of Britain. . . . Canadians would have to fight British vessels, if they wanted to be neutral during a war. We would have to

---

[19] Canadian House of Commons, *Official Report of Debates,* 1939, Vol. I, p. 52.
[20] J. P. E.
[21] Canadian House of Commons, *Official Report of Debates,* 1939, Vol. III, pp. 65–66.

intern British sailors who came to seek refuge in any of Canada's ports. . . . We have contracts and agreements with Britain for the use of the dry docks at Halifax and Esquimalt. . . . Could Canadians in one section of the country compel other Canadians in other sections to remain neutral and to enforce such neutrality even against their own King . . . ? For the sake of unity we cannot be neutral in Canada." [22]

To sum up, in September 1939 neutrality was considered impossible in all parts of the British Commonwealth outside of Eire. Other reasons apart, it was impossible because each dominion recognized at once that its own existence was directly at stake in the war.

5. The Working of the Constitutional Bonds and the Machinery of Cooperation

We must turn now from this negative aspect to something positive, the actual working of the constitutional bonds and the machinery of cooperation under the stress of the war. This involves especially a consideration of the working of the Crown as an institution, the functioning of the diplomatic and conference machinery of the Empire, the conduct of foreign policy, and the machinery for the coordination of defense.

I · KING AND CROWN

The Crown is the keystone of the constitutional structure of the British Commonwealth of Nations — as of that of each of its constituent parts (with the partial exception of Eire), including the Indian Empire and the colonies. Each executive authority, whether the Cabinet in the United Kingdom, or a dominion cabinet, or the executive council in a colony, exercises its power directly or indirectly in the name of the Crown.[23] A cabinet minister anywhere in the Empire is a "Minister of the Crown." Executive acts are performed in the name of the King-in-Council, or on behalf of the King by the governor-general-in-council or the colonial governor-in-council. In each part of the Commonwealth the legislative power is more than Parliament; it is the King-in-Parliament. A law is enacted by the King, or his representative, "by and with the advice and consent" of the Houses of Parliament.

[22] *Ibid.*, Special War Session, p. 67.

[23] Compare the famous phrase of Sir Robert Borden in his Peace Conference Memorandum (*Canadian Parliament Papers*, 41 J., 1919), "The Crown is the supreme executive in the United Kingdom and in all the Dominions, but it acts on the advice of different Ministries within different constitutional units."

The far-reaching powers given to ministers of the Crown, under the wartime emergency legislation, by each Parliament — subject always to the retention of full power of public criticism by the Parliament — have increased the importance of the Crown as a unifying factor in the British Empire. But the Crown is more than an instrument of executive and legislative power. An even more important function is indicated in the words of the Statute of Westminster: " the Crown is the symbol of the free association of the members of the British Commonwealth of Nations." British subjects throughout the length and breadth of the Commonwealth and beyond it " are united by a common allegiance to the Crown." They are identified with one another, become members of one another psychologically, through the common symbol as well as the common person. Such a symbol might play a part as a unifying factor, though it were but the figure of a person who never existed, such as Uncle Sam. When the symbol is embodied in a real person, that person himself must inevitably play a part in the working of the institution.

The fact that, as perspective now shows, the abdication of King Edward VIII had no adverse effect upon the unity of the Empire, indicates the vitality of the institution of the monarchy irrespective of the personality of the King. After the first shock there was an upsurge of unity throughout the Commonwealth around the new King. The coronation ceremony was of great political and psychological importance in consolidating the Empire. For the first time in such a ceremony, all the peoples participated through the radio in what was in a sense a vast family rededication to the Empire and the higher purposes which it served in the world. The peoples gathered round the radio from the villages in the highlands of Scotland to the lonely sheep stations in the Never Never of Australia. The peoples heard the King reply firmly to the question put to him in the new coronation oath, which for the first time mentioned separately Canada, Australia, New Zealand, and South Africa.

> Will you solemnly promise and swear to govern the peoples of Great Britain Ireland Canada Australia New Zealand and the Union of South Africa, of your Possessions and the other Territories to any of them belonging or pertaining, and of your Empire of India, according to their respective laws and customs? [24]

---

[24] Speaking of the new oath at the Imperial Conference of 1937, the Prime Minister of Canada said, " For the first time in this great ceremony it was recognized that the relationship between the King and his people of Canada is direct and immediate."

The direct relationship of the King to Canada was heightened by his visit with the Queen in June 1939. Of the political importance of this visit on the very eve of the war there is much evidence. Conventional words had a sudden poignant vivid reality when M. Lapointe, the French-Canadian statesman, said in the House on September 9: " Our King, Mr. Speaker, is at war and this Parliament is sitting to decide whether we shall make his cause our own." [25] Or when, in the Quebec elections in October 1939, which turned largely on the issue of complete participation in the war, he appealed " to the feeling of loyalty to the Crown on the part of French-Canadians generally, a feeling which was so markedly intensified by the Royal visit." [26]

When the war broke the King spoke over the microphone, directly to his people throughout the British Empire. " I send," he said, " to every household of my people this message spoken with the same depth of feeling for each one of you as if I were able to cross your threshold and speak to you myself." The peoples who listened were lifted out of themselves and united with an intensity that is perhaps unattainable by large groups of human beings except through their common identification with a chief. The spirit of hundreds of messages received in London in the early days of the war is typified in one from Lord Craigavon, Premier of Ulster: " Though Ulster be but a small link in the chain which encircles and binds the Empire, she is, by virtue of her strategical position and her hardy Northern stock, *a strong link — a link that will neither break nor bend before the King's enemies. We are King's men. We will be with you to the end.*" [27]

II · IMPERIAL WAR CONFERENCE AND CABINET

While the King is the symbol of unity, it is the King's Ministers who carry on the work of government; and between the Ministers of the Crown in the different parts of the British Commonwealth there must be consultation and collaboration. The system of " consultative cooperation," whereby the British Commonwealth handles its common concerns and coordinates its common action in war and peace, includes many elements. But the element which by general consent would be placed first is the system of regular meetings between the cabinets, represented by

---

[25] Canadian House of Commons, *Official Report of Debates*, Special War Session, p. 65.
[26] *Round Table*, December 1939, p. 188.
[27] *National Review*, London, March 1940, p. 293.

the prime ministers or their deputies, in the Imperial Conference with its wartime variants of Imperial War Conference and Imperial War Cabinet.

The League of Nations was likewise a system of frequent conferences of governments, and it developed this procedure beyond the point it has attained in the British Commonwealth. This was the League's one strength: it had little or none of the many other elements that gave vitality and strength to the British Commonwealth. It is these other elements that have to be remembered when we try to account for the fact that the Empire could carry on without any Imperial Conference in the first two and a half years of the present war. This failure to use what appeared to be the chief political instrument of the British Commonwealth is all the more difficult to understand when we remember that the leaders of the Axis met in frequent conference, that the Supreme War Council met at intervals up to the collapse of France, and that even Roosevelt and Churchill met in the Atlantic Conference of August and at Washington at Christmas 1941, and that the Tripartite Conference of Great Britain, the U.S.A., and the U.S.S.R. met in Moscow in September 1941, with the German Army not far from the gates.

No adequate explanation is to be found in the fact that the prime ministers of the dominions had far greater tasks to handle in this war than in the last. This war is being organized and fought in widely separated regions — as a battle for the world. The dominions are no longer mere distant reservoirs of man power, but great arsenals of munitions and stores and centers of air power. And in addition to their armies stationed in Europe and the Near East, they have had to mount guard in some cases against the enemy on their frontiers.

These differences in the strategic situation, as well as factors like the independent status of the dominions, the new diplomatic system of the British Commonwealth, the daily meetings of the high commissioners with the Dominions Secretary, and new technical means of communication such as radio broadcasting and the airplane, make it difficult to draw a parallel between the First and Second World Wars. But in the first war there was a like initial delay — two and a half years — in the holding of an Imperial Conference. From 1914 to early in 1917 there were frequent visits to London of cabinet ministers, including most of the prime ministers. The Imperial War Conference met in the spring of 1917, and again in 1918. The first two sessions of the Imperial War Cabinet were held during these Imperial War Conferences; its third session began after the Armistice on November 20, 1918, and held twelve meetings before the end of the year and others in the first half of 1919.[28]

The Imperial War Cabinet and the Imperial War Conference were both meetings of Governments, the former being more directly concerned with the most urgent business of the war. Neither was an executive organ, despite the use of the somewhat misleading word *cabinet*. The Imperial War Cabinet was, as Sir Robert Borden, the Canadian Prime Minister, put it, " a Cabinet of Governments. Every Prime Minister who sits around that board is responsible to his own parliament and to his own people; the conclusions of the War Cabinet can only be carried out by the parliaments of the different nations of our Imperial Commonwealth." [29] As the Australian Prime Minister expressed it, " the government of the dominion . . . always remained in the dominion." [30]

But it is characteristic of the flexibility of British institutions that dominion prime ministers and ministers from time to time attended the British War Cabinet, so that there must have been days when the secretaries had to be careful to ascertain which of the two Cabinets they were recording, since there was little in the room, or the persons present, or the topics under discussion, which would distinguish one Cabinet from the other. From 1917 onwards, General Smuts sat continuously in the British War Cabinet and represented South Africa in the Imperial War Cabinet when in session. And, as the report of the British War Cabinet for 1918 indicates, after the close of the second session of the Imperial War Cabinet, " several meetings of the British War Cabinet were attended by such representatives of the Dominions as still remained in the United Kingdom." Indeed, as the terms of the invitation clearly showed, when the dominion prime ministers were summoned in December 1916 to come to a Conference in London, it was regarded as " a series of special and continuous meetings of the War Cabinet." [31]

As in substance there was little or no difference between Imperial (War) Cabinet and Imperial (War) Conference, it might have been expected that the use of the term Cabinet would not be objected to by the dominions after the war was over. But there were elements in the dominions which disliked and even feared the term *Cabinet* or *Council*, since under cover of it there might somehow creep in a power to make

[28] *Report of the War Cabinet*, 1918. Cmd. 325.
[29] *Ibid.*
[30] W. M. Hughes, *The Splendid Adventure*, quoted in Scott, *Official History of Australia in the War of 1914–1918*, Vol. XI, p. 756.
[31] *Round Table*, London, June 1917.

binding decisions. From the earliest days of the Imperial Conference there had been a persistent refusal on the part of the dominions to allow the Imperial Conference to develop into anything more than a periodical meeting of Governments. Anything in the nature of an Imperial council, any development likely to give the conference a more permanent character, was rejected out of hand. A permanent secretariat was rejected by the Conference of 1907. A suggestion by the Colonial Secretary of a standing committee of the Conference composed of the Colonial Secretary and the Dominion High Commissioners was rejected in 1911.[32] (It was destined to reappear again as a daily meeting of an entirely informal character held in the room of the Secretary of State for the Dominions during the great crises which preceded the present war and during the war itself.) There were undoubtedly some hopes in England that as a result of the experience of the war this objection on the part of the dominions might be overcome sufficiently to give the Imperial Conference somewhat greater authority and permanence. This hope was so definite that the British Prime Minister on May 17, 1917, told the House of Commons of the view taken by the members of the Imperial War Cabinet that " the holding of an annual Imperial Cabinet to discuss foreign affairs and other aspects of Imperial policy will become an accepted convention of the British Constitution." The same expectation can be traced in the phraseology used in the report of the British War Cabinet in 1918 in which " the establishment as a permanent institution of the Imperial Cabinet system " is mentioned, and also in the words of the official announcement in November 1920 of the summoning of the Imperial Conference of 1921 in which it was described as a " meeting on the lines of the Imperial War Cabinet meetings." Such phraseology was dropped from the official report of the Imperial Conference of 1921 in deference to the wishes of the dominions. It was characteristic that the " natural remedy for . . . giving the Imperial War Cabinet continuity by the presence in London of oversea Cabinet Ministers definitely nominated to represent the Prime Ministers in their absence," which was proclaimed in a resolution of the Imperial War Cabinet on July 30, 1918,[33] dropped completely out of sight and was never heard of again.

The same difficulties were manifest in the period from 1921 to 1941. The British Government was acutely aware of the deficiencies of the Imperial Conference system and its inability to provide for the " con-

---

[32] Cmd. 5741, 1911.
[33] Cmd. 325, 1918.

tinuous consultation in all important matters of common Imperial concern," which the Imperial War Conference had agreed in 1917 was essential. The Chanak incident in 1922, the difficulties in connection with the ratification of the Treaty of Lausanne in 1924, the inability to secure effective consultations on the Geneva Protocol, and the Locarno Treaties in 1924-25, were all illustrations of this deficiency. As the Prime Minister, Ramsay MacDonald, pointed out in his telegram to the Dominions on June 23, 1924, the " present system of consultation . . . has two main deficiencies. . . . It renders immediate action extremely difficult. . . . Conclusions reached at and between Imperial Conferences are liable to be reversed through changes of Government." [34] But the exchange of telegrams between the Governments led to no permanent results — not even the holding of more frequent Imperial Conferences, which was probably the most important method of meeting the deficiencies. An Australian proposal for a " permanent Imperial Secretariat " was never adopted. Mr. Mackenzie King, the Canadian Prime Minister, warned Mr. Ramsay MacDonald off dangerous ground by cabling, " We regard the Imperial Conference as Conference of Governments of which each is responsible to its own Parliament . . . and in no sense as Imperial Council determining the policy of the Empire as a whole." [35] It is characteristic of this discussion, and similar discussions on the same problem in later years, that the British Government saw the problem of coordinating the actions and policies of the Governments of the British Commonwealth with greater clarity and objectivity than the dominions.

In his opposition to the holding of an Imperial War Cabinet or Conference in the first two years of this war, the Canadian Prime Minister, Mr. Mackenzie King, tended to refer to it as if it would be a continuously meeting body, whereas the Imperial War Cabinet and Conference were never permanent bodies and held only occasional sessions. In his interview with the press on arrival in London in 1941 he justified his opposition to the meeting of an Imperial War Cabinet on the ground that " important decisions should not be made by one man but by a government as a whole." [36] But in fact the Imperial War Cabinet and Conference had not made decisions without reference to their constituent Governments. His opposition to such a cabinet or conference probably colored somewhat the remarkable tribute which he then proceeded to

---

[34] Cmd. 2301, 1925.
[35] *Ibid.*
[36] *The Times,* London, August 22, 1941.

pay to the existing system of communications and consultation between the Governments of the British Commonwealth. " A perfect continuous conference of Cabinets now exists," he said, " and there has never been a time when relations were closer between the Governments. Not a single point of difference has arisen on any essential subject since the outbreak of war." Six months before in the Canadian Parliament he had spoken of the existence of a " real but invisible Imperial Council made possible by these means of constant and instantaneous conference." This tribute was no doubt in a measure well founded. It was supported by the statement made by Mr. Malcolm MacDonald, British High Commissioner to Canada, in an interview with the Canadian press on May 20, 1941, that the system of intra-Empire communication between the heads of Governments in Britain, Canada, Australia, and South Africa had been speeded up so much that " it almost seems as though the four leaders were sitting around one table."

But in fact it was just this coping stone, the final meeting of the leaders round a table, that was missing. In all its lower ranges, in the matter of efficiently organized foreign offices and Empire diplomatic system, of military and naval liaison, of the exchange of information, the perfection of complete systems of intra-Empire air transport and cables and telephone, the structure of the Empire was far more solidly and efficiently organized than ever before in its history.

In the judgment of the British Government and of several of the dominion Governments, especially Australia, it was necessary for the effective conduct of the war and the formulation of war and peace aims to hold an Imperial War Cabinet or Conference, since no consultations by telephone or cable could substitute for the discussion round one table of the highly complex issues involved. The question of holding such a meeting was raised in the British House of Commons on September 21, 1939; and again on October 4, when Mr. Eden revealed that the Government had inquired whether the other Governments would be ready to send a cabinet minister to London for consultations. The result was the visit to London of cabinet ministers from each of the dominions for informal consultations in November and December 1939. This was followed by a number of visits by individual ministers from each of the dominions at intervals during 1940 and 1941. No less than seven Canadian ministers visited London prior to the visit of the Prime Minister; so that there has almost always been one Canadian minister in Britain since the early months of the war. The Australian Prime Minister,

Mr. Menzies, visited London in April and May 1941, followed some weeks later by the Prime Minister of New Zealand, whose visit overlapped with that of Mr. Mackenzie King in August 1941. Each of the prime ministers attended meetings of the British War Cabinet and Mr. Menzies attended also the Defense Committee of the Cabinet during the campaigns in the Balkans and Libya.[37]

A further serious effort was made, during the long visit to London of the Australian Prime Minister, to hold an Imperial War Conference. Mr. Churchill gave the House of Commons on June 24, 1941, the results of his inquiries. " As I have told the House," he said, " we very much desire such a Conference." Negative replies were received from Mr. Mackenzie King and General Smuts regretting their inability to attend a conference in the near future. For a short time in August the presence simultaneously in London of the Canadian and New Zealand Prime Ministers and of Lord Halifax, the British Ambassador to Washington, seemed to offer the possibility of convening an Imperial Conference. But the desire of the Australian Prime Minister to proceed to London, to represent Australia at the War Cabinet and in any conference, was thwarted by factions in the Australian Parliament, which brought about his resignation at the end of August. This situation illustrates a perpetual difficulty in the working of the Imperial Conference system, involving as it does the absence of a Prime Minister from the helm in his own Cabinet and Parliament, at times when such absence may be highly inconvenient.

There is a strong case for the holding of a small Conference of Parliaments parallel with an Imperial War Conference. Like the Conference held in 1937, it could be attended by a small representative delegation from each Parliament headed by a cabinet minister who would also sit in an Imperial War Conference of governments. It is of special importance that leaders of the opposition parties in the parliaments should also attend, as was the case in the Empire Parliamentary Conferences held in London in 1935 and 1937. The Parliamentary War Conference held in London in 1916 was of considerable importance from the point of view of forming and consolidating public opinion in the dominions, especially in Canada. A strong all-party delegation from the Canadian Parliament did visit London in October 1941 to confer with their col-

---

[37] The Canadian Air Minister also attended the War Cabinet early in August. It is of interest to note, as illustrating the elasticity of British constitutional procedure, that Mr. Harry L. Hopkins attended a meeting of the British War Cabinet on his arrival in London on July 17, 1941. M. Daladier, as French Prime Minister, was also present at the War Cabinet early in the war. General Smuts attended for five weeks late in 1942.

leagues at Westminster on war matters and to study the war effort of
Great Britain and its relation to Canada. This was to be followed in De-
cember by similar delegations from Australia, New Zealand, and South
Africa. The first two turned back; only the South Africans came. An
effort was to have been made to bring these delegations together in a
Parliamentary War Conference in England or in Canada. Out of this it
was hoped would come a meeting between the leaders of the United
States Congress and the British Parliament such as was proposed in
May 1942.

The friction between Canberra and London between December 1941
and March 1942 [38] showed that the political machinery of the British
Commonwealth was not functioning smoothly. Both the Australian and
New Zealand Governments asked for the creation of an Imperial
War Cabinet in London and an Inter-Allied Pacific War Council in
Washington. These requests were put forward early in January and
answered by Mr. Churchill in his speech in the House of Commons
on January 27. "We have always," he said, "been ready to form an
Imperial Cabinet containing the Prime Ministers of the four dominions." Unfortunately, he continued, it had not been possible for all of
them to be present at one and the same time; but at every opportunity
dominion prime ministers had sat in the British War Cabinet and the
Defense Committee. In the last three months the Australian Government, he pointed out, had been represented on the War Cabinet by Sir
Earle Page. The British Government had now agreed to the specific
requests of the Australian and New Zealand Governments, that their
accredited representatives should have the " right to be heard in the War
Cabinet in the formulation and direction of policy "; [39] and similar facilities would be available to Canada and South Africa. The invitation was
extended to India a little later. " The presence," Mr. Churchill continued, " at the Cabinet table of Dominion representatives who have no
power to take a decision and can only report to the governments, evidently raises some problems, but none I trust which cannot be got over
with goodwill here. It must not, however, be supposed that in all circumstances the presence of Dominion representatives for certain pur-

---

[38] See Chapter VIII, Part II.

[39] The Australian Minister of External Affairs stated in the House on February 25, 1942, that
the Australian Advisory War Cabinet's interpretation that " the right to be heard in the United
Kingdom War Cabinet ' in the formulation and direction of policy ' " carried with it " membership in the War Cabinet," was judged by Mr. Churchill as " not in accordance with constitutional
practice."

poses in any way affects the collective responsibility of His Majesty's servants to the Crown and to Parliament."

As Canada and South Africa had not felt able to avail themselves of Mr. Churchill's offer, the Australian Government did not push the matter further. Their representative (Sir Earle Page) continued to attend meetings of the British War Cabinet and Defense Committee " whenever matters which were considered by the British Prime Minister to be of direct and immediate concern to Australia were under consideration." Sir Earle Page had " the right to be heard in the formulation and direction of policy," but had no power to commit his Government without referring back to it. His authority to speak for Australia was limited by the fact that he was not even a member of the Australian Cabinet. The essence of the Imperial War Cabinet of 1917–19, on the other hand, was that it brought together prime ministers or their deputies, that is those charged with the responsibility for leadership in their cabinets and parliaments, and able therefore in no small measure to commit their governments.

Pacific War Councils [40] have since been set up in London and Washington. That in Washington, both because of its membership and because it exists alongside the Anglo-American combined war machinery (the Combined Chiefs of Staff Group, the Munitions Assignments Board, the Combined Shipping Adjustment Board, and the Combined Raw Materials Board, the Combined Food Board, and the Combined Production and Resources Board), seemed destined to play a larger part than the London body, with which it maintained close liaison.

These parallel councils were in one sense anomalies, because they purported to deal with only a segment of an indivisible world war, for handling of which there was no general council of the United Nations, nor even an Imperial War Cabinet or Conference. The Combined Chiefs of Staffs Group which was the nearest thing to a war council on the plane of strategy, since it dealt with the war as a whole, was confined to strategy. It was not concerned with politics. Moreover, like the five other joint boards, it was purely Anglo-American in composition without representation of the U.S.S.R. or any other allied nation.[40a] The incompleteness and complexity of the Inter-Allied machinery was in part due to the geographical separation of the three great partners, and the

---

[40] See Chapter VIII, Part II.

[40a] A Canadian representative was included in the Combined Production and Resources Board in September 1942.

fact that two of them were on the periphery and separated from some or all of the war zones by immense distances.[41]

So far, then, the war has tested the Imperial Conference system and found it wanting. There have never been more contacts on the ministerial and official plane, and the communications system has never functioned as well as now. But the final coordination of the Conference has been lacking. The prime ministers of four of the dominions have individually attended odd meetings of the British War Cabinet. They have never conferred together as a group in conference, face to face. For their direct contacts with each other the prime ministers of the Empire have relied largely upon pentagonal telephone conversations from the five corners of the earth, when something more effective than the long-distance telephone was needed to defeat the unified strategy of the Axis. They have failed to achieve all the political, strategical, and psychological advantages offered by meetings of an Imperial Conference or Cabinet. Of these advantages not the least are those affecting morale. Such meetings of the leaders of the British Commonwealth of Nations furnish symbols

---

[41] The following extract from the ministerial statement by Dr. Evatt in the House at Canberra on February 25 illustrates the complexity of the machinery. Though the subsequent setting up of the parallel Pacific War Council in Washington might seem to add to the cumbersomeness of the procedure, as he described it, the close relation of the Council to the Combined Chiefs of Staffs Group was a compensating factor:

" A hypothetical case will illustrate the way in which this Pacific Council (London) fits into the general machinery. Let us assume that the Supreme Commander requires guidance or direction from the " higher authority " in relation to the supply of reinforcements or the like. The procedure is something like this: —

(a) The Supreme Commander in the Pacific telegraphs his question to a Combined Chiefs of Staff Committee which has been set up in Washington as the agency to represent the United States and United Kingdom Services. The Commander also telegraphs to the Chiefs of Staff Committee in London, which is a United Kingdom body.

(b) Both in London and in Washington, the telegrams are remitted to Joint Planning Staffs for examination.

(c) The Joint Planning Staffs submit reports to the Chiefs of Staff in London and the Chiefs of Staff Committee in Washington respectively, and the two staff authorities proceed to resolve any points of difference between them.

(d) When this has been done the British Chiefs of Staff submit a report to the Far Eastern (Pacific) War Council in London.

(e) Any differences of view between the members of the Council and the Chiefs of Staff are argued out in the Council.

(f) The agreed views of the Council are then telegraphed to the Chiefs of Staff Committee in Washington. If members of the Council differ the British Prime Minister is to " focus " the divergent views and communicate with Washington.

(g) If the Chiefs of Staff Committee in Washington accepts them, they are presented to the President who then issues the necessary executive order.

(h) If there is a difference of view between London and Washington, the President informs Mr. Churchill, who remits the matter to the Pacific War Council.

(i) Then, presumably, the whole matter returns to stage (e) and is thrashed out again."

of unity and determination. The leaders themselves are stimulated, and the sluggish and weak are fortified by the strong. The morale of the peoples is heightened. Fresh and more effective weapons for psychological war against the enemy are forged. By forgoing meetings of an Imperial War Conference or Cabinet, the dominions atrophy the central political institution of the British Commonwealth to which they have attached the greatest importance in the past. They deny their national status by throwing upon the British War Cabinet most of the responsibility for the higher political and strategic direction of the war. It is difficult to believe that such a situation can continue for long. The higher direction of the war effort of the British Commonwealth requires something in the nature of meetings at not too great intervals of an Imperial War Conference or Cabinet or Supreme War Council — the name matters little. And some such body is not less essential to coordinate the common efforts of the British democracies and India in the building up of a stable peace. The fault lies not so much with the system of the Imperial Conference itself, which despite all its difficulties can be worked. Provided command is maintained over the sea and the air above it — a condition threatened by Japan in the Pacific and the Indian Oceans in 1942 — conferences can be held at relatively short intervals without necessarily involving, even for the most distant parts of the Empire, more than several weeks' absence for the prime ministers or their deputies. In any case the right of any dominion prime minister who is able to visit London, to sit *ex-officio* — as a member by right without need of special invitation — in the War Cabinet, might be recognized.[42]

The main obstacles are to be found, when traced down to their roots, less in material factors than in mental attitudes. Even this brief record of the difficulties experienced by the British democracies in the last two generations, in bringing themselves to accept modest steps towards a more unified common direction of their foreign affairs and defense, should serve as a warning to those who have an easy optimism regarding the rate of progress which is possible towards world government.

III · COMMON EMPIRE FOREIGN POLICY

Broadly speaking, the effect of the war on the foreign policies of the members of the British Commonwealth has been to weave them together more than ever as strands in a single rope. When, in the interval between the two great wars, the strain at times slackened, the strands

---

[42] This suggestion was made by the *Times,* London, August 25, 1941.

might loosen and even fray out; but only to draw together when the strain increased in a crisis. It is not untrue to say that there existed a common, joint British Commonwealth of Nations foreign policy in the crises leading to this war, as there existed a single British Empire foreign policy before 1914.

The relative weakness of the dominions was increased by the rapid mechanization of war. They had enough sense of reality to know that there was no magic in their new equality of status with Great Britain which could make it possible to have the independence of policy which is the exclusive privilege of only the greatest of the Great Powers. They understood well enough the fundamental truth which they had " frankly recognized " in the Balfour Report of 1926; namely, that in the sphere of foreign affairs as in the sphere of defense, " the major share of the responsibility rests now, and must for some time continue to rest, with His Majesty's Government in Great Britain."

As that report pointed out, and subsequent developments have made still more clear, the special circumstances and geographical conditions of each country in the Commonwealth make it inevitable that there should be certain differences of approach and emphasis in the matter of foreign policy on the part of each government. If, in the words recently used by an Australian Prime Minister, Australia is a " principal " bearing " primary risks and primary responsibilities " in matters affecting the Pacific and the Far East, the same is true of England in relation to Europe, as Sir Austen Chamberlain pointed out in justification of the British policy expressed in the Locarno Treaties. It is true also of Canada in relation to the United States; but here there is no question of any primary risk, but only of an enviable security which has enabled Canada to profess a detachment to which the less secure dominions cannot hope to aspire.

Because of Australia's special interest in the Far East, the Australian Minister of External Affairs could on occasion talk of " the formulation and application of (Australia's) Far Eastern policy." [43] But the phrase meant little more than that her " Near North " is for Australia to a much greater degree than for any other dominion a region of special interest in the general field of common Empire foreign policy. This point was never for a moment forgotten at the five centers (namely, Canberra, London, Washington, Tokyo, Chungking) where Australian ministers and diplomats were shaping and carrying out Australia's

---

[43] Declaration in the Australian House of Representatives, November 28, 1940.

Far Eastern policy in the closest consultation with British ministers and diplomats. It was at the same time Australia which at the Imperial Conference of 1937 boldly used such phrases as " common Empire policy," " British Empire Foreign Policy," and " consistent and united Empire Policy." The only other dominion which could use such language was New Zealand.

Yet a broad general survey of the foreign policy of the British Commonwealth, in the interval between the two great wars, shows that the divergencies between Britain and the dominions were comparatively few and, in the long run, of no great importance. Such divisions as did occur arose largely from the discrepancies between the *theory of equal status* and the *reality of unequal stature*. In theory, the dominions had equal status with Great Britain; but in practice her enormously greater stature, as a Great Power with world interests, forced her into independent action and commitments without the dominions. The difference of stature led to some differences in matters of procedure such as representation at international conferences and the signing and ratification of treaties. The sensitiveness of the dominions in questions involving their status tended to give undue publicity to differences of this kind which were not really matters of substance.

From the end of the First World War and until about 1921 foreign policy was one and indivisible for all practical purposes. The report of the Imperial Conference of 1921 [44] has a number of phrases which reveal this conception of a unitary " foreign policy of the British Empire." In the Washington Arms Conference, 1921, and the treaties of Naval Limitation issuing from it, the naval forces of the members of the British Commonwealth of Nations were treated as a complete unity for international purposes, and all the members of the British Commonwealth signed and ratified as members of the group. Exactly the same procedure was followed in the subsequent treaties for the limitation and reduction of naval armament signed at London, April 22, 1930, and March 25, 1936 (except that Eire took part only in the 1930 treaty). There were a number of other instances of complete group action, such as the signing and ratification of the Paris Pact of 1928 and the accession in 1931 to the General Act of 1928. It is true that the principle of diplomatic unity had broken down badly at the time of the Chanak incident in 1922, but this was not followed by any serious consequences. The divergencies over the Lausanne Treaty of 1923 and the Locarno Treaties

[44] Cmd. 1474, 1921.

of 1925 were more apparent than real. In the case of the Locarno Treaties, Great Britain was able merely to keep the dominions informed but without full consultation in an Imperial Conference, although it tried to secure one. It had to enter into guarantees to which the dominions were not formally parties because, as Sir Austen Chamberlain put it in the House of Commons on November 18, 1925, " We live close to the Continent . . . we must make our decision." But the dominions were aware that they were likely to be involved in any ultimate consequences that might come from the Locarno Treaties.

Until the archives are thrown open, we can have no complete picture of the attitudes of the different dominions in matters of foreign policy prior to the present war. But from the information available, it is clear that, whereas Canada willingly received the information on foreign policy supplied by the Foreign Office, she preferred, and was even grateful, not to be " consulted "; she was very sparing in any expression of her own views, and in particular of saying expressly that she concurred with the views of the British Foreign Office; and she rarely put forward suggestions of her own. On the other hand Australia (and no doubt New Zealand, although the information published in her case is somewhat less full) repeatedly concurred in actions about to be taken by the British Government, and frequently gave her views when asked to do so. But it was only occasionally that she raised on her own initiative points for consideration by London and asked for an answer.

The procedure of endorsing the British Government's action used by Australia and New Zealand in connection with the declaration of war against Germany [45] was adopted on a number of important occasions by these dominions in the years immediately preceding the present war. For example, in connection with the signing of the Anglo-Italian agreement on November 16, 1938, and the recognition at the same time of the Italian conquest of Abyssinia, Mr. Neville Chamberlain announced the receipt of telegrams from the prime ministers of South Africa and Australia approving the intention to put the agreement into force. On the same day the Australian Prime Minister, Mr. Lyons, announced in the Australian House that " the Government has been in consultation with the Government of Great Britain and has expressed the opinion that the sooner the Agreement (with Italy) is concluded the better for the two countries immediately concerned and probably for the peace of

---

[45] See above, pp. 20–21.

the world." [46] The procedure here was parallel to that of the declaration of war in the sense that when the British Government informed the dominions that it intended to act, the Australian Cabinet indicated its concurrence and requested the British Government to associate Australia with the action taken. But on this occasion New Zealand refrained from concurrence. She never recognized the Italian conquest of Ethiopia, and now that Haile Selassie is back in Addis Ababa, events have caught up with her.

But the greatest occasion of a concerted foreign policy was at the outbreak of the war itself and in the events immediately preceding it. The false start at Munich was in a high degree an act of common foreign policy. Appeasement then was a policy to which all the Dominion Cabinets were as fully committed as Britain itself.[47] In the swiftly moving events following upon the German occupation of Czechoslovakia in March 1939, the dominion governments expressly or silently concurred at every point in the successive steps taken by the British Government, such as the momentous decision of the pact with Poland. The dominions had the fullest information regarding this treaty, although in form it was " an agreement of Mutual Assistance between the United Kingdom and Poland," and its obligations did not formally involve the dominions.

Although the British Government may not have possessed from a single dominion the formal assurance in advance that it would enter the war simultaneously with Great Britain, it knew by a thousand signs and indications that most if not all of the family of nations would act together, whatever the procedures might be, or the initial difficulties they might have to pass through in making their decisions. Mr. R. G. Casey, the Australian Minister at Washington, stated in a speech given on March 20, 1941, that: " Australia, on her own decision, declared herself in a state of war with Germany on the same day as Great Britain — and without any prior knowledge on Britain's part that we would do so — or even the slightest hint from Britain that we *should* do so." Nevertheless the British Prime Minister was able *before* the war, on September 1, 1939, to say to the House of Commons with complete confidence: " We shall enter (the war) with a clear conscience, with the support of

---

[46] *Parliamentary Debates,* Session 1937–38, p. 1110.

[47] E.g., the speech of the Australian Prime Minister in the House on September 28, 1938, in which he suggested that this policy had indeed been pressed by Australia upon the British Government.

the dominions and the British Empire, and with the moral approval of the greater part of the world." [48] To those who think of the British Commonwealth in terms of formal relationships and established procedures, this situation must remain an incomprehensible mystery. But it will offer no difficulty to those who realize that the key to an understanding of the British Commonwealth is the relationship of members of a family to one another.

During the war itself consultation, concurrence, and cooperation have been more complete than at any time since the war of 1914–18. The policy of the British Commonwealth of Nations, apart from Eire, has been one and indivisible. The veil was lifted for an instant by Mr. Churchill in his speech to the House of Commons on June 18, 1940, to reveal the working of the Empire machinery at the time of the fall of France and the evacuation of Dunkirk. It was the most critical moment in the history of the Empire. The speech showed Great Britain discussing whether it was possible to carry on, and then moving forward once more in the van of the British Commonwealth with " invincible resolve." " We have fully informed all the self-governing dominions and we have received from all Prime Ministers messages couched in the most moving terms, in which they endorse our decision and declare themselves ready to share our fortunes and persevere to the end." Gone with the winds of disaster were all delicate distinctions between information and consultation and endorsement!

In the offer as a free gift of naval bases in Newfoundland and Bermuda, and the exchange of other naval bases on the British Atlantic islands for fifty destroyers (August and September 1940), negotiations were conducted between Great Britain and the United States as principals, with Canada represented only by an observer. To safeguard her special position, and her right of acting as a principal in any further negotiations in relation to Newfoundland (which lies athwart her front door and is an integral part of her defense), a protocol to the bases agreement was drawn up at her instance. [49]

The Far East forms another chapter in this joint foreign policy. The closing and the opening of the Burma Road in the fall of 1940 revealed the United States in close consultation not only with Great Britain but also with other parts of the British Commonwealth most immediately

---

[48] J. P. E., Vol. XX, p. 823.
[49] March 27, 1941. Cmd. 6259. See Grant Dexter in *Proceedings of the Fourth Conference on Canadian-American Affairs*, 1941.

concerned, such as Australia. The closing of the road was decided upon " after full consultation with the (Australian) Commonwealth and the other Dominion Governments." The decision to reopen it after October 18, 1940, " was taken with the full concurrence of the Commonwealth Government and after close consultation with the United States Government whose interest in this area is closely allied to our own." [50] It is indeed likely that when the full facts are known the foreign policies of the United States and Great Britain in relation to the Far East will be shown to have been, at least since the outbreak of the war, to all intents and purposes first parallel and then joint. A number of illustrations of such joint action could be given. They would cover the joint aid to China, joint or parallel diplomatic or economic action against Japan, and the planning of concerted defense measures. For several years a joint policy towards Japan was followed, which President Roosevelt defined as " keeping war out of the South Pacific for our own good, for the good of the defense of Great Britain and the freedom of the seas." [51] The freezing of all Japanese assets in all parts of the British Commonwealth and the United States which was announced on July 25, immediately after this remark by the President, was a signal illustration of this joint foreign policy of the English-speaking peoples. As soon as Britain was informed that the American action had been taken, a " parallel measure " was put into effect throughout the whole British Empire including India, Burma, and the colonies. All commercial treaties between any part of the British Empire and Japan were simultaneously denounced. It was a joint policy of economic sanctions against Japan.

The announcement on August 14 of the meeting of President Roosevelt and Winston Churchill and the text of the Atlantic Charter, together with the text of the joint Roosevelt-Churchill message to Stalin made public the next day, indicated how far-reaching the joint policy and action of Great Britain and the United States had become. Moreover, it indicated that in the stress of this great crisis, it had been found necessary for Great Britain to enter into and carry through negotiations of the utmost importance to the whole British Commonwealth, without it being possible for the dominions to participate directly. The dominion prime ministers had indeed been informed in advance of the Atlantic Conference, and they received the text of the declaration well in

---

[50] Sir Frederick Stewart, Minister of External Affairs in the Australian House, November 28, 1940, *Current Notes of the Ministry of External Affairs,* December 1, 1940.

[51] *New York Times,* July 24, 1941.

advance of its publication; but they were not invited to attend the meeting.[52]

The dominions had individually expressed their concurrence in the Atlantic Charter and the action following it. They were to give formal approval in the second meeting of the Council of Allied Governments in London on September 24 in St. James's Palace. The resolutions adopted by that Council, as on the occasion of its first meeting on June 12, 1941, constituted a joint act in a common British Empire foreign policy. It was an act, as Winston Churchill put it in his speech on June 12, of " the servants of the ancient British monarchy and the accredited representatives of the British dominions beyond the seas, of Canada, Australia, New Zealand and South Africa, of the Empire of India, of Burma and of our colonies in every quarter of the globe."

Here too something more than a joint Empire policy was involved. The common policy extended to all the Allies and to the U.S.S.R. But in relation to the U.S.S.R., as in relation to the United States, Great Britain was forced to take action with which the other nations of the British Commonwealth could not be formally associated. On occasion it was not even possible to consult them in advance. Mr. Churchill's important speech a few hours after Russia's entry into the war had to be delivered without the possibility of consultation with the dominions; and the Anglo-Soviet Pact signed on July 12, 1941, in Moscow was in form a pact between " His Majesty's Government in the United Kingdom " and the U.S.S.R. But as Winston Churchill announced to the House of Commons three days later, it was " a solemn agreement between the British and Russian Governments carrying with it the full assent of the British and Russian people and of the great dominions of the Crown for united action against a common foe."

More and more as Britain and America assumed the leadership of the United Nations, Britain found it necessary to take action with which the dominions were not formally associated, though rarely if ever without informing them of the action intended. The pattern which, therefore, emerges so far in the war is that of rings within rings. There is an inner ring of the common foreign policy of the British Commonwealth; a second, middle ring of common foreign policy of the English-speaking peoples grown still more definite with the entry of the United States into the war. A third, outer ring began to take shape in 1940 and 1941 in the

---

[52] The reason was not merely that the conference was a personal one, but that a wider conference would have made the necessary secrecy impossible.

group of Allied nations in London under British leadership; it widened with the entry of the U.S.S.R. into the war and came full circle when Japan's entry on the side of the Axis united the Far Eastern and the European wars into a single world war. Thus was born the United Nations.

IV · EMPIRE DIPLOMATIC SYSTEM

The war has seen a marked development of the system whereby the Governments of the British Commonwealth are represented in one another's capitals by high commissioners. The direct relations between ministers of the Crown in different parts of the Empire by means of personal visits and by telephone, telegram, and dispatch, are now supplemented by a well developed intra-Empire diplomatic system.

The conditions of war make it important that the contact between governments through diplomatic representatives should be closer and more speedy than in peace. The diplomatic representatives must be men of such standing and experience that they can act with the utmost speed in establishing direct contact between cabinet and cabinet and in getting things done with the least possible red tape. It is for this reason that London, in its relation with the dominions during the war, has changed over from career men (mainly high officials of the Dominions Office) as high commissioners to high commissioners of cabinet rank, who might even, in special cases, continue to hold their status of minister of the Crown in their new post. It was the same consideration which determined the action of the British Government in appointing Lord Halifax, a member of the War Cabinet, as Ambassador in Washington. Though Ambassador, he formally retains his rank as a member of the War Cabinet; and when he returned on a visit to England in August 1941 he resumed, as Mr. Churchill had indicated on his appointment, " his full functions and responsibilities as a Minister of the Crown." [53] In the same way, Mr. Malcolm MacDonald, who for nearly a decade had been Secretary of State for the dominions or colonies, was sent as High Commissioner to Ottawa, Sir Ronald Cross, formerly Minister of Shipping, to Canberra, and Lord Harlech (Mr. Ormsby-Gore), formerly Secretary of State for the Colonies, to Pretoria. The United Kingdom is also represented by high commissioners in Dublin and Wellington.

This tendency was carried further in 1941 by the stationing, in two important areas of regional defense, of ministers of cabinet rank, but

[53] Speech to the Pilgrims, January 9, 1941.

without portfolio, to represent and advise the War Cabinet, and to co-ordinate political, military, and economic arrangements in connection with the war. Mr. Duff-Cooper was sent to Singapore to improve co-ordination among British territories and civil and military authorities in the Far East. Captain Oliver Lyttelton was sent in a similar capacity to the Near East.[54] His successor, Mr. R. G. Casey, former Australian Federal Treasurer and Minister in Washington, was made on appointment Minister of State with a seat in the British War Cabinet.

The same tendency to appoint Cabinet ministers to key positions is shown by the action of the Australian Government in sending to Washington Mr. Casey, whose status was that of second in command in the Cabinet, and the sending by New Zealand to a similar post of its Deputy Prime Minister, Mr. Walter Nash. By a special act of the New Zealand Parliament both Mr. Nash and Mr. Langstone, the New Zealand High Commissioner in Ottawa, retained their seats in the Cabinet.

While, from a formal point of view, the change-over to high commissioners of Cabinet rank may not be great, its practical importance is very considerable. As an official put it privately in Ottawa, Mr. Malcolm MacDonald can lift the receiver of the telephone without hesitation and talk directly with Mr. Mackenzie King and Mr. Winston Churchill; whereas a man whose career had been that of an official might think twice before taking any such step. But such arrangements are likely to be of a temporary character, not carried on beyond the period of the war, since men of Cabinet rank will probably wish to return again to their political careers. The war has brought about a considerable expansion of the functions and the personnel of the High Commissioner's Office in Ottawa, necessitating the creation for the first time of a new post of Deputy High Commissioner.

These British high commissioners are appointed by the Dominions Office, and not, as ambassadors are, by the King on the advice of the Foreign Office. Their functions are of a quasi-diplomatic character; and in some cases, as in Ottawa, they have on their staffs officials seconded from the Foreign Office as well as the Dominions Office. The high commissioners, by whom the members of the British Commonwealth are represented in one another's capitals, form a kind of private Empire diplomatic system distinct from the diplomatic representatives of foreign powers. In the *Annual Report of the Canadian Secretary of State for*

---

[54] See below p. 72. Lord Swinton went to West Africa as Resident Minister in June 1942; and in December, Mr. Harold Macmillan to North Africa and Col. J. J. Llewellin to Washington — each as a Resident Minister of Cabinet rank.

External Affairs (1940) " the Representatives in Canada of Other Governments of His Majesty " are listed in one annex; while a separate annex is devoted to " Diplomatic Representatives in Canada," comprising the ministers of the United States, France, Japan, Belgium, and the Netherlands (to which are being added ministers for China, the Argentine, Brazil, and Chile). For the purpose of precedence, the high commissioners rank in relation to one another in the order in which their countries appear in the Statute of Westminster, 1931 (namely, United Kingdom, Dominion of Canada, Commonwealth of Australia, Dominion of New Zealand, Union of South Africa, Eire), and not in accordance with the date of formation of the office or of appointment of the individual. In Ottawa, as in London, high commissioners are exempt from the payment of customs and income taxes; they do not possess, however, the general legal immunities to which foreign diplomatic representatives are entitled.[55]

As regards the high commissioners of the dominions in London, the war has accentuated a change already marked in the prewar years. Whereas formerly they were mainly concerned with financial and trade matters, they now deal also with political issues, especially in relation to foreign affairs, the conduct of negotiations with the British Government, and defense. With the creation of the Pacific War Council on February 9, 1942, in which the dominions have been represented by their high commissioners, the political character of this office became marked.

The work of the dominion high commissioners in London has expanded in connection with defense and matters of an economic and financial character relating to the war. Their work has increased also as a result of the creation of separate dominion organizations to deal with dominion troops and air forces in England, and, in the case of Canada, the stationing in England of a representative (with staff) of the Department of Munitions and Supply. But this expansion is of less importance comparatively than in the First World War. This is partly because of the very frequent visits of Canadian Cabinet ministers to London and the transaction by them of the most important business connected with the war.[56] In this war, too, transactions involving Canada and the United Kingdom are being carried out in considerable measure in Ot-

[55] *The British Empire*, Royal Institute of International Affairs, p. 188. The accrediting of Mr. S. M. Bruce as Australian Minister to the Netherlands Government in London gives him a double status as member of both the Empire and the foreign diplomatic corps.

[56] The fact that 246 diplomatic bags were sent by Canada House in London to Ottawa during 1940, in comparison with 84 during 1939 illustrates the increase in the business of the high commissioners' offices. *Annual Report of the Canadian Secretary of State for External Affairs, 1940*.

tawa rather than in London. In Ottawa there is for this purpose almost the beginnings of a skeleton British Civil Service, with representatives from a number of government departments empowered with a greater autonomy and authority to make decisions than would normally be the case. This is true to a far greater degree in Washington, where there is a whole series of special missions and other agencies staffed by large numbers of British and dominion officials from a variety of government departments and empowered to make on-the-spot decisions of considerable importance. Close relations are maintained with the ministries in London by cables numbering several hundreds a day. Ministerial coordination and supervision are maintained to some extent through the British Supply Council presided over by the Resident Minister who with the Ambassador, Lord Halifax, exercises general jurisdiction over this organization. From the point of view of munitions and supply, Ottawa and Washington are playing a greater part than was the case in 1914–18; so also are Delhi, Canberra, Wellington, and Pretoria.

The closeness and the frequency of the contacts of the dominion high commissioners in London with members of the British Government, as well as with one another, have increased considerably during the war. It has been the custom during the war for the high commissioners of the dominions to meet together daily each afternoon with the Secretary of State for the Dominions, and in his room at the Dominions Office. The value of this development is that the Dominions Secretary, who since February 1942 has been a member of the War Cabinet, informs the Cabinet of any point arising in his discussions with the high commissioners pertinent to the matters under consideration by the Cabinet. But this is perhaps of less importance than the other purposes which these meetings serve. The Dominions Secretary also reports back to the high commissioners for transmission to their governments on the matters discussed and the decisions taken in the War Cabinet relating to the conduct of the war. He is able also to make known to the high commissioners the views of the British Government on any matter. These daily meetings are entirely informal and without minutes and secretaries.

How far these daily meetings of Dominions Secretary and high commissioners can fulfill some of the functions of an Imperial Conference depends on the standing of the high commissioners and their power to represent the views of their governments. Most of them are not at present men of Cabinet rank. Some can usually express only their personal views. Only one or two are able to speak habitually for their governments.

The functions and the importance of this new element in Commonwealth machinery fluctuate according to circumstances and are thus difficult to assess. They vary from time to time and from high commissioner to high commissioner. While the holding of daily meetings became a fixed practice during the war, it originated some years before the war. The practice appears to have begun about the time of Mr. Malcolm MacDonald's tenure of the Dominions Office. In all the international crises, as well as during the abdication crisis, daily meetings of the high commissioners were held in the Dominions Office; sometimes twice a day. During the Munich crisis long meetings were held beyond midnight. With the war, crises became continuous and the meetings became a matter of daily routine. Among the other wartime functions falling upon the offices of the high commissioners in London is participation in the Empire Clearing House set up in April 1942 to cooperate with the Combined Raw Materials Board in Washington.

The development of a system of high commissioners as between the dominions themselves is one of permanent importance which would have come in any case even without the stimulus of the war. South Africa sent an " Accredited Representative " to Ottawa in 1938. This was followed in 1939 by the appointment of a high commissioner from Eire. On September 11, 1939, a week after the outbreak of the war, the Prime Minister of Canada announced in the House of Commons the decision of the Government to appoint high commissioners in Australia, New Zealand, South Africa, and Eire. In welcoming this development on September 12 the spokesman of the Australian Government explained to Parliament that this was not merely a crisis measure but " a natural corollary in the present structure of the British Commonwealth to the exchange of High Commissioners between the Dominions and the United Kingdom." [57] Canada is as yet the only dominion which has completed its intra-Empire system of diplomatic representation, the others being represented only in London and Ottawa.

The announcement on July 21, 1941, by the India Office in London of an exchange of representatives between India and the United States " in the special circumstances of the war," together with the announcement some weeks previously of an agreement for the exchange of ministers between the United States and New Zealand, completed the chain of British Empire diplomatic representation at Washington. When this development began fifteen years ago with the appointment of a minister

[57] *J. P. E.*, Vol. XX, p. 941.

of the Irish Free State, followed by ministers of Canada and South Africa, the opinion was current in Washington that it would weaken the structure of the British Empire. The British Ambassador, in announcing to the Secretary of State of the United States the proposed arrangements for appointment of a minister of the Irish Free State in Washington, indicated that they " would not denote any departure from the principle of the diplomatic unity of the Empire." [58] This phrase, " diplomatic unity of the Empire," was qualified five years later in 1929 in a letter by the British Ambassador in Berlin to the German Minister of Foreign Affairs by the words, " that is to say the principle of consultative cooperation amongst all His Majesty's Representatives, as amongst His Majesty's Governments themselves, in matters of common concern." The British Ambassador then expressed the trust of His Majesty's Government in the Irish Free State that the establishment of an Irish legation would not only promote cordial relations between the Irish Free State and Germany " but also between Germany and the whole British Commonwealth of Nations." [59] These formulae have now become standard. The experience of nearly two decades has shown that the existence of dominion ministers at Washington has not impaired this principle. As Mr. Menzies has put it, the appointment of ministers in foreign capitals has been an addition to, and not a subtraction from, the diplomatic strength of Britain.

The interdependence of the countries of the Commonwealth has been strengthened rather than weakened by the close contacts with Washington due to the present war. The American Government has found it both convenient and necessary to deal with the British Commonwealth as a whole in many matters such as the allocation to different countries of material under the Lend-Lease Act. The British Commonwealth organization, which was built up for this purpose before American entry into the war, was the British Supply Council in North America; under it was the British Purchasing Commission, with subsidiary organizations, such as the Empire and Allied Requirements Committee on which were representatives of every country in the Empire.

This tendency for Britain to act on behalf of the dominions as leader of the British democracies in relation to the United States of America

---

[58] Letter of Sir Esmé Howard dated July 24, 1924; A. Lawrence Lowell and H. Duncan Hall, *The British Commonwealth of Nations,* World Peace Foundation, 1927.

[59] Letter of the British Ambassador in Berlin to the German Minister of Foreign Affairs, June 9, 1929, regarding the appointment of an Irish Minister. A. Berriedale Keith: *Speeches and Documents on the British Dominions, 1918–1931.*

was strongly emphasized by the setting-up of the Anglo-American war organization at Washington, and the parallel organization in London, in January 1942 as a result of the agreement between President Roosevelt and Mr. Churchill.[60] This organization, comprising the Combined Chiefs of Staffs Group, the Munitions Assignments Board, the Combined Shipping Adjustment Board, and the Combined Raw Materials Board, was Anglo-American; the dominions were not represented directly, though they had ready access to it through special liaison officers and representation on various committees. The Commonwealth Supply Council (incorporating the Empire Clearing House), composed of representatives of all Empire governments, was set up later in London to plan and coordinate certain aspects of Commonwealth production and requirements in cooperation with the Combined Boards in Washington.

Twenty years of participation in international affairs by the dominions has created something which did not exist in 1914, and which has added to the strength and cohesion of the British Commonwealth. It has built up in the dominions what formerly existed only in Britain, a body of men possessing a wide experience of the world outside their own countries, of cabinet ministers and ex-ministers, members of Parliament, diplomats and officials in the various government departments, and men holding responsible positions in commerce, journalism, and other fields. Their training ground has been partly in the international political and technical gatherings in Geneva under the League of Nations and International Labor Office, partly in international conferences held in London and elsewhere, partly in Imperial conferences, in conferences of Empire parliaments held under the auspices of the Empire Parliamentary Association in each of the capitals of the Empire, in intra-Imperial committees or conferences of a technical character and in the foreign services of each part of the Empire. Voluntary organizations for the scientific study of international affairs, such as the closely interconnected Institutes of International Affairs in each part of the Empire, have also played their part in this process.

V · EMPIRE COMMUNICATIONS AND EXCHANGE OF INFORMATION ON FOREIGN AFFAIRS

Despite the war, and the difficulty of communication involved in it, the stream of information, by cable and in documentary form, flowing out from Whitehall, continues during the war in greater volume

---

[60] Cmd. 6332, 1942. See above, pp. 37 and 50.

than ever. The extent of the documentation involved at moments of the greatest pressure was indicated by the Secretary of State for the Dominions, Mr. Malcolm MacDonald, on November 1, 1938, in the House of Commons. He gave the House information regarding the working of the system as laid down by Imperial Conferences, whereby " the Dominion Governments were kept constantly informed by telegraph of the information at the disposal of the United Kingdom Government as well as of the Government's policy regarding foreign affairs." The number of circular telegrams so sent to each of the Dominion Governments on foreign affairs since the beginning of 1938 (ten months) had been 398, of which some 150 were sent during the month of September alone.[61] As indicated above, this is more than an information service containing all the information available to the British Government, including the most secret. In dispatching a document the Foreign Office may ask whether the dominions have any views to express and, on occasion, whether they concur in an action which London proposes to take.

Since the building up of this system at the end of the First World War, the dominions have made available to the Foreign Office such information on foreign affairs as they had available from their own sources. They have also, though somewhat spasmodically, made such information available from time to time to each other. The interchange of high commissioners between Ottawa and the other Dominion capitals has begun to increase the exchange of information on foreign affairs between the governments.

This system of interchange of confidential state documents and information on foreign affairs is unique. There is no parallel to it anywhere in the field of international relations. It did not and could not exist between the members of the League of Nations. Only rarely and in a limited degree have allied nations been able to put all their cards in each other's hands. The system even goes beyond any confidential interchanges between a foreign office, like the State Department of the United States, and its ambassadors and ministers in foreign capitals. That this stream of documents should issue constantly from London to half a dozen capitals in the British Empire (with somewhat smaller streams passing in the reverse direction and between each two of these capitals), and that leakages of confidential documents or information should be exceedingly rare, is a remarkable tribute to the administrative efficiency

---

[61] *J. P. E.*, Vol. XX, p. 29.

and the quality of the personnel of the civil services and ministers of the Crown concerned. Such a system could not possibly exist in a society whose members did not have complete confidence in each other's good faith and good will. It could exist, therefore, only as between nations in an intimate family group such as the British Commonwealth.

After Dunkirk and the fall of Singapore, there was some interruption in the air-mail services, which now form one of the most important parts of the communications system of the British Commonwealth; (there were no such services in the First World War). These services still function regularly by commercial planes or bombers between all dominion capitals and London and cover many of the colonial territories in Asia and Africa. Indeed, there is now available, by means of the bombers being flown across the Atlantic and the return ferry service for pilots, a daily air-mail service which brings Ottawa as close to London for air-mail purposes as it is to Washington. And on both sides of the Atlantic full advantage is being taken of this service for the transport of state documents as well as ministers and officials on missions in connection with the war. The air-mail services available to some of the other dominions are less frequent than before the war, but adequate enough when supplemented by an extensive use of the cable and telephone. It is the fixed practice of the foreign offices of the British Commonwealth and their foreign services, for reasons of secrecy and security, to entrust diplomatic bags only to ships and planes of British and dominion registry. On occasion, however, official documents may be sent by other channels, e.g., American ships or clipper planes, entrusted to a " safe hand," i.e., a person, usually an official, carrying an official letter indicating that he is charged with responsibility for the delivery in person of state documents. For the same reason of secrecy, only a limited use is made of the telephone as a means of official communication between capitals of the British Commonwealth, or between them and their embassies or legations abroad. But on special occasions where the prime ministers have had to discuss matters of a complex and urgent character the telephone has been used freely and effectively.

All this serves to emphasize that the British is a maritime Empire. It came into being because Britain was a sea power. Its peculiar organization is in no small degree due to the fact of its being a maritime Empire; and safe communications by ships, by submarine, cable, and by air services using the same sea lanes as the ships use, and the same ports upon them, are vital to its continued existence.

The war has revealed some small difficulties in the organization of the existing machinery of cooperation which it should be comparatively easy to remedy. Even before the war, complaints were sometimes made that the machinery for the transmission of information from the Foreign Office to the external affairs departments and vice versa was too unwieldy, and that it occasioned frequent delay both in the transmission of information to the dominions and the transmission of dispatches from the departments of external affairs of the Dominions to the Foreign Office. These channels, at the London end, comprise the Dominions Information Department of the Foreign Office, and the Foreign Affairs Department of the Dominions Office, with subsidiary channels through the high commissioner of the dominion concerned and, in the case of Australia, through the liaison officer maintained in London by the Department of External Affairs. At the dominion end the inward communications go directly, except in the case of Australia, to the external affairs department. With the appointment of British high commissioners in the dominion capitals, there has developed a tendency, especially during the war, for London to use its high commissioners in the dominions as a channel for the transmission of documents or information, particularly those involving discussion, to the Prime Minister or the department of external affairs. In the case of Australia there is an additional complication due to the fact that the External Affairs Department is not administered by the Prime Minister, as in Canada, South Africa, and New Zealand, but as a separate ministry. Outgoing communications from Australia pass through the Prime Minister's Department to the Dominion's Office in London, and this additional complication has caused some criticism in Australia.

Apart from the purely official and departmental methods of communication which facilitate cooperation between the governments of the Empire in the conduct of foreign affairs, other steps towards unity of policy are the appearance of the Empire Parliamentary Association's quarterly foreign affairs report and the formation in each dominion parliament of an all-party study group on international affairs. Though groups of this character were established shortly before the war in the parliaments of the Australian Commonwealth, New Zealand, and the Union of South Africa, under the auspices of the Empire Parliamentary Association, it was not until the war had started and a further stimulus had been given to the study of external relations, that a similar group was formed in the Canadian Parliament at

Ottawa. These groups receive special information relating to the war and international affairs and they meet from time to time to hear confidential talks from experts specially qualified to deal with some aspect of foreign affairs. Both in helping forward the war effort and in providing machinery which will tend towards uniformity of action in dealing with international affairs and post-war problems, the groups may serve a most important purpose. The linking together of these groups by personal contact and conference, and through the Canadian group or the Parliament at Westminster, the forging of a link with the foreign affairs committees of the American Congress, are possible wartime developments.

While some of the sources of authoritative information, such as the reports previously sent by ambassadors or ministers from enemy countries or enemy-controlled countries, have now dried up, these have in some measure been replaced by reports gathered by the intelligence services. One new source of information is available which did not exist in any previous war, namely, the reports of the Monitoring Service of the British Broadcasting Corporation and the secret intelligence reports based upon the analysis by experts of the material received by the Monitoring Service. The purpose of these reports, which supplement the work of the ordinary intelligence service, is to work back from the words used as instruments of war by the Axis propaganda ministries and their satellites in occupied territory. In the matter of defense against the psychological war of the enemy and in the conduct of the counter-offensive, the dominions are necessarily dependent on Great Britain. Great Britain alone is in a position to maintain a central Empire staff in the radio war, and armies of listeners, translators, and central intelligence officers. The dominions have neither the resources nor the physical possibility of receiving in their territories one of the most essential parts of the total enemy propaganda, namely, that constituted by the long and medium wave broadcasts of the European stations, nor can they receive the Russian broadcasts other than short wave. A branch Monitoring and Broadcasting Service of the B.B.C. was, however, set up late in 1941 at Singapore, which received all broadcasts from Asiatic countries available in Singapore and itself broadcast in some sixteen languages.

Empire broadcasting as a means of informing and strengthening the public opinion on which the foreign policy of a democracy must rest, has played an extremely important part in this war. In the years immediately before the war, and during the war itself, the Empire Broadcasting Service of the British Broadcasting Corporation has increased enormously in importance. On an all-Empire hook-up the voices of the King and of political leaders reach into every household. Hundreds of thousands of short wave sets are tuned in daily all over the Empire to the B.B.C. short wave programs, particularly the news broadcasts. For example, these broadcasts are listened to by a very large portion of the English-speaking population of South Africa, particularly in their rebroadcast form over the South African stations. Three of the B.B.C. news bulletins and some of the talks in English are rebroadcast daily by South African stations. At the request of the Australian Broadcasting Commission, two of the B.B.C. news bulletins were rebroadcast daily by the Singapore station. The dominions themselves have been extending their short wave transmissions; Australia has set up a powerful station capable of transmissions throughout the world. Rebroadcasting facilities are also being developed in a number of the British colonies in the shape of medium wave transmissions.

We have traced here only part of the machinery of cooperation which knits together the Empire. There is, in a sense, far more than one Empire diplomatic system; there are many different systems of liaison. There is the system of military, air, and naval attachés of different parts of the Empire operating to maintain liaison for the defense services in London, Washington, and Ottawa. With the setting-up of the Pacific War Councils in London and Washington, and of the joint Anglo-American bodies to deal with strategy, shipping, supplies, the service liaison maintained by the dominions in London and Washington has been greatly extended by appointment of high-ranking officers to carry out these functions.

The importance of such liaisons between the principal departments dealing with external relations was emphasized by Sir Earle Page, Australian representative in the British War Cabinet, in a statement issued in London on January 14, 1942. The statement sums up the conclusions emerging from a close examination of the working of the system of Empire consultation. The chief defect in the machinery he found to be that consultations on the political or horizontal plane, i.e., between cabinet ministers, were not backed up by enough consultations on the vertical or administrative plane. Close and continuous contact between Government departments in London and the dominions " at a lower plane than the ministerial level and at a stage when foreign policy and strategy are still in a fluid form " is essential, he thought to insure effective consultations between the Prime Ministers or their deputies. The remedy he suggests is " a more active and complete system of liaison covering not only foreign policy (such as the Australian liaison officer attached to the Foreign Office) but also the three fighting services, as well as supply and economic relations." There was a great deal of consultation on the administrative plane between London and Washington from January 1942 onwards — probably more than within the Empire, owing to the large number of British officials stationed at Washington. Adequate consultation on this plane is essential as a permanent element in the peacetime machinery of the Empire as well as in Anglo-American relations.

There is growing also an important liaison between the councils of scientific and industrial research in different parts of the Empire and in the United States. For example, Great Britain has such a liaison officer attached to the National Research Council in Canada. In view of the importance of science from the point of view of the war, scientific missions have been dispatched by Great Britain and Australia to the United States, and American scientific missions have been sent to London. Moreover, there are the beginnings of a system of scientific attachés at the legations in certain of the capitals. In 1941, Canada sent a scientific attaché to Canada House in London, and an Australian scientific attaché was sent to the Legation in Washington.[62]

The machinery involved in the coordination of the production and distribution of the supplies required for the conduct of the war, and the coordination of the economic war now being waged on a common world front by each part of the Empire, would require a chapter of its own. How intricate is the problem of such coordination even within the limits of each part of the Empire is shown in some of the chapters which follow.

6. Coordinated Defense and Unity of Command

I · THE SYSTEM OF COORDINATED DEFENSE AND ITS WORKING

The British Commonwealth in normal times has no centralized defense system, no common navy, army, or air force, except in so far as

---

[62] Great Britain sent Dr. Darwin, Director of the National Physical Laboratory " as Director of a Central Intelligence Office working under the direction of the British Supply Council in North America to collaborate with United States research bodies." This mission is closely linked with Canada. The United States sent Dr. Conant, the President of Harvard University, to establish " a corresponding mission in Great Britain." Lord Hankey, 118 H. L. Deb., 5 s., c. 993.

the forces of the United Kingdom, and above all the Navy, are able to provide some measure of defense for the whole Empire. But, even in times of peace, the forces of the whole Empire are coordinated in such a way that, if the nations take a decision to make war together, these forces can intermesh smoothly and without friction, to form a common navy, a common air force, and a common army. In time of war, unified command of the armed forces in the field, including air and naval forces, is a matter of course. But even in time of war there is no centralized command or control with authority over all the land or air forces, or even of all the naval forces, of the British Empire. The unified command set up for the forces operating together in the field does not extend to those in the home bases, especially in the dominions. Even the forces of India and the dependent Empire, although under the supreme authority of Great Britain, cannot be considered as merely reinforcements of the British Army; but rather as localized systems of defense in a world-wide complex.

The basic principles of the defense systems of the various parts of the Empire are twofold: First, that each part shall provide in the first instance, as far as it is able to do so, for its own local defense; second, that its forces shall take part in the common defense of the British Commonwealth, when and to the extent its government and legislature so decide. The conception that the defense forces of one member should be available for the defense of the other parts of the Commonwealth is more highly developed in some places than in others. Only in the case of Great Britain is it taken completely for granted that the forces of the United Kingdom shall be available for the defense of the Empire as a whole.

The defense system of the British Empire consists therefore of a number of separately organized forces under the control of autonomous states; although there is a strong assumption that because of their family bond and common interests they will assist one another in time of need, they have not made express commitments in advance to render such assistance. Such a system necessitates a high degree of liaison and coordination if it is to work at all. The system worked out in the British Commonwealth, especially at the Imperial Defense Conferences of 1909 and 1911, of planning defense to ensure in advance such a high degree of coordination that the separate forces can be fitted instantly together and become parts of a homogeneous Imperial army and navy, is one of its most interesting and effective institutions. This system is in operation in all parts of the British Empire, except Eire, which decided not to train and equip its forces on the common lines. Under the Anglo-Egyptian Treaty of Alliance signed on August 26, 1936, the system was extended in part to Egypt.[63]

In time of peace the higher political liaison between the defense forces of the Empire is secured largely through the Imperial conferences, which devote a large part of their discussions to defense matters, and sometimes through special Imperial defense conferences. During the war there has been continuous consultation by telephone, cable, and visits by the responsible ministers, including the exchange of special missions.[63a] The Defense Committee of the British War Cabinet (the wartime form of the Committee of Imperial Defense), expanded from time to time to include visiting dominion ministers, has been the principal coordinating agency during the war. On the side of strategy and technique, liaison is maintained by constant consultations between the defense and supply ministries and the general staffs, especially at London.

In reporting to the House of Commons on the "astonishing story of comradeship in arms of the free citizens of the British Empire" in the African campaigns of this war, Lord Croft, Under-Secretary of State for War, said, "These campaigns had been truly Imperial, and troops of the Commonwealth of Australia, New Zealand, the Union of South Africa, Rhodesia, the African Colonies and the Sudan, along with the British troops and fine divisions from India had written great fresh chapters in British military history."[64]

Not the least part of the "astonishing story" was the fact that these units from the five ends of the earth, composed of different races and traditions, should have fitted instantly together and worked like a single well-oiled machine. No mere unity in the high command could have achieved such a result. Despite differences of external appearance in color, language, headdress, and uniform, each force had been trained with the idea that it was destined to form part of a single army. They had learned from the same army manuals. Their training and discipline had been on common lines. Their higher officers had been trained in the same higher staff colleges; they shared a common military doctrine and tradition, and many of them knew each other. As far as possible

---

[63] A letter attached to the treaty provides that " in view of the possible necessity of cooperative action between the British and Egyptian forces, the armament and equipment, land and air, of the Egyptian forces shall not differ in type from those of the British forces."

[63a] See above, pp. 47–55.

[64] *J. P. E.*, Vol. XXII, p. 185.

their equipment was on standard lines; the same rifles and machine guns and artillery, taking the same spare parts and the same ammunition. An Australian and a New Zealander, a Sikh, a South African, and a Scotch Highlander, could go to the same ammunition dump and find cartridges that fitted all the rifles and the machine guns and field artillery. The cartridges were the standard .303 — not the .300, with the little difference on the rim, taken by the standard American rifle. As these two cartridges are not interchangeable, American troops, fighting alongside of the Empire forces in Australia and elsewhere, have to be supplied from separate ammunition dumps.

The Committee of Imperial Defense. In the matter of its Imperial defense organization on the strategic and the technical side, the British Commonwealth was far from being planless and improvised. Even before 1914 there was a high degree of unified planning and uniformity of administrative practice in its defense system. On the naval side the British Admiralty planned for the defense of the Empire as a whole, its guiding principle being that of the strategic unity of the Empire on the basis of sea power. But it was the Committee of Imperial Defense which planned for all aspects of defense for the whole Empire. In this body the Empire possessed an efficient organization, typically British in its absence of a written constitution, and in its power to achieve far-reaching results with the minimum of formal machinery and an almost complete absence of publicity. It was the Committee of Imperial Defense which before 1914 planned with remarkable precision and incorporated in the War Book the action to be taken in the event of war. From time to time official reports and speeches have thrown some light upon its working. Lord Balfour and Lord Haldane referred to it in speeches in the House of Lords, in June 1926. They revealed that the chiefs of staff, who had already learned through their work in the committee to consult not merely from the point of view of their own departments but of " the common defense of the Empire," would now have this duty formally imposed upon them by the Warrant of their appointment. Lord Haldane, as one who had had almost a lifelong contact with the Committee, not only on its political side, but also with its technical subcommittees,[65] gave some details of its working in relation to the dominions. The Committee, he pointed out, had purposely been kept purely advisory in character, subject only to the Prime

---

[65] At that time they numbered about thirty, and they have since been multiplied.

Minister, in order that the dominions should feel perfectly free to co-operate with it. Not being afraid of encroachment on their autonomy by an Imperial executive authority, they would be able to send their staff representatives to take part freely in the deliberations of the Committee when summoned to it. Since the war of 1914–18, representatives of Australia and New Zealand have frequently been present at the meetings of the Committee and have asked for and received advice on their defense problems. The other dominions, such as Canada, at least in recent years, refrained for political reasons from attending meetings of the Committee. But without being represented at its sessions the Defense Departments of both Canada and South Africa appear to have consulted freely with it. Here, as in the case of the higher political machinery of the Empire, the still lingering traces of political immaturity, from a psychological point of view, revealed in the attitude of the Dominions, had prevented the building up of an entirely adequate system of defense cooperation. During the present war, as at the beginning of the last war, the Committee of Imperial Defense has become the Defense Committee of the Cabinet.[66]

Unity in the Higher Command. An important element in the efficient coordination of Empire defense in time of peace has been supplied by the interchange of officers between the different defense forces and the common training provided by the Imperial Defense College. Before and during the war, officers from the three services of the United Kingdom have been attached to units in the dominions and vice versa. Part of the training of some Australian and New Zealand officers has been secured in the army in India. These interchanges have extended not only to the army but also to the navies and air force. The Imperial Defense College was set up in 1927. " Its purpose," in Lord Haldane's words in the speech referred to above, " was the training of the super-staffs, the higher elements of the staffs in the three Services," in the principles of Imperial strategy in their broadest aspects. The College has played an important part in the training of military, naval, and air officers from all the dominions (except Eire) and from India. Civilian officials, e.g., the Secretary of the Defense Department in Australia, have also passed through

---

[66] The Committee consists in normal peace times of the Prime Minister and persons summoned by him to the meetings. In practice, the ministers for the various defense departments and their principal advisors, the Chancellor of the Exchequer and the secretaries of State for Home Affairs, Foreign Affairs, the Dominions and Colonies, and India, are usually summoned to attend plenary sessions of the Committee.

the training of the College. The leaders of the armies of Great Britain and the dominions are thus largely men who have passed through the Imperial Defense College as instructors or students. For example, the two senior generals in the Canadian Army, Lieutenant-General Mc-Naughton and Major General Crerar, worked together in the Imperial Defense College with General Sir Archibald Wavell, Commander-in-Chief in India, Sir Alan Brooke, Commander of the Home Forces in England, with whom the Canadian Corps is serving, and General Sir John Dill, formerly Chief of the Imperial General Staff, later a member of the Combined Chiefs of Staffs Group in Washington. They were not only trained together, but came to form an inner group as experts in the new mechanized warfare, sharing identical strategical and tactical views. These are factors of incomparable importance from the point of view of the future campaigns of the war in the different areas in which the various Imperial Armies must operate.

The system of unity of command adopted in the present war in the different campaign areas is much the same as that adopted in the war of 1914–18. The system as it applied to the Australian forces in the different areas was summed up as follows by the Acting Prime Minister of Australia: [67]

> The General Officer Commanding Australian Imperial Force in Malaya commanded and administered all Australian Imperial Force units located in Malaya. Operational control was exercised by him, subject to the orders of the General Officer Commanding Malaya. The command and administration of the Australian Imperial Force, Middle East, was exercised by the General Officer Commanding, Australian Imperial Forces, Middle East, on the same basis. The Royal Australian Air Force units located at Singapore were under the operational control and direction of the Commander-in-Chief, Far East.

The situation appears to be in principle the same in respect of all the dominion military and air forces operating in Great Britain and in the other areas mentioned. As the Canadian Prime Minister explained to the men of the First Canadian Division on August 26, 1941, the retention of the Canadian troops in England was due solely to strategic reasons and not to any limitation imposed upon their use by the Canadian Government. "So far," he explained, "as the disposition of troops is concerned, the Canadian Government places no restriction

[67] *J. P. E.*, XXII, p. 268.

whatever upon any decision that may be made, other than that the Government itself shall have the opportunity of knowing what is contemplated and an opportunity of expressing its views." [68] This may be said to sum up the situation in respect of all the dominions. The principal difference between the situation in the present war and the First World War is the adherence, from the outset, as regards the military forces, and as far as practicable in respect of the air forces, to the principle of organizing dominion forces in their own separate divisions, army corps, and air squadrons.

It is not yet possible to judge how far this situation will be modified by the entrance of the United States into the war. In Australia supreme command over land and sea forces of the United Nations in the South Pacific was assumed by General MacArthur in mid-March with Lieutenant General George H. Brett of the United States Army in command of all air forces operating in Australia. A week later, Lieutenant General Sir Thomas Blamey (Australian) was appointed Commander in Chief of the United Nations land forces in Australia.

II · THE COMMON EMPIRE NAVY AND THE WORLD CHAIN OF NAVAL AND AIR BASES

The dominions have always steadfastly refused to accept the principle of a single Imperial navy, although none of them has maintained naval forces of sufficient strength to give them adequate naval defense without the assistance of the British Navy. The dominion ministers rejected an Admiralty memorandum circulated to the Imperial War Conference of 1918 proposing " a single navy at all times under a central naval authority." But they agreed, in a joint memorandum of reply, that the principles of coordination already being followed — namely, " the character of construction, armament and equipment, and the methods and principles of training, administration, and organization, should proceed upon the same lines in all the navies of the Empire." [69] These principles have been followed without deviation. The principle of unity of command in time of war had already been accepted in the Naval Agreement of 1911; and in accordance with this Agreement the ships of the Royal Australian Navy and of the New Zealand Division of the Royal Navy (now the Royal New Zealand Navy) were transferred to the control of the British Admiralty at the outbreak of the war. The same ap-

[68] *New York Times,* August 28, 1941.
[69] H. Duncan Hall, *The British Commonwealth of Nations,* 1920, p. 303.

pears to have been the case with the ships of the Royal Canadian Navy operating in the Atlantic convoys, in the Caribbean and in the convoying of Australian troops. In the case of Canada, as of Australia, some of the ships have continued to operate in the waters adjacent to their shores under the immediate control of the dominion naval authorities. Units of the South African naval force cooperated with the Royal Navy in the Mediterranean off the northern coast of Africa. The Royal Indian Navy has operated under Admiralty control from the outset of the war.

In the matter of naval forces, the principle of strategic unity has been more closely adhered to than in any other branch of defense. The Royal Navy itself has always been regarded by Great Britain, and also consciously or half-consciously by the dominions, as available for the defense of all parts of the British Empire in the seven seas. This was well expressed in the important speech of the First Lord of the Admiralty, Sir Samuel Hoare, in announcing the policy of building a navy able to operate in the Eastern as well as the Western Hemisphere. " The Empire was," he said, " an oceanic Empire with world-wide communications. . . . As it was the duty of the Navy to keep open the trade routes and communications of the Empire, it was essential that the Navy should be able to carry out their duty in both the Eastern and the Western Hemisphere." [70]

How close is the coordination between the Royal Navy and the Royal Australian Navy is shown by the following details: The Australian Navy operates in time of peace under the control of the Commonwealth Naval Board. The First Naval Member of the Board is a British naval officer selected in Britain after consultation between the two governments, to serve on the Board under the Australian Government. In matters of organization, promotion, training, etc., the Royal Australian Navy operates in accordance with the King's Regulations and Admiralty Instructions. It uses only the British naval manuals for tactical training. Some of its higher officers have always hitherto been senior British naval officers. At the outbreak of the war three of its six cruisers were commanded by British naval officers. Its adherence to a common doctrine is further facilitated by the training of its higher officers in the Royal Naval Staff College and the Imperial Defense College. The Royal Australian Naval College near Melbourne trains cadets who pass later through the naval torpedo, navigation, and signal schools at Greenwich

[70] *The Times*, London, December 3, 1937.

and Portsmouth in England.[71] Officers move freely back and forth between the Australian and the British Navies. Australian officers in the present war have commanded ships of the Royal Navy in the North Sea, and British officers command ships of the Australian Navy. Ships as well as officers are interchangeable. A British ship may become part of the Australian Navy on the Australian station and a ship of the Australian Navy may operate in the British Navy (in the Home Fleet or in the various stations, such as the Mediterranean, China, and the East Indies). When so serving in time of peace or war the Australian ship is under the command of the Commander-in-Chief of the station, subject to the general strategic control of the Admiralty. Two cruisers of the Australian Navy served thus with the Royal Navy in the Mediterranean during the sanctions crisis of 1935–36.

The principle of standardization and interchangeability of equipment is carried out in great detail. The uniforms are exactly the same except that Australian naval officers have the word " Australia " in addition to the " Royal Navy " on their buttons. Promotion in one navy carries with it corresponding rank in the other navy. But standards of pay are different — and the rum ration, traditional in the British Navy, is not apparently standard in the Australian Navy.

" The United States Navy," Mr. Churchill said on January 27, 1942, " is linked in the most intimate union with the Admiralty, both in the Atlantic and the Pacific. We shall plan our naval movements together literally as if we were one fleet." But the extreme difficulty of securing strategic and tactical coordination between the squadrons of different powers, never designed to operate as a single fleet, is shown in the disaster suffered by the United Nations in the Battle of Java Sea.

The World Chain of Naval and Air Bases. It has always been recognized, as witness many passages in the reports of Imperial Conferences, that defense of sea and air communications, and the bases necessary for this purpose, are peculiarly matters of common concern. The naval forces of this oceanic Empire could not carry out their functions of keeping the sea lanes open without a vast chain of major and minor naval bases encircling the globe — with links at points such as: Portsmouth, Belfast, Halifax, Esquimalt, Bermuda, the Falkland Islands,

---

[71] The ratings in the New Zealand Division of the Royal Navy (who are New Zealanders) receive their technical training as seamen, gunners, gun layers, gunners mates, at training establishments in Australia. Incidently, it may be noted here that the majority of the New Zealand army officers have been trained in the past at the Royal Military College at Duntroon, Australia.

Freetown, Gibraltar, Malta, Aden, Bombay, Trincomalee, Singapore, Hong Kong, Kilindini, Darwin, Albany, Melbourne, Sydney, Auckland, Suva. These give the Royal Navy an effectiveness in the exercise of sea power on a world-wide scale which could not be attained by the American Navy without similar bases, even if it were several times as large as the Royal Navy. The Atlantic Naval Bases Agreement, whereby the American Navy secured a fringe of protecting bases off its entire Atlantic coast, has a certain counterpart in agreements between different members of the British Commonwealth; for example, the agreement between Great Britain and South Africa regarding the maintenance of a British Naval Base at Simonstown, at the Cape of Good Hope, and the agreements with Canada for the use of the ports of Halifax and Esquimalt. By virtue of such agreements the British Commonwealth becomes in the matter of sea power to some extent an alliance with a certain contractual basis. The First Lord of the Admiralty informed Parliament on March 25, 1941, that a complete coordinated system for the repair of naval vessels in all the main seaports of the dominions, India, and the colonies, has been developed during the course of the present war. This world-wide chain of defensive bases and repair facilities has been greatly strengthened by the throwing open to the British Navy since 1941 of the repair facilities of all the main American ports.

The importance of having a chain of air bases with adequate fueling facilities, comparable to the naval bases of the Empire, was recognized in the Imperial Conference of 1926. Such chains of bases now exist, linking up the different parts of the Empire and following in part the principal shipping routes. During the war the airdromes and airports used by the Empire Air-Mail Services have been enlarged for military purposes and considerably increased in number. If victorious, the British Empire will emerge from the war with its system of sea and air communications — by land as well as by sea — vastly strengthened and far more important to its continued existence than ever before. For reasons of military necessity full details are not yet available regarding the important further developments which have taken place since 1938, and especially during the war, to make the Pacific south of the Equator an Empire air stronghold, particularly in the area between Northern Australia, New Guinea, Fiji, and New Zealand, and also to develop strategic air routes in the region of the Indian Ocean. When the United States entered the war these naval and air bases in all parts of the world and their repair facilities were thrown open to its armed forces.

The British Commonwealth Air Training Plan. The British Commonwealth Air Training Plan [72] is the outcome of intra-Imperial discussions which began in 1938. It is controlled by a sort of Commonwealth air cabinet composed of representatives of Canada, Great Britain, Australia, and New Zealand, acting either through their high commissioners in Canada or their air liaison officers, who link up with their own air councils or boards in different parts of the Empire. The plan consists of much more than the great organization in Canada. In its wider sense, it includes the preliminary training schools in Australia, New Zealand, and Great Britain in which the contingents receive their elementary training before passing through the central training schools in Canada. In addition to its participation in the plan, Australia trains large numbers of airmen outside the British Commonwealth Plan. South Africa has its own air training scheme, which since October 1940 has been training a certain number of British pilots. India also has its own air training organization. The former Australian Prime Minister, Mr. Menzies, justly said early in 1941 that the British Commonwealth Air Training Plan was the greatest piece of Empire cooperation yet evolved in the war.

Its importance is far greater than the mere output of pilots, observers, and air gunners. It is of profound significance to the Commonwealth from a political and psychological point of view. The psychological importance of the plan consists in the bringing together from the various parts of the Empire of an elite of young men, the few to whom, in Mr. Churchill's words, the many owe so much, and binding them to one another by the ties of common training, and the spirit of fellowship arising from their dedication to a common purpose. In the air force as in the navy there is a far closer intermingling than between the more separate units of the armies.

III · THE PROBLEM OF INDUSTRIAL STANDARDS

Behind the system of coordination of defense and uniformity of equipment lies the whole problem of industrial standards in the British Commonwealth. With the exception of Canada, which follows American standards, British engineering standards are generally observed throughout the British Commonwealth.[73] In view of the dependence of modern armies upon highly standardized equipment manufactured by mass

---

[72] See Chapter V.
[73] See *Report of the Imperial Conference on Standardization*, Cmd. 3716, 1930.

production, the problem of building up and maintaining common engineering standards between a group of countries cooperating in a common defense system is of vital importance.

The absence of such standardization between Britain and America, for example, affects the whole range of mechanized equipment from the bore of the guns to the component parts of armored vehicles, tanks, and airplanes. When war vessels of Britain or America enter each other's ports in any part of the world, they cannot use the ammunition stored there, since this is made to fit guns of different calibre and firing mechanism. Every British or Australian mechanic likely to be called on to service an American plane in England or Egypt or India or Australia has to provide himself with two kits of tools in the matter of wrenches, etc. — one to fit English standard nuts and bolts and another for American. The problem of getting grounded planes into the air by rushing the necessary spare parts to them is already one of considerable difficulty even for British planes. To provide the same service for American planes all over the world, far from the parent factories and without the special regional repair factories provided for the different types of British planes, is an extremely complex problem. The difficulty arising from lack of uniformity in engineering standards and designs has affected above all the manufacture of aircraft and tanks.

While in general the principle of uniformity of equipment has been maintained in the great mass of army equipment for the various Empire forces, it has broken down in some measure in the matter of aircraft and tank manufacture. The difficulty has been most serious in Canada, where factories had to be retooled in order to manufacture British planes such as the Hurricane in accordance with British designs and specifications. In order, however, to obtain full-scale mass production and to utilize in full the whole engineering resources of Canada, it has been found necessary to abandon the uniform Empire standards and to go over increasingly to American standards. Efforts are being made, however, by British and American experts to secure the greatest possible degree of standardization through the use of standard designs and interchangeable parts in airplanes, tanks, and other mechanized military equipment. The problem of conflicting standards is not, of course, one which is confined to the relations between American and British industries. It exists also in greater or lesser measure within British and American industry and even between their defense services; for example, between the American navy and the army. Only far-sighted and continuous effort will secure the degree of industrial standardization necessary to secure the colossal output of defense goods required during the war.

IV · THE NEW REGIONALISM IN DEFENSE AND SUPPLY

One of the most striking developments of the present war, which is without real parallel in the war of 1914–18, and which is likely to leave some permanent traces on the postwar structure of the British Empire, has been the development of a new regionalism in Empire defense. At first sight this seems paradoxical because it has come at a time when the mechanized war on land, at sea, and above all in the air, has given the Empire a greater strategical unity than ever before. But in fact it is nothing more than an extension of one of the basic principles of Empire defense — that the primary responsibility of each member (as of all states in all periods of history) is its own defense. The speed and range of modern weapons of war have made it necessary for whole regions comprising a number of states and territories to combine in regional mutual security systems. A regional organization of defense is also made necessary by the quantity and variety of raw materials and manufacturing skills required in modern war, which are beyond the capacity of single states however great.

The new regionalism in the British Commonwealth is an early symptom of the inevitable changes in the states system of the world involved in new technical developments. It is the certain forerunner of the grouping of many of the smaller and weaker states of the world into regional federations. The process may be seen at work in all parts of the world. The agreement between the governments of Poland, Czechoslovakia, Yugoslavia, and Greece announced at the International Labor Conference in November 1941, foreshadows a possible regional federation of all Eastern Europe between Germany and Russia. Canada and the United States, by the Ogdensburg Agreement and the Hyde Park Declaration [74] and other acts of long-term collaboration are deliberately building a permanent system of joint North American military and economic defense. The leasing by the United States from Britain of a whole chain of naval bases to form a protective screen from Newfoundland out as far as Bermuda and down as far as British Guiana, is but another aspect of North American continental regional defense. So is the similar protective screen developed from Kodiak Island through

---

[74] See Chapter V.

Hawaii to Samoa. The " Western Hemisphere " conception is that of a regional grouping of North and South America for defense and other common purposes.[75]

The Eastern Group Supply Council [76] at Delhi represents a different type of regional organization, with the coordination of war production in the British territories of the Eastern Hemisphere as its principal function. The corresponding military organization for the actual purchase and distribution of armaments and other military equipment — the Central Provision Office — supplies a far-flung series of local provision offices extending into Australasia, the Middle East, and Africa. The experience gained here, and in the similar large-scale planning of production and supply by combined boards in Washington and London, may be of significance in the solution of postwar economic problems.

Perhaps the most interesting and highly developed of such regional organizations is the Middle East Supply Centre at Cairo, which coordinates the non-military supplies with military requirements in the area including Egypt and the Sudan, Iraq and Persia, Palestine, Cyprus, Malta, Ethiopia, and the British East African Colonies and Mandated Territory. The Middle East Supply Centre was established during the summer of 1941 by Mr. Oliver Lyttelton, Minister of State in the British War Cabinet, and its first purpose was to facilitate shipping and transport.[76a] Mr. Lyttelton had been charged by the War Cabinet to concert " the measures necessary for the prosecution of the war in that theatre other than the conduct of military operations." His Middle East War Council included representatives of the commanders-in-chief, representatives of the governments of the various territories concerned, and representatives of various British embassies and legations in the region.

The importance of this regional political and supply organization was increased by the presence of American military missions in Cairo and Basra, the building of a great American supply base in Eritrea, and the development of trans-African supply routes by air and road from the Atlantic to the Red Sea. With the entry of the United States into the war the M. E. S. C. organization became combined Anglo-American, not

---

75 Malaya, Burma, Australia, New Zealand, and the island groups in the Southern Pacific formed an obvious region for defense within the British Empire, and it had been expanded at the beginning of 1941 to include the Dutch East Indies and the Free French island possessions. See Chapter VIII.

76 See Chapter XI.

76a The Supply Centre operates under the control of a small Executive Committee, and has its own secretariat, director, and secretary-general. Its functions, however, are those of supervision and coordination of civilian supply, production, etc., rather than direct administration.

only in respect of its central organs, but also of its local offices in certain territories.

Coordination between different regional areas from a political and strategical point of view is maintained through the War Cabinet in London, and by special missions.

Regionalism in defense does not necessarily imply regionalism in foreign policy. The very fact that in Britain, the Near and Middle East, and Southeastern Asia truly Imperial armies, comprising at least token forces of most parts of the British Empire, have been operating is an indication that behind the regional defense lies unity of foreign policy. The arrival at Hong Kong in mid-November 1941 of a Canadian force was accompanied by a significant declaration by the Canadian Prime Minister, strongly emphasizing this point: "Defense against aggression," he said, "actual or threatened, in any part of the world is today a part of the defense of every country which still enjoys freedom," and he went on to state that it was in accordance with this principle that Canada had joined the Imperial army defending the British Empire in the Far East.

7. *The Foundations of the Empire — The Psychological Bonds and Governing Ideas*

I · "WHENCE COMES THE COHESION OF THE BRITISH EMPIRE?"

Whence comes the cohesion of the Brit. Emp.?
1. Patriotism. Loyalty. Custom.
2. Religion. Race. Pride in various manifestations. Habit. Language.
Mere law is the weakest of all bonds.

These words, jotted down by Lord Balfour a few weeks before his death, were revealed in a letter to the London *Times* on December 14, 1936. They form the theme on which this chapter must close, though it has been implicit in all that has been written above. But the emphasis of the chapter so far has been mainly upon institutions and the more concrete ideas and material relations. If the economic bonds, which are of the greatest importance, have been omitted it is mainly because they receive some attention in the other chapters of this book. We must turn now to the imponderables, the emotional forces and their accompanying ideas, which escape only too easily through the coarse meshes of the normal analysis with its emphasis upon certain formal or abstract categories. The British Commonwealth, whether in peace or war, can never be understood either by friend or enemy, or would-be impartial scientific observer, unless he has an understanding of these imponderables.

If this element is studied in the speeches of the leaders and statesmen of the British Commonwealth, it will be seen how largely it figures implicitly or explicitly in them. When King George VI tried at the London Guildhall to sum up his visit to Canada and the United States, he emphasized as his " first and deepest impression " that " even in this age of machines and mass production, the strength of human feeling is still the most potent of all the forces affecting world affairs." Mr. Churchill's speeches are full of understanding of this point. So also are the speeches of General Smuts — as when he said, in the Union Parliament in 1928, that the British Commonwealth was not held together like Empires in the past by law and sovereign authority: " Here," he said, " is an entirely new condition — no central force, but psychology, which is more powerful, the soul of a group of nations." Mr. Mackenzie King realized the importance of these imponderables when he explained in 1937 that the Imperial conference system worked easily because of " an antecedent and substantial measure of readiness to work towards common ends." It was indeed this basic psychological condition that alone made the machinery workable.

II · THE FAMILY BOND, ITS VALUE, AND CONSEQUENCES

The basic fact of the British Commonwealth is that it is a family of nations. The relations of its peoples to one another are those of the members of a family. This is not, as it is often taken to be, a mere analogy but a living reality. Only in this fact have we any key to the meaning of the words of the Official Historian describing Australia's response in 1914: " A warm, enthusiastic response to the magnetism of kinship thrilled the country as it had never been touched before in its most profound emotions." [77] Only in this fact is the real key to be found to the spontaneous and unpledged going together of the members of the British Commonwealth into war, or to those messages received by Winston Churchill from the Prime Ministers of all the dominions in the dark hours after Dunkirk — " messages couched in the most moving terms, in which they endorse our decision to go on and declare themselves ready to share our fortunes and persevere to the end."

---

[77] Scott, *Official History of Australia in the War of 1914–1918*, Vol. XI, p. 862.

In these phenomena there is something far more than the fact, better understood perhaps by political thinkers in earlier generations than in our own,[78] that the private family situation and the feelings, ideas, and traditions associated with it have a profound influence on the lives of men in the wider society of the State, influencing their relations as individuals to authority, and affecting their group loyalties and antagonisms and their political ideas and philosophy. In the British Commonwealth there is superimposed upon this normal situation characteristic of all societies, an additional factor — the family relation of the members of the Commonwealth to one another and the ideas and emotions appropriate to this relation. Each member nation of the family has its individuality due to many historical factors; but each has its own characteristic set of relations with, and emotional attitudes towards, the other members of its family of nations. This general set of emotional relations affects somewhat differently each citizen. His private family pattern may play a part in determining just where he fits into the general supernational family pattern — whether he exaggerates or underemphasizes a particular trend such as the independent status of his dominion in relation to the Mother Country, or the character and degree of loyalty of which his nature is capable.

It is easy to see how this family relation developed. The " great Dominions of the Crown " were not States built primarily by the conquest of subject peoples. English, Scotch, Welsh, Irish, settlers went to the new lands, taking with them from their homeland common ideas, traditions, ideals, and loyalties, all that makes up the character of a people, the cultural heritage of their mother countries.

Out of this common inheritance the dominions have developed their own individual societies. They have passed through a first phase of dependence on the Mother Country; their second phase was that of adolescence with its growing independence and self-reliance, its tendency to over self-assertion, its emphasis upon status and repudiation of the authority of the Mother Country, combined with an inability to accept the full responsibilities of autonomy. The third phase into which they now enter is characterized by an adult willingness and ability to accept responsibility, and unwillingness to remain dependent, combined with a reasonable acceptance of the family bonds without undue self-assertion or subservience. But if the Mother Country from which

---

[78] E.g., Sir Henry Maine, *Ancient Law*.

they sprang were to disappear, with all the loss of prestige involved for their common legal and political systems, the inner structure of each of the daughter societies would be profoundly affected.

It is only when we regard dominion nationalism in this light that we can understand its essential difference from nationalism of the normal type. At least in the wide sphere of the British Commonwealth nationalism is no selfish self-regarding thing. It is rather a nationalism like that of Britain itself, which, as it achieves the mental maturity that should go with adult stature, becomes increasingly aware of the need of subordinating itself freely to the requirements of life in the family of British nations.

Only when the history of the relations of Britain with the dominions is examined from this point of view (and such a history still has to be written) can the magnitude of the achievement of British statesmanship in building the new British Commonwealth of Nations be appreciated. The successful handling by Britain of this most difficult of all psychological transitions, after the initial disaster of 1776, demanded endless patience, a skill on the part of the much maligned Colonial Office, a degree of political maturity and wisdom in the successive British governments and parliaments, which have been rarely shown in history.[79]

Legal Consequences of the Family Bond. It is in this light only that we can measure aright the meaning and importance of legal conceptions such as the *inter se* doctrine. By this doctrine the family group of the British Commonwealth has established in some measure a private system of international law which refuses to recognize the relations between its members as being of the same character as the relations between normal states. For example, legal agreements between its members are not regarded as being in the nature of international treaties. In this light also must be considered the private system of commercial treaty relations involved in Imperial preference. These are regarded as lying outside the scope of most-favored-nation clauses in commercial treaties with foreign powers, because they are treated as private arrangements between members of an inner family circle. So also the private family arrangements regarding defense, which are implicit in the treaties

---

[79] It is characteristic that a Colonial Office Official, Sir Charles Lucas, in *Greater Rome and Greater Britain,* 1912, should have written one of the few essays on the "family analogy" in the British Commonwealth. See also W. Y. Elliott, *The New British Empire,* 1932, Chapter IV.

for limitation of naval armaments, and the private Empire diplomatic system.[79a] One can see this family conception actually working in the mind of an eminent constitutional lawyer, Sir John Latham, former Attorney General of the Commonwealth of Australia, now Chief Justice of the High Court of Australia. Speaking on the Statute of Westminster in the Australian Parliament on July 17, 1931, he said, " I regard the relations of the self-governing parts of the Empire, *inter se,* as corresponding closely in the political world to the relations of the members of a family in the personal world. I do not want the relations of myself and my children to be determined by rules written in a book, to which each of us must refer to discover who is right and who is wrong. I do not desire such things to be made rigid by legal rules and enactments." In this passage perfect expression is given to the psychological assumption on which the whole law is built and without a knowledge of which it cannot be understood.

III · THE FUNDAMENTAL ASSUMPTION OF MUTUAL AID

As an illustration of the basic political ideas which spring from this family bond we may take what might be called the conception of mutual security. The mutual security system of the British Commonwealth cannot be regarded as merely the outcome of the conception of a common interest in a system of collective security between independent states with which the League of Nations has made us familiar. A common interest may exist without people realizing it or being able to achieve it. The psychological bonds uniting the members of the League were too weak to enable this idea and the necessary political institutions to take root. It was an idea not yet able to command enough of the will and the instinctive emotional forces of the peoples to permit it to become a living reality.

The mutual security system of the British Commonwealth, on the other hand, has a solid psychological basis. It is no artificial creation, but the outgrowth of the family bonds uniting its members. Its roots lie deep back in the history of the Empire. It has behind it a long experience which has been embodied in a set of ideas and ethical principles,

---

[79a] The habit whereby the members of the British Commonwealth of Nations constitute " one family " when convenient, and independent sovereignties when equally convenient, has called forth protests from other countries, particularly as regards " *inter se* " exemptions from international covenants and from the most-favored-nation clause in commercial treaties. See my *New British Empire* and Robert Stewart, *Treaty Making Relations of the British Commonwealth of Nations.* W.Y.E.

such as the plain and simple principle that if you would command the loyal support of others, you must be loyal to them. It is the principle expressed by Charles James Fox in his letter to Talleyrand on March 26, 1806. In reply to the latter's inquiry as to a possible basis for peace, Fox pointed out that England "would not treat, still less conclude upon anything but in concert with her allies, especially the Emperor of Russia." "England," Fox wrote, "cannot neglect the interest of any of her Allies." [79b] If loyalty to your allies, how much more loyalty to the fellow members of your family of nations in the British Commonwealth! And it is striking that in September 1939 in the supreme hour when the dominion governments had to take their decisions, it was this simple principle of ethics that stood out in their minds.

Those who expressed this feeling most clearly in September 1939 were leaders like General Smuts and Colonel Reitz in South Africa and M. Lapointe, the French-Canadian leader; and by expressing it they showed how fully they had entered into the British Commonwealth as members of the common family. " I think that we should do our duty," said General Smuts to his Parliament; " we should do the proper thing and align ourselves with our friends, and we should ward off and prevent those dangers which are almost sure to overtake this country in the future, if we now isolate ourselves and have afterwards to face our ordeal alone." As M. Lapointe before the outbreak of the war put it, " If Canada has to rely on allies . . . those allies will have to rely on Canada." It was the certainty on the part of the dominions that in the event of war Great Britain would come unhesitatingly to their assistance, that made the great difference between the British Commonwealth and all other international associations like the League of Nations or groupings based upon multilateral or bilateral treaties of mutual assistance. Only certainty can breed certainty. Without it there can be no collective security, and it is a plant of slow growth.

IV · COMMON CITIZENSHIP AND COMMONWEALTH LOYALTY

The Prime Minister of Canada in his tribute at the Imperial Conference of 1937 to King George V said, " His conception of the Empire was always proclaimed in terms of the loyalties of the home and the affections of family life." And the speeches of leading statesmen in the Empire have been full of this same conception. The tributes of loyalty made by all the Imperial Conferences to His Majesty the King have

---

[79b] *Papers relative to the Discussion with France in the Year 1806,* London, 1807, No. 5.

been no mere empty formulae, but have expressed the inner reality of the British Commonwealth. The prayer of the Imperial Conference in 1937 that " Your Majesties may long be spared to strengthen the ties of affection and loyalty which unite all the peoples of the British Commonwealth under the Crown," as indeed all previous " loyal resolutions " from 1887 onward, expressed the family ties binding the peoples of the Commonwealth through the symbol of the Crown " as Head of this great family of peoples." The Imperial Conference was itself a gathering of the heads of the family, and the majority of Imperial Conferences have been associated with great events in the life of the Sovereign — such as the Golden Jubilee of 1887, the Diamond Jubilee of 1897, the Coronation of 1911, the Jubilee of 1935, and the Coronation of 1937.

Out of the spreading from the center by migration without breach of family ties, and with the continuance unbroken of the allegiance to the common Crown, there has come the most significant of all the institutions of the British Commonwealth; namely, common citizenship, the " common status " of " British Subject " as distinguished from the " particular (national) status." [80] The psychological importance of this institution of " common citizenship " as the basis and the symbol of the supernational loyalty and patriotism uniting British subjects all over the Commonwealth to each other, and particularly to the United Kingdom, cannot be overemphasized. This wider loyalty varies in degree and character with individuals. For whole groups of peoples, such as the French-Canadians and the Dutch South Africans, it exists in a lesser degree, or it may be even replaced in the case of some groups and individuals by antagonism towards the Commonwealth. Yet it must always be remembered that the British Commonwealth is a family of affiliated peoples almost as much as it is of kindred peoples.

The " common citizenship," and the feeling of a common patriotism extending out to the whole family of nations, remains the most important single factor to be taken into account in explaining, in Lord Balfour's phrase, " the cohesion of the British Empire." If there had been a breach of continuity of allegiance, a breaking of the family tie, with the profound psychological disturbances which may accompany such a change, the British Commonwealth as described here could never have existed. British, Canadians, Australians, New Zealanders, South Afri-

---

[80] Report of the Imperial Conference, 1937. Eire has legislated to eliminate the " common status," so far as its nationals are concerned, substituting for it what may be called a reciprocal citizenship.

cans, even Indians from British India, and most of the sixty millions
of colored peoples in the colonial Empire, are not in law aliens to one
another. They are fellow citizens in a vast supernational family of
kindred and affiliated peoples.

It is inevitable that the picture of a highly complex situation boldly
sketched in this last section should be oversimplified and overidealized.
It has been objected that the British Commonwealth, because of its lack
of a more centralized organization, failed to foresee and to arm itself in
time against the aggression of the Axis powers. But this surely was the
common failure of many democracies, whatever their form of organization. And it is not clear that if the British Commonwealth had had a
federal organization it would have shown greater foresight or resolution in advance, or have met the crisis when it actually arose with less
internal friction. " In this war the British Commonwealth has functioned as a unitary state almost as smoothly as if we had been provinces
in a federation." These are the words in which high officials from
Britain, Canada, and Australia summed up to the writer their judgment
on the working of the machinery of the British Commonwealth during
the war. Yet it is not clear that this loose type of organization will continue to be entirely adequate, or that it would be effective between
states not bound by the strong psychological bonds that unite the members of the Commonwealth to one another.

It is in these bonds that the secret of the British Commonwealth lies.
Its greatest leaders from Edmund Burke to Winston Churchill have
understood. In one of his prophetic speeches five months before the war
began the latter said:

> " Some foreigners mock at the British Empire because there are no parch-
> ment bonds or hard steel shackles which compel its united action. But
> there are other forces far more compulsive to which the whole fabric
> spontaneously responds. These deep tides are flowing now. They sweep
> away in their flow differences of class and party. They override the vast
> ocean spaces which separate the Dominions of the King."

CHAPTER III

The British War Administration

PART ONE

WARTIME ADMINISTRATION IN GERMANY AND GREAT BRITAIN[1]

by Heinrich Brüning

✿

1. The General Problem of War Administration

A comparison of wartime administration in different countries, especially in Great Britain and any of the larger continental European countries, will always be a difficult task. The problems of different countries in regard to raw materials, production, supply, and rationing varied greatly even before the use of such enormous quantities of military equipment and munitions as are required by modern warfare. Wherever

---

[1] In asking Dr. Heinrich Brüning, Littauer Professor of Government in the Graduate School of Public Administration, Harvard University, to contribute to the present volume I have imposed very heavily on his friendship. The following chapter is his current revision of a lecture comparing the organization of war controls of industry in Germany and Great Britain, which originally formed the basis of discussion in a seminar that he and I conducted together at Harvard, and which he has now kindly placed at my disposal. The chart of British administrative organization which accompanies it is based on work done by members of the same seminar, particularly by Miss Nix, who acted as secretary of the seminar — W.Y.E.

adequate supplies of food stuffs, feeding stuffs, and industrial raw materials were home-produced, or where their regular importation was unhindered, and where there was abundant man power and industrial capacity, problems of rationing, allocation, or priorities were practically non-existent. All that was necessary was clear and farsighted strategic planning combined with the right timing of orders for supply by the defense forces, and the close coordination of the military operations and supply of all the defense forces under one supreme command. All these are problems which have arisen in earlier wars.

At the beginning of the First World War almost all the belligerents expected it to be of the same character. They entered hostilities without any idea of, or preparation for, a long war, which exhibited before its close all the main characteristics of total war. Every country began with the administrative machinery, the methods of strategic planning, and the organization of supply to which it had been accustomed for more than half a century. The separate defense forces ordered their own ammunition and arms, uniforms, and food supplies through their separate and long established procurement offices. In some countries it was, however, realized very soon that the indiscriminate mobilization of miners and farm hands was threatening future fuel and food supplies. The blockaded countries were forced to recognize, too, that their available supplies of food and of agricultural requirements, as well as of industrial raw materials, were insufficient for a war of longer than twelve months.

Without some control of the market in these countries prices would have risen enormously, and hoarding would have produced widespread discontent and led to the disappearance of certain essential goods. Rationing, the fixing of maximum prices, and the control and requisitioning of raw materials were unavoidable. New industrial capacity had also to be found in addition to existing ammunition and arms plants, and skilled workmen who had been mobilized had soon to be released from the army for work in essential war industries. Plants of little or no importance for military supply had to be converted to war production or closed down, and their workmen took the places of the skilled men released from the army. As more firms changed over to war production and by various methods of organization more skilled labor was made available, step by step, without any comprehensive plan, an increasing number of raw materials were controlled directly, and their utilization by particular manufacturers determined in advance.

During the first half of the last war hardly any government tackled these problems with foresight or a full understanding of their magnitude. The control of various commodities and the organization of supply were improvised and somewhat haphazard. In some countries special, semi-independent organizations were formed outside the direct control of the government or the defense forces. Individual merchants and manufacturers competed with one another for raw materials and semi-finished goods. What was worse was that in almost every country the army and navy placed orders in competition with one another, without regard to cost or to whether the raw materials and man power available in a given period would permit their fulfillment. Without complete control and allocation of materials the distinguishing of certain orders as urgent and the issuing of various forms of priority certificates defeated their own purpose. They led only too easily to the creation of bottlenecks of every kind and prevented the full and steady employment of available capacity and man power, especially when priority orders were placed not directly by government departments but through interested agents and intermediate contractors.

There were severe drawbacks in basing production primarily on priority certificates. Certificates were issued in excess of the raw materials and semi-finished products available in a given period. It frequently happened that a manufacturer was able to secure with priority certificates all but one or more of the materials he required when, because of a temporary scarcity, he was without any possibility of obtaining the rest. This was doubly disastrous for the war effort, since the raw materials and semi-finished goods he had already acquired were wasted. Under the crude priority system, half of the necessary materials for a given type of armament might lie unused in one firm, and the other half in another, the materials, capacity, and labor of the two firms thus having no part in the productive process.

The situation was aggravated by the fact that until late in the war there was not in any country a sufficiently close relation between the planning of military operations and the estimation of the future supply requirements of the defense forces. For this the continual strategic miscalculations and tactical surprises of the last war were largely responsible. It was not of first importance to the Allies, whose relatively free disposal of the raw materials of the world was limited only by the shipping tonnage available to them; but the position of the blockaded powers was very different.

Their very limited supply of raw materials threatened to diminish in proportion to the enormous consumption of ammunition and increasing demands of mechanized warfare. In Germany it was soon discovered that military requirements had to be adapted not so much to productive capacity as to the supply of raw materials available. To exaggerate, one can say that the strategy of the Central Powers, especially during the second half of the war, when the employment of industrial capacity had reached an optimum, was dictated by the limited supply of raw materials. For the Allies, on the other hand, the amount of raw materials imported at any given time could be planned in accordance with strategic decisions.

In fact, of course, the Central Powers succeeded in spite of the blockade in importing considerable amounts of raw materials throughout the war. But the army and navy were forced, nevertheless, to coordinate their demands and to submit definite plans for fixed periods in advance. This was originally due to the efforts of the civilian administration and of a number of industrialists who did not share the optimistic views of some military and naval leaders about armament requirements and the possibilities of supply, and who succeeded in persuading the War Ministry that plans should be made as if for a war of unlimited duration. Civilian consumption had to be restricted and adapted to a bare minimum, and the production of civilian goods was concentrated in factories that could not be readily converted to war production.

Once that had been accomplished, and in the expectation that the war would last for at least three years after 1915, a formula was worked out to give the possible supply of any commodity for any period. This formula was:

$$D \text{ (supply for a number of months)} = \frac{M \text{ (supply on hand)}}{V \text{ (monthly consumption)} - Z \text{ (monthly production and import)}}.$$

The use of this formula for different materials made it possible to state when the demands of the defense forces were submitted exactly how far they could be satisfied and what would be left for civilian consumption. The production program for three years was divided into six-month periods, and the supplies of raw materials available in each month calculated. The program had to be so coordinated and the allocation of supplies to different firms so organized that each firm would have all the different raw materials it required at any time.

In the face of sudden changes in the military situation, changes had to be made in the plan of production, as they did with the Allies also. In Germany there was a certain rigidity, whatever changes occurred, due to the strict limitation of supplies. This meant of course that the strategic planning of the Central Powers was restricted by the conditions of long range planning of production to a degree that more than offset their strategic advantage of operating on interior lines of communication.

This was a reversal of Germany's position in the only two wars of the preceding hundred years in which all her military forces had been mobilized. The War of 1866 was somewhat like a civil war, and lasted seven weeks. The only real foreign war, in 1870, lasted only seven months, and was carried out on a basis of careful planning, coordination, and synchronization of supply with strategy in advance by the regular procurement branch of the Army. The outbreak of war in 1914, on the contrary, followed an increase in the size of the Army to which the organization of supply had not yet been fully adapted, so that all the trained man power available could not be put to use in the first six months of the war.

For two years before the outbreak of war in fact, the General Staff were so much preoccupied with reorganization and with fear of war against the combined forces of Russia, France, and Great Britain that General Moltke, in contrast to Admiral von Tirpitz, supported von Bethmann-Hollweg in his endeavors to reach an understanding with Great Britain. The Chancellor went so far as to reject urgent demands by the General Staff for increased economic preparedness, which he feared might endanger peaceful relations with England. The same difficulty of combining preparedness with appeasement was experienced in Great Britain before the present war.

All these experiences of the First World War formed the background of much discussion and the basis of critical studies in Germany after 1932. The results were embodied in the Four Years' Plan, in which the whole organization of military supply was built up behind a screen of other purposes, and in decrees issued at the outbreak of the Second World War providing for the coordination of strategic and economic planning, the civilian administration, and the various agencies of industry, agriculture, and the Nazi Party. Similarly in Great Britain many years before the outbreak of the present war the Committee of Imperial Defense prepared a plan and a skeleton organization for the mobilization of the economic resources of the Empire. This too was based on the experience of the last war and on plans adopted but not yet carried fully into effect when the breakdown of the Central Powers occurred in 1918.

It is therefore wrong to suppose that the chief of the Imperial General Staff and the able officers and civil servants collaborating in the Committee of Imperial Defense did not take into consideration with regard to organization in wartime the full impact of the danger of war with the Axis and Japan. It would be more correct to say that they were filled with apprehensions similar to those of the German General Staff and a few top ranking civil servants before 1914. They were handicapped, as the German General Staff was before 1914, by the fact that the Government did not fully appreciate the gravity of the situation and that too many people in influential positions were unwilling for defense preparations to be consolidated in peacetime.[1a] Plans for preemptive purchasing of a number of essential commodities such as, for example, metal alloys, which were proposed in 1937, would very likely if they had been adopted have rendered impossible the whole subsequent policy of the Nazis. When leading officials of a country that has been victorious in one war continue to occupy the same positions in a second, they are strongly inclined to rely on exactly the same methods which formerly proved successful, an average human reaction which has invited calamity throughout history.

There can be no doubt, however, that some of the major problems of modern total war were studied by the Committee of Imperial Defense and preparations made to meet them in the years immediately preceding the present war. This is true especially of the tentative organization of administration and supply on a regional basis in case communications should be interrupted by air attack. The coordination of certain aspects of civil administration, military organization, and supply was also considered, and before the outbreak of war certain outstanding civil servants were placed in political or administrative positions in which their experience and gifts could be brought to bear on these problems of organization in case of war.

Both Great Britain and Germany had learned that one of the most important conditions of victory would be the successful coordination of strategic planning, supply, and civil administration which was lack-

---

1a Cf. the summary in the leading article, " Conduct of Foreign Policy," *The Times,* London, January 4, 1943.

ing in the last war. That is the problem to be discussed in this paper. It resolves itself into two related questions: how do the German and the English systems provide for general coordination of the war effort at the top? and how do they provide for coordination in detail at the regional and local levels? This of course involves the relations between political authorities, administrative officers, the defense forces, and associations of industry, trade, and agriculture at every stage of development. Special attention will be paid to the functions of the civil service, which are very different in Great Britain and Germany, but which in both countries have undergone essential modifications during the last war and the present one.

During the last war the executive functions of the German civil service with regard to supply were different from, and to some extent less important than, what they had been in earlier wars. The development of military and semi-independent organizations for the control and distribution of different commodities pushed the civil service somewhat into the background. With the exception of certain very able and farsighted men in top positions, some of whom became leading figures in the semi-independent war agencies created *ad hoc,* the civil service was not prepared to assume the tremendous burden of organization which resulted from the technical revolution of the last war. Only the top ranks of the civil service were concerned with these new problems, and its regional and local officers were affected, at most, indirectly. In the creation of agencies outside the civil service for the particular problems of the war there was little difference between practice in Germany and other Continental countries and in England.

Industrialists and business men occupied leading public positions in every country during the last war, because the methods and training of the regular civil service were not appropriate to the control and detailed allocation of particular commodities. Neither was there in any country a sufficient number of army and navy officers trained for such tasks, although both the British and the German navies occupied exceptional positions in this respect. In Germany the position of all the armed forces with regard to the organization of production has been greatly changed in the present war.

The Treaty of Versailles, like any knock-out peace imposed upon a virile nation, had unexpected consequences here and in other respects. Because of the compulsory reduction of the total number of officers in the German Army to 10,000, several hundred able young staff officers had to find some other livelihood. Thus they studied economics or science and technology at the universities, or entered business firms and there learned the details of organization and production as they could not have done in any other way. These people were later available for the administration of the Four Years' Plan. In industry they had risen in twenty years to top positions, where they combined with their earlier general staff or other military training wide experience of a particular business. There is a parallel in England in the case of former high officials of the Admiralty who now hold leading positions in industry.

Although in the course of the war there have been further parallels in the evolution of the British and the German administrative systems, there are essential differences between them resulting from historical causes. It must be emphasized from the beginning that a totalitarian form of government does not in itself make for easier and better planning or a higher degree of efficiency in administration, and that the functioning of the wartime administration in Germany to date has been largely due to the long established traditions of the Army and the civil service. That a democracy, under a federal form of government, is capable of the simplest and most efficient organization is demonstrated by the example of Switzerland, even though she has certain particular advantages of tradition and geography.

Hardly any other country combines decentralized administration with the highest degree of military preparedness in peacetime so successfully. The Swiss army organization has always received the highest tribute from the German General Staff; it was the model after which General Groener and other leading officers tried to organize the German Army on a purely defensive basis before their removal from power. The central government at Berne works largely through the agency of industrial associations and the cantonal governments. Thus it is kept in contact with reality and with the people, and escapes the great danger of over-centralized administration — blueprint thinking, with the habit of referring every question to some central office by correspondence, a method which stultifies imagination and initiative.

It is crucial for any country at war to avoid this danger, which is common, if one examines the facts, to all forms of government. What is most important is the supreme coordination of the main lines of policy, strategy, and supply. It is only the manner in which this is achieved that varies with the form of government and with the character, imagination, and driving force of leading figures in a country. What is next in importance is a system of administration in which execution in detail is decentralized, either through associations of industry, commerce, and agriculture, or regionally and locally, and in which flexibility, which is so essential in total war, is ensured. Regional administration cannot be successful without definite planning and the close coordination of every phase of the war effort at the center. The necessary harmony and firmness of will at the center depends, correspondingly, on coordination at the regional level of the execution by different branches of the administration of decisions reached at the top.

Above all it is necessary for the responsibilities of every branch and every member of the administration to be clearly defined in such a way as to prevent their interference in tasks that are not theirs. Those bearing final responsibility at the top must have some guarantee, which will not preclude the free adaptation of general instructions to varying circumstances by subordinate officials, that the different branches of the war organization are in gear at every level. Only so will they be free to plan ahead and to meet unforeseeable problems quickly and positively.

Clear cut responsibility is easier to achieve on paper than in fact, especially in a total war affecting every branch of production. It presupposes great self-restraint, not least on the part of those in central positions. This should not be confused with exclusive departmentalism; it is very dangerous for any official to ignore the relation of his own definitely prescribed functions to others'. Neither does a precise delimitation of his responsibilities relieve any one of the task of anticipating his possible duties under suddenly changed strategic conditions. Without such self-restraint and consideration of future contingencies, a man of great push and pull whose job is to speed up the production of a particular weapon may succeed only at the expense of other, equally essential types of production. This has happened more than once in several of the belligerent countries.

What the results of a sharp definition of functions will be depends largely on the balance struck between the enumeration of specific tasks and reliance on the discretion of executive officers. Constructive initiative should not be curbed, but neither can irresponsibility be tolerated. Too informal a method of procedure, especially at the level of supreme coordination, may end in muddling in spite of a clear distribution of authority on paper. The establishment of the essential conditions of successful administration, in wartime particularly, requires men of great administrative experience. It is in fact only through experience that the right combination of centralization in planning and decentralization in execution can be recognized. Experience without evenness of temperament is of course worthless, and in this respect the demands of war are more exacting than those of peace, since war administration involves a combination of the various methods of different professional types.

For the problems arising in every stage of total war to be solved promptly and efficiently, there must be close cooperation between political leaders, army and navy officers, the civil service, and business men and technicians, as well as a clear demarkation of their functions. The patriotism felt in wartime is sometimes expected to make cooperation spontaneous, and certainly it makes it much easier. The mentality and the methods of these different types, as well as their attitudes toward any given question, are nevertheless very different. Differences of experience and lifelong routine necessarily produce differences of outlook. One of the most difficult problems of wartime administration is the amalgamation, as far as that is possible, of these different and sometimes antagonistic conceptions.

There is no formula for its solution. Unless it is solved, however, the best-made plans are irrelevant. This is the lesson of the defeat of France. The law drafted by the French General Staff for the mobilization of the entire nation in case of war and adopted by Parliament in 1938 was unquestionably comprehensive, thorough, and systematic. It had little beneficial effect either when war occurred or in the prewar period. For want of vision and energy, and, even more, for want of close cooperation among political leaders, the defense forces, the bureaucracy, and business, much irretrievable time for arms production was lost, and the elaborate organization created meanwhile lacked the right spirit for the best combination of the different talents required.

Men who have spent their lives in politics always tend to choose the alternative that promises to excite least opposition at the moment. As they are accustomed to registering the slightest oscillations of public opinion, they are inclined to support measures that will produce the most favorable immediate emotional reaction. In wartime, if not in peacetime as well, this is a very dangerous method. The experience of history is certainly that farsighted and constructive measures are for the most part contrary to current tendencies, and therefore initially unpopular. If this were not the case, the successful accomplishments of the greatest political leaders would not have been attended by so much suffering and pain. These men, while accepting unpopularity, vitriolic abuse, and slander, neglected no opportunity to further those policies which alone could bring about lasting results.

Civil servants as a class, in many European countries, are trained too much to carry out instructions by a routine based upon regulations and precedents. They cannot approach their problems like a business man buying and selling on the open market in the particular interests of a single firm. They must establish uniform procedures of general applicability. In contracting for urgently needed supplies they cannot offer a premium for quick delivery without having some legal basis for it, or without some assurance that it will not create a precedent upsetting the oldest traditions of public expenditure. "Business looks forward, law looks backward," E. M. H. Lloyd writes in his admirable book *Experiments in State Control*.[2] With regard to business, the statement is, of course, intended only in the sense of this particular antithesis.

Even civil servants, like those employed by the German state railways, who enjoy great freedom of initiative are not safe from the risk of a routine conduct of business in accordance with established rules. Thus in long years of service, especially if it is in the same department of one ministry, they may easily lose what native imagination they possess. Seeing that constructive efforts are often frustrated by the expression of popular reactions in parliament or by over-cautious and unimaginative cabinet ministers, they learn to be slow in suggestion and to attend strictly to their explicit duties. Where they are a closed group, recruited on the basis of examination and promoted in accordance with seniority, they may, in addition, be unfit for tasks of economic organization which require firmness of purpose and flexibility in execution, as well as practical business experience.

When, as in wartime, the civil service assumes business functions, business men must assume the role of civil servants and accustom themselves to semi-governmental procedure. They bring with them to the tasks of war administration many qualities not ordinarily found among public servants. If they have risen to the top of great business concerns by merit, they have learned the technique of administration and the division of responsibility at different levels in detail. They calculate exactly the effect of any decision down to the lowest level of any branch of a firm. Civil servants share this advantage only in countries where they are frequently transferred between central administrative departments and the subordinate regional and local administration.

---

[2] *Experiments in State Control at the War Office and the Ministry of Food,* Oxford, 1924.

Business men are able to select the best man for a particular job without reference to general budgetary provisions or fixed rules of promotion. A man who fails to do well can be readily and easily exchanged. Successful business men must have vivid imagination as well as the genius and courage to make momentous decisions. Without being accustomed to take great risks they would not have attained leadership. They are not bound as civil servants are by precedent. They may learn, too, to establish definite responsibility for different agents in the execution of a decision once taken. They have often great technical experience or know what experts can give quick and accurate advice in technical matters. Finally, they may know how to deal informally with their staffs without sacrificing fixed responsibility and efficiency, although this has not been so in all cases during the last war or the present one. These are a few of the factors that make their services indispensable in wartime.

They suffer, on the other hand, from the handicap of unfamiliarity with politics, or rather, with parliamentary methods and political criticism. They may feel hampered, too, by the formalities of bureaucratic organization. Lack of military experience may put them at a disadvantage in their dealings with the defense forces. They may be unable, as they were in many European countries in the last war, to accustom themselves to the abruptness and icy objectivity with which general staff officers may change their supply specifications with changed military conditions, perhaps upsetting carefully planned and organized production just at its peak.

Business men in war administration may also suffer from too narrow a conception of their functions. Placing the orders of one large firm in a normal market is essentially different from the organization of production for total war. The possible implications of every step for the economy as a whole and for later adaptation to changed military conditions must be taken into consideration. This can be done only if those occupying top positions in the organization of production are initiated into strategic plans and conditions and have natural gifts sufficient to grasp their full importance. Another handicap for the business man who accepts a coordinating administrative position may be his tendency to concentrate on the aspect of any problem that is most familiar to him, leaving other considerations to the attention of specialists. When this is the case there will not be the uniform coordination of effort in every phase of production which, as the experience of the last and the present wars shows, officers trained in general staff duties can, with few exceptions, achieve. The real problem of the business man and the civil servant in war administration is that in making decisions that must determine future military supplies they run the risk of being blamed at some time for influencing strategy adversely. The natural desire to avoid such responsibility is a very important factor in organization. When the coordination of strategy and supply is substituted for unified direction, the chiefs of staff or commander-in-chief on the one hand and those civilians who are responsible for military supplies on the other almost inevitably find themselves concerned in one another's functions.

It has been very popular from time to time, in England especially, but also in other European countries, for journalists and politicians to abuse the " brass hats." This attitude is generally ill-founded. There are brass hats in every army, but their prominence may be due to the fact that in peacetime budgetary considerations have left little opportunity for quick promotion in the army, or for able young men, especially those whose intelligence and character would predestine them for careers in the military or naval staffs, to enter the armed forces. The right training of officers for staff work stimulates not only the qualities required for strategic planning or for a quartermaster's work, but also those required for general administrative functions in total war. It is in fact the question of training which is decisive. Good military training, while it includes the precise execution of orders, also makes for quick and bold decision. It should instill that calmness and courage in the face of unexpected difficulty which is essential to the unravelling of a confused situation.

Frequent transfers between the general staff and line commands provide the same opportunities to discover how plans and decisions made at the top are worked out in practice as are enjoyed by civil servants who are transferred between the central departments and the regional administration, and usually by business leaders. Whatever experience staff officers in the army and navy may gain of branches of the service in which they have not specialized enlarges their vision and reduces the danger of routine decisions. Any one who is forced from time to time to leave behind him most of what he has learned and to learn something different will gain in initiative and constructive imagination.

Staff officers who have studied problems of communication, executed great engineering projects as they have done in the United States, entered large engineering or business establishments, or carried out the organization of particular branches of public administration, bring to their war service experience and qualities which fit them to solve the problems of coordination in production not only at the top but also at the regional and local levels. Trained officers of the British Admiralty are to be found in peacetime in private naval construction firms and in the administration of dockyards and ports, and in wartime throughout industry. Such experience has been denied to the British Army, except for its procurement officers and the directors of the Royal Ordnance Factories.[3] For the rest, only the few army officers who held ranking positions in the colonial administration have had any general experience of administration. The lack of officers who combine general staff training with technical and industrial knowledge is a greater handicap in the present war than ever before, and is more dangerous, since Germany has, in consequence of the effects of the peace treaty already stated, a large number of such officers.

To sum up, one may say that in any country, whatever its political traditions or its available productive capacity, man power, and raw materials, there are two major problems of administrative organization for total war. The first is the coordination of strategic planning, supply, and civil administration at the top. The second is the coordination of production throughout the country. Only coordination at the regional and local levels will make the avoidance of bottlenecks possible as far as may be. Only if such coordination is efficient and assured can elaborate correspondence be eliminated. Bottlenecks occur not only in production but also in administration at the points where the burden of responsibility is greatest, and unless those who must make critical long-range decisions are freed of the burden of detail their vision will be obscured.

Closely related to these two problems is the organization of mass production in such a way as to secure the maximum flexibility consistent with volume. This, indeed, is the crux of modern war. Flexibility in design and volume of production are, as Captain Lyttelton has said, essentially opposed. The modern production engineer demands the manufacture of a given type as steadily as possible. This becomes more essential with every increase in the dilution of labor, as the employment of less skilled labor necessitates more elaborate tooling in order to simplify the manual actions to be performed. The most enormous output

---

[3] Great progress in the centralization of Army purchasing was made in Great Britain only during the second half of the nineteenth century.

secured by these means may, however, prove to be of no value in a military showdown. It is as true today as in the last war that the superiority of a particular tactic of offense or defense is only temporary. A type of airplane well adapted to tactical cooperation with large tank and motorized infantry masses may not prove to be of great value in large scale bombing, as was shown by the failure of the German attack on Great Britain in the months following Dunkirk.

The question is less vital to a country holding the strategic initiative than to its opponents. As soon as the Axis powers are forced, as the British Government has been several times, and as the United States Government has been, to adapt themselves suddenly to entirely changed conditions created by the initiative of their foes, the German organization may be seriously disturbed.

The changes made in the German supply organization in the spring of 1942 were probably occasioned not by the shortage of certain raw materials alone but by the continued absorption of German forces in Russia, the necessity of constructing new weapons of defense against threatened mass bombing, and the necessity of producing bombers comparable to the British and American in armor and striking power.

As war production approaches the maximum in all countries, the advantage of the possession of the strategic initiative may be reduced. The scope of strategic genius may be increasingly restricted, but strategic genius and tactical evolution will nevertheless continue to necessitate changes in the types of armament produced and in the organization of supply. The disturbing effect of such changes will be minimized where diplomacy and strategy are most closely combined, where the quickest advantage is taken of the results of technical observation of the performance of different weapons on the battlefield, and where the organization of supply is most flexible.

For Napoleon it was still possible to bring about the necessary coordination wholly in his own master mind. In the First World War, the only war for a century in which problems comparable to those that faced Napoleon arose, such coordination was not achieved in any country, and certainly it is doubtful whether any individual today can assume the role Napoleon performed for many years so successfully. The closer the coordination of the war effort at the top, and the greater the initiative permitted below, without danger to central executive control, the freer those who carry the burden of final decision will be to devote themselves to constructive planning and to the general direction of the gigantic war machinery. When maximum production is finally attained everywhere there will be an inevitable similarity between the administrative methods adopted in different countries, just as there was at the end of the last war. The wide variations of organization in different countries during the transitional period are largely explained by the beginning of preparation for war at different times and by differences in administrative tradition.

2. The German System of War Administration

I · THE TRADITIONS OF THE CIVIL SERVICE

Even in the greatest emergency of a total war, no government can create an administrative organization independently of the long established traditions of the country. Though this applies most directly to Great Britain, it is much more true of Nazi Germany than is generally realized. Napoleon could not have created the most perfectly centralized war organization the world had yet seen if it had not been for the complete centralization of the French administration under Richelieu and Mazarin. What he did was to revive their form of government, after the Revolution had destroyed all those traditional institutions which were least conformable to authoritarian military rule. There is one essential general aspect of this question. *The traditions of a country that owes its power to naval supremacy will differ in many ways from those of continental states.* Thus the role and the influence of the army and the civil service in normal times is much greater in almost every continental European country than in the Anglo-Saxon countries. In this respect there is no difference in principle between the German administration and the French. Since the beginning of the seventeenth century the political, military, and administrative evolution of these two countries has been determined by considerations which were all but unknown to England. Since this difference affects the present organization of the war effort in Germany and England as well as normal methods of administration, a few further comments may be in place.

The similarities of type among the administrations of different continental European countries are due in part to the fact that when a new and more efficient administration has been developed in one country principally for purposes of war, neighboring countries are forced to imitate it if they wish to survive. This was the case in many countries under the impact of the French military expansion in the seventeenth and eighteenth centuries. In most of them, including the greater part of Germany, there had for centuries been only a very loose central administration, the functions of administration remaining for the most part with the territories and towns. This changed as a result of the increasing predominance of a highly centralized administration in France during the one hundred fifty years preceding the Napoleonic era. The events of that period resembled today's. Then the success of the French administration in subordinating every other purpose to the expansionist policies of Richelieu and Mazarin compelled the countries chiefly threatened by them to imitate the French system. The military organization of old Prussia, of course, was dependent both on the French model and on an older, highly developed administrative system.

It was, however, the crushing expansion of the Napoleonic regime that led to the establishment nearly everywhere of centralized bureaucratic machinery especially adapted to the tasks of wartime. When Prussia was defeated in 1806 and forced into very much the position of Vichy France in 1940, farsighted patriots realized that Napoleon would be defeated only by the same kind of organization to which his success was largely due. The conception of the modern general staff appeared for the first time in Prussia, where it was combined, in the most critical period, with the French prefectural system and, contrary to the Napoleonic precedent, with a new and very democratic type of conscription. The subsequent development of a permanent general staff, culminating only under the elder Moltke, can be traced back in its essential lines to Napoleonic principles.

In peacetime the general staff had not only to plan the military operations required by any possible emergency, but also to plan the organization of supply in close connection with possible military operations. A form of civilian administration ensuring the organization of the civilian needs of the country in wartime and their coordination with military requirements was needed in addition. It cannot be doubted that the Napoleonic model of administration by *préfets* had great influence on the shaping of the civilian administration in Germany during the one hundred years between the Napoleonic Wars and the First World War, although the fact has been neglected for reasons of national pride. In Prussia, for example, and other German federal states a tendency to imitate the French prefectural system without regard for existing traditions prevailed in the years before the Allied victory over Napoleon. Attempts to effect a compromise between this system and older methods of administration have continued until the present war, in which the Napoleonic model has again, increasingly, prevailed.

The *federal tradition* has indeed been very strong throughout German history, and has demonstrated its power of survival again and again. Thus the decentralization of executive responsibility became a leading maxim of German administration. It had led to a combination of local self-government with devolution of the functions of the central government which was on the average, before the Nazis came into power, very happy. In this respect Germany differs greatly from both England and France.

In England after the Norman Conquest political power was far more centralized than in any other European country, and any tendency toward even limited regional autonomy was prevented. Neither was the delegation of the executive powers of the Crown for any large area to an officer responsible only to the central government, uniting in the hands of one man control over all the administrative problems of the region, fully accepted over any period of time. Because of the divergence in historical evolution, there are no precise and equivalent terms by which the fundamental differences in the methods of carrying out the policy of the central government on the Continent and in Great Britain can be expressed.

In France political and administrative centralization was established finally in the Napoleonic era. The existence of the *préfets* as agents of the central government did not imply any devolution of power to institutions of true regional self-government. The *préfet* in the Napoleonic conception was responsible only for the execution in his department of the instructions issued by the ministries in Paris, and the scope of representative government in the municipalities was as restricted as it was until the 1890's in England. In Germany, on the other hand, the vitality of politics and administration is strongest in the municipalities and the federal states. Every far-reaching increase of the power of the national government has been accepted grudgingly. It was only because of the experience of the two hundred years until the end of the Napoleonic Wars, in which Germany was the battlefield of foreign powers struggling for the domination of Europe, that the powers secured from the states by the national government in 1871, which, contrary to the popular impression abroad, were very slight, could be obtained.

Even under the Bismarckian constitution the importance of the federal states remained much greater in most branches of administration than that of the central government. In this respect Germany's constitutional and administrative problems resembled those of the United States, and the relation of the central government to the federal states was much the same. The central government could communicate with the self-governing municipalities or counties only indirectly through the administrations of the federal states, as the Swiss government does through the administrations of the cantons. The functions of the central government were about the same as those of the national executive in Washington during the same period; until 1920 even the right to impose and collect income taxes was reserved to the municipalities and the federal states. The powers of the Emperor were less than those of a president of the United States.[4]

Until 1919 there was no German cabinet. There were instead permanent secretaries in the different departments of the central government and a Chancellor, who was responsible for the whole policy of the government, but whose actual power ordinarily depended on the fact that he was also Prime Minister of Prussia. The Federal Council (*Bundesrat*), the members of which were appointed by the governments of the federal states, had much greater powers of control than has the Senate of the United States. The Chancellor had to obtain the approval of the Federal Council in advance for legislation introduced into the Reichstag. The larger federal states had their own armies and their own war ministers, though not separate general staffs. The only official access of the general staff to the Chancellor was through the Prussian war minister.

Within the federal states there was devolution of administrative power to provincial and district governors, whose functions were partly executive and partly those of control over self-governing provincial and local representative bodies.[5] The principle of this organization was to allow the greatest possible initiative to institutions of local self-government and to self-governing institutions of industry, trade, and agriculture, while ensuring general coordination by a single official in each district. To the stranger it seemed complicated, but it effectively com-

---

[4] The strength of his position depended on his constitutional powers in Prussia, the largest of the federal states.

[5] Prussia, which until 1938 comprised nearly two-thirds of the German population, was, and remains, divided into provinces and subdivided into districts. Some of the other federal states are no larger than Prussian provinces or administrative districts.

bined highly developed regional and local self-government with centralization at the top. It prevented the danger of over-centralization such as prevailed in France and prevented the rise of genuine local self-government there.

One of the greatest advantages of the German compromise was that every civil servant was trained to consider the *regional coordination of different branches of administration* as important as the work of the central departments. Civil servants in regional and local administration had to deal directly with people throughout the country in their daily lives, and not primarily with legislative provisions and statistical reports. They were expected to submit new problems as they arose to their superiors up to the central department, but they were left great freedom and discretion in carrying out the policy of the department in detail within the framework of existing legislation and administrative regulations. Under this system the social and industrial problems resulting from the rapid expansion of industry and the development of public utilities, almost all of which have been brought wholly or partly under the influence of government planning since the last decade before the First World War, were met, on the average, very constructively. The employment of technical experts as civil servants in the government-owned railways, mines, and forests, and the fact that cities elected men of professional training as mayors for terms of twelve years produced civil servants of broader vision, greater knowledge of general conditions, and greater initiative and adaptability than is possible under the narrower tradition of a civil service dominated by treasury officials with their exclusive emphasis on fiscal control.

Greater centralization and some curtailment of the powers of the federal states were necessitated by the problems arising from the last war and, even more, from the effects of the treaty of peace. In modern history at least, the accumulation of huge war debts generally leads to an increase in the power of the central government over the national resources and in its administrative functions, particularly in connection with taxation and unemployment, at the expense of the federal states. The Weimar Constitution created an opportunity for greatly increased centralization, without, however, providing any consistent redistribution of functions of national and state administration. Unfortunately, a tendency therefore prevailed for central ministries to set up separate agencies of their own throughout the country, thus destroying the established balance in regional administration. Much friction, duplication, and dissatisfaction was the outcome.[6] There were two undesirable consequences of particular importance, which impaired some of the best traditions of German administration.

Chiefs of the financial and the labor administration were appointed in each province with rank approximately equal to the provincial governor's, but dependent directly upon the central ministries. Thus there was no longer one man in each regional administrative unit responsible for the coordination of every aspect of administration within his area, as had been proved essential for efficient administration in the past. To have one such man who knows the different branches of administration as well as the people and the special conditions of his region greatly simplifies and facilitates the constructive solution of many problems. He must of course be endowed with vision, experience, and tact, and must have authority to make as many decisions as possible on the spot without reference to the central departments. Under such an arrangement, the responsibility of the central departments is normally limited to legislative planning and to issuing general instructions to the single responsible head of the entire administration of each region. Thus they are spared a voluminous correspondence about minor details and the impossible task of considering particular cases requiring immediate and flexible decision. Otherwise, the decision by central ministries of a multitude of individual cases not involving major questions of principle will be based only upon routine and precedent and will lead to the development of a purely legalistic method of administration. Members of the staff of a central ministry are always haunted in deciding questions in relation to special local conditions by the fear of creating a precedent that would be inappropriate to conditions in another part of the country.

The absence of a more systematic distribution of functions between the national and state administrations at the regional level, a problem which exists under every federal constitution, endangered another advantage of the older form of German administration — the exchange of civil servants among ministries, as well as between central ministries and the regional and local administration. A balance between centralization and decentralization, between planning and legislation and execu-

---

[6] Nevertheless, in grave situations in which the emergency powers of the president were invoked, the system was able, because of the traditions which remained alive in the civil service, to meet the greatest demands. A complete revision of the structure of prices, wages, and rents, for instance, was carried through in two months at the beginning of 1932 without the opening of any new administrative office or the appointment of any additional personnel. Cooperation between the central, state, and local administrations was perfectly satisfactory.

tion in detail is possible only when civil servants are frequently exchanged between the central, regional, and local administrations. Over a long period of time it became an established conviction in German administration that no one who had not held responsible positions in regional and local administration would ever do well in a central ministry. When young civil servants enter ministries without much experience and remain there permanently, they will become specialists and will in the long run offer routine objections to every constructive proposal. They will be unable to appreciate the effect of legislation and executive orders under different conditions in different parts of the country. Similarly, no one who remains always in the regional or local administration will appreciate the broader legislative problems of the central ministry. His outlook will be narrowed, and his reports and actions will hardly contribute to the constructive solution of national problems.

Thus an exchange of personnel between the different branches of administration is essential. After a high civil servant has assisted in the formulation of major legislation, nothing is better for him than to go into the regional administration. There he has time and opportunity to observe the detailed operation of the legislation. He comes into contact with individual citizens and with the actualities of life. Certainly he will return to the central ministry with a more practical conception and with fresh suggestions. Without such an exchange of personnel between the different levels of administration one of the main purposes of regional administration, the correction of abstract and theoretical tendencies by practical experience, will be frustrated.

When there is constant interchange of detailed practical experience and of central planning, the economic, political, and psychological reactions to legislation are transmitted from the bottom of the administration to the top as effectively as orders and instructions are transmitted from the top to the bottom, with mutual loyalty and understanding. This is parallel with the practice of the old German general staff. No officer was left on the staff for more than a few years without interruption. They were frequently transferred for a year or more to positions in the Army where they could test the plans they had formed and develop new ones on the basis of practical experience.

In both cases there is a further advantage incidental to the practice of transferring personnel. One of the greatest problems of administration is the wording of the instructions of central departments and of administrative orders for the execution of particular legislation. Such orders must be legally exact, but without stifling the initiative of the subordinate officer. The right combination of precise direction with a margin of discretion generally results only from actual experience in regional administration and consequent recognition of the necessity of adapting instructions to local conditions.

This has been, in essence, the ideal of the best civil servants and of political leaders in Germany in the past. An administration of this kind, if its members are capable, united in feeling, and zealous in their work and have learned to avoid publicity, may ensure some continuity of long range policy and, even under an extreme democratic constitution, may stabilize violent oscillations of public opinion. There is of course a latent danger that the bureaucracy may involve cabinet members in actions that are in the end detrimental to democracy. It is one of the major functions of parliament to prevent this by the presence of its best members in the cabinet.

There are other dangers. The German civil service, except for a relatively short period, was exclusive. That is to say, people without normal civil service training were unacceptable to it. Although the civil service itself was recruited from more or less all classes of the population, an able business man, for example, would not have felt at home in it or have been able to adjust himself to its procedure. This is one reason why, in the last war and the present war, so few industrialists have been able to assume functions of control over production and distribution inside the regular ministries. It is one explanation of the creation of semi-public institutions for the control of production, and for other purposes for which business or industrial experience is indispensable, in which business men can work in cooperation with the regular civil service without actually entering the ministries. This adjustment is much easier, as will be described later, under the British system of administration. Another handicap after the last war was that the regional organization of administration in the federal states was still too much influenced by methods developed when the problems of administration were very different, and when communication was not so easy as it is today. In the years 1930–32 the financial basis was laid down for a new integration of the whole administrative system, which could have been carried out in detail at the end of 1932.

These proposals were not, however, put into practice. The administration of justice and the police have been transferred from the federal states to the central government. The other administrative departments in the states have been subordinated to the corresponding ministries of the national government in Berlin. The state parliaments have been abolished, and the town councils have become little more than Nazi Party meetings under the leadership of the mayors. Otherwise, from the practical point of view of actual administration, the Nazis have left everything more or less as they found it. Certainly until the outbreak of war, and even now, the German administration, in comparison with the British, has not been so frictionless as is generally assumed. There is much unnecessary duplication of work in parallel organizations. Foreigners studying " new " organizations of industry, trade, and agriculture, often fail to realize that in the eight years of its absolute domination the Nazi Party has not achieved a constructive reorganization of the entire civil administration. This is of course the normal result of totalitarian government, unless the dictator is at once a military, political, and administrative genius. Revolutions are always prolific in abstract schemes of organization which fascinate the uninitiated onlooker by their apparent simplicity and by the ruthlessness of their imposition. Most of the innovations of the Nazis, the pseudo-corporative organization of agriculture for instance, are nothing but the amalgamation of existing private or public institutions, the organization of which was outwardly complicated but in fact exceedingly efficient. The continued working of these pseudo-corporative institutions, as well as many other organizations under Nazi supervision paralleling the regular civil service, is due only to people with a large experience and a great ethical tradition, who have, however, no powers of independent decision.

The coordination of the war effort suffers in many ways from overelaboration, resulting not, as in Great Britain, from the absence of any effective coordination at the regional level, but from the existence of too many parallel institutions. But one thing is certain — with the help of the Gestapo and other coercive Party organizations any plan once decided on is carried out ruthlessly in the smallest detail and in the most obscure community. Not only are legislation and regulations rigidly enforced in certain directions, but Nazi Party executives are also uninhibited by the law or decisions of the courts.

This is an enormous difference from the conditions of the last war. The German civil service and the courts were then all too reluctant to exercise their constitutional powers. Appreciating the difficulties with which every citizen was confronted, even the commanding generals in the corps areas made the least possible use of their rights of coercion.

The civil administration and the courts were so lenient in this respect that the number of minor violations tolerated had a cumulative effect and gradually undermined the authority of the law and the administration. Recent major administrative changes limiting the responsibility of the civil service may not be altogether unwelcome to it. The civil service, like the Army, perhaps, prefers to remain anonymous in the conduct of the war, leaving to the Nazi Party the onus of inflicting hardship and privation and even of failure.

From outside it cannot be seen how far the influence of the German Army and civil service has actually diminished in the past nine years. That they have had any influence in political questions since January 1938 is hardly possible. It is very important for any understanding of the situation in Germany to realize that there has been a constant struggle on the part of the Nazi Party to establish its own members in leading positions in the bureaucracy and to have the functions of general staff officers in the civil administration transferred to leading party members. Recent changes in this direction have resulted in a somewhat less consistent organization of production than existed during the first part of the war. To judge from newspaper reports, the power of the S.S. organization under Himmler's supreme command is now predominant in the whole police and civilian defense administration. Young Party members seem now to feel that they have learned enough of the tradition and technique of administration to replace experienced leading civil servants, contrary to the tendency which prevailed at the outbreak of war. Certain branches of industry have also been granted greater autonomy and self-government lately than they ever before enjoyed, in Imperial Germany, under the Weimar Republic, or under the Nazi regime.

Before the outbreak of war the consequences of substituting blueprint schemes for efficient private organizations and of the Nazi craving to duplicate established public institutions by party institutions of their own must have caused concern among military leaders and also among a few central figures in the Nazi Party. This is the reason for the promulgation at the outbreak of war of decrees scrapping many of the Nazi experiments in administration. The tendency of such decrees was to prevent any interference with the normal processes of public administration by Party leaders bearing no definite and open responsibility within the administration. The supervisory powers of the civil administration over the semi-public organizations of industry and agriculture were in addition transformed in most cases to specific executive powers. Within the administration, in the most influential positions especially, there had of course been many compromises with the ambitions of the Nazi Party. Party members in the Cabinet and in the positions of governors and presidents in the regional and federal administration hold final control in many respects.

II · THE CENTRAL DIRECTION OF THE WAR EFFORT

The form of coordination of every aspect of the war effort at the top and at the regional level adopted in August 1939, in which a few major changes were made later, clearly shows an effort to avoid irresponsible interference by Nazi Party agencies without reducing the Party's controlling influence and to prevent the conflicts of authority which contributed to Germany's defeat in the last war. During and before the last war the federal form of government imposed severe handicaps on the German war machinery.

The organization of supply at the beginning of the last war was the responsibility principally of the Prussian War Minister, and to a lesser extent of the war ministers of other large federal states. All of them received statements of military requirements from the Great General Staff at Imperial General Headquarters. It was soon found necessary to concentrate the functions of the war ministers of other states with regard to supply in the Prussian War Minister in Berlin, and this was accompanied by the establishment of a number of separate controls either under the authority of the Prussian War Minister or semi-independently.

There was much friction in the coordination of naval and strictly military demands, and between the Chancellor, who was responsible for foreign policy and all internal questions not of a purely military character, and the Chief of the General Staff there was even more. Until Hindenburg and Ludendorff came to the High Command in 1916 the Chief of the General Staff had not always sufficient authority to ensure that the procurement program of the Navy was not undertaken in competition with that of the Army. It was only in 1916, with the adoption of the so-called Hindenburg Program, that this problem of organization was temporarily solved. Final decisions in all cases of conflict were supposedly made by the Emperor on the advice of the Chancellor. This was constitutionally correct, and had been practical in the time of William I, when Germany had no Navy, and when no conflagration like that of 1914 could be foreseen. Except in the period before the last war, when he supported the Chancellor's objections to military preparations which might prove further obstacles to peaceful understanding in Europe, the Emperor's decision was only nominal.

At present Hitler actually enjoys the power which during the last war writers in foreign countries mistakenly attributed to the Emperor. He is Commander-in-Chief of all the defense forces; he must reconcile considerations of strategy and of foreign policy; he controls the various coercive institutions of the Nazi Party, including the *S.S.* and the Gestapo, which are under Himmler's executive direction. Beyond this, full responsibility for the coordination of the entire war effort was delegated by Hitler in August 1939 to a committee of the *Supreme Defense Council,* which had been established in peacetime under the chairmanship of Goering, who is also chairman of the special committee.

Hitler is represented on this executive committee in his capacity as Commander-in-Chief of all the defense forces by Field Marshal Keitel as Chief of Staff, and in his capacity as President and Chancellor of the Reich by the permanent directors of the President's Office and the Chancellery. Since Hitler has also assumed nominal command of the Army, the former commander, General Brauchitsch, who was originally a member of the Supreme Defense Council, has not been replaced. The only additional members of the committee are the Minister of the Interior, who is responsible for the whole civilian administration, and the Economic Commissioner-General, who is also Minister of Economics and President of the *Reichsbank.*

Neither the Foreign Minister nor the Minister of Food and Agriculture belongs to the executive committee of the Supreme Defense Council. The fact that the Minister of Finance is also excluded serves to illustrate the difference in character between the Defense Council and the present British War Cabinet. All this means that Goering has supreme executive authority for the coordination of the war effort outside foreign policy, strategy, and the activity of Nazi Party organizations. Goering's position is counter-balanced by that of Himmler, who, as has been said, receives instructions from Hitler directly. He is not a member of the executive committee of the Supreme Defense Council; his controlling powers, rather, are parallel to those of the Defense Council and independent of it.

Before sketching the main lines of organization down to the local level, it is important to emphasize certain essential characteristics of the administration in order to gain a better understanding of the British war administration by way of comparison. As chief of the *O.K.W.* (*Oberkommando der Wehrmacht,* High Command of all the Defense Forces) Field Marshal Keitel is effectively responsible for all the functions which Ludendorff performed only during certain periods of the last war, and then only *de facto,* not formally. He is at the same time Chief of Staff for all the defense forces and Minister of Defense. The Chiefs of Staff of the separate forces are subordinate to him, and he has a Deputy Chief of Staff, Colonel-General Jodl, with the special function of maintaining liaison between Hitler and the *O.K.W.* Thus Field Marshal Keitel is nominally responsible not only for the long-range strategic planning of the three defense forces, but also, as Minister of Defense, for the coordination of the supply of all three forces.

This, in combination with the fact that he and his staff are in close touch with every day's military events, is a very great advantage indeed. It guarantees coordination at the top, which, as we shall see, has not been achieved to the same extent in England. There can be no question that final decision as to the strategic plans of all the defense forces and the general allocation of supplies among them for at least two years ahead must rest with one man. He alone can at once issue the necessary instructions when a sudden reverse prevents the execution of prearranged plans and when expectations of success are disappointed. Officers of his staff decide not only changes in specifications but also the allocation of available industrial capacity and raw materials among the three defense forces in the light of strategic plans for more than a year ahead and corresponding tactical requirements.

For this purpose authority over armament production and over supply in general was concentrated at the outbreak of war in a twin department of the *Oberkommando der Wehrmacht,* the *Rüstungs- und Wehrwirtschaftsamt.* This was split up in the spring of 1942 into separate departments — the *Rüstungsamt* for technical specification and procurement, and the *Wehrwirtschaftsamt* for the coordination of all the economic factors in the conduct of the war. Both departments remained under the direction of the same general who had previously directed the united department. These two departments, as will be more fully described later, had even before the war their own regional staffs, which remain united as before under the authority of the commanding generals in the corps areas, and their inspectors in every important firm engaged in any way in the manufacture of armament.

Agricultural commodities are controlled in the Ministry of Food and

Agriculture, and other commodities by the Minister of Economics. The *Reichsstellen,* or controls, for different commodities in the Ministry of Economics were to a large extent directed until the beginning of 1942 by general staff officers, and the head of the coordinating materials department in the ministry was also a staff officer. In the Ministry of Transport general staff officers have until recently been responsible for the coordination of rail and motor traffic and for the organization and expansion of road haulage. Officers of the *Wehrwirtschaftsamt* may also attend the meetings of so-called *Hauptvereinigungen* which exist for every important agricultural commodity in the Ministry of Food and Agriculture. These last combine the functions of marketing organizations with the planning of the particular food products and feeding stuffs to be grown on every farm and the local enforcement of the program.

A large part of the production of armament and of the supply of raw materials for armament production is also controlled under the Four Years' Plan, which again includes in its organization officers of the *Rüstungsamt* and the *Wehrwirtschaftsamt* of the *O.K.W.* The office of the Price Commissioner, whose powers are dictatorial, is also included in the organization of the Four Years' Plan. Goering, as chairman of the executive committee of the Supreme Defense Council, as president of the organization of the Four Years' Plan, as chairman of the General Economic Council, and to a lesser extent as Air Minister, was originally responsible for the entire economic war effort, although until the spring of 1942 officers of the supply department of the *O.K.W.* exercised the actual direction.

The changes introduced, particularly in the control of certain materials and in the priority and allocation machinery, in March 1942 increase the difficulty of determining from outside the exact role of the *Economic Commissioner-General.* Since the beginning of 1940 he has been pushed somewhat into the background. He is primarily Goering's deputy-chairman of the *General Economic Council,* which is in effect a civil servants' coordinating committee. Its members are the permanent under-secretaries of the Ministries of Economics, Agriculture, Labor, Transportation, and the Interior, the National Forest Office, and the Four Years' Plan, the Reich Price Commissioner, a representative of the Nazi Party, and the general directing the *Rüstungsamt* and the *Wehrwirtschaftsamt.* The functions of the Economic Commissioner-General, apart from the direction of the *Reichsbank,* seem to consist in adjusting civilian consumption and foreign trade, through the commodity controls in the Ministry of Economics, to the requirements laid down by the supply departments of the *O.K.W.*

During the past year there has certainly been some diminution of the influence of general staff officers in the economy as a whole. The war administration is now less streamlined than before, and a graph illustrating the present organization would seem almost as complicated at the top as a chart of the British organization. The reorganization was necessitated by certain problems of production which had arisen in England before, and its result seems to have been to restrict the coordinating functions of the Economic Commissioner-General to those sections of the economy not directly concerned in the manufacture of armament and munitions.

The recent reorganization, which resembles in some respects the present organization in Great Britain, is best explained by a fact which is too often ignored. In the organization of production for total war there are parallel phases which occur in different countries at different times and different intervals. While Germany had an advantage over Great Britain in the construction of capacity for the mass production of armaments beginning in 1934, certain problems in the administration of the priority system and the more elaborate allocation of supplies which became acute in Great Britain immediately after the Battle of France arose in Germany more than a year later, after the Russian campaign of 1941.

The first, tentative period of rearmament began in Germany late in 1934. It entailed some control over production and the supply of labor, but it consisted primarily in the creation of new capacity for the mass production of tools and gauges, munitions, guns, and airplanes. It also included the further rapid expansion of synthetic oil and rubber capacity and the mining of low-grade ores.[7] This phase occupied three years. The program was not in every respect successful. The first mass production of airplanes in Germany, begun in 1936, was a partial failure and most of the planes so produced had to be scrapped in 1938. Even the type of plane put into production in 1938 proved unsuitable, as has been mentioned, for attack on Great Britain. With four years of experimen-

---

[7] The substitution of low-grade for high-grade ores is possible only to a limited extent. The coke required for the production of a ton of pig iron from low-grade German ore is about two and one-half or three times the amount required with high-grade ore, a serious drawback, since German coke production and transportation facilities before the occupation of Belgium were insufficient.

tation and production since the Nazis had come into power, only one tank division had been equipped by the spring of 1937. It was only during that year that the plans of the three years before were put fully into execution. Until the occupation of Czechoslovakia,[8] however, their limited productive capacity and supplies of raw materials, with the exception of stocks of grain, rubber, and oil, acquired largely with foreign credits, did not permit the Nazis to run the risk of war in their foreign policy. The pace of the Nazi rearmament could not have been kept up through 1937 if it had not been for the Anglo-German clearing agreement of October 1934.

During this period a system of *commodity control* was evolved in the Ministry of Economics, not primarily for the purpose of armament production, but rather because of the lack of foreign exchange. The method was not very different from that introduced in other countries at the outbreak of war. Agricultural production and marketing had been similarly organized, not on a permanent basis but *ad hoc,* before the Nazis came into power.[9] The Nazi platform had included the reorganization of the German economy on a corporative basis and a promise to the farmers of complete autarchy. Their promises have been realized in blueprint schemes of organization, within which older and very efficient voluntary associations in agriculture, trade, and industry have continued to function.

Exceptions to this statement must be made for the agricultural marketing organizations (*Hauptvereinigungen*) and for organizations in the flour milling industry and for the manufacture of " ersatz " products, all of which seem to have been fairly effective. They provided the model for the semi-corporative institutions for the control of certain branches of industry introduced in the early spring of 1942. In general, however, it is true that legislation for the corporative organization of various trades was given practical effect only where the lack of foreign exchange

---

[8] At the beginning of 1939 Germany had five tank divisions. The German occupation of Czechoslovakia, which had a higher armament capacity in proportion to its population than any other country in the world, however, changed the balance of military power in forty-eight hours. Czechoslovakia's army was, in addition, one of the most modern in respect to mechanical equipment. With this captured equipment Germany was able to transform four light armored divisions into tank divisions, thus raising the number of German tank divisions available at the outbreak of the war to nine.

[9] By 1932 Germany was virtually self-sufficient in all essential agricultural products except fat. The effort of the Nazis to achieve complete autarchy has been a failure, and is partly responsible for present difficulties of food supply.

made some form of strict organization inevitable and where there were available people with great experience of voluntary industrial association for more or less similar purposes.

The early introduction of control over certain commodities in order, to repeat the fact again, to conserve foreign exchange was greatly facilitated by the existence in a number of industries of long established forms of organization which combined a legislative origin and a certain amount of government control with all the flexibility of private management.[10] Neither the functions nor the form of these organizations was essentially altered until the spring of 1942. Most private *cartels,* despite the contrary opinion sometimes expressed abroad, have also survived, although deprived of certain vital functions. The Nazis, in effect, revived the cartel policy introduced in 1931 and abandoned in July 1932. The compulsory cartels formed principally for the expansion of *ersatz* industries were a Nazi innovation, as was the use of private cartels by the Price Commissioner to keep prices at approximately the level established by the Fourth Major Decree of December 1931.[11]

Wages were in general frozen at about the level established by the same Decree. In order to hold them at this level while employment was rapidly increasing during the first phase of rearmament, regional *Treuhänder der Arbeit* (Labor Trustees) were appointed under a *Reichstreuhänder der Arbeit.* They exercised dictatorial powers over wages and hours, and severe restrictions were imposed on the movement of labor between plants and industries.

All this is to say that the lack of foreign exchange brought about an

---

10 The coal syndicate, for example, was originally based upon voluntary agreements in the different coal producing areas, where production quotas were established for each mining firm. These regional syndicates were placed by later legislation under the final control of a coal commissioner, who was advised by representatives of mine owners, miners, and consumers. The potash industry was similarly organized under legislation so that overproduction was prevented and competition on the world market facilitated. The government not only controlled these industries from above but was also a member of the different syndicates, since, as in many other Continental countries, mines had been owned and operated by the government from time immemorial. This was especially true of the later development of the potash industry in Germany. The employment in government mines of civil servants with special technical training made practical as well as legal control of the syndicates possible.

11 Because of the loss of the major part of Germany's reserve of gold and foreign exchange, which at its postwar height was insufficient to cover her short-term foreign indebtedness, prices, wages, rents, and the rate of interest were fixed by decree in December 1931. As a part of the burden of taxation was shifted at the same time from real property to sales taxes, the entire basis of economic life was revised. These drastic measures were made possible only by their synchronization. The Nazis later had only to freeze price relations as they found them. Since 1933 there has been only a slight rise in the price index. This is, of course, a statistical illusion, since the quality of many goods has seriously deteriorated, and the real cost of living has risen considerably.

organization of scarcity such as nations normally accept only in war-time. Before the mass production of armament began in Germany control of production, prices, and wages had reached a degree to which many belligerent nations were unwilling to submit even during the first phase of the war itself. Neither this control alone nor any old or new form of voluntary or compulsory organization could have made it possible for the Nazis to wage war for more than a year, since it could not overcome the actual dearth of important raw materials, especially iron ore, resulting from Germany's loss of territory after the last war. The occupation of Norway, however, ensured a regular supply of high-grade iron ore from Sweden throughout the year. The armistice with France similarly ensured supplies of other types of iron ore and of various other essential materials.

In attempting to apply the legislation of 1934 for the corporative re-organization of the whole economy, the Nazis were confronted with the same difficulties as the Weimar Republic in attempting to implement existing provisions of the Constitution, which had been influenced by the Soviet Revolution. These earlier constitutional provisions were bound to fail, since their tendency was to replace voluntary industrial associations which solved the particular problems with which they were concerned exceedingly well according to the flexible principles of private management by institutions the functions of which would be rigidly defined by legislation. That would have meant depriving existing employers' and employees' associations of all vitality, and the subjection of very different industries to a uniform scheme of organization. There will always be conflicts of interest between industries for mass production, for which a national form of organization is preferable, if they can be brought within any organization, and smaller industries, to which a regional form of organization is better adapted. In this respect there has been even less approach to a balanced organization during the past ten years than under previous Governments which pursued a more cautious policy of non-interference.

The picture of economic organization in Nazi Germany is thus very complicated for an outsider. There is almost universal conflict between ideological blueprint forms of organization and others which have grown out of practical problems of production. This must have caused great toil and trouble to general staff officers and to old civil servants, particularly in connection with the utilization of all available industrial capacity to meet the requirements of the prolonged Russian campaign.

In Great Britain the more efficient utilization of existing capacity became a necessity even before the completion of plant expansion for the mass production of armament. In Germany, on the other hand, production in the period between the Battle of France and the Russian campaign was characterized by a rather loose dispersal of orders throughout industry in Germany and the occupied territories. Subcontracting reached a maximum in the summer of 1941. The increased demand for tanks, guns, and munitions in 1941 could no longer be met by the further dispersal of contracts. In addition, bottlenecks had occurred because the bureaucratic methods employed by the *Reichsstellen* in dealing with larger firms contracting directly with the *Rüstungsamt* were not appropriate in dealing with smaller firms. The amount of clerical work involved in the centralized control of materials for a great number of small firms threatened to become a serious hindrance to the full utilization of capacity and prompt delivery on contracts.

This explains why in the spring of 1942 new controls were organized and a newly appointed *Minister of Armament and Munitions* was entrusted with the control, standardization, and rationalization of armament production with the aim of concentrating production and man power in plants operating under the most favorable conditions of equipment and organization, transport facilities, and safety from bombing attack. He was charged in addition with the technical improvement of the design and manufacture of weapons and the oversight of armament priorities. Subsequently he has assumed the practical management of the Four Years' Plan. His full title is now *Generalbevollmächtigter für Rüstungsaufgaben und Beauftragter für den Vierjahresplan* (Commissioner-General for Armament and Executor of the Four Years' Plan). The appointment to such a position of an architect and engineer, not a staff officer, who had been responsible for important construction work before and during the war, indicates the preponderant importance at this stage of the war of purely technical aspects of production from the design of weapons to the rationalization and concentration of war industry. This new organization was intended to concentrate the executive control of armament production in the hands of one man who was acquainted with technical problems in the different stages of production, the same purpose for which, at almost the same time, Mr. Lyttelton was appointed Minister of Production in Great Britain.

The appointment of a Minister of Armament and Munitions seemed at first to introduce into the otherwise streamlined organization of supply in Germany an element of complication suggestive of the division of responsibility in Great Britain among the Deputy Chief of the Imperial General Staff, the Minister of Production, and the Admiralty and Ministries of Supply and Aircraft Production. As his powers became known, however, it was made apparent that by superseding in some respects the military elements that formerly exercised exclusive control of war production he was able to unite in his own hands all technical and administrative decisions affecting armament production without sacrificing the existing organizations of the *O.K.W.* and the Economic Commissioner-General. The former departments of the *O.K.W.* are closely meshed with the new ministry. The functions of the *Rüstungsamt* of the *O.K.W.* remain unchanged, but the *Rüstungsamt* itself is incorporated in the Ministry of Armament and Munitions. The same general remains chief of the *Rüstungsamt* and also chief of the *Wehrwirtschaftsamt*, which is directly subordinate to the *O.K.W.*

There can be no doubt that in the final phase of total war less efficient plants must be eliminated from production. The speed of production in different firms must be at least sufficiently uniform to ensure that the delivery of particular supplies essential to the opening of a new campaign will not be delayed by a few firms which may represent only a small fraction of total production. This is the sphere of the Minister of Armament and Munitions. His responsibility does not end with technical standardization of the design of weapons and their component parts, but includes the rationalization of every stage of manufacture to secure the maximum output.

It is for this reason that the *Rüstungsamt*, while remaining under the orders of the *O.K.W.*, has been transferred to the Ministry of Armament and Munitions. The *Rüstungsamt* places its own contracts as before, and the execution of contracts is inspected by its own regional and local officers, whose position in the regional administration has, however, as will be seen later, been somewhat changed since the establishment of the new ministry. Probably these officers receive more definite and more practical instructions in their dealings with the managers of armament plants because of the new relation of the *Rüstungsamt* to the Ministry of Armament and Munitions. An order by the Minister of Armament and Munitions for the increased supply of scrap suggests one of the reasons for the reorganization. Before and during the war the *Rüstungsamt* had accumulated enormous reserves of component parts of weapons and vehicles, which have been rendered obsolete by changes in design and are to be scrapped. Orders for newly standardized component parts are evidently to be placed by the Ministry of Armament and Munitions rather than the *Rüstungsamt* itself, and the minister will be responsible for their timing in such a way that reserves can be built up without the waste of production formerly entailed.

At the same time that the *Rüstungsamt* was incorporated in the Ministry of Armament and Munitions so-called *Hauptausschüsse* (Main Committees) for the major armament industries were established in the ministry, for the standardization of articles of mass production and rationalization of industry, and *Ringe,* technical committees covering all engineering production, for the standardization of component parts. This indicates clearly the principal function of the new minister. He is responsible for the best technical provision to meet the total requirements of the *Rüstungsamt* and for bringing designers and engineers into the closest possible contact with the *O.K.W.* in the statement of specifications. The same designers and engineers are concerned with the increase of output by the technical improvement of individual plants. Under the *Hauptausschüsse* there are special committees for specific problems, such as the design and production of tanks, in which officers with actual experience in battle of the use of the weapon in question meet with designers and engineers. For questions concerning both one or more of the committees of the *Hauptausschüsse* and one of the technical *Ringe,* a common expert chairman is appointed.

Here too the principle of ensuring coordination through the assumption by one individual of several closely related functions has been followed in each industry. In the iron and steel industry, for example, one man is chairman of the *Hauptausschuss* for iron and steel in the Ministry of Armament and Munitions, head of the iron and steel control in the Ministry of Economics, in which allocations of iron and steel are made for firms not working on armament orders, and leader of the new *Reichsvereinigung* [12] for iron and steel production, including the mining of iron ore, trade in iron and steel and scrap, and the supply of coal and coke for blast furnaces. He is appointed leader of the *Reichsvereinigung* by Goering; as chairman of the *Hauptausschuss* he is responsible to the Minister of Armament and Munitions; for the functions

---

[12] It is hard to know whether to call these institutions cooperative associations or corporations, as their legal character is dangerously vague.

remaining to the iron and steel control in the Ministry of Economics he is responsible to the Economic Commissioner-General. He is in addition a member of the Armament Council in the Ministry of Armament and Munitions, consisting of six high-ranking officers representing the three defense forces and nine industrialists. While the Ministry of Armament and Munitions was established with a view to the rationalization of all industry, its primary concern is with articles employed in warfare or, like railway engines, essential to the maintenance of war production. The Minister of Economics, or Economic Commissioner-General, is responsible for the production of articles, like textiles and shoes, both for military use and for civilian consumption and export.

This division of responsibility at the cabinet level, alien to the German tradition, is the consequence of a radical change from a form of control based on raw materials to one based on the major branches of industry, or rather on pre-Nazi associations, both private and statutory. With the vitality of all natural growth, they have survived the Nazi blueprint era either on a national or regional, a vertical or horizontal basis. These associations have now become executive public authorities. They are responsible in varying degree for planning, market regulation, and the allocation of materials within their industries and, in conjunction with the committees for their industries in the Ministry of Armament and Munitions, for increasing production by rationalization.

That explains the new term *Lenkungsbereich* (managerial control), which has replaced the former *Reichsstelle* (the English " control "). The directors of every *Lenkungsbereich* are leading members of the industries concerned, and they have been given control over related materials required in a single industry, such as iron and non-ferrous metals, with the aim of reducing the total number of central controls. It is a realistic adaptation to specific difficulties of supply, to established private organizations, and to the need for a system of control geared into the Ministry of Armament and Munitions. It is an essentially sound devolution of responsibility for the synchronized allocation of all the materials any firm requires, and also for ensuring the best use of the man power and materials available, to unbureaucratic private organizations with full executive authority.

When plans for the requirements of the *O.K.W.*, based on the strategic forecast, and for those of the civilian population have been agreed to in detail for a year or more in advance by the Minister of Armament and Munitions and the Minister of Economics, the director of each

Lenkungsbereich receives a branch plan for his industry together with block allocations (*Globalkontingente*) of the necessary materials. He has then to determine corresponding plans and reallocations for the different groups or cartels in his industry. They in turn are responsible not only for well timed allocations of materials to individual firms but also for the saving of material and labor by improved methods of production.[13] With the supervision of the Price Commissioner under the Four

---

[13] Under the *Reichsstellen* materials were sometimes allocated on the basis of quotas fixed in the period of rearmament before the war. A new method of allocation has been introduced in the industries for which *Reichsvereinigungen* have been established. Allocations of non-ferrous metals and iron and steel, for example, are now made in four main groups; these include contracts for standardized component parts placed by the Ministry of Armament and Munitions, contracts placed by the *Rüstungsamt,* production for the machine tool industry, and all other production, divided into a number of different categories, for which allocations are made through the non-ferrous metals control in the Ministry of Economics.

The Ministry of Armament and Munitions, the *Rüstungsamt,* the machine tool industry, and the non-ferrous metals control keep statistical accounts, like bank deposit accounts, with the *Rüstungskontor GmbH* (limited liability company with relatively low capitalization), an agency of the Ministry of Armament and Munitions, which serves as a clearing house for the amounts of materials consumed in any quarter of the year. The *Rüstungskontor* has also for prime contractors in each classification statistical accounts which presumably show the extent to which their capacity is being utilized and the size of their inventories at any given moment.

In placing a contract any government department issues with it a voucher for the allocation of the necessary materials. This voucher the prime contractor must present for validation to the *Rüstungskontor GmbH.* The *Rüstungskontor* is thus enabled not only to keep the total of orders placed in any category within the total amount of materials allowed for it, but also to control the timing of individual contracts in accordance with a general quarterly and yearly schedule of production and to prevent any department from getting out of line with the national program. It can at the same time prevent the placing of contracts with any manufacturer in excess of his capacity and can guarantee the availability of all the different materials required for the completion of any given order.

When the *Rüstungskontor* has approved a contract, it returns to the prime contractor a second, "transfer" voucher. This he delivers with his orders for semi-finished materials to his subcontractors, who must secure their own raw materials. The control of contracts in relation to capacity and to the amount of materials available in this second stage is not the concern of the *Rüstungskontor,* but of the new *Reichsvereinigungen.* Thus the transfer voucher must in turn be submitted for validation to the *Reichsvereinigung.* By this system the allocation of raw materials to individual firms in accordance with their capacity and with the total amount of raw materials available in any quarter is separated in most cases from the central control of production as a whole, which does not usually extend beyond prime contractors. It was discovered in the last war that between business practices and government accounting methods there is often a gulf which can be bridged only by a more or less independent institution combining essential characteristics of both. The *Rüstungskontor* represents such an attempt to reconcile bureaucratic control and efficient management.

Years before the war private *Auftragsbörsen* (contract exchanges) were organized on a regional basis under the control of the long established public offices (*Ausgleichsstellen*) that provided for the participation of small contractors and artisans in government work. The purpose of the new *Auftragsbörsen* was to bring representatives of the great armament firms into contact with smaller manufacturers. Plans and specifications were exhibited so that smaller manufacturers could see how their tools and labor force could be best employed. These regional exchanges continue to function, and in October 1942 the first nation-wide *Auftragsbörse* was held for two weeks in Berlin by the Ministry of Armament and Munitions. Firms were invited to attend by the

Years' Plan, they also control prices. The principal model has been the organization of the paper industry since the outbreak of war. Cartels which had survived only as blanket cartels to be revived in peacetime have been dissolved, and the functions of active cartels now include the executive direction of their members' particular operations. Thus the manufacturer no longer applies for his materials to several central controls, but simply to his private industrial association or cartel or to the regional commissioner of the *Lenkungsbereich*. Form-filling and the necessity of writing, telephoning, and travelling to Berlin have been minimized, and the personnel of the central controls has been cut in half.

In certain industries for which materials remain under the control of the Ministry of Economics this system is still in its introductory stages and has not been fully developed. In a second group of industries the direction of each *Lenkungsbereich* lies outside the Ministry of Economics in the hands of a leading industrialist. In the machine industry, for example, a former president of the long established association of machine manufacturers, in close contact with technical committees in the Ministry of Armament and Munitions, has full responsibility for allocations of materials, combined with executive authority over the rationalization and concentration of production, through subordinate associations for different branches of the industry.

A third and most important stage of development has been reached by the six corporative *Reichsvereinigungen* for iron and steel, coal, shoe manufacture, and different textile fibres. The *Reichsvereinigungen* for iron and steel and coal have evolved from semi-public, pre-Nazi organizations. Except for the fact that capital in the industries has not changed hands, they resemble the old I. G. Farben Combine in the chemical industry and the Soviet industrial trusts. Individual firms must follow the instructions given by directors of the *Reichsvereinigung* in accordance with plans formed in the *Hauptausschuss* of the industry in the Ministry of Armament and Munitions. They are told what to produce and how, and the price is fixed on the basis of the production costs of the best equipped plants. Where differences in cost are too great for this, group

---

Hauptausschüsse in the ministry and by the ministry's regional armament committees, and the requirements of the new system of standardization were emphasized. Products were grouped so that firms in the same category with bottlenecks either in labor or in tools could exchange orders among themselves. The principle is the same as that of the district capacity exchanges in Great Britain, with the difference that in Germany the organization has been expanded to a national scale.

prices are fixed for manufacturers of the same products under approximately the same conditions of cost.[14] The clerical labor involved in cost accounting separate contracts with individual firms is thus eliminated. Plants unable to produce on this basis are closed down or scrapped. The *Reichsvereinigungen* are responsible not only for the maximum utilization of capacity, materials, and labor and for the synchronization of deliveries by their member firms, but also for the definition of market areas with a view to the national saving of transportation. In this they have the benefit of the accumulated experience of private industrial associations, syndicates, or cartels.

III · THE REGIONAL COORDINATION OF THE WAR EFFORT

The coordination of every aspect of the war effort at the regional level was based until late summer 1942 mainly on the conditions of the last war. The principal regional divisions of the country for the wartime functions of administration were the eighteen *corps areas,* not the federal states or the provinces. In the last war commanding generals were appointed in these areas immediately after mobilization, with political powers similar to those provided for in case of war in most European countries. For the purpose of coordination their staffs included industrialists, agriculturalists, and journalists, all for the most part in their capacity as reserve officers. Under certain conditions the commanding generals also exercised control over the civil administration in order to prevent friction between the regular administration and the military organization in the corps areas.

As the war continued, and especially after 1916 when economic problems became increasingly complex, there was much criticism of the activities of the commanding generals in the corps areas. It became clear that while in a shorter war they might have accomplished the task of coordinating the entire war effort successfully, they had not all training or imagination enough to control the civil administration over a long period of time without seriously impairing its initiative. In the present war the corps area commanders have consequently held no political powers. Their responsibility has been limited to military questions, which include the organization of supply.

The *Rüstungsamt* and the *Wehrwirtschaftsamt* of the *O.K.W.* had

---

14 The result has been a reduction in prices in the industries immediately concerned and in the prices of products in which these materials are used. Steady maximum production has also made possible the reduction of certain other cartellized prices.

until the summer of 1942 their own regional departments under the control of the commanding generals in every corps area. Their function was to coordinate the different factors in production and to keep the actual progress of production in gear at the regional level with central plans for production. These departments and the *Rüstungs-* and *Wehrwirtschaftsinspektoren* under them had to keep in close contact with the regional and local civil administration. In fact, the regional *Wehrwirtschaftsämter* established in every corps area in the period of rearmament and modelled on those of the last war were transformed into executive bodies (*Bezirkswirtschaftsämter*) comprising representatives of every government and Party institution connected with war economics and meeting under the chairmanship of provincial or state governors. The executive functions of regional officers of the *Rüstungsamt* and *Wehrwirtschaftsamt* were concerned only with war production. Inspectors of the three defense forces in every corps area were responsible for the discovery of new capacity for armament production, for remedying technical deficiencies in production, and for reporting labor shortages to the chief labor officers of the region.

Thus from the *O.K.W.* and the Supreme Defense Council down to the local level of administration and in individual plants the military element predominated in the organization of supply. The full importance of the military personnel has not been evident, however, to the general public, and it does not imply any influence in political questions or executive responsibility for the regional coordination of the different branches of civil administration with the military administration.

For the latter purpose, special *defense commissioners* were appointed at the outbreak of war in each corps area as controlling agents of the Supreme Defense Council. They have been drawn increasingly from among Nazi Party leaders, until by the end of 1942 all Party *Gauleiter* had become defense commissioners.[14a] They are in close regular contact with the generals commanding the corps areas. Each defense commissioner is advised by a board comprising the governors of the federal states or provinces [14b] wholly or partly included in his corps area, the local Party leaders, the district presidents (permanent heads of the civil administration in their areas), the chief of the regional organiza-

---

[14a] Thus there are now 42 commissioners instead of the original 17. Whenever the boundaries of the *Gaue,* which are identical with the old Parliamentary constituencies, do not coincide with those of the corps area, one of the commissioners in the area is made responsible for the others and is stationed in the town in which the corps area headquarters are situated.

[14b] In some cases the governor of the federal state and the *Gauleiter* are identical.

tion of labor supply, and the *Treuhänder der Arbeit,* who fixes wages and hours of work for the region.

The defense commissioner is responsible for the regional coordination of military, administrative, and Party institutions in the total war effort of his region. He must keep every branch of the civil administration, including public and semi-public organizations for production and distribution, the military organization, and the organs of the Nazi Party working together in each corps area. The necessary administrative duties of the defense commissioners are discharged not through separate regional defense offices but through the established offices of provincial governors in Prussia and officials of comparable rank in the other federal states and, in the territories annexed since the autumn of 1938, of *Gauleiter.*

Since provincial and state governors for the most part serve as the regional officers of the Economic Commissioner-General and are also from an administrative point of view agents of the General Economic Council, all executive functions outside the military organization and the Nazi Party are concentrated in their hands under the supervision of the defense commissioners. This salient fact must be emphasized in any accurate picture of the regional organization. It means that in spite of the introduction of regional defense commissioners traditional administrative organization and accumulated experience have been preserved in wartime. The defense commissioners, although all routine correspondence between military and civilian authorities must pass through their hands, have no staffs of their own. They use the permanent staffs of provincial and state governors.[14c]

Thus all communications between the Supreme Defense Council and its members, and likewise the General Economic Council and its members, and the civil administration in the country at large pass exclusively through the hands of experienced permanent officials. Apart from the S.S. and Gestapo and, more recently, the civilian defense organization, all of which are under Himmler's direct control, only the courts, the customs and revenue offices, the state railway offices, and the six new corporative industrial organizations controlled by the Ministry of Armament and Munitions have any direct communication with central ministries. This represents a major simplification of the work of the central

---

14c Under the administrative jurisdiction of the Minister of the Interior.

ministries, and it enormously facilitates coordination at the regional level as well as among the different central ministries.

Any remnants of self-government either in municipal institutions or in semi-public chambers of commerce and industry disappeared at the outbreak of war. Every such organization has become an executive instrument of the provincial governor and a cog in the war machine. The provincial or state governor, in his capacity as regional economic commissioner, can issue instructions to every public and private economic organization. That is to say, through the provincial governor the Minister of Economics, the Minister for Food and Agriculture, or the chief of the Forest Service can dissolve or amalgamate or subordinate to the regular civil administration any of the organizations, either long established or newly introduced by the Nazis, under his partial supervision and control.

In each province or comparable administrative area the governor has, in addition to the provincial economic office (*Bezirkswirtschaftsamt*), which developed from the regional *Wehrwirtschaftsamt* of the O.K.W., a provincial office for food and agriculture (*Landesernährungsamt*) and another for forestry and timber products. The corporative oganizations of agriculture are subordinate to these offices and act as their agents. Below the provincial food and economic offices there are offices in every county and town. The food offices are responsible both for local production and for distribution. The economic offices coordinate production within their areas, with the special function of increasing capacity. Prices not fixed by the central Price Commissioner or in the corporative organizations of industry are controlled by these offices.

During 1942 private chambers of commerce, industry, and handicrafts have been combined to a large extent in *Gauwirtschaftskammern*. This is one step toward the still unrealized Nazi ideal of making the *Gau* the general administrative unit, as some are for labor supply and wage regulation. It represents an achievement for the Party, followed up as it has been by further inroads into the civil administration. It is a reversal of the tendency at the outbreak of war to scrap Party organizations paralleling the normal administration, though with the help of the Gestapo the Party has always been able to control individual members of the civil service and the Army. At present the prevailing tendency is for Party functionaries to succeed to key posts in the administration.

The new *Gauwirtschaftskammern* coordinate every aspect of production in small industrial units, in which there is not, as there is in the new *Reichsvereinigungen,* immediate contact with the Ministry of Armament and Munitions. Their task is to speed up rationalization outside the six new industrial organizations, and, since they are also political bodies, it is to be supposed that the power of the Party is behind them. They are not yet, however, organs of the Party. Their areas correspond to those of the labor administration and of the *Treuhänder der Arbeit*. The chairmen of the new chambers, who must be active industrialists, are appointed by the district Party leaders; they have authority to dissolve existing chambers of commerce and industry whenever they consider it necessary in order to save personnel or for closer coordination.

The organization of the supply of labor has until recently followed the outlines established before the Nazis came into power. The boundaries of the regional administration of employment exchanges and of all other questions of employment, including public work creation, were never identical with those of the provinces, but were determined rather by economic conditions. The same principles were applied in defining the jurisdiction of the regional arbitrators of wage and hour disputes, who have been succeeded under the Nazi regime by the *Treuhänder der Arbeit*. The central allocation of labor supply has recently been transferred from the high civil servant whose responsibility it had been for fourteen years to a prominent Nazi Party district leader. One of his first tasks was to work out new wage scales to replace established piece rates.[15]

The German transport system has hardly been changed by the Nazis. For many decades the railways and canals have been owned by the state and administered under a very flexible system of decentralization. Until 1919 there was a general staff officer in every regional office of the state railways, and this arrangement was reintroduced by the Nazis.

---

[15] The purpose of the new rates is to induce highly skilled workers to give up work that, with new tooling, can be performed by unskilled or semi-skilled workers. The former system of piece rates has been revised on the basis of " value units " of work. The least skilled process has a value of six units, while in mining, for example, the performance of the most highly skilled work has a value of forty-seven. White collar work is valued at from thirteen to seventy-five units, according to the different processes involved. The new rates mean that the output of skilled workmen may be increased without abnormal increases in their wages and in the cost of production. Imported labor from occupied countries, on the other hand, may be more strictly controlled from the point of view of efficiency, and among foreign workers the discrepancy between the least and most highly valued processes of white collar work may be reduced.

The government had obtained power to coordinate the railway system and road traffic, in order to prevent ruinous competition by an economic allocation of freight to the railways and to motor carriers, in 1931. For more than forty years regional syndicates and cartels had limited transportation costs in their industries by placing orders for all standardized products with the supplier nearest the particular purchaser, and this system is apparently now being extended. The utter neglect of the railways in favor of road transportation by the Nazis has, however, made it necessary to establish a more comprehensive organization. During the past winter a number of local freight officers for the different means of transport were appointed, with functions like those of the regional and local officers appointed in Great Britain by the Ministry of Transport and by the different supply ministries at the outbreak of war.

The pattern of regional organization drawn above underwent a further change in the late summer of 1942 when the Minister of Armament and Munitions formed regional armament committees in every corps area. These committees included the regional armament inspectors of the *O.K.W.* and representatives of the regional defense commissioners, the regional economic offices, the *Hauptausschüsse* and *Ringe* in the Ministry of Armament and Munitions, and of the *Gauwirtschafts-kammern* (District Economic Chambers) of the area. It is not clear from reports published abroad whether the regional organization of the *Rüstungsamt* has been replaced, or whether it has expanded into the new armament committees, as the regional organization of the *Wehrwirtschaftsamt* of the *O.K.W.* was expanded in the first phase of the war into the provincial economic offices.

The new organization represents a great extension of the power of the Minister of Armament and Munitions at the expense of the Ministry of Economics, the Economic Commissioner-General, the employment exchanges, and, possibly, the military supply department. The armament committees must equate the demands for man power by the armed forces and by industry on a regional basis. It is also intended to introduce a regional control of individual plants that will eliminate all direct contact between manufacturers and central government departments and thus reduce bureaucratic work. The armament committees may be described as a combination of the separate British man power boards and regional production boards, given real executive responsibility and brought into close contact at the regional level with the ad-

ministration of economic questions and with the military administration.

This very brief survey of the German wartime administration reveals several characteristics. The most important, although somewhat
modified by the establishment of the Ministry of Armament and Munitions and its regional committees, has been the consistent military
coordination of the entire war effort. The problem of the coordination
and synchronization of strategy and supply has been solved as efficiently
as the interference of Party leaders permits. As far as General Keitel has
Hitler's approval, he is responsible for steering the whole war machine.
As chief of the *Oberkommando der Wehrmacht* he determines the
main lines of strategy and supply for a year or more in advance once
Hitler has decided the largest questions of military and foreign policy.
The functions of the Supreme Defense Council are, as has already been
pointed out, in all likelihood limited to coordination as among the defense forces, the organizations of the Nazi Party, and the civil administration.

It is true that the coordinating influence of general staff officers in
regional administration has been reduced. Nevertheless, the fact that
the supply department of the *O.K.W.* has remained since its incorporation in the Ministry of Armament and Munitions under the single direction of the same general who controls the economic planning department of the *O.K.W.* and the fact that general staff officers remain
in control of certain essential war commodities in the Ministry of Economics and continue to occupy, although to a lesser extent than formerly, both executive and advisory positions throughout the transport
system show that the organization of the *O.K.W.* has at least remained
intact.

It may be assumed that the regional coordination of every aspect of
the war effort, although nominally the responsibility of the regional defense and regional economic commissioners and also, with regard to
production, of the armament committees of the Ministry of Armament
and Munitions is still largely dominated by the staffs of the commanding generals in the corps areas. They are undoubtedly informed by the
O.K.W. of the general lines of strategy and of supply requirements
many months in advance. The *O.K.W.*, on the other hand, can get direct, reliable, and detailed reports on the functioning of the supply organization, the production and distribution of food, the work of the
civil administration, and the actions of Nazi Party agencies at any time

from the staffs of corps area headquarters, the armament inspectors in particular plants or districts, and the regional liaison officers of its economic planning department. Through the corps area headquarters the urgency of various demands made by the military program is impressed on the local institutions of the civil administration and the Nazi Party.

This line of military authority converges in the offices of the regional defense commissioners, which are also the offices of state or provincial governors, with lines running from the Supreme Defense Council, the General Economic Council, the Economic Commissioner-General, and the Ministries of Economics and Agriculture. Thus the traditional concentration of responsibility for the entire administration of a large area in one man has been maintained. As far as the civil administration is concerned the function of the defense commissioner is not one of coordination merely. He has the power of decision over all questions that affect only his region. Thus the central ministries are spared a daily inundation of correspondence and the impossible task of considering innumerable particular cases. The commissioners report to the Supreme Defense Council and to its individual members and may make suggestions concerning any phase of the war effort. They may also request the fuller interpretation of legislation or executive orders.[15a]

Certainly in the *O.K.W.* and its regional organization everything appears to have been done to provide a constructive balance between centralization and devolution, between long range planning and flexible execution, without sacrificing clear responsibility or coordination. Final judgment is, of course, better reserved even in this respect until the system has been tested under other conditions than the generally favorable ones resulting from the fact that the Axis until the autumn of 1942 held the strategic initiative.

Whatever the present influence of the Army and civil service may be either centrally or at the regional level, the German administration is still characterized by concentration of responsibility for major decisions and devolution of authority over execution in detail. The system as such is certainly very well conceived. In spite of the increasing political control exercised, secretly or openly, by the Gestapo and other Nazi Party agencies, and admitting the possibility that some general staff officers

---

[15a] The Supreme Defense Council may appoint a special defense commissioner with overriding powers for any corps area.

may not be equipped for their tremendous responsibilities, it is impossible to deny the great advantages of the organization.

How far this system actually results in coordination at every level in the face of the ambition of every Nazi Party leader to duplicate the functions of existing institutions and the consequent plethora of parallel organizations can hardly be judged from outside. Neither can the effect that the constant threat of intervention by the Gestapo must have on the nerves of those who are doing constructive work. Certainly this threat must paralyze that free and spontaneous initiative which was shown in Great Britain after Dunkirk to be so important in unforeseen emergencies.

In any comparison between the German administration and others, three points should be remembered. First, because of the suppression of public criticism in Germany, failures are not registered outside. Secondly, Germany's long possession of the strategic initiative made the organization of supply much simpler than it can be in a country constantly on the defensive, particularly if in such a country circumstances make it inadvisable to reveal the full extent of military reverses. In the latter case frequent, sudden changes of plan for which no explanation can be offered create a general sense of frustration. Thirdly, changes in the organization of supply correspond to different phases of war production, which do not occur simultaneously in different belligerent countries. Much criticism of wartime administration in Great Britain and the United States is attributable to a failure to appreciate this difference in time periods.

It may be said, finally, that the German wartime administration is characterized by planning from the top down to every municipality and firm and by the greatest possible delegation of responsibility for execution in detail to decentralized administrative institutions either of the Army, the civil administration, organizations of industry and agriculture, or the Nazi Party. The practical obstacles that will always arise to the realization of preconceived plans could not, indeed, be overcome if it were not for the existence of a large number of civil servants trained in the close coordination of different branches of administration at the regional level. Without such coordination central planning will lack the necessary flexibility in application. This is the chronic problem of German administration. It is characteristic of the German mind to crave abstract perfection. Before the Nazis came into power their blueprint schemes of organization won great popularity. In nearly every case these schemes have gone awry in practice, like every previous attempt to introduce an artificial consistency into the system of administration.

The tendency of the British mind is just the opposite, and " planning " finds little favor. Administrative organization is evolved gradually by induction and by trial and error. Every ministry, and perhaps each department of a ministry, expands its own activities as the occasion arises without concern for the functioning of the administration as a whole if the departmental chief is able to accomplish his immediate object. In comparing wartime administration in Great Britain and Germany it is important to bear this temperamental difference in mind.

3. The British System of War Administration

I · ADMINISTRATIVE TRADITION AND THE REGIONAL PROBLEM

In the preceding discussion two main lines of the present German war administration have been emphasized. General Headquarters (the *Oberkommando der Wehrmacht*) is finally responsible for strategy and supply. It controls the entire war effort directly or indirectly through its departments for general production planning and procurement, through their regional and local officers, and through the commanding generals in the corps areas. Thus the *O.K.W.* combines functions which in the last war General Headquarters performed only uncertainly and irregularly. The Army has, on the other hand, lost all influence in questions of internal and international politics in comparison with its position in the last war. This is the natural result of an expansionist, totalitarian form of government. The civil service has similarly lost all political influence, although it has been able to save certain administrative methods and traditions. The Army and the civil service may occasionally be able to prevent a disastrous political decision if they are warned of it in time, but they cannot look for support to Parliament or to public opinion, and key positions in the civil administration are almost all in the hands of Nazi Party members.

In England, despite the inclusive emergency powers voted to the Government in May 1940,[16] the Prime Minister remains accountable to Parliament for the general lines of policy, and each minister remains accountable for the policy of his department. How far Parliament can actually control the policy of the Prime Minister in time of war is doubtful. The Prime Minister and his small War Cabinet must sometimes

---

[16] See Appendix I.

take decisions of the gravest consequence in a few hours; Parliament may later call attention to, but can hardly correct, the results. It can, however, control the administration of each department of state as long as the minister remains unconditionally responsible to Parliament for the policy of his department and the actions, or inaction, of all its employees in Whitehall and in the country at large. This is the mainstay of British Parliamentary government.

It is also the major reason for the difficulty of regional coordination even now, when in spite of the absence of any established tradition the paramount importance of such coordination is universally admitted. The heads of departments are individually responsible for the execution of every decision of the War Cabinet. Thus the machinery of each department extends down to the local level and into individual firms. Even for executive functions that are similar or overlapping this principle is maintained, so that, to take an example, in an emergency the Ministry of Food may operate canteens for a particular locality, while the Ministry of Labor operates canteens for the factories in that locality.

Since a more detailed description of the British wartime administration, analogous to the preceding description of the German administration, is given elsewhere,[16a] the discussion here will be concentrated on the problem of coordination among the executive departments in the central government and in the country at large and on the influence of the civil service and the defense forces and its compatibility with the responsibility of the Prime Minister and the ministerial heads of departments. The role of *the civil service* in England, which was already very large in the last war, has greatly increased since then, and the range of its functions has been widely extended. Although there has been a sharp distinction between British and Continental tradition in this respect ever since many of the older traditions of Continental administration were broken under the impact of Napoleonic totalitarianism, more recent changes in the importance and the functions of the civil service in England and on the Continent have, despite temporary variations, followed somewhat parallel lines.

The influence of the German civil service declined during the last war and in the years immediately following. During the years between 1923 and 1925, when the disastrous effects of the extreme inflation and of stabilization at too high a rate of exchange made themselves fully felt, the civil service and the Army acquired a preponderance of actual

[16a] See Chapter III, Part II, p. 179.

power, which decreased again during the three outwardly prosperous years before 1929. In 1931 and 1932 the likelihood was that the relations of the civil service to the cabinet and to parliament would evolve in the same direction in Germany and in Great Britain. Everywhere in Europe in fact the influence of the civil service, although parliaments opposed it and attempted to obscure it, increased during the '30's. The case will be the same in any grave and prolonged financial and economic crisis. This is why one should expect the importance of the permanent civil service everywhere in the world to increase in the face of complicated problems of reconstruction in the postwar period. In many countries a new equilibrium may have to be established between the civil service, the cabinet, and parliament. A reverse tendency may be looked for only when the world enters a period of prosperity based on internal and international freedom of trade and enterprise.

There are many reasons for the growth of the influence of the civil service in periods of structural economic crisis. Emergency legislation, whatever its constitutional basis, often changes the character of law. Whenever measures have to be taken hurriedly and frequently legislation is bound to assume increasingly the form of decrees or executive orders; this has been more or less the case everywhere. The fact itself is evidence that the problems of legislation had become too complex, and changed too abruptly, for the normal parliamentary technique to be appropriate. Parliaments have striven to maintain their rights of criticism and ultimate control. For the rest they have had in many countries to accept their inability to compete with the accumulated experience, the routine, and the possibilities of long-range planning enjoyed by civil servants who may have devoted the imagination and effort of a lifetime to the solution of a particular problem.

In the light of the experience of all Europe in the interval between the two wars, it can be said without exaggeration that whatever the form of government the bureaucracy has provided a major element of stability. In the last analysis the bureaucracy alone has been in a position to guarantee some continuity in periods of emergency. Under a weak government it may enjoy great powers of initiative and exercise real, if not open, leadership; under a strong government it is restricted to executing orders and instructions. When the policy of a particular cabinet or prime minister seems dangerous, the bureaucracy may find means of indicating that it is not to be identified with the policy of the government, thus preparing the way for its own ascendancy to effective leadership when the government falls without its help. Trained in an old tradition, the bureaucracy is a permanent "brain trust," and not the servant of one government alone or of an unbalanced parliamentary majority. Thus whatever changes in personnel it may undergo, it survives as a body. It gradually accumulates a detailed knowledge of facts and personalities, as well as of the law, which gives its members enormous weight behind the scenes.

This is especially true everywhere of treasury officials. In any ministry, however, civil servants can support or handicap a policy by eliminating, in the first case, or introducing, in the second, a multitude of factual and legal objections. A minister may be generously supplied with information or starved out by the bureaucracy. No newcomer in office can do without its help, especially if he has been shifted frequently in different cabinets from one department to another.

A continuous merry-go-round of cabinet ministers such as occurred in France necessarily increases the power of the civil service in practice, without producing any constructive result. Constant changes in legislation and ambition on the part of a government to associate its regime with as many paragraphs in the statute book as possible, most pronounced in a totalitarian system, will greatly enhance the importance of the civil service. Even in a democratic state like France legislation gradually assumed in normal times, just as in emergencies, the character of administrative decrees, and the authority of Parliament consequently suffered. Most nations naturally fear such an evolution. There are outbursts in almost every parliament from time to time, after the event, against the influence of the civil service. For this the parliament itself is frequently to blame, since the preponderance of actual power in the civil service often results from an attempt to accomplish through frequent legislation functions which should be purely administrative.

It would be wrong to suppose that these are the only reasons for the power of the bureaucracy, or that its influence is always the same, or that it does not meet with strong resistance. The influence that the bureaucracy enjoys is ultimately due to the skill, the routine, and the endurance found in all institutions of long-established tradition. The bureaucracy in Germany, after periods of sterility in which it was the object of bitter criticism, has recovered its influence again and again by finding the will and vigor to reform itself, and has vied with Parliament in discovering administrative abuses and eliminating unnecessary duplication of effort and confusion. It was prepared to adopt efficient new methods of administration from private business and from the municipalities. It constantly measured popular reactions and responded to them by issuing administrative orders or by preparing legislation to be introduced to Parliament before the different political parties, conscious of the same reactions, had decided how to respond to them. In its best periods it was not directed by Parliamentary criticism but rather took the initiative in the passage by Parliament of measures that were sound for the country as a whole but not to begin with popular politically.

All this may be said, too, of the *English civil service* in the last war and again in the economic crisis in the early '30's. Until then the economic and administrative problems of Great Britain had been much simpler than those of almost any other European country. With a stable currency, more or less free trade, and the absence of state ownership and operation of transportation facilities, mines, or forests, government interference in the economy was largely limited to financial control. The civil service was not required to exercise any initiative except in the preparation of legislation in response to Parliamentary pressure. The policy of non-interference was easily compatible with extreme centralization of power, first in the Crown and later in Parliament. Fiscal and judicial control were all that was required for the enforcement of acts of Parliament. The experience of patronage in the seventeenth and eighteenth centuries also created suspicion of any activity by government officers.

Thus in English administration, contrary to Continental administrative practice, there has been until recently *no intermediate executive institution between the central government and the local authorities.* There are separate health officers, employment officers, factory inspectors, inland revenue and customs collectors of course, and officers of the departments of the Admiralty concerned with the royal dockyards, naval construction, engineering, ordnance, etc. The War Office has maintained ordnance factories and permanent depots for the regular and territorial armies in peacetime. There has, however, been no specific executive institution between the county councils or municipalities and the central administration. The county councils have only limited executive functions, which are defined by Parliamentary legislation.

There has been no office like that of the German provincial or district governor or, to take a somewhat different example, the French *préfet,* all of whom have general executive powers in their administrative areas.

In the absence of any such intermediate institution between Whitehall and the municipalities, changing conceptions of the government's role in economic planning and, more especially, the direct intervention of the government in economic life in wartime have led to the over-elaboration of the machinery of each of the central executive departments both at the top and in its subordinate branches.

There are other reasons for the rising influence of the civil service. The experience of the past fifteen years has shown that the increasing selection of members of Parliament by party machines rather than by the electorate has not served to improve the quality of Parliamentary representation. The fact that ranking members of the present Cabinet, with influence second only to the Prime Minister's, have been drawn from the civil service is indicative of the growing importance of the purely administrative functions of government and of administrative training. Whatever the future evolution may be, however, the tradition that has characterized relations between the civil service, the Government, and Parliament in England since the disappearance of the system of patronage is still very strong.

Why is it that, except for a few smaller countries, it is only in the Anglo-Saxon countries that this conception of the restricted role of the civil service in relation to parliament and the Government survives so strongly? It cannot be assumed that it is only because their love of an easy-going life of individual freedom is more pronounced than that of other nations. Except in wars and grave emergencies, a free and unregulated existence is most satisfactory to human nature everywhere. The Anglo-Saxon countries are conspicuous, however, for the performance of many tasks of a purely administrative character not by an effectively organized professional administration under the control of cabinet ministers, but by special commissions and committees and by semi-judicial institutions.

The explanation may be that extreme individualism and a loosely organized administration is possible in a country that has not suffered from foreign invasion for many generations and even appears from its geographic position to be immune. It is fair to state that in the long run *the nature of administration in peacetime,* and consequently the manner in which the requirements of war are met, *generally depends upon the probability of foreign invasion.* Great Britain has been able to rely in safety through four hundred years on her sea frontiers.

Alertness, naval preparedness, and the prompt adaptation of strategic plans to changes in the balance of naval power are all that is required for her security in normal times. This leads, rightly, to the control of peacetime armament in accordance with the demands of naval supremacy and the tactical development of sea warfare. It leads further to the independent organization of naval supply and to priority for naval contracts over those of the other defense forces. For the same reason, the views of the Admiralty usually tip the scales in considerations of British foreign policy. Great Britain's position has been changed by air armament and technical progress in the range, speed, and carrying capacity of airplanes. Even when the necessity of quick, simultaneous armament in the air and on the sea was recognized in 1937, however, priority was maintained for the orders placed independently by the Admiralty.

The peacetime role of the army in a country with sea frontiers is necessarily a minor one. In Great Britain the strength of the Army is generally reduced immediately after the conclusion of peace to what is required for skeleton forces in India and the Colonies, the protection of the lifelines of the British Empire, and the staffing of ordnance depots. Parliament cannot be induced to support a large army, or even a skeleton organization that could be rapidly expanded in case of war. As far as regards supply, the Army is the Cinderella of the defense forces in peacetime and during the first phase of a war.

As long as the Navy is able and ready to meet any threat of attack, military and civilian administration can remain loosely organized. Thus Parliament and the Cabinet will appear at least to direct the whole policy of the country, without the existence of a large civil service either at the top or at a subordinate, regional level, and without much planning ahead. Legislation is executed under the supervision of government inspectors by municipalities, and to a more limited extent by county councils or special commissions created *ad hoc*. Certain changes made in this picture by the administrative provisions for social security do not alter it essentially.

There is little incentive in such a situation, while the navy or air force can guarantee the flow of necessary imports, to the planning of armament production in peacetime. Any urgent arrangements can be made by cabinet ministers and their staffs on the one side and private associations in industry, trade, and agriculture on the other. In such an administrative system the permanent civil service is confined for the most part to the central ministries, and its methods conform to the pattern of treasury control. Political control over administration remains to parliament, and legal control, to the regular courts.

The condition of countries with open land frontiers is, and always will be, quite different. The necessity for a central direction of every branch of the administration in strict accordance with a general policy increases in proportion to the "openness" of the frontiers. In eastern Europe, where there are vast plains, and where rivers often fail to provide a natural barrier against attack, the tendency towards centralization is greatest. Military requirements, as a result either of long-established tradition or of repeated experience, have generally had an important influence on the normal method of administration. There are exceptions to this rule. In France, for example, Revolutionary and Napoleonic totalitarianism was at least as much responsible as considerations of military necessity for the centralization of the administration. The two factors combined to make the Napoleonic prefectural system the prototype of extremely centralized bureaucracy.

Such long range economic planning as was attempted in many countries after the last war can hardly succeed without a permanent body of experienced civil servants and without coordination at the regional level of most of the functions of administration. Otherwise an executive officer of one department may be ignorant of activities corresponding to his own by agents of other departments, or even of other divisions of his own department, in the same district. With one man responsible for the coordination of the activities of different departments within his region, instructions are passed down to the lowest ranks of the administration easily and quickly, and with some guarantee that they will be carried out as originally intended. Through such an official the central authorities will also discover whether a general instruction is impracticable, and why, more directly than through scattered agents of every branch of administration in each region. Members of an intermediate regional administration trained in peacetime in such duties of coordination as have already been described can contribute their knowledge of the population, of industrialists, farmers, and traders, to the solution of problems of military supply in wartime. In an era of total warfare this thorough knowledge of local conditions is especially important.

The absence of a regional administration of the Continental type in Great Britain has been a serious and admitted drawback in this war. It is extremely difficult for higher civil servants in Whitehall to ascertain how Government policy operates in detail in the country at large. Human reactions to executive directions will always make themselves felt more slowly than under the Continental system of administration. This means a waste of time, material, labor, and, even more, of human energy and imagination. Deficiencies are discovered by the ministries for the most part by accident, through the medium of Parliamentary criticism or of the enormous number of visits to the ministries made daily by industrialists and by labor and farm leaders. The physical capacity of the higher civil servants is inevitably overtaxed, and this leads to the loss of their freshness, initiative, and imagination.

In wartime it means, too, that collaboration at the top between the civil service and the defense forces, in so far as it is dependent on a clear appreciation of conditions in the country, is defective. It is extremely difficult to form a picture of a nation's war effort from the correspondence of the separate departments of every ministry with municipalities, county councils, special local committees, and trade associations. Problems in the allocation of man power and industrial capacity can hardly be solved by this method. Since the Admiralty has had its own organization for the supervision of individual plants, and the Air Ministry has adopted a similar organization, there has been much friction and wasted effort both at the top and at the regional and local levels.

The British supply system and the whole organization of production was perhaps too much influenced in the first phase of the war by the system of raw material control developed during the last war. At that time people with business experience in a particular trade were appointed government purchasing agents. Little interference from central ministries was required, and wide discretion could be left to subordinate officers. In most cases ministers and high permanent officials were concerned only with decisions of major importance and with the enforcement of certain indispensable regulations ensuring uniformity of practice or preventing injustice and corruption.

Once leading officials in a ministry have secured a legal basis for action, they must formulate regulations to be observed uniformly. If their application in detail can be left without risk to subordinates with business experience, as is the case in the control of particular commodities, the higher officers have then to intervene only when a breakdown threatens and when new problems of general concern arise. In the solution of intricate questions of industrial capacity and man power which occur in each new phase of war production, and which vary in every part of the country and concern different ministries, this easy method is hardly applicable. This is especially so in the case of small firms not represented in any influential trade association. There the questions to be decided include the best possible use of their capacity, the advisability of their closing down, whether to withdraw their labor supplies or to increase them, and, finally, what raw materials and semi-finished products they may acquire, and when. Such problems can be solved only on the spot by officials whose instructions are broad enough to leave them a margin of freedom in deciding each case quickly on its merits, and who do not have to stop half-way because of a conflict of jurisdiction.

Such instructions must be formulated with a view to their application under widely varying circumstances. They must state what may and may not, rather than what should, be done. Good administration is an art very difficult to acquire. Breadth of vision and legal exactness in the central ministries must be combined with adaptability to special needs at the regional and local levels. This problem was solved by the German civil service in its best periods by the constant interchange of personnel between the different levels of administration.

Even such a tradition and training may prove inadequate without regular coordination between different departments at the regional level. If such coordination is lacking, and if the regional and local officers of different departments are not all imbued with similar principles, it may well happen that the constructive efforts of the regional officers of one department are frustrated by rigid insistence on precedent in another. This danger is increased when the experience of regional and local officials is limited to a single department, or when, as is the case with the British Admiralty in relation to the other supply departments, the regional organization of one department enjoys an established routine while the organization of other departments has been hastily expanded. Between regional officers with great experience of administration in one department and inexperienced or unimaginative officers in other departments there is bound to be friction and delay. The distinct and independent regional organizations of each ministry and each department within a ministry may be appropriately compared to threads strung in a loom without a shuttle.

At this point in the discussion it will have become clear why in every region one man of vision and experience and legal knowledge enough to reconcile the conflicting conceptions and methods of different departments is required to exercise over the officers of every department in his region the control exercised at the top by the central offices of each department separately. He can avoid duplication and delay and the establishment of overlapping agencies. Only the existence of regional officials responsible for the coordination of every phase of the war effort within their areas and with power to make quick decisions on the spot can prevent the national administration from becoming topheavy. It will spare the heads of departments in the central ministries the burden of enormous correspondence and constant committee meetings, which forces them to neglect their proper functions of general planning and control, however admirably fitted for them by training and experience they may be.

This is a great disadvantage of the British war administration in comparison with the German, in which all correspondence between regional officers and the Supreme Defense Council, the Economic Commissioner-General, or the central departments is handled by the permanent staffs of provincial and state governors. Such highly trained officials can unravel complications or decide special cases and so spare officials in the central departments as much time as possible for planning and general direction. The position of the *regional defense commissioners* in the twelve areas into which Great Britain has been divided for purposes of defense may seem analogous to that of the German defense commissioners; it was indeed hoped that the regional defense commissioners might perform the same function of coordination.

That would have meant that they assumed full responsibility in their regions for every part of the war effort outside the control of the Army, Navy, and Air Force. It would have meant, too, that any central department could obtain from the regional commissioners at any time a complete statement of the practical effect of its orders. By meeting from time to time with the principal ministerial committees of the Cabinet, the regional commissioners could have gained some insight into the most urgent problems of production and of interdepartmental cooperation, which can never be achieved by correspondence. In fact, however, the executive powers of the regional defense commissioners have been limited for the most part to the hypothetical cases of invasion or the interruption of communications with London by bombing attacks.

Without any responsible coordination at the regional level, each ministry has created its own more or less independent regional organization. There is not regular contact between the regional officials of all the departments and the regional defense commissioners, not to mention the absence of any jurisdiction by the regional defense commissioners over the officers of different departments. Nor have the regional officers of the various departments within the same region much contact with one another. Wherever there is coordination in any particular respect, as in the *area supply boards,* the officers of each department retain the right to refer any decision back to their own ministry. This of course entails renewed consultation among the different departments concerned at the top if corresponding instructions are to be issued to the different regional officers. The consequence is an enormous duplication of labor and loss of time both at the regional level and, where it is more important, at the top.

It appears, furthermore, that when regional coordination of the different departments concerned with production was first attempted through the area supply boards, the chairmen were retired naval officers and civil servants. That is to say, each of them had behind him very likely the training of a lifetime in a single branch of administration, which did not help him to understand the often very different methods of other services. Civil servants are for the most part exchanged between ministries only after they have reached the top positions of undersecretary or principal. Short of that, they become specialists in a particular routine. The great disadvantage of this training for any interdepartmental coordination is that civil servants in the lower ranks have no opportunity to acquire an understanding of the implications of one ministry's policies for the work of other ministries.

In local administrative agencies like the employment exchanges under the Ministry of Labor there will be a large number of officials who are acquainted only with the limited problems of their own offices and have no comprehensive knowledge of national issues. Thus they gradually forget the reasons for which their own branch of administration was originally established. There were many complaints, for example, at the beginning of the war that the officers of the employment exchanges had come during the prolonged economic crisis to confine their activities to the payment of the dole and no longer concerned themselves with the organization of the labor market or the causes of unemployment in different localities. From this one must conclude that the regional officers (divisional controllers) who existed, by exception from the practice of most other departments, in the Ministry of Labor failed to inspire the subordinate local officers with any constructive purpose. The particular functions and training of the divisional controllers of the Ministry of Labor during the prewar period are not clear, however, to the outsider.

In judging the whole present need for regional organization in the British civil service, one should remember that the evolution away from strict Treasury control toward greater initiative in civil service training has been comparatively recent and rather slow. Great Britain has had at her disposal in the last war and at present not only highly trained and farsighted Treasury officials, who have few equals in Europe, but also ranking civil servants with varied experience in responsible positions in different executive departments and in the colonies. It is on civil servants of this type that the main burden of coordination of the war effort at the top and at the regional level has fallen. Even the outsider sees that the tasks of Sir John Anderson, who rose in the home civil service to an Indian governorship before entering the House of Commons and the Cabinet, of the present War Secretary, who also held a responsible position in India before he became under-secretary of the War Office, and of many permanent under-secretaries and directors of divisions within ministries demand the highest personal qualifications. It is mainly because men of exceptional qualifications were available that the administration was kept in gear in the confusion of the suddenly changed strategic situation resulting from the defeat in France.

The existence of a limited number of such first class civil servants of very wide experience does not by itself completely alter long-standing traditions of the civil service determined by the form and incidence of *Treasury control*. Treasury control, for historical reasons and because of certain characteristics of the British Parliamentary system, is the most significant element of British administration. This is true to some extent in other countries as well, since the influence of every parliament originated with, and in the final analysis depends upon, the right to vote revenue and appropriations. Nowhere else, however, has this fact remained so plainly evident or received so much formal expression as in England, and nowhere else has the treasury exercised such strict control over local government through the administration of grants-in-aid.

The Chancellor of the Exchequer has played a predominant role in the Cabinet and in Parliament. Even the Prime Minister holds office as the nominal First Lord of the Treasury. The character and functioning of the entire civil service is largely decided by the Treasury's traditional control over expenditure and revenue. Since the office of head of the civil service was created it has been held by the permanent under-secre-

tary of the Treasury. One can say without oversimplification that the traditional functions of Treasury officials have been the most important influence on the character and mentality of the civil service. This has been
largely due, of course, to the principle of government non-interference
in economic life except by fiscal control.

In many other European countries, although the influence of the
treasury remained predominant in administration, other conceptions
as well have evolved during the centuries in which the state has owned
and managed mines and forests. Such tasks require special training in
addition to normal civil service training. The whole outlook of civil
servants so employed came to differ widely from that of treasury officials, who exercise a restrictive control over administration by checking
expenditure. They were concerned rather with increasing the revenue
of state owned properties or services by improved management. This
entailed the combination of two different types of administration and
made a restricted departmental outlook impossible.

Wherever the standards of the civil service were high, regional and
local officers were expected to display initiative and creative imagination
as well as a sense of definite responsibility. There were experts on all
questions available in the civil service for important positions in the
central ministries or elsewhere in the country whenever new problems
of administration arose. They had the advantage of not having spent
their lives in central offices, remote from realities and from the people
whose conduct formed the object of legislation, and they were frequently exchanged between departments. Civil servants trained in the
old treasury style, or those who have spent their lives in one department, rising slowly by seniority, cannot have the same knowledge of
varying local conditions or the same adaptability.

Civil servants of the type developed in England under the system
of Treasury control while it was the first ambition of the Chancellor
of the Exchequer to present a budget without increased taxation, or
even perhaps with a reduction of the income tax, are of course no longer
to be found in the top ranks. Since the last war, and especially since 1931,
the scope and the personal breadth of vision of leading officials in the
British Treasury have been unrivalled, on the average, in most other
countries. They cannot be blamed for the present difficulties arising
from older traditions and methods of training in the civil service.

The indisputable fact is that for treasury control of expenditure, which
is one of the vital functions of administration everywhere, men of a par-

ticular type, indifferent to the glamour of novel proposals for spending money, are needed. Unless they are hard and skeptical in this respect they will fail in their duty. The consequence, however, is in many cases an unimaginative rigidity. Elaborate formality on the part of the treasury may entail greater eventual expenditure than the ready acceptance of measures the original cost of which is apparently high. None of this matters if there is a balance in the administrative service as a whole between progressive and enterprising civil servants in other branches of the administration and more cautious, in the lower ranks possibly even pedantic, civil servants in the treasury. The danger lies in training an entire civil service on the model of the latter type and in confining the activity of the civil service exclusively to central departments.

Thus such outbursts against the civil service as occurred in the House of Lords in February and March 1941 and in the press overshoot the mark. In this case it is only natural that equally bitter criticism should since have been directed against politicians as a class. The shortcomings of the wartime administration in the first phase of the war should in fact be attributed to the British political system as a whole, which, with its very agreeable traditions and particularities, works so smoothly in normal times.[16b]

It is easy to understand why, when strict departmental traditions still survive in the older generation, efforts to coordinate even the placing of orders for armament by the different supply departments at the regional level have not been wholly successful. The very great reluctance of English business to accept any bureaucratic interference has deprived the civil service of much experience of economic problems. This is one reason why, for example, in the summer of 1942 prominent in-

---

[16b] The problem has been stated very well in a discussion of the *Sixteenth Report* of the House of Commons Select Committee on National Expenditure in *The Economist* of November 7, 1942. There a demand is made for a redistribution of responsibility among civil servants as a preliminary to the more logical distribution of functions among departments recommended by the Haldane Committee in 1918. " On the one hand, civil servants, even in key positions, are not encouraged or even expected to make decisions on their own responsibility, without a frustrating process of reference back, discussion, argument, self-justification, and self-protection. On the other hand, the existing rigid system of recruitment, appointment, grading and promotion frequently makes it impossible for the right men to be placed in the right positions." The author adds that " the entry of temporary civil servants from the outside world of business, scholarship, and the professions has shown what can be done to fit men to jobs, even with the existing inhibitions and frustrations." In the German administration much of the same criticism, which would formerly have been unjustified, may now be made of certain branches of the civil service which have been deprived under the centralized Nazi system of their old willingness to accept grave responsibility and to exercise initiative of their own.

dustrialists instead of civil servants were appointed regional controllers for the new Ministry of Production.

This is not symptomatic of a *malaise* peculiar to Great Britain. The administrative functions of individual industrialists and of corporative organizations in certain industries have been extended in Germany, too, as stated above, at the expense of the established administration. The use of a similar form of corporative organization for the self-government of whole industries in England has been widely discussed during 1942. To appreciate the whole problem of British administration, one must realize that the tradition confining the civil service almost exclusively to Whitehall is very strong, and that the regional officers who have been appointed by various departments have had little assistance in evolving some means of coordinating their efforts with those of the representatives of other departments in the same regions. They proceed in accordance with the emergency motto " Il faut se débrouiller."

It would be quite wrong to suppose that this method results in chaos. It merely fails to produce the maximum result possible when it may be most necessary. It does assure the Admiralty, where regional and local officers of long standing know the specific problems of shipbuilding and naval supply, of its maximum share of the industrial capacity and skilled labor of the country. Any department under a minister as indifferent to the inhibitions imposed by the necessity of general coordination as Lord Beaverbrook may likewise succeed in getting its share, but probably only at the sacrifice of steady production for all the defense forces and the adjustment of the whole production of the country to long-range strategic plans. With pulling and hauling between ministries, the task of coordination and mediation falling to the top civil servants becomes necessarily harder.

Suspicion of any intermediate administrative institution between the local authorities, which, it must always be remembered, have never enjoyed as much " home rule " as municipalities in pre-Nazi Germany or in the United States, and Whitehall is deeply rooted in the British nation. Hence any discussion of the possibility of making the office of regional defense commissioner permanent, and entrusting such regional commissioners with a large degree of responsibility in peacetime as a counterweight to over-centralization, has subsided. The Minister of Home Security, under whom the regional defense commissioners hold office, has said that if the regional commissioners were given executive powers over the different branches of administration at the regional level, the opposition of local authorities would be such that they would find no cooperation. The establishment of a permanent responsible regional organization and the development of a large civil service in the country would, it is true, entail some alteration of the British political system.

The results of this instinctive opposition to any effective regional institution for coordinating the independent activities of the regional officials of various ministries as they appear in the initial slowness with which plans decided on by the Cabinet are carried out is often overlooked. The inductive method, which is applied within each ministry as well as in interdepartmental coordination, takes time. Eventually of course the machinery of each department is improved, suitable positions are found for capable men, and, which is even more important, definite responsibility is established. Individual cooperation among the officers of different departments may then result in as effective coordination as is secured in Germany by the concentration of authority in each region, but the British system in comparison with the German is exposed to the disadvantage of a time lag.

An organization established by the method of trial and error, while it will not be systematic, will be practical and will be free from the dangers of conformity to an artificial pattern which exist at present in Germany. It may be surmised that the recent organization of *Gauwirtschaftskammern,* for example, was not due to necessity but rather to the Nazi hobby of streamlining everything on paper. Since the *Gaue,* while they are more or less identical with the regions of the labor administration, do not correspond to the corps areas or to the regional divisions of the provincial economic offices, further reorganization will be necessary before the various subdivisions of administration can be made to present an appearance of perfect congruity. There is the risk that in this process great experience and very valuable traditions may be sacrificed to political ambition and superficial uniformity.

The contrary is true of the British system. In the Ministry of Food, for example, rationing to consumers is based on county and municipal committees, which are grouped in regions corresponding to the civil defense regions. For more general purposes of distribution, however, the country is divided into eight areas, determined by purely practical considerations of transport, and local groups of wholesalers are forbidden to deal with retailers outside their areas. For the purchase of particular commodities from producers and their distribution to wholesalers, again, the various controls in the ministry have their own area divisions, which correspond to the centers of supply. This solution is very complicated on paper, but to all appearances very satisfactory in practice.

The adjustment of the supply of labor to present and future industrial capacity is of course much more difficult. The employment exchanges, which had, as has already been mentioned, atrophied with respect to certain of their functions, have been adapted to the present emergency in so far as they receive instructions locally from man power officers and from special labor supply officers for the industries to which Essential Work Orders have been applied, and regionally from the regional controllers of the Ministry of Labor. As far as can be judged, the somewhat casual system of consultation between labor supply officers introduced in the summer of 1940 has been replaced by closer coordination within smaller districts of the work of man power officers, who control military recruiting as well as the transfer of labor, and who receive instructions from the regional controllers of the ministry. The latter must have some knowledge of general problems of production and of the plans agreed on centrally by the supply ministries.

Responsibility for the coordination of the work of regional officers of the different supply departments now rests with the regional controllers of the Ministry of Production, who are, as has already been mentioned, not civil servants but business men and industrialists. The problem resulting from the existence of an independent and long established supply organization in the Admiralty has not of course been solved. Neither have the regional controllers of the Ministry of Production any executive authority over the representatives of other departments. In shipbuilding, where the functions of the Admiralty are definitely preponderant, the employment and release of labor and the allocation of capacity and materials as between naval and merchant shipbuilding and repairs are under direct Admiralty control.

II · CABINET RESPONSIBILITY AND COORDINATION

These few instances may perhaps convey an impression of the working of the British system. There can be no doubt that the maximum utilization of capacity is attained more slowly than under the German system. It is also true that the British system may be more flexible in emergencies. The method of proceeding at the regional level by trial and error may, however, entail great difficulties unless there is comprehensive planning in the Cabinet and close coordination among the executive departments in all military and supply problems. In the present German system, in which the best possible arrangements are made for such planning at the center, deficiencies at the regional level, where they exist, are less dangerous than in England. The commanders of the corps areas with their supply departments (*Rüstungsämter*) and the defense commissioners, whose staffs have a long training in regional coordination, can find the easiest way out of any difficulty. It is doubtful whether the regional controllers of the British Ministry of Production, business men familiar for the most part with one type of production, can be similarly efficient, especially since they have no executive powers. It is also doubtful whether the best British regional defense commissioners could assume the role of their German counterparts even if the Government desired it, since the British civil service has no tradition in the coordination of the functions of different departments at the regional level. The fact that a special regional commissioner for the supervision of communications in the London area was appointed in 1940 in addition to the existing defense commissioner and his deputies is evidence of this.

Had the British defense commissioners the function of coordinating every aspect of the war effort in their regions, it would nevertheless be difficult for them to obtain definite instructions from the Government, since every minister is anxious, because of his responsibility to Parliament, to keep all executive power in his department in his own hands. This factor also affects the method of cooperation among Cabinet ministers and top civil servants in the central ministries.

One main consideration should dominate the organization of wartime administration at the top and at the regional level — a right balance between centralization in planning and supervision and flexibility in detailed execution and adaptation to new tasks or changed conditions. When organization is too rigid and planning too conventional there is a danger that in sudden emergencies or under the strain of unforeseen developments the whole machinery may break down. The farther executive centralization is carried, the more that danger increases. But if there is no definite prearranged relation between central and regional administration, many valuable months and years may be lost in wartime by muddling through.

In the first part of this war, time counted heavily, since Germany had been able to begin the mass production of armaments at the end of 1936. Modern techniques of mass production necessitate a comparatively long interval between the designing and testing of a weapon and capacity production. Thus any country entering a war with a three years' lead in armament production and capacity has a great initial advantage over an opponent that will reach capacity production only later.

These factors must be borne in mind in an analysis of *coordination of central departments* in Great Britain, since they have contributed to make the tasks of wartime administration much heavier. The immediate difficulties increased when war actually broke out; they increased threefold after the Battle of France. This explains to some extent why necessary measures were delayed, why Cabinet members were constantly shifted, and why the organization of the Cabinet and the administrative services has undergone such frequent drastic changes. Ministers or committees which seemed energetic and efficient in one phase of the war failed when confronted with different problems of unexpected magnitude in the next. The methods and the personnel of committees that had developed a satisfactory routine after initial experimentation suddenly proved useless. Committees appointed for a particular purpose survived after having lost their original functions. Excellent team work achieved over long periods of regular collaboration and personal acquaintance failed in the face of novel and complex problems demanding greater imagination and physical vitality.

Whether or not advantage is taken of a nation's gifts of improvisation will depend on the constructive imagination of its political leaders and civil servants. The inventiveness of any nation varies from generation to generation. It is usually heightened after defeat. Whether or not political and military leaders and civil servants of imagination and initiative are available, however, the wartime problems of precise definition of responsibility and coordination of the main lines of foreign policy, strategy, and supply are the same.

There must be a small *war cabinet* or defense council to support and to control the prime minister's policy. Such a cabinet must be responsible for the general lines of strategy and of economic organization, and for the coordination of the whole administration as well as for the solution of specific problems as they arise. It cannot consider details, but it must make definite plans. It must be composed of people capable of quick decision, each of whom exercises direct supervision over a certain branch of administration. It must have team spirit. The *prime minister* should be freed as much as possible from the burden of detail. When particular cases that have acquired major importance are brought to his attention he must dispose of them decisively. He cannot indulge in procrastination by paper compromises that have no practical result. His mind must be kept fresh to anticipate the requirements of the immediate and the more distant future. All this means that he must have great experience, knowledge, imagination, courage, and strength.

He must exercise initiative in the general conduct of the war, and must also have the gift of putting the right man in the right place. He must refrain from occupying himself with everyone's business. His task is to keep his eyes and ears open, to inspire and direct the efforts of his colleagues, parliament, and the public. He must avoid the excitement of popular emotion by continual sensations, and he must express burning passion as well as serene calm and balance of mind. Such a figure cannot be found in every nation at every major crisis. Nor will he be able if he is in power to discover at once the collaborators he needs.

In the latter respect the British Prime Minister's difficulties are greater than any which exist in totalitarian states or in the United States. The President of the United States is restricted in his appointments only by the necessity in some cases of obtaining senatorial approval, which is assured in any grave emergency. He can appoint able and experienced men to direct the most important war agencies and assure them of a comparatively long tenure of office, which is one of the essential conditions of constructive leadership. They need not be members of his Cabinet, which therefore does not become so large that it is necessary to form a super-Cabinet, as is the case in England. When the President wishes to do so, he will have relatively little difficulty in conferring on one man full responsibility for the control of production, prices, and labor in relation to the war effort and in defining his functions as broadly as he chooses. He can decide whether to make the Cabinet the highest coordinating authority by including such a man in it, or whether to become himself the final arbiter by establishing independent agencies outside the regular departments. He may confine himself to acting as the impartial chairman of the Cabinet, or may hold Cabinet meetings only rarely, deciding the main lines of policy himself in consultation with individual Cabinet members or the heads of special agencies, or even with personal advisers.

Constitutionally the President of the United States could create a simpler, more sharply defined, and more centralized organization at the top than exists in Germany. He might, of course, encounter opposition in Congress if he attempted to put any military officer in the same dominating position that Marshal Keitel and his staff occupy under Hitler. Congressional control over legislation is much more active than Parliamentary control in England. At the beginning of a war, however, when popular emotion is strong enough to prevent any Congressional opposition, the President will have no difficulty in securing full powers. As enthusiasm subsides, he may of course have to meet greater resistance. In England, on the other hand, Parliament has been increasingly prepared as the country's danger has increased to confer any power desired on the Government, wisely confining itself to the function of constructive criticism.

Even with his present enormous powers, the British Prime Minister labors under difficulties which do not exist to any comparable extent in the United States. They result from the complexity of the interests of the world-wide British Empire, from deeply ingrained constitutional traditions, and, finally, from the necessity of maintaining a balance of power between the members of a coalition Government. In an empire scattered over all the earth the number and complexity of the questions involved in the efficient coordination of strategy and foreign policy, the timing of military action, the seizure of favorable strategic opportunities in spite of the possible consequences for foreign policy, and the coordination of the plans of the three defense forces is obviously overwhelming. The dominions of the British Commonwealth are bound only in a loose federal union by common allegiance to the Crown, and identity of interest in one part of the world does not necessarily imply identity of interest elsewhere. Strategic opportunities may be neglected in one theatre because to take advantage of them would involve political complications in another. Great Britain in fact enjoys complete freedom of strategic movement only after the entire world is arrayed in two or more opposing camps, and the complete and effective participation of all the dominions is assured.

The effect of existing British constitutional and political traditions in conditions like the present is to burden the Prime Minister, whose role in normal times is that of the chairman of a committee, with such a number of particular vital decisions that it is extremely difficult for him to find the necessary freedom for the planning and initiation of general lines of policy. His problems of organization arise in part from the fact that the head of every executive department in the British Government must be a member of the House of Commons or the House of Lords. For historical reasons, and because of a largely traditional division of functions which has little relation to the specific problems of this war, the Government includes more than twenty-five ministers of Cabinet rank. Each minister is responsible to Parliament for all the executive functions of his department, and this has led, as has been mentioned, to duplication and overlapping in administration in the country at large. The essential problem of coordination among departments in Whitehall and their officers in different parts of the country has thus assumed such proportions that it obscures the definite ministerial responsibility upon which the whole system of British Parliamentary government rests.

One manifestation of this is the rank growth of interdepartmental committees. Another is the formation of a super-Cabinet and super-ministries, though without any clear distinction between executive and coordinating functions and so without achieving the essential purpose of such super-groupings. A successful combination of closely related executive functions in a single ministry has been achieved only in the case of the Ministry of War Transport. Between the Ministries of Agriculture and Food, for example, there is cooperation but not unified direction, with little regular contact between their agencies in the country at large. None of the attempts made thus far to solve the problems of coordination of supply and of the strategy of the three defense forces, and thus to relieve the Prime Minister of very exacting duties, seems to have been wholly successful, although great progress has been made during 1942.

The difficulties inherent in long established traditions have been increased by the necessity of securing a balance of power in the Ministry and in the War Cabinet among the different Parliamentary parties in the coalition Government. *Government by coalition* in wartime has several drawbacks. The influence of very able ministers over their own parties is weakened by the absence of any active opposition to consolidate support within the Government for necessary measures. The lack of an official opposition for the expression of dissatisfaction in a long and disappointing war results also in the election of independent, non-party candidates who may upset established Parliamentary practice. By far the most important weakness, however, is that the Prime Minister is not free to select ministers for the departments in which they are most likely to be successful. Members of Parliament of long political experience have had to be appointed to positions in the Government for which administrative talents and experience should have been the only qualification. Others have been given sinecure Cabinet offices with nominal functions of general coordination. In fact the full burden of coordination of civil and of military affairs rests on a former civil servant holding political office and a general without executive powers performing the function of liaison between the Prime Minister and the service and supply departments, although it may be assumed that during 1942 the Minister of Production has acquired an increasing share of responsibility.

To anticipate a problem about which more must be said later, it is clear that a successful ministry of production must have executive responsibility for general economic planning, for supply for all the defense forces and the synchronization of production with strategy, and for the distribution of labor. That such responsibility has not been established is due not only to constitutional considerations, but also to the fact that very likely no one has seemed ready to assume these functions of supreme executive control, that if someone did the two major coalition parties would hardly agree to submit all these questions to his decision, and that there is no administrative organization for the coordinated execution of the instructions of such a ministry in the country at large.

The alternative to appointing ministers on the basis of their importance in their own parties rather than of their personal capacities is the appointment as ministers of civil servants, business men, industrialists, and trade unionists who are not members of Parliament and for whom seats in the House of Commons must be found or peerages created. By this means important offices have been increasingly neutralized from the political point of view. The War Office and the Ministries of Food, Production, Supply, War Transport, and Labor are now, and the Ministry of Works and Buildings and the Board of Trade have been, in the hands of men who entered the Government either before or immediately after having become members of Parliament for the express purpose of taking administrative office. Thus the constitutional position has been saved, and the civil service and the defense forces seem still to be subordinate to ministers who are members of and responsible to Parliament. This is, however, the outward constitutional aspect; it forms a legal screen for the actual preponderance of the defense forces and the civil service in planning and administration. Much misunderstanding of the British wartime administration and much exaggerated criticism of its coordination may be attributed to the existence of this screen, which also complicates any outline of executive functions.

Either under a coalition government or under a one-party government the gradual replacement of ministers who are not up to the jobs to which they have been assigned and for which they may have no inclination by other members of Parliament or by outsiders is a long and tedious process. Every British Prime Minister in the past has had to make ministerial appointments from among the members of his party in Parliament with a view to strengthening his hold over the party as a whole. He must consider prestige established and rewards earned in opposition. Members of Parliament who have been most conspicuous in criticism of a previous government and are consequently popular in the country may not be by any means the best people for important administrative offices. They may be devoid of creative imagination, energy, initiative, or administrative genius. Their efforts may be concentrated in Parliamentary or public brilliance. They may aspire to political longevity and therefore oppose beneficial but controversial measures, without hesitating at the same time to create differences in Parliament and the country if that promises to advance them on the ladder leading to the position of Chancellor of the Exchequer or even Prime Minister. The problem is not, of course, peculiar to Great Britain.

None of this mattered when the power of England was uncontested and her wealth expanding, and when even major political errors could be repaired without the loss of too much power and prestige. That was the ideal period for political leaders who were brilliantly gifted for parliamentary debate but amateurs in administration and therefore happy to refer any difficult question to the judiciary, to a special commission, or to some legalistic expert in the Cabinet. It passed during the last war. England's difficulties have been largely due to her return for some time between the last war and the present one to that easy-going and certainly most agreeable system. The most farsighted and energetic members of Parliament were pushed into the background lest they should spoil the picture of modest but steady progress.

Years ago it became evident that this method was unsatisfactory. Unprecedented tasks in organization and administration had to be performed in a very short time in 1931–32, and again after the need for rapid rearmament was recognized in 1936. Under the fire of Parliamentary criticism Cabinets were continually reshuffled. The Prime Minister was not free, however, any more than the present Prime Minister is, to choose the best men for the most exacting tasks. That was made the more difficult by the fact that the British Parliament, in contrast to many other European Parliaments, is very moderate in its criticism of ministers and is prepared to condone the blunders of anyone who openly confesses his mistakes or omissions. In the long run this is certainly a great advantage for the dignity of Parliamentary traditions, but for a Prime Minister of great imagination and initiative who is also loyal to the members of his old team, the difficulty of transferring Cabinet ministers who don't do well is not lessened by the very humane attitude of Parliament.

Thus the Prime Minister must always try to compensate for the deficiencies of particular Cabinet ministers by matching them with permanent under-secretaries who possess just the qualities they themselves lack. This is one of his most anxious tasks, and the eventual coordination of the war effort may depend upon his success. It requires enormous patience, tact, and keen judgment of personal qualities and temperaments. Problems will certainly arise on the civil service side as well; there is none too large a selection of civil servants eligible for under-secretaryships in any country.

Men with creative imagination, initiative, and willingness to undertake grave responsibility are not normally of a type also willing to remain in the background, patiently performing an enormous amount of daily work, drafting legislation and watching over its passage, without being able to determine at any point the manner in which the minister will carry it through the Cabinet committees, the Cabinet, and, finally, Parliament. The civil servant's only possibility of action is to prepare the ground for a constructive policy privately among his colleagues. Except for the " Chief Advisers " of the Government, who were appointed for the first time during the crisis of 1931, civil servants do not normally participate in Cabinet meetings. It may be assumed that even the chief advisers attended Cabinet meetings only occasionally. Their position in the administration is, in addition, somewhat anomalous, and many permanent under-secretaries may very well have taken exception to it.

The fact that Mr. Lloyd George when he was Prime Minister during the last war waived the traditional exclusion of everyone outside the Cabinet from Cabinet meetings was a great step toward bringing the views of ranking civil servants directly before the Prime Minister and Cabinet.[17] The methods of the War Cabinet were influenced, as every

---

[17] In other European governments in which civil servants have frequently been invited to attend formal Cabinet meetings, persons who did not belong either to the military or the civil

administrative institution in Great Britain has been, by the model of court procedure. Thus the War Cabinet reserved the right to call in at any time departmental chiefs, either ministers or civil servants, and outside experts, each of whom was expected to give his opinion frankly when asked for it, even if it differed from that of his superior or superiors.

The appearance of complexity and rigidity presented by the chart of the British administration at the back of this book may be misleading, since a long established informality of procedure makes the dependence there indicated of almost every department on the decisions of others non-existent in practice. There are certain dangers in this agreeable informality, especially when critical decisions have to be taken quickly. Although the *Cabinet Secretariat* circulates a record of decisions taken in Cabinet meetings to the different departments, there is no regular control over the execution of these decisions by individual ministers. In Germany, on the other hand, and similarly in many other Continental countries, the permanent secretary of the Chancellery has always been responsible for the exact application of Cabinet decisions by the departments affected.[18] This is of course a reflection of the position of the German Chancellor under the Bismarckian constitution, which, in spite of the changes made by the Weimar Constitution, was partially revived in practice later.

Where no established tradition governs the precise formulation of Cabinet decisions and the control of their execution, an additional bur-

---

service have nevertheless been rigidly excluded. Where parliamentary under-secretaries are not appointed to the executive departments from among the members of Parliament, the influence of the permanent under-secretaries is of course much more evident to the public. In Germany, for example, although the permanent secretaries of departments did not normally attend Cabinet meetings, they could do so either at the request or with the permission of the Chancellor. They could also at the Chancellor's request meet as often as and in whatever manner he decided either among themselves or with their respective ministers. There was, however, an established routine for such meetings. Flexibility and immediate access to the greatest knowledge and experience available were combined with clear-cut responsibility, the Chancellor having always the initiative in the establishment of such committees and final responsibility for their decisions. The Parliamentary duties of Cabinet members were lightened, in comparison with the British system, by the fact that higher civil servants could also answer questions in Parliament and could participate in debates whenever their ministers so instructed them, or when they were appointed by the government as commissioners for the discussion of a particular bill. This of course increased the influence of the civil service without increasing its formal responsibility. Higher civil servants, however, participated regularly and openly in much of the work of preparation and coordination which they perform only informally and in private in Great Britain.

[18] The decisions of the Supreme Defense Council are now communicated directly to the generals commanding the corps areas as well as to the defense commissioners, so that their full and accurate application is doubly guaranteed.

den is thrown on ranking civil servants. They frequently have to agree among themselves as to general lines of policy as well as on more specific questions. This partly explains the *duplication of ministerial committees by committees of civil servants.* Another reason is the amalgamation at the outbreak of war of the established interdepartmental organization of the *Committee of Imperial Defense* with other committees of the Cabinet. The existence of the Committee of Imperial Defense made it very easy in peacetime to bring Cabinet ministers, high civil servants, and military officers around the same table to develop common lines of action and a team spirit which could come fully into play at the outbreak of war. The fact that the first permanent secretary of the Cabinet, Lord Hankey, also one of the ablest public servants Great Britain has had, was for a generation secretary of the Committee of Imperial Defense as well was undoubtedly a very important factor in its success.

At first glance the transition from the work of preparation in the Committee of Imperial Defense to the organization of the first War Cabinet seems to have been well conceived and easily effected. It was facilitated by Mr. Chamberlain's use long before the outbreak of war of an *" inner Cabinet."* The Chancellor of the Exchequer became chairman of the Economic Policy Committee, which dealt with the most general economic questions, while three other major coordination committees concerned primarily with civilian questions have retained the form they had at the outbreak of war until today. The great problem of the coordination of strategy and supply, on which most subsequent criticism and change has centered, appeared to have been solved by the appointment of Lord Chatfield as chairman both of the Military Coordination Committee and the Ministerial Priority Committee.

The combination of responsibility for strategic planning, the actual conduct of the war, and the general allocation of man power, materials, and industrial capacity was in itself very farsighted. Lord Chatfield's position was as close an approximation to Marshal Keitel's as there has yet been in Great Britain, and probably as close as the traditions of English politics permit. The Prime Minister apparently considered his own functions to be those of a committee chairman and general coordinator, leaving him time for a certain minimum of initiative in policy and for participation in the relatively frequent meetings of the House of Commons during that period. Whether even a Prime Minister of a different type from Mr. Chamberlain would have found the calm and the freedom from daily business which is essential for the leader of a vast Empire in modern total war by a more precise delegation of executive responsibility may be doubted.

This organization might have been successful if the war had continued as Mr. Chamberlain seemed before the Battle of France to expect, and if there had been more men with imagination and driving force in leading positions. The first favorable impression, however, must be largely discounted on closer examination. To place the supreme coordination of all economic questions, with the exception of priorities in armament production and the allocation of materials, under the Chancellor of the Exchequer, was a concession to the traditional control of the Treasury over the whole administration which could not, with all respect to the abilities of high civil servants in the Treasury, be called constructive in view of the scale of the economic problems which were to be met.

Lord Chatfield's resignation as Minister for the Coordination of Defense in April 1940 on the ground that the tasks for which he was appointed before the war had been assumed by the Prime Minister and War Cabinet is also symptomatic. Possibly the War Office and the Air Ministry objected to the general determination of questions of priority by an Admiral of the Fleet. Perhaps, again, the Admiralty preferred after the occupation of Norway that the First Lord of the Admiralty, bearing full constitutional responsibility for naval policy, should preside over the two ministerial committees concerned with military operations and supply in order to ensure the cooperation of the three forces and their intelligence services in future; or perhaps difficulties occurred over the failure of any action to prevent the German occupation of Norway. Possibly, too, it had become clear that the task of coordination was one for a dynamic personality enjoying great political prestige. In succeeding Lord Chatfield as chairman of the Military Coordination and Ministerial Priority Committees Mr. Churchill, while remaining First Lord of the Admiralty, became in effect minister of defense in preparation for his succession to the premiership.

It is true that a small War Cabinet consisting of strong personalities could have assumed the functions performed by the Minister for the Coordination of Defense, and that this would have been a logical concentration of responsibility. The reasons given for Lord Chatfield's resignation, however, in connection with subsequent discussion in the press, indicated that although there had been a formal transition from the organization of the Committee of Imperial Defense to wartime administration, there was no clear realization of the fact that methods which had been appropriate for prewar planning and for the first stage of mobilization were no longer suitable for the actual direction of operations after war had begun. Moreover, the arrangement by which Mr. Churchill as Prime Minister became also Minister of Defense, responsible for the coordination of strategic planning and of supply in accordance with it, was suited to his dynamic temperament and to the situation immediately resulting from the defeat in France.

Mr. Churchill's intention was very likely to achieve the same highly concentrated direction of the main lines of policy, strategy, and the war economy which has been achieved, to date at least, in Germany in the present war. His position, however, created the impression that he was trying to accomplish still more than this, under constitutional traditions which permitted him to do even less. The difference between the central direction of the war in England and in Germany is that Hitler is finally responsible only for the most general coordination of strategy, foreign policy, and the pressure exercised in various directions by institutions of the Nazi Party. More than that is beyond the power of any man in a war of the magnitude of the present one.

In Germany formal responsibility for the coordination of military operations and the organization of supply rests, as has been emphasized before, with Marshal Keitel as chief of the *O.K.W.* His are functions which can be fully assumed only after the outbreak of war, but for them to be performed effectively there must be some practical experience of coordination under a single executive authority. No one without long military training in positions of definite responsibility will be able to establish an ascendancy over the three defense services. The danger of entrusting responsibility for coordination to a civilian is of course that he will be swayed by his own temperamental inclinations or by some strategic predilection or, on the other hand, act as an impartial arbiter, which means that he will form no plan except by compromise. In Germany consultation among the heads of the three forces before a final decision is reached does not end in a compromise of their separate views,[18a] a risk inseparable from the making of final decisions in committee.

The German system has been designed to avoid the difficulties which have beset the British Government, and which beset the German Gov-

---

[18a] Although the necessity of compromise with Hitler's personal views must be remembered.

ernment during the last war. Then the problem was to coordinate effectively the constitutional and traditional functions of the Emperor, largely nominal though they were, and those of the chiefs of staff of the Army and Navy, the war minister, and the Chancellor, who was responsible for everything except purely strategic decisions. At present the organization of the *Oberkommando der Wehrmacht* extends, as has been mentioned, into the regional and local administration and into individual factories. The *O.K.W.* has no real decision in foreign policy, and it can be assumed that in other connections there is friction between the organizations of the *Wehrmacht* and those of the Nazi Party. Except for broad strategic decisions dependent on foreign policy, however, Hitler's authority is nominal. That is why he has given increasing coercive powers to Himmler's organizations and has appointed a figure like Keitel to accept the military consequences of his foreign policy.

For any outsider to decide how well-founded much of the criticism of Mr. Churchill's conduct of business may be is very risky. His obvious difficulties may very well have arisen much more from the intrinsic nature of British administration and politics than from the personality of the Prime Minister. Here again the position is very different from that in the United States. The President of the United States is, under the Constitution, the Commander-in-Chief of the Army and Navy, and also, in practice, the final coordinator of the civil administration. This is the role Mr. Churchill may have tried to emulate.

In Great Britain there is *no Commander-in-Chief* of the three armed forces; the Imperial General Staff is in fact an Army staff only. Final decisions, before they are endorsed by the War Cabinet must therefore be reached by the three chiefs of staff together. The Prime Minister, and in some cases the War Cabinet, may have to decide, as Lord Hankey has pointed out, between conflicting proposals and demands by the three chiefs of staff. The Prime Minister's burden would be greatly relieved, and he would escape a very large part of the most earnest criticism directed against him, if there existed a chief of the joint staff of the three forces or a single commander-in-chief. Actual responsibility for military operations would then rest with the chief of staff, and the responsibility of the Prime Minister and the War Cabinet would be largely formal. Such a situation would, however, be contrary to all British tradition. It is also doubtful whether it would have been tenable without a particularly happy selection of the chief of staff, or, in any case, as long as Great

Britain remained on the strategic defensive without the possibility of a general strategic initiative.

The problem of selecting a suitable commander-in-chief or chief of staff for the three defense forces is especially complex in England, where the role of the Admiralty is traditionally preponderant. In peacetime the Navy provides the nerve system of the British Empire, and the Army figures only in wartime. A chief of the joint staff would have to have been, like General Wavell, in independent command of a campaign and to have made on the spot under very critical conditions decisions affecting the combined action of the three defense forces. In any government the position of political leaders refusing to support a plan of operations agreed on by the three forces and presented by a supreme chief of staff would become very precarious.[19]

There is, of course, no ideal solution of the relationship of political and military leaders. In wartime one sees a cloud of melancholy over political leaders who must accept responsibility for decisions that are not their own in purely strategic questions. The same cloud hangs over military leaders who are bound by political decisions to undertake or to abandon military operations against their professional judgment. Throughout history nations have owed the achievement of their aims more to the existence of political and military leaders who have shared the same qualities of vision, stability of purpose, and loyalty without unduly interfering in one another's spheres of action than to either military strength and skill or political genius alone.

One thing may be said with certainty about the *supreme coordination of British strategy*. Although the Prime Minister's burden is alleviated to a certain extent by the fact that the former secretary of the Committee of Imperial Defense, Major-General Ismay, serves as his personal chief of staff and attends the meetings of the Chiefs of Staff Committee, his total responsibilities are nevertheless greater than can be borne with complete success by any man. If the functions performed by General Ismay were to be assumed by a military leader with definite and open responsibility for strategic decisions, the Prime Minister would in fact be able to exercise a much more effective direction of the essential coordination of strategy and supply than at present. Such a solution the British na-

---

[19] Germany's defeat in the last war is of course an illustration of the possible consequences of such a situation. The Chancellor was constantly threatened by the resignation of the extremely popular nominal Chief-of-Staff, Hindenburg, and his First Quartermaster-General, Ludendorff. Although the Chancellor kept a liaison officer at General Headquarters, he was frequently forced to accept decisions effectively taken without his knowledge.

tion has not yet been prepared to accept. The decision of military questions by military experts to the extent that it was possible until 1942 in Germany would indeed affect the relation of the British Government to Parliament, and would be incompatible with the direct responsibility to Parliament of the three defense ministers and the Prime Minister.

There are two other aspects of the problem of supreme coordination which require some comment. First, the tasks of an officer serving as *permanent military secretary to the Cabinet,* or in some other capacity preparing the ground for intimate understanding between the statesmen who are finally responsible for policy and the chiefs of staff of the defense forces, are very delicate and trying. Whether he makes any contribution to victory or not will depend on his military vision and judgment, his tact, self-effacement, and loyalty. He holds no formal responsibility or executive authority, but his actual influence may be enormous. To bring about agreement between soldiers and politicians in military questions may not always be his most difficult problem. It may be harder for him to reconcile temperamental differences, between sanguineness on the one side and on the other inflexible detachment from emotional considerations such as results only from a lifelong discipline in rejecting comforting illusions as well as depressing doubt. In extreme emergencies everything depends on constant self-control and the ability to overcome misgivings, which paralyze initiative.

Such an intermediary between the defense forces and the Government must also expect military experts to dismiss the strategic conceptions of other people as dilettantism. On the other hand, an amateur of genius and decision may have great military vision without having a grasp, which is indispensable, of what General Wavell has called the " logistics " of warfare. The results of action decided on by a man of this type in opposition to the professional advice of military leaders may of course be disastrous. Briand's determination in confronting Marshal Joffre with a choice between holding Verdun to the last man and resigning his command and Clemenceau's action in 1917 in restoring the morale of the French Army are rare exceptions to the many cases of failure due to the intervention of civilians in strategy. President Lincoln's attitude of unwavering support for the commanding general is usually the safer course.

These considerations are more relevant to the eventual outcome of a war than almost any others. Yet texts of constitutional theory and administrative practice seldom mention them. Neither do they express any realization of the increasing isolation of statesmen who in critical periods must make vital decisions every hour, perhaps for years, in the face of conflicting advice. This psychological factor makes the delegation of definite responsibility for the general coordination of each group of closely related aspects of administration to a few individuals all the more desirable.

The Prime Minister should ideally have the assistance of a chief of the joint staff of the defense forces, of a super-minister for the complex organization of industrial production, labor supply, supplies of raw materials, and price control, and of another super-minister for agricultural production and food supplies. They should be able to issue directions which would be put into effect by existing departmental machinery down to the regional and local levels of administration, but they should themselves have no administrative responsibilities. Only so can they enjoy the necessary serenity and freedom to formulate the general principles of policy and to supervise their application. They are the people who, with the Chancellor of the Exchequer, if he is not unimaginative, the Foreign Secretary, and another minister responsible for home affairs, should constitute the War Cabinet. The Prime Minister could then, except in sudden emergencies, reasonably hope for success in his double task of acting as final arbiter in case of conflict and at the same time directing the enormous war machine.

Until the present, however, there has been no one in England to perform the functions of Marshal Keitel, nor is there any single directive power comparable to the influence of the *Oberkommando der Wehrmacht,* which pervades every level of the German administration. The executive authority of the present British *Minister of Production* is limited, and he can at best anticipate such differences among the production departments as the Production Executive had formerly to mediate after they arose. The *Joint Production Staff* under the chairmanship of the Minister of Production is composed of representatives of the armed forces and executive officers of the supply departments. The Minister of Production has no more executive authority over its members than his regional officers have over the officers of the supply departments in the consultative area supply boards over which they preside. The *Minister of Production* is a member of the War Cabinet, but if he is invited to attend the meetings of the Defense Committee of the Cabinet only from time to time, as was the Minister of Supply during 1940, his chances of success will be limited, and he may end only as the chairman of another of the succession of coordinating committees. The minister must have vision enough to foresee future bottlenecks in production and energy enough to prevent their occurrence, and he must also be fully initiated into the strategic situation and plans of future operations. Only so will he be able to instill into the supply departments an appreciation of future requirements and their implications for present production. He must, further, have the means of ascertaining how far his intentions are given effect by the different departments. Certainly the personal achievements of the present minister since taking office have been great.[19a]

The position of the *Treasury*, since it has been divorced from questions of supply, leaves little to be desired, and is certainly very different from what it was at the beginning of the war, when Sir John Simon presided over the Economic Policy Committee of the Cabinet. The presence of the Chancellor of the Exchequer in the War Cabinet and of Treasury officials in every interdepartmental coordinating committee ensures the observance of the financial policy to which the Chanceller of the Exchequer is committed. This policy is also decided in close consultation with a small permanent advisory committee of the leading financial experts of the country.

In general, however, *interdepartmental liaison* and the substitution of consultation for clear direction is still a predominant characteristic of the wartime administration. A major cause for this is the average quality of the ministers appointed in accordance with the demands of the coalition form of government and the members of Parliament selected by the party machines. The story of the transformations of the British Government in the past two years is largely the history of men appointed in order to preserve a balance of power in the Cabinet to positions for which they were not suited, instead of to positions in which their political prestige and experience might perhaps have served them well. " The War Cabinet was called or forced into existence," as has been written in a leading article in the London *Times,* " by the very need which is negatively expressed and exemplified in the multitude of committees." [20]

Certain *standing committees,* like the interdepartmental priority committee for the allocation of raw materials, have to all appearances arrived at perfectly satisfactory solutions, or at least at the definition of an intelligible policy. Coordination in execution in this respect is assured

---

19a 'Some changes in the organization of the Ministry of Production at the end of 1942 closely approximate the organization of the German Ministry of Armament and Munitions. But here again the tendency in Great Britain, as English critics have pointed out, has been rather to a better coordination among departments than to a clarification of executive responsibility.

20 July 22, 1942.

by the issue of all specific allocations through the Ministry of Supply, where a record can be kept of the total consumption of materials for the purposes of different government departments. In the control of raw materials the British system is as efficient as the German system and in many ways simpler, a fact which is of course partly explained by the comparative ease with which imported commodities can be controlled as they enter the country and the absence in Britain of many of the complications of *ersatz* production.

There is no doubt that a number of *standing committees* could be dispensed with if the War Cabinet itself consisted of ministers with authority over groups of related executive departments, able to plan ahead and to issue definite instructions so that the heads of particular departments, and more especially the civil service, could see their own places in the general plan and could be held to account for the performance of specific functions. In an editorial entitled, " The Inner Cabinet," the *Times* [20a] has described this aspect of the problem as follows:

". . . The Ministries of Defense, Production, Food, Fuel, and War Transport all broadly exemplify a right functional principle of arrangement. . . . The advantages of a basic regrouping of the functions of central government are many and impressive. There would be an immediate gain in efficiency by making clearer the lines of authority, and by concentrating responsibility. It is a common complaint that on many matters requiring administrative decision the variety of departments to be consulted and the numbers of ministers whose responsibility is affected combine to make delay and timidity characteristic qualities of official action. . . . The present division of work between departments is not based on a conscious specialization of function but is mainly the product of historical development and political manoeuvre. . . . It cannot be too firmly emphasized that all the major administrative experiments of the war in this field have been applications of the method first suggested by the Haldane committee (in 1918), and that these experiments have been most successful when a genuine reallocation has taken place and reform has not stopped short at a token combination of offices."

There is interdepartmental consultation among the responsible heads of departments and civil servants about particular problems in the administration of every country. That is not the same thing as the institution of standing committees to which questions too various for *ad hoc* bodies are regularly referred. Such a system is fatal to individual responsibility and to constructive policy, since the chair-

---

20a January 4, 1943.

man of a committee is only too readily inclined to decide in favor of the majority opinion or to take a mean of the opinions expressed. Committees are too often the graves of enterprise and of good will. In any administration general direction must come first, and the detailed application of clearly enunciated principles and the coordination of closely related aspects of administration in committees must be only supplementary. It is not to be expected of human nature that effective direction will ever result from the dilution of individual responsibility and its transference to a collective body. In wartime the use of consultative committees should be limited to the arrangement of such details as are left in any case to high-ranking civil servants. To quote the *Times* again, "The fault lies not so much with the natural propensities of the civil service as with defects in its political leaders."[21]

Immediately below, or parallel to, the War Cabinet there are two supreme coordinating committees, the *Defense Committee* under the chairmanship of the Prime Minister and the *Coordinating Committee for Home Affairs* under the chairmanship of the Lord President of the Council.[21a] The present efficient coordination of every aspect of the national effort not directly concerned with military operations or supply in the latter committee could hardly have been achieved if it had not been for the presence in Parliament and the Government of this very able and experienced former civil servant. The Defense Committee is concerned both with military operations and supply; it receives reports from the Chiefs of Staff Committee in the former connection and the Joint Production Staff in the latter. Despite the efforts that have been made during 1942 to bring the technical design of weapons and the organization of production into closer relation with the particular requirements of the fighting forces, no fully satisfactory solution of the problem of the coordination of strategy and supply has been achieved.

The number of standing ministerial committees that have been formed and dissolved in England in the past three years contrasted with the continuity of certain interdepartmental committees of civil servants, shows where the difficulty has lain. It is, of course, not healthy for people to owe positions of great responsibility in such a grave emergency to political influence, and to rely in actual decisions on their experienced permanent staffs, while permanent officials have no opportunity to

---

[21] July 22, 1942.

[21a] This does not prevent the members of the Defense Committee from meeting, sometimes with other ministers, for special purposes in groups like the U-Boat Committee, of which the Prime Minister is chairman.

make suggestions or offer warnings directly to the War Cabinet without being expressly invited to do so. It may be taken for granted, therefore, that it is because of a high team spirit among the top officials of different departments that the system works. In certain branches of the war administration there is no doubt that a stabilization admitting of only minor improvements has been achieved.

As every belligerent country approaches capacity production, changes of policy and the adaptation of production to suddenly changed circumstances, especially under conditions of mass production, become more and more difficult. The organization of production may become very effective after maximum productivity is reached, but with every vital tactical change there will be an interval while production is shifted during which no strategic action can be undertaken. In this respect, especially, the present war has given rise to problems which are entirely new. The complexity of mass production is such that flexibility in changing over to new types of weapons may become more decisive than total output, or than strategic genius. It is here that the best routine elaborated in any department may fail. For this reason some form of regional organization to free local initiative from the restrictions of centralized bureaucratic control and to increase flexibility in the performance of any program is more urgent now than ever before.

There are two facts to be stressed in any final judgment of different systems of war administration. For many of the technical problems resulting from the peculiar character of modern warfare there is no perfect solution. This point the critics of any government frequently overlook. The recent administrative reorganization in Germany shows that no system, however well conceived in advance, will survive throughout a war of the technical character of the present one without undergoing radical and sudden alterations.

Critics of the statesmen who must bear the full responsibility for the conduct of the war also overlook the fact that a parliament by granting emergency powers to the Government and supporting, sometimes grudgingly, the policy of the head of the Government does not by this assure the success of his policy. Particularly if the prime minister is supported by a coalition of political parties because of his personal prestige, he will face something of the eternal Cromwellian problem of the absence of any strong opposition.[22] A man with a clear appreciation of present and fu-

---

[22] *The Economist*, July 11, 1942, p. 33. Cf. Lord Beaverbrook's speech in the House of Lords, February 9, 1943.

ture needs, who understands the organizational problems of administration in wartime and knows how to delegate definite responsibility in such a way as to ensure conformity with the main lines of his policy and flexibility in detail, and is not deflected from his purpose by the influence of his own emotions, can get whatever he wants from a parliament. Popular feeling and constructive criticism may no longer have their normal influence on the prime minister's policy if there is not the force of a strong opposition behind the criticism and advice offered. If the prime minister is a dominant figure he can secure himself against opposition by including the leading members of all parties in his cabinet. Nevertheless, he will bear the same responsibility as a dictator in a totalitarian government, without being able to override traditional constitutional obstacles to the fulfillment of his aims. Thus the British Prime Minister is not free either to appoint ministers or to define their functions without regard to political considerations. Although the responsibility of every minister to Parliament for the policy of his department relieves the Prime Minister of legal responsibility for the supervision of the entire administration, the extent of his actual responsibility increases correspondingly with the relaxation of Parliamentary control over the Government's policy. Criticism which fails to take into account this concentration of actual power and responsibility for which there is no suitable provision in the traditional constitutional system is often misdirected against individuals.

There is another thing which any critic of the British administration should in fairness recognize. There are two main types of administration. In many countries, in Germany especially, the Government and the civil service are expected to lead the nation in exercising foresight and constructive initiative. Up to a certain point it is very advantageous for members of the Government to have considered every possible emergency in advance and to have prepared practical measures to meet them. This may easily result, however, in rigidity and over-organization. The individual citizen becomes inclined to look for miracles from the government, and he loses self-confidence, resourcefulness, and the faculty of positive criticism. He fails to realize that his reliance on the wisdom of the Government implies increasing interference by the state in his personal affairs and daily life, and this he resents when it occurs. This is especially so, of course, when he is deprived of every opportunity of criticism, as under a totalitarian government.

The British Government, on the contrary, ordinarily waits upon public opinion, considering only the most urgent necessities of the hour. To this tempo the civil service has been forced to adapt itself. The haphazard trend of British politics has largely preserved the traditional constitutional balance among different institutions, but it has often brought the country to the brink of catastrophe in great emergencies. Even, in normal times it has resulted in a refusal to tackle crucial economic and social problems. The leisurely atmosphere established throughout the country under the British political system is so highly valued that its consequences for national and, often, international security are overlooked. This system does, on the other hand, preserve a spirit of moderation and compromise in politics, and it protects the freshness of men's nerves. Citizens are more capable of improvisation in extreme emergencies, and can bring better support to the policy of the Government where the grinding of the administrative machinery is not always heard. In such an atmosphere the effects of a series of unexpected defeats are more easily overcome. The final test of any political and administrative system is whether it encourages and provides ample scope for individual initiative in a national effort firmly directed from above under well defined executive responsibility, and this final test can be made only after unforeseen reversals of the military position. In war it is the immediate positive reaction to the unexpected that is decisive.

PART TWO

THE ORGANIZATION OF SUPPLY IN GREAT BRITAIN

by Claire Nix

1. Preparation and Precedent

Several main considerations underlay the defense policy of the British Empire after the First World War. The disarmament of Germany, the consequences of the revolution in Russia, and the building up of a Continental military system including France, the nations of the Little Entente, and, more loosely, Poland resulted in French hegemony in Europe. For the British Government it was undesirable that this hegemony should result in such a consolidation of power that England's position would become insecure in the event of a threat to her Empire in another part of the world. Thus the complete elimination of Germany as a military factor by France and her allies, and likewise the disturbance of any economic and political stability in Germany by demands for reparations on the one hand and the agitation of the Third International on the other, had to be prevented.

The fact that Japan, by her alliance with England and her participation in the war against the Central Powers, had enormously improved her strategic position in the Pacific, and had emerged from the war with large reserves of capital and industrial capacity became a leading consideration of British naval policy. The cancellation of the Japanese alliance was an expression of the uncertainty of the Admiralty and the Foreign Office about the future in the Pacific, in China, and in India. Whether the dominions would again support England to the same extent as in the First World War was also long in doubt. The industrial capacity of the United States could be taken into account, but it was again doubtful whether the United States would be prepared to join in a struggle in which the safety of the British Empire might be involved. People in England who saw clearly ahead were undoubtedly alarmed for the future in case of a major conflict and undoubtedly watched Japanese policy with increasing suspicion after the occupation of Manchukuo.

Throughout these years desire to reduce the burden of public expenditure had dictated a policy of disarmament. The total defense expenditures of Great Britain were reduced by almost four-fifths between 1919–20 and 1922–23, and remained at approximately the same level from 1923 to 1936. The fixing of an international ratio for naval rearmament was designed both to prevent a naval race like that which preceded the First World War, and in which it would have been difficult for Great Britain to maintain supremacy over the United States and Japan, and also to prevent the formation of French and Italian fleets which might together become a threat to Great Britain. England had to prevent the preponderance of any group of countries with which she might possibly find herself in opposition. Until 1931 her policy consisted in cautiously balancing potential blocks of power, without any distinct tendency and without positive support of general disarmament.

The idea that England must by any means avoid the employment of such large forces as in the last war in any future Continental struggle prevailed over a long period; the Army was considered chiefly in relation to the defense of the dominions and colonies. From 1927 a very enlightened belief in the future of mechanized warfare, which the British Army inaugurated in 1917, was common, and the importance of air warfare was also appreciated. The proportion of total defense expenditure devoted to the Air Force was doubled between 1923 and 1930. In the design of tanks and airplanes Great Britain led every other country. No definite conception of their combined use developed, although the possibility was clearly envisaged while Field Marshal Lord Milne was Chief of Staff.

The Manchukuo crisis found Great Britain totally unprepared. Nor did it result in any close coordination between the policies of Great Britain and the United States. It was more than doubtful then whether a strong line would be followed by strong action on the part of the United States. At the same time that the economic crisis necessitated the reduction of Army expenditure, in 1932 and '33, the Committee of Imperial Defense began to study the questions of production and organization in case of war with Japan, which might produce a regrouping of powers. There was no idea at that time, or even during 1933 and the greater part of 1934, of the possibility of a rapid German rearmament.

The lack of many essential industrial materials within the German frontiers of 1919 made any threat from that quarter unlikely. Not even the military occupation of the demilitarized zone of the Rhineland by the Nazis in 1936 was seen to alter the situation essentially, since an agreement on naval rearmament had just been reached between Great Britain and the Nazis. Action then by Great Britain, had it been contemplated, would have been hampered by the position in the Mediterranean created by the Italian campaign in Ethiopia. A consciousness of growing danger existed, but it was hoped that the League of Nations could be mobilized, and that the threat of sanctions would be enough to prevent the expansion of any European power. Within the British Cabinet there was no accepted policy towards Italy, nor any willingness to come to a definite understanding with France about a policy to be pursued in the Mediterranean. This would in any case have been difficult with continual changes of government in France. Until 1937 the pace of German rearmament was not considered alarming. The certainty that Germany was far behind in beginning her rearmament and that she could be deprived of essential materials by a naval blockade supported the conviction that immediate action was unnecessary. Neither was there much desire for action in other governments in countries which were either still suffering from the effects of the financial and economic crisis or just beginning to recover.[23]

These facts help to explain Great Britain's difficulties in the organization of production and supply after the beginning of British rearmament in 1936. The problem of preparation for a total war was not considered in its entirety. Certain plans made in the Committee of Imperial Defense for the Empire, in the first place, could be put into effect only when events ensured the participation of the different dominions, and remained in large part on paper. In Great Britain defense expenditures in 1936, '37, and '38 amounted altogether to £1,250,000,000. The manufacture of ammunition was begun early, even railway repair shops being used for the purpose. Careful consideration was given to the immunization of new plants against bombing attacks; they were constructed partly underground and located chiefly in Lancashire, South Wales, and in the region of the Bristol Channel. By the fall of 1939 there were thirteen government ordnance factories in operation and three under construction. In the summer of 1942 there were forty-two.

Until the winter of 1938–39, however, government expenditure for new plant was devoted almost exclusively to the creation of capacity for aircraft manufacture. Great progress was made in the development of airplane types, but the actual increase of production corresponded only to the rate of training of pilots permitted by different supplementary budgets. Much of the capacity planned in the three years before the war came into production only at the end of 1939. In addition to the financing of new plant by the Air Ministry, most conspicuously in the construction of " shadow " factories for airplane manufacture in conjunction with automobile plants, manufacturers were offered special

---

[23] These statements concerning British foreign policy are made for their relevance to the organization of supply, and are necessarily much simplified from the political point of view. As the policy of the editors has been to allow perfect freedom of expression of opinion to each contributor, they are to be taken only as personal judgments. Attention should certainly be invited, however, to the attitude of the British Government of this period toward the Spanish War. Note should also be taken of the now pretty well documented Tory error of unwillingness to understand the inevitable association between Fascism and military expansion. It was a widely shared delusion that peace could be kept in such a world. — W. Y. E.

depreciation allowances in taxation and in government contracts for new additions to plant and were guaranteed the capital cost of expanded capacity for airplane production still unused after a given period of time.

The storage of reserves of a limited number of commodities such as wheat, fats, whale oil, petroleum, and fertilizers was undertaken in the year before the war [24] on a modest scale and consequently with little disturbance of the markets. At the outbreak of war in 1939 ordinary reserves of rubber and tin had been depleted by the exchange of these two materials for United States cotton. The very large stocks of cotton goods held in England in consequence were for the most part destroyed in the bombing of 1940. The dispersal of large firms engaged in air-craft and tank manufacture into a number of small, in some cases dupli-cate, plants, which was undertaken in 1940, was designed not only to ensure continuous production in spite of enemy bombing but also to protect supplies of materials by scattering them.

The prewar phase of rearmament was in general characterized by hesitation to undertake full production and to organize the whole econ-omy for the manufacture of armament in peacetime. Certainly fear of the dislocation of production and the consequences for the recovery of English trade which might result from a full dress rearmament, if war were after all avoided predominated. There was government planning of potential capacity, not of actual production.

This was in part a natural consequence of the purely consultative character of the *Committee of Imperial Defense*. Although 95 percent of the recommendations of the specialized interdepartmental subcom-mittees of the Committee of Imperial Defense may be of a detailed or technical nature requiring only the executive sanction of the particular departments concerned, the guiding principle of the committee's com-position has been the reservation of all decisions of " policy " to the Cabinet as a whole. The principle of Cabinet responsibility is of course the explanation of the customary establishment of more or less informal standing or temporary committees of ministers and civil servants to consider problems affecting several departments or on special issues. It is also the objection offered to every proposal to concentrate authority over strategic planning, for example, or the organization of production, in any one minister whose decisions would to some extent determine the functioning of other departments. When executive action on a very large scale is required, joint Cabinet responsibility, while greatly increasing

[24] By the Board of Trade under the Essential Commodities Reserves Act, 1938.

the importance of the Prime Minister's position, also necessitates an elaborate organization of consultation between departments.

When the Committee of Imperial Defense was established in 1904 the Prime Minister was made its chairman so that its relation to the Cabinet should be as close as possible. Such an advisory committee has the advantage of flexibility of membership, ministers, civil servants, and private persons being equally eligible to participate in its meetings.[25] Before the last war its procedure was in one respect more formal than that of the Cabinet, as a small staff of Army and Navy officers kept a permanent record of the discussions of the committee and its subcommittees and regularly informed the departments concerned of conclusions reached. The committee was absorbed by the Cabinet, meeting as a War Committee or War Council of ministers, at the beginning of the last war, and the small staff of the committee became the Cabinet Secretariat.

Mr. Lloyd George broke the Asquith coalition Government in 1916 with the demand that a committee of three ministers be made responsible for the military conduct of the war, Mr. Asquith proposing in reply a second, corresponding, ministerial committee for "national organization." The *War Cabinet* as organized at the beginning of 1917 consisted only of Mr. Lloyd George as Prime Minister, three ministers without portfolio, and the Chancellor of the Exchequer, who was also leader of the House of Commons. Two more ministers without portfolio were added in the course of the war. War Cabinet committees including ministers who were not War Cabinet members, civil servants, and others were appointed for special questions and also for such general problems as "man power policy" and "demobilization," and were frequently superseded by other committees of slightly different personnel. People of all sorts appeared before the War Cabinet itself, which disposed of conflicting claims very much like a bench of judges.

The Cabinet resumed its normal form at the end of 1919, retaining from the period of the war only its permanent secretariat, which remained more or less identical with the secretariat of the Committee of

---

[25] In 1939 meetings of the main Committee of Imperial Defense were attended by any of the following: the Prime Minister, the Minister for the Coordination of Defense, the Chancellor of the Exchequer, the Home Secretary, the Lord Privy Seal, the Secretaries of State for Foreign Affairs, Dominion Affairs, Colonies, and India and Burma, the First Lord of the Admiralty, the Secretaries of State for War and Air, the Chiefs of Naval Staff, of the Imperial General Staff, and of Air Staff, the Permanent Secretary to the Treasury, and the Secretary to the Cabinet. Major-General H. L. Ismay, *The Machinery of the Committee of Imperial Defense,* in The Journal of the Royal United Service Institution, Vol. LXXXIV, No. 534, May 1939.

Imperial Defense. The reporting of Cabinet committee and subcommittee meetings by this secretariat, combined with the fact that Treasury officials attend all committee and subcommittee meetings, and that all proposals for legislation are examined before being submitted to the Cabinet in the Home Affairs Committee, which includes the law officers, provides some coordination of the extensive committee organization.

The subcommittees of the Committee of Imperial Defense itself before the present war fell into five main groups for strategy and planning, organization for war (including civil defense), man power, supply, and technical experiment and research.[26] The most important of the first group was of course the committee of the three chiefs of staff for the Navy, the Army, and the Air Force, with subordinate joint staff committees, which very largely retain their prewar organization. In the second group the Principal Supply Officers Committee dealt with industrial capacity and raw materials in time of war. Actual contracts were and are, however, placed separately by the contracts divisions of the supply ministries. The heads of these divisions meet under the chairmanship, since 1940, of a Treasury official in the *Contracts Coordination Committee,* where forms of contracts are standardized.[26a]

The duty of presiding over the Committee of Imperial Defense in the Prime Minister's absence was allotted in March 1936 to a newly created *Minister for the Coordination of Defense,* who also met with the chiefs of staff and presided over the Principal Supply Officers Committee. The minister's department consisted of two secretaries and

---

26 Ismay, *op. cit.*

26a The Treasury has no responsibility for rates of profit allowed in contracts placed by the different ministries. Two separate branches of the Contracts Coordinating Committee are concerned with works contracts and with other contracts for more general purposes. To avoid delay in Treasury approval of particular contracts after the introduction of a program of rearmament in 1936, a Treasury Inter-Service Committee including officers of the three services was empowered to approve expenditure in advance of formal Treasury approval and to report total defense expenditure.

The commonest form of government contract has become the " fixed price " contract, with a specific price agreed to in advance, usually on the basis of investigation by accountants belonging to the government department concerned, of the cost of production of the same article under similar circumstances. For urgent work of which there is little previous experience the " cost plus " contract, under which the manufacturer receives the actual cost of production, whatever it may be, plus an agreed percentage as profit, is still employed. " Maximum price " and " target price " contracts have been devised to supply the incentive to reduction of cost of production which is lacking in the " cost plus " contract. Under the " target price " contract the manufacturer is penalized for exceeding the estimated cost of production and receives a premium when actual cost is less than the estimate.

clerical assistance.[27] Sir Thomas Inskip (Lord Caldecote), the first Minister for the Coordination of Defense, described his office as that of liaison between the chiefs of staff and the Cabinet and Parliament. His coordinating functions were extended to include civil defense after the appointment of Sir John Anderson as Lord Privy Seal with special responsibility for civil defense in November 1938. In February 1939 the former First Sea Lord, Admiral of the Fleet Lord Chatfield, himself became Minister for the Coordination of Defense. That he was primarily concerned with strategic coordination is evidenced by the fact that Mr. W. S. Morrison, then Chancellor of the Duchy of Lancaster, became his associate, acting as chairman of the Supply Officers Committee, as well as answering for the coordination of defense in the House of Commons.

At the outbreak of war Mr. Chamberlain's Cabinet was reduced, as a *War Cabinet,* to nine members, four of whom had no particular departmental responsibilities. The Minister for the Coordination of Defense became chairman of a *Committee on Military Coordination,* to which the defense ministers and the chiefs of staff belonged, and to which the organization of the Chiefs of Staff Committee was subordinate, and also of a *Ministerial Priority Committee,* to which the interdepartmental supply organization was subordinated. The other major committees of the Cabinet for war purposes were the *Civil Defense Committee,* the *Food Policy Committee,* and the *Economic Policy Committee,* under the chairmanship of the Chancellor of the Exchequer. In subsequent reorganizations of the Cabinet in April and May 1940, October 1940, January 1941, May 1941, and January and February 1942 the Chancellor of the Exchequer has lost his dominating position, and the dual responsibility for the coordination of strategy and of supply which was initially united in Lord Chatfield has been divided and redistributed.

The overall organization of supply naturally followed the lines that had developed at the end of the last war. In all the planning of the Committee of Imperial Defense, however, the United States with its productive capacity remained an uncertain factor. The United States attitude of neutrality made it doubtful that American resources, without which those who were responsible for England's preparation realized that the defeat of the Central Powers in 1918 would have been impossible, would be available again. Great Britain had to rely on her own

---

[27] His budget was £7,789.

capacity and that of the dominions and colonies. This fact must affect any judgment of the British organization of production. If it had been sure that airplanes and tanks, for example, could have been provided immediately from the United States, much capacity in England could have been made available for other purposes, and the direction of English industry would have been somewhat different.

A second difference in the position in this war from that at the end of the last arises of course from the unexpected German victory over France, after which Great Britain remained more or less on the defense strategically, unable even to occupy the very large part of the German Army available for action in other theatres. Thus even with the best plans and most detailed organization of production the actual result would always have been inadequate to the needs of the moment until the United States, having entered the war, should reach optimum production.

At the beginning of the last war there was no idea in England, or any other of the belligerent countries, of the eventual consumption of munitions and equipment. It was only gradually, and especially so in England, that the necessity of organizing production on the basis of strategic plans prepared at least a year in advance was recognized. In the recruitment of man power for military purposes and for industry, in the distribution of raw materials, and in the conversion of industrial capacity to war production a wholly empirical extension of public control was accomplished by a constant increase of the executive powers of the central government.[28]

The transfer of labor to war industries and recruiting for the armed forces were divided between employment exchanges, which were incorporated in the *Ministry of Labor* in 1917, and successive directors of recruiting or national service. A Ministry of National Service, later combined with the Ministry of Labor, was established for military recruiting in 1917, when the question of man power, following the introduction of conscription in 1916, had become acute. The chief executive officer of the exchanges in the Ministry of Labor provided liaison by serving also as director of labor supply in the Ministry of National Service.

The reservation of individual workmen in essential occupations was originally put at the discretion of prime contractors for the Admiralty,

---

28 Most measures of government control of the economy between 1914 and 1918 were effected by order-in-council under the Defense of the Realm Act of 1914, the Munitions of War Act of 1915, and on the basis of a theory of the royal prerogative which was invalidated by the House of Lords in 1920, when actions taken on this basis were indemnified by act of Parliament.

War Office, or Ministry of Munitions. It was later transferred to the labor department of the Ministry of Munitions and then to the skilled trade unions, being fixed early in 1917 with recruiting officers in the twelve areas into which the country was divided for the manufacture of munitions. Central and local committees on reservation, containing trade union representatives and officials of the government departments concerned with supply, were set up to advise these recruiting officers. Under the Munitions of War Act prohibiting strikes and lockouts in war production, an interdepartmental Committee on Production including officials of the supply departments and the Home Office [29] became the tribunal for the arbitration of wage disputes. Its awards were consistently made on the basis of the cost of living. For the practical application of its decisions the Committee was dependent on negotiations between employers and employees.

Great Britain's dependence on imports of all basic food stuffs and most industrial materials, while it necessitates the central control of supplies in a war emergency, also makes control comparatively easy to impose. In the last war prices of jute, hemp, leather, hides, shoes, wool, flax, woolen and linen textiles were fixed by the War Office as the largest or the exclusive buyer, and distribution was determined by the licensing of dealers. Sugar, cereals, meat, oils and fats, and dairy produce were brought gradually under the control first of the Board of Trade and then of the *Ministry of Food,* which came into existence in the summer of 1917 when imports had been drastically reduced by the submarine campaign. Iron and steel, other industrial metals, explosives, and, for a time, coal supplies were similarly controlled by the Ministry of Munitions. As the import of various other commodities was licensed by the Board of Trade, more than 90 percent of imports into Great Britain at the end of 1917 were controlled by five government departments.

The *Ministry of Munitions* was established in May 1915 to provide for the armaments requirements of the War Office or the Admiralty, but in fact assumed responsibility only for War Office contracts, the Admiralty retaining its separate procurement organization. In its final form the Ministry was organized in more than fifty departments for different types of armament, grouped in ten general directorates. For the supervision of munitions contracts, the country was divided into twelve Munitions Areas. Within these areas the Ministry relied primarily on the initiative of fifty district Boards of Management com-

---

[29] Which was responsible for the regulation of conditions of work.

posed of manufacturers, principally in the engineering industry. These boards not only distributed contracts among the engineering firms in their districts but also operated, on behalf of the Ministry, "national factories" in which local engineering capacity could be pooled. In the industries under War Office control, too, regional boards within the industries, including in some cases representatives of labor, decided the proportion of work on government orders, for export, and for civilian requirements in different firms and the amount of reserve stocks to be held.

The issue of priority certificates for government orders was centralized in the priority department of the Ministry of Munitions. It was supplemented by the, sometimes fully independent, allocation of materials by the agencies controlling particular commodities and by licensing. It was only with the shipping crisis of 1917 that any determination in advance of the total requirements of production became necessary and that the definition of different classes of contracts in order of urgency was attempted. Until the end of the war all production plans remained subject to overriding considerations of the amount of shipping tonnage available. General priority orders early in 1917 established three categories of work: the first including the manufacture of armaments on government contract, merchant shipbuilding, and work especially certified by the Ministry of Munitions or the Board of Trade; the second including necessary repairs and replacements, certified exports, and other work certified by government departments as "necessary to the efficient conduct of the war," or to the effect that the requisite materials were available; all remaining civilian work falling into the third. A further refinement of three degrees of urgency for prime government contracts was introduced a year later.

All the government departments concerned with production were represented from an early period of the war on an informal "priority committee" in the Ministry of Munitions. This committee's authority varied in different departments and was lowest in the Admiralty, where conflicting priority certificates were sometimes issued independently. A *War Priorities Committee of the Cabinet* was formed only at the end of 1917, and then in a manner characteristic of the War Cabinet's methods of improvisation. The organization of airplane manufacture, the allocation of available resources between the Royal Flying Corps and the Royal Naval Air Service, and the question of combined operations had been referred successively to two independent boards without executive functions. A committee of ministers appointed in the autumn of 1917 to consider the priority that should be allowed to airplane production reported after one meeting that the duty assigned to it could be performed only by a standing committee on priorities for all war production. Thus, with the approval of the War Cabinet, the War Priorities Committee came into being under the chairmanship of General Smuts. It comprised the First Lord of the Admiralty, the Secretary of State for War, the Minister of Munitions, the recently created Secretary of State, Royal Air Force, and the Minister of National Service. Since the committee's purpose was to mediate conflicting demands it worked through interdepartmental boards for every major commodity in short supply. These boards and, in addition, a business men's committee on priorities in civilian industry and a committee on general services, or utilities, were subordinate to an interdepartmental Joint Priority Board, which relieved the main committee of ministers and the duplicate committee of civil servants of all but final decisions of particular importance. Special sub-committees considered priorities for shipping tonnage, labor supply, and building construction.

This more comprehensive organization was imposed so late on an economy already over-taxed that its working until the unforeseen cessation of hostilities in 1918 hardly affords a basis for critical judgment. In his excellent survey of commodity controls in the last war E. M. H. Lloyd writes that the absence of " an Economic General Staff " continued to be felt until the end of the war.[30] The futility of establishing the relative importance of particular products without uniform control of the materials of production had at least been demonstrated, and at the beginning of the present war emphasis was consequently placed on the " allocation " of raw materials to the requirements of the different armed services.

2. Evolution Since 1939

Supplies of *essential materials* are monopolized under the Ministry of Supply,[31] the Ministry of Food,[32] the Ministry of Aircraft Produc-

---

[30] E. M. H. Lloyd, *Experiments in State Control at the War Office and the Ministry of Food,* Oxford, 1924.

[31] The Ministry of Supply controls: chrome ore, magnesite, wolfram; cotton; fertilizer; flax; iron and steel; iron and manganese ores; leather and tanning materials; molasses and industrial alcohol; non-ferrous metals; paper; silk and rayon; sulphur and pyrites; timber; wool; dyestuffs.

[32] The Ministry of Food controls: animal feeding stuffs; bacon and hams; butter and cheese;

tion,[33] and, since November 1940, the Ministry of Works and Buildings. The Admiralty (for merchant and naval shipbuilding and naval ordnance), the production departments of the Ministry of Supply (for the equipment and munitions of the Army), since May 1940 the Ministry of Aircraft Production, the War Office (for Army construction and provisions), the construction departments of the Ministry of Works and Buildings (for most other government construction), the Ministry of Home Security (for the civil defense requirements of local authorities), and the Board of Trade (for civilian industry) are the principal competitors for their use. The act which established the Ministry of Supply in July 1939 also conferred on the government full legal powers to demand priority for the completion of government contracts before others and when necessary to take temporary possession of firms. Power to require firms to accept government contracts was conferred at the end of May 1940.

Why a *Ministry of Supply* should not have been created earlier in the defense program is hard to say. The Government had not decided to prepare as if for war, and the production of much greater stores of armament seemed idle while there was a shortage of trained officers and men in the Army, especially in the mechanized forces. Without compulsory service the organization of production for armament in time of peace will always be considered doubtfully. The results of the recruitment of volunteers for the Army begun in 1936 were negligible. Under these conditions provisions for an eventual increase of production if war occurred were considered sufficient. Conscription was introduced only after the occupation of Prague, and the formation of the Ministry of Supply to meet the increased requirements of the Army immediately followed it.

The definition of the new ministry's functions as those previously discharged by the procurement branches of the War Office, and by the Board of Trade in acquiring stocks of commodities, disappointed those advocates of the appointment of a minister to direct the adjustment of all industry to the requirements of defense who had hoped to find in the Ministry of Supply a ministry of economic planning. To most of the Government a ministry of the latter sort must have seemed ultimately undesirable in its economic implications, immediately dan-

canned fish; canned fruit and vegetables; cereals; cocoa; condensed milk; dried fruits; imported eggs; meat and livestock; oils and fats; potatoes; sugar; tea; imported fresh fruit and vegetables.

33 The Ministry of Aircraft Production controls: aluminum; bauxite; fabrication of aircraft materials.

gerous in the possible range of its errors, and certainly contrary to the prevailing "judicial" conception of administration. The Minister for the Coordination of Defense held that the relations with industry already established separately by the Admiralty and the Air Ministry could not be improved by establishing such a planning ministry, and when the issue arose again in 1940, as it continued to do until after Captain Lyttelton was made Minister of Production in the spring of 1942, the Prime Minister argued that the responsibility of the Chancellor of the Exchequer for the stability of the currency in fact extended over the entire economy, and that a minister charged with the direct supervision of production would inevitably infringe upon the authority of the Treasury.

Consequently in the Admiralty, where alone contracting firms were systematically supervised by regional and local officers in peacetime, a closed organization of production for naval requirements extending into individual plants, and including the control of shipbuilding labor, has been maintained. Had the course of the war been what was expected in 1939, with prolonged fighting in northern France, while the Admiralty enforced the blockade, transported troops across the Channel, or made preparations for invasion elsewhere on the Continent, all its demands might have been met under this arrangement. In the suddenly changed conditions of 1940, however, when the tanks, trucks, artillery, and even machine guns of the British Expeditionary Force were lost, and when all available capacity was required for the manufacture of pursuit planes, the independent activity of different ministries became an obstacle to the organization of existing capacity for maximum production.

The *controllers of commodities in the Ministry of Supply,* who were appointed at the outbreak of war, are, like the controllers in the Ministry of Food, members of the controlled trades. Some of their staffs, although now paid by the government in an effort to reduce the cost of control, originally received their salaries from the trade associations, to which the government paid a fee for this service. Many of the central offices of the controls are located in the trading centers, the wool control for example, in Bradford, and the cotton control in Manchester. The first task of the controls was to fix the prices of the materials in question. In this connection costs were initially determined by trade association accountants, the ministry undertaking no independent investigation of profits until the spring of 1941. Besides the raw material controls, there are in the Ministry of Supply production directorates for munitions, tanks and transport, equipment and stores, and tools.

The various controls distribute supplies to individual firms in accordance with the contracts they have undertaken. Orders by or, in the case of certain civilian manufacture, authorized by particular government departments are so designated through each stage of subcontracting. In the manufacturer's application to the controls for supplies all government orders enjoy, in principle, the same urgency,[34] since changing proportions of the total available supplies of the controlled materials are allocated in advance to the use of each of the departments, and the contracts placed by any department should not require for their completion more than the quota of materials allowed to the department. In this respect there are no varying degrees of priority among authorized contracts.[35] The *Priorities Department of the Ministry of Supply,* which issues the priority authorizations for all government contracts, is in a position to estimate the total consumption of every department.

There was no correspondingly strict allocation of plant capacity to different and conflicting requirements. That would have necessitated intimate contact by the contracting departments with varying local conditions, for which no administrative provision was made. This is not a handicap to the Ministry of Aircraft Production, for example, when dealing with a few large producers of aircraft frames. In various other aspects of munitions production, however, it has resulted in the overloading of many plants and the neglect of others equally well or better equipped. Its disadvantages are most apparent in competition between the departments for engineering facilities, which are widely scattered.

The particular allocation of materials to each department is agreed upon in an interdepartmental committee of civil servants from the departments concerned. This committee is one of five *priority committees* concerned with materials and production, man power, industrial capacity, works and buildings, and transport respectively. Officials of the Pri-

---

[34] The very slight proportions of controlled materials remaining in excess of allocations to government departments are licensed by the controls to individual applicants.

[35] There are, however, general supplementary priority directions. See below, p. 183. During 1940 the interdepartmental committee on works and buildings priority established definite classes of construction with graded claims on building labor, and particular construction projects were assigned to one or another of these classes, a reversion to the discredited priority system of the last war. The result was that by the time the Ministry of Works and Buildings was created at the end of 1940 work had been undertaken 30 percent to 40 percent in excess of total building capacity.

orities Department in the Ministry of Supply keep records of their discussions and maintain some contact between them. The Materials and Production Committee is a combination of two committees on materials and on production which existed in the first period of the war, and the Man Power Committee is likewise a combination of two earlier committees on labor and on the distribution of man power between production and the armed forces. The Industrial Capacity Committee came into existence in the summer of 1940. Subcommittees of the main priority committees, like the Allocation of Traffic Subcommittee and the Works Contracts Subcommittee, are responsible for more detailed coordination. The looseness of this interdepartmental organization and the importance of purely personal factors may be illustrated by the fact that the chairmanship of the Materials and Production Committee, which was originally held, quite logically, by the then Parliamentary secretary of the Ministry of Supply, remained with the same gentleman when he became Parliamentary secretary of the Ministry of Aircraft Production, and later of the Ministry of War Transport, and is now held by the Minister of Works and Buildings, who was formerly director of a department in the Ministry of Supply concerned with total supplies of raw materials.

By agreement between the supply departments a circular instruction to industry to give first, second, and third priority to the production of a few specified articles and to any work for the armed forces or the merchant marine that could by this means be completed within a given short period of time was issued [36] in the crisis of 1940. The strict application of these directions necessarily interrupted existing production schedules, and a revised general instruction issued in November 1941 contained a proviso that the three higher degrees of priority did not apply to " machine tools, plant, or materials." Certificates are, however, issued for particular articles which are to be added to or removed from the list of those receiving the higher ratings, and in these certificates it may be stipulated that the special priority shall include machine tools, plant, and materials.

The distribution of transport facilities in accordance with the urgency of the various claims upon them has been greatly facilitated by the unification of control over shipping and railway movements, motor transport, and canals in a single *Ministry of War Transport* since April

---

[36] By the Ministry of Supply on behalf of the Admiralty, War Office, Air Ministry, and Ministry of Aircraft Production.

1941. The interdepartmental Allocation of Traffic Subcommittee meets in the ministry with the heads of its different divisions. Rail traffic is directed, very much as in the last war, by a *Railway Executive Committee* which includes the managers of the large railway companies and the London Passenger Transport Board. Initial agreements between the ministry and the companies provided for a minimum revenue for the entire railway system to be guaranteed by the government and a maximum permitted revenue, but in 1941 the payment of fixed rentals by the government was substituted for the earlier agreements. Shipping owners, on the other hand, operate their own vessels, which have been requisitioned by the ministry, as well as vessels built since the beginning of the war on the ministry's account [37] in return for fixed commissions under the direction of the *Shipping Operations Control,* a more bureaucratic agency than the Railway Executive. Most of the staff of the shipping divisions of the Ministry of War Transport performed the same or similar duties in the Marine Department of the Board of Trade before the war and in the short lived Ministry of Shipping instituted after the outbreak of war.

Several thousand motor vehicles have been chartered by the Ministry of War Transport and employed in the carriage of goods for which government departments are responsible. A larger pool of privately operated vehicles has been organized in regional offices paralleling those of the official pool. With the increasing scarcity of motor fuel and rubber it has been the policy of the Ministry to transfer all the freight possible from road to rail carriage. This has necessitated compensation of road haulage operators if adequate numbers of vehicles were to be maintained. At the end of 1942 the Government made proposals in which all vehicles employed in long-distance freight carriage were brought under unified control in a scheme closely resembling the control of shipping, with the difference that the owners of transport vehicles accepted in the national pool receive standard payments based on their prewar earnings whether or not the vehicles are in current operation.

In the field of exports and purchases abroad a committee corresponding to the interdepartmental priority committees was formed under the chairmanship of the under-secretary of the Ministry of Economic Warfare, who had been Chief Economic Adviser to the Government since 1931, in the first months of the war. With the subsequent exten-

---

[37] Since May 1942 tonnage built on government account has been allocated to individual shipping owners in proportion to their losses for purchase after the war.

sion of the blockade to cut off the greater part of the European market, this committee has become known as a *committee on world surpluses,* and in 1941 the Minister Without Portfolio, who was then the minister concerned with general questions of postwar reconstruction, presided over it. The division of the Ministry of Economic Warfare concerned with international problems of postwar trade, and the under-secretary, were transferred to the Board of Trade when the Minister Without Portfolio left the Government early in 1942.

At the same time a newly appointed Paymaster General, who has since succeeded to the position of Minister Without Portfolio, but without becoming a member of the War Cabinet, was charged with the general consideration of " reconstruction." Responsibility for the physical aspects of planning was transferred at the beginning of 1942 from the Ministry of Health to the Ministry of Works and Buildings, which was retitled Ministry of Works and Planning. The publication of two major reports on rural and urban development during 1942 led to the establishment early in 1943 of an independent Ministry of Town and Country Planning, the precise functions of which must, of course, depend on the adoption of a definite policy by the Government.

There has been no formal coordination of the *price fixing* powers vested in different departments of the government, outside of two interdepartmental committees on agricultural and food prices. These include representatives of the Ministry of Labor, which is concerned with the cost of living of wage earners, the Ministry of Agriculture, the Departments of Agriculture for Scotland and Northern Ireland, and the Ministry of Food, the interests of the Ministries of Agriculture and Food being opposed as those of seller and buyer. Maximum prices for consumer goods are fixed, subject to review by a referee appointed by the Lord Chancellor, by the Board of Trade.[38]   The Board acts in consultation with a representative, advisory Central Price Regulation Committee, which receives complaints of excessive prices on behalf both of the Board of Trade and the Ministry of Food.

The fixing of maximum prices for consumer goods was followed, at the same time that all imports were brought under a licensing system in June 1940, by the drastic *limitation of supplies.* This was at first effected by orders forbidding wholesalers to supply retailers with more than a given percentage of their purchases in the corresponding period of the previous year. The assumption made in fixing percentages was

---

[38] Under the Prices of Goods Act, 1939 and the Goods and Services (Price Control) Act, 1940.

that a reduction of turnover by 75 percent would not threaten the continued existence of the consumer goods industries. The compulsory concentration of consumer production in the most efficient, " nucleus " firms, to operate at capacity while other firms in the same industries were closed or continued to operate only as selling and distributing organizations, was introduced in March 1941.[39] Firms that are closed down receive compensation from a levy on the earnings of those remaining in operation, a species of rationalization with which the British shipbuilding industry was familiar before the war. So that the plant capacity released would actually be transferred to essential uses, the acquisition of new factory and storage space outside the engineering and munitions industries was licensed under a Controller of Factory and Storage Premises, who became responsible for the allocation of storage accommodation among the different government departments.

The direct rationing of clothing and footwear to consumers began in the summer of 1941. The " telescoping " of retail trade has been a corollary of the limitation of civilian supplies, but there has been no government support for the rationalization of distribution comparable to the concentration of consumer industries. A committee representing retail traders reported in the summer of 1942 that during the war the number of " very large " and " large " shops had increased by 4 percent, although individual shops within these groups had lost 25 to 30 percent of their space and personnel, while the number of " small " and " very small " shops had decreased by 11 percent and 19 percent respectively. The response of the Board of Trade has been to guarantee establishments falling into the " small " category new stock equal to fixed percentages of their total turnover in given periods earlier in the war and immediately before the war.

Separate measures of price fixing, preemptive purchasing abroad, labor regulation, and procurement obviously require some correlation, if only for the negative purpose of ensuring their conformity with the financial policy of the Treasury. The direction of the main lines of production in accordance with strategic necessity, by such decisions as those in May 1940 that airplanes were of first importance, in the summer of 1941 that tanks were, and in the spring of 1942 that shipbuilding should take precedence of everything else, also requires more inclusive authority than a consultative committee of civil servants can have. It is

---

[39] By July 1942, 250,000 workers and above 55,000,000 sq. feet of factory space had been released under schemes of concentration.

in these broad aspects of planning and decision that the organization of interdepartmental coordination has most often proved defective.

At the beginning of the war " economic policy " was decided in the Treasury. In addition to the ministerial committee on economic policy under the Chancellor of the Exchequer, an interdepartmental committee of civil servants met under the chairmanship of the late Lord Stamp,[40] who was appointed Economic Adviser to the War Cabinet. He worked in the Treasury with a staff of four economists (the Economic and Financial Survey). Questions arising in the work of the interdepartmental priority committees were referred for decision to the ministerial Priority Committee under the Minister for the Coordination of Defense. The latter office ceased to exist in April 1940,[41] and the First Lord of the Admiralty (Mr. Churchill) became chairman of the Priority Committee and of the ministerial Committee on Military Coordination.

After the formation of the Churchill Government in May 1940 the War Cabinet was reduced to six members,[42] excluding the service ministers, and the Prime Minister assumed also the title of *Minister of Defense*. When Mr. Churchill, while still First Lord of the Admiralty, assumed the chairmanship of the two principal ministerial coordinating committees, the secretary of the Committee of Imperial Defense, Lieutenant-General H. L. Ismay, became his principal private secretary. This position he has continued to hold, with the additional title of Chief of Staff to the Prime Minister and Minister of Defense. His position more or less corresponds to that of the Chief of Staff to the Commander-in-Chief in the United States, and he represents the Prime Minister in the Chiefs of Staff Committee. The " Ministry of Defense " consists solely of General Ismay's office and a " statistical department " [43] under Lord Cherwell as scientific adviser.

---

[40] The chairman of the London, Midlands, and Scottish Railway, he had also been chairman of the standing committee of the Economic Advisory Council responsible for reports to the Government.

[41] See above, Part I, p. 157.

[42] The Prime Minister, the Lord Privy Seal, the Foreign Secretary, the Lord President of the Council, the Minister Without Portfolio, and the Minister of Aircraft Production. The Cabinet was enlarged to eight members in October 1940 by the inclusion of the Chancellor of the Exchequer and the Minister of Labor. In subsequent reshufflings of the leaders of the Labor and Conservative Parties until the end of 1942 the posts of Minister of Aircraft Production, Minister Without Portfolio, and Lord Privy Seal were eliminated from the War Cabinet, and the posts of Minister of Production, Secretary of State for Dominion Affairs, and Home Secretary were included in it.

[43] Cf. 373 H. C. Deb. 5 s., col. 1275. Lord Cherwell at the end of 1942 entered the Government as Paymaster General, his functions remaining unchanged.

The Committee on Military Coordination became by the change of Government the *Defense Committee of the Cabinet,* and its jurisdiction was extended to include questions of supply. The ministerial Priority Committee was replaced, in an inferior position, by the so-called *Production Council* under the chairmanship of the Minister Without Portfolio (Mr. Greenwood), whose career in opposition had in no way prepared him for an executive role. He became at the same time chairman of a revised Economic Policy Committee which was designed as the long-range planning branch of the Production Council. The membership of these last two committees was flexible enough to include on occasion any member of the Government. The occasion, however, was seldom, as meetings were held only once or twice a month. The Chancellor of the Exchequer was promoted to a " *Supreme Coordinating Committee* " of four ministers over whom the Lord President of the Council, then the former Prime Minister, Mr. Chamberlain, presided. After Mr. Chamberlain was succeeded as Lord President of the Council by Sir John Anderson in October 1940, the Supreme Coordinating Committee became in fact the final authority short of the War Cabinet in home affairs, its position corresponding to that of the Defense Committee in military affairs.

An expansion of production was promised by the formation in January 1941 of ministerial Import and Production " Executives " under the chairmanship of the Ministers of Supply [44] and Labor respectively. [45] The Production Council, and with it the Economic Policy Committee, disappeared. Lord Stamp resigned as the Cabinet's economic adviser shortly thereafter, presumably finding no place for his advice. The imports of different departments from North America had been regulated as far as necessary during 1940 by an interdepartmental committee under the parliamentary secretary of the Ministry of Shipping. As they increased in importance a *North American Supply Committee* was constituted by the Ministers of Supply and Aircraft Production and the First Lord of the Admiralty. (The resulting organization may be clarified by the chart inserted at the back of this book.)

In addition to the Production and Import Executives there remained the Defense Committee of the Cabinet — including the Prime Minister

---

44 After June 1941, the President of the Board of Trade.

45 The Import Executive consisted of the Ministers of Supply, Food, War Transport, and Aircraft Production, the First Lord of the Admiralty, and the President of the Board of Trade. The Production Executive consisted of the Ministers of Labor, Supply, Aircraft Production, and Works and Buildings, the First Lord of the Admiralty, and the President of the Board of Trade.

as chairman, the Lord Privy Seal and leader of the House of Commons (Mr. Attlee), the Foreign Secretary, the three service ministers and the chiefs of staff, the Minister of Aircraft Production, and, from time to time, the Minister of Supply — which dealt with war production as well as with military operations. When Lord Beaverbrook, who, as Minister of Aircraft Production, had been a member of the War Cabinet, resigned in May 1941, the office of " Minister of State " was invented for him, and he was made deputy chairman of the Defense Committee for supply problems, the Lord Privy Seal becoming deputy chairman for military operations. This delegation of the Prime Minister's functions as Minister of Defense lasted only a few weeks, until Lord Beaverbrook became Minister of Supply. He was succeeded as Minister of State by Captain Lyttelton, who was dispatched immediately to Cairo, with the duty of organizing the supplies of the armies in the Near East.[46]

Consultation among departments in the Production Executive and the subordinate interdepartmental priority committees was duplicated in production boards in the *twelve regions* into which England, Scotland, and Wales are divided for purposes of civil defense.[47] The area of each of the five home commands of the Army corresponds to the areas of two or three of these regions. They were created by legislation in March 1939, when *regional defense commissioners* were appointed to exercise the full authority of the central government in the event that communications between any region and the central government should be destroyed by enemy action. Some precedent for the regional division existed in the munitions areas of the last war, in the normal organization of the employment exchanges into nine geographic divisions, and in the appointment of Admiralty inspectors of naval construction and engineering for particular areas, which varied with the location of the particular industries.

Officers of every important ministry except those concerned with external affairs, and of several departments of some ministries, have since been appointed in each of the civil defense regions or areas, although

---

[46] See Chapter II, p. 72.

[47] Scotland, Northern, Northeastern, North Midlands, Eastern, London, Southeastern, Southern, Southwestern, Midlands, Northwestern, and Wales. In the regional supply organization the London and Southeastern regions are combined, and Northern Ireland, which has its own civil defense organization, is included in the supply organization. The London and Southeastern regions are also combined in the organization of the Ministry of Labor, which does not include Northern Ireland. The indiscriminate use of the terms " area," " region," " division," and " district " for the same administrative unit has created some confusion.

their offices are not all established in the same town in any region.[48]
Their powers vary widely from the direct executive authority of the
regional controllers of labor or transport to the "liaison" between the
central ministry and local agencies provided by the regional officers of
the Ministry of Agriculture. Within the Ministry of Supply particularly,
the regional officers of different departments have frequently ignored or
opposed one another's endeavors. Authority over the different departmental representatives lies with the regional defense commissioners
only in such emergencies as have not yet occurred.[49]

The immediate functions of the defense commissioners have been
limited to supervising the civil defense measures of local authorities, the
expenses of which are borne by the Home Office (since the beginning
of the war, the Home Office and Ministry of Home Security), and the
special aspects of air raid precautions for which the Ministry of Health
is responsible. The distribution of *emergency services* illustrates very
well the necessity for local and regional as well as central coordination
of the work of different departments. The civil defense services proper,
which are operated by local authorities, are subject to Home Office supervision, as are fire services, which were nationalized under a Fire Service
Department of the Home Office in 1941. The Ministry of Health, however, supervises conditions in shelters and rest centers and first aid services. The Board of Education is responsible for the evacuation of school
children, and the Ministry of Health, for the evacuation of others.
County authorities are responsible for the reception of evacuated school
children; and local authorities, for the reception of other evacuees.[50]
The Ministry of Food operates canteens outside the factories, and the
Ministry of Labor, canteens inside the factories. For the emergency
repair of air raid damage, the Ministry of Works and Buildings maintains dumps of building materials at strategic points. Repairs to private
dwellings under a certain maximum sum are licensed by local authorities, and repairs to factories are decided by local Emergency Reconstruction Panels including local manufacturers and local or regional

48 In the Northeastern region, for example, the offices of the regional defense commissioner,
the regional controller of labor, and the regional representative of the Ministry of Works and
Building are in Leeds and the area supply board in Sheffield. In Scotland the area supply board
is located in Glasgow and the regional defense commissioner and labor controller in Edinburgh.

49 For this reason the relations between the regional defense commissioners and the regional
officers of the different departments of the government have been indicated on the chart of
British administration at the back of this book with broken lines.

50 Indeed, the Ministry of Food, through the reports of local rationing committees, maintains the only complete census of population movements.

officers of the different supply departments. The regional defense commissioner decides the allocation of the total supplies released for repairs as between dwelling and factory reconstruction.

A short rehearsal of the wartime functions of different ministries will be enough to suggest the number of agencies of the central government, many of them affecting the lives of the population directly, which come into contact at the regional level. The powers of the *Ministry of Agriculture* have been largely delegated with respect to the increase of production to *War Agricultural Executive Committees* appointed by the minister, in districts which do not coincide with local government areas, and through them to local War Agricultural Committees including representatives of every parish.[51] The most important growers of the typical products of the area meet in the district committees under the chairmanship of a land officer of the ministry. They can require land that is not under cultivation to be plowed up, take possession of and operate " substandard " farms, allow grants for drainage improvements on behalf of the ministry to individuals and to county catchment boards, and extend credit to farmers for improvements, and they operate or let agricultural and drainage machinery owned by the ministry.

These committees come under the general supervision of land commissioners in the Ministry of Agriculture and of the eleven regional liaison officers already mentioned. Since the Agricultural Research institutes in England are responsible not to the Ministry of Agriculture but to the Agricultural Research Committee of the Privy Council, the ministry has suffered from a lack of scientifically trained personnel, which is not felt in Scotland, where the executive officers of the Agricultural Executive Committees are all officials of the Scottish Agricultural Colleges. Roughly parallel county committees, all of which include members of the corresponding District War Agricultural Executive Committee, have been established, with local subcommittees of their own, for the direction of the additional agricultural labor mobilized in the Women's Land Army.

The separation of production and marketing in the Ministry of Agriculture and purchasing in the *Ministry of Food* is an obvious handicap to the development of a consistent program, the more particularly since most agricultural subsidies are now borne by the Ministry of Food. The food ministry is responsible not only for central purchasing and

---

[51] This subdivision does not exist in Scotland where there are forty Agricultural Executive Committees.

distribution but also for rationing under the two heads of food and feeding stuffs. Its organization for the *rationing of feeding stuffs* consists of twelve divisional committees of manufacturers of feeding stuffs, wholesalers, and farmers, with executive officers from the ministry, and county feeding stuffs committees representing both farmers and traders. Although the areas of the feeding stuffs committees do not correspond to those of the agricultural committees, their relations are necessarily close, and their membership is overlapping. For *food rationing* there are more than fifteen hundred local food committees representing traders, consumers, and the local authorities, with the town clerk usually serving as executive officer. Food control officers of the ministry in each of the civil defense areas deal with many of the unforeseen problems of distribution resulting from war conditions. Complaints of excessive food prices or violations of price fixing orders reach the ministry through seventeen local Price Regulation Committees, again representative of consumers, traders, and local authorities, appointed by the Board of Trade early in the war. Although these committees were not concerned originally with food prices, but with the prices of other consumers' goods, they received such frequent complaints of food prices that they were given the alternative title of Food Price Investigation Committees. This fortuitous arrangement has the advantage of ensuring the conformity of recommendations made by the Central Price Regulation Committee to the Board of Trade on the one hand and the Ministry of Food on the other.

The trades organized in the *commodity controls* of the Ministry of Food have their own area divisions. Under the meat and livestock control, for example, there are eight Area Wholesale Meat Supply Associations and a Meat Importers National Association with twelve branch offices. The most severe criticism of the ministry has been for its failure to correct extravagance in distribution. The existence of national marketing boards for products like bacon and milk has not always contributed to the reduction either of duplication of facilities or of the number of separate processes in distribution. The compulsory pooling [52] of certain commodities and the definition of fixed areas for the distribution of others at the beginning of the war entailed so much waste and inconvenience that they were quickly withdrawn, and it was only in the early summer of 1942 that considerations of transport and personnel led the ministry to attempt a similar and more successful restriction of

---

[52] Elimination of trade names and substitution of standard grades at uniform prices.

distribution. Retailers in eight areas into which the country is divided for this purpose must draw their supplies from wholesalers in the same area. In other products such as margarine, bread, cake and biscuit, bacon, sugar, sweets, and flour, which the retailer and, in the last case, the baker frequently obtain direct from the manufacturer, they are restricted to purchases regardless of brand from the firms nearest. At the same time the retail distribution of milk was restricted to standard grades to be supplied to assigned districts by dairy companies in proportion to their share in the total consumption of the locality. In this connection the Ministry of Food departed from its established method of control through representatives of the trade controlled to make General Sir Robert G. Finlayson partly responsible for the administration of the milk scheme.

The allocation of available transportation facilities in the *Ministry of War Transport* requires a more unified regional organization. Twelve regional transport commissioners are responsible for the supervision not only of the divisional transport officers of the ministry, who are concerned with road traffic, but also of the district officers of railway companies, the actual operation of which is otherwise little affected by a nominal government control, and of the local transport officers of the Ministries of Aircraft Production and Food, the Admiralty, and the Ministry of Supply, the latter acting also on behalf of the Ministry of Agriculture,[53] and for the provision of additional facilities to satisfy requirements arising from the transfer of labor or industry. The regional transport commissioners also control the rationing of gasoline by officers of the Petroleum Department of the Board of Trade. A large part of the motor vehicles originally operated by the Road Haulage Branch of the ministry were taken over from a pool for the transport of meat supplies established by the Ministry of Food; most of the others were employed in connection with the clearance of ports. The ministry's pool of trucks was organized in six large areas and fourteen smaller divisions, but since all long-distance haulage has come under government control the divisions have been brought into conformity with the twelve civil defense areas. Canals are similarly organized into six areas, in each of which a committee of canal owners, representatives of other forms of transportation, and transport officers of different government departments has authority to allocate particular traffic to the canals. The canal

---

[53] Partly for the reason that the Ministry of Supply is responsible for the distribution of fertilizers.

systems of the six regions are coordinated through an advisory Central Canal Committee of which the Parliamentary secretary of the Ministry of War Transport is chairman.

The greatest transportation problems in England in wartime arise, of course, from the fact that goods are delivered in large convoys which are directed by the Admiralty to the ports that seem safest from attack. The collection of cargoes for and the quick distribution of cargoes brought in by numbers of ships the departure and arrival of which cannot be made known in advance, as well as the actual unloading and turnaround of the ships, is the concern of the *Port and Transit Control* of the ministry. The head of this department belongs, with the directors of the liner, ship management, and short sea shipping divisions of the ministry and the controller of commercial shipping, to the Shipping Operations Control. The loading of ships abroad with a view to expediting the discharge of their cargoes in England is superintended by officers of the Ships Distribution (Diversion) Section of the ministry. Within each port executive committees composed of the naval officers in command of the ports, shipping and railway agents, motor transport operators, representatives of dock labor, of traders, and of the government importing departments have been formed more or less spontaneously. In certain most congested ports the Ministry of Transport is the employer of all dock labor.[54] Regional port directors for the Clyde areas, the northwestern English ports, the Bristol Channel ports, and the ports of the eastern coast have been appointed by the minister to concentrate the efforts of the port committees and to coordinate their work with that of the central controls.

The functions of regional representatives of the *Board of Trade* are apparently limited to assisting manufacturers in the export trade to obtain transportation and to advising them how best to secure from the Board authorization of applications for supplies and labor.[55] The Controller of Factory and Storage Premises in the Board of Trade has his

---

[54] See Chapter IV, Part II, p. 244.

[55] Manufacturers of the same or closely similar articles have formed "Export Groups" through which applications to the Board can be made. There is a central Industrial and Export Council of which the President of the Board of Trade is chairman, and the Secretary of the Department of Overseas Trade, vice-chairman, and which includes Parliamentary secretaries of the Ministries of Supply and Labor, representatives of the Treasury, the Ministry of Economic Warfare, and the Foreign Office, the controllers of wool, cotton, and factory and storage space, and representatives of industry, commerce, finance, and labor. While the Council, which dates from February 1940, has met on a monthly basis, it has had sub-committees which met more frequently, and a small executive committee in permanent session. The functions of the Council, in spite of its large official membership, are advisory.

own representatives in the twelve regions, who must work in cooperation with the twelve licensing offices for private building maintained by
the Ministry of Works and Buildings. With the transfer of the powers
of the Ministry of Transport over electricity supplies to the Board of
Trade late in 1941, a new division was formed for the administration of
gas and electricity, and eleven regional Fuel and Power Commissioners were appointed. These officers were transferred to the *Ministry of
Fuel, Light, and Power,* which also absorbed the Department of Mines
under the Board of Trade, upon its creation in June 1942. They will be
responsible for the rationing of fuel to consumers. Regional controllers
of the Ministry of Fuel in eight coal mining areas exercise the government's recently assumed powers over the operation of coal mines and are
responsible for the actual output of the mines in their regions.

The organization of the *Ministry of Labor* [56] is unique in the delegation of the authority of all the central departments of the ministry over
the activities of their local agents and inspectors to a single controller
in each of the defense regions. Within his region he is responsible for
recruiting, training, the transfer of labor to work of urgent importance,
conditions of work, and the welfare of working people. Labor supply
inspectors, whose task is to secure the maximum use of the minimum
labor, report (except for the industries under Essential Work Orders)
to man power officers, whose task is the allocation of available man
power as between industry and the armed forces, and the directors of
employment exchanges, to whom particular applications for labor are
made. The regional controllers of labor have thus been better able than
any other regional officers to recognize bottlenecks in production, and
so far as they are due to lack of labor to remedy them. While periodical
instructions are issued by the Ministry of Labor in agreement with the
supply departments as to the types of production, or even the particular
firms, to which special priority in labor supply is to be granted, the regional controllers themselves may give first preference to any firms in
their regions in which comparatively small numbers of workmen are
required or which seem to them for any reason to deserve exceptional
treatment.

Since the beginning of the war officers of the departments concerned
with production, transportation, and trade have met in *regional supply
boards*. These were originally headed by the representatives of the munitions department of the Ministry of Supply. The director of the depart-

[56] See Chapter IV, Part II, p. 241.

ment was a former engineer-in-chief of the Admiralty, and it may be supposed that his appointees, " engineer ex-admirals," had the advantage of familiarity with regional supply organization in the only department in which it normally existed. That their organization was ineffective in planning the fullest use of capacity or coordinating the orders of the different supply departments is due in the first place to the absence of any general responsibility for production in the Ministry of Supply and in the second place to the very limited authority of the regional officers of the departments, who were concerned for the most part with the " progressing " of orders placed by their departments centrally. Agreement among the representatives of the supply departments in any region as to the placing of particular contracts in that region by any one of their departments was sought for the first time in July 1942.

Advisory committees of representatives of employers and labor, appointed by the Minister of Supply, were attached to the first regional boards. In the reorganization of the government in the crisis of 1940 control of the boards was secured briefly by the Ministry of Labor, and then returned to the Ministry of Supply. Six representatives of industry and labor were, however, added to the membership of each board, and the chairmen and vice-chairmen were chosen from among them. It is doubtful whether in some regions the members appointed ever assembled before 1941.

The role of the boards remained advisory, not executive, and in that capacity they reported after the establishment of the Production Executive in 1941 to its Industrial Capacity Subcommittee, or, presumably, to the chairman of the committee, the Parliamentary secretary of the Ministry of Supply. By the middle of 1941 the area boards included officers of the Ministry of Supply and the raw materials department of the Ministry of Supply, the controller's department of the Admiralty,[57] the Ministry of Aircraft Production, the Ministry of War Transport, the Ministry of Labor, the Ministry of Works and Buildings, the Board of Trade, and the regional committees of the Machine Tool Control in the Ministry of Supply. Something of what they might have accomplished is illustrated by the success of capacity exchanges or clearing centers established principally in the London area, but also under some other boards, for the use of small manufacturers. The creation late in 1941 in the Ministry of Supply of a division of regional control to supervise the regional

---

[57] The Third Sea Lord, who is a member of the Board of Admiralty, is responsible for naval supply, and is called the Controller of the Admiralty.

and local activity of agents of different divisions of the ministry was also symptomatic of an increasing effort to make the best use of existing capacity.

The necessity for a more coherent regional organization of war production and for the closer application of technical resources to the tactical requirements of the armed forces was recognized in the formation of the *Ministry of Production* in March 1942. This date roughly marks the end of the construction of new capacity for armament production, the conversion of existing capacity to armament production, the recruitment of additional labor for armament work, or the release of labor from non-essential work for armament production. The importation of raw materials was at the same time restricted by sinkings and by lack of shipping tonnage. The conditions of production were thus narrowed, and any further increase of output depended on the more efficient use of the factors already engaged.[57a] The beginning of a great expansion of capacity for armament production in the United States also made it possible for British production to be concentrated to a certain extent on articles better produced, for reasons of quality, technique, materials, or transport in England than in the United States.

The central organization of supply under the Ministry of Production bears more resemblance to the organization under the Minister for the Coordination of Defense in 1939 than to that of the Production Council in 1940 or the Import and Production Executives in 1941. The latter bodies have given way to a *Joint Production Staff* corresponding to the Chiefs of Staff Committee. Its members have more authority than civil servants ordinarily can, and more knowledge of specific problems than is ordinarily expected of ministers.

The administration of the service departments is distinguished from that of other ministries by the fact that all major departmental decisions are taken jointly in the Board of Admiralty, the Army Council, or the Air Council by the responsible minister and the service or civil service heads of the various divisions. In the Ministry of Supply, the *Supply Council,* and in the Ministry of Aircraft Production, the *Air Supply Board,* likewise include the heads of important departments of each ministry. Although they are much more informally constituted, they too are designed to prevent difficulties from arising in the direction of highly technical services by temporary civilian ministers. The chair-

---

[57a] Cf., for example, Mr. Oliver Lyttelton's address to the Institution of Production Engineers, London, October 23, 1942.

man of the Supply Council is appointed for the purpose of general co-ordination in the ministry and has no particular executive responsibilities. The Joint War Production Staff is thus composed of the Assistant Chiefs of the Imperial General and the Naval Staffs, the member of the Air Council concerned with supply, the chairman of the Supply Council in the Ministry of Supply, the member of the Board of Admiralty concerned with production, and the highest official of the Ministry of Aircraft Production, meeting under the chairmanship of the Minister of Production or his chief adviser.

The Joint Production Staff, like the Chiefs of Staff Committee, is executive. There are subordinate to it, as there are to the Chiefs of Staff Committee, joint planning groups of representatives from different departments. These groups are sometimes formed *ad hoc* and are concerned with the production of particular weapons, their members working under the direction of the Department of Programs and Planning, which has been transferred from the Ministry of Supply to the Ministry of Production. Others, under the chairmanship of the special industrial adviser of the Ministry of Production, are standing committees concerned with more general questions of production efficiency and economy of man power.

The analogous Joint Planning Staff and Joint Intelligence Subcommittee under the *Chiefs of Staff Committee* and the Vice-Chiefs of Staff Committee are permanent bodies, and their members constitute a " joint staff " in addition to the staffs of the three services. The Joint Planning Staff consists of the directors of plans of the three services, but its subsections [58] include besides officers of the three forces liaison officers from the Ministry of War Transport, the Ministry of Economic Warfare, and the Ministry of Home Security. The Joint Intelligence Subcommittee also includes officials of the Foreign Office and the Ministry of Economic Warfare, and the Ministry of Economic Warfare is represented in the intelligence section for operations.

Responsibility for the *design of weapons* remains with the Ministries of Supply and Aircraft Production, to which the departments of scientific research in the War Office and the Air Ministry were transferred when the separate production ministries were established, and with the production department of the Admiralty. There are departments

---

[58] Strategical Planning Section, Executive Planning Section, and Future Operational Planning.

of scientific research and development in the Admiralty, the Ministry of Supply, and the Ministry of Aircraft Production. There is also an independent Department of Scientific and Industrial Research under the supervision of the Lord President of the Council, which is responsible for the work of the National Physical Laboratory and of the national Scientific Advisory Council. The Prime Minister as Minister of Defense has his own scientific adviser. A Scientific Advisory Committee in the Ministry of Supply and an Aeronautical Research Committee in the Ministry of Aircraft Production include scientists who hold government offices. The Aeronautical Research Committee is in addition interdepartmental, including besides the director of research and development in the Ministry of Aircraft Production and the supervisor of the Royal Aeronautical Research Establishment the director of meteorological research in the Air Ministry and the director of scientific research in the Ministry of Supply.

The new appointment of a scientific adviser to the War Office in the spring of 1942 suggests in itself that collaboration between the service and production ministries in meeting particular requirements has left something to be desired. At the same time the post of Deputy Chief of the Imperial General Staff for organization and equipment was created, the D.C.I.G.S. becoming a member of the Supply Council in the Ministry of Supply. An advisory board comprising officers from the War Office and the Ministry of Supply had been established in 1940 for the design and production of tanks. To this has now been added a Weapon Development Committee under the D.C.I.G.S. The appointment of a deputy to the Chief of the Imperial General Staff was followed in August 1942 by the appointment of a Deputy First Sea Lord to direct the administrative work of the Naval Staff in relation to training and material, and later of a Fifth Sea Lord as Chief of Naval Air Equipment. In the Ministry of Aircraft Production a Chief Naval Representative, who is a naval captain, and a staff of naval officers supervise the supply of naval aircraft. The reporting of the tactical performance of different weapons to the production ministries by qualified officers in the field was not organized systematically before the summer of 1942 and was only occasional.

The *Minister of Production*, unlike the ministers of the several supply departments, is a member of the War Cabinet. His executive powers are limited to the allocation of raw materials and machine tools, and upon this his influence over the supply departments must depend. The allocation of labor and the allocation of capacity for shipbuilding and repairs, over which the Admiralty retains complete control, have been specifically exempted from his jurisdiction. Even the Machine Tool Control and the Raw Materials Department, which, in contrast to the individual controls, is concerned with total supplies rather than with distribution to particular plants, have remained as before in the Ministry of Supply, certain of their officers being included also on the staff of the Ministry of Production. The Machine Tool Controller, for example, is also the head of a department in the Ministry of Production which supervises the actual progress of the procurement programs of the different supply departments. There is an industrial division in the Ministry of Production for the correction of defects of organization in individual firms and the improvement of facilities for armament production. It acts mainly at the request of other supply departments, and an advisory panel of industrialists and trade unionists, the successor of the Production Executive's Central Joint Advisory Committee, is attached to it.

The existing purchasing organizations of the Ministry of Supply, the Ministry of Aircraft Production, and the Admiralty in the United States were not disturbed by the creation of the Ministry of Production. In November 1942, however, the post of Minister Resident in Washington for Supply, " responsible to " the Minister of Production was established. The minister appointed, who had been employed since 1939 in the Ministry of Supply, the Ministry of War Transport, and the Ministry of Aircraft Production, must superintend the work of the British staffs of the five combined American and British boards and of various special British missions. On the overall Combined Production and Resources Board, with offices in Washington and London, British interests are represented by the Ministry of Production alone. Under the Production and Resources Board it has been possible to establish a technical " Combined Committee " for the standardization of steel production in Great Britain and North America, the members of which severally represent two combined boards and departments of the United States, Canadian, and United Kingdom Governments. Here again the Ministry of Production represents the interests of the other supply ministries in Great Britain.

To the growing list of regional officers, regional representatives of the Ministry of Production, all successful company directors, have been added. The *regional controllers of production,* who have in fact no executive authority over the regional representatives of other departments, have become the chairmen of the area production boards. Each board as reconstituted contains besides the regional representatives of the Ministry of Production, the Admiralty, the Ministry of Supply, the Ministry of Aircraft Production, the Ministry of Labor, and the Board of Trade, three representatives of employers and three of employees appointed by the Minister of Production, one of whom is the vice-chairman of the board and a member of its executive committee. The technical directors of capacity clearing centers in smaller districts are also appointed now by the Ministry of Production. The function of the regional controllers of production, as of their ministry, is to coordinate the activities of the different production departments. Their success, since every departmental regional officer remains accountable to his own department and can appeal any decision to it, must ultimately depend on the degree of authority which the Ministry of Production establishes centrally, although any prestige which the regional controllers enjoy locally may contribute to the ministry's authority. Indeed their appointments seem to have been made with a view to that end. The vice-chairmen of the eleven regional boards meeting together constitute a National Production Advisory Council. The officials chiefly concerned with regional organization in the Ministry of Production, the Admiralty, the Ministries of Supply, Aircraft Production, and Labor, and the Controller of Machine Tools also meet regularly in the Ministry of Production.

The existence of the Ministry of Production has at least resulted in the better definition of the aims of the supply departments and a more practical organization of coordination. When the Minister of Production was appointed it was stated that his role in relation to the supply departments would resemble that of the Minister of Defense in relation to the armed services. The actual organization of the Ministry of Production has served, however, to emphasize the barrenness of the comparison. The Minister of Production cannot override the other production departments. He tries presumably to form an independent estimate of the demands that may be made on them and of their common resources and to focus effort where it is most necessary or will be most profitable. Here the analogy between the Ministry of Production and an ideal defense ministry ends. The aim of the production departments is to satisfy the requirements of the armed forces; for this the systematic coordination of effort and the fixing of definite responsibility are essential. In the exertion of military power, on the other hand, the planned selection of strategic objectives is of the first importance. Success will not follow from the most perfect coordination of separate efforts without central decision and direction.

In Great Britain this central decision rests with three interlocking committees: the committee of the three Chiefs of Staff, who have " an individual and collective responsibility for advising on defense policy as a whole," to which the Prime Minister and his deputy belong; the Defense Committee of the Cabinet, which includes the Chiefs of Staff, and of which the Prime Minister is chairman; and finally the War Cabinet, to which the Chiefs of Staff may have direct access. Although it may be assumed that domestic questions are sifted very finely through the supreme coordinating committee on home affairs before they reach the War Cabinet, it remains doubtful whether the direction of military operations by the War Cabinet can be more than general or sporadic. The critics of this organization, who include among other distinguished officers the secretary of the Committee of Imperial Defense for thirty years and the last Minister for the Coordination of Defense, claim that it leads not to coordinated strategic planning, but to compromise, which is the opposite. A Minister of Defense of great military experience who was not Prime Minister, and who bore full responsibility for strategic planning, would enjoy a greater freedom of appeal to the War Cabinet against the three Chiefs of Staff or any one of them than can the Prime Minister himself, who must appear in any difference of opinion as both advocate and judge.[58a]

In summing up this brief outline of the British war administration one generalization unavoidably presents itself. The range and the vital importance of the government's wartime functions have led to the replacement of parliamentarians in most critical positions in the administration by experts, that is, by former civil servants and men of experience in private enterprise or organization. The Lord President of the Council and chairman of the supreme coordinating committee for home affairs and the Secretary of State for War are former civil servants. The Ministers of Production, Supply, Food, War Transport, and the former Minister of Aircraft Production are all business men. The Minister of Labor was a leading trade union executive. The great administrative problem before them is to avoid duplication between departments and between the regional and central levels of administration and to substi-

---

[58a] Cf. especially the debates in the House of Lords April 15, May 5, and May 20, 1942.

tute clear direction for consultation. The solution under rapidly changing conditions cannot be easy.[59]

---

[59] Some few remarks must be made in explanation of the chart of British wartime administration attached at the back of this book. Any schematic arrangement of an administration in which executive authority is strictly departmentalized is difficult. It is necessary, however, to give some impression of the interconnections of ministerial and civil servce committees. Since the regional and local functions of each ministry are exercised separately, the number of lines between ministries and local officers creates an exaggerated impression of complexity. The Regional Defense Commissioners exercise a tentative control over the officers of other departments in the event of grave emergency, and their relations to the officers of other departments in their regions have therefore been indicated by broken lines. The position of members of the Ministry and of standing ministerial committees has been indicated by black boxes. The position of standing committees of civil servants and of advisory committees has been indicated by broken black boxes. Wherever possible executive authority has been indicated by solid connecting lines, and a consultative relation by broken lines of connection. Different colors have been used to connect the major ministerial committees with their subcommittees and with the departments represented in them: black for home affairs; green for food policy; purple for the Import Executive; blue for the Production Executive; and red for defense and civil defense. These colors have been carried through the organization of the departments most closely concerned in the work of the committees, but other colors have been used to distinguish the departmental organization of other ministries included in the same committees: brown for the Ministry of Labor under the Production Executive; and orange for the Ministry of Transport under the Import Executive. Below some of the ministers who are included in coordinating committees, such as the Lord Privy Seal, the Minister Without Portfolio, and the Lord President of the Council there is of course no departmental organization.

The arrangement of ministerial committees shown is roughly that from January 1941 to February 1942. Since then successive changes have been made in the personnel of the War Cabinet. A Minister of Production has been appointed, and the Joint Production Staff under him has replaced both the Import and the Production Executives. The Regional Production Boards now report directly to the Ministry of Production. The chairmanship of the interdepartmental committee on world surpluses has since been transferred to the Board of Trade. The chart also fails to include the independent Ministry of Fuel, Light, and Power created in June 1942, and the Ministry of Town and Country Planning established in February 1943.

CHAPTER IV

The British War Economy

PART ONE

THE FINANCE OF BRITAIN'S WAR EFFORT

by William S. McCauley

1. Some Elementary Principles

The emphasis of mobilization economics on real resources of production quite properly relegates finance to a secondary position. But in democratic countries there is great danger that the problems of war finance may be pushed too far into the background of public consciousness. The objective of industrial mobilization for war is the devotion of as large a proportion of the national resources as possible to the production of weapons of war. It is not money that buys armaments, but men who, with the aid of machines, transform materials. The limits of the defense effort will be set by the availability of the real ingredients of production rather than by lack of money. Finance must, nevertheless, play an important role in the shifting of a large proportion of the nation's plant from the production of peacetime goods to the manufacture of armaments. This is especially true of capitalistic countries like Britain and the United States, where the absence in the early phases of the war effort of governmental machinery for the direct allocation of industrial capacity and the restriction of consumption has required greater reliance on financial policies to convert the economy to war production.

The objectives of mobilization finance should be threefold. The first objective, of course, is the provision of funds for defense expenditure. No government with a modern banking system at its disposal need fear a shortage of purchasing power over productive resources. Money can be created; and the danger of war finance is that reliance will be placed too largely on the creation of new funds instead of the transfer of money already in the hands of the public.

The second objective is for finance to become an adjunct of armament policy in facilitating the transfer of manufacturing plant from civilian to military production. This entails prohibitive taxation of the sale of non-essential goods not subject to direct governmental control.

The third and most important aim of armament finance is to preserve economic stability by imposing on the public the sacrifices required for the *large-scale* output of armaments. This necessity for public sacrifice is too little understood in countries accustomed to the existence of idle men and unused plant. It is true that in a capitalist economy which seldom operates at more than 80 percent of capacity initial expenditure on armaments may employ otherwise idle resources, so that no sacrifice in the standard of living is required. But as armament expenditure absorbs an increasing proportion of the national income full capacity is reached, and abundance and waste are superseded by scarcity and economy. At this point the consumption of civilians decreases as the consumption of the government increases. If the economy is not to be disrupted by a competitive scramble for goods, by sharply rising prices, and by social conflict, financial policy must be combined with price, wage, and rationing policy to reduce the consumption of civilians in order that the consumption of the government may continue to grow.

The three general methods of transferring purchasing power from citizens to the government are taxation, borrowing, and currency inflation. Taxation is, of course, the most desirable, as it leaves no heritage of debt. It is, however, impossible to increase revenue from modern tax systems as quickly as expenditure increases. The sharpest limitation on drastic increases in taxation is their effect on the business community. Sudden changes in the tax structure may upset specific calculations so that a downward spiral is the result. Until the economy reaches full capacity, small increases in taxation are wiser.

Because of this, and because of the magnitude of modern war expenditure, governments resort to large-scale borrowing from the public and the banks. Borrowing has many advantages. There need be no time lag before receipts are realized. People generally prefer making loans to paying taxes, however similar the economic effect in diverting purchasing power may be. A defense bond represents wealth, while a tax receipt does not. The possession of fixed-price government securities becomes less attractive when prices are rising, but this disadvantage can be overcome by strict control of the capital market to discourage investment in other securities.

The amount that can be borrowed is limited, however, to the genuine gross savings of the community, plus whatever can be raised from the savings of other nations. The replacement of depreciated plant can be suspended, and private investment at home or abroad forbidden. The amount of new savings can be increased by various controls that restrict consumption, such as price-fixing, rationing, and limitation of output. If foreign loans cannot be floated, existing foreign assets can be exchanged for foreign savings. But even with the adoption of measures to increase new savings and to realize past savings (by the sale of foreign assets), the sum the government can hope to raise by borrowing is definitely limited.

In an economy where wages, costs, prices, and production are not rigidly controlled by the government, there is no alternative to a resort to inflation when the Treasury's outlay exceeds its income from taxes and loans. Inflation is here defined as the restriction of civilian consumption by means of increased prices due to the creation and expenditure of new money by the government when the economy is near full capacity. It must be emphasized that borrowing in itself does not necessarily produce inflation, for if amounts loaned to the government would otherwise have been spent by the public, there is no net addition to the income of the economy. It is evident that when the government contributes more to the national income in expenditure than it withdraws in taxes and loans there will be an increase in the quantity of money while the quantity of actual resources remains fixed, or is reduced. In this case purchases by the government are in competition with those by the public, and prices rise, thereby diminishing the purchasing power of money. Wages and other costs rise subsequently, providing additional cause for further price rises in ascending plateaus of price-wage increases.

The fundamental problem of wartime finance is easily stated. As an economy approaches capacity, with employment of the unemployed, payment of overtime, and greater industrial activity, the total national income is increased. But as a growing proportion of production is devoted to armaments, the total supply of consumers' goods is reduced. Inflation is implicit in any situation in which total purchasing power is augmented while the amount of goods offered for sale is diminished.

To avoid inflation, the government must adopt one of two alternatives. Either the excess of private purchasing power over the amount of goods available for civilian consumption must be captured by the Treasury through taxation or borrowing, or a comprehensive control of prices and distribution must be imposed by the government. Otherwise, this surplus of purchasing power will be spent in pushing up prices, at the expense of economic stability and social justice.

2. British Defense Finance

On the basis of these general principles, we can turn to a study of the problems of British finance from the beginning of rearmament in 1936 until after the passage of the Lend-Lease Act in 1941. It is first necessary to understand the magnitude of Great Britain's transformation from a nation at peace to a fortress of war. As Chart I indicates, in 1935 the British spent for defense only 2.7 percent (£136.9 millions) of their national income; this percentage had risen just before the outbreak of war in 1939 to 13.4. But during the fiscal year 1941–42 domestic defense expenditure was expected to absorb at least 42 percent of the nation's domestic income.

The consequent reduction in the standard of living of the English people can be illustrated in another way. In 1935 forty-five million Britishers had more than £4,900 millions to spend on civil consumption and the upkeep and expansion of industrial plant. But in 1941 the public had £3,400 millions, 20 percent less. On the other hand, the domestic expenditure of the government had risen nearly five times from £776 millions to £3,700 millions.[1] Although this increased outlay was from a national income two-fifths larger (because of fuller employment and higher prices), a sizeable diversion of economic resources had also been undertaken.

To understand how this diversion was achieved, we must survey the financial policies of the Treasury. Any such survey falls naturally into

---

[1] See Chart I.

Chart I

British Budget Expenditure and Deficits 1935-1941
£ Millions

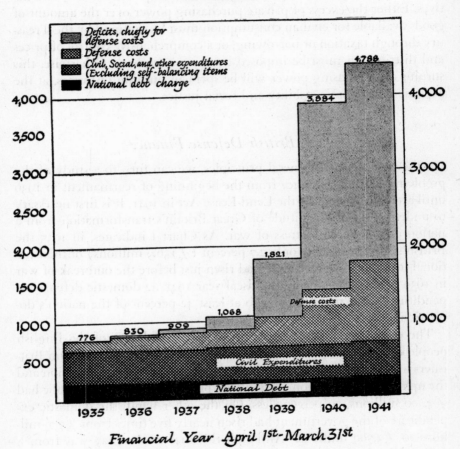

Financial Year April 1st-March 31st

two phases. The first is the stage of rearmament finance beginning in 1936 and lasting through the fiscal year 1938. The second is the period of war finance dating from the Budget of April 1939.

In the initial phase of British rearmament the dominant spirit was one of financial conservatism. In the middle '30's Britain was the only major country enjoying the orthodoxy of a balanced budget. While the United States, France, and Germany experienced large yearly deficits, the criteria of British finance were economy and retrenchment. This unique financial stability was the result of two favorable conditions. The first was internal economic recovery, producing larger revenues; the second was the conversion of the internal debt, reducing interest charges on the budget by one-third. The recovery Budgets of 1934 and 1935 included slight reductions in taxation and the restoration of expenditures that had been eliminated during the depression.

By 1936, when the British Government first markedly increased defense expenditure, it was apparent that the happy period of orthodoxy was drawing to a close. The Chancellor of the Exchequer, Neville Chamberlain, proposed to pay for the first year's rearmament without resort to borrowing, but he warned that to finance future defense outlays exclusively from taxation " would seriously cripple the industry of this country." [2] In 1937 the Government announced its plan of spending £1,500 millions on rearmament in the next five years. Parliament was asked for authority to borrow £400 millions of this amount. The same Government that had refused to increase the public debt by undertaking a productive program of public works at the depth of the depression was now compelled to borrow for rearmament at the peak of the business cycle. The Treasury was beset by a double sin: it was not only incurring deficits; it was incurring them at the wrong time.

To offset this double economic heresy, the provisions of the loan were curiously orthodox. It must be explained that the Government did not view the rearmament program as preparation for war. It was hoped that within five years the armed forces could be expanded and equipped, and that the costs of defense would then be limited to replacement and maintenance. Expenditure was expected to rise to a peak, perhaps in 1939, and to taper off when expansion was completed. The terms of the Defense Loan provided that borrowed funds would be devoted to the payment of the non-recurrent costs of rearmament; tax revenues would provide for

---

[2] 311 H. C. Deb., c. 54.

the recurrent costs of maintenance. The Treasury planned to repay the principal and interest of the loan after the five-year period of borrowing in thirty annual installments.

The Government's decision to increase the national debt to pay for rearmament was opposed by the Labor and Liberal Parties, but supported by financial and business opinion. The latter was reluctant to accept the heavy tax increases necessary for the full cost of rearmament to be met from current revenue. That does not mean that taxes were not raised during the years of rearmament; they were substantially. But in view of the strength of economic recovery in Great Britain the Government could have relied more on taxation than it did.

The British tax structure rests on two principal supports: (1) the personal income tax and (2) customs and excise taxes. Indirect duties on commodities like tea, tobacco, beer, and wine reach the low income groups which are not subject to direct taxation on earnings. Beginning in 1936 the standard rate of income tax was pushed higher year by year, and in 1938 it stood at 5s. 6d. This was a shilling above the 1935 rate and just under the record high of 6s. in 1919. The yield from income tax (including surtax) increased as a result of improved business conditions as well as heavier tax rates by £109.3 millions between 1935 and 1938.

Indirect levies were likewise increased; the tea duty was raised twice in 1936 and 1938, and in 1938 the tax on petroleum oil and alcohol was raised a penny a gallon. By 1938 customs and excise taxes were supplying £340.5 to the Treasury, £37 millions more than in 1935. But because of the greater reliance on income tax the proportion of total tax revenues derived from indirect commodity taxes fell from 48.7 percent in 1935 to 44.4 percent in 1938.

In the 1937 Budget the Chancellor of the Exchequer introduced a graduated tax on excess profits called the National Defense Contribution. The proposal satisfied no one. The Labor and Liberal Parties, who were the most frequent critics of " profiteering," opposed the tax because of its small estimated yield of only £25 millions *per annum*. Business interests in the Conservative Party feared, with some justification, that the tax would penalize prosperity, for it was to be levied on profits earned in excess of those earned in a standard period from 1933 to 1935.[3] Hostility to the tax was so acute that Mr. Chamberlain's first act upon

---

[3] An alternative method of profits valuation was permitted. It subjected to tax profits in excess of 6 percent of the assessed value of a company. 322 H. C. Deb., April 20, 1937, c. 1616.

becoming Prime Minister was to withdraw it and to substitute for it a flat levy on profits.[4]

As a result of tax revisions and of the growth of national income as business activity expanded, the budgetary revenue of 1938 was £927.3 millions, or nearly £149 millions above that of 1935. The Government expected defense costs in 1937 to amount to £278 millions and total budget costs to rise to £942 millions, of which £80 millions were to be met from loans. Actually, expenditures fell short of the estimate, and only £64.9 millions of Defense Loan were used. But in 1938 the political tension resulting from the Austrian and Czech crises in that year raised defense costs beyond expectations to £400 millions, out of a total budgetary expenditure of £1,068 millions. Of this, £128 millions were met from loans, which raised to £193 millions the amount of defense expenditure met by borrowing in two years.

To secure these funds the Government offered two series of Defense Loans to the public. In April 1937 an issue of £100 millions 2½ percent National Defense Bonds (redeemable 1944–48) was floated. This financial operation was poorly timed and was therefore not well received by the investment market. The loan was overpriced (issued at 99½) in comparison with the quotations of other gilt-edge securities, and in addition the City was profoundly disturbed by the National Defense Contribution Profits Tax announced just a few days before. Consequently an unusually large proportion of the loan was taken up by the public funds for later release to the market. A year later, in June 1938, a second issue of 3 percent National Defense Bonds (redeemable 1954–58) was opened for subscription. It was offered at 98 and, in contrast to the 1937 loan, was oversubscribed.

There is considerable evidence that the British Treasury geared the amount of its defense borrowing, and consequently the tempo of rearmament, to the surpluses accumulating yearly in the extra-budgetary funds. These public and semi-public funds generally received an excess of revenue from savings and pension payments over expenditure of about £75 millions in a moderately prosperous year, and this surplus was invested in government securities.[5] It was customary for the public

---

[4] This was a 5 percent levy on company profits, 4 percent on those of individuals and partnerships. It was to run for five years and was expected to produce 18 millions a year revenue.

[5] The extra-budgetary funds are administered by the National Debt Office and include: (1) the National Health Insurance Fund, (2) the Pensions Fund, (3) the Unemployment Insurance Fund, (4) the Post Office Savings Bank, (5) the Trustee Savings Bank, (6) miscellaneous sums managed by the National Debt Commissioners. For an analysis of the assets of these Funds, see N. F. Hall, "Some Technical Aspects of the Finance of Rearmament," *Economica*, May 1937.

funds to cooperate in the financial policy of the Treasury. The effect of this cooperation was to stabilize the gilt-edge securities market and to make the Treasury less dependent in the conduct of its financial operations on prevailing conditions in the investment market.

In 1937, when the Chancellor of the Exchequer, Neville Chamberlain, thought it possible to keep yearly deficits down to an average of £80 millions over the five years of "emergency" defense expenditure, the Treasury no doubt hoped to draw substantially on the revenues of these public funds in the flotation of public issues. A large part of the 1937 Defense Loan was, as we have seen, absorbed by these funds, but in the depression of 1938 these agencies were less able to take up government securities. This explains the more favorable terms of the 1938 Defense Loan. By 1939 the Government's borrowing operations would be so enormous that the extra-budgetary funds could make only a minor contribution to the flotation.

We can conclude that in the first period of rearmament financing through the fiscal year 1938–39 the financial position of the British Government was not unsatisfactory. It is true that the budget was unbalanced, but although the deficits were growing in size, they were not so large that they could not be financed without undue disturbance of the investment market. But in 1939 Britain experienced the first billion-pound Budget, and the trend of all segments of governmental expenditure was upward. As the national debt increased, the burden of interest charges became heavier. The costs of civil government, of social services, of subsidies were rising, and by 1939 the rapidly increasing expenditure for defense would dominate the whole British economy as well as the budget.

3. Wartime Finance

The year 1939 was the first year of war finance. The Government's efforts to arrive at stable estimates for expenditure were without success. British defense costs spiraled upward with each new threat of war, and finally with the fact of war. In February 1939 the Government stated that its outlay on defense in the fiscal year 1939–40 would be at least £580 millions. When Sir John Simon presented the Budget late in April the sum had risen to £630 millions. By late July Supplementary Estimates for the Defense Forces and the Ministry of Supply carried the figure to £749 millions. The outbreak of war added additional millions, and in the course of the fiscal year total expenditures reached £1,817 millions, of which £768 millions were borrowed.[6]

Large as this figure was in comparison with peacetime spending, it was less than half the amount the Government expended in 1940–41. Under the pressure of total war, one budget after another proved inadequate. Chancellors of the Exchequer tended to underestimate the costs of the conflict consistently. In April 1940, in the expectation of a war of stagnation, Sir John Simon presented his "Budget of Delusions," in which Britain's expenditure for 1940 was estimated at £2,667 millions, of which £2,000 millions were to be devoted to the war.

The idea that England could defeat Hitlerism by spending two-thirds of what the Nazis spent passed with the defeat of France.[7] Great Britain was then left alone to meet the financial burden of the war. After the formation of the Churchill Government in May 1940, the new Chancellor of the Exchequer, Sir Kingsley Wood, presented a second Budget in July 1940, which added another £800 millions to expenditure, raising war costs to £2,800 millions out of a total outlay of £3,467 millions. But by the end of the fiscal year 1940–41, actual expenditure amounted to £3,884 millions, of which about £3,200 millions were spent on the war.

The most notable aspect of these figures of expenditure is the relatively small proportion met from tax revenue, even after drastic increases in both direct and indirect taxation. The budgetary deficit for the fiscal year 1939–40 mounted from the £380 millions anticipated in February 1939 to £768 millions by the close of the year in April 1940. During the fiscal year ending March 31, 1941, the deficit reached the total of £2,475 millions, and during 1941–42, £2,702 millions. Revenue from taxes, which covered 87 percent of expenditure in 1938, furnished 36 percent of the Treasury's expenditure in 1940–41, 41 percent in 1941–42, and 50 percent in 1942–43.[7a]

The rising cost of the conflict to the British people can be more clearly illustrated perhaps by the following table, which shows the Government's *daily* expenditure and deficit during the war. The outlay on sup-

---

[6] On September 2, 1939, a Vote of Credit of £500 millions brought the estimated expenditure for 1939–40 to £1,933.3 millions, allowing for economies of £20 millions in the Civil Departments. Defense expenditure was to account for £1,249 millions of this. Actual outlay was £1,816.9 millions, which was £116.4 millions short of the estimate. This total does not include £4.2 millions outside the permanent debt charge.

[7] *The Economist* estimated that German war expenditure in 1940 was at the rate of about £3,000 millions *per annum*. May 4, 1940, p. 806.

[7a] When ordinary revenue reached a total of £2,819,850,783.

ply services, largely devoted to the war, rose from £3.9 millions a day in October 1939 to £11.8 millions in 1941 and £13.1 millions in 1942.

DAILY EXPENDITURES, REVENUES, AND DEFICITS [8]
(£ millions)

		Expenditure			
		Supply	Total	Revenue	Deficit
Oct.	1939	3.9	4.8	2.3	—2.5
Jan.	40	5.7	6.2	6.8	+ .6
Oct.	40	9.9	11.0	3.2	—7.8
Jan.	41	12.1	12.6	8.3	—4.3
Oct.	41	11.8	13.1	5.0	—8.0
Jan.	42	12.8	13.0	10.9	—2.1
Oct.	42	13.1	13.6	5.7	—7.9

The Treasury's increasing reliance on non-tax resources was exhausting Britain's holdings of foreign securities as well as driving the British economy into the disturbances of inflation. Since 1939 four budgets had been adopted, three of them wartime budgets, and all including heavy increases in tax schedules. The standard rate of income tax was raised from 5 shillings, 6 pence in 1938 to 8 shillings, 6 pence in July 1940. Surtaxes were sharply increased by about 25 percent, varying of course with the level of income, and estate duties were raised by 30 percent. Indirect taxes on beer, wines, alcoholic spirits, sugar, tobacco, matches, and entertainments were heavily increased. The tax on motor cars was raised from 15 shillings to 25 shillings per unit of horsepower. The charges for telephone, telegraph, and postal services were advanced in order that these state enterprises could contribute as tax collectors to the Treasury. In addition, two new taxes were introduced into the fiscal system: the Excess Profits Tax and the Purchase Tax.

Mr. Chamberlain had promised the House of Commons in the spring of 1939 that special steps would be taken to penalize profiteering resulting from the defense program. In June Sir John Simon introduced the Armaments Profit Duty, a 60 percent tax on the profits of armament firms holding defense contracts of over £200,000 in excess of profits earned by them in a standard period.[9] In the first emergency war budget of September 1939, the Armaments Profit Duty was succeeded by the Excess Profits Duty, which followed the same general principles,

---

[8] London and Cambridge Economic Service, *Bulletins.*

[9] This standard period was based on the more prosperous years 1935, 1936, and 1937, and the major objection made by business firms to the "depression standard" of the ill-fated National Defense Contribution profits tax of 1937 was thus avoided.

except that the new tax was levied on the profits of all firms. Although the rate was lifted to 100 percent after the formation of the Churchill Government, the yield in 1940 was only £96 millions.

The Excess Profits Duty was a revival of a tax employed in the First World War to divert the extraordinary profits of defense industries to the Treasury. But the Purchase Tax first announced in Sir John Simon's Financial Statement of April 1940 was an innovation in the British tax structure. This tax was levied not on retail sales, as is usually the case, but on wholesale transactions between a registered list of wholesalers and their retail dealers. As eventually modified by Sir Kingsley Wood, the Purchase Tax provided for a 33⅓ percent levy on luxury goods and a 16⅔ percent tax on more essential commodities. Food, drink, tobacco, and gasoline, which were already subject to heavy taxation, as well as children's clothing were exempt. As several months were required to compile a register of 40,000 traders and to overcome other administrative complexities, the tax did not become effective until the autumn of 1940. This accounts for its small yield of £26 millions during the year 1940–41. The yield for 1941–42, including £8 millions in arrears for the previous year, was £98 millions.

Even with the addition of these new duties and heavier rates for older taxes, the increased yield to the Treasury was dangerously inadequate. In the fiscal year 1940 the *increase* in government expenditures over 1938 was £2,816 millions, and the growth in tax revenue was scarcely one-sixth of this, or £476 millions. The return from the purchase tax could not be increased without imposing an inequitable burden on the consuming public and thereby raising the cost of living. Luxury taxes, if high, would so restrict consumption as to furnish little revenue, and if moderate, would fail to penalize non-essential industry. Excess Profits Duty could not be expected to produce more than £100 millions a year, unless price inflation multiplied industrial profits, and this the Government was anxious to avoid.

A fundamental shift in the British tax structure was required in order to provide a larger revenue and to avoid a continuing spiral of inflation. But this did not mean that the chief economic sacrifice could be borne by the rich alone. Even if all individual incomes above £2,000 a year had been confiscated by the Government, they would have amounted only to £60 millions a year. And, as J. M. Keynes demonstrated in his book *How to Pay for the War,* little more than £600 millions could be made available by the absorption of all individual income above £500 a year.[10]

The only substantial source of revenue would be a tax on the lower and middle income groups of the population, considerably increasing the contribution of the group with earnings of from £250 to £500 a year. It was to make some such sacrifice acceptable to this lower income group that Mr. Keynes devised his scheme for compulsory savings, or " deferred pay." Essentially, it was a plan by which increased taxation of small incomes in wartime would be compensated by postwar rebates to be financed from a capital levy. The Keynes savings plan was compulsory, but there was the prospect of future return. The virtues of the plan were that in wartime private consumption would be restricted and inflation thereby averted, while repayment in peacetime would stimulate purchasing power, thereby counteracting postwar deflation.

One other revenue proposal was frequently advocated, a tax on services. The expenditures of the English public on services of various kinds — transportation, lodging, domestic service — are largely neglected by the British tax structure. *The Economist* estimated that, after the exemption of essential professional services like medical treatment, a stiff turnover tax on services might yield about £150 millions a year.[11]

In the absence of any such fundamental revision of the tax structure, revenues were alarmingly insufficient.[12] In the two years of war finance from April 1939 to April 1941, the Government spent a total of £5,071 millions, of which only £2,458 millions were raised from taxation. This left a total deficit of £3,243 millions, 57 percent of the Government's outlay. The question immediately arises: how did the Treasury meet this enormous deficiency of revenue? The answer is that it did so by means of an increase in the National Debt, but that is only half the answer. It is not complete until we know two things: first, how did the Treasury conduct such gigantic borrowing operations; second, what were the available sources from which the funds were raised?

To answer the first question, a brief survey of the loan policy of the Treasury will suffice. It is apparent that the borrowing of £768 millions in 1939–40, and of £2,475 millions in 1940–41 called for a very different technique than was required for the smaller deficits of previous years. In the spring of 1939 Britain's economy was still suffering from the business recession of 1938, and any large issue of Defense Loan would have

---

[10] Keynes' income figures are, however, based on prewar rates of taxation.
[11] February 22, 1941, p. 235.
[12] See Chart I.

disturbed the investment market. In all probability the prices of gilt-edge securities would have fallen, and the rate of interest would have risen to the disadvantage of the Treasury.

It is generally admitted that as an economy approaches full employment the supply of savings increases, for company profits and the incomes of institutions are augmented in the larger national income. In addition, it must be emphasized that government expenditure financed from deficits ultimately creates the supply of savings to pay for itself. Payments made to contractors in time become wages, interest, and profits, and after percolating through the economy come to rest in the hands of persons or companies who do not spend their receipts immediately, who save. As these savings accumulate, the holders become anxious to invest them in profitable assets, and if no new investments are available, the funds will be shifted into gilt-edge securities. The prices of gilt-edge will rise, the rate of interest will fall, and an exceptionally favorable borrowing position will be created for the Exchequer. The Government can borrow funds in the form of long-term loans, which will be respent, resaved, and again lent to the Government.

Two conditions are essential to the success of such a plan. First, the Government must be able to meet preliminary expenditures until market conditions favor the issue of a public loan. This the Exchequer could do, by borrowing from the short-term money market through the issue of Treasury bills, while withholding public loans until savers were eager to invest in new government securities. The second essential condition was for the Exchequer to exercise control over the capital market, preventing opportunities for new investment and encouraging new savings to enter gilt-edge. When the banking system reached a position of high liquidity, new defense loans could be launched.

In April 1939 the amount of Treasury bills held by the public was about £150 millions below the level of previous years, and the banks were in need of additional short-term paper. The Treasury was in the fortunate position of being able to meet a large part of its deficit for 1939 at low interest by the sale of Treasury bills, which would in turn help to satisfy the appetite of the money market. By the end of the fiscal year 1939–40 the total amount of Treasury bills had risen to £1,427.7 millions, an increase of £535.3 millions over March 31, 1939.[13]

In November 1939 the Government sought to tap the savings of low

---

[13] The amount of Ways and Means Advances by public departments had increased by £33.6 millions from £27.9 millions on March 31, 1939 to £61.5 millions on March 31, 1940. The total Floating Debt was £1,489.2 millions on the latter date.

income groups by the issue of two small securities. One was a series of National Savings Certificates, carrying compound interest slightly in excess of 3 percent, offered in small lots at fifteen shillings each. The second was a 3 percent Defense Bond, purchasable in multiples of £5, with individual holdings limited to £1,000. But these were designed solely to interest the small investor, who was being urged by the National War Savings Campaign to lend to the Government, and produced only £122 millions in the fiscal year 1939.

Not until March 1940 did the Treasury consider gilt-edge prices sufficiently high for major long-term borrowing. Then a £300 millions issue of 3 percent War Loan, redeemable in nineteen and one-half years, was announced. This was oversubscribed, and was followed up on June 25, 1940, with the issue of 2½ percent National War Bonds (five to seven years) of unlimited amount. On January 2, 1941 a new issue of 3 percent Savings Bonds (1955–65) and a second series of 2½ percent National War Bonds were announced, followed in August 1941 by a third series of 2½ percent National War Bonds. Tax Reserve Certificates acceptable in payment of taxes due not less than two months nor more than two years from the date of purchase were issued in December 1941 at 1 percent interest. The amounts raised by these loans during the three financial years ending March 31, 1942, are shown in the following table.

GOVERNMENT WAR BORROWING, APRIL 1939–MARCH 1942 [14]
(£ millions)

Increase in Long Term Debt	1939–40	1940–41	1941–42	1939–42
National Savings Certificates and 3% Defense Bonds	109	360	409	878
3% War Loan	98	202	3	303
2½% National War Bonds	...	592	724	1,316
3% Savings Bonds	...	89	577	666
3% National Defense Loan 1954–58 issued to National Debt Commissioners	...	75	45	120
Tax Reserve Certificates	...	...	192	192
Miscellaneous	2	36	9	47
Total	209	1,354	1,959	3,522
Increase in Floating Debt				
Treasury Bills	535	784	404	1,723
Ways and Means Advances	33	110	24	167
Treasury Deposits by banks	...	430	67	497
Total [14a]	568	1,324	495	2,387
Total Increase in Internal Debt	777	2,678	2,454	5,909

[14] Compiled from *The Economist*, annual national debt figures.

[14a] The total floating debt, to be distinguished from the total increase since 1939 given here, was £4,029,000,000 at the end of 1942.

Allowance must also be made for other borrowing operations of the Treasury such as the 1940 Conversion Loan and debt repayment to arrive at the net total of the actual deficit. The top limit of Defense Loans of £400 millions authorized in 1937 was raised to £800 millions in February 1939. In November 1939 the National Loans Bill permitted unlimited borrowing by the Treasury.

One of the most significant aspects of these figures is the abnormal dependence of the Treasury on short-term borrowing. Between March 31, 1939 and March 31, 1941 the Floating Debt increased by £1,896 millions to a total of £2,813.4 millions, and this expansion accounted for 55 percent of the Government's total borrowing during those two years. But nearly half of the additional Floating Debt in the hands of public funds and the exchange equalization fund, and nearly a fourth of the increase represented funds deposited by the banks with the Treasury, for which they received deposit receipts. This was a new development arising from the direct cooperation of the banking system with the Exchequer. Considering that nearly three-fourths of this expansion of the Floating Debt represented (1) Treasury bills in the hands of governmental agencies, (2) Ways and Means Advances by public departments, and (3) Treasury Deposit Receipts with the banks, the volume of bills " foisted on the banks " does not appear to have been excessive.

As a result of these combined long-term and short-term borrowing operations, Great Britain's gross National Debt stood at about £11,420 millions on March 31, 1941, and £14,070 millions on March 31, 1942. This was an increase of £6,369.6 millions above the postwar low point of March 31, 1935.

If the growing total of the debt was discouraging, there was some encouragement in the fact that the new loans were being raised at an average rate of interest of less than 2 percent, in contrast to the rate of 5 percent during World War I. This was due chiefly to the effective control of the capital market by the Treasury, the second essential condition of successful borrowing operations. All private investment not contributing directly to the war effort was in effect excluded.

In peacetime Treasury " influence " had been sufficient to insure the cooperation of investment houses, but after the outbreak of war formal machinery was set up. The existing Foreign Transactions Committee was called the Capital Issues Committee, and was asked to advise the Treasury on all applications for new investment issues. The Treasury's consent was required for all capital issues, with certain minor exceptions. Applications for foreign issues were required to show " urgent necessity and special circumstances," and proof was required that issues of domestic loans were " advisable in the national interest."

These regulations place the capital market at the service of the Treasury, and their effectiveness can be judged from the figures in the table below, which indicate that of £1,088.7 millions borrowed in 1940 only £17.9 millions were on private account. The expansion of plant required for increasing war production was financed almost entirely by the Government.

TOTAL BORROWING[15]

(INCLUDING "PERMISSION TO DEAL") NEW BASIS

(Millions of pounds)

Years	Govt.	Home Corpo-rations	Others	Total home	Empire	Foreign	Total issues
1936	60.2	82.1	306.1	448.4	33.8	1.2	493.9
1938	75.9	27.7	110.1	213.7	53.7	5.7	458.0
1939	36.8	12.1	66.2	115.1	25.5	2.2	142.8
1940	1070.8		16.6	1087.4	1.3		1088.7
1941	1497.5		8.0	1505.5	4.2	.1	1509.8
1942	1457.1		9.2	1466.3	.8	.1	1467.2

The second aspect of the problem, the origin of these borrowed funds, must now be considered. Apart from taxation, there are two general sources of revenue on which a government can draw — holdings of gold and foreign assets, and the gross savings of the nation.

It is evident that a government with command of the seas can convert its own gold reserves and the foreign securities or credits held by citizens of the nation into foreign exchange with which to pay for purchases abroad. But this conversion of capital assets is reflected in the items of the national debt. A private citizen receives cash or government bonds in return for the foreign securities he surrenders to the government. And in Great Britain when the exchange equalization fund sells its gold reserves to the Treasury it reinvests the proceeds of the sale in Treasury bills. British gold and foreign holdings at the beginning of the war could be expected, with favorable selling conditions, to produce at least a billion pounds of foreign exchange.[16]

But by far the more important source of funds to be diverted to gov-

---

[15] *The Economist,* January 6, 1940, p. 27; January 4, 1941, p. 16; January 3, 1942, p. 18; January 9, 1943, p. 52.

[16] For an analysis of British resources see Part III, Eric Roll, *Great Britain's Overseas Trade.*

ernment expenditure is represented by the gross savings of the nation. *Gross* savings may be defined for purposes of war finance as the part of the national income not spent in consumption. It comprises three elements: (1) replacement savings; (2) net new savings; (3) compulsory social savings. Replacement saving is the customary devotion of a part of current proceeds to the replacement of obsolete plant and the general maintenance of productive facilities. In a national crisis productive equipment may be allowed to deteriorate, and depreciation allowances can be diverted to the government. Net saving is the part of the annual national income normally available for investment in new business enterprise or new capital. By social savings are meant the surpluses of the health, old age, and unemployment insurance funds and other extrabudgetary funds, which are invariably invested in government obligations.

It was probable that in every year of full employment about £800 millions (on the basis of prewar prices) of gross savings would be available to take up Government loans. There are no official statistics to indicate prewar savings in prosperous years. Colin Clark estimates that in 1934 *net* savings were £461.4 millions.[17] This seems rather high for a year of moderate industrial activity, but it is likely that Britain's net savings from all sources would be between £450 and £500 millions in a year of high business activity.

To this £450 or £500 millions must be added another £400 millions of replacement savings. Not all replacement of course can be neglected even in time of war, but perhaps £300 millions of this could be diverted to government securities. The prewar savings of the extrabudgetary funds amounted, as mentioned above, to about £75 millions a year. This source might easily yield from £125 to £150 millions in wartime, as the result of decreased payments of unemployment insurance and the larger returns produced by a higher level of employment.

This brings the total real savings that might possibly be absorbed by government borrowing to between £700 and £900 millions.[18] This to-

---

[17] Colin Clark, *National Income and Outlay*, p. 190. J. M. Keynes, *op. cit.*, p. 22, considered £400 millions if anything, too low. In 1926 Mr. Coates told the Colwyn Committee that British net savings were about £500 millions a year, *Report of the Committee on National Debt and Taxation*, Cmd. 2800/1927, p. 17. *The Economist*, January 6, 1940, p. 22, gave total borrowing in 1936 as £493.9 millions. Investment issues are another expression of savings.

[18] Colin Clark, "The Determination of the Multiplier from National Income Statistics," *Economic Journal*, September 1939, estimates total investment, including depreciation allowances, at £760 millions for 1936 and £830 millions for 1937. *The Times*, February 22, 1939 gave larger figures for the same years: £877 millions and £893 millions.

tal could be considerably increased by sharp wartime reductions of personal consumption. Inflation, too, would increase the amount of savings as the money profits of industry were increased.

In April 1941 the Treasury published in a White Paper [19] an explanation of its financial operations during the first eighteen months of the war, and the practice of issuing an explanatory white paper when the budget is introduced now seems to be established. As the White Paper showed, government expenditure in the first twelve months of the war was £2,597 millions, and after the deduction of £1,148 millions tax revenue a deficit of £1,499 millions remained. This deficit was met in part by a draft on overseas assets of £542 millions, of which the prewar assets of the exchange equalization fund furnished £184 millions and overseas balances held in London and the sale of foreign securities the remaining £358 millions. This left a total of £907 millions to be financed from domestic resources out of gross savings, of which net savings (institutional and personal) produced £592 millions, replacement savings, £60 millions, and social savings (the extra-budgetary funds), £113 millions. Tax accruals accounted for £140 millions.

In the third six-month period of the war there was a striking increase of 60 percent in war expenditure, to an annual rate of £4,150 millions. Two significant and serious aspects of British deficit finance become apparent. The first is the rapid exhaustion of British overseas assets in the period after Dunkirk, and before the passage of the Lend-Lease Act. The draft on foreign resources in six months was £479 millions, of which £204 millions came from the Exchange Equalization Account. By March 1941 Britain had used up £1,021 millions of foreign assets, and the Treasury was scraping the bottom of its chest. By September 1, 1941, Britain's holdings of dollar assets had fallen to $1,527,-000,000.

Equally serious was the clear evidence of inflation in the figures for personal savings and draft on domestic capital assets, which had reached annual rates of £640 and £480 millions respectively. The voluntary savings campaign, in combination with rationing and price control of course increased the volume of personal savings, just as lack of men and materials for plant replacement increased replacement savings. But even allowing for these factors, it is unlikely that savings could have risen to such an extent without the inflationary creation of bank credit.

[19] *An Analysis of the Sources of War Finance* and *An Estimate of the National Income and Expenditure in 1939 and 1940.*

4. *Wartime Inflation*

There is no doubt that a proportion of British government borrowing has been financed by an expansion of bank credit. The inflationary technique of the last war has been used again. The table below clearly illustrates the extent to which the banking system has participated in the financing of the war.

CREATION OF CREDIT TO FINANCE DEFENSE EXPENDITURE[20]
(nearest £ millions)

	August 1939	August 1940	August 1941	August 1942	August 39–42
Bank Deposits	2,162	2,481	2,997	3,305	1,143
Treasury Deposits Receipts	...	26	469	634	634
Investments	570	682	935	1,082	512
Cash and Balances with Bank of England	224	273	316	351	127
Discounts	272	430	266	283	11
Loans and Advances	954	919	838	784	—170

The rise in bank deposits in the first year and a half of war indicates the extent to which bank credit was being expanded to help meet the budgetary deficits of the Government. Deducting a rough £20 millions to account for items in transit (bank checks, etc.), it can be stated safely that the creation of credit up to September 1940 amounted to at least £300 millions, and through February 1941, to £525 millions. The increase in Treasury deposits receipts and bank investments represents almost entirely funds placed at the disposal of the Treasury. But these increases do not reveal the full extent of the banks' support of armament finance. For the reduction in discounts and loans and advances was much less than would be expected from the curtailment of civil business and the drop in personal loans. A marked redistribution took place in loans and discounts, so that the bank credit extended to firms engaged on defense contracts and holders of Treasury bills was multiplied several times. Credit was being manufactured to pay for the war.

The effect of this additional credit was naturally to stimulate a rise in prices. Chart II on prices, wage rates, and bank deposits shows clearly the sharp rise in the cost-price structure after the outbreak of war, following a period of surprising stability in the years of rearmament. The volume of currency in circulation increased from £529,498,805 in Au-

---

[20] These figures are taken from the monthly averages given in *The Economist*. They apply only to the Clearing Banks, but the adjustments required to account for items in transit do not affect the general proportions.

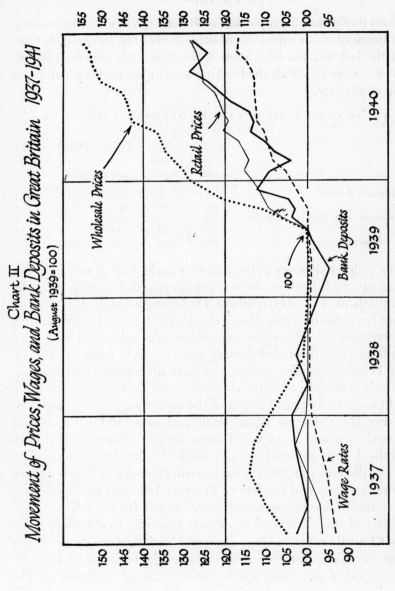

Chart II

Movement of Prices, Wages, and Bank Deposits in Great Britain   1937-1941

(August 1939=100)

Wholesale Prices

Retail Prices

100

Bank Deposits

Wage Rates

1937   1938   1939   1940

Wholesale Prices, Board of Trade General Index.   Wage Rates, London & Cambridge Economic Service Index.
Retail Prices, Ministry of Labour Cost of Living Index.   Bank Deposits, The Economist Clearing Banks Monthly Averages.

gust 1939 to £667,257,551 in August 1941 and £830,016,655 in August 1942, or almost 60 percent in three years.

The first government borrowing for rearmament of £100 millions in 1937 may have been slightly deflationary in effect, as the budgetary deficit for the fiscal year was only £36 millions. But the effect of the deficit of £141 millions in 1938 was probably like that of a public works program. That the increase of defense expenditure through 1939 stimulated the exceedingly rapid recovery that characterized the months before the war is undeniable. In the spring of 1939 Britain's economy was approaching full employment, and there was imminent danger of inflation when war came.

After September 1939 the character of the British economy was divided. The armament industries showed the general symptoms of full employment, labor scarcity, rising wages, rising costs. Many non-essential fields of work, on the other hand, especially the luxury and white-collar trades, experienced falling demand with consequent unemployment and, in some cases, falling wages. But despite the existence of unemployment side by side with capacity output, the general movement of wages and of wholesale and retail prices was sharply upward. By February 1941, wholesale prices had risen 48.9 percent above those of August 1939, retail prices, 27.2 percent, and wage rates, 17.1 percent.[21]

These price increases can be divided roughly into two periods, from September 1939 through February 1940, and from then until the present. In the first period prices advanced rapidly; both wholesale and retail prices rose 10 percent in the first two months of the war. The causes of this were not primarily monetary. Since Britain imports most of her industrial raw materials, and the larger part of her food stuffs, the depreciation of the pound by 14 percent (from $4.68 to $4.03) at the beginning of the war, increased shipping charges, and higher cargo insurance premiums quickly affected the price level. This initial rise in living costs was followed by widespread wage increases, which in turn contributed to increased costs of production.[22] But the effect of these initial economic forces was largely exhausted by February 1940.

The continued, if slower, price spiral from the spring of 1940 on was largely due to the Government's financial policy, or lack of policy. Neither the Chamberlain nor the Churchill Governments had any compre-

---

[21] Subsidies paid by the Treasury to stabilize the retail prices of certain foods are estimated at more than £58 millions for 1940–41.

[22] The wage rates of many trade unions were linked to the Ministry of Labor's Cost of Living Index, so that wages and retail prices rose together.

hensive price-wage policy, and both encountered strong trade union opposition to the suggestion that wages be controlled. Excess Profits Tax of 100 percent and cost-plus contracts deprived plant managers of incentive to keep costs down, and wage demands were readily granted. In the armament industries workers' earnings increased twice as much as the rise in actual wage rates through the payment of overtime and bonuses.[23]

This increased income was not withdrawn from consumption through taxation or borrowing by the Government. Instead, the creation of bank credit to cover government expenditures added to the volume of consumer income competing for a reduced amount of goods. The rise in the price level through February 1941 was between 25 percent and 30 percent, and at least a third of this was the direct result of the use of bank credit to finance government deficits. If further maladjustment was to be avoided, heavier taxation, compulsory savings, extensive rationing, and more stable wage rates were essential.

The first two requirements were met in the Budget of April 1941, in which government expenditure for the fiscal year 1941–42 was estimated at £4,206.7 millions. Income tax was raised from 8 shillings, 6 pence a pound to 10 shillings. A system of compulsory savings ("deferred pay") was introduced; exemption allowances for income tax were lowered, and the additional income tax paid was to be credited to the taxpayer in the Post Office Savings Bank, to be repaid as savings after the war.[24] These two revisions of the income tax were expected to produce an additional £250 millions in a full year.

In June 1941 rationing was extended to all clothing. In July the Government expressed in a White Paper its opposition in principle to further wage increases. Sir Kingsley Wood had announced in his 1941 Budget speech that the Treasury intended to subsidize retail prices in order to hold the Cost of Living Index at 25 per cent or 30 percent above the prewar level, and it was hoped that this would offset claims for wage increases to protect the standard of living of the workers.

As a result of these measures the tempo of inflation was definitely retarded by the middle of 1941. There was evidence that the public was holding large sums of money idle and that the velocity of circulation of

---

[23] Between October 1938 and July 1940 earnings in the vehicle and aircraft industries increased by 58 percent, in the shipbuilding industry, by 51 percent, in the engineering trades, by 40 percent, London and Cambridge Economic Service's *Report on Current Economic Conditions, Memorandum No. 85,* February, 1941, p. 9.

[24] The provisions of the Excess Profits Tax were modified at the same time to permit one-fifth of the duty's being returned to the taxpayer as savings after the war.

money was falling. From June 1941 to September 1942 wholesale commodity prices rose only 5 percent, retail prices, 1 percent, and wage rates 9.5 percent.

In conclusion, it is necessary to evaluate British financial policy since 1936 on the basis of the three principles of defense stated in the beginning. First, it is evident that the British Treasury was able to provide funds with which to pay for armaments, but at the cost of exhausting Britain's assets of gold and foreign securities, and by the considerable creation of credit.

Secondly, British financial policy can be criticized for not having assisted, especially in the prewar period, in the shifting of the economy from civil to armament production. The facilities of the automotive industry should have been diverted to the aero-engine and aircraft industries, and the tax power could have been used to this end. The horsepower tax of 1939 did not serve this purpose; it penalized the use of cars and not their production. The Purchase Tax, with its high rates of 33⅓ percent on luxuries, may have freed some economic resources for wartime uses, but it was too unselective to be of specific assistance. Moreover, it did not become effective until a year after the outbreak of war.

But the most important criticism of the Treasury must be for its failure to preserve the greatest possible economic stability in the country, the third objective of war finance. Chancellors of the Exchequer moralized repeatedly on the evils of inflation, but for the first year and a half of war the sacrifices necessary to avoid inflation were not imposed on the public in the form of taxation or compulsory loans. There are good reasons for not increasing taxes in a period of recession, like the first part of 1939, or in the middle of the fiscal year, when the war began, but by April 1940 the British public were willing to make heavier sacrifices than they were asked to bear. Since the costs of the war were constantly underestimated, tax revenues that were inadequate for estimated expenditure were disastrously so for actual expenditure. The Treasury's deliberate policy of indecision did not provide for the withdrawal of sufficient income from civilian consumption to prevent inflation. The British people, and especially the low income group, were forced to bear the burden of a greater rise in prices than the increase of non-monetary costs necessitated. The adoption of compulsory savings in 1941 marked what was in fact the first War Budget.

PART TWO

THE PROBLEM OF LABOR SUPPLY

by William S. McCauley

One of the major omissions of the Chamberlain Government was its failure to meet the problem of labor supply in a war economy. At the end of the First World War, approximately five million persons were engaged in the production of war materials for the armed forces. With the greater mechanization of modern armies and the growing complexity of industrial production, it was apparent by 1939 that eight million persons would be required in British war industry if Britain were to emerge victorious from the present war.

The transfer of such an enormous number from peacetime employment, or unemployment, to essential war work called for a great effort of national planning on the part of Britain's industry and labor under the leadership of the Government. Yet throughout the years of rearmament and war from 1936 into 1940, the National Government refused to assume the responsibility for creating and training the requisite labor supply and for distributing it in the armament industries as needed. As a result Britain experienced the phenomena of intense labor scarcity in key armament industries side by side with a number of unemployed exceeding one and one-half million. More than any other one factor, the shortage of skilled workers in vital armament industries impeded Britain's efforts to rearm.

1. The Years of Rearmament before the War

First of all we must examine the condition of the British labor market during the years of rearmament from mid-1936 to August 1939. During this period there was a chronic shortage of certain specialized types of skilled labor. Private contractors engaged on armament work for the Government reported their inability to secure sufficient welders, electricians, mechanics, lathe-turners, fitters, grinders, machine-setters, naval and aircraft draftsmen, machine-tool craftsmen, and technicians for scientific and optical instruments.

A shortage of aircraft workers was the major bottleneck restricting the expansion of the R.A.F. The 1939 Estimates of the Air Ministry called for an expenditure on aircraft and engines of nearly £56,000,000 more than in 1938. But in August 1939, there were only 15,500 persons listed as unemployed in the three fields of motor vehicles, cycles, and aircraft, and their combined output — assuming they might all find jobs — was estimated to be less than £11,000,000, only one-fifth of what was required.[25]

Unprecedented demands for skilled craftsmen were made by the armed forces as well as by civil industry. It is a characteristic of modern defense forces that a large proportion of the men enlisted must have some training as mechanics, welders, draftsmen, engineers, and electricians. The authorized strength of the British Army, Navy, and Air Force increased more than 386,000 men between March 1935 and July 1939, and a large number of these (no statistics are available) were skilled workers drawn from the civilian labor market.

Of course, the greatest demand for skilled labor came from civil industry, and during the four prewar years from 1935 to 1939 there was a notable expansion in the total employment of the heavy industries most affected by rearmament. In all fields related to the production of armaments, the number of workers employed increased by 769,440 between July 1935 and July 1940. As would be expected, employment in the aircraft industry showed the most sensational expansion, a growth of 360 percent. Employment in explosives manufacture increased by 114 percent; in metal manufacture (including iron and steel), by 50 percent; in the manufacture of scientific instruments, by 38 percent; and in the engineering industry, by 28 percent. There are no statistics available to show the increase in employment for defense work, but aside from the aircraft industry, the larger part, probably two-thirds, of this expansion was for civilian production.

During the first two years of rearmament, in 1936 and 1937, the

---

[25] The 1935 Census of Production placed the gross output per worker in the motor vehicles, cycles, and aircraft industries at £612 per year. Accounting for price increases, by 1939 this might have been raised to £700 a year. *The Economist*, May 6, 1939, p. 297.

British economy was rising to new peaks of prosperity, and the requirements of civil industry were competing with defense work. The business recession, initiated in the fall of 1937, lasted through 1938 and undoubtedly set free some trained workers in the engineering and automobile industries for employment in expanding defense work, somewhat relieving the scarcity of labor. But in the prewar months of 1939, the situation in the labor market became serious again. The Government's prospective deficit of £511 millions in the financial year 1939–40 represented a total expenditure requiring the direct and indirect employment of 1,900,000 additional workers. Yet the total number of unemployed in April 1939 was only about 1,700,000. The establishment of priority for defense work and the allocation of labor to the most urgent production were essential if rearmament was not to be impeded.

Such measures, however, were not adopted. Both trade union leaders and politicians continued to explain away the fact of a labor shortage by referring to the large volume of unemployment in Britain. It is true that throughout the 1930's the number of unemployed ranged from one and one-half million to two million workers. But to assume that the registered unemployed represented a reservoir of " labor " that could be drawn upon to satisfy the needs of rearmament was to accept a statistical mirage for reality.

The Ministry of Labor's Register of Unemployed Persons is deceptive for three reasons. In the first place it gives only a formal number of persons who may be out of jobs, but not in any real sense available for work. In a normal month there are about 700,000 persons who are only passing between jobs, who are too old and infirm to work, or who have had no working experience whatever. These people should be considered as unemployables instead of as available unemployed. If this 700,000 is deducted from the total of about 1,500,000 unemployed in the month of May, 1939, less than 800,000 remains.

There is a second reason why even this residual figure brought little comfort to defense contractors in search of employees, for the largest part of Britain's unemployed were occupationally maladjusted for armament work. In August 1939 there were nearly 450,000 unemployed in the textile, coal mining, shipbuilding, and building and construction industries, while at the same time there were only 58,000 workless in the major armament and engineering trades. In Britain it is generally assumed that the point of effective full employment is reached when the percentage of unemployment in an industry falls to 5 percent, for a moderate labor reserve is necessary for employers' requirements to be met readily. Yet by August 1939, and in some cases throughout the years of rearmament, the percentage of unemployment in war industries was noticeably below 5 percent, while other industries had surpluses of 10 percent to 17 percent. Loom tenders, coal miners, and brick layers were not adaptable to work as aircraft fitters, engine mechanics, and draftsmen.

There was a third element of deception in the Ministry of Labor's figures, for even the small reserves of labor in the war industries were so maldistributed regionally as to be largely unavailable for defense work. The heaviest demands for armament workers were in the Midlands and the southern regions of Great Britain, and these were the sections of greatest labor scarcity with unemployment of 5 percent or less. The large surplus of idle workers was to be found in the depressed areas with declining export industries, in Wales, Scotland, Northern Ireland, and the north of England, where unemployment ranged from 11 percent to 19 percent. Within particular armament industries reserves of labor were as badly dispersed. In July 1939, *The Economist* found that for one prosperous armament industry unemployment in one administrative area was only 2 percent, while in a neighboring area it was 22.7 percent.[26]

Armchair economists forget when speaking of "full employment" that there is no such thing as demand for or supply of labor in general. Instead, there are demands for *specific* types of workers at particular points of employment. To utilize the hidden reserves of untrained or maldistributed labor, the British Government would have had to adopt a comprehensive man power program.

Such a program would have recognized that in modern war industrial man power is of equal importance with military man power, that the fighting forces are only the cutting edge of a highly synchronized industrial machine. First of all, the Government would have had to draft a plan of the future requirements in man power of both the armed forces and the defense industries. On the basis of such a program the Government should have arranged for cooperation between trade unions and employers to insure that adequate numbers of workmen would be available where needed. This would have entailed measures to absorb the unemployed in war work by intensified sub-contracting, the enlargement of the existing labor force by the admission of unskilled

[26] " Tapping Labour Resources," *The Economist*, July 22, 1939.

workers and unemployed women, an adequate training program to equip new workers for the simpler processes of war production, and a schedule of priorities for the use of labor where civilian employment was competitive with defense work.

These were the essential ingredients of a labor policy, but at no time in the years of rearmament from 1936 to 1939 did the British Government appear to recognize them. In the first place, the National Government rejected responsibility for the supply of labor required by the defense program. The Prime Minister said in March 1936, " As the defense scheme comes into being . . . problems will certainly arise with regard to the supply of the particular kinds of skilled labor which will be required . . . I regard these as essentially problems which should be faced and settled by the industries themselves." [27] This " hands off " attitude persisted through the first few months of the war.

The Government might plead that discussion between organized labor and organized management was the traditional method of settling internal questions in British industry, but as a result of the Government's refusal to accept full responsibility for the supply of labor, its meager efforts to transfer, dilute, and train workers were disastrously inadequate. We have seen that there were small surpluses of unemployed workers who might have been transferred to areas where labor was scarce. It is astonishing that the Ministry of Labor never made a survey of the registered unemployed to find what numbers might be experienced and available for armament work. Neither did the Government seek to overcome the natural immobility of labor by compensating workers for the cost of moving from one region to another.

Reliance was placed solely on the existing machinery of the Ministry of Labor's Employment Department with its 1,626 employment exchanges and offices scattered throughout the country. All unemployed persons registered at the exchanges, and employers reported all vacancies to them. This machinery had proved invaluable in the last war and could have played an important role in preparation for this one. But in the postwar years many employers had become prejudiced against the efficiency of the exchanges and preferred to find their own labor, while many exchanges found the payment of the dole their only function. Although the Ministry of Labor gave information on the availability of labor when requested, the employment exchanges were not fully

---

[27] 309 H. C. Deb. 5 s., col. 1840.

utilized, nor did they help to coordinate the letting of contracts by the service departments. Only about 30 percent of job vacancies were filled through the ministry's employment offices.

The Labor Department did provide allowances for the transfer each year of about 18,000–20,000 unemployed men from the distressed regions. Nothing was done, however, to expand this program to meet the specific needs of defense industry and the number of men so transferred actually decreased in 1938. The Government made some efforts, not conspicuously successful, to encourage the construction of munition plants in the depressed areas and to extend subcontracting. A number of Royal Ordnance Factories were built in the depressed regions, but the defense services did not exert sufficient pressure on private contractors to disperse their plants.

If the Government's efforts to facilitate the transfer of unemployed were ineffective, the measures taken for the dilution of labor by the admission of the unskilled were even more so. Conferences in April 1938 between the leaders of industry, labor, and the Government called for a "speed up" of armament production, and this was in effect a request for the engineering unions to dilute their ranks with unskilled workers. The two principal trade unions concerned in armament manufacture, the Confederation of Shipbuilding and Engineering Trades, and the Amalgamated Engineering Union insisted that the sacrifice of union standards implied by dilution should be accompanied by a Government pledge to restore the prevailing conditions at the expiration of the emergency. The unions pointed, in addition, to the regional reserves of unemployed engineers and shipbuilders and questioned the urgency of dilution at a time when unemployment was growing during the 1938 recession. The Chamberlain Government made no effort to meet these requests by the unions. No guarantee of the eventual restoration of union standards was given, and no steps were taken to absorb the surplus unemployed. Consequently, the trade unions refused the Government's request for dilution.

The unions' stubborn refusal to accept dilution may be condemned in the light of events. Nevertheless, the major responsibility must rest on the Ministry of Labor for failing to prepare a program to put the unemployed engineers to work and to guarantee the restoration of suspended trade union practices. Such a pledge of restoration was given by the Government in the Treasury Agreement of 1915 to secure the unions' consent to dilution in the First World War.

Among the unemployed there were thousands of workers who had little prospect of regular employment and with some training in the basic skills might have been rehabilitated for the armament industry. This would have required a scheme of labor training, both in government schools and in the factories; but the Government's training program was as timid as its action with regard to dilution. This was another case in which the Ministry of Labor had facilities at hand that might have been utilized to speed the rearmament program. In 1935 the Labor Ministry had established a few training centers in the depressed areas to rehabilitate the unemployed for work in some trade. Six-month courses were given in the basic elements of such crafts as plumbing, metal work, and draftsmanship. But throughout the years of rearmament this training was continued only as a minor social service for the submarginal worker. In 1939 the total capacity of the Ministry's fourteen training centers was only 8,739 persons. During the entire year of 1938 less than 14,000 men completed courses, and only a portion of these were trained for work related to defense industry.

Neither did the Ministry of Labor take steps to develop a program to train apprentices in the factories. Each employer was left to meet his own needs although individual employers, not knowing the future scope of the Government's program, could not foresee the labor needs of industry as a whole, and business men were naturally reluctant to divert their limited supplies of machines and craftsmen to the task of instructing apprentices who when trained might find work elsewhere. The development of a training program in the factories and training centers was a task for the Government, and this task, during the years of rearmament, was not undertaken.

Neither did the Government establish a system of labor priorities whereby skilled workers engaged in civilian work might have been shifted to more important defense work. The chief limitation on the expansion of the aircraft industry was the scarcity of trained workers, but even here, where priority was most urgent, the Government refused to call in engineering labor engaged on other work. The Air Ministry explained this inaction by stating in 1937 that:

> If you were to pick skilled men from other engineering industries, and draft them into the aircraft industry, it would cause a tremendous dislocation in the general engineering industry.[28]

---

[28] 321 H. C. Deb. 5 s., cols. 1774–5.

The policy of "business as usual" was never better stated. It overlooked the fact that in defense economics the shortage of available resources necessitates some planned readjustment of civilian production unless the defense program itself is to suffer from maladjustment.

2. *The War — Phase I*

With the outbreak of war in September 1939 positive action on the part of the Government was more urgent, for the dimensions of the labor problem were more vast. The general objective of British wartime labor policy, easily stated, but difficult of attainment, was to increase production with about one-half the number of *men* employed in peacetime. First of all, perhaps 5,000,000 men must be withdrawn from industry for the three fighting services, the merchant marine, and civil defense. Second, given the greater technical requirements of mechanized forces, it was probable that before victory could be won at least 10,000,000 persons must be employed in the armament industries, compared to the 5,000,-000 so engaged in the last war.[29] Third, Britain's export trade had to be maintained and, if possible, augmented in order to obtain the foreign exchange with which to pay for essential imports. Hence this gigantic transfer of 15,000,000 people to war purposes had to be made largely at the expense of Great Britain's domestic standard of living without impairing the health of the population as a whole.

To replace men drawn into the armed forces and to provide the labor required by expanding war industries, millions of idle persons had to be brought into active employment. There were three chief sources of man power to be drawn upon, (1) the unemployed, (2) nonworking women, and (3) white-collar employees engaged in the nonessential service trades. As for the unemployed, it was conceivable that a training and transfer program might cut the total number of workless persons from the 1,500,000 of October 1939 to about 500,000. The large number of nonworking women, however, represented the greatest single resource of new labor. It was estimated that in Britain there were from three to four million unoccupied women (widows, wives, etc.) who might be brought into industry and the professions, to release men for fighting service or the more strenuous types of war work. In the First World War over 1,660,000 women found employment and at least twice

---

[29] *The Economist*, February 3, 1940, p. 189.

as many would probably be called into war work in this conflict. Finally, in the white-collar services there were at least 10,000,000 persons, about half the employed population of Britain, and from 2,000,000 to 4,000,000 of them could be shifted into war work by the restriction of their opportunities for civil employment.

These three sources together could provide the eight to ten million additional armament workers who would be needed in British industry by the end of the war. Of course, the transfer of such a large number of persons would take years, but the program could be carried out in phases, with perhaps two million people a year being brought into war production.

Unfortunately, for the first eight months of the war the Chamberlain Cabinet failed to formulate any program for the distribution of man power between the fighting front and the home front in such a way as to create the strongest possible army with the greatest possible equipment. With the exception of the calling-up of men for the armed forces, which was systematically carried out, the Government's efforts (1) to stabilize the labor market, (2) to expand the labor force by dilution, (3) to transfer and (4) to train workers, were insufficient in scope and ineffective in execution. Its one creditable performance was the mobilization of military man power. Immediately on the declaration of war on September 3, 1939, the National Service (Armed Forces) Act, 1939, was enacted. This superseded the Military Training Act of May to 1939, by which conscription had been introduced, and extended liability for compulsory military service to all men between 18 and 41 years of age. The calling-up proceeded smoothly, and by May 9, 1940, approximately 4,500,000 men had been asked by the Ministry of Labor and National Service to register, and 1,500,000 of them had joined the Army.

Early in 1939 the Schedule of Reserved Occupations had been established to prevent the enlistment in the Regular Army of trained workers required in war industries, and in this it was partially successful. But the actual mobilization of industrial man power, on the other hand, was neglected. One of the most crucial requirements of British industry was for some stability in the labor market, which had become increasingly chaotic since early in 1939. The scarcity of engineering labor and the efforts of the defense services to speed output by offering cost-plus contracts encouraged employers to offer attractions to the skilled craftsmen of other contractors. Labor scouts were sent out; a system of auctioning trained workers between different firms developed. Workers in the machine tool industry, the pivotal defense industry and one long suffering from labor shortages, left their jobs to accept better paid work in aircraft factories.

To prevent competitive bidding, Parliament had passed the *Control of Employment Act* in September 1939. This statute empowered the Minister of Labor to issue special orders prohibiting employers from advertising for workers or hiring (and rehiring) them without the consent of the Ministry of Labor. For all practical purposes, however, the Control of Employment Act remained a dead letter. Since it was an enabling act, it became effective only when special orders applying its provisions to particular occupations were issued by the Minister of Labor, and during the first seven months of the war, despite the increase of labor turnover, Ernest Brown issued no orders. Then the first *Control of Employment (Advertisement) Order* in April 1940 was applied to the building and contracting industries.

Six days before the outbreak of war, on August 28, 1939, the Amalgamated Engineering Union reached an agreement with the Engineering Allied Employers' National Federation permitting the entrance of less skilled male labor into the engineering and aircraft industries. This agreement, however, did not permit large-scale dilution, for the admission of new workers was hedged with numerous restrictions protecting local union privileges. Local committees composed of trade union and employer representatives were established to approve applications for additional labor. A national joint committee was established to adjust the differences in case of disagreement by these local committees. In addition, provision was made for the return to " normal " union practices after the emergency, and a record was to be kept of all modifications of union standards.

Seven months of war elapsed before the Ministry of Labor decided in March 1940 to take a partial census of the number of workers employed in the three major armament industries of (1) engineering, (2) motor vehicles and aircraft, and (3) shipbuilding and repairing.[30] To frame a major transfer program, the Government should have known not only the number of persons already employed in the war trades, but,

---

[30] All employers in these fields were asked to make returns to the Ministry of Labor by April 10, 1940 (and henceforth quarterly) of the number of persons engaged on work for the Government and the export and domestic markets and of the relative number of skilled and unskilled men, women, and juveniles employed. *Ministry of Labour Gazette*, April 1940, p. 105. The data received was not made public.

chiefly, the number employed in other industries who might be shifted into war work.[31]

In spite of the Minister of Labor's announced intention to intensify the labor training program, there were only 7,000 men enrolled in the government training centers in April 1940, and they were pursuing five-to six-month courses. At this rate the training centers could turn out 15,000 semi-skilled workers a year. For the inadequacy of the British program to be appreciated, it should be compared with the labor training program in Nazi Germany, where 16,000 instructors in 200 training camps of the Labor Front were prepared to train over 1,000,000 workers a year for German industry.

Given the Chamberlain Government's failure to enlarge appreciably the supply of munition workers by dilution, transfer, and training, British industry had to work longer and harder for armament output to be speeded up. In Britain there is no general Wage-Hour Act limiting the hours of employment for all workers. Instead, agreements between trade unions and employers customarily limit weekly working hours for men to from 44 to 48 hours a week, depending on the trade. Only for women and juveniles are maximum working hours set by law, at 48 and 44 hours respectively. During the rearmament years, and especially after the beginning of the war, the engineering, shipbuilding, and construction trade unions frequently agreed to considerable overtime. The statutory restrictions on the employment of women and young people engaged on defense contracts were likewise relaxed by the Home Office [32] after the war broke out. At first the supply departments authorized their contractors to work up to sixty hours a week. Subsequently, all munition factories desiring to employ women overtime were required to gain the permission of the factory inspectors, and this permission was readily given.

It was estimated that in December 1939 overtime in the engineering

---

[31] It is true that on September 5, 1939, the National Registration Act was enacted which provided that the entire population of the United Kingdom must be enrolled on the National Register. The purpose of the law however was not principally to procure man power information but to provide the Government with population statistics (to supplement the 1931 census) in order to facilitate the administration of conscription, evacuation, and wartime insurance.

Plans were made before the war for a Central Register of " scientific, technical, professional, and higher administrative personnel," and a Supplementary Register was established in December 1939 for persons in the same general categories whose careers had been interrupted by the war, and who were not qualified for the Central Register. The Central and Supplementary Registers were merged in March 1942 in an Appointments Department of the Ministry of Labor.

[32] The Factory Acts were administered by the Home Office until June 1940, when the factory inspectorate was transferred to the Ministry of Labor.

industry averaged twelve hours a week for the country as a whole, and was as high as thirty hours a week in some factories. This general resort to overtime was bound to increase costs as well as to react unfavorably on the health of British workers and on the productivity per head of British industry. But in the absence of a much larger number of workers to divide the total work effort there was no prospect of reduced working hours. Instead, the disastrous days of Dunkirk directly ahead were to call for greater sacrifices and still longer hours.

One scheme devised by the Ministry of Labor deserves special comment, for it indicates the fruitful achievements that were possible when the Government formulated a positive plan and called upon industry and labor for full cooperation. This was the organization of mobile squads of stevedores to be shunted from one port to another to overcome the congestion of dock facilities resulting from the diversion of British shipping. Joint committees of employers' and dock workers' representatives were set up in every port. The Transport and General Workers' Union compiled lists of dockers willing to be transferred to other ports upon notification from these committees that additional labor was needed. These volunteers were guaranteed a traveling and a living allowance and a minimum daily wage for a limited time by the Ministry of Labor.

Information for an exact appraisal of the Chamberlain Government's labor policy in the first eight months of war is not available, for statistics of actual employment in British industries were no longer published after the outbreak of war. Figures of unemployment are, however, available, and some conclusions can be drawn on this basis. The number of unemployed in Great Britain and Northern Ireland in August 1939 was 1,295,000. The dislocation of foreign and domestic markets by the blockade, evacuation, and the blackout created some additional unemployment after the outbreak of war. But after eight months of war there were only 254,000 fewer unemployed than in August 1939. Even this reduction of unemployment was chiefly accounted for not by the armament industries, but by coal mining, textile manufacture, building and contracting, clothing manufacture, and transport. When allowance is made for the men called to military service after June 1939, total employment is found to have decreased by about 1,050,000 between June 1939 and April 1940.[33]

---

[33] This represents a net decrease in the productivity of the British economy of from 5½ to 8½ percent. Since many men called to the colors were not engaged in registered occupations, the actual reduction of industrial employment may have been as low as 5%.

It is apparent that the labor policies of the Chamberlain Government were disastrously inadequate to the needs of industry in total war. Demand for armament workers was concentrated in the Midlands and the north of England. There was at no time any sufficient program for the transfer of unemployed workers or workers employed in nonessential trades to the six key industries of engineering, vehicle and aircraft manufacture, metal manufacture, other metal industries, chemical manufacture, and shipbuilding. At no time in the first phase of the war did the British economy approach the full employment of its resources of labor. Trade union disputes persisted, and wages were allowed to rise as rapidly as the unions could push them up, thereby stimulating the upward spiral of costs and prices.

3. The War — Phase II

With the formation of the Churchill Cabinet in May 1940, Ernest Bevin, former secretary of the Transport and General Workers Union, and one of Britain's outstanding labor leaders, was appointed Minister of Labor. It is to his credit that the Ministry of Labor was converted from an impassive registry of economic statistics to a true ministry of labor supply. The new Minister had more to do than to repair the omissions of his predecessor, for the task of British industry was enormously enlarged by the defeat of France. A more efficient distribution of man power between military and industrial requirements was urgent. The Army was to be expanded by 1,500,000 men, and the manufacture of armaments was expected to absorb another 1,000,000 within a year. The (second) Emergency Powers Act of May 1940 [34] conferred new powers over property and services on the Government, and the Minister of Labor sought in a series of decrees issued under the Act to increase the output of the existing labor force, to stabilize the chaotic labor market, and to bring new workers into the armament factories.

The Chamberlain Government's use of the Control of Employment Act, 1939, had been negative; it restricted the future engagement of workers by employers. But Regulation 58A under the Emergency Powers Act of May 1940 empowered the Minister of Labor " to direct any person in the United Kingdom to perform such services . . . as may be specified." [35] This gave Ernest Bevin practically unlimited powers.

---

[34] See Appendix I.
[35] *Ministry of Labour Gazette,* June 1940, p. 156.

During the remaining months of 1940, however, the Government was reluctant to take recourse to these powers; Mr. Bevin was opposed to any form of industrial conscription for British workers. As a result many essential measures depending on compulsion were long delayed, especially the transfer of workers from other industries to war work.

There was no doubt good reason for this reluctance " to make a nation of industrial slaves." Before large sections of British workers could be transferred out of civil industry, it was necessary to devise adequate machinery to administer the task.

As a first step in administrative reorganization, a joint consultative committee, composed of fourteen members, labor and industry each having seven representatives, was appointed to discuss with the department such problems as the regulation of wages, the postponement of holidays, the prohibition of strikes, and arrangements for the health and welfare of the workers.[36] Next Mr. Bevin established under his own chairmanship an advisory Labor Supply Board consisting of four newly appointed Directors of Labor Supply, two chosen from industry and two from the trade unions.

The regional organization of labor supply was based on the existing employment exchanges, which act for all purposes directly under the authority of the eleven Divisional Controllers who are the principal representatives of the Ministry of Labor in their regions. A staff of several hundred labor supply inspectors reported to twenty-seven labor supply committees, composed of officials of the ministry, which were set up in the engineering centers. Advisory panels in particular industries, such as iron and steel and shipbuilding, were associated with the committees. The labor supply inspectors were empowered to enter any plant to investigate requests for additional workers, to supervise training facilities, and to ensure the most advantageous use of skilled labor. These first labor supply committees gave way a year later to forty-four Man Power Boards, which are also official in their composition, and which combine responsibility for recruitment for the armed forces and the provision of labor for essential work.

For the immediate future output could be increased only by calling on the existing force of workers to increase their total effort. In the

[36] It was in effect a smaller and more workable subcommittee drawn from the membership of the National Joint Advisory Council of thirty representatives. This Joint Council was appointed in October, 1939, by the Chamberlain Government, after consulting the British Employers Federation and the General Council of the Trades Union Congress. *Ministry of Labour Gazette,* August, 1940, page 203.

disastrous days of Flanders and Dunkirk England's survival was at stake, and on May 22, 1940, Herbert Morrison, the Minister of Supply, ordered all Royal Ordnance Factories and private firms engaged on defense contracts to work twenty-four hours a day seven days a week. All holidays, both public and personal, were cancelled or ordered postponed for the period of the crisis. In the armament, engineering, shipbuilding, and munitions industries labor responded to this appeal and worked twelve-hour shifts, seventy to eighty-four hours a week without interruptions.

After two months of such strenuous effort, however, there was growing evidence that British workers were suffering from nervous and physical strain. Absenteeism was common. Employees arrived late; women workers especially suffered from illness and fatigue. In late July the Ministry of Labor issued a bulletin, setting forth certain general principles which should govern overtime employment. There it was stated that maximum war production must be maintained and in fact increased, but that the strain on workers of the seventy-eighty-hour week " must be relieved by an immediate reduction of hours." [37] Although a shortage of available labor might prevent a shortening of the work week to the optimum hours, which experience indicated to be in the region of fifty-six hours a week, it was none the less urgent to limit working hours to an average of sixty hours a week until the training of additional labor would permit a further reduction. Furthermore, the Ministry of Labor intended to enforce again after August 1 the limitations on hours of women and young persons, as provided in the Factory Acts.

The shortage of labor in British armament industries prevented the general adoption of these recommendations. In the absence of compulsory rulings applying to any industry as a whole, which the Ministry of Labor refused to make, individual employers found it difficult to reduce hours. The supply departments were urging contractors to speed deliveries and were offering payment on a cost-plus basis. Moreover, workers were anxious to obtain high overtime wage rates, and if one employer restricted overtime, workers would drift away to more lucrative jobs. Consequently, long hours and Sunday work persisted in many defense industries throughout 1940 and 1941. In May 1941 labor fatigue and truancy were still disturbing factors in the armament industries. Re-

---

[37] *Hours of Work and Maximum Output*, July 25, 1940, Ministry of Labor and National Service, pp. 2–3.

medial measures were left to the officers of the Factory and Welfare Department established in the summer of 1940 to supervise the welfare of workers outside as well as within the factories.

It was sought to increase the output of industry by eliminating the loss of work days due to strikes as well as lengthening the working week. During the first phase of the war strikes had continued at about their prewar rate, 70 to 90 a month. Although many of these disputes occurred in the aircraft and engineering trades, none was sufficiently serious for the Chamberlain Government to risk alienating the uncertain support of the trade unions by prohibiting strikes. But Mr. Bevin could walk where his predecessor had feared to tread. In June the Consultative Committee, on which the labor unions were represented, unanimously recommended that during the war emergency " it is imperative that there should be no stoppage of work owing to trade disputes." [38] The Committee urged that existing arbitration boards and facilities for collective bargaining continue to be used in all industrial disputes, but that where no agreement could be reached disputes should be referred to an arbitration tribunal whose decisions would be binding. These recommendations were embodied in the *Conditions of Employment and National Arbitration Order* in July 1940. Strikes and lockouts were prohibited; and a five-man National Arbitration Tribunal was established. Union standards of employment were imposed upon all employers in an industry whether or not they recognized trade unions.

Strikes have, however, continued to occur about as frequently as before they were prohibited. In the prewar years, 1935–1939, the monthly average of strikes was 78, and in May 1940 there were 92. In the crisis month of June workers voluntarily suspended strikes, and the number of disputes dropped to 30, but in July, the month strikes were banned, the total began to mount until in October 1940 it reached 92, more than for any month of 1939. But the number of workers involved and the work days lost were much lower than in pre-Flanders months. Disputes affected smaller numbers of persons and were settled more rapidly.

These disputes arose principally from demands for wage increases. Employers were surprisingly willing to meet such demands, for the original 100 percent Excess Profits Tax and cost-plus contracts have diminished the incentive to keep costs down. As a result most strikes have

[38] *Ministry of Labour Gazette*, August, 1940, page 210.

been settled quickly, generally by direct negotiation between the unions and employers or through the machinery set up under the Industrial Courts Act of 1919. In the first year of its existence the National Arbitration Tribunal had granted 144 awards. Although the prohibition of strikes had not prevented strikes, as World War I experience had indicated would be the case, the statement of industrial policy, which the report of the Consultative Committee was in effect, was useful in focusing the attention of the workers on the necessity of avoiding work stoppages whenever possible.

Arrangements for shunting dock workers from one port to another were strengthened during the summer of 1940. In the four great shipping areas of Liverpool, London, Newcastle, and Edinburgh local committees were superseded by regional Port Labor Inspectors directly responsible to the Ministry of Labor. These inspectors were given broad supervisory powers over dock workers, who were required to register with, and could receive employment only through, the Port Labor Inspectors. A wider reorganization of the conditions of dock labor was introduced in the Merseyside, Manchester, and Preston areas in March 1941, and later in the Clydeside area. First, all dock workers in those areas were henceforth to be employed and paid directly by the Government — by the Minister of Transport — although they would continue to work for private employers, who would be registered and supervised by the Regional Port Directors of the Ministry of Transport. Second, all dock workers were guaranteed a minimum of forty-four hours of work a week at a minimum wage, with the prospect of considerable overtime employment. The scheme was voluntary, but all dockers accepting work under it were required to accept any engagement to which they might be assigned by the Port Labor Inspectors. Dockers' wages, plus a percentage to defray administrative expenses, were to be paid by the employers into a central fund from which the Minister of Transport would pay the dockers. The purpose of these changes was to " decasualize " dock labor by substituting steady pay for the intermittent employment characteristic of dock work. The Government's direct responsibility was increased in August 1941 by the formation of a National Dock Labor Corporation. The Corporation, under a board of directors of eight members, two appointed by the Minister of Labor as his representatives and three each nominated by the employers and unions concerned, was to promote, finance, and administer schemes of employment, and to arrange for the transfer of dockers from one port to another. These reforms in the conditions of dock work will in all probability be continued in peacetime.

All these measures to lengthen the work week, to provide for the health of the workers, to prevent loss of time by strikes, and to facilitate the transfer of shipbuilding and dock labor were aspects of a primary objective — to increase production by a better utilization of existing supplies of labor. The second general objective of labor policy was to bring some order into the labor market. Under the powers of Regulation 58A, the *Undertakings (Restriction of Engagement) Order* was issued in early June 1940. This provided that in the engineering or shipbuilding industries no employer could hire workers except through the local Employment Exchange or under an approved arrangement between employer and union organizations. Workers normally employed in coal mining or agriculture, forestry, or horticulture could not be engaged in any other industry except by special permission of the local Labor Office. In July national minimum wages for agricultural labor were raised by about 35 percent.

All these "poaching" regulations were intended to stop the movement of labor from the poorly paid agricultural and mining trades to more lucrative jobs and the uncontrolled movement of labor within armament industry. They were only partially effective. They were difficult to enforce and were frequently evaded by employers; they did not prevent individual workers from quitting one job and finding another; nor did they enforce work discipline in the plants.

Stronger and more direct measures were announced in March 1941 in the form of "Essential Work Orders." These apply only to particular industries and make the right of employers to discharge workers, and the right of workers to quit their jobs, subject to the permission of a national service officer and at least a week's notice. Special tribunals representing both labor and management have been established under independent chairmen to hear appeals from workers and employers against the decisions of service officers. In addition, the employer is required to guarantee basic weekly minimum wage rates. Conditions and terms of work must accord with the standards set for the industry by collective agreements, and the plant management must make satisfactory provision for the welfare of employees. These Orders effectively tie the worker to his job, while at the same time attempting to establish satisfactory wages and working conditions for the employees.

Essential Work Orders have been issued for the principal defense industries, shipbuilding and ship repairing, the merchant marine, coal mining, building and civil engineering, dock transport, chemicals and iron and steel. They have been criticized for removing the employer's sanction of discharge to enforce discipline and for the delay inherent in the appeal procedure. Nevertheless, they have served to stabilize the labor market and have curtailed mobility of labor and laxness of discipline.

The third major objective of the Government's labor policy was to increase the total number of workers engaged in armament production. The most immediate source of additional workers was, of course, the unemployed. Several means existed to bring them into industry. First, the Schedule of Reserved Occupations, which, within certain age limits, exempted persons from enlistment in the armed forces, was revised. As the schedule was originally drawn up, nearly 4,500,000 men — far too many — were included. The chief weakness of the plan was that men were exempted according to categories, electricians and shipbuilders, for instance, and not according to actual employment in vital war work.

Various minor revisions were made in the Schedule during the latter half of 1940, and in April 1941 a Revised Schedule of Reserved Occupations, which embodied two basic changes, was issued. The ages of reservation in many trades were raised by from 5 to 10 years, the changes to become effective in three successive two-month periods. The second change was the introduction of a category of " protected work " within the reserved occupations, with a lower reservation age for workers employed on work of special importance in the war effort. Firms included in five general classes of essential work were listed on a Register of Protected Establishments.

From July 1940 anyone refusing work of national importance was disqualified from receiving unemployment benefits. In areas and industries with heavy unemployment panels representing employers, employees, and the general public were set up to review the unemployment registers and attempt to place workers unemployed for more than a month in industry or civil defense work. In September 1940 all evacuated persons without jobs were asked to register at the employment exchanges in their new districts.

In addition, the Ministry of Labor took steps to mop up hidden reserves of labor in the armament industries. By mid-June 1940 the percentage of unemployed in all engineering industries was only 1.8 percent, in the production of motor vehicles and aircraft, 1.5 percent, in the chemical industry, only 2.5 percent. For this small margin an Industrial Registration Order, requiring the registration of all men over the age of twenty-one who were employed in certain engineering, armament, and heavy goods industries but not engaged entirely on government contracts, was issued. All men under sixty-five years of age who had worked in any of these specified fields for one year at any time since January 1929 were likewise asked to register. As a result of these orders, surprisingly large numbers of skilled workers not wholly employed in war work were made available. In the northwestern administrative area alone a reserve of 61,000 men was discovered. Many of these were qualified engineers retained on the payrolls of inactive firms which disliked losing their staff of trained personnel to other companies. The Ministry of Labor's inspectors frequently investigated such cases and ordered the transfer of men from one company to another.

Finally, the Government sought to bring into war production whatever trained men were available either in the armed forces or among the growing population of refugees resident in England. In the military interlude following the collapse of France, about 3,000 skilled mechanics were temporarily combed out of the British Army for munition work.[39] Some effort to utilize the special talents of European refugees in Britain was long overdue when the formation of an International Labor Force, designed to register and find employment for all anti-Fascist aliens was announced in August 1940.

All these measures were helpful in the short run, but they could at best furnish only a small part of the estimated demand of the war industries for two million additional workers. As explained above, the chief sources of new labor were nonworking women and persons employed in nonarmament industries. May 22, 1940, the unions principally concerned with the employment of women in the engineering industry had agreed with the Engineering and Allied Employers National Federation to relax the previous restrictions on even the temporary admission of women into the engineering fields. In general, women were to receive equal pay with men for equal work, but where they lacked experience for the job, they were to undergo several probationary stages, totalling thirty-two weeks, before they received equal pay. The opening late in 1940 and early in 1941 of newly completed Royal Ordnance Fac-

---

[39] Previously under Ernest Brown about 33,000 skilled men not required for technical work had been released by the War Office.

tories required hundreds of thousands of women and girls. In November 1940 the Prime Minister appealed for one million people to enter the munition factories voluntarily within the next nine months.

A vast expansion of the Government's labor training program was necessary to facilitate this transfer of workers. The Ministry of Labor's training scheme was accelerated to turn out 200,000 instead of 15,000 trainees a year. In addition, the technical schools and colleges of the country introduced shorter and more intensive courses for 50,000 a year. This acceleration of labor training was unfortunately restricted by the Government's reluctance to divert skilled technicians and machine tools from production to instruction. The greatest training ground of all was in the factories, but although industrial management did train workers for their own immediate needs, they were under constant pressure from the Supply Departments to use their facilities fully to increase production. An official plan for training in the factories, with compulsory quotas of trainees for each plant and payment of private industry for the service, might have given useful results. A voluntary scheme of in-factory training was notably unsuccessful. The Government's failure to adopt such a compulsory labor training program undoubtedly impaired its other efforts to expand the supply of workers available for employment.

Throughout 1940 there was little resort to the unlimited powers conferred on the Minister of Labor and no resort to industrial conscription of labor. But by January 1941 Britain had reached the point of full employment where further expansion of war production could be achieved only by the contraction of civil output. The number of wholly unemployed persons in Britain was only 521,000 in January 1941, and as most of these were in fact unemployable, it was doubtful if the figure would be reduced very rapidly. The planned compulsory transfer of large numbers of workers from nonessential trades could no longer be postponed. Both the restriction of civil industry and the conscription of industrial labor were necessary.

It is true that many of the Government's policies since the outbreak of war had been restrictive of civil business. The savings campaign, heavy income and purchase taxes, and rationing had all reduced private purchasing power. In addition the Board of Trade's *Limitation of Supplies Orders* of June and November 1940 had reduced the supplies of raw materials available to certain industries with a view to decreasing both consumption and employment. But none of these measures was directly coordinated with demand for labor in the armament industries. On the contrary, they produced conspicuous waste of labor. In general, the firms affected continued to operate at reduced, and usually inefficient, levels of output. Consequently, a disproportionately small number of workers were actually discharged from their positions. Neither was there any assurance that the persons thrown out of work would actually find their way into armament employment.

For these shortcomings to be overcome there had first to be an overall plan whereby the reduced output of civil industry would be concentrated in a few firms working at capacity while the remaining firms were closed down and their facilities and employees made available for the production of armaments. The equipment and especially the workers thus disemployed had then to be conscripted and allocated for war work.

The Churchill Government adopted this twofold policy early in 1941. In March the Board of Trade announced its scheme " to concentrate production in a reduced number of factories working full time." [40] The program of concentration applied to more than thirty consumer-goods industries — textiles, cotton, woolens, silk, hosiery, pottery, cycles, plastics, musical instruments, and a host of others. The Government encouraged the trade associations in the industries concerned to formulate voluntary schemes of the particular firms to be closed out, and wherever possible make arrangements for their compensation. The Government stated its intention of using compulsion if voluntary programs were not forthcoming. The surviving nucleus firms in industries were granted some protection. They would receive available government contracts, and their supplies of raw materials, labor, and plant would be safeguarded as far as the circumstances of the war permitted. It was estimated that from 500,000 to 700,000 workers would ultimately be released for transfer to war work.[40a]

So that the labor released should be absorbed in armament trades, Great Britain accepted industrial conscription. On March 16, 1941 the Minister of Labor declared that all men between the ages of forty-one and forty-five, and all women of twenty and twenty-one years of age, if not already in war employment must register for it by mid-April. Persons registering were subsequently to be interviewed, and after their capabilities had been determined they were to be directed to report for

[40] *Concentration of Production*, March 1941, Cmd. 6258.
[40a] For the actual result, see Chapter III, Part II, p. 186.

training and eventual employment in shipyards, engineering works, and armament plants. The facts that in total war a nation's man power is indivisible and that the organization of those who produce is as essential to victory as the organization of those who fight had been faced. After eighteen months of war, Britain had at last an integrated policy for the utilization of man power.

During 1941, as further munitions plants came into production and the armed forces expanded, the crisis of man power became increasingly acute. In December 1941 the Government acted to relieve the crisis by introducing the National Service (No. 2) Bill. This statute extended the age of men subject to armed service, supplanted the Schedule of Reserved Occupations, and made women subject to compulsory service for certain branches of defense work.

The age of men liable to military and civil defense was raised from 41 to 51, and lowered from 19 to 18½ years, thereby bringing 2,750,000 more men within conscription. The Government stated its intention of posting men over 40 years of age to sedentary work and permitting the release of younger men for combat work. The Schedule of Reserved Occupations, which established exemption by occupational age-blocs, was replaced by a system of individual deferment. Beginning on January 1, 1942 the age of reservation was to be raised by one-year steps at monthly intervals, exemption was to be granted only to persons actually engaged in work of national importance.

The most striking provision of the Act at the time, though its later more extensive application has been accepted without sensation, was that women likewise were subject to conscription. Married women, and mothers with children under 14 years of age were exempt for the time being, although they could be directed into industrial employment under previous orders. Women between the ages of 20–30 years were to be called up immediately and directed into the Women's Auxiliary Services, civil defense, or factory work. Britain was approaching full mobilization of her man power resources.

The concentration of nonessential industries provided an example for the subsequent, inevitable concentration of war work in the most efficient " production units," which was begun in the autumn of 1942. The corresponding reallocation of labor among firms already holding defense contracts became Great Britain's most acute industrial problem. The licensing of new undertakings was restricted, with the aim of checking the trend of labor into congested areas, and less essential enterprises were compulsorily transferred from certain centers of specialized work.

To conclude, it is evident that it was not until after the formation of the Churchill Cabinet and the appointment of Ernest Bevin as Minister of Labor that the British Government assumed responsibility for the supply of labor to the armament factories. Even then it was nine months before the adoption of any coherent man power policy involving the allocation of labor. Bevin's primary objective in the summer of 1940 was an immediate increase in the output of weapons. For this purpose, overtime was accepted as an effective short-run policy. It was not until the late summer of 1940 that much progress was made in putting unemployed to work, and not until early 1941 that the organized compulsory transfer of workers was accepted.

PART THREE

GREAT BRITAIN'S OVERSEAS TRADE

by Eric Roll

The problems of foreign trade in time of war form only a part of the wider question of the proper economic organization of a country's war effort. That, in its turn, is inseparable from the whole complex of military, diplomatic, political, and social considerations which have to be taken into account when a nation is to be mobilized for war. But foreign trade deserves separate treatment here for at least two reasons. The economic life of Great Britain has for centuries been built up on a basis of vast economic relations — commercial and financial — with the outside world. And there is not a single important aspect of the British war economy which can be discussed without at once raising problems of an international character. The second reason arises out of this: most of the major decisions on war policy have their foreign trade aspect. Just as the war itself cannot be analyzed except in terms of a prolonged process, Britain's wartime overseas trade must also be viewed against the background of its development in the years preceding the outbreak of war. This survey begins, therefore, with a brief sketch of the trends in Britain's international economic relations during the period between the First World War and the Second.

1. The Background

Britain suffered particularly heavily from the decline of world trade which followed the war of 1914–18. In 1924, when much of the immediate postwar disturbance had disappeared, the volume of Britain's imports was about 2.5 percent higher than in 1913; but exports were still only three-quarters of their prewar volume. But by 1929, the peak year of the postwar period, the volume of exports was still 17 percent below the 1913 figure, while imports, due largely to relatively low food prices, were about 18 percent higher than before the war. Exports formed a continually declining proportion of national output. From 30 percent in 1907, they fell to 25 percent in 1924 and to 21 percent in 1930.

The picture presented by merchandise trade is strengthened when the rest of Britain's international transactions are considered. For more than a century, Britain has had capital invested overseas. For nearly a century she has been receiving each year large sums as payment of interest and repayment of capital on those foreign investments. These sums, together with the large annual net income she draws from abroad for the services of her shipping, her banks, and other financial institutions, have enabled her to finance larger purchases of goods from abroad than would have been possible from the proceeds of her merchandise exports alone. Since 1857 Britain has had a continuous series of annual import surpluses. But these have been more than offset by the other items mentioned. And although adequate statistics are not available for the earlier period, it is fairly certain that in every year between 1857 and 1931 Great Britain has had a current surplus on her balance of international payments. This has been available for the purpose of adding to her foreign investments.

The balance of payments on current account in the postwar period shows a fairly definite trend, interrupted only during a short part of the period. From 1920 to 1925 the annual surplus on all current items shows a continuous decline: from £252 million in the former year to £9 million in the latter. The next three years show an upward movement, due to the diminution of the import surplus which was brought about by the expansion of exports in that period of stabilization. In 1929, the current surplus reached £138 million. But this improvement was short-lived: in the following year the surplus had again fallen to £28 million; and in 1931 a deficit appeared for the first time. This was of the substantial amount of £104 million. The restrictive measures adopted in that year caused the deficit to diminish to £51 million in 1932 and made the balance even in 1933. But since then there has been only one year, 1935, in which Britain has had a current surplus. In each of the two last years before the present war broke out, there has been a current deficit of about £55 million.

These figures seem to indicate the presence of a long process of deterioration in Britain's current international transactions. A similar trend is revealed in Britain's position as an international creditor. In 1913, British subscriptions to new overseas issues exceeded repayments to the United Kingdom on account of past loans by £243 million. In 1928, this difference was only £108 million. And since the depression there have been only two years in which the difference has been a positive quantity. Overseas capital issues in London have fluctuated between a high of £143 million in 1928 and a low of £20 million in 1935. Since 1931, they have been increasingly strictly controlled by the government, with the result that the average of the ten years 1930–39 was £39.4 million as compared with £116 million for the preceding decade.[41]

The crisis of 1931 and the lengthy depression which followed it led to the adoption of a number of now familiar defensive and palliative measures, including the abandonment by Great Britain of her century-old policy of free trade. It has been argued, with justice, that the long-run effects of the adoption by Britain, the greatest international commercial and financial center, of such measures of restrictive economic nationalism would be to aggravate the economic difficulties of the world and to contribute to the intensification of political friction. The immediate result of these measures, however, was to improve Britain's in-

---

[41] It is not possible to measure the decline of British investments abroad precisely, owing to the difficulties of collecting comprehensive data and of fluctuations in market values. One indication may be obtained by Sir Robert Kindersley's estimate of the nominal amount of quoted foreign securities held by British residents. This shows a decline from £3,438 million in 1929 to £3,292 million in 1938. Moreover, it would appear that repayment has affected the most easily realizable assets and has left the composition of the remaining total less favorable than it used to be.

ternational economic position by arresting for a time the long process of deterioration. We find, for example, that while the volume of world trade fell between 1929 and 1934 by 22.5 percent, Britain's share in it rose from 13.05 percent to 13.85 percent. Perhaps the most striking single indication of the measure in which Britain succeeded in turning her international transactions in her favor is to be found in the figures for the terms of trade.[42] Taking 1930 as 100, this index rose to 110.3 in 1931, 110.8 in 1932, and 115.2 in 1933. This improvement is somewhat compensated for by a diminution in the total volume of foreign trade in these years. But, on the other hand, the subsequent decline in the terms of trade — to 112.1 in 1934 and 109.4 in 1935 — is more than offset by a rise in the volume of trade. It is true that the following three years showed a fresh decline in the terms of trade. But in 1937, they were still above the 1930 figure (in 1938 there was another substantial improvement); and if the volume index is taken into account, the rise was continuous from 1932 onward.

This improvement, whatever its more remote significance and consequences, reflects essentially the drive towards bilateralism in British trade. The inevitable depression phenomenon of agricultural prices falling more rapidly than the prices of manufactured goods was one factor in Britain's favor. In a buyer's market for food and raw materials, Britain, as one of the world's chief buyers of these products, was able to obtain good terms. The depreciation of sterling did not counteract this favorable development, but strengthened it, since a large number of Britain's suppliers followed the pound. With the creation of the Sterling Area, which excluded Canada but included some countries not in the British Empire, Great Britain carved out a trading area in which all the strong factors of her economic position showed up to their full advantage and the weaknesses could be minimized. The Ottawa Agreements brought much of the Canadian trade into line; and similar arrangements could thereafter be attempted with the remainder of the non-sterling world.

Since this alignment of British foreign trade is of great importance in relation to wartime problems, it may be worth while to summarize its effect. The following table shows the changes in the distribution of

---

42 This measurement, specifically designed to show changes in the gain derived by a country from each unit of its foreign trade, reveals an interesting movement in the years following the depression. The net terms of trade are given by the ratio of the average price of exports to the average price of imports. They are an index of the changes in the amount of imports that are obtained for each unit of exports.

British trade as between the British Empire and European and non-European foreign countries.

Area	Percent of total imports from		Percent of total exports to	
	1929	1938	1929	1938
British Empire	29.4	40.4	44.5	49.9
Non-European foreign countries	32.5	26.1	22.7	18.2
European foreign countries	38.1	33.5	32.8	31.9

This table may be supplemented by the following figures which illustrate the effects of the creation of the Sterling Area:

Area	Percent of total imports from		Percent of total exports to	
	1929	1938	1929	1938
11 non-British free exchange countries	40.9	33.5	25.5	24.2
12 countries in the Sterling Area	31.9	36.2	38.3	44.5
4 former " Gold Bloc " countries	12.8	8.6	10.9	8.5

The composition of Britain's trade did not change greatly during the period reviewed. The protectionist policy diminished somewhat the proportion of finished goods within the group of manufactured imports in favor of semi-finished products. The exigencies of rearmament and the laying-in of reserves of food and raw materials are also revealed in a proportionate rise of the relevant imports in the last two prewar years. The share of manufactured exports declined slightly in favor of raw materials (mainly coal), and an important decline occurred in the value of re-exports, reflecting the diminished importance of British *entrepôt* trade in a world in which she and her competitors were engaged on an energetic drive towards bilateralism.

It is important to keep in mind the changes in the geographical distribution of British trade in the years before the war, because these changes — and the strains and stresses which they either followed or preceded — were responsible for many problems of wartime policy. The measures which brought about the greater concentration of trade within the Empire and the Sterling Area were designed to counter the weakened economic position of Britain, and while not so definitely bilateral in intention as measures adopted by Germany, particularly towards her neighbors in southeastern Europe, they were also of a monopolistic character. As such, they of necessity produced some friction. Within the Empire itself complaints were not unknown, and many modifications of the original Ottawa Agreements had to be introduced.

South Africa, for example, claimed that her purchases from Britain had risen more than those of any other country in the world, while her sales to Britain had declined. India, on the other hand, was increasing her exports to Britain, but diminishing her imports, particularly in cotton manufactures, from Britain. For Canada and Australia the picture was somewhat similar: a rise in the proportion of exports to Britain unaccompanied by any rise in the proportion of imports from Britain.

Those countries, notably France, which for a time formed the Gold Bloc, sharply reduced the proportion of their trade with Britain.[43] Trade with Germany and Italy, the countries with which Britain was to be at war, had declined in the last prewar decade. In the latter case, it was about halved both for exports and imports percentages. The proportion of British imports from Germany declined more heavily than that of British exports to Germany, though less heavily than the proportion of re-exports. In the countries of southeastern Europe, in which German methods of bilateral trade and payments agreements were most energetically pursued, British trade declined less than is often thought. This was due less to any very determined British counteraction than to the fact that the proportion of trade which Britain did with those countries had always been very small. In addition, imports and exports of Czechoslovakia, Italy, and Austria, from and to southeastern Europe were more similar to those of Germany and were, therefore, more affected by the German drive than those of Britain.

As far as the rest of the world was concerned, the movement of British trade seems to have been closely related to the development of individual trade agreements. In the case of trade with the three Scandinavian countries and Finland, with which trade agreements were concluded in 1933, there has been a sharp rise in the proportions. The same is true of Poland and the Baltic states. In the trade with the United States there was until 1938 a heavy decline of imports from that country with a small decline in exports and a considerable decline in re-exports. But the short record of the trade agreement concluded between the United Kingdom and the United States in 1938 suggests that, but for the war, the experience of the other trade agreements might have been repeated. The South American proportions declined for exports but rose slightly for imports, the decline in the proportion of exports being

---

[43] This reduction was not markedly reversed after the abandonment by these countries of their former gold parity, thus possibly indicating the greater importance of trade agreements as against currency factors in influencing the direction of trade.

particularly marked in the case of Brazil and Chile, where both Germany and the United States were able to expand. With Argentina, Britain has traditionally very close financial and commercial ties. Here, recent trade and payments agreements succeeded in maintaining the percentage of British exports, but were unable to prevent a fall in the share of British imports. The effect of the trade agreement with Russia conformed to the general pattern. The general course of the percentage of imports from Russia was steady, but that of exports, and much more that of re-exports, was upward.

Thus the general picture is one of a fair measure of success in the adoption of new policies. It offsets to some extent the impression of long-run weakness presented by British trade in the whole postwar period.

2. The War Developments

I. The general problems of the organization of the economy of a capitalist state for the purpose of waging war have been analyzed and debated at length for the last few decades, and particularly during the last two years. It is neither possible nor desirable to recapitulate this discussion here. In its simplest and most abstract terms the general economic problem of war is one of securing the necessary supplies. The scale on which the problem of supply appears in wartime lifts it out of the domain of public finance — budgeting, taxation, etc. — and causes it to affect profoundly every aspect of the existing economic structure.

In the last war, the technique in all belligerent countries was essentially an indirect one, although as the war progressed more direct measures were increasingly applied. The agencies of government appeared in the market as buyers equipped with purchasing power raised in part through taxation but mainly through borrowing. Their greater monetary resources, combined with some direct measures designed to discourage the purchase and production of non-war goods, enabled these governmental agencies to " bid away " goods, and the resources needed to make these goods, from their peacetime uses. It was largely through such inflationary processes, placing the burden on the mass of consumers, that the essential shifting of production and the necessary industrial concentration were achieved. It was no doubt due to the still largely fluid and competitive relations between different sections of capitalist enterprise, and to the relations between them and labor, that these indirect means had to be used. And since in 1914 monopolization of industry and integration of leading sections of it with finance and the state were much more highly advanced in Germany than in Britain, measures of direct control were adopted there earlier and to a greater extent.

The roles of inflation and of direct control, which in 1914–18 was used only tardily and mainly as an adjunct to inflationary finance, have now been in a sense reversed. In the present war, the methods of finance and the use of the market mechanism very soon became only supplementary to direct intervention.

The evolution of measures of domestic regulation during the course of the war has been in the direction of steadily increasing control. To-day, the formal possibility exists of establishing completely centralized control of the whole economic activity of the United Kingdom. And to a large extent this possibility has become a reality. This is not the place to discuss the significance of these measures, but it must be remembered that however far-reaching they may be, they do not fundamentally alter the economic structure. Essentially, reliance is still placed on the operation of the capitalistic process. Even though the rights and powers of many sections of private enterprise have been restricted by the action of the state, private property, individual enterprise, the profit motive, and the working of the market mechanism are still basic. In the field of foreign trade to which we now turn, it has also been clear that the competition of divergent interests has by no means been wholly eliminated by the vast apparatus of control which has been created.

II.   Before we enumerate the measures for the regulation of Britain's foreign transactions, it is useful to look again at the international economic position which Britain occupied at the outbreak of the war. That position was generally recognized to be a strong one in spite of intermittent difficulties. Britain's foreign trade in 1938 still formed in value over 26 percent of world trade. She was by far the most important carrying nation, possessing the world's largest mercantile marine (18 million tons, as against the second largest, 9 million tons). Above all, she was still the world's largest foreign investor, her holdings being estimated at well over £3,000,000,000.

Probably the best single factor to take for an estimate of available economic strength is the amount of British assets in the United States at the outbreak of war. These were estimated to have been as follows: [44]

---

[44] Federal Reserve Board *Bulletin*, January 1941.

(in $000,000)

Central Gold Reserves	$ Balances	Readily marketable securities at market value	Total
2,000	595	1,080	3,675
(1914:165)	(1914:2,600–3,800		2,765–3,965)

A number of other resources might be added to this table. For example, British direct and other not immediately marketable investments in the United States were estimated at $1,185,000,000; and Canadian assets amounting to over $1,500,000,000, two-thirds of which were easily realizable, could also be regarded as available to the British Empire for war purposes. The American assets of other British countries should also be taken into account. The substantial French assets, amounting to over $3,500,000,000, could, until the French collapse, be counted as part of the financial strength of the Allies. When it is remembered that Germany's dollar assets amounted to only about $255,000,000 [45] as compared with a 1914 total of perhaps $1,000,000,000, the financial power of Britain appears in its true proportions.

The measures which were taken in the field of international trade fall into three classes. There are first the simple corollaries of domestic measures for the centralization of economic control. There are measures which supplement and reinforce domestic policy directed to the husbanding of resources. And finally there are the measures of active economic warfare. It is not necessary to list all of the very numerous new measures which have been adopted since the outbreak of war, some in the form of new legislation, others as regulations under the defense emergency powers, but the most important ones may be mentioned. The following fall mainly into the first category. The *Currency (Defense) Act* authorizes the use of the Exchange Equalization Account for war purposes. The *Import, Export and Customs Powers (Defense) Act* gives the Board of Trade the power to prohibit or regulate the import and export of all goods. The *Ships and Aircraft (Transfer Restrictions) Act* gives powers over the transfer of ships and aircraft to the Board of Trade and the Secretary for Air. The *Import Duties (Emergency Provisions) Act* allows the Treasury to act as if the (now suspended) Import Duties Advisory Committee had made a recommendation.

In the class of active economic warfare, there is the *Trading with the*

---

[45] According to the estimate of the U. S. Department of Commerce.

Enemy Act which imposes severe penalties for carrying on transactions with, or for the benefit of, the enemy; and the declaration of the blockade of German-occupied areas. The *Trading with the Enemy Act* follows the principles adopted in the last war, but it has a wider application, and its stringency has been increased by subsequent orders. The blockade, while again based on old-established principles, is much more broadly conceived and more comprehensive than it has ever been before. Not only is the Ministry of Economic Warfare charged with supervising the execution of the original, almost all-inclusive prohibition of imports into Germany; since the latter part of November 1939 and the use by Germany of the magnetic mine in shipping lanes, German exports, too, fall under the prohibition which is enforced by the British Navy and its contraband control. An elaborate machinery has been set up for checking the imports and exports of neutral countries against their peacetime quantities and estimated current requirements so as to prevent any leakage in the blockade of the enemy by way of those neutral countries.

The purpose of economic warfare is to deprive the enemy of materials essential for the prosecution of the war. This is done either directly by stopping his imports, or indirectly by preventing him from exporting and so obtaining the funds with which to pay for imports. It will depend on the whole military and diplomatic situation whether such a physical blockade is sufficient to achieve this purpose. At the outbreak of the present war, the existence of a large number of neutrals made it clear that active economic warfare would involve more than the imposition of a blockade and the use of appropriate economic and military means for enforcing it. The British blockade was supplemented from the very beginning by a carefully planned program of trade agreements with neutrals for which the " dog in the manger " was the inspiration. In addition to assurances that British exports would not find their way to the enemy, the agreements provided for large purchases from neutrals in order to prevent their products from being sold to the enemy.

These agreements have been very numerous and have covered single transactions and trade in particular commodities as well as the entire volume of trade with an individual country. It is not possible to list them all here or to discuss their details, since the rapidly changing diplomatic and military situation has caused, and is causing, continual modifications in them. Indeed, some agreements have remained dead letters because they were overtaken by events. But a few individual trade negotiations and agreements may be mentioned to illustrate some of the above-mentioned principles of economic warfare. We shall see presently that a number of important additional considerations were involved in these trade agreements; and we shall also discuss some of the difficulties which Britain encountered in her efforts to push this trade policy.

Within the first eight months of war Britain had concluded agreements with, among others, Turkey, Rumania, Greece, Belgium, Luxemburg, Switzerland, Spain, Norway, Sweden, and a number of South American countries. Apart from provisions relating to foreign exchange and payments (which are discussed below), the general framework of these treaties is broadly similar. While no details have been made public, it is known that all included reference to specific commodities and the quantities in which these were to be exchanged between the parties. For example, the pact with Turkey, signed on February 3, 1940, provided for the sale by Britain of airplanes, machinery, cotton, and other war materials in exchange for Turkish supplies of raw materials, including tobacco and dried fruit. The treaty with Spain, concluded a few weeks later, was designed to enable Spain to obtain such products as coal and machinery from Britain as well as important supplies (including oil) from the Sterling Area, while Britain was to expand her imports from Spain particularly of iron ore, pyrites, and fruit. The agreement with Switzerland, signed towards the end of April, was an interesting example of joint action between Britain and France. Like the agreements with Luxemburg and Belgium, it was entered into by the Allies jointly and was regarded as indicative of the greater concessions which they could jointly offer, and the greater pressure which their cooperation could exert. This agreement, too, provides for the sale to Switzerland of certain raw materials and some finished goods required by Swiss industry in return for purchases of various manufactures. Both this treaty and that with Spain contained clauses assuring Britain that her exports would not be re-exported to Germany.

III. It is to be remembered that many of the problems which formed the subject of negotiations were not connected with the blockade. For one thing, as has already been pointed out, Britain tried for a considerable time to enlarge her export markets, particularly in South America. In addition, much negotiation has been made necessary by the severe limitations upon certain non-essential imports and the criticism which these have called forth from former suppliers. More complex are the kinds of prohibitions or restrictions resulting not so much from the drive to confine imports to goods essential for the prosecution of the war, or from regulation of trade for political reasons, as from the need to achieve the optimum use of existing foreign balances and of funds accruing from current exports. These particular prohibitions and restrictions must, therefore, be considered in relation to foreign exchange policy in general.

The control of foreign exchange dealings, which constitutes one of the most powerful single means of foreign trade regulation even in time of peace, has been used as a vital supplement to the measures of direct wartime intervention. Since such control is comprehensive, it illustrates the chief trade problems of war more clearly than any other instrument of policy. It is, therefore, worthwhile to trace the evolution of Britain's exchange policy in some detail.

The pound sterling had been under pressure since early in 1938. But from the end of 1938 until the end of August 1939 (and particularly from March to August 1939) the rate maintained comparative stability round a figure of $4.68 as the result of continuous intervention by the British Exchange Equalization Account and a consequent very heavy loss of gold and foreign exchange resources. The approach and outbreak of the present war caused a steep fall in sterling. The rate slipped to $4.12 on August 28 when the authorities abandoned their support. It recovered at the end of the month but fell again to $4.075 on September 5. On that day, exchange control was instituted and an official rate established.

The first phase of British wartime exchange control lasted until January 8, 1940. Its measures can be briefly summarized as follows. The immediate step taken by the monetary authorities was the establishment of an official foreign exchange market, maintained by the Bank of England and by authorized dealers, in which official buying and selling rates for sterling were fixed. These rates were $4.02 — $4.06 to begin with; were later narrowed to $4.02 — $4.04; and later still the range was further reduced to $4.02½ — $4.03½. A series of regulations were issued designed to bring the bulk of foreign exchange transactions within the official market. Residents in the United Kingdom were obliged to sell to the authorities any funds they possessed or afterwards acquired in ten specified currencies at the officially established rates; and they were not allowed to deal in these currencies outside the official market.[46] The purposes for which foreign exchange could be obtained from the authorities (imports, payments of past debts, travelling expenses, etc.) were carefully circumscribed and made subject to a stringent system of licensing. The regulations were designed to make capital exports by residents impossible. By an earlier order, holders of securities in the specified currencies were required to register their holdings with the authorities and power was taken to order the sale of these holdings to the authorities. This power was exercised on February 8, 1940, with respect to 60 securities; and on April 14, 1940, another 112 securities were added to the list.

Combined with the regulation of imports, the exchange control set up a series of priorities of import sources and gave a general preference to imports invoiced in sterling. In the first place, all imports were discouraged (except, of course, those vital materials of war which the government itself had to obtain from abroad). Next to the preference for United Kingdom goods stood that for products of the Empire (including Canada). In the trade with these countries, sterling was the currency used; and in any case, the Empire had also instituted exchange control which was closely coordinated with that of Britain. France figured next as a preferred source of imports. Indeed, while the alliance lasted, France was fast becoming an integral part of the economic system of the British Empire.[47]

The fourth place in the list of sources of imports under the scheme of trade and exchange control was occupied by countries with whom Britain had concluded special treaties, such as Sweden, Spain, Turkey, Rumania and countries in South America. These treaties regulated the disposal of sterling exchange which the countries concerned were acquiring through their exports to Britain. Some examples may be mentioned to illustrate the principles involved. The agreement with Spain provided in the first place for a loan. The British Government agreed to lend £1.5 million which, added to the £2 million of Spanish funds accumulated in Britain and immobilized in the clearing account since 1936, would be applied to liquidate one-half of the £7 million of past

[46] These specified currencies were: United States dollars, Netherlands guilders, Dutch East Indies guilders, Swiss francs, belgas, Canadian dollars, French francs, Swedish kroner, Norwegian kroner and Argentine pesos.

[47] Of this tendency, the currency agreement between Britain and France concluded in December 1939 was the most visible symptom. It pegged the exchange at 176.5 francs to the pound and postponed the transfer of any balance in the transactions between the two countries until after the war.

debts to Britain frozen in Spain. The British Government also agreed to lend a further sum of £2 million to finance fresh Spanish purchases in the Sterling Area. The payments agreement proper in this treaty stipulated that the service on the above loan (consisting of interest until 1942 and thereafter of repayment of principal in ten equal annual instalments) should be the first charge on the sterling proceeds of Spanish exports. Of the balance, 45 percent was to be applied to the purchase of goods and the payment of shipping freights in the United Kingdom. Another 45 percent was reserved for purchases from United Kingdom firms of goods from specified parts of the Sterling Area. The remaining 10 percent was available for such payments as insurance premiums and royalties.

The treaty with Norway was said to have consisted of an agreement for a pound for pound clearing, thus reserving all sterling proceeds of Norwegian exports for purchases in the Sterling Area. Such a provision would be impossible in the case of a country whose balance of payments with the whole Sterling Area was normally in that country's favor, unless recourse was had to the more extreme measures of the German technique of bilateralism. Britain recognized this difficulty in her agreement with Sweden. This treaty allowed Sweden the use of sterling balances for purchases in two specified non-sterling markets, Belgium and Brazil, whose balances of payments with Sweden were complementary to those with the countries in the Sterling Area. Such concession means the loss of some exchange, and Britain has naturally been anxious to avoid it wherever possible.

Canada, although a part of the Empire, stood only fifth on the list, because she lay within the dollar currency area. A modification in this situation was, however, introduced when the Canadian exchange regulations were amended so as to permit exports to countries in the Sterling Area to be invoiced in Canadian dollars or in sterling (the general rule being that all exports had to be invoiced in United States dollars or in freely convertible currencies). Moreover, the bulk of the trade with Canada has been the subject of special arrangements.

Sixth and last on the list were the countries with free currencies with which no special payments or clearing agreement had been concluded. Of these, by far the most important was the United States. Since the United States is also the most important source of supply for most of the essential war materials, notably airplanes, the British authorities have been particularly assiduous in their efforts to husband their American dollar resources. This has been done by administration of the general import licensing regulations, by special prohibitions and restrictions, as well as by the exercise of the exchange control. In addition, there has been an increasing tendency to concentrate all British trade with the United States (or, at any rate, all British purchases in the United States) in the hands of government agencies.

The subsequent development of the British exchange regulations can be seen in retrospect as a tightening up of the control through a gradual restriction of both the supply and demand of sterling outside the officially established channels. This development is most usefully discussed in connection with the conflicting views regarding the most effective exchange and trade policy in wartime. At this point, therefore, a brief summary of the main changes since January 1940 may suffice.

The original regulations were far from completely watertight. In the first place, a free market continued to exist for all currencies other than the ten specified ones. This, however, was comparatively unimportant. What was much more important was that supplies of, and demands for, sterling could arise and meet outside the official market. One part of the supply came from non-residents who held sterling balances at the outbreak of war and who, although they could not obtain foreign exchange from the authorities, could liquidate their holdings if they could find other non-residents willing to buy these sterling balances. This supply was replenished by the proceeds of those foreign exports to Britain which were invoiced in sterling — as most of them were, especially those from countries with weak currencies. The foreign exporter could liquidate his sterling by selling it to some other non-resident account. The demand for this supply of non-resident sterling balances came from all those who had commitments in sterling to meet. Since the bulk of British exports had normally been invoiced in sterling and nothing in the first phase of exchange control interfered with that practice, there was a continuous demand for sterling from foreign buyers of British goods. With a stream of offers coming from non-residents anxious to liquidate their sterling holdings, even at a rate lower than the official one (of which they could not take advantage), and a demand originating from importers of British goods, a market for sterling outside the official one arose. In this free market, the one in New York being the most important, sterling was quoted at a fluctuating and often very considerable discount, and through it much exchange was lost to the authorities.

The first step towards abolishing this free market was taken in an order which from January 8, 1940 made very much more difficult than before the transfer of sterling from resident to non-resident accounts. Ten specific kinds of permitted transactions were laid down, and authorized exchange dealers were required to satisfy themselves by documentary evidence that any application was covered by the list. This restriction of the supply was followed by an order on March 7, 1940, which greatly reduced the demand for free sterling. It was laid down that as from March 25, 1940, all British exports of whisky, furs, rubber, tin, jute, and diamonds had either to be invoiced in United States dollars or, if invoiced in sterling, the authorities had to be satisfied that the sterling had been obtained from official sources, i.e., at the official rate. Since the six commodities constituted an important part of the exports from the Sterling Area, particularly to the United States, this meant that the demand for free sterling was severely curtailed.

The next landmark was June 7, 1940, when simultaneously a new and drastic diminution of the supply and demand of free sterling was brought about. Sales of British securities by non-residents (a source of disposable non-resident sterling balances) were prohibited. At the same time, it was decreed that all British exports to the United States and Switzerland had to be paid for in United States dollars, Swiss francs or official sterling.

The scope of the free market was so greatly reduced by these means that on June 11, 1940, the British authorities felt justified in asking the New York foreign exchange market to cooperate with them in making the official rate universally applicable. By July 18, 1940, the negotiations to this end had been concluded, and a scheme was announced by which virtually all transactions involving payments between Britain and the United States were to be settled through registered accounts and at the official rate. As a coping stone to this finished building of exchange control, there was added on August 21, 1940, an order prohibiting the import into the United Kingdom of British bank notes. While this order was designed to prevent the Germans from benefitting from any British notes seized in the territories occupied by them, it also closed one of the few remaining small loopholes in the system of exchange control.

The fact that exchange control is now practically all-inclusive, makes a discussion of some of the problems of policy somewhat academic. Nevertheless, the issues raised in the course of the evolution of the control are not without their practical importance for the future and form an important part in the whole scheme of trade policy in wartime. To the general problems of this policy we must now turn.

3. The Problem of Policy

I. In this section an attempt is made to deal briefly with the broader issues of wartime trade policy in the light of the factual summary already given. The subject cannot be discussed here exhaustively; and even a short analysis of its chief points is difficult. Policy in wartime is surrounded by secrecy. Details of agreements actually concluded are seldom published; and little information is made available on the course of negotiations with other countries. Reasons for particular actions and measures have been given from time to time; but they have rarely been either simultaneous with action or fully exhaustive when they have been publicly stated. Such official reticence on foreign trade matters is only to be expected, since policy in the economic sphere is regarded as being no different in essence from military policy. But the commentator's function is, as a result, often little more than guesswork.

Again, the concrete conditions of the war have been changing very rapidly, particularly after the comparative calm of the first six or seven months; critical comments on policy as it appears to be at any moment, as well as proposals for new measures, have, therefore, become inappropriate almost as soon as they have been made. Finally, it must be remembered that there are no " pure " foreign trade problems; they are to be regarded as one aspect only of a complex of problems of which all the parts are intimately linked together.

There is much interplay between economic, military, and diplomatic considerations in determining policy. An obvious example is that of the blockade. It is clear that the military and naval possibilities will be the first to be taken into account. Thereafter two questions arise: How far has military effectiveness to be supplemented, and by what means? and to what extent do diplomatic and economic considerations make it advisable not to do everything that military power makes practicable? Even recondite connections, though they may sometimes be ignored by those who make policy, should not be overlooked by the student. It is well to remember that foreign trade is peculiarly fitted to be thought of in connection with the major issues of the war. The future of the domestic economic and social structure, the machinery of political control, the future of the colonies, the relations with the dominions, the whole complex of problems embraced by the term imperialism, no less than the narrower trade problems, as, for example, the future of sterling or London's financial position after the war, obtrude themselves strongly into any study of the appropriate technique of wartime foreign trade.

One of the most striking expressions of the intimate connection between different parts of war policy is to be found in the long *versus* short war debate. As will be shown below, the slow evolution of a 100 percent exchange control and the slowness with which foreign assets were apparently liquidated in the early stages of the war, are examples of policies which were in part influenced by a belief in a long war of slowly gathering momentum. A strong belief, on the other hand, that the war would be short and intensive should have led to the placing of all the emphasis on military factors. Existing reserves of food in Britain would then have been considered adequate and no question about securing a continuous stream of food from abroad would have arisen. The ultimate effects of the war upon the position of London as an international financial center or upon Britain's share of exports markets would not have weighed seriously in the determination of day-to-day trade policy. Probably, too, there would have been less incentive to respect meticulously the feelings of neutrals in the application of the blockade.

Nevertheless, some basic economic facts remain even when all allowance has been made for the close interdependence of all aspects of war policy. Apart from the necessities of the blockade, we may say that dependence upon foreign supplies of certain goods is the most important of these basic facts. The amount of food, of raw materials, and of manufactured war materials, such as airplanes and munitions, that has to be imported is not an unchangeable magnitude. It will depend in part upon certain objective conditions (shipping space, efficiency of the convoy system, damage to domestic industry resulting from bombing, etc.). But it will also be affected by policy; and this, in its turn, will be influenced both by expectations (for example, about the duration of the war) as well as by decisions on such points as what amount of consumers' goods production is to be maintained, to what extent food is to be imported for the purpose of building up reserves, or how quickly available foreign exchange is to be used up. However, given a number of definite objective conditions and decisions on matters of policy, there will be a determinate amount of foreign goods which will have to be imported. This determines foreign exchange needs, and so provides one part of the data upon which exchange and export and import policy are based. The other part of the data by the means of which policy will be determined is to be looked for in any desires that may exist to achieve certain more distant objectives as, for example, the safeguarding of foreign markets in the postwar future.

II. It is unlikely that in practice the problem has always presented itself to those in power in quite this way. But for purposes of analysis, some such logical approach will be found a convenient method. The first expression of the trade problem would thus be financial. The questions to be asked would be: What funds are immediately available for foreign purchases? how can they best be mobilized? and at what rate, and in what manner, are they to be used up? We have already seen the data available for answering this question, that is, the actual amount of British-owned dollar assets. The liquid foreign balances of British nationals were acquired by the government, as we have seen, immediately after the outbreak of war; and the exchange control, even in its early incomplete form, channeled all foreign exchange newly acquired by residents into government uses. The compulsory sale to the government of foreign securities held by residents followed after a considerable interval. The first list of February 1940 was confined to minor issues that were not very actively dealt in; but the second list was much more comprehensive and important. The gradualness of the application of the government's powers in this field was designed to make the acquiescence of those affected more certain and to avoid friction in important respects. The initial purchase of minor and inactive securities, combined with declarations that "orderly selling" was the policy of the British authorities, was designed to reassure the New York market that it would not be upset by any hasty British action. The authorities also showed themselves anxious to act by agreement rather than decree in allowing alien residents to apply for exemptions from the order to sell foreign securities, and in exempting altogether certain American holders who were resident in Britain.

The question of the rate at which these foreign assets have been used is a separate one. It is not possible to state with complete precision what the pace of liquidation has been. On this point, a distinction must be drawn between the earlier part of the war when a somewhat lax exchange control coincided with the absence of extensive military operations and the later stage.[48] A particularly well-informed writer made an estimate in May 1940 of the British gold and foreign exchange loss during the first six months of the war. The method was to estimate the foreign exchange needs in terms of the excess of current imports from hard currency countries over exports productive of " good " foreign exchange, and to deduct from that the estimated gold and foreign exchange receipts (mainly from newly produced gold of the sterling Empire and liquidation of foreign holdings and cash balances). The result was an estimated loss of gold or foreign exchange reserves, during the first six months, of $250,000,000.

It was pointed out that, while such a depletion was small in itself, it was kept at a low level by so rapid a liquidation of assets that the British authorities were unlikely to allow it to proceed for long. In the light of this interpretation, the tightening-up of exchange control which set in with the order of March 7, 1940, and which was quickly completed, could be regarded as a means of husbanding foreign assets more carefully and of covering a larger part of the current exchange outflow by current exchange acquisitions. This may well represent a fairly accurate description of the attitude of the British authorities at that stage of the war. The loopholes left in the original exchange control machinery were substantial, and considerable criticism was voiced in Britain of the waste of exchange resources which the British authorities were permitting. In the United States criticism was directed mainly against the apparent reluctance of the British authorities to make full and immediate use of their foreign investments for purchases of war materials in the United States.

The official British answer was never publicly stated, but it can nevertheless be presumed to have been in some such terms as these. Britain had to try and preserve as much of her foreign investments as possible for the sake of the postwar future. Britain, it could be argued, would then be badly in need of foreign supplies of food, materials for reconstruction, and industrial raw materials, and she would need the income from these foreign investments to finance many of her imports from abroad.

By the early months of 1941 the picture of Britain's relative financial strength was greatly altered. The intensification of the war had brought

---

[48] It has, for example, been suggested that voluntary liquidation of American securities from British sources, prior to the execution of the Government's scheme, amounted to $95,000,000 during the first three months of the war. This gives an indication of the amount of foreign exchange reaching the authorities from one source.

about a considerable change in the extent of British foreign investments and in the official attitude concerning their liquidation. In January 1941 the Secretary of the Treasury of the United States presented to the House Committee on Foreign Affairs in the course of its hearings on the Lend-Lease Bill, a statement of Britain's financial position. According to official statements, the net amount which the Sterling Area had to meet in gold and dollars during the first sixteen months of the war was $3,281,000,000. Of this total, $965,000,000 was covered by gold newly mined or dishoarded in the area, leaving a net drain on resources held at the outbreak of war of $2,316,000,000. This represented about half the prewar total. Allowing for minor differences of estimation and for minimum reserves necessary for the maintenance of current business, it was found that between $1,700,000,000 and $1,800,000,000 remained available to cover an estimated minimum net debit balance for 1941 of $1,500,000,000.

There has been some controversy over these figures and over the obvious political implication which they hold. With that controversy we are not here concerned. But whatever view one may take of the true extent of financial resources remaining available to Britain for purchases in the United States, it must be clear that considerable resources have in fact already been used up. The rapidly rising cost of the war, the increasing need for American supplies, the greater difficulty of producing exports and of transporting them, are all tending to increase the absolute demand for, as well as its relation to the current supply of, dollars. The total picture of this change in the relative financial position of Britain and the United States is fortified by such partial details as the sale of British direct investments in the United States, which was initiated in March 1941 by the disposal of the British holdings in the American Viscose Corporation, valued at $100,000,000.

The question of the future disposal of what resources remain is also very controversial. Leaving aside the more obviously political arguments, there are still profound economic problems involved in the possibility of a complete exhaustion of Britain's foreign assets. This is not the proper place for a discussion of these problems, since they are essentially problems of the postwar future. One's view of them will depend on the kind of postwar world which one posits or desires. If the premise is that of a restoration of an international trading system based to a large extent on countries which maintain a system of capitalist enterprise, then the transfer of Britain's foreign investments to the United

States must raise a vast problem of readjustment of traditional American economic policy. It can be easily seen how difficult it would be to fit such facts as the traditional American protectionist policy and the small experience of (and, possibly, aversion to) foreign lending, to say nothing of the fairly constant export surplus and the small relative importance to the United States of her foreign trade, with a newly acquired position of being the world's largest foreign creditor.

III.   The most economical use of foreign resources readily available as a capital fund is only one of the problems of international war finance. In the case of countries with negligible foreign assets this problem does not even arise. Equally important is the maximization of current foreign receipts and their most economical use. This is the problem of export trade and exchange policy. We have seen the steps by which a solution of this problem was in fact reached. A brief summary of conflicting theories of the matter may now be added.

Much of the early discussion of the British exchange control was concerned with pointing out deficiencies in the mechanism and the waste of foreign exchange which resulted. It could be argued that the policy of granting import licenses more readily when the imports were invoiced in sterling created a continuous supply of sterling for the free market. Since sterling could be freely transferred from one non-resident to another, there was, as one writer said, a " basic contradiction " between the desire to husband dollar resources (through exchange control) and the desire to preserve the international character of sterling (by putting a premium on the invoicing of imports in sterling). Of a similarly contradictory character, it was said, was the action of allowing sterling to depreciate after the institution of control. Before control is established, a fall in the value of the currency acts as a deterrent to the export of capital. Afterwards, the control itself should be effective enough to stop such exports, which, it was claimed, was not the case. Such criticism seems logical enough. But when it is remembered that the authorities had to keep more than one objective in view, the difficulty of the situation can be more clearly realized. A contradictory policy becomes, then, merely the expression of an essentially contradictory situation.

One alternative before the British Government at the outbreak of war was to institute a full-fledged system of trade and exchange control which would have been fairly similar to that existing in Germany.

This would have meant the blocking of all balances in Britain and the creation of a number of different pounds at widely differing rates. It would have necessitated an aggressive drive towards a comprehensive system of bilateral trade agreements, and all the political and economic friction with neutrals which that would have involved. It would have roused considerable antagonism in the United States, at any rate in the short run, while in the long run it might well have destroyed forever the international financial position of London.

It is not the purpose of this study to examine the question whether the authorities were wise, especially in view of the course which the war subsequently took, to have let the above-mentioned considerations weigh in the determination of policy. But it seems certain that these considerations were in fact taken into account. Any realistic study must recognize that the British Government could not be expected, at the outset of the war when the exact alignment of all the different forces was still quite obscure, to take irrevocable, "logical" decisions on such fundamental issues as the whole future of British world financial supremacy. It can be, and has been, argued that the conditions in which the present war arose were such that Britain had to recognize the economic supremacy of the United States. As a condition of winning the war against Germany, Britain had to resign herself to a loss of her predominant position in international finance. Whether that is a true analysis of world economic forces or not, it would be naïve to suppose that the British authorities would accept and act upon such an assumption at the outset, and at a time when the United States was still neutral.

An explanation of the incompleteness and slow development of exchange control can be given in some such terms as these. To allow a free market in sterling to develop was to effect a compromise between completely prohibiting the withdrawal of foreign balances (which would have been fatal to London's international status), and making foreign exchange freely available at the official rate to all those non-residents who wished to withdraw their funds (which would have been far too costly). By creating a supply of free sterling and not interfering with the demand for it from foreign buyers of British goods, a liquidation of the "hottest" foreign balances in London could be effected without benefit of the official rate. It must, moreover, be remembered that the Sterling Area, with the addition at that time of France and her Empire, was excluded from this mechanism owing to the existence of coordinated exchange control and the special agreement with France.

London remained, therefore, the international banker and international debtor as far as that area was concerned. In relation to the non-sterling world, London became a short-term creditor; and this division made for greater elasticity and technical financial strength.

It may be that it was not necessary to go so far as to increase the supply of free sterling by favoring sterling-invoiced imports. But here, too, the authorities' desire seems clearly to have been to delay doing anything that would undermine the international status of sterling until they were absolutely forced to do so. In any case, the whole policy was a transitional one designed mainly to gain time. It made it possible to conclude special arrangements with individual large holders of sterling, and to explore the possibility of additional clearing agreements with different countries. We have also seen that from an early stage measures designed to tighten the control and to reduce the scope of the free market were introduced.

To explain the initial actions of the authorities in this way is to emphasize the difficulty of the situation which confronted the British Government. It is not intended to deny either that the actions lacked consistency or that they involved a considerable cost. The most important of the undesirable results of temporization was its effect upon the domestic price structure. The toleration of a free market for sterling undoubtedly increased the influence which depreciation had on the internal economic situation. It greatly encouraged inflationary tendencies, and has even been regarded by some as the chief cause of inflationary developments. The correlation between the British-American wholesale prices ratios and the pound/dollar free rate of exchange in the early months of the war is certainly very striking. While it is not possible to ascribe precise weights to all the influences at work, depreciation played an important part in giving wholesale prices that upward impetus which by January 1941 had carried them to a level 47.4 percent above the average of 1938.

The later evolution of exchange control has been in the direction of that greater completeness which critics demanded. This is true not only of the mechanism of control itself, but of the general principles of trade policy. The purpose of exchange control is not only to husband gold and foreign exchange, but also to make the country's terms of trade (that is, the ratio between the cost of imports and the proceeds of exports) as favorable as possible. Many writers have suggested (partly under the influence of the long history of German exchange control) that this aim might be achieved by maintaining, or even raising, the external value of sterling. One commentator has suggested that the best value of sterling would be nearer $5 than $4.

The reasons for this argument were as follows. Assuming that because of war-induced shortages, diversion of resources, and physical and economic limitation of shipping space, exports could not be increased, or even maintained at their prewar level, it must follow that depreciation could not give British exports a competitive advantage. Assuming further that foreigners' demand schedule for British goods had remained unchanged, the most effective policy for cheapening essential imports and avoiding inflation would be to raise the value of sterling by rigorous rationing of imports and consumption.

An examination of the relative depreciation of sterling in different countries was used to show the increased cost of imports due to depreciation; while the geographical distribution of British exports demonstrated that foreign demand for British goods, so far from falling, was likely to rise. All these data could then be made to support the policy of raising the dollar value of sterling.

The weakness of this proposal lies in the fact that once the pound had been allowed to depreciate, it would have required more than strict import control and rationing of consumption to raise the rate again. It seems clear that the cost of appreciation in terms of gold, foreign exchange, and foreign assets would have been very considerable. It was, therefore, a question of deciding whether the loss of goods due to the use of gold and other assets for the purpose of raising the exchange rate would have been more than offset by the gain of imports arising from a high value pound. It is doubtful whether a case can be made out for answering this question in the affirmative, especially in view of the increasing tendency — due to the very exigencies of the war — for imports to be more and more the subject of special deals, and for the decisive influence of the sterling rates in this respect to disappear.

The argument which has just been examined has the merit that it emphasizes the fallacy of assuming too lightly that depreciation of sterling would greatly encourage British exports. Of greater significance, however, are those proposals which affect the whole system of wartime trade policy. These generally begin with a statement of the undesirable features of exchange depreciation. The conditions of production and transport in wartime, it is said, make depreciation ineffective as a means for balancing trade. Sharp depreciation, moreover, leads to domestic inflation and decreases the value of income from foreign assets, most of which, in Britain's case, are in sterling. Another disadvantage among the many that could be cited is that the indirect tax on imports which depreciation represents is particularly unjust at a time when only vital necessities are supposed to be imported.

It is further pointed out that the elasticity of the demand for British goods varies from one country to another; that, therefore, the maximization of the terms of trade demands a policy of discrimination. Such a policy can be best executed by means of an extensive system of clearing agreements in which the value of the pound is fixed at as high a level as is politically practicable. This would cheapen imports and increase the proceeds of those exports with regard to which Britain is in a more or less monopolistic position. It has been argued that this policy would even increase the demand for competitive British exports in spite of the high pound, since the clearing partners would be forced (as many of them were under the German system) to spend funds accruing to them through their exports to Britain on the purchase of British goods.

The chief objection to this argument is derived from wider political, rather than from purely economic considerations. In the first place it must be remembered that, as has been frequently pointed out, the British Government would be slow to do anything which meant an irrevocable departure from that foreign trade mechanism through which London exercised its dominant position. The analogy of the supposed (but often controverted) success of German bilateralism would hardly be sufficient, since the conditions in which Britain was placed were quite different from those which caused Germany to adopt her clearing agreements policy. Britain's international position, which made it impossible for her to profit from the repudiation of debts, the structure of trade within the Empire, the possibility of intra-Imperial friction, the effect of any given policy on the United States, these and many other points would influence the decisions of the British Government. In particular, it may be pointed out that too aggressive a drive towards bilateralism (for example, in South America) would hardly have been well received by the United States, whose State Department had for long been committed to the defense of the most-favored-nation clause. And the United States itself, which was rapidly becoming Britain's most important supplier, was unlikely to join in a clearing agreement of the type envisaged.

Nevertheless, British policy did evolve slowly and cautiously in the way advocated by the protagonists of bilateralism. The number and range of trade and clearing agreements increased; and the order of March 7, 1940, which took six quasi-monopolistic commodities out of the depreciated free sterling market, can be regarded as a partial substitute for a clearing agreement with the United States. It increased the proceeds of exchange from the export of an important range of commodities and preserved for a time whatever stimulating effects the depreciated rate may have had on the export of competitive goods. The raising of the sterling price of monopolistic commodities, such as tin, which also happen to be greatly in demand in wartime, was another means of achieving the results of the German type of clearing agreement without provoking undue opposition.

Thus, in its practical working-out, exchange policy illustrates once again the close connection between the technical-economic, and the economico-political problem of warfare. A more detailed study than the present would, therefore, have examined Britain's relations with neutral countries in the light of the attitude of these countries to all the economic and political issues raised by the war. Britain had, for example, not concluded a trade agreement with the Soviet Union when that country was attacked by Germany, although negotiations had been going on for a considerable time. In the case of the United States, on the other hand, the absence of a comprehensive special wartime trade agreement did not prevent close cooperation. There was undoubtedly some friction, in the early stages, on such matters as the censorship of mails, the blockading of German exports, the problem of the exchange, British trade policy in South America, and many others; though no detailed official statement on these has ever been issued. But the general course of the measures adopted by the United States even in the early stages was characterized first by acquiescence in most of the major lines of British policy, including particularly the blockade, and later by active cooperation on an ever increasing scale. This cooperation was exemplified by the shipping provisions of the Neutrality Act and the raising of the embargo on arms shipments. Without such a broad conception of neutrality, the task of British economic warfare would have been made considerably more difficult.

4. Lend-Lease and After

On March 11, 1941 the Congress of the United States passed an Act "Further to promote the defense of the United States, and for other purposes." Its effect was immediately to alter Britain's wartime trade and, perhaps, to affect profoundly her postwar international economic relations. On June 22, 1941 Germany attacked the Soviet Union. That country became Britain's ally; and some of Britain's most difficult problems of trade and economic warfare were at once removed. In addition, entirely new prospects were opened up for the future alignment of international trade. On December 7, 1941 Japan attacked Pearl Harbor. Shortly thereafter the United States formally became a belligerent and Britain's ally; and within a few months great strides were made in the setting up of joint machinery for coordinating the economic activities of the two countries. These three great landmarks in the development of the present war mark the road which has led towards an increasingly planned and controlled international economic life of the United Nations and more particularly Great Britain.

Nothing illustrates these developments more than the great change in Britain's export policy. During the year 1941, the tendencies operative from the very beginning of the war were much accelerated. At the beginning of the year, British exports were still being fostered by an export drive which was served by all the usual means of advertising, good-will missions and the like, especially in South America and especially in regard to traditional export commodities such as cotton textiles. "Buy British" and "Britain delivers the goods" were the slogans heard at that time. Exchange pressure was particularly great, and it buttressed with the argument of national welfare a deep-seated commercial interest.

Even at that time, however, the more far-sighted observers realized that the export drive was bound to come up against powerful wartime obstacles, and that it could not for long be relied on as a contribution to solving Britain's exchange problem. Man power shortages became more and more acute. Material shortages became more and more acute. And facilities, too, were soon so strained that a concentration of civilian output in a few plants, with a conversion of the suitable remaining ones to direct war production, became an established policy. Finally, shipping movements and productive changes in other countries also made it increasingly difficult to harmonize import needs with the export drive. Military developments and the decline in import capacity due to sinkings necessitated diversions of mercantile tonnage in accordance with basic raw material and food import requirements, thus frequently making nugatory the efforts to expand exports.

The exchange problem was, of course, aggravated by these developments, and it was clear that a vicious circle was created which somehow had to be broken. Lend-Lease was the solution. It opened up to Britain a vast import potential which was not tied to Britain's ability to supply dollars for her overseas purchases. It immediately relieved the exchange pressure and permitted that relaxation in Britain's export drive which was in any case called for by fundamental wartime supply problems.

Lend-Lease took "the dollar-sign" out of U. S.-British trade and transferred the problem of international exchange between the two countries onto an entirely different level. It did, of course, put in a different light the fundamental problem of the economic relations of the two countries, and it created a major problem of postwar settlement. But for the purpose of the successful prosecution of the war, at any rate, it did tear aside the monetary veil, and it thus meant a very considerable step in the direction of a general realization of the basic supply problems of war.

Lend-Lease had another, somewhat slower but even more direct effect on Britain's export policy. From the very beginning of operations under Lend-Lease, it became obvious that substantial political difficulties might be encountered if Britain's exports were not consciously re-directed in the light of the newly-created import reservoir which, in the first instance, at any rate, was being financed by the American taxpayer. The British Government was fully conscious of this problem and showed great anxiety to prevent any cause being given for accusations that Lend-Lease was being used as a convenient means for strengthening or enlarging British export markets. On September 10, 1941 the British Government issued a White Paper which contained a declaration of its export policy. According to this declaration, the British Government does not permit the use of Lend-Lease goods for the furtherance of private interests, but only for the prosecution of the war effort. The British Government declares that British exports are restricted to the irreducible minimum necessary to supply or obtain materials essential to the war effort. Finally, the British Government declares that subject to certain exceptions, due to the difficulty of physical segregation or to the need to supply Empire and Allied countries, Lend-Lease goods and goods in short supply in the United States, would not enter into Britain's export trade.

Nor were Britain's imports unaffected by the developments of the war and by the institution of Lend-Lease. The latter allowed the creation of more rational import programs based on the all-important supply and shipping considerations rather than on the, in wartime, meaningless availability of foreign exchange. In general, it meant a vast increase in imports from the United States. The great increase in food imports from the United States illustrates best perhaps the supremacy of the need for shipping economy over the more normal commercial factors in international trade. As for the concentration of imports on goods essential for the prosecution of the war, the more recent developments of the war have merely intensified a tendency which, happily, had been in existence from the very beginning. What few nonessential imports remained, were completely eliminated after the fall of France. Strategic developments have, of course, also resulted in considerable shifts in sources of supply. The war in the Pacific, in particular, has cut out many imports and has in many instances resulted in changes in the geographical distribution of trade.[49]

As might be expected, so great a change in the relations between the United States and Britain as that occasioned by Lend-Lease could not take place without some measure of friction. Criticism has existed on both sides. Frequently it was misinformed or political in the narrowest sense. But occasionally there was also some genuine fear that vested commercial interests or undue concern with their relative postwar position was interfering with the countries' pursuit of the most rational and effective war policy. It is easy to see how the question of British policy outlined in the White Paper might become the basis of charges by both sides that foreign trade was being manipulated in accordance with ulterior motives.

It would be foolish to shut one's eyes to the existence of such criticism, particularly since it is now a thing of the past. Since the entry of the United States into the war, a number of developments have occurred which have immeasurably strengthened the tendency for emphasizing direct supply considerations which was inaugurated by the Lend-Lease Act. In the first place, there has been a substantial conversion of U. S.

---

[49] It is not possible to give figures, since statistics of the changes here discussed are now, quite properly, secret.

industry to war production with a consequent decline in the possibility of holding or winning export markets. Secondly, imports are increasingly controlled by war necessities. Thirdly, and perhaps most important of all, shipping has become as much an overriding factor for the United States — and for the other United Nations — as it was for Great Britain. This again meant that commercial motives of trade had to fall into the background. It is hardly possible now for Britain and the United States to accuse each other of trying to get new markets. They have too good an appreciation of each other's supply and production problems. It is, for example, notorious that Britain's exports to South America have fallen considerably while her imports from South America have increased, with a consequent large increase in the sterling balances held by South American countries. Even if she wanted to, it would not be possible for the United States to exploit this situation, since on grounds both of scarcities of man power and materials and of shipping shortage, the United States must strictly limit the goods which she can make available to South America.

This increasing congruence of the trading interests and possibilities of the two countries is becoming crystallized in the various combined boards created in Washington. Shipping, raw materials, food, production and resources, no less than military planning, come now increasingly within the purview of joint British and American organizations. There is, moreover, an increasing liaison with other United Nations. And, no doubt, before very long an even more direct joint planning by the two countries of their foreign trade — in so far as it is still of a civilian and commercial character — will be achieved and economic warfare in the narrower sense will thus become a joint effort. The British navicert, and the American export licensing system are already fully coordinated.

One powerful inducement to this general coordination, which is also a symptom of the progress already made, is the increase in what is often popularly referred to as " Reverse Lend-Lease." The present aid rendered by Great Britain and the British Empire consists both of goods — particularly of food and other material for U. S. forces overseas — and of services. No public statements have been made of the exact value of this reciprocal aid, but indications have been given that it is very considerable indeed. A general awareness of this aid and of the increase in U. S. production facilities called forth by British war orders of over $3,000,000,000 placed in the United States prior to Lend-Lease helps to remove the last traces of friction which Lend-Lease may have created. Reciprocal aid, moreover, is a powerful new concept and instrument of international exchange.

The United States has now signed so-called "Master Agreements" with a number of countries receiving Lend-Lease aid. That with Great Britain was concluded early in 1942. It is couched in only general terms as regards the "consideration" which is to be rendered for the Lend-Lease aid received. It does, however, bind the signatories to a mutual observance after the war of trade policies designed to work for "the expansion, by appropriate international and domestic measures, of production, employment, and the exchange and consumption of goods, which are the material foundations of the liberty and welfare of all peoples." The two nations also agree "to remove discrimination from trade, to work for the reduction of trade barriers, and to seek generally the attainment of the purposes set out in the Atlantic Charter." [50]

In addition, the United States concluded agreements for reciprocal aid with the United Kingdom, Australia, New Zealand, and Fighting France. These agreements, together with the protocol aid obligations towards Russia undertaken by the United Kingdom and the United States and the Canadian gift of $1,000,000,000 to the United Kingdom for the purchase of Canadian produce, may be cited as a few other outstanding symptoms of the emergence of a more complex mutual aid system among the Allies. The transformation of the original one-way flow of Lend-Lease from the United States to the United Kingdom into a more general system of mutual aid among all the Allies and the establishment of combined boards between the United Kingdom and the United States encourage one to hope that the basis has been laid for a brighter postwar future.

---

[50] See Appendix II.

CHAPTER V

Political Developments in Canada

by Gwendolen M. Carter

1. Before the Outbreak

In the last decade, doubt was often expressed that Canada would participate if another European war broke out in which Great Britain was engaged. This doubt was based on the independence of action of the senior Dominion, on Canada's geographical security and its proximity to the United States, and on the fear known to exist that participation in another conflict would strain Canadian unity to the breaking point. It underestimated both the strength of the British tie and Canadian awareness of the menace implicit in Nazism. The consciousness of a direct challenge in September 1939 bound surface divisions into a new and closer unity and in time resolved Canada's most delicate external problem, its close relations with the British Commonwealth of Nations and the United States.

These close relations are evident in economic life, where Canada's adverse balance of trade with the United States, the greatest source of its imports, is customarily met through its favorable sterling balance; in defense, where its geographical position makes it a pivot in the two defense systems of the British Navy and the Monroe Doctrine; in political and cultural fields, where the proximity of the United States is balanced by the British Commonwealth relationship and the less tangible links of tradition and sentiment. They provide external security but force Canada, for the preservation of its separate existence and individuality, to maintain a careful balance in external relations and to guard its internal unity.

Although different economic interests and racial backgrounds among Canada's 11½ million people have been reflected in policy, there has been no controversy over the continuance of the British connection, which all groups have accepted.

In the formative period before World War I, however, the relationship was interpreted somewhat differently by the two major parties, the Liberal, which under the leadership of Sir Wilfred Laurier dominated Quebec Province, and the Conservative, with a nucleus of "imperially minded" Canadians. The Liberals, though accepting the responsibility of Canada to go to the assistance of Great Britain in any major conflict, emphasized freedom of action, with the corollary that Canada had no right to influence British policy. The Conservatives supported a more positive policy of contributing aid to Britain, which they coupled with a claim to be consulted on British external policy.

The outbreak of war in 1914 found the Conservatives in office, but the wholehearted support of Laurier and the Liberals was pledged for the conflict. Unfortunately tactless handling of French-Canadian recruiting, their smaller proportion of enlistments, and other sources of internal friction caused growing feeling between English- and French-speaking Canadians which culminated in a struggle in 1917 over conscription for overseas service. In the ensuing election, parties divided on racial lines, an English-speaking Government facing a French-speaking Opposition. In the months following only wise leadership on both sides prevented active trouble. The experience was to cast a heavy shadow over future Canadian policy. A deep suspicion of the Conservative Party's external policy lasted long in Quebec and in some western communities. Over and above this were fears never wholly dissipated in the postwar period: fear on the part of French Canada lest it should find itself again in isolation from the rest of the country, and fear of the permanent destruction of Canadian unity should such an issue again arise.

Despite the smallness of the Canadian military establishments in 1914, Canada raised an army of over 600,000 men. It also made itself a base of supply for munitions during World War I. This activity was largely the result of the efforts of the Imperial Munitions Board, an agency of the British Government set up in 1915, under whose direction

Canadian factories produced huge quantities of shells, some 3,000 airplanes, and a considerable number of ships. The sudden industrial expansion, which raised Canadian exports of manufactured goods to Great Britain from a value of $8,500,000 in 1913–14 to $339,000,000 in 1916–17, came at a moment when the Canadian economy could best respond to it. The opening of the prairies in the decade preceding World War I had concentrated Canadian activities on construction. The end of this period was in sight when the new military demands stimulated the transfer of Canadian resources to production. In the four years of the war Canada emerged as an industrial country.

The postwar reaction common to all belligerents was intensified in Canada by the memory of the conscription crisis. Canadian policy became marked by unwillingness to assume obligations which might imply participation in another conflict.

At the time of the Treaty of Lausanne it was maintained that there was a moral freedom of obligation under pacts which Canadian plenipotentiaries had not negotiated or signed. Parallel with efforts to avoid commitments were those to secure a more independent status; Canada led the movement which resulted in separate dominion membership in the League of Nations. By contrast, in the field of Anglo-American relations with which it is vitally concerned, Canada made one small but possibly decisive contribution through its opposition at the 1921 Imperial Conference to the renewal of the Anglo-Japanese Alliance which, it feared, might extend to Great Britain the tension existing between the United States and Japan. Through this opposition the way was paved for the British acceptance of the invitation to the Washington Conference, out of which evolved the new conception of relations in the Pacific area embodied in the Four-Power Treaty.

The course of events after the failure of the attempt to enforce collective security in 1936 shattered Canada's aloofness and led it " inevitably closer " to Great Britain and to the United States.

Collaboration was at first implicit rather than explicit. In the matter of form, Canada avoided commitments, especially in its relations with Great Britain. There was, for example, no attendance at the meetings of the Committee of Imperial Defense, a fact which inevitably complicated cooperation later on. In relation to the United States, responsibilities were immediate, for Canada like many other states had neglected its defenses in the postwar period. Further curtailment of defense expenditure during the depression left the country with virtually no formal means of protection. Even before President Roosevelt declared at Chautauqua in 1936, "We can defend ourselves, and we can defend our neighbourhood," the Canadian Government recognized the necessity of reorganizing Canada's defenses so that it might be able to assume its own responsibilities in continental defense.

The comprehensive plan adopted for this purpose placed priority upon the fortification of coastal areas, the Pacific being given precedence, indicated the Air Force as Canada's first line of defense and the Navy as the second, provided a reorganization of the non-permanent militia along more modern and realistic lines, and sponsored a small armament industry to make Canada more self-sufficient. The program was moderate in scope, but by September 1939 Canada, although by no means fully prepared, was in a better position to provide its own protection than on the eve of any previous war.

Despite the obvious emphasis on home defense, the program had not gone unchallenged by those groups which feared to be involved in British wars. Although the plans were introduced and carried through by the Liberal Ministry, some of this opposition came from Liberals. The election of 1935 had brought this party its greatest majority since Confederation, 180 seats out of 245 in the federal House of Commons. But its members included diverse elements, one-third sitting for French-speaking constituencies and others representing varied industrial and agricultural interests. Such a combination taxed even the powers of its veteran leader, the Right Honorable Mackenzie King, a skilled though cautious parliamentarian. His control of his party was made still more difficult by the personal antagonism of the Liberal Premier of Ontario, Mr. Hepburn, and by the success in 1936 in the Liberal stronghold of Quebec of a party supporting local nationalism and provincial rights, the *Union Nationale* under M. Duplessis, who threatened to work with Mr. Hepburn for the discomfiture of Mr. King. Even more outspoken was the opposition to the defense program voiced by members of the C.C.F. (Cooperative Commonwealth Federation) Party, a small but well-organized group pledged to a moderate socialist program aiming to unite farmers and the urban laboring class. In contrast, the few comments of the Conservative Party, which formed the official Opposition, although it was composed only of thirty-nine members, favored closer cooperation with British defense plans, particularly through building up the Navy.

The logic of events gradually developed a more unified opinion.

When President Roosevelt emphasized closer continental relations in the face of danger abroad, in a speech of August 18, 1938, at Queen's University, Kingston, Ontario, there was general approval throughout Canada. Agreement on joint responsibilities for continental defense prepared the way for other measures of Canadian-American collaboration. Negotiations were reopened over the St. Lawrence Waterway scheme, there was further investigation of possible routes for an Alaska Highway, an invitation to an Inter-American Travel Conference was accepted (the first time the Canadian Government had participated in such inter-American activity), and the Canadian tariff structure was substantially modified to facilitate the Anglo-American Trade Agreement of November 1938.

The Canadian Ministry cautiously avoided committing itself on European events in the period which culminated in the Czechoslovakian crisis in the fall of 1938, but this was, in part, because though it was aware of the dangers of the situation, the country at large was not. The occupation of Prague brought from Mr. King a forecast of particular importance in view of his customary reluctance to make specific statements, " If there were a prospect of an aggressor launching an attack on Britain with bombers raining death on London, I have no doubt what the decision of the Canadian people and Parliament would be. We would regard it as an act of aggression, menacing freedom in all parts of the British Commonwealth." The announcement of the German-Soviet Pact helped to convince most of French-speaking Canada of the need for a united front. In September 1939 there was general agreement that Canada itself must decide the part it should play in any war in which Great Britain was involved, that its contribution would be largely economic, and its military effort relatively small, that there should be no conscription for overseas service. Events were to modify considerably the last two of these points, but the general agreement at this time was in itself of the greatest importance.

On August 22, 1939, following news that the British Parliament had been summoned, Mr. King informed the leaders of the opposition parties of the seriousness of the situation and received from them expressions of the fullest support. The War Measures Act of 1914, which had never been repealed, was brought into operation, and a number of Orders-in-Council began the process of bringing Canada to a war footing. Parliament was called for September 7, and the Prime Minister announced that if the Government of the United Kingdom became involved in war in an effort to resist aggression, the Canadian Government would seek authority for effective cooperation by its side. Thus, when Great Britain declared war upon Germany on September 3, it was clear that Canada would soon come to its support.

2. The Early Stages of the War

The fulfillment of the pledge that Canada should participate in war only by action of its own Parliament delayed its formal entry but not its preparation for conflict.[1] Parliament met for formal consideration of active participation in the war on September 7. It was not yet clear what means would be taken to bring the country to a status of active belligerency, but on September 9 it was announced that acceptance of the Speech from the Throne would be regarded as approving immediate participation. On the same evening the address was adopted without a division. Immediately following adjournment, the Cabinet met and approved an Order-in-Council authorizing the Prime Minister to advise the King to approve the proclamation declaring a state of war. On Sunday morning, September 10, Canada was formally at war with Germany.

Canada was the only dominion which took this procedure in adopting active belligerency. The form was important for the unity and effectiveness of the Canadian effort, for it threw responsibility directly upon all members and parties within the House. At the same time it assured groups throughout the country that the Government did not intend to precipitate action on its own initiative. On the major issue of participation in war all parties agreed.

Over the type and extent of Canadian participation considerable divergence of opinion was expressed. Mr. King's own survey of Canada's probable major activities emphasized responsibility for the defense of Canada, Newfoundland, Labrador, and British and French territory in the Western Hemisphere. He foresaw overseas aid primarily through air personnel. But there was general acceptance by both Conservatives and Liberals that other direct military aid might be sent abroad. Emphasis was also laid in general on the voluntary character of contributions. M. Lapointe, Minister of Justice and Mr. King's chief French-Canadian lieutenant, made it clear that he and the other Cabinet members from Quebec made their support of the Government conditional

[1] See below, Chapter VII, p. 330.

on exclusion from the military program of conscription for overseas service.

Parliament was kept in session only long enough to pass the War Appropriations Bill of $100,000,000 for the prosecution of war activities, and taxation measures which indicated that the Government intended to follow a " pay-as-you-go " policy.[2] It was then adjourned indefinitely, to the disappointment of many of its members. The Government, however, with support pledged by the other parties, preferred to work through Orders-in-Council. In the succeeding weeks it laid the foundations for military and economic aid and developed administrative instruments for limiting the effect on the civilian population of war conditions.

The fact that Canada had not assumed active belligerency until after the calling of Parliament and the formal vote on the Address had been satisfying to most French-Canadian nationalists, while the interest of English Canadians in the same procedure brought a new sense of unity. But a dangerous threat to this growing understanding arose with the announcement on September 25 that the *Union Nationale* Premier of Quebec, M. Duplessis, was calling a general election, to secure a mandate to resist certain war measures. M. Lapointe and the other Federal Cabinet members from Quebec came to the support of the provincial Liberal Party, pointing out that they would treat the results as a vote of confidence in themselves and would resign if M. Duplessis were returned. Quebec was thus faced with the loss of its representation in the Federal Government if it supported M. Duplessis' program. Beyond this, the success of the Liberal Party, which was brought into office in Quebec at the election on October 25, was the expression of a general desire for the maintenance of Canadian unity.

As early as September 19 the public learned that an expeditionary force had been decided upon after consultation with the British Government. In addition it was planned to send as many trained aviators, doctors, engineers, and technicians as possible to be absorbed into British units. The Navy was ready when war began to take its part in the transatlantic convoy system, and on September 16 the first convoy sailed. Close collaboration led to Canadian and British warships being interchangeable as need demanded. In addition to this support there was the Air Force, which was seen from the beginning to be one of Canada's most important contributions to the allied war effort. The strate-

---

[2] See Chapter VI, pp. 310, 314.

gic situation of Canada for air training had already been recognized in an agreement announced in the spring of 1939, to give advanced flying training to fifty airmen a year from the United Kingdom. A plan of far wider scope for a great training center in Canada for airmen from the United Kingdom, Australia, and New Zealand, as well as from the Dominion, was proposed by the British Government and worked out in detail by technical missions sent to Canada by the other countries.

The British Commonwealth Air Training Plan, as agreed on in November and announced in December 1939, provided for the training in Canada of about 35,000 pilots, observers, and wireless-operator air gunners a year by the time the scheme reached its maximum proportions. About 20 percent of these were to come from the United Kingdom, Australia, and New Zealand for advanced training, while 80 percent of the personnel was to be recruited in Canada. The R.A.F. was to supply some of the training staff, but when the organization was in full operation most of the approximately 40,000 men required to man it were to be provided by Canada out of those first trained under the plan. Costs of the scheme were divided roughly in proportion to the number of men trained for each government. Most of the aircraft required were to be supplied by Great Britain as its contribution, although elementary trainers and certain other planes were to be built in Canada. Of the total cost, amounting, it was estimated, to $600,000,000 for the period of the agreement, to March 31, 1943, $350,000,000 was to be Canada's share.[3] In marked contrast to the practice during the First World War, when the Imperial Air Force undertook its own recruiting and training in Canada independently of the Dominion authority, the program was to be administered by the Canadian Government and to be under the control of the R.C.A.F. with the advice and assistance of a Supervisory Board nominated by the participating governments.[4]

The huge proportions of the plan made necessary vastly increased facilities for air training before it could come into full operation. When

---

[3] By May 1941 the cost estimate had risen to $824,000,000, of which Canada's share was $531,000,000, or more than its total revenue in a normal year. A new agreement extending the plan to March 31, 1945 was negotiated in May 1942. The cost from July 1942 through March 1945 is estimated at $1,500,000,000, of which Canada's share will be $750,000,000.

[4] The Supervisory Board is under the Chairmanship of the Minister of National Defense, and includes the Minister of Finance, the Minister of Transport, representatives of the Governments of the United Kingdom, Australia and New Zealand, the Deputy Minister for Air of the Department of National Defense, and the Chief of the Air Staff. Contact with the Canadian Government is maintained by the Board through its Chairman, and with the Royal Canadian Air Force through the Chief of the Air Staff.

fully organized the training was to be carried on in ninety-three schools which covered every aspect of air force work. Sixty new air fields were needed, and about twenty others had to be enlarged.

To indicate the scope of the task, it is necessary only to enumerate some of the special training demanded by the complex character of air operations. Adequate staffs for the flying schools necessitate highly skilled flying instructors and also officers of administration, equipment and accounting, wireless engineering, and armament, as well as operators, instructors, and armorers, each of whom requires special training in specially equipped schools. Provision had to be made for the training of mechanics to do the work of checking, overhauling, and repairing the aircraft used by the pilot pupils, while supplementary repair depots, equipment units, and schools for training motor-boat crewmen and aircraft inspectors had to be organized.

Recruits are assembled in manning depots where they receive two weeks' drill and a general introduction to air force work. The next stage is carried on in the initial training schools, where a course of five weeks is given in such subjects as air force law, mathematics, flight theory, mechanics, air armament, and physical training. After this the recruits are divided into three groups as pilots, observers, and wireless-operator air gunners.[5] In each branch extensive instruction in the special field is coupled with sufficient training in the others to make it possible to take over those duties in case of emergency.

Pilots begin in the elementary flying training schools with a seven weeks' course of instruction in the ground school and in the air. This is followed by ten weeks with intermediate and advanced training squadrons, flying service types of aircraft. Some of these schools concentrate on instruction in piloting fighter planes and others on training bomber pilots.[6] At this later stage, the Canadians are joined by the Australians, New Zealanders, and British, sent for advanced training under the plan after receiving elementary instruction in their own countries.

Observers, who chart the course of the plane and also aim the bombs on raids, spend fourteen weeks at an observers' school learning air nav-

---

[5] Prospective pilots must be between 18 and 31, while observers and wireless-operator air gunners must be between 18 and 33. Pilots and observers must have passed junior matriculation (University entrance) or equivalent, and wireless-operator air gunners must have completed successfully two years of High School.

[6] Originally, student pilots concluded with two weeks at a bombing and gunnery school for instruction in the use of machine guns and in bombing technique but this was later omitted. All the periods of training given are those in effect at the end of 1941 and represent some increase over the periods originally allowed.

igation, aerial photography and reconnaissance duties such as sketching, observation, and spotting enemy positions and concentrations, following this with six weeks at the bombing and gunnery school for special training in the use of bomb-sighting devices, as well as the handling of machine guns, and ending with four weeks in advanced air navigation. Wireless-operator air gunners, who maintain touch with home bases and handle the armament, begin their specialized training with twenty weeks in a wireless school, followed by four weeks in the bombing and gunnery school concentrated upon the use of machine guns and training in repairing them. After the completion of this training the three groups form an air crew pool, from which some are chosen as instructors and the rest assembled at embarkation depots. Once overseas, they receive operational training preparatory to active service.[7]

After the first enthusiasm, realization of the length of time required to bring the Air Training Plan under way soon brought criticism upon the Government for not having foreseen and begun to meet the need when the issue of training British pilots first arose. To this was added considerable criticism of the slowness of recruiting, inadequacies in the equipment of the soldiers, and above all the smallness of the orders coming to industry from abroad. While Canadian Government contracts from July 1, 1939, to March 31, 1940, totaled $176,000,000, the orders of the British Supply Board in Canada between October 20, 1939 and March 31, 1940, amounted only to $70,000,000 of which the major portion was not placed until the first quarter of 1940. Moreover, there was irritation at British slowness in releasing plans and patents, and at the difficulty of meeting apparently rigid specifications for which Canadian firms were not equipped. Impatience over the gap between the desire to give help and the opportunities being offered foreshadowed a vigorous indictment of the sins of omission and commission of the Liberal Ministry in the Parliamentary session, scheduled to open January 25, 1940. To the disapproval expressed in the statements of the federal Opposition leaders was added a vote of censure in the Ontario legislature on January 18, which was jointly sponsored by Mr. Hepburn, the Liberal Premier, and Colonel Drew, the Conservative opposition leader, and carried by a decisive majority of forty-four to ten. To the dismay of the Opposition leaders, Mr. King presently declared that this made it necessary to go to the country for a nation-wide vote of confidence. Despite protests at hav-

---

[7] Active service is undertaken in the R.A.F. or R.C.A.F. In May 1942 R.C.A.F. Headquarters overseas was given general supervision over R.C.A.F. personnel attached to the R.A.F.

ing to fight an election without having had a full discussion of the war effort, Mr. King, waiting only to defend his policy in general terms, decided upon a dissolution the evening of the day Parliament met.

The two months' campaign succeeding the sudden dissolution of Parliament centered about the extent of Canada's effort in the war. It was in the main a clear-cut battle between the two major parties, the Conservatives charging that more should have been done, particularly in preparation for the Air Training Plan, and Mr. King standing on the record of his Government and the unity it had commanded. The election on March 26 provided the somewhat unexpected result of a substantial increase to 53 percent of the popular vote for the Liberal Party as well as the retention of its overwhelming majority within the House. There was still impatience over the smallness of war orders from outside. But in the situation existing in March 1940 many groups felt it was neither wise nor necessary to ask Canada to increase its own war contribution. Beyond the satisfaction of at least a majority of the voters with what had been done was the feeling that the King Ministry provided the best possibility of preserving national unity through its hold upon the two great racial entities of the country and their support of its policies.

Events were beginning to move, however, in a direction which made the continuation of previous policies impossible. The occupation of Denmark and of Norway gave the military situation a new character. But from April on there was a growing appreciation in Canada of the need of Hemisphere defense and of extending increased aid abroad. The demands made upon British resources by the outcome of the Battles of Flanders and of France made it necessary to turn for as many additional supplies as possible to Canada. The pent-up impatience of a people which had found it difficult to understand why full use had not been made of its resources received a sudden outlet. This helps to explain the immediacy of the response to the new situation.

3. The Response to the German Westward Drive

The response of Canadian public opinion to the Norwegian campaign was in some respects more immediate than that in Britain. Satisfaction with the Government's program of limited participation was replaced in many quarters with demands for increased aid. To these, the attacks on Holland and Belgium gave a new intensity. On May 15 the German Army broke through the French lines, an ominous background for the first session of the dominion Parliament the following day. From the party point of view the Liberal Ministry, with the national election behind it and commanding 183 out of a total of 245 seats, appeared in a stronger position than in even the previous Parliament. The Conservative Party was numerically small, as was the C.C.F. Party, returned at its former strength of eight members, and the Social Credit group, reduced in numbers to eleven. The spur to action was not party activity but overseas events and national concern.

In an atmosphere of great tension, Mr. King announced to the House accelerated recruiting, with a full corps abroad as its eventual aim, and the organization of a veterans' home guard and reserve companies of veterans. The British Commonwealth Air Training Plan was to be speeded up with the aim of completing during 1940 the training establishments planned for construction in two years.

When this decision was taken the elementary training establishments were just coming into operation. The plan of using civilian flying facilities for this stage had been adopted from British experience. Each flying club throughout Canada was offered the sponsorship of a company to be incorporated with a capital of from $35,000 to $50,000 to operate an elementary flying school. The Government furnished the buildings and loaned aircraft, while the companies provided the management.[8]

Serious curtailment of the schedule was threatened by lack of advanced training planes, a large number of which had been expected from Great Britain but could not be sent. Full-scale elementary training was, however, continued and other aspects of the Plan accelerated in the hope that aircraft would eventually be forthcoming. The production of advanced trainer air frames that could take United States engines was begun in Canadian factories. A number of trainers intended originally for France were secured through the British Purchasing Commission in the United States, and some shipments from Britain were resumed in July, with the net result that there was no alteration of the form of the Training Plan and its pace was increased.

As the Battle of Flanders was lost and the withdrawal from Dunkirk

---

[8] For each four weeks period during which a group of seventy pupils was trained, the company received a fee of approximately $1400 to cover instruction, food and maintenance of the aircraft. In order to prevent excessive profits it was eventually decided that no company should be allowed to pay a dividend of more than 5 percent on the subscribed capital. The company's books are supervised and new arrangements are made about twice a year on the basis of the profits of the preceding period.

began, Canada extended all possible aid. The second R.C.A.F. contingent was sent abroad, arriving May 29. After the withdrawal from Dunkirk Canadian troops of the division already in England were landed in France, only to be immediately evacuated. Canadian destroyers were serving with the British Navy in United Kingdom waters. All available equipment was rushed overseas, including fighter planes in use by the R.C.A.F. Airplanes on order in Canada and in Great Britain were released for British use and bombers en route to Canada for use in the Air Training Plan were sent back to the United Kingdom. At the request of the British Government, Canadian troops were sent to the West Indies, to free British regular troops garrisoned there, and to Iceland.[9]

In no place did the separate French peace bring more potential complications than to Canada with its large French-speaking population. But under the leadership of Cardinal Villeneuve, M. Lapointe, and Premier Godbout of Quebec, the French-speaking elements threw their continued support behind the cause which they had adopted as their own.

Secure in this support, the Ministry assumed emergency powers to mobilize human and material resources for the defense of Canada under the new National Resources Mobilization Act. Stressing that the mobilization of man power would relate " solely and exclusively to the defense of Canada on our own soil and in our own territorial waters," [10] the Prime Minister repeated his pledge against conscription for overseas service at the same time that the Ministry of National Defense announced provision for compulsory military training. This training, largely because of the restricted training facilities available, was limited to one month. Subsequently the period of training was extended, but in any case, unlike the selective service plan later adopted in the United States, the measure was intended only to be supplementary to the main Canadian recruitment which is on a voluntary basis.

The seriousness of the issues faced in the new international situation stimulated demands for a national government to give united direction to a united effort and a war cabinet whose members would be free from departmental duties. Though the Prime Minister argued that the election returns had given a national mandate to the Liberal Party, he made tentative moves to satisfy these demands. Some well-known Con-

---

[9] On June 10, 1940, Italy declared war on Britain and France, and the following day the King approved the proclamation declaring a state of war between Canada and Italy " as and from the tenth day of June.

[10] House of Commons, *Official Report of Debates*, June 18, 1940.

servative business men who were not in Parliament were asked to take portfolios in the Government. Following their refusal, a limited number of the Liberal ministers were designated a War Committee,[11] and four of the leading figures of Opposition groups were offered associate membership in this body or, as an alternative, regular consultations with ministers. Leaders of the Conservative Party felt slighted, however, by the offers made to non-Parliamentary Conservatives and also considered that acceptance of either plan would hamper their freedom of action without giving them sufficient share in the formulation of policy. The leader of the C.C.F. Party also declined the proposals, and no further effort along these lines was made by the Prime Minister.

While Canada's defenses were being strengthened, as much as possible was spared for the overseas effort to which public opinion was almost wholly directed. Unknown to the public, however, discussions concerning Canada's place in the scheme of North American defense were being carried on in continuation of private conversations between President Roosevelt and Prime Minister King during the previous three and a half years. They were based on the cooperation between Canadians and Americans already evident in the Permanent International Joint Commission and the more recent plans for the Alaska Highway and the St. Lawrence Seaway. But they had far-reaching implications not only for Canadian-American relations but also for those between the United States and all parts of the British Commonwealth.

On August 18 announcement was made, during a meeting of the President and the Prime Minister at Ogdensburg, of an organization for joint defense which potentially brought Canada and the United States closer together than they had ever been before and made it virtually inevitable that such close relations should be permanent. The joint statement gave only the bare facts that a permanent joint board on defense, consisting of four or five members from each country, most of them from the services,[12] would be set up at once, to commence immediate studies relating to sea, land and air problems, including personnel and matériel and to consider " in the broad sense " the defense of the northern half of the Western Hemisphere. The Board's first report was made on October 4, and the public was told that a Boston-Halifax defense

---

[11] See below, Chapter VII, pp. 359–362.

[12] The Honorable Fiorello H. LaGuardia was made head of the United States section, and Colonel O. M. Biggar, C. C., of the Canadian section. Other members included representatives of the army, navy, and air services of both countries, and a secretary from both the Department of State and Department of External Affairs.

line of ships and airplanes was planned capable of meeting an invasion five hundred miles at sea.

The Permanent Joint Board on Defense is a consultative body, with no executive power. Its reports are confidential. It appears, however, that it considers the whole field of North American defense and that its advice has been followed closely. Though the full extent of its influence cannot be known, the significance of the first permanent defense board of its kind is undeniable.

The Ogdensburg Agreement was not an isolated move. Almost simultaneously Mr. Churchill announced the offer to the United States of ninety-nine-year leases for air and naval bases in Newfoundland and Bermuda. To this gift was added an agreement, announced September 3, whereby the right to acquire similar bases in the Bahamas, Jamaica, St. Lucia, Trinidad, Antigua, and British Guiana was acquired in consideration of the transfer to Great Britain of fifty over-age destroyers. Six of these destroyers became units of the Canadian Navy and were already commissioned by the end of September.

Behind the negotiations resulting in the offer of bases Canadian initiative may well lie. At least it is known that the offer of the Newfoundland base was made to the United States with Canada's special approval. Canadian troops had been garrisoning Newfoundland since the beginning of the war, but because of its limited sea power Canada needed further assistance in protecting that area. That responsibility was shared with the United States in an area so vital to Canadian defense was the best indication of the permanence of the defense relations signalized in the Ogdensburg Agreement.[13]

The consummation of the British-American arrangement gave a new perspective to the Ogdensburg Agreement. The fear that attention to the defense of Canada would detract from aid abroad gave way to a realization that they were part of a common problem and that the only question was one of proportion. The widening impact of war caused by the German drive to the west had demanded an intensification of effort in every sphere. The results could be measured not only in terms of men and matériel but also of planned cooperation on a scale unimagined before the great emergency was faced.

---

[13] Canada's special interest in Newfoundland was recognized in the Protocol added to the Bases Agreement, March 27, 1941 (Cmd. 6259).

4. Consolidation of Effort

For the year from June 1940 to June 1941, Canada was Great Britain's strongest ally and the one closest to it geographically. During this period, and indeed, throughout 1941, Canada held first place as an outside source of supply for British war needs, except in airplanes. Further aid in guarding the convoys of the North Atlantic was provided with Canadian naval expansion and the extension of American aid in this sphere. In September 1940 Canadian forces on active service at home and abroad amounted to nearly 200,000 men, of whom 161,000 were in the Army, 11,149 in the Navy, and 26,500 in the Air Force. In the next nine months unspectacular but steady development virtually doubled the size of the Navy, bringing the mobilized strength to more than 20,000 by July 1, 1941, and to over 200 vessels.

In air training a new development was the establishment, in the autumn of 1940, of R.A.F. air schools in Canada under the direction of the British Air Liaison Mission at Ottawa. They were later integrated with the larger training plan. The Commonwealth Air Training Plan was also expanding, and by July 1, 1941, all but 12 of its schools were in operation. For the first time, all available applicants were being accepted and installed in schools immediately after enlistment. It was planned to recruit 36,000 men in 1941, 7 to 10 percent of this number coming from the United States by midsummer. Training of other personnel was keeping pace, so that the twenty-five Canadian squadrons to join the R.A.F. in 1941 would be served by Canadian ground-crew and administrative staff.

In the dark days following Dunkirk, the Canadian division had been the most fully trained and equipped of the forces in England which might have had to meet invasion. It remained a matter of consistent policy to continue to send new Canadian units to Great Britain. On Christmas Eve 1940, the formation of a Canadian army corps overseas was announced, just a day before the eighth contingent reached the United Kingdom, and brought the Second Division to full strength. In the summer much of the Third Division joined them, and Canada's first tank brigade. By July, there were approximately 220,000 in the active Army, of whom about 100,000 were overseas.

The period of training under the compulsory military service program was extended from one month to four in February 1941. Before the first group under the four-month plan concluded their service, it was announced that all called up for training would be retained for the duration. About one-half of the trainees have volunteered for active service, and the rest are posted to home defense duties to relieve men of the active Army for overseas. Other relief was provided by the recruitment of a Canadian Women's Army Corps, parallel to Women's Auxiliary forces in the other branches, to take over such duties as those of drivers, cooks, clerks, and messengers. By July, the Reserve Army numbered about 170,000, approximately one-half of whom were on fulltime duty.

In the field of supply, the elaborate plant extension construction program [14] begun after the fall of France was bearing results but at the same time confronting serious scarcities which threatened to limit it. Within the country there was a shortage of skilled labor, of some raw materials, and of machine tools. As Canada turned more and more to the United States to make up its deficiencies in matériel, another even more serious block threatened — an exhaustion of Canadian funds with which to continue purchases in the United States. Since December 1940 Canada had borne the full burden of expenditure in the United States both for components for its own individual war contribution and for those needed for British orders from Canada.

The Lend-Lease Act of March 12, 1941, solved the serious situation which had been caused by Great Britain's financial stringency. Canada, however, preferred not to accept Lend-Lease aid if some other way could be found to meet its problems. That way became known through a joint statement by President Roosevelt and Prime Minister King, made on April 20, known as the Hyde Park Declaration. Though little publicized, it had far-reaching implications. It extended to the field of supply the principle of joint planning to provide not only for Hemisphere defense but also for aid to Great Britain and " the other democracies."

To meet Canada's immediate need for exchange there was to be more extensive buying by the United States of Canadian raw materials and supplies. Canadian purchases from the United States for use in British war orders were to come under Lend-Lease. This provided considerable relief and the possibility of more nearly balancing exports and imports. In the long run it appeared that not all of Canada's deficit in the United States could be met by these means and that some movement of gold and disposal of assets would continue to be necessary. The great change in the situation, however, was the acceptance of the " economic interde-

---

[14] See Chapter VII, p. 337.

pendence of Canada and the United States as the foundation of the programme of war production in both countries." [15] This meant not only that subsequent problems would be met by joint action but that efforts would be made to prevent them from arising.

The general principle was accepted that each country was to provide the other " with the defense articles which it is best able to produce, and, above all, produce quickly." The increasing duplication in war materials being produced by the two countries was thus to be restrained and future expansion to be planned jointly. A Material Coordinating Commission was formed in April 1941 consisting of officials of the Office of Production Management and of members of Canada's Wartime Industry Control Board. Its special responsibilities were to collect and exchange information on raw material supplies in the United States and Canada, and to consider their maximum utilization. Wider still in scope were the Joint Economic Committees set up in June 1941 by the two countries to explore the possibility of a greater degree of economic cooperation in fields not already covered by other agencies. Their responsibilities were extended also to studying possibilities of reducing " the probable postwar dislocation " resulting from the changes the two economies were undergoing. A Joint War Production Committee established in November 1941 at the recommendation of the Joint Economic Committees now coordinates the war production of the two countries and authorizes the free movement of essential supplies. In the ensuing year diplomatic conversations led to an agreement on steps to establish freer trade between Canada and the United States and with other nations after the war.

The Hyde Park Declaration and the measures which followed it were logical extensions of the planned cooperation announced at Ogdensburg in August 1940. The interrelation of military matters and war production was clear. It was from members of the Joint Defense Board that the proposals for the Material Coordinating Committee and the Joint Economic Committees came. With their acceptance in implementation of the Hyde Park Declaration, collaboration in meeting the needs of Hemisphere defense was extended to the whole field of war production. Beyond this was the agreement that wartime cooperation should be continued for wider purposes in peacetime.

---

[15] Mr. King in the House of Commons, April 28, 1941.

5. The Impact of Widening War

The new widening of the war which added Russia, Japan, and the United States to the major powers engaged brought Canada from the periphery of the war to its center. Canada's declaration of war against Japan came a few hours before those of the United States and Great Britain. Closer on both Atlantic and Pacific coasts than the United States to the main Axis powers, Canada seriously faced for the first time the possibility of enemy attack. With the slack of its man power and its productive capacities already taken up, Canada became confronted with a new urgency by the conflicting demands of home activities and overseas aid.

The first great widening of conflict, the outbreak of the Russo-German war on June 22, 1941, raised special problems for Canada. It was not clear immediately that French Canada would be ready to accept the Soviet Union as an ally. The question lay largely in the attitude to be adopted by the Catholic hierarchy. But throughout the war, its influence had been placed on the side of national unity, and this attitude was to be maintained in the new crisis. Under its ecclesiastical and political leaders, French Canada, though maintaining its inherent dislike of Communism, agreed to cooperate with the rest of Canada and its allies in aiding Russia against their common enemy.

The Far Eastern war has turned much public attention to the protection of Canada's Pacific coast, which is virtually linked by Alaska and the Aleutian Islands to the Asiatic mainland. Fortunately, nature facilitates its defense, for along most of its six hundred miles of extent, mountains rise sheer out of the water making a natural barrier from 50 to 100 miles in width and rising to a height of 7,000 to 10,000 feet. Only two passages exist which might serve an invader from the sea, the Fraser Valley, through which Canada's two transcontinental railways run, and the more northerly Skeena Valley, where a trunk line terminates at Prince Rupert. Both areas, particularly that around Vancouver, are fortified and guarded by Canadian troops. Beyond its immediate territory, however, were responsibilities for the Alaska panhandle bordering northern British Columbia and the Yukon and for aiding communications between the State of Washington and Alaska. To serve both purposes, the Canadian Government, on the recommendation of the Permanent Joint Board on Defense, had already built a chain of air bases which, linked with existing Trans-Canada Airlines facilities, made possible the rapid transfer of fighter planes to Alaska as well as the maintenance of a coastal patrol. When the intensity of the Pacific conflict led to a shortage of shipping with which to transport supplies to Alaska and raised the danger of submarine attack, it was determined to build a highway to Alaska linking the air bases. Although much of the road goes through unbroken country, it was completed in November 1942.[16]

In British Columbia are centered practically all of Canada's Japanese, who number just under 25,000. Already in January 1941 a voluntary registration of Japanese had been conducted. In the first week after Pearl Harbor, registration was made compulsory. In January 1942 special regulations limited their movements. In February, in a move parallel to the Pacific coast arrangements in the United States, enemy aliens were ordered to evacuate British Columbia west of the Cascade Range of mountains by April 1.

The success of Japanese arms in the East and the menace of the Nazi war machine in Europe faced Canadians in the spring of 1942 with two great problems concerning the use of their resources. Both concerned the distribution of Canadian man power. There were those, particularly, but not exclusively, in Quebec, who felt that the new dangers accentuated the need for home defense. In contrast was the outspoken support of the new Conservative leader, Mr. Arthur Meighen, for conscription for overseas service.[17] The second division was between those who felt that all available man power should be placed in the armed forces and those who maintained that Canada's greatest contributions were in the field of supply and that care should be taken to keep adequate personnel both in industry and agriculture.

With his usual habit of compromise, Mr. King chose the middle way in regard to both controversies. Home defense forces, particularly of the R.C.A.F., are being strengthened. There is no slackening in the steady voluntary recruitment which had brought the armed forces to 422,000 at the end of 1941 (295,000 in the Army, 100,000 in the Air Force, and 27,000 in the Navy) and is expected to bring them to 600,000 by March 1943. But in the light of the new situation abroad, Mr. King asked to be released by a nation-wide plebiscite on April 27 from the pledge not to draft soldiers for overseas service.[18] Following the plebiscite Mr. King

---

[16] The expenses of construction are borne by the United States Government, and the road will become part of the Canadian highway system after the war.

[17] Mr. Meighen was replaced as leader of what is now to be called the Progressive Conservative Party in December 1942 by Mr. John Bracken.

[18] The plebiscite resulted in a 64 percent vote in favor of releasing the Government from its

introduced a Government measure in the House of Commons to delete clause 3 of the National Resources Mobilization Act under which men called up for compulsory military service could not be sent overseas. In so doing, he declared that " we are obtaining men for overseas service at the present time as rapidly as we can train them." With the passing of the measure, the Government was empowered to institute conscription for overseas service when it was found necessary.

On the other issue of the distribution of man power between the armed services and the needs of industry and agriculture, Mr. King has also chosen a middle course. Compulsory military service for home defense has been extended to all men between the ages of twenty-one and forty, selection to be by lot. To increase the numbers available for service or for war industry, entry into a large number of occupations has been prohibited for men over seventeen and under forty-five years of age. The increasing needs of industry are to be met by bringing in women and older men. Employment in agriculture is to be more or less stabilized. Farmers' sons and agricultural laborers need not undertake compulsory military service if they are considered essential workers in agriculture. No man employed in agriculture may accept other service without permission except to enlist in the armed forces.

In its fourth year of war, Canada is reaching full utilization of its human and material resources. Its most spectacular contribution, the British Commonwealth Air Training Plan, is now associated with the American air training program through the Combined Committee on Air Training in North America.[19] All of Canada's own war contribution, and practically all of what it has supplied Great Britain, has been financed by Canadians. In 1942 a direct gift has been made to Great Britain of a billion dollars worth of munitions, raw materials, and food stuffs. In addition an interest-free loan of $700,000,000 has been extended for the duration of the war, and $295,000,000 worth of Dominion securities have been repatriated. Additional burdens are imposed by heavy buying in the United States, which continues to confront Canada with a deficit, which amounted to $142,000,000 in 1941. Canada's own war expenses for 1942 will exceed by far what it spent in the whole of World War I.

---

pledge not to impose conscription for overseas service. The civilian vote was 2,670,088 in the affirmative and 1,547,724 in the negative, while the military vote was 251,118 to 60,885. All provinces except Quebec had a majority for the affirmative.

[19] Set up in May 1942, following an Air Training Conference in Ottawa in which fourteen of the United Nations were represented.

Beyond all this, history may designate Canada's share in developing collaboration with the United States and in extending it to Great Britain as its most significant achievement. In so far as it has been, to quote Prime Minister Churchill in Ottawa in December 1941, " a potent magnet drawing together those in the new world and in the old," Canada has made a decisive contribution not only to the war but also for the future.

CHAPTER VI

Canada's Economic War Policy

by B. S. Keirstead

Introduction

The Canadian economy on which such heavy new demands and responsibilities have fallen was not organized for war, and from the military point of view it had certain obvious weaknesses. There were, however, elements of strength, sources of great potential power, once the
transition to a war organization had been accomplished. Besides her
great export surpluses of grain and other agricultural produce, Canada
possessed both metallurgical and manufacturing industries of first-rate
importance and was the fifth ranking commercial power in the world.
Her metallurgical output includes coal, in which she has satisfied more
than 50 percent of her requirements, iron and steel, now developed to
the point of being nearly adequate to the support of her war industries,
an annual oil production of 10,000,000 barrels, and nickel, aluminum,
copper, zinc, silver, and gold,[1] in all of which she has large export
surpluses. In addition she has the greatest per capita development of
hydroelectric power in the world, which will be even higher when the
St. Lawrence Waterways Project is executed. Canadian nickel mines
produce 85 percent of the world output.

Canadian manufacturing, small compared with that of the United

---

[1] Annual gold production is $200,000,000.

States, has nevertheless replaced agriculture as the largest industrial source of income, and has put Canada among the first ten manufacturing countries in the world. With a gross peacetime value productivity of over $3,500,000,000 and a " value added " of more than $1,500,000,000, Canadian manufacturing was equipped to make an important contribution to the war needs of the British Commonwealth. The internal organization of manufacturing industry, characterized by the large-scale firm, has made for the maximum strength in time of war. The concentration of ownership and the comparatively small number of firms to an industry, all of considerable size, a phenomenon not without evil social implications in peacetime, has permitted the rapid organization and complete control of industry for war purposes. It has meant, further, that mass production methods were familiarly in use, and it has facilitated the rapid and most economic expansion of industrial plants in sectors already well served by reservoirs of hydroelectric power. We may notice also the advantages that accrue from close proximity to the United States. Many Canadian firms are branches of American business.[2] They have " entered into the fruits " of American labor in industrial research, scientific methods, and efficient management. Technically, Canadian business has been able to enjoy a similar order of superiority to that enjoyed by the United States. Moreover Canada is able readily to draw on the United States for supplies of precision instruments, and she is able partly to rely on the American engineering and chemical industries. This, however, cannot entirely be entered on the credit side.[3]

Finally one should mention the human qualities without which all natural wealth is not a real and active but merely a potential and passive asset. The Canadian population is a mixed one in which the British elements, amounting to about 50 percent, predominate. Then follow the French, about 30 percent, and people of other European stock, mainly German, Scandinavian, Italian, Polish, and Slav, about 20 percent. In general the population is of a high level of health, intelligence, and training. In morale, in labor skills, in productivity, it would rank very high compared with European peoples. But the depression years have left their mark. Canadian governments, dominion and provincial, with few exceptions, have been notorious for their indifference to social wel-

---

[2] Canada is normally the largest purchaser of the United States, and United States investments in Canada are larger than in any other country.

[3] See below, p. 322.

fare and there have been conditions of malnutrition, disease, and dire poverty, conditions which have been neglected as in few other advanced nations. It has taken the crisis of a dangerous war to illuminate the evils of social neglect.

Of the weaknesses of Canada as a military nation must first be set her complete lack of defense preparations. In 1938, her last peacetime year, her estimates for defense were $32,000,000, and in 1939 the ordinary budgetary defense provision was $34,000,000, sums which represented rather less than 1 percent of the total national incomes of those years. One may set this percentage against the German provision which in 1939 totalled 50 percent of the whole national income. Even in Britain 25 percent of the national income was devoted to war by the peacetime budget of 1939. Canada had few industries engaged in direct war production, and her basic industries were all engaged along peacetime channels. To maintain her small peacetime navy she had bases at Halifax and Esquimalt and a shipbuilding industry, which had little experience in the construction of war vessels. The Royal Canadian Air Force depended rather on British aircraft production than on the infant industry that was just being established in Canada. Her army of 4,000 men used weapons and equipment standardized throughout the British Empire and supplied mainly by Great Britain, although Canada did maintain the Dominion Arsenals.

Hence the Canadian economy started, so to speak, from scratch in the race of belligerents to maximize their war production. The changeover to a full war basis, difficult under any circumstances, was rendered all the more difficult for Canada by certain other weaknesses in her economic position. Canada's has always been an exposed economy; approximately 30 percent of her total net production is normally exported. Her chief industries are far more dependent than any important American industry on export markets. Many of these were shut off or reduced with the outbreak of war, either because they were in enemy territory or because of British rationing and the establishment of Admiralty shipping priorities. The immediate effect, particularly on the wheat-growing west, was one of extreme dislocation and market depression which served to increase the confusion attendant on the shift of industry to a war basis.

Further, the Canadian economy is a regional one. Manufacturing industry is concentrated in southeastern Ontario and western Quebec.

Also in Ontario and Quebec in the northern areas and about the Great Lakes are the metallurgical industries, based on the rich mineral deposits of the Laurentian shield. The prairies are agricultural, primarily dependent on the wheat economy and consequently desirous of good export markets and low prices on manufactured goods. British Columbia is a prosperous maritime economy with mining, forestry, specialized agriculture and horticulture, secondary manufactures, and a great Pacific trade. The Maritime Provinces on the Atlantic seaboard are comparatively poor with a diversified, not very abundant, agriculture, small-scale manufactures, some small share in the Atlantic trading, but primarily dependent on the forest and metallurgical industries and fishing.[4] These different economic regions with various and often conflicting interests have given rise to serious problems affecting the federal structure of Canada. It has always been difficult to find some compromise for the general opposition between a national policy directed towards the greatest economic efficiency conceived in pecuniary or production concepts and one directed towards national welfare conceived as a general level of well-being in the least well-favored as in the best-favored regions. In wartime this opposition takes the form of setting the greatest possible efficiency of industrial war effort against the needs and welfare of some of the nonindustrial regions.

Finally we must notice a noneconomic source of weakness which, though coming from without the field of economics, had direct consequences on Canadian economic development for war. Economic war planning must be integrated with general strategy. The economy must be geared to produce the supplies as and when they are strategically required. Now the Anglo-French grand strategy was defensive. The Allies meant to stand behind the natural sea defenses of Britain and the Maginot line of France, gradually weakening Germany by blockade, and in the meantime organizing and mobilizing their own industrial resources. They enjoyed at that time an overwhelming advantage in potential economic strength. This strategy gave Canada ample time to accomplish a slow transition to a war economy, avoiding the worst

---

[4] The treatment in the text is necessarily oversimplified and compressed. Quebec Province has a peasant population dependent on mixed agriculture and parts of Ontario are well-known for horticulture, dairy farming, gardening, and mixed farming. In the western provinces of the prairies are found mining both of coal and metallic minerals and the oil industry of Turner Valley. The statement that metallurgical industries are concentrated in the central provinces must be qualified in the light of the gold, silver, copper, and zinc production of British Columbia and the iron and coal industry of Nova Scotia.

confusion of a revolutionary change-over. It also meant that the Canadian economy could be geared to the British, with standardized equipment and with British airplane engines, wartime tools, and engineering components. Canada could specialize in raw material production and in those lines of manufacturing, such as motor vehicles, in which she enjoyed advantages, while drawing on Britain for those goods in which the more mature industrial economy enjoyed a comparative advantage. When this strategical assumption was overturned by the German success against France, the whole economic plan had to be changed. England had need of all her own tools, armor steel, every item of equipment. Nothing could be spared for Canada, who had to improvise equipment for her own forces, revolutionize her industrial plans, and find either within her own boundaries or in the United States sources of supply for the equipment, tools, and so forth she had expected to get from England. Thus the military crisis led to some of the most difficult problems that Canada has had to face in preparing her economy for war.[5]

1. The First Phase (September 1939–May 1940)

It is, of course, essential in modern war that military and economic strategy be part of one "master plan" or "grand strategy." But the academic or newspaper critics who believe that an entire war can be set out, so to speak, in a blueprint and handed over as a whole to the military, naval, and economic architects to turn into reality, have failed to understand the essential nature of warfare. You are not, in war, operating on a passive substance which you can mould to your plans, not dealing, to change the metaphor, with a constant, or even with a variable whose mutations can be plotted or "projected" with certainty along some regular curve. The very essence of war is the resistance of the enemy, his ability to thwart your plans, divert your intentions, defeat and confound your schemes. The first test, therefore, of any "grand strategy," is elasticity; the decisive trial of the strategist, adaptability. It is true that military and economic planning must be part of a whole, that fiscal and monetary policy must serve supply, that supply and the proper allocation of the agents of production must be so organized that various supply departments do not bid against or thwart one another, and that all this economic planning must be directed to serving the military requirements so that decisive weight can be thrown against the enemy where he

---

[5] See Chapter VII, p. 337.

is weakest when he is least well prepared. But it is equally true that the military strategy must provide for alternatives, must be ready to modify the disposition of forces so as to frustrate the enemy's strokes, to counterattack if the suitable moment comes. Thus the needs of the military are fluid, subject to change. It is essential that the economic program be such as to meet these fluid needs, and that supply departments be not so rigidly confined to a "master plan" as to be unable to meet *ad hoc* problems as and when they occur.

All this is especially relevant to Canada, because, as a minor power (in the early days of the war), she had but little part in making the master plan and had rather to accept the part therein assigned to her, which was to specialize in the production of those war goods in which she enjoyed a comparative advantage. In general Canada, under the original scheme, was relied upon to produce food stuffs, raw materials, and nonferrous metals. She undertook, as well, to provide for the establishment of the Air Training Plan, and Canadian manufacturing industry was to supply her own forces with clothing, various items of personal equipment, and certain small arms and ammunition. Her motor vehicle industry was called upon to supply both the Canadian and, in part, the British forces, and some explosives were made, and plant construction was started for the expansion of munitions and explosives supply.

Immediately following the declaration of war [6] Parliament was summoned in special session and voted the sum of $100,000,000 for national defense.[7] Certain additional taxes were imposed, notably a 20 percent surtax on all taxable income under the Income War Tax Act,[8] and an Excess Profits Tax,[9] and certain minor indirect taxes chiefly directed against luxury goods. On the whole the Government, however, decided not to impose heavy taxation at that stage. Canada had a large amount of unemployment and of under-employment both of men and of capital. Inasmuch as heavy taxation tends to have a regressive effect, the Govern-

---

[6] See Chapter V, p. 288.

[7] An Act for granting to His Majesty aid for National Defense and Security, September 11, 1939.

[8] An Act to amend the Income War Tax Act, September 12, 1939.

[9] The Excess Profits Tax Act, September 12, 1939; this Act provided for two schedules of rates at the option of the taxpayer. Schedule A was a graduated tax beginning at 10 percent of profits in excess of 50 percent and not exceeding 10 percent of the capital employed, and rising to 60 percent of profits and not exceeding 25 percent of capital. Schedule B imposed a straight levy of 50 percent on all "profits in excess of the average annual income of the taxpayer . . . for the four years 1936, 1937, 1938 and 1939. . . ."

ment proposed, until its spending program was under way, to stimulate employment and industrial expansion by short-term loans from the commercial banks.

This policy was followed with satisfactory results. Though there was the usual recession both in prices and employment immediately after the outbreak of war, and though there was considerable dislocation in agriculture, the commercial pick-up and industrial expansion followed at once. The Government borrowed $200,000,000 from the commercial banks on two-year notes at 2 percent, and the Bank of Canada's assets increased between August and November by $107,000,000 as a result of open market buying. This increase in reserves enabled the banks to increase their deposits by just over $300,000,000. The stimulus to business activity was reflected in all the indices of retail and wholesale turnover, industrial production, and prices, though these indices showed a considerable sag in the early months of 1940. When, in the spring of that year, the Government floated a public loan of $200,000,000 and increased its own spending, there was a renewal of business expansion, which then continued throughout the year and was apparent in industries producing for civilian consumption as well as in the heavy and armaments industries.[10]

Apart from these no extraordinary powers were assumed by the Government for economic control. It was presumed that the monetary policy and government borrowings would stimulate enterprise and that government expenditures would direct labor and capital into war channels. The free price mechanism was relied upon to function as the agency through which public, like private, demand would gain effect.

2. The Crisis (May 1940 and After)

When the storm broke and the German armies marched through Holland, Belgium, and then accomplished in twenty-one days the complete defeat of the army which inherited the tradition of Jena and defended the principles of 1789, the whole ordering and marshaling of the strength of the British Empire was thrown into confusion. The invasion of England was imminent, and the military equipment of England was a mass of burning, charred, or broken metal strewed along the plains from Antwerp to Dunkirk.

That there was confusion is to be expected, that mistakes were made

---

[10] See Table I, p. 315.

may be presumed; yet when the ministers met the House of Commons during the critical days of May and June there was neither hysteria nor a sense of frustration. No attempt was made to formulate a new war plan on the grand lines of the old. Immediate *ad hoc* problems of supply had to be tackled as they arose. Gradually, however, as the immediate demands were satisfied, and as the summer passed without invasion, a new policy began to be formulated.

I · SUPPLY

The immediate problem was of supply. It is, perhaps, usual to look on this as a matter of production, and to regard as distinct questions, fiscal and monetary policy, labor policy, and capital allocation. There is a convenience in this method for it is almost essential to impose classifications to order and elucidate a complicated question. Nevertheless the problem of supply is a complex involving all economic relationships. It consists in obtaining labor and capital in the war industries in sufficient quantities to provide the required production. Where there are scarcities, the labor and capital must be apportioned so that the most urgent needs are first filled, and so that great accumulations of half-finished material, shells for instance, are not piled up waiting such components as fuses, the production of which waits on a supply of skilled labor that has been too rapidly consumed in the manufacture of steel for shell casings. Thus on examination the supply problem is seen to include the planning not simply of production within this or that industry, but the ordering, as between various branches, of the supply of capital and labor disposal. Thus war supply is only a special case of the general economic problem of allocating scarce means to manifold ends. The labor and capital must be found by training and transferring the unemployed or those employed on unnecessary peacetime pursuits. This means that production must be expanded to the limit of the national capacity and that civilian demand must be reduced, and reduced if possible without affecting the morale, health, or efficiency of the population. Involved is the whole question of war finance, of industrial and price controls, of rationing, and of monetary action. Thus, in reviewing the problem of supply and its treatment in Canada throughout the period of crisis after May in 1940 to midsummer, 1941, we must keep steadily in mind, even if we are obliged to pursue but one thread of thought at a time, that economic policy had ultimately to be conceived and developed as a whole.

First must come, though it has been often neglected, the continuation of the Canadian supply of raw materials. Canadian agriculture had to supply foods for an England deprived of Scandinavian and Dutch sources, and the wheat economy, with its European market depleted, had to yield place, at least in part, to the production of hogs, stock, and dairy produce. The shift from wheat could not be either immediate or in any proportion to the decline of the market, and, to save the prairies from utter destitution, the Government had, at considerable public expense, to undertake to store and to market millions of bushels of unsold wheat. Canadian copper, nickel, and aluminum production had to support, as they have adequately done, the war needs of the Empire, and gold production was increased to finance the purchase of United States supplies. Canadian steel had to make the war industries as self-sufficient as possible.[11]

Despite all difficulties, the Canadian industrial effort of 1940 was a considerable achievement. In the industries in which there existed, prior to the war, plant, experienced management, and skilled labor, fast schedules were set and exceeded. The British Army of the Nile was carried forward to crush Italian power in North Africa in Canadian built motor vehicles; its supply was maintained by Canadian trucks. The Canadian Active Army of four divisions with reinforcements and Corps troops and an even larger number of men in the Reserve Army were clothed and supplied by Canadian industry.[12]

During 1941 the military demands were further increased and it was made known that Canadian industry had developed to the point where it was possible to raise and equip armored divisions in Canada. Before the end of 1941 Canada had promised to send to England an armored brigade to act with the first and second divisions of the Canadian Army Corps now in England, and also to dispatch the third infantry division and a full armored division.[13] Keels for the first destroyers to be constructed in Canada were laid down in early summer, 1941.

In the industries in which there had been little if any previous Canadian experience, chiefly tanks and military aircraft, the difficulties were

---

[11] Steel production in 1940 and 1941 has been 43 and 77 percent above 1939.

[12] Canada also undertook to build weapons of the following categories: 40-mm. Bofors anti-aircraft guns; 3.7-inch anti-aircraft guns; 25-pounder guns and carriages; Colt-Browning aircraft machine guns; Colt-Browning tank machine guns; 6-pounder guns for tanks; 2-pounder anti-tank guns and carriages; 4-inch guns and mountings; 12-pounder guns and mountings; 4-inch naval guns; 6-inch naval guns; Lee-Enfield rifles.

[13] About 10,000 vehicles are required for an infantry division.

greater and deliveries were not always made on schedule. Some 3,000 tanks were ordered in Canada in 1940, but actual production was postponed until early in 1941. Airplane manufacture in Canada was for the most part concentrated on trainer aircraft, though some bombers and some Hurricane fighters were ordered for the Royal Air Force and a few flying boats for the Royal Canadian Air Force.[14]

In sum, the Canadian accomplishment in production may best be realized by comparing the advance in the production indices of 1940 over 1939 with the advance of 1930 over 1925. In twelve months under Government direction and the stimulus of war as much was accomplished as during five years of the greatest peacetime industrial expansion modern capitalism has experienced under the stimulus of private profit. But in 1940 the progress was made under conditions of a changeover in the type of product and of machine tools and the adaptation of labor skills that amounted to an industrial revolution.

II · FISCAL POLICY

The supply departments thus set out requirements and, in the main, fulfilled them by an enormous transition and expansion of Canadian industrial production. How were the labor and capital obtained and directed to carry out this war program? The Government, as we saw, stimulated industrial expansion by its fiscal and monetary policy in the early months of the war. It carried forward about $200,000,000 in cash from its long-term borrowings into the fiscal year of 1940 and thus maintained the slightly inflationary policy it had initiated. But in the June 1940 budget it was clear the Government meant to begin the fiscal restriction of consumers' demand. Wars must be paid for out of current income in the sense that the weapons and munitions of war have to come out of the current production of the nation. How they are paid for does not affect this basic truism. If the Government pays for them by taxing the public it simply takes away the amount of the tax from potential consumers or from potential investors who might otherwise invest in peacetime capital and it spends the proceeds in purchasing war goods or wartime capital equipment. Fewer consumers' goods or peacetime capital goods are bought and consequently the demand for labor and capital in the peacetime trades falls off, and the agents of production are directed into the war industries. A tax, levied according

---

[14] By the spring of 1942 over 300 airplanes were being turned out every month.

to ability to pay, imposes the sacrifices of consumers' satisfactions roughly according to ability to bear sacrifices.

A long-term loan may likewise impose certain sacrifices of consumers' goods. It is generally not subscribed from current income but from accumulated savings, although the average investor, if he reduces his accustomed liquid balance at the bank, is apt to curtail expenditure until he re-establishes it in whole or in part. Thus a loan may result in some restriction in consumers' demand, and to a greater extent in a restriction of demand for peacetime capital goods. But on the whole a loan is not effective, as a tax is, in imposing regular sacrifices of consumption. Also a loan means that though a sacrifice of at least potential satisfactions is made by the class with bank balances, this class obtains a claim on the community as a whole which must eventually be met. Hence it is a mistake to consider loans as an alternative to taxation. The ideal of war finance is to restrict consumers' demand and to increase production. Until the mystical limit of full employment is achieved, loans tap idle resources and give the Government spending power and the central bank lending power that can be used to increase production. Thus war finance must strike the right balance between taxing and borrowing, increasing the proportion to be carried by taxation as the economy approaches full employment.

TABLE I. DOMINION REVENUES AND EXPENDITURES, 1938–42 *
($000,000's)

	1938–39	1939–40	1940–41	1941–42 †
War Expenditures	72	207	795	1,414
Total Expenditures	552	680	1,249	1,893
Total Revenues	502	562	873	1,481
Deficit	51	119	377	413

* Canadian House of Commons, *Official Report of Debates*, Vol. LXXX, " Appendix to The Budget, 1942–43," p. 10.
† Estimated.

The Canadian budget for the fiscal year 1940–41,[15] which was introduced in June after the collapse of France, reflected in part the new role which Canada had then to play in the war. It forecast war expenditures of at least $700,000,000 with possibly another $150,000,000 required before the end of the year; $200,000,000 for the repatriation of Canadian securities held in England, thus providing England with Canadian dollar exchange; and ordinary government expenditures of

---

[15] See Table I.

$448,000,000. To meet this total of expenditures of $1,500,000,000 the Government had in hand a cash balance of $200,000,000 carried forward from the previous fiscal year; and it proposed to raise by taxation $760,000,000; by war savings certificates (voluntary small-scale loans subscribed over a period of time with the same general effect as taxation of reducing consumers' demand) about $50,000,000; and the balance of about $500,000,000 by borrowing. Actually tax revenues were more elastic and expenditures were rather less than the budget forecast, so that something under $400,000,000 was all that was required from borrowing, an amount which was subscribed in one appeal to the public.

The new taxation was restrictive, although there was nevertheless a considerable expansion in the production and consumption of consumers' goods. The taxation of the 1940–41 budget must be regarded as having limited the expansion of consumption rather than as having imposed an actual curtailment. New direct income taxes amounting to $35,000,-000 from the new National Defense Contribution Tax and an increase of $58,000,000 in the personal income tax which resulted from a sharp increase in rates, and increased indirect taxation, most of which was transferred to the consumer, amounting in all to $86,000,000, confiscated for the state something less than a third of the total increase in the national income. The new Excess Profits Tax yielded $100,000,000, and this definitely restricted the ability of corporations to invest their profits in increased plant facilities for ordinary peacetime production.

The budget was designed to shift an increasingly large share of the productive resources of the country into war channels; but it was not a restrictive budget in the sense of imposing an actual reduction in the consumption of ordinary peacetime goods and services. It did, of course, reduce the consumption of certain classes, particularly those of middle and higher incomes, though it would be a serious error to suppose that any severe sacrifices were borne by the upper income groups. On the other hand previously unemployed and under-employed workers and their families were able to restore their scale of living to something like a minimum standard of health and comfort. The general expansion in the consumers' goods industries indicates one of the weaknesses of this method of relying on the price system for the necessary redistribution of productive resources in a war economy. It takes very heavy taxation and a long period of time before any considerable redistribution of resources occurs, particularly if general economic expansion is going on, and, further, there are certain obstacles to this redistribution which the price mechanism is by itself incapable of surmounting. These obstacles are the technical difficulties of adapting plant, the occupational immobility of labor, and the unwillingness of industrialists to make large investments in wartime plant without some guarantee against a dead loss on the investment when the war emergency is over.

These considerations led many Canadian observers, most of whom no doubt approved the Government's middle of the road budget, to hope that the budget would be followed by direct devices to overcome these obstacles, and that the Government would use some of the extraordinary powers over capital and labor which it had taken to itself under wartime legislation, powers which included the right to expropriate property, to direct an industry or, if the industry failed to accept direction, to take over the management for the duration of the war, to set and fix prices including wages, to establish priorities and ration the consumption of raw materials, and to mobilize labor for war work.[16] During 1940 the Government did make some progress in the direct approach to these problems, but that there was some disappointment was evident both from criticism in the House of Commons and in the newspaper and periodical press.

The military situation demanded with the utmost urgency the most rapid possible development of Canadian industry and expansion of Canadian munitions and war output. In wartime the price mechanism is not only slow to give effect to military demands, it cannot even properly reflect them in many instances, because with no competitive market there is no way of making economic valuations. If a decision is to be made between ten airplanes and ten tanks it is not an economic one but a strategic one, and strategic, not pecuniary, considerations must determine the allocation of steel as between the airplane and the tank industries. Similarly, who is to say that $1.25 a day represents a soldier's marginal productivity? Wage payments as between army and industry are certainly no guide for the proper distribution of man power, and the

---

[16] An Act respecting a Department of Munitions and Supply, September 12, 1939.

An Act to confer certain powers upon the Governor-in-Council for the mobilization of National Resources in the present war, June 21, 1940.

An Act to amend the Department of Munitions and Supply Act, June 14, 1940.

An Act to amend the Department of National Defense Act, July 8, 1940.

An Act respecting a Department of National War Services, July 12, 1940.

An Act respecting the payment of compensation for the taking of certain property for war purposes, August 1, 1940.

price system in the labor market ought not to be relied on as the method of drawing labor from peacetime to wartime employment. Exactly the same argument holds true with even greater force in the field of capital.

One looked, therefore, to the budget for the year 1941-42 for a more realistic conception of the needs of total war, and certainly few Canadians have complained that taxation was too light. The budget proposed to raise a total of $2,670,000,000 including the financing of British purchases in Canada, purchases which must of course come out of the Canadian real income for the present. Of this total, the Government proposed to raise $1,450,000,000 by taxation, about $200,000,000 from such government trust accounts as the Unemployment Insurance fund and from the sale of war savings certificates, and the balance of about $1,000,000,000 by borrowing. The increase in direct taxation was heavy and practically put a limit to any increase in spending from the new incomes created by the war, and it also provoked a sharp curtailment in the spending capacity of the middle and upper incomes. In terms of aggregate social income the effect was to produce a slight curtailment as over 1940 in the consumption of consumers' goods but to leave the level of consumption rather higher than in 1939. This means in effect that there were more incomes being earned than there were in peacetime and that in general the working class were able to improve their standard of living, particularly during the year 1940, but that this improvement was stabilized by the 1941 budget at the 1940 level.

Sacrifices have been made by the upper income groups who have had to reduce their level of consumption, nevertheless the upper income groups are still left with large spending surpluses. A man with an income of $20,000 a year may look upon the tax of $9,000 as very heavy, but actually a bachelor (for we are considering the tax on single persons) with a net income, after paying taxes, of $11,000 cannot be said to be undergoing privation. In a country with everything at stake in a total war it ought to be possible to set a maximum net income and if this were done at a level, say, of $5,000 there is no question but that a very considerable reduction amounting probably to $200,000,000 or $300,000,000 could be effected in consumers' spending on luxuries and comforts. In a siege economy in the third year of war this might have been possible, and there were some Canadians who felt that the Government could well have imposed these additional sacrifices and to this extent have increased its share of contributions to the Commonwealth war effort. However this may be, the 1941 budget definitely put an end to the expansion in the production of consumers' goods and it diverted to the supply of war needs nearly one-half of the national income.[17]

The Excess Profits Tax of 1940 was continued for the fiscal year 1941–42, though in a form somewhat amended to remove seeming injustices, and yielded $140,000,000, so that a very definite restriction was placed on new investment by private corporations. The tax levied a 75 percent rate on all profits in excess of the 1936–39 average plus a straight 18 percent corporation tax on gross profits or a 40 percent tax on all profits, whichever is higher. The Excess Profits Tax Act was amended however to provide for "hard" cases. This tax and the very heavy public borrowing[18] were certain to have the desired effect of curtailing private investment;[18a] but as the Minister of Finance himself said there will be required "also the careful limitation of our commercial and industrial investment to such plant and equipment as will aid in carrying on the war and as is necessary to the maintenance of essential services."[19] Thus the administration came at length to the admission that the price system even under the stimulus of stringent taxation was too slow and ineffective a mechanism for the direction and allocation of wartime investment. Mr. Ilsley announced that an Order-in-Council had been passed "making it necessary for any person or firm erecting or extending building structures for industrial and commercial use or installing machinery and equipment to apply for and obtain a license."[20] The responsibility for administration is vested under the Order-in-Council in the Director-General of Priorities under the Department of Munitions and Supply.[21]

The budget for 1942–43, which was not presented until June 1942 envisaged a total expenditure of $3,900,000,000, or about two-thirds of the national income. Revenues of $2,145,000,000 were anticipated on the basis of increased tax yields and refundable taxes, leaving $1,755,000,000 to be met by borrowing. It was estimated that about one-third of this figure would come from government cash balances, Unemployment In-

---

[17] There are some who have said that whereas America, even before she entered the war, had lent goods to Britain under Lend-Lease, Canada, her partner in the British Commonwealth, was making her pay cash for everything she received. This is not true. See below, p. 322.

[18] In the case of the first Victory Loan of 1941 a total of over $700,000,000 at a time when notice deposits were at a peak of $1,800,000,000.

[18a] Ordinarily gross investment, derived mainly from the profits of industry, is about $1,000,000,000 a year in Canada, of which some $300,000,000 represents new capital investment.

[19] Honorable J. L. Ilsley, budget speech, April 25, 1941, House of Commons, *Official Report of Debates,* unrevised edition, Vol. LXXIX, No. 60, p. 2550.

[20] *Ibid.*

[21] See Chapter VII, pp. 337, 340–342.

surance funds, and corporate investors, but "a very large balance should," according to the Minister of Finance, "be provided by individual purchases of War Savings Certificates and bonds."

In the new budget personal income taxes and the National Defense Tax were combined and made deductible at the source, and their incidence increased. There was an attempt to mitigate the severity of the new tax rates by making a portion of them refundable in the postwar period, with 2 percent accrued interest. This refundable tax has come to be known by common consent as "Forced Savings." The same principle was applied to the Excess Profits Tax, which was raised to 100 percent, 20 percent being refundable — a provision designed to afford protection in the form of increased reserves to industries, especially smaller industries, in the postwar period. Taxation on luxuries was intensified and extended, and was clearly intended less to increase revenue than to restrict consumption, thus affording a supplementary form of commodity rationing.

III · DIRECT CONTROL

The direct control over investment by means of a licensing system introduced in 1941 culminated a gradual development of regulatory powers. During the first phase of the war Canadian fiscal policy had been based on the assumption that the economic objective of maximum mobilization of resources for total war could be attained largely without the aid of direct restrictive controls over consumer behavior and without direct compulsory controls over industry. Such control was to be kept at a minimum, being regarded as inimical to Canadian industrial traditions and unnecessary so long as the economy remained considerably below full employment. 1941 was a period of transition at an ever accelerating rate from indirect to direct government restriction of consumers and compulsion of producers.

The Wartime Prices and Trade Board, set up at the beginning of the war, was designed to provide for the regular supply and stable price of consumers' necessities.[21a] It could not meet the problems of raw material rationing and capital priorities. In the early months of the war controllers under the Ministry of Supply were put directly in charge of steel,

---

21a In order to maintain ceiling prices and to prevent the drain of certain commodities to the United States, the Board has found it necessary, notably in the case of beef, to buy up output at American prices and distribute at the ceiling price in Canada, the American ceiling having proved elastic.

timber, oil, coal, and certain other basic metals. Their duties were to maintain an adequate supply and see that it was properly apportioned among war industries. For the most part they were able to achieve their results by informal methods, because on the whole industry was either glad to cooperate or was willing to do so rather than see the controllers forced to use the powers they possessed. General coordination and planning of their activities were provided by the Wartime Industries Supply Board, supplemented by the Wartime Requirements Board.[22]

Further the Government engaged directly in investment both on its own account and on account of the British Government. Fiscal policy made available to the Government a large share of the annual Canadian savings, thus reducing the ordinary demand for producers' goods and machinery. In place of this demand there is the vastly increased demand of the war industries for capital goods. But as in the United States, producers hesitated to embark on large construction to meet a war demand which will be of temporary nature and leave them at the war's end with an overexpanded plant. To meet this difficulty and provide for new fixed capital where needed the Government has allowed in some cases for the amortization of new plants by permitting contractors on war account to charge in their prices an amortization write-off calculated on a two- or four-year depreciation, an extravagant way of solving the problem. The Government in effect pays for new plant in its orders over two or four years, but in the end the plant belongs to the corporation. Another method is for the Government to build new plant, lease it to the industry, and retain ownership after the war. This gives the Government a direct interest in, and control over, war industry and promises interesting developments in the postwar period.[23]

IV · FOREIGN EXCHANGE

Another control over capital has been the control of foreign investment and foreign exchange. In the summer of 1940 the Foreign Exchange Control Board registered all Canadian-held securities in the United States, took over Canadian-owned American dollar balances, prohibited pleasure travel in the United States and, in December, under power of the Foreign Exchange Conservation Act,[24] prohibited certain types of imports. The obvious result was to cut off the consumers' im-

---

[22] See Chapter VII, pp. 340, 341.
[23] For more detailed description and recent figures, see Chapter VII, p. 337.
[24] The Foreign Exchange Conservation Act, December 1940.

ports from the United States, setting free exchange for the purchase of war goods and machinery. There may be far more important long-run results. Canada is ceasing to be in England's debt as her own government acquires ownership of bonds and stocks of her industries formerly held by British individuals. At the end of the fiscal year 1940–41 Britain's deficit with Canada on real trade was approximately $800,000,000. During that year Canada provided London with exchange to the amount of 42.4 percent of the total by the repatriation of Canadian securities held in Britain and to the amount of 26.2 percent of the total by allowing sterling balances to accrue to Canadian account in London. The remainder was met by the transfer of gold. In January 1942 accumulated Canadian sterling credits in London were converted into an interest-free loan. This was followed by a free gift of $1,000,000,000 from Canada to Great Britain. The exhaustion of this gift early in 1943 was marked by the establishment of a Canadian War Supplies Allocation Board to correspond to the United States Lend-Lease Administration in the distribution of Canadian supplies among the United Nations.[25]

Economically and financially Canada has increased steadily her position as a North American country and a dependency of the United States, and this in the very act of asserting her political allegiance to the intercontinental system of the Commonwealth and the unity of her political destiny with that of Britain. Until the Hyde Park Agreement Canada's foreign exchange problem was simply that of obtaining American dollars. It is not that she has an unfavorable balance in all foreign trade, but most of her favorable balance is in sterling and one of the major preoccupations of the war administration has been to find ways and means of financing American imports.

The Foreign Exchange Control Board [26] with its regulatory powers over the issuance of foreign exchange has thus had as its chief object the conservation of American exchange rather than the stabilization of the Canadian dollar, though that has been a secondary and indeed complementary function. Its activities and the effect of the War Exchange Conservation Act have very definitely reduced Canadian civilian spending in the United States, but it is unlikely that the figure for Canadian purchases in the United States of $950,000,000 for the fiscal year 1941–42 can be reduced, because of this amount $428,000,000 is for war pur-

---

25 At the same time the Canadian Government purchased $200,000,000 of British Government investments in the Canadian munitions industry.

26 See Chapter VII, p. 352.

chases and $238,000,000 is for the payment of interest and dividends to United States investors.

V · LABOR POLICY

The war industries were calculated in 1940 to require 200,000 additional skilled workers, and many additional skilled craftsmen were enlisted in the R.C.A.F. and other branches of the armed forces. Unemployment in Canada greatly exceeded this amount in total, but of the unemployed the majority were unskilled or had lost their skills. By the time of the seasonal upswing in late summer when employment figures were at their height, unemployment in all the skilled trades reporting through trades unions had sunk as low as 4 percent, the lowest figure since the boom days of the 'twenties. In certain skilled trades a shortage of labor made its appearance. Obviously in a country with considerable total unemployment, local and trade shortages could be met by training young workers, rehabilitating older workers, and arranging for a transfer of workers both from place to place and from trade to trade. In the successful accomplishment of such a program the enthusiastic support of both labor and management would be essential.

The Government seemed rather slow to realize the growing gravity of the shortage of labor and policy to grapple with this problem was not devised until late in 1940. The Administration took considerable pride in the passage of the Unemployment Insurance Act which, for the first time,[27] guaranteed Canadian workers a certain security in case of unemployment, a forward-looking measure, indeed, but not one conceived to meet the needs of a war economy facing not a scarcity of jobs but a scarcity of workers. To fill this want the Government relied chiefly on the Youth Training Program which it conducted in cooperation with the provinces. For the major part of 1940 this program was operating at a rate of about 24,000 "trainees" a year, and there were some few in training in industry. To the problem of supplementing this admittedly inadequate program by the rehabilitation of older workers and the training of women, the Government's attitude can best be given in the words of the Minister of Labor who said, "I would not want to say that definite representations had been made to industry to

---

[27] Labor legislation under the British North American Act was regarded as falling within the jurisdiction of the provinces rather than the Dominion. A constitutional amendment was necessary to obtain the Unemployment Insurance Act. This constitutional difficulty has been one of the obstacles standing in the way of progressive social legislation in Canada.

employ older men. I think that is something which industry will have to take upon itself. As demand increases and supply diminishes industry will almost automatically be required to take on older men and women." [28]

Thus the Government, throughout most of 1940, trusted to the price system, the attraction of higher wages, to provide it with the requisite skilled labor in the defense industries. In spite of the powers enjoyed under the National War Services Act, it did not establish any labor priorities or, until late in the year, develop a policy of planned transfer.

Moreover, the Government's policy raised certain cricitisms in labor circles. There was some labor dilution, and considerable sacrifice was being asked of union standards of hours and conditions of work. The Government made a statement of principle to the effect that these standards should be restored after the war, but the unions, as in Britain,[29] wanted a legislative guarantee. Some labor spokesmen also felt that the Government was less reluctant to issue legislation working in a different way, such as an order-in-council extending the compulsory provisions of the Industrial Disputes Investigation Act to all war industries. The Defense of Canada Regulations in the hands of certain provincial attorneys-general had been used in a manner that aroused resentment and opposition in Labor circles and alarmed the defenders of civil liberties, although the Canadian Trades and Labor Congress approved the Regulations in principle.[30]

All this, coupled with the growing pressure on the available supply of labor, led to a sharp shift in policy in the latter part of 1940. The Youth and Emergency Training Programs were " stepped up " to train 50,000 workers a year, and this was increased in 1941–42 to over 90,000. A national policy of " upgrading " was introduced whereby young workers were taught to perform certain skilled functions, thus relieving the skilled men of all but the most essential and difficult parts of their task. Transfer has been worked out on a national scale through Dominion bureaus spread through the country.

---

[28] Honorable N. A. McLarty, Minister of Labor, House of Commons, *Debates,* Nov. 28, 1940, Vol. LXXIX, No. 15, p. 532. The National Elective Service plan announced March 24, 1942, introduces a more positive program in this respect. See Chapter V, p. 303 and Chapter VII, pp. 346, 347.

[29] See Chapter IV, p. 233.

[30] A new Order-in-Council, P. C. 892, removed one of the most objectionable interpretations of the Defense of Canada regulations, viz.: that which made picketing in defense industries illegal and the Government has declared as a matter of policy that the rights of workers to Trades Union organizations and collective bargaining should be recognized by industry.

Government policy indeed seemed to have been based on the assumption that the industrial unrest which developed throughout Canada in 1941 was chiefly a matter of wages, whereas many authorities on labor problems and indeed the Department of Labor statistics on the causes of strikes, indicated that the question of union recognition was the major issue in many of the important industrial disputes. A firmer stand on the question of union recognition might prove much more effective. In other ways the Government had not been unmindful of the rights and needs of the workingman. Indeed some industrialists felt that the Government leaned backward in its efforts to be fair to labor. When workers went on strike contrary to the provisions of the Industrial Disputes Investigation Act — that is to say, previous to the appointment of a Board of Conciliation — the Department of Labor ordinarily took the attitude that they were unaware that the Act had been extended to cover all defense industries, and handled the workers in a conciliatory spirit. On the other hand, when a prominent corporation engaged in defense work in the city of Hamilton refused to submit a dispute to a Board of Conciliation, the Government promptly stepped in and took over the factory, an episode which occupied the better part of the front page of the *Financial Post* for two weeks.

The Government's initial attempt at wage regulation was set out in Order-in-Council P.C. 7440. The object of this Order was probably twofold: (a) to prevent a wage spiral with inflationary effects, and (b) to safeguard workers against rises in the cost of living and at a minimum level of comfort. The Order provided that wages should not be increased above the 1926–29 level (or any year previous to 1940 where the level was higher than the 1926–29 average) but should be stabilized at that rate and that Boards of Conciliation should not entertain demands for wage increases above that level except in cases where it was shown that the cost of living had increased by 5 percent since August 1939, in which event cost of living bonuses at a flat amount uniform for all workers regardless of earnings should be paid to cover the increase in the cost of living.[31] In October 1941 the Order was extended to constitute a wage ceiling in practically all industries. The effect has been to establish a minimum real wage, but to reduce the differential accruing

---

[31] The order made exception for employments in which wages were unduly depressed, but since this phrase was not defined it was not surprising to find a Board of Conciliation established the precedent that wages no matter how low they might be could not be raised above the 1926–29 level.

to the more highly skilled workers. The policy has therefore not commended itself to the trade unions, which for the most part represent such workers.

By the third year of war Canada had attained full industrial employment; in Mr. King's words, there was " no slack left " in the industrial economy. The main diversion of resources from civilian to war purposes had been accomplished, and the Government's problem was now twofold: to continue to drain off excess purchasing power in the hands of the public so as to prevent inflation; and to provide for war industries a maximum amount of labor, material, and capital. The second objective could only be attained by limiting supplies of labor, material, and capital to nonessential industries. In the field of labor the Government made no attempt to sweep man power into the armed forces or war production by direct conscription, but rather like a monumental vacuum cleaner proceeded to draw them in by suction. Men of military age and physically fit were prohibited to enter almost any occupation outside farming and food production. In addition, a policy of bringing women into industry was put forward as " the most important single feature of the program." Discouraged by the drain on their labor supply, the reduction of their market by prohibitive taxation on their products and the reduction of purchasing power in the hands of the public, and by the restriction of supplies through various control boards, all nonessential industries were reducing production by 1942. Five hundred of them had been eliminated, and progressive mortality was to be expected.

Conclusion

Under the pressure of modern war the dominant role of government in the economy becomes an accomplished and accepted fact. Planning, at first *ad hoc* and admitted only when necessity drove, promises, before the war is over, to embrace in its scope the entire economic life of the nation. What is implied for the future of Canada, the British Commonwealth, and North America remains obscure and must do so until the issue of the war is decided. But, while none in Canada doubts the ultimate outcome, most believe that the war will be long drawn out, and that, during its course, many of the tendencies already well established will become definitely set. Canada's position in finance, vis-à-vis England, will be permanently changed; she will be the creditor country, England the debtor. Again Canada will be a much more self-sufficient, a less exposed, a more industrialized, economy. The internal balance of the economy will be shifted more favorably to the industrial heart in Ontario; the external trading position may well be revolutionized. The extension of government ownership and interference in the free market will both obstruct a reversion to "free capitalism" and complicate the division of jurisdiction as between Dominion and provinces.

Already the regional effects of the war are apparent. Efficient prosecution has precluded any "equitable" provincial distribution of war orders, so that industrial Ontario has been the great beneficiary of the war development, while the prairie wheat economy leans heavily on the Dominion Government's purchase and storage of wheat. The concentration of industry in the central areas and its great development during the war mean the growth of economic power in these central provinces. Only a growth in the powers of the federal government can offset this, can use it for the protection of social welfare throughout the Dominion as a whole. Every month of war intensifies this problem.

Some notion of the problems this will breed when peace comes can be had from a consideration of the opposition of Ontario to the report of the Royal Commission on Dominion-Provincial Relations. This Commission, appointed before the war, was to study the financial and constitutional arrangements obtaining between the Dominion and provinces and to make recommendations for changes which would be in the interest of greater national unity and welfare. The report recommended very moderate increases in the federal power and greater financial aid by the Dominion to the provinces to equalize social welfare standards. When the provincial premiers met in Ottawa in January 1941 to consider the recommendations with the Dominion officials, the Premier of Ontario, Mr. Hepburn, refused even to discuss them.[32] His attitude was responsible for the postponement of the whole matter, much to the confusion of the Dominion Government, which was looking to the recommendations of the report for a consolidation of taxes and an equalization of war tax burdens throughout the country.

In connection with the new tax provisions of 1941 the Dominion Government concluded an agreement with the provinces whereby the latter relinquished their right to impose a provincial or municipal income tax, in consideration of appropriate subventions in lieu from the Dominion Government. The Dominion Government also assumed control of the Succession Duties, previously an exclusively provincial tax field. Thus

[32] He received the support of the Premiers of British Columbia and Alberta.

in two important fields the fiscal freedom of the provinces was limited
by the federal government, a limitation which constituted a significant
change in the British North America Act governing Dominion-provincial relations. This followed along the lines suggested by the Royal
Commission on Dominion-Provincial Relations, but whereas the
Rowell-Sirois Report had recommended that fiscal changes should be
accompanied by an assumption on the part of the federal government
of responsibility for a minimum standard of national social services, the
actual change made was purely fiscal.[33]

With the economy increasingly dominated by Ontario the political
problems of a regional federalism promise to become no less difficult or
dangerous. Meantime national unity in the war effort continues. The
Dominion Government is increasingly the biggest buyer, the biggest
entrepreneur, the biggest investor in the nation, and as long as the
war continues the forces which the war releases will be operative to
increase the dominant role of government in economic life. We have
seen why this must be. Whether it results finally in a greater social
democracy, a greater security for the common citizen within a more
unified Canada, or whether it leads to regional dominance and the
growth of disintegrating centrifugal forces with, perhaps, attempted
authoritarianism as a solution, remains for history and the issue of the
war to determine.

---

[33] Unfortunately, the subventions made to provincial governments to compensate them for
their loss of revenue were based on calculations of revenue for 1940, which were inadequate in
1941 in view of advancing costs and increasing demands on provincial and municipal social
services.

CHAPTER VII

The Organization and Work of the Canadian War Administration

by Gwendolen M. Carter

Introduction

The organization of the Canadian war administration demonstrates the ability of the democratic system to add new agencies and controls affecting almost every aspect of life without losing its essence of responsibility to the electorate. This has remained true despite the variety of new functions which have been undertaken, the pragmatic character of the development and the rapidity with which it has been carried through. Marked changes have occurred particularly in the great increase of federal responsibilities. But within the Dominion Government, the concentration of authority in the Cabinet, the politically responsible organ of the parliamentary system, insures control. Despite the greatly increased powers of the executive, Parliament remains 'active, and exercises power of free criticism.

The centralizing tendencies induced by war demands are reversing an earlier constitutional trend. The British North America Act (1867), which provides the constitutional structure for Canada, allots enumerated powers to the provinces in property and civil rights, education, the incorporation of companies whose activity is confined to the province, municipal institutions, control of public works and undertakings, and in general all things of a local nature; to the Dominion it allots regulation of trade, postal service, currency, census and statistics, provisions for military and naval defense, and criminal law and procedure. Concurrent powers exist in immigration and agriculture, the federal government being the superior legislative authority in both. The intention of the Fathers of Confederation was to avoid the weakness exemplified by the American Civil War and by vesting residual powers in the federal government to develop a strong central power. In a curious analogy to American constitutional development, judicial decisions (for Canada, by the Judicial Committee of the Privy Council) reversed somewhat the intended process so that the provinces possess more power than was originally intended. The general power of the Dominion to regulate trade and commerce became restricted by judicial interpretation to cover only regulations for political purposes such as trade in arms. Uniformity in ways of settling industrial disputes, in developing water power, and formulating general company law became virtually impossible.

Such a constitutional development has resulted in less centralized direction in Canada than in any comparably industrialized country. While the size of the provinces and the variety of their problems have given some justification to decentralization, it has raised dangers to national unity and to economic progress which were becoming increasingly obvious during the past decade.

The exigencies of war would have intensified these dangers had not an instrument under which the federal government could assume direction of the life of the country in time of war emergency existed in the War Measures Act of 1914. This was brought into operation on August 2, 1939, by proclamation of the Governor in Council.[1] The Act authorized measures deemed " necessary or advisable for the security, defence, peace, order and welfare of Canada," and in particular extended the powers of the Governor in Council to: " (a) Censorship and the control and suppression of publications, writings, maps, plans, photographs, communications and means of communication; (b) Arrest, detention, exclusion and deportation; (c) Control of the harbours, ports and territorial waters of Canada and the movements of vessels; (d) Transportation by land, air, or water and the control of the transport of

---

[1] That is, by executive act. The Governor-General acts only on the advice of his Canadian ministers. Hence, the executive authority in Canada as in Great Britain is centered in the Cabinet, though executive orders (orders-in-council) are issued in the name of the Governor.

persons and things; (e) Trading, exportation, importation, production and manufacture; (f) Appropriation, control, forfeiture and disposition of property and of the use thereof."

Under this Act and other statutes four new departments of Munitions and Supply, National Defense for Air, National War Services, and National Defense for the Navy have been set up. Besides these, there are numerous specialized agencies, including the Foreign Exchange Control Board, the Wartime Prices and Trade Board, the Agricultural Supplies Board, the Canadian Shipping Board, the Censorship Coordination Committee, and the Bureau of Public Information. Each of the special agencies is responsible to a minister, though it is not part of his department. An elaborate series of Cabinet committees, which will be described in more detail below, provides attention for the fields in which these agencies work, but the major coordination and direction is secured through the War Committee and the Cabinet as a whole.

The Canadian war administration has developed empirically as the strain on a particular aspect of the economy became obvious, or as new needs demanded new controls and direction. It has grown piecemeal with the course of the war and the exhaustion of surpluses. In the first stage of the war it was largely protective in character. The Wartime Prices and Trade Board was set up to protect the civilian consumer against hoarding, profiteering, and curtailment of necessary supplies. The Foreign Exchange Control Board was established to prevent a flight of capital from Canada and to limit uncertainties as to Canada's financial position. Censorship was introduced to prevent harmful dissemination of information. In general the ordinary business mechanism was allowed to function within the limits of foreign exchange control. In industrial supply, the only change before April 1940 was to give wider powers to the purchasing organization. In the supervision of exports and imports, the chief organizational innovation was to appoint special boards and administrators to deal directly with similar bodies or officials in Great Britain. Particular arrangements were necessary from the beginning for transportation because of the scarcity of shipping and because of dangers to it, and the Transport Controller and the Canadian Shipping Board were both active in this period.

The German break-through to the west precipitated the second stage, in which the Department of Munitions and Supply was set up to take over direction of industrial production, and the Department of National Defense separated into three departments, for the Army, Navy, and Air

Force. The Department of National War Services was established to assist in mobilizing the resources of the nation. The third stage, developing throughout 1941, was marked less by the appearance of new organs than by extension of the duties and powers of existing ones. The fourth stage, in which Canada now finds itself, is that of integrating the machinery developed to deal with varied problems which have now become obviously part of a single effort. The instruments responsible for war and civilian supply, the Wartime Industries Control Board and the Wartime Prices and Trade Board, are coordinating their policy through interlocking membership. The comprehensive price control and wage stabilization program adopted in October 1941 brings the closest relation between the price structure, supply, and labor. This program has introduced the most drastic controls yet adopted by a democratic nation.

In wartime the ends of a society become simplified by the singleness of the task at hand. Its facets are many but direction is given by strategic necessities. In contrast the technical organization required is complex, because the compulsion comes from outside and its demands are not limited by the resources easily available. In its fourth year of war, the Canadian Government faces the responsibility of maintaining the smooth working of an elaborate system of control which may be affected by outside forces such as price rises in the United States. How successfully it can be expected to meet future demands may be judged in part by the history of its growth and achievements.

The pattern adopted for detailed analysis of the existing organization and work of the war administration considers first the services of national defense and the organization and problems of wartime supply in the fields of industry and agriculture. Transportation belongs to this as a vital element in linking Canada to the European battle front. Next are examined the agencies of financial control and civilian supply which seek to prevent the concentration upon war needs from disorganizing the life of the country. Finally there is an evaluation of the supervision and coordination of the wartime administration. In describing the organization of the war administration a disproportionate emphasis will inevitably fall upon the special wartime agencies and departments. It must be remembered that they are additions to an existing governmental organization and that the effectiveness of their efforts rests to a considerable extent upon the aid and cooperation extended by the older departments.

Despite the limitation on federal action, very considerable progress had been made since the First World War in building up an efficient federal administration. Perhaps the chief difference between the administrative situation in 1914 and in 1939 lay in the improvement of the caliber and experience of the civil service. It is not too much to say that the achievements of the existing civil service in maintaining ordinary functions, participating in new ones, and providing a large measure of co-ordination to the whole, have been fundamental to the successful work of the war administration.

1. National Defense

At the outbreak of war, the defense services were consolidated in the Department of National Defense organized under the National Defense Act of 1922 which had brought together the former Department of Militia and Defense, the Department of Naval Service, and the Air Board under one Minister. He was advised by a Defense Council, and in 1936 this was made advisory to a Defense Committee of the Cabinet consisting of the Prime Minister and several senior ministers. Just before war, the Defense Committee was reorganized as the Emergency Council (Committee on General Policy), and subsequently became the War Committee in the Cabinet reorganization of July 1940.

Under the pressure of war, it was decided to set up separate ministries for the Air Service and for the Navy, the former on May 22, 1940, and the latter on July 8, 1940. The work of the Department of National Defense was thus divided between three ministers, each of whom is responsible for the direction of his service and for its administration. The Department of National Defense (for the Army) is divided into four branches, comprising: the General Staff; the Master General of the Ordinance, including the sections of the chief accountant, chief ordnance mechanical engineer, and directors of ordnance services (mechanization, technical stores, general stores, and administration); the Quartermaster-General, under whom are the Director of Engineering Services, responsible for works and buildings, fortifications and equipment, and the Director of Supplies, responsible for supplies and accommodation and transport, on land and sea; and the Director of Organization, who deals with administration and personnel, including enlistments, discharges, administration, and discipline. Each of the three defense services has a somewhat comparable organization and some duplication is inevitable, particularly in auxiliary services such as the medical service and the women's auxiliary services.

There is no organization in Canada comparable to the British Committee of Imperial Defense. Coordination between the three services is maintained through the Minister of National Defense, who is the final authority on any matter involving more than one service. There is also an Associate Minister of National Defense, endowed with the same powers. This latter office is at present held by the Minister of National Defense for Air. These arrangements have made it possible to secure decentralization and at the same time to preserve the essential unity of the services without establishing an outside coordinator.

Working closely with the Department of National Defense is the Department of National War Services set up on July 12, 1940, to assist in carrying out the purposes of the National Resources Mobilization Act of June 21, 1940, for "the mobilization of all the effective resources of the nation, both human and material, for the purpose of the defense and security of Canada." The immediate responsibilities of the new department were to conduct the national registration from which was secured the data for the newly introduced compulsory military training for Canadian youth; to organize and promote different forms of voluntary assistance to the war effort; and to coordinate existing public information services of the government and use them with any necessary additions to secure "the utmost aid from the people of Canada in the national emergency which has arisen." The National War Services Department is also responsible for individual notifications to report for compulsory training. Until the trainees reach camp they are under the Department of National War Services and upon their arrival become the responsibility of the Department of National Defense. The War Services Department has organized the National Salvage Campaign, and supervises all organizations collecting for war charity. It is also responsible for most of the services distributing information. In addition to the Office of the Director of Public Information, the Canadian Broadcasting Corporation, the Travel Bureau, the National Film Board, and the Motion Picture Bureau have been placed under its supervision.[2]

---

[2] The Bureau of Information was originally set up under the Prime Minister's office, then transferred to the Department of Labor, to the Secretary of State, and, in July 1941, to the Department of National War Services.

2. Munitions and Industrial Supply

I · EARLY PURCHASING ORGANIZATION

Arrangements for service purchasing differ in Canada from those used in the United States, where the different services outline their requirements and place their own contracts. The principle of centralized buying was accepted by Canada in July 1939, when the Defense Purchasing Board was set up, following an investigation of the absence of competitive bids for a contract to manufacture Bren machine guns. This central purchasing agency expanded by September 15, 1939, into five buying units directed by experienced purchasing agents drawn from the staff of the Canadian National Railway, and from the Contracts Branch of the Department of National Defense, which was transferred to the Board.

In November the War Supply Board superseded the Defense Purchasing Board. It was empowered to act in Canada on behalf of the British Government as well as for the Canadian Government, and on February 23, 1940, was authorized to act in Canada on behalf of the French Government. The War Supply Board reported to the Minister of Finance at first but was soon made responsible to the Minister of Transport, Mr. C. D. Howe, later Minister of Munitions and Supply.

Increase in the volume of purchases necessitated the reallocation of much of the work to ten purchasing sections,[3] which were united in the General Purchasing Division directed by a general purchasing agent. Final testing was carried on by technical experts in the Department of National Defense. Local purchasing offices were established in Halifax, St. John, Quebec, Montreal, Ottawa, Toronto, Winnipeg, Calgary, and Vancouver for provision of supplies to adjacent military, air force, or naval depots.

Ordinary purchasing routine has not been feasible for the complicated new articles, which since June 1940 have formed an increasingly larger part of production. These are ordered generally on a cost plus fixed fee basis from whatever firm can make them. Various measures have been taken to overcome the objectionable features of the cost plus contract and these include " target " price contracts, " ceiling " price contracts, and management fee contracts. For other goods, requisitions are

---

[3] Clothing, aircraft, machinery, wood products, motor vehicles, fuel and paint, medical supplies, food stuffs, naval and militia stores, and barracks stores.

received from the three branches of the Department of National Defense and distributed to the various sections of the General Purchasing Division. Invitations to tender are either advertised or sent out to firms which might be interested in the order. Final approval for contracts over $5,000 must be given by Order-in-Council. If a contract is placed by agreement instead of tender, the price is investigated by the division expert and subsequently by the head of the purchasing section concerned and the general purchasing agent. In most major contracts and in all contracts awarded without tender, the department reserves the right to examine the books of the contractor in order to insure that the price is fair and reasonable.

In addition to general purchasing, six specialized divisions for Aircraft, Ships, Explosives and Chemicals, Construction, Plant Survey and Production Follow-up, and Overseas Munitions were established in October 1939. The Aircraft Division awarded all contracts on behalf of the Canadian, British, and French Governments, and placed the orders for aircraft and other requirements of the British Commonwealth Air Training Plan. The Construction Division took over from the Department of National Defense all construction work in progress. The Plant Survey and Production Follow-up Division was the continuation of a survey, begun by the Department of National Defense in 1936, which by March 1940 had completed over 2,200 plant inspections. The Overseas Munitions Division handled all purchases made by the British Supply Board in Canada. The work done through these six divisions of the War Supply Board was largely preliminary in character. Much information became available and some small-scale expansion in building was arranged but the general emphasis remained on purchasing.[4]

II · THE DEPARTMENT OF MUNITIONS AND SUPPLY

The establishment of a Department of Munitions and Supply with exclusive authority over the procurement of munitions was provided for by legislation passed in September 1939.[5] But it was not until April 1940

---

[4] During its lifetime the Defense Purchasing Board awarded contracts totalling some $43,000,-000 of which $24,868,498 consisted of purchase of railway equipment for the Canadian National and Canadian Pacific Railways. The War Supply Board placed orders of approximately $133,-350,000. Thus the total for the period from July 14, 1939, to March 31, 1940, was $176,152,714.

[5] Department of Munitions and Supply Act. The Department received wide powers for the organization of industry, including the power to appoint controllers for industrial administration. Supplies could be acquired and holders forced to accept fair and reasonable prices, a wide interpretation being given to the term " supply " to include anything likely to be useful in the prosecution of the war and in the economic life of the country.

that this was brought into effect by proclamation, and the Honorable C. D. Howe was appointed Minister. The establishment of the department on April 9, the day of the invasion of Denmark and Norway, coincided with changes in the war situation which brought a new perspective on what Canada's contribution might be.[6] The Purchasing Branch and the production divisions of the War Supply Board were taken over by the Department of Munitions and Supply, under which they expanded in size and function. Some of their activities have since been undertaken by government-owned companies.

The new department was faced with a much more complex task than that of placing service orders. It became necessary to increase plant capacity to meet the vastly enlarged orders. In consequence, heavy commitments have been made by both the Canadian and the British Governments for capital expenditures for plant extensions.

The government-financed plant construction program is largely concerned with providing additional facilities for the increased production of explosives and chemicals, armaments, ammunition and its components, automotive products, aircraft, machine tools, and base metals.[7] The capital commitments are split three ways, approximately 35 percent being paid by the Canadian Government, 26 percent by the British Government, and 39 percent by joint account. Plants financed by Great Britain sell to Canada its requirements of their output, and plants financed by the Canadian Government similarly sell to Great Britain.

The necessary enlargement of plant facilities was provided under four different arrangements, in two of which the Crown retained title. In some cases, private interests enlarged facilities and paid the cost themselves, a government board determining the sums which they were able to write off for depreciation on any profits which accrued. In other cases, expansion costs were met in the unit price of the first order, subsequent orders being filled at the normal rate. Where the government undertakes the responsibility of financing, it subsequently owns the plant or plant extension and its equipment. In general, private interests operate the plant for a management fee, the government obtaining the output

---

[6] The new situation was reflected in the great increase in the number and value of contracts. During the first quarter of 1940, approximately 1,901 contracts were awarded per month; in the second quarter of 1942, 18,029. By June 1942, the total of contracts placed amounted to $4,877,063,532.

[7] Capital commitments for this construction increased rapidly. By the end of September 1940, they amounted approximately to $235,000,000; by the end of June 1941, to $511,256,321; and by the end of June 1942 to $690,000,000.

at cost. In some special cases, however, the government has set up Crown companies, in which it has retained the management itself.

The Crown companies, now [7a] twenty-two in number, are a novel device for meeting special supply problems where the lowest price can be obtained only by private purchasing or where there are special administrative or manufacturing problems. They are incorporated, but their shares are held by the Minister of Munitions and Supply, and they are subject to Treasury control. Although they are responsible to the Government through the Department of Munitions and Supply, they are organized like private business concerns and each operates as a separate entity under its own president and board.

Four of these companies, the Allied War Supplies Corporation, the Citadel Merchandising Company, Ltd., Wartime Housing, Ltd., and Wartime Merchant Shipping, Ltd., are largely concerned with the administration, supervision, and planning of the programs for explosives and munitions, machine tools, houses to be erected in overcrowded defense areas, and cargo ships respectively. The Citadel Merchandising Company maintains a representative in Washington, attached to the British Purchasing Commission, who centers all orders for machine tools from private manufacturers working on the war program and clears the export licenses.

Five companies undertake specialized tasks in regard to machine tools and ships. Cutting Tools, Ltd., is responsible for salvaging old cutting tools and Machinery Service, Ltd., created on December 22, 1941, employs a group of skilled civilian enemy aliens to repair, rebuild, design and manufacture machinery, machine tools, jigs, and dies. Toronto Shipbuilding Company, Ltd., operates the former Dufferin Shipbuilding Company, which was one of the larger shipbuilding units of Canada and was taken over by the government in order to expand its facilities and output; Trafalgar Shipbuilding, Ltd., arranges priorities for material required in the program being carried on by the Shipbuilding Branch of the department; the Park Steamship Company supervises and controls the operation of newly built Canadian cargo vessels. Five of the Crown companies manufacture along specialized lines: Research Enterprises, Ltd., making optical glass and special instruments; Small Arms, Ltd., manufacturing the Lee-Enfield rifle; Federal Aircraft, Ltd., directing production of the Anson airplanes; National Railway Munitions, Ltd., manufacturing weapons; and Atlas Plant Extension, Ltd.,

---

[7a] August 1942.

manufacturing special alloy steels. Aero Timber Products, Ltd., which controls the production and use of airplane spruce, was incorporated in June 1942, and Veneer Log Supply, Ltd., in July.

Three companies, the Plateau Company, Ltd., Melbourne Merchandising, Ltd., and Fairmont Company, Ltd., are for the purchase of commodities. Considerable secrecy has been maintained in regard to their purchasing efforts since their function is to acquire certain materials essential to the war effort without allowing it to be apparent that the government is in the market. Fairmont Company, Ltd., did, however, purchase large stocks of rubber in 1940; the Melbourne Company purchases wool; and the Plateau Company administers the Order-in-Council " freezing " all raw silk not required for war purposes. These commodity companies operate on a self-sustaining basis, the cost of operating being added to the selling price of the product. Two companies formed in March 1942 are responsible for the production of scarce materials: the Polymer Corporation, Ltd., to produce synthetic rubber; and Wartime Metals Corporation to produce metallic magnesium and any other emergency projects in the field of war metals.[8]

Still another company, War Supplies, Ltd., was formed to aid the implementation of the Hyde Park Agreement. Through its Washington officers, War Supplies, Ltd., acts as the channel for the transfer of these purchase orders from the various United States Government departments to Canada, where the orders are then handled by the Department of Munitions and Supply.

This use of government corporations by the Department of Munitions and Supply has not gone uncriticized. There is appreciation that the form appeals through its familiarity to the business men who direct it and that it facilitates decentralization, which has been important in a period of rapid growth. It is not clear, however, that the work could not be done as well or, in the case of purchasing, better by a branch of a government department. Whether in view of the independence of action and secrecy of proceedings of the government corporations, a greater degree of responsibility is secured by the use of this form than by giving managerial direction to a private concern is an open question. Whether there is a comparable degree of initiative is also difficult to decide. It must be noted that the presidents of the Crown companies in-

---

[8] It may be noted that the main project of Wartime Metals Corporation arises out of a new method developed at the National Research Council in Ottawa for extracting magnesium metal from dolomite.

clude men of exceptional drive and experience, and the use of this form may make it easier to secure outstanding people.

In addition to supervising production, the Department of Munitions and Supply has had to widen its responsibilities to include control of essential commodities used in production. Controllers have been appointed for steel, lumber, oil, metals other than steel and iron, machine tools and machinery, power and electrical equipment, ship construction and repairs, motor vehicles, chemicals, transit, construction and supplies. This last term has been redefined frequently since the Controller of Supplies was appointed in August 1941, to cover a variety of scarce goods, and since September 1941 covers certain services as well. Each controller has extensive powers to direct the industry by buying, selling, storing, or transporting any commodity in the industry; fixing prices; issuing and cancelling licenses to do business; inspecting premises; and taking possession of any commodity or means of production, storage, or transport used by the industry.

In general it has not been necessary for them to use their coercive powers, and their work has been largely that of advice and adjustment. The controllers are responsible to the Minister of Munitions and Supply. Upon their appointment, they become members of the Wartime Industries Control Board, a clearing house through which points of conflict as to functions may be adjusted and matters affecting the various controls coordinated.

The work of the individual controllers has been far more significant than their published orders suggest. Direction and coordination go on continuously behind the scenes with largely satisfactory results. As with so much of the work of direction, however, the activities of the directors themselves have lacked coordination. To August 1941 the Wartime Industries Control Board had hardly acted even as a clearing house for information. A less indefinite arrangement was secured in August through assigning specific coordinating functions to the Board, and through appointing the Director-General of Priorities as its chairman. Not having the detailed responsibilities of a controller, he can survey the fields administered from a more general standpoint, and with more awareness of the interrelation of actions taken.

In this administrative reorganization the work of the Wartime Industries Control Board was also linked more closely to that of the Wartime Prices and Trade Board, which is responsible for civilian supply and price control. The chairman of each Board was made a member of the other. The simultaneous appointment of a Controller of Supplies provided a channel whereby the Wartime Industries Board may extend its control to other commodities which are not supervised by an administrator, and like rubber and silk are used extensively in war production. Thus a comprehensive integration of the programs for war and civilian supply was secured.

The need for general information on war requirements and for determining priorities gave rise in November 1940 to a new body known as the Wartime Requirements Board, under Mr. H. R. McMillan, formerly Timber Controller. It was empowered to obtain from any source, and more particularly from each of the fighting services, information concerning commitments, and current and future requirements; to co-ordinate and analyze this information; to formulate plans in relation to priorities; and to supply information to the controllers and departments of the Department of Munitions and Supply. The Board was responsible to the Minister of Munitions and Supply, but reported direct to the War Committee of the Cabinet. Its powers were advisory and investigatory, but an organization with executive powers, the Priorities Branch, was established to work under and in conjunction with it. Due to disagreements between the head of the War Requirements Board, who subsequently resigned, and the Minister of Munitions and Supply, the Board has not played so active a role as was expected.

Its place as arbiter of priorities was taken by the departmental organ, the Priorities Branch, which has two parts: the Priorities Division and the Construction Control Division. Its work is to implement the production and acquisition of war requirements and also to give priority aid, where necessary, to certain important civilian projects. Civilian needs are thus balanced with war requirements in so far as it is possible to do so.

War requirements are primarily a problem for the services, and their relative importance is decided in the first instance by the Army, Navy and Air Force experts, through the Inter-Service Priorities Committee. Their requirements and those of the United Nations are listed in order of importance and urgency. In addition, preferences are established for work on projects closely related to the war program — such as transportation, production of power, and fuel — and on those contributing materially to the export trade, particularly with the United States, such as the mining industry and the pulp and paper industry. Generally speaking, the Priorities Officer in the Priorities Branch of the Department of Munitions and Supply is responsible for the determination of preference ratings on all items, including raw materials, and, subject to the approval of the minister, he has sole authority for issuing priority orders or certificates.

The administration of the priorities system was initially on an informal rather than a formal or automatic basis, and public statements were not made as to classifications or categories. In general it was applied only where it was the sole means of overcoming serious delays in delivery. Since early in 1941, when President Roosevelt authorized a special arrangement extending American priorities to Canadian Government contracts and sub-contracts in the United States, the development of the Canadian priorities system has been closely related to that of the American. Contracts for Canadian war requirements in the United States receive the same ratings as comparable contracts authorized by the United States Army and Navy Munitions Board.

The Civilian Construction Control is part of the priorities organization, since it is a means of controlling civilian activities which may interfere with war requirements. Under its direction new construction, rehabilitation of plants or buildings, and the installation of new equipment not at the moment essential for the war effort are postponed. The stated intention of the control is " to postpone all avoidable non-war expenditures," and one of its additional purposes is to create a backlog for the construction industry after the war.

Unlike ordinary government departments, the Department of Munitions and Supply is not highly centralized. In its early months it was run by an executive committee, in which the heads of the various branches and other senior executives participated with the minister. As the number of branches increased the committee was abandoned. Thereafter the directors-general of the branches have had direct access individually to the minister, who, rather than the deputy minister, is to be regarded as the executive head of the department.[9]

---

[9] The following outline gives the organization of the Department of Munitions and Supply as of July 25, 1942:

Minister, Hon. C. D. Howe
   Executive Assistants
   Special Adviser on Production

ADMINISTRATION
Deputy Minister, G. K. Sheils
   Executive Assistants (Financial, General, Procurement)
General Counsel
Liaison with Department of Labor

Liaison with Department of Trade and Commerce
Director of Protection of Petroleum Reserves
United Kingdom Representative (London)
Member War Contracts Depreciation Board

One of the real problems of the department has been that so many of its members, coming often from a background of competitive business, have found it difficult to see their particular part of the work in terms of the whole. This puts heavy responsibilities on the minister and has sometimes made difficult the coordination with other branches of the war administration. Moreover the character of the department's work naturally places the emphasis on completion of construction or production as rapidly as possible rather than on the maintenance of labor standards, and the department policy in the latter regard has been generally unsatisfactory. On the other hand the decentralization of departmental organization limited administrative bottlenecks in a time of rapid growth and drawing upon business experience aided greatly in undertaking at short notice heavy responsibilities in specialized fields.

Wartime Administrator of the Port of Halifax
Representative of Transport Controller
Branches:
Economics and Statistics
Legal
Publicity

PRODUCTION
Coordinator of Production, H. J. Carmichael
Financial Adviser to Department, F. H. Brown
Director of Aluminum Production and Inter-Governmental Distribution
Requisitions and Progress Division
Branches:
Aircraft Production
Ammunition Production
Army Engineering Design
Arsenals and Small Arms Production
Automotive Production
Chemicals and Explosives
Communications and Fire Control Production
Defense Projects Construction
Gauge and Cutting Tool Production

FINANCE
Assistant Deputy Minister, J. P. Pettigrew
Liaison with Land and Expropriations
Liaison with Treasury
    Chief Treasury Officer
    Chief Cost Accountant
Purchase Investigators
Branches:
Comptroller's
Personnel and Organization
Secretary's

Washington Office

General Purchasing
Gun Production
Industrial Security
Industry and Sub-Contract Coordination
Munitions Contracts
Naval Armament and Equipment
Scrap Disposal
Shipbuilding
Tank Production
United States Purchases

III · THE INSPECTION BOARD OF THE UNITED KINGDOM AND CANADA

The need for inspection services has developed in ratio to the increase in production. Beginning with a few inspection officers in the Department of National Defense and one member of the British Purchasing Commission, there has been a steady enlargement until the personnel engaged in this task numbered 7,000 by July 1941. In November 1940 it was decided to join the Canadian and British inspection services and in January 1941 the Inspection Board of the United Kingdom and Canada took over all responsibilities in this regard for both governments. A branch of the Board operated in the United States for the same purpose. The Inspection Board of the United Kingdom and Canada carries out the inspection of all war equipment purchased in Canada for the United Kingdom War Office. Some of the items which they inspect, such as clothing and small arms, are on order for the Air Ministry and the Admiralty as well as for the War Office.[10]

SUPPLY
Priorities Branch
Wartime Industries Control Board
   Chairman, R. C. Berkinshaw
   Controllers:

Aircraft	Power
Chemicals	Ship Repairs and Salvage
Construction	Steel
Machine Tools	Supplies
Metals	Timber
Motor Vehicles	Transit
Oil	Transport

   Departmental Production Committee Representative
   Wartime Prices and Trade Board Representatives

CROWN COMPANIES

Aero Timber Products, Ltd.	Plateau Co., Ltd.
Allied War Supplies Corp.	Polymer Corp., Ltd.
Atlas Plant Extension, Ltd.	Research Enterprises, Ltd.
Citadel Merchandising Co., Ltd.	Veneer Log Supply, Ltd.
Cutting Tools and Gauges, Ltd.	Small Arms, Ltd.
Fairmont Co., Ltd.	Toronto Shipbuilding Co., Ltd.
Federal Aircraft, Ltd.	Trafalgar Shipbuilding Co., Ltd.
Machinery Service, Ltd.	War Supplies, Ltd.
Melbourne Merchandising, Ltd.	Wartime Housing, Ltd.
National Railways Munitions, Ltd.	Wartime Merchant Shipping, Ltd.
Park Steamship Co., Ltd.	Wartime Metals Corp.

[10] Admiralty equipment is inspected by the British Admiralty Technical Mission in Ottawa, and all aircraft are inspected by the representative in Montreal of the British Air Commission, Washington.

3. Labor

In the light of the great industrial expansion, major importance accrues to securing a coordinated policy on labor. This is complicated in Canada by the division of authority between the Dominion and the provinces, the understaffing of Dominion and provincial labor departments, the divisions between trade union groups and the general weakness of union organization, the attitude towards labor of employers' organizations such as the Canadian Manufacturers' Association, the lack until recently of a national system of employment offices and the divergent purposes in regard to labor of the Departments of National Defense, Munitions and Supply, Agriculture and Labor. In addition, the absence of labor representation on many government boards and the internment of some labor leaders have led to bitterness which has interfered with smooth relations.

The Labor Department developed a more forward policy during 1941, but it lacked the comprehensive organization needed for increasingly pressing problems. Two organs which had been established to meet special problems were the Interdepartmental Committee on Labor Coordination, an advisory body of senior civil servants set up on October 25, 1940, and the National Labor Supply Council, which was set up in June 1940 to exercise a general supervision over government labor policy, but has become a purely advisory board. The latter reports to the Ministry of Labor and the former to the Committee on Labor Supply of the Cabinet, of which the Minister of Labor is chairman.

Early in the war all disputes in war industries were placed under the Industrial Disputes Investigation Act of 1907, which had been drafted originally to cover disputes in mines and industries connected with public utilities. It requires that every means of mediation and conciliation be exhausted before action is taken. Negotiation between employers and employees is mandatory. Following this, notice must be given of intention to act. Either or both parties then ask the Minister of Labor to appoint a Board of Conciliation and Investigation, which he is supposed to do within fifteen days. The Board of Conciliation and Investigation consists of three members of whom one is recommended by the employees, one by the employer, and the third by the two first chosen. The findings of the Board are not binding on either party, but they must be made public in the *Labor Gazette,* organ of the Labor Department. If the employees reject the board's recommendation, they are free to strike after a majority vote taken under the auspices of the department. In nearly all cases both parties abide voluntarily by the board's opinion. Recently provision has been made for an intermediate stage through the appointment of an investigator to determine whether or not a Board of Conciliation is necessary.

An attempt to regulate wages in war industries by keeping them from going above the levels reached before 1940 was made under Order-in-Council in December 1940.[11] On October 18, 1941, a more comprehensive program of wage stabilization was announced as part of the attempt to secure general stabilization of prices and wages. Under this program all wages and salaries have been stabilized at the rate established before November 7, 1941. Those receiving salaries of more than $3,000 a year are not paid cost-of-living bonuses, but those under that amount may be.[12] Basic wage rates may not be increased or decreased by employers without permission. Restrictions on the movements of workers in war industries have also been introduced, and no application may be accepted from them by any other employers, except in the case of a skilled tradesman not working at his trade. The movement of male labor from agriculture or into a large number of specified services and industries has been prohibited except by special permit from the National Selective Service.

Inspection and enforcement of this program is provided by the joint staffs of the Dominion and provincial departments of labor. They are supervised by a newly created National War Labor Board and nine Regional Labor Boards (one in each province) on which government, labor and employers are represented. Only these boards may authorize changes in wage scales, and permission is given only when the wage level is found to be below that in similar occupations in comparable localities.[13]

On March 24, 1942 an extended National Selective Service plan for mobilizing Canadian labor was announced.[14] The Minister of Labor

---

[11] See Chapter VI, p. 325.

[12] All adult male employees and all other employees employed at basic wage rates of $25 or more a week receive cost-of-living bonuses at the rate of 25 cents a week for each one percent rise in the cost-of-living index. Male employees under twenty-one years of age and female workers employed at basic wage rates of less than $25 a week receive one percent of their basic weekly wage rates. The bonus is paid by the employer, and the rate is adjusted every three months. The first bonus was awarded in July 1942.

[13] Promotion of salaried officials, if it involves a salary increase, must be approved by the Minister of National Revenue.

[14] See Chapter V, p. 303.

and under him the Director and Associate Director of National Selective Service are primarily responsible for the plan. Regional officers were to be appointed and to be advised and assisted by voluntary unpaid citizens' committees.

A central registry has been established in the Department of Labor for the necessary data for the working of the program. This will be based primarily on the records of the 1940 national registration and the unemployment insurance files, and may be supplemented by further surveys. To avoid duplication, administrative responsibility for national registration has been transferred from the Department of National War Services to the Department of Labor, but the calling up of men for compulsory military service continues to be the responsibility of National War Services. The actual mobilization of industrial man power will be effected in the main through the Employment Service of Canada. A record of professional technicians has been compiled by the Wartime Bureau of Technical Personnel set up within the Department of Labor. Under the new regulations employment of engineers, college teachers of engineering science, research scientists, physicists, geologists, mathematicians, and architects is subject to the approval of this Bureau.

4. Food Supply

Canadian agriculture, largely dependent as it is upon exports, suffered severely from the depression and from prewar autarchical policies in Europe, particularly in the totalitarian states. At the outbreak of war, it was far from having recovered the favorable position it held in 1928, nor in general have the demands of war restored this position. Exclusion from continental markets after the German break-through to the west and the need of conserving British shipping have severely limited exports except in a few products, most notably hogs and cheese. Agricultural policy has had to seek expansion in these fields and at the same time plan for reduction in others, particularly wheat.

On September 9, 1939, a special body to supervise Canadian agriculture during the war was set up as the Agricultural Supplies Committee, subsequently renamed the Agricultural Supplies Board. This body is composed of senior members of the Department of Agriculture, and its work is virtually indistinguishable from that of the department. The membership of three special committees — the Seed Supply Committee, the Fertilizer Supply Committee, and the Pesticide Supply Committee — which assist the board [15] is also drawn from the permanent service. Much of the work of the board is carried on in cooperation with provincial committees which are representative of provincial and Dominion field staffs and producer organizations.

The policy of the board, as of the Department of Agriculture, has been conservative. Its purpose is to keep Canadian agriculture functioning to supply the food and fiber needs of Canada and the Allies without unnecessarily complicating the return of the Canadian farmer to a normal program when peace comes. Its work is difficult since British imports are restricted as far as possible to concentrated, storable, and relatively cheap food stuffs that are not difficult to handle and of which sufficient quantities cannot be produced in the United Kingdom. Essential food products in general order of preference are wheat and other cereals, dairy products, bacon and other cured meats, canned and frozen fish, poultry and eggs, canned fruit and canned vegetables.

Canada's surplus production of wheat, despite the fact that the British demand for it is about 160,000,000 bushels a year, places a heavy drain upon dominion resources, since farmers are guaranteed 70 cents a bushel for A-1 quality.[16] Because wheat is such an important item in Canadian agriculture, there has long existed a special statutory organ, the Wheat Board, which gives it exclusive attention. In an effort to reduce the surplus in 1941, farmers were offered bonuses of $2 an acre for the whole or any part of the 1940 wheat acreage transferred to coarse grains, $4 an acre for acreage out of wheat and put in summer fallow, and $2 an acre for placing fiber in the soil to provide a better seed bed for future wheat growing and in the meantime sowing grass on the reduced wheat acreage. Quotas of delivery to the Wheat Board were compulsorily limited to 65 percent of the 1940 deliveries. Through this drastic program, it was hoped that there would be not only reduction of acreage but also a stimulus to dairy products through the increased growing of grass. The cost to the government nevertheless remains very high. For some other surplus products the government has guaranteed from 80 to 85 percent of the prevailing price on about 80 percent of the amount affected by blockade restrictions.

In contrast to the surplus production in many fields there has been

---

[15] The ingredients of fertilizers and pesticides are normally imported into Canada from European sources.

[16] A good crop in 1940 coupled with the loss of continental markets resulted in a carry-over of 575,000,000 bushels which necessitated a great expansion of storage space. There were in April 1942 more than 467,000,000 bushels on hand.

steadily increasing demand from Great Britain for specialized products which fitted its particular requirements. One feature of the British agreement in November 1939 to purchase 5,600,000 lbs. of Canadian bacon and ham per week for the next year was that the purchases must be made through a single agency.[17] The Bacon Board was therefore established to insure that regular and sufficient supplies would be available for export as required. It is also responsible for the maintenance of prewar quality through price differentials as between grades and of a fair relationship between hog and bacon prices. The Bacon Board has power to license packers, to require any packer to give priority to the pricing and delivering of bacon required to fill the export quota and to fix the minimum price to be paid by packers for hogs. A Bacon Advisory Committee reviews the policy of the Board.

A special agreement, administered by the Dairy Products Board, also exists for cheese. There is also a special arrangement for condensed milk, but cheese is preferred.[18] There is no arrangement for butter, lest it interfere with the quantity of cheese delivered. In addition to the Dairy Products Board a Special Products Board was established in the spring of 1941 to deal with egg and poultry export orders and also with orders for any other agricultural product for which handling arrangements had not already been provided.

The British have tried to secure the agricultural agreements at prewar prices f.o.b. (which means that they meet the increased shipping costs), and this has created some difficulty, since agricultural costs vary more than those of raw materials. The department might have pressed for higher prices, but it was difficult to do so in a general situation of surplus, particularly as the period was also one of United States surpluses and low prices. At the time of the passing of the Lend-Lease Act, considerable fear was expressed in Canada that the new arrangement would result in the British taking from the United States the agricultural supplies which until that time had been secured from Canada. Great quantities of food stuffs are taken from the United States, but the United

---

[17] The contract for the period ending October 31, 1940, called for the delivery of 291.2 million lbs. of bacon, and actually 331 million lbs. were delivered. For the next year it was arranged to ship 425.6 million lbs. at a lower price. The agreement for the year ending October 31, 1942 called for the delivery of 600,000,000 lbs., more than was shipped in the ten years between 1927 and 1936.

[18] 90,000,000 lbs. of cheese were delivered in 1939–40. Since then the British have been prepared to take all that can be produced. 115,000,000 lbs. were shipped in the year ending March 31, 1942.

Kingdom has been under political pressure from the Canadian Government to take as much as possible from Canada.

The amount of food and agricultural produce which Canada can provide depends to some extent on the policy adopted by the Department of Agriculture. Demand is high within restricted fields, and there are possibilities of expansion to aid in counterbalancing the potential dangers of existing heavy surpluses. On October 18, 1941, the Prime Minister announced the intention of the Government to apply the principle of the price-ceiling to agricultural prices, as an integral part of the general program of price and wage stabilization. Maximum prices for certain farm products are based on the maximum market prices during the four-week period ending October 11. In March 1942 agricultural workers were forbidden to accept any other occupation without special permission. These efforts to stabilize agricultural employment and prices might well be coupled with a more forward policy of stimulating the production of needed commodities by subsidies so as to meet demand for them when it arises.

5. Transportation. Canadian Shipping Board and Transport Controller

To make available to Great Britain and its Allies the supplies which Canada produces, it has been necessary to keep close supervision over transportation within and outside the country. The Canadian railway transportation system, overdeveloped for peacetime uses, is a distinct asset in the war situation. In contrast, Canadian shipping is comparatively small, though increasing. While the latter is under ultimate Canadian control there is a well-integrated division of responsibility, in accordance with which the Canadian Government has control over the ports while the British direct the movement of ships to and from them. This has worked fairly well, though during most of the war closer cooperation between Canadian and British authorities and more precise recognition of spheres of influence would have been desirable.

In November 1939 a Transport Controller was appointed within the Department of Transport with general power over internal and external transportation arrangements. Applications for priority of transportation for troops, naval forces, materials, and supplies on behalf of the Canadian, British, or Allied Governments, are made through the Department of Transport and determined by the Transport Controller. Before this all vessels of more than 500 gross tons had been licensed by the Minister of Transport, acting through an advisory Ship Licensing Board, which was also empowered to requisition and reroute shipping. The Canadian Shipping Board, which since January 1940 has been associated not with the Ministry of Transport but with the Department of Trade and Commerce, was set up in December 1939 to assist in providing ocean transport for Canadian trade. It maintains close contact with the movements of all Canadian shipping through its own Ship Licensing Committee.

Since Canadian ships have all been placed on " dangerous routes," Canada has been dependent for necessary services in " safe trades " on neutral shipping. The Shipping Board has had great difficulty in procuring neutral shipping space, and since the extension of naval conflict to the Pacific, the shipping problem has become progressively more difficult.

6. Financial Control and Civilian Supply

I · THE FOREIGN EXCHANGE CONTROL BOARD

Foreign exchange control is the most radical of the measures which have been adopted to prevent a dislocation by wartime conditions of Canada's internal structure and external economic relations. Its initial purpose was to prevent a flight of capital from Canada and by curbing the uncertainties of its financial situation to strengthen internal morale. Subsequently, with the new stage following the German break-through, the pressure of heavy government expenditure threatened depreciation, and more rigid restrictions on outflow of capital had to be made.

Canada was in a particularly difficult position because exchange control in the Sterling Area at the outbreak of war made it impossible to convert a favorable sterling balance into dollars to meet an adverse balance of trade with the United States. Britain's increasingly heavy purchases in Canada were, furthermore, financed by the repatriation of Canadian securities held in the United Kingdom and the accumulation of sterling balances in London, or by credits extended by Canada to the United Kingdom.[19] Thus the problem of buying in the United States has become ever more difficult, as Canada has a steadily increasing adverse balance to meet out of capital resources.

---

[19] See Chapter VI, p. 322.

The Foreign Exchange Control Board, set up on September 15, 1939, is not itself a policy-making body but an instrument for carrying out Government policy on exchange matters. It has broad powers to take control over all foreign exchange held or owned by any resident of Canada; it may license all imports and exports and if necessary control or limit their quantities, and it has also the power to fix exchange rates. Its membership, under the chairmanship of the Governor and Deputy Governor of the Bank of Canada (a statutory body with which the Board works closely), is drawn from key members of the civil service.[20]

The regulation of capital exports involves supervision of all transactions between residents of Canada and non-residents.[21] Most of the vast amount of administrative work occasioned by transactions between Canada and the United States is carried on in Ottawa, though a special office has been set up in Vancouver to handle the special exchange problems of the Pacific Coast. Routine work is carried on through five sections: the Foreign Exchange Section, which works with the chartered banks on matters concerning the purchase and sale of foreign exchange; the Securities and Insurance Section, for security questions; the Canadian Payment Section, for exports; the General Section, dealing with trust and loan companies, private problems, and miscellaneous subjects; and the Commercial Section, for relations with corporations and businesses other than financial companies. The latter is subdivided into five divisions: the Examiners Division, with branch offices in Toronto and Montreal, which audits monthly returns of some two thousand companies with permits to operate foreign currency bank accounts and special export-import licenses; the Investigators Division for investigating work in the field, and also the returns to the Examiners Division; the Approvals Division for applications to pay dividends to nonresident shareholders; the Grain Division; and a General Division for miscellaneous problems. Thus a careful check is kept on all aspects of the situation and the effect of the stringent regulations is as far as possible equalized.

The successful working of foreign exchange control is in considerable part due to the secrecy preceding its introduction, the comprehensiveness of the regulations, which paralleled at the time of their introduction

20 It includes the Deputy Minister of Finance, the Commissioner of Customs, the Chief Inspector of the Post Office Department, the Director of Commercial Intelligence Service, Department of Trade and Commerce, and the Under-Secretary of State for External Affairs.

21 It should be noted that there are no restrictions on transfers from American holdings of Canadian dollars or on capital payments made under the terms of a contract dated prior to September 16, 1939, where the contract stipulates payment in a foreign currency, as, for example, in the case of maturing Canadian bonds which are payable in United States dollars.

the arrangements arrived at in Great Britain after a year of experimentation, and the possibility of drawing on the facilities of the Bank of Canada in its operations. Such evasions of its rules as have occurred have been in the main from ignorance, and in general the regulations have been accepted cooperatively.

II · THE WARTIME PRICES AND TRADE BOARD

The Wartime Prices and Trade Board was established within a few hours of the British declaration of war, to aid in the transition from a peace to a wartime economy. All civilian " necessaries of life," with the exception of wheat and fish, which were already regulated by statutory bodies,[22] were placed under its supervision. Subject always to the approval of the Governor-in-Council, it was given power to license producers or dealers, fix prices, ration commodities, buy and sell goods, commandeer supplies, and place embargoes on exports. Its function as a supervising agent to prevent hoarding and the charging of exorbitant prices on food, fuel, and other necessities, has loomed large in the public's view of the Board, but is subsidiary to the wider responsibility of securing supplies and arranging their equitable allocation. It has functioned in fact as a civilian board of supply, and its work has been increasingly concerned with planning on a long-range scale.

Members of the Board were drawn from the permanent service, and the policy has been to use where possible the facilities of other organizations such as the Dominion Bureau of Statistics rather than to duplicate their functions. The Board's work has been carried on through investigations into the distribution and sale of a wide range of commodities, through a constant check on retail prices to assure that they are in line with prices of raw materials and wholesale prices, through conferences with representatives of the industries, and through the appointment of administrators who organize and direct supplies in particular fields. The Board has in general relied on investigation and publicity rather than its coercive powers and has been able to depend upon the voluntary cooperation of industry and the public, both of which fear a repetition of the inflation of the last war.

The Board's practice of appointing special administrators in certain fields requiring detailed and continuous attention was early established, and has subsequently been adopted by the Department of Munitions and Supply. The administrators have all been selected from outside the fields

---

[22] The Wheat Board and the Salt Fish Board.

for which they are made responsible, serve on a dollar-a-year basis with their expenses met, and are assisted by technical advisers who are the best experts in the field that could be secured. General lines of policy are worked out by the Board in consultation with the Cabinet on the one hand and the administrator on the other. It is the administrator's responsibility, with the assistance of his technical adviser, and in frequent consultation with the industry, to work out these policies in day-to-day activities. In addition to supervising the distribution and allocation of supplies in Canada, the administrators conduct any necessary negotiations with the United Kingdom controllers for the regular supply of imports.

The work of the administrators, as of the Board as a whole, has a particular interest because it was concerned so early with the organization of supply, and because it met so satisfactorily the initial problems in its field. A good illustration of this is to be found in the handling of wool supplies, about which there was immediate concern. The purchase by the United Kingdom of the entire Australasian wool clip for the duration of the war and subsequent prohibition of export of all wool from Australia, New Zealand, and Great Britain temporarily cut off the normal source of 75 percent of the Canadian wool supply. On September 18, 1939 a Wool Administrator was appointed to coordinate the industry and to allocate the supply and production in accord with need. The Wool Administrator, unlike the Sugar Administrator,[23] does not buy supplies but supervises buying and distribution. On November 24 the Board issued an order temporarily fixing a maximum price for the grades of wool most urgently needed, particularly for uniforms, the only definite price-fixing action the Board undertook in the first months of its existence. Subsequently negotiations with the Wool Control Scheme resulted in increased releases of supplies, and through constant attention satisfactory conditions have been maintained. Other administrators have been appointed for coal, hides and leather, oils, and rentals, the latter in consequence of the extension of the powers of the Board in September 1940 over rent for housing accommodation. This was necessitated by the influx of population and the consequent housing shortage in certain areas in which military or wartime industrial expansion had taken place.

---

[23] Under whom all raw sugar for Canadian use is purchased from the United Kingdom Sugar Control and resold to Canadian refineries, the price for raw sugar being agreed upon each year by the United Kingdom and Canada.

The Wartime Prices and Trade Board was also used by the Government to see that manufacturers did not take advantage of the imposition in June 1940 of a 10 percent War Exchange Tax on imports from non-British countries. The Board has also carried on investigations in regard to the incidence of import prohibitions and excise taxes under the regulations of December 2, 1940, to see that there is no increase in prices of similar goods produced in Canada. But during the first two years of the war the Board used its power sparingly, except in regard to rents. In this respect a definite policy of price-fixing was pursued. The satisfaction it has given depends on the selection of the localities, the time of introduction, and the rate of the ceiling. In general the work has been approved, and no serious restraint appears to have been exercised on private building.[24]

The accomplishments of the Board as described so far comprise the first stage of its activities when it concentrated upon meeting the needs of civilian supply and preventing profiteering. In policing prices it acted on complaints rather than on its own initiative and in general it dealt with cases rather than with broad problems. But the work of the Board and its administrators was an important factor in preventing the cost of living index from rising more than 9.6 percent from the outbreak of war until June 1941, in spite of depreciation of the Canadian dollar, increased taxation on many food stuffs, and the increase of costs on overseas supplies. As scarcities became serious and the United States moved also toward scarcities and price rises, more comprehensive planning and coordination of action became necessary.

Between June and October 1941 the cost of living index rose another 6 percent. Emphasis shifted to the problem of controlling inflation, and the Wartime Prices and Trade Board entered the second stage of its activities with major responsibilities for administering a new program of price stabilization and control. In the middle of August, the Wartime Prices and Trade Board was transferred from the Minister of Labor to the Minister of Finance. At the end of the month, the Board's responsibilities were extended to cover all prices, control being thereby central-

24 For certain designated areas the Board fixed rentals at the levels of January 2, 1940, and for others subsequently added, at the level of January 2, 1941. If there was no lease at the given date, maximum rental is determined by the administrator. Hearings to determine a satisfactory policy have been held in a number of places. For the more detailed investigation dependence was had at first on local rentals committees, and subsequently on county or district court judges or other persons appointed by the rentals administrator. Rentals for new housing are fixed only on application of landlord or tenant. The provision of needed housing has been undertaken by a Crown company under the Department of Munitions and Supply, Wartime Housing Ltd.

ized in the Department of Finance with which the Board remains associated. In addition, the Board's responsibilities for supply were extended to "all goods and services" not coming under the jurisdiction of the Wartime Industries Control Board.

Under the new orders the powers of the Wartime Prices and Trade Board included the authority to fix minimum as well as maximum prices and markups, and to prohibit the purchase, sale, or supply of "any goods and services" at variance with such prices. It could also prescribe the terms and conditions under which any goods or services might be sold or supplied. This included regulation of "installment-buying." Complete authority was given to license the suppliers of "any goods or services." To carry out these responsibilities the Board received extensive powers of investigation and regulation. In October the Board instituted a system of licenses for dealers in food and clothing. To curtail purchases it severely restricted consumer credit by making the minimum down payment on a long list of goods 33⅓ percent of the cash price and twelve months the limit within which installments had to be paid.

At the same time that the responsibilities of the Wartime Prices and Trade Board were extended, its organization was coordinated more closely with that of the Wartime Industries Control Board. This made possible more comprehensive planning for and organization of the whole field of supply. A closely integrated organization had thus been secured before fresh responsibilities were laid on the Wartime Prices and Trade Board by the elaborate program for stabilization of prices and wages announced on October 18, 1941 and brought into effect on December 1, 1941.

This program set as a "ceiling" above which prices were not to rise — the highest price of each seller during the four weeks' basic period, September 15 to October 11, 1941. This ceiling covers the prices of all goods except a few which are expressly exempt, and thirteen specified essential services such as electricity and gas. It does not include most professional services. Sales to the Department of Munitions and Supply are exempt, as are exports, sales of personal belongings and of securities. Certain other exceptions take into account normal seasonal fluctuations in price or export of fresh fruit and vegetables, fish, livestock and certain farm products sold by farmers to dealers and processors. These prices are carefully watched, however, and if they rise unreasonably may be put under the ceiling.

The Wartime Prices and Trade Board has the major responsibility for administering the price ceiling. For this purpose it has set up certain additional machinery including administrators and directors from the membership of each industry and trade; and coordinators for textiles, foods, metals, and paper products. In addition it has appointed administrators for the retail and the wholesale trade and for services. The controllers of the Department of Munitions and Supply act as administrators for the Board in respect to the prices of commodities under their jurisdiction. For local supervision of the program regional offices have been established by the Board throughout Canada. It has also set up a Consumers' Branch to watch over the interests of consumers and to coordinate the work of recently established Women's Regional Advisory Committees.

The decision was taken to impose a general price ceiling because it was felt that it could be most quickly imposed, was not discriminatory, involved fewer administrative difficulties, because there would be no uncontrolled group of prices to disturb the program for others, and because it would justify general wage stabilization. Set prices are not imposed for all commodities throughout the country, but individual ceilings determined by the prices charged during the base period are established for every store.

Certain problems inevitably arise, some due to " time lags," others to increased costs due for example to the Pacific war or to future costs-of-living bonuses.[25] In some cases the retail ceiling price will be lower than the price the retailer will have to pay for future supplies. Wholesalers may face similar difficulties in relation to manufacturers' prices, and manufacturers in relation to their costs. The attempt is being made to have all sections of the trade concerned absorb a part of increased cost in accordance with their ability to reduce their profits. Also, unnecessary costs of production and distribution are to be cut out. To supervise this the Wartime Prices and Trade Board established a Division of Simplified Practice to cooperate with their administrators and with the advisory committees which have been set up in each trade. A number of recent orders have provided for conservation of scarce materials, for standardization and for the elimination of competitive practices.

When industries find it impossible to maintain supplies at prices under the ceiling, government assistance may be given, either through a subsidy or through reduction or remission of taxes. Subsidy payments

---

[25] The first cost-of-living bonus was awarded in July 1942. In December, to keep the index steady, subsidies were introduced for several commodities such as milk, tea, coffee, and oranges.

(decided upon by the Wartime Prices and Trade Board) are handled through the Commodity Prices Stabilization Corporation, a government corporation. Recently, temporary subsidies for milk and shoes were provided, but the chief need will be in connection with imports. Thirty classes of unessential goods have been listed as ineligible for subsidy. Consumers' purchases of certain scarce commodities have also been limited.

As in its earlier work, the Wartime Prices and Trade Board is relying extensively upon the voluntary cooperation of business, farmers, labor and consumers. Penalties for violation of its rules may be imposed on both buyers and sellers. There is an Enforcement Administration which cooperates with existing government officials such as the weights and measures inspectors of the Department of Trade and Commerce. So far, however, cooperation on the part of both sellers and consumers has been generously extended. This has been a decisive factor in the successful establishment of the drastic experiment of general price control.

7. Coordination and Control

Coordination and supervision of the new agencies is secured through the Cabinet structure. The new departments are under responsible ministers, and the independent boards are responsible to particular ministers and through them to the Cabinet. Although associated with existing government departments,[26] the agencies are not branches or sections of them and the direct relationship is through the ministers. While the

---

26 Department of Finance: The Foreign Exchange Control Board, National Loan Committee, National War Savings Committee

Department of Labor: Wartime Prices and Trade Board (transferred, Aug. 1941, to Department of Finance). National Labor Supply Council

Department of Agriculture: Agricultural Supplies Committee (Agricultural Supplies Board) Bacon Board, Advisory Committee to Bacon Board, Dairy Products Board

Department of Fisheries: Wartime Fisheries Advisory Board, Lobster Controller and Advisory Board

Department of Munitions and Supply: The Wartime Industries Control Board

Department of Trade and Commerce: The Canadian Shipping Board, Inventions Board

Department of Transport: Transportation Controller, Advisory Boards recommending compensation for requisitioned boats

Department of Secretary of State: Voluntary Service Registration Bureau, Internment Operations, Custodian of Enemy Property, Censorship Coordination Committee (also with National Defense, Postmaster-General, Transport)

Department of Justice: Registrar-General of Alien Enemies, Advisory Committee on Enemy Aliens, Committee on Emergency Legislation

Department of National Defense: Dependents' Allowance Board

Department of National War Services: Office of the Director of Public Information, War Charities Advisory Board

Prime Minister's Office: Advisory Committee on Economic Policy

detailed programs and the timing of action are decided by the boards themselves, recommendations for action must come before the Cabinet, and some of the powers of the agencies, price-fixing for example, are exercisable only with the approval of the Governor-in-Council in each instance. A recommendation can come before Council only through a minister who must sign and, therefore, make himself responsible for it.

While the Cabinet as a whole bears formal responsibility, it operates in part through the War Committee and subcommittees charged with responsibility in special spheres of activity. The War Committee, whose particular functions will be considered below, concentrates on matters of war policy and defense. In the early period, it reviewed decisions of the war agencies, particularly in regard to activities in which more than one department was involved, but subsequently, as the agencies became better established, the review has become more formal.

I · COMMITTEES OF THE CABINET

The subcommittees, ten in number, are designed to provide specialized attention for particular fields of activity. Shortly before the outbreak of war, five subcommittees for supplies, legislation, public information, finance, and internal security were set up. In a reorganization on December 5, 1939, committees were established on War Finance and Supply, Food Production and Marketing, Fuel and Power, Shipping and Transportation, Price Control and Labor, Internal Security, Legislation, and Public Information, in addition to which are the usual standing committee on Wheat and another subsequently set up on Demobilization and Reestablishment. The special war agencies and some statutory bodies with particular war functions are grouped under seven of these committees [27] but report to the minister of the department with

---

[27] Committee on War Finance and Supply: Foreign Exchange Control Board, Inventions Board, Wartime Industries Control Board

Committee on Food Production and Marketing: Agricultural Supplies Board, Bacon Board, Advisory Committee to the Bacon Board, Dairy Products Board, Wartime Fisheries Advisory Board, Lobster Controller, and Advisory Board

Committee on Shipping and Transportation: Canadian Shipping Board, Transport Controller

Committee on Price Control and Labor: Wartime Prices and Trade Board, National Labor Supply Council, Inter-Departmental Committee on Labor Coordination

Committee on Internal Security: Custodian of Enemy Property, Registrar-General of Alien Enemies, Director of Internment Operations, Dependents' Allowance Board, Administrator of War Charities Act, Advisory Committee on Enemy Aliens

Committee on Legislation: Committee on Emergency Legislation

Committee on Public Information: Voluntary Service Registration Bureau, Censorship Coordination Committee, Public Information Office

which they are associated rather than to the chairman of the committee under which they are placed. All committees are organized under the chairmanship of the minister most concerned and include three to five of his colleagues whose departments are particularly interested in the subject.

The extent to which the committees have been used has varied according to the particular minister who acted as its convener. In cases where ministers are also in the War Committee, discussion may be carried on there instead of in the specialized committee. For example, the War Finance and Supply Committee functioned fairly regularly when Mr. Ralston was Minister of Finance, but after he was succeeded by Mr. Ilsley the committee was used very little and matters which would have been discussed there were taken direct to the War Committee. The Food Production and Marketing Committee has been used fairly systematically, and as always the Wheat Committee has been active. The Committee on Fuel and Power has scarcely met and that on Shipping and Transportation not frequently. The Committee on Price Control and Labor meets from time to time to consider recommendations on policy put forward by the Wartime Prices and Trade Board, the National Labor Supply Council and the Inter-Departmental Committee on Labor Coordination. The Committee on Internal Security, concerned with drafting the Defense of the Realm Act, and the Committee on Legislation, which prevents overlapping between new legislation and that already in existence, were more active at the beginning of the war than subsequently. Not very much has been done through the Committee on Public Information. The most recently established committee of the Cabinet, that on Demobilization and Reestablishment, has functioned steadily since the problems with which it is concerned began to attract attention.

II · WAR COMMITTEE OF THE CABINET

The most important of the Cabinet committees and the real center of power in the Government is the War Committee. This body, formally established in July 1940, assumes the major responsibility for directing not only war policy but also general affairs. Matters concerning departments not represented in the War Committee are considered fully in Cabinet Council, and formal action on everything must be taken by the Cabinet through the Privy Council. But the War Committee comprises a quorum in itself if it needs to take instant action. Its decisions pass the larger body with little question and it is accepted as chief coordinator of all activity.

A somewhat similar executive committee has existed since 1936, first as the Defense Committee and after August 1939 as the Emergency Council (Committee on General Policy). The War Committee, however, assumes more general direction of affairs than did either of the other bodies and its control of war policy is virtually complete.

This central position of the War Committee raises two questions which are vital for the successful working of the war administration: its control over the activities of government and the measure of planning and coordination which it is able to undertake. Both are dependent on the effectiveness of the War Committee itself and on the instruments of coordination which it can use.

The size of the War Committee, numbering ten officially,[28] is a handicap in giving concentrated direction and unnecessary for supervision. Reduction of its numbers would run counter to the tradition, which has made the Cabinet so unwieldy, of representing geographical divisions in the executive organ, but would increase its efficiency. As far as functional representation is concerned the War Committee might well be reduced to five members — the Prime Minister, and the Ministers of Justice, Finance, National Defense, and Munitions and Supply. In fact, some such limitation in numbers appears to be evolving empirically. The late leader of the Government in the Senate, M. Dandurand, rarely attended meetings in the months before his death; one of the ministers of National Defense is nearly always abroad; and it does not seem that the new Minister of National War Services is included. This means that usually six or seven attend, making a more manageable number.

The aid of a secretariat is now a regular feature of the War Committee routine. Before the war, some minutes were taken at meetings of the Defense Committee and records are now kept of Cabinet decisions. The most complete minutes are kept of the War Committee, and in addition the clerk of the Privy Council frequently draws up its agenda, circulates

---

[28] War Committee: Prime Minister (Minister of External Affairs)
                Leader of the Government in the Senate
                Minister of Justice
                Minister of Finance
                Minister of National Defense
                Minister of Mines and Resources
                Minister of Munitions and Supply
                Minister of National Defense for Air
                Minister of National Defense for Naval Services
                Minister of National War Services

documents, and sends a record of decisions to the ministers concerned.

Outside of the War Committee and Cabinet responsibilities, each member of the War Committee carries heavy administrative responsibilities (the Prime Minister is also Minister of External Affairs) which entail a serious burden. On the other hand this makes the direct supervision of key departments and agencies possible. The idea of a War Cabinet freed of administrative duties has found little favor in Canada, and it is unlikely that such an expedient will be tried. The burden of parliamentary routine could be somewhat lightened, however, by the use of Parliamentary under-secretaries. This was tried in a modest way during the last war and could lessen the load of overworked ministers for more vital duties of coordination and planning.

While these changes would enable the War Committee to fulfill better its tasks of supervision, coordination and planning, it is clear that it must be able to draw on other coordinating bodies for information and advice. Two bodies of this character have been established of which the second, the Wartime Requirements Board, set up in November 1940 to provide the War Committee with information on current and future requirements, has had little active function. The first, the Advisory Committee on Economic Policy, has had very considerable importance and will be described briefly before a general consideration of the needs of the new situation of growing scarcities is undertaken.

III · THE ADVISORY COMMITTEE ON ECONOMIC POLICY

The Advisory Committee on Economic Policy was set up in September 1939, and is composed of important officials from different departments and boards.[29] It reports direct to the War Committee, particularly

---

[29] Chairman, Dr. W. C. Clark, Deputy Minister of Finance
Assistant to Chairman, Dr. W. A. Mackintosh, Special Assistant to Deputy Minister of Finance
Graham F. Towers, Governor of the Bank of Canada
H. D. Scully, Commissioner of Customs (Steel Controller)
H. B. McKinnon, Chairman of the Tariff Board and of the Wartime Prices and Trade Board
G. S. H. Barton, Deputy Minister of Agriculture
Charles Camsell, Deputy Minister of Mines and Resources
L. D. Wilgress, Deputy Minister of Trade and Commerce
R. H. Coats, Dominion Statistician
Colonel H. DesRosiers, Associate Deputy Minister of National Defense
N. A. M. Robertson, Under-secretary of State for External Affairs
R. A. C. Henry, Economic Adviser, Department of Munitions and Supply
Bryce Stewart, Deputy Minister of Labor
Secretary, R. B. Bryce, Department of Finance

on general economic problems. In the beginning, reports of the special agencies were frequently referred to it, but this became less common as the agencies developed. The almost constant reference of general questions to it during the first fifteen months of war slackened greatly after December 1940 and the Committee met less frequently than was common in the earlier period. It is still important, however, as a clearing house for information and for discussion of general policies, and its work has aided greatly in reducing overlapping and friction.

The reduced importance of the Advisory Committee appeared to be the result of a deliberate policy on the part of the War Committee of preventing other organs from becoming too powerful. By virtue of its membership, however, it will retain a significant position unless superseded by some comparable institution. It is clear that outstanding officers from different branches of the service who have specialized knowledge of departmental work, as well as of the new agencies, can accomplish much through the rather informal meetings of the Committee. When Dr. Mackintosh was brought to Ottawa from Queen's University as a special adviser to the Deputy Minister of Finance, he acted also as assistant to him in his capacity as chairman of the Advisory Committee. With the secretary, he drafted most of its reports as well as carrying a good deal of responsibility for general direction. The fact that his lack of specific administrative duties makes him freer to undertake such important functions suggests the value of including more advisers of similar status.

IV · A MINISTRY OF ECONOMIC AFFAIRS?

Since August 1941, the Canadian war administration has been moving steadily in the direction of greater integration of its technical services. Finance has been used as a coordinating power. The transfer of the Wartime Prices and Trade Board to the Minister of Finance and the greatly extended responsibilities of the board under the price control program are evidence of this. The close working together of the Wartime Prices and Trade Board and the Wartime Industries Control Board has secured a more integrated direction of war and civilian supply.

It may still be asked whether a Ministry of Economic Affairs would not be valuable in aiding the War Committee to make its decisions on general economic policy. The special responsibility of such a ministry would be to study continuously the war activity in all its aspects. It could draw upon the facilities of existing departments but its research workers should not have administrative responsibilities. Such an organ would have two marked advantages over the Advisory Committee: its members could devote their full attention to the specialized work, and it would have a minister participating in the War Committee, who would see that the information collected was made use of in the meetings and that proposals which the investigations had indicated to be valuable were given full consideration.

After three years of war, it is possible to see that the early demands of war gave rise to a multiplicity of new committees, boards, and departments highly diversified in form and function but unified by the dual purposes of furthering the war contribution and of easing the strain upon domestic life and economy. Lack of a general plan resulted in overlapping and a somewhat clumsy organization, but the decentralization permitted the agencies to adapt themselves to circumstances and to new demands. Their flexibility and that of old and new government departments led to some striking individual contributions in complex situations, while supervision and a general coordination was achieved through the unremitting efforts of ministers and key men in the civil service. Close coordination was developed with Great Britain and the United States largely through the personal relations of " opposite numbers," only a small proportion of which were institutionalized in such bodies as the Materials Coordinating Committee, the Joint Economic Committees and the War Production Committee. The resulting structure is firmly integrated both within Canada and as regards Canadian relations with the United States and Great Britain.

CHAPTER VIII

Australia at War

PART ONE

AUSTRALIA'S WAR EFFORT

by Fred Alexander

✲

1. Before the Outbreak

During the first four decades in the life of the Commonwealth of Australia, which was formally inaugurated on January 1, 1901, by the federation of the colonies of New South Wales, Victoria, South Australia, Queensland, Western Australia, and Tasmania, the attitude adopted by the Australian people on issues affecting other parts of the British Commonwealth or foreign countries altered surprisingly little. Differences in emphasis revealed themselves from time to time, before as well as after the First World War; during the second half of the thirties, as will be shown below, these differences became sufficiently marked to suggest the possible emergence of a new Australian nationalism with an autonomous and distinctively Australian foreign policy. The Australian international outlook nevertheless continued to be influenced in September 1939, as it had been in January 1901, by three main factors, geographic, racial, and economic. These three factors, when taken together and passed through the mill of local politics, gave to the Australian people an outlook on world affairs which differed appreciably from that of

Canadians or South Africans on the one hand and that of New Zealanders on the other, and which to some extent determined in advance the Australian attitude to the war against Nazi Germany.

Of the three factors mentioned, geographic situation was the most obviously influential. Isolation in the southwest Pacific encouraged Australians in their preoccupation with the local problems of a partially developed island-continent and prevented the rapid growth of an informed public opinion on international affairs in distant parts of the world. Public interest in foreign affairs outside the southwestern Pacific — in which field Australians have at all times maintained a careful watch upon the activities of foreign nations, whether France in the first half of the nineteenth century, or Germany in the 'eighties or Japan in later times — was at the best spasmodic and as a rule half-hearted. Yet the exposed position of Australia, together with a traditional and uncritical acceptance of the British Navy as the first line of Australian defense, retarded the growth of an avowedly isolationist policy.

In similar fashion, the racial homogeneity of the Australian nation, albeit grossly exaggerated by statistical juggling into the oft-quoted estimate of "98 percent British," made British sentiment a force which acted as a powerful brake upon the autonomist tendencies inherent in dominion nationalism. Even without the small minority of non-British immigrants, the peculiarly Australian amalgam of English, Scotch, Welsh, and Irish tended to create a national viewpoint which was Australian rather than either English or Scotch or Irish, but its political implications were checked by a persistent sentiment for the Mother Country, which was deep-rooted and widespread even if most Australians were not as conscious of its influence as their New Zealand neighbors were said to be. Racial sentiment thus reinforced the prevailing conception of strategic necessity.

During the first four decades after federation, moreover, Australian national sentiment found an outlet in industrial and social progress without the corresponding growth of a strong sense of economic rivalry with Great Britain, which might have made Australian nationalism a more powerful centrifugal force within the British Commonwealth. Foreign observers might talk of the financial domination of London and might cite in confirmation the visit to Australia of Sir Otto Niemeyer of the Bank of England at the beginning of the economic depression. But financial dependence on London did not prevent the growth of Australian manufacturing industries inside a tariff wall which penalized English exporters only less severely than foreign manufacturers. Meanwhile, the United Kingdom remained the most important market for wool, wheat, and meat, staple raw materials upon which Australian prosperity depended.

On the whole, domestic politics in Australia from 1901 to 1939 did little to strengthen the potentially centrifugal tendencies in Australian nationalism. All political parties gave more than lip service to the ideals of Australian nationhood, but none ventured to proclaim distinctively Australian foreign or defense policies which seriously threatened the unity of the British Commonwealth. The fact is clearly evident in the record of the various political groups which were the antecedents of the United Australia Party and the Country Party, the two anti-Labor parties which together controlled the House of Representatives and the Senate in the Federal Parliament of September 1939. Each of these parties still accepted the application to Australia of the view presented by Prime Minister S. M. Bruce in 1923, that " when one part of the Empire is at war, the whole Empire is at war." The statement also holds for the Australian Labor Party, despite occasional indications to the contrary which make a survey of Labor's attitude to foreign relations and defense essential to an understanding of the Party's attitude in September 1939, and after.

It was a Labor Government, the first Fisher administration, which secured the passage, in 1909, of legislation imposing compulsory military training for home defense. Labor also joined with other parties in the Federal Parliament in supporting the establishment of an Australian Navy as a mark of Australian nationhood. Confusion regarding Labor's defense and foreign policies began during the First World War, when Prime Minister W. M. Hughes and other leading members of the Labor Party, which had obtained a majority in both the House of Representatives and the Senate at the elections of 1914, favored extension of the compulsory system by advocating conscription for overseas service. The majority of the Labor Party inside and outside Parliament refused to accept this lead; their determined opposition was the chief reason for the defeat of two conscription referenda, in 1917 and 1918 respectively. Throughout the campaigns, Labor spokesmen on anti-conscription platforms vigorously denied charges of disloyalty to the Imperial cause, for which, in fact, 329,000 Australian volunteers (out of a total Australian population which was then only five millions) fought overseas between 1914 and 1918. The charges, however, were repeated; the suspicion and bitterness engendered during the two conscription campaigns carried over into the postwar period and helped to color Labor's attitude on foreign affairs throughout the two decades of peace.

Only one Labor Government held office between November 1918 and September 1939. During their first postwar decade in opposition individual Labor members occasionally gave an isolationist twist to speeches on foreign affairs. The Scullin Labor administration of 1929-32 also drastically reduced the armed forces of Australia. In this, however, the Government's special severity in retrenchment was not without precedent and was largely the result of the demand which came with the economic depression for reduction in government expenditure as well as in wages and in interest, a demand which eventually caused a split in Labor ranks and brought into being the United Australia Party and a coalition Government with the former Labor leader, Mr. Joseph A. Lyons, as Prime Minister.

During its second long postwar period in opposition, the Australian Labor Party gave its critics fresh grounds for charges of isolationist "disloyalty" threatening the unity of the British Commonwealth. In 1935-36, for example, the Labor Party in the Federal Parliament opposed Australia's collaboration in applying League sanctions to Italy in the Ethiopian incident. Uncertainty as to the Party's attitude in the event of a war involving Great Britain was partly responsible for Labor's defeat in the 1937 election campaign and prevented the defense program of the Party, under its new leader, Mr. John Curtin, from receiving the attention it deserved during and after that campaign.

The history of Australian defense policy before and after the establishment of the Commonwealth had been one of vacillation. A well considered policy, consistently applied over a lengthy period, had been lacking; expert opinion had been divided between preparations for resistance to large-scale invasion and short-term protection against more scattered raids, pending the arrival of overseas naval forces; the general public remained uncertain as to the precise objectives to be met by increased expenditure on armaments. The situation was further complicated by the fact that Australia's defenses had suffered severely during the fifteen years following the Armistice of 1918. All branches of the national defense had been affected by postwar economies.

The efficiency of the land forces of Australia had been lowered by a series of changes in periods of training and in methods of recruitment. These began with the advent of war in 1914, three years after the original scheme of compulsory military training had become effective. The period of training was permanently reduced in 1922; compulsory service was suspended in 1929, partly for financial reasons.

Australia's air defenses were also in an unsatisfactory condition in 1937. The Royal Australian Air Force had been constituted as an independent body in 1923, as the successor to the Commonwealth Air Force of 1921 and to the Australian Flying Squadron which had served abroad with distinction during the First World War. Its equipment, training, and administration had, however, been very severely criticized by Sir John Salmond, a British expert who had been commissioned to report on this arm of the services in 1928. The Salmond Plan for additions and improvements which would enable the R.A.A.F. not only to meet military and naval requirements but also to serve as an additional defense against hostile raids and attacks, was accepted by the Bruce-Page Government, but the Air Force shared in the economies suffered by all branches of the defense forces in 1929–30.

The naval forces at the command of the Australian Government in the mid 'thirties had also been weakened. The Australian Navy had shared in the reductions made by all signatories of the Washington Treaties of 1922. Ships in commission had been reduced from twenty-five in 1921 to thirteen in 1928. By January 1929, however, in consequence of a gradual developmental program adopted in 1924, Australia possessed twenty-five vessels of war. As a result of the Scullin Government's retrenchment of 1929–30 only six vessels of this naval unit were retained in commission and the total seagoing strength of the Navy was reduced between 1929 and 1932 from 5,300 to 3,527 men.

Though financial interest rather than a fixed defense policy had been the main cause of the drastic reductions of 1929–30, basic differences in policy, as well as party factiousness, underlay Labor's opposition to the Lyons Government's rearmament program, which began with the breakdown of the Disarmament Conference and the evidence of disturbed political conditions in Europe and the Far East. In September 1933, a three-year plan affecting military, naval, and air forces was announced. In 1934, the defense estimates rose from £A3,500,000 to £A5,270,000; in 1935, a further increase to £A7,350,000 was voted. This rearmament program was accepted without public enthusiasm. To the Australian people war still seemed very remote. Experts also continued to be divided on two main issues: the relation of the naval to the other arms of the national defense and the method of recruitment. On each of these matters the Labor Opposition in the Federal Parliament had decided views.

On the first issue, one school of experts held that Australia's security was so bound up with the maintenance of communications by sea with the outside world that naval expenditure must be a first charge upon Australian defense funds. Protection of trade routes outside Australian waters must needs be left to the British Navy; but it was argued that Australia could make an important contribution by undertaking what might be termed the outward defense of the Empire in the Pacific area. The opposing school admitted the importance of overseas trade routes but discounted the danger of serious and vital interference with all of them. Members of this school placed greater emphasis on the danger of attack upon certain of the vital industrial urban centers of eastern Australia in the event of the Singapore base falling into enemy hands. This second school accordingly favored diversion of funds from naval to military and air expenditure. Its members included some who regarded the resumption of compulsory service as a condition precedent to effective military preparedness.

Advocates of a return to compulsory service were to be found among the Government's supporters in the Federal Parliament as well as among the experts, but any form of conscription was politically impossible in 1937, so strong was the hold which the memory of the conscription referenda of 1917 and 1918 still exercised in Australian politics, and so slight was the public conception of the serious threat to Australia's security. The alignment of political forces did, however, sharpen the divergence of technical opinion on the naval question. When Mr. Lyons led the Australian Delegation to the Imperial Conference of 1937, he took with him the outlines of a new defense program which aimed to spread increased expenditure, which had risen to £A11,500,000, over all three services but which accepted the argument that the Navy was the first line of Australian defense.

On this point, the new defense program was vigorously assailed by the Labor Opposition. Mr. Curtin invited the Government and the people of Australia to face the possibility that a British Government which was hard pressed in Europe would be unable or unwilling to send sufficient reinforcements to the Indian Ocean and Pacific squadrons based on Singapore to give Australia adequate protection from invasion by a first-class naval power in the Pacific. Labor's answer to the Government's defense program was to advocate a mobile and well-equipped mechanized land force and a substantially increased air force, maintained by the output of Australian factories. Thus the issue in the campaign for the triennial elections to the Federal Parliament, which were held in October 1937, concerned the relative merits of naval and air armaments as the first line of Australian defense.

This issue was not squarely faced by the Australian people. The Lyons Government was returned to office, despite serious losses in the Senate, with a reduced but a working majority in the House of Representatives, to which, in accordance with Australian constitutional practice, the Federal Government is responsible. The election was, however, a vote against the Labor Party rather than against Labor's defense policy. The latter suffered from its association with the confused foreign policy pursued by the official leaders of the party in previous years and from the divergent views of certain minority Labor groups, which ranged from support for collective security to extreme forms of isolationism.

Australia thus entered upon the critical year of Munich with its people unprepared for the gravity of the crisis which lay ahead. That the Government was seized of the importance of rearmament was shown by a sharp increase in the 1937–38 defense expenditure and in a new three-year program announced by the Prime Minister in March 1938, for which it was anticipated that a sum of £A43,000,000 would be required. The manner in which the money was to be distributed over the several arms of the national defense continued to receive criticism at the hands of Mr. Curtin, while some of the Labor rank and file went further and questioned the wisdom of entrusting control of increased armaments to a Government whose foreign policy they regarded as virtually directed from Downing Street and subservient to " Fascist " interests at home and abroad.[1] The Prime Minister's declarations on foreign policy were of the vaguest. When the Czech crisis of May brought the threat of war near enough for all to see, the Government did its best to discourage " provocative " comment or discussion, particularly over the radio.

The Government's desire to avoid any provocative action during the mounting tension in Europe was, however, due to more than a desire not to embarrass Mr. Chamberlain. It was, in fact, very largely the result of the Lyons Government's interpretation of the situation in the Far

---

[1] The Labor Party supported a motion of no confidence on the defense program. In the course of the debate their leader said, " Any increase of defense expenditure after the Munich Pact, so far as Australia is concerned, appears to me to be an utterly unjustifiable and hysterical piece of panic propaganda." (Ed.)

East and its realization of the very grave position in which Australia would be placed, with its existing defenses, if members of the British Commonwealth were brought to war with Germany and Italy, and the Anti-Comintern Pact of 1936 were to become a military alliance involving Japan. In this policy the Lyons Government had the support of some influential Australians outside official circles, who were well-informed on international affairs. Their doubts of the efficacy of collective action against aggression were strengthened by their experience of Japanese aggression in China, and were also combined with a belief that Japan had had genuine economic grievances in the postwar high tariff world and by a recognition that Australia had very recently emerged from an economic brush with Japan following the trade diversion incident of 1936–37, in which neither wisdom nor material advantage had rested with the Australian Government.

Rapid progress in Australian manufactures, accompanied by a high standard of living for industrial workers, had been made possible during the first postwar decade by high world prices for raw materials and by easy borrowing on the London market. Australia's export trade to Japan had also increased until, in 1928–29, the latter country was Australia's third best customer. Hopes of developing markets in the East Indies and elsewhere in the Pacific had led to the appointment of trade commissioners from whose activities some results had been obtained. Nor were the effects of the economic depression in Australia as serious as at one time had seemed likely.

The trouble out of which the trade diversion decision sprang immediately was the intelligible desire of Japanese exporters to offset restrictions on their cheap goods in many foreign (including some British colonial) markets by increased sales in British dominions with which the balance of trade was adverse to Japan. When the Japanese pressed for a trade agreement on these lines the Australian Government refused. With a suddenness, a temerity, and a disregard for some who might well have claimed the right to be consulted, the Government announced a new trade policy, in May 1936. New customs duties and a licensing system were to be introduced, ostensibly to divert imports from countries which were " bad customers," such as the United States, to those with which the balance of trade was less unfavorable to Australia. But the moment chosen for the announcement, immediately after the abortive Japanese trade negotiations, made it seem that the main objective of the new policy was to force the consent of Japan (which, incidentally, was a " good customer ") to a new trade agreement by which she would continue to buy Australian wool and wheat but would accept a limitation upon the sale of cheap Japanese textiles on the Australian market.

It was soon apparent that the trade diversion policy was a grave blunder both economically and politically. The best that can be said is that efforts were made to rectify the policy as soon as possible and to prevent permanent losses resulting from it. Its most damaging economic effect upon Australia was the encouragement it gave to Japanese manufacturers to turn to staple fiber instead of wool to avoid undue dependence on any foreign nation. The Australian Government was given a sharp reminder of the importance to Australia's economic well-being, as well as to its security, of peace and stability in the Pacific. This was a return to the position that had prompted the Government's abortive proposal at the Imperial Conference of 1937 for a Pacific non-aggression pact. Renewed political interest in the Pacific during 1938 also revived earlier suggestions for the establishment of an Australian Legation at Washington and one at Tokyo as a beginning in direct diplomatic representation abroad, in respect to which Australia had failed to follow the lead of her sister dominions, Canada and South Africa.

In all the circumstances of May to September 1938, therefore, it is scarcely surprising that the Chamberlain Government's attitude during the crisis which culminated in the Munich Agreement was generally supported in Australia. How much influence Mr. Lyons and his colleagues exercised upon British policy in the crisis has yet to be fully revealed, but both the Government and the Labor Opposition endorsed the British action at Munich.

The Munich incident may nevertheless be regarded by future writers as the turning point in the history of Australian foreign policy. Hopes persisted that the Munich settlement would produce permanent peace but there was general recognition that no risks should be taken. The Federal Government speeded up and extended its already augmented defense program of March 1938; the cooperation of state premiers was obtained in the establishment of a National Defense Council; the militia was increased; belated provision was made for the strengthening of the Air Force; and a compulsory register of men between the ages of 18 and 64 was taken. In April 1939, a decisive step in economic preparation for effective defense was made by the creation of a new ministerial department of Supply and Development under the former Federal Treasurer, Mr. Richard G. Casey, who was charged with the coordination of industrial and defense activity. In the same month, a Pacific Defense Conference of representatives of Great Britain, Australia, and New Zealand met in the capital of the latter dominion.

By this time, Hitler's invasion of Prague had prepared the Australian people for the worst. The shock of the actual events of September was, however, cushioned in advance for Australians by the isolation of Japan which accompanied the conclusion of the Russo-German Pact of August. In the weeks that preceded the outbreak of war in Europe there was no doubt that the Australian Government would have general support in following the British Government into war, but it was impossible to predict the spirit in which the Australian people would enter the conflict or the extent to which political and strategic conditions, both at home and abroad, would permit a wartime effort comparable with that of 1914–18.

At the beginning of September 1939, a new Prime Minister of only four months' standing, Mr. Robert G. Menzies, faced a Parliament in which his own United Australia Party was in a minority. The Labor Opposition, which might at any moment play upon the personal antipathy to Mr. Menzies of certain Country Party members and thus force a general election, was still accused of harboring elements disloyal to the Empire. Its leaders, moreover, seemed uncertain in their own conception of Australia's wartime role and were, not unnaturally, anxious regarding the social consequences of the conflict. The extent of British naval assistance which would be available in Australian waters in certain eventualities depended upon the outcome of the first real test of air and naval strength in European waters. The efficiency of Australia's own defensive rearmament was yet unproved, the validity of the theory on which it was based was untested. Most important of all, none could tell how the Australian people would respond to a new test of the responsibilities of nationhood after two decades of peace, during which the rank and file of Australians had shown relatively little interest in outside politics.

Such was the state of affairs in Australia when, on the evening of Sunday, September 3, 1939, a meeting of the Federal Executive Council approved the issue of a proclamation declaring the existence of a state of war in Australia — approximately one hour after the British Prime Minister had announced that Great Britain was at war with Germany.[1a]

[1a] For a discussion of the procedure involved in the declaration of war, see Chapter II, pp. 20 f.

2. *The First Eight Months of War*

In the first few months after the outbreak of war, domestic political complications were much less serious in Australia than might have been expected. The basic reason lay in the fact that the nation at large approved the Government's action in declaring Australia's position at once, without hesitation. The actual declaration of a state of war by Government proclamation without prior parliamentary authorization was, moreover, in keeping with the official Australian interpretation of British Commonwealth unity in vital matters.[2] It was clear that such political differences as were likely to arise regarding the war would concern the manner and not the fact of Australia's participation in it.

Events helped the new Prime Minister. In the early days of the national emergency, firmness rather than finesse was called for. There was no doubt that the Prime Minister proved a steadying influence in the crisis. In his first wartime address in Parliament he coupled an appeal for a united war effort with an avowal of his desire to interfere as little as possible with the machinery of constitutional government and with the democratic way of life:

> However long this conflict may last, I do not seek a muzzled opposition. Our institutions of Parliament, and of liberal thought, free speech and free criticism, must go on. It would be a tragedy if we found that we had fought for freedom and fair play and the value of the individual human soul, and won the war only to lose the things we were fighting for.

In the circumstances, the continuance in office of the Menzies Government, and its effective preparation for the conduct of Australia's war effort without the delay and disorder which would accompany an early appeal to the electors, depended on the attitude adopted by the majority of the Labor Party, with its controlling position in the House of Representatives, and on the skill with which its leader succeeded in serving his Party without endangering the interests of the nation. Mr. Curtin's responsibilities were no less heavy and his difficulties no less acute than those which faced the Prime Minister. A journalist by profession, Mr. Curtin's personal experience as an active anti-conscriptionist in Victoria, during the campaigns of 1917–18, and as editor of the *Westralian Worker,* in the early postwar years, was sufficient to remind him of the

---

[2] Cf. the 1923 declaration of Mr. S. M. Bruce, cited above, p. 367.

havoc which conflicting loyalties may play with the Labor machine in a national emergency.

With the outbreak of war, however, it was clear that very skillful direction would be needed if Labor was to face the electors as one united party in the campaign for the triennial elections to the Federal Parliament, which the Constitution required not later than January 1941. Upon the Labor leader in the Federal Parliament also fell the chief responsibility for seeing that the Party's wartime record was such as to insure Labor reasonable prospects at the polls or, at the worst, to prevent disastrous defeat in a " win-the-war " election. Six months after the outbreak of war, it was apparent that the Federal Labor leader had been unable to maintain the united front he desired; he did, however, succeed in gradually weaning the majority of his Party from the impliedly isolationist policy of 1937, to a position where, if office were thrust upon him by some turn of the political wheel, he and his colleagues would be able to carry on the wartime administration of the country without alienating the nation and without irretrievably splitting the Party as had been done during the First World War of 1914–18, when Mr. William M. Hughes was its leader. Meanwhile, Mr. Curtin maintained a degree of cooperation with the Prime Minister, notwithstanding major differences in the outlook of the two men on both foreign and domestic issues and despite the evident determination of the Labor leader to take no action which could be held disloyal to his Party.

The Prime Minister made little effort to exploit the prevailing sentiment; in the weeks following the outbreak, he refrained from emotional appeals and avoided action likely to provoke an outburst from Labor members of Parliament whose prewar utterances had committed them to opposition to an overseas expeditionary force, and who had not yet adjusted themselves to the facts of the wartime situation. When, on September 15, the Government announced its decision to enlist a volunteer force of 20,000, it was stated that the men would be recruited for service " at home or overseas." Not until November 1 did the Prime Minister indicate that " the second A.I.F." would be sent abroad; even then, the announcement was qualified by the proviso " unless circumstances made such a course impracticable." By the end of November, when it was officially disclosed that the second A.I.F. would go overseas early in 1940, the Prime Minister had completed the initial stages of administrative reform aimed at facilitating the war effort.

The first important administrative change was the formation in mid-

September of a War Cabinet of six members, the Prime Minister, the Attorney-General, the Minister for Supply and Development, the Minister for Defense, the Minister for External Affairs, and the Minister for Commerce, which was to work within the larger Cabinet. The powers of the Executive in its various forms had also been considerably increased by the passage in September of the National Security Act,[3] which authorized the issuing of Government Regulations to secure " the public safety and the defense of the Commonwealth of Australia and the Territories of the Commonwealth," subject to a limiting clause which precluded the use of such a regulation for " the imposition of any form of compulsory naval, military or air force service, or any form of industrial conscription, or the extension of any existing obligation to render compulsory service." On November 11, it was announced that, instead of one Ministry for Defense, three departments of the Army, Navy, and Air Force respectively had been created with separate ministers, but all three, together with the Minister for Supply, to work under the general direction of the Prime Minister in his capacity as Minister for Defense Coordination. What was formerly the Secretariat of the Department of Defense, charged with responsibility for coordinating the three services under the Minister of Defense, became the Department of Defense Coordination. The Secretary of the Department of Defense, who was also Secretary of the War Cabinet, became permanent head of the new Department of Defense Coordination. Extension of the activities of each of the three arms of the national defense was decided upon at the beginning of November. Compulsory military service was reintroduced for home defense, and was calculated to raise the strength of the militia forces to a figure not less than 75,000, out of a total population of 7,000,000. The first trainees, who were to spend three months in camp during 1940, were to consist of unmarried men who would reach the age of 21 during the year ending June 30, 1940.

The Royal Australian Navy, which, as in August 1914, the Commonwealth Government transferred to the control of the British Admiralty on the outbreak of war, then consisted of the following ships in commission, exclusive of survey ships and minesweepers: two 10,000 ton " County " class heavy cruisers, 8 inch guns; three modified " Leander " class cruisers, 6 inch guns; one remodelled cruiser, 5000 tons, 6 inch guns; two sloops; five destroyers including a flotilla leader. These forces were to be strengthened by the construction in Australia of three

---

[3] Act No. 15 of 1939.

"Tribal" class destroyers and four local defense vessels suitable for anti-submarine or mine-sweeping work. The Government chartered other vessels for the latter type of work and a number of ships were converted into armed merchantmen.

Australia's air program had two objectives. The first was to provide sufficient aircraft and trained personnel to insure effective resistance to raids or other action by sea-borne aircraft;[4] the second was to assist the British air effort. The acceptance of the British Commonwealth Air Training Plan led, however, to modifications of the project for a strong expeditionary air force. Instead, Australia accepted responsibility under the plan for what the Prime Minister announced on December 15 as "a first objective" of 26,000 men comprising 10,400 pilots and 15,600 observers and wireless operators and air gunners. A corresponding number of ground personnel were to be provided, the great majority of all men to be fully trained in Australia under a local training scheme which would reach its peak in 1942. It was later announced that, in all, 28,500 men were to be contributed by Australia by June 1941, and 57,473 by March 1943. A small proportion only of these men — two-ninths — would receive the final stages of their advanced training in Canada. At the beginning of November 1939 the air development program was also accelerated so that nineteen squadrons of the Royal Australian Air Force would be in active operation by June 1940.

Provision of airplanes to meet the needs of the R.A.A.F. both in training and in action presented one of the most serious problems before the Australian Government. Experimental prewar production of Wirraways — light planes suitable both for training and for resisting sea-borne aircraft — had reached the point where an output of one Wirraway per day was expected by the end of 1939; 100 privately owned aircraft were acquired; more than 1000 other ships were ordered, some to be built in whole or in part in Australia, some to be obtained elsewhere.

From the first, the Government realized that the war would be won as much in the factory as on the field. The creation in April 1939 of the Ministry of Supply[5] was an indication that an effort would be made to

---

[4] Australia's air transport was developed far beyond that of any country comparable in population and extent of territory. In 1939 there were forty commercial services in operation with a total route mileage of 29,500. There were four well-developed transcontinental air routes. The number of airdromes and emergency landing fields was 500 in 1939, and a great expansion has of course taken place during the war, especially in the northern areas. — Ed.

[5] See above, p. 373.

turn to account the material development of the preceding decade, in the supply not only of personal equipment for individual soldiers but also of munitions and armament of all types. Of the 1939–40 estimated expenditure of £A59,500,000, less than £A8,000,000 [6] was to be spent abroad. This was hailed as an indication of the extent to which Australia had become self-sufficient in the supply of its defense requirements. Additional factories were built for the manufacture of explosives and rifle ammunition, Bren guns and 25 pounder field guns, two pounder anti-tank guns, shells, air bombs, naval mines, and depth charges. The administrative organization rendered necessary by these activities led in November to the creation of an " Economic Cabinet," consisting of the Prime Minister, the Minister for Supply and Development, the Minister and Assistant Minister for Commerce, the Minister for Customs, and the Treasurer.

Economic problems of equal importance arose out of the need to supervise closely the marketing arrangements for Australian exports, which had exceeded £A150,000,000 annually in the years preceding the war. Though only two percent of Australian exports had gone to Germany in the year 1938–39, the extension of German control over other European countries had the effect of cutting off more and more markets for Australian exports until the percentage of the export trade affected had risen to 15 after nine months of hostilities. With this possibility already in view at the beginning of the war it was evident that every effort should be made to retain the valuable United Kingdom market which in peacetime absorbed more than half of the total exports of Australia.

Machinery for this purpose was provided by marketing control boards set up under the National Security Act, which negotiated on behalf of the Australian Government with the Government of Great Britain. Of the contracts agreed upon — which involved sales totalling approximately £A100,000,000 — special publicity was given to the wool agreement. The British Government purchased the entire Australian wool clip for the period of the war and one year thereafter at an average price which represented an increase of approximately one-third on the average price obtained by Australian wool producers in the open market in the previous year. This gave security to producers even if some were

[6] When the estimated expenditure rose to £A75,000,000 (March 1940) and again to £A179,-000,000 (September 1940) the amounts to be expended abroad were given as £A14,000,000 and £A33,924,759 respectively.

dissatisfied with the amount of the increase in price, and others doubted whether the provisions for resale by the British Government of supplies in excess of its needs would effectively preserve the Australian market in neutral countries, notably in the United States.

Frozen meat exports, handled after, as before, the outbreak of war by the Australian Meat Board, were maintained. Short-term butter, cheese, and eggs contracts were concluded with the British Government, and no trouble was anticipated in maintaining exports of dried and canned fruits. The unsold portion of the surplus of the 1939 raw sugar crop was also bought by the British Government at a price satisfactory to growers. It was not, however, possible to make equally satisfactory arrangements for the two important exports of wheat and fresh fruit or for wine.

Wheat presented a more difficult problem than wool because of the excess of production over consumption of wheat in the British Empire. The Australian Wheat Board, with some 195,000,000 bushels to be disposed of in 1939–40, had sold 92,500,000 bushels by March 1940 and had reasonable expectations of sales of another 18,000,000, but the board was faced with the certainty of a surplus and also with the problem of storing much of the wheat sold pending removal as shipping space was provided from time to time by an Australian liaison officer working with the British Ministry of Shipping.[7]

The fresh fruit situation was much more serious. In peacetime, the annual export of apples to Great Britain and the European Continent averaged nearly 5,000,000 bushels. Little more than half of the total apple and pear yield was consumed in Australia. Fresh fruit was not included by the British Government among its wartime list of essential commodities. It was recognized, therefore, that the difficulty of securing shipping space would be considerable; it was also feared that the indiscriminate dumping of fresh fruit on the Australian home market would not only depress fruit prices but might also react on the Government's efforts to maintain prices as nearly as possible on their prewar level. As a result of a conference between the Australian Apple and Pear Organization Board and representatives of the state governments, a scheme for orderly marketing of fruit was brought into operation. By zoning of markets and a nationwide " Eat more fruit " campaign it

---

[7] The marketing problem was solved by the fact that owing to dry conditions the 1941 wheat crop was 83,200,000 bushels, the lowest since 1919–20 (the crop for 1940 was a record, 210,-277,000 bushels). The result was a carry-over of only sixteen million bushels, far below the average. (Ed.)

was hoped that fruit growers might receive something from sales in addition to the amount of 2s. per bushel for apples and 3s. per bushel for pears which the Government advanced to growers and which would barely cover costs of production.

Price-fixing plans had been prepared before hostilities broke out. The Prices Commission, with the cooperation of the state and federal governments, sought to achieve the two objectives of preventing wartime profiteering and of permitting such reasonable increases in retail prices as would encourage a continuation of normal peacetime business activities. The cooperation of the business community was obtained, with the result that, after ten months of war, the Commission was able to state that, despite increases of 35 percent in landed costs of imports, 23 percent in the prices of exports and 10 percent in interstate shipping rates, the index of retail prices had risen less than 2 percent. Government control of capital investment was also established. Regulations were promulgated requiring that all projected issues of new or additional capital were to be submitted to the Treasurer, who was provided with special advisory assistance for this purpose.

The immediate problems involved in financing the war effort concerned overseas rather than domestic expenditure, especially expenditure in non-sterling countries. The ordinary peacetime necessity of retaining balances in London to service the interest on Australia's loan indebtedness to Great Britain [8] presented no serious problem in view of the wool purchase and the agreements noted above. It was also decided that purchases by the Australian Government for the equipment and maintenance of expeditionary forces abroad should be met temporarily by loans from the British Government. Even as late as May 2, 1940, when the Federal Treasurer brought down preliminary proposals for the 1940–41 budget, he announced, " with reluctance," that the Government had decided to defer for the present the question for providing funds in Australia to meet any portion of the overseas expenditure in 1940–41.

Provision for expenditure in non-sterling countries, on the other hand, was early recognized as an urgent matter of vital importance. The unfavorable peacetime balance of trade between Australia and the United States [9] was met by drawing on sterling credits in London. The increase in the London demand for dollar exchange, which inevi-

---

[8] The annual interest in 1936–37 was £A18,111,150.
[9] The 1938–39 figures were: Exports £3,614,038; Imports £14,647,305.

tably followed the placing by the British Government of extensive
orders for war materials in the United States, had been foreseen in Australia before the outbreak of war. Defense (Monetary Control) Regulations were promulgated by the Governor-General in Council on August
23, 1939, and were subsequently embodied in amended regulations issued in November under the National Security Act. Though the nature
and extent of the currency restrictions thus imposed varied from time
to time, their purpose throughout was to conserve Australian reserves
of foreign currencies and to prevent the importation of commodities
not essential to the war effort. Australian owners of certain American
stocks were ordered to sell their holdings within six months and to
lodge the proceeds with the Commonwealth Bank; arrangements were
made with American companies for the retention in Australia of a portion of their Australian profits; the issue of dollar credits by private
banks was restricted and was placed in the control of the Commonwealth
Bank; importing of certain specified nonessential goods was prohibited
and the maximum amount of other imports limited; a system of licensing exports was also introduced on May 1, 1940, to prevent the export
of goods required for defense purposes.[10]

The methods adopted by the Government for financing domestic war
expenditure also did little to bring home to the Australian taxpayer
the actual or potential gravity of the wartime situation. The revised
estimates of November 1939 increased the amount for Defense and War
Services to £A62,014,000. The Government declared its general financial policy as designed to finance the war effort by a "balanced program of taxation, borrowing from the public and borrowing from
the banking system," with a deliberate weighting of the balance towards
borrowing with the assistance of the banking system during the early
months of the war, so as to add nothing to the temporary dislocation of
the economic system due to the passage from a peace to a war economy.
The Government was enabled so to weight the balance by the fact that
during the years immediately preceding the war the Commonwealth
Treasurer had resisted the temptation to accept easy methods of financing federal expenditure without recourse to taxation. Against the estimated expenditure within Australia for the years 1939–40 and 1940–
41, which totalled £A125,000,000, provision had yet to be made in

---

[10] For a detailed survey of the restrictions see A. V. Janes, "History of Exchange Control
in Australia," *The Economic Record*, Vol. XVI, June 1940. The whole of this issue of *The Economic Record* is worth consulting for the economic side of the Australian war economy in its
first nine months.

May 1940 for £A70,000,000. Of this amount, the Treasurer proposed to raise only £A20,000,000 by additional taxation, the balance to be obtained by public loans.[11] Of the £A20,000,000, customs, excise, and sales taxes accounted for £A10,300,000. Less than £A8,000,000 was to be raised by income taxation and of this amount only £A3,000,000 by taxation on individuals, which would be felt mainly by taxpayers in the middle income group. This softening of the impact of the war upon the Australian economy may have been financially sound; together with other influences, however, it helped to create a false sense of security among the Australian people.

Among these influences, geographical situation, as ever, played an important part in conditioning the Australian outlook. The main center of conflict was far removed from Australia; the continued neutrality of the Japanese Government and the evidently anti-Nazi sentiments of the Roosevelt administration emphasized the existing tranquillity of the Pacific scene. Wishful thinking, especially on the subject of American opinion — on which few Australians were well-informed — encouraged the belief that there was slight risk of an extension of the war into Australian waters.

Meanwhile, the political calm which had been maintained on the home front during the first few months of the war had also come to an end. In January a vacancy in the House of Representatives was created by the resignation of the member for Corio, the Rt. Hon. Richard G. Casey, Minister of Supply, who was appointed as Australia's first Minister to the United States.[12] The Labor Party chose to make the issue of the by-election the defense policy of the Government — a challenge which the Prime Minister accepted.

The resulting defeat for the Government, and the election as Labor member for Corio of a former Captain in the first A.I.F. was not as clear an indication of the nation's attitude to the Prime Minister's war and defense policies as might at first sight appear. Other matters entered into the Corio campaign, including a rash decision of the Government to begin the manufacture of motor cars — engines as well as chassis — in Australia.[13]

---

[11] The issue of War Savings Certificates by the Government was begun a few months earlier. Certificates were issued in denominations of £1, £5 and £10, bearing 3¼ percent interest and maturing in 7 years, with a maximum of £250 worth to any one person.

[12] See below, p. 392.

[13] The manner in which a virtual monopoly was granted by the Government during the parliamentary recess to one company, to be formed by the influential Australian Consolidated

Mr. Curtin was not allowed to enjoy his Party's triumph at Corio and to look forward with confidence to the result of the federal elections a few months later. The unity of the Labor movement which he had striven so hard to maintain was seriously threatened by a " Hands off Russia " resolution of the Easter Conference of the Labor movement of New South Wales.[14] The resolution was at once disavowed by Mr. Curtin, who pointed out that only the Federal Labor Conference could direct the Party in matters affecting the federal platform. The damage had, however, been done, and later in the year Labor was to face the electors of New South Wales not as one party, but as three.

The Corio election, moreover, had brought the United Australia Party and the Country Party back into an uneasy alliance against their common opponent of many years. Mr. Menzies, recognizing his weakened position after the by-election, was forced to modify his formal refusal to accept Country Party members of his Cabinet other than those chosen by himself. An agreement was reached whereby the leader of the Country Party (Mr. Archie Cameron) became Deputy Prime Minister, and, in joint consultation, the Prime Minister and Deputy Prime Minister selected six Country Party members, three of whom were to serve as Ministers, three as Assistant Ministers. On March 21, the Prime Minister announced the reconstruction of the War Cabinet and the Economic Cabinet, the former to consist of two Country Party and seven United Australia Party members, the latter of two Country Party and five United Australia Party members. For the time being, the agreement strengthened the Government's position in the Federal Parliament but the Government's future and the future of its wartime program were far from being assured.

Too much still depended on two men, the Prime Minister and the leader of the Opposition, the influence of each of whom had been weakened in recent months. The administrative burdens of the Prime Minister had steadily increased. Moreover, continuance of the satisfactory working results which had emerged from the mutual respect and

---

Industries, Ltd. provided the Labor opposition with an effective weapon with which to belabor the Government in the Corio campaign. After prolonged public and parliamentary criticism, the chairman of A. C. I. announced, in June 1940, that plans for the production of motor cars in Australia had been deferred " probably until the end of the war."

[14] The war policy adopted by the Conference included the following statements:

" The Conference makes it clear that, while being opposed to Australian participation in oversea conflicts, it is also opposed to any effort of the anti-Labor Government to change the direction of the present war by an aggressive act against any other country with which we are not at war, including the Soviet Union."

restraint which the head of the Government and the leader of the Opposition had displayed towards one another since the outbreak of the war was seriously threatened. Mr. Curtin himself was no longer sure of the support of all members of his Party. And a general election with all its confusion and its conflicting loyalties loomed ahead.

3. From the Blitzkrieg of May to the Elections of September 1940

While none could foresee the rapidity with which the collapse of Belgium and France would follow the German invasion of the Low Countries on May 10, the Australian Government was not slow to realize the gravity of the situation in the middle of that month. Speaking in the House of Representatives at Canberra on May 22, 1940, the Prime Minister bluntly stated that " as British people we have reached a stage of emergency without precedent in the history of the Empire."

The most important administrative measure taken to meet the emergency was the reorganization of the work of munitions supply in Australia by the appointment of a Director-General of Munitions who, the Prime Minister announced, would be " freed from all hampering regulations," and given the utmost authority " not only to get things done with the existing government machinery but to press into service civil factories, or all or any of the mechanical resources of these factories." The Director-General's status was to resemble that of the chiefs of staff and he was to have direct contact with the Prime Minister as the head of the War Cabinet. The Government congratulated itself on obtaining the services as Director-General of Munitions of Mr. Essington Lewis, managing director of the Broken Hill Proprietary Company, Ltd., one of the largest and most powerful concerns in Australia. An Assistant Director-General was appointed and directors (most of them experienced business executives) for each branch of Munitions Supply — Aircraft, Explosives, Ordnance, Gun Ammunition, Materials, Machine Tools, Finance, and Labor Supply and Regulation. Supplementary organizations were set up in each of the States.

The first political test of Labor's attitude to the new war situation following the *Blitzkrieg* in western Europe came on June 20, when the Prime Minister introduced a bill to amend the National Security Act of the previous year to bring it into line with the Emergency Powers Act passed through the British Parliament on May 22 and a similar New

Zealand Act. On the day before the amending bill was brought before Parliament, a special conference of the Federal Labor Party had revised its war policy in terms which permitted the leader of the Opposition to support the amending bill despite the fact that the measure removed all except one of the limitations which had been set up to the 1939 Act, including the safeguard against " industrial conscription." The sole remaining limitation was the proviso to section 13A of the Act " that nothing in the section shall authorize the imposition of any form of compulsory service beyond the limits of Australia," the term " Australia " being defined to include the " Territories of the Commonwealth of Australia." On a division, the amending measure was passed by the House of Representatives by 61 votes for and 9 against.

While the war policy adopted by the special June Conference of the Australian Labor Party revealed considerable changes as the result of the greater emergency, it also made clear that the Party had no intention of sinking its individuality in the national war effort. These changes in policy were made palatable to members of the Labor movement not only by recognition of the emergency. Stress was also laid on the importance which the Labor Party had itself allotted, before and since the outbreak of war, to the strengthening of Australia's air defenses and to the local manufacture of munitions.

The most notable change was the acceptance of compulsion in training for home defense and provision of reinforcements for the expeditionary forces overseas. Mr. Curtin and all Labor spokesmen were, however, adamant in their refusal to participate in a National Government. The matter was considered by the special conference of the Australian Labor Party in the third week of June, but the farthest the conference was prepared to go was to authorize Mr. Curtin and his parliamentary colleagues to participate in a National War Council " to advise the Government in respect to the conduct of the war and in preparing for the postwar reconstruction."

The Labor proposal for a War Council did not appeal to the Government which, in the absence of a partisan opposition, was able to carry on with its fairly comfortable majority of 9 in the House of Representatives. The main political concern of Mr. Menzies arose from the fact that all members of the House of Representatives and half the members of the Senate must face a General Election not later than January 1941. Towards the end of July the Prime Minister confirmed reports that the Government proposed to move for an increase in powers of the federal legislature to enable Parliament, if necessary, to extend its own life. The method of obtaining the desired power, which was fully canvassed in the press, was by resolution, carried by both Houses, requesting the British Parliament to pass legislation amending in this respect the Commonwealth of Australia Constitution Act, the statute which brought the federation of the Australian colonies into being. " The view of the Government," Mr. Menzies said, " is that the next election should occur within its due period, unless circumstances make it impossible or dangerous to Australia's war effort to have an election campaign, but if such circumstances arise and no power to postpone the election exists (as the case now is under the Constitution) Parliament will simply be unable to prevent it, and the consequences may be disastrous."

In his original announcement, Mr. Menzies had intimated that he would not proceed with the matter until after consultation with the leader of the Opposition and with Mr. Beasley, leader of the Australian Labor Party (Non-Communist). On August 6, a discussion between the Prime Minister and the party leaders made it clear that unanimity would not be obtained. The Country Party was favorable in principle, but the opposition of the Labor Party killed the proposal. The Prime Minister announced that polling would take place on September 21; both Houses concluded their sittings on August 22, and members prepared for a whirlwind electioneering campaign.[15]

The policies for which the several parties sought the electors' approval reflected the course of events since the outbreak of war. For the historian of Australia's war effort, the campaign of September 1940 thus serves as a test not merely of the nation's judgment of the Menzies Government's administrative record but also of the considered attitude of the Australian people towards the war and the respective war policies advocated by the five parties [16] which faced the electors. The Prime Minister rested

---

[15] While political negotiations with the Labor Party were hanging fire, the Government had made some progress in associating trade unions with the war effort. As early as April 11 an agreement had been reached with the Amalgamated Union of Engineers for dilution of labor in munitions factories and became effective on May 1. The Prime Minister's negotiations for the formation of a Trade Union Advisory Panel were long drawn out but eventually led to the creation of a Panel representative of the Australian Workers' Union, Amalgamated Engineering Union, Maritime Transport Council, Federated Enginedrivers' and Firemen's Association, Road Transport Union, Textile Workers' Union, Arms Explosives and Munitions Workers' Union with the declared objective of advising and guiding the Government in matters affecting the trades unions engaged in defense work. The Panel as constituted was, however, opposed by the powerful Australian Council of Trade Unions.

[16] United Australia Party, Country Party, Australian Labor Party, Australian Labor Party (Non-Communist) and Australian Labor Party (New South Wales).

the Government's case for return to office on its record in organizing the military, naval, and air forces for overseas and for home service and in directing the economic activities of the nation so that a maximum of assistance should be given to the war effort with the minimum of dislocation of the lives of private citizens. In his policy speech of September 2, Mr. Menzies emphasized the fact that his Government had raised and equipped " the better part of 130,000 men " for the A.I.F. — " and many thousands in addition for the Navy and Air Force." Establishment of a home defense army of nearly 100,000 men made, he declared, " a force immeasurably greater and more efficient than anything we have had before."

The course of events since the German attack on Norway and on the Netherlands had on the whole confirmed, though in some respects it had weakened, the marketing position of the first few months of the war. While some primary producers might not share the satisfaction expressed by the Prime Minister in his policy speech with the results of the Government's system of marketing controls, Mr. Menzies was able to cite the impressive annual figure of £A120,000,000 for contracts concluded for the sale of primary produce. Few, moreover, were likely to challenge his claim that careful attention to retail prices had prevented the rapid increase in the cost of living which had been one of the features of the war of 1914–18 in Australia.

Restrictions on imports were not popular. Some measure of the extent to which the Australian public still failed to appreciate the gravity of the war situation was given by its reluctance to accept serious restrictions on gasoline consumption. Australia's dependence on external supplies of motor fuel was generally recognized. Commendable progress was being made with the distillation of petrol from shale and in the use of producer gas, but the need for storage against possible interference with overseas supplies of gasoline in the event of an extension of active hostilities to the Pacific areas, together with the necessity of conserving dollar exchange, made some restrictions on local consumption of motor fuel inevitable.[17] The proposal was nevertheless fought vigorously and the

17 The Glen Davis Plant in N.S.W. was producing 35,000 gallons of petrol daily by the end of August 1940, but distillation was difficult and expensive. In July 1941 a plan was announced to produce from wheat 10,000,000 gallons of power alcohol, the use of which in automobiles would be made compulsory. In his speech on June 17, 1941, Mr. Menzies announced the cutting of gasoline rations for Australia from 20,000,000 gallons to 12,000,000 gallons a month. The cut as actually introduced a few days later reduced the ration for private cars from 38 miles per week to 20 miles per week. (Ed.)

Government was compelled to amend the rationing schedules which were promulgated on July 11, 1940. Under the amended schedules, the amount of petrol supplied depended on the mileage limit fixed for the class of motor vehicle operated. This limit ranged from 4,000 miles per annum for cars used for non-business purposes to 15,000 miles per annum for cars used for special business, with additional provisions for certain classes of vehicles such as taxicabs and omnibuses.

The Labor Party's policy, on its constructive side, was divisible into two parts: that which concerned the prosecution of the war and that which concerned social standards and peacetime policy. In his war program, Mr. Curtin took his stand on the planks of the platform adopted by the special Federal Labor Conference of June, declaring that " the Australian Labor Party stands inflexible in support of the British cause."

In his immediate social program, the Labor leader sought to outbid the Prime Minister for popular support by promising increases in soldiers' pay, in old-age and in invalid pensions, provision for pensions for widows with dependent children, and a family allowance for families with more than two children under sixteen. Mr. Curtin advocated reconstruction of the Australian Wheat Board and increased rates of payment for the first 3,000 bushels of each farmer's crop. Against the Labor program for social amelioration the Prime Minister set a policy which " means hard times, discomfort, sacrifice, loss, . . . the use of the public and private credit resources of the country to the utmost; much Government control; no profiteering; the forgetting of private interests."

The result of the election was not clear. While the Government had a sweeping victory in the returns for the Senate, its majority in the House of Representatives, on which it depended for continuance in office, was reduced from nine to one (exclusive of the Speaker).

In the circumstances, two, possibly three, inferences should be drawn from the country's verdict on September 21, 1940. The first was that the nation supported the war policy applied in its name by the Menzies Government. On the other hand, the faithful support of the official Labor Party by a very considerable minority of the Australian people indicated that the nation did not desire continued participation in the war to distract attention any more than was absolutely necessary from ideals of social justice, in the attainment of which Australia had already made great progress in the past and of which the Labor Party was the most vigorous advocate. A third inference was permissible: that, while a considerable section of the Australian people expressed at one and the same time its desire for continuation of the war effort and its confidence in Mr. Curtin and his colleagues of the Opposition, the nation as a whole could not be said to have given anyone a mandate for the formation of a national government in which Labor might in course of time lose its identity and weaken itself in the struggle for social reconstruction when the war was over. The problem which Mr. Menzies and Mr. Curtin had to face, therefore, was to effect the greatest possible cooperation in a joint war effort without prejudice to differences in domestic policy on which it was clear that the views of Mr. Curtin's party were widely respected and supported in the country even in the critical wartime situation.

The elections had, if anything, emphasized the significance of personal factors in the political scene. In the first place, the position of Mr. Menzies was greatly strengthened by his overwhelming victory in his own constituency of Kooyong in the State of Victoria. Paradoxically, Mr. Curtin's standing was also improved by the fact that he narrowly escaped defeat — for some days, indeed, was thought to have been defeated — in his electorate of Fremantle, Western Australia. The threatened defeat of Mr. Curtin had the effect of directing attention to his self-effacing services both to his Party and to the nation. His defeat when it was thought to be inevitable was generally deplored; when Mr. Curtin was eventually returned by the results of the soldiers' vote for his electorate, the leader of the Opposition was able to exercise an even greater influence within and without the ranks of his Party than before the elections. The failure of the New South Wales Labor group led by Mr. J. R. Hughes to win a single seat in the new Parliament and the weakening of the representation of the " Non-Communist " group led by Mr. Beasley also strengthened Mr. Curtin's position. Among several new members of the Federal Parliament Mr. Curtin also obtained the support of Dr. H. V. Evatt who had taken the virtually unprecedented course of retiring from the Bench of the High Court of Australia — the highest judicial position open to an Australian lawyer — to contest and win the constituency of Barton, New South Wales.

When the final count of the votes had been made — including the overseas soldiers' vote — and the United Australia and the Country Party Government led by Mr. Menzies was seen to have a majority of two members only in the House of Representatives, from one of whom the Speaker would be taken, it was apparent that two courses were possible for the Prime Minister. He had either to take the risk and the heavy responsibility of preparing to seek another more decisive election at an early date or of coming to some arrangement with the two Labor parties which would insure that his tenuous hold on a majority in the House was not constantly threatened by factious Opposition tactics.

Mr. Curtin had made it a condition precedent to formal negotiations that Mr. Menzies should give an assurance that, in the event of some form of Labor cooperation, the Government would implement some at least of the social, financial, and industrial planks in Labor's electoral program. Mr. Menzies proposed that the Opposition parties should accept " half the seats in a National Government or, failing a National Government, half the seats in some form of National or War Council, with executive functions." The Prime Minister's proposals were submitted to the Official Labor Caucus on October 22. The Labor Party adhered to its pre-election decision not to join a National Government and also rejected the proposal for membership in a War Council with executive powers. Instead, it proposed an Australian War Advisory Council representative of all political parties and " empowered to investigate and to advise and assist the Government in its war efforts," the members of the Council being " sworn to respect all confidences."

In this form the Labor proposal was accepted by the Prime Minister. It was agreed that the Advisory War Council should consist of four members of the existing Government parties, three Official Labor members and one Labor (Non-Communist) member, and that it should sit under the presidency of the Prime Minister or his deputy. Meanwhile, Mr. Menzies rearranged his own Cabinet, one major change being the dropping of Mr. Archie Cameron, who had been replaced as leader of the Country Party by Mr. A. W. Fadden, who therefore became Deputy Prime Minister.[18] Sir Earle Page, the former leader of the Country Party, also rejoined the Government as Minister for Customs. The Prime Minister reduced the size of his War Cabinet in view of the constitution of the Advisory War Council, which was duly set up by the end of October with Mr. Curtin, Mr. F. M. Forde (Deputy Leader of the Labor Party) and Mr. N. J. O. Makin as the three official Labor representatives, and Mr. Beasley as the " Non-Communist " member of the Council. With the machinery of Government thus reorganized, ministers and their semi-official collaborators from the Opposition parties

---

[18] Other changes were forced upon the Prime Minister by a tragic air crash of August which had caused the death of the Minister for the Army, the Air Minister, and the Vice-President of the Executive Council, in addition to the Chief of the General Staff.

renewed their attack upon the many problems of the Australian wartime effort.

The weakening of the French position in Indo-China confirmed the immediate prewar trend of Australian thinking towards the Pacific. In the early months after the outbreak of hostilities, there had been a widespread feeling that, whatever the result of the war, it would have the effect of changing appreciably the economic association between Australia and European countries. The emergence of a European politico-economic bloc, while it would not completely destroy Australia's trade relations with Great Britain, would throw Australia more directly upon her own resources and upon the markets of her own geographic hinterland, making closer relations with other Pacific countries highly desirable. When the course of the war increased the threat to Great Britain, and Australian security was seen to be more seriously threatened by the conversion of the anti-Comintern agreement into a military alliance, with Japan likely to seize the first opportunity for a drive to the South, political and strategic rather than economic considerations influenced Australian thinking in regard to the Pacific. In the circumstances, increased attention was given to the future policy of the United States in the Pacific and to the possibility of closer relations between the Australian and the American democracies.

The question of direct Australian diplomatic representation in the leading Pacific countries with which Australia had important political and economic associations had long been the subject of discussion in Canberra. The decision to open the first Australian Legation abroad, in Washington, D.C., had been taken before the outbreak of hostilities. The Menzies Government was not deterred from its purpose by the war, and in March 1940 the first Australian minister arrived in Washington. Corresponding steps were taken to strengthen relations between Australia and Canada by the appointment of high commissioners in Ottawa and Canberra respectively. In April 1939, the Menzies Government had also announced its decision to appoint a minister to Japan. For this important position the Chief Justice of the High Court, Sir John Latham, was given leave from the High Court in August 1940 to establish the first Australian Legation in Tokyo.

By such steps the Menzies Government gave expression to the growing conviction of the Australian people that, whatever the nature of the postwar economic organization of the world, Australia would of necessity find its future linked not only with Great Britain but also with the other countries of the Pacific. In short, the exigencies of the war situation had served at once to strengthen the traditional economic and strategic ties of the British connection and yet to emphasize the significance of Australia's own regional associations, responsibilities, and liabilities.

PART TWO

AUSTRALIA AND THE WAR WITH JAPAN
(1941 TO MARCH 1943)

by H. Duncan Hall

✡

1. The Eve of the War — 1941

In the first eleven months of 1941, ending in war with Japan on December 7, Australia underwent internal political changes which brought the Labor Party into power both in the Commonwealth and in the most important of the states, New South Wales; she expanded greatly her war production; her fighting forces received their first great baptism of fire in this war, in Greece, Crete, North Africa, and Syria. With armed forces entrenched in Malaya, she passed through three periods of suspense in expectation of Japan's drive south that came finally like a typhoon out of the China Sea in the twelfth month of the year.

The Prime Minister, Mr. Menzies, by his great personal qualities, won an outstanding place in Empire councils during his mission to Britain from February to May. When he returned to Australia at the end of May, his personal position seemed stronger than ever and even his political critics paid tribute to the quality of leadership which he displayed. Yet three months after his return he was forced to resign; and his resignation led to the defeat of the Coalition Government and the coming into power of the Labor Party under Mr. John Curtin. The success of the Labor Party in the elections in New South Wales in May had been a warning that the hold of the Ministry over the country was weakening. The crisis came to a head on August 26, and after two days of confused political discussions in which faction fights within the Coalition Government appeared to have played an important part, Mr. Menzies was forced to resign, his place being taken, without other change in the composition of the Ministry, by the leader of the Country Party, Mr. A. W. Fadden.

This political crisis, which had lasted for several weeks during a period of grave tension in Australia's external affairs, discredited the Coalition Government sufficiently to bring about its downfall in a vote of no confidence in the House a few weeks later. The Labor Ministry, announced by the new Prime Minister, Mr. Curtin, on October 6, was composed largely of right-wing members of the Party. It consisted of nineteen ministers, the number to which the Cabinet of Mr. Menzies had been increased in the ministerial reorganization made at the end of June after his return from his visit abroad.

The new Ministry continued the essential elements of the reorganized war program as announced by Mr. Menzies in his important broadcast to the Australian people on June 17. The Government had then proposed " to set up an authority with wide powers to take over factories and plants, or, if necessary, to close factories in whole or in part, with powers like those recently announced in the United Kingdom by the Board of Trade." Among the new authorities created were ministries for tank and armored vehicle production and for aircraft production and a Shipping Commission to requisition and supervise the operation of all Australian shipping, the actual management of the ships remaining with the owners.[19] For the more effective use of internal transport, principally under the control of the State Railway Commissioners and Road Boards, a rail and road transport coordinating authority was set up.[20] " The chairmen of the Shipping Board, the railways authority and the roads authority, will together," Mr. Menzies said, " make up a Commonwealth Transport Authority." A Coal Commission to direct national coal production, consumption, and distribution was also to be established.

---

[19] Sixty-three ships engaged in the coasting trade were requisitioned immediately, to be operated by the Australian Shipping Control Board as a national mercantile marine.

[20] Australian rail communications (although cursed with a break of gauge at a dozen points of strategic importance, which military leaders have sought in vain to remove since before the First World War) are on an extraordinary scale for a country with a population less than that of New York City. In 1939 there were 27,973 miles of track.

A Director-General of Supply with wide powers was also to be appointed together with an authority to control and coordinate the supply of labor. A proposal to prohibit strikes and lockouts and business combinations slowing down war production was also made; but this met with such opposition from Labor that it was not carried into effect until the Labor Government was forced by the Japanese attack on the outer ramparts of Australia to adopt, early in 1942, the drastic policy of complete conscription of labor. In addition, standing parliamentary committees were to be attached to government departments in order to bring the legislature in the fullest possible degree into active contact with the different branches of the war administration. Other steps proposed were a further drastic cutting of nonessential imports, both sterling and non-sterling, as part of an effort to divert private spending to the financing of the war effort.

The magnitude of the Australian effort to make itself an arsenal of democracy was revealed more fully during the year. In the first two years of the war, its munitions expenditure was estimated at £A120,-000,000, compared with a total munitions expenditure in the year before the war of under £A4,000,000. Australian forces abroad were equipped to an important degree with arms of Australian manufacture including armored vehicles, machine guns and light artillery and supplies, and munitions of all kinds.[21]

As a result of a policy of decentralization, a chain of small-arms ammunition factories was being extended right round the Commonwealth. In 1940 some sixty or seventy million rounds of small-arms ammunition were exported to the United Kingdom and were used by the R.A.F. in the Battle of Britain. The complicated 3.7 anti-aircraft gun was produced in 1940 within ten months of the receipt of the blueprints, from which 70,000 tools had to be made before actual production could begin. There were fifty factories making machine tools, compared with three before the war, and eighty-five firms making high precision gauges, compared with five before the war. There has been during the war a great expansion in metallurgical industries; at an earlier stage of the

---

[21] The decision to set up and to equip from Australian factories a complete armored division at a cost of £A30,000,000 was an illustration of the range of Australian arms production. Such a division requires hundreds of tanks, as well as armored vehicles, mobile artillery units, etc., as well as reserves. Part of the equipment was to be Bren guns and carriers, anti-aircraft and anti-tank guns and howitzers (all of which were already being produced), tanks (in mass production early in 1943), mobile anti-aircraft units, sound detector apparatus, of which manufacture had begun or was about to begin at the end of 1941.

war four hundred thousand tons of Australian steel were exported to Great Britain in addition to large quantities supplied to various other parts of the British Empire and the Netherlands Indies. In October 1941 the new Labor Minister announced that Australia was to make available immediately, for British-Soviet use on the trans-Iranian railway, sorely needed standard-gauge locomotives and freight cars.

The Australian airplane industry had its thousandth plane in the air in September 1941, and production of two to three hundred planes a month was predicted for 1942 and 1943. Six-hundred-fifty-horsepower and 1100-horsepower airplane engines are now being manufactured. Beaufort bombers began to come off the production lines, and the first squadron reached Singapore in December some days after Japan struck. The delivery of Australian-built training planes to the Netherlands Indies had begun in 1941. Aluminum sheet production was being expanded and plans were well advanced for the manufacture of aluminum from local bauxite or alunite. Over fifty naval vessels, including three cruisers and several destroyers, were under construction in Australian yards; and a program for the building over a five-year period of sixty merchant ships of 9,200 tons each was under way. Marine engines were being built for them. An optical instrument industry entirely new to Australia and involving the manufacture of practically all types of complicated optical instruments, including about 150 types required in modern war, was established in 1941. All this in a country that at the outbreak of war had only 25,000 skilled engineers.

In November 1941 the total number employed directly and indirectly in the making of arms and munitions was stated to be 210,000 as compared with 5,000 at the time of the fall of France. It was planned to transfer another 160,000 from civil to war industry in 1942. Although the possibilities of the production of armaments and war supplies in Australia far exceeded those of any other country in the Eastern Supply Group,[22] at the end of 1941 it seemed to be approaching its maximum output of munitions; yet in reality it was on the eve of an immensely greater expansion. The consequence for the future of Australia of this immense program of wartime industrial production is incalculable. If Australia escapes actual devastation in war, she will emerge from it one of the highly industrialized small powers of the world, far better able to defend herself than before.

War expenditure for 1941 to 1942 was over £A300,000,000, more than

---

[22] See Chapter XI, p. 467; also Chapter II, p. 72.

Australia's total war expenditure in the five financial years of the First World War, which amounted to £A270,059,000. The personnel of the Royal Australian Air Force, which included less than 500 pilots at the outbreak of the war, had reached 70,000 early in 1942. Air Force pilots and air crews were being turned out at the rate of more than 20,000 per year, being drawn as needed from the pool formed by the more than 200,000 who had applied for enlistment in the R.A.A.F. The total of the Australian armed forces overseas in the three services was put at from 170,000 to 250,000; the Royal Australian Navy, at well over 20,000. The militia and home garrisons totalled 200,000; the Home Guard (A.I.F. veterans), 50,000. The total Australian armed forces at home and abroad were about 450,000 in the fall of 1941.

With 450,000 in the armed forces and 210,000 directly or indirectly in arms and munitions production, even on the limited scale of a war largely confined to one hemisphere with Japan neutral, the problem of man power had become serious. The only important margin of expansion still left seemed to be the employment of women in industry, thus freeing men for new war industry. About 750,000 women were employed, and it was thought this figure might be expanded to an estimated total of 1,000,000 in two years' time. The drawing off into the armed forces and munitions of agricultural and other labor already threatened a decline of production. Group farming was the reply — the collective organization of men and machines to farm a whole district as a unit.[23]

An agreement between Great Britain and Australia regarding the general principles of policy to be pursued in respect of the surplus stocks of Australian produce during and immediately after the war was published in June 1941.[24] In principle, Great Britain agreed to purchase the Australian produce that could be shipped. Reserve stocks of storable foodstuffs were to be created up to a certain quantity to meet probable demand during and after the war; and the cost of acquiring and holding these stocks was to be shared equally between the two governments. This agreement (and the identical agreement between Britain and New Zealand) has an important bearing on postwar world reconstruction on the economic side.

In anticipation of a Japanese drive south, there was intense activity in the fields of defense and diplomacy at Singapore and in London,

---

[23] Certain classes of agricultural work were made reserved occupations.
[24] Appendix V.

Washington, Manila, and Canberra. The Australian Prime Minister and general staff officers visited London early in the year, attending meetings of the British War Cabinet and its Defense Committee. Important diplomatic discussions between the Australian Minister to the United States, the British Ambassador, and the American Secretary of State took place during the year in Washington, and staff conferences and consultations in Manila. In Singapore and Canberra there were important regional defense conferences in which the British Commander-in-Chief in the Far East conferred with Australian, New Zealand, and Dutch ministers and general staff officers.[25]

In April it was announced that Australia and New Zealand had decided to establish a Permanent Joint Committee, which appeared to resemble the Permanent Joint Canadian American Defense Committee; it was to consist of two ministers from each country, who were to discuss common defense and economic problems and coordinate the interests of the two countries in these fields.[26] In June the New Zealand Minister of National Services stated that Australia had promised to put New Zealand on the same basis for supplies as any Australian state.

Australia also played a leading part in the Eastern Group Conference at Delhi in November 1940 and in the permanent Eastern Group Supply Council and the permanent Central Provision Office, set up early in 1941.[27] Australia's role was to supply equipment and supplies (training planes, naval craft, armored vehicles, shells, small arms and ammunition, boots, woolens, canned meat, etc.) to India, Burma, Malaya, and the armed forces in the area served by the Council.

Australia's war situation from a strategic point of view was quite different from that of the other dominions. Like England, she saw the enemy poised and ready to strike near her frontiers.[28] She alone of the members of the British Commonwealth had her armed forces dispersed over five continents. She felt, thus, more acutely than the others the need of a unified strategy in the higher direction of the war, and

---

[25] On February 1, 1942, an exchange of ministers with the Netherlands was announced. The Australian High Commissioner in London was accredited to the Dutch Government in London and a consul-general appointed to Java. An exchange of ministers with the U.S.S.R. took place early in 1943.

[26] A joint Australian and New Zealand report on common strategy was made to London in February 1942.

[27] See Chapter XI, p. 467.

[28] On several occasions after the outbreak of war with Japan the Australian Prime Minister and Foreign Minister referred to the failure of two earlier attempts on their part to secure the negotiation between Britain and Russia of a mutual assistance pact whereby they would agree to make war in common against Japan if one of them were attacked by her.

restraint which the head of the Government and the leader of the Opposition had displayed towards one another since the outbreak of the war was seriously threatened. Mr. Curtin himself was no longer sure of the support of all members of his Party. And a general election with all its confusion and its conflicting loyalties loomed ahead.

3. From the Blitzkrieg of May to the Elections of September 1940

While none could foresee the rapidity with which the collapse of Belgium and France would follow the German invasion of the Low Countries on May 10, the Australian Government was not slow to realize the gravity of the situation in the middle of that month. Speaking in the House of Representatives at Canberra on May 22, 1940, the Prime Minister bluntly stated that " as British people we have reached a stage of emergency without precedent in the history of the Empire."

The most important administrative measure taken to meet the emergency was the reorganization of the work of munitions supply in Australia by the appointment of a Director-General of Munitions who, the Prime Minister announced, would be " freed from all hampering regulations," and given the utmost authority " not only to get things done with the existing government machinery but to press into service civil factories, or all or any of the mechanical resources of these factories." The Director-General's status was to resemble that of the chiefs of staff and he was to have direct contact with the Prime Minister as the head of the War Cabinet. The Government congratulated itself on obtaining the services as Director-General of Munitions of Mr. Essington Lewis, managing director of the Broken Hill Proprietary Company, Ltd., one of the largest and most powerful concerns in Australia. An Assistant Director-General was appointed and directors (most of them experienced business executives) for each branch of Munitions Supply — Aircraft, Explosives, Ordnance, Gun Ammunition, Materials, Machine Tools, Finance, and Labor Supply and Regulation. Supplementary organizations were set up in each of the States.

The first political test of Labor's attitude to the new war situation following the *Blitzkrieg* in western Europe came on June 20, when the Prime Minister introduced a bill to amend the National Security Act of the previous year to bring it into line with the Emergency Powers Act passed through the British Parliament on May 22 and a similar New

Zealand Act. On the day before the amending bill was brought before Parliament, a special conference of the Federal Labor Party had revised its war policy in terms which permitted the leader of the Opposition to support the amending bill despite the fact that the measure removed all except one of the limitations which had been set up to the 1939 Act, including the safeguard against " industrial conscription." The sole remaining limitation was the proviso to section 13A of the Act " that nothing in the section shall authorize the imposition of any form of compulsory service beyond the limits of Australia," the term " Australia " being defined to include the " Territories of the Commonwealth of Australia." On a division, the amending measure was passed by the House of Representatives by 61 votes for and 9 against.

While the war policy adopted by the special June Conference of the Australian Labor Party revealed considerable changes as the result of the greater emergency, it also made clear that the Party had no intention of sinking its individuality in the national war effort. These changes in policy were made palatable to members of the Labor movement not only by recognition of the emergency. Stress was also laid on the importance which the Labor Party had itself allotted, before and since the outbreak of war, to the strengthening of Australia's air defenses and to the local manufacture of munitions.

The most notable change was the acceptance of compulsion in training for home defense and provision of reinforcements for the expeditionary forces overseas. Mr. Curtin and all Labor spokesmen were, however, adamant in their refusal to participate in a National Government. The matter was considered by the special conference of the Australian Labor Party in the third week of June, but the farthest the conference was prepared to go was to authorize Mr. Curtin and his parliamentary colleagues to participate in a National War Council " to advise the Government in respect to the conduct of the war and in preparing for the postwar reconstruction."

The Labor proposal for a War Council did not appeal to the Government which, in the absence of a partisan opposition, was able to carry on with its fairly comfortable majority of 9 in the House of Representatives. The main political concern of Mr. Menzies arose from the fact that all members of the House of Representatives and half the members of the Senate must face a General Election not later than January 1941. Towards the end of July the Prime Minister confirmed reports that the Government proposed to move for an increase in powers of the federal

the desirability of an Imperial War Cabinet on which she would be represented by her Prime Minister or his deputy or of an Imperial Conference.[29] That this wish was not realized in 1941 was due not so much to any real opposition in London, where the idea was welcomed, but to the fact that the Canadian Government did not support it.

Without any diminution of the Australian war effort in the matter of men and supplies, directed steadily through Suez, to Egypt, and the Near East, the attention of Australia was focused more and more during the year upon the region between Northern Australia and Singapore. An all-weather strategic highway across the central Australian desert to link the northern port of Darwin with the south and east of Australia was begun in October, 1940, a few days after Japan joined the Axis, and completed to Darwin early in 1941. Steps were taken to double the 2,000-mile telegraph line between Adelaide and Darwin to provide trunk telephone connection for the first time between Darwin and the rest of Australia. A powerful garrison was transported to Darwin, now the base from which Australian planes, munitions, and armies gathered in the more sheltered regions of the south and east of Australia could be launched against any force attacking from the north. Darwin had no docking facilities, but was an oil fueling depot and an air base. Late in January 1942 a second transcontinental roadway was completed to link Adelaide and Perth, thus strengthening the strategically weak " island " of Western Australia, one of the main keys to naval power in the Indian Ocean.

Though dependent for its ultimate safety on the British Navy and the security of Britain, Australia was fast becoming a powerful fortress in its own right. It was garrisoned by a trained army equipped by its own factories, and rapidly becoming mechanized. A ring of radio-location stations gradually being built round its shores began to give it eyes far out at sea to warn against surprise attack. But better than new mechanical inventions against such surprises was reputation. The legend spread throughout the entire world of the valor and fighting skill of the Anzacs, renewed in this generation by their sons in Greece and Crete, in Libya and at Tobruk, warned would-be enemies to think twice before committing themselves to the conquest of the thinly populated island continent. But the country had been stripped of equipment to make good the heavy losses of the A.E.F. in these campaigns and faced Japan without military planes — either fighters or bombers.

---

[29] See Chapter II, p. 35.

2. *Australia as United Nations Base*

The first four months of Australia's war with Japan were the most critical in her history. The sea-walls had cracked. In four months of war, Japan took Singapore and Java, crashed through the barrier of the Netherlands Indies into the Indian Ocean, the Timor Sea, and the Coral Sea.[30] Australia's outer ramparts were invaded on January 23, 1942, with the occupation of Rabaul and attacks on New Guinea. The bombing of Darwin on February 19 brought war at last to the only continent that had never known it.

But, as the Japanese struck at the North, with repeated bombings of Port Moresby, Thursday Island, Darwin, and other points along the northern coast of Australia, the vanguard of an American army arrived in the South. An American General, who had already become a world figure, arrived dramatically in Australia to take over command, at the request of the Australian Government, of the United Nations forces in the Southwest Pacific, including Australia but not New Zealand. Time alone will show the full significance of these events. They are incidents in the general strategy of an indivisible war extending to all continents.

The fact that an American and not a British army went to Australia was not due to any greater will on America's part to come to the aid of Australia. Britain's contribution to the defense of Australia in the period before December 7, and even more before June 22, 1941, when she faced the Axis alone, had been immense. The defense of Malaya was the defense of Australia. Britain had in Malaya an army several times greater than the Australian forces. Before America's entry into the war, Britain dispatched to Singapore several of the most powerful units of the British Navy. The defense of Suez and the Near East was part of the defense of Australia. The main body of the Australian Imperial Force stationed in Syria, alongside a British and Indian army, was playing almost as vital a part in the defense of Australia as the Australian and American troops were later to play on the beaches of Northern Australia. The entry of the United States made possible a sharing of this great burden.

The arrangement whereby an American army went to Australia resulted from the decisions on the grand strategy of the war taken by

---

[30] The Australian casualties in the Malayan campaign were announced on March 13, 1942, as 17,301, the great majority taken prisoners at the fall of Singapore.

Mr. Churchill and President Roosevelt, in consultation with the dominions, in December 1941 and early January 1942. Then it was agreed to put aside political considerations, and to distribute forces in the common war in such a way as to secure the maximum result in the shortest time. Britain was to concentrate on the defense of the northwestern, and the United States, of the southern end of the common battle line. This decision was dictated primarily by two facts. The first was that Britain was already heavily engaged in the northern areas and could not divert forces from them without risking an Axis break-through. The withdrawal of the Australian garrison at Tobruk seriously delayed the British Libyan offensive and perhaps spoiled the chance of getting through to Tripoli before the Japanese struck at Pearl Harbor on December 7.[31] The second fact was that the distance of Britain from Australia is almost twice that of the United States of America; so that the transport of an American army involves only about half the amount of shipping. As it was the lack of ships that was most likely to lose the war for the United Nations, this factor was of capital importance.

A corresponding arrangement was made at the same time in the matter of the naval forces in the Southern Hemisphere. As Mr. Churchill stated on January 27, the British Navy was to be primarily responsible for the Indian Ocean, and therefore for the west coast of Australia, while " the eastward approaches to Australia and New Zealand have been called the Anzac area and are under United States command " and responsibility. New Caledonia, a vital strategic point midway between New Guinea and New Zealand, received an American garrison, and by the middle of March 1942 substantial American forces had arrived in Australia. By the end of April and in May the air reinforcements were sufficient to gain mastery of the air over New Guinea, and by midsummer the American Navy had fought the great battles of the Coral Sea, the Solomons, and Midway.

All this movement of forces to Australia and New Zealand was planned and supervised day by day by the Anglo-American Combined Chiefs of Staff Group in Washington, with the assistance of other joint Anglo-American boards, including the Munitions Assignments Board, the Combined Shipping Adjustment Board, and the Combined Raw Materials Board. The Australian Government was kept informed of

---

[31] Further withdrawal then became necessary to reinforce Singapore and Burma. Substantial forces were brought back from the Near East at the end of March 1942. The Ninth Division, which had formed the British spearhead at El Alamein, returned to Australia early in 1943 for action against Japan.

these developments through its service liaison officers and its Minister in Washington.

The Government left no stone unturned, as was its duty to its people, to make certain that Australia's need of aid was fully understood in London and Washington. The decision to allow the United States to give sole aid on land without even token British forces and planes was bad political psychology. " We are Britain's sons," Mr. Curtin said in a broadcast to America. British aid to her sons in the Near East, Singapore, India, and the Indian Ocean was immense, but invisible and unknown to the public; the eleven precious destroyers lent by the Royal Navy were unseen; so were the British Beaufighters in the skies over New Guinea and the British Spitfires over Darwin. There was no visible aid and comfort. And the absence of such aid from the Mother Country could not fail to create in many people an uneasy sense of being let down. The result was in some cases a deep psychological disturbance, out of all proportion to the real facts.

The second point on which the Australian Government concentrated was a demand, many times repeated, for full and equal participation of Australia in any councils in London, Washington, or Singapore which might be set up to decide the political and strategical war policy. The formation of the short-lived War Council under Mr. Duff Cooper at Singapore was proposed by the Australian Government. In January 1942 repeated requests were made to the British Government for full representation of Australia in an Imperial War Cabinet in London, for the setting up of an inter-allied Pacific War Council, and for full Australian participation in the Combined Chiefs of Staff Group in Washington dealing with the broad strategy of the Pacific war.

Divergence of views, and sharp discussion before agreement is reached, do not necessarily mean that a family is divided against itself. Such situations have been frequent in the family life of the British Commonwealth even in time of war. The personality of the leaders, above all the individual and characteristic reaction of each to the family relationship of the Empire, may play an important part in such a situation. The tendency on the part of some dominion statesmen to combine devotion to the Mother Country with opposition to the existing British Government is as old as British colonization.[32] Such ambivalence is all the more likely to flourish if there are no direct personal relationships. Unlike the Labor Cabinet in New Zealand, the Australian

---

[32] See Chapter II, p. 75.

Labor Cabinet, in power after long years in opposition, had no personal relations with the British Cabinet. This fact was in itself a sufficient justification for the request which Australia made for representation in an Imperial War Cabinet.[33]

In January 1942 Mr. Churchill announced the agreement between himself and President Roosevelt for the " setting up of a Pacific War Council in London on a ministerial plane comprising Great Britain, Australia, New Zealand, and the Dutch East Indies, assisted by the British Chiefs of Staff and the great staff organizations beneath them." " The united view of the British Commonwealth and the Dutch," he continued, " would be transmitted on the Chiefs of Staff level to the Combined Chiefs of Staff sitting in Washington." The first meeting of the Council, with Mr. Churchill as chairman, was attended by the Dutch Prime Minister, the Australian and New Zealand High Commissioners in London, the British Foreign Secretary, the Secretary of State for India, the British Deputy Prime Minister, and the three British Chiefs of Staff. China became a member of the Council shortly after. The function of the Council was formally that of advice rather than executive decision.

The arrangement whereby the Pacific War Council met in London without American representation, while the Combined Chiefs of Staff Group dealing with strategy met in Washington without direct dominion participation was open to criticism, and as a result of pressure from Australia and New Zealand the United States and British Governments agreed to the setting up of a Pacific War Council in Washington. It met on April 1, with President Roosevelt as chairman, and was attended by representatives of the United States, the United Kingdom, Canada, Australia, New Zealand, China, and the Netherlands Indies. The Council was to be parallel to the Pacific War Council in London, with provision for liaison between the two. But the latter had still no representative of the United States or Canada, while the Washington Council had no representative of India. It was described by President Roosevelt as a consultative body dealing with broad questions of policy and not with fighting strategy and the immediate allocation of supplies.

The Australian and New Zealand plea for direct representation on

[33] The misunderstandings that arose regarding the appointment on March 19, 1942 of Mr. R. G. Casey, the Australian Minister to Washington, as British Minister of State at Cairo to coordinate the British Commonwealth war effort in the Near and Middle East offer a clear illustration of the kind of difficulty which might easily have been avoided by the setting up of an Imperial War Cabinet.

the Combined Chiefs of Staff Group and its three subsidiary Anglo-American bodies dealing with munitions, shipping, and raw materials was thus rejected. But Australia and New Zealand (like Canada) sent joint staff missions, with officers from the three services, to act as liaison with the Chiefs of Staff Group and as advisers to their representatives on the Pacific War Council. What were to be the ultimate consequences for the British Empire of the defense of Australia by an American army could not be foreseen. But it was clear that this dramatic entry of America into Australia's history was the beginning of far closer bonds between Australia, New Zealand, and the United States of America. These two dominions seemed likely in future to serve, like Canada, as bonds of union between Britain and the United States. But Australia's ties with Britain show no signs of diminishing. As Mr. Menzies put it on February 7, 1942, " the overwhelming bulk of Australians are utterly and soundly British, and nothing is further from their thoughts than to appear to be reproaching Great Britain at this critical time."

On February 19, 1942, sweeping government regulations to regiment the man power and material resources of the country were issued. The sale or transfer of capital without government authorization, except for obvious war purposes, was prohibited. (Government bonds and notes were excepted.) Prices and wages were pegged at their existing levels, provision being made for the continuance of cost of living adjustments in wage rates at the discretion of the Commonwealth Court of Conciliation and Arbitration. All transfers of labor were placed directly under the Minister of Labor. Profits in all enterprises with capital above $5,000 were limited to 4 percent of capital employed,[34] though this limitation has subsequently been repealed as impossible of uniform application, and the direct control of individual costs has proved more effective. The Commonwealth Bank, subject to the Federal Treasurer, was to determine interest rates for different classes of investment in relation to the bond rate.

The Defense Coordination Minister could direct any person to perform any duty in relation to his trade, business, or profession deemed necessary. It became illegal for employers and employees to be absent from their work. This was equivalent to a prohibition of strikes and lockouts. Industrial tribunals were to continue to settle disputes and to deal with hours and conditions of labor. The system involved the compulsory registration of all persons. As a Government spokesman put

---

[34] As defined by the War-Time (Company) Tax Assessment Act.

it on February 18, " the government has now assumed supreme power over the private life and property of every individual Australian." It now possessed full power to close nonessential industries and to transfer labor to war industries. Total mobilization of man power for service in the army and industry, a *levée en masse,* has probably been carried as far in Australia as in any other belligerent country.

Several new pieces of machinery were added to the war organization. An Industrial Relations Council, presided over by an Arbitration Court Judge and comprising eight employer and eight labor members, was set up at the beginning of January to advise with a view to securing the maximum war production. An Allied Works Council with Mr. E. G. Theodore as Director General was set up to deal with defense works other than munitions production. The Director was armed with wide powers for the compulsory recruitment through the army of the man power needed to construct urgent defense works such as airdromes and strategic roads. Civilians up to the age of sixty could be called up for such work at award rates of pay. A mobile labor army of over 50,-000 constructed in a year 5,000 miles of strategic roads and hundreds of full-scale airdromes and flight strips. Production for civil needs was cut so ruthlessly that by August 1942 two-thirds (511,000 out of 705,000) of the factory workers were on government or private defense work. In addition there was the labor army mentioned above, and the fighting forces had been expanded to about 650,000. A United Nations Supply Council was also set up. Its function was to coordinate Australian supplies required by the United Nations (especially the United States). A large-scale supply agreement with the United States — involving a two-way Lend-Lease arrangement — was negotiated at meetings of the Council in the latter part of March 1942.

The constitutional relation of the Commonwealth Government and the state governments was vitally affected by the Commonwealth Government's assumption, in the summer of 1942, of the exclusive right to levy income tax for the period of the war. It was argued that as the burden of taxation increased it should be more equitably distributed than could be the case with varying state rates of taxation. The state governments are reimbursed from the proceeds of the uniform tax amounts equal to the average of their income tax receipts for the two years before.

Meanwhile the Opposition had become more and more closely associated with the conduct of the war through the increased importance of the Advisory War Council of five Labor leaders and five Opposition party leaders. The Council met frequently, and dealt with important issues of policy. The Government adopted the policy of implementing all unanimous decisions of the Council. Out of this there may be developing a new mechanism for maintaining continuity of foreign policy despite changes of Government.

The invasion of Australia involved for Japan a greater and more risky effort than any she had undertaken.[35] Australia's coastline of 12,000 miles was open at a thousand points to invasion; but if the enemy were to invade any part of the thousands of miles of virtually undefended coastline in the North and Northwest he would have against him the continental distances and appalling difficulties of communications through arid country under heavy attack by enemy bombers. The country accepted the threat of invasion without flinching and in a resolute and aggressive spirit. The early plan of falling back on a defense line north of Brisbane, emptying the North of food for any Japanese invading army by vast cattle drives southwards, was soon abandoned. By March 1943 an offensive movement had carried the United Nations armies, with Australians making up 80 percent of the ground troops, a thousand miles forward, across the Owen Stanley Range, to the northern coasts of New Guinea. The insular stronghold of democracy had been held. Protected on the left flank by the armed force of Britain and on the right by the United States, it was being organized by the United Nations as the southern anchor of their power, the base from which the task of pushing the enemy back out of his island conquests could later be undertaken.

[35] For a study of this problem see H. Duncan Hall, " The Invasion of Australia," *Atlantic Monthly*, April 1942 and *New York Times*, January 11 and May 3rd.

CHAPTER IX

The Dominion of New Zealand at War[*]

by F. L. W. Wood

1. Domestic Politics and Relations with Britain

In 1939 as in 1914 New Zealand proudly claimed to have been the first dominion to declare itself at war by Britain's side; and this alacrity fitly epitomized her century of political and economic evolution. She has always lacked some of the most potent of those factors which helped to foster nationalism in her fellow dominions by giving a sense of difference from England. Unlike Canada and South Africa, she has a population which is homogeneous. Her Maori race — now some 90,000 — has never lacked grievances, but it has long exercised equality of citizenship, and European immigrants rapidly became assimilated to a self-consciously British stock. Nor did New Zealand's early colonists include any coherent group which brought to the new world a traditional sense of grievance. Their memories were not of Irish distresses and evicted crofters but of a solid and potentially pleasant life which could be recreated, free from old-world stresses, amid colonial abundance. New Zealand's climate, soil and scenery were ideal for those determined to live like Englishmen. Games, books, educational methods and social traditions all came straight from Home, and so did the voluminous news printed by numerous journals modeled on the format of the *Times*. A steady

---

* Events from January 1941 to early 1943 have been dealt with by the editor, H. D. H.

stream of immigrants kept personal bonds numerous and strong, while in later years habits of travel refreshed the affection of the well-to-do for a Mother Country whom they had learnt to regard with sentimental optimism as the source of all good things, whether cultural or material.

During the past seventy years, indeed, and particularly since the development of refrigeration in the 1880's, economic self-interest powerfully reinforced sentiment. New Zealand became one of the great exporting countries of the world: lately she has exported goods worth £70,000,000 per year (about £40 per head of the population), or not far short of half her total production. Four-fifths of these exports went to England, and most of them had no alternative market. New Zealand had in fact organized herself to produce butter, cheese, wool, and meat on the assumption that Britain's appetite for these things was insatiable. Organization to meet this visionary demand depended not only on technical efficiency in farming, but on capital; and capital was provided without stint or forethought by a London market eager for investments. To this day, therefore, New Zealand's production, commerce, shipping, and insurance are very largely financed, but not controlled, by British capital. Large-scale "borrowing for development" by the state began seventy years ago. Since then it has been carried on with enthusiasm by Governments of all political complexions, so that by 1932 New Zealand had, with London's benevolent approval, accumulated a public debt in England of nearly £160,000,000 — more than £100 per head of the population.

Commercial and financial dependence on a kindly Mother Country was not, on nineteenth and early twentieth century assumptions, undesirable; for with dependence went security. Between 1919 and 1939, however, it became evident to experts if not to public opinion that the rigidity of the economic bond with Britain had disadvantages. For example, it was seen to transmit depressions to New Zealand with exaggerated effect; hence some experiments in price control to give her some protection from fluctuations on the English market, leading to Labor's scheme of guaranteed prices for dairy products, and its ambition to "insulate" the country, as far as possible, from overseas depressions. Again, it became clear that British demand for New Zealand's exports would not be unlimited after all. The falling birth rate and attempts to revive British agriculture gave plain warning, and, even after the depression, New Zealand faced the possibility of quotas and falling prices. Consequently there was talk (so far fruitless) of exploring new markets, and of developing local industries to give New Zealand's economy a better balance. Here again, though the ground was prepared by the collection of information, not much had been achieved by 1939 save a certain expansion due to local prosperity. Finally, in 1938–39 New Zealand was read a sharp lesson in the disadvantages of being a large-scale debtor who is unwilling or unable to repudiate.

During the Labor Government's first term, suspicion of its domestic policy felt (rightly or wrongly) by British and New Zealand investors led to a big withdrawal of capital, which some estimates put at over £20,000,000 during four or five years. In 1938 withdrawal became a flight of capital, ten to fifteen million pounds being sent out of the country in the second half of the year. This made necessary exchange control and drastic restriction of imports. Next year the moral was pressed home, for a large loan had to be converted in London. Times were in any case bad for such operations, but London's particular suspicions of New Zealand led to the demand that £17,000,000 of capital should be repaid in five years. Repayment at this rate involved further drastic cuts in New Zealand's imports (which are also British exports) and so reacted on her domestic situation. It can be argued that the crisis would have been avoided if the Government had realized the inevitable consequences of its financial policy and imposed exchange control in good time; and it is easy enough to understand the grounds for London's action. All the same, it was plain to those interested that New Zealand's indebtedness made the reactions of British investors, who presumably knew little about New Zealand issues, vitally important for her domestic policy. Significantly enough, however, this aspect was not greatly stressed, for the two political parties agreed in blaming each other for what had happened. With time, however, this difficulty was overcome. Government control of imports was designed to cut down imports to absolutely essential requirements. During the war the restrictions have been extended to imports from all parts of the British Commonwealth, not merely to conserve New Zealand's sterling funds but also to lessen the demands made upon the productive capacity of Great Britain.

In short, the checkered economic history of the years 1919–39 did nothing to weaken New Zealand's sentimental and economic link with Britain. Commercial agreements were negotiated directly with some foreign countries, beginning with Japan in 1928, but did not lessen her fundamental dependence on the British market. Again, the Government acquired great power over overseas trade and the financial system through the guaranteed prices scheme, the establishment of the Reserve Bank (1934), and the enforcement of exchange-control; but these powers were deliberately used to buttress existing trade with Britain rather than to pursue business in new and unlikely places. In this the Government undoubtedly reflected the country's instinct, and showed that, right up to the present time, the forces of sentiment and economic interest have acted in harmony to bind New Zealand closely to the British system.

It is notable, however, that these forces operated slowly, if surely, and did not produce their consummation till the sense of dangerous isolation became their ally in the twentieth century. In the early days of colonization New Zealand had her own views on Imperial and foreign affairs, and was not notable for loyalty to British leadership. On the contrary, instinctive belief in the permanence of *pax Britannica* permitted a turbulent independence of spirit which could frankly contemplate separation from an ungrateful motherland, and even, in hostility to Britain, junction with the United States. However, confidence was shaken by the Russian scares of the 1880's, and it died away in the tension that preceded the First World War. Nor was there any powerful neighbor on whom an isolated dominion could rely. She had lost touch with the United States, and cooperation with Australia became less and less attractive. The Australian colonies, with whom New Zealand had once ranked as equal, combined in 1900 to form a federal commonwealth. To suspicious eyes this looked big and close enough to crush New Zealand's individuality if she should be foolish enough to enter into too close an association. Australia was, moreover, a trade competitor, and after all lacked the power to guarantee security in the Pacific. Therefore, reacting against Australian nationalism, New Zealand clung all the more earnestly to the Mother Country, whose navy gave security, and whose cultural and political attraction was exercised across 12,000 miles of friendly ocean. Thus was the way prepared for enthusiastic participation in the First World War, and for that following period when New Zealand's sense of her own insignificance and of the wisdom and goodness of Britain reached a climax. This was the period of so-called "Mother-complex." While Canada, South Africa, and Ireland fought successfully for dominion status, and the right to independence in foreign affairs, New Zealand strove passionately to preserve the Imperial connection as an organic reality.

The appearance of exaggerated subservience to British leadership in foreign affairs provoked reaction, and the Labor Party became spokesman of that minority which urged New Zealand to form views in such matters, and which championed the cause of collective security. Taking power at last at the end of 1935, the Party proceeded, in foreign as in domestic affairs, to carry out a policy based on conditions during its previous long years of opposition. For the first time New Zealand formed vigorously expressed views on foreign policy which were out of harmony with those of the British Government, and, until checked by the chilly atmosphere of crisis in 1938, she was an acknowledged crusader for collective security and other unpopular policies.[1] In 1938, however, it became clear that war and peace hung in the balance, and that in the first instance at least war would be waged in Europe. Facing this fact, the New Zealand Government apparently concluded that it would be unfair to clamor for a policy the drawbacks of which would be borne by others. Thus, though there is no reason to think that New Zealand changed her mind on collective security, or ceased to advocate it in Imperial discussions, she no longer crusaded in public. Nor was this evolution rejected by public opinion. In September 1938, for example, New Zealand was in the middle of a general-election campaign. Though the Czech crisis raised in an acute form the whole question of collective security, the Government gave no lead to public opinion beyond making it clear that New Zealand would in any event stand by Britain. And the public was content. The issues were not discussed in the press or on the platform, and election propaganda went on undisturbed. New Zealand seemed to have returned to her traditional attitude towards foreign affairs: frank loyalty to British leadership, tempered by confidential comment. In the following year no one asked whether the guarantee to Poland had been given with dominion approval, and though it was noted with uneasiness that the " Tokyo Agreement " of July 1939 had apparently been concluded without full consultation with all the Pacific dominions, no public protest was made.

Thus by 1939 the cycle in New Zealand's foreign policy was complete, and with the outbreak of war she associated herself with Britain instantly and without question. The Prime Minister's words, " Where Britain goes we go. Where she stands we stand," summed up the feeling

---

[1] See for example the remarkable memorandum forwarded to the League of Nations in 1937 by the New Zealand Government containing observations on the amendment of the Covenant. New Zealand also refused to fall into line with the rest of the Empire in recognizing the Italian conquest of Ethiopia. (Ed.)

of the country. The decision was made by her own Cabinet, for the British declaration of war was apparently not held to involve New Zealand automatically.[2] Some argued that the responsibility should have been thrown on Parliament, which in fact unanimously endorsed Cabinet's action; but prompt and wholehearted support of Britain was clearly in accord with the wish of the great majority of citizens and with recent pronouncements by Government spokesmen. Even those ministers who had opposed the "Imperialist" war of 1914 showed no hesitation. In 1938 and 1939 they had gone very close to saying that Britain's wars were of necessity New Zealand's, and with the declaration of war they threw themselves into the work of war organization. In particular, they vigorously denounced those small elements in the population which questioned the majority view that New Zealand's fate was inextricably bound up with that of Britain. The Communist paper was suppressed, pacifist speakers were disciplined through the courts, and there was something like a purge in the civil service, all on the ground that, since New Zealand was at war, she must prevent any action which would weaken her military efficiency.

In supporting Britain to the limit the Government undoubtedly commanded the widest support not only from the conservative Opposition, but from the great majority of the Labor Party, which is traditionally anti-Imperialist, and which remembers bitterly the appeasement phase of British policy. At Easter 1940, for example, the annual conferences of the Federation of Labor and of the Labor Party adopted an interesting statement on the war position. According to this statement, the British Government had at length adopted the policy urged for years by the Labor movements throughout the British Commonwealth, so that to support even Mr. Chamberlain in his belated resistance to Hitlerism was an elementary act of good faith — and of self-preservation.

General agreement on the basic war issue, however, did not clarify the obscurity of domestic politics, which arose primarily from a struggle for power within the Government party. Labor won a sweeping victory in the election of 1938, partly because of the unique command over public opinion of its leader, Mr. Savage. He stood for a humanitarian and undoctrinaire socialism which was strictly in line with New Zealand tradition, and which his confident and kindly personality was ideally fitted to present from the platform and over the radio. However, the very size of Labor's majority made possible some vocal criticism against

---

[2] See Chapter II, p. 21.

his leadership. His Cabinet, virtually unchanged since Labor took office in 1935, was composed of the Party's elderly stalwarts, and no steps had been taken to introduce younger blood into high places. Thus there was persistent criticism in Labor's ranks. This was partly personal, claiming changes in the Cabinet and greater control over the Cabinet by caucus (the Parliamentary Party as a whole).

This conflict arose before the war and was undisturbed by it, for there was no disagreement on the need to resist Hitlerism; but it was greatly confused by the illness of Mr. Savage. He underwent a serious operation just before the war and died at Easter 1940. During the intervening months passions rose, and for a time it seemed that the Party might split asunder in personal wrangles. In the end Mr. Fraser, Mr. Savage's able and moderate Deputy, became Prime Minister, and the older group remained in charge.

Even so, clear political stability was not reached. On the one hand, the new Prime Minister had not yet found that ready access to public confidence that would make him an obvious wartime leader. On the other hand, some of the criticisms brought against his predecessor, which were backed by a strong and active minority, had not yet been met. For example, many who agreed that Hitlerism must be fought complained that in their eagerness to support Britain the Government had not sufficiently safeguarded the dominion's independence of judgment in matters of high policy, and that they were too sensitive to local criticisms of their war effort. The demand was accordingly made for more democratic frankness both as between members of the Commonwealth and on the home front: a demand in line with the Party's caucus's apparent intention to exercise a greater control over policy in general. In November Mr. Fraser was re-elected leader for three years. In December, as promised, the composition of the Cabinet was submitted to caucus and some changes made in its membership.

The war, in its earlier stages, did not solve the problem of leadership in the Labor Party; nor did it lead to suspension of party politics. The opposition, while eager to fight Hitler or any other enemy of Britain, complained that Labor was pushing its private policy of socialism under the thin disguise of war-emergency measures, and it demanded things which the Government was pledged to refuse: notably conscription of man power and a coalition national government. Parliament had been prorogued since the early days of the war but with the German breakthrough in the West it was called together again, and in June passed what was popularly known as the " all-in " legislation. This followed Mr. Churchill's similar Act in Britain and gave the Government potentially absolute control over men, money, and industry.

Finally, in July, a curious compromise War Cabinet was set up. The existing Cabinet continued intact for the ordinary functions of government, but there was superimposed upon it a War Cabinet of five: three key ministers — Messrs. Fraser (Prime Minister), Nash (Deputy Prime Minister and Minister of Finance), and Jones (Minister of Defense), and two leaders of the Opposition, Messrs. Hamilton and Coates. The War Cabinet was given full charge of the war effort.[3] While it apparently worked smoothly and usefully, on the political side it gave an additional weapon to those leftists who accused the Labor Government of undue truckling to conservatism. It was assisted by an advisory war council made up of representatives of political, commercial, and workers' organizations.

In November 1940 the Opposition changed its leadership, and it has been suggested that one object was to regain some of the freedom of opposition criticism which was lost when the former leader of the Opposition joined the War Cabinet; the Prime Minister said that in his view the leader of the Opposition must be a member of the War Cabinet, if it was to have a national character.[4]

2. The War Organization and the War Effort

The war effort thus elaborately supervised was in part military and in part economic. On the military side, the understanding before the outbreak of the war was that the primary duty of the Pacific dominions would be to protect themselves, and presumably detailed plans were discussed at the Pacific Defense Conference between the representatives of Britain, Australia, and New Zealand who met in Wellington on New Zealand's initiative in April 1939. But in the upshot the whole war situation was altered for a time by the abstention of Japan and Italy, and popular sentiment, governed by memories of the First

---

[3] Though it contains leading members of the opposition the War Cabinet has full executive authority in all war matters. It is not an advisory body like the Australian Defense Council. Although policy is left to the War Cabinet, administration remains in the hands of the Labor ministers. An attempt to expand the War Cabinet into a war administration with seven Labor and six National Party members failed in October 1942.

[4] On October 15, 1941, the Prime Minister announced the postponement for a year of the General Election which was due in the normal course in 1941. In October 1942 the Government decided to hold an election twelve months later. (Ed.)

World War, thought of war efforts in terms of trained man power sent overseas. The natural result was that an expeditionary force was rapidly organized, and New Zealand undertook to maintain a division abroad, which has for long been stationed in the Middle East. Any damage to Territorial organization resulting from the drawing off of this expeditionary force was energetically repaired in 1940, when, following the military disasters in France, the whole Territorial Force was called up for intensive training. From July 1940 onwards the men needed for home or overseas service were found by ballot under the conscription law. Service in the Home Guard is compulsory. It provides static defense in home districts, the members giving army service on a shift basis which does not interfere with their civil occupations.

By the first half of 1942 New Zealand had become an armed camp. Her total man power and woman power was organized in the armed forces, in the civil defense organizations and the emergency services. She had some 60,000 men abroad in the three services — army, navy, and air force.[5] Over 5,000 of her airmen were serving abroad in separate New Zealand fighter, bomber, or torpedo-bomber squadrons, or with the R.A.F. in the various combat zones. R.N.Z.A.F. patrols kept watch over the Pacific islands, five widely scattered groups of which (including Fiji and Samoa) were garrisoned by New Zealand forces. Her air force at home was over 12,000 airmen. It was based on over 200 airdromes, most of them constructed since 1936. Her annual air quota to the British Commonwealth Air Training Plan was 5,000 airmen. Her naval personnel was over 4,500 men. Units of her small navy (containing two cruisers, the *Achilles* and the *Leander,* and a number of auxiliary vessels) distinguished themselves in the battle of the River Plate with the *Admiral Graf Spee,* and in the Mediterranean and the Indian Ocean; and throughout the war they did silent service in convoy work and minesweeping.

Her armed forces in New Zealand were well over 150,000 men. These included over 50,000 men in the Home Guard. How far total mobilization had gone is shown by the fact that in June 1942 one out of every six males of military age was in the actual battle line; that nearly one in three of the total male population of New Zealand was trained and equipped for combat duties or was being trained; that over half of the

---

[5] New Zealand casualties in the Eastern Mediterranean area were given in May 1942 as 13,000. Only a limited number of officers were brought back to New Zealand for training purposes after the outbreak of war with Japan.

total males aged 20 to 60 years were mobilized in the armed forces. Those that were not in the armed forces were in the Civilian Defense Organization or organized in the Emergency Services. There were 60,000 in the Women's War Service Auxiliary.

In the matter of munitions and war supplies New Zealand's contribution was necessarily small. She was mainly a primary producing country without an iron and steel industry. In the early months of the war she continued to look to Britain for military supplies.[6] But when France collapsed, and Britain, besieged, was in desperate need of supplies to replace the losses at Dunkirk, New Zealand's light engineering industry was swiftly and successfully geared to war production. With the railway workshops as a basis nearly sixty firms were turned over to the manufacture of some seventy different types of munitions. These included trench mortars and mortar bombs, high explosive bombs, Bren-gun carriers, light-armored cars, hand grenades, small arms ammunition, steel helmets. Minesweepers and parts of training aircraft were also built. For some supplies, particularly steel, New Zealand was able to turn to Australia, but even in 1942 the main source of supplies for her essential requirements in steel and armaments was still Great Britain and the United States.

A small country, which even before the war had a more centralized form of government than the other dominions, New Zealand gave far-reaching powers to its Government for the conduct of the war without hesitation. At the outbreak of war a number of domestic economic controls were set up along lines previously planned. Each important branch of supply and production was placed under the supervision of a Controller with wide powers. There were also set up two advisory councils, with ministerial chairmen, to provide an effective link between the Government and those actually operating industry. The National Council of Primary Production represented farming interests and workers and had numerous local branches to keep in touch with farming problems and farmers' grievances. The Industrial Emergency Council was nominated equally by the Employers' Federation and the Federation of Labor, and considered all cases where modification of labor conditions, such as the extension of hours of work, seemed necessary in the public interest. Parallel with these economic controls, the state took wide cen-

---

[6] But as a result of the early wartime expansion of exports to Great Britain, New Zealand's favorable annual balance of trade was £24.7 in June 1940, an improvement of £16 over the position a year before.

sorship powers, together with the right virtually to govern by regulation; and these wide powers were made wider still during 1940.

On the whole the Government made sparing use of its potential dictatorship. It had already a firm grip on the country's economy before the war, so in most cases the new powers were not needed; moreover, its deliberate wartime policy was to cooperate with industry rather than bludgeon it. Consequently the new controls were little before the public eye, except where inescapable circumstances forced the Government into action. For example, shortage of non-sterling exchange led to severe gasoline rationing, at Britain's urgent request, while lack of structural steel threw power into the hands of the Building Controller. For similar reasons the importance of the Factory Controller proved to be considerable. His main function was at first to apportion government contracts among private firms. But the importance of government orders in some trades became very great. Moreover, it was natural for those officials controlling the importation and rationing of industrial raw materials to act to some extent in consultation with the Factory Controller. Thus quietly, and without apparent friction, steadily increasing influence fell to the Controller and to those officials with whom he was in constant if sometimes informal contact. Even this modest development took place in the second year of war rather than in the first, and for the most part life proceeded much as usual. A considerable change-over from butter to cheese production, following a request from Britain, was organized almost entirely by persuasion and provision of the necessary financial assistance.

As the armaments manufacture of Britain and the United States increased and the strain on overseas shipping became greater, the problem of supply grew more and more serious. To insure continuity of production, arrangements were made by the Government for the accumulation by manufacturers of stocks of some of the basic materials. In some cases the Government made bulk purchases to put in stock. The practice of issuing certificates of essentiality was begun for some commodities; import licenses covering as much as a year were issued. A Supply Council was set up in 1941 with powers to operate under the general control of the War Cabinet and the Minister of Supply, mainly with the object of planning production on a long-term basis and obtaining supplies for the armed forces. By this means manufacturers could be given longer-term contracts, and could be assured of the necessary materials for carrying them out. These arrangements were of special importance to a country with so few of the raw materials required by defense industry.

The emergency powers of the Government were not fully used until the entry of Japan brought war close to the shores of New Zealand. The first of a number of farreaching orders issued then declared certain industries essential to the war effort, placing on all employers and employees an obligation to maintain production. No employee in such industries could terminate his engagement or transfer to another employment. Nor could he be discharged without the consent of the Government working through its man power officials. The obligation to serve in the armed forces if called of course remains. A further order restricts the flow of workers into nonessential industries. Retail shops, other than those engaged in the distribution of food, drugs, and fuel, fall into this category. By this and other measures (enrollment in the Emergency Corps, registration of all those with engineering experience, etc.), the whole of the male population was brought within the scope of the National Service Department. In marshaling the man power and woman power of the dominion the Government acted on the principle of " a post for everyone and everyone trained for his post."

Over 160,000 men were drawn off from production into the armed forces. This was more than one-third of the total number of males gainfully employed in normal times. Despite this decrease in the labor force, harder work, longer hours, and the employment of women in industry pushed up production in farm and factory continuously to points never before attained in the history of the country. A further step was the appointment of a Director of Production. He was given wide powers to insure the most effective use of material and machines for the production of munitions and war supplies. He himself was an executive officer of the Supply Council, and one of his principal tasks was the coordination of the work of the eleven controllers attached to the Ministry of Supply.

The Japanese threat to the shores of New Zealand greatly increased the importance of local defense works. A Commissioner of Defense Construction was appointed with the role of commander-in-chief of the building and construction trade. He was empowered to move workers from any part of the country to particular jobs; to take over material and equipment for urgent defense works; to take over the management of concerns; to set the price at which contract work was to be done.

To facilitate the working of this plan labor awards were set aside. A flat rate of £5/5s. a week was guaranteed with allowances for traveling and board. Hours of work were extended from forty to fifty-four per week. Similar extensions took place in all war industries. Award conditions were varied, statutory holidays suspended. With a non-party national War Cabinet pledged to the principle of equality of sacrifice and service, and with employers and employees fully represented in war advisory councils, it was possible to carry through these changes in the social structure without friction.

Though her military contribution has been considerable for a small country, it was generally agreed in the earlier stages of the war that New Zealand could best help the British Commonwealth through her characteristic exports of wool and food. In September 1939 she offered to Britain her whole surplus of these goods, and after lengthy negotiations agreements were concluded in which a fine balance between good business and Imperial sentiment concealed from the public eye a real threat to the dominion's economy. The British Government promised to buy all surplus wool for the duration of the war and one year after, together with fixed quantities of butter, cheese, and meat: quantities which were subject to revision from year to year. The details were fair enough in the first instance. The quantities fixed practically covered the season's surplus, and the prices were above the figures for 1939. However, no satisfactory arrangements were made for revision. New Zealand suggested that if the price-level of Britain's exports to New Zealand rose by 10 percent, then the prices paid for New Zealand's exports should be correspondingly revised; but nothing was promised. Other dangers for New Zealand lurked in the background. It was possible that war conditions might do much to persuade overseas manufacturers that staple fiber was just as good as wool, and housewives that vitaminized margarine at 8d. per lb. was better than butter at 1s. 7d. If these things should happen, the prewar nightmare of falling markets might become real with sudden and devastating effect. Indeed, the only one of New Zealand's normal exports for which the demand seemed likely to increase was cheese, which offers cheap and concentrated nourishment for low-paid workers. The catastrophe of Denmark and Holland did indeed postpone the economic threat to New Zealand. For the year ending September 1941 the British Government agreed " to purchase, shipped or unshipped, 248,000 tons of meat, 120,000 tons of butter, and all the cheese available." The meat contract for the first year of the war was 300,000 tons. For the first two full years of the war New Zealand shipped to the United Kingdom 254,000 tons of butter, 210,000 tons of cheese, 598,000 tons of meat and 1,600,000 bales of wool. On making this agreement the British Government promised that the general arrangement would be continued throughout the war, and that every effort would be made to provide ships: a vital point, since all British shipping was centrally controlled. However, in spite of this more generous treatment, it was clear that New Zealand's trading position in the long view was entirely dependent on the fortunes of the war. As witness the British Government's announcement in January 1941, that for the time being meat imports from the dominion must be cut down drastically, owing to shipping difficulties. The vastly increased cold-storage space, which was provided locally, could not be more than a temporary remedy for such a stoppage.

On June 27, 1941, the texts of identical agreements between the governments of the United Kingdom, and Australia and New Zealand, were issued in London.[7] The agreements set out the principles governing the cooperation between the governments in the matter of the surplus produce of Australia and New Zealand for the period of the war. The United Kingdom Government agrees to purchase produce of each country that can be shipped in any one season. Reserve stocks of storeable foodstuffs are to be created to meet demand during or after the war, the costs being shared equally between the governments.

As the Honorable Walter Nash, the Minister of Finance, explained to Parliament in his budget speech, this agreement " provides a definite basis on which the future financial obligations of our export trade with the United Kingdom will be determined. Secondly it creates a broad framework within which our future primary production must be organized and directed." Having promised to sell in bulk to Britain, the New Zealand government had to buy from its own producers. This meant applying to wool and meat a procedure roughly similar to that already evolved for butter and cheese, and virtually completed the government's control over the whole of the country's overseas trade. Dairy produce had for some years been bought by the Marketing Department at the point of shipment; the only change was that it was now resold to the British Government instead of to trading interests. Wool, previously sold at auction, was appraised under the wartime arrangement by the men formerly employed as wool buyers by private firms but now acting as government valuers. Meat was still handled by the normal agencies such as freezing works, which now acted for the government in buying from farmers and delivering frozen meat ready for shipment. These arrangements worked extremely well, the main point of friction

---

[7] See Appendix V.

being the vociferous discontent of the dairy farmers' organizations in the earlier phase of the war with the prices for butter and cheese. As regards wool and meat the Marketing Department simply paid out on the basis of prices to be collected from Britain, but dairy farmers claimed that under the guaranteed price procedure they should be paid according to local costs irrespective of prices received.

Nevertheless in a world full of grim uncertainties the policy of the Government gave the dairy industry stability. As Mr. Nash pointed out, it protected the farmers against " the major risks " and gave them financial security to carry on their operations with confidence. A number of other steps announced by him in his budget speech were aimed at protecting the pastoral industries from " the major economic shocks arising from the war "; these included fertilizer subsidies and railway rebates. Owing to increasing shipping difficulties, especially in the third year of the war, the Government made arrangements to facilitate the change-over from butter to cheese. The goal set in 1942 was 153,000 tons — more than the total cheese imports of the United Kingdom in peace years. A special war costs allowance was also made to the dairy industry to compensate for increased manufacturing costs. This was to be accompanied by a corresponding increase in the wages of dairy farm workers.

New agreements with Great Britain made in accordance with the surpluses agreement of June 1941, in respect of meat, butter, and cheese, were announced in February 1942. The general effect of the agreements was to stabilize or reduce the quantities of meat and butter produced. To offset the need for less production of meat and butter the Minister of Marketing called for " a greater production of wheat, linen-flax, cheese and possibly other milk products such as whole milk powder."

If the Government's first principle was to help Britain to the limit, its second was to preserve New Zealand's social experiment with as little change as possible. This fact, together with the Government's view on war finance, was made clear in the Budget of June 1940. About £20,-000,000 was to be borrowed from the British Government for overseas war expenses in 1940-41, but for the rest, the war should be paid for out of revenue so as to avoid leaving a deadweight burden to posterity. The Government had previously turned its face against the suggestion that the war should be financed by cutting down ordinary expenditure. It was willing in principle to economize to the bone where this could be done without injury to the social structure, but it had already shown clearly that in practice it found the field for socially desirable economy narrow indeed. The result was that ordinary expenditure increased slightly to stand at £37,000,000. This, with total war expenditure of £37,500,000 and public works at £20,589,000, makes a total expenditure of nearly £100,000,000. To meet this large total, taxation rates were increased again on every section of the community, and it was estimated that special taxes would provide £14,120,000 towards war expenditure in New Zealand. The remainder would apparently be borrowed, together with about £15,000,000 for public works; this last being a reduction of about £4,000,000 on the amount borrowed for this purpose in 1939.

The Budget showed the gap separating the ideas of the Cabinet from those of the Opposition on the one hand and of its own leftist critics on the other. For the Opposition the basic principle of war finance should be economy in all other directions. Any other course, in its view, led to straight-out inflation, and it pointed to alarming danger signals in the size of the state's overdraft with the Reserve Bank and in the increasing note circulation. To the leftists, on the other hand, war taxation on lower incomes and borrowing were alike evil, for they both sacrificed the happiness of human beings to the shibboleths of discredited financial orthodoxy. Their solution was, therefore, " debt free money " to be issued by the Reserve Bank. Talk of inflation, said a spokesman of this group, was a capitalist dodge; it could not happen under a socialist government. And apart from such theorists a powerful trade union movement was unfailingly vocal in defense of working conditions and real wages.

Between such conflicting advice the Government steered the difficult course of moderation in a sea of trouble. On the one hand, they refused to cut social services. The 40-hour week remained intact, except where a few carefully safeguarded extensions for war purposes seemed unavoidable. Wage rates were maintained, and in August 1940 the Arbitration Court gave an all round 5 percent increase in award wages, based on increased cost of living since 1937. On the other hand, the possibility of inflation was for the Government no bogey to be exorcised by bland nonrecognition. Mr. Nash, Minister of Finance, had always argued that new bank credit is not inflationary when matched by increased consumer's goods on which credit could be spent. But in 1940, he argued, import restrictions and war stringencies were actually cutting down the goods available to the people at a time when heavy war spending must increase their purchasing power. Therefore, the duty of the wise administrator was plain. Secondary industry should be stimulated to supply as many as possible of the missing consumer-goods; and, indeed, in spite of the absorption of men into the Army, all important industries except motor assembly reported substantial increases in production in 1940. However, in the official view, there were technical limits to the pace of such expansion, while the supply of industrial equipment was limited by sterling funds, and in any case a considerable proportion of the increased production was absorbed by the Army. In these circumstances the Government's case was that bank credit should be used sparingly; and purchasing power must be cut down to safe levels by taxation and by loans, which might be made compulsory for the well-to-do, at nominal rates of interest. This must have been a distasteful policy to a Government elected to raise purchasing power; but wars produce odd necessities in dependent communities.

Eighteen months later, in June 1942, the full effects of the war had become more manifest. Mr. Nash, now New Zealand Minister in Washington, estimated the total war expenditure for the year at £NZ133,-000,000, three times the war expenditure in 1941. Of this sum £46,000,-000 was to be expended on war account overseas. Of the total war expenditure approximately £40,000,000 was expected to be obtained from revenue, £8,000,000 from national savings and departmental funds, and £28,000,000 by war loans. " The total national expenditure for this year under all headings," he said, " amounts to the enormous sum, for New Zealand, of £188,000,000, an amount in excess of New Zealand's total national income only a few years ago." Despite heavy taxation, war loans, and large contributions to patriotic funds, savings continued at a fair level. Net savings registered in bank deposits for the year ending in March 1942 were £32,000,000. While food supplies remained adequate, luxuries had almost disappeared; many goods formerly imported were no longer available or were severely rationed. As in Australia, only enough gasoline was allowed for 40 miles a month, just sufficient to keep cars in running order — as a strategic reserve. As a result of the decrease of imports and the heavy demands of the armed forces, the supply of goods available for civilian consumption in 1942 was estimated by Mr. Nash as 30 percent less than usual, while the spending power of the community was 10 percent higher. Taxation had reached a maximum rate of 90 cents in the dollar on incomes equivalent to $12,000. In accordance with the principle of " pay as you go " more than half of the war cost had been met up to that date out of revenue.

As a result of price control and other measures, retail price increases from September 1939 to June 1942 were kept down to an average of less than 10 percent above the prewar level — only about a third of the retail price increases in the United Kingdom. Rents as well as prices were rigidly controlled. Prices for a range of 38 items of food, clothing, footwear, light, and public utilities were stabilized. In order to keep prices at this level, subsidies were paid for bread, sugar, and coal, commodities for which New Zealand had been in part dependent on imports. To meet the rise in cost of living the 5 percent increase of wages in October 1940 was repeated in April 1942. On each occasion a cost of living bonus at a flat rate of £13 per year was granted to government employees on the low income levels.[8] Regulations issued on December 15, 1942, marked an important further step to secure stabilization. The freezing of rents was made complete; wages and all other forms of remuneration including salaries and fees were frozen at existing levels. A new quarterly cost-of-living index was set up. The Arbitration Court was empowered to adjust wages in the event of a rise or fall in the index beyond a fixed percentage. The list of stabilized prices was extended to cover 110 commodities which go into the average family budget. Prices of the major items entering into farm costs, such as power, transport, fertilizers, etc., were also fixed.

Even in the third year of the war, Mr. Nash claimed that " in spite of the heavy added burden of war expenditure there has been no wholesale retrenchment in the field of social services. . . . No general retreat . . . in fact some notable advances." These included the widening of the scope of family allowances to cover the first child instead of the third, and an increase of the allowance payable for each child from 4s. to 6s. per week; and the provision of free medical (general practitioner) and pharmaceutical benefits irrespective of income.[9]

The immediate effect of the war was, of course, to tighten considerably New Zealand's already intimate bonds with the Mother Country. On the economic side she embraced the inevitable with enthusiasm, and willingly gave her whole export trade into Britain's keeping. On the political side, again, it may be doubted whether the situation left New Zealand much freedom of choice. After all, Britain had taken up arms

---

[8] In judging the significance of figures given here (or in Chapter VIII), it should be remembered that, measured in terms of purchasing power, the New Zealand (or Australian) pound is worth two or three times its nominal fixed dollar exchange value. (H. D. H.)

[9] The shortage of doctors due to the war delayed the full application of this scheme.

in the name of principles unanimously approved by New Zealanders, however much some of them might question whether those principles had really guided British policy in the past, and anything like a desertion of Britain in these circumstances would have been a denial of all New Zealand's history.

This attitude was criticized by radicals, but the Cabinet may have preserved a greater degree of independence in judgment than appeared on the surface. If so, it probably represented " average opinion," in so far, that is, as a conflict of undigested individual wills may ever be represented. The " general will " has in fact matured somewhat during the last twenty-five years. It is still dominated by loyalty to the British connection, but alongside of that loyalty there has grown up an increasing appreciation of the facts of world politics. There was an increasing minority which realized, even before Japan's final plunge into the war, that New Zealand, though bound to Europe by trade and tradition, was a Pacific country; and that the Pacific was no more likely than Europe itself to keep forever its nineteenth century framework.[10]

---

[10] Japan's southward drive in the spring and summer of 1942 opened a new phase in the political and military history of New Zealand, linking her far more closely than ever before with the United States of America. Her old instinctive friendship for the United States had become more conscious as the war developed. The first diplomatic appointment in New Zealand's history was the naming of a minister to Washington early in 1942 in the person of Mr. Walter Nash. As a result of the Roosevelt-Churchill decisions of January 1942, New Zealand was placed in the American operational sphere. American armed forces were stationed in the country and an American naval force under Vice-Admiral Ghormley was based on Auckland. The aid of the United States was enthusiastically welcomed by New Zealanders, but without any feeling that Britain had " let them down." Already in May 1942 British military equipment was reaching the country in unprecedented quantities. With the double aid of Great Britain and the United States New Zealand faced her future with confidence and resolution — with much of her armed power abroad, with her coasts blacked out, her beaches guarded, and trenches dug in her cities. (Ed.)

CHAPTER X

The Union of South Africa in the War

by Lucretia Ilsley

✵

1. Party Politics, 1932–41

This chapter deals first with the background of the political crisis which was occasioned by South Africa's entry into the war, then with the crisis itself and the political realignments resulting from it. The Union's war effort is next considered from the military and economic viewpoints. At the beginning of the war the United Party Fusion, led by Prime Minister Hertzog and General Smuts, was shattered on the issue of neutrality. To appreciate the significance of the Fusion and its breakdown, it is essential to recall the struggle of 1932 over the abandonment of the gold standard, which led ultimately to the formation of the United Party.

From 1924 until February 1933, General Hertzog, head of the Afrikaans-speaking Nationalist Party, was Prime Minister of the Nationalist-Laborite Pact Government, while the South African Party, composed of both Afrikaans- and English-speaking elements under the leadership of General Smuts, formed the Opposition. As the effects of the depression became apparent in South Africa, the Pact Government was confronted with increasingly serious problems. Prices for diamonds, wool, and other agricultural products fell, and the hardships of the farmers were intensified by a severe drought. The gold industry, by contrast, remained prosperous and contributed to the financial stability of the country.

In the fall of 1931 came the Central European banking crisis and the resulting departure of Great Britain from the gold standard, events which inevitably caused repercussions in South Africa. During the next fifteen months the question of whether South Africa should remain on gold became the outstanding political issue which was debated with increasing vehemence in Parliament and outside. The Hertzog Government stood firm for gold, while the South African Party, after some initial hesitancy, advocated action similar to that taken in Great Britain. Among the Government's supporters were Afrikaans-speaking farmers who, in spite of their economic plight, hesitated for political reasons to denounce the gold standard. At first the gold mining interests approved the Government's policy. Within a few months, however, leaders of this group reversed their position on the ground that abandonment of the gold standard would make it profitable to work low-grade ores and thus prolong the life of the mines by 50 percent. The Government's tenacity in clinging to gold in the face of growing opposition was probably motivated in considerable part by its Nationalist aspirations to demonstrate that South Africa was not merely an economic satellite of Great Britain. Speculation on probable devaluation caused a flight from the South African pound; but the Government, in the face of its outspoken commitments for gold, seemed unable to take decisive action to remedy the situation.

Finally, in December a *deus ex machina* appeared in the person of Tielman Roos, former Minister of Justice in the Pact Government. Roos suddenly announced his resignation from the Appellate Division of the Supreme Court, together with his intention of leading a movement for a national government on non-racial lines which would devalue the currency. This dramatic incident gave such impetus to the flight from the pound that between two and three million pounds of foreign exchange had to be supplied by the South African Reserve Bank within three days. In the face of this crisis the Government, on December 28, decided to go off gold.

Aside from bringing to a head the issue of the gold standard, the Roos movement had important political repercussions. While the Government was denouncing Roos for betrayal of the Nationalist cause, General Smuts was trying to effect a coalition between the Roosites and the South African Party, but negotiations broke down because Smuts could not accept Roos as Prime Minister. Smuts thereupon tried to render the Roos movement harmless by introducing in the House of Assembly a motion for the formation of a national government. The Prime Minister at first rejected the idea and with the support of the Roosites brought about the defeat of General Smuts's motion. Private negotiations between Hertzog and Smuts continued, however, and culminated in the announcement on February 28, 1933, of a Coalition between the Nationalist and South African Parties under the premiership of General Hertzog. The principles on which the Coalition was based included maintenance of the Union as a national unit on the basis of the sovereign independence guaranteeed by the Statute of Westminster and protection of the Union's capital assets.

At the general election on May 17, the Coalition won 138 out of 150 seats in the House, while the Roosites, who had made the Coalition possible, secured only 2. Thus the economic depression and the monetary problems arising from it had as a significant consequence the reconciliation of two political enemies of long standing and the inauguration of a period of greater cooperation between the two European races in South Africa.

As a step toward welding the Coalition into Fusion, the Government in 1934 found it expedient to appease Nationalist sentiment by the passage of legislation which defined more explicitly South Africa's status in the British Commonwealth. The Status of the Union Act declares that all sovereign legislative power for the Union is vested in the Union Parliament alone. It further states that all executive power over internal and external affairs is vested in the King, acting on the advice of his South African ministers, but administration of this power may be carried on either by the King or by the Governor-General, as his representative, upon the advice of Union ministers.[1]

During lengthy parliamentary debates the Government took the position that the Status Bill did not go beyond the constitutional resolutions of 1926–30 and the Statute of Westminster. There was, however, a divergence of opinion between Prime Minister Hertzog and his deputy, General Smuts, regarding interpretation of the aforesaid constitutional measures. Throughout the debates the Prime Minister remained silent, but shortly before the introduction of the Status Bill he had written to

---

[1] The Royal Executive Function and Seals Act, 1934, provides further that if the signature of the King to a measure cannot be obtained, the Governor-General may execute and sign on behalf of the King.

a leader of the Nationalist Party that since 1926 he had never doubted the reality for South Africa of sovereign independence, divisibility of the Crown, and the twin rights of neutrality and secession, although, he added, too close definition of these rights might be confusing. General Smuts asserted in the House that the pending legislation did not touch these contentious points, on which he held views less advanced than those of the Prime Minister, but merely affirmed the existing constitutional position. The group of extreme Nationalists led by Dr. D. F. Malan voted for the status legislation because they professed to see in it divisibility of the Crown and sovereign international status. A small faction of the South African Party with strong British sympathies, headed by Col. C. F. Stallard, unsuccessfully fought the bills as an attempt to impair the prerogative of the Crown.

In December 1934, a few months after the adoption of the Status and Seals Acts, the Coalition was transformed into Fusion by the formation, under the leadership of Prime Minister Hertzog and General Smuts, of the United South African National Party. Dr. Malan and his followers decided to reject the Fusion, and taking up the cause of Afrikanderism with the slogan, " A republic, not necessarily in our time," became the Nationalist Opposition. At the opposite pole, Col. Stallard organized as the Dominion Party that group which opposed the trend away from the Commonwealth which they saw in the adoption of the legislation on status. At the general election of May 1938, the Fusion Government appealed for a further mandate on the grounds of national unity, and its record of achievement as shown by general recovery and increasing revenue. Election results showed that the United Party was still in a strong position, as it won 111 out of 150 seats, losing only 6 seats to the two extreme groups.

Before the political crisis which immediately preceded South Africa's entry into hostilities with Germany is discussed, a brief survey of Union foreign policy in the latter part of the decade prior to the conflict may contribute to an understanding of the disintegration of the Fusion on the neutrality issue. After the collapse of the Disarmament Conference in 1934, the South African Government continued to uphold collective security despite Nationalist insistence on South Africa's right to neutrality. Italy's Ethiopian adventure aroused fears in South Africa that the attack on a native state might have unfavorable repercussions among Union natives and might encourage Germany to future action. The Government and a large section of public opinion gave strong support to League sanctions against Italy, although protests were heard from the Nationalist Opposition. It may be noted that the Italian shipping subsidy [2] remained in force despite the imposition of sanctions by the Union. When the League Assembly voted to recommend abandonment of sanctions, the South African delegate, Mr. ter Water, abstained from voting after an emphatic protest. General Hertzog officially upheld the League system to the extent that in April 1939 he opposed a Nationalist demand for South African withdrawal. In the fall of 1939 South Africa was elected to membership on the League Council.

When Germany's remilitarization of the Rhineland in 1936 demonstrated that collective security had failed to preserve the *status quo* of Versailles, public sentiment in the Union was divided with regard to German colonial claims. The Fusion Government's official position with regard to Southwest Africa, expressed in a communiqué of December 1936, was that transfer of the mandate to another power would not be considered. Notwithstanding this declaration, which enjoyed widespread support in United and Dominion Party circles, in March 1937, the Prime Minister asserted in Parliament that the psychological aspect of Germany's case should not be overlooked, and that while in favor of retaining Southwest Africa for the Union, he was prepared to take Germany's legal claim into account.

A tour of European capitals undertaken by the Minister of Defense, Mr. O. Pirow, during the post-Munich era, aroused suspicion that he was promoting a scheme for appeasing Germany with a colonial area in West Africa to be carved from the possessions of Great Britain, France, Belgium, and Portugal. Although disavowing that he had ever negotiated with any government or individual about such a transfer of territory, Mr. Pirow in June 1939 declared that the problem of compensating Germany must be faced. Dr. Malan announced in May 1939 that the Nationalist Party would resist any attempt to use the connection between the Union and the mandate as a pretext for dragging South Africa into war.

If there was divided opinion in South Africa over the question of German colonial demands, the issue of neutrality revealed a deeper cleavage, which antedated the Fusion. In organizing the Coalition of 1933, Prime Minister Hertzog and General Smuts had reached a compromise

---

[2] A subsidy of £150,000 per annum was granted to Italian shipping lines in 1934 for a five-year period. Since the grant failed to effect any marked expansion of Union trade in West Africa and the Mediterranean, it was not renewed upon its expiration in February 1939.

on this controversial point. It was then agreed that the Union was not automatically bound to enter into a war involving the Commonwealth, but would participate only if Parliament should so decide when the occasion arose. Since the South African Government, under the Smuts-Churchill Agreement of 1922, had assumed responsibility for the land defenses of the British naval base at Simonstown, there was a question as to the compatibility of the Coalition's attitude on neutrality with this Agreement. Asserting that Union neutrality was possible despite the Agreement, General Hertzog in 1935 compared Simonstown with Gibraltar. Later he took the rather questionable position that South African neutrality would not be contravened by granting military assistance to a belligerent in accord with a previous agreement.

As European political tension increased in the summer of 1938, the issue of neutrality came to the fore in South Africa. Prime Minister Hertzog steadfastly refused to make any public commitments regarding the Union's attitude in a hypothetical European struggle, but from subsequent disclosures by Generals Hertzog and Smuts, it now appears that the inner Cabinet favored neutrality during the Czech crisis which culminated in the Munich Agreement. European political developments after Munich failed to deflect Prime Minister Hertzog and several of his colleagues from their neutral policy. But with the Nazi attack on Poland a public decision could no longer be avoided.[3]

Prime Minister Hertzog announced his stand for neutrality at a Cabinet meeting called only on September 3, after Parliament had been summoned in special session. General Smuts and other Cabinet members who advocated Imperial cooperation tried vainly to persuade General Hertzog at least to bring the issue before the caucus of the United Party. On September 4 the Prime Minister introduced into the House of Assembly a motion favoring neutrality, without impairment of Union obligations resulting from the Simonstown Agreement, membership in the League of Nations, and free association in the British Commonwealth. At the close of the debate, in which the two leaders of the Cabinet eloquently set forth their conflicting views, General Smuts and his supporters brought about the defeat of the motion by a margin of 13 votes.[4] By the same majority, the House adopted the

---

[3] On August 25, 1938, General Smuts had stated in the House that if England were attacked, he could not imagine South Africa's withdrawal from the friendly bonds uniting the two countries, but that the Union Parliament would decide whether South Africa would go to war.

[4] It may be recalled that when on September 9, 1914, the Botha Government introduced into the House of Assembly an address assuring His Majesty of the Union's cooperation in maintain-

Smuts amendment, calling for the severance of relations with Germany and continued cooperation with the British Commonwealth.[5]

South Africa's subsequent entry into the war was achieved at the cost of a change of political leadership and a rupture of the United Party. General Hertzog, supported by Dr. Malan, leader of the Nationalist Opposition, recommended a dissolution of Parliament and upon the Governor-General's rejection of his advice resigned the premiership with an appeal to his followers to confine their activities within constitutional limits. The question of the constitutionality of Sir Patrick Duncan's action in refusing a dissolution to General Hertzog has become something of a political issue in South Africa. Although General Hertzog at first admitted that the Governor-General had acted constitutionally, several months later he joined with Dr. Malan in criticizing General Smuts for having accepted office without a mandate from the people. Constitutionality aside, it appears from the political viewpoint that dissolution would probably have increased factional bitterness and would have placed the Union in the uncertain position of remaining neutral during an election campaign in which the German Minister and his friends would undoubtedly have aided the Nationalist cause.

The new Government, formed by General Smuts on September 6, included both English and Afrikaans-speaking leaders of the United Party who were loyal to Smuts and also the heads of the Dominion and Labor Parties. Its first act was to advise the Governor-General to issue a proclamation of a state of war with Germany.[6]

In the months after the opening of the war, there occurred a disintegration of the United Party Fusion, which left General Smuts in control of the party machinery, and subsequently, a realignment of opposition groups. Protracted negotiations between the more extreme Nationalists under Dr. Malan and the Hertzogites finally culminated at the end of January 1940 in the formation of the Reunited Nationalist or People's Party (commonly known as the " or " Party), a title which reflected the unwillingness of the two factions to merge their identity.

---

ing the integrity of the Empire, General Hertzog, then leader of a Nationalist minority group, proposed an amendment to the effect that while the House favored measures to defend Union territory, " any act in the nature of an attack on German territory in South Africa would be in conflict with the interests of the Union and of the Empire." The House voted favorably upon the address, rejecting General Hertzog's amendment by a vote of 92 to 12. Hertzog accepted the position of the majority in that he refrained from supporting the subsequent Nationalist rebellion.

[5] See Chapter II, p. 25, notes 17 and 18.

[6] See Chapter II, p. 23.

One obstacle to agreement was the Malanite Nationalists' demand that republicanism be made a tenet of the new party, which while acceptable to some Hertzogites, including Mr. Pirow, aroused opposition from the moderates, among whom were General Hertzog himself and his chief deputy, Mr. Havenga. In taking the position that " a republican form of government separated from the British Crown is best suited to the traditions and aspirations of the South African people," the " or " Party apparently accepted the Nationalist view. As a sop to the moderates, it was conceded that a republic should be achieved not merely by a parliamentary majority, but by a special mandate from the voters.

This reluctant union proved to be short-lived. The issue of republicanism was brought into the open by Dr. N. J. van der Merwe who, shortly before his death in the summer of 1940, organized a mass meeting at Bloemfontein " to consider active constitutional steps to establish a republic." General Hertzog thereupon issued a statement in which he expressed the strongest possible disapproval of the meeting. The former Premier characterized the republican movement as extremely unwise under the existing circumstances and warned the public against irresponsibility. Internal discord within the Opposition was further intensified by the personal antagonism between General Hertzog and Mr. C. R. Swart, successor of Dr. van der Merwe as Nationalist leader in the Orange Free State, which had long been General Hertzog's political stronghold.

Rupture of the " or " Party occurred in November 1940, when the party congress of the Free State adopted principles which would give the English section only language and cultural rights in the future republic. This was interpreted by General Hertzog as a manifestation of lack of confidence in his leadership, and he thereupon resigned from the leadership of the party, subsequently advising his own supporters not to vote for Mr. Swart's candidacy in a forthcoming local election. These events were followed by the announcement in December that General Hertzog and Mr. Havenga, who had followed him out of the Reunited Nationalist Party, were resigning from Parliament with the intention of retiring to private life.[7] In January 1941, however, the Afrikaner Party came into existence with ten Hertzogite members of the House and four Senators as its nucleus. This organization subscribes

---

[7] Mr. Swart defeated his opponent of the United Party in the Winberg by-election in January 1941. Nationalist candidates were elected over opponents of the Afrikaner Party to the seats vacated by General Hertzog and Mr. Havenga.

to the principle of equality between Afrikaner and English elements and to General Hertzog's anti-war policy as well. General Hertzog accepted the position of honorary chief of the new party, which is not as yet an important political element in the country.[7a]

General Hertzog's retirement and the withdrawal of the moderate Hertzogites from the " or " Party did not result in unanimity among the left-wing Nationalists. Dr. Malan's leadership seemed to be facing keen competition both from Mr. Pirow and from the Ossewa Brandwag (Oxwagon Fire Watch). Mr. Pirow's brand of republicanism was advertised as " South African Christian National Socialist " in character. While declaring himself against dictatorship in South Africa, the former Minister for Defense has said that the present constitution must go and that the franchise should be restricted to persons with " a certain degree of Afrikaner sentiment." [8]

Probably more significant politically than Mr. Pirow's " new order " is the Ossewa Brandwag, which originated in 1938 ostensibly as a non-political, cultural association of Afrikaners dedicated to Voortrekker ideals. Since October 1940, when it entered into an agreement with the Reunited Nationalist Party, the Ossewa Brandwag has assumed an increasingly important role in South African politics.[9] According to compact, the two organizations were to cooperate but to refrain from interference in each other's affairs. As the Ossewa Brandwag has a secret military organization on Nazi lines, its professed republicanism is obviously not democratic in character. Its Commandant-General, Dr. J. F. J. van Rensburg, who assumed leadership in January, 1941 (after resigning the post of Administrator of the Free State), is known to be an admirer of Nazism.

It is apparent that for some time prior to the opening of the present war, the Nazis were developing a " fifth column " in South Africa and its mandated territory.[10] Nazi propaganda was spread by broadcasting from Zeesen, by diplomatic and trade agents, as well as by the activities of German colonists who, at the close of World War I, remained in

---

[7a] Mr. Havenga was unanimously elected to succeed General Hertzog as head of the party after the latter's death in November 1942.

[8] Early in 1942 Dr. Malan issued a draft constitution based on racial ascendancy and restricting the franchise to those who might be " expected to assist in building up the nation." (Ed.)

[9] In February 1941 Dr. Malan asserted that the Ossewa Brandwag numbered between 300,000 and 400,000 members. Opponents of the organization claim these figures include women and children.

[10] General Smuts has revealed that in the spring of 1939 a contemplated *Putsch* by Nazi agents and South African Black Shirts in Southwest Africa was thwarted by official precautions.

Southwest Africa. Shortly after the beginning of hostilities, the South African authorities interned over a thousand Nazi agents and Nazi sympathizers. At the end of June 1940, it was reported that in the past few weeks more than 3,000 persons, including all Germans not previously arrested, as well as 200 Italians, had been interned in South Africa and Southwest Africa. Among Union nationals taken into custody were a number of men who had been holding responsible positions in the government service and in business.

Convinced that the Ossewa Brandwag's activities were subversive in character, the Smuts Government in November 1940 forbade the police to be members of the society.[11] After serious riots occurred in Johannesburg between Union soldiers and Brandwagian sympathizers, the Government, in February 1941, further prohibited all public servants from joining the Ossewa Brandwag. In February 1941 a more stringent National Security Code was issued.

In view of the lack of unanimity for South African participation in the war, it is of interest to review the trend of public opinion towards the Smuts Government and its war policy. With regard to the attitude of the general public at the outbreak of the war, it has been estimated by Colonel Reitz (who, as Minister of Native Affairs, may be considered as an *ex parte* authority) that 50 percent of the Afrikaans-speaking population favored participation in the war. Since the Afrikaans element constitutes roughly 60 percent of the European population and the British 40 percent, Colonel Reitz's statement would imply that 70 percent of the people favored entering the war. This proportion may be contrasted with the vote of 80 to 67 by which the Smuts amendment for belligerency was carried in the House.

General Hertzog brought about a trial of the Government's strength when Parliament met in January 1940 by a motion to restore peaceful relations with Germany. This was defeated by an increased Government majority of twenty-two votes, which was due in part to Nationalist abstentions. In August 1940, although he had thrown cold water on the Nationalist outburst of republicanism in July, General Hertzog introduced a second motion favoring immediate peace negotiations with Germany and Italy,[12] and this was rejected by a majority of eighteen

---

[11] The Minister of Justice informed the House of Assembly on January 26, 1942, that over 300 Johannesburg policemen had been arrested as members of the organization. An outbreak of sabotage in Johannesburg and elsewhere early in 1942 was ascribed mainly to enemy agents working from Portuguese East Africa. (Ed.)

[12] War with Italy was brought about by a proclamation of the Governor-General issued

votes. The Prime Minister had received shortly before from United Party supporters a "Peace Through Victory" petition bearing over 600,000 signatures. A Nationalist motion to secede from the British Empire in January 1942 was rejected by a majority of forty-two votes in the House of Assembly, and by twenty votes to five in the Senate.

It is unsafe to prophesy how soon the broken ranks of the Opposition will coalesce. The Nationalist Party in August 1941 condemned both the "new order" of Mr. Pirow and the Ossewa Brandwag. General Hertzog's sensational statement in October 1941 that Nazism was in keeping with Afrikaner tradition was immediately repudiated by Mr. Havenga, the leader of the Afrikaner Party. It seems likely that the several Nationalist and Hertzogite elements will ultimately have to choose between the United Party of General Smuts and the authoritarianism of the Ossewa Brandwag.

It is not too much to say that the political future of South Africa depends on Britain's military success. If British resistance seems to weaken, it is likely that defeatists of the Opposition will press the issues of republicanism and secession, as well as peace. With regard to the legal aspect of secession, Keith in 1934 expressed the opinion that in strict law there seemed to be no obstacle to passage of a Union act of secession.[13] From the external viewpoint, it is fairly safe to predict that in case of a German victory, the Union would have been the first dominion (if exception is made for Eire) over which Hitler attempted to extend his sway. The principal gold-producing country in the world, with its mandated territory of Southwest Africa, a strategic gateway to the Indian Ocean — South Africa would have been a major prize for the Nazis. And the Fuehrer would have found a welcome in the Union from that minority of whom General Smuts has said, "They dream of a republic and would welcome it even from the hands of a Hitler."[14] On the other hand, if England is victorious, General Smuts's war policy will undoubtedly appear as justified in the eyes of many South Africans who have favored neutrality.[15]

June 12, and dating belligerency from June 11. The Opposition condemned this declaration of war without parliamentary sanction in their peace campaign during the summer of 1940. (Ed.)

[13] A. B. Keith, "Notes on Imperial Constitutional Law," *Journal of Comparative Legislation & International Law*, Vol. XVI, November 1934, p. 291.

[14] Speech on Empire Day, May 24, 1940.

[15] In 1942 and 1943 the German attack on Soviet Russia, the belligerency of the United States, and United Nations successes helped to consolidate public opinion in South Africa behind the war effort, though a considerable section of the Afrikaans-speaking population held aloof. (H. D. H.)

2. *The Union's War Effort in Its Military Aspects*

Turning from party politics to the Union's war effort, we find that for at least two cogent reasons the Smuts Government adopted a policy of limited participation, which, in contrast to the Union's policy of 1914, excluded military action in the European theatre of the war.[16] In the first place, the Government's pledge not to send troops overseas undoubtedly made the status of belligerency acceptable to many South Africans who would otherwise have favored neutrality. Furthermore, as a result of Mr. Pirow's inactivity as Minister of Defense in the Fusion Cabinet, Prime Minister Smuts, who also holds the Defense portfolio, found the Union in a state of military unpreparedness in September 1939. After the Smuts Cabinet took office, the defense forces had to be equipped not only to assume responsibility for the land and air defense of the Union, but also to cooperate with British troops on the East African and Egyptian fronts.

Although disavowing any idea of a Monroe Doctrine for Africa, the new Prime Minister immediately pledged assistance to British colonies in southern Africa — " northern outposts of the Union " — and further stated that Mozambique should be able to rely on South African aid. Since there was opposition, particularly among the Nationalists, to the idea of ordering troops to serve outside the Union, General Smuts in November 1939 stated that only volunteers would be sent beyond the frontiers to protect African colonies. At the end of March 1940, however, in accordance with an invitation issued by the Government a voluntary oath was taken by nearly the whole of the defense forces to serve " anywhere in Africa." Many of the members of the forces in taking the oath crossed out the words " in Africa," leaving only the word " anywhere." A few weeks later it was officially announced that no new volunteers would be accepted for the defense forces unless they were prepared to give a similar pledge. In May the few members of the defense forces who had refused to sign the new oath, binding them to serve outside the Union, were given permission to terminate their service with the forces. Some 40 percent of the forces raised in South Africa by voluntary recruitment have been of Afrikaner stock.

South Africa's war effort may be better understood if the framework

---

[16] This was based upon a resolution of Parliament under which troops would not be sent " overseas," which was interpreted to mean outside the African continent. General Smuts assured Parliament on March 26, 1941, that troops would not be sent farther without Parliament's consent. In February 1943 Parliament agreed to overseas service for South African forces. (Ed.)

of her defense organization is recalled. Defense legislation (Union acts of 1912 and 1922) provides for compulsory registration of all youths between the ages of 17 and 25, who are liable for peacetime training over a period of four years. A minimum of 50 percent of those liable are required by law to take this training with the defense forces, while the remaining number must enroll as members of Defense Rifle Associations for four years' training. Lack of training facilities and a shortage of modern equipment meant that the total number of registrants in any year were never called up for training. A five-year plan for building up the South African land and air forces was inaugurated in 1934, and in 1936 another five-year plan, calling for larger forces and more modern equipment, was superimposed upon it. Rearmament was not taken very seriously until the Munich crisis aroused Parliament to authorize larger defense expenditures.

At the outbreak of the war, when Mr. Pirow followed General Hertzog into opposition, and the Defense portfolio was assumed by Prime Minister Smuts, it became apparent that the defense plans in most respects had not advanced beyond the paper stage. According to statements by General Smuts, the Active Citizen Force in training at the opening of the war totalled 18,700 men, one-third the number reported by Mr. Pirow. Reserves and rifle associations were unorganized and modern equipment for all services was woefully lacking. The Air Force was in possession of only a very few modern training planes, and the planes turned over to the Air Force in September 1939 by South African Airways were mostly German Junkers. For the defense expansion program £3,000,000 had been provided by the 1939–40 budget in addition to the defense vote. When Mr. Pirow left office not more than £290,000 had been spent on the expansion program.

A War Measures Act passed early in 1940 validated a number of emergency actions taken by the Smuts Government at the outbreak of the war. Strong objections in Parliament prevented the inclusion of a proposed omnibus clause giving the Government practically unlimited power in the war sphere. Several months later, when the legality of General Smuts's order commandeering rifles of private individuals was contested, the Government found itself hampered by lack of power which the omnibus clause would have conferred, and the War Measures Act had to be amended to include such a clause with retroactive effect. Owing to the neglect in recent years of the machinery of the Defense Act, the Defense Department relied upon volunteers until

May 24, 1940, when a system of selection was instituted. By November 1941 the total strength of the armed forces of the Union was 163,400 men of all ranks. This does not include 10,000 in women's auxiliary defense corps nor 57,000 non-Europeans in the labor and pioneer corps.[17]

The strength of the S.A.A.F. stood at about 22,000 in August 1941 and was expected by General Smuts to reach in time 50,000. Although it decided not to participate in the British Commonwealth Air Training Plan in Canada, the Union Government offered to train air personnel from Great Britain and British African colonies. Owing to the fall of France, the British Air Ministry was forced to delay acceptance of this proposal, but by October 1940 British airmen were in training in the Union.

As for coastal and naval defense, the Smuts Government is honoring South Africa's obligations under the Smuts-Churchill Agreement of 1922 to provide for the land defense of the Simonstown naval base. Coastal defenses are considered adequate except in case of attack by a battle fleet. A South African Seaward Defense Force for mine sweeping and patrol service has been organized. Early in 1941, when German reinforcements greatly strengthened the position of the Axis in North Africa, it was announced that units of the South African Seaward Defense Force were cooperating with the Royal Navy in the Mediterranean off the northern shores of Africa and in the Red Sea. As in the past, however, the burden of Union naval defense rests upon the Africa station of the British Navy.

3. The Economic Structure and the War Effort

From the economic viewpoint the period from 1933 to 1939 was one of recovery for South Africa, and so far as the gold mining industry was concerned, an era of growing prosperity. Gold mining has long occupied a predominant position in the South African economy. The main attraction for foreign capital,[18] it accounts ordinarily for about 70 percent of the Union exports and provides employment for about one-half of the total working population occupied in mining and manufacturing. The industry, it is estimated, contributes £140,000,000 in

---

[17] Editor.

[18] S. H. Frankel, *Capital Investment in Africa*, 1938, pp. 102–105. Of the £200,000,000 new capital invested in the Rand mines between 1887 and 1932, roughly £120,000,000 came from overseas. By comparison £20,000,000 of overseas capital was invested in the diamond industry during those years.

earning and spending power in a year, equaling 33 to 40 percent of the national income.[19] In addition, heavy taxation of the gold mining industry is the backbone of the Union's economic policy for fostering other industries, and especially agriculture.

Gold mining held its own during the depression, and, in fact, improved its position when the gold standard was abandoned. The industry then experienced the greatest boom in its history; more capital was invested in new mines between 1932 and 1936 [20] than in any other four-year period. The rise in the price of gold, with unit working costs remaining relatively unchanged, made it profitable to crush low-grade ores and the Government encouraged this by increasing the rate of surtax with the increase in profit per ton of ore crushed.

The annual volume of gold production on the Rand increased by 21.5 percent between 1932 and 1940, when the output totalled more than 14,000,000 fine ounces valued at £117,900,000, a figure more than double that of 1932, due to the steady rise in the sterling price per ounce. The Government income from gold mining taxation rose from £4,265,000 in the fiscal year 1932–33 to approximately £26,500,000 in 1940–41, accounting for about one-sixth of the total revenue in the former period and two-fifths in the latter.

Wartime conditions brought an added tax burden to the gold mining industry in the form of a levy on profits derived from the rise in the price of gold. It was immediately announced on August 30, 1939, that the Union Government would appropriate all proceeds arising from the sale of gold in excess of 150s. per ounce. The London price of gold was within a short time fixed by the British Government at 168s. per ounce. In preparing its budget for 1940–41, the Government yielded to protests of the mining industry, thus relieving producers of low-grade ore, and substituted for the levy a special war contribution from the mines of 9 percent of their taxable income. This contribution was raised to 11 percent later in the fiscal year and to 16 percent for the year 1941–42.

Among the problems which have confronted the gold mining industry has been the shortage of native labor. The industry, presently employing more than 300,000 native workers, has found difficulty in recruiting adequate native labor within the Union, and has been regu-

---

[19] Professor Reedman estimates the national income at present as between £360,000,000 and £420,000,000. Quoted in *Commercial Opinion*, March 1941, p. 294.

[20] Frankel, *op. cit.*, p. 98.

larly compelled to secure natives from other African territories. Employment of natives increased during the last decade from 203,473 on December 1930 to 346,726 on December 31, 1940. While it was possible to increase the number of Union and adjoining protectorate natives employed from 131,000 to 244,000 during that period, east coast natives and natives from tropical areas had to be secured in ever larger numbers. It is here that the largest reservoir of native labor may be found in the future.[21]

In comparison with gold, diamond mining has been a declining industry for many years, and though the 1938 production of 1,200,000 carats showed an increase in volume of 181.3 percent above the low point of 1934, it was still only about a third of the production of 1929. A new stimulus has been given by the war demand for industrial diamonds, but they account normally only for about one-fifth of the value of diamond sales. The general outlook for the industry was considerably darkened when, through the invasion of the Low Countries, cutting and polishing transactions were practically stopped.

Agriculture, which was severely depressed in the period immediately preceding departure from the gold standard, experienced only a measure of recovery. Largely because of unfavorable natural conditions, South African agriculture suffers from excess costs to the extent that in the years preceding the outbreak of the present war there was no important agricultural commodity except wool which was not dependent on the maintenance of an artificial internal price structure or some form of protection.[22] A White Paper issued on March 15, 1939, stated that in the preceding eight years Government expenditure for agricultural subsidies amounted to approximately £20,000,000, of which about one-eighth would be repaid. Half the total had been expended on export subsidies and one-fifth on interest subsidies.

At the beginning of the war, marketing schemes [23] were in force for maize, wheat, dried fruit, and tobacco in addition to dairy products and livestock and meat, while several new schemes were under consideration. Export bounties have been granted to individual products, as for example, dark tobacco, butter, and maize. Maize is produced mainly

---

[21] There were over 22,000 natives from those areas employed at the end of 1940. An agreement of 1940 with the Portuguese Government increased the number of Mozambique natives contracted for 12 or maximal 18 months' employment in Union mines from 80,000 to 100,000.

[22] Wool production in 1938–39 was still one-fifth below the production of 1932–33.

[23] Under the Marketing Act of 1937 (Amended 1938) which established general conditions for the operation of control boards.

for domestic consumption. The export of its surplus is made possible by a levy on the internal price. Wheat production has been stimulated by a subsidization scheme which guarantees the producer a fixed price well above the world market level, while at the same time imports have been restricted by a licensing system. But in normal years the production still falls short of domestic requirements.[24] The war stimulated exports of cane sugar,[25] which reached a high of 340,000 tons and an increase in value of around £1,000,000 in 1940.

Prior to the present war, the outlook of secondary industries in the Union for future expansion appeared restricted on several grounds, among which the question of an adequate labor supply has been of main importance. The characteristic feature of the South African labor markets is the wide spread in the wages of the skilled or European group, the semiskilled group composed of poor whites and Asiatics, and the unskilled or native group. The wages of the second group vary from 30 to 75 percent and of the third group from 15 to 30 percent of the skilled rate. Though the unemployed European farmers come to the cities to seek employment, they cannot maintain anything like a European standard of living at the low rates paid for unskilled labor. On the other hand, there is not sufficient cheap native labor available to form the necessary base of the labor force. Furthermore, development of an extensive local market has been restricted by the lack of purchasing power of the unskilled poor whites and natives; while due to excessive costs and the remoteness of potential markets, the prospects for promoting the export of South African manufactured goods in peacetime were slight.

The war, however, has changed the whole outlook considerably, although the question of a sufficient labor supply remains precarious and the shortage of skilled labor has been keenly felt in an industrially undeveloped country, suddenly faced with a tremendous expansion. A special Controller of Industrial Man Power was appointed in February 1941. The cost problem is of lesser importance for defense production and for the production of goods no longer obtainable through imports. New enterprises have opened up in many manufactures, quite a number of which will be established on a permanent basis. By the establishment of the Industrial Development Corporation which began to

[24] Since the outbreak of the war, export of wheat and wheat products, which was of some importance in only one year, 1937, has been prohibited except under permit.
[25] The Agreement limits output to 476,488 tons per annum, while the Union's annual export quota under the International Sugar Agreement of 1937 was set at 230,000 tons.

function in October 1940 with a capital of £5,000,000, the Government has created an instrument for the advancement of loans to heavy industries.

The Union has been in the rather fortunate position of amassing budget surpluses, even though in peacetime the population enjoyed a relatively small income tax (2s. in the pound maximum) and a rebate of 30 percent on the income tax. That the individual taxpayer's burden

TABLE I

UNION REVENUES AND EXPENDITURES *

Fiscal Year (Ending March 31)	REVENUES			EXPENDITURES				
	Total	† From Gold Mining in '000 £	In percent of total revenues	Total	Land and Agriculture in '000 £	Assistance to Farmers	Total Agriculture	In percent of total expenditures
1933	28,442	2,338	8.2	22,714	1,302	2,759	4,061	17.9
1934	37,625	10,648	28.3	27,282	1,603	3,731	5,334	19.5
1935	38,730	9,205	23.8	29,551	2,951	2,969	5,920	20.0
1936	39,676	10,594	26.7	30,136	2,082	3,036	5,118	17.0
1937	43,087	13,921	32.3	30,796	2,162	2,348	4,510	14.6
1938	43,611	9,456	21.7	32,629	2,294	1,610	3,904	12.0
1939	44,076	9,204	20.9	35,095	2,752	1,506	4,258	12.1

* *Official Yearbook of the Union of South Africa.*
† From income tax, state ownership credited to income tax (1933–37), excess profits duty (1934–36), gold profits surtax (1936–37). The larger part of the income from state ownership is credited to the loan account.

was comparatively light was mainly due to heavy reliance on the gold mines as a large contributor to the revenue of the state. This financial consideration has been responsible for the reluctance of the Smuts Government to reduce gold mining in favor of strategic minerals. By keeping the tax load of the individual income taxpayer relatively low and by paying large sums as assistance to the struggling farmers, the Government distributed the wealth accruing to the mines over the whole of the population.[26]

With regard to public debt, the significant development since 1933 has been the constant trend toward substituting internal debt for external debt. While in 1933 61 percent of the total gross debt was external, the relationship was more than reversed in 1940, when 64 percent of the

[26] See Table I.

total indebtedness was internal.[27] The successful internal flotation of two Union defense loans in October and November 1940 illustrates the Union's growing economic independence.

TABLE II
UNION OF SOUTH AFRICA PUBLIC DEBT
In '000 £ *

31st of March	GROSS DEBT					SINKING FUND	NET DEBT
	Total	External Debt	In per- cent of of Total Gross Debt	Internal Debt	In per- cent of Total Gross Debt		
1933	272,134	165,656	60.87	106,478	39.13	21,789	250,345
1934	274,311	165,037	60.17	109,274	39.83	23,277	251,034
1935	274,115	156,676	57.16	117,439	42.84	24,064	250,052
1936	251,087	122,654	48.85	128,433	51.15	4,680	246,407
1937	254,937	103,973	40.78	150,964	59.22	5,710	249,227
1938	262,618	101,123	38.51	161,495	61.49	6,780	255,838
1939	278,876	101,123	36.26	177,753	63.74	7,885	270,991
1940	291,449	106,103	36.41	185,346	63.59	6,426	285,023
1941	335,997	98,142	29.21	237,856	70.79	7,638	328,359

* *Official Yearbook of the Union of South Africa.*

Foreign trade plays the most prominent role in South African economic life; the Union maintained a favorable trade balance even in the black year of 1932. At present South Africa's exports of manganese, chromite, coal, iron ore, asbestos, and other essential materials are of great strategic value both to Great Britain and to the United States.

South Africa has sent by far the greater part of her exports to the United Kingdom and imports far more from her than from any other country. During recent years Britain supplied over 40 percent of the Union's imports and received about 80 percent of the Union's exports including specie.[28] The Ottawa Agreement of 1932 failed to increase the latter very high percentage.[29] South Africans in general have not been enthusiastic about intra-Commonwealth preferences. It has been charged that the Agreements have led to sharp competition between Empire

---

[27] See Table II.
[28] See Table III.
[29] In 1936 about 50 percent of Union nongold exports to the United Kingdom were on a preferential footing. In 1937–38 the preference given by the United Kingdom on Union merchandise was valued at £ 2,374,000. This preference, calculated in relation to the *total* of South African merchandise exports to the United Kingdom, amounts to about 16 percent.

TABLE III

VALUE OF SOUTH AFRICAN EXPORTS *
(including ship stores and specie)

Year	Total	Percentage of total exports going to			
	(£'000)	U.K.	Other Br. Countries	Germany	U.S.A.
1932	68,938	81.42	5.59	2.12	.49
1933	95,275	82.10	4.67	2.15	.80
1934	82,074	80.16	5.98	2.46	.70
1935	102,293	81.42	5.07	3.71	.63
1936	113,770	82.75	4.23	2.06	.93
1937	125,380	78.26	5.60	3.97	1.07
1938	105,885	79.52	5.94	4.67	.71

VALUE OF SOUTH AFRICAN IMPORTS *
(including Government stores, excl. specie)

Year	Total	Percentage of total imported from			
	(£'000)	U.K.	Other Br. Countries	Germany	U.S.A.
1932	32,673	46.27	11.17	7.62	12.99
1933	49,121	50.32	9.6	6.60	12.28
1934	66,259	48.75	9.87	5.04	16.33
1935	75,301	48.64	9.69	5.17	16.93
1936	86,282	46.30	9.40	5.71	18.72
1937	103,368	42.56	9.36	6.56	19.57
1938	95,859	43.25	10.08	8.00	17.41

* *Official Yearbook of the Union of South Africa.*

producers in the United Kingdom market and to a lesser degree in Canada. A larger proportion of total Union imports has been brought within the scope of tariff preferences.[30] Trade between the Union and the rest of the Commonwealth has been comparatively small. The possibilities of colonial markets for South African exports have as yet hardly been explored.

Germany was South Africa's second best customer from December 1934 (when the first clearing agreement between the Union and Germany was signed) through 1939, except in 1936 when France occupied

---

[30] In 1936 39 percent of British and 15 percent of colonial imports into the Union enjoyed preferential margins compared with 34 and 9 percent in 1932. British and colonial suppliers increased their share in the preferential sector of the Union market from 53 to 59 percent and from 7 to 40 percent respectively, but the British share in the nonpreferential category declined from 44 to 40 percent between 1932 and 1936. Van Biljon, *State Interference in South Africa,* 1938, pp. 202, 203. In 1938 the preference given by the Union to the United Kingdom was valued at £1,377,677. This preference, calculated in relation to *total* British exports to the Union works out at about 4 percent.

that position. Following Great Britain and the United States, Germany has ranked third as a source of South African imports since 1932 and maintained that position in 1939, even though trade relations were severed in September. Under successive clearing agreements the debits and credits were made to balance at the ratio of 1:1, but at the outbreak of the war there was a substantial balance in favor of the Union. As regards trade with the United States, South Africa has had a large adverse balance. Since the opening of the war, however, increased American purchases of South African wool, manganese, and chrome ore have improved the Union's position. The United States held third place as a buyer of Union produce before the war and second place as a source of Union imports.

The war has made governmental regulation of foreign trade necessary. The Government immediately assumed control of the purchase, sale, and holdings of foreign currency, foreign securities, and gold, and at the end of June 1940, of the foreign exchange proceeds of all exports. Provision for the prohibition of imports and exports of any specified goods were part of the National Emergency Regulations of September 14, 1939.[31] The entire economy of the Union is dependent upon the exchange of the Union's production for manufactured products used in domestic consumption and raw materials and semi-manufactured goods essential to the Union's own industry. Every effort has been made to maintain her foreign trade. Loss of Germany as a buyer and a supplier was a serious disruption. Other difficulties were the lack of shipping space and the increasing freight and insurance rates.

Wool formed by far the largest share of exports to Germany, which had taken more than a third of all wool exports. This loss was for the most part compensated for by large sales to the United States and Japan, which could no longer obtain Australian wool. To protect the wool market, the United Kingdom in October 1939 agreed to purchase an undisclosed quantity at the same basic price guaranteed to Australia of

---

31 A system of permits for the control of imports and exports was brought into operation on September 11, 1941. Permits had to be obtained for all imports, with a few minor exceptions, from countries outside the Commonwealth. The issue of the permit was dependent on the importance of the imports from the point of view of the prosecution of the war. Private purchases of certain classes of commodities from the United States would no longer be possible under this arrangement, but arrangements were being made whereby the Government itself in conjunction with other countries in the Commonwealth could obtain supplies of such commodities for essential purposes under the Lend Lease Act. A system of permits was also to be introduced for the export of goods to destinations outside the British Commonwealth, and in the case of a number of specific commodities within the Commonwealth itself. (Ed.)

10.75d. per pound, which was 30 percent above the average price realized for the Union clip of the previous season. For the season 1940–41 an agreement with the United Kingdom was announced in August 1940 according to which for the duration of the war and one year afterward, Britain will buy and market the entire clip, as she did the Australian clip of the preceding season. The price guarantee remains the same as in the first agreement. As wool exports in 1940 were valued at £2,219,000, the farming population of the Union is thus assured of a considerable money income.[32]

All gold exports are purchased by the Bank of England, which also bears the insurance cost. This arrangement gives the Union treasury an additional revenue of roughly £2,000,000 a year. The war may have a stimulating effect upon Union coal trade. There is a possibility of developing new markets in South American countries which find it difficult to buy coal in Europe. Shipments have already been made to the Argentine. Furthermore, the diversion of shipping from the Suez Canal to the route around the Cape has increased sales of bunker coal.

Serious difficulties have arisen for the deciduous fruit export. Britain licensed imports during the first war months, and lack of refrigerated shipping space has forced a ban on almost all imports of fruit to Great Britain. An experimental shipment to the United States proved unsuccessful, as the price realized did not cover the expenses. The Union Government has granted a special subsidy to the deciduous fruit growers and is attempting to assist the farmers by encouraging a canning industry.

The Union's rich resources in gold, diamonds, copper, manganese, chrome, and tin are of high wartime value. So is her surplus wool and foodstuff production. Her rich deposits of iron are not sufficiently developed to satisfy more than her own needs. The steel ingot capacity of the government-controlled South African Iron and Steel Corporation (ISCOR), and three smaller companies, accounted in the summer 1940 for 42 percent of the domestic requirements. Efforts are being made to increase the steel production. A new branch plant of ISCOR and expansion of the existing works will bring the total production to two-thirds of the domestic consumption.

Production of ammunition began in 1936, when a government ammunition factory was opened. Educational orders for armament equip-

---

[32] The entire sugar export and three-quarters of the 1940 citrus crop were also taken by Britain.

ment were advocated by the Chief of Staff in 1937, but apparently not much was done in that direction. General Smuts stated that in September 1939 there was not sufficient artillery ammunition for one day's fighting. In November 1939 a War Supplies Directorate was formed with the function of organizing the procurement and manufacture of war materials. Wide powers were conferred on the Director-General of this body for the purchase and production of goods and the establishment of factories.

The South African boot industry has been able to meet the Union's needs and to fill large orders for the British Army. But the clothing industry was unable, in April 1940, to supply the army with 250,000 uniforms, and orders for cloth had to be placed in the United States and India, the uniforms to be made up, however, in Union factories.

It is evident that the Union's industrial rearmament got a rather late start. But it must be remembered that other parts of the defense program fared no better. For each of the fiscal years 1937–38, 1938–39, and 1939–40, the regular defense vote was only £1,800,000. At the time of the Munich crisis an additional £6,000,000 was appropriated, to be expended over a period of three years. £1,000,000 was appropriated from the loan account in 1938–39, the first authorization for defense expenditure from loan funds during the period of rearmament. The budget of 1939–40 provided, in addition to the defense vote, £3,000,000 for the defense expansion program.

The total defense expenditure in 1939–40 amounted to £5,600,000 while the February budget for 1940–41 contained a total defense appropriation of £14,000,000. To meet the increased expenditure, heavier taxes were introduced. As a special war contribution, the gold mining industry was to pay on its taxable income an additional 9 percent from which £3,500,000 was expected. The diamond mines were to contribute £30,000. Furthermore, withdrawal of the 30 percent rebate on the income tax accounted for £1,800,000 revenue. An excess profit tax of 10s. in the pound on profits (except in gold and in diamond mining) in excess of the average of the three years prior to the war was expected to bring in £8,000,000.

Italy's entrance into the war necessitated far larger defense expenditure by the Union than had been provided in the main budget for 1940–41. A first supplementary budget, presented at the special session of Parliament in August 1940, called for an additional defense expenditure of £32,000,000, of which £4,800,000 was to be obtained from increased revenue, £23,600,000 from loan account, while the remainder was taken care of by saving on other votes and higher than estimated revenue under the main budget. To provide the needed revenue, the war contribution of the gold mining companies was raised from 9 to 11 percent while the normal income tax which had been 1s. in the pound and the supertax operating on incomes exceeding £2,500 a year were increased by 20 percent. Postal charges were advanced and heavier taxes placed on gasoline, tires, cigarettes, and liquor. The Government intended borrowing from the public £18,000,000. When the lists were closed ahead of the anticipated time, this amount was oversubscribed by £10,000,000.

A second supplementary budget of January 1941 brought the total defense expenditure for the fiscal year to £60,000,000; the additional £14,000,000 was debited to the loan account but could be financed in part by further savings on other votes. In the fiscal year 1941–42 defense expenditures were £72,000,000. Income and excess profit taxes were again raised, as were customs duties and excises, while the special contribution from the gold mines was fixed at 16 percent of their taxable income. This was increased to 20 percent for the year 1942–43, when defense expenditures were estimated at £80,000,000.

Since 1941 the Union has produced small-arms ammunition and TNT for export to Great Britain and the Middle East as well as for her own needs. The defense equipment now being manufactured in South Africa includes certain types of light artillery, shells, bombs, cordite, anti-tank armor-piercing ammunition, infantry mortars and ammunition, steel helmets, steel airplane hangars, armored car bodies made of South African armor plate, and portable bridges. Airplane frames and airplane engines, automobile engines and chassis, and more complicated forms of artillery have to be imported. Under the Eastern Group supply arrangements spare parts for the repair of damaged tanks and planes are transported from South Africa to the Middle East by air. There are also naval and mercantile marine repair bases at Simonstown, Capetown, and Durbam.

The attempt since the outbreak of the war to build up an efficient secondary industry may change the whole economic structure of South Africa. This development is still in its infancy, and it is highly uncertain which industries will be strong enough at the close of the war to fulfill civilian requirements for which goods have hitherto been imported. It seems probable, however, that after the war the Union will no longer be classed with countries primarily producing raw materials for export. The fact which General Smuts recognized in the first year of the war, that the decision to declare war had been " a turning point in the history of South Africa," has become increasingly plain with the progress of events.[33]

---

[33] South Africa's future in Africa and her place in the British Commonwealth and in world affairs are all involved. That South Africa is likely to play a positive role in these events more important than that which a small state might normally expect to play, is indicated by several factors. The first is her strategic position as one of the pivotal points of world sea and air power — not only in this war but in any postwar international security system set up by the United Nations. Powerful British and American forces for the defense of India, the Near East, and Egypt making the passage of the Cape of Good Hope have brought South Africa more closely than ever into contact with Britain and the United States. The second factor is the important part played by South African armed forces in the liberation of Ethiopia and the battles of Libya and Tunisia. This reinforces her claim to a voice in the common affairs of the African continent, in which in recent years she has taken a constantly increasing interest. The third factor is the quality of her leadership — her possession in General Smuts of one of the three or four men who have achieved the stature of world statesmen. His visit to London in the fall of 1942 to sit in and confer with the War Cabinet, his famous speech before the unique joint meeting of both Houses of the British Parliament held in his honor, his pronouncements on the place of the British Commonwealth in world affairs, all pointed to his playing once more, as in 1918–19, a leading role in a new world settlement. The strengthening of his position in his own country was shown when, in February 1943, Parliament carried his motion to free South African forces for service overseas by a majority twice as great as that which brought South Africa into the war in 1939. The lengthening arm of air power from the north, the Japanese threat to Madagascar on the east, the vicious U-boat wolf-packs off Capetown pointed unmistakably to South Africa's entry into the full stream of world politics and to the need of redoubling, to a point beyond the power of her small population, of the guard over the world's richest gold fields and its most important cape. (H. D. H.)

CHAPTER XI

India and the War

Introduction

India's central geographic position, her wealth of natural resources, her expanding industries, and her large reserves of man power go to make up her great strategic importance. " India is the pivotal defence center of the mid-East," said Sir Girja Shankar Bajpai, India's first envoy to the United States, on his arrival in New York.

About two-thirds of the British Commonwealth lies in a huge semicircle around the Indian Ocean, a semicircle which curves from South Africa up through the East African colonies, across the southern coasts of Asia and down to Australia and New Zealand. Midway on the arc of the semicircle lies the subcontinent of India. From around the Cape of Good Hope, from the Red Sea and from the Persian Gulf, up from New Zealand and Australia, ships converge on India's ports, and from her ports they put out again laden with Indian produce and manufactures. India's airports are relatively short flights from Egypt, Iraq, or Darwin.

India is thus the natural collecting and distributing center for all the Allied territories in the Eastern Hemisphere. India is the central base for operations in the Middle or Far East. From India troops and supplies can readily be dispatched around the Mediterranean, to East or South Africa, or through Iraq and Iran.

The ships that put out from India's ports are laden with varied cargos. There are convoys of supply ships for the armed forces. America's defense program calls for manganese ore and mica from India's mines. The black sea sands of Travancore yield the rarer industrial minerals, ilmenite and monazite. Indian kyanite, sillimanite, and magnesite provide furnace linings in many of the world's great industrial plants. India has a virtual monopoly of jute — her most important raw material contribution to the United Nations — of the burlap made from jute, and of lac, and she is the world's major source of hides and skins. Vegetable oils, raw drugs, and timber are among her other products.

Nor does India export only raw materials. Ranked by the International Labor Office as one of the eight leading industrial countries of the world, she manufactures annually thousands of millions of yards of textiles: cotton, jute, and woolens. The Tata Iron and Steel plant at Jamshedpur is the largest in the British Commonwealth. By far India's greatest resource is of course her immense man power. About one-fifth of the peoples of the world live in India. The 1941 census estimates the population at 389,000,000.

There is no political party or group in India which has not publicly proclaimed its abhorrence of Nazi, Fascist, and Japanese aggression, and no group or party has shown the least desire to pin their hopes for the realization of their political aspirations to an Axis victory.[1] The communal rivalries and differences of religion, race, and culture in India at first glance appear to offer an ideal field for the favorite preliminary technique of Nazi propagandists, the exploitation of minority grievances, nor has this possibility been overlooked by the Nazis or the Japanese. In the summer of 1940, however, when a bitter opponent might have seized the chance to administer a *coup de grâce* to Britain, the political deadlock in India came nearer to a settlement than ever before. This does not mean, of course, that all elements in India are democratic in their political conceptions; the Hindu caste system is based on a hierarchical principle which has no close parallel in Western or in Moslem traditions.

India's unique contribution to world politics has been the development of the technique of passive resistance as a political weapon. *Satyagraha,* or nonviolence, first employed by Mr. Gandhi in his struggle for the rights of Indians in South Africa, has long been the official policy of the National Congress Party,[1a] the largest and best organized party in India. At times Mr. Gandhi has restricted the practice of pas-

---

[1] Mahatma Gandhi's statement after his interview with the Viceroy at the outbreak of war in September 1939 — "I told His Excellency that my own sympathies were with England and France from the purely humanitarian standpoint." — is often quoted in this connection.

[1a] Some popular misunderstanding has arisen from the name of the "Indian National Congress," which is not a legislative body but a political party.

sive resistance to specified individuals or even to himself, when he felt that the movement was degenerating or when, as earlier in the present war, he did not wish to embarrass the British Government by a mass civil disobedience program. His own faith in the efficacy of nonviolence, which is based on his experience of a regime guaranteeing personal freedom and equality before the law, has never been shaken. So strong is Mr. Gandhi's hold on the Congress Party that nonviolence has remained its official policy through the third year of the war.

1. India's Relations with Britain and the British Commonwealth

At the outbreak of war, the new constitution provided by the Government of India Act, 1935, had been in effect in British India for almost two and a half years. In eight of the eleven self-governing provinces, ministers of the National Congress Party controlled the administration, and had inaugurated numerous social and economic reforms. More than one Congress premier has testified to the sympathetic and loyal cooperation he received from the Governor of his Province and the members of the Indian Civil Service, although only a few years earlier the Congress Party had been an illegal organization. Negotiations between the Viceroy and the Indian States, comprising about one-fourth of India's population, with a view to bringing into operation the provisions of the constitution for the federation of the provinces of British India and the Indian States were in progress.

Not only were the States reluctant to surrender the powers sought for the central administration, but both the Congress Party and the Moslem League, the second largest party in India, were also opposed to the scheme of federation. Under the federal provisions of the 1935 Act a proportion of seats in the Central Legislature had been reserved for Moslems, Sikhs, and other minorities. The Congress Party strongly objected to these reservations, maintaining that all seats should be open to the election of any candidate whatever his creed. The All-India Moslem League, whose leader is Mr. Jinnah, retorted that the reason for this attitude was obvious: Hindus with a population of approximately 256,000,000 would form the vast majority of the electorate and the Moslems and other minorities would form a permanent minority. While the Moslems also considered their own interests insufficiently safeguarded by the reservation of seats for minorities provided for in the 1935 Act, it would at least have rendered government by coalition essential, and it is arguable that this would have provided the basis for a solution of India's communal problem.

When Britain declared war, the Viceroy, Lord Linlithgow, immediately proclaimed that, " A state of war exists between his Majesty and Germany." India was thus at war. This was constitutionally correct, but nationalist sentiment was deeply offended that the consent of India's political leaders had not first been obtained, and the Legislature not consulted. The majority of the Congress Party leaders adopted a resolution, drafted by Pandit Jawaharlal Nehru, condemning both Nazi aggression and British " imperialism," and making cooperation in the war conditional on a statement of war and peace aims by the British Government and an immediate grant of independence to India. The Moslem League, too, expressed sympathy for Poland, England and France, but asked for " an assurance that no declaration regarding the question of constitutional advance for India should be made without the consent and approval of the All-India Moslem League."

Meanwhile the Viceroy was holding a series of interviews with the leaders of every political party and representatives of every shade of opinion, and as a result he made two offers on behalf of Britain. The first was a promise to reconsider the whole question of the constitution at the end of the war; the second was a proposal to form a consultative committee representing all parties, to cooperate with him in the conduct of the war.[2]

The Viceroy's proposal was rejected by the Congress Party, and as a sign of protest the Working Committee of the Party ordered the eight provincial Congress ministries to resign. In one province, Assam, a coalition government was soon formed; Orissa formed an alternative ministry in November 1941; the administration of the other provinces was undertaken by the Governors with advisory councils, in accordance with the Act of 1935. In no case were reforms instituted by the Congress Party ministries interrupted.

A conciliatory statement by Mr. Gandhi early in 1940 aroused hopes that an agreement might be reached, but in March 1940, at the annual party conference, the Congress Party reiterated its demand for complete independence and for a constituent assembly to draft a new constitution elected on a basis of adult suffrage. This would of course result in preponderant Hindu representation. The resolution added that the with-

---

[2] Cmd. 6121, 1939.

drawal of Congress ministries from the provinces "must naturally be followed by civil disobedience." At the same time the Moslem League, meeting at Lahore, widened the breach by demanding that any new constitution should divide India and create independent Moslem states in the northwest and east where Moslems are in a majority.

The suggestion for the partition of India and the creation of a Moslem state, Pakistan,[3] was not new, but it had never before been put forward as a serious political demand. Since its adoption in March 1940, Mr. M. A. Jinnah, the president of the Moslem League, has been increasingly insistent that it is the only solution of the constitutional problem the Moslem League will accept. The growth of political consciousness among the Moslems of India is due to a variety of causes. From the time of the Government of India Act of 1935 it has been apparent that great powers were to be transferred in the near future to Indians, and it was a natural corollary that the Moslems, like other parties, should seek to muster their electoral strength.[3a] Again, the conviction that Moslem interests suffered in provinces where popular Congress ministries held office served to mobilize a mass of " floating " Moslem opinion into the ranks of the All-India Moslem League.

In July the Congress passed a resolution demanding complete independence for India and the establishment of a provisional nationalist government as measures which would "enable the Congress to throw in its full weight in the efforts for the effective organization of the defense of the country." Although Pandit Nehru in an explanatory statement made it perfectly clear that the resolution envisaged only defense measures for an independent India, and did not imply active participation in the war effort, it was the closest approach to cooperation yet made by the Congress.

The British Government found it impossible at that time to meet the Congress Party demand.[4] But on August 8, 1940 the Viceroy issued a statement reaffirming that the British Government's objective for India was dominion status, and announcing that the Government was ready to replace the Act of 1935 immediately after the war by a new constitution to be drafted by Indians, which " should originate from Indian con-

---

[3] Pakistan is said to be derived from the initial letters of the territories affected, i.e., Punjab, Afghanistan (North West Frontier Province), Kashmir, and Sind.

[3a] From one point of view, the increased tension of communal relations in recent years and the constant jockeying for position may be taken as evidence of faith in British promises of Indian independence.

[4] 364 H. C. Deb. 5s., c. 875.

ceptions of the social, economic, and political structure of Indian life," the only condition being that it must not be unacceptable to large and powerful elements in India's national life.[5]

At the same time, the Viceroy was authorized to enlarge his Executive Council by inviting a number of representative Indians to join, and to create a new, representative War Advisory Council. The response to this offer was not encouraging. The Moslem League approved in principle, but hedged its acceptance with so many conditions that no agreement could be reached. The Congress Party rejected the Viceroy's proposal and, apparently repenting its temporary defection, returned to its old attitude. On September 17, 1940, the All-India Congress Committee reaffirmed the party's faith in nonviolence and requested Mr. Gandhi to assume its leadership. The Viceroy announced in November 1940 that, failing to obtain the cooperation of the chief parties, he would not proceed with the proposals, but that the offer remained open.

Mr. Gandhi had meanwhile been informed that he and his followers would be accorded the rights of conscientious objectors in Britain, that is, absolved from the duty of fighting but not permitted to dissuade soldiers from fighting or war workers from working. Since the Congress Party insisted on the right to urge Indians not to enlist or to work in munitions factories, a campaign of civil disobedience was opened. Mr. Gandhi, who had repeatedly declared that he had no desire to embarrass the British Government, directed the campaign, which he designated individual civil disobedience, as distinct from the mass movement advocated by some of his supporters.

The plan of campaign showed Mr. Gandhi's desire to avoid embarrassing India's war effort while registering his protest against the conditions in which that war effort was being carried out. Mr. Gandhi nominated a Congress Party member, who thereupon sent word to the local authorities that at a stated time and place he proposed to offer *satyagraha,* i.e., to preach nonviolence and urge noncooperation in the war effort. At the time and place appointed, Mr. Gandhi's nominee arrived to find the police waiting for him; he began his speech or shouted a few *satyagraha* slogans, and was arrested. Nevertheless, the arrest, however deliberately courted, of such prominent Nationalists as Pandit Jawaharlal Nehru, Maulana Abdul Kalam Azad, the President of the Congress Party, and former provincial premiers and presidents of

---

[5] Cmd. 6219, 1940. The Secretary of State for India on April 22, 1942, referred to this as " recognition in advance of India's status as a dominion."

the party could not fail to be an acute embarrassment. Failure to act would have implied one law for obscure individuals and another for well-known leaders.

Among moderate elements in the country there was a sense of frustration at the twofold political deadlock. Under the chairmanship of Sir Tej Bahadur Sapru a conference of moderates met in Bombay in March 1941 and submitted a series of suggestions to the Government. These included recommendations that for the duration of the war the Viceroy's Council should be composed exclusively of Indians, acting on a basis of collective responsibility, and that this government should occupy the same position in intra-Imperial and international affairs as the governments of the dominions. In rejecting the Sapru proposals as impracticable, the Secretary of State for India emphasized that they had been repudiated by the president of the Moslem League, while the secretary of the Hindu Mahasabha Party had declared that his party would not cooperate in any scheme in which the numerical majority of Hindus was not reflected in the composition of the council.

The Viceroy then returned to his proposals of August 8, 1940, and even though the major parties held aloof it was announced on July 22, 1941 that a number of Indian statesmen had consented regardless of party affiliations to serve on the Executive Council, which was enlarged from seven to twelve members. Eight of the twelve portfolios were held by nonofficial Indians, who thus for the first time outnumbered Europeans on the Council. At the same time a National Defense Council was set up, an advisory body of about thirty members, all of them Indians except for one representative of the European commercial community and one Anglo-Indian. A Defense Committee of the legislature had already been formed to keep the members of the legislature in touch with the work of the Defense Department. Sir Gurunath Bewoor, a distinguished Indian civil servant, was appointed additional secretary of the Defense Department, hitherto regarded as " a European preserve."

The new administrative measures encountered a good deal of criticism, chiefly because the portfolios of Defense and Finance were not entrusted to Indians. The Sikh community protested that it was given no representation. The Moslem League ordered the Premiers of Bengal, the Punjab, and Assam to resign from the National Defense Council, on the ground that they had been appointed not *ex officio* but as members of the Moslem League, without the consent of that body. They did resign, the Premier of Bengal resigning simultaneously from the Moslem League in protest. The only woman member of the Defense Council and the new Law Member of the Executive Council defied Mr. Jinnah by refusing to resign, and were expelled from the Moslem League for five years. The Member for Indians Overseas anticipated similar disciplinary action by resigning from the National Congress Party.

It should be noted that the nonofficial Indian majority of the Executive Council exercises decisive control over the Government of India's policy as a whole. It is true that the Viceroy could under certain circumstances overrule his Council, but to this the nonofficial majority would have a simple and extremely effective retort: resignation, accompanied by publication of the reasons which led them to do so. Such a crisis would be acutely embarrassing to the Viceroy as a public confession of the imposition of Britain's will against Indian wishes and he would naturally strive to the utmost to avoid such an outcome. All the nonofficial members of the Viceroy's Council were distinguished in Indian business and political life, and some of them had been closely associated at different stages in their careers with the Congress Party. The inclusion of nine representatives of the Indian States in the National Defense Council was another significant step, which was expected to make it easier for representatives of the States and of British India to cooperate in peace as well.

Till December 1941, the political deadlock remained unchanged. The Moslem League rested upon its demand for a separate Moslem state. The Congress Party had not officially deserted its policy of nonviolence, but the number of prisoners dwindled, and those who had been released showed no desire to court rearrest. On December 3, the Government announced the release of Pandit Nehru, of Maulana Azad, the President of the Congress Party, and of those " whose offences have been formal or symbolic in character." The dramatic sequel of Sir Stafford Cripps' mission is told in the final section of this chapter.

2. Indian Defense

For many years before the outbreak of war in 1939 India differed in no way from the rest of the British Commonwealth in being unprepared for defense in comparison with the potential enemy. In 1938,[6] however,

---

[6] In November 1937 a grant of £600,000 was made, to be spread over three years beginning April 1938. In September 1938 a further capital grant up to £500,000 was voted, as well as an increase by £500,000 of the annual grant of £1,500,000 in aid of military expenditure.

a grant was made by the British Parliament for the mechanization of the Indian Army, and an expert committee under Lord Chatfield was sent from Britain to India to investigate both the military and the financial aspects of the modernization of the Indian Army.

Hitherto responsibility for the defense of India had been divided between India and Great Britain. India had been responsible for the "minor danger" of the maintenance of internal security and the protection of her frontiers, while Britain assumed responsibility for the "major danger" of an attack by a great power upon India or upon the Commonwealth through India. The Chatfield Committee in its report departed from this principle, on the grounds that India was now more vulnerable to attack in forms not envisaged when the principle was formulated, and that India was therefore directly interested in defense measures extending beyond her local frontiers. The Committee recommended that the forces maintained by India should not only be adequate for purely local defense but should include what were termed "external defense troops."

It was for the purpose, therefore, of the defense of India's external "bastions" that on the outbreak of war Indian troops were dispatched to Egypt and Malaya to guard those vital approaches to India, the Suez Canal, and Singapore, while smaller units were sent to Hong Kong, Aden, and Burma. In December 1939 a small Indian contingent landed in France, a self-contained unit consisting almost entirely of pack transport companies. For Indian forces the main theater, however, was the Middle East, and General Wavell stated in August 1941 that "for more than a year after the outbreak of war the Fourth Indian Division and the Seventh Armored Division (of the British Army) formed the main, almost the only, bulwark of the defense of Egypt on the west."[7]

India entered the war with an army of about 170,000 Indian soldiers.[8] By the beginning of 1942 more than a million had volunteered, for in India conscription for military service is applied only to men from the United Kingdom. It had long been a grievance in some parts of India that the Army was recruited from the so-called "martial races" of Northern India, but thanks to the understanding of Sir Claude

[7] Indian Information, Vol. IX, p. 236. "After the Battle of Sidi Barrani was won, two Indian Divisions, supported by Sudanese troops, carried out that brilliant campaign in Eritrea and Abyssinia. . . . In Cyrenaica, and at Tobruk, an Indian Motor Brigade was of very great value, doing most gallant work. In East Africa, the Western Desert, and in Syria, the 4th Indian Division contributed greatly to success and enhanced the reputation of Indian troops. Indian troops helped restore our position in Iraq and assisted our occupation of Syria."

[8] There were about 50,000 British troops in India.

Auchinleck, during his term as Commander-in-Chief, the basis of recruitment was widened and new regiments formed. At the same time facilities for the training of Indian officers were increased. In the course of 1941, the intake of Indian officers was 600 and it was expected that this would be raised to 2,000 a year.

The Royal Indian Navy at the outbreak of war consisted of eight vessels, intended primarily for patrolling India's long coastline. This small force has been expanded by the addition of many sloops and patrol craft and of anti-submarine vessels and mine sweepers. Italy's entry into the war meant arduous and continuous naval work in escort and patrol duty in the Indian Ocean, the Red Sea, and the Persian Gulf. During the East African campaign Indian naval units cooperated with conspicuous efficiency in landing troops and supplies on the hostile coast of Eritrea, and at the recapture of Berbera in British Somaliland the first troops to land were carried by Indian warships. Ships of the Royal Indian Navy, manned by Indian officers and ratings, have taken part in the Battle of the Atlantic. They have played an important part in the patrol of the Indian Ocean, and participated in the battle off Java. Nor should India's 40,000 merchant seamen be forgotten.

The Indian Air Force on the outbreak of war consisted of headquarters and two flights, with a complement of sixteen officers and 152 air ratings.[9] Within a year the first squadron, an Army Cooperation Squadron, had been fully equipped and a second squadron was being trained. Ten civil flying clubs were transformed into training schools, and the Directorate of Civil Aviation undertook the training of 300 pilots and 2,000 mechanics a year. An Indian Air Force Volunteer Reserve was formed for defense duties mainly on coastal patrol, and was immediately overwhelmed with recruits. With the exception of a few technical experts, the personnel of the Indian Air Force Volunteer Reserve is entirely Indian.

The size of the Indian forces in future depends essentially upon the amount of equipment and material becoming available from Indian industry and from British and American sources. By the middle of 1942 recruits were being accepted by the Indian Army at the rate of 70,000 a month, while many volunteers were refused for lack of equipment. India's effort during the first two years of the present war exceeded by astronomical figures in every direction the whole of her effort between 1914 and 1918.

---

9 Units of the Royal Air Force were also stationed in India.

3. Economic and Financial Mobilization

Even with aid from the British Exchequer,[10] the war has meant a heavy increase in the Indian budget, an increase which has been met by additional taxation, defense loans, and a defense savings movement. An excess profits tax of 66 2/3 percent has been imposed, and a surcharge of 25 percent on income tax and surtax introduced in a supplementary budget in November 1940 was increased to 33 1/3 percent in the 1941–42 budget. Two 3 percent defense loans have been floated as well as a three-year interest-free loan for those persons anxious to assist the war effort without receiving interest. There are many such in India, including some with religious scruples against interest. For the small investor, Post Office ten-year defense savings certificates were introduced, giving a tax-free yield of 3 1/8 percent.[11]

The calling in of sterling securities by the British Treasury enabled the Government of India to undertake a great program of debt repatriation, i.e., the cancellation of sterling debt and its replacement by rupee loans. By the beginning of 1943, out of a total sterling debt (inclusive of railway stock, debentures, and annuities) amounting in 1936–37 to £360,000,000, £294,000,000 had been repatriated.

At the beginning of the war the control of foreign exchange was put in the hands of the Reserve Bank of India. All dealings in foreign exchange were required to be transacted through authorized dealers, comprising the exchange banks and a few joint stock banks. No restrictions were placed on transactions in Empire currencies, except Cana-

---

10 It was announced in the House of Commons on February 29, 1940, that the "Indian budget should provide during the war for:

" (a) the normal cost of India's prewar Forces whether they are employed within or outside India, adjusted from time to time in accordance with the trend of prices, etc.; and

" (b) the cost of special defense measures undertaken by India in Indian interests during the war.

"In addition a contribution as recommended by the Chatfield Committee will be made towards the extra costs of certain troops while employed outside India. All defense expenditure over this amount incurred by the Government of India will be met by the British Exchequer. This arrangement will be made retrospective to 1st April, 1939, and will take account of sums issued from grants-in-aid provided for re-equipment in the Estimates of the current year." 357 H. C. Deb. 5s., c. 2255–6.

11 Reckoning the rupee as 30 cents, total subscriptions to Indian Defense Loans up to February 7, 1942 were $370,116,000. This should be compared with the average prewar budgets of the Government of India and eleven provincial governments combined of $480,000,000.

dian, Newfoundland, and Hong Kong dollars, but sales of non-Empire currencies were restricted to genuine trade purposes. In March 1940 a scheme was introduced to control the foreign exchange proceeds of exports to countries on hard currencies (i.e., countries nominally on the gold standard). Originally relating only to jute and rubber, the scheme was later extended to all commodities. The licensing of imports for the conservation of foreign exchange was also introduced in March 1940. An ordinance of July 1940, in conformity with practice in other parts of the Commonwealth, called for the registration of dollar securities held by Indian nationals, and certain specified American securities were acquired by the Government of India in the spring of 1941.

In general the monetary authorities have kept money as cheap as possible through the expansion of currency to meet the increased requirements of trade and industry and through the purchase of securities in the open market to avoid the dangers of inflation of the last war.[12] With an abrupt rise in prices in September 1939 the Government of India gave the provincial governments power to fix the extent of the rise in prices of necessary commodities at each stage of production and distribution. Price control conferences at which certain guiding principles were formulated were later held in Delhi under the chairmanship of the Commerce Member of the Executive Council, Sir A. Ramaswami Mudaliar.

It was found undesirable to control any tendency for agricultural products to rise, and the primary stage of production was therefore left uncontrolled. In the secondary stage of distribution, the conferences decided that control of the wholesale markets ought to be left to the central government, while profits in the retail market could be controlled by the provincial authorities. The central control did not mean that wholesale prices would be uniform throughout the country; the action of the Government would be to regulate the price in each area according to the circumstances prevailing there. Where price control on any large scale is necessary in a province, a controller of prices is appointed at the headquarters of the province. With him is associated an advisory board representing producers, commercial bodies, traders, consumers, and other interests affected.

In view of shortages created by the demands of the fighting services

---

[12] After a steady advance for the first four months of the war, prices have gradually declined. The peak was reached in the first week of January, 1940, when prices rose to 39 percent above the prewar level.

and war industries and by restrictions on trade, an Economic Resources Board, also under the presidency of Sir A. Ramaswami Mudaliar, was established in October 1939. The Board has no executive functions, but acts as a clearing house of economic and statistical information, discussion and advice, and coordinates the work of all departments concerned with the development and conservation of India's resources. Various trades and industries affected by the loss of European markets, or otherwise concerned with the development of India's potentialities as a supply center, were represented on an Export Advisory Council, which met regularly under Sir A. Ramaswami Mudaliar to plan the expansion of export trade and to seek alternative markets.

4. War Industries

Since the First World War the growth of manufacturing in India, thanks to protective tariffs and the stimulus exerted on domestic industries by the Indian Stores Department, has assumed the proportions of an industrial revolution. The Indian Stores Department took every opportunity to assist Indian manufacturers to improve the quality of their products, and preference was invariably given to supplies of indigenous manufacture. Thus in September 1939 the Army could turn not only to the Ordnance Factories, which play a much greater role than government arsenals in most countries and provide an example for private undertakings, but also to a flourishing steel industry built up over many years by Indian capital and enterprise, and great cotton and woolen mills. All the armies of the Middle East march on India-made boots, and Indian timber provides railway ties, piles, and telegraph poles as well as packing cases and hutting. By July 1942 India was manufacturing 80 percent of her total war requirement. She had also sent overseas large quantities of ammunition and had undertaken the manufacture of armored fighting vehicles, while aircraft assembly plants had been established, and Indian shipyards were producing various types of small craft. Lack of machine tools, the simpler types of which are now being manufactured in India, has been one of the chief obstacles to the development of new industries, as formerly almost all machine tools were imported.

On April 1, 1940, the Board of Scientific and Industrial Research was set up to advise the Government on the coordinated development of India's industries, particularly potential new enterprises related to the war effort. It has not only been able to suggest improved methods in existing industries, but has insured the production in India of such wartime articles as anti-gas fabrics, solid fuel for a portable cooking outfit, and an unbreakable container for dropping gasoline or water supplies from the air without parachutes.

The Indian workman adapts himself readily to the use of precision tools, but technical experience as well as natural aptitude is required. Thus in June 1940 the first compulsory war service in India was introduced for skilled labor and accepted throughout the continent without difficulty. National Service Labor Tribunals were set up in specified areas to administer the calling up for work in munitions factories of technicians not already engaged in work of national importance. For munitions work 10,000 men were thereby made available. Indian technicians have also been sent in small parties of fifty to Great Britain for intensive training over periods of six months. One of the purposes of the British Minister of Labor in this arrangement was obviously to send the workmen back to India with some knowledge of trade unionism and other labor organizations in Britain.

To consider the postwar readjustment of industry and labor the Government of India appointed in the middle of 1941 a Reconstruction Coordination Committee. The committee began its work through four sub-committees for labor and demobilization, disposals and contracts, public works and government purchases, and international trade policy.

5. Supply

For some years before the war the Government of India had maintained an organization known as " The Principal Supply Officers' Committee." Its chief functions were to investigate wartime requirements and the resources available to meet them, taking into consideration the needs not only of the defense services but of communications, public utilities, essential industries, and civilian supplies. During 1938 special consideration had been given to the needs of the iron and steel industry, oil refinery, textiles, government workshops, and shipping.

The way was thus paved for the creation on August 26, 1939 of a Department of Supply, which was added to the portfolio of the Law Member of the Executive Council. At the same time a Director-General of Supply was appointed and a War Supply Board established. The function of the Board was to ensure an adequate supply of war materials. At first largely an advisory body, it was reconstituted in November 1939 and given executive powers.

The Department of Supply and the War Supply Board were not concerned with supplies for normal trading purposes, but procured the essential materials for firms engaged on war contracts, for utility services, and for concerns of national importance. Priority arrangements were made for essential imports, and close liaison was maintained with Indian industrial interests. The actual procurement of armaments and ammunition, army clothing, and saddlery for the armed forces was not at first the responsibility of the Supply Department, but of the Master-General of Ordnance.

By the summer of 1940 the new demands upon India's productive capacity had so increased that it was thought best to put all the supply organizations under unified control. A new War Supply Board was formed in July 1940, with the Supply Member of the Executive Council as president and the former Director-General of Supply as vice-president. The Board worked through two branches, for munitions production and supply. The Director-General of Munitions Production was responsible for armaments and ammunition, steel production and all metals; the Director-General of Supply had charge of all other war supplies: foodstuffs, textiles, leather, lumber, and miscellaneous stores. The two directors-general were stationed, respectively, at Calcutta and New Delhi. The Indian Stores Department and the Contracts Directorate at New Delhi remained responsible for the actual purchase of all stores. In the provinces there were provincial purchase branches, industrial planning officers, and the agents of the controllers appointed for particular commodities, such as steel and machine tools. Since a great part of India's industry is situated in Bengal and Bihar, it was found that these arrangements resulted in excessive centralization at Delhi and the organization was therefore modified in December 1940. Responsibility was decentralized by converting the two Directorates-General into self-contained units, one of them at Calcutta, and empowering the directors-general to take decisions, with the concurrence of their financial advisers, without financial restrictions on all matters within their jurisdiction.

A War Transport Board was constituted on September 8, 1939, to control and coordinate transport by rail, road, and sea. Constant supervision is maintained on the movements of both civil supplies and essential war material. The Communications Member of the Executive Council originally presided over the Board, on which the Commerce, Finance, Defense, and Supply departments were also represented. In the middle of 1942 the Board was reconstituted as a separate "portfolio" in the Executive Council.

To meet some of the intricate problems arising in the course of letting and adjusting war supply contracts, an Advisory Panel of Accountants was established by the Government of India in June 1941. The Panel's duties were to advise on general accountancy questions relating to the terms of contracts for war supplies, such as those terms bearing on system of payments, elements of costs, profit percentages, the extent of check to be applied on the accounts of contractors, and similar problems. Six Indians and four Europeans were nominated to the Panel, which held its first meeting in Delhi in July 1941.

The collapse of France and the entry of Italy into the war meant the diversion of shipping from the Mediterranean to the Cape of Good Hope route. The British Commonwealth countries east and south of Suez were thereby cut off to a certain extent from the Mother Country and had to place more reliance on their own resources. In order to coordinate their war effort, the Viceroy, Lord Linlithgow, invited representatives of the various parts of the British Commonwealth in the Eastern Hemisphere to a conference at Delhi. The Eastern Group Supply Conference which met from October 25 to November 25, 1940, under the chairmanship of an Indian, Sir Muhammad Zafrullah Khan, was an event of capital importance in the development of the British Commonwealth and a landmark in the war. It promised a new solidarity between all the parts of the Commonwealth round the shores of the Indian Ocean out of which a permanent regional organization might develop. It was attended by delegates from Australia, New Zealand, South Africa, India, Southern Rhodesia, Kenya, Uganda, Tanganyika, Northern Rhodesia, Nyasaland, Zanzibar, Burma, Ceylon, Malaya, Hong Kong, and Palestine. Great Britain was represented by a special mission, which had been sent to India to discuss the production of munitions and other war stores both for Indian needs and for the forces in the Middle East. Delegates from the Netherlands East Indies also attended the Conference as observers.

The interchange of information at the Conference revealed opportunities hitherto unsuspected by many of the delegates, and from the "plus" and "minus" items in each country's capacity it was possible to map the actual and potential war resources of the entire Eastern Group.

While the Conference was still in session it had been possible, by correlating surpluses in equipment with existing requirements, to supply important deficiencies without waste of time or undue call on shipping space.

To continue the work of coordinating supply and planning production on a permanent basis the Eastern Group Supply Council was established, with headquarters at Delhi, on February 14, 1941. The chairman of the Council represents the United Kingdom and the colonies, and the other five members include representatives of India, Australia, South Africa, and New Zealand and an army officer, the controller-general of army provision (Eastern Group).

Side by side with the Eastern Group Supply Council, which is a civil organization, there has been set up in Delhi a Central Provision Office under military control. The military member of the Supply Council is in charge of the office and is the link between the two organizations. His staff consists of about forty to fifty officers drawn from the forces of Great Britain, India, and the dominions concerned. Delhi is thus the seat of two councils, one civilian and one military, through which the industrial activities and military equipment of two-thirds of the British Commonwealth are coordinated.

The Central Provision Office acts as an agency for the armed forces, and also maintains contact with the countries participating through local provision offices. Its functions are to estimate the immediate and future needs of the armed forces in the Middle and Far East that cannot be met locally and to inform the Supply Council of them. The Provision Office also assumes responsibility for the holding and distribution of military stores, which includes the coordination of all shipping requirements for the conveyance of supplies throughout the Eastern Group. The Supply Council in its turn meets the demands of the Provision Office by drawing on available resources in the group countries, maintains information about the actual and potential productive capacity of each member, and arranges for new production through the supply departments of the cooperating countries.

Thus, if the army of the Middle East, for example, or one of the local provision offices, requires supplies which cannot be obtained locally, a demand is made on the Central Provision Office. The Central Provision Office informs the Eastern Group Supply Council, which determines from what country it will be best to obtain the supplies, and asks the government of that country to place the necessary contracts. Delivery of supplies is arranged by the Central Provision Office. By the close collaboration between the two organizations in Delhi, the forces of the Eastern Group are provisioned through a system which makes the fullest use of the industrial capacity of each unit, conserves shipping space, and makes due allowance for the general strategic position.

An American Technical Supply Mission visited India in the spring of 1942, the first United States Minister to India having been appointed in July 1941.[12a] As a result of its recommendations the executive direction of India's economic war effort was placed with a committee of the Viceroy's Executive Council known as the War Resources Committee. This committee was to be responsible for implementing the production program of the government. Its decisions were made binding on all authorities.

6. The Indian States

The foregoing survey has dealt almost exclusively with the war effort of British India. But there is another India, comprising two-fifths of the area and one-fourth of the population, the India of the Indian States. At the outbreak of war the different Princes published loyal messages placing their services and resources at the disposal of the Crown.

Since 1888 certain of the states have maintained Indian States' Forces, troops trained by their own officers, in consultation with the Indian Army authorities, and armed by the British Government, ready to take their place beside units of the Indian Army. By 1938 the Indian States' Forces numbered over 45,000. The Bikaner Camel Corps and some other units from the states are serving overseas; a Jammu and Kashmir Mountain Battery distinguished itself in the East African campaign; units from Jaipur, Patiala, Udsipur, Bhopal, Travancore, Jodhpur, and Indore, are serving outside their own states, thereby releasing units of the Indian Army for overseas. The states are collaborating with British India to recruit and train for the Indian Army new motor transport and signalling units, labor companies are being raised in Kapurthala and Tehri-Garwhal, and among the flying clubs that are training pilots for the Indian Air Force are those of Jodhpur and Hyderabad.

Many states are equipped to take part in the industrial war effort. Railway workshops in Bikaner and Jodhpur have undertaken the mak-

---

[12a] In April 1942 India and China exchanged diplomatic representatives. The Indian Agent-General in China was to stand in the same relation to the British Ambassador in China as any dominion Minister.

ing of munitions, surveys have been made of the industrial resources of several states, and the output of the factories of Mysore has greatly increased. States' subjects are eligible for technical training under various schemes of the British Indian authorities. The Indian member of the Eastern Group Supply Council speaks for the Indian States as well as for British India. Very large individual money gifts have been made to the government by the rulers and by the people of the states, usually for a definite object, such as a fighter squadron or a naval vessel, and large contributions are also made to the Viceroy's War Purposes Fund, which is applied to relief as well as armament.

When restrictions on finance and trade were imposed in British India, some apprehension was felt that unscrupulous traders might evade them by transferring their activities to the Indian States. But the princes have cooperated with the Government of India by adopting in their territories the same financial, import and export regulations as in British India, thereby ensuring uniformity of policy throughout India.

7. The Mission of Sir Stafford Cripps

With the crisis in Indian affairs arising out of the Japanese advance early in 1942, it was announced that Sir Stafford Cripps, who had recently accepted a seat in the Churchill Cabinet, enjoying " the full confidence of His Majesty's Government," would undertake a mission to India. He arrived in New Delhi on March 23. Invitations had been issued previously to the Indian political parties and other groups to select representatives to discuss draft proposals unitedly agreed upon by the British War Cabinet. Sir Stafford first met the members of the Executive Council, the Commander-in-Chief, the governors of the provinces, and then began negotiations with representative political leaders.[13]

The stated purpose of the draft proposals issued by Sir Stafford was " the creation of a new Indian Union which shall constitute a dominion associated with the United Kingdom and the other dominions by a common allegiance to the Crown, but equal to them in any respect, in

---

[13] Pandit Jawaharlal Nehru, Maulana Abul Kalan Azad, for the Congress Party, Mr. M. A. Jinnah for the Moslem League, Mr. V. D. Savarkar, president of the Hindu Mahasabha, Sir Tej Bahadur and the Rt. Hon. M. R. Jayakar as spokesmen for the nonparty group, Sir Jogendra Singh, speaking for the Sikhs, Dr. Ambedkar and Mr. Rajah for the scheduled castes, Mr. N. M. Joshi for Labor; Mr. Fazl-ul-Huq, premier of Bengal, Khan Bahadur Allah Baksh, premier of Sind, a committee representative of the Chamber of Princes, and Mr. Gandhi, who came especially from Wardha, were among those with whom Sir Stafford consulted.

no way subordinate in any aspect of its domestic or external affairs." Since these proposals have continued to form the basis of much discussion, they are here given in full:

(a) Immediately upon the cessation of hostilities, steps shall be taken to set up in India, in the manner described hereafter, an elected body charged with the task of framing a new Constitution for India.

(b) Provision shall be made, as set out below, for the participation of the Indian States in the constitution-making body.

(c) His Majesty's Government undertake to accept and implement forthwith the Constitution so framed subject only to: —

(i) the right of any Province of British India that is not prepared to accept the new Constitution to retain its present constitutional position, provision being made for its subsequent accession if it so decides.

With such nonacceding Provinces, should they so desire, His Majesty's Government will be prepared to agree upon a new Constitution, giving them the same full status as the Indian Union, and arrived at by a procedure analogous to that here laid down.

(ii) the signing of a Treaty which shall be negotiated between His Majesty's Government and the constitution-making body. This Treaty will cover all necessary matters arising out of the complete transfer of responsibility from British to Indian hands; it will make provision, in accordance with the undertakings given by His Majesty's Government, for the protection of racial and religious minorities; but will not impose any restriction on the power of the Indian Union to decide in the future its relationship to the other Member States of the British Commonwealth.

Whether or not an Indian State elects to adhere to the Constitution, it will be necessary to negotiate a revision of its Treaty arrangements, so far as this may be required in the new situation.

(d) The constitution-making body shall be composed as follows, unless the leaders of Indian opinion in the principal communities agree upon some other form before the end of hostilities: —

Immediately upon the result being known of the provincial elections which will be necessary at the end of hostilities, the entire membership of the lower houses of the Provincial legislatures shall, as a single electoral college, proceed to the election of the constitution-making body by the system of proportional representation. This new body shall be in number about one-tenth of the number of the electoral college.

Indian States shall be invited to appoint representatives in the same proportion to their total population as in the case of the representatives of British India as a whole, and with the same powers as the British Indian members.

(e) During the critical period which now faces India and until the new Constitution can be framed His Majesty's Government must inevitably bear the responsibility for and retain control and direction of the defense of India as part of their world war effort, but the task of organizing to the full the military, moral, and material resources of India must be the responsibility of the Government of India with the cooperation of the peoples of India. His Majesty's Government desire and invite the immediate and effective participation of the leaders of the principal sections of the Indian people in the counsels of their country, of the Commonwealth and of the United Nations. Thus they will be enabled to give their active and constructive help in the discharge of a task which is vital and essential for the future freedom of India.

Mr. Amery's previous offer to accept any constitution drawn up by Indians which was not rejected by some substantial and powerful section of Indian opinion had been criticized in India on the ground that it enabled the Moslem minority to impede India's independence for ever; the first aim of the Cripps plan was to meet this objection by providing that rejection of the constitution by any province need not impede India's independence because it could have separate autonomy. On the other hand, in order not to stimulate the formation of separate states but to promote the unity of India, it was essential to offer some strong inducement to the minorities in general, and to the Moslems in particular, to partake in the work of the constitution making body. Hence the provision allowing for separate autonomy was inserted to allow the minorities a margin of bargaining power.

The first practical difficulty encountered was over defense, and this occupied most of the discussions with the Congress Party. The demand from the Congress Party stated that the defense of India should be placed in Indian hands. No suggestion was made that the Commander-in-Chief of the armed forces should be an Indian, but the party asked that his functions as Defense Member should be transferred to an Indian. This would have entailed " a long and difficult reorganization " of the Defense Secretariat, and it was countered with a proposal to create a new department under the Commander-in-Chief as war member for the governmental relations of general headquarters and naval and air head-quarters, leaving the other functions of the existing Defense Department to an Indian member.

The Congress objections appeared to take no account of an offer of nominations by the nationalist parties for the Pacific War Council or of the fact that all the departments of government would have been in Indian hands, so that, through the Departments of Supply and Finance particularly, they could have exercised a powerful brake on any policy of the Commander-in-Chief of which they disapproved.

The nationalized Executive Council, representing the great political parties, would have had positive power, and if the Viceroy had attempted to oppose it he would have faced the risk of a major political crisis, uniting against him all or some of the most powerful political forces in India. While such a nationalized Viceroy's Council would not of course have meant responsible government, the measure of power in fact transferred would have been very real and very great. Until the very last night of the negotiations the Congress Party raised no general issues or discussions on " responsible government "; until then all negotiations were attempts to find a new formula for clause (e) — defense — of the draft.

Sir Stafford Cripps' own explanation of the rejection of his proposals was that " the plan broke down on the question of to whom the proposed interim Indian National Government was to be responsible," the Congress Party reiterating in their final statement that they could not accept the British Government's contention that any interim Indian Government must remain responsible either to the Viceroy or to the British Government.[14] The Congress, the Hindu Mahasabha, the Sikhs, the Moslem League, and the depressed classes were agreed in rejecting, for varying reasons, the suggestion to allow provincial independence. The Secretary of State for India, however, after Sir Stafford Cripps had reported to the House of Commons the failure of his mission, made a concluding statement that the Viceroy would welcome any " practical suggestions " from Indian leaders to implement the War Cabinet's proposals for independence.

Significant administrative changes followed in July 1942. The Viceroy's Executive Council was enlarged to fifteen members, with separate departments for War and for Defense. The Commander-in-Chief, Sir Archibald Wavell, remained War Member. Coordination between the

---

14 Cf. dispatch by Mallory Brown, *Christian Science Monitor*, April 23, 1942.

defense forces and other departments of the government, defense legislation, the recruitment of man power, the administration of cantonment
areas, the acquisition of land for defense purposes, the provision of oil
supplies, and the care of prisoners of war were, however, vested in the
new Indian Defense Member, Sir Firoz Khan Noon, who had been
High Commissioner for India in London from 1936 to 1941.[15] At the
same time two Indian members, Sir A. Ramaswami Mudaliar, who remained a member of the Viceroy's Council without portfolio, and the
Maharaja Jam Saheb of Nawanagar, Chancellor of the Chamber of
Princes, were appointed to the War Cabinet in London and the Pacific
War Council. Their status in the British War Cabinet has apparently
been exactly comparable to that of the representatives of any of the
dominions.[16]

The foregoing chapter on India was the product of many mishaps, including the going astray
of material prepared in the winter of 1941–42 by Mr. Pargat Singh Muhar which never reached
the editors, possibly through loss in the mails or through censorship. His earlier contributions to
the chapter had become too far out of date to be useful except for background. As it has now been
written the chapter represents on the whole a non-official British view of India, which closely
reflects the official view and is interesting for that reason.

To an American editor two things become of major interest. One is that a situation of the
complexity of the Indian one does not lend itself to solution in the forum of American public
opinion. Our national interest is at stake in seeing that a secure base is maintained for operations
for the relief of China and for a counterattack through Burma and for the holding of Ceylon and
of India proper. It is therefore to our interest that no government antipathetic to the war effort
should be set up in India, and some doubt has been raised by Mahatma Gandhi's statements as
to his own attitude in this respect.[17]

On the other hand, it is clear that India is far larger even than the much publicized figure of
Gandhi, and that a growing nationalism has now touched nearly all elements of the population,
even those which are, from the point of view of literacy, hardly comparable with modern elec-
torates elsewhere. It has reached even the groups which formerly inclined to support the British
raj as a matter of self-interest. To speak of democracy in India is perhaps to anticipate, but to
speak of nationalism in India is certainly to deal with a fact.

The second point for an American is that our own interest lies in convincing the Asiatic peoples
that this war is a genuine war for freedom. It is obvious that China views the solution of the
Indian problem as a measure of the sincerity of the professions of the United Nations. It is to our
interest to see that this problem does not go by default merely because of the breakdown of Sir

---

[15] At the beginning of 1943 a new Food Department was added to the Government of India. Because of the cutting off of supplies of rice from Burma, the demands of the armed forces,
and unfavorable weather conditions in several provinces it was necessary to concentrate various
functions of food purchase and distribution which had formerly been scattered in several departments in this one.

[16] The Maharaja of Nawanagar, on a trip to India in February 1943 described his position
in the War Cabinet to the Indian press. He had received no instructions from the Secretary of
State for India, and his only instructions from the Viceroy had been to do what he thought best
" in the interest of the Indian States, India as a whole, and the Empire. . . . Political questions
did not come before the War Cabinet, whose business was the conduct of the war." *The Times,*
London, February 19, 1943.

[17] See Appendix VI.

Stafford Cripps' efforts to work out a solution along the lines of Churchill's willingness to concede dominion status after the war.

Without attempting to indicate the outlines of British policy at this time, it would seem an act of statesmanship to offer India self-government on any terms that could be arrived at by substantially unanimous agreement among conflicting communal and other interests in India, subject always to the retention of military and, if necessary, police control in areas of military importance. The psychological effects of such an offer at this time would be enormous. If, as has often been averred, Indians cannot get together, there would at least be no harm in an examination of the reasons why. If Indians are capable of finding a formula for the setting up of a constitution, or for the constructive combination of their efforts until the formation of a constitution can be undertaken, there can be no doubt of the effect upon morale, not only in India but among the other peoples of the East.

There is a natural reluctance on the part of the British at a time of great danger to concede military control or civil control that might endanger military success. There is also, however, such a thing as political warfare, and it is in this light that the independence of India presents problems of immediate and pressing importance. — W. Y. E.

The dominions, like the United States, rarely make official public reference to India. But knowing the Empire as " a school of government that inevitably leads to self-government," they have no doubt that Britain will carry out her pledge to India when Japan is defeated. They feel that swapping the horses of government in mid-stream, in face of enemy fire from the banks, would be all too likely to break down India's internal peace and undermine the fine discipline of the Indian Army of 2,000,000 volunteers, destined to play a vital part in Japan's defeat.

From experience the dominions know that national unity and federation are not easy to achieve. These cost the dominions decades of hard effort, and success was due to a positive nationalism — not mere negative opposition to Britain, but a substantial agreement and identity of purpose among the peoples, parties, and creeds of the newly emerging states. Of this they see little sign in India. They see instead a baffling maze of races, languages, states, and principalities, in population equal to Europe and three times the remainder of the British Commonwealth of Nations, and cleft to the roots by ancient incompatibilities of caste, creed, and different levels of domestication. Their liberal sympathies call for quick action; but their reason tells them that more haste is less speed. — H. D. H.

CHAPTER XII

Fighting Ulster and Neutral Eire

by H. Duncan Hall

The scope of this book does not admit of more than a short note upon the role either of Neutral Eire or of that part of Ireland which is not neutral in the common war of all the democracies for the preservation of their liberties. The story of Ulster's contributions, if it could be told in detail, would show that with her population of about 1,280,000 she has played a part in the common war effort hardly less than that of the smaller dominions.

It would be hard to imagine a greater contrast than that between the mental atmosphere of Belfast and Dublin during the war. To the people of Belfast the war was the one thing that mattered; the issues were crystal-clear; everything they held dear was at stake; they stood or fell with Britain and the Empire. But from Dublin the war looked strangely different — remote and confused; political neutrality was accompanied by a curious mental paralysis, a neutralism which blurred the sharp edges of facts as well as of moral and political principles. It was not easy to deduce from the speeches of political or even of spiritual leaders in Dublin that most of the people of Erie shared the general detestation of Nazi tyranny and its attack upon the foundations of the common Christian civilization of the West. Tens of thousands of them had indeed enlisted as individuals in the armed forces of the British Commonwealth;[1] they were no doubt glad that they could serve in a common

---

[1] Reports said some 100,000 with another 180,000 in war work in Britain.

cause with fellow Irishmen from Ulster in some of the famous old Irish regiments whose very names summoned up so much of the military history of the British army. Many of them had already given their lives; nearly one-fifth of those lost on H.M.S. *Courageous* at the beginning of the war bore Irish names.

But the people of Eire as a whole were war-weary people, for whom the First World War was followed by a civil war that lasted years after the Armistice. The preoccupation of some was to avoid war at almost all cost, in order to save, as they thought, the remnant of four million people which constitutes the Mother Country of the Irish race. To many of them it seemed possible to answer in the affirmative the incredulous question asked by President Roosevelt on December 30, 1940: If the Nazis won, " would Irish freedom be permitted as an amazing pet exception in an unfree world? "

The debate on external affairs in the Dail on April 23, 1941, showed something of this mood. It seemed to show that the representatives of Eire gathered together in the Dail hardly shared the tremendous preoccupations and anxieties of Northern Ireland, of Britain, of the British overseas dominions, and of the United States. The debate left no doubt of the almost unanimous acceptance in the Dail of the policy of neutrality, not of the active American type, but of a type which in many cases went so far as to wash its hands of the deeper issues of the war, denying through its principal leaders that any clear-cut religious or moral issues were involved. Thus the plea made by Mr. J. M. Dillon, deputy leader of the opposition party — the United Ireland Party — in the debate on July 17, 1941, fell on deaf ears. The Parliament of Eire, he said, " should ascertain precisely what cooperation Great Britain and the United States of America may require to insure success against the Nazi attempt at world conquest and, as expeditiously as possible, to afford to the United States and Great Britain that cooperation to the limit of our resources. . . . The Atlantic life line joining these two champions of democracy and civilization is no stronger than its weakest link. . . . A gap is opening in that life line. . . . We can close that gap." His suggestion was repudiated by most of the other speakers in the debate, including the leaders of all parties; and he was forced some six months later to resign on this issue from his own party.

This and other debates on external affairs revealed that the division was not one between Catholic Ireland and Protestant Ulster, but rather one between the chief leaders of Catholic Ireland and the colonies of

Irish Catholics in England and all parts of the British Commonwealth. The contrast between the views of the leaders of the Irish Catholic community was revealed in two declarations made some five months later — one by the head of the Catholic Church in Dublin, and the other from across the narrow waters in the war-torn city of Liverpool. From the head of the Catholic Church in Dublin came the demand for a negotiated peace. From Liverpool the Irish Catholic Archbishop Downey spoke of the intrepid flock standing amidst the debris of one of his churches crying, "We shall build it again." "They had seen," he said, "their sanctuary reduced to ruins that the sanctuary of their souls might not be defiled." And he called for a relentless prosecution of the war "against the oppressors of humanity." Time alone could show what the real view of Catholic Ireland was upon these grave issues. In the debate referred to, a private member gave a warning that "if a vote came before the House on the moral issue, even the Prime Minister might be surprised at the result."

On the economic side both parts of Ireland have made an important contribution to the war. With the swallowing up by the Axis of Denmark, the value of the contribution of Eire as the nearest important supplier of food to Britain was greatly enhanced. Even before the war nearly the whole of Eire's external trade was with Britain. During the war she continued to export to Britain virtually the whole of her exportable surplus of foodstuffs. Her secondary industries, patiently fostered over the past decade by de Valera's Government, suffered from a shortage of raw materials. Virtually without a mercantile marine (her few ships having been freely sunk, with apologies, by German submarines), she was dependent on what supplies Britain could afford from those fought through the U-boat wolf-packs by British and American convoys. In the matter of supplies of vital raw materials, Eire received from Britain at least as favorable treatment as other neutrals.

Of Ulster's contribution on the material side not much needs to be said. It has been of considerable importance in the matter of war industries, particularly the shipbuilding of Belfast, and of man power for the armed forces of the United Kingdom of which Ulster forms a part. All controls, such as the rationing of gasoline, food, and clothing, operating in the United Kingdom extend to Northern Ireland, and are carried out through the departments of the Government of Northern Ireland. Though service in the defense forces and in civil defense had to remain on a voluntary basis, a number of men volunteered for service in the army, particularly in such Irish regiments as the Royal Inniskilling Fusiliers, the Royal Ulster Rifles, the Royal Irish Fusiliers, the North Irish Horse, and the Irish Guards. In addition, numbers of men served in all branches of the Royal Navy and the R.A.F., as well as in the Merchant Marine. The Home Guard, set up in the summer of 1940, was about 30,000 strong a year later.

Virtually the whole of industry in Ulster served directly or indirectly the needs of war production. In the matter of shipbuilding, hundreds of thousands of tons of shipping were launched annually from the yards of Messrs. Harland and Wolff. The Belfast shipyards made a very important contribution in the matter of naval vessels, including the aircraft carrier, H.M.S. *Formidable,* and the heavy cruiser, H.M.S. *Belfast.* Other spheres in which the industry of Belfast contributed to war production were in the manufacture of various types of aircraft, tanks, iron and steel, shells, artillery, gun mounts, etc. The linen industry constituted an important element in the wartime export trade of the United Kingdom.

But the most important contribution of Ulster has been strategic. The intense loyalty of at least two-thirds of her citizens, and the good will of some at least of the remaining third, have rendered fully available to the British Commonwealth Ulster's vital strategic situation. So important is this contribution that the loss of Northern Ireland might well have meant the loss of the war. The strategic position has been well put by a writer in the *Round Table* of March 1941: "Throughout the centuries one continuous thread can be detected running through the variegated web of British military and naval policy; it is the strategical indivisibility of the British Isles. The defense of Ireland is the defense of Britain. Elizabeth knew it; Cromwell knew it; William of Orange . . . knew it; and so did Pitt and Castlereagh; so, too, in our time did Mr. Lloyd George. . . ." It was the unvarying view of Britain that the latter expressed in 1921 in these words: " The security of this country depends on what happens on this breakwater, this advance post, this front trench of England." [1a]

Britain's enemies also knew it at each critical epoch in her history — Philip of Spain, Napoleon, the German General Staff in 1916; and again in 1939, when on August 31 the German minister in Dublin called hopefully upon Mr. de Valera to assure him that the German Government would respect Eire's neutrality. Britain depends for its life upon the sea lanes to the Atlantic, running north and south of Ireland. The sur-

[1a] H. C. Deb. 14 Dec. 1921.

render in 1938 of the two Southern British bases, Cobh and Berehaven, followed by the neutrality of Eire and the German occupation of France, cut the southern lane — and halved the problem of the German submarine commanders. " It is, therefore," as the writer cited above pointed out, " through the narrow waters of the North Channel that the bulk of our shipping must make the western ports of Britain under the protection of the Royal Navy and the Royal Air Force, only because and only as long as six of the thirty-two counties of Ireland still render allegiance to the British Crown." How great was the cumulative effect of the loss of the three Irish bases was shown when Japan's entrance into the war threw a sudden enormous strain on the shipping resources of the United Nations. The loss of Ulster, whether by enemy action or a policy of appeasing Eire, might have meant the loss of the Battle of the Atlantic. It might also have made Ireland into a second Crete, whereby she would have become the classical example of how a small neutral country can destroy a great power by leaving its flank wide open to the enemy.

It was to prevent such a catastrophe, involving perhaps the destruction of England and certainly of ill-defended Eire, that a fully-equipped British mechanized army stood poised for many months upon the Ulster boundary, ready to sweep down the entire length of Eire to destroy an enemy force landed on its southern coast. It was joined by an American force in January 1942.

The policy of appeasement in 1938 renounced naval and air bases in Eire which were essential to the defense of the British Isles. But for the passionate loyalty of less than a million Ulstermen, that policy might well have had a fatal sequel. It might have bowed to the insistence of the Government of Eire and sacrificed Ulster and with it the port of Belfast. The leaders of Ulster steadfastly opposed any step involving, as the present Prime Minister, Mr. J. M. Andrews, said on July 7, 1940, the " further dismemberment of the United Kingdom," and the giving-up by the people of Northern Ireland of their British citizenship " to become citizens of Eire, which was really a republic standing neutral in the war and harbouring the Empire's enemies." The heavily overstaffed legations and consulates which neutral Eire permitted the enemies of the Empire and the United Nations to maintain in Dublin proved invaluable to the intelligence services of the Axis. The war offered no stranger contrast than that between the stream of enemy messages pouring out of these legations to Berlin, Rome and Tokyo, and the messages going from Belfast to London and the whole British Commonwealth. The burden of them was the message of Ulster's veteran Prime Minister, the late Lord Craigavon, " We are King's men. We will be with you to the end."

There were not wanting in the Dublin Parliament voices which recognized these facts and the impossibility of taking any step that would run counter to the deep feeling of loyalty binding the majority of the people of Ulster to the rest of the British Commonwealth.[2] But Mr. de Valera himself had never wavered in peace or in war in his relentless opposition to what, in his letter to the Secretary of State for Dominion Affairs on April 5, 1932, immediately after coming into power, he called " the outrage of Partition and the alienation of the most sacred part of our national territory." In that letter partition was coupled (as always in his mind) with the British naval bases established in the three Irish ports which he declared gave Britain the power " to make our neutrality a mockery."

The only terms on which apparently he felt he could accept the ending of partition were the withdrawal of Ulster, like the three ports, into the neutral zone of Eire, thus removing her from the common defense system of the British Commonwealth. Thus he stated in an interview on July 5, 1940, in the darkest hour of the war, a little more than a fortnight after Dunkirk: " In face of the present emergency Ireland should be whole and undivided," the Northern Parliament becoming " subject to the Parliament of All Ireland instead of to the British Parliament. . . . The determination of policy and defense measures were possible only on such a basis, and such measures must be founded on neutrality." [3]

In the face of this policy the possibility of a joint defense scheme between Northern Ireland and Eire, which at that time had been under discussion, fell to the ground. In the judgment of the leaders of Ulster acceptance of Mr. de Valera's proposals must mean the withdrawal of Ulster, as Lord Craigavon put it, from " full partnership in the United Kingdom and the British Empire," as well as, in the words of one of his colleagues, from " the fight for liberty, justice, and civilization." Nevertheless, because of the opposition of Eire, the Ulster leaders were forced nine months later to abandon a proposal for conscription, which the Northern Ireland Cabinet regarded as the only means whereby it could

---

2 E.g., J. M. Dillon, then Deputy Leader of the United Ireland Party in the Dail, February 15, 1939, and July 16, 1941, and Senator MacDermot in the Seanad on January 26, 1939.
3 As reported in *The Times*, London, July 9, 1940.

play its full part in the war as an integral part of the Empire. They repudiated strongly the claim which Mr. de Valera made in the Dail May 26, 1941, to speak, as the Prime Minister of Northern Ireland put it, " in the name of the people of this area. . . . All matters connected with Northern Ireland are completely outside the jurisdiction of the Eire Government and so they shall remain." [4]

The entry of the United States into the war, as a result of the direct attack of the Axis upon her, made no difference in Dublin's determination to remain neutral — " Irish neutrality is unchanged; our policy of state remains unchanged," Mr. de Valera said on December 14, 1941. The landing of the American armed force in Ulster at the end of January 1942 led on January 27 to a protest by Mr. de Valera in the sharpest terms against this violation of the national sovereignty and the neutral status of Ireland. In defiance of President Wilson's principle of self-determination and a 3-to-1 vote of the Irish people, Britain, Mr. de Valera said, had partitioned Ireland: " The partition of Ireland was no different from the partition of Poland. Nor are the events that flow from it less than those Abraham Lincoln foresaw from the projected partition of the United States. . . . Maintenance of the partition of Ireland is as indefensible as aggression against all nations, which it is the avowed purpose of Britain and the United States to bring to an end." At the same time Dublin once more repeated the warning often given before that any attempt to seize ports, no matter by whom, would be resisted by force. The Premier of Northern Ireland replied on January 28, welcoming the American Army, and repudiating Mr. de Valera's claim to sovereignty over Ulster. " Northern Ireland," he said, " is in the fight for freedom and intends to see it through." That he did not speak for an important part of the Catholic minority in Ulster was shown by the statement of Cardinal MacRory, Archbishop of Armagh and Primate of Ireland, on September 26, 1942. The Cardinal referred to partition as a " flagrant and intolerable injustice against Catholics doomed to live under the narrow and unjust domination of the Belfast Parliament and Executive." " When I read," he continued, " day after day, that this war is being fought for the rights and liberties of small nations and then think of my own corner of my country overrun by British and United States soldiers against the will of the nation, I confess I sometimes find it hard to be patient." [5]

---

[4] *J. P. E.*, Vol. XXII, p. 367.
[5] As reported in the *New York Times*, September 28, 1942.

It would hardly be fair to deduce from such words that only a matter of patience and tactics separated the Cardinal and Mr. de Valera from the Irish Republican Army, which continued to wage its underground war by violence against the Government of Northern Ireland and the invader — both American and British. The I.R.A.'s program of violence was generally frowned on by the hierarchy, and Mr. de Valera's government waged war ceaselessly upon it.

Such statements were, indeed, a striking example of the tragedy of Anglo-Irish relations. Some Irishmen, brooding over the past, went on living in a private world quite different in its proportions and scale of values from the normal world. Thus the setting up in 1920 of the Parliament of Northern Ireland in accordance with the freely-expressed will of two-thirds of the people of the area, though against the will of the other third, became equivalent in the minds of some of Eire's leaders to the partition of Poland, the American Civil War, and the violent rape by the Axis of fifteen free nations.

In the dire hour of common need ghosts of the past rose up before the eyes of official Dublin, obscuring all the clear lines of reality, Britain's fight for freedom, America's peril, even the fate of all the colonies of Mother Ireland. Nation after nation, including all Overseas Ireland, became members of the United Nations. But Eire remained outside brooding over the past. It was a theme for the epic and saga; it recalled an incident in the Burnt Njal Saga. The hero, Gunnar of Lithend, in his death-fight held off a great band of enemies that besieged his house, and had slain many of the attackers. But one of them climbed up unnoticed and slashed his bowstring. Gunnar then turned to his wife, Hallgerda, "'Give me two locks of thy hair, and ye two, my mother and thou, twist them together into a bowstring for me.' 'Does aught lie upon it?' she said, 'My life lies on it,' he said; 'for they will never come to close quarters with me if I can keep them off with my bow.' 'Well!' she said, 'now I will call to thy mind that slap on the face which thou gavest me; and I care never a whit whether thou holdest out a long while or a short.'"

The end of the story of Eire and Britain was not yet revealed. In the early months of 1942 neutral Eire was reported to be receiving weapons sorely needed by those fighting to the death for their liberties in Russia, at Singapore, in Java and Burma. Ships of war and transports that might have saved Singapore were tied up in the Atlantic because of the neutrality of Eire. But Dublin was still haunted by ghosts. From it came hints of a possible settlement that had little relation to reality — the ending of partition by American pressure on Ulster and Britain. It was a settlement that could hardly be bought except at the cost of civil war in Ireland and a crisis in Anglo-American relations. It ignored the deep gulf of distrust dug already between Ulster and Eire by the policy of neutrality. Union with an Eire which had already shown that it was capable of insisting on neutrality in a life and death struggle involving the whole British Commonwealth, could only mean permanently removing Ulster from the mutual security system of the British Commonwealth, and so undermining the central citadel of the British Isles and jeopardizing all the United Nations.

In December 1921 Mr. Lloyd George commended the Irish Treaty to the House of Commons. Speaking to a House still under the shadow of the First World War, he expressed the faith in which the whole of the British Commonwealth had welcomed this charter of Irish freedom: " There are still dangers lurking in the mists. Whence will they come? . . . Who knows? But when they do come I feel glad to know that Ireland will be there by our side, and that the old motto that ' England's danger is Ireland's opportunity ' will have a new meaning." In the Second World War — which was the thing lurking not far ahead in the mists — many thousands of individual Irishmen justified this faith; but into the fourth year of the war the Irish Government had given no sign. One minister, Dr. James Ryan, on January 10, 1942, had hinted at forces seething underneath: " When the position becomes acute there will be some who will favour departing from neutrality. . . . There may possibly be a stampede." When would the position become acute . . . ? — Malaya and the Netherlands Indies gone; Japan at the gates of India; two million Irishmen in Australia standing guard to prevent the Japanese from bursting over the northern boundary; the German Army on the Volga; and the transport of American armies and supplies for the United Nations still held up for lack of facilities that Eire, if it had been a member of the United Nations, could have furnished. Or was Eire's choice already final — to remain in its backwater, watching in uneasy silence the tide flooding back to the ocean, bearing on its crest all the ships of the United Nations to their appointed tasks of founding the new world of tomorrow?

Appendix I

✲

EMERGENCY POWERS (DEFENCE) ACT,
1939

An Act to confer on His Majesty certain powers which it is expedient that His Majesty should be enabled to exercise in the present emergency; and to make further provision for purposes connected with the defence of the realm. (24th August 1939.)

BE it enacted by the King's most Excellent Majesty, by and with the advice and consent of the Lords Spiritual and Temporal, and Commons, in this present Parliament assembled, and by the authority of the same, as follows:

1. (1) Subject to the provisions of this section, His Majesty may by Order in Council make such Regulations (in this Act referred to as " Defence Regulations ") as appear to him to be necessary or expedient for securing the public safety, the defence of the realm, the maintenance of public order and the efficient prosecution of any war in which His Majesty may be engaged, and for maintaining supplies and services essential to the life of the community.

(2) Without prejudice to the generality of the powers conferred by the preceding subsection, Defence Regulations may, so far as appears to His Majesty in Council to be necessary or expedient for any of the purposes mentioned in that subsection,

(a) make provision for the apprehension, trial and punishment of persons offending against the Regulations, and for the detention of persons whose detention appears to the Secretary of State to be expedient in the interest of the public safety or the defence of the realm;

(b) authorise
(i) the taking of possession or control, on behalf of His Majesty, of any property or undertaking; (ii) the acquisition, on behalf of His Majesty, of any property other than land;

(c) authorise the entering and search of any premises; and

(d) provide for amending any enactment, for suspending the operation of any enactment, and for applying any enactment with or without modification.

(3) Defence Regulations may provide for empowering such authorities, persons or classes of persons as may be specified in the Regulations to make orders,

rules and byelaws for any of the purposes for which such Regulations are authorised by this Act to be made, and may contain such incidental and supplementary provisions as appear to His Majesty in Council to be necessary or expedient for the purposes of the Regulations.

(4) A Defence Regulation, and any order, rule or byelaw duly made in pursuance of such a Regulation, shall have effect notwithstanding anything inconsistent therewith contained in any enactment other than this Act or in any instrument having effect by virtue of any enactment other than this Act.

(5) Nothing in this section shall authorise the imposition of any form of compulsory naval, military or air force service or any form of industrial conscription, or the making of provision for the trial by courts martial of persons not being persons subject to the Naval Discipline Act, to military law or to the Air Force Act.

(6) In this section the expression " enactment " includes any enactment of the Parliament of Northern Ireland.

2. (1) The Treasury may by order provide for imposing and recovering, in connection with any scheme of control contained in or authorised by Defence Regulations, such charges as may be specified in the order; and any such order may be varied or revoked by a subsequent order of the Treasury.

(2) Any charges recovered by virtue of such an order as aforesaid shall be paid into the Exchequer of the United Kingdom or, if the order so directs, be paid into such public fund or account as may be specified in the order.

(3) Any such order as aforesaid shall be laid before the Commons House of Parliament as soon as may be after it is made, but, notwithstanding anything in subsection (4) of section one of the Rules Publication Act, 1893, shall be deemed not to be a statutory rule to which that section applies.

(4) Any such order as aforesaid imposing or increasing a charge shall cease to have effect on the expiration of the period of twenty-eight days beginning with the day on which the order is made, unless at some time before the expiration of that period it has been approved by a resolution of the Commons House of Parliament, without prejudice, however, to the validity of anything previously done under the order or to the making of a new order.

In reckoning any period of twenty-eight days for the purposes of this subsection, no account shall be taken of any time during which Parliament is dissolved or prorogued, or during which the Commons House is adjourned for more than four days.

(5) Without prejudice to the preceding provisions of this section, any Defence Regulations may provide —

(a) for charging, in respect of the grant or issue of any license, permit, certificate or other document for the purposes of the Regulations, such fee not exceeding five pounds as may be prescribed under the Regulations with the approval of the Treasury; and

(b) for imposing and recovering such charges as may be so prescribed in respect of any services which, in pursuance of such Regulations, are provided on behalf of His Majesty, or under arrangements made on behalf of His Majesty, other than services necessary for the performance of duties imposed by law upon the Crown;

and all sums received by way of such fees or charges as aforesaid shall be paid into the Exchequer of the United Kingdom or, if the Treasury so direct, be paid into such public fund or account as they may determine.

3. (1) Unless the contrary intention appears therefrom, any provisions contained in, or having effect under, any Defence Regulation shall —

    (a) in so far as they specifically impose prohibitions, restrictions or obligations in relation to ships, vessels or aircraft, or specifically authorise the doing of anything in relation to ships, vessels or aircraft, apply to all ships, vessels or aircraft in or over the United Kingdom and to all British ships or aircraft, not being Dominion ships or aircraft, wherever they may be; and

    (b) in so far as they impose prohibitions, restrictions or obligations on persons, apply (subject to the preceding provisions of this subsection) to all persons in the United Kingdom and all persons on board any British ship or aircraft, not being a Dominion ship or aircraft, and to all other persons being British subjects except persons in any of the following countries or territories, that is to say, —

    (i) a Dominion,

    (ii) India, Burma and Southern Rhodesia,

    (iii) any country or territory to which any provisions of this Act can be extended by Order in Council, and

    (iv) any other country or territory, being a country or territory under His Majesty's protection or suzerainty:

Provided that Defence Regulations may make provision whereby the owner, manager or charterer of any British ship or aircraft, being a person resident in the United Kingdom or a corporation incorporated under the law of any part of the United Kingdom, is subjected to restrictions in respect of the employment of persons in any foreign country or territory in connection with the management of the ship or aircraft.

(2) In this section the expression "Dominion ship or aircraft" means a British ship or aircraft registered in a Dominion, not being a ship or aircraft for the time being placed at the disposal of, or chartered by or on behalf of, His Majesty's Government in the United Kingdom; and, for the purposes of subsection (1) of this section, any ship or aircraft registered in India, Burma or Southern Rhodesia, not being a ship or aircraft for the time being placed at the disposal of, or chartered by or on behalf of, His Majesty's Government in the United Kingdom, shall be treated as if it were a Dominion ship or aircraft.

(3) Subsection (1) of this section shall apply in relation to British protected persons, as that subsection applies in relation to British subjects.

4. (1) His Majesty may by Order in Council direct that the provisions of this Act other than this section shall extend, with such exceptions, adaptations and modifications, if any, as may be specified in the Order,

    (a) to the Isle of Man or any of the Channel Islands,

    (b) to Newfoundland or any colony,

    (c) to any British protectorate,

    (d) to any territory in respect of which a mandate on behalf of the League of Nations has been accepted by His Majesty, and is being exercised by His Majesty's Government in the United Kingdom, and

(e) (to the extent of His Majesty's jurisdiction therein) to any other country or territory being a foreign country or territory in which for the time being His Majesty has jurisdiction;

and, in particular, but without prejudice to the generality of the preceding provisions of this section, such an Order in Council may direct that any such authority as may be specified in the Order shall be substituted for His Majesty in Council as the authority empowered to make Defence Regulations for the country or territory in respect of which the Order is made.

(2) His Majesty may by Order in Council make, or authorise the making of, provision whereby persons offending against any Defence Regulations may be apprehended, tried and punished in the United Kingdom, or any of the countries or territories specified in the preceding subsection, whether section one of this Act extends to that country or territory or not.

5. (1) If and so far as the provisions of any Act for purposes of defence passed by the Parliament of the Commonwealth of Australia or by the Parliament of the Dominion of New Zealand purport to have extra-territorial operation as respects —

(a) ships or aircraft registered in the said Commonwealth or Dominion, or

(b) the employment of persons in relation to British ships or aircraft by owners, managers or charterers of such ships or aircraft who are persons resident in the said Commonwealth or Dominion or corporations incorporated under the law of the said Commonwealth or Dominion or any part thereof,

the said provisions shall be deemed to have such operation.

(2) No law made for purposes of defence by the Indian Legislature or the Federal Legislature of India or by the Legislature of Burma shall, on the ground that it would have extra-territorial operation, be deemed to be invalid in so far as it makes provision whereby any owner, manager or charterer of a British ship or aircraft who is a person resident in India or Burma or a corporation incorporated under the law of India or Burma or any part thereof, is subjected to restrictions in respect of the employment of persons in relation to the ship or aircraft.

Nothing in this subsection shall be taken to prejudice the effect of section ninety-nine of the Government of India Act 1935, or section thirty-three of the Government of Burma Act, 1935.

(3) If and so far as the provisions of any law for purposes of defence made by the Legislature of Southern Rhodesia purport to have extra-territorial operation as respects

(a) aircraft registered in Southern Rhodesia, or

(b) the employment of persons in relation to British aircraft by owners, managers or charterers of such aircraft who are persons resident in Southern Rhodesia or corporations incorporated under the law of Southern Rhodesia,

the said provisions shall be deemed to have such operation.

6. (1) If, as respects any proceedings before a court (whether instituted before or after the commencement of this Act), the court is satisfied that it is expedient,

in the interests of the public safety or the defence of the realm so to do, the court

> (a) may give directions that, throughout, or during any part of, the proceedings, such persons or classes of persons as the court may determine shall be excluded;
>
> (b) may give directions prohibiting or restricting the disclosure of information with respect to the proceedings.

The powers conferred by this subsection shall be in addition to, and not in derogation of, any other powers which a court may have to give such directions as aforesaid.

(2) If any person contravenes any directions given by a court under the preceding subsection, then, without prejudice to the law relating to contempt of court, he shall be liable, on summary conviction, to imprisonment for a term not exceeding three months or to a fine not exceeding one hundred pounds or to both such imprisonment and such fine, or, on conviction on indictment, to imprisonment for a term not exceeding two years or to a fine not exceeding five hundred pounds or to both such imprisonment and such fine.

(3) The operation of subsection (4) of section eight of the Official Secrets Act, 1920, shall be suspended during the continuance in force of this Act.

7. Every document purporting to be an instrument made or issued by any Minister or other authority or person in pursuance of any provision contained in, or having effect under, Defence Regulations, and to be signed by or on behalf of the said Minister, authority or person shall be received in evidence, and shall, until the contrary is proved, be deemed to be an instrument made or issued by that Minister, authority or person; and *prima facie* evidence of any such instrument as aforesaid may, in any legal proceedings (including arbitrations), be given by the production of a document purporting to be certified to be a true copy of the instrument by, or on behalf of, the Minister or other authority or person having power to make or issue the instrument.

8. (1) Every Order in Council containing Defence Regulations shall be laid before Parliament as soon as may be after it is made; but, notwithstanding anything in subsection (4) of section one of the Rules Publication Act, 1893, such an Order shall be deemed not to be a statutory rule to which that section applies.

(2) If either House of Parliament, within the next twenty-eight days on which that House has sat after such an Order in Council as aforesaid is laid before it, resolves that the Order be annulled, the Order shall thereupon cease to have effect except as respects things previously done or omitted to be done, without prejudice, however, to the making of a new Order.

(3) Any power conferred by the preceding provisions of this Act to make an Order in Council shall be constructed as including a power to vary or revoke the Order.

9. The powers conferred by or under this Act shall be in addition to, and not in derogation of, the powers exercisable by virtue of the prerogative of the Crown.

10. (1) In this Act the expression " Dominion " means any Dominion within the meaning of the Statute of Westminster, 1931, except Newfoundland, and includes any territory administered by His Majesty's Government in such a Dominion.

(2) References in this Act to British aircraft shall be constructed as references to aircraft registered in any part of His Majesty's dominions, in any British protectorate or in any territory in respect of which a mandate on behalf of the League of Nations has been accepted by His Majesty and is being exercised by the Government of any part of His Majesty's dominions.

(3) For the avoidance of doubt it is hereby declared that any reference in this Act to Defence Regulations includes a reference to regulations made under any provision of this Act, as extended to any country or territory by an Order in Council under this Act, and that any reference in this Act to any country or territory includes a reference to the territorial waters, if any, adjacent to that country or territory.

11. (1) Subject to the provisions of this section, this Act shall continue in force for the period of one year beginning with the date of the passing of this Act, and shall then expire:

Provided that, if at any time while this Act is in force, an address is presented to His Majesty by each House of Parliament praying that this Act should be continued in force for a further period of one year from the time at which it would otherwise expire, His Majesty may by Order in Council direct that this Act shall continue in force for that further period.

(2) Notwithstanding anything in the preceding subsection, if His Majesty by Order in Council declares that the emergency that was the occasion of the passing of this Act has come to an end, this Act shall expire at the end of the day on which the Order is expressed to come into operation.

(3) The expiry of this Act shall not affect the operation thereof as respects things previously done or omitted to be done.

EMERGENCY POWERS (DEFENCE) ACT,
1940

An Act to extend the powers which may be exercised by His Majesty under the Emergency Powers (Defence) Act, 1939. (22nd May 1940.)

WHEREAS by the Emergency Powers (Defence) Act, 1939, His Majesty was enabled to exercise certain powers for the purpose of meeting the emergency existing at the date of the passing of that Act:

And whereas by reason of the development of hostilities since that date it has become necessary to extend the said powers in order to secure that the whole resources of the community may be rendered immediately available when required for purposes connected with the defence of the Realm:

Now therefore be it enacted by the King's most Excellent Majesty, by and with the advice and consent of the Lords Spiritual and Temporal, and Commons, in this present Parliament assembled, and by the authority of the same, as follows:

1. (1) The powers conferred on His Majesty by the Emergency Powers (Defence) Act, 1939, (hereinafter referred to as the " principal Act ") shall, notwithstanding anything in that Act, include power by Order-in-Council to make such Defense Regulations making provision for requiring persons to place themselves, their services, and their property at the disposal of His Majesty, as appear to him to be necessary or expedient for securing the public safety, the defence of the Realm, the maintenance of public order, or the efficient prosecution of any war in which His Majesty may be engaged, or for maintaining supplies or services essential to the life of the community.

(2) In paragraph (d) of subsection (2) of section one of the principal Act and in subsection (4) of that section the expression " enactment " shall mean any enactment passed before the commencement of this Act.

(3) Subsection (1) of section eleven of the principal Act (which relates to the duration of that Act) shall have effect as if for the words " one year," where those words first occur, there were substituted the words " two years."

2. This Act may be cited as the Emergency Powers (Defence) Act, 1940, and this Act and the Emergency Powers (Defence) Act, 1939, may be cited together as the Emergency Powers (Defence) Acts, 1939 and 1940.

EMERGENCY POWERS (DEFENCE) (NO. 2) ACT, 1940

An Act to remove doubts as to the extent of the powers which may be exercised by His Majesty under the Emergency Powers (Defence) Act, 1939. (1st August 1940.)

WHEREAS by the Emergency Powers (Defence) Act, 1939, His Majesty was enabled to exercise certain powers for the purpose of meeting the emergency existing at the date of the passing of that Act, but the said powers did not enable provision to be made for the trial by courts martial of persons not being subject to the Naval Discipline Act, to military law, or to the Air Force Act:

And whereas by reason of the development of hostilities since that date it has become expedient to remove doubts as to the extent of the said powers in order to secure that provision for the trial of such persons by special courts may be made where necessary:

Now, therefore, be it enacted by the King's most Excellent Majesty, by and with the advice and consent of the Lords Spiritual and Temporal, and Commons, in this present Parliament assembled, and by the authority of the same, as follows:

1. (1) It is hereby declared that the powers conferred on His Majesty by the Emergency Powers (Defence) Act, 1939 (hereinafter referred to as " the principal Act ") to make by Order in Council such Defence Regulations as appear to him to

be necessary or expedient for securing the public safety, the defence of the realm, the maintenance of public order, and the efficient prosecution of any war in which His Majesty may be engaged, include power to make provision for securing that, where by reason of recent or immediately apprehended enemy action the military situation is such as to require that criminal justice should be administered more speedily than would be practicable by the ordinary courts, persons, whether or not subject to the Naval Discipline Act, to military law, or to the Air Force Act, may, in such circumstances as may be provided by the Regulations, be tried by such special courts, not being courts martial, as may be so provided.

(2) After paragraph (a) of subsection (2) of section one of the principal Act there shall be inserted the following paragraph —

"(aa) make provision for the apprehension and punishment of offenders and for their trial by such courts, not being courts martial, and in accordance with such procedure as may be provided for by the Regulations, and for the proceedings of such courts being subject to such review as may be so provided for, so, however, that provision shall be made for such proceedings being reviewed by not less than three persons who hold or have held high judicial office, in all cases in which sentence of death is passed, and in such other circumstances as may be provided by the Regulations: "

and in the said paragraph (a) the words " for the apprehension " trial and punishment of persons offending against the Regulations " and " are hereby repealed.

Appendix II

✦

THE ATLANTIC CHARTER

The President of the United States of America and the Prime Minister, Mr. Churchill, representing His Majesty's Government in the United Kingdom, being met together, deem it right to make known certain common principles in the national policies of their respective countries on which they base their hopes for a better future for the world.

FIRST, Their countries seek no aggrandizement, territorial or other;

SECOND, They desire to see no territorial changes that do not accord with the freely expressed wishes of the peoples concerned;

THIRD, They respect the right of all peoples to choose the form of government under which they will live; and they wish to see sovereign rights and self-government restored to those who have been forcibly deprived of them;

FOURTH, They will endeavour, with due respect for their existing obligations, to further the enjoyment by all States, great or small, victor or vanquished, of access, on equal terms, to the trade and to the raw materials of the world which are needed for their economic prosperity;

FIFTH, They desire to bring about the fullest collaboration between all nations in the economic field with the object of securing, for all, improved labor standards, economic advancement and social security;

SIXTH, After the final destruction of the Nazi tyranny, they hope to see established a peace which will afford to all nations the means of dwelling in safety within their own boundaries, and which will afford assurance that all the men in all the lands may live out their lives in freedom from fear and want;

SEVENTH, Such a peace should enable all men to traverse the high seas and oceans without hindrance.

EIGHTH, They believe that all of the nations of the world, for realistic as well as spiritual reasons, must come to the abandonment of the use of force. Since no future peace can be maintained if land, sea or air armaments continue to be employed by nations which threaten, or may threaten, aggression outside of their frontiers, they believe, pending the establishment of a wider and permanent system of general security, that the disarmament of such nations is essential. They will likewise aid and encourage all other practicable measures which will lighten for peace-loving peoples the crushing burden of armaments.

Franklin D. Roosevelt
Winston S. Churchill

Dated August 14, 1941.

DECLARATION BY UNITED NATIONS

A joint declaration by the United States of America, the United Kingdom of Great Britain and Northern Ireland, the Union of Soviet Socialist Republics, China, Australia, Belgium, Canada, Costa Rica, Cuba, Czechoslovakia, Dominican Republic, El Salvador, Greece, Guatemala, Haiti, Honduras, India, Luxembourg, Netherlands, New Zealand, Nicaragua, Norway, Panama, Poland, South Africa, Yugoslavia.

The governments signatory hereto,

Having subscribed to a common program of purpose and principles embodied in the joint declaration of the President of the United States of America and the Prime Minister of the United Kingdom of Great Britain and Northern Ireland dated August 14, 1941, known as the Atlantic Charter, being convinced that complete victory over their enemies is essential to defend life, liberty, independence and religious freedom, and to preserve human rights and justice in their own lands as well as in other lands, and that they are now engaged in a common struggle against savage and brutal forces seeking to subjugate the world, *Declare:*

1. Each government pledges itself to employ its full resources, military or economic, against those members of the tripartite pact and its adherents with which such government is at war.

2. Each government pledges itself to co-operate with the governments signatory hereto and not to make a separate armistice or peace with the enemies.

The foregoing declaration may be adhered to by other nations which are, or which may be, rendering material assistance and contributions in the struggle for victory over Hitlerism.

Done at Washington, January first, 1942.

TREATY OF ALLIANCE IN THE WAR AGAINST HITLERITE GERMANY AND HER ASSOCIATES IN EUROPE

and of Collaboration and Mutual Assistance Thereafter Concluded between the Union of Soviet Socialist Republics and the United Kingdom of Great Britain and Northern Ireland.

His Majesty the King of Great Britain, Ireland and British Dominions beyond the Seas, Emperor of India, and the Presidium of the Supreme Council of the Union of Soviet Socialist Republics;

Desiring to confirm the stipulations of the agreement between His Majesty's Government in the United Kingdom and the Government of the Union of Soviet

Socialist Republics for joint action in the war against Germany signed at Moscow, July 12, 1941, and to replace them by a formal treaty;

Desiring to contribute after the war to the maintenance of peace and to the prevention of further aggression by Germany or the States associated with her in acts of aggression in Europe;

Desiring, moreover, to give expression to their intention to collaborate closely with one another as well as with the other United Nations at the peace settlement and during the ensuing period of reconstruction on a basis of the principles enunciated in the declaration made Aug. 14, 1941, by the President of the United States of America and the Prime Minister of Great Britain, to which the Government of the Union of Soviet Socialist Republics has adhered;

Desiring finally to provide for mutual assistance in the event of attack upon either high contracting party by Germany or any of the States associated with her in acts of aggression in Europe;

Have decided to conclude a treaty for that purpose and have appointed as their plenipotentiaries;

His Majesty the King of Great Britain, Ireland and the British Dominions Beyond the Seas, Emperor of India, for the United Kingdom of Great Britain and Northern Ireland:

The Right Hon. Anthony Eden, M. P., His Majesty's Principal Secretary of State for Foreign Affairs;

The Presidium of the Supreme Council of the Union of Soviet Socialist Republics:

M. Vyacheslav Mikhailovich Molotov, People's Commissar for Foreign Affairs.

Who, having communicated their full powers, found in good and due form, have agreed as follows:

PART ONE

Article I

In virtue of the alliance established between the Union of Soviet Socialist Republics, the high contracting parties mutually undertake to afford one another military and other assistance and support of all kinds in the war against Germany and all those States which are associated with her in acts of aggression in Europe.

Article II

The high contracting parties undertake not to enter into any negotiations with the Hitlerite Government or any other government in Germany that does not clearly renounce all aggressive intentions, and not to negotiate or conclude, except by mutual consent, any armistice or peace treaty with Germany or any other State associated with her in acts of aggression in Europe.

PART TWO

Article III

1. The high contracting parties declare their desire to unite with other like-minded States in adopting proposals for common action to preserve peace and resist aggression in the post-war period.

2. Pending adoption of such proposals, they will after the termination of hostilities take all the measures in their power to render impossible a repetition of aggression and violation of the peace by Germany or any of the States associated with her in acts of aggression in Europe.

Article IV

Should one of the high contracting parties during the post-war period become involved in hostilities with Germany or any of the States mentioned in Article III, Section 2, in consequence of an attack by that State against that party, the other high contracting party will at once give to the contracting party so involved in hostilities all the military and other support and assistance in his power.

This article shall remain in force until the high contracting parties, by mutual agreement, shall recognize that it is superseded by the adoption of the proposals contemplated in Article III, Section 1. In default of the adoption of such proposals, it shall remain in force for a period of twenty years and thereafter until terminated by either high contracting party as provided in Article VIII.

Article V

The high contracting parties, having regard to the interests of the security of each of them, agree to work together in close and friendly collaboration after the re-establishment of peace for the organization of security and economic prosperity in Europe.

They will take into account the interests of the United Nations in these objects and they will act in accordance with the two principles of not seeking territorial aggrandizement for themselves and of non-interference in the internal affairs of other States.

Article VI

The high contracting parties agree to render one another all possible economic assistance after the war.

Article VII

Each high contracting party undertakes not to conclude any alliance and not to take part in any coalition directed against the other high contracting party.

Article VIII

The present treaty is subject to ratification in the shortest possible time and the instruments of ratification shall be exchanged in Moscow as soon as possible.

It comes into force immediately on the exchange of the instruments of ratification and shall thereupon replace the agreement between the Government of the Union of Soviet Socialist Republics and His Majesty's Government in the United Kingdom signed at Moscow July 12, 1941.

Part One of the present treaty shall remain in force until the re-establishment of peace between the high contracting parties and Germany and the powers associated with her in acts of aggression in Europe.

Part Two of the present treaty shall remain in force for a period of twenty years. Thereafter, unless twelve months' notice has been given by either party to terminate the treaty at the end of the said period of twenty years, it shall continue in force until twelve months after either high contracting party shall have given notice to the other in writing of his intention to terminate it.

In witness whereof the above-named plenipotentiaries have signed the present treaty and have affixed thereto their seals.

Done in duplicate in London on the twenty-sixth day of May, 1942, in the English and Russian languages, both texts being equally authentic.

Anthony Eden
V. Molotov

Appendix III

AGREEMENT BETWEEN THE GOVERNMENTS OF THE UNITED
STATES OF AMERICA AND OF THE UNITED KINGDOM
OF GREAT BRITAIN AND NORTHERN IRELAND
*on the Principles Applying to Mutual Aid in the Prosecution of the
War Against Aggression, Authorized and Provided for by the Act of
March 11, 1941.*

WHEREAS the Governments of the United States of America and the United
Kingdom of Great Britain and Northern Ireland declare that they are engaged in
a cooperative undertaking, together with every other nation or people of like mind,
to the end of laying the bases of a just and enduring world peace securing order
under law to themselves and all nations;

And whereas the President of the United States of America has determined, pursuant to the Act of Congress of March 11, 1941, that the defense of the United
Kingdom against aggression is vital to the defense of the United States of America;

And whereas the United States of America has extended and is continuing to extend to the United Kingdom aid in resisting aggression;

And whereas it is expedient that the final determination of the terms and conditions upon which the Government of the United Kingdom receives such aid and
of the benefits to be received by the United States of America in return therefor
should be deferred until the extent of the defense aid is known and until the progress of events makes clearer the final terms and conditions and benefits which will
be in the mutual interest of the United States of America and the United Kingdom
and will promote the establishment and maintenance of world peace;

And whereas the Governments of the United States of America and the United
Kingdom are mutually desirous of concluding now a preliminary agreement in regard to the provision of defense aid and in regard to certain considerations which
shall be taken into account in determining such terms and conditions and the making of such an agreement has been in all respects duly authorized, and all acts, conditions and formalities which it may have been necessary to perform, fulfill or execute prior to the making of such an agreement in conformity with the laws either
of the United States of America or of the United Kingdom have been performed,
fulfilled or executed as required;

The undersigned, being duly authorized by their respective Governments for
that purpose, have agreed as follows:

497

Article I

This Government of the United States of America will continue to supply the Government of the United Kingdom with such defense articles, defense services, and defense information as the President shall authorize to be transferred or provided.

Article II

The Government of the United Kingdom will continue to contribute to the defense of the United States of America and the strengthening thereof and will provide such articles, services, facilities or information as it may be in a position to supply.

Article III

The Government of the United Kingdom will not without the consent of the President of the United States of America transfer title to, or possession of, any defense article or defense information transferred to it under the Act or permit the use thereof by anyone not an officer, employee, or agent of the Government of the United Kingdom.

Article IV

If, as a result of the transfer to the Government of the United Kingdom of any defense article or defense information, it becomes necessary for that Government to take any action or make any payment in order fully to protect any of the rights of a citizen of the United States of America who has patent rights in and to any such defense article or information, the Government of the United Kingdom will take such action or make such payment when requested to do so by the President of the United States of America.

Article V

The Government of the United Kingdom will return to the United States of America at the end of the present emergency, as determined by the President, such defense articles transferred under this Agreement as shall not have been destroyed, lost or consumed and as shall be determined by the President to be useful in the defense of the United States of America or of the Western Hemisphere or to be otherwise of use to the United States of America.

Article VI

In the final determination of the benefits to be provided to the United States of America by the Government of the United Kingdom full cognizance shall be taken of all property, services, information, facilities, or other benefits or considerations provided by the Government of the United Kingdom subsequent to March 11, 1941, and accepted or acknowledged by the President on behalf of the United States of America.

Article VII

In the final determination of the benefits to be provided to the United States of America by the Government of the United Kingdom in return for aid furnished under the Act of Congress of March 11, 1941, the terms and conditions thereof shall be such as not to burden commerce between the two countries, but to promote mutually advantageous economic relations between them and the betterment of world-wide economic relations. To that end, they shall include provision for agreed action by the United States of America and the United Kingdom, open to participation by all other countries of like mind, directed to the expansion, by appropriate international and domestic measures, of production, employment, and the exchange and consumption of goods, which are the material foundations of the liberty and welfare of all people; to the elimination of all forms of discriminatory treatment in international commerce, and to the reduction of tariffs and other trade barriers; and, in general, to the attainment of all the economic objectives set forth in the Joint Declaration made on August 12, 1941, by the President of the United States of America and the Prime Minister of the United Kingdom.

At an early convenient date, conversations shall be begun between the two Governments with a view to determining, in the light of governing economic conditions, the best means of attaining the above-stated objectives by their own agreed action and of seeking the agreed action of other like-minded Governments.

Article VIII

This Agreement shall take effect as from this day's date. It shall continue in force until a date to be agreed upon by the two Governments.

Signed and sealed at Washington in duplicate this 23ᵈ day of February 1942.

For the Government of the United States of America:

Sumner Welles,
Acting Secretary of State of the
United States of America.

For the Government of the United Kingdom
of Great Britain and Northern Ireland:

Halifax
His Majesty's Ambassador Extraordinary
and Plenipotentiary at Washington

Appendix IV

MEMORANDUM OF AGREEMENT REGARDING INTERNATIONAL TRADE IN WHEAT

1. Officials of Argentina, Australia, Canada and the United States, wheat exporting countries, and of the United Kingdom, a wheat importing country, met in Washington on July 10, 1941 to resume the wheat discussions which were interrupted in London by the outbreak of war in September 1939 and to consider what steps might be taken towards a solution of the international wheat problem.

2. The discussions at Washington, which extended over a period of many months, have made it clear that a satisfactory solution of the problem requires an international wheat agreement and that such an agreement requires a conference of the nations willing to participate which have a substantial interest in international trade in wheat. It was also recognized that pending the holding of such a conference the situation should not be allowed to deteriorate. The Washington Wheat Meeting has recorded the results of its deliberations in the attached Draft Convention in order to facilitate further international consideration of the subject at such time as may be possible and to provide a basis for such interim measures as may be found necessary.

3. The Washington Wheat Meeting has recognized that it is impracticable to convene at the present time the international wheat conference referred to above. Accordingly, the five countries present at that Meeting have agreed that the United States, so soon as after consultation with other countries it deems the time propitious, should convene a wheat conference of the nations having a substantial interest in international trade in wheat which are willing to participate, and that the Draft Convention above mentioned should be submitted to that conference for consideration.

4. In the meantime there should be no delay in the provision of wheat for relief in war-stricken and other necessitous areas so soon as in the view of the five countries circumstances permit. Likewise it is imperative that the absence of control measures over the accumulation of stocks in the four countries now producing large quantities of wheat for markets no longer available should not create insoluble problems for a future conference. Accordingly, the five countries have agreed to regard as in effect among themselves, pending the conclusions of the conference

referred to above, those arrangements described in the attached Draft Convention which are necessary to the administration and distribution of the relief pool of wheat and to the control of production of wheat other than those involving the control of exports.

5. If the conference contemplated above shall have met and concluded an agreement prior to the cessation of hostilities, no further action will be needed by the countries represented at the Washington Meeting. However, if this is not the case, it will be necessary, in order to prevent disorganization and confusion in international trade in wheat, to institute temporary controls pending the conclusions of the conference. Accordingly the five countries agree that in the period following the cessation of hostilities and pending the conclusion of a wheat agreement at the conference referred to the arrangements described in the attached Draft Convention which relate to the control of production, stocks and exports of wheat and to the administration thereof will be brought into effect among themselves. Those arrangements will come into effect on such date as may be unanimously agreed. Announcement of that date will be made within six months after the cessation of hostilities.

6. Pending the conclusions of the conference contemplated above, the five countries, on the cessation of hostilities or such earlier date as they may agree, will regard as in effect among themselves the arrangements described in the attached Draft Convention for the control of the prices of wheat. The determination of prices required to be made in accordance with those arrangements will be made by unanimous consent. If no determination of prices has been made on the cessation of hostilities, the five countries will, pending such determination but for a period not exceeding six months, maintain as the export price of wheat the last price negotiated by the United Kingdom for a bulk purchase of wheat from the principal country of supply; equivalent f.o.b. prices will be calculated for wheats of the other exporting countries and will be adjusted from time to time to meet substantial changes in freight and exchange rates.

7. In taking any decisions under this Memorandum and the arrangements of the Draft Convention which it brings into operation each of the five countries will have one vote, and a two-thirds majority will be required for decision except as otherwise provided herein.

8. The provisions of this Memorandum will be superseded by any agreement reached at the proposed wheat conference or by any arrangements which the five countries and other interested countries may make to deal with the period pending such a conference. In any event they are to terminate two years from the cessation of hostilities.

> ARGENTINA
> AUSTRALIA
> CANADA
> THE UNITED KINGDOM
> THE UNITED STATES

Washington,
April 22, 1942.

Appendix V

�֍

STATEMENT OF POLICY IN REGARD TO AUSTRALIAN SURPLUSES[1]

His Majesty's Governments in the United Kingdom and the Commonwealth of Australia, in consultation, have agreed upon the following statement of principles for dealing, on a basis of co-operation, with the surplus produce of the Commonwealth for the period of the war.

His Majesty's Government in the United Kingdom fully recognise the grave difficulties created for Australian industries by the shortage of shipping. They are anxious to continue taking all the Australian produce that can be shipped. They also appreciate the serious effect upon Australia's economic and financial structure which these difficulties are causing. With a view to minimizing these effects and preventing the impairment of Australia's war effort, the United Kingdom Government are prepared to join with the Commonwealth Government in co-operative arrangements to ease the burden falling on Australia during the war, framed on lines that will not prejudice the post-war position.

The Governments have agreed that the following principles should be applied as a basis for such co-operation:

1. The United Kingdom Government to purchase the Australian produce that can be shipped and to pay for such produce at the price and upon such terms and conditions as are from time to time agreed with the Ministry of Food.
2. The Australian industries to make every effort to adapt their production to shipping possibilities, e.g., deboning, canning or pressing meat.
3. Alternative markets to be developed wherever possible.
4. Reserve stocks of storable foodstuffs to be created up to certain quantities to be agreed.
5. The quantities to be stored to be determined in relation
   (a) to probable demand during or after the war;
   (b) to the importance of the industry to Australia.
6. The financial burden of acquiring and holding these reserve stocks, pending their disposal, to be shared equally between the two Governments.
7. The payments to be made for produce acquired for the reserve stocks to be

---

[1] Cmd. 6287, 1941.

agreed between the two Governments. While it will be necessary to take due account of such matters as costs of storage, depreciation, etc., it is intended that the payments shall be fixed on such a basis as will so far as practicable achieve the objective of keeping the industry operating efficiently, avoiding the creation of unmanageable surpluses.

8. The detailed application of the above principles to be referred to competent representatives from the two countries.

The Commonwealth Government will be ready to collaborate in any discussions which may be convened within the British Commonwealth or internationally to consider marketing or related problems.

Appendix VI

✲

CHRONOLOGICAL EXCERPTS FROM SPEECHES AND DOCUMENTS ILLUSTRATING THE INDIAN POLITICAL CRISIS FROM APRIL TO OCTOBER, 1942

April 28. — Sir Stafford Cripps in describing the course of his mission in the House of Commons:

"But do not let the House or the people of this country imagine that all the results of the War Cabinet's action and my mission are on the debit side . . . the content of the scheme has put beyond all possibility of doubt or question that we desire to give India self-government at the earliest practicable moment and that we wish her to determine for herself the form which that government shall take . . . no responsible Indian leader has challenged our sincerity upon that point. I think it would be accurate to say that this is the first time that such an assertion could be truly made, and it is a most important and significant fact for our future relationships. . . .

". . . It is in fact the past exercising its influence upon all parties that has proved too strong for us, and we must now leave the leaven of better understanding to work quietly toward an ultimate and satisfactory solution of the political problem. . . ."[1]

April 30. — Resignation from Working Committee of All-India Congress Party of Chakravarthi Rajagopalachari, former Premier of Madras, to work for agreement between the Moslem League and the Congress Party on the basis of the acceptance of "Pakistan."

May 2. — Resolution passed by Committee of All-India Congress Party at Allahabad meeting:

"The present crisis, as well as the experience of negotiations with Sir Stafford Cripps, make it impossible for Congress to consider any schemes or proposals which retain even a partial measure of British control and authority in India. . . . It is on the basis of independence alone that India can deal with Britain or other nations.

"The committee repudiates the idea that freedom can come to India through interference or invasion by any foreign nation. . . . In case invasion

---

[1] As reported in *The Times*, London, April 29, 1942.

504

takes place, it must be resisted. Such resistance can only take the form of non-violent non-cooperation. . . ." [2]

July 2. — Appointment of Indian members of British War Cabinet and Pacific War Council and increase of Viceroy's Council to fifteen members.

July 14. — Resolution passed by Working Committee of All-India Congress Party at Wardha meeting:

" Events . . . confirm the opinion of Congressmen that British rule in India must end immediately, not merely because foreign domination, even at its best, is evil in itself and a continuing injury to the subject people, but because India in bondage can play no effective part in defending herself and in affecting the fortunes of war that are desolating humanity. . . .

" This frustration (Cripps negotiations) resulted in a rapid and widespread increase of ill-will against Britain, and a growing satisfaction at the success of Japanese arms.

" The Working Committee view this development with grave apprehension, as this, unless checked, will inevitably lead to the passive acceptance of aggression. The Committee hold that all aggression must be resisted. . . .

" Congress representatives have tried their utmost to bring about a solution of the communal tangle. But this is made impossible by the presence of a foreign Power, and only after ending foreign domination and intervention can . . . the people of India, belonging to all groups and parties, face India's problems and solve them on a mutually agreed basis.

" The present political parties, formed chiefly with a view to attracting the attention of and influencing British power, will then probably cease to function. . . .

" On the withdrawal of British rule from India responsible men and women of the country will come together to form a provisional Government, representative of all important sections of the people of India, which will later evolve a scheme whereby a constituent Assembly can be convened in order to prepare a constitution for the Government of India acceptable to all sections of the people.

" The representatives of free India and Great Britain will confer together for the adjustment of future relations and for the cooperation of the two countries as allies for a common cause in meeting aggression. . . .

" Congress is . . . agreeable to the stationing of the armed forces of the allies in India should they so desire in order to ward off and resist Japanese or other aggression and to protect and help China.

" The proposal for the withdrawal of British power from India was never intended to mean the physical withdrawal of all Britons from India, and certainly not those who would make India their home and live there as citizens and as equals with others. If such a withdrawal takes place with good will, it would result in establishing a stable provisional Government in India, and cooperation between this Government and the United Nations in resisting aggression and helping China. . . .

---

[2] As reported in *The Times,* London, May 4, 1942.

" Should . . . this appeal fail . . . Congress will then reluctantly be compelled to utilize all the non-violent strength it has gathered since 1920, when it adopted non-violence as part of its policy. . . . Such a widespread struggle would inevitably be under the leadership of Mr. Ghandi. . . ." [3]

Resolution referred to meeting of Committee of All-India Congress Party in August.

July 19. — Statement by Pandit Nehru that Congress Party demands not limited to British India.

July 20 — August 4. — Opposition to Wardha resolution expressed by United Provinces Liberal Federation, All-India Scheduled Castes Conference, Radical Democratic Party, Hindu Mahasabha, and Nationalist League (member of National Democratic Union). Opinion of the *Hindu* (Madras) and the *Indian Social Reformer* that Congress Party should have waited for assured support of whole country and for agreement with Moslem community.

July 30. — Statement by Mr. L. S. Amery, Secretary of State for India, in House of Commons in reply to question concerning future protection of British commercial interests in India:

" His Majesty's Government made it clear in connection with the recent offer that a guarantee of special protection for British commercial interests in India would not be a condition for the acceptance of whatever constitution India might evolve after the war, and that any such provisions would more properly be a matter for negotiation with the future Government of India." [4]

Statement by M. A. Jinnah, President of the Moslem League:

" The program of Gandhi and his Hindu Congress has been to blackmail the British and coerce them into establishing a system of government and transfer of power which would establish a Hindu Raj immediately under the aegis of a British bayonet, thereby throwing the Moslems and other minorities and interests at the mercy of the Congress Raj. . . . Gandhi asked for an immediate declaration of independence and freedom for India, with the right for the people to frame their own constitution by a constituent assembly elected by adult franchise — which meant a 75 percent Hindu majority. . . . In 1939 Gandhi asked the Congress Ministries to resign, thereby making the working of a constitution impossible. Then he set upon another method based on the same line of coercion. Under the guise and slogan of ' freedom of speech,' he launched his individual civil disobedience after the August declaration of 1940. . . .

" It was the policy of the British Government that clearly encouraged Gandhi. The British Government had concentrated its attention on the Congress view. . . .

" It was quite obvious for two reasons the British Government dare not surrender to Gandhi's demands. Firstly, because it would be going against the solemn resolve of 100,000,000 Moslems that they stand for ' Pakistan ' and will never submit to a Hindu Raj or any unitary central government with a

---

[3] As reported in *The Times*, London, July 16, 1942.
[4] As reported in *The Times*, London, July 31, 1942.

Hindu majority; and secondly, it would be the grossest breach of faith with the Moslems if the British Government disregarded all its declarations that it could not contemplate the transfer of its present responsibilities to any system of government whose authority was directly denied by large and powerful elements of India's national life.

"Gandhi cannot believe that immediately the British withdraw, the representatives of various parties and interests would at once agree and set up a provisional government for this subcontinent. What is there to prevent them from agreeing now? . . .

"Moslems of India have not the slightest objection to the British withdrawing from India today. But what Moslems fear is that in their dire distress and shaken condition the British may commit the blunder of appeasing the Congress at the cost of Moslem and other minorities. . . ." [4a]

August 4 — Appeal by Sir Tej Bahadur Sapru (Liberal) to leaders of all parties to call joint conference to avert civil disobedience.

Publication by Government of India after raid on Congress Party headquarters of text of resolution originally proposed by Gandhi at Allahabad meeting of Working Committee of Party:

"India's participation in the war has not been with the consent of the representatives of the Indian people. It was purely a British act. If India were freed her first step would probably be to negotiate with Japan. The Congress is of opinion that if the British withdrew from India, India would be able to defend herself in the event of Japanese or any aggressor attacking India.

". . . The Princes need have no fear from unarmed India.

"The question of majority and minority is a creation of the British Government, and would disappear on their withdrawal. . . .

"This committee desires to assure the Japanese Government and people that India bears no enmity either towards Japan or towards any other nation. India only desires freedom from all alien domination. But in this fight for freedom the committee is of opinion that India, while welcoming universal sympathy, does not stand in need of foreign military aid . . . the committee hopes that Japan will not have any designs on India. But if Japan attacks India and Britain makes no response to its appeal the committee would expect all those who look to Congress for guidance to offer complete non-violent non-cooperation to the Japanese forces and not render any assistance to them. . . .

". . . At present our non-cooperation with the British Government is limited. Were we to offer them complete non-cooperation when they are actually fighting it would be tantamount to placing our country deliberately in Japanese hands. Therefore not to put any obstacle in the way of the British forces will often be the only way of demonstrating our non-cooperation with the Japanese. Neither may we assist the British in any active manner. . . .

"It is not necessary for the committee to make a clear declaration in regard to the scorched earth policy . . . it can never be the Congress policy to destroy what belongs to or is of use to the masses.

[4a] As reported by Reuter.

". . . Whether the British remain or not it is our duty always to wipe out unemployment, to bridge the gulf between rich and poor, to banish communal strife, to exorcise the demon of untouchability, to reform dacoits and save the people from them. If crores of people do not take a living interest in this nation-building work, freedom must remain a dream and unattainable by either non-violence or violence.

" The All-India Congress Committee is of opinion that it is harmful to India's interests and dangerous to the cause of India's freedom to introduce foreign soldiers in India. . . .

". . . Japan's quarrel is not with India. She is warring against the British Empire." [5]

August 5. — Statement by Chakravarthi Rajagopalachari:

". . . the only way to save India is to form an interim popular government at once. All suspicions and legalities should be scrapped and full power transferred to such an interim government, subject only to the maintenance of the present war policy and international relations.

". . . I am sure the statesmen of Britain have knowledge of the present feeling of the people of India and also of the peril inherent in the situation. They have imagination and experience enough to see whom the people would trust and whom they would not. . . ." [6]

August 7. — Introduction of civil disobedience resolution to meeting of Committee of Congress Party at Bombay. Statement by Maulana Azad, president of the party:

". . . It is absurd to suggest that we want anarchy and the complete absence of government in the country. What we want is a change of administration. It is also wrong to say that we want the British and American armies to leave India. . . . The slogan " Quit India " means nothing more and nothing less than the complete transfer of power to Indian hands. . . ." [7]

Statement by Gandhi:

". . . We shall get our freedom by fighting. It cannot fall from the skies. I know full well that the British will have to give us our freedom when we have made sufficient sacrifices and proved our strength. . . .

" There is one principle in the fight which you must adopt. Never believe — as I have never believed — that the British are going to fail. . . .

" Sardar Patel is reported to have said that the (civil disobedience) campaign may be over in a week. . . . If it ends in a week it would be a miracle. . . .

" Once independence is obtained, whoever is capable of taking power will do so. . . ." [8]

Order by Government of India prohibiting the closing of food shops and restaurants between specified hours.

---

[5] As reported in *The Times,* London, August 5, 1942.
[6] As reported in *The Times,* London, August 6, 1942.
[7] As reported in *The Times,* London, August 8, 1942.
[8] Ibid.

August 8. — Resolution adopted by Committee of Congress Party:

" . . . The committee has viewed with dismay the deterioration in the situation on the Russian and Chinese fronts. . . . This increasing peril makes it incumbent on all those who strive for freedom and who sympathize with the victims of aggression to examine the foundations of the policy so far pursued by the allied nations which have led to repeated and disastrous failures. . . .

" A free India will assure this success (of freedom and democracy) by throwing all her great resources into the struggle for freedom and against the aggression of Nazism, Fascism, and Imperialism. This will not only affect materially the fortunes of the war but bring all subject and oppressed humanity to the side of the United Nations. . . .

" . . . Only the glow of freedom now can release that energy and enthusiasm in millions of people which will immediately transform the nature of the war. The All-India Congress Committee therefore repeats with all emphasis its demand for the withdrawal of British power from India.

" On the declaration of India's independence, a provisional Government will be formed, and free India will become the ally of the United Nations. . . . A provisional Government can only be formed by the cooperation of the principal parties and groups in the country. . . .

" Its primary functions must be to defend India and resist aggression with all the armed as well as the non-violent forces at its command, together with its allied Powers, and to promote the well-being and progress of workers in the fields and factories and elsewhere to whom essentially all power and authority must belong.

" The provisional Government will evolve a scheme for a constituent assembly. . . . This constitution, according to the Congress view, should be a federal one with the largest measure of autonomy for federating units, and with residuary powers vesting in these units.

" . . . Freedom for India must be a symbol of, and prelude to, the freedom of all other Asiatic nations under foreign domination.

" Burma, Malaya, Indo-China, the Dutch East Indies, Persia, and Iraq must also attain their complete freedom. It must be clearly understood that such of these countries as are under Japanese control now, must not subsequently be placed under the rule or control of any other colonial Power.

" . . . the committee is of opinion that the future peace and security and ordered progress of the world demand a world federation of free nations. . . .

" In view of the war, however, a federation to begin with must inevitably be confined to the United Nations. . . .

" The earnest appeal by the Working Committee to Great Britain and the United Nations has so far met with no response. . . .

" But the committee feels that it is no longer justified in holding the nation back from endeavoring to assert its will against the imperialist and authoritarian Government which dominates it. . . . The committee resolves therefore to sanction . . . the starting of a mass struggle on non-violent lines on the widest possible scale. . . .

" Such a struggle must inevitably be under the leadership of Gandhi, and the committee requests him to take the lead and guide the nation in the steps to be taken. . . ." [9]

Statement by Gandhi:

" We shall make every effort to see the Viceroy before starting the movement." [10]

Statement by Governor-General of India in Council:

". . . The Governor-General in Council has been aware . . . for some days past of the dangerous preparations by the Congress Party for unlawful, and in some cases violent, activities directed, among other things, to interruption of communications and public utility services, the organization of strikes, tampering with the loyalty of Government servants, and interference with defence measures, including recruitment.

". . . To a challenge such as the present there can be only one answer. The Government of India would regard it as wholly incompatible with their responsibilities to the people of India, and their obligations to the allies, that a demand should be discussed the acceptance of which would plunge India into confusion and anarchy internally and would paralyse her effort in the common cause of human freedom. . . .

". . . The Congress Party is not India's mouthpiece, yet, in the interests of securing their own dominance, and in pursuit of a totalitarian policy, its leaders have consistently impeded efforts made to bring India to full nationhood. But for the resistance of the Congress Party to constructive endeavors, India might even now be enjoying self-government.

". . . They (the Government of India) urge the people of India to unite with them in resistance to the present challenge of a party. . . ." [11]

Orders by Government (1) prohibiting publication of " factual news " about civil disobedience movement not obtained from official or authorized sources and (2) empowering provincial governments to supersede local authorities.

August 9. — Arrest of Gandhi and all members of Working Committee of Congress Party who took part in the Bombay meeting. Committee of Congress Party and provincial committees declared illegal associations by Government.

Broadcast statement by Mr. L. S. Amery, Secretary of State for India:

". . . What we are really concerned with is not a demand which no one can take seriously, but the action which Congress has resolved upon. . . .

" There was abundant ground for punitive action, but the Government of India have confined themselves to action which is essentially preventive. What they have in fact done is to disconnect Mr. Gandhi and his confederates, to cut out the fuse leading from the arch-saboteurs to all the inflammable and explosive material which they hoped to set alight all over India.

---

[9] As reported in *The Times,* London, August 7, 1942.

[10] As reported in *The New York Times,* August 9, 1942.

[11] As reported in *The Times,* London, August 10, 1942.

"By their prompt and resolute action the Government of India have saved India and the allied cause from a grave disaster. . . ."[12] Beginning of rioting.

August 19. — Appeal by president of Hindu Mahasabha for:

"(1) Immediate declaration by the British Parliament that India is raised to the position of a completely free and equal partnership — as equal and free as Britain herself in the Commonwealth. (2) During wartime this declaration of India's independence should be implemented by complete Indianization of the Viceroy's Executive Council, the decisions of which should be binding on the Viceroy; the only exceptions being those of military and strategical matters and the suppression of any internal anarchy. (3) Indianization of the Army as rapidly as possible. (4) Provincial governors to have executive councils similar to that of the Viceroy. (5) A conference to be called immediately at the end of the war to frame a national constitution for India and to give full effect to the declaration of independence."[13]

August 20. — Resolution passed by Working Committee of Moslem League making acceptance of Pakistan the condition of participation in any national government.

August 21. — Resignation from Viceroy's Council of Sir Ramaswami Aiyar in order to oppose with complete freedom the Congress Party's "mass action that if unchecked was bound to hamper India's progress and war effort and those of the Indian States in whose well-being and fortune he was vitally interested."[14]

August 24. — Statement by Sir Stafford Cripps for *New York Times:*

". . . The action against Mr. Gandhi and his followers was a decision of the Government of India, supported fully by, but not proposed or initiated by, the British Government."[15]

Statement by Sir Firoz Khan Noon, Defense Member of Viceroy's Council at Aligarh Moslem University:

". . . During his term of office the Viceroy had not on a single occasion overruled him or rejected his advice. . . . On many occasions controversial questions had come before the Executive Council. In no case had the Viceroy vetoed the decision of the majority. . . .

"The political unity of India was the great aim which every Indian ought to have in view. . . . His suggestions were that British India should be divided into five Dominions consisting of 1. Bengal and Assam; 2. the Central Provinces, the United Provinces, and Bihar; 3. Madras; 4. Bombay; and 5. the Punjab, Baluchistan, Sind, and the North-West Frontier.

". . . for certain matters central authority and united effort by the Dominions were essential. These were defense, customs, foreign relations, and

---

[12] Ibid.
[13] As reported in *The Times,* London, August 19, 1942.
[14] As reported in *The Times,* London, August 22, 1942.
[15] As reported in *The Times,* London, August 24, 1942.

currency. For the administration of these four subjects only there should be a central authority, consisting of delegates nominated by the five Dominion Governments. If at any time any Dominion were dissatisfied with the working of the central authority, it should be entitled to secede, but there should also be provision for the seceding Dominion to return to the centre when the point of difference was removed. . . ." [16]

September 12. — Statement by Mr. Churchill in the House of Commons:

". . . The broad principles of the declaration made by His Majesty's Government, which formed the basis of the Lord Privy Seal's mission to India, must be taken as representing the settled policy of the British Crown and Parliament. . . .

" The good offices of the Lord Privy Seal were rejected by the India Congress Party, but that does not end the matter. The Congress Party does not represent all India. It does not represent the majority of the people of India. It does not represent the Hindu masses. It is a political organization, part of a party machine sustained by certain manufacturing and financial interests. Outside that party, and fundamentally opposed to it, are 90,000,000 Moslems, who have their rights of self-expression, 50,000,000 depressed classes . . . and 95,000,000 subjects of the Indian Princes, to whom we are bound by treaty. In all there are 235,000,000 in these three groups out of a total of about 390,000,000 in India. This takes no account of large elements among the Hindus, Sikhs, and Christians who deplore the present policy of the Congress Party.

". . . The Congress Party has now abandoned, in many respects, the policy of non-violence Mr. Gandhi has inculcated in them. It has come into the open as a revolutionary movement designed to paralyse communications by rail and telegraph, and generally to promote disorder, the looting of shops, sporadic attacks on the Indian police, accompanied from time to time by revolting atrocities — the whole having the intention or, at any rate, the effect of hampering the defense of India against the Japanese invader. . . .

" It may well be that these activities of Congress have been aided by Japanese ' Fifth Column ' work on a widely extended scale and with special direction to the strategic points. . . .

" It is fortunate indeed that the Congress Party has no influence with the martial races on whom the defence of India, apart from the British forces, largely depends. Many of these are divided by unbridgable religious gulfs from Hindu Congress and would never consent to be ruled by them. Nor shall they ever be against their will so subjugated. . . .

". . . I may add that large reinforcements have reached India, and the number of white soldiers now in the country, although very small compared with its size and population, is larger than at any time in the British connection. I therefore feel entitled to report to the House that the situation in India at this moment gives no occasion for undue despondency or alarm." [17]

---

[16] As reported in *The Times*, London, August 27, 1942.
[17] As reported in *The Times*, London, September 11, 1942.

September 13. — Statement by M. A. Jinnah that " Congress Party's civil disobedience movement not merely a declaration of war against the British Government, but also a war against the Moslem League, which had not been consulted. . . . Mr. Churchill's reference to the Moslem League as opposing the Congress Party did not mean that the League supported the Government."

September 15. — Statement by Sir Reginald Maxwell, Home Member of Viceroy's Council, in Legislative Assembly:

" The extent of the damage caused and the extreme seriousness at one time of the situation in the whole of Bihar except the most southern districts and the eastern part of the United Provinces had perhaps not been generally appreciated. . . . A large part of the railway systems in this area was put out of action. For a considerable period Bengal was almost completely cut off from northern India, while communications with Madras were interrupted by damage done to the railways in that Presidency. . . .

" There were some aspects of the disturbances which in his view negatived the idea that they were spontaneous. Attacks on railways and communications had started simultaneously in various parts of India. Special implements were used. . . . There was evidence also that the saboteurs had technical knowledge . . . strategic importance of the areas affected and the objects of attack. . . . On the other hand, the ordinary characteristics of spontaneous disturbances were largely absent — looting was less than expected, hartals were not observed to the extent that seemed likely, and the selective nature of the acts of sabotage was brought into relief by the fact that there had been little or no sabotage of industrial plant or machinery. . . .

" . . . The police had been through a very trying ordeal. They had been compelled on many occasions to fire on riotous mobs and gangs of saboteurs, and often in defense of their lives. Thirty-one policemen so far had been reported killed. . . . British and Indian troops had been called out in not less than 60 places, and on a number of occasions they stood by. . . ." [18]

His preliminary figures indicated that in $5\frac{1}{2}$ weeks of rioting 340 persons had been killed and 850 wounded by police, and 318 killed and 153 wounded by British Indian troops, and that 49 police, civil servants, and soldiers had been killed by mobs.[19]

September 16. — Statement by Sir T. B. Sapru (Liberal) and M. R. Jayaker (non-party group) urging attempt to form an Indian national government.

September 23. — Statement in Indian Council of State by the Leader of the House in reply to the question whether the Government of India were prepared to reopen negotiations for the formation of a composite Government:

" That was primarily a question for the Governor-General and the British Government, rather than for the Government of India. . . . Constitutional questions did not come within the purview of the Executive Council." [20]

---

[18] As reported in *The Times,* London, September 16, 1942.
[19] As reported in *The Times,* London, September 17, 1942.
[20] As reported in *The Times,* London, September 24, 1942.

September 28. — Allah Baksh, Premier of Sind (subsequently dismissed) and President of All-India Independent Moslem Conference renounced British title and honors.

October 9. — Statement by Mr. L. S. Amery, Secretary of State for India in the House of Commons:

". . . Indian nationalism, the desire to see India's destiny directed by Indian hands free from all external control, is not confined to any one party in India. It is shared by all. To that aim we in this country have solemnly pledged ourselves before India and before the world. In the name of his Majesty's Government I repeat that pledge today. . . .

". . . We have . . . come to the conclusion that no constitution imposed from without can meet the case. It is for those who have to live under the constitution to find the compromises and concessions which will enable them to work it. It is those who frame the constitution for themselves who will bring to it the good will without which it can never succeed. It is on that principle that his Majesty's Government based the draft declaration of policy which Sir S. Cripps took out to India to discuss with Indian political leaders. . . .

". . . The limitation of any interim Government to the framework of the existing constitution was in any case a necessity so long as the final responsibility for waging the war rested with his Majesty's Government, for it is upon the whole machinery of Government, and not merely upon the Commander-in-Chief's department, that India's war effort depends. . . .

" To understand why the Congress Party executive under Mr. Gandhi's influence was determined to wreck any settlement however generous to India, I must ask the House to go back for a moment to the whole course of Congress policy in recent years. Originally a constitutional party with a programme of evolution towards complete self-government, Congress had in the last generation, and especially since it had come under Mr. Gandhi's autocratic influence, become a party of revolution. . . .

" What I wish to make clear to the House is that . . . this rebellion, to use Gandhi's own words . . . was deliberately resolved upon in order to defeat the generous policy put forward by his Majesty's Government. . . .

" It is idle to suggest that anything could possibly have resulted from negotiations after the passing of the All-India Congress Committee's resolution except the more complete organization of plans for dislocating communications and making rebellion effective. . . .

" The firmness of the Government, loyally supported by the civil service, the police, and when it became necessary, the army, has broken the back of the movement. . . . The forces of law and order will for months to come have to be unceasingly vigilant, and will need all the support that the Government of India and this House can give them. . . .

" For all this tragic business the responsibility and the whole responsibility must rest with Mr. Gandhi and the Congress leaders. . . .

". . . So far as Congress is concerned, its leaders have by their action put themselves out of court. There can be no question of the Government of India entering upon negotiations with them or allowing others to do so so long as there is any danger of a recrudescence of the troubles for which they have been responsible, or until they have made it clear to the authorities that they have abandoned the whole policy of securing control of India by illegal and revolutionary methods and are prepared to come to an agreed settlement with the rest of their fellow-countrymen. . . ." [21]

October 21. — Statement to the press by Chakravarthi Rajagopalachari:

". . . The Viceroy should immediately invite the most popular and responsible Indian leaders to form a Government. Thereafter the Viceroy should arrange for direct elections to the provincial Legislatures and indirect elections to the Central Legislature from provincial Legislatures. . . .

". . . it was a calumny to say that Mr. Jinnah and the League wanted partition of the country today. What Mr. Jinnah wanted was that in a postwar decision that issue should not be prejudged. It would be open to the provisional Government which he proposed to give such an assurance in the clearest possible terms. . . . The Viceroy should select for the Government five Congress men whom the Viceroy thought would be likely to head the poll at the election — including persons now in prison — and ask Mr. Jinnah to join the Government with as many men of his choice as he liked. . . . The Congress Party and Moslem League nominees should add to themselves, say, three persons representative of any important interests left out. . . .

". . . The Viceroy could easily envisage the kind of Legislature that the Government would have to face, and could make his selection accordingly. If the Government did not get the confidence of the Legislature, the Viceroy, acting for the Crown, could dismiss the one or dissolve the other.

". . . Britain's temporary hold on India today was, by its own admission, only for the purpose of the war, and should therefore be exercised in such a way as to help the war. . . ." [22]

April 2, 1943. — Letter to American Defense, Harvard Group, by Sumner Welles, Under Secretary of State:

" You also mention our ' failure to mediate in Indian affairs ' as a criticism of the Department of State. The present military situation in the Far East is one in which all of us, including the people of India, face grave perils. The future constitutional status of India is a tremendously complicated and delicate problem. The United States Government is, of course, anxious to give full assistance to its solution. The people of India have been most solemnly assured that as soon as the necessities of war permit they will be given the opportunity to choose freely the form of government they desire. Wise men, vitally concerned both with the welfare of the people of India and with the defeat of our enemies, may differ as to the possibility of fighting the war and solving India's historic problems at the same time. But to make active intervention in the Indian situation a test of liberalism, as some have done, presupposes a definition of liberalism which, I must confess, is beyond my comprehension." [23]

---

[21] As reported in *The Times,* London, October 9, 1942.
[22] As reported in *The Times,* London, October 22, 1942.
[23] U. S. State Department *Bulletin,* Vol. VIII, No. 199, April 17, 1943.

Index

i

THE TEXT OF THIS BOOK IS SET IN GRANJON,
a type named in compliment to ROBERT GRANJON, type-
cutter and printer — Antwerp, Lyons, Rome, Paris — active
from 1523 to 1590. The boldest and most original designer
of his time, he was one of the first to practise the trade of
type-founder apart from that of printer.

This type face was designed by GEORGE W. JONES, who
based his drawings upon a type used by CLAUDE GARAMOND
(1510–61) in his beautiful French books, and more closely
resembles Garamond's own than do any of the various modern types that bear his name.

This book was composed, printed, and bound by THE
PLIMPTON PRESS, Norwood, Mass.

THE PROSE WORKS OF

*W*ILLIAM *B*YRD

OF *W*ESTOVER

THE PROSE WORKS OF

*W*ILLIAM *B*YRD

OF *W*ESTOVER

Narratives of a Colonial Virginian

Edited by

Louis B. Wright

THE BELKNAP PRESS OF

HARVARD UNIVERSITY PRESS

Cambridge, Massachusetts

1966

$\mathcal{P}$REFACE

$\mathcal{A}$ NEW edition of the literary prose works of William Byrd II of Westover has long been needed. For many years an edition collated with the original Westover Manuscripts was impossible because that document was in private hands and could not be seen. But in 1962 the Virginia Historical Society acquired the folio volume of the Westover Manuscripts from the owners and immediately made it available. The present editor wishes to thank the Virginia Historical Society for its courtesy in providing a microfilm copy of the manuscripts for purposes of comparison. Mr. John Jennings, the director of the Virginia Historical Society, has been particularly helpful.

In preparing the text for publication, we have modernized eccentricities of spelling, punctuation, and capitalization, but we have changed no words nor tampered with Byrd's grammar. The text is as precisely accurate as human fallibility permits. Although we cannot be certain that we have not erred in interpreting Byrd's handwriting here and there, we have made every effort to achieve accuracy.

The spelling of proper names has raised problems, for Byrd himself was not consistent. Where proper names have a modern accepted form, we have followed the practice of regularizing them. But where Byrd's spelling indicates a variation in pronunciation, or a form different from the modern word (as distinct from a mere eccentricity of spelling), we have retained the form as Byrd wrote it.

The notes prepared by William K. Boyd identifying persons mentioned in the *Secret History*, which Boyd edited in 1929, are still valid, and we have reprinted many of them verbatim with proper credit to him.

PREFACE

A study of the provenance and relations of the manuscripts, made by Mrs. William Leonard, is reproduced in the Appendix. I am indebted to Mrs. Leonard for her careful study of these manuscripts. Mr. Whitfield Bell of the American Philosophical Society and Mr. Francis Berkeley of the University of Virginia have supplied information and data useful in explaining the relationship of the various manuscripts. I am grateful to the staff of Harvard University Press for their invariable helpfulness. I am greatly in the debt of Miss Virginia LaMar, chief editor of the Folger Publications, for assistance in solving various problems and in the preparation of the notes. To Mrs. John Bates and to Mrs. John Hendrickson I wish to express my appreciation for their transcription of manuscripts and the typing of difficult copy.

Louis B. Wright

February 5, 1965

CONTENTS

ILLUSTRATIONS

INTRODUCTION

WILLIAM BYRD AS A
MAN OF LETTERS

ONE of the most urbane writers of the colonial period in British America was William Byrd of Westover in Virginia, the second of his name in the colony, whose narrative, *The History of the Dividing Line betwixt Virginia and North Carolina, Run in the Year of Our Lord 1728,* has become a classic of early American literature. Byrd never permitted this account to be printed in his lifetime, but he allowed various friends in both Virginia and England to read it in manuscript. This document, along with others written by Byrd, remained unpublished until 1841, when Edmund Ruffin brought out at Petersburg, Virginia, a volume bearing the title *The Westover Manuscripts: Containing the History of the Dividing Line betwixt Virginia and North Carolina; A Journey to the Land of Eden, A.D. 1733; and A Progress to the Mines. Written about 1728 to 1736, and Now First Published.*

Although Ruffin was the first to print Byrd's principal prose writings, they were known to some of the author's contemporaries and to others in a later period. Thomas Jefferson, for example, interested himself in trying to have the Westover Manuscripts published. Byrd was not one to hide his light under a bushel, but he was a perfectionist about his writing, and he was unwilling to turn over the manuscript to a publisher until he had given it an ultimate polishing. As a proud and dandified colonial gentleman, eager to retain the good opinion of aristocratic friends in England, he felt a certain diffidence about rushing into print like any common scribbler. As was the way of dilettantes of letters, he preferred to have his writings circulate genteelly in manuscript until such time as he could bring them out in a manner befitting a gentleman.

He may also have enjoyed arousing the curiosity of his friends about his literary efforts. For example, Peter Collinson, the English naturalist and virtuoso, who corresponded with many Americans, was

I

eager to see Byrd's narrative, which he had heard about, and wrote to ask if he could borrow a copy. In a letter written in 1736, Byrd made an excuse that the treatise was not yet finished, but he would send him the journal if he promised to let only Sir Charles Wager see it. Another naturalist, Mark Catesby, however, saw a copy and praised Byrd for it, to which the author replied in 1737: "I am obliged to you for the compliment you are pleased to make to my poor performances. 'Tis a sign you never saw them that you judge so favorably . . . It will seem like a joke when I tell you that I have not time to finish that work. But 'tis very [certain] I have not, for I am always engaged on some project for improvement of our infant colony. The present scheme is to found a city at the falls of the James River, and plant a colony of Switzers on my land upon Roanoke." [1]

That Byrd was hoping to publish his book appears from a letter that he wrote to Collinson on July 5, 1737, saying that he expected to finish his history during the next winter; he asked Collinson's aid in having illustrations made of animals that he described. We do not know why Byrd did not complete the manuscript and send it to press. For a man who was constantly reading and writing, it is incredible that he could not find time to put the last finishing touches on the document. Either his sense of perfection or his aristocratic notions about committing his work to print prevented the publication.

William Byrd's attitude toward his writings was conditioned by his social milieu and his own personal predilections. Few men of his generation so perfectly reflected the society in which they moved as did William Byrd of Westover, one of the most cultivated members of the landed ruling class of Virginia and a social aspirant in the drawing rooms of the aristocrats of early Georgian England. Byrd was wealthy, well-read, well-traveled, and socially acceptable in any society. He chose to be a social climber in England and to cultivate the friendship of titled Englishmen. But the social aspirations which he displayed in his years in England were not merely evidences of personal vanity; the contacts that he so sedulously cultivated were neces-

---

[1] Cited by John Spencer Bassett, *The Writings of Colonel William Byrd of Westover in Virginia* (New York, 1901), p. lxxix.

sary to him as the agent for the colony of Virginia, an office that he held on various occasions. And they were useful to him in his search for a rich wife, a pursuit that occupied some of his time abroad. It was necessary for him to be mindful of those things expected of a gentleman and a beau in the reigns of the first two Georges.

William Byrd the writer was the son of William Byrd I, himself a wealthy planter, landowner, and Indian trader. The father had come to Virginia sometime before 1670, in which year, as a youth of eighteen, he inherited from his uncle, Thomas Stegge, Jr., a considerable estate which Stegge had acquired by way of trade. Trade was in the blood, for William Byrd I's father had been a goldsmith of London, and Stegge had probably induced his nephew to come to Virginia to help him with his own trade with the Indians. Certainly the nephew quickly adapted himself to the life that his uncle had planned for him and became one of the most important traders in Virginia. He employed pack trains to travel to the back country with trading goods — beads, pots, pans, blankets, rum, guns, lead for bullets, and anything else in demand from the natives — and these pack trains brought back a rich freight of beaver skins, mink, otter, and other furs, as well as deerskins and an occasional buffalo robe. How far Byrd's traders penetrated into the interior can never be known, for these pioneers were closemouthed about their activities, but it is fairly certain that they reached the mountain region. With his profits, Byrd added land to his estate.

Always with an eye on the main chance, William Byrd I made a good match in 1673 with Mary Horsmanden, daughter of Warham Horsmanden, a royalist from East Anglia. Mary was already the widow of Samuel Filmer. The couple's first child, a son born on March 28, 1674, was named William after his father. In time Mary bore Byrd three other children, all daughters. All of the children were sent to England to be educated under the direction of their maternal Grandfather Horsmanden, of Purleigh, in Essex. The youngest, Ursula, at the age of seventeen married Robert Beverley, the historian, and died at the birth of her first child.

The future author of the *Dividing Line* left for England when he was a child of seven and did not return until 1696, when he was a young man of twenty-two. Thus in education he was an Englishman. During his formative youth he lived through the later years of Charles II's reign, saw the events of the Glorious Revolution of 1688, and remained in London until the middle years of William III's reign. His education was that of a son of a prosperous family well connected with the gentry. His grandfather placed him in Felsted Grammar School in Essex under a famous schoolmaster, Christopher Glasscock. It was this school that Oliver Cromwell had chosen for his sons, not because of its political point of view but because of its reputation for sound classical learning. Byrd's grandfather, though a royalist, evidently concurred in this faith in the school, and Byrd's father wrote to the headmaster to express his own "hearty thanks" for the lad's excellent instruction. The elder Byrd hoped that the boy would not "be discouraged in his fair proceedings." That young Byrd received a good grounding in the classics and acquired a taste for learning was demonstrated throughout his life. In his later diaries he constantly reports reading Latin, Greek, and Hebrew and occasionally mentions his own efforts at translating something from the classics. Christopher Glasscock found an apt pupil and left a profound impression upon him.

Byrd's father, a realistic businessman as well as a member of the aristocratic landed class in Virginia, had no notion of making a mere scholar of his son and heir. He realized that when the youth eventually inherited his estate he would have heavy responsibilities that required a knowledge of business as well as the cultivation expected of a gentleman. In this period, Virginia had no towns, and each great tobacco planter shipped tobacco directly from his own docks to his factor in London or Bristol; furthermore, he frequently bought tobacco from small farmers and sold them goods imported from England. Added to these normal transactions, William Byrd I had the responsibility of an extensive Indian trade that he had developed. All of these multifarious duties would in time devolve upon his only son, who had to be trained for his tasks. To this end, when William was sixteen, Byrd instructed his London factors, the merchant house of Perry & Lane, to send the boy to Holland for additional experience in business and trade. Apparently young Byrd did not like Holland, for he wrote his father asking permission to return to London. Whereupon Byrd replied that he had instructed Perry & Lane "to employ you about business wherein I hope you will endeavor to acquaint yourself that you may be no stranger to it when necessity will require you to attend to it." [2]

For two years after his return from Holland in 1690, young Byrd employed his time in the countinghouse of Perry & Lane learning what he could about the tobacco trade and the ways of business in the later years of the seventeenth century. But since his father did not intend his heir to become merely another London merchant, he saw to it that the youth entered the Middle Temple in April 1692, where in due course he was admitted to the bar.

The life of an incipient lawyer in one of the Inns of Court in the last decade of the seventeenth century was not dedicated exclusively to poring over Coke's *Reports* and other volumes interpreting English law. Some of the most illustrious families in Great Britain were represented in the membership of the Inns of Court, and many writers and other intellectuals of the day frequented the Inns, where they formed lasting friendships.

Byrd found the life congenial. Not only did he meet many Englishmen whose acquaintance served his ends in later years, but he found there other colonials with whom he formed useful friendships. Many years later, in 1735, Byrd wrote to Benjamin Lynde of Salem, Massachusetts, then a dignified judge, to recall their mutual escapades in the Middle Temple:

If I could persuade our captain of the guard ship to take a cruise to Boston at a proper season, I would come and beat up your quarters at Salem. I want to see what alteration forty years have wrought in you since we used to intrigue together in the Temple. But matrimony has atoned sufficiently for such backslidings, and now I suppose you have so little fellow feeling left for the naughty jades that you can order them a good whipping without any relenting. But though I should be mistaken, yet at least I hope

[2] Cited in Louis B. Wright, *The First Gentlemen of Virginia* (San Marino, Calif., 1940; paperback edition, University Press of Virginia, 1964), p. 321. This volume gives an account of the social background of Byrd and his contemporaries in Virginia.

your conscience with the aid of threescore-and-ten has gained a complete victory over your constitution, which is almost the case of, sir, your, &c.[3]

Almost but not quite, in Byrd's case, one should note incidentally, for in his diary for February 25, 1741, when he was sixty-seven, he notes that he "played the fool with Sarah, God forgive me. However, I prayed and had coffee." Other similar entries indicate that the habits of the gay life that he led at the Middle Temple lingered into old age.

Byrd's life at the Middle Temple served as a sort of literary apprenticeship, for, although he himself was not actively pursuing the profession of letters, he made the acquaintance at this time of several important writers, among them Charles Boyle (later the Earl of Orrery), William Congreve, William Wycherley, and Nicholas Rowe. Rowe was to become the first biographer of Shakespeare and the editor of his works. With such companions as these Byrd could hardly have avoided developing a taste for contemporary literature and the theater. We know from entries in his diaries that he frequently went to see plays, though, unlike Samuel Pepys, he rarely mentions the name of the play or his reaction to the performance.

Among his friends and acquaintances were also some who were interested in science, and Byrd managed to get himself elected to membership in the Royal Society on April 29, 1696. That a youth of twenty-two not yet known for any scientific accomplishments or literary activities should have been elected to this body of virtuosi argues some influence in high place, which, indeed, was true, for Byrd had cultivated the friendship of Sir Robert Southwell, Principal Secretary of State for Ireland, who served as president of the Royal Society from 1690 until 1696.

Byrd had a peculiar genius for picking the right people to be his friends, and his choice of Southwell illustrated this skill in the young Virginian. It was through Southwell's influence that Byrd met Sir Hans Sloane, Sir William Petty, and other scientific minds of the day. Byrd himself had a curiosity about natural philosophy and found

[3] Cited by Louis B. Wright in the introduction to *William Byrd of Virginia: The London Diary, 1717–1721*, edited by Louis B. Wright and Marion Tinling (New York, 1958), pp. 9–10. This introduction provides a succinct life of William Byrd incorporating recent discoveries concerning his career and background.

William Byrd As a Young Man

*(This painting, by an unknown artist, is believed to be the
earliest of the known portraits of Byrd; it may have been
painted in London between 1692 and 1695, while Byrd was
a member of the Middle Temple. Formerly at Westover, it
now hangs in the Capitol at Williamsburg.)*

Westover As It Appears Today

Bookplate of William Byrd II

association with these men to his liking. He valued highly his membership in the Royal Society, and was much distressed in later years when his name happened to be omitted from a published list of members. To complain of this slight, he wrote to Sir Hans Sloane in 1641:

I take it a little unkindly, Sir, that my name is left out of the yearly list of the Royal Society, of which I have the honor to be one of its ancientest members. I suppose my long absence has made your secretaries rank me in the number of the dead, but pray let them know I am alive and by the help of ginseng hope to survive some years longer.[4]

Soon after his election, Byrd felt a compulsion to demonstrate his own qualifications by submitting a paper entitled "An Account of a Negro Boy That Is Dappled in Several Places of His Body with White Spots. By Will. Byrd, Esq., F.R.S.," which he read to the Society on November 17, 1697, and had published in the *Philosophical Transactions* (XIX, 781–782, London, 1698). It is not recorded that his essay made any important contribution to an understanding of albinism, but it did give evidence of his concern with natural phenomena.

During his years at the Middle Temple, Byrd probably tried his hand at writing light verse and translating bits from the classics, for we have evidence in the diaries of a later date that he amused himself from time to time in this way. At any rate, in one of his notebooks in the University of North Carolina Library he has left a short translation of the story of the Matron of Ephesus from the *Satyricon* of Petronius Arbiter. He may have been the collaborator of William Burnaby, a Middle Temple colleague, in the translation of Petronius published in 1694, *The Satyr of Titus Petronius Arbiter, a Roman Knight, with Its Fragments Recovered at Belgrade, 1688, Made English by Mr. Burnaby of the Middle Temple, and Another Hand.* In view of Byrd's long-continued interest in Petronius, as evidenced by his entries in the diaries, his may have been the other hand.

Besides these literary and scientific friends, Byrd also cultivated other men of prominence, including Charles Wager, knighted in 1709 and created First Lord of the Admiralty in 1733; John Campbell, who in 1703 became the second Duke of Argyll and in 1715 commanded

[4] Cited *ibid.*, p. 10.

the Hanoverian troops against the Jacobite rebels in Scotland; and John Percival, created Earl of Egmont in 1733 and an associate of General James Oglethorpe in the development of the colony of Georgia. With these and other important English aristocrats, Byrd kept up a correspondence long after his student days in London. Later he had the portraits of some of his titled English friends painted so that he could hang their likenesses in his house at Westover and impress his Virginia neighbors.

The education available to a well-bred young Virginian backed by a county family in Essex extended far beyond books and moot courts at the Middle Temple. Moving in the most sophisticated circles of London society, Byrd acquired the cultivation, the polish, the manners, and the vices of the beaux of his time. He also made the contacts that later would prove invaluable to him when he was appointed to represent his colony before the Board of Trade and other official bodies in England.

The senior William Byrd back in Virginia, anxious about his heir who had been absent so long, in 1696 called him home. To establish him properly among the best people, he contrived to have his son elected to the House of Burgesses as a representative from Henrico County. The young lawyer from the Middle Temple, more Englishman than Virginian, showed a quality of easy adaptation to his new environment that was characteristic of Byrd throughout his life. However much he enjoyed London and England, and though he spent many years there in his youth and afterward, he was able to resume plantation life without any evidence of unhappiness.

A Virginian with so many useful contacts in London could not hope to remain long at home, for the colonials had frequent need of an advocate in England. Consequently Byrd found himself on the way back to London in 1697, within a few months after he had served his first term in the House of Burgesses. The journey was dictated by a combination of personal business for his father and political activities for the Virginia Assembly and Governor Edmund Andros of Virginia. In April 1697 he presented an address from the Virginia Assembly to the Board of Trade, and in December he served as attorney for

Andros at a hearing called at Lambeth Palace by the Archbishop of Canterbury and the Bishop of London to consider complaints made by James Blair, Commissary of the Bishop of London in Virginia, that the Governor was blocking the Commissary's efforts to support the College of William and Mary and to improve the clergy in his jurisdiction.[5] This was the beginning of a long feud with James Blair, a stubborn Scot, who managed to get Andros recalled despite an able defense made by the twenty-three-year-old attorney.

During the next few years Byrd remained in London and, as agent for the colony, carried out various political missions. In a long controversy between the colony and Governor Francis Nicholson involving the respective prerogatives of the Virginia Assembly and the Governor, Byrd represented the Assembly against Nicholson,[6] who at last in 1705 was recalled. Nicholson during his governorship aroused the indignation of the Virginians by opposing the growing and processing of cotton and flax, which he feared might injure the English market for textiles. The Virginians, on their part, claimed that shipping was so difficult in time of war that they stood in danger of going naked unless they themselves took steps to produce textiles. Byrd and his brother-in-law, Robert Beverley the historian, both argued in behalf of the Virginia point of view, and Byrd made representations before the Board of Trade, but the London mercantilists were obdurate in their opposition. Though Byrd was not altogether successful in his efforts in behalf of the colony, he gained useful experience. Nicholson, however, achieved a modicum of revenge upon Byrd by dividing the office of auditor and receiver-general of quitrents, an office that the senior Byrd had held for years and had expected his son to inherit; this action resulted in a financial loss to the Byrds.

Although young Byrd was more at home in London than in Virginia, he was obliged to return to the place of his birth in 1705 to look after the inheritance that his father left at his death on December 4,

---

[5] For an account of this affair, see Louis B. Wright, "William Byrd's Defense of Sir Edmund Andros," *The William and Mary Quarterly*, 3rd Ser., 2:47–62 (January 1945).

[6] Details of this episode may be found in Louis B. Wright, "William Byrd's Opposition to Governor Francis Nicholson," *The Journal of Southern History*, 11:68–79 (February 1945).

1704. It was a princely estate that included more than twenty-six thousand acres of land. The home plantation at Westover alone contained fourteen thousand acres, with a comfortable manor house of wood, which William Byrd II rebuilt in brick. In addition to the land on the James at Westover, Byrd owned land farther up the river on the present site of Richmond.

The heir of this legacy quickly assumed the responsibilities and the privileges that had been his father's. He obtained the office of receiver-general of the colony's revenues and in 1709 took his seat on the Council of State, the highest official body in the colony and the goal of every member of the aristocratic ruling class.

In the meantime, on May 4, 1706, he married Lucy Parke, daughter of Daniel Parke, Governor of the Leeward Islands, a marriage that mingled affection with stormy quarrels. Parke had married a daughter of Philip Ludwell and owned land in Virginia. Lucy's sister Frances, who married John Custis, proved such a shrew that Custis had engraved on his own tombstone an epitaph declaring that his bachelor days were the only peace he knew before death. Byrd's father-in-law, who was killed in an insurrection in the Leeward Islands, left to Byrd's wife a legacy of £1,000, but to Custis' wife he bequeathed his lands, which Byrd had hoped to get. All his life, William Byrd was greedy for land.

Parke also left debts which had to be paid for out of the sale of a portion of his estate. Seeing an opportunity to obtain at least part of Parke's Virginia land, Byrd agreed to obligate himself to pay Parke's debts in exchange for the lands that would have to be sold. This agreement was a disaster for Byrd, who did not bother to ascertain in advance the extent of Parke's indebtedness. As a result he found himself burdened with financial obligations that persisted through most of his life.

For this period, when Byrd was adapting himself to the life of a Virginia planter, we have ample documentation in the first portion of his diary covering the years 1709–1712.[7] In the daily entries we can

[7] *The Secret Diary of William Byrd of Westover, 1709–1712*, edited by Louis B. Wright and Marion Tinling (Richmond, Va., 1941). An abridgment of this

follow the routine of a young married man eager to establish himself as a member of the ruling hierarchy with all the material wealth that went with his position. He is conscientious about his duties to the commonwealth, ambitious to improve his estate, attentive to all the details of managing his plantation, and concerned with maintaining his intellectual and literary interests. A passage for June 4, 1709, picked at random, illustrates his routine:

I rose at 5 o'clock and read a chapter in Hebrew and some Greek in Josephus. I said my prayers and ate milk for breakfast. I danced my dance [setting-up exercises that he took regularly]. My man Jack was pretty well. We made some wine of the common cherry for an experiment. It was extremely hot this day. I was out of humor with my wife for not minding her business. I ate roast shoat and sallet for dinner. In the afternoon I read some Latin and some Greek in Homer. In the evening Mr. C—s came to see me, who is a man of good understanding, and Ned Randolph brought me a letter from Mr. Bland in which he told me that the Lord Lovelace was dead at New York. We took a walk. I said my prayers and had good health, good thoughts, and good humor, thanks be to God Almighty.

This entry, like hundreds of others in his diaries, shows Byrd's devotion to learning, for throughout a long lifetime he kept up his Hebrew, Latin, and Greek, besides French, Italian, and Dutch, which he also read. In addition, it suggests an innate piety that remained with him through life, whatever his occasional lapses from moral rectitude may have been. His prayers were constant, and he had a taste for sermons as reading matter. For example, on Christmas night, 1710, he notes, "In the evening I read a sermon in Mr. Norris but a quarrel which I had with my wife hindered my taking much notice of it. However we were reconciled before we went to bed, but I made the first advance."

In August of 1709 Byrd notes that he is busy arranging books in his library, which was already one of the best in the colonies. Clearly he had spent many hours in England visiting bookshops. Eventually he collected more than 3,600 titles, a number only equaled at this time by the library of Cotton Mather in Boston. Curiously, these two men, so alien from one another in most ways, bought and read many

volume appears as *The Great American Gentleman: William Byrd of Westover in Virginia. His Secret Diary for the Years 1709–1712* (New York, 1963).

books on the same subjects. Byrd's library contained some 150 works of divinity, about the same as the number of his law books. Of Greek and Roman classics, in their original languages, he had nearly 300 titles, and he had probably the best collection of belles lettres, including contemporary drama, in the British colonies. Like other colonial libraries, Byrd's collection also had a number of utilitarian books, including an assortment of medical and scientific works. He fancied himself something of a physician and was constantly prescribing some remedy for his servants and neighbors. Byrd's library was the source of much pleasure and pride; he sometimes expressed annoyance because a chance visitor took him from his books; at other times he was delighted to show off his library, as on July 12, 1710, when he noted a visit by Dr. William Cocke and added, "The Doctor, who is a man of learning, was pleased with the library."

Byrd was too busy with plantation affairs and politics to turn his attention to many literary efforts during these years, but on at least one occasion his facility with the pen got him into trouble. During a meeting of the House of Burgesses in Williamsburg in November 1710, Byrd took it upon himself to write a satire of some of the members and their actions. On November 24, 1710, he notes:

I directed a letter to Nat Burwell with a lampoon in it and threw it into the capitol and Mr. [John] Simons found it and gave it him, which put the House of Burgesses into a ferment, but I discovered to nobody that I had a hand in it . . . About 4 o'clock we went to dinner and I ate boiled pork. Then we went to the coffeehouse where I played at cards and I lost my money but was diverted to see some of the burgesses so concerned at the lampoon.

The peace of anonymity and the enjoyment of the Burgesses' discomfiture ended with an untoward incident on November 26, which disclosed the authorship of the satire. After a session at the coffeehouse, Byrd writes: "Before we had been there long, in came George Mason [grandfather of the author of the Virginia Bill of Rights] very drunk and told me before all the company that it was I that wrote the lampoon and that Will Robertson dropped it. I put it off as well as I could but it was all in vain for he swore it." Previously the Burgesses had voted "that a scandalous paper lately found be privately kept by the clerk and that the author thereof, if discovered, be liable to the censure of this House."[8] The clerk kept the document so privately that this evidence of Byrd's literary quality has been lost to posterity.

Byrd's political ambitions led him in 1710 to attempt to procure the office of lieutenant governor for himself. The titular governor was the Earl of Orkney, who, like many who held colonial sinecures, was an absentee who ruled by deputy. The lieutenant governor of Virginia was therefore actually *de facto* governor, and the office was worth a high fee. An age which regarded as commonplace the sale of commissions in the army and navy and the auction of almost any office in the government saw nothing improper in William Byrd's bid of £1,000 for the lieutenant governorship of Virginia. Unhappily, the Duke of Marlborough, a veteran of the wars, declared that none but a soldier ought to govern a plantation overseas, and Byrd was disappointed. The appointment went to Alexander Spotswood, with whom Byrd had many political and personal controversies but at last managed to establish a friendship.

By late 1714 or early 1715 Byrd was again in England. Personal and public business dictated the journey; Byrd went with a mandate from some of the ruling hierarchy to complain to the Board of Trade about Spotswood's alleged usurpation of the rights of the colonists. A constant battle went on in Virginia between the Burgesses and Council and the Crown's representative concerning the respective prerogatives of each.

Byrd found quarters in a flat off the Strand and sent for his wife, who died the next year, 1716, of smallpox. A year later, his daughter Evelyn came over, followed by her younger sister, Wilhelmina, in 1719. Because a widower's quarters in London were not suitable for two daughters, he placed them with friends and relatives, but he himself carefully supervised their bringing-up. Byrd remained in England until late in 1720. These years are also well documented by an extant diary.

[8] *Journals of the House of Burgesses of Virginia*, edited by H. R. McIlwaine (Richmond, Va., 1918–19), volume for 1702–1712, p. 281.

Much of Byrd's energy in this period was expended in pursuit of an heiress. Between fortune-hunting by day and the search for less honorable game by night, Byrd managed to lead a full life — which he carefully records in his diary, even to the occasional rebuffs that he suffered.

The heiress whom Byrd selected as the most promising was one Mary Smith, daughter of John Smith, a commissioner of excise, a wealthy and proud citizen of London with lands in Lincolnshire. She lived in Beaufort Street, across from Byrd's own quarters, from which he could occasionally wave to the elusive object of his affection and interest. The course of this courtship can be charted in the diary and in a series of faintly disguised letters in which Byrd designates Mary as Sabina and her father as Vigilante. The ardent lover of forty-three reveals in his letters the conventional swing between happiness and dejection, depending upon the expression of favor or coolness shown by the coquettish Mary. In the end her father demanded a financial statement from her colonial suitor and rejected him outright in favor of a more opulent baronet. Byrd's envious disappointment was not eased when Mary's father died three days after her marriage and the baronet came into possession of her fortune.

During this period of courtship, Byrd was not without other, less reticent feminine consolation, as he often notes in his diary. For a time he kept as mistress a certain Mrs. A-l-c, to whom he paid a fee of two guineas a visit, until at last he brought himself to dismiss her for infidelity. Not one to waste an opportunity for an amour, on October 4, 1718, he makes this entry: "Then I went to visit Mrs. A-l-n and committed uncleanness with the maid because the mistress was not at home. However when the mistress came I rogered her and about 12 o'clock went home and ate a plum cake for supper. I neglected my prayers, for which God forgive me." With no more discrimination than James Boswell was later to show, Byrd was not above picking up a stray wench in St. James's Park and consummating the affair in the weeds nearby. As a result he was forced to undergo a course of treatment for gonorrhea, but even this only temporarily curbed his zest for illicit amours.

Although Byrd was consistently promiscuous during his years in London, he was not without conscience and, after recording some notable encounter, he frequently appends this phrase, "may God forgive me." And in spite of his amorous activities, he was extraordinarily busy about other matters. He carefully cultivated politicians who could be of help to Virginia and Virginians and was a frequent visitor to coffeehouses where merchants and politicians could be found, the Virginia Coffeehouse, Will's Coffeehouse, and St. James's Coffeehouse being his favorite haunts. He also took part in various social affairs, masquerade balls, theater parties, and visits to the Spanish Ambassador's, where there was habitual gambling. Byrd does not appear to have been lucky, and records more losses than winnings. He also conscientiously visited his daughters and was periodically engaged in business conversation with Micajah Perry, the leading merchant in the Virginia trade and Byrd's own factor. On November 17, 1718, as agent for the colony of Virginia, Byrd had an audience with King George I.

Byrd had been earnestly laying petitions before the Board of Trade and had made an appeal to the Crown to prevent Governor Spotswood from establishing courts of oyer and terminer and appointing the judges, a move that the Virginia ruling class believed would curtail their own rights and liberties. In the end the King upheld Spotswood, and Byrd had to agree that the Council would quit feuding and make peace with the lieutenant governor. Spotswood was anxious to have Byrd removed from the Council on the grounds of his long absence from Virginia, but Byrd received assurances that as the price of peace he would have the support of the Board of Trade in keeping his place on the Council.

The diary for 1717–1721 frequently records that Byrd was writing something, although the writer usually does not specify what form of composition was engaging his interest. On June 18, 1718, he notes:

Then we went to Mrs. D-n-s where we drank tea and ate sweet biscuits. I read several things to them out of my book and we stayed till 10 o'clock and then took leave. Then we went to the coffeehouse and read the news and about eleven I went home and said my prayers.

The next day he recorded that "after dinner I wrote some English till five." He was busy "writing English" during this period, but what he put into "his book" remains a matter of conjecture.

During a stay at the fashionable watering place of Tunbridge Wells in the summer of 1719, however, Byrd was slightly more specific about his literary activities. On August 24, 1719, he makes this entry in his diary:

> I rose about 7 o'clock and read a chapter in Hebrew and some Greek. I neglected my prayers, and had milk for breakfast. I danced my dance and read some English and then wrote some verses upon four ladies . . . About 10 o'clock I took a walk and met with a woman and kissed her exceedingly. Then I went home and said my prayers.

The verses that he was writing appeared under the pseudonym of "Mr. Burrard," in a thin little volume entitled *Tunbrigalia: or, Tunbridge Miscellanies, For the Year 1719* (London, 1719). Ladies to whom Byrd addressed compliments in verse in this volume included the Duchess of Montague, Lady Hinchinbrooke, Lady Percival, Lady Ranelagh, and other fashionable visitors to Tunbridge Wells.[9] Much of his effort in this period was devoted to satirical and occasional verse. On August 4, 1719, he notes: "I wrote some verses to ridicule Mr. Buckhurst's panegyrics." On several consecutive days, August 16–19, he continued to report that he "wrote some English," without specifying what, but on August 25 he

> wrote verses all the morning till 1 o'clock and then went upon the Walk . . . After dinner Molly the fruit girl came and Mr. C-r-v-n and I kissed her. Then I went home and wrote some English till six and then returned to the Walk and won a little at the ace of hearts . . . About twelve I went home and neglected to say my prayers.

Some of Byrd's literary efforts in this period were evidently devoted to a prose description of Virginia, for on November 20, 1719, he made this comment: "I went to Lord Islay's where I stayed till 12 o'clock and then went to the Duke of Argyll's but he was from home; but I

[9] These verses have been reprinted in *Another Secret Diary of William Byrd of Westover, 1739-1741*, edited by Maude H. Woodfin and Marion Tinling (Richmond, Va., 1942), pp. 397-409.

left the description of Virginia for him and gave my Lord Islay another." Islay was the Duke of Argyll's brother, and Byrd was cultivating both of them assiduously. In the preface to the 1741 edition of John Oldmixon's *The British Empire in America*, the author states that he has used a history of Virginia "written with a great deal of spirit and judgment by a gentleman of the province, . . . Colonel Byrd, whom I knew when I was in the Temple." A number of years after Byrd left his description of Virginia with the Duke of Argyll, Samuel Jenner published in Berne, Switzerland, a descriptive volume on Virginia, based on notes provided by Byrd and bearing the title *Neu-gefundenes Eden* (1737), which has been translated and published by R. C. Beatty and W. J. Mulloy as *William Byrd's Natural History of Virginia* (Richmond, 1940). This book, frankly a promotional tract to lure settlers to Byrd's lands on the North Carolina border, may have been an adaptation of the work that he supplied the Duke of Argyll and John Oldmixon. At any rate, Byrd was interested in writing about Virginia even before his longest extant narrative, the account of running the dividing line between Virginia and North Carolina, was composed.

Although Byrd must have found it hard to tear himself away from the pleasant life of London and Tunbridge Wells, at length he found it necessary to think of Virginia, and on November 24, 1719, he embarked at Dover with two English maids, Annie and Hannah, upon whom from time to time he laid amorous hands. On February 2, 1720, his ship rounded the Virginia capes and came to anchor. Weary of the sea and unwilling to wait until a favorable wind might take them to his own dock at Westover, Byrd had the captain put him ashore and traveled overland to Westover, which he reached on February 13.

During the next year, Byrd busied himself with many details of plantation life. His garden and his library were his particular delights, and he apparently spent considerable effort in restoring or remodeling the plantation house, for the diary mentions the arrival of a shipload of shingles and the payment to a bricklayer for his work. As a member of the Council, Byrd took part in the political affairs of the colony and during this period managed to patch up his relations with Governor Spotswood, with whom he had long conducted a political feud.

The diary continued to note that the author was "writing English," and we know from specific entries that Byrd was engaged in preparing a treatise on the plague. On March 26, 1721, for instance, Colonel Nathaniel Harrison came over for Sunday morning breakfast at Westover and Byrd "read some of my plague book to him." On April 4, 1721, he turned over the manuscript to a ship captain bound for London, with instructions to deliver it to his agent, Micajah Perry, who apparently saw to its publication. That year there appeared in London *A Discourse Concerning the Plague with Some Preservatives Against It. By a Lover of Mankind*, "printed for J. Roberts near the Oxford Arms in Warwick Lane." From the style it is evident that the "Lover of Mankind" who wrote the *Discourse* was William Byrd. If this indeed is Byrd's treatise, it is the only complete book that he saw through the press during his lifetime.

The Discourse Concerning the Plague must have been pleasing to Virginia tobacco planters, for it concludes with an eloquent declaration of the virtue of tobacco as a panacea against infection. "I am humbly of opinion," the author writes,

that when there is any danger of pestilence, we can't more effectually consult our preservation than by providing ourselves with a reasonable quantity of fresh, strong scented tobacco. We should wear it about our clothes and about our coaches. We should hang bundles of it round our beds, and in the apartments wherein we most converse. If we have an aversion to smoking, it would be very prudent to burn some leaves of tobacco in our dining rooms lest we swallow infection with our meat. It will also be very useful to take snuff plentifully made of the pure leaf to secure the passages to our brain. Nor must those only be guarded but the pass to our stomachs should be also safely defended by chewing this great antipoison very frequently.[10]

In 1721 Byrd received another appointment as agent for the colony of Virginia, and in the summer of that year he sailed again for England, where, as it turned out, he would remain for the next five years. Since we have no diary entries for these years, we cannot follow him

[10] *Ibid.*, p. 442.

closely, but a few records and letters indicate his activities. He made representations before the Board of Trade on various matters and was busy about his own affairs, particularly about his father-in-law's debts that he had agreed to pay. He also renewed his search for an heiress, but in the end, after pursuing various prospects, he married Maria Taylor, of Kensington, who brought him no fortune. Nevertheless, she made him a good wife, displayed a far more equable disposition than his first wife, Lucy, and bore him four children, including William, his son and heir.

In 1726 Byrd came back to Westover, where he remained for the rest of his life. Again, although he was thoroughly at home in England, he showed no reluctance to resuming his life on a Virginia plantation and quickly fell into the routine of a member of the ruling aristocracy of the province. To his friends in London he described his life as something approaching a pastoral idyl. "Thus, my Lord," he wrote to the Earl of Orrery on July 5, 1726, "we are very happy in our Canaans if we could but forget the onions and fleshpots of Egypt." His daughters, Evelyn and Wilhelmina, whom he also brought back to Virginia, found it somewhat harder to adjust; Byrd comments in a letter on February 2, 1727, "My young gentlewomen like everything in the country except the retirement; they can't get the plays, the operas, and the masquerades out of their heads; much less can they forget their friends." [11]

As a duty to the colony of Virginia, Byrd accepted in 1728 the headship of a commission appointed to settle a long-standing boundary dispute between Virginia and North Carolina. The Virginia commissioners planned to meet a similar commission appointed by North Carolina and actually to survey the line and make a map plainly showing the border. The survey was made in the spring and autumn of 1728, and it was upon the experiences of this expedition that Byrd based *The History of the Dividing Line betwixt Virginia and North Carolina, Run in the Year of Our Lord 1728*, his most extensive literary work.

This account, published by Edmund Ruffin in 1841 from a manu-

[11] Cited in *London Diary*, p. 38.

script copied by an amanuensis and corrected by Byrd himself, was expanded from rough notes that Byrd made on the spot. Other members of the party perhaps kept notes that Byrd may have consulted in the preparation of his own narrative. He also wrote another literary account of the expedition with the title *The Secret History of the Line*, which was not published until W. K. Boyd's edition in 1929 from the original manuscript preserved in the library of the American Philosophical Society in Philadelphia.[12] In this version Byrd is franker in some of his comments than in the *History*. In the *Secret History* he uses descriptive pseudonyms for the participants in the expedition, and this gives him license to report their shortcomings with considerably more freedom than he employs in the *History*.

Two other, much briefer reports, hardly more than rough notes, exist in manuscript. They apparently were sent to London as early reports on the survey. One, called "a Journal of the Dividing line . . . [by] Colo. Byrd & Others," is preserved in the British Museum, and the second, entitled "A Journal of the proceedings of the Commissioners . . . ," is in the Public Record Office in London. Neither is in Byrd's handwriting. The first, by "Colonel Byrd and others," is short, ungrammatical, and much abbreviated. The second, the "Journal of the Proceedings," appears to be a somewhat expanded version of the first and must have been the official report submitted by Byrd. A study of these two reports indicates that Byrd used them in expanding his account into the two "literary" narratives, the *History* and the *Secret History*.

In the present edition of Byrd's literary prose, the editor has made an effort to eliminate corruptions that crept into earlier texts. Ruffin's edition was carelessly printed on cheap newsprint paper. The next edition, that by Thomas H. Wynne, *History of the Dividing Line and Other Tracts from the Papers of William Byrd of Westover, in Virginia, Esquire* (2 vols., Richmond, 1866), was more carefully compared with the manuscript, but it too has many errors that have been perpetuated in later editions, even the editions by Boyd and the

---

[12] *William Byrd's Histories of the Dividing Line betwixt Virginia and North Carolina*, edited by William K. Boyd (Raleigh, N.C., 1929).

handsomely printed version edited by John Spencer Bassett, *The Writings of Colonel William Byrd of Westover in Virginia* (New York, 1901). Although no editor can hope to avoid misreadings, the present edition at least has had a careful collation with the earliest extant version of Byrd's writings, known as the Westover Manuscripts, acquired in 1962 by the Virginia Historical Society, and with the manuscript of the *Secret History* in the American Philosophical Society. A hiatus in the *Secret History* manuscript has been supplied by the collation of two fragments, one in the Huntington Library and another in the Blathwayt Papers at Colonial Williamsburg. Another manuscript of the *History* exists in the American Philosophical Society, evidently a fair copy made by an amanuensis, probably from a lost original. The two manuscript versions of the *History*, that in the Westover Manuscripts and that in the American Philosophical Society, have many slight variations in phraseology. Corrections in the Westover Manuscripts in a hand that looks like Byrd's indicate that the author himself revised this version. It is this manuscript that is the basis of the present edition.

An attempt was made by the American Philosophical Society beginning about 1816 to publish Byrd's *History of the Dividing Line.* The project originated with the gift to the Society in 1815 of a manuscript of the *History*, presented by Mrs. E. C. Izard, a great-granddaughter of the author. The task was undertaken by the Literary Committee, consisting of Peter S. DuPonceau, J. Correa de Serra, and Dr. Caspar Wistar, who recommended its publication because of the "important and curious information that it affords" and the information on "the state of civilization of these states about the middle of last century."[13] Since the Committee discovered that their manuscript had several pages missing, they sought the help of Mrs. Izard and Thomas Jefferson in locating other copies of the document that might supply the missing pages. On January 27, 1817, Jefferson wrote that he had borrowed a manuscript and would supply the gaps, but it turned out that the manuscript in his possession was that of the *Secret*

---

[13] A more detailed discussion of the manuscripts in the American Philosophical Society and the early plans for publication will be found in the Appendix.

History; later he forwarded this manuscript to the Society with the permission of the *de facto* executor of the Byrd estate, Benjamin Harrison, who offered to help find a copy of the *History* that might supply the lost leaves. The manuscript of the *Secret History* was never returned and remains to this day in the library of the American Philosophical Society. In January 1818, Harrison wrote Jefferson that he had located the manuscript of the *History* in the possession of George Evelyn Harrison at Brandon and would lend it to Jefferson to copy the required pages, provided that Jefferson would undertake not to let it leave his hands. Whereupon Jefferson again wrote to DuPonceau that he would have the pages copied, which he did. For reasons that do not appear, the American Philosophical Society did not carry through its intention of publishing the *History of the Dividing Line* and the matter was allowed to drop, to be revived in 1834, when a committee was appointed to determine whether any portion of the Byrd material might be published in the Society's *Transactions*. After reading the documents, the committee reported that "the style and manner in which they are written forbid their publication as a whole, and . . . even extracts or a review of them, though they might amuse elsewhere, would not be in their place in the *Transactions* of our Society." Someone, whether this committee or an earlier editor, went through the manuscript and "improved" the diction by substituting more elegant words for homely expressions. Even so, the style was too racy for the staid dignity of the American Philosophical Society in the year 1834.

The document that the philosophers of 1834 found improper for their transactions is indeed a brisk, uninhibited, entertaining, and sometimes satirical account of the joint expedition of the Virginia and North Carolina commissioners who surveyed the boundary in 1728. As one would expect from the pen of a man who had been the friend and associate of writers of Restoration and Augustan London, Byrd's prose is sophisticated and urbane. It reads as if it might have been written by a Londoner, for Byrd automatically chooses similes that are reminiscent of his life in England. For example, in describing a bivouac, he says the men lay around their campfire "like so many

Knights Templars," a figure suggested by the effigies on the tombs in the Temple Church, where he had walked many times while a resident in the Middle Temple; two horses that had strayed were found standing "as motionless as the equestrian statue at Charing Cross." These similes came naturally to one who had had long experience in England; furthermore Byrd was probably consciously writing with an English audience in mind.

His satirical commentary on some of his fellow commissioners from North Carolina and upon North Carolinians generally has not endeared the writer to sensitive citizens of that commonwealth. When the North Carolina commissioners arrived, Byrd observed that they had come "better provided for the belly than the business" and "not above two men . . . would put their hands to anything but the kettle and the frying pan." His commentary upon the laziness of the North Carolinians has been often cited:

Surely there is no place in the world where the inhabitants live with less labor than in North Carolina. It approaches nearer to the description of Lubberland than any other, by the great felicity of the climate, the easiness of raising provisions, and the slothfulness of the people . . . The men, for their parts, just like the Indians, impose all the work upon the poor women. They make their wives rise out of their beds early in the morning, at the same time that they lie and snore till the sun has risen one-third of his course and dispersed all the unwholesome damps. Then, after stretching and yawning for half an hour, they light their pipes, and, under the protection of a cloud of smoke, venture out into the open air; though if it happen to be never so little cold they quickly return shivering to the chimney corner. When the weather is mild, they stand leaning with both their arms upon the cornfield fence and gravely consider whether they had best go and take a small heat at the hoe but generally find reasons to put it off till another time. Thus they loiter away their lives, like Solomon's sluggard, with their arms across, and at the winding up of the year scarcely have bread to eat. To speak the truth, 'tis a thorough aversion to labor that makes people file off to North Carolina, where plenty and a warm sun confirm them in their disposition to laziness for their whole lives.

Of Edenton, Byrd is equally satirical:

There may be forty or fifty houses, most of them small and built without expense. A citizen here is counted extravagant if he has ambition enough to aspire to a brick chimney. Justice herself is but indifferently lodged, the courthouse having much the air of a common tobacco house. I believe this is the only metropolis in the Christian or Mahometan world where there is neither church, chapel, mosque, synagogue, or any other place of worship of any sect or religion whatsoever. What little devotion there may happen to be is much more private than their vices. The people seem easy without a minister as long as they are exempted from paying him. Sometimes the Society for Propagating the Gospel has had the charity to send over missionaries to this country; but, unfortunately, the priest has been too lewd for the people, or, which often happens, they too lewd for the priest. For these reasons these reverend gentlemen have always left their flocks as arrant heathen as they found them.

Byrd's narrative displays the keen and amused observations of a man interested in the world about him. Indeed, wherever he found himself, whether in the center of London society or on the borders of the Dismal Swamp, Byrd was never bored; he always found something in his environment to attract his attention, to entertain him, and to be worth a comment. As a member of the Royal Society and a virtuoso himself, he was fascinated by the curiosities of nature that he encountered on the survey of the border. His observations are still of use to students concerned with the plant and animal ecologies of colonial Virginia and North Carolina. When Byrd discovered some new or interesting animal or plant, it usually called forth a comment that reflected his past reading and his stored knowledge. From Pliny, Olaus Magnus, and other writers, he had picked up traditional lore about animals that found its way into the *History*. For instance, he tells a tale that had often appeared in earlier writers of the squirrel's ingenuity in crossing a stream by launching a chip and hoisting its tail as a sail; and he relates a bit of ancient lore about the alligator, which swallows rocks in order to sink to the bottom more readily.

As a practical explorer and planter, Byrd was eager to find good land for exploitation, minerals that would be profitable, and plants and animals that might prove beneficial. After describing a buffalo that the party's hunters discovered, Byrd commented: "Buffaloes may be easily tamed when they are taken young . . . If we could get into a breed of them they might be made very useful, not only for the dairy, by giving an ocean of milk, but also for drawing vast and cumbersome weights by their prodigious strength."

Of all the plants that Byrd found on the survey, he became more enthusiastic about ginseng than any other. Indeed, he remained for the rest of his life an advocate of ginseng as a sort of panacea and restorative. At one point in the *History*, he remarked:

> Though practice will soon make a man of tolerable vigor an able footman, yet, as a help to bear fatigue, I used to chew a root of ginseng as I walked along. This kept up my spirits and made me trip away as nimbly in my half-jack boots as younger men could do in their shoes. This plant is in high esteem in China, where it sells for its weight in silver. Indeed, it does not grow there but in the mountains of Tartary, to which place the Emperor of China sends ten thousand men every year on purpose to gather it. But it grows so scatteringly there that even so many hands can bring home no great quantity. Indeed, it is a vegetable of so many virtues that Providence has planted it very thin in every country that has the happiness to produce it . . . It grows also on the northern continent of America, near the mountains, but as sparingly as truth and public spirit . . . Its virtues are that it gives an uncommon warmth and vigor to the blood and frisks the spirits beyond any other cordial. It cheers the heart even of a man that has a bad wife and makes him look down with great composure on the crosses of the world. It promotes insensible perspiration, dissolves all phlegmatic and viscous humors, that are apt to obstruct the narrow channels of the nerves. It helps the memory and would quicken even Helvetian dullness . . . However, 'tis of little use in the feats of love, as a great prince once found, who, hearing of its invigorating quality, sent as far as China for some of it, though his ladies could not boast of any advantage thereby.

Byrd's language is simple, direct, concrete, and idiomatic; his sentences are usually short and unencumbered with awkward constructions; and his paragraphs frequently build up to some striking statement or humorous comment. For instance, a routine account of the party's arrival at a lone farmhouse where they planned to spend the night gives a crisp and entertaining bit of information in a short paragraph:

> We had but two miles more to Captain Embry's, where we found the housekeeping much better than the house. Our bountiful landlady had set

her oven and all her spits, pots, gridirons, and saucepans to work to diversify our entertainment, though after all it proved but a Mahometan feast, there being nothing to drink but water. The worst of it was we had unluckily outrid the baggage and for that reason were obliged to lodge very sociably in the same apartment with the family, where, reckoning women and children, we mustered in all no less than nine persons, who all pigged lovingly together.

Byrd's commentary on the Indians that the party met holds more than passing interest, for in it he argues for miscegenation as the way to solve the Indian problem, an argument that his brother-in-law Robert Beverley also made in the *The History and Present State of Virginia* (1705). Speaking of the poor success of the whites in Christianizing the Indians, Byrd remarks:

I am sorry I can't give a better account of the state of the poor Indians with respect to Christianity, although a great deal of pains has been and still continues to be taken with them. For my part, I must be of opinion, as I hinted before, that there is but one way of converting these poor infidels and reclaiming them from barbarity, and that is charitably to intermarry with them, according to the modern policy of the Most Christian King in Canada and Louisiana. Had the English done this at the first settlement of the colony, the infidelity of the Indians had been worn out at this day with their dark complexions, and the country had swarmed with people more than it does with insects. It was certainly an unreasonable nicety that prevented their entering into so good-natured an alliance. All nations of men have the same natural dignity, and we all know that very bright talents may be lodged under a very dark skin. The principal difference between one people and another proceeds only from the different opportunities of improvement. The Indians by no means want understanding and are in their figure tall and well proportioned. Even their copper-colored complexion would admit of blanching, if not in the first, at the farthest in the second, generation. I may safely venture to say, the Indian women would have made altogether as honest wives for the first planters as the damsels they used to purchase from aboard the ships. 'Tis strange, therefore, that any good Christian should have refused a wholesome, straight bedfellow when he might have had so fair a portion with her as the merit of saving her soul.

Both for content and style, Byrd's *History* is a landmark in colonial writing. Few other contemporary documents are so "civilized," so entertaining, and so modern in tone and point of view.

The *Secret History* is hardly more than half as long as the *History* and was probably written first and designed for a more restricted group of readers. Although it disguises the names of the participants under such names as Steddy (Byrd himself), Meanwell (William Dandridge, one of the Virginia commissioners), Firebrand (Richard Fitzwilliam, another of the Virginia commissioners), and Dr. Humdrum (Peter Fontaine, the chaplain), the document is much more explicit than the *History* about the characteristics of the individuals taking part in the expedition, their quarrels and conflicts of interest, and various episodes including incidents involving violence to women on the frontier. The *Secret History* contains some preliminary letters exchanged between the Virginia and North Carolina commissioners and other documents not included in the *History*.

That the Virginians and North Carolinians would not work in harmony might have been predicted from the beginning. For one thing, they were trying to settle a long-standing quarrel: the controversy over the boundary that had exacerbated feelings on both sides for many years. Both Virginia and North Carolina claimed certain territory in the border region, and both jurisdictions had from time to time tried to collect taxes from the inhabitants of the disputed territory.[14] The second charter granted to North Carolina (1665) declared that the boundary should run "from the north end of Currituck River or Inlet upon a straight westerly line to Weyanoke Creek, which lies within or about the degrees of 36 and 30' northern latitude, and so west in a direct line as far as the South Seas." The problem in 1728 was to locate "Weyanoke" Creek, which had lost its identity with the passage of years. It was finally agreed that Nottoway River was meant, and the survey was run that way. But this agreement did not come without argument, which is related in the *Secret History*.

The *Secret History* shares with the *History* its racy quality and idiomatic expression. The uninhibited frankness gives additional

[14] Boyd, *William Byrd's Histories*, pp. xvi ff, gives a succinct account of the boundary dispute.

piquancy to this narrative, particularly in Byrd's characterization of his associates. For instance:

We found Shoebrush [John Lovick, one of the North Carolina commissioners] a merry good-humored man, and had learnt a very decent behavior from Governor Hyde, to whom he had been *valet de chambre*, of which he still carried the marks by having his coat, waistcoat, and breeches of different parishes. Puzzlecause [William Little, another North Carolina commissioner] had degenerated from a New England preacher, for which his godly parents designed him, to a very wicked but awkward rake.

Byrd's observations during this survey whetted his appetite for frontier land to such a degree that he obtained from North Carolina 20,000 acres at the confluence of the Dan and Irvin rivers. Much later he acquired another 6,000 acres adjoining this property. To this territory he gave the name of the Land of Eden. Between 1730 and 1738, Byrd acquired 5,211 acres at the confluence of the Dan and Staunton rivers. Finally, in 1742 he took up 105,000 acres of frontier land on the borders of North Carolina and about the same time bought a plantation on the Meherrin River consisting of 2,429 acres. By the time of his death in 1744, Byrd was the owner of a total of 179,440 acres; to the end of his life, the appetite for land remained unsatisfied. He even conceived a project to drain the Great Dismal Swamp and turn it into a vast plantation for hemp and other products. To advance this project Byrd wrote, apparently soon after the completion of the survey of the dividing line, "A Description of the Dismal," which was published by Edmund Ruffin at Petersburg in the *Farmer's Register*, IV (1836). At the time, Ruffin reported that "The manuscript, in our charge, is the original, in the handwriting of the author — and though time worn, and requiring much care to handle without injury, is perfectly legible. It is here copied literally." Apparently the fragile manuscript has been lost. Ruffin's version was edited in 1922 by Dr. Earl Gregg Swem and issued in an edition of sixty-one copies by Charles F. Heartman of Metuchen, New Jersey. The whole document consists of only thirty-two pages of large print. Byrd includes descriptive material that he used in the *History of the Dividing Line* and adds some estimates of cost, with a copy of a petition to the King asking him to grant to the petitioners the "large bog . . . that corrupts the air of all the neighboring country by the noxious vapors that perpetually ascend from it." After estimating the expense in money and slaves, Byrd remarks that "we may safely conclude that each share will then [after the draining of the swamp] be worth more than ten times the value of the original subscription, besides the unspeakable benefit it will prove to the public."

Nothing came of Byrd's project to drain the Dismal Swamp, but the scheme continued to excite the activity of his heirs and successors. George Washington was concerned with a plan to drain the swamp which was under discussion both before and after the Revolution. In fact, it was the continued talk of draining the Dismal Swamp that prompted Edmund Ruffin to take an interest in Byrd's manuscripts and to print the first edition of the *History of the Dividing Line*. His initial intention was evidently to extract only those portions dealing with the Dismal Swamp, but his interest was captured by the document as a whole.

Two shorter pieces of prose from Byrd's pen, similar in tone to the *History of the Dividing Line*, have appeared in editions of Byrd's works since Ruffin's time. They are *A Journey to the Land of Eden in the Year 1733* and *A Progress to the Mines in the Year 1732*. The previous versions of Byrd's prose have printed them in this reverse chronological order, which is the way they appear in the Westover Manuscripts. In the present edition they are printed in their chronological order.

In the early autumn of 1732 Byrd made the journey that he described in *A Progress to the Mines*. On September 18, he set out from Westover accompanied by Mrs. Byrd and their young son "in the chariot." After a picnic lunch on the road, his companions turned back and Byrd continued alone on horseback to the site of Richmond, where he found his water mills idle because of a drought. He continued his journey by easy stages to Fredericksburg and Germanna, where Colonel Alexander Spotswood, the former governor and Byrd's political rival, was operating iron mines which Byrd wished to see.

He writes in an easy, gossipy manner of his adventures along the way. At Tuckahoe, the Randolph plantation near Richmond, he was graciously received by the Widow Randolph, who told him a sad story of her daughter's elopement with an uncle's overseer, an Irishman without "one visible qualification except impudence to recommend him to a female's inclination." Marooned at Tuckahoe by a three days' rainstorm, he found a copy of *The Beggar's Opera* in the Randolph library and read it aloud to the family. "Thus we killed the time and triumphed over the bad weather," he adds.

His next stop after leaving Tuckahoe was at the house of Charles Chiswell, "a sensible, well-bred man, and very frank in communicating his knowledge of the mystery of making iron, wherein he has had long experience." Byrd's interest was now in the smelting of iron, but some years before he had other designs on the Chiswell family. In his diary for November 2, 1709, he had noted:

I played at [r–m] with Mrs. Chiswell and kissed her on the bed till she was angry and my wife also was uneasy about it, and cried as soon as the company was gone. I neglected to say my prayers, which I should not have done because I ought to beg pardon for the lust I had for another man's wife.

Now, nearly a quarter of a century later, he comments sadly on the ravages of time, perhaps recalling that earlier romantic moment:

I had not seen Mrs. Chiswell in twenty-four years, which, alas! had made great havoc with her pretty face and plowed very deep furrows in her fair skin. It was impossible to know her again, so much the flower was faded. However, though she was grown an old woman, yet she was one of those absolute rarities, a very good old woman.

Byrd no longer had eyes for Mrs. Chiswell, but he talked earnestly with his friend Mr. Chiswell about iron smelting, a secret to stop the fermentation of any liquor, and a method of keeping weevils out of wheat and other grain. He enjoyed the hospitality of the Chiswells and "after saying some very civil things to Mrs. Chiswell for my handsome entertainment, I mounted my horse and Mr. Chiswell his phaeton, in order to go to the mines at Fredericksville [Fredericksburg]."

Byrd's destination was Colonel Spotswood's home at Germanna, which he reached on September 27.

> This famous town consists of Colonel Spotswood's enchanted castle on one side of the street and a baker's dozen of ruinous tenements on the other, where so many German families had dwelt some years ago, but are now removed ten miles higher, in the fork of Rappahannock, to land of their own,

he comments. The hospitality of Colonel and Mrs. Spotswood was unbounded, and Byrd enjoyed his stay at Germanna visiting a man with whom he was now happily reconciled and on terms of intimate friendship. The passages telling of his days at Germanna provide a charming picture of life in Virginia in the first third of the eighteenth century.

Byrd was prompted to write *A Journey to the Land of Eden in the Year 1733* by his experiences in surveying lands that he had acquired in the border region. During the survey of the dividing line, he had had an opportunity to observe the quality of the terrain on the border, and the sight had aroused his land-hunger. From the North Carolina commissioners, who had received frontier land in payment for their services, Byrd bought the 20,000 acres at the confluence of the Dan and Irvin rivers which he christened "the Land of Eden." It was to survey this estate that he set out with a party of friends on September 11, 1733. From this time onward until the end of his life he was eagerly seeking to acquire more frontier land and trying to induce colonists to settle on his holdings.

The people whom Byrd preferred for his lands were Swiss, and he made persistent efforts to lure Swiss settlers to his new Eden. In the years following the acquisition of land on the Dan River on the North Carolina side of the border, he had taken up even larger holdings on the Virginia side in the Dan and Roanoke valleys, and it was for these lands that he sought colonists. Byrd was emphatic in his preference for Swiss instead of the Scotch-Irish who were threatening to swarm down from Pennsylvania "like the Goths and Vandals of old." [15] A

[15] Richmond C. Beatty and William J. Mulloy (eds.), *William Byrd's Natural History of Virginia or The Newly Discovered Eden*, edited and translated from a German version (Richmond, Va., 1940), p. xxii.

correspondence with a certain Mr. Ochs about Swiss colonists began hopefully, but Ochs was not able to deliver any Switzers.

A more promising effort was made in July 1736, when Byrd made a contract with Samuel Jenner, of Berne, an authorized agent of the Helvetian Society, for the sale of 33,400 acres on the Roanoke River. He gave a receipt to Samuel Tschiffeli on January 9, 1737, for £3,000 in payment for this land. To promote the enterprise, Byrd supplied Jenner with notes for the description of Virginia that was published in Berne in 1737 with the title *Neu-gefundenes Eden*. Byrd's name was translated in Jenner's document as Wilhelm Vogel. His description of the delights of life in Virginia and the prosperity to be expected in so fruitful a country would do credit to the most zealous real estate promoter. Some 250 emigrants left Switzerland in the winter of 1738, but they suffered shipwreck off the coast of Virginia and only a few "unhappy wretches," Byrd reported, survived to reach his lands. Although he again tried to get Swiss or German settlers, he failed to attract an appreciable number of these colonists and was at last driven to seek Scots.

The narrative of his visit to the border lands in *A Journey to the Land of Eden* is informative, lively, and entertaining. The party surveyed Byrd's North Carolina holdings and then explored his other lands on the Roanoke River. On September 19, after a strenuous day of paddling up and down the river, Byrd returned to camp and apparently spent the evening drawing plans for cities that he expected to create on the James and Appomattox rivers. "When we got home," he comments,

we laid the foundation of two large cities: one at Shacco's, to be called Richmond, and the other at the point of Appomattox River, to be called Petersburg. These Major Mayo offered to lay out into lots without fee or reward. The truth of it is, these two places, being the uppermost land of [the] James and Appomattox rivers, are naturally intended for marts where the traffic of the outer inhabitants must center. Thus we did not build castles only, but also cities in the air.

While Major Mayo was out with a surveying party, Byrd and some of his other companions spent time in camp occupying themselves as best they could. On October 9 the author comments that he "never spent a day so well during the whole voyage," for on that day he managed to pull "an impertinent tooth" in his upper jaw, as he explains in some detail:

Toothdrawers we had none amongst us, nor any of the instruments they make use of. However, invention supplied this want very happily, and I contrived to get rid of this troublesome companion by cutting a caper. I caused a twine to be fastened round the root of my tooth, about a fathom in length, and then tied the other end to the snag of a log that lay upon the ground in such a manner that I could just stand upright. Having adjusted my string in this manner, I bent my knees enough to enable me to spring vigorously off the ground as perpendicularly as I could. The force of the leap drew out the tooth with so much ease that I felt nothing of it, nor should have believed it was come away unless I had seen it dangling at the end of the string . . . This new way of toothdrawing, being so silently and deliberately performed, both surprised and delighted all that were present, who could not guess what I was going about.

Byrd possessed a sense of satirical humor that found expression in much of his writing. The foibles of his associates on the expedition to survey the dividing line, the qualities of the people whom he observed in London or in Virginia, the shortcomings of those who incurred his disfavor, might become the subject of commentary in one of his journals or in letters that he carefully composed as if for purposes of publication.

Byrd's letters are particularly interesting, not only for their biographical significance but for their literary quality. Although he did not intend to publish his correspondence, he obviously was so unwilling to see these manifestations of his literary skill perish that he carefully copied them. In a notebook in the University of North Carolina library, reproduced by Miss Maude H. Woodfin in her edition of *Another Secret Diary*, Byrd preserved a considerable body of his correspondence, but he disguised the names of the persons addressed under such fanciful appellations as "Charmante," "Sabina," "Vigilante," "Cleora," "Erranti," "Belinda." Miss Woodfin managed to identify a number of these addressees. Some of the letters are cast in the form of the eighteenth-century "character," essentially an informal descriptive essay, and included among the letters are two or three characters that are strictly literary exercises. One of these, entitled "Inamorato L'Oiseaux," [16] is a self-portrait of Byrd himself. Miss Woodfin thinks the use of the plural form, "L'Oiseaux" was a slip of Byrd's pen when he copied it in his notebook.

The character that Byrd painted of himself is revealing and substantially accurate. He begins with a description of his amorous nature that is confirmed by his diaries. "Never did the sun shine upon a swain who had more combustible matter in his constitution than the unfortunate Inamorato. Love broke out upon him before his beard, and he could distinguish sexes long before he could the difference between good and evil," he comments at the beginning of the little essay. "This foible has been an unhappy clog to all his fortunes and hindered him from reaching that eminence in the world which his friends and abilities might possibly have advanced him to," he adds. Unwilling to subdue his spirit to the requirements of ambition, he recognizes the limitations upon his attainments that the pursuit of pleasure has imposed. "Diligence gives wings to ambition by which it soars up to the highest pitch of advancement. These wings Inamorato wanted, as he did constancy, which is another ingredient to raise a great fortune." This passage helps to explain why Byrd made no more of his literary efforts than he did. His interest in his writing flagged, and he did not have the drive required to make him complete any great work. He was willing to content himself with pretty little essays, light verses, and satirical pieces to entertain his friends. He remained essentially a dilettante of letters, albeit a brilliant one.

One characteristic bit of light foolery is reprinted by Miss Woodfin from a manuscript in the Huntington Library. Entitled "The Female Creed," [17] it dates from about 1725 and is a satire on the credulities and weaknesses of women, with veiled references to particular women whom Byrd knew in London. A somewhat ribald piece without much merit, it was probably written to entertain some of Byrd's English

---

[16] Woodfin, *Another Secret Diary*, pp. 276–282.
[17] *Ibid.*, pp. 447–475.

cronies. Nevertheless it is revealing as an example of the type of composition that Byrd found pleasure in writing.

That he was an inveterate writer is abundantly evident from the surviving pieces from his pen: his diaries, which he evidently kept throughout his life, though many portions have been lost; his numerous letters, which he took care to preserve; his notebooks, like the ones at the University of North Carolina which Miss Woodfin has edited; and his commonplace books, which we now have evidence that he kept.

Why Byrd — or anyone — should keep the kind of diaries that he kept remains a mystery of human nature. In them he entered the stark and banal doings of each day with a minimum of comment upon them. He also recorded the intimate details of his sex life in as matter-of-fact a manner as he would mention the arrival and departure of guests. For reasons that puzzle us, Byrd felt a compulsion to write, even to write down his most trivial or most intimate actions. He also felt impelled to keep everything that he wrote. Unhappily, large sections of his diaries have been lost and may never be recovered, and notebooks containing letters and memoranda have disappeared.

A commonplace book that Byrd kept between the years 1722 and 1732 has recently come to light and has been acquired by the Virginia Historical Society. Through the kindness of the Director, Mr. John Jennings, it has been made available for study. In Byrd's own handwriting, it reveals matters that caught his interest in reading or in chance conversations. Here he jotted down the items that he wanted to remember, perhaps for his own conversational purposes or for use in his writing. The book is a hodgepodge of miscellaneous quotations and curious information, much of it ribald. It contains proverbs, words of advice, anecdotes, recipes, cures for venereal diseases, rules for good health, pious moralizing, gossip about Charles II and other prominent characters, bits of verse, quotations from Greek and Roman writers, and almost anything that Byrd thought worth remembering. It also contains four letters dating from 1722 and addressed to "Charmante," whom Miss Woodfin identified as Lady Elizabeth Lee, granddaughter of Charles II; Byrd had sought in vain to persuade her to marry him, but she chose to marry in 1731 Edward Young, the poet and the author of *Night Thoughts.*

Elizabeth Lee's refusal of Byrd's hand infuriated him and moved him to write this message to posterity at the end of the last letter copied in his commonplace book:

These passionate billets were writ to a lady who had more charms than honor, more wit than discretion. In the beginning she gave the writer of them the plainest marks of her favor. He did not only hint his passion to her but also confirmed it by many a close hug and tender squeeze, which she suffered with the patience of a martyr. Nay, that she might have no doubt of his intentions, he put the question to her in the plainest terms, which she seemed to agree to, not only by a modest silence but by permitting the same familiarities for more than a month afterwards.

Byrd continues in this vein and blames his bad fortune upon a rival who found it necessary "to work underground and blow him up by a mine." Elizabeth Lee did not marry Young for his virtue, Byrd suggests, but

for the worst quality any husband can have — for his wit. That I own he has his share of, yet so overcharged and encumbered with words that he does more violence to the ear than a ring of bells, for he's altogether as noisy, without having so many changes. But if he had never so much wit, a wife may be sure the edge of it will be turned mostly against herself.

This comment prompts Byrd to make some observations upon the hazards of displaying too much wit.

Wit is a dangerous quality, both for the owner and everyone that has the misfortune to belong to him. He that is curst with wit has commonly too much fire to think, too much quickness to have any discretion . . . In one word, wit rarely makes a man either happier or better, and much seldomer makes him rich than immortal. Wit in a man, like beauty in a woman, may please and divert other people but never does its owner any good.[18]

The commonplace book is filled with facts, anecdotes, and curious bits of lore that Byrd gleaned in his reading. Some of it is ribald and bawdy, some of it is pious and moralistic, and all of it reflects the diversity of his reading. As in the diaries, he rarely specifies the title

[18] Commonplace Book, Virginia Historical Society, pp. 91–92.

of the book that is the source of the information that he copies. An entry that may reflect Byrd's own hesitancy about publishing his work reads: "Socrates had a modesty which would much better become most of our modern authors, for, being asked why he would not oblige the world with some of his works, replied, ''Twould be a pity to spoil so much paper.'" In another characteristic passage on the same page of the commonplace book, he quotes Aristotle but gives no source: "Aristotle had a despicable opinion of human nature, by saying that man was the very center of frailty, the jest of fortune, the emblem of inconstancy, the prey of time, and the shuttlecock of envy and compassion, and for the rest, nothing but phlegm and melancholy." This observation is followed by a short paragraph reading: "Approach not the tremendous throne of God with any petition for prosperity, but pray for such a portion of grace and wisdom as may enable you in all conditions to behave in a manner suitable to the dignity of your nature and the firmness of your dependence." [19]

This commonplace book is a revelation of the diversity of Byrd's interests and his curiosity about everything, ranging from abstract matters of religion to practical questions affecting life on a Virginia plantation. He describes the diagnostic skill of Dr. John Radcliffe, the most eminent physician in the reign of Queen Anne, and provides some sensible rules of health (which his diaries indicate that he tried to follow). As he indicated in his character of himself, he recognized his own amorous proclivities and was fascinated by these manifestations in others, as entries in the commonplace book show. The contemplation of the frailties of men and women results in a curious jumble of quotations, proverbs, advice, and even recipes in the commonplace book. "In matters of love, the only sure way to conquer is to run away, according to Cato," Byrd observes. "'In spite of all the virtue we can boast, / The woman that deliberates is lost.' Nor is this the case with the women only, but the men find it as true as they in every instance of temptation." He cites various methods by which men have sought to gain supremacy over their emotions. Some have worn "a leaden girdle upon their loins and strewed their

[19] *Ibid.,* p. 40.

beds with white roses," he states. "They have also eat sour lemons and abundance of lettuce to cool their concupiscence."[20] This problem constantly occupied Byrd's attention and resulted in a variety of curious entries in the commonplace book.

This collection of miscellaneous observations and quotations provides additional insights into Byrd's character, his tastes, and his literary interests. In itself it is not a literary document of much value, but it supplies clues to an understanding of one of the most entertaining men in colonial America. The study of Byrd's writings makes us wish that he had shown less of the modesty that he recommended for "our modern authors" and had devoted more of his time to writing for publication. If he had, we can be certain that colonial literature would have been much richer — and far more amusing.

[20] *Ibid.*, p. 84.

THE SECRET HISTORY
OF THE LINE

*T*HE Governor and Council of Virginia in the year 1727 received an express order from His Majesty to appoint commissioners who, in conjunction with others to be named by the government of North Carolina, should run the line betwixt the two colonies. The rule these gentlemen were directed to go by was a paper of proposals formerly agreed on between the two governors, at that time Spotswood and Eden.[1] It would be a hard thing to say of so wise a man as Mr. Spotswood thought himself that he was overreached, but it has appeared upon trial that Mr. Eden was much better informed how the land lay than he. However, since the King was pleased to agree to these unequal proposals, the government of Virginia was too dutiful to dispute them. They therefore appointed Steddy[2] and Merryman[3] commissioners on the part of Virginia to execute that order and Astrolabe[4] and Capricorn[5] to be the surveyors. But Merryman dying, Firebrand[6] and Meanwell[7] made interest to fill his place. Most of

[1] See the Appendix, pp. 322–336.   [2] William Byrd.

[3] Boyd (*William Byrd's Histories of the Dividing Line betwixt Virginia and North Carolina*, edited by William K. Boyd [Raleigh, N.C., 1929]): "Nathaniel Harrison (1677–1727) of Wakefield, Surry County, member of the House of Burgesses (1699–1706) and of the Council (1713–1727), County Lieutenant of Surry and Prince George in 1715 and after, and Auditor of Virginia in 1724."

[4] William Mayo. Boyd: Mayo was "a native of Wiltshire, England, who arrived in Virginia about 1723 from the Barbadoes, whither he had migrated prior to 1712. During 1717–1721 he made a survey of the Barbadoes and also a map, preserved in the library of King's College. He was one of the justices of Goochland County and was very active as a surveyor in that county and the colony at large, laying off for Byrd the City of Richmond and aiding in establishing the boundaries of the Northern Neck. He died in 1744. Mayo's River is named for him. See Brown's *The Cabells and Their Kin*."

[5] John Allen. Boyd: "See 'Virginia Council Journals,' Sept. 12, 1727. (*Virginia Magazine of History and Biography*, Vol. XXXII, p. 242.) He was probably that John Allen of Surry County who married Elizabeth Bassett, daughter of William Bassett of the Virginia Council, and sometime a student of William and Mary. His will was proved in 1741. See 'Allen Family of Surry County' in *William and Mary College Quarterly*, Vol. VIII, p. 110."

[6] Richard Fitzwilliam. Boyd: "In 1719 he was Collector of Customs for the Lower District of James River. (*Calendar of Treasury Books and Papers, 1714–1719*, p. 481.) On November 21, 1727, he was appointed 'Surveyor General of all the Duties and Importations' for the Carolinas, Maryland, Virginia, Pennsylvania, the Bahama Islands and Jamaica. (*Ibid.*, 1729–30, p. 470.)"

[7] William Dandridge. He was a partner of Governor Spotswood in commercial

the Council inclined to favor the last, because he had offered his services before he knew that any pay would belong to the place. But Burly,[8] one of the honorable board, perceiving his friend Firebrand would lose it if it came to the vote, proposed the expedient of sending three commissioners upon so difficult and hazardous an expedition. To this a majority agreed, being unwilling to be thought too frugal of the public money. Accordingly, they were both joined with Steddy in this commission. When this was over, Steddy proposed that a chaplain might be allowed to attend the commissioners, by reason they should have a number of men with them sufficient for a small congregation and were to pass through an ungodly country where they should find neither church nor minister; that, besides, it would be an act of great charity to give the gentiles of that part of the world an opportunity to christen both them and their children. This being unanimously consented to, Dr. Humdrum[9] was named upon Steddy's recommendation.

Of all these proceedings notice was dispatched to Sir Richard Everard, Governor of North Carolina, desiring him to name commissioners on the part of that province to meet those of Virginia the spring following. In consequence whereof that government named Jumble,[10] Shoebrush,[11] Plausible,[12] and Puzzlecause,[13] being the flower

---

enterprises in 1717 and in 1740 took part in the naval operations against the Spanish at St. Augustine. In 1728 he was a member of the Virginia Council.

[8] Boyd: "Rev. James Blair, Commissary of the Bishop of London in Virginia from 1685 until his death in 1743. A veritable 'King Maker,' for he was responsible for the recall of three governors, Andros, Nicholson, and Spotswood. In 1697 Byrd represented Governor Andros before the Archbishop of Canterbury and the Bishop of London in the controversy between Andros and Blair, and lost his case."

[9] Boyd: "Rev. Peter Fontaine (1691–1757), one of the six children of James Fontaine, a Huguenot refugee . . . Peter was educated at Dublin, Ireland, and after officiating at Wallingford, Weyanoke, Martin's Brandon, and Jamestown, became rector of Westover Parish, Charles City County, of which Byrd was a parishioner."

[10] Christopher Gale. Boyd: "Chief Justice, a native of Yorkshire, England, and eldest son of Rev. Miles Gale, rector of Wighby . . . By 1703 he was a Justice of the General Court and in 1712 was appointed Chief Justice, an office which he held until 1731, except for an intermission from 1717 to 1722 when he was in England, and a briefer one in 1724–25 . . . He was Collector of the Customs at Edenton."

[11] John Lovick. A deputy of the Proprietors and a member of the Council from 1718 to 1731; secretary to the Council and also Secretary of the province from

and cream of the Council of that province. The next step necessary to be taken was for the commissioners on both sides to agree upon a day of meeting at Currituck Inlet in order to proceed on this business, and the fifth of March was thought a proper time, because then Mercury and the moon were to be in conjunction.

It was desired by Sir Richard that the commissioners might meet on the frontiers sometime in January to settle preliminaries, and particularly, that it might be previously agreed that the present possessors of land in either government should be confirmed in their possession, though it should not happen to fall within the government that granted it. This the Governor of Virginia disagreed to, not thinking it just that either the King or the Lords Proprietors should grant away land that did not belong to them. Nor was this proposal made on the part of Carolina purely out of good nature, but some of the Council of that province found their own interest concerned; and particularly the Surveyor General must in justice have returned some of his fees, in case the people should lose the land he surveyed for them as belonging to the Proprietors when in truth it belonged to the King.

Soon after the commissioners for Virginia wrote the following letter to the worthy commissioners of North Carolina:

Gentlemen:

We are sorry we can't have the pleasure of meeting you in January next, as is desired by your governor. The season of the year in which that is proposed to be done, and the distance of our habitation from your frontiers,

---

1722 to 1730. He held other governmental posts including that of Surveyor General, to which he was appointed in 1732.

[12] Edward Moseley. Boyd: Moseley was "a member of the boundary commission of 1710, the preeminent political leader of North Carolina from his appearance in public affairs in 1705 until his death in 1749 . . . He was a member of the Council under four administrations, being President of that body and Acting Governor in 1725 . . . He was one of the commissioners chosen in 1709 to establish the boundary, and in 1723 he was made Surveyor General. Later he was one of the commissioners to establish the South Carolina boundary and also the boundary of the Granville District."

[13] William Little. Boyd: "a native of Massachusetts and a graduate of Harvard, class of 1710. While visiting in England he met Chief Justice Gale and was persuaded by him to move to North Carolina. He settled at Edenton and in 1726 married Justice Gale's daughter, Penelope. In 1725 he was appointed Attorney General and in 1726 Receiver General of Quit Rents. He was also Clerk of the General Court and in 1732 became Chief Justice, an office he held for one year."

43

we hope will make our excuse reasonable. Besides, His Majesty's order marks out our business so plainly that we are persuaded that there can be no difficulty in the construction of it. After this, what imaginable dispute can arise amongst gentlemen who meet together with minds averse to chicane and inclinations to do equal justice both to His Majesty and the Lords Proprietors? in which disposition we make no doubt the commissioners on both sides will find each other.

We shall have full powers to agree at our first meeting on what preliminaries shall be thought necessary, which we hope you will likewise be, that an affair of so great consequence may have no delay or disappointment.

It is very proper to acquaint you in what manner we intend to come provided, that so you gentlemen who are appointed in the same station may, if you please, do the same honor to your government. We shall bring with us about twenty men, furnished with provisions for forty days. We shall have a tent with us and a marquee for the convenience of ourselves and servants. We shall be provided with as much wine and rum as just enable us and our men to drink every night to the success of the following day. And because we understand there are many gentiles on your frontier who never had an opportunity of being baptized, we shall have a chaplain with us to make them Christians. For this purpose we intend to rest in our camp every Sunday, that there may be leisure for so good a work. And whoever of your province shall be desirous of novelty may repair on Sundays to our camp and hear a sermon. Of this you may please to give public notice, that the charitable intentions of this government may meet with the happier success.

Thus much, gentlemen, we thought it necessary to acquaint you with and to make use of this first opportunity of signifying with how much satisfaction we received the news that such able commissioners are appointed for that government, with whom we promise ourselves we shall converse with prodigious pleasure and execute our commissions to the full content of those by whom we have the honor to be employed.

We are, gentlemen, your most humble servants,

Firebrand   Steddy

Meanwell

Williamsburg
The 16th of December, 1727

To this letter the commissioners of Virginia the latter end of January received the following answer:

Gentlemen:

We have the honor of your favor from Williamsburg, dated the sixteenth of December, in which you signify that the proposals already agreed on are so plain that you are persuaded there can no difficulty arise about the construction of them. We think so too; but if no dispute should arise in construing them, yet the manner of our proceeding in the execution we thought had better be previously concerted, and the end of the meeting we proposed was to remove everything that might lie in the way to retard the work, which we all seem equally desirious to have amicably concluded. We assure you, gentlemen, we shall meet you with a hearty disposition of doing equal justice to either government; and as you acquaint us you shall come fully empowered to agree at our first meeting to settle all necessary preliminaries, we shall endeavor to have our instructions as large. Your governor in his last letter to ours was pleased to mention our conferring with you by letters about any matters previously to be adjusted. We therefore take leave to desire by this messenger you will let us know after what manner you purpose to run the line — whether you think to go through the Great Swamp, which is near thirty miles through and thought not passable; or, by taking the latitude at the first station, to run a due-west line to the swamp and then to find the said latitude on the west side the swamp and continue thence a due-west line to Chowan River; or to make the second observation upon Chowan River and run an east line to the Great Swamp. We shall also be glad to know what instruments you intend to use to observe the latitude and find the variation with in order to fix a due-west line. For we are told the last time the commissioners met their instruments varied several minutes, which we hope will not happen again, nor any other difficulty that may occasion any delay or disappointment after we have been at the trouble of meeting in so remote a place and with such attendance and equipage as you intend on your part. We are at a loss, gentlemen, whether to thank you for the particulars you give us of your tent, stores, and the manner you design to meet us. Had you been silent, we had not wanted an excuse for not meeting you in the same manner; but now you force us to expose the nakedness of our country and tell you we can't possibly meet you in the manner our great respect to you would make us glad to do, whom we are not emulous of outdoing, unless in care and diligence in the affair we came about. So all we can answer to that article is that we will endeavor to provide as well as the circumstances of things will admit; and what we want in necessaries we hope will be made up in spiritual comfort we expect from your chaplain, of whom we shall give notice as you desire and doubt not of making a great many boundary Christians. To conclude, we promise to make ourselves as agreeable to you as possibly we can; and we beg leave to assure you that it is a singular pleasure to us that you gentlemen are named on that part to see this business of so great concern and consequence to both governments determined, which makes it to be undertaken on our parts more cheerfully, being assured your characters are above any artifice or design.

We are your most obedient, humble servants,

| Plausible | Jumble |
| Puzzlecause | Shoebrush |

This letter was without date, they having no almanacs in North Carolina, but it came about the beginning of January. However, the Virginia commissioners did not return an answer to it till they had consulted their surveyor, honest Astrolabe, as to the mathematical part. When that was done, they replied in the following terms:

Gentlemen:

We should have returned an answer sooner had not the cold weather and our remote situation from one another prevented our meeting. However, we hope 'tis now time enough to thank you for that favor and to assure you that though we are appointed commissioners for this government we incline to be very just to yours. And as the fixing fair boundaries between us will be of equal advantage to both, you shall have no reason to reproach us with making any step either to delay or disappoint so useful a work. If the Great Swamp you mention should be absolutely impassable, we then propose to run a due-west line from our first station thither and then survey round the same till we shall come on our due-west course on the other side, and so proceed till we shall be again interrupted. But if you shall think of a more proper expedient, we shall not be fond of our own opinion. And though we can't conceive that taking the latitude will be of any use in running this line, yet we shall be provided to do it with the greatest exactness. In performing which, we shall on our part use no graduated instrument,[14] but our accurate surveyor, Astrolabe, tells us he will use a method that will come nearer the truth. He likewise proposes to discover, as near as possible, the just variation of the compass, by means of a true meridian to be found by the North Star. We shall bring

[14] Boyd: "The 'graduated instrument' was doubtless the surveyor's pole, 16½ feet long. By sighting the north star with this, latitude could be crudely calculated. The 'better method' referred to was perhaps the astrolabe."

with us two or three very good compasses, which we hope will not differ much from yours, though if there should be some little variance, 'twill be easily reconciled by two such skillful mathematicians as Astrolabe and Plausible.

In short, gentlemen, we are so conscious of our own disposition to do right to both colonies, and at the same time so verily persuaded of yours, that we promise to ourselves an entire harmony and good agreement. This can hardly fail when justice and reason are laid down on both sides as the rule and foundation of our proceeding. We hope the season will prove favorable to us, but, be that as it will, we intend to preserve fair weather in our humor, believing that even the Dismal may be very tolerable in good company.

We are without the least artifice or design, gentlemen, your most humble servants,

S. F. M.

It was afterwards agreed by the commissioners on both sides to meet on the north shore of Currituck Inlet on the fifth day of the following March in order to run the dividing line. In the meantime, those on the part of Virginia divided the trouble of making the necessary preparations. It fell to Steddy's share to provide the men that were to attend the surveyors. For this purpose, Mr. Mumford [15] recommended to him fifteen able woodsmen, most of which had been Indian traders. These were ordered to meet at Warren's Mill, armed with a gun and tomahawk, on the twenty-seventh of February, and furnished with provisions for ten days. Astrolabe came on the twenty-sixth in order to attend Steddy to the place of rendezvous.

[27.] [16] The next day they crossed the river, having first recommended all they left behind to the divine protection. Steddy carried with him two servants and a sumpter horse for his baggage. About twelve o'clock he met the men at the new church near Warren's Mill. He drew them out to the number of fifteen, and, finding their arms in good order, he caused them to be mustered by their names as follows:

---

[15] Boyd: "Robert Mumford (Munford), Justice and Colonel of Militia in Prince George County, vestryman of Bruton Parish, and member of the House of Burgesses in 1720–22." He acted as Byrd's lawyer and business manager.

[16] The date has been added from the *History* (p. 171).

Peter Jones	Thomas Jones	John Ellis
James Petillo	Charles Kimball	John Evans
Thomas Short	George Hamilton	Robert Hix
Thomas Wilson	Steven Evans	Thomas Jones, Jr.
George Tilman	Robert Allen	John Ellis, Jr.

Here, after drawing out this small troop, Steddy made them the following speech:

Friends and fellow travelers:

It is a pleasure to me to see that we are like to be so well attended in this long and painful journey. And what may we not hope from men who list themselves not so much for pay as from an ambition to serve their country. We have a great distance to go and much work to perform, but I observe too much spirit in your countenances to flinch at either. As no care shall be wanting on my part to do every one of you justice, so I promise myself that on yours you will set the Carolina men whom we are to meet at Currituck a constant pattern of order, industry, and obedience.

Then he marched his men in good order to Capricorn's elegant seat,[17] according to the route before projected, but found him in doleful dumps for the illness of his wife. She was really indisposed, but not so dangerously as to hinder a vigorous man from going upon the service of his country. However, he seemed in the midst of his concern to discover a secret satisfaction that it furnished him with an excuse of not going upon an expedition that he fancied would be both dangerous and difficult. Upon his refusing to go for the reason above-mentioned, Steddy wrote to the Governor how much he was disappointed at the loss of one of the surveyors and recommended Astrolabe's brother[18] to supply his place. At the same time he dispatched away an express to young Astrolabe to let him know he had named him to the Governor for his service. But, not knowing how it would be determined, he could promise him nothing; though if

[17] Bacon's Castle. This seventeenth-century house, built about 1650, was never occupied by Nathaniel Bacon, despite the name. At the time of Bacon's Rebellion it was the home of Major Arthur Allen, grandfather of Capricorn, but it was seized and fortified by one of Bacon's followers. The name was given it at a later date. It still stands, the only Jacobean house in Virginia. See Richard L. Morton, *Colonial Virginia* (Chapel Hill, 1960), I, 273–274 and n. 44.

[18] Boyd: "Joseph Mayo, of 'Powhatan Seat,' on the James River, below Richmond."

he would come to Norfolk at his own risk he should there be able to resolve him. This was the best expedient he could think of for the service at that plunge, because Capricorn had in the bitterness of his concern taken no care to acquaint the Governor that he was prevented from going. However, Dr. Arsmart,[19] who had been to visit Mrs. Capricorn, let the Governor know that he was too tender a husband to leave his spouse to the mercy of a physician.

Upon this notice, which came to the Governor before Steddy's letter, it was so managed that the learned Orion[20] was appointed to go in his room. This gentleman is professor of the mathematics in the College of William and Mary but has so very few scholars that he might be well enough spared from his post for a short time. It was urged by his friends that a person of his fame for profound learning would give a grace to the undertaking and be able to silence all the mathematics of Carolina. These were unanswerable reasons, and so he was appointed. The Reverend Doctor Humdrum came time enough to bless a very plentiful supper at Capricorn's. He treated his company handsomely, and by the help of a bowl of rack punch his grief disappeared so entirely that if he had not sent for Arsmart it might have been suspected his lady's sickness was all a farce. However, to do him justice, the man would never be concerned in a plot that was like to cost him five pistoles.[21]

28. The table was well spread again for breakfast, but, unfortunately for the poor horses, the key of the cornloft was mislaid; at least the servant was instructed to say as much. We marched from hence in good order to the Widow Allen's,[22] which was twenty-two

[19] The fragment of the "Secret History" in the Huntington Library has the name "Dr. Nicolas" crossed out, with "Dr. Arsmart" written above it. This would probably be Dr. George Nicholas, who emigrated to Williamsburg from Lancashire in 1700 after training as a surgeon. He married Elizabeth Carter Burwell, daughter of Robert "King" Carter and widow of Nathaniel Burwell. See *Dictionary of American Biography* under Robert Carter Nicholas, the doctor's eldest son.

[20] Alexander Irvine, professor of mathematics at the College of William and Mary (1729–1732).

[21] A pistole was a Spanish gold coin worth 16s. 6d. to 18s.

[22] Boyd: "The maiden name of this hospitable lady was Bray. She was thrice married: first to Arthur Allen, second to Arthur Smith, finally to —— Stith. In 1753 she donated £125 for a free school in the upper part of Isle of Wight County and her will revealed a bequest of £120, the interest from which was to be used for the education of 'any six poor children.' See *William and Mary College Quarterly*, Vol. VI, pp. 77–78."

miles. She entertained us elegantly and seemed to pattern Solomon's housewife, if one may judge by the neatness of her house and the good order of her family. Here Firebrand and Meanwell had appointed to meet Steddy but failed; however, the tent was sent hither under the care of John Rice, of the kingdom of Ireland, who did not arrive till twelve o'clock at night. This disorder at first setting out gave us but an indifferent opinion of Firebrand's management.

29. From hence Steddy sent a letter to the Governor with an account of his march to that place and of the steps he had taken about Astrolabe's brother. At ten in the morning he thanked the clean widow for all her civilities and marched under the pilotage of Mr. Baker to Colonel Thomas Godding's.[23] By the way Steddy was obliged to be at the expense of a few curses upon John Rice, who was so very thirsty that he called at every house he passed by. The cavalcade arrived at Colonel Godding's about four o'clock after a pleasant journey of thirty miles. But Steddy found himself exceedingly fatigued with the march.

In passing through the upper part of the Isle of Wight, Mr. Baker remarked the dismal footsteps made by the hurricane, which happened in August, 1626. The violence of it did not extend in breadth above a quarter of a mile but in that compass leveled all before it. Mr. Baker's house was so unlucky as to stand in its way, which it laid flat to the ground and blew some of his goods above two miles.

Colonel Godding was very hospitable, both to man and beast, but the poor man had the misfortune to be deaf, which hindered him from hearing any parts of the acknowledgments that were made to him; he pressed everybody very kindly to eat, entreating 'em not to be bashful, which might be a great inconvenience to travelers. The son and heir of the family offered himself as a volunteer the overnight[24] but dreamt so much of danger and difficulties that he declared off in the morning.

[23] Boyd: "The Baker family was prominent in Isle of Wight County, Lawrence Baker being a vestryman of New Port Parish from 1724 to 1737 and James Baker, Clerk of the County Court, 1732–1734. Colonel Thomas Godding was Colonel Thomas Godwin of Nansemond County."
[24] The night before.

MARCH

1. About nine in the morning the Colonel was so kind as to set all his guests over the south branch of Nansemond River, which shortened their journey seven or eight miles, and from thence his son conducted them into the great road. Then they passed for several miles together by the north side of the Great Dismal and after a journey of twenty-five miles arrived in good order at Major Crawford's[25] over against Norfolk Town. Just before they got hither, the lag commissioners overtook them and all the men were drawn up to receive them. Meanwell was so civil as to excuse his not meeting Steddy at Mr. Allen's as had been agreed, but Firebrand was too big for apology.

It was agreed to leave the men and the heavy baggage at Major Crawford's (having made the necessary provision for it) and pass over to Norfolk only with the servants and portmantles,[26] that the townsmen might not be frightened from entertaining them. Here they divided their quarters, that as little trouble might be given as possible, and it was Steddy's fortune, after some apprehensions of going to the ordinary,[27] to be invited by Colonel Newton.[28] To show his regard to the church, he took the chaplain along with him.

Mrs. Newton provided a clean supper without any luxury about eight o'clock and appeared to be one of the fine ladies of the town and, like a true fine lady, to have a great deal of contempt for her husband.

2. This morning old Colonel Boush[29] made Steddy a visit with the tender of his service. There was no soul in the town knew how the land lay betwixt this place and Currituck Inlet, till at last Mr. William Wilkins,[30] that lives upon the borders, drew a rough sketch

[25] Boyd: "Major William Crawford, a member of the County Court of Norfolk in 1728. See *Lower Norfolk County, Virginia, Antiquary*, Vol. I, p. 80."
[26] Portmanteaux, baggage.
[27] Tavern or inn.
[28] Boyd: "George Newton, Lieutenant-Colonel of Militia in Norfolk County, one of the trustees of the Town of Norfolk in the transfer of land owned by the town to Norfolk Academy. In 1744 he was a member of the County Court of Norfolk (*Lower Norfolk County, Virginia, Antiquary*, Vol. I, pp. 78–81, 117.)"
[29] Boyd: "Samuel Boush, member of the County Court of Norfolk in 1728. Today there is a Boush Avenue in Norfolk."
[30] Boyd misread the last name as "Williams," but at a later mention of the man he identifies him as "probably William Wilkins, Justice of Norfolk County in 1728."

that gave a general notion of it. The light given by this draft determined the commissioners to march to the landing of Northwest River and there embark in a piragua [31] in order to meet the commissioners of Carolina at Currituck.

It was really a pleasure to see twelve or fourteen sea vessels riding in the harbor of this city and several wharves built out into the river to land goods upon. These wharves were built with pine logs let into each other at the end, by which those underneath are made firm by those which lie over them. Here the commissioners were supplied with two kegs of wine and two of rum, 178 pounds of bread, and several other conveniencies.

Our good landlord entertained Steddy and the chaplain at dinner, but Firebrand refused because he was not sent to in due form. In the evening the commissioners were invited to an oyster and a bowl by Mr. Sam Smith, a plain man worth £20,000. He produced his two nieces, whose charms were all invisible. These damsels seemed discontented that their uncle showed more distinction to his housekeeper than to them.

We endeavored to hire two or three men here to go along with us but might for the same price have hired them to make a trip to the other world. They looked upon us as men devoted, like Codrus [32] and the two Decii,[33] to certain destruction for the service of our country. The parson and I returned to our quarters in good time and good order, but my man Tom broke the rules of hospitality by getting extremely drunk in a civil house.

3. This being Sunday, we were edified at church by Mr. Marston [34] with a good sermon. People could not attend their devotion for staring at us, just as if we had come from China or Japan. In the meantime, Firebrand and Astrolabe, not having quite so much regard for the Sabbath, went to the Northwest Landing to prepare vessels for our

---

[31] A type of canoe. The manuscript spells this word "periagua" or "periauga."

[32] A legendary king of Sparta, who sacrificed his life rather than allow it to be the price of his country's surrender to Dorian invaders.

[33] Presumably Gaius Messius Quintus Trajanus Decius, Roman Emperor A.D. 249–251, and his son, both of whom were killed in a battle with the Goths.

[34] Boyd identifies him as the Reverend Richard Marsden, of Lynnhaven Parish, Princess Anne County.

transportation to Currituck. I wrote to the Governor an account of our progress thus far, with a billet-doux to my wife. The wind blew very hard at southwest all day; however, in the evening Steddy ordered the men and horses to be set over the South Branch [35] to save time in the morning. My landlady gave us tea and sweetened it with the best of her smiles. At night we spent an hour with Colonel Boush, who stirred his old bones very cheerfully in our service. Poor Orion's horse and furniture were much disordered with the journey hither. His instrument would not traverse nor his ball rest in the socket. In short, all his tackle had the air of distress. Over against the town is Powder Point,[36] where a ship of any burden may lie close to and the men-of-war are used to careen.

4. About eight o'clock in the morning we crossed the river to Powder Point, where we found our men ready to take horse. Several of the grandees of the town, and the parson among the rest, did us the honor to attend us as far as the great bridge over South River. Here we were met by a troop under the command of Captain Wilson,[37] who escorted us as far as his father's castle near the Dismal. We halted about a quarter of an hour and then proceeded to Northwest Landing. Here Firebrand had provided a dinner for us, served up by the master of the house, whose nose seemed to stand upon very ticklish terms.

After dinner we chose ten able men and embarked on board two piraguas under the command of Captain Wilkins,[38] which carried us to the mouth of Northwest River. By the way we found the banks of the river lined with myrtles and bay trees, which afforded a beautiful prospect. These beautiful plants dedicated to Venus and Apollo grow in wet ground, and so does the wild laurel, which in some places is intermixed with the rest. This river is in most places about one hun-

---

[35] Of Elizabeth River, on which Norfolk is located.
[36] Now a suburb of Norfolk called Berkeley.
[37] Boyd suggests Captain Willis Wilson, Jr., who was in 1744 a member of the County Court of Norfolk, but Byrd later mentions a Captain James Wilson (p. 84), and further references to Captain Willis Wilson suggest that he is a different man.
[38] One cannot be certain whether this is the same man as the William Wilkins mentioned earlier or, indeed, whether the name is a mistake for Wilson.

dred yards over and had no tide till the year 1713, when a violent tempest opened a new inlet about five miles to the southward of the old one, which is now almost closed up and too shallow for any vessel to pass over. But the new inlet is deep enough for sloops.

We were four hours in rowing to the mouth of the river, being about eighteen miles from the landing. Here we took up our lodging at one Andrew Duke's, who had lately removed, or rather run away, hither from Maryland. We were forced to lie in bulk upon a very dirty floor that was quite alive with fleas and chinches and made us repent that we had not brought the tent along with us. We had left that with the rest of the heavy baggage at Captain Wilson's under the guard of seven men. There we had also left the Reverend Doctor Humdrum, with the hopes that all the gentiles in the neighborhood would bring their children to be christened, notwithstanding some of them had never been christened themselves. Firebrand had taken care to board his man Tipperary with Captain Wilson, because by being the squire of his body he thought him too much a gentleman to diet with the rest of the men we left behind. This indignity sat not easy upon their stomachs, who were all honest housekeepers in good circumstances.

5. At break of day we turned out, properly speaking, and blest our landlord's eyes with half a pistole. About seven we embarked and passed by the south end of Knott's Island, there being no passage on the north. To the southwards at some distance we saw Bell's and Church's Islands. About noon we arrived at the south shore of old Currituck Inlet, and about two we were joined by Judge Jumble and Plausible, two of the Carolina commissioners; the other two, Shoe-brush and Puzzlecause, lagged behind, which was the more unlucky because we could enter on no business for want of the Carolina commission which these gentlemen had in their keeping. Jumble was brother to the late Dean of York,[39] and if His Honor had not formerly been a pirate himself, he seemed intimately acquainted with many of them. Plausible had been bred in Christ's Hospital and had a tongue

[39] This is not literally true. The purport of Byrd's remark is not clear. See *Dictionary of National Biography* under Thomas Gale, Dean of York, and Miles Gale (father of the Chief Justice).

as smooth as the Commissary, and was altogether as well qualified to be of the Society of Jesus. These worthy gentlemen were attended by Boötes [40] as their surveyor, a young man of much industry but no experience.

We had now nothing to do but to reconnoiter the place. The high land ended in a bluff point, from which a spit of sand extended itself to the southeast about half a mile. The inlet lies between this spit and another on the south side, leaving a shoal passage for the sea not above a mile over. On the east are shoals that run out two or three miles, over which the breakers rise mountains high with a terrible noise. I often cast a longing eye toward England and sighed.

This night we lay for the first time in the woods, and, being without the tent, we made a bower of the branches of cedar, with a large fire in front to guard us from the northwester, which blew very smartly. At night young Astrolabe came to us and gave great jealousy to Orion. His wig was in such stiff buckle that if he had seen the devil the hair would not have stood on end. This night we found the variation to be 3° west, by a due meridian taken from the North Star.

6. We were treated at breakfast by the commissioners of Carolina, who, coming from home by water, were much better provided for the belly than the business. At noon we found the latitude to be 36° 31′, according to Astrolabe, but Orion, to prove his skill in the mathematics by flat contradiction, would needs have it but 36° 30′. Captain Wilkins furnished us with excellent oysters, as savory and well-tasted as those in England.

About three o'clock Messrs. Shoebrush and Puzzlecause made a shift to come to us, after calling at every house where they expected any refreshment; after the necessary compliments and a thousand excuses for making us wait for them so long, we began to enter upon business. We had a tough dispute where we should begin; whether at the point of high land or at the end of the spit of sand, which we with good reason maintained to be the north shore of Currituck Inlet, ac-

[40] Boyd identifies him as Samuel Swann (1704-1772), son of Major Samuel Swann and nephew of Edward Moseley. He was a member of the North Carolina Assembly from Perquimans County from 1725 to 1734, from Onslow County, 1734-1762, and was Speaker from 1742 to 1762.

55

cording to the express words of His Majesty's order. They had no argument to support our beginning at the high land but because the former commissioners for Virginia submitted to it. But if what they did was to be a rule for us, then we ought to allow no variation of the compass because those gentlemen allowed of none.

This controversy lasted till night, neither side receding from its opinion. However, by the lucky advice of Firebrand, I took Plausible aside and let him know the government of Virginia had looked upon him as the sole obstacle to the settling the bounds formerly, and if we should break off now upon this frivolous pretense he would surely bear the blame again. At the same time I showed him a representation made to the late Queen by Colonel Spotswood greatly to his disadvantage. This worked so powerfully upon his politic that he without loss of time softened his brethren in such a manner that they came over to our opinion. They were the rather persuaded to this by the peremptory words of our commission, by which we were directed to go on with the business though the Carolina commissioners should refuse to join with us therein. However, by reason of some proof that was made to us by the oaths of two credible persons that the spit of sand was advanced about two hundred yards to the southwards since the year 1712, when the proposals between the Governors Eden and Spotswood were agreed upon, we thought it reasonable to allow for so much and accordingly made our beginning from thence.

Upon the high land we found one kind of silk grass and plenty of yaupon, which passes for tea in North Carolina, though nothing like it. On the sands we saw conch shells in great number, of which the Indians make both their blue and white peak,[41] both colors being in different parts of the same shell.

7. We drove down a post at our place of beginning and then crossed over to Dosier's Island, which is nothing but a flat sand with shrubs growing upon it. From thence we passed over to the north end of Knott's Island, our line running through the plantation of William Harding. This man had a wife born and bred near Temple Bar and still talked of the walks in the Temple with pleasure. These poor people bestowed their wood and their water upon us very freely.

[41] A variant of "peag" or "wampum"; see pp. 178 and 218.

We found Shoebrush a merry, good-humored man and had learnt a very decent behavior from Governor Hyde, to whom he had been *valet de chambre*, of which he still carried the marks by having his coat, waistcoat, and breeches of different parishes. Puzzlecause had degenerated from a New England preacher, for which his godly parents designed him, to a very wicked but awkward rake.

I had almost forgot to mention a marooner [42] who had the confidence to call himself an hermit, living on the south shore of Currituck near the Inlet. He has no other habitation but a green bower or arbor, with a female domestic as wild and as dirty as himself. His diet is chiefly oysters, which he has just industry enough to gather from the neighboring oyster banks; while his concubine makes a practice of driving up the neighbor's cows for the advantage of their milk.

Orion seemed to be grievously puzzled about plotting off his surveyor's work and chose rather to be obliged to the Carolina commissioners than to Mr. Mayo for their instruction, which it was evident to everybody that he wanted. The truth of it is, he had been much more discreet to loiter on at the College and receive his salary quietly (which he owes to his relation to the pious Commissary) than to undertake a business which discovered he knew very little of the matter.

8. We quitted our camp about seven and early dispatched away the large piragua, with the heavy baggage and most of the men, round the south end of Knott's Island. About nine we embarked ourselves on board the lesser piragua, under the pilotage of Captain Wilkins, and steered our course toward the north end of the island. This navigation was so difficult by reason of the perpetual shoals that we were often fast aground, but Firebrand swore us off again very soon. Our pilot would have been a miserable man if one half of that gentleman's curses had taken effect. It was remarkable to see how mild and unmoved the poor man was under so much heavy displeasure, insomuch that the most passionate expression that escaped him was, "Oh, forever and after!" which was his form of swearing.

We had been benighted in that wide water had we not met a canoe that was carrying a conjurer from Princess Anne to Carolina. But, as all conjurers are sometimes mistaken, he took us at first for pirates,

[42] Buccaneer or pirate, hence a disreputable person.

and, what was worse for him, he suspected afterwards that we were officers that were in pursuit of him and a woman that passed for his wife. However, at last being undeceived in both these points, they suffered us to speak with them and directed us in the course we were to steer. By their advice we rowed up a water called the Back Bay as far as a skirt of pocosin [43] a quarter of a mile in breadth. Through this we waded up to the knees in mud and got safe on the firm land of Princess Anne County.

During this voyage, Shoebrush, in champing a biscuit, forced out one of his teeth, which an unlucky flux had left loose in his head. And though one of his feet was inflamed with the gout, yet he was forced to walk two miles as well as the rest of us to John Heath's, where we took up our quarters. Amongst other spectators came two girls to see us, one of which was very handsome and the other very willing. However, we only saluted [44] them, and if we committed any sin at all, it was only in our hearts.

Captain White,[45] a grandee of Knott's Island, and Mr. Moss, a grandee of Princess Anne, made us a visit and helped to empty our liquor. The surveyors and their attendants came to us at night, after wading through a marsh near five miles in breadth which stretches from the west side of Knott's Island to the high land of Princess Anne. In this marsh several of the men had plunged up to the middle; however, they kept up their good humor and only made sport of what others would have made a calamity.

9. In the morning we walked with the surveyors to the line, which cut through Eyland's plantation, and came to the banks of North River. Hither the girls above-mentioned attended us, but an old woman came along with them for the security of their virtue. Others rose out of their sickbeds to see such rarities as we were.

One of our piraguas set the surveyors and five men over North River. They landed in a miry marsh, which led to a very deep pocosin. Here they met with beaver dams and otter holes which it was not

[43] Swamp, a word of Algonquian origin.
[44] Kissed.
[45] Boyd: "Reference is doubtless to Capt. Solomon White of Princess Anne County. There is no record of a Moss family in that County."

practicable to pass in a direct line, though the men offered to do it with great alacrity, but the surveyors were contented to make a traverse.

While they were struggling with these difficulties, we commissioners went in state in the other piragua to Northwest River and rowed up as high as Mr. Merchant's.[46] He lives near half a mile from the river, having a causeway leading through a filthy swamp to his plantation. I encamped in his pasture with the men, though the other commissioners indulged themselves so far as to lie in the house. But it seems they broke the rules of hospitality by several gross freedoms they offered to take with our landlord's sister. She was indeed a pretty girl, and therefore it was prudent to send her out of harm's way. I was the more concerned at this unhandsome behavior because the people were extremely civil to us and deserved a better treatment.

The surveyors came to us at night, very much jaded with their dirty work, and Orion slept so sound that he had been burnt in his blanket if the sentry had not been kinder to him than he deserved.

10. This being Sunday, we rested the men and surveyors, though we could not celebrate the Sabbath as we ought for want of our chaplain. I had a letter from him informing me that all was well, both soul and body, under his care. Captain Wilkins went home to make his wife a visit and brought me a bottle of milk, which was better than a bottle of Tokay. Firebrand took all occasions to set Orion above Astrolabe, which there was no reason for but because he had the honor to be recommended by him. I halted as bad as old Jacob, without having wrestled with anything like an angel. The men were concerned at it and had observed so much of Firebrand's sweet temper that they swore they would make the best of their way home if it pleased God to disable me from proceeding on the business. But I walked about as much as I could and thereby made my hip very pliable.

We found Captain Willis Wilson here, whose errand was to buy pork, which is the staple commodity of North Carolina and which with pitch and tar makes up the whole of their traffic. The truth of it

[46] Boyd: "There was a Willoughby Merchant, justice of Princess Anne, at this time."

is, these people live so much upon swine's flesh that it don't only incline them to the yaws [47] and consequently to the downfall of their noses, but makes them likewise extremely hoggish in their temper, and many of them seem to grunt rather than speak in their ordinary conversation.

11. We ordered the surveyors early to their business, with five of the men to attend them. They had a tiresome day's work of it, wading through a deep pocosin near two miles over, in which they frequently plunged up to the middle. In the meantime, we commissioners rowed up the river in our piragua much more at our ease and dropped anchor at Mossy Point, near a deserted pork store belonging to Captain Willis Wilson. After the men had swept out a cartload of dirt, we put our baggage into it for fear of rain. Then we sent our piragua in quest of the surveyors; and Firebrand, believing nothing could be well done without him, went in it himself, attended by Puzzlecause, though he did no other good but favor us with his room instead of his company.

In the meanwhile, Shoebrush and I took a walk into the woods and called at a cottage where a dark angel surprised us with her charms. Her complexion was a deep copper, so that her fine shape and regular features made her appear like a statue *en bronze* done by a masterly hand. Shoebrush was smitten at the first glance and examined all her neat proportions with a critical exactness. She struggled just enough to make her admirer more eager, so that if I had not been there, he would have been in danger of carrying his joke a little too far.

The surveyors found us out in the evening very much fatigued, and the men were more off their mettle than ever they had been in the whole journey, though without the least complaint. I took up my lodging in the camp but was driven into the house about midnight without my breeches, like Monsieur Broglie,[48] by a smart shower of rain. Here we all lay in bulk the rest of the night upon a dirty and wet floor without taking cold.

[47] A contagious disease, common in warm and tropical climates, somewhat resembling syphilis.

[48] Byrd possibly refers to François Marie, duc de Broglie, who served in the French army during the War of the Spanish Succession and in later battles in Italy. On the night of September 14, 1734, his quarters on the Secchia were raided and he narrowly escaped capture. If Byrd has this incident in mind, the reference was obviously added much later than the original composition of his narrative.

12. Complaint was made to me this morning that the men belonging to the piragua had stole our people's meat while they slept. This provoked me to treat them *à la dragon*, that is, to swear at them furiously, and by the good grace of my oaths I might have passed for an officer in His Majesty's guards. I was the more out of humor because it disappointed us in our early march, it being a standing order to boil the pot overnight that we might not be hindered in the morning.

This accident and necessity of drying our bedclothes kept us from decamping till near twelve o'clock. By this delay the surveyors found time to plot off their work and to observe the course of the river. Then they passed it over against Northern's Creek, the mouth of which was very near our line. But the commissioners made the best of their way to the bridge and, going ashore, walked to Mr. Ballance's plantation.

I retired early to our camp at some distance from the house, while my colleagues tarried withindoors and refreshed themselves with a cheerful bowl. In the gaiety of their hearts, they invited a tallow-faced wench that had sprained her wrist to drink with them, and when they had raised her in good humor they examined all her hidden charms and played a great many gay pranks. While Firebrand, who had the most curiosity, was ranging over her sweet person, he picked off several scaps as big as nipples, the consequence of eating too much pork. The poor damsel was disabled from making any resistance by the lameness of her hand; all she could do was to sit still and make the fashionable exclamation of the country, "Flesh alive and tear it!" and, by what I can understand, she never spake so properly in her life.

One of the representatives of North Carolina made a midnight visit to our camp, and his curiosity was so very clamorous that it waked me, for which I wished his nose as flat as any of his porcivorous countrymen.

13. In the morning our chaplain came to us and with him some men we had sent for to relieve those who had waded through the mire from Currituck. But they begged they might not be relieved, believing they should gain immortal honor by going through the Dismal. Only Petillo desired to be excused on the account of his eyes. Old Ellis petitioned to go in the room of his son, and Kimball was deprived from

that favor by lot. That grieved him so that he offered a crown to Hamilton to let him go in his room, which the other would not listen to for ten times the money.

When this great affair was settled, we dismissed all the men to their quarters at Captain Wilson's except the nine Dismalites. Of these we sent five with the surveyors, who ran the line to the skirts of the Dismal, which began first with dwarf reeds and moist, uneven grounds. We discharged our piraguas, and about noon our good friend Captain Wilkins conducted us to his own house and entertained us hospitably. We made the necessary disposition for entering the Dismal next morning with nine of our men and three of Carolina, so many being necessary to attend the surveyors and for carrying the bedding and provisions. The men were in good spirits, but poor Orion began to repent and wish he had slept in a whole skin at the College rather than become a prey to the turkey buzzard. These reflections sunk his courage so low that neither liquor nor toast could raise it. I hardly knew how to behave myself in a bed, after having lain a week in the open field and seeing the stars twinkle over my head.

14. This morning early the men began to make up the packs they were to carry on their shoulders into the Dismal. They were victualed for eight days, which was judged sufficient for the service. These provisions, with the blankets and other necessaries, loaded the men with a burden of fifty or sixty pounds for each. Orion helped most of all to make these loads so heavy by taking his bed and several changes of raiment, not forgetting a suit for Sundays, along with him. This was a little unmerciful, which with his peevish temper made him no favorite.

We fixed them out about ten in the morning, and then Meanwell, Puzzlecause, and I went along with them, resolving to enter them fairly into this dreadful swamp, which nobody before ever had either the courage or curiosity to pass. But Firebrand and Shoebrush chose rather to toast their noses over a good fire and spare their dear persons.

After a march of two miles through a very bad way, the men sweating under their burdens, we arrived at the edge of the Dismal, where the surveyors had left off the night before. Here Steddy thought proper to encourage the men by a short harangue to this effect: "Gentlemen, we are at last arrived at this dreadful place, which till now has been thought unpassable, though I make no doubt but you will convince everybody that there is no difficulty which may not be conquered by spirit and constancy. You have hitherto behaved with so much vigor that the most I can desire of you is to persevere unto the end. I protest to you, the only reason we don't share in your fatigue is the fear of adding to your burdens (which are but too heavy already), while we are sure we can add nothing to your resolution. I shall say no more but only pray the Almighty to prosper your undertaking and grant we may meet on the other side in perfect health and safety." The men took this speech very kindly and answered it in the most cheerful manner with three huzzas.

Immediately we entered the Dismal, two men clearing the way before the surveyors to enable them to take their sight. The reeds, which grew about twelve feet high, were so thick and so interlaced with bamboo briers that our pioneers were forced to open a passage. The ground, if I may properly call it so, was so spongy that the prints of our feet were instantly filled with water. Amongst the reeds here and there stood a white cedar, commonly mistaken for juniper. Of this sort was the soil for about half a mile together, after which we came to a piece of high land about one hundred yards in breadth.

We were above two hours scuffling through the reeds to this place, where we refreshed the poor men. Then we took leave, recommending both them and the surveyors to Providence. We furnished Astrolabe with bark and other medicines for any of the people that might happen to be sick, not forgetting three kinds of rattlesnake root made into doses in case of need.

It was four o'clock before we returned to our quarters, where we found our colleagues under some apprehension that we were gone with the people quite through the Dismal. During my absence Firebrand was so very careful in sending away the baggage that he forgot the candles.

When we had settled accounts with our landlord, we rode away to Captain Wilson's, who treated us with pork upon pork. He was a great lover of conversation, and rather than it should drop, he would repeat the same story over and over. Firebrand chose rather to litter the floor than lie with the parson, and, since he could not have the best bed, he sullenly would have none at all. However, it broiled upon his stomach so much that he swore enough in the night to bring the devil into the room, had not the chaplain been there.

15. We sent away the baggage about eight o'clock under the guard of four men. We paid off a long reckoning to Captain Wilson for our men and horses, but Firebrand forgot to pay for the washing of his linen, which saved him two shillings at least. He and his flatterer, Shoebrush, left us to ourselves; intending to reach Captain Meade's[49] but, losing their way, they took up at Mr. Pugh's, after riding above fifty miles, and part of the way in the dark. How many curses this misadventure cost them I can't say, though at least as many as they rode miles. I was content to tarry to see the men fixed out and jog on fair and softly along with them, and so were Meanwell and Puzzlecause. One of our men had a kick on the belly by a horse, for which I ordered him to be instantly blooded, and no ill consequence ensued. We left Astrolabe's Negro sick behind us.

About eleven we set off and called at an ordinary eight miles off, not far from the great bridge. Then we proceeded eight miles farther to honest Timothy Ives's,[50] who supplied us with everything that was necessary. He had a tall, straight daughter of a yielding, sandy complexion, who having the curiosity to see the tent, Puzzlecause gallanted her thither, and might have made her free of it had not we come seasonably to save the damsel's chastity. Here both our cookery and bedding were more cleanly than ordinary. The parson lay with Puzzlecause in the tent to keep him honest or, peradventure, to partake of his diversion if he should be otherwise.

16. We marched from hence about nine, always giving our baggage the start of us. We called at John Ives's for a taste of good water, which is as rare in these parts as good doctrine. We saw several pretty girls

[49] Boyd: "Andrew Meade . . . a member of the House of Burgesses, 1727–1734, and of the County Court, and . . . Senior Captain of Militia. See Baskerville's *Andrew Meade of Ireland and Virginia*."
[50] The last name is Ivy in the *History* (p. 192). In the American Philosophical Society manuscript of the "History" the name has been corrected from Ives's to Ivy's. The scribe may have been influenced by the John Ives mentioned below.

here as wild as colts, though not so ragged, but dressed all in their own industry. Even those could not tempt us to alight, but we pursued our journey with diligence.

We passed by Mr. O'Shield's and Mr. Pugh's, the last of which has a very good brick house, and arrived about four at Captain Meade's. Here amongst other strong liquors we had plenty of strong beer, with which we made as free as our libertines did with the parson. The Carolina commissioners did not only persecute him with their wit but with their kisses too, which he suffered with the patience of a martyr. We were no sooner under the shelter of that hospitable house but it began to rain, and so continued to do great part of the night, which put us in some pain for our friends in the Dismal. The journey this day was twenty-five miles, yet the baggage horses performed it without faltering.

17. It rained this morning till ten o'clock, which filled us all with the vapors. I gave myself a thorough wash and scrubbed off a full week's dirt, which made me fitter to attend the service which our chaplain performed.

I wrote to the Governor a particular account of our proceedings and had the complaisance to show the letter to my colleagues. These worthy gentlemen had hammered out an epistle to the Governor, containing a kind of remonstrance against paying the Burgesses in money, and prevailed with our landlord to deliver it.

At night we had a religious bowl to the pious memory of St. Patrick, and, to show due regard to this saint, several of the company made some Hibernian bulls, but the parson unhappily outblundered all, which made his persecutors merry at his cost.

18. It was not possible to get from so good a house before eleven o'clock, nor then neither for our servants. When Firebrand asked his man why he lagged behind, he expressed himself with great freedom of his master, swearing he cared for no mortal but his dear self and wishing that the devil might take him if he ever attended him again in any of his travels.

We made the best of our way to Mr. Thomas Speight's,[51] who ap-

[51] Boyd: "Mr. Thomas Speight, of Perquimans County, member of the North Carolina Assembly in 1725 and Associate Justice of the General Court, 1726–28."

peared to be a grandee of North Carolina. There we arrived about four, though the distance could not be less than twenty-five miles. Upon our arrival our poor landlord made a shift to crawl out upon his crutches, having the gout in both his knees. He bid us welcome, and a great bustle was made in the family about our entertainment. We saw two truss[52] damsels stump about very industriously, that were handsome enough upon a march.

Our landlord gave us much concern by affirming with some assurance that the Dismal could not be less than thirty miles in breadth. All our comfort was that his computation depended wholly on his own wild conjecture. We ordered guns to be fired and a drum to be beaten to try if we could be answered out of the desert, but we had no answer but from that prating slut, Echo.

The servants tied the horses so carelessly that some of them did our landlord much damage in his fodder. I was the more concerned at this because the poor man did all he could to supply our wants.

Firebrand and the parson lay single, while some were obliged to stow three in a bed. Nor could lying soft and alone cure the first of these of swearing outrageously in his sleep.

19. We dispatched men to the north and south, to fire guns on the edge of the Dismal by way of signal, but could gain no intelligence of our people. Men, women, and children flocked from the neighborhood to stare at us with as much curiosity as if we had been Morocco ambassadors. Many children were brought to our chaplain to be christened, but no capons, so that all the good he did that way was gratis. Major Alston and Captain Baker made us a visit and dined with us.

My landlord's daughter, Rachel, offered her service to wash my linen and regaled me with a mess of hominy, tossed up with rank butter and glyster sugar.[53] This I was forced to eat to show that nothing from so fair a hand could be disagreeable. She was a smart lass, and, when I desired the parson to make a memorandum of his christenings that we might keep an account of the good we did, she asked me very

[52] Shapely.
[53] Probably a scribal error for "caster sugar."

pertly who was to keep an account of the evil? I told her she should be my secretary for that if she would go along with me. Mr. Pugh and Mr. O'Shield helped to fill up our house, so that my landlady told us in her cups that now we must lie three in a bed.

20. No news yet of our Dismalites, though we dispatched men to every point of the compass to inquire after them. Our visitors took their leave, but others came in the evening to supply their places. Judge Jumble, who left us at Currituck, returned now from Edenton and brought three cormorants along with him. One was his own brother,[54] the second was brother to Shoebrush,[55] and the third, Captain Genneau, who had sold his commission and spent the money. These honest gentlemen had no business but to help drink out our liquor, having very little at home. Shoebrush's brother is a collector and owes his place to a bargain he made with Firebrand. Never were understrappers[56] so humble as the North Carolina collectors are to this huge man. They pay him the same colirt[57] they would do if they held their commissions immediately from his will and pleasure, though the case is much otherwise, because their commissions are as good as his, being granted by the same commissioners of His Majesty's Customs. However, he expects a world of homage from them, calling them his officers. Nor is he content with homage only, but he taxes them, as indeed he does all the other collectors of his province, with a hundred little services.

At night the noble captain retired before the rest of the company and was stepping without ceremony into our bed, but I arrived just time enough to prevent it. We could not possibly be so civil to this free gentleman as to make him so great a compliment, much less let him take possession, according to the Carolina breeding, without invitation. Had Ruth or Rachel, my landlord's daughters, taken this liberty, we should perhaps have made no words, but in truth the captain had no charms that merited so particular an indulgence.

21. Several persons from several parts came to see us, amongst which

[54] Edmund Gale.
[55] Boyd: "Thomas Lovick, of Chowan County, Collector of the Customs."
[56] Underlings.
[57] Probably a scribal misreading for "courtesy."

was Mr. Baker and his brother, the surveyor of Nansemond, but could tell us no tidings from the Dismal. We began to be in pain for the men who had been trotting in that bog so long, and the more because we apprehended a famine amongst them. I had indeed given them a warrant to kill anything that came in their way in case of necessity, not knowing that no living creature could inhabit that inhospitable place.

My landlord thought our stay here as tedious as we did, because we eat up his corn and summer provisions. However, the hopes of being well paid rendered that evil more supportable. But complaint being made that the corn grew low, we retrenched the poor men's horses to one meal a day.

In the evening Plausible and Puzzlecause returned to us from Edenton, where they had been to recover the great fatigue of doing nothing and to pick up new scandal against their governor.

22. Our disagreeable Carolina visitors were so kind as to take their leave; so did Mr. O'Shield and Captain Foot, by which our company and my landlord's trouble were considerably lessened. We went out several ways in the morning and could get no intelligence. But in the afternoon Boötes brought us the welcome news that the surveyors and all the people were come safe out of the Dismal. They landed, if one may so call it, near six miles north of this place about ten this morning, not far from the house of Peter Brinkley. Here they appeased their hungry stomachs and waited to receive our orders. It seems the distance through the desert where they passed it was fifteen miles. Of this they had marked and measured no more than ten but had traversed the remainder as fast as they could for their lives. They were reduced to such straits that they began to look upon John Ellis' dog with a longing appetite, and John Evans, who was fat and well-liking,[58] had reason to fear that he would be the next morsel.

We sent Astrolabe's horses for him and his brother, and Firebrand ordered Peter Jones, with an air of authority, to send his horse for Orion, but he let him understand very frankly that nobody should ride his horse but himself. So, not finding his commands obeyed by

[58] Thriving.

68

the Virginians, he tried his power amongst the Carolina men, who were more at his devotion and sent one of their horses for his friend, to save his own. He also sent him a pottle [59] bottle of strong beer particularly,[60] without any regard to Astrolabe, though the beer belonged to the other commissioners as much as to him.

We also sent horses for the men, that they might come to us and refresh themselves after so dreadful a fatigue. They had, however, gone through it all with so much fortitude that they discovered as much strength of mind as of body. They were now all in perfect health, though their moist lodging for so many nights and drinking of standing water, tinged with the roots of juniper, had given them little fevers and slight fluxes in their passage, which as slight remedies recovered.

Since I mentioned the strong beer, it will be but just to remember Captain Meade's generosity to us. His cart arrived here yesterday with a very handsome present to the commissioners of Virginia. It brought them two dozen quart bottles of excellent Madeira wine, one dozen pottle bottles of strong beer, and half a dozen quarts of Jamaica rum. To this general present was added a particular one to Meanwell of Naples biscuit from Mrs. Meade. At the same time we received a very polite letter, which gave a good grace to his generosity and doubled our obligation. And surely never was bounty better timed, when it enabled us to regale the poor Dismalites, whose spirits needed some recruit. And indeed we needed comfort as well as they, for though we had not shared with them in the labors of the body, yet we made it up with the labor of the mind, and our fears had brought us as low as our fatigue had done them. I wrote a letter of thanks to our generous benefactor, concluding with a tender of the commissioners' service and the blessing of their chaplain.

23. The surveyors described the Dismal to us in the following manner: that it was in many places overgrown with tall reeds interwoven with large briers, in which the men were frequently entangled, and that not only in the skirts of it but likewise toward the middle. In

[59] Half-gallon.
[60] That is, for Orion particularly, and for no one else.

other places it was full of juniper trees, commonly so called though they seem rather to be white cedars. Some of these are of a great bigness, but, the soil being soft and boggy, there is little hold for the roots, and consequently any high wind blows many of them down. By this means they lie in heaps, horsing upon one another and bristling out with sharp snags, so that passage in many places is difficult and dangerous. The ground was generally very quaggy, and the impressions of the men's feet were immediately filled with water. So, if there was any hole made, it was soon full of that element, and by that method it was that our people supplied themselves with drink. Nay, if they made a fire, in less than half an hour, when the crust of leaves and trash were burnt through, it would sink down into a hole and be extinguished. So replete is this soil with water that it could never have been passable but in a very dry season. And, indeed, considering it is the source of six or seven rivers without any visible body of water to supply them, there must be great stores of it underground. Some part of this swamp has few or no trees growing in it but contains a large tract of reeds, which being perpetually green and waving in the wind, it is called the Green Sea. Gallbushes grow very thick in many parts of it, which are evergreen shrubs bearing a berry which dyes a black color like the galls of the oak, and from thence they receive their name.

Abundance of cypress trees grow likewise in this swamp and some pines upon the borders toward the firm land, but the soil is so moist and miry that, like the junipers, a high wind mows many of them down. It is remarkable that toward the middle of the Dismal no beast or bird or even reptile can live, not only because of the softness of the ground but likewise because 'tis so overgrown with thickets that the genial beams of the sun can never penetrate them. Indeed, on the skirts of it cattle and hogs will venture for the sake of the reeds and roots, with which they will keep themselves fat all winter. This is a great advantage to the bordering inhabitants in that particular, though they pay dear for it by the agues and other distempers occasioned by the noxious vapors that rise perpetually from that vast extent of mire and nastiness. And a vast extent it is, being computed at a medium ten miles broad and thirty miles long, though where the line passed it 'twas completely fifteen miles broad. However, this dirty Dismal is in many parts of it very pleasant to the eye, though disagreeable to the other senses, because there is an everlasting verdure which makes every season look like the spring. The way the men took to secure their bedding here from moisture was by laying cypress bark under their blankets, which made their lodging hard but much more wholesome.

It is easy to imagine the hardships the poor men underwent in this intolerable place, who, besides the burdens on their backs, were obliged to clear the way before the surveyors and to measure and mark after them. However, they went through it all not only with patience but cheerfulness, though Orion was as peevish as an old maid all the way, and the more so because he could persuade nobody to be out of humor but himself. The merriment of the men and their innocent jokes with one another gave him great offense; whereas if he had had a grain of good nature he should have rejoiced to find that the greatest difficulties could not break their spirits or lessen their good humor. Robin Hix took the liberty to make him some short replies that discomposed him very much: particularly, one hot day, when the poor fellow had a load fit for a horse upon his back, Orion had the conscience to desire him to carry his greatcoat. But he roundly refused it, telling him frankly he had already as great a burden as he could stagger under. This Orion stomached[61] so much that he complained privately of it to Firebrand as soon as he saw him but said not one syllable of it to me. However, I was informed of it by Astrolabe but resolved to take no notice, unless the cause was brought before us in form, that the person accused might have the English liberty of being heard in his turn. But Firebrand said a gentleman should be believed on his bare word without evidence and a poor man condemned without trial, which agreed not at all with my notions of justice.

I understood all this at second hand, but Meanwell was let into the secret by the parties themselves with the hopes of perverting him into their sentiments; but he was stanch and they were not able to

[61] Resented.

71

make the least impression upon him. This was a grievous balk, because if they could have gained him over, they flattered themselves they might have been as unrighteous as they pleased by a majority. As it happens to persons disappointed, it broiled upon our gentlemen's stomachs so much that they were but indifferent company, and I observed very plain that Firebrand joked less adays and swore more anights ever after. After these misfortunes, to be formally civil was as much as we could afford to be to one another. Neither of us could dissemble enough to put on a gay outside when it was cloudy within. However, these inward uneasinesses helped to make the rest of our sufferings the more intolerable. When people are joined together in a troublesome commission, they should endeavor to sweeten by complacency [62] and good humor all the hazards and hardships they are bound to encounter and not, like married people, make their condition worse by everlasting discord. Though in this, indeed, we had the advantage of married people, that a few weeks would part us.

24. This being Sunday, the people flocked from all parts, partly out of curiosity and partly out of devotion. Among the female part of our congregation there was not much beauty; the most fell to Major Alston's daughter, who is said to be no niggard of it. Our chaplain made some Christians but could persuade nobody to be married, because every country justice can do that job for them. Major Alston and Captain Baker dined with us.

In the afternoon I equipped the men with provisions and dispatched them away with Astrolabe and Boötes to the place where they were to return into the Dismal, in order to mark and measure what they had left unfinished. Plausible and Shoebrush took a turn to Edenton and invited us to go with them, but I was unwilling to go from my post and expose the men to be ill treated that I left behind. Firebrand had a flirt at Robin Hix, which discovered much pique and no justice, because it happened to be for a thing of which he was wholly innocent.

25. The air was chilled with a northwester, which favored our Dismalites, who entered the desert very early. It was not so kind to

[62] Complaisance, courtesy.

Meanwell, who unseasonably kicked off the bedclothes and catched an ague. We killed the time by that great help to disagreeable society, a pack of cards.

Our landlord had not the good fortune to please Firebrand with our dinner, but, surely, when people do their best, a reasonable man would be satisfied. But he endeavored to mend his entertainment by making hot love to honest Ruth, who would by no means be charmed either with his persuasion or his person. While the master was employed in making love to one sister, the man made his passion known to the other; only he was more boisterous and employed force when he could not succeed by fair means. Though one of the men rescued the poor girl from this violent lover but was so much his friend as to keep the shameful secret from those whose duty it would have been to punish such violations of hospitality. Nor was this the only one this disorderly fellow was guilty of, for he broke open a house where our landlord kept the fodder for his own use, upon the belief that it was better than what he allowed us. This was in compliment to his master's horses, I hope, and not in blind obedience to any order he received from him.

26. I persuaded Meanwell to take a vomit of ipecacuanha, which worked very kindly. I took all the care of him I could, though Firebrand was so unfriendly as not to step once upstairs to visit him. I also gave a vomit to a poor shoemaker that belonged to my landlord, by which he reaped great benefit. Puzzlecause made a journey to Edenton and took our chaplain with him to preach the Gospel to the infidels of that town and to baptize some of their children. I began to entertain with my chocolate, which everybody commended but only he that commends nothing that don't belong to himself. In the evening I took a solitary walk that I might have leisure to think on my absent friends, which I now grew impatient to see. Orion stuck as close to his patron Firebrand as the itch does to the fingers of many of his country folks.

27. Though it threatened rain both yesterday and today, yet Heaven was so kind to our friends in the Dismal as to keep it from falling. I persuaded Meanwell to take the bark, which he did with good effect,

though he continued very faint and low-spirited. He took Firebrand's neglect in great dudgeon and, amidst all his good nature, could not forbear a great deal of resentment; but I won his heart entirely by the tender care I took of him in his illness. I also gained the men's affection by dressing their wounds and giving them little remedies for their complaints. Nor was I less in my landlord's books for acting the doctor in his family, though I observed some distempers in it that were past my skill to cure. For his wife and heir apparent were so inclined to a cheerful cup that our good liquor was very unsafe in their keeping. I had a long time observed that they made themselves happy every day before the sun had run one third of his course, which no doubt gave some uneasiness to the old gentleman, but custom, that reconciles most evils, made him bear it with Christian patience.

As to the young gentleman, he seemed to be as worthless as any homebred squire I had ever met with and much the worse for having a good opinion of himself. His good father intended him for the mathematics, but he never could rise higher in that study than to gauge a rum cask. His sisters are very sensible, industrious damsels, who, though they see gentlemen but seldom, have the grace to resist their importunities and, though they are innocently free, will indulge them in no dangerous liberties. However, their cautious father, having some notion of female frailty from what he observed in their mother, never suffers them to lie out of his own chamber.

28. I had a little stiffness in my throat, I fancy by lying alone, for Meanwell, being grown restless by his indisposition, chose to lie by himself. The time passed heavily, which we endeavored to make lighter by cards and books. The having nothing to do here was more insupportable than the greatest fatigue, which made me envy the drudgery of those in the Dismal.

In the evening we walked several ways, just as we drew in the day, but made a shift to keep within the bounds of decency in our behavior. However, I observed Firebrand had something that broiled upon his stomach, which though he seemed to stifle in the day, yet in the night it burst out in his sleep in a volley of oaths and imprecations.

yet in the Night it burst out in his Sleep in a Volley of Oaths & Imprecations. This being my Birth day, I adored the Goodness of Heaven, for having indulg'd me with so much Health & very uncommon happiness, in the Course of 54 Years in which my Sins have been many, & my Sufferings few, only Opportunitys great, but my Improvements small. Firebrand & Meanwell had very high Words, after I went to Bed, concerning Astrolabe, in which Conversation Meanwell shew'd most Spirit, & Firebrand most Arrogance & Ill Nature.

29. I wrote a Letter to the Governor which I had the Complaisance to shew to my Collegues to prevent Jealousies & Fears. We received Intelligence that our Surveyors & people finish'd their business in the Dismal last Night, & found it no more than 5 Miles from the Place where they left off. Above a Mile before they came out, they were led up to the Knees in a Pine Swamp. We let them rest this day at Peter Brinkleys, & sent Orders to them to proceed the next Morning. Bootes left them & came to us with intent to desert us quite, & leave the rest of the Drudgery to Plausible, who had indulg'd his Old Bones hitherto. Our Parson return'd to us with the Carolina Commissioners from Edenton, where he had preach'd in their Court-house, there being no Place of Divine Worship in that Metropolis. He had also Christen'd 19 of their Children, & pillag'd them of some of their Cash, if Paper money may be allow'd that Appellation.

30. This Morning all the ill-humour that Firebrand had so long kept broiling upon his Stomach broke out. First he insisted that Young Astrolabe might go no longer with the Surveyors to be a Spy upon Orion's

---

A Page from the Manuscript of *The Secret History of the Line* in the American Philosophical Society Library

This being my birthday, I adored the goodness of Heaven for having indulged me with so much health and very uncommon happiness in the course of fifty-four years, in which my sins have been many and my sufferings few, my opportunities great but my improvements small.

Firebrand and Meanwell had very high words after I went to bed concerning Astrolabe, in which conversation Meanwell showed most spirit and Firebrand most arrogance and ill nature.

29. I wrote a letter to the Governor, which I had complaisance to show to my colleagues to prevent jealousies and fears.

We received intelligence that our surveyors and people finished their business in the Dismal last night and found it no more than five miles from the place where they left off. Above a mile before they came out, they waded up to the knees in a pine swamp. We let them rest this day at Peter Brinkley's and sent orders to them to proceed the next morning. Boötes left them and came to us with intent to desert us quite and leave the rest of the drudgery to Plausible, who had indulged his old bones hitherto.

Our parson returned to us with the Carolina commissioners from Edenton, where he had preached in their courthouse, there being no place of divine worship in that metropolis. He had also christened nineteen of their children and pillaged them of some of their cash, if paper money may be allowed that appellation.

30. This morning all the ill-humor that Firebrand had so long kept broiling upon his stomach broke out. First he insisted that young Astrolabe might go no longer with the surveyors to be a spy upon Orion. I told him that volunteers were always employed upon the side, that he was very useful in assisting Orion, who had reason to be satisfied with having his defects so [well] [63] supplied. Then he complained of the rudeness of Robin Hix to Orion and proposed he might be punished for it. To this I answered that if Orion had any accusation to make against Robin Hix, it had been fair to make it openly before all the commissioners, that the person accused might have an opportunity to make his defense, and ought not to whisper his complaints in pri-

[63] So illegible that the reading is doubtful.

vate to one gentleman, because it looked like suspecting the justice of the rest. That word "whispering" touched him home and made him raise his voice and roll his eyes with great fury, and I was weak enough to be as loud and choleric as he. However, it was necessary to show that I was not to be dismayed either with his big looks or his big words, and, in truth, when he found this, he cooled as suddenly as he fired. Meanwell chimed in with my sentiments in both these points, so that we carried them by a fair majority. However, to show my good humor and love of peace, I desired young Astrolabe to concern himself no more with the surveying part, because it gave uneasiness, but only to assist his brother in protracting and plotting of the work. After this storm was over, Firebrand went with Shoebrush to Mr. O'Shield's for some days, and his going off was not less pleasing to us than the going off of a fever.

31. This was Sunday, but the people's zeal was not warm enough to bring them through the rain to church, especially now their curiosity was satisfied. However, we had a sermon and some of the nearest neighbors came to hear it. Astrolabe sent word that he had carried the line seven miles yesterday but was forced to wade up to the middle through a mill swamp. Robins sent his mate hither to treat with my landlord about shipping his tobacco; they roll it in the night to Nansemond River, in defiance of the law against bringing of tobacco out of Carolina into Virginia, but 'twere unreasonable to expect that they should obey the laws of their neighbors who pay no regard to their own. Only the masters of ships that load in Virginia should be under some oath or regulation about it.

Sunday seemed a day of rest indeed, in the absence of our turbulent companion, who makes every day uneasy to those who have the pain of his conversation.

APRIL

1. We prepared for a march very early, and then I discharged a long score with my landlord and a short one with his daughter Rachel for some smiles that were to be paid for in kisses. We took leave in form of the whole family and in eight miles reached Richard Par-

ker's, where we found young Astrolabe and some of our men. Here we refreshed ourselves with what a neat landlady could provide and christened two of her children, but did not discharge our reckoning that way. Then we proceeded by Somerton Chapel (which was left two miles in Virginia) as far as the plantation of William Speight, that was cut in two by the line, taking his tobacco house into Carolina. Here we took up our quarters and fared the better for a side of fat mutton sent us by Captain Baker. Our lodging was exceedingly airy, the wind having a free circulation quite through our bedchamber, yet we were so hardy as to take no cold, though the frost was sharp enough to endanger the fruit. Meanwell entertained the Carolina commissioners with several romantic passages of his life with relation to his amours, which is a subject he is as fond of as a hero to talk of battles he never fought.

2. This morning early Captain Baker came to make us a visit and explained to us the reason of the present of mutton which he sent us yesterday. It seems the plantation where he lives is taken into Virginia, which without good friends might prejudice him in his surveyor's place of Nansemond County. But we promised to employ our interest in his favor.

We made the best of our way to Chowan River, crossing the line several times. About a mile before we came to that river we crossed Somerton Creek. We found our surveyors at a little cottage on the banks of Chowan, over against the mouth of Nottoway River. They told us that our line cut Blackwater River about half a mile to the northward of that place, but, in obedience to His Majesty's order in that case, we directed them to continue the line from the middle of the mouth of Nottoway River. Accordingly, the surveyors passed Chowan there and carried the line over a miry swamp, more than half a mile through, as far as an Indian old field.

In the meantime, our horses and baggage were ferried over the river a little lower to the same field, where we pitched our tent, promising ourselves a comfortable repose; but our evil genius came at night and interrupted all our joys. Firebrand arrived with his most humble servant, Shoebrush, though, to make them less unwelcome, they brought a present from Mr. O'Shield's of twelve bottles of wine and as many of strong beer. But to say the truth, we had rather have drunk water the whole journey to have been fairly quit of such disagreeable company.

Our surveyors found by an observation made this night that the variation was no more than 2° 30' westerly, according to which we determined to proceed in the rest of our work toward the mountains.

Three of the Meherrin Indians came hither to see us from the place where they now live about seven miles down the river, they being lately removed from the mouth of Meherrin. They were frightened away from thence by the late massacre committed upon fourteen of their nation by the Catawbas. They are now reduced to a small number and are the less to be pitied because they have always been suspected to be very dishonest and treacherous to the English.

3. We sent away the surveyors about nine o'clock and followed them at ten. By the way Firebrand and Shoebrush, having spied a house that promised good cheer, filed off to it and took it in dudgeon that we would not follow their vagaries. We thought it our duty to attend the business in hand and follow the surveyors. These we overtook about noon, after passing several miry branches where I had like to have stuck fast. However, this only gave me an opportunity to show my horsemanship, as the fair-spoken Plausible told me.

After passing several dirty places and uneven grounds, we arrived about sunset on the banks of Meherrin, which we found thirteen and a quarter miles from the mouth of Nottoway River. The county of Isle of Wight begins about three miles to the east of this river, parted from Nansemond by a dividing line only. We pitched our tent and flattered ourselves we should be secure from the disturber of our peace one night more; but we were mistaken, for the stragglers came to us after it was dark, with some danger to their necks because the low grounds near the river were full of cypress snags as dangerous as so many *chevaux de frise*.[64] But this deliverance from danger was not enough to make Firebrand good humored, because we had not been so kind as to rejoice at it.

[64] Defensive barriers, often made of sharpened stakes.

4. Here we called a council of war whether we should proceed any farther this season, and we carried it by a majority of votes to run the line only about two miles beyond this place. Firebrand voted for going on a little longer, though he was glad it was carried against him. However, he thought it gave him an air of industry to vote against leaving off so soon, but the snakes began to be in great vigor, which was an unanswerable argument for it.

The river was hardly fordable and the banks very steep, which made it difficult for our baggage horses to pass over it. But thank God we got all well on the other side without any damage.

We went to a house just by the riverside, belonging to a man who learnedly called himself Carolus Anderson, where we christened his child. Then we proceeded to Mr. Kinchen's, a man of figure in these parts, and his wife a much better figure than he. They both did their utmost to entertain us and our people in the best manner. We pitched our tent in the orchard, where the blossoms of the apple trees mended the air very much. There Meanwell and I lay, but Firebrand and his flatterers stuck close to the house.

The surveyors crossed this river three times with the line in the distance of two and a half miles and left off about half a mile to the northward of this place.

5. Our surveyors made an elegant plat of our line from Currituck Inlet to the place where they left off, containing the distance of seventy-three miles and thirteen poles.[65] Of this exact copies were made and, being carefully examined, were both signed by the commissioners of each colony. This plat was chiefly made by Astrolabe, but one of the copies was taken by Plausible; but Orion was content with a copy which the parson took for him. However, he delivered me the minutes which he had kept of our proceedings by order of the commissioners.

The poor chaplain was the common butt at which all our company aimed their profane wit and gave him the title of "Dean Pip," because instead of a pricked line he had been so maidenly as to call it a pipped line. I left the company in good time, taking as little pleasure

---

[65] A pole is a measure identical with a rod (16½ feet). The *History* (p. 216) says seventy-three miles and thirteen chains (a measure of four rods).

in their low wit as in their low liquor, which was rum punch. Here we discharged six of the men, who were near their own habitations.

6. We paid our scores, settled our accounts, and took leave of our Carolina friends. Firebrand went about six miles with us as far as one Corker's, where we had the grief to part with that sweet-tempered gentleman and the burr that stuck to him, Orion. In about ten miles we reached a muster field near Mr. Kindred's house, where Captain Gerald was exercising his company. There were girls enough come to see this martial appearance to form another company and beauties enough among them to make officers of.

Here we called and christened two children and offered to marry as many of the wenches as had got sweethearts, but they were not ripe for execution. Then we proceeded ten miles farther to Bolton's Ferry, where we passed Nottoway River at Mr. Symonds' quarter. From hence we intended to proceed to Nottoway Town to satisfy the curiosity of some of our company, but, losing our way, we wandered to Richard Parker's plantation, where we had formerly met with very kind entertainment. Our eyes were entertained as well as our stomachs by the charms of pretty Sally, the eldest daughter of the family.

7. This being Sunday, we had a sermon, to which very few of the neighbors resorted, because they wanted timely notice. However, some good Christians came and amongst them Molly Izard, the smartest damsel in these parts. Meanwell made this girl very vain by saying sweet things to her, but Sally was more engaging, whose wholesome flesh and blood neither had nor needed any ornament. Nevertheless, in the afternoon we could find in our hearts to change these fair beauties for the copper-colored ones of Nottoway Town.

Thither we went, having given notice by a runner that we were coming, that the Indians might be at home to entertain us. Our landlord showed us the way, and the scouts had no sooner spied us but they gave notice of our approach to the whole town by perpetual whoops and cries, which to a stranger sound very dismal. This called their great men to the fort, where we alighted and were conducted to the best cabins. All the furniture of those apartments was hurdles covered with clean mats. The young men had painted themselves in a hideous manner, not for beauty but terror, and in that equipage entertained us with some of their war dances. The ladies had put on all their ornaments to charm us, but the whole winter's dirt was so crusted on their skins that it required a strong appetite to accost them. Whatever we were, our men were not quite so nice but were hunting after them all night. But though Meanwell might perhaps want inclination to these sad-colored ladies, yet curiosity made him try the difference between them and other women, to the disobligation of his ruffles, which betrayed what he had been doing.

Instead of being entertained by these Indians, we entertained them with bacon and rum, which they accepted of very kindly, the ladies as well as the men. They offered us no bedfellows, according to the good Indian fashion, which we had reason to take unkindly. Only the Queen of Weyanoke told Steddy that her daughter had been at his service if she had not been too young.

Some Indian men were lurking all night about our cabin, with the felonious intent to pilfer what they could lay their hands upon, and their dogs slunk into us in the night and eat up what remained of our provisions.

8. When we were dressed, Meanwell and I visited most of the princesses at their own apartments, but the smoke was so great there, the fire being made in the middle of the cabins, that we were not able to see their charms. Prince James's princess sent my wife a fine basket of her own making, with the expectation of receiving from her some present of ten times its value. An Indian present, like those made to princes, is only a liberality put out to interest and a bribe placed to the greatest advantage.

I could discern by some of our gentlemen's linen, discolored by the soil of the Indian ladies, that they had been convincing themselves in the point of their having no fur.

About ten we marched out of the town, some of the Indians giving us a volley of small arms at our departure. We drank our chocolate at one Jones's, about four miles from the town, and then proceeded over Blackwater Bridge to Colonel Henry Harrison's,[66] where we

---

[66] Boyd: "Henry Harrison (1691–1732) . . . member of the House of Burgesses in 1715 and later years, and of the Council in 1730."

were very handsomely entertained and congratulated one another upon our return into Christendom.

9. We scrubbed off our Indian dirt and refreshed ourselves with clean linen. After a plentiful breakfast, we took our leave and set our faces toward Westover. By the way we met Bowler Cocke and his lady, who told me my family was well, Heaven be praised.

When we came to the new church near Warren's Mill, Steddy drew up his men and harangued them in the following manner: "Friends and fellow travelers, it is a great satisfaction to me that after so many difficulties and fatigues you are returned in safety to the place where I first joined you. I am much obliged to you for the great readiness and vigor you have showed in the business we went about, and I must do you all the justice to declare that you have not only done your duty but also done it with cheerfulness and affection. Such a behavior, you may be sure, will engage us to procure for you the best satisfaction we can from the government. And besides that, you may depend upon our being ready at all times to do you any manner of kindness. You are now, blessed be God, near your own dwellings and, I doubt not, willing to be discharged. I heartily wish you may, every one, find your friends and your families in perfect health, and that your affairs may have suffered as little as possible by your absence."

The men took this speech very kindly and were thankful on their part for the affectionate care we had taken of them during the whole journey. Upon the whole matter, it was as much as we could do to part with dry eyes. However, they filed off to Prince George court, where they entertained their acquaintance with the history of their travels; and Meanwell with the two Astrolabes passed over the river with me to Westover, where I had the pleasure of meeting all my family in perfect health, nor had they been otherwise since I left them. This great blessing ought to inspire us all with the deepest sentiments of gratitude, as well as convince us of the powerful effect of sincere and hearty prayers to the Almighty in all our undertakings.

Thus ended our progress for this season; and it should be remembered that before we parted with the commissioners of North Carolina we agreed to meet again at Kinchen's on the tenth of September to continue the line from thence toward the mountains—upon this condition, nevertheless, that if the commissioners on either side should find it convenient to alter the day, they should give timely notice to the other.

I had been so long absent from home that I was glad to rest myself for a few days, and therefore went not down to Williamsburg till the seventeenth of April. And then I waited upon the Governor to give an account of my commission but found my reception a little cooler than I thought my behavior in the service had deserved. I must own I was surprised at it, till I came to understand that several stories had been whispered by Firebrand and Orion to my disadvantage.

Those gentlemen had been so indiscreet as to set about several ridiculous falsehoods, which could be proved so by every man that was with us, particularly that I had treated Orion not only without ceremony but without justice, denying him any assistance from the men and supporting them in their rudeness to him. And because they thought it necessary to give some instance of my unkindness to that worthy gentleman, they boldly affirmed that I would not send one of the men from Captain James Wilson's to Norfolk Town for his horse, which he had left there to be cured of a sore back. The Father of Lies could not have told one more point-blank against the truth than this was, because the author of it knew in his own conscience that I had ordered one of the men to go upon this errand for him, though it was more than fifty miles backward and forward, and though his own servant might as well have gone, because he had at that time nothing to hinder him, being left behind at Wilson's where the men were and not attending upon his master. And this I could prove by Meanwell, who wrote the order I signed for this purpose, and by Dr. Humdrum, who received it and thereupon had sent one of the men to Norfolk for him.

Nor were these gentlemen content with doing this wrong to me, but they were still more and more unjust to Astrolabe, by telling the Governor that he was ignorant in the business of surveying, that he had done nothing in running of the line but Orion had done all, which was as opposite to truth as light is to darkness or modesty to impudence. For, in fact, Astrolabe had done all and Orion had done nothing but what exposed not only his awkwardness in the practice but his ignorance in the theory. Nor was this a bare untruth only with regard to Astrolabe, but there was malice in it; for they had so totally prepossessed the Commissary with his being ignorant in the art of surveying that, contrary to his promise formerly given, he determined not to make him surveyor of Goochland, nor had he yielded to it at last without the interposition of the Governor. So liable is human nature to prepossession that even the clergy is not exempt from it.

They likewise circulated a great many other ridiculous stories in the gaiety of their hearts, which carried a keener edge against themselves than Steddy and therefore merited rather my contempt than resentment. However, it was very easy when Meanwell and I came to town not only to disprove all their slander but also to set everything in a true light with regard to themselves. We made it as clear as noonday that all the evidence they had given was as much upon the Irish [67] as their wit and their modesty. The Governor was soon convinced and expressed himself very freely to those gentlemen and particularly to Orion, who had with great confidence imposed upon him. He was also so fully persuaded of Astrolabe's abilities that he perfectly constrained the Commissary to appoint him surveyor of Goochland, to the mortification of his adversaries.

As soon as I could complete my journal, I sent it to Firebrand for his hand if he found it right, but after many days he returned it to me unsigned, though he could make no objection. [68] I gave myself no further trouble about him but desired Mr. Banister [69] to give it to the Governor, subscribed by Meanwell and me. Upon his asking Firebrand why he would not grace the journal with his hand, his invention could find no other reason but because it was too poetical. However, he thought proper to sign this poetical journal at last, when he found it was to be sent to England without it.

[67] In the manner of the Irish.

[68] This is the "Journal of the Proceedings," in the Public Record Office, P.R.O. CO5/1321.

[69] Boyd: "John Banister, collector of the Customs for the Upper James District, son of Rev. John Banister, naturalist and entomologist, who arrived in Virginia about 1678. The Banister plantation was near Petersburg."

Sometime in June, Plausible made me a visit and let me know in the name of his brother commissioners of North Carolina that it was their common request that our meeting to continue the line might be put off to the twentieth of September and desired me to communicate their sentiments to the other commissioners for Virginia. I begged he would make this request in writing by way of letter, lest it might be called in question by some unbelievers. Such a letter he wrote, and a few days after I showed it to Firebrand and let him know Meanwell and I had agreed to their desire and intended to write them an answer accordingly. But he, believing this alteration of the day to have been made in compliment to me (because he knew I had always been of this opinion), immediately sent away a letter, or rather an order, to the commissioners for Carolina, directing them to stick to their first day of meeting, being the tenth of September, and to disown their order to Plausible to get it put off. A precept from so great a man, three of these worthy commissioners had not the spirit to disobey but meanly swallowed their own words and under their hands denied they had ever desired Plausible to make any such motion. The renegade letter of these sycophants was afterwards produced by Firebrand to the Governor and Council of Virginia. In the meantime, I sent them an epistle signed by Meanwell and myself that we, in compliance with their desire delivered by Plausible, had agreed to put off our meeting to the twentieth of September. This servile temper in these three Carolina commissioners showed of what base metal they were made and had discovered itself in another pitiful instance not long before.

Firebrand, despairing of a good word from his Virginia colleagues, with great industry procured a testimonial from his Carolina flatterers, as well for himself as his favorite Orion. And because the compliment might appear too gross if addressed to himself, it was contrived that the gentlemen above-mentioned should join in a letter to the Commissary (with whom, by the way, they had never before corresponded), wherein without rhyme or reason they took care to celebrate Firebrand's civility and Orion's mathematics.

This certificate was soon produced by the good Commissary to our Governor, who could not but see through the shallow contrivance. It appeared ridiculous to him but most abject and monstrous to us, who knew them to be as ill judges of the mathematics as a deaf man could be of music. So that, to be sure, it was a great addition to the character of our professor to have the honor of their testimonials. And though we should allow men of their education to be critics in civility, yet at first these very men complained of Firebrand's haughty carriage, though now they have the meanness to write to the Commissary in commendation of his civility. These are such instances of a poor spirit as none could equal but themselves in other passages of their behavior.

And though the subject be very low, yet I must beg leave to mention another case in which not only these but all the Council of North Carolina discovered a submission below all example. They suffered this Firebrand to come in at the head of their Council, when at his first admission he ought to have been at the tail. I can't tell whether it was more pretending in him to ask this precedence or more pitiful in them to submit to it. He will say, perhaps, that it befitted not a gentleman of his noble family and high station to sit below a company of pirates, vagabonds, and footmen; but, surely, if that be their character, he ought as little to sit among them at all. But what have they to say in their excuse for prostituting the rank in which the Lords Proprietors had placed them, since the person to whom they made this compliment has no other title to the arms he bears and the name he goes by but the courtesy of Ireland? And then for his office, he is at most but a publican and holds not his commission from His Majesty but from the Commissioners of the Customs. So they had no other reason to give this man place but because their own worthlessness flew in their faces.

Sometime in July, I received a letter from Firebrand, in which he accused me of having taken too much upon me in our last expedition by pretending to a sole command of the men, that then the number of our men was too great and brought an unnecessary charge upon the public, that nine or ten would be sufficient to take out with us next time, of which he would name three. This was the sum and substance of his letter, though there were turns in it and some raillery which he intended to be very ingenious and for which he belabored his poor brains very much. I did not think this epistle worth an answer but fancied it would be time enough to dispute the points mentioned therein at our next council.

It happened in August, upon the news of some disturbance among the Indians, that the Governor called a small council composed only of the councilors in the neighborhood, judging it unnecessary to give us the trouble of a journey who lived at a greater distance. At this council assisted only Firebrand, the Commissary, and three other gentlemen. Neither Meanwell nor I were there nor had any summons or the least notice of it. This Firebrand thought a proper occasion to propose his questions concerning the reduction of the number of our men and the day when we were to meet the Carolina commissioners. He was seconded by his friend the Commissary, who surprised the rest of the council into their opinion, there being nobody to oppose them nor any so just as to put off the question till the two commissioners that were absent might be heard in a matter that concerned them.

However, these unfair and shortsighted politics were so far from prospering that they turned to the confusion of him that contrived them. For, having quickly gained intelligence of this proceeding, I complained of the injustice of it in a letter I wrote to the Governor, and he was so much convinced by my reasons that he wrote me word he would call a general council the week following to overhaul that matter again. Indeed, he had been so prudent at the little council as to direct the clerk not to enter what had been there determined upon the council books, that it might not stand as an order but only as matter of advice to us commissioners.

Upon receipt of this letter, I dispatched an express to Meanwell, acquainting him with this whole matter and entreating him to call upon me in his way to the next council. When he came, we consulted what was fittest for us to do after such treatment; and, upon weighing every circumstance, we resolved at last that since it was not possible for us to agree with Firebrand we would absolutely refuse to go with him upon the next expedition lest His Majesty's service might suffer by our perpetual discord.

Full of this resolution, we went down to Williamsburg and begged the Governor that he would be pleased to dispense with our serving any more with Firebrand in running the line, because he was a person of such uneasy temper that there were no hopes of preserving any harmony amongst us. The Governor desired we would not abandon a service in which we had acquitted ourselves so well but finish what we had began, though he owned we were joined by a gentleman too selfish and too arrogant to be happy with him. I replied that since he did me the honor to desire me to make another journey with him, I would do it, but hoped I might have twenty men and have the sole command of them to prevent all disputes upon that chapter. He thought what I asked was so reasonable that if I would propose it to the Council, I might easily carry it.

According to the Governor's advice, Meanwell and I yielded to put it to the Council; and when it was met and our business entered upon, I delivered myself in the following terms: "I humbly conceive that the business of running the line toward the mountains will require at least twenty men if we intend to follow it with vigor. The chain carriers, the markers, and the man who carries the instrument after the surveyor must be constantly relieved. There must be five in number always upon duty, and where the woods are thick, which will frequently be the case, there should be two more men to clear the way and open the prospect to the surveyors. While this number is thus employed, their arms must be carried and their horses led after them by as great a number. This will employ at least ten men constantly, and, if we must have no more, who must then take care of the baggage and provisions, which will need several horses, and in such pathless woods each horse must be led by a careful man or the packs will soon be torn off their backs. Then, besides all these, some men should be at leisure to hunt and keep us in meat, for which our whole dependence must be upon the woods.

Nor ought we in an affair of so much consequence be tied down to so small a number of men as will be exactly requisite for the daily business; some may be sick or lame or otherwise disabled. In such an exigence must we return home for want of spare hands to supply such misfortune? Ought we not to go provided against such common disasters as these? At this rate we should lose more in the length of time than we should save by the shortness of our number, which would make our frugality, as it often happens, an extravagant expense to us.

Nor would it be prudent or safe to go so far above the inhabitants without a competent number of men for our defense. We shall cross the path which the northern Indians pass to make war upon the Catawbas and shall go through the very woods that are frequented by those straggling savages, who commit so many murders upon our frontiers. We ought therefore to go provided with a force sufficient to secure us from falling into their hands.

It may possibly be objected that the Carolina men will increase our number, which is certain, but they will very little increase our force. They will bring more eaters than fighters, at least they did so the last time, and, if they should be better provided with arms now, their commissioners have so little command over the men that I expect no good from them if we should be so unfortunate as to be attacked.

From all which I must conclude that our safety, our business, and the accidents that attend it will require at least twenty men. And, in order to make this number more useful, there ought to be no confusion in the command. We are taught both by reason and experience that when any men in arms are sent on an expedition they ought to be under the command of one person only. For should they be commanded by several claiming equal power, the orders given by so many might happen to be contradictory, as probably they would happen to be in our case. The consequence of which must follow that the men would not know whom to obey. This must introduce an endless distraction and end in defeating the business you are sending us about.

It were ridiculous to say the command ought to rest in the majority, because then we must call a council every time any orders are to be issued. It would be still more absurd to propose that such persons claiming equal power should command by turns, because then one commander may undo this day what his colleague had directed the day before, and so the men will be perplexed with a succession of jarring orders. Besides, the preference and distinction which these poor fellows might have reason to show to one of these kings of Brentford [70] may be punished by the other when it comes to his turn to be in power. This being the case, what men of spirit or common sense would list themselves under such uncertain command where they could not know whom to please or whom to obey?

For all which reasons, sirs, I must conclude that the command of the men ought to rest in one person, and if in one, then without controversy in him who has the honor to be first in commission."

The Council, as well as the Governor, was convinced by these arguments and unanimously voted twenty men were few enough to go out with us and thought it reasonable that the command of them should be given to me as being the first in commission. Firebrand opposed each of these points with all his eloquence, but to little purpose, nobody standing by him — not so much as his new ally, the Commissary. He seemed at first to befriend him with a distinction which he made between the day of battle and a day of business, but, having no second, he ran with the stream. However, in pure compassion to poor Firebrand, for fear he should want somebody to run of his errands for him, it was agreed he should have three men to fetch and carry for him.

I had the same success in getting the day of meeting which the Carolina commissioners desired might be put off till the twentieth of September, notwithstanding Firebrand produced letters from Messrs. Jumble and Shoebrush that they had not desired their colleague Plausible to procure our rendezvous to be deferred. I confronted these letters with that epistle I had from Plausible which flatly contradicted them. Thus it was evident there was a shameful untruth on one side or the other; but if we consider the characters of the men and the

[70] In Buckingham's play *The Rehearsal* there are two kings of Brentford ruling simultaneously. The character Bayes (author of the play within the play, a satire on John Dryden) explains in Act I, sc. ii: "The chief hinge of this play, upon which the whole plot moves and turns . . . is that I suppose two kings of the same place; as, for example at Brentford . . . Now the people have the same relation to 'em both, the same affections, the same duty, the same obedience, and all that; are divided among themselves in point of devoir and interest, how to behave themselves equally between 'em: these kings differing sometimes in particular, though in the main they agree."

influence of Firebrand over those two, whose brothers were collectors, one may guess where it lies, especially since this was not the first time their pens had been drawn in his service.

However, these letters did no service. But the Governor declared he would write to Sir Richard Everard that we should meet the commissioners of his government on the twentieth of September with twenty men. How much the pride of Firebrand was mortified by so entire a defeat in every one of his points may be easily guessed by the loud complaint he made afterwards how inhumanely the Council had treated him and by the pains he took with the Governor to get the order of Council softened with relation to the command. But remembering how unjustly he had reproached me with having taken too much upon me in our former trip, I insisted upon the order of Council in the fullest extent. Upon seeing me so sturdy, he declared to the Governor he could not go on such dishonorable terms and swore to others he would not; but interest got the better of his oath and honor too, and he did vouchsafe to go at last, notwithstanding all the disgraces which he thought had been put upon him. From hence we may fairly conclude that pride is not the strongest of his passions, though strong enough to make him both ridiculous and detestable.

After these necessary matters were settled, I ordered one thousand pounds of brown biscuit and two hundred pounds of white to be provided and six baggage horses to carry it, at the rate of three bags containing two hundred pounds each horse. As for meat, I intended to carry none but to depend entirely upon Providence for it. But because the game was not like to be plentiful till we got above the inhabitants, I directed all the men to find themselves with ten days' provision. I augmented my number of men to seventeen, which, together with three which Firebrand undertook to get, made up the complement of twenty. For these I provided ammunition after the rate of two pounds of powder a man, with shot in proportion. On the sixteenth of September, Meanwell and Astrolabe came to my house in order to set out with me the day following toward the place of rendezvous.

SEPTEMBER

17. About ten in the morning I, having recommended my wife and family to the protection of the Almighty, passed the river with Messrs. Meanwell and Astrolabe to Mr. Ravenscroft's landing.[71] He was so complaisant as to accompany us as far as the new church,[72] where eight of our men were attending for us, namely, Peter Jones, George Hamilton, James Petillo, Thomas Short, John Ellis, Jr., Richard Smith, George Tilman, and Abraham Jones. The rest were to meet us at Kinchen's, which lay more convenient to their habitations. Only I had ordered three of them who were absent to convoy the bread horses thither the nearest road they could go, namely, Thomas Jones, Thomas Jones, Jr., and Edward Powell, to the last of which the bread horses belonged.

We proceeded with the eight men above-mentioned to Colonel Henry Harrison's, where our chaplain, Dr. Humdrum, was arrived before us. We were handsomely entertained and after dinner furnished ourselves with several small conveniences out of the store. Then we took a turn to the cold bath, where the Colonel refreshes himself every morning. This is about five feet square and as many deep, through which a pure stream continually passes, and is covered with a little house just big enough for the bath and a firing room. Our landlord, who used formerly to be troubled both with the gripes and the gout, fancies he receives benefit by plunging every day in cold water. This good house was enough to spoil us for woodsmen, where we drank rack punch while we sat up and trod on carpets when we went to bed.

18. Having thanked the Colonel for our good dinner, we took leave about ten, not at all dismayed at the likelihood of rain. We traveled after the rate of four miles an hour, passing over Blackwater

[71] Boyd: "Reference is to the Maycox plantation, across the James from Westover, which was purchased in 1723 by Thomas Ravenscroft. In the late eighteenth century it passed into the ownership of David Meade who made it one of the famous show places of Virginia. See Tyler, *Cradle of the Republic*, p. 212."
[72] Boyd suggests that this was a chapel built in 1723, the contractor being a Mr. Thomas Jefferson, and cites William Meade, *Old Churches, Ministers, and Families* (Philadelphia, 1857), I, 440.

Bridge and, ten miles beyond that, over another called Assamoosick Bridge. Then we filed off to Richard Parker's plantation, where we had been kindly used in our return home. We found the distance twenty-four miles, going a little astray for want of a guide, and there fell a sort of Scots mist all the way. We arrived about five o'clock and found things in much disorder, the good woman being lately dead and those that survived sick. Pretty Sally had lost some of her bloom by an ague but none of her good humor. They entertained us as well as they could, and what was wanting in good cheer was made up in good humor.

19. About ten this morning we wished health to Sally and her family and forded over Nottoway River at Bolton's Ferry, the water being very low. We called upon Samuel Kindred again, who regaled us with a beefsteak and our men with cider. Here we had like to have listed a mulatto wench for cook to the expedition, who formerly lived with Colonel Ludwell.[73] After halting here about an hour, we pursued our journey, and in the way Richard Smith showed me the star root,[74] which infallibly cures the bite of the rattlesnake.

Nine miles from thence we forded over Meherrin River near Mr. Kinchen's, believing we should be at the place of meeting before the rest of the commissioners. But we were mistaken, for the first sight my eyes were blest with was that of Orion and, finding the shadow there, I knew the substance could not be far off.

Three commissioners on the part of North Carolina came that night, though Jumble and Puzzlecause were ordered by their governor to stay behind lest their General Court might be delayed. But they came notwithstanding, in the strength of their interest with the Council, but seemed afraid of being pursued and arrested. They put on very gracious countenances at our first greeting, but yet looked a little conscious of having acted a very low part in the epistles they had written. For my part, I was not courtier enough to disguise the sentiments I had of them and their slavish proceeding and therefore

[73] Colonel Philip Ludwell II, of Green Springs, James City County, member of the Council, trustee of the College, and vestryman of Bruton Parish.
[74] The star grass or colicroot, a shrub bearing white or yellow flowers, the roots of which were used medicinally.

could not smile upon those I despised. Nor could I behave much better to Firebrand and his echo, Orion; nevertheless, I constrained myself to keep up a stiff civility.

The last of these gentlemen, remembering the just provocation he had given me, thought it necessary to bring a letter from the Governor recommending him to my favor and protection. This, therefore, had the air of confessing his former errors, which made me, after some gentle reproofs, assure him he should have no reason to complain of my treatment. Though I carried fair weather to Firebrand, yet Meanwell could not, but all ceremony, notice, and conversation seemed to be canceled betwixt them. I caused the tent to be pitched in the orchard, where I and my company took up our quarters, leaving the house to Firebrand and his faction.

20. This morning Meanwell was taken a-purging and vomiting, for which I dosed him with veal broth and afterwards advised him to a gallon of warm water, which finished his cure. We herded very little with our brother commissioners, and Meanwell frankly gave Jumble to understand that we resented the impertinent letters he and some of his colleagues had writ to Virginia. He made a very lame apology for it, because the case would not bear a good one.

He and his brethren were lamentably puzzled how to carry their baggage and provisions. They had brought them up by water near this place and had depended on fortune to get horses there to carry them forward. I believe too they relied a little upon us to assist them, but I was positive not to carry one pound weight. We had luggage enough for our own horses, and, as our provisions lightened, the shortness of their provenders would require them to be lightened too. I was not so complaisant to these worthy gentlemen as Firebrand, for he brought a tent for them out of the magazine at Williamsburg to requite the dirty work they had been always ready to do for him. At last they hired something like a cart to carry their lumber as far as it could go toward Roanoke River.

In the evening six more of our men joined us, namely, Robert Hix, John Evans, Stephen Evans, Charles Kimball, Thomas Wilson, and William Pool, but the three men that conducted the bread horses came not up as yet, which gave me some uneasiness though I concluded they had been stopped by the rain. Just after sunset Captain Hix and Captain Drury Stith [75] arrived and made us the compliment to attend us as far as Roanoke. The last of these gentlemen, bearing some resemblance to Sir Richard Everard, put Messrs. Jumble and Puzzlecause into a panic lest the knight was come to put a stop to their journey.

My landlord had unluckily sold our men some brandy, which produced much disorder, making some too choleric and others too loving, so that a damsel who came to assist in the kitchen would certainly have been ravished if her timely consent had not prevented the violence. Nor did my landlady think herself safe in the hands of such furious lovers and therefore fortified her bedchamber and defended it with a chamber pot charged to the brim with female ammunition. I never could learn who the ravisher was, because the girl had walked off in the morning early, but Firebrand and his servant were the most suspected, having been engaged in those kind of assaults once before.

21. In the morning Meanwell joined us. We sent away the surveyors about nine, who could carry the line no more than three and a half miles, because the low grounds were covered with thickets. As soon as we had paid a very exorbitant bill and the Carolina men had loaded their vehicle and disposed of their lumber, we mounted and conducted our baggage about ten miles. We took up our quarters at the plantation of John Hill, where we pitched our tent with design to rest there till Monday. This man's house was so poorly furnished that Firebrand and his Carolina train could not find in their hearts to lodge in it, so we had the pleasure of their company in the camp. They perfumed the tent with their rum punch and hunted the poor parson with their unseemly jokes, which turned my stomach as much as their fragrant liquor. I was grave and speechless the whole evening and retired early; by all which I gave them to understand I was not fond of the conversation of those whose wit, like the commons at the university and Inns of Court, is eternally the same.

[75] Boyd: "Colonel Drury Stith, Sheriff of Charles City County in 1719-20 and 1724-25. He removed to Brunswick County and was its first County Clerk."

22. This being Sunday, we had a large congregation, and though there were many females, we saw no beauty bright enough to disturb our devotions. Our parson made eleven Christians. Mr. Hill made heavy complaint that our horses did much damage to his cornfield; upon which I ordered those that were most vicious that way to be tied up to their good behavior. Among these, Humdrum's and Astrolabe's were the greatest trespassers. After church I gave John Ellis a vomit for his ague, with good success, and was forced myself to soften my bowels with veal broth for a looseness. I also recommended warm water to Captain Stith for the colic, which gave him immediate ease.

In the afternoon our three men arrived with the six bread horses, having been kept so long behind by the rain, but thank God it had received no damage. I took a walk with Plausible and told him of the letters his colleagues had writ to falsify what he had told me concerning their request to put off the time of our meeting. He justified his own veracity but showed too much cold blood in not being piqued at so flagrant an injury.

Firebrand and his followers had smelt out a house about half a mile off, to which they sent for the silver bowl and spent the evening by themselves, both to their own satisfaction and ours. We hoped to be rid of them for all night, but they found the way to the camp just after we were gone to bed, and Firebrand hindered us from going to sleep so soon by his snoring and swearing.

23. We continued in our camp and sent the surveyors back to the place where they left off. They could run the line no more than four miles by reason that it was overgrown with bushes.

I sent several of the men out a-hunting, and they brought us four wild turkeys. Old Captain Hix killed two of them, who turned his hand to everything notwithstanding his great age, disdaining to be thought the worse for threescore-and-ten. Beauty never appeared better in old age, with a ruddy complexion and hair as white as snow.

It rained a little in the evening but did not hinder our rum commissioners from stepping over to John Hill's to swill their punch, leaving the tent clear to us. After midnight it rained very hard, with a storm of thunder and lightning, which obliged us to trench in our tent to cast off the water. The line crossed Meherrin five times in all.

24. So soon as the men could dry their blankets, we sent away the surveyors, who made a shift to carry the line seven miles. But we thought it proper not to decamp, believing we might easily overtake the surveyors before tomorrow night. Our shooters killed four more wild turkeys. Meanwell and Captain Stith pretended to go a-hunting, but their game was eight fresh-colored wenches, which were not hard to hunt down. The neighbors supplied us with pretty good cheese and very fat mutton. I ordered a view of John Hill's damage in his corn-field and paid him for six barrels on that account.

Firebrand instructed one of the three men which he listed on the public service to call him master, thereby endeavoring to pass him on the Carolina commissioners for his servant, that he might seem to have as many servants as Steddy; but care was taken to undeceive them in this matter and expose his vanity. The Carolina men lived at rack[76] and manger without any sort of economy, thereby showing they intended not to go very far with us, though we took care to set them a better example.

Our chaplain had leave to go home with Robert Hix, who lived no more than six miles from this place, to christen his child, and the old Captain went along with them. We had the comfort to have the tent to ourselves, the Knights of the Rum Cask retiring in the evening to the house and wasting the liquor and double-refined sugar as fast as they could.

25. Our surveyors proceeded to run little more than seven miles. Firebrand and his gang got out this morning before us on pretense of providing our dinner; but they outrid the man that carried the mutton, and he, not knowing the way, was lost, so that instead of having our dinner sooner, we run a hazard of having none at all. We came up to them about four o'clock and thanked them for the prudent care they had taken. This was a sample of these gentlemen's management whenever they undertook anything.

We encamped near Beaver Pond Creek, and on our way thither Peter Jones killed a small rattlesnake. The surveyors made an end

[76] A "rack" was a framework to hold fodder for animals.

very near where we lay. Orion was exceedingly awkward at his business, so that Astrolabe was obliged to do double duty. There being no house at hand to befriend us, we were forced to do penance at the tent with the topers.

26. This morning we dispatched the surveyors early, and they ran about ten and a half miles. By the way the men that were with him killed two large rattlesnakes. Will Pool trod upon one of them without receiving any hurt, and two of the chain carriers had marched over the other, but he was so civil as to bite neither of them; however, one of these vipers struck at Wilson's horse and missed him. So many escapes were very providential, though the danger proves that my argument for putting off our business was not without foundation.

We marched upon the line after the surveyors and about four o'clock encamped upon Cabin Branch, which is one of the branches of Fontaine Creek.

Before we set off this morning, we christened two children. One of them was brought by a modest lass, who, being asked how she liked Captain Stiff, replied, "Not at all, nor Captain Limber neither," meaning Orion.

We saw abundance of ipecacuanha in the woods and the fern rattlesnake root,[77] which is said to be the strongest antidote against the bite of that viper. And we saw St.-Andrew's-cross [78] almost every step we went, which serves for the same purpose. This plant grows on all kinds of soil everywhere at hand during the summer months, when the snakes have vigor enough to do mischief. Old Captain Hix entertained us with one of his trading songs, which he quavered out most melodiously, and put us all into a good humor.

27. We sent away the surveyors before ten o'clock and followed with the baggage at eleven. But Firebrand thought proper to remain with three of the Carolina commissioners till their cart came up and took it ill that we tarried not with them likewise. But I could not compliment away our time at that rate. Here they made broad hints

[77] Boyd: "An herb of the chicory family. Its milky juice was taken internally and its leaves when steeped were applied externally in the treatment of snake wounds."
[78] Boyd: "A small plant of the St. Johns-wort family, so called because its petals open into shape like the St. Andrews cross."

to carry some of their luggage for them; I would put not such hardships upon our men, who had all enough to carry of their own, so we
left them there to make the best shift they could and followed the
line with all diligence.

We passed Pea Hill Creek and, sometime after, Lizard Creek,
which empties itself into Roanoke River. Here we halted till our
chaplain baptized five children. Then we proceeded to Pigeon Roost
Creek, where we took up our quarters, having carried the line above
nine miles.

28. We hurried away the surveyors, who could run no more than
six miles because of the uneven grounds near Roanoke River. We
did not follow with the baggage till ten, being stayed to christen six
children and to discourse a very civil old fellow, who brought us two
fat shoats for a present. The name of our benefactor was Epaphroditus
Bainton, who is young enough at sixty years of age to keep a concubine and to walk twenty-five miles in a day. He has forsworn ever
getting on a horse's back, being once in danger of breaking his neck
by a fall. He spends most of his time in hunting and ranging the
woods, killing generally more than one hundred deer in a year. He
pretends to skill in the virtues of many plants, but I could learn
nothing of that kind from him.

This man was our guide to Major Mumford's plantation, under the
care of Miles Riley, where we were regaled with milk, butter, and
many other refreshments. The Major had ordered some wine to be
lodged here for us and a fat steer to be at our service, but the last we
refused with a great many thanks.

From hence we continued our journey to the canoe landing upon
Roanoke River, where young Mumford and Mr. Walker met us.
Here we ferried over our baggage and our persons, ordering the men
with the horses to the ford near a mile higher which leads to the
trading path. Here my old friend Captain Hix took his leave, committing us to our kind stars.

We were set ashore at another plantation belonging to Major
Mumford, under the management of a man they called Nat. Here
was another fat steer ordered for us, which we thankfully accepted

of for the sake of the men. We pitched the tent near the house, which supplied all our wants. Poor Miles Riley received a kick from one of the horses, for which I ordered him to be instantly blooded and hindered all bad consequences. I interceded with Plausible in behalf of the Virginians whose land was left by the line in Carolina, and he promised to befriend them. George Hamilton killed a snake with eleven rattles, having a squirrel in his belly which he had charmed and only the head of it was digested. Also the chain carriers killed another small one the same day.

29. Being Sunday, we had a sermon, but 'twas interrupted with a shower of rain which dispersed our congregation. A little before noon the Carolina baggage came up, and the servants blessed us with the news that their masters would come in the evening. They also informed us they lay last night at John Young's and had hired him and his brother to assist them upon the line; that for want of horses to carry their luggage they had left some of it behind.

Our chaplain baptized five children, and I gave Thomas Wilson a vomit that worked powerfully and carried off his fever. I wrote to the Governor a full and true account of all our proceedings and sent the letter by Mr. Mumford, who took his leave this evening.

About four in the afternoon Firebrand and his Carolina guards came to us, as likewise did some of the Saponi Indians. I had sent Charles Kimball to Christanna [79] to persuade two of their most able huntsmen to go the journey to help supply us with meat. I had observed that our men were unfortunate gunners, which made me more desirous to have some that had better luck. Out of five which came I chose Bearskin and another, who accepted the terms I proposed to them. From this time forward the Carolina men and their leader honored us with their company only at dinner, but mornings and evenings they had a distinct fire, to our great comfort, at which they toasted their noses. Indeed, the whole time of our being together, our dear colleague acted more like a commissioner for Carolina than Virginia

[79] A fort established by Governor Spotswood in 1714 on the south side of Meherrin River between Emporia and Lawrenceville in what is now Brunswick County. Here the Saponi Indians were to be introduced to Christianity under the instruction of Charles Griffin, as Byrd mentions in the *History* (p. 220).

and not only herded with them perpetually but in every instance joined his politics with theirs in their consultations. No wonder then they acted so wisely in their conduct and managed their affairs with such admirable prudence. It rained the whole night long and held not up till break of day.

30. The tent and baggage was so wet that we could not get them dry till twelve o'clock, at which hour we sent the surveyors out and they carried the line about four and a half miles, which we computed was as high as any inhabitants. But we moved not till two with the baggage. We passed over Hawtree Creek two miles from our camp, marching over poisoned fields. By the way a very lean boar crossed us and several claimed the credit of killing it, but all agreed 'twas stone-dead before Firebrand fired, yet he took the glory of this exploit to himself, so much vanity he had that it broke out upon such paltry occasions.

Before we set off this morning, Orion came to me with a countenance very pale and disordered, desiring that Astrolabe might have orders never to concern himself when it was his turn to survey, because, when he needed to be relieved, he chose rather to be beholden to Boötes than to him. I could by no means agree to this request, telling him that none was so proper to assist one Virginia surveyor as the other. I let him know too that such a motion savored more of pique and peevishness than reason. However, I desired him to ask the opinion of the other commissioners, if he was not satisfied with mine, but he found it proper to ask no more questions.

Puzzlecause had a sore throat which incommoded him very much indeed, for he could not swallow so much as rum punch without pain. But I advised him to part with twelve ounces of blood, which opened the passage to his stomach. I recommended the bark to Boötes for an ague and gave one of the Carolina men a dose of ipecacuanha for the same distemper as I did to Powell, one of our own men.

OCTOBER

1. We sent out the surveyors early, and by the benefit of clear woods and even ground they carried the line twelve miles and twelve

poles. One of our baggage horses being missing, we decamped not till noon, which gave Firebrand and his crew an opportunity to get the start of us about an hour. However, we came up with the surveyors before them. We forded over Great Creek not far from the place where we encamped and passed Nutbush Creek about seven miles from thence. And five miles further we quartered near a branch which we called Nutbush Branch, believing it ran into the creek of that name. One of the Indians killed a fawn, which, with the addition of a little beef, made very savory soup. The surveyors, by the help of a clear night, took the variation and found it something more than 2° 30′; so that it did not diminish by approaching the mountains, or by advancing toward the West, or increasing our distance from the sea, but continued much the same we found it at Currituck.

2. The surveyors got out about nine o'clock and advanced the line about nine miles. We followed with the baggage at eleven and passed at three miles distance from our camp Massamony Creek, an Indian name signifying "Paint Creek," from red earth found upon the banks of it, which in a fresh tinges the water of that color. Three miles farther we got over Yapatsco or Beaver Creek with some difficulty, the beavers having raised the water a great way up. We proceeded three and a quarter miles beyond this and encamped on the west side of Ohimpamony Creek, an Indian name which signifies "Fishing Creek."

By the way Firebrand had another occasion to show his prowess in killing a poor little wildcat, which had been crippled by two or three before. Poor Puss was unhappily making a meal on a fox squirrel when all these misfortunes befell her. Meanwell had like to have quarreled with Firebrand and his Carolina squadron for not halting for me on the west side of Yapatsco, having been almost mired in crossing that creek, while they had the fortune to get over it at a better place. The Indians killed two deer and John Evans a third, which made great plenty and consequently great content in Israel.

3. We hurried away the surveyors by nine, who ran something more than eight and a half miles. We followed them at eleven and crossed several branches of excellent water. We went through a large level of very rich, high land, near two miles in length and of unknown

breadth. Our Indian killed one deer and William Pool another, and this last we graciously gave to the Carolina men, who deserved it not because they had declared they did not care to rely upon Providence.

We encamped upon Tewahominy or Tuscarora Creek. We saw many buffalo tracks and abundance of their dung, but the noise we made drove them all from our sight. The Carolina commissioners with their leader lagged behind to stop the cravings of their appetites; nor were we ever happy with their conversation but only at dinner, when they played their parts more for spite than hunger.

4. The surveyors got to work a little after nine and extended the line near eight miles, notwithstanding the ground was very uneven. We decamped after them about eleven, and at five miles distance crossed Bluewing Creek, and three miles beyond that we forded Sugartree Creek and pitched our tent on the west side of it. This creek received its name from many sugar trees which grow in the low grounds of it. By tapping the sugar tree in the spring, a great quantity of liquor flows out of it, which may be boiled up into good sugar. It grows very tall and the wood of it is very soft and spongy.

Here we also found abundance of spice trees, whose leaves are fragrant and the berry they bear is black when dry and hot like pepper. Both these trees grow only in a very rich soil.

The low ground upon this creek is very wide, sometimes on one side, sometimes on the other, but on the opposite side the high land advances close to the creek. It ought to be remembered that the commissioners of Carolina made a compliment of about two thousand acres of land lying on this creek to Astrolabe, without paying any fees.

Robert Hix saw three buffaloes but, his gun being loaden only with shot, could do no execution. Boötes shot one deer, and the Indians killed three more and one of the Carolina men four wild turkeys. Thus Providence was very plentiful to us and did not disappoint us who relied upon it.

5. This day our surveyors met with such uneven ground and so many thickets that with all their diligence they could not run the

line so far as five miles. In this small distance it crossed over Hycoo-tomony Creek[80] no less than five times. Our Indian, Ned Bearskin, informed us at first that this creek was the south branch of Roanoke River, but I thought it impossible, both by reason of its narrowness and the small quantity of water that came down it. However, it passed so with us at present till future experience could inform us better.

About four o'clock this afternoon Jumble advanced from the rest of his company to tell me that his colleagues for Carolina wanted to speak with me. I desired, if they had anything to communicate, that they would please to come forward. It was some time before I heard any more of these worthy gentlemen, but at last Shoebrush, as the mouth of the rest, came to acquaint me that their government had ordered them to run the line but thirty or forty miles above Roanoke, that they had now carried it near fifty and intended to go no further. I let them know it was a little unkind they had not been so gracious as to acquaint us with their intentions before; that it had been neighborly to have informed us with their intentions before we set out how far they intended to go, that we might also have received the commands of our government in that matter; but since they had failed in that civility, we would go on without them, since we were provided with bread for six weeks longer. That it was a great misfortune to lose their company, but that it would be a much greater to lose the effect of our expedition by doing the business by halves. That though we went by ourselves, our surveyors would continue under the same oath to do impartial right both to His Majesty and the Lords Proprietors; and though their government might choose perhaps whether it would be bound by our line, yet it would at least be a direction to Virginia how far His Majesty's land extended to the southward.

Then they desired that the surveyors might make a fair plat of the distance we had run together, and that of this there might be two copies signed by the commissioners of both governments. I let them know I agreed to that, provided it might be done before Monday

[80] Now Hyco River.

noon, when, by the grace of God, we would proceed without loss of time because the season was far advanced and would not permit us to waste one moment in ceremony to gentlemen who had showed none to us. Here the conversation ended till after supper, when the subject was handled with more spirit by Firebrand. On my repeating what I had said before upon this subject, he desired a sight of our commission. I gave him to understand that since the commissioners were the same that acted before, all which had heard the commission read, and since those for Carolina had a copy of it, I had not thought it necessary to cram my portmanteau with it a second time, and was therefore sorry I could not oblige him with a sight of it. He immediately said he would take a minute of this, and, after being some time in scrabbling of it, he read to this effect: that being asked by him for a sight of my commission, I had denied it upon pretense that I had it not with me; that I had also refused the commissioners of Carolina to tarry on Monday till the necessary plats could be prepared and exchanged but resolved to move forward as soon as the tent should be dry, by which means the surveyors would be obliged to work on the Sunday. To this I answered that this was a very smart minute, but that I objected to the word "pretense," because it was neither decent nor true that I denied him a sight of our commission upon any pretense but for the honest reason that I had it not there to show. Most of the company thinking my objection just, he did vouchsafe to soften that expression by saying I refused to show him the commission, alleging I had not brought it.

Soon after, when I said that our governor expected that we should carry the line to the mountains, he made answer that the Governor had expressed himself otherwise to him and told him that thirty or forty miles would be sufficient to go beyond Roanoke River. Honest Meanwell, hearing this and, I suppose, not giving entire credit to it, immediately lugged out his pencil, saying in a comical tone that since he was for minutes, egad, he would take a minute of that. The other took fire at this and without any preface or ceremony seized a limb of our table, big enough to knock down an ox, and lifted it up at Meanwell while he was scratching out his minutes. I, happening to see him brandish this dangerous weapon, darted toward him in a moment to stop his hand, by which the blow was prevented; but while I hindered one mischief, I had like to have done another, for the swiftness of my motion overset the table and Shoebrush fell under it, to the great hazard of his gouty limbs. So soon as Meanwell came to know the favor that Firebrand intended him, he saluted him with the title he had a good right to, namely, of son of a w — e, telling him if they had been alone he durst as well be damned as lift that club at him. To this the other replied with much vigor that he might remember, if he please, that he had now lifted a club at him.

I must not forget that when Firebrand first began this violence, I desired him to forbear or I should be obliged to take him in arrest. But he telling me in a great fury that I had no authority, I called to the men and let him know if he would not be easy I would soon convince him of my authority. The men instantly gathered about the tent ready to execute my orders, but we made a shift to keep the peace without coming to extremities. One of the people, hearing Firebrand very loud, desired his servant to go to his assistance. "By no means," said he, "that's none of my business, but if the gentleman will run himself into a broil, he may get out of it as well as he can."

This quarrel ended at last, as all public quarrels do, without bloodshed, as Firebrand has experienced several times, believing that on such occasions a man may show a great deal of courage with very little danger. However, knowing Meanwell was made of truer metal, I was resolved to watch him narrowly to prevent further mischief. As soon as this fray was composed, the Carolina commissioners retired very soon with their champion, to flatter him, I suppose, upon the great spirit he had showed in their cause against those who were joined with him in commission.

6. This being Sunday, we had prayers but no sermon, because our chaplain was indisposed. The gentlemen of Carolina were all the morning breaking their brains to form a protest against our proceeding on the line any further without them. Firebrand stuck close to them and assisted in this elegant speech, though he took some pains to persuade us he did not. They were so intent upon it that we had not their good company at prayers.

The surveyors, however, found time for their devotions, which helped to excuse their working upon their plats when the service was over. Besides, this, being a work of necessity, was the more pardonable.

We dined together for the last time, not discovering much concern that we were soon to part. As soon as dinner was over, the protesters returned to their drudgery to lick their cub into shape. While I was reading in the tent in the afternoon, Firebrand approached with a gracious smile upon his face and desired to know if I had any commands to Williamsburg, for that he intended to return with the Carolina commissioners; that it was his opinion we had no power to proceed without them, but he hoped this difference of sentiment might not widen the breach that was between us; that he was very sorry anything had happened to set us at variance and wished we might part friends. I was a little surprised at this condescension but humored his inclinations to peace, believing it the only way to prevent future mischief. And as a proof that I was in earnest, I not only accepted of these peaceable overtures myself but was so much his friend as to persuade Meanwell to be reconciled to him. And at last I joined their hands and made them kiss one another.

Had not this pacification happened thus luckily, it would have been impossible for Meanwell to put up the indignity of holding up a club at him, because in a court of honor the shaking of a cudgel at a gentleman is adjudged the same affront as striking him with it. Firebrand was very sensible of this and had great reason to believe that in due time he must have been called to an account for it by a man of Meanwell's spirit. I am sorry if I do him wrong, but I believe this prudent consideration was the true cause of the pacific advances he made to us, as also of his returning back with his dear friends of Carolina, though there might have still been another reason for his going home before the General Court. He was, it seems, left out of the instructions in the list of councilors, and as that matter was likely to come upon the carpet at that time, he thought he might have a better chance to get the matter determined in his favor when two of his adversaries were absent. Add to this the lucre of his attendance during the General Court, which would be so much clear gain if he could get so much interest as to be paid as bountifully for being out four weeks as we for being ten out upon the public service. This I know he was so unconscionable as to expect, but without the least shadow of reason or justice.

Our reconciliation with Firebrand naturally made us friends with his allies of Carolina, who invited us to their camp to help finish their wine. This we did, as they say, though I suspect they reserved enough to keep up their spirits in their return, while we that were to go forward did from henceforth depend altogether upon pure element.

7. This morning I wrote some dispatches home, which Firebrand was so gracious as to offer to forward by an express so soon as he got to Williamsburg. I also wrote another to the Governor, signifying how friendly we parted with our brother commissioner. This last I showed to my colleagues to prevent all suspicion, which was kindly taken.

The plats were countersigned about noon, and that which belonged to Virginia we desired Firebrand to carry with him to the Governor. Then the commissioners for Carolina delivered their protest, signed by them all, though I did not think Plausible would have joined in so ill-concerted a piece. I put it up without reading, to show the opinion I had of it, and let the gentlemen know we would endeavor to return an answer to it in due time. But that so fine a piece may be preserved, I will give both that and the answer to it a place in my journal. The protest is in the following words:

We, the underwritten commissioners for the government of North Carolina, in conjunction with the commissioners on the part of Virginia, having run the line for the division of the two colonies from Currituck Inlet to the southern branch of Roanoke River, being in the whole about 170 miles and near 50 miles without the inhabitants, being of opinion we had run the line as far as would be requisite for a long time, judged the carrying of it farther would be a needless charge and trouble. And the grand debate, which had so long subsisted between the two governments about Weyanoke River or Creek, being settled at our former meeting in the spring, when we were ready on our parts to have gone with the line to the outmost inhabitants (which if it had been done, the line at any time after might have been continued at an easy expense by a surveyor on each side, and if at any time hereafter there should be occasion to carry the line on farther than we have now run it, which we think will not be in an age or two, it may be done in the same easy manner without the great expense that now attends it); and on a conference of all the commissioners, we, having communicated our sentiments thereon, declared our opinion that we had gone as far as the service required and thought proper to proceed no farther; to which it was answered by the commissioners for Virginia that they should not regard what we did, but if we desisted, they would proceed without us. But we, conceiving by His Majesty's order in council they were directed to act in conjunction with the commissioners appointed for Carolina, and having accordingly run the line jointly so far and exchanged plans, thought they could not carry on the bounds singly, but that their proceedings without us would be irregular and invalid and that it would be no boundary, and thought it proper to enter our dissent thereto. Wherefore for the reasons aforesaid, in the name of His Excellency the Palatine and the rest of the true and absolute Lords Proprietors of Carolina, we dissent and disallow of any farther proceedings with the bounds without our concurrence and, pursuant to our instructions, do give this our dissent in writing.

Plausible   Jumble

Puzzlecause   Shoebrush

October 7th, 1728

To this protest the commissioners for Virginia made the following answer:

Whereas on the seventh day of October a paper was delivered to us by the commissioners of North Carolina in the style of a protest against our carrying any farther without them the dividing line between the two governments, we, the underwritten commissioners on the part of Virginia, having maturely considered the reasons offered in the said protest why those gentlemen retired so soon from that service, beg leave to return the following answer.

They are pleased to allege in the first place by way of reason that, having run the line near fifty miles without the inhabitants, it was sufficient for a long time and in their opinion for an age or two. To this we answer that they, by breaking off so soon, did very imperfectly obey His Majesty's order, assented to by the Lords Proprietors. The plain meaning of that order was to ascertain the bounds betwixt the two governments as far toward the mountains as we could, that neither the King's grants may hereafter encroach upon the Lords Proprietors nor theirs on the right of His Majesty. And though the distance toward the mountains be not precisely determined by the said order, yet surely the west line should be carried as near to them as may be, that both the land of the King and of the Lords may be taken up the faster, and that His Majesty's subjects may as soon as possible extend themselves to that natural barrier. This they will do in a very few years when they know distinctly in which government they may enter for the land, as they have already done in the more northern parts of Virginia; so that 'tis strange the Carolina commissioners should affirm that the distance of fifty miles beyond the inhabitants should be sufficient to carry the line for an age or two, especially considering that a few days before the signing of this protest Astrolabe had taken up near two thousand acres of land, granted by themselves, within five miles of the place where they left us. Besides, if we reflect on the goodness of the soil in those parts and the fondness of all degrees of people to take up land, we may venture to foretell, without the spirit of divination, that there will be many settlements much higher than these gentlemen went in less than ten years and perhaps in half that time.

The commissioners of North Carolina protested against proceeding on the line for another reason: because it would be a needless charge and trouble, alleging that the rest may be done by one surveyor on a side in an easy manner when it shall be thought necessary. To this we answer that frugality of the public money is a great virtue, but when the public service must suffer by it, it degenerates into a vice, and this will ever be the case when gentlemen execute the orders of their superiors by halves. But had the Carolina commissioners been sincerely frugal for their government, why did they carry out provisions sufficient to support themselves and their men for eight weeks when they intended to tarry out no longer than half that time? This they must confess to be true, since they had provided five hundred pounds of bread and the same weight of beef and bacon, which was sufficient allowance for their complement of men for two months if it had been carefully managed. Now after so great an expense in their preparations, it had been but a small addition to their charge if they had endured the fatigue a month longer. It would have been at most no more than what they must be at whenever they finish their work, even though they think proper to entrust it to the management of a surveyor, who must have a necessary strength to attend him both for his attendance and defense.

These are all the reasons these gentlemen think fit to mention in their protest, though in truth they had a much stronger argument for their retiring so abruptly, which because they forgot, it will be but neighborly to help them out and remind them of it. The provisions they brought along with them, for want of providing horses to carry it, was partly left behind upon a high tree to be taken down as they returned, and what they did carry was so carelessly handled that after eighteen days, which was the whole time we had the honor of their company, they had by their own confession no more left than two pounds of bread for each man to carry them home.

However, though in truth this was an invincible reason why they left the business unfinished, it was none at all to us who had at that time biscuit sufficient for six weeks longer. Therefore, lest their want of management should put a stop to His Majesty's service, we conceived it our duty to proceed without them and have extended the dividing line so far west as to leave the mountains on each hand to the eastward of us. This we have done with the same fidelity and exactness as if those gentlemen had continued with us. Our surveyors acted under the same oath which they had taken in the beginning and were persons whose integrity will not be called in question. However, though the government of North Carolina should not hold itself bound by the line we made in the absence of its commissioners, yet it will continue to be a direction to the government of Virginia how far the King's lands reach toward Carolina and how far His Majesty may grant them away without injustice to the Lords Proprietors. To this we may also add that, having the authority of our commission to act without the commissioners of North Carolina in case of their disagreement or refusal, we thought it necessary on their deserting to finish the dividing line without them, lest His Majesty's service might suffer by any neglect or mismanagement on their part. Given under our hands the seventh of December, 1728.

Meanwell   Steddy

Though the foregoing answer was not immediately returned to the protest, as appears by the date, yet it can't be placed better in this journal than next to it, that the arguments on each side may be the better compared and understood.

Thus, after we had completed our business with our dear friends of Carolina and supplied 'em with some small matters that could be spared, they took their leave and Firebrand with them, full of professions of friendship and good will — just like some men and their wives who, after living together all their time in perpetual discord and uneasiness, will yet be very good friends at the point of death when they are sure they shall part forever.

A general joy discovered itself through all our camp when these gentlemen turned their backs upon us; only Orion had a cloud of melancholy upon his face for the loss of those with whom he had spent all his leisure hours. Before these gentlemen went, he had persuaded Puzzlecause to give him a certificate concerning the quarrel betwixt Firebrand and Meanwell, not because he was ignorant how it was, because he was sitting by the fire within hearing all the time of the fray, but because he should not be able to tell the truth of the story for fear of disobliging his patron, and to disguise and falsify the truth, besides making himself a liar, would give just offense to Meanwell. In this dilemma he thought it safest to persuade Puzzlecause to be the liar by giving him a certificate which softened some things and left out others and so, by his New England way of cooking the story, made it tell less shocking on the side of Firebrand. This was esteemed wonderful politic in Orion, but he was as blameable to circulate an untruth in another's name and under another's hand as if it had been altogether his own act and deed, and was in truth as much resented by Meanwell when he came to hear it.

Because Firebrand desired that one of the men might return back with him, I listed one of the Carolina men to go on with us in his room, who was indeed the best man they had. One of our horses being missing, we quitted not our camp till two o'clock. This and the thick woods were the reason we carried the line not quite three miles. We crossed Hycootomony Creek once more in this day's work and encamped near another creek that runs into it called Buffalo Creek,[81] so called from the great signs we saw of that shy animal.

Now we drank nothing but the liquor Adam drank in Paradise and found it mended our appetite, not only to our victuals, of which we had plenty, but also to women, of which we had none. It also promoted digestion, else it had been impossible to eat so voraciously, as most of us did, without inconvenience.

Tom Short killed a deer, and several of the company killed turkeys. These two kinds of flesh, together with the help of a little rice or French barley, made the best soup in the world. And what happens

[81] Buffalo Mineral Springs, in Halifax County, is believed to have received its name from Byrd's description of the buffalo he saw nearby.

very rarely in other good things, it never cloys by being a constant dish. The bushes, being very thick, began to tear our bread bags so intolerably that we were obliged to halt several times a day to have them mended. And the Carolina men pleased themselves with the joke of one of the Indians, who said we should soon be forced to cut up our house (meaning the tent) to keep our bags in repair. And what he said in jest would have happened true in earnest if I had not ordered the skins of the deer which we killed to be made use of in covering the bags. This proved a good expedient, by which they were guarded and consequently our bread preserved.

I could not forbear making an observation upon our men, which I believe holds true in others, that those of them who were the foremost to stuff their guts were ever the most backward to work and were more impatient to eat their supper than to earn it. This was the character of all the Carolina men without exception.

8. We hurried the surveyors out about nine and followed ourselves with the baggage about eleven, yet the woods were so thick we could advance little better than four miles. I spirited up our men by telling them that the Carolina men were so arrogant as to fancy we could make no earnings of it without them.

Having yet not skins enough to cover all our bread bags, those which had none suffered much by the bushes, as in truth did our clothes and our baggage, nor indeed were our eyes safe in our heads. Those difficulties hindered Tom Jones from coming up with some of the loaded horses to the camp where we lay. He was forced to stop short about a mile of us, where there was not a drop of water, but he had the rum with him, which was some comfort. I was very uneasy at their absence, resolving for the future to put all the baggage before us.

We were so lucky as to encamp near a fine spring, and our Indian killed a fat doe, with which Providence supplied us just time enough to hinder us from going supperless to bed. We called our camp by the name of Tear-Coat Camp by reason of the rough thickets that surrounded it. I observed some of the men were so free as to take what share of the deer they pleased and to secure it for themselves while others were at work, but I gave such orders as put a stop to those irregularities and divided the people into messes, among which the meat was fairly to be distributed.

9. The surveyors went to work about nine, but because the bushes were so intolerably thick, I ordered some hands to clear the way before them. This made their business go on the slower; however, they carried the line about six miles by reason the thicket reached no farther than a mile and the rest of the way was over clear woods and even grounds. We tarried with the rear guard till twelve for our absent men, who came to the camp as hungry as hawks, for, having no water to drink, they durst not eat for fear of thirst, which was more uneasy than hunger.

When we had supplied our wants, we followed the track of the surveyors, passing over two runs of excellent water, one at three and the other at four miles' distance from our last camp. The land was for the most part very good, with plenty of wild angelica growing upon it. Several deer came into our sight but none into our quarters, which made short commons and consequently some discontent. For this reason some of the men called this Bread-and-Water Camp, but we called it Crane Camp, because many of those fowls flew over our heads, being very clamorous in their flight. Our Indian killed a mountain partridge, resembling the smaller partridge in the plumage but as large as a hen. These are common toward the mountains, though we saw very few of them, our noise scaring them away.

10. We began this day very luckily by killing a brace of turkeys and one deer, so that the plenty of our breakfast this morning made amends for the shortness of our supper last night. This restored good humor to the men, who had a mortal aversion to fasting. As I lay in my tent, I overheard one of them, called James Whitlock, wish that he were at home. For this I reproved him publicly, asking him whether it was the danger or the fatigue of the journey that disheartened him, wondering how he could be tired so soon of the company of so many brave fellows. So seasonable a reprimand put an effectual stop to all complaints, and nobody after that day was ever heard so much as to wish himself in Heaven.

A small distance from our camp we crossed a creek which we called Cockade Creek, because we there began to wear the beards of wild turkey cocks in our hats by way of cockade. A little more than a mile from thence we came to the true southern branch of Roanoke River, which was about 150 yards over, with a swift stream of water as clear as crystal. It was fordable near our line, but we were obliged to ride above 100 yards up the river to the end of a small island and then near as far back again on the other side of the island before we could mount the bank. The west side of this fine river was fringed with tall canes a full furlong in depth, through which our men cleared a path broad enough for our baggage to pass, which took up a long time. The bottom of the river was paved with gravel, which was everywhere spangled with small flakes of mother-of-pearl that almost dazzled our eyes. The sand on the shore sparkled with the same. So that this seemed the most beautiful river that I ever saw. The difficulty of passing it and cutting through the canes hindered us so much that we could carry the line little more than three miles.

We crossed a creek two and a half miles beyond the river, called Cane Creek from very tall canes which lined its banks. On the west side of it we took up our quarters. The horses were very fond of those canes, but at first they purged them exceedingly and seemed to be no very heartening food.

Our Indian killed a deer and the other men some turkeys, but the Indian begged very hard that our cook might not boil venison and turkey together because it would certainly spoil his luck in hunting and we should repent it with fasting and prayer. We called this south branch of Roanoke the Dan, as I had called the north branch the Staunton before.

11. We hurried away the surveyors at nine and followed with the baggage about eleven. In about four and a half miles we crossed the Dan the second time and found it something narrower than before, being about 110 yards over. The west banks of it were also thick set with canes, but not for so great a breadth as where we passed it first. But it was here a most charming river, having the bottom spangled as before, with a limpid stream gently flowing and murmuring among

the rocks, which were thinly scattered here and there to make up the variety of the prospect. The line was carried something more than two miles beyond the river, in which distance the thickets were very troublesome. However, we made a shift to run six and a half miles in the whole, but encamped after sunset. I had foretold on the credit of a dream which I had last Sunday night that we should see the mountains this day, and it proved true, for Astrolabe discovered them very plain to the northwest of our course, though at a great distance. The rich land held about a mile broad on the west side the river. Tom Jones killed a buck and the Indian a turkey, but he would not bring it us for fear we should boil it with our venison against his ridiculous superstition. I had a moderate cold, which only spoiled my voice but not my stomach. Our chaplain, having got rid of his little lurking fevers, began to eat like a cormorant.

12. The surveyors were dispatched by nine, but the thick woods made the horses so hard to be found that we did not follow with the baggage till after twelve. The line was extended something more than five miles, all the way through a thicket. We judged by the great number of chestnut trees that we approached the mountains, which several of our men discovered very plainly. The bears are great lovers of chestnuts and are so discreet as not to venture their unwieldy bodies upon the smaller branches of the trees which will not bear their weight. But after walking upon the limbs as far as is safe, they bite off the limbs, which falling down, they finish their meal upon the ground. In the same cautious manner they secure the acorns that grow on the outer branches of the oak. They eat grapes very greedily, which grow plentifully in these woods, very large vines wedding almost every tree in the rich soil. This shows how natural the situation of this country is to vines.

Our men killed a bear of two years old which was very fat. The flesh of it hath a good relish, very savory, and inclining nearest to that of pork. The fat of this creature is the least apt to rise in the stomach of any other. The men for the most part chose it rather than venison; the greatest inconvenience was that they eat more bread with it. We, who were not accustomed to eat this rich diet, tasted it at first with some squeamishness but soon came to like it. Particularly, our chaplain loved it so passionately that he would growl like a wildcat over a squirrel.

Toward the evening the clouds gathered thick and threatened rain, and made us draw a trench round the tent and take the necessary precautions to secure the bread, but no rain fell. We remembered our wives and mistresses in a bumper of excellent cherry brandy. This we could afford to drink no oftener than to put on a clean shirt, which was once a week.

13. This being Sunday, we rested from our fatigue and had a sermon. Our weather was very louring, with the wind hard at northwest with great likelihood of rain. Every Sunday I constantly ordered Peter Jones to weigh out the weekly allowance of bread to each man, which hitherto was five pounds. This with plenty of meat was sufficient for any reasonable man, and those who were unreasonable I would by no means indulge with superfluities. The rising ground where we encamped was so surrounded with thickets that we could not walk out with any comfort; however, after dinner several of the men ventured to try their fortune and brought in no less than six wild turkeys. They told us they saw the mountains very distinctly from the neighboring hills.

In the evening I examined our Indian, Ned Bearskin, concerning his religion, and he very frankly gave me the following account of it. That he believed there was a supreme being that made the world and everything in it. That the same power that made it still preserves and governs it. That it protects and prospers good people in this world and punishes the bad with sickness and poverty. That after death all mankind are conducted into one great road, in which both the good and bad travel in company to a certain distance where this great road branches into two paths, the one extremely level and the other mountainous.[82] Here the good are parted from the bad by a flash of lightning, the first filing to the right, the other to the left.

[82] William Strachey's relation of the beliefs of the Powhatan Indian tribes concerning an afterlife has some points of resemblance with Bearskin's religion. See William Strachey, *Historie of Travell into Virginia Britania*, edited by Louis B. Wright and Virginia Freund (London, 1953), pp. 102–103.

The right-hand road leads to a fine warm country where the spring is perpetual and every month is May. And, as the year is always in its youth, so are the people, and the women beautiful as stars and never scold. That in this happy climate there are deer innumerable, perpetually fat, and the trees all bear delicious fruit in every season. That the earth brings forth corn spontaneously, without labor, which is so very wholesome that none that eat of it are ever sick, grow old, or die. At the entrance into this blessed land sits a venerable old man, who examines everyone before he is admitted, and if he has behaved well, the guards are ordered to open the crystal gate and let him into this terrestrial paradise.

The left-hand path is very rough and uneven, leading to a barren country where 'tis always winter; the ground was covered with snow and nothing on the trees but icicles. All the people are old, have no teeth, and yet are very hungry. Only those who labor very hard make the ground produce a sort of potato, pleasant to the taste but gives them the dry gripes and fills them full of sores which stinks and are very painful. The women are old and ugly, armed with sharp claws like a panther, and with those they gore the men that slight their passion. For it seems these haggard old furies are intolerably fond. They talk very much and very shrill, giving most exquisite pain to the drum of the ear, which in that horrid climate grows so tender that any sharp note hurts it.

On the borders sits a hideous old woman whose head is covered with rattlesnakes instead of tresses, with glaring white eyes sunk very deep in her head. Her tongue is twenty cubits long, armed with sharp thorns as strong as iron. This tongue, besides the dreadful sound it makes in pronouncing sentence, serves the purpose of an elephant's trunk, with which the old gentlewoman takes up those she has convicted of wickedness and throws them over a vast high wall, hewn out of one solid rock, that surrounds this region of misery to prevent escapes. They are received on the inside by another hideous old woman, who consigns them over to punishments proper for their crimes. When they have been chastised here a certain number of years according to their degrees of guilt, they are thrown over the wall again and driven once more back into this world of trial, where, if they mend their manners, they are conducted into the above-mentioned fine country after their death. This was the substance of Bearskin's religion, which he told us with a freedom uncommon to the Indians.

14. It began to rain about three o'clock this morning, but so gently that we had leisure to secure the bread from damage. It continued raining all night and till near noon, when it held up; the clouds looked very heavy and frightened us from all thoughts of decamping. Meanwell and I lay abed all the morning, believing that the most agreeable situation in wet weather. The wind, blowing hard at northeast, made the air very raw and uncomfortable. However, several of the men went hunting in the afternoon and killed three deer and four turkeys, so that the frying pan was not cool till next morning. The chaplain, disdaining to be useful in one capacity only, condescended to darn my stockings; he acquired that with his other university learning at the College of Dublin. At six it began to rain again and held not up till nine, when the clouds seemed to break away and give us a sight of the stars. I dreamt the three Graces appeared to me in all their naked charms; I singled out Charity from the rest, with whom I had an intrigue.

15. The weather promising to be fair, we hurried away the surveyors as early as we could but did not follow with the baggage till one o'clock, because the thick woods made it difficult to find the horses. I interposed very seasonably to decide a wager betwixt two of the warmest of our men, which might otherwise have inflamed them into a quarrel.

In about a mile's march we passed over a large creek, whose banks were fringed with canes. We called it Sable Creek from the color of its water. Our surveyors crossed the Dan twice this day. The first time was 240 poles from our camp and the second in 1 mile and 7 poles farther, and from thence proceeded with the line only 59 poles, in all no more than 1 mile and 300 poles. The difficulty they had in passing the river twice made their day's work so small.

The baggage did not cross the river at all but went round the bent of it; and in the evening we encamped on a charming piece of ground that commanded the prospect of the reaches of the river, which were about fifty yards over and the banks adorned with canes. We pitched the tent at the bottom of a mount, which we called Mount Pleasant for the beauty of the prospect from thence.

This night Astrolabe's servant had his purse cut off, in which he lost his own money and some that my man had put into his keeping. We could suspect nobody but Holmes of the kingdom of Ireland, who had watched, it seems, that night for several of the men, without which he could not have had an opportunity. He had also the insolence to strike Meanwell's servant, for which he had like to have been tossed in a blanket. Astrolabe's horse fell with him in the river, which had no other consequence but to refresh him and make the rest of the company merry. Here the low ground was very narrow, but very dry and very delightful.

16. The surveyors got to work about nine, and we followed with the baggage at eleven. They carried the line about four and a half miles and were stopped by the river, over which they could not find a ford. We passed a small creek near our camp, which had canes on each side on which our horses had feasted. The constant current in the river may be computed to run about two knots, and we discovered no falls over which a canoe might not pass.

Our journey this day was through very open woods. At three miles' distance we crossed another creek, which we called Lowland Creek from a great breadth of low ground made by this creek and the river, which ran about a fourth of a mile to the northward of us. We were obliged to go two miles higher than where our line intersected the river, because we could not find a ford.

In our way we went through several large Indian fields where we fancied the Sauro Indians [83] had formerly planted corn. We en-

---

[83] The Cheraws, also variously known as the Saraws, Saras, Sauras. This Siouan tribe lived on the Yadkin River in the seventeenth century, but in 1700 they settled on the Dan, near the southern boundary of Virginia, with a second village thirty miles higher on the south side of the Dan; the latter was known as Upper Saura Village and the other Lower Saura Village. The Iroquois forced them to move southeast to join the Keyauwee in about 1710, and later they moved to the vicinity of the Pee Dee River. See John R. Swanton, *The Indians of the Southeastern United States* (Washington, D.C., 1946), pp. 109-110.

camped near one of these Indian cornfields, where was excellent food for our horses. Our Indian killed a deer, and the men knocked down no less than four bears and two turkeys, so that this was truly a land of plenty both for man and beast. Dr. Humdrum at this camp first discovered his passion for the delicious flesh of bear.

17. The surveyors moved early and went back at least two miles on the south side of the river before they could get over. Nor was it without difficulty and some danger that they and we crossed this ford, being full of rocks and holes and the current so swift that it made them giddy. However, Heaven be praised, we all got safe on the other side; only one baggage horse stumbled and sopped a little of the bread.

The puzzle in crossing the river and the thick woods hindered our surveyors from carrying the line farther than 2 miles and 250 poles to the banks of Cascade Creek, so called from several waterfalls that are in it. We encamped the sooner because it threatened rain, the wind strong at northeast.

In our way to this place we went over abundance of good land, made so by the river and this creek. Our dogs catched a young cub, and the Indian killed a young buck. Near the creek we found a very good kind of stone that flaked into thin pieces fit for pavement.

About a mile southwest from our camp was a high mount that commanded a full prospect of the mountains and a very extensive view of all the flat country, but being with respect to the mountains no more than a pimple, we called it by that name.

18. The weather clearing up with a brisk northwester, we dispatched the surveyors about nine, who carried the line about 6 miles and 30 poles to a branch of the Dan, which we called the Irvin. We did not follow with the baggage till twelve. We crossed Cascade Creek over a ledge of rocks and marched through a large plain of good land but very thick woods for at least four miles together. We met with no water in all that distance. A little before sunset we crossed the Irvin at a deep ford where the rocks were so slippery the horses could hardly keep their feet. But by the great care of Tom Jones, we all got safe over without any damage to our bread.

We encamped on a pleasant hill in sight of the river, the sand of which is full of shining particles. Bearskin killed a fat doe and came across a bear which had been killed and half devoured by a panther. The last of these brutes reigns king of the woods and often kills the poor bears, I believe, more by surprise than fair fight. They often take them napping, bears being very sleepy animals, and though they be very strong, yet is their strength heavy, and the panthers are much nimbler. The Doctor grutched the panther this dainty morsel, being so fond of bear that he would rise before day to eat a griskin [84] of it.

19. About nine the surveyors took their departure and advanced with the line 5 miles and 135 poles; nor was this a small day's work, considering the way was more uneven and full of thickets than ever. We did not follow them till twelve, because some of the bread horses were missing. Astrolabe would have fain sent out two of the men to find out where the Dan and the Irvin forked, but I would not consent to it for fear they should fall into some disaster, we being now near the path which the northern Indians take when they march against those of the south.

Something more than four miles from our camp we crossed Matrimony Creek, which received its name from being very noisy, the water murmuring everlastingly amongst the rocks. Half a mile beyond this creek we discovered five miles to the northwest of the line a small mountain, which we called the Wart.

We would willingly have marched to a good place for our horses, which began to grow very weak, but, night coming on, we were obliged to encamp on very uneven ground, so overgrown with bushes and saplings that we could with difficulty see ten yards before us. Here our horses met with short commons, and so should we too if we had not brought a horseload of meat along with us. All that our hunters could kill was only one turkey, which helped however to season the broth.

20. This being Sunday, I washed off all my week's dirt and refreshed myself with clean linen. We had prayers and a sermon. We began here to fall from five to four pounds of bread a man for the following week, computing we had enough at that rate to last a month longer. Our Indian had the luck to kill a monstrous fat bear, which

[84] Chop or steak.

came very seasonably, for our men, having nothing else to do, had eat up all their meat and began to look very pensive. But our starved horses had no such good fortune, meeting with no other food but a little wild rosemary that grows on the high ground. This they love very well if they had had enough of it, but it grew only in thin tufts here and there. Tom Short brought me a hatful of very good wild grapes, which were plentiful all over these woods.

Our men, when the service was over, thought it no breach of the Sabbath to wash their linen and put themselves in repair, being a matter of indispensable necessity. Meanwell was very handy at his needle, having learnt the use of that little implement at sea, and flourished his thread with as good a grace as any merchant tailor.

21. Our surveyors got to work about nine and carried the line 4 miles and 270 poles, great part of that distance being very hilly and grown up with thickets, but we could not follow them till after two. Both Hamilton and his horse were missing, and though I sent out several men in quest of them, they were able to find neither. At last, fearing we should not overtake the surveyors, I left Tom Jones and another man to beat all the adjacent woods for them. We passed through intolerable thickets, to the great danger of our eyes and damage of our clothes, insomuch that I had enough to do to keep my patience and sweet temper. With all our diligence we could fight our way through the bushes no farther than two and a half miles before sunset, so that we could not reach the surveyors. This was a sensible grief to us, because they had no bedding with them and probably no victuals. And even in the last article we were not mistaken, for though our Indian killed a bear, he had left it on the line for us to pick up. Thus our dear friends run a risk of being doubly starved both with cold and hunger. I knew this would ill agree with Orion's delicate constitution, but Astrolabe I was in less pain for, because he had more patience and could subsist longer upon licking his paws.

We had the comfort to encamp where our horses fared well, and we drank health to our absent friends in pure element. Just as it was dark, Tom Jones brought poor Hamilton to us without his horse. He had contrived to lose himself, being no great woodsman, but pretended that he was only bogged. He looked very melancholy for the loss of his horse till I promised to employ my interest to procure him satisfaction. For want of venison broth for supper we contented ourselves with some greasy soup *de jambon*, which, though it slipped down well enough, sat not very easy on our stomachs. So soon as we encamped, I dispatched John Evans to look for the surveyors, but he returned without success, being a little too sparing of his trouble. We saw a small mountain to the northwest, which we called the Wart.

22. This morning early, I sent John Evans with Hamilton back to our last camp to make a farther search for the stray horse, with orders to spend a whole day about it. At the same time I dispatched Richard Smith to the surveyors with some provisions to stop their mouths as well as their stomachs. It was eleven o'clock before we could get up all the horses, when we followed our surveyors and in a mile and a half reached the camp where they had lain. The woods were extremely thick in the beginning of this day's march but afterwards grew pretty open. As we rode along we found no less than three bears and a half a deer left upon the line, with which we loaded our light horses.

We came up with the surveyors on the banks of the western branch of the Irvin, which we called the Mayo. Here they had halted for us, not knowing the reason why we stayed behind so long. And this was the cause they proceeded no farther with the line than 1 mile and 230 poles. About a mile before we reached this river we crossed a small creek, which we called Miry Creek because several of the branches of it were miry. We passed the Mayo just below a ledge of rocks, where Meanwell's horse slipped and fell upon one of his legs and would have broke it if his half-jacks [85] had not guarded it. As it was, his ankle was bruised very much, and he halted several days upon it.

After the tent was pitched, Astrolabe, Humdrum, and I clambered up a high hill to see what we could discover from thence. On the brow of the hill we spied a young cub on the top of a high tree at supper upon some acorns. We were so indiscreet as to take no gun with us and therefore were obliged to halloo to the men to bring one.

[85] Boots like jack boots but of shorter length.

125

When it came, Astrolabe undertook to fetch the bear down but missed him. However, the poor beast, hearing the shot rattle about his ears, came down the tree of his own accord and trusted to his heels. It was a pleasant race between Bruin and our grave surveyor, who, I must confess, runs much better than he shoots; yet the cub outran him, even downhill, where bears are said to sidle lest their guts should come out of their mouths. But our men had better luck and killed no less than six of these unwieldy animals.

We sent our horses back to Miry Creek for the benefit of the canes and winter grass, which they eat very greedily. There was a waterfall in the river just by our camp, the noise of which gave us poetical dreams and made us say our prayers in meter when we awaked.

23. Our surveyors moved forward and proceeded with the line 4 miles and 69 poles. At the distance of 62 poles from our camp we passed over another branch of the Irvin with difficulty, about half a mile from where it forked. It was extremely mountainous great part of the way, and the last mile we encountered a dreadful thicket interlaced with briers and grapevines. We crossed a large creek no less than five times with our line, which for that reason we called Crooked Creek; the banks of it were steep in many places and bordered with canes. With great luck for our horses we encamped where these canes were plentiful. This refreshment was very seasonable after so tiresome a journey, in which these poor beasts had clambered up so many precipices.

About sunset Evans and Hamilton came up with us, but had been so unlucky as not to find the horse. Our men eat up a horseload of bear, which was very unthrifty management, considering we could meet with no game all this day. But woodsmen are good Christians in one respect: by never taking care for the morrow but letting the morrow care for itself, for which reason no sort of people ought to pray so fervently for their daily bread as they.

24. The men feasted so plentifully last night that some of them paid for it by fasting this morning. One who had been less provident than the rest broke his fast very oddly. He singed all the hair off of a bearskin and boiled the pelt into broth. To this he invited his par-

ticular friends, who eat very heartily and commended the cookery by supping it clean up.

Our surveyors hurried away a little after eight and extended the line 6 miles and 300 poles. We did not follow them till about eleven and crossed a thicket two full miles in breadth without any great trees near it.

The soil seemed very rich and level, having many locust and hickory saplings. The reason why there are no high trees is probably because the woods in these remote parts are burnt but seldom. During those long intervals the leaves and other trash are heaped so thick upon the ground that when they come to be set on fire they consume all before them, leaving nothing either standing or lying upon the ground.

Afterwards our way was mountainous and the woods open for about two and a half miles, then level and overgrown with bushes all the remaining distance. The line crossed Crooked Creek ten times in this day's work, and we encamped upon a branch of it where our horses fared but indifferently. The men came off better, for the Indian killed two bears, on which they feasted till the grease ran out of their mouths. Till this night I had always lain in my nightgown, but upon trial I found it much warmer to strip to my shirt and lie in naked bed with my gown over me. The woodsmen put all off, if they have no more than one blanket to lie in, and agree that 'tis much more comfortable than to lie with their clothes on, though the weather be never so cold.

25. The surveyors got to work soon after eight and run the line 4 miles and 205 poles. We did not follow them till near two, by reason Holmes's horse could not be found. And at last we were forced to leave Robin Hix and William Pool behind to search narrowly for him.

The woods were so intolerably thick for near four miles that they tore the very skins that covered the bread bags. This hindered us from overtaking the surveyors, though we used our utmost diligence to do it. We could reach but four miles and were obliged to encamp near a small run, where our horses came off but indifferently. However, they fared very near as well as their masters, for our Indian met with no game, so we had nothing to entertain ourselves with but the scanty remnant of yesterday's plenty. Nor was there much luxury at the surveyors' camp either in their lodging or diet.

However, they had the pleasure, as well as we, to see the mountains very plain both to the north and south of the line. Their distance seemed to be no more than five or six miles. Those to the north appeared in three or four ledges rising one above another, but those to the south made no more than one single ledge, and that not entire but were rather detached mountains lying near one another in a line. One was prodigiously high and the west end of it a perpendicular precipice. The next to it was lower but had another rising out of the east end of it in the form of a stack of chimneys. We could likewise discern other mountains in the course of the line but at a much greater distance. Till this day we never had a clear view of any of these mountains, by reason the air was very full of smoke. But this morning it cleared up and surprised us with this wild prospect all at once. At night the men brought Holmes's horse.

26. We had ambassadors from our hungry surveyors setting forth their wants, which we supplied in the best manner we could. We moved toward them about eleven and found them at the camp where they lay, near a rivulet which we judged to be the head of Deep River, otherwise called the north branch of Cape Fear.[86] We resolved to encamp here because there was great plenty of canes for the poor horses, which began to grow wondrous thin. However, the surveyors measured three hundred poles this day, which carried the line to the banks of the rivulet. The last line tree they marked is a red oak with the trees around it blazed.

We determined to proceed no farther with the dividing line, because the way to the west grew so mountainous that our jaded horses were not in condition to climb over it. Besides, we had no more bread than would last us a fortnight at short allowance. And the season of the year being far advanced, we had reason to fear we might be intercepted by snow or the swelling of the rivers which lay betwixt us and

[86] It seems unlikely that the party was far enough south to have encountered the head of Deep River in Forsyth County, North Carolina. Boyd suggested that the survey ended at "Peter's Creek, on the border of Stokes County, North Carolina."

home. These considerations checked our inclinations to fix the line in the ledge of mountains and determined us to make the best of our way back the same track we came. We knew the worst of that and had a straight path to carry us the nearest distance, while we were ignorant what difficulties might be encountered if we steered any other course.

We had intended to cross at the foot of the mountains over to the head of James River, that we might be able to describe that natural boundary. But prudence got the better of curiosity, which is always the more necessary when we have other men's welfare to consult as well as our own. Just by our camp we found a pair of elk's horns, not very large, and saw the track of the owner of them. They commonly keep more to the northward, as buffaloes do more to the southward.

In the afternoon we walked up a high hill north of our camp, from whence we discovered an amphitheater of mountains extending from the northeast round by the west to the southeast. 'Twas very unlucky that the mountains were more distant just at the head of our line toward the west by thirty or forty miles.

Our chaplain attempted to climb a tree, but before he got six feet from the ground fear made him cling closer to the tree than love would make him cling to a mistress. Meanwell was more venturesome but more unfortunate, for he bruised his foot in a tender place, by which he got a gentle fit of the gout. This was an improper situation to have the cruel distemper in and put my invention upon contriving some way or other to carry him back. In the meanwhile, he bathed his foot frequently in cold water to repel the humor if possible, for, as the case was, he could neither put on shoe nor boot.

Our men killed two bears, a buck, and a turkey — a very seasonable supply and made us reflect with gratitude on the goodness of Providence. The whole distance from Currituck Inlet, where we began the line, to this rivulet where we ended it, was 241½ miles and 70 poles.[87] In the night the wind blew fresh at southwest with moderate rain.

[87] The recording of distances seems to have been rather careless, or they were carelessly transcribed by the copyist. This total appears on p. 153 as 241¼ miles, 70 poles. The *History* (p. 268) gives the total distance traveled as 240 miles and 230

27. This being Sunday, we gave God thanks for protecting and sustaining us thus far by his divine bounty. We had also a sermon proper for the occasion. It rained small rain in the morning and looked louring all day. Meanwell had the gout in form, his foot being very much swelled, which was not more pain to him than it was disturbance to the rest. I ordered all the men to visit their horses and to drive them up that they might be found more easily the next morning. When the distribution of bread was made among the men, I recommended good husbandry to them, not knowing how long we should be obliged to subsist upon it. I sat by the riverside near a small cascade fed by a stream as clear as liquid crystal, and the murmur it made composed my senses into an agreeable tranquillity. We had a fog after sunset that gave an unpleasant dampness to the air, which we endeavored to correct by a rousing fire. This, with the wetness of the ground where we encamped, made our situation a little unwholesome; yet, thank God, all our company continued in a perfect health.

28. We ordered the horses up very early, but the likelihood of more rain prevented our decamping. And we judged right, for about ten o'clock it began to rain in good earnest. Meanwell made an excellent figure with one boot of leather and the other of flannel. So accoutered, he intended to mount, but the rain came seasonably to hinder him from exposing his foot to be bruised and tormented by the bushes.

We kept snug in the tent all day, spending most of our time in reading; and Dr. Humdrum, being disturbed at Astrolabe's reading *Hudibras* aloud, gabbled an old almanac three times over to drown one noise with another. This trial of lungs lasted a full hour and tired the hearers as much as the readers.

Powell's ague returned, for which I gave him the bark, and Pool took some Anderson's pills to force a passage through his body. This man had an odd constitution: he eat like a horse, but all he eat stayed with him till it was forced downwards by some purging physic. Without this assistance his belly and bowels were so swelled he could

poles (3,795 feet), or less than 241 miles. The journals of the expedition sent to England give still different mileage for the total distance.

hardly breath. Yet he was a strong fellow and used a world of exercise. It was therefore wonderful the peristaltic motion was not more vigorously promoted. Page was muffled up for the toothache, for which distemper I could recommend no medicine but patience, which he seemed to possess a great share of. It rained most part of the night.

29. In the morning we were flattered with all the signs of a fair day, the wind being come about to the northwest. This made us order the horses to be got up very early, but the tent horse could not be found; and 'tis well he stopped us, for about ten all our hopes of fair weather blew over and it rained very smartly for some time. This was all in favor of Meanwell's gouty foot, which was now grown better and the inflammation assuaged. Nor did it need above one day more to bring it down to its natural proportion and make it fit for the boot.

Being confined to the tent till dinner, I had no amusement but reading. But in the afternoon I walked up to a neighboring hill, from whence I could view the mountains to the southward, the highest of which our traders fancied to be the Katawa Mountain,[88] but it seems to be too northerly for that.

Our men went out a-driving and had the luck to kill two bears, one of which was found by our Indian asleep and never waked. Unfortunate Hamilton, straggling from the rest of the company, was lost a second time. We fired at least a dozen guns to direct him by their report to our camp, but all in vain: we could get no tidings of him. I was much concerned lest a disaster might befall him, being alone all night in that doleful wilderness.

30. The clouds were all swept away by a kind northwester, which made it pretty cold. We were all impatient to set our faces toward the east, which made the men more alert than ordinary in catching their horses. About seven our stray man found the way to the camp,

---

[88] The *History* (p. 274) reads "Kiawan" Mountain, a name that probably derives from that of the Keyauwee Indians. Boyd identified this as Pilot Mountain in Surry County, North Carolina, which seems probable. The Indians may have fancied they were seeing Shepherd Mountain, in Randolph County, near which the site of an Indian village was found in 1936. The name, like that of Pilot Mountain, may indicate that it was used by the Indians as a landmark.

being directed by the horses' bells. Though he had lain on the bare ground without either fire or bedclothes, he catched no cold.

I gave order that four men should set off early and clear the way, that the baggage horses might travel with less difficulty and more expedition. We followed them about eleven, and, the air being clear, we had a fair prospect of the mountains both to the north and south. That very high one to the south with the precipice at the west end we called the Lover's Cure, because one leap from thence would put a sudden period both to his passion and his pain. On the highest ledge, that stretched away to the northeast, rose a mount in the shape of a maiden's breast, which for that reason we called by that innocent name. And the main ledge itself we called Mount Eagle. We marched eleven miles from the end of the line and encamped upon Crooked Creek near a thicket of canes. In the front of our camp was a very beautiful hill which bounded our prospect at a mile's distance, and all the intermediate space was covered with green canes. Firewood was scanty with us, which was the harder because 'twas very cold. Our Indian killed a deer that was extremely fat, and we picked his bones as clean as a score of turkey buzzards could have done.

By the favor of a very clear night we made another essay of the variation and found it much the same as formerly, 2° 30'.

This being His Majesty's birthday, we drank his health in a dram of excellent cherry brandy but could not afford one drop for the Queen and the royal issue. We therefore remembered them in water as clear as our wishes. And because all loyal rejoicings should be a little noisy, we fired canes instead of guns, which made a report as loud as a pistol, the heat expanding the air shut up within the joints of this vegetable and making an explosion.

The woods being cleared before us by the pioneers and the way pretty level, we traveled with pleasure, increased by the hopes of making haste home.

31. We dispatched away our pioneers early to clear away the bushes but did not follow them till eleven o'clock. We crossed Crooked Creek several times, the banks of which, being very steep, jaded our poor horses very much. Meanwell's baggage horse gave out the first,

and next to him one of the bread horses, so that we were obliged to drop them both by the way. The second time we crossed Crooked Creek, by endeavoring to step off my horse's back upon the shore, I fell all along in the water. I wet myself all over and bruised the back part of my head, yet made no complaint but was the merriest of the company at my own disaster. Our dreamer Orion had a revelation about it the night before and foretold it fairly to some of the company.

The ground was so mountainous and our horses so weak that with all our diligence we could not exceed four miles. Indeed, we spent some time in crossing the Dan and the Mayo, the fords being something deeper than when we came up. We took up our camp at Miry Creek and regaled ourselves with one buck and two bears, which our men killed in their march. Here we promoted our chaplain from the deanery of Pip to the bishopric of Beardom. For as those countries where Christians inhabit are called Christendom, so those where bears take up their residence may not improperly go by the name of Beardom. And I wish other bishops loved their flock as entirely as our Doctor loves his.

NOVEMBER

1. The pioneers were sent away about nine o'clock, but we were detained till near two by reason John Evans his horse could not be found, and at last we were obliged to leave four men behind to look for him. However, we made a shift to go six miles and by the way had the fortune to kill a brace of does, two bears, and one turkey. Meanwell's riding horse tired too by the way, so that we were obliged to drop him about a mile short of the camp. Many more of our horses were so weak they staggered under their riders, so that in compassion to the poor animals we walked great part of the way, notwithstanding the path was very rough and in many places uneven. For the same good-natured reason we left our bears behind, choosing rather to carry the venison, for which our bishop had like to have mutinied. We endeavored about noon to observe the latitude, but our observation was something imperfect, the wind blowing too fresh. By such a one as we could make, we found the latitude no more than 36° 20'.

In this camp our horses had short commons and, had they been able to speak like Balaam's ass, would have bemoaned themselves very much.

2. We lost all the morning in hunting for Powell's mare, so that it was two o'clock before we decamped. Our zeal to make the best of our way made us set out when it was very like to rain, and it rained in good earnest before we had marched a mile. We bore it patiently while it was moderate and repassed Matrimony Creek about one and a half miles from our camp. But soon after the rain fell more violently and obliged us to take up our quarters upon an eminence, that we might not be drowned.

This was the only time we were catched in the rain upon the road during the whole journey. It used to be so civil as to fall in the night, as it did while Herod was building the temple, or on a Sunday, or else to give us warning enough to encamp before it fell. But now it took us upon the way and made our lodging uncomfortable, because we were obliged to pitch the tent upon wet ground. The worst circumstance of all was that there was hardly any picking for the horses, which were now grown so lean and so weak that the turkey buzzards began to follow them. It continued raining till three o'clock in the morning, when, to our great joy, it cleared up with a northwester.

3. It was my opinion to rest in our camp, bad as it was, because it was Sunday, but everybody was against me. They urged the danger of starving the horses and the short march we made yesterday, which might justify making a Sabbath Day's journey today. I held out against all these arguments on account of resting the horses, which they greatly needed, as well as because of the duty of the day, till at last the chaplain came with a casuistical face and told me it was a case of necessity that obliged us to remove from a place that would famish all our horses, that charity to those poor animals would excuse a small violation of the Fourth Commandment. I answered that the horses would lose as much by the fatigue of traveling as they would gain by the bettering their food, that the water was raised in the river Irvin and we should be forced to stay till it was fallen again, and so should gain no distance by traveling on the Sunday. However, on

condition the Doctor would take the sin upon himself, I agreed to move three or four miles, which carried us to the banks of the Irvin.

By the way our Indian killed four deer and a bear. When we came to the river, we found the water three or four foot higher than when we came up, so that there was no likelihood of getting over under two days. This made good my argument and put our hasty gentlemen into the vapors, especially Orion, who was more impatient than anybody. I could find no other reason for it but because he had dreamt that Colonel Beverley [89] was dead and imagined his absence might hinder him from making interest for his place of Surveyor General.

In the evening we perceived the water began to fall in the river, which gave some of the company the vain hopes of getting over the next day.

4. In the morning we measured the marks we had set up at the river and found the water had not fallen above a foot; by this we were convinced that we should be obliged to halt there a day longer. We sent some men to endeavor to bring up two horses which tired on Saturday, but the horses were too well pleased with their liberty to come along with them. One of these manumitted horses belonged to Abraham Jones, and, being pricked in the mouth, he bled himself quite off his legs.

There being great plenty in our camp, the men kept eating all day to keep them out of idleness. In the evening it looked very dark and menaced us with more rain, to our great mortification, but after a few drops, I thank God, it blew over. Orion sighed heavily while it lasted, apprehending we should take up our winter quarters in the woods.

John Ellis, who was one of the men we had sent to bring up the tired horses, told us a romantic adventure which he had with a bear on Saturday last. He had straggled from his company and treed a young cub. While he was new priming his gun to shoot at it, the old gentlewoman appeared, who, seeing her heir apparent in distress, came up to his relief. The bear advanced very near to her enemy, reared up on her posteriors, and put herself in guard. The man pre-

[89] William Beverley, son of Robert Beverley the historian, and Byrd's nephew.

135

sented his piece at her, but, unfortunately, it only snapped, the powder being moist. Missing his fire in this manner, he offered to punch her with the muzzle of his gun, which Mother Bruin, being aware of, seized the weapon with her paws and by main strength wrenched it out of his hand. Being thus fairly disarmed and not knowing in the fright but the bear might turn his own cannon upon him, he thought it prudent to retire as fast as his legs could carry him. The brute, being grown more bold by the flight of her adversary, immediately pursued, and for some time it was doubtful whether fear made one run faster or fury the other. But after a fair course of forty yards, the poor man had the mishap to stumble over a stump and fell down at his full length. He now would have sold his life a pennyworth, but the bear, apprehending there might be some trick in this fall, instantly halted and looked very earnestly to observe what the man could mean. In the meantime, he had with much presence of mind resolved to make the bear believe he was dead by lying breathless on the ground, upon the hopes that the bear would be too generous to kill him over again. He acted a corpse in this manner for some time, till he was raised from the dead by the barking of a dog belonging to one of his companions. Cur came up seasonably to his rescue and drove the bear from her pursuit of the man to go and take care of her innocent cub, which she now apprehended might fall into a second distress.

5. We found this morning that the river had fallen no more than four inches the whole night, but a northwester had swept away all the clouds. About ten we resolved to pass the river, which we did very safely, thank God, only Tom Short's horse fell with him and sopped him all over. In the distance of six miles we crossed Cascade Creek and from thence proceeded in near three miles to the Dan, which we forded with some difficulty because the water was deeper than when we came over it before. Unfortunate Mr. Short was ducked a second time by the fall of his horse but received no hurt. My horse made a false step so that his head was all under water but recovered himself with much ado.

Having day enough left, we proceeded as far as Lowland Creek, where we took up our quarters and had great plenty both of canes and winter grass for the horses, but Whitlock's horse tired two miles off and so did one of Astrolabe's. The truth of it is we made a long journey, not less than fourteen miles in the roundabout distance we came, though it did not exceed ten upon the line. I favored my steed by walking great part of the way on foot; it being level and well cleared made the fatigue more tolerable. The Indian killed a young buck, the bones of which we picked very clean, but want of bear made Dr. Humdrum less gay than he used to be where that delicious food was plenty.

6. We set not out till near twelve and passed over very uneven ground, though our comfort was that it was open and clear of bushes. We avoided crossing the Dan twice by going round the bent of it. About three we passed by Mount Pleasant and proceeded along the riverside to Sable Creek, which we crossed, and encamped a little beyond it near the banks of the Dan. The horses fared sumptuously here upon canes and grass.

Hamilton wounded a buck, which made him turn upon the dogs and even pursue them forty yards with great fury. But he got away from us, choosing rather to give the wolves a supper than to more cruel man. However, our other gunners had better fortune in killing a doe and a two-year-old cub. Thus Providence supplied us every day with food sufficient for us, making the barren wilderness a theater of plenty.

The wind blew very cold and produced a hard frost. Our journey this day did not exceed five miles, great part of which in compliment to my horse I performed on foot, notwithstanding the way was mountainous and the leaves that covered the hills as slippery as ice.

7. After dispatching away our pioneers at eight o'clock, we followed them at ten. The ground was very hilly and full of underwood, but our pioneers had helped that inconvenience. Our journey was eight miles by the lines but near ten by our path, which was not quite so straight. The hunters were more fortunate than ordinary, killing no less than four deer and as many turkeys. This made them impatient to encamp early, that they might enjoy the fruits of their good luck.

We arrived at two o'clock on the banks of the Dan, where we

marked out our quarters, where the horses had as great plenty as ourselves. However, they were now grown so weak that they staggered when we dismounted, and those which had been used to the stable and dry food throve least upon grass and canes and were much sooner jaded than the rest.

8. The pioneers took their departure about nine, and we set out upon their track at ten and found the ground rising and falling all the way between the two fords of the river. The first of these we passed at first setting-out, but Robin Hix and the Indian undertook to go round the bent of the river without crossing it all. This they performed, making the distance no more than twelve miles. About a mile from our camp they met with a creek whose banks were fortified with high cliffs, which gained it the name of Cliff Creek. Near three miles beyond that they forded over another creek, on whose margin grew plenty of canes. And this was called Hix's Creek from the name of the discoverer. Between these two creeks lies a level of exceeding good land, full of large trees and a black mold.

We that marched upon the line passed over Cane Creek something more than four miles from the camp, and three miles beyond that we forded the Dan for the last time, passing through a forest of canes before we got at it. It was no small joy to us to find ourselves safe over all the waters that might retard our journey home. Our distance upon the line was seven miles, and where we encamped afforded good forage for the horses, which we had favored by walking the greater part of the way. The Indian brought us the primings[90] of a fat doe, which he had killed too far off for him to carry the whole. This and two turkeys that our men shot made up our bill of fare this evening.

9. Dr. Humdrum got up so early that it made him quite peevish, especially now we were out of the latitude of fat bear, with which he used to keep up his good humor. It was necessary to hurry out the pioneers by eight o'clock, because great part of the journey was overgrown with bushes. However, about five miles of this day's work were very open and tolerably level. The distance in all was twelve

[90] Prime parts.

miles by the line, though we made fifteen of it by picking our way. Of this I footed it at least eight miles, notwithstanding my servant had scorched my boots by holding them too near the fire. The length of our march harassed the horses much, so that Page was obliged to leave his two miles short of our journey's end, and several others had much ado to drag one leg after another.

In less than half a mile from the Dan we crossed Cockade Creek, so called from our beginning there to wear the turkey beard in our hats by way of cockade. This we made one of the badges of a new order called the Order of Maosti, signifying in the Saponi language a turkey's beard. The other badge is a wild turkey in gold with the wings expanded and a collar round its neck, with this motto engraven upon it: *vice coturnicum.*[91] As most orders have been religious in their original, so this was devised in grateful remembrance of our having been supported in the barren wilderness so many weeks with wild turkeys instead of quails.

From thence we continued our march to Buffalo Creek, on which we encamped. Here our horses made better cheer than we, for the Indian killed nothing but one turkey. However, with what remained of our former good fortune, this was sufficient to keep famine out of the camp.

10. This being Sunday, we observed the Fourth Commandment; only our hunters went out to provide a dinner for the rest, which was matter of necessity. They fired the woods in a ring, which burning inwards drove the deer to the center, where they were easily killed. This sport is called fire-hunting and is much practiced by the Indians and some English as barbarous as Indians. Three deer were slaughtered in this manner, of which they brought one to the camp and were content only to prime[92] the other two. Besides these, Thomas Short brought in a doe, which made us live in luxury.

William Pool complained that though his stomach was good and he eat a great deal yet he hardly ever went to stool without the help of physic. This made him very full and uneasy, giving him pains both

[91] "In place of quail." Byrd refers to the Lord's provision of quail to feed the starving Children of Israel in the Wilderness (Ex. 16:13).

[92] Select the best parts.

in his stomach and bowels. First I gave him a dose of Anderson's pills, which afforded him very little ease. Then I prescribed a small dose of ipecacuanha to be taken in hot broth well seasoned with salt, which took off the emetic quality and turned it downwards. This not only employed him and gave him ease but brought him to be very regular in his evacuations, by being now and then repeated. Page went out in quest of his horse and brought him to the camp pretty well recruited. The absence of most of the men diminished our congregation so much that we who remained behind were contented with prayers. I read a great deal and then wrote a letter with design to send an express with it so soon as we got amongst the inhabitants.

11. By the favor of good weather and the impatience of being at home, we decamped early. But there was none of the company so very hasty as Orion. He could not have been more uneasy even though he had a mistress at Williamsburg. He found much fault with my scrupulous observing the Sabbath. I reproved him for his uneasiness, letting him understand that I had both as much business and as much inclination to be at home as he had, but for all that was determined to make no more haste than good speed.

We crossed Hycootomony Creek twice in this march and traversed very thick and very uneven woods as far as Sugartree Creek. This was no more than seven miles but equal in fatigue to double that distance on good ground. Near this creek our men killed a young buffalo of two years old that was as big as a large ox. He had short legs and a deep body, with shagged hair on his head and shoulders. His horns were short and very strong. The hair on the shoulders is soft, resembling wool, and may be spun into thread. The flesh is arrant beef; all the difference is that the fat of it inclines more to be yellow. The species seems to be the same, because a calf produced betwixt tame cattle and these will propagate. Our people were so well pleased with buffalo beef that the gridiron was upon the fire all night. In this day's march I lost one of the gold buttons out of my sleeve, which I bore the more patiently because that and the burning of my boots were all the damage I had suffered.

12. We could not decamp before eleven, the people being so much

engaged with their beef; I found it always a rule that the greater our plenty the later we were in fixing out. We avoided two miles of very uneven ground by leaving the line on our left and keeping upon the ridge. Something less than three miles' distance from the camp we passed over Bluewing Creek and five miles beyond this over that of Tewahominy. Thence we traversed a very large level of rich, high land near two miles in breadth and encamped on a branch three and a half miles beyond the last-named creek, so that our whole distance this day was more than eleven miles.

Here was very scanty fare for the horses, who could pick only here and there a sprig of wild rosemary, which they are fond of; the misfortune was there was not enough of it. John Ellis killed a bear in revenge for the fright one of that species had lately put him into. Nor was this revenge sweeter to him than a griskin of it was to the Doctor, who of all worldly food conceives this to be the best. Though, in truth, 'tis too rich for a single man and inclines the eater of it strongly to the flesh, insomuch that whoever makes a supper of it will certainly dream of a woman or the devil, or both.

13. This morning I wrote a letter to the Governor, intending to dispatch it away by an express from the outermost inhabitants. We mounted about ten, and after proceeding three miles crossed a large branch and two miles farther reached Ohimpamony Creek. Beyond that three and a quarter miles we came to Yapatsco or Beaver Creek. Here those industrious animals had dammed up the water in such a manner that we could with difficulty ford over it. However, we all got happily over and continued our march three miles farther to Massamony Creek, so that the day's journey was in all eleven and a quarter miles. But to make the horses some amends, we encamped in the midst of good forage. Both Meanwell's horses could hardly carry their saddles, no more being required of them; nor was it much better with many others in the company. On our way we had the fortune to kill a deer and a turkey, sufficient for our day's subsistence; nor need anyone despair of his daily bread whose faith is but half so big as his stomach.

14. About eight in the morning, I dispatched two men to Miles

Riley's and by the way to hire John Davis to carry my letters to Major Mumford's with all expedition. I also gave them orders to get a beef killed and likewise some meal ground to refresh the men on their arrival amongst the inhabitants.

We decamped after them at eleven o'clock and at the end of seven and a quarter miles crossed Nutbush Creek. From thence we proceeded about four miles farther to a beautiful branch of Great Creek, where we arrived in good order about four o'clock in the afternoon. We encamped on a rising ground that overlooked a large extent of green reeds with a crystal stream serpenting through the middle of them. The Indian killed a fawn and one of the other men a raccoon, the flesh of which is like pork, but truly we were better fed than to eat it. The clouds gathered and threatened rain, but a brisk northwester swept them all away before morning.

15. We were ready to march about ten o'clock and at the distance of six miles passed Great Creek. Then, after traversing very barren grounds for near five miles, we crossed the trading path used by our traders when they carry goods to the southwest Indians. In less than a mile from thence we had the pleasure to discover a house, though a very poor one, the habitation of our friend Nat on Major Mumford's plantation. As agreeable a sight as a house was, we chose our tent to lie in as much the cleanlier lodging. However, we vouchsafed to eat in the house, where nothing went down so sweetly as potatoes and milk. In order for that, a whole ovenful of potatoes were provided, which the men devoured unmercifully.

Here all the company but myself were told that my little son was dead. This melancholy news they carefully concealed from me for fear of giving me uneasiness. Nothing could be more good-natured and is a proof that more than thirty people may keep a secret. And what makes the wonder the greater is that three women were privy to this my supposed misfortune.

I drew out the men after dinner and harangued them on the subject of our safe return in the following terms:

"Friends and fellow travelers, it is with abundance of pleasure that I now have it in my power to congratulate your happy arrival among the inhabitants. You will give me leave to put you in mind how manifestly Heaven has engaged in our preservation. No distress, no disaster, no sickness of any consequence has befallen any one of us in so long and so dangerous a journey. We have subsisted plentifully on the bounty of Providence and been day by day supplied in the barren wilderness with food convenient for us. This is surely an instance of divine goodness never to be forgotten, and, that it may still be more complete, I heartily wish that the same protection may have been extended to our families during our absence. But lest amidst so many blessings there may be some here who may esteem themselves a little unfortunate in the loss of their horses, I promise faithfully I will do my endeavor to procure satisfaction for them. And as a proof that I am perfectly satisfied with your service, I will receive your pay and cause a full distribution to be made of it as soon as possible. Lastly, as well to gratify your impatience to see your several families as to ease the expense of the government, I will agree to your discharge so fast as we shall approach the nearest distance to your respective habitations."

16. It was noon before we could disengage ourselves from the charms of Madam Nat and her entertainments. I tipped her a pistole for her civilities and ordered the horses to the ford, while we and the baggage were paddled over in the canoe. While the horses were marching round, Meanwell and I made a visit to Cornelius Keith, who lived rather in a pen than a house with his wife and six children. I never beheld such a scene of poverty in this happy part of the world. The hovel they lay in had no roof to cover those wretches from the injuries of the weather, but when it rained or was colder than ordinary the whole family took refuge in a fodder stack. The poor man had raised a kind of a house, but for want of nails it remained uncovered. I gave him a note on Major Mumford for nails for that purpose and so made a whole family happy at a very small expense. The man can read and write very well and by way of a trade can make and set up quernstones,[93] and yet is poorer than any Highland Scot or bogtrotting Irishman. When the horses came up, we moved forward to Miles

[93] Grinding stones for hand mills.

143

Riley's, another of Major Mumford's quarters. Here was a young steer killed for us and meal ground, and everything also provided that the place afforded. There was a huge consumption of potatoes, milk, and butter, which we found in great plenty.

This day I discharged Robin Hix, Thomas Wilson, and Charles Kimball, allowing them two days to reach their homes. I also dismissed our honest Indian Bearskin, after presenting him with a note of £3 on Major Mumford, a pound of powder with shot in proportion. He had, besides, the skins of all the deer he had killed in the whole journey and had them carried for him into the bargain. Nothing could be happier than this honest fellow was with all these riches, besides the great knowledge he had gained of the country. He killed a fat buck, great part of which he left us by way of legacy; the rest he cut into pieces, toasted them before the fire, and then strung them upon his girdle to serve him for his provisions on his way to Christanna Fort, where his nation lived.

We lay in the tent, notwithstanding there was a clean landlady and good beds, which gave the men an opportunity of getting a house over their heads after having for two months had no covering but the firmament.

17. Being Sunday, besides performing the duties of the day, we christened Thomas Page, one of our men who had been bred a Quaker, and Meanwell and I were his gossips.[94] Several of the neighbors came, partly out of curiosity and partly out of devotion. Amongst the rest came a young woman which lives in comfortable fornication with Cornelius Cargill and has several children by him. Meanwell bought a horse of this man, in which he was jockeyed. Our eyes as well as our taste were blest with a sirloin of roast beef, and we drank pleasure to our wives in a glass of shrub. Not content with this moderate refreshment, my friends carried on the joke with bombo made of execrable brandy, the manufacture of the place. I preached against it, though they minded me as little at night as they had Humdrum in the morning, but most of them paid for it by being extremely sick. This day I discharged John Holmes and Thomas Page with a reasonable allowance of days for their return home.

[94] Godparents or sponsors.

144

18. This day we endeavored to set out early but were hindered by Powell's not finding some of his horses. This man had almost [95] been negligent in that particular but amongst the inhabitants was more careless than ordinary. It was therefore thought high time to discharge him and carry our baggage as well as we could to Cornelius Cargill's, who lived about seven miles off, and there hire his cart to transport it as far as Major Mumford's. We made the best shift we could and, having crossed Mrs. Riley's hand with a pistole, we moved toward Cargill's, where we arrived about two o'clock. Here we put the heavy baggage into the cart, though I ordered mine to continue on my own horses lest some disaster might happen to this frail vehicle. Then, appointing a guard to attend the baggage, we proceeded five miles farther to George Hix's plantation, where preparation was made to entertain us.

By the way we met John Davis, that brought me letters from home and from Major Mumford in answer to those I had sent to them by this express. He had indeed been almost as expeditious as a carrier pigeon, for he went from Miles Riley's on Saturday, and he met us this day, being Monday, early in the afternoon, three miles before we got to George Hix's. By the letters he brought I had the pleasure to hear that all my family was well, that my heir apparent had been extremely ill but was recovered; nevertheless, the danger he had been in gave birth to the report that he was dead. All my company expected that now the bad news would be confirmed. This made Meanwell take a convenient station to observe with how much temper I should receive such melancholy tidings. But not finding any change in my countenance, he ventured to ask me how it fared with my family. And I must gratefully own that both he and the whole company discovered a great deal of satisfaction that the report proved false. They then told me with how much care they had concealed from me the fame of his being dead, being unwilling to make me uneasy upon so much incertainty.

We got to George Hix's before four o'clock, and both he and his

[95] So in the manuscript, possibly in error for "always." The fragment of the "Secret History" in the Blathwayt Papers at Colonial Williamsburg has the word "ever" crossed out in this place and a partially blotted word that may be either "almost" or "always" written above it.

lively little wife received us courteously. His house stands on an eminence, from whence is a good prospect. Everything looked clean and wholesome, which made us resolve to quit the tent and betake ourselves to the house.

All the grandees of the Saponi nation waited here to see us, and our fellow traveler, Bearskin, was amongst the gravest of them. Four ladies of quality graced their visit, who were less besmeared with grease and dirt than any copper-colored beauties I had ever seen. The men too had an air of decency very uncommon, and, what was a greater curiosity, most of the company came on horseback. The men rode more awkwardly than sailors, and the women, who sat astride, were so bashful they would not mount their ponies till they were quite out of sight.

Christanna Fort, where these Indians live, lies three miles from George Hix's plantation. He has considerable dealings with them and supplies them too plentifully with rum, which kills more of them than the northern Indians do and causes much disorder amongst them.

Major Mumford was so good as to send me a horse, believing that mine was sufficiently jaded, and Colonel Bolling [96] sent me another. With the last I complimented Orion, who had marched on foot good part of the way from the mountains. When we saluted Mrs. Hix, she bobbed up her mouth with more than ordinary elasticity and gave us a good opinion of her other motions. Captain Embry, who lives on Nottoway River, met us here and gave us an invitation to make our next stage at his house. Here I discharged John Evans, Stephen Evans, William Pool, George Tilman, George Hamilton, and James Petillo, allowing them for their distance home. Our course from Miles Riley's inwards held generally about northeast and the road level.

19. We dispatched away the cart under a guard by nine o'clock,

[96] Boyd: "Colonel John Bolling (1700–1757), son of Major John Bolling (1676–1729) and grandson of Robert Bolling (1646-1709) who came to Virginia in 1660 and married Jane Rolfe, grand-daughter of John Rolfe and Pocahontas. The residence referred to was 'Cobbe' in Chesterfield, now Henrico County. See 'The Ancestors and Descendants of John Rolfe' (Virginia Mag. Hist. and Biog., Vol. XXII, p. 103)."

and, after complimenting our landlord with a pistole for feeding us and our horses, we followed about eleven. About a mile from the house we crossed Meherrin River, which, being very low, was not more than twenty yards wide. About five miles farther we passed Meherrin Creek, almost as wide as the river. From thence eight miles we went over Sturgeon Run, and six miles beyond that we came upon Waqua Creek, where the stream is swift and tumbles over the rocks very solemnly; this makes broad, low grounds in many places and abundance of rich land.

About two miles more brought us to our worthy friend Captain Embry's habitation, where we found the housekeeping much better than the house. In that the noble Captain is not very curious, his castle containing of one dirty room with a dragging door to it that will neither open nor shut. However, my landlady made us amends by providing a supper sufficient for a battalion. I was a little shocked at our first alighting with a sight I did not expect. Most of the men I discharged yesterday were got here before us and within a few good downs of being drunk. I showed so much concern at this that they had the modesty to retire.

Mr. Walker met us here and kindly invited us to his house, being about five miles wide of this place. I should have been glad to accept of his civility but could not with decency put a slur upon our good friend the Captain, who had made abundant provision for us. For this reason we chose to drink water and stow thick in a dirty room rather than give our black-eyed landlady the trouble of making a feast to no purpose. She had set all her spits, pots, frying pans, gridirons, and ovens to work to pamper us up after fasting so long in the wilderness. The worst point of her civility was that she made us eat part of everything, which obliged two of the nine that lay in the room to rise at a very unseasonable time of night.

20. Mr. Walker came to us again in the morning and was [97] so kind as to bring us some wine and cider along with him. He also lent Meanwell [a] horse for himself and me another for one of my

[97] The text from "so" here through "thankful" (p. 149) is supplied from the fragment in the Blathwayt Papers preserved by Colonial Williamsburg, Inc.

men. We had likewise a visit from Colonel Bolling, who had been surveying in the neighborhood. Our landlord, who is a dealer in rum, let me have some for the men and had the humility, though a captain, to accept of a pistole for our entertainment. I discharged John Ellis and James Whitlock at this place.

It was twelve o'clock before we could get loose from hence, and then we passed Nottoway River just below Captain Embry's house, where it was about fifteen yards over. This river divides Prince George County from Brunswick. We had the company of Colonel Bolling and Mr. Walker along with us, who could not heartily approve of our Lithuanian custom of walking part of the way.

At the distance of eleven miles we crossed Stony Creek, and five miles farther we went over Gravelly Run, which is wide enough to merit the name of a creek. We passed by Sapony Chapel and after thirty good miles arrived safe at Colonel Bolling's, where we were entertained with much plenty and civility. Among abundance of other good things he regaled us with excellent cider.

While Meanwell and I fared deliciously here, our two surveyors and the Reverend Doctor, in compliment to their horses, stuck close to the baggage. They reached no farther than eighteen miles and took up their quarters at James Hudson's, where their horses were better provided for than their masters. There was no more than one bed to pig into, with one cotton sheet and the other of brown Osnaburgs,[98] made browner by a month's perspiration. This mortified Orion to the soul, so that the other two were happy enough in laughing at him; though I think they ought all to have been perfectly satisfied with the man's hospitality who was content to lie out of his own bed to make room for them.

21. These gentlemen quitted their sweet lodging so early that they reached Colonel Bolling's time enough for breakfast. Mr. Mumford's pretty wife was very ill here, which had altered her pretty face beyond all knowledge. I took upon me to prescribe to her and my advice succeeded well, as I understood afterwards.

About eleven o'clock we took leave and proceeded to Major Mum-

[98] A kind of coarse linen originally made in Osnabrück.

ford's, when I discharged the cart and the few men that remained with me, assuring them that their behavior had engaged me to do them any service that lay in my power. I had no sooner settled these affairs but my wife and eldest daughter[99] arrived in the chair to meet me. Besides the pleasure of embracing them, they made me happy by letting me understand the rest of the family were extremely well. Our treatment was as civil as possible in this good family. I wrote a letter to send by Orion to the Governor, and the evening we spent giving an account of our travels and drinking the best cider I ever tasted.

22. I sent away Meanwell's baggage and my own about ten o'clock, he intending to take Westover in his way home. When we had fortified ourselves with a meat breakfast, we took leave about twelve. My wife and I rode in the chair and my daughter on an easy pad she had borrowed. Mrs. Mumford was so kind as to undertake to spin my buffalo's hair in order to knit me a pair of stockings. Orion took the nearest way to Williamsburg, Astrolabe to Goochland, and Humdrum to Mount Misery. We called on Mr. Fitzgerald to advise him what method to take with his sick child, but nature had done the business before we came.

We arrived at Coggins Point about four, where my servants attended with boats in order to transport us to Westover. I had the happiness to find all the family well. This crowned all my other blessings and made the journey truly prosperous, of which I hope I shall ever retain a grateful remembrance. Nor was it all that my people were in good health, but my business was likewise in good order. Everyone seemed to have done their duty, by the joy they expressed at my return. My neighbors had been kind to my wife, when she was threatened with the loss of her son and heir. Their assistance was kind as well as seasonable, when her child was threatened with fatal symptoms and her husband upon a long journey exposed to great variety of perils. Thus, surrounded with the most fearful apprehensions, Heaven was pleased to support her spirits and bring back her child from the grave and her husband from the mountains, for which blessings may we be all sincerely thankful.

[99] Evelyn Byrd.

149

THE NAMES OF THE COMMISSIONERS TO DIRECT THE RUNNING OF THE
LINE BETWEEN VIRGINIA AND NORTH CAROLINA

Steddy
Firebrand } Commissioners for Virginia
Meanwell

Judge Jumble
Shoebrush
Plausible } Commissioners for North Carolina
Puzzlecause

Orion
Astrolabe } Surveyors for Virginia

Plausible
Boötes } Surveyors for North Carolina

The Reverend Doctor Humdrum   Chaplain

NAMES OF THE MEN EMPLOYED ON THE PART OF VIRGINIA TO RUN
THE LINE BETWEEN THAT COLONY AND NORTH CAROLINA

On the first expedition	*On the second expedition*
1. Peter Jones	Peter Jones
2. Thomas Short	Thomas Short
3. Thomas Jones	Thomas Jones
4. Robert Hix	Robert Hix
5. John Evans	John Evans
6. Stephen Evans	Stephen Evans
7. John Ellis	John Ellis
8. Thomas Wilson	Thomas Wilson
9. George Tilman	George Tilman
10. Charles Kimball	Charles Kimball
11. George Hamilton	George Hamilton
12. Robert Allen	Edward Powell
13. Thomas Jones, Junior	Thomas Jones, Junior
14. John Ellis, Junior	William Pool

15. James Petillo
16. Richard Smith
17. John Rice

James Petillo
Richard Smith
Abraham Jones
18. William Calvert
19. James Whitlock
20. Thomas Page [100]

ACCOUNT OF EXPENSE OF RUNNING THE LINE BETWEEN

VIRGINIA AND NORTH CAROLINA

To the men's wages in current money	£277	10	0
To sundry disbursements for provisions, etc.	174	1	6
To paid the men for seven horses lost	44	0	0
	£495	11	6
The sum of £495 11s.6d. current money reduced at 15% to sterling amounts to	£430	8	10
To paid Steddy	142	5	7
To paid Meanwell	142	5	7
To paid Firebrand	94	0	0
To paid the Chaplain Humdrum	20	0	0
To paid Orion	75	0	0
To paid Astrolabe	75	0	0
To paid for a tent and marquee	20	0	0
	£1000	0	0 [101]

This sum was discharged by a warrant out of His Majesty's quit-rents from the lands in Virginia.

THE DISTANCES OF PLACES MENTIONED IN THE FOREGOING HISTORY

OF THE DIVIDING LINE BETWEEN VIRGINIA AND NORTH CAROLINA

	M	Q	P [102]
From Currituck Inlet to the Dismal	21	2	16
The course through the Dismal	15	0	0

[100] The *History* lists twenty-one men on the second expedition, including John Ellis, Jr., who is omitted from this list.

[101] The total is actually £999 rather than £1,000.

[102] The "Q" possibly stands for *quarentena*, a measure equaling a furlong (forty rods, perches, or poles). The "P" probably stands for *perca* or poles. But the totals of the columns (224 miles, 71 furlongs, 2,084 poles) do not convert to a figure equaling the total given. See note 86 for comment on discrepancies in figures.

To the east side of Blackwater River	20	1	43
We came down Blackwater to the mouth of Nottoway 176 poles, from whence to Meherrin	13	2	46
To Meherrin River again		1	67
To Meherrin River again	2	0	40
To the ferry road	1	2	60
To Meherrin again			22
To Meherrin the fifth and last time	2	3	66
To the middle of Jack's Swamp	11	0	25
To a road	1	2	52
To Beaver Pond Creek the first time	3	3	8
To a road from Bedding Field southward	11	0	37
To Pea Hill Creek	3	1	33
To a road	2	0	30
To Lizard Creek		3	38
To Pigeon Roost Creek	3	1	72
To Cocke's Creek	2	3	24
To Roanoke River		2	48
To the west side of Do [ditto]			49
To the Indian trading path	8	0	20
To Great Creek	4	3	28
To Nutbush Creek	7	0	6
To Massamony Creek	7	1	4
To Yapatsco Creek	3	0	30
To Ohimpamony Creek	3	1	38
To Tewahominy Creek	8	2	54
To Bluewing Creek	4	3	10
To Sugartree Creek	2	3	10
To Hycootomony Creek	3	1	76
To the same			18
To the same		2	64
To the same		2	66
To the same again			42 [?]
To Buffalo Creek	1	8	40
To Cockade Creek	11	3	6 [?]
To the south branch of Roanoke called the Dan		1	26
To the west side including the island			34
To Cane Creek	2	2	42
To Dan River the second time	4	1	38
To the west side of Do [ditto]			24

To Dan River the third time	8	0	68
To the northwest side aslant			53
To the Dan River the fourth time	1	0	7
To the west side			21
To Lowland Creek	3	2	50
To Dan River the fifth time	1	0	18
To the northwest side aslant			66
To Cascade Creek	2	3	10
To Irvin River, a branch of the Dan	6	0	30
To Matrimony Creek	4	0	31
To Miry Creek	7	1	68
To Mayo River, another branch of the Dan		1	36
To Dan River the sixth and last time		1	2
To Crooked Creek the first time	2	1	77
To Ne plus ultra Camp	13	0	35
To a red oak, marked on three sides with four notches and the trees blazed about it, on the east bank of a rivulet supposed to be either a branch of Roanoke or Deep River		3	60
The whole distance	241	2	70

HISTORY OF THE
DIVIDING LINE

*betwixt Virginia and North Carolina
Run in the Year of Our Lord 1728*

$\mathcal{B}$EFORE I enter upon the journal of the line between Virginia and North Carolina, it will be necessary to clear the way to it by showing how the other British colonies on the main have, one after another, been carved out of Virginia by grants from His Majesty's royal predecessors. All that part of the northern American continent now under the dominion of the King of Great Britain and stretching quite as far as the Cape of Florida went at first under the general name of Virginia.

The only distinction in those early days was that all the coast to the southward of Chesapeake Bay was called South Virginia and all to the northward of it North Virginia.

The first settlement of this fine country was owing to that great ornament of the British nation, Sir Walter Raleigh, who obtained a grant thereof from Queen Elizabeth, of ever-glorious memory, by letters patent dated March 25, 1584.

But whether that gentleman ever made a voyage thither himself is uncertain, because those who have favored the public with an account of his life mention nothing of it. However, thus much may be depended on, that Sir Walter invited sundry persons of distinction to share in his charter and join their purses with his in the laudable project of fitting out a colony to Virginia.

Accordingly, two ships were sent away that very year, under the command of his good friends Amadas and Barlow,[1] to take possession of the country in the name of his royal mistress, the Queen of England.

These worthy commanders, for the advantage of the trade winds, shaped their course first to the Caribbee Islands, thence, stretching away by the Gulf of Florida, dropped anchor not far from Roanoke Inlet. They ventured ashore near that place upon an island now called

[1] Philip Amadas and Arthur Barlow. The latter wrote a narrative of their experiences, which was printed by Richard Hakluyt in *Principal Navigations* (1589), pp. 728–733. D. B. Quinn has recently reprinted it in *The Roanoke Voyages* (London, 1955), I, 91–117 (Hakluyt Society, 2nd Ser., CIV).

Colleton Island,[2] where they set up the arms of England and claimed the adjacent country in right of their sovereign lady, the Queen; and this ceremony being duly performed, they kindly invited the neighboring Indians to traffic with them.

These poor people at first approached the English with great caution, having heard much of the treachery of the Spaniards and not knowing but these strangers might be as treacherous as they. But at length, discovering a kind of good nature in their looks, they ventured to draw near and barter their skins and furs for the baubles and trinkets of the English.

These first adventurers made a very profitable voyage, raising at least a thousand per cent upon their cargo. Amongst other Indian commodities, they brought over some of that bewitching vegetable, tobacco. And this being the first that ever came to England, Sir Walter thought he could do no less than make a present of some of the brightest of it to his royal mistress for her own smoking. The Queen graciously accepted of it, but finding her stomach sicken after two or three whiffs, 'twas presently whispered by the Earl of Leicester's faction that Sir Walter had certainly poisoned her. But Her Majesty, soon recovering her disorder, obliged the Countess of Nottingham and all her maids to smoke a whole pipe out amongst them.

As it happened some ages before to be the fashion to saunter to the Holy Land and go upon other Quixote adventures, so it was now grown the humor to take a trip to America. The Spaniards had lately discovered rich mines in their part of the West Indies, which made their maritime neighbors eager to do so too. This modish frenzy, being still more inflamed by the charming account given of Virginia by the first adventurers, made many fond of removing to such a Paradise.

Happy was he, and still happier she, that could get themselves transported, fondly expecting their coarsest utensils in that happy place would be of massy silver.

This made it easy for the Company to procure as many volunteers as they wanted for their new colony, but, like most other undertakers who

---

[2] Named for Sir John Colleton, one of the Lords Proprietors. The name has now become corrupted to "Colington."

have no assistance from the public, they starved the design by too much frugality; for, unwilling to launch out at first into too much expense, they shipped off but few people at a time, and those but scantily provided. The adventurers were, besides, idle and extravagant and expected they might live without work in so plentiful a country.

These wretches were set ashore not far from Roanoke Inlet, but by some fatal disagreement or laziness were either starved or cut to pieces by the Indians.

Several repeated misadventures of this kind did for some time allay the itch of sailing to this new world, but the distemper broke out again about the year 1606. Then it happened that the Earl of Southampton and several other persons eminent for their quality and estates were invited into the Company, who applied themselves once more to people the then almost abandoned colony. For this purpose they embarked about an hundred men, most of them reprobates of good families and related to some of the Company who were men of quality and fortune.

The ships that carried them made a shift to find a more direct way to Virginia and ventured through the capes into the Bay of Chesapeake. The same night they came to an anchor at the mouth of Powhatan, the same as James River, where they built a small fort at a place called Point Comfort.

This settlement stood its ground from that time forward, in spite of all the blunders and disagreement of the first adventurers and the many calamities that befell the colony afterwards. The six gentlemen who were first named of the Company by the Crown and who were empowered to choose an annual president from among themselves were always engaged in factions and quarrels, while the rest detested work more than famine. At this rate the colony must have come to nothing had it not been for the vigilance and bravery of Captain Smith, who struck a terror into all the Indians round about. This gentleman took some pains to persuade the men to plant Indian corn, but they looked upon all labor as a curse. They chose rather to depend upon the musty provisions that were sent from England; and when they failed they were forced to take more pains to seek for wild fruits in the woods than they would have taken in tilling the ground. Besides, this exposed them to be knocked in the head by the Indians and gave them fluxes into the bargain, which thinned the plantation very much. To supply this mortality, they were reinforced the year following with a greater number of people, amongst which were fewer gentlemen and more laborers, who, however, took care not to kill themselves with work. These found the first adventurers in a very starving condition but relieved their wants with the fresh supply they brought with them. From Kecoughtan[3] they extended themselves as far as Jamestown, where, like true Englishmen, they built a church that cost no more than fifty pounds and a tavern that cost five hundred.

They had now made peace with the Indians, but there was one thing wanting to make that peace lasting. The natives could by no means persuade themselves that the English were heartily their friends so long as they disdained to intermarry with them. And, in earnest, had the English consulted their own security and the good of the colony, had they intended either to civilize or convert these gentiles, they would have brought their stomachs to embrace this prudent alliance.

The Indians are generally tall and well proportioned, which may make full amends for the darkness of their complexions. Add to this that they are healthy and strong, with constitutions untainted by lewdness and not enfeebled by luxury. Besides, morals and all considered, I cannot think the Indians were much greater heathens than the first adventurers, who, had they been good Christians, would have had the charity to take this only method of converting the natives to Christianity. For, after all that can be said, a sprightly lover is the most prevailing missionary that can be sent amongst these or any other infidels.

Besides, the poor Indians would have had less reason to complain that the English took away their land if they had received it by way of a portion with their daughters. Had such affinities been contracted in the beginning, how much bloodshed had been prevented and how populous would the country have been, and, consequently, how considerable! Nor would the shade of the skin have been any reproach at

[3] Modern Hampton, Virginia.

this day, for if a Moor may be washed white in three generations, surely an Indian might have been blanched in two.

The French, for their parts, have not been so squeamish in Canada, who upon trial find abundance of attraction in the Indians. Their late grand monarch thought it not below even the dignity of a Frenchman to become one flesh with this people and therefore ordered 100 livres for any of his subjects, man or woman, that would intermarry with a native.

By this piece of policy we find the French interest very much strengthened amongst the savages and their religion, such as it is, propagated just as far as their love. And I heartily wish this well-concerted scheme don't hereafter give the French an advantage over His Majesty's good subjects on the northern continent of America.

About the same time New England was pared off from Virginia by letters patent bearing date April 10, 1608. Several gentlemen of the town and neighborhood of Plymouth obtained this grant, with the Lord Chief Justice Popham at their head.

Their bounds were specified to extend from 38 to 45 degrees of northern latitude, with a breadth of one hundred miles from the seashore. The first fourteen years this company encountered many difficulties and lost many men, though, far from being discouraged, they sent over numerous recruits of Presbyterians every year, who for all that had much ado to stand their ground, with all their fighting and praying.

But about the year 1620 a large swarm of dissenters fled thither from the severities of their stepmother, the church. These saints, conceiving the same aversion to the copper complexion of the natives with that of the first adventurers to Virginia, would on no terms contract alliances with them, afraid, perhaps, like the Jews of old, lest they might be drawn into idolatry by those strange women.

Whatever disgusted them I can't say, but this false delicacy, creating in the Indians a jealousy that the English were ill affected toward them, was the cause that many of them were cut off and the rest exposed to various distresses.

This reinforcement was landed not far from Cape Cod, where for their greater security they built a fort and near it a small town, which, in honor of the proprietors, was called New Plymouth. But they still had many discouragements to struggle with, though by being well supported from home they by degrees triumphed over them all.

Their brethren, after this, flocked over so fast that in a few years they extended the settlement one hundred miles along the coast, including Rhode Island and Martha's Vineyard.

Thus the colony throve apace and was thronged with large detachments of Independents and Presbyterians who thought themselves persecuted at home.

Though these people may be ridiculed for some pharisaical particularities in their worship and behavior, yet they were very useful subjects, as being frugal and industrious, giving no scandal or bad example, at least by any open and public vices. By which excellent qualities they had much the advantage of the southern colony, who thought their being members of the established church sufficient to sanctify very loose and profligate morals. For this reason New England improved much faster than Virginia, and in seven or eight years New Plymouth, like Switzerland, seemed too narrow a territory for its inhabitants.

For this reason, several gentlemen of fortune purchased of the company that canton of New England now called Massachusetts Colony. And King James confirmed the purchase by his royal charter dated March 4, 1628.[4] In less than two years after, above one thousand of the Puritanical sect removed thither with considerable effects, and these were followed by such crowds that a proclamation issued in England forbidding any more of His Majesty's subjects to be shipped off. But this had the usual effect of things forbidden and served only to make the willful Independents flock over the faster. And about this time it was that Messrs. Hampden and Pym, and, some say, Oliver Cromwell, to show how little they valued the King's authority, took a trip to New England.[5]

[4] The charter was, of course, confirmed by Charles I, not James, and dated March 4, 1628 (Old Style).
[5] Byrd here repeats an unconfirmed tale that was already in circulation in the seventeenth century. Hampden and Pym were among the recipients of a grant of

In the year 1630, the famous city of Boston was built in a commodious situation for trade and navigation, the same being on a peninsula at the bottom of Massachusetts Bay.

This town is now the most considerable of any on the British continent, containing at least 8,000 houses and 40,000 inhabitants.[6] The trade it drives is very great to Europe and to every part of the West Indies, having near 1,000 ships and lesser vessels belonging to it.

Although the extent of the Massachusetts Colony reached near 110 miles in length and half as much in breadth, yet many of its inhabitants, thinking they wanted elbowroom, quitted their old seats in the year 1636 and formed two new colonies: that of Connecticut and New Haven. These King Charles II erected into one government in 1644[7] and gave them many valuable privileges, and among the rest that of choosing their own governors. The extent of these united colonies may be about seventy miles long and fifty broad.

Besides these several settlements, there sprang up still another, a little more northerly, called New Hampshire. But that, consisting of no more than two counties and not being in condition to support the charge of a distinct government, was glad to be incorporated with that of Massachusetts, but upon condition, however, of being named in all public acts, for fear of being quite lost and forgot in the coalition.

In like manner New Plymouth joined itself to Massachusetts — except only Rhode Island, which, though of small extent, got itself erected into a separate government by a charter from King Charles II soon after the Restoration and continues so to this day.

These governments all continued in possession of their respective rights and privileges till the year 1683, when that of Massachusetts was made void in England by a *quo warranto*.

In consequence of which, the King was pleased to name Sir Ed-

land at Saybrook, Connecticut, made in March 1632 by the Earl of Warwick, President of the New England Council. Pym in particular interested himself in furthering overseas settlement where freedom of religion could be practiced. There is no evidence, however, that either Pym or Hampden ever actually visited New England.

[6] Byrd's figures are exaggerated. Boston had a population of 10,567 according to a census of 1722, 13,000 by a census of 1730. See Evarts B. Greene and Virginia D. Harrington, *American Population before the Federal Census of 1790* (New York, 1932), p. 22.

[7] Actually as of April 23, 1662.

mund Andros his first governor of that colony. This gentleman, it seems, ruled them with a rod of iron till the Revolution, when they laid unhallowed hands upon him and sent him prisoner to England.

This undutiful proceeding met with an easy forgiveness at that happy juncture. King William and his royal consort were not only pleased to overlook this indignity to their governor but, being made sensible how unfairly their charter had been taken away, most graciously granted them a new one.

By this some new franchises were given them as an equivalent for those of coining money and electing a governor, which were taken away. However, the other colonies of Connecticut and Rhode Island had the luck to remain in possession of their original charters, which to this day have never been called in question.

The next county dismembered from Virginia was New Scotland, claimed by the crown of England in virtue of the first discovery by Sebastian Cabot.[8] By color of this title, King James I granted it to Sir William Alexander by patent dated September 10, 1621.

But this patentee never sending any colony thither, and the French, believing it very convenient for them, obtained a surrender of it from their good friend and ally, King Charles II, by the Treaty of Breda. And to show their gratitude, they stirred up the Indians soon after to annoy their neighbors of New England. Murders happened continually to His Majesty's subjects by their means, till Sir William Phips took their town of Port Royal in the year 1690. But as the English are better at taking than keeping strong places, the French retook it soon and remained masters of it till 1710, when General Nicholson wrested it once more out of their hands.

Afterwards the Queen of Great Britain's right to it was recognized and confirmed by the Treaty of Utrecht.

Another limb lopped off from Virginia was New York, which the Dutch seized very unfairly on pretense of having purchased it from Captain Hudson, the first discoverer. Nor was their way of taking possession of it a whit more justifiable than their pretended title. Their West India Company tampered with some worthy English skippers,

[8] Really John Cabot, although his son, Sebastian, may have been with him.

who had contracted with a swarm of English dissenters to transport them to Hudson River, by no means to land them there but to carry 'em some leagues more northerly.

This Dutch finesse took exactly and gave the Company time soon after to seize Hudson River for themselves. But Sir Samuel Argall, then Governor of Virginia, understanding how the King's subjects had been abused by these republicans, marched thither with a good force and obliged them to renounce all pretensions to that country. The worst of it was, the knight depended on their parole to ship themselves for Brazil but took no measures to make this slippery people as good as their word.

No sooner was the good governor retired but the honest Dutch began to build forts and strengthen themselves in their ill-gotten possessions; nor did any of the King's liege people take the trouble to drive these intruders thence. The civil war in England and the confusions it brought forth allowed no leisure for such distant considerations. Though 'tis strange that the Protector, who neglected no occasion to mortify the Dutch, did not afterwards call them to account for this breach of faith. However, after the Restoration the King sent a squadron of his ships of war, under the command of Sir Robert Carr, and reduced that province to his obedience.

Some time after, His Majesty was pleased to grant that country to His Royal Highness the Duke of York by letters patent dated March 12, 1664. But to show the modesty of the Dutch to the life, though they had no shadow of right to New York, yet they demanded Surinam, a more valuable country, as an equivalent for it, and our able ministers at that time had the generosity to give it them.

But what wounded Virginia deepest was the cutting off Maryland from it by charter from King Charles I to Sir George Calvert, afterwards Lord Baltimore, bearing date the twentieth of June, 1632. The truth of it is, it begat much speculation in those days how it came about that a good Protestant king should bestow so beautiful a grant upon a zealous Roman Catholic. But 'tis probable it was one fatal instance amongst many other of His Majesty's complaisance to the Queen.

However that happened, 'tis certain this province afterwards proved a commodious retreat for persons of that communion. The memory of the Gunpowder Treason Plot was still fresh in everybody's mind and made England too hot for papists to live in without danger of being burnt with the Pope every fifth of November; for which reason legions of them transplanted themselves to Maryland in order to be safe, as well from the insolence of the populace as the rigor of the government.

Not only the Gunpowder Treason but every other plot, both pretended and real, that has been trumped up in England ever since, has helped to people His Lordship's propriety. But what has proved most serviceable to it was the grand rebellion against King Charles I, when everything that bore the least tokens of popery was sure to be demolished and every man that professed it in jeopardy of suffering the same kind of martyrdom the Romish priests do in Sweden.

Soon after the reduction of New York the Duke was pleased to grant out of it all that tract of land included between Hudson and Delaware Rivers to the Lord Berkeley and Sir George Carteret by deed dated June 24, 1664. And when these grantees came to make partition of this territory, His Lordship's moiety was called West Jersey and that to Sir George, East Jersey.

But before the date of this grant the Swedes began to gain footing in part of that country, though after they saw the fate of New York, they were glad to submit to the King of England on the easy terms of remaining in their possessions and rendering a moderate quitrent. Their posterity continue there to this day and think their lot cast in a much fairer land than Dalecarlia.[9]

The proprietors of New Jersey, finding more trouble than profit in their new dominions, made over their right to several other persons, who obtained a fresh grant from His Royal Highness dated March 14, 1682.[10]

Several of the grantees, being Quakers and Anabaptists, failed not to encourage many of their own persuasion to remove to this peaceful region. Amongst them were a swarm of Scots Quakers, who were not tolerated to exercise the gifts of the spirit in their own country.

[9] A region in west-central Sweden.
[10] March 14, 1683, New Style.

Besides the hopes of being safe from persecution in this retreat, the new proprietors inveigled many over by this tempting account of the country: that it was a place free from those three great scourges of mankind, priests, lawyers, and physicians. Nor did they tell them a word of a lie, for the people were yet too poor to maintain these learned gentlemen, who everywhere love to be well paid for what they do and, like the Jews, can't breathe in a climate where nothing is to be got.

The Jerseys continued under the government of these proprietors till the year 1702, when they made a formal surrender of the dominion to the Queen, reserving, however, the property of the soil to themselves. So soon as the bounds of New Jersey came to be distinctly laid off, it appeared there was still a narrow slip of land lying betwixt that colony and Maryland. Of this William Penn, a man of much worldly wisdom and some eminence among the Quakers, got early notice and, by the credit he had with the Duke of York, obtained a patent for it dated March 4, 1680.[11]

It was a little surprising to some people how a Quaker should be so much in the good graces of a popish prince, though, after all, it may be pretty well accounted for. This ingenious person had not been bred a Quaker but, in his early days, had been a man of pleasure about the town. He had a beautiful form and very taking address, which made him successful with the ladies, and particularly with a mistress of the Duke of Monmouth. By this gentlewoman he had a daughter, who had beauty enough to raise her to be a duchess and continued to be a toast full thirty years. But this amour had like to have brought our fine gentleman in danger of a duel, had he not discreetly sheltered himself under this peaceable persuasion.[12] Besides, his father having been a flag officer in the navy while the Duke of York was Lord High Admiral might recommend the son to his favor. This piece of secret history I thought proper to mention to wipe off the suspicion of his having been popishly inclined.

This gentleman's first grant confined him within pretty narrow

[11] March 14, 1681, New Style.

[12] Boyd: "This is a piece of gossip not found elsewhere; it calls to mind other calumnies against Penn perpetuated by Macaulay, which are refuted in Dixon's *William Penn*, pp. 338–357." *William Byrd's Histories of the Dividing Line betwixt Virginia and North Carolina*, edited by William K. Boyd (Raleigh, N.C., 1929).

bonds, giving him only that portion of land which contains Bucking-ham, Philadelphia, and Chester Counties. But to get these bounds a little extended, he pushed his interest still farther with His Royal Highness and obtained a fresh grant of the three lower counties called Newcastle, Kent, and Sussex, which still remained within the New York patent and had been luckily left out of the grant of New Jersey. The six counties being thus incorporated, the proprietor dignified the whole with the name of Pennsylvania.

The Quakers flocked over to this country in shoals, being averse to go to Heaven the same way with the bishops. Amongst them were not a few of good substance, who went vigorously upon every kind of improvement; and thus much I may truly say in their praise, that by diligence and frugality, for which this harmless sect is remarkable, and by having no vices but such as are private, they have in a few years made Pennsylvania a very fine country. The truth is, they have observed exact justice with all the natives that border upon them; they have purchased all their lands from the Indians, and though they paid but a trifle for them it has procured them the credit of being more righteous than their neighbors. They have likewise had the prudence to treat them kindly upon all occasions, which has saved them from many wars and massacres wherein the other colonies have been indiscreetly involved. The truth of it is, a people whose principles forbid them to draw the carnal sword were in the right to give no provocation.

Both the French and Spaniards had, in the name of their respective monarchs, long ago taken possession of that part of the northern continent that now goes by the name of Carolina; but, finding it produced neither gold nor silver, as they greedily expected, and meeting such returns from the Indians as their own cruelty and treachery deserved, they totally abandoned it. In this deserted condition that country lay for the space of ninety years, till King Charles II, finding it a derelict, granted it away to the Earl of Clarendon and others by his royal charter dated March 24, 1663. The boundary of that grant toward Virginia was a due-west line from Luck Island (the same as Colleton Island), lying in 36 degrees of north latitude, quite to the South Sea.

But afterwards Sir William Berkeley, who was one of the grantees and at that time Governor of Virginia, finding a territory of thirty-one miles in breadth between the inhabited part of Virginia and the above-mentioned boundary of Carolina, advised the Lord Clarendon of it. And His Lordship had interest enough with the King to obtain a second patent to include it, dated June 30, 1665.

This last grant describes the bounds between Virginia and Carolina in these words: "To run from the north end of Currituck Inlet due west to Weyanoke Creek, lying within or about the degree of thirty-six and thirty minutes of northern latitude, and from thence west in a direct line as far as the South Sea." Without question this boundary was well known at the time the charter was granted, but in a long course of years Weyanoke Creek lost its name, so that it became a controversy where it lay. Some ancient persons in Virginia affirmed it was the same with Wiccacon, and others again in Carolina were as positive it was Nottoway River.

In the meantime, the people on the frontiers entered for land and took out patents by guess, either from the King or the Lords Proprietors. But the Crown was like to be the loser by this uncertainty because the terms both of taking up and seating land were easier much in Carolina. The yearly taxes to the public were likewise there less burdensome, which laid Virginia under a plain disadvantage.

This consideration put that government upon entering into measures with North Carolina to terminate the dispute and settle a certain boundary between the two colonies. All the difficulty was to find out which was truly Weyanoke Creek. The difference was too considerable to be given up by either side, there being a territory of fifteen miles betwixt the two streams in controversy.

However, till that matter could be adjusted it was agreed on both sides that no lands at all should be granted within the disputed bounds. Virginia observed this agreement punctually, but I am sorry I can't say the same of North Carolina. The great officers of that province were loath to lose the fees accruing from the grants of land, and so private interest got the better of public spirit — and I wish that were the only place in the world where such politics are fashionable.

All the steps that were taken afterwards in that affair will best ap-

pear by the report of the Virginia commissioners, recited in the order
of the council given at St. James's, March 1, 1710, set down in the
appendix.[13]

It must be owned, the report of those gentlemen was severe upon
the then commissioners of North Carolina, and particularly upon Mr.
M[oseley]. I won't take upon me to say with how much justice they
said so many hard things, though it had been fairer play to have given
the parties accused a copy of such representation, that they might have
answered what they could for themselves.

But since that was not done, I must beg leave to say thus much in behalf of Mr. Moseley: that he was not much in the wrong to find fault
with the quadrant produced by the surveyors of Virginia, because that
instrument placed the mouth of Nottoway River in the latitude of 37
degrees, whereas by an accurate observation made since it appears to
lie in 36° 30' 30", so that there was an error of near 30 minutes, either
in the instrument or in those who made use of it.

Besides, it is evident the mouth of Nottoway River agrees much
better with the latitude wherein the Carolina charter supposed Weyanoke Creek (namely, in or about 36° 30'), than it does with Wiccacon Creek, which is about fifteen miles more southerly.

This being manifest, the intention of the King's grant will be pretty
exactly answered by a due-west line drawn from Currituck Inlet to
the mouth of Nottoway River; for which reason 'tis probable that
was formerly called Weyanoke Creek and might change its name
when the Nottoway Indians came to live upon it, which was since the
date of the last Carolina charter.

The Lieutenant Governor of Virginia, at that time Colonel Spotswood, searching into the bottom of this affair, made very equitable
proposals to Mr. Eden, at that time Governor of North Carolina, in
order to put an end to this controversy. These, being formed into preliminaries, were signed by both governors and transmitted to England,
where they had the honor to be ratified by His late Majesty and
assented to by the Lords Proprietors of Carolina.

Accordingly an order was sent by the late King to Mr. Gooch, afterwards Lieutenant Governor of Virginia, to pursue those preliminaries

[13] See pp. 322–336.

exactly. In obedience thereunto he was pleased to appoint three of the council of that colony to be commissioners on the part of Virginia, who, in conjunction with others to be named by the Governor of North Carolina, were to settle the boundary between the two governments upon the plan of the above-mentioned articles.

Two experienced surveyors were at the same time directed to wait upon the commissioners: Mr. Mayo, who made the accurate map of Barbados, and Mr. Irvin, the mathematic professor of William and Mary College. And because a good number of men were to go upon this expedition, a chaplain was appointed to attend them, and the rather because the people on the frontiers of North Carolina, who have no minister near them, might have an opportunity to get themselves and their children baptized.

Of these proceedings on our part, immediate notice was sent to Sir Richard Everard, Governor of North Carolina, who was desired to name commissioners for that province to meet those of Virginia at Currituck Inlet the spring following. Accordingly he appointed four members of the council of that province to take care of the interests of the Lords Proprietors. Of these, Mr. Moseley was to serve in a double capacity, both as commissioner and surveyor. For that reason there was but one other surveyor from thence, Mr. Swann. All the persons being thus agreed upon, they settled the time of meeting to be at Currituck, March 5, 1728.

In the meantime, the requisite preparations were made for so long and tiresome a journey; and because there was much work to be done and some danger from the Indians in the uninhabited part of the country, it was necessary to provide a competent number of men. Accordingly, seventeen able hands were listed on the part of Virginia, who were most of them Indian traders and expert woodsmen.

FEBRUARY 1728

27. These good men were ordered to come armed with a musket and a tomahawk or large hatchet and provided with a sufficient quantity of ammunition. They likewise brought provisions of their own for ten days, after which time they were to be furnished by the govern-

ment. Their march was appointed to be on the twenty-seventh of February, on which day one of the commissioners met them at their rendezvous and proceeded with them as far as Colonel Allen's. This gentleman is a great economist and skilled in all the arts of living well at an easy expense.

28. They proceeded in good order through Surry County as far as the Widow Allen's, who had copied Solomon's complete housewife exactly. At this gentlewoman's house the other two commissioners had appointed to join them, but were detained by some accident at Williamsburg longer than their appointment.

29. They pursued their march through the Isle of Wight and observed a most dreadful havoc made by a late hurricane, which happened in August, 1726. The violence of it had not reached above a quarter of a mile in breadth but within that compass had leveled all before it. Both trees and houses were laid flat on the ground and several things hurled to an incredible distance. 'Tis happy such violent gusts are confined to so narrow a channel, because they carry desolation wherever they go. In the evening they reached Mr. Godwin's, on the south branch of Nansemond River, where they were treated with abundance [of] primitive hospitality.

March 1. This gentleman was so kind as to shorten their journey by setting them over the river. They coasted the northeast side of the Dismal for several miles together and found all the grounds bordering upon it very full of sloughs. The trees that grew near it looked very reverend with the long moss that hung dangling from their branches. Both cattle and horses eat this moss greedily in winter when other provender is scarce, though it is apt to scour them at first. In that moist soil, too, grows abundance of that kind of myrtle which bears the candleberries. There was likewise here and there a gallbush, which is a beautiful evergreen and may be cut into any shape. It derives its name from its berries turning water black, like the galls of an oak. When this shrub is transplanted into gardens, it will not thrive without frequent watering.

The two other commissioners came up with them just at their journey's end, and that evening they arrived all together at Mr. Crawford's, who lives on the south branch of Elizabeth River over against Norfolk. Here the commissioners left the men with all the horses and heavy baggage and crossed the river with their servants only, for fear of making a famine in the town.

Norfolk has most the air of a town of any in Virginia. There were then near twenty brigantines and sloops riding at the wharves, and oftentimes they have more. It has all the advantages of situation requisite for trade and navigation. There is a secure harbor for a good number of ships of any burden. Their river divides itself into three several branches, which are all navigable. The town is so near the sea that its vessels may sail in and out in a few hours. Their trade is chiefly to the West Indies, whither they export abundance of beef, pork, flour, and lumber. The worst of it is, they contribute much toward debauching the country by importing abundance of rum, which, like gin in Great Britain, breaks the constitutions, vitiates the morals, and ruins the industry of most of the poor people of this country. This place is the mart for most of the commodities produced in the adjacent parts of North Carolina. They have a pretty deal of lumber from the borders on the Dismal, who make bold with the King's land thereabouts without the least ceremony. They not only maintain their stocks upon it but get boards, shingles, and other lumber out of it in great abundance.

The town is built on a level spot of ground upon Elizabeth River, the banks whereof are neither so high as to make the landing of goods troublesome or so low as to be in danger of overflowing. The streets are straight and adorned with several good houses, which increase every day. It is not a town of ordinaries and public houses, like most others in this country, but the inhabitants consist of merchants, ship carpenters, and other useful artisans, with sailors enough to manage their navigation. With all these conveniences it lies under the two great disadvantages that most of the towns in Holland do by having neither good air nor good water. The two cardinal virtues that make a place thrive, industry and frugality, are seen here in perfection; and so long as they can banish luxury and idleness the town will remain in a happy and flourishing condition.

173

The method of building wharves here is after the following manner. They lay down long pine logs that reach from the shore to the edge of the channel. These are bound fast together by cross pieces notched into them, according to the architecture of the log houses in North Carolina. A wharf built thus will stand several years, in spite of the worm, which bites here very much, but may be soon repaired in a place where so many pines grow in the neighborhood.

The commissioners endeavored in this town to list three more men to serve as guides in that dirty part of the country but found that these people knew just enough of that frightful place to avoid it. They had been told that those nether lands were full of bogs, of marshes and swamps, not fit for human creatures to engage in, and this was reason enough for them not to hazard their persons. So they told us, flat and plain, that we might e'en daggle through the mire by ourselves for them.

The worst of it was, we could not learn from anybody in this town what route to take to Currituck Inlet; till at last we had the fortune to meet with a borderer upon North Carolina, who made us a rough sketch of that part of the country. Thus, upon seeing how the land lay, we determined to march directly to Prescot Landing upon Northwest River and proceed from thence by water to the place where our line was to begin.[14]

4. In pursuance of this resolution we crossed the river this morning to Powder Point, where we all took horse; and the grandees of the town, with great courtesy, conducted us ten miles on our way, as far as the long bridge built over the south branch of the river. The parson of the parish, Mr. Marston, a painful apostle from the Society,[15] made one in this ceremonious cavalcade.

At the bridge these gentlemen, wishing us a good deliverance, returned, and then a troop of light horse escorted us as far as Prescot Landing upon Northwest River. Care had been taken beforehand to provide two piraguas to lie ready at that place to transport us to Cur-

[14] In the *Secret History* Byrd relates the activities of the party in Norfolk on March 2 and 3, omitting the detailed description of the town given here (see pp. 51–53).
[15] The Society for the Propagation of the Gospel in Foreign Parts.

rituck Inlet. Our zeal was so great to get thither at the time appointed that we hardly allowed ourselves leisure to eat, which in truth we had the less stomach to by reason the dinner was served up by the landlord, whose nose stood on such ticklish terms that it was in danger of falling into the dish. We therefore made our repast very short and then embarked with only the surveyors and nine chosen men, leaving the rest at Mr. W[ilso]n's to take care of the horses and baggage. There we also left our chaplain, with the charitable intent that the gentiles round about might have time and opportunity, if they pleased, of getting themselves and their children baptized.

We rowed down Northwest River about eighteen miles, as far as the mouth of it, where it empties itself into Albemarle Sound. It was really a delightful sight, all the way, to see the banks of the river adorned with myrtle, laurel, and bay trees, which preserve their verdure the year round, though it must be owned that these beautiful plants sacred to Venus and Apollo grow commonly in a very dirty soil. The river is in most places fifty or sixty yards wide, without spreading much wider at the mouth. 'Tis remarkable it was never known to ebb and flow till the year 1713, when a violent storm opened a new inlet about five miles south of the old one; since which convulsion the old inlet is almost choked up by the shifting of the sand and grows both narrower and shoaler every day.

It was dark before we could reach the mouth of the river, where our wayward stars directed us to a miserable cottage. The landlord was lately removed bag and baggage from Maryland, through a strong antipathy he had to work and paying his debts. For want of our tent, we were obliged to shelter ourselves in this wretched hovel, where we were almost devoured by vermin of various kinds. However, we were above complaining, being all philosophers enough to improve such slender distresses into mirth and good humor.

5. The day being now come on which we had agreed to meet the commissioners of North Carolina, we embarked very early, which we could the easier do, having no temptation to stay where we were. We shaped our course along the south end of Knott's Island, there being no passage open on the north. Farther still to the southward of us we

discovered two smaller islands that go by the names of Bell's and Church's Isles. We also saw a small New England sloop riding in the sound a little to the south of our course. She had come in at the new inlet, as all other vessels have done since the opening of it. This navigation is a little difficult and fit only for vessels that draw no more than ten feet water. The trade hither is engrossed by the saints of New England, who carry off a great deal of tobacco without troubling themselves with paying that impertinent duty of a penny a pound.

It was just noon before we arrived at Currituck Inlet, which is now so shallow that the breakers fly over it with a horrible sound and at the same time afford a very wild prospect. On the north side of the inlet the high land terminated in a bluff point, from which a spit of sand extended itself toward the southeast full half a mile. The inlet lies between that spit and another on the south of it, leaving an opening of not quite a mile, which at this day is not practicable for any vessel whatsoever. And as shallow as it now is, it continues to fill up more and more, both the wind and waves rolling in the sands from the eastern shoals.

About two o'clock in the afternoon we were joined by two of the Carolina commissioners, attended by Mr. S[wan]n, their surveyor. The other two were not quite so punctual, which was the more unlucky for us because there could be no sport till they came. These gentlemen, it seems, had the Carolina commission in their keeping, notwithstanding which they could not forbear paying too much regard to a proverb fashionable in their country — not to make more haste than good speed.

However, that we who were punctual might not spend our precious time unprofitably, we took the several bearings of the coast. We also surveyed part of the adjacent high land, which had scarcely any trees growing upon it but cedars. Among the shrubs, we were showed here and there a bush of Carolina tea called yaupon, which is one species of the phillyrea. This is an evergreen, the leaves whereof have some resemblance to tea but differ very widely both in taste and flavor. We also found some few plants of the spired-leaf silk grass, which is likewise an evergreen, bearing on a lofty stem a large cluster of flowers

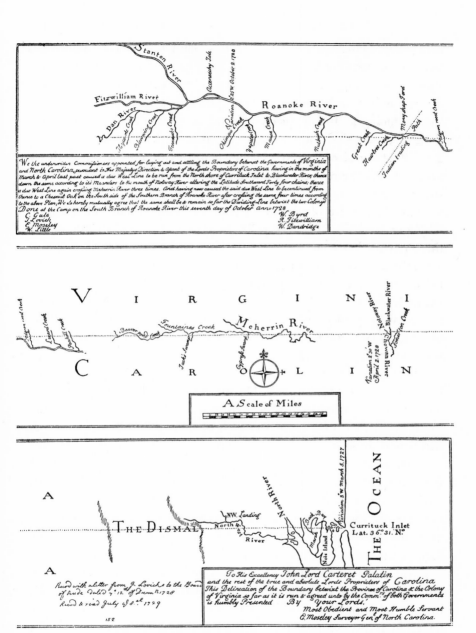

Surveyor's Map of the Dividing Line Submitted to the Board of Trade

(*reproduced here in three sections*)

of a pale yellow. Of the leaves of this plant the people thereabouts twist very strong cordage.

A virtuoso might divert himself here very well in picking up shells of various hue and figure and amongst the rest that species of conch shell which the Indian peak is made of. The extremities of these shells are blue and the rest white, so that peak of both these colors are drilled out of one and the same shell, serving the natives both for ornament and money, and are esteemed by them far beyond gold and silver.

The cedars were of singular use to us in the absence of our tent, which we had left with the rest of the baggage for fear of overloading the piraguas. We made a circular hedge of the branches of this tree, wrought so close together as to fence us against the cold winds. We then kindled a rousing fire in the center of it and lay round it like so many Knights Templars. But, as comfortable as this lodging was, the surveyors turned out about two in the morning to try the variation by a meridian taken from the North Star and found it to be somewhat less than three degrees west.

The commissioners of the neighboring colony came better provided for the belly than the business. They brought not above two men along with them that would put their hands to anything but the kettle and the frying pan. These spent so much of their industry that way that they had as little spirit as inclination for work.

6. At noon, having a perfect observation, we found the latitude of Currituck Inlet to be 36° 31'.

Whilst we were busied about these necessary matters, our skipper rowed to an oyster bank just by and loaded his piragua with oysters as savory and well-tasted as those from Colchester or Walfleet, and had the advantage of them, too, by being much larger and fatter.

About three in the afternoon the two lag commissioners arrived and, after a few decent excuses for making us wait, told us they were ready to enter upon business as soon as we pleased. The first step was to produce our respective powers, and the commission from each governor was distinctly read and copies of them interchangeably delivered.

It was observed by our Carolina friends that the latter part of the

Virginia commission had something in it a little too lordly and positive. In answer to which we told them 'twas necessary to make it thus peremptory lest the present commissioners might go upon as fruitless an errand as their predecessors. The former commissioners were tied down to act in exact conjunction with those of Carolina and so could not advance one step farther or one jot faster than they were pleased to permit them. The memory of that disappointment, therefore, induced the government of Virginia to give fuller powers to the present commissioners by authorizing them to go on with the work by themselves, in case those of Carolina should prove unreasonable and refuse to join with them in carrying the business to execution. And all this was done lest His Majesty's gracious intention should be frustrated a second time.

After both commissions were considered, the first question was where the dividing line was to begin. This begat a warm debate, the Virginia commissioners contending, with a great deal of reason, to begin at the end of the spit of sand, which was undoubtedly the north shore of Currituck Inlet. But those of Carolina insisted strenuously that the point of high land ought rather to be the place of beginning, because that was fixed and certain, whereas the spit of sand was ever shifting and did actually run out farther now than formerly. The contest lasted some hours with great vehemence, neither party receding from their opinion that night. But next morning Mr. M[oseley], to convince us he was not that obstinate person he had been represented, yielded to our reasons and found means to bring over his colleagues.

Here we began already to reap the benefit of those peremptory words in our commission, which in truth added some weight to our reasons. Nevertheless, because positive proof was made by the oaths of two credible witnesses that the spit of sand had advanced two hundred yards toward the inlet since the controversy first began, we were willing for peace's sake to make them that allowance. Accordingly we fixed our beginning about that distance north of the inlet and there ordered a cedar post to be driven deep into the sand for our beginning.

While we continued here, we were told that on the south shore not far from the inlet dwelt a marooner that modestly called himself a hermit, though he forfeited that name by suffering a wanton female to cohabit with him. His habitation was a bower covered with bark after the Indian fashion, which in that mild situation protected him pretty well from the weather. Like the ravens, he neither plowed nor sowed but subsisted chiefly upon oysters, which his handmaid made a shift to gather from the adjacent rocks. Sometimes, too, for change of diet, he sent her to drive up the neighbor's cows, to moisten their mouths with a little milk. But as for raiment, he depended mostly upon his length of beard and she upon her length of hair, part of which she brought decently forward and the rest dangled behind quite down to her rump, like one of Herodotus' East Indian Pygmies. Thus did these wretches live in a dirty state of nature and were mere Adamites, innocence only excepted.

7. This morning the surveyors began to run the dividing line from the cedar post we had driven into the sand, allowing near three degrees for the variation. Without making this just allowance, we should not have obeyed His Majesty's order in running a due-west line. It seems the former commissioners had not been so exact, which gave our friends of Carolina but too just an exception to their proceedings. The line cut Dosier's Island, consisting only of a flat sand with here and there an humble shrub growing upon it. From thence it crossed over a narrow arm of the sound into Knott's Island and there split a plantation belonging to William Harding.

The day being far spent, we encamped in this man's pasture, though it lay very low and the season now inclined people to aguish distempers. He suffered us to cut cedar branches for our enclosure and other wood for firing, to correct the moist air and drive away the damps. Our landlady, in the days of her youth, it seems, had been a laundress in the Temple and talked over her adventures in that station with as much pleasure as an old soldier talks over his battles and distempers and, I believe, with as many additions to the truth.

The soil is good in many places of this island, and the extent of it pretty large. It lies in the form of a wedge: the south end of it is several miles over, but toward the north it sharpens into a point. It is a plentiful place for stock by reason of the wide marshes adjacent to it and because of its warm situation. But the inhabitants pay a little dear for this convenience by losing as much blood in the summer season by the infinite number of mosquitoes as all their beef and pork can recruit in the winter.

The sheep are as large as in Lincolnshire, because they are never pinched by cold or hunger. The whole island was hitherto reckoned to lie in Virginia, but now our line has given the greater part of it to Carolina. The principal freeholder here is Mr. White, who keeps open house for all travelers that either debt or shipwreck happens to cast in his way.

8. By break of day we sent away our largest piragua with the baggage round the south end of Knott's Island, with orders to the men to wait for us in the mouth of North River. Soon after, we embarked ourselves on board the smaller vessel, with intent, if possible, to find a passage round the north end of the island.

We found this navigation very difficult by reason of the continued shoals and often stuck fast aground; for though the sound spreads many miles, yet it is in most places extremely shallow and requires a skillful pilot to steer even a canoe safe over it. It was almost as hard to keep our temper as to keep the channel in this provoking situation. But the most impatient amongst us stroked down their choler and swallowed their curses, lest, if they suffered them to break out, they might sound like complaining, which was expressly forbid as the first step to sedition.

At a distance we descried several islands to the northward of us, the largest of which goes by the name of Cedar Island. Our piragua stuck so often that we had a fair chance to be benighted in this wide water, which must certainly have been our fate had we not luckily spied a canoe that was giving a fortuneteller a cast from Princess Anne County over to North Carolina. But, as conjurers are sometimes mistaken, the man mistrusted we were officers of justice in pursuit of a young wench he had carried off along with him. We gave the canoe chase for more than an hour and when we came up with her threatened to make them all prisoners unless they would direct us into the right channel. By the pilotage of these people we rowed up an arm of the sound called the Back Bay till we came to the head of it. There we were stopped by a miry pocosin full half a mile in breadth, through which we were obliged to daggle on foot, plunging now and then, though we picked our way, up to the knees in mud. At the end of this charming walk we gained the terra firma of Princess Anne County. In that dirty condition we were afterwards obliged to foot it two miles as far as John Heath's plantation, where we expected to meet the surveyors and the men who waited upon them.

While we were performing this tedious voyage, they had carried the line through the firm land of Knott's Island, where it was no more than half a mile wide. After that they traversed a large marsh, that was exceeding miry and extended to an arm of the Back Bay. They crossed that water in a canoe which we had ordered round for that purpose and then waded over another marsh that reached quite to the high land of Princess Anne. Both these marshes together make a breadth of five miles, in which the men frequently sank up to the middle without muttering the least complaint. On the contrary, they turned all these disasters into merriment.

It was discovered by this day's work that Knott's Island was improperly so called, being in truth no more than a peninsula. The northwest side of it is only divided from the main by the great marsh above-mentioned, which is seldom totally overflowed. Instead of that, it might by the labor of a few trenches be drained into firm meadow, capable of grazing as many cattle as Job in his best estate was master of. In the miry condition it now lies, it feeds great numbers in the winter, though when the weather grows warm they are driven from thence by the mighty armies of mosquitoes, which are the plague of the lower part of Carolina as much as the flies were formerly of Egypt (and some rabbis think those flies were no other than mosquitoes).

All the people in the neighborhood flocked to John Heath's to behold such rarities as they fancied us to be. The men left their beloved chimney corners, the good women their spinning wheels, and some, of more curiosity than ordinary, rose out of their sick beds to come and stare at us. They looked upon us as a troop of knights-errant who were running this great risk of our lives, as they imagined, for the public weal; and some of the gravest of them questioned much whether we were not all criminals condemned to this dirty work for offenses against the state. What puzzled them most was what could make our men so very light-hearted under such intolerable drudgery. "Ye have little reason to be merry, my masters," said one of them, with a very solemn face. "I fancy the pocosin you must struggle with tomorrow will make you change your note and try what metal you are made of. Ye are, to be sure, the first of human race that ever had the boldness to attempt it, and I dare say will be the last. If, therefore, you have any worldly goods to dispose of, my advice is that you make your wills this very night, for fear you die intestate tomorrow." But, alas, these frightful tales were so far from disheartening the men that they served only to whet their resolution.

9. The surveyors entered early upon their business this morning and ran the line through Mr. Eyland's plantation, as far as the banks of North River. They passed over it in the piragua and landed in Gibbs's marsh, which was a mile in breadth and tolerably firm. They trudged through this marsh without much difficulty as far as the high land, which promised more fertility than any they had seen in these lower parts. But this firm land lasted not long before they came upon the dreadful pocosin they had been threatened with. Nor did they find it one jot better than it had been painted to them. The beavers and otters had rendered it quite impassable for any creatures but themselves.

Our poor fellows had much ado to drag their legs after them in this quagmire, but, disdaining to be balked, they could hardly be persuaded from pressing forward by the surveyors, who found it absolutely necessary to make a traverse in the deepest place to prevent their sticking fast in the mire and becoming a certain prey to the turkey buzzards.

This horrible day's work ended two miles to the northward of Mr. Merchant's plantation, divided from Northwest River by a narrow swamp which is causewayed over. We took up our quarters in the open field not far from the house, correcting by a fire as large as a Roman funeral pile the aguish exhalations arising from the sunken grounds that surrounded us.

The neck of land included betwixt North River and Northwest

River, with the adjacent marsh, belonged formerly to Governor Gibbs[16] but since his decease to Colonel Bladen,[17] in right of his first lady, who was Mr. Gibbs's daughter. It would be a valuable tract of land in any country but North Carolina, where, for want of navigation and commerce, the best estate affords little more than a coarse subsistence.

10 The Sabbath happened very opportunely, to give some ease to our jaded people, who rested religiously from every work but that of cooking the kettle. We observed very few cornfields in our walks and those very small, which seemed the stranger to us because we could see no other tokens of husbandry or improvement. But upon further inquiry we were given to understand people only made corn for themselves and not for their stocks, which know very well how to get their own living. Both cattle and hogs ramble into the neighboring marshes and swamps, where they maintain themselves the whole winter long and are not fetched home till the spring. Thus these indolent wretches during one half of the year lose the advantage of the milk of their cattle, as well as their dung, and many of the poor creatures perish in the mire, into the bargain, by this ill management. Some who pique themselves more upon industry than their neighbors will now and then, in compliment to their cattle, cut down a tree whose limbs are loaded with the moss afore-mentioned. The trouble would be too great to climb the tree in order to gather this provender, but the shortest way (which in this country is always counted the best) is to fell it, just like the lazy Indians, who do the same by such trees as bear fruit and so make one harvest for all. By this bad husbandry milk is so scarce in the winter season that were a big-bellied woman to long for it she would tax her longing. And, in truth, I believe this is often the case, and at the same time a very good reason why so many people in this province are marked with a custard complexion.

The only business here is raising of hogs, which is managed with

---

[16] Boyd: "John Gibbs, of the Currituck region, who, in 1690, claimed to be Governor of North Carolina and resisted the authority of Philip Ludwell, the appointee of the Proprietors."
[17] Boyd: "Martin Bladen (1680–1746), Whig politician, and member of the Board of Trade from 1717 to his death. His wife was Mary Gibbs."

the least trouble and affords the diet they are most fond of. The truth of it is, the inhabitants of North Carolina devour so much swine's flesh that it fills them full of gross humors. For want, too, of a constant supply of salt, they are commonly obliged to eat it fresh, and that begets the highest taint of scurvy. Thus, whenever a severe cold happens to constitutions thus vitiated, 'tis apt to improve into the yaws, called there very justly the country distemper. This has all the symptoms of the pox, with this aggravation, that no preparation of mercury will touch it. First it seizes the throat, next the palate, and lastly shows its spite to the poor nose, of which 'tis apt in a small time treacherously to undermine the foundation. This calamity is so common and familiar here that it ceases to be a scandal, and in the disputes that happen about beauty the noses have in some companies much ado to carry it. Nay, 'tis said that once, after three good pork years, a motion had like to have been made in the House of Burgesses that a man with a nose should be incapable of holding any place of profit in the province; which extraordinary motion could never have been intended without some hopes of a majority.

Thus, considering the foul and pernicious effects of eating swine's flesh in a hot country, it was wisely forbid and made an abomination to the Jews, who lived much in the same latitude with Carolina.

11. We ordered the surveyors early to their business, who were blessed with pretty dry grounds for three miles together. But they paid dear for it in the next two, consisting of one continued frightful pocosin, which no creatures but those of the amphibious kind ever had ventured into before. This filthy quagmire did in earnest put the men's courage to a trial, and though I can't say it made them lose their patience, yet they lost their humor for joking. They kept their gravity like so many Spaniards, so that a man might then have taken his opportunity to plunge up to the chin without danger of being laughed at. However, this unusual composure of countenance could not fairly be called complaining.

Their day's work ended at the mouth of Northern's Creek, which empties itself into Northwest River; though we chose to quarter a little higher up the river near Mossy Point. This we did for the convenience of an old house to shelter our persons and baggage from the rain, which threatened us hard. We judged the thing right, for there fell an heavy shower in the night that drove the most hardy of us into the house. Though indeed our case was not much mended by retreating thither, because, that tenement having not long before been used as a pork store, the moisture of the air dissolved the salt that lay scattered on the floor and made it as wet withindoors as without. However, the swamps and marshes we were lately accustomed to had made such beavers and otters of us that nobody caught the least cold.

We had encamped so early that we found time in the evening to walk near half a mile into the woods. There we came upon a family of mulattoes that called themselves free, though by the shyness of the master of the house, who took care to keep least in sight, their freedom seemed a little doubtful. It is certain many slaves shelter themselves in this obscure part of the world, nor will any of their righteous neighbors discover them. On the contrary, they find their account in settling such fugitives on some out-of-the way corner of their land to raise stocks for a mean and inconsiderable share, well knowing their condition makes it necessary for them to submit to any terms. Nor were these worthy borderers content to shelter runaway slaves, but debtors and criminals have often met with the like indulgence. But if the government of North Carolina have encouraged this unneighborly policy in order to increase their people, it is no more than what ancient Rome did before them, which was made a city of refuge for all debtors and fugitives and from that wretched beginning grew up in time to be mistress of great part of the world. And, considering how Fortune delights in bringing great things out of small, who knows but Carolina may, one time or other, come to be the seat of some other great empire?

12. Everything had been so soaked with the rain that we were obliged to lie by a good part of the morning and dry them. However, that time was not lost, because it gave the surveyors an opportunity of platting off their work and taking the course of the river. It likewise helped to recruit the spirits of the men, who had been a little harassed with yesterday's march. Notwithstanding all this, we crossed the river

before noon and advanced our line three miles. It was not possible to make more of it by reason good part of the way was either marsh or pocosin. The line cut two or three plantations, leaving part of them in Virginia and part of them in Carolina. This was a case that happened frequently, to the great inconvenience of the owners, who were therefore obliged to take out two patents and pay for a new survey in each government.

In the evening we took up our quarters in Mr. Ballance's pasture, a little above the bridge built over Northwest River. There we discharged the two piraguas, which in truth had been very serviceable in transporting us over the many waters in that dirty and difficult part of our business. Our landlord had a tolerable good house and clean furniture, and yet we could not be tempted to lodge in it. We chose rather to lie in the open field, for fear of growing too tender. A clear sky, spangled with stars, was our canopy, which, being the last thing we saw before we fell asleep, gave us magnificent dreams. The truth of it is, we took so much pleasure in that natural kind of lodging that I think at the foot of the account mankind are great losers by the luxury of feather beds and warm apartments.

The curiosity of beholding so new and withal so sweet a method of encamping brought one of the Senators of North Carolina to make us a midnight visit. But he was so very clamorous in his commendations of it that the sentinel, not seeing his quality either through his habit or behavior, had like to have treated him roughly. After excusing the unseasonablness of his visit and letting us know he was a parliament man, he swore he was so taken with our lodging that he would set fire to his house as soon as he got home and teach his wife and children to lie like us in the open field.

13. Early this morning our chaplain repaired to us with the men we had left at Mr. Wilson's. We had sent for them the evening before to relieve those who had the labor oar from Currituck Inlet. But to our great surprise, they petitioned not to be relieved, hoping to gain immortal reputation by being the first of mankind that ventured through the Great Dismal. But the rest being equally ambitious of the same honor, it was but fair to decide their pretensions by lot. After For-

tune had declared herself, those which she had excluded offered money to the happy persons to go in their stead. But Hercules would have as soon sold the glory of cleansing the Augean stables, which was pretty near the same sort of work. No sooner was the controversy at an end but we sent those unfortunate fellows back to their quarters whom chance had condemned to remain upon firm land and sleep in a whole skin. In the meanwhile, the surveyors carried the line three miles, which was no contemptible day's work, considering how cruelly they were entangled with briers and gallbushes. The leaf of this last shrub bespeaks it to be of the alaternus family.

Our work ended within a quarter of a mile of the Dismal above-mentioned, where the ground began to be already full of sunken holes and slashes, which had, here and there, some few reeds growing in them. 'Tis hardly credible how little the bordering inhabitants were acquainted with this mighty swamp, notwithstanding they had lived their whole lives within smell of it. Yet, as great strangers as they were to it, they pretended to be very exact in their account of its dimensions and were positive it could not be above seven or eight miles wide, but knew no more of the matter than stargazers know of the distance of the fixed stars. At the same time, they were simple enough to amuse our men with idle stories of the lions, panthers, and alligators they were likely to encounter in that dreadful place. In short, we saw plainly there was no intelligence of this *Terra Incognita* to be got but from our own experience. For that reason it was resolved to make the requisite dispositions to enter it next morning. We allotted every one of the surveyors for this painful enterprise, with twelve men to attend them. Fewer than that could not be employed in clearing the way, carrying the chain, marking the trees, and bearing the necessary bedding and provisions. Nor would the commissioners themselves have spared their persons on this occasion but for fear of adding to the poor men's burden, while they were certain they could add nothing to their resolution.

We quartered with our friend and fellow traveler, William Wilkins, who had been our faithful pilot to Currituck and lived about a mile from the place where the line ended. Everything looked so very clean and the furniture so neat that we were tempted to lodge withindoors. But the novelty of being shut up so close quite spoiled our rest, nor did we breathe so free by abundance as when we lay in the open air.

14. Before nine of the clock this morning the provisions, bedding, and other necessaries were made up into packs for the men to carry on their shoulders into the Dismal. They were victualed for eight days at full allowance, nobody doubting but that would be abundantly sufficient to carry them through that inhospitable place; nor indeed was it possible for the poor fellows to stagger under more. As it was, their loads weighed from sixty to seventy pounds, in just proportion to the strength of those who were to bear them. 'Twould have been unconscionable to have saddled them with burdens heavier than that, when they were to lug them through a filthy bog which was hardly practicable with no burden at all. Besides this luggage at their backs, they were obliged to measure the distance, mark the trees, and clear the way for the surveyors every step they went. It was really a pleasure to see with how much cheerfulness they undertook and with how much spirit they went through all this drudgery. For their greater safety, the commissioners took care to furnish them with Peruvian bark,[18] rhubarb, and ipecacuanha, in case they might happen, in that wet journey, to be taken with fevers or fluxes.

Although there was no need of example to inflame persons already so cheerful, yet to enter the people with the better grace, the author and two more of the commissioners accompanied them half a mile into the Dismal. The skirts of it were thinly planted with dwarf reeds and gallbushes, but when we got into the Dismal itself we found the reeds grew there much taller and closer and, to mend the matter, were so interlaced with bamboo briers that there was no scuffling through them without the help of pioneers. At the same time we found the ground moist and trembling under our feet like a quagmire, insomuch that it was an easy matter to run a ten-foot pole up to the head in it without exerting any uncommon strength to do it. Two of the men whose burdens were the least cumbersome had orders to march before with their tomahawks and clear the way in order to make an opening

[18] Cinchona, used as a specific for malaria and other fevers.

for the surveyors. By their assistance we made a shift to push the line half a mile in three hours and then reached a small piece of firm land about a hundred yards wide, standing up above the rest like an island. Here the people were glad to lay down their loads and take a little refreshment, while the happy man whose lot it was to carry the jug of rum began already, like Aesop's bread carriers, to find it grow a good deal lighter.

After reposing about an hour, the commissioners recommended vigor and constancy to their fellow travelers, by whom they were answered with three cheerful huzzas, in token of obedience. This ceremony was no sooner over but they took up their burdens and attended the motion of the surveyors, who, though they worked with all their might, could reach but one mile farther, the same obstacles still attending them which they had met with in the morning. However small this distance may seem to such as are used to travel at their ease, yet our poor men, who were obliged to work with an unwieldy load at their backs, had reason to think it a long way; especially in a bog where they had no firm footing but every step made a deep impression which was instantly filled with water. At the same time they were laboring with their hands to cut down the reeds, which were ten feet high, their legs were hampered with briers. Besides, the weather happened to be warm, and the tallness of the reeds kept off every friendly breeze from coming to refresh them. And indeed it was a little provoking to hear the wind whistling among the branches of the white cedars, which grew here and there amongst the reeds, and at the same time not to have the comfort to feel the least breath of it.

In the meantime the three commissioners returned out of the Dismal the same way they went in and, having joined their brethren, proceeded that night as far as Mr. Wilson's. This worthy person lives within sight of the Dismal, in the skirts whereof his stocks range and maintain themselves all the winter, and yet he knew as little of it as he did of *Terra Australis Incognita*. He told us a Canterbury tale of a North Briton whose curiosity spurred him a long way into this great desert, as he called it, near twenty years ago, but he, having no compass nor seeing the sun for several days together, wandered about till he was almost famished; but at last he bethought himself of a secret his countrymen make use of to pilot themselves in a dark day. He took a fat louse out of his collar and exposed it to the open day on a piece of white paper, which he brought along with him for his journal. The poor insect, having no eyelids, turned himself about till he found the darkest part of the heavens and so made the best of his way toward the North. By this direction he steered himself safe out and gave such a frightful account of the monsters he saw and the distresses he underwent that no mortal since has been hardy enough to go upon the like dangerous discovery.

15. The surveyors pursued their work with all diligence but still found the soil of the Dismal so spongy that the water oozed up into every footstep they took. To their sorrow, too, they found the reeds and briers more firmly interwoven than they did the day before. But the greatest grievance was from large cypresses which the wind had blown down and heaped upon one another. On the limbs of most of them grew sharp snags, pointing every way like so many pikes, that required much pains and caution to avoid. These trees, being evergreens and shooting their large tops very high, are easily overset by every gust of wind, because there is no firm earth to steady their roots. Thus many of them were laid prostrate, to the great encumbrance of the way. Such variety of difficulties made the business go on heavily, insomuch that from morning till night the line could advance no farther than one mile and thirty-one poles.

Never was rum, that cordial of life, found more necessary than it was in this dirty place. It did not only recruit the people's spirits, now almost jaded with fatigue, but served to correct the badness of the water and at the same time to resist the malignity of the air. Whenever the men wanted to drink, which was very often, they had nothing more to do but make a hole and the water bubbled up in a moment. But it was far from being either clear or well tasted and had, besides, a physical effect from the tincture it received from the roots of the shrubs and trees that grew in the neighborhood.

While the surveyors were thus painfully employed, the commissioners discharged the long score they had with Mr. Wilson for the men and horses which had been quartered upon him during our expedition to Currituck. From thence we marched in good order along the east side of the Dismal and passed the long bridge that lies over the south branch of Elizabeth River. At the end of eighteen miles we reached Timothy Ivy's plantation, where we pitched our tent for the first time and were furnished with everything the place afforded. We perceived the happy effects of industry in this family, in which every one looked tidy and clean and carried in their countenances the cheerful marks of plenty. We saw no drones there, which are but too common, alas, in that part of the world. Though, in truth, the distemper of laziness seizes the men oftener much than the women. These last spin, weave, and knit, all with their own hands, while their husbands, depending on the bounty of the climate, are slothful in everything but getting of children, and in that only instance make themselves useful members of an infant colony.

There is but little wool in that province, though cotton grows very kindly and, so far south, is seldom nipped by the frost. The good women mix this with their wool for their outer garments; though, for want of fulling, that kind of manufacture is open and sleazy. Flax likewise thrives there extremely, being perhaps as fine as any in the world, and I question not might with a little care and pains be brought to rival that of Egypt; and yet the men are here so intolerably lazy they seldom take the trouble to propagate it.

16. The line was this day carried one mile and an half and sixteen poles. The soil continued soft and miry but fuller of trees, especially white cedars. Many of these, too, were thrown down and piled in heaps, high enough for a good Muscovite fortification. The worst of it was, the poor fellows began now to be troubled with fluxes, occasioned by bad water and moist lodging, but chewing of rhubarb kept that malady within bounds.

In the meantime, the commissioners decamped early in the morning and made a march of twenty-five miles, as far as Mr. Andrew Meade's, who lives upon Nansemond River. They were no sooner got under the shelter of that hospitable roof but it began to rain hard and continued so to do great part of the night. This gave them much pain for their friends in the Dismal, whose sufferings spoiled their taste for the good cheer wherewith they were entertained themselves. However, late that evening these poor men had the fortune to come upon another terra firma, which was the luckier for them because the lower ground, by the rain that fell, was made a fitter lodging for tadpoles than men. In our journey we remarked that the north side of this great swamp lies higher than either the east or the west, nor were the approaches to it so full of sunken grounds.

We passed by no less than two Quaker meetinghouses, one of which had an awkward ornament on the west end of it that seemed to ape a steeple. I must own I expected no such piece of foppery from a sect of so much outside simplicity. That persuasion prevails much in the lower end of Nansemond County, for want of ministers to pilot the people a decenter way to Heaven. The ill reputation of tobacco planted in those lower parishes makes the clergy unwilling to accept of them, unless it be such whose abilities are as mean as their pay. Thus, whether the churches be quite void or but indifferently filled, the Quakers will have an opportunity of gaining proselytes. 'Tis a wonder no popish missionaries are sent from Maryland to labor in this neglected vineyard, who we know have zeal enough to traverse sea and land on the meritorious errand of making converts. Nor is it less strange that some wolf in sheep's clothing arrives not from New England to lead astray a flock that has no shepherd. People uninstructed in any religion are ready to embrace the first that offers. 'Tis natural for helpless man to adore his Maker in some form or other, and were there any exception to this rule, I should suspect it to be among the Hottentots of the Cape of Good Hope and of North Carolina.

There fell a great deal of rain in the night, accompanied with a strong wind. The fellow feeling we had for the poor Dismalites, on account of this unkind weather, rendered the down we laid upon uneasy. We fancied them half-drowned in their wet lodging, with the trees blowing down about their ears. These were the gloomy images our fears suggested, though 'twas so much uneasiness clear gains. They happened to come off much better, by being luckily encamped on the dry piece of ground afore-mentioned.

17. They were, however, forced to keep the Sabbath in spite of their teeth, contrary to the dispensation our good chaplain had given them. Indeed, their short allowance of provision would have justified their making the best of their way without distinction of days. 'Twas certainly a work both of necessity and self-preservation to save themselves from starving. Nevertheless, the hard rain had made everything so thoroughly wet that it was quite impossible to do any business. They therefore made a virtue of what they could not help and contentedly rested in their dry situation.

Since the surveyors had entered the Dismal, they had laid eyes on no living creature: neither bird nor beast, insect nor reptile came in view. Doubtless the eternal shade that broods over this mighty bog and hinders the sunbeams from blessing the ground makes it an uncomfortable habitation for anything that has life. Not so much as a Zeeland frog could endure so aguish a situation. It had one beauty, however, that delighted the eye, though at the expense of all the other senses: the moisture of the soil preserves a continual verdure and makes every plant an evergreen; but at the same time the foul damps ascend without ceasing, corrupt the air, and render it unfit for respiration. Not even a turkey buzzard will venture to fly over it, no more than the Italian vultures will over the filthy Lake Avernus, or the birds in the Holy Land over the Salt Sea where Sodom and Gomorrah formerly stood.

In these sad circumstances the kindest thing we could do for our suffering friends was to give them a place in The Litany. Our chaplain, for his part, did his office and rubbed us up with a seasonable sermon. This was quite a new thing to our brethren of North Carolina, who live in a climate where no clergyman can breathe, any more than spiders in Ireland.

For want of men in holy orders, both the members of the council and justices of the peace are empowered by the laws of that country to marry all those who will not take one another's word; but, for the ceremony of christening their children, they trust that to chance. If a parson come in their way, they will crave a cast of his office, as they call it; else they are content their offspring should remain as arrant pagans as themselves. They account it among their greatest advantages that they are not priest-ridden, not remembering that the clergy is rarely guilty of bestriding such as have the misfortune to be poor. One thing may be said for the inhabitants of that province, that they are not troubled with any religious fumes and have the least superstition of any people living. They do not know Sunday from any other day, any more than Robinson Crusoe did, which would give them a great advantage were they given to be industrious. But they keep so many Sabbaths every week that their disregard of the seventh day has no manner of cruelty in it, either to servants or cattle.

18. It was with some difficulty we could make our people quit the good cheer they met with at this house, so it was late before we took our departure; but to make us amends our landlord was so good as to conduct us ten miles on our way, as far as the Cypress Swamp, which drains itself into the Dismal. Eight miles beyond that we forded the waters of Corapeake, which tend the same way as do many others on that side. In six miles more we reached the plantation of Mr. Thomas Speight, a grandee of North Carolina. We found the good man upon his crutches, being crippled with the gout in both his knees. Here we flattered ourselves we should by this time meet with good tidings of the surveyors but had reckoned, alas! without our host: on the contrary, we were told the Dismal was at least thirty miles wide in that place. However, as nobody could say this on his own knowledge, we ordered guns to be fired and a drum to be beaten, but received no answer, unless it was from that prating nymph, Echo, who, like a loquacious wife, will always have the last word and sometimes return three for one. It was indeed no wonder our signal was not heard at that time by the people in the Dismal, because, in truth, they had then not penetrated one third of their way. They had that morning fallen to work with great vigor and, finding the ground better than ordinary, drove on the line two miles and thirty-eight poles. This was reckoned an Herculean day's work, and yet they would not have stopped there had not an impenetrable cedar thicket checked their industry.

Our landlord had seated himself on the borders of this Dismal for the advantage of the green food his cattle find there all winter and for the rooting that supports his hogs. This, I own, is some convenience to his purse, for which his whole family pay dear in their persons, for they are devoured by mosquitoes all the summer and have agues every spring and fall, which corrupt all the juices of their bodies, give them a cadaverous complexion and, besides, a lazy, creeping habit, which they never get rid of.

19. We ordered several men to patrol on the edge of the Dismal, both toward the north and toward the south, and to fire guns at proper distances. This they performed very punctually but could hear nothing in return nor gain any sort of intelligence. In the meantime, whole flocks of women and children flew hither to stare at us with as much curiosity as if we had lately landed from Bantam or Morocco. Some borderers, too, had a great mind to know where the line would come out, being for the most part apprehensive lest their lands should be taken into Virginia. In that case they must have submitted to some sort of order and government; whereas, in North Carolina, everyone does what seems best in his own eyes. There were some good women that brought their children to be baptized, but brought no capons along with them to make the solemnity cheerful. In the meantime, it was strange that none came to be married in such a multitude, if it had only been for the novelty of having their hands joined by one in holy orders. Yet so it was that though our chaplain christened above an hundred, he did not marry so much as one couple during the whole expedition. But marriage is reckoned a lay contract in Carolina, as I said before, and a country justice can tie the fatal knot there as fast as an archbishop.

None of our visitors could, however, tell us any news of the surveyors, nor indeed was it possible any of them should at that time, they being still laboring in the midst of the Dismal. It seems they were able to carry the line this day no farther than one mile and sixty-one poles, and that whole distance was through a miry cedar bog, where the ground trembled under their feet most frightfully. In many places, too, their passage was retarded by a great number of fallen trees that lay horsing upon one another.

Though many circumstances concurred to make this an unwholesome situation, yet the poor men had no time to be sick, nor can one conceive a more calamitous case than it would have been to be laid up in that uncomfortable quagmire. Never were patients more tractable or willing to take physic than these honest fellows, but it was from a dread of laying their bones in a bog that would soon spew them up again. That consideration also put them upon more caution about their lodging. They first covered the ground with square pieces of cypress bark, which now, in the spring, they could easily slip off the tree for that purpose. On this they spread their bedding, but, unhappily, the weight and warmth of their bodies made the water rise up betwixt the joints of the bark, to their great inconvenience. Thus they lay not only moist but also exceedingly cold, because their fires were continually going out. For no sooner was the trash upon the surface burnt away but immediately the fire was extinguished by the moisture of the soil, insomuch that it was great part of the sentinel's business to rekindle it again in a fresh place every quarter of an hour. Nor could they indeed do their duty better, because cold was the only enemy they had to guard against in a miserable morass where nothing can inhabit.

20. We could get no tidings yet of our brave adventurers, notwithstanding we dispatched men to the likeliest stations to inquire after them. They were still scuffling in the mire and could not possibly forward the line this whole day more than one mile and sixty-four chains. Every step of this day's work was through a cedar bog, where the trees were somewhat smaller and grew more into a thicket. It was now a great misfortune to the men to find their provisions grow less as their labor grew greater; they were all forced to come to short allowance and consequently to work hard without filling their bellies. Though this was very severe upon English stomachs, yet the people were so far from being discomfited at it that they still kept up their good humor and merrily told a young fellow in the company, who looked very plump and wholesome, that he must expect to go first to pot if matters should come to extremity. This was only said by way of jest, yet it made him thoughtful in earnest. However, for the present he returned them a very civil answer, letting them know that, dead or

alive, he should be glad to be useful to such worthy good friends. But, after all, this humorous saying had one very good effect, for that younker, who before was a little inclined by his constitution to be lazy, grew on a sudden extremely industrious, that so there might be less occasion to carbonade him for the good of his fellow travelers.

While our friends were thus embarrassed in the Dismal, the commissioners began to lie under great uneasiness for them. They knew very well their provisions must by this time begin to fall short, nor could they conceive any likely means of a supply. At this time of the year both cattle and hogs had forsaken the skirts of the Dismal, invited by the springing grass on the firm land. All our hopes were that Providence would cause some wild game to fall in their way or else direct them to a wholesome vegetable for subsistence. In short, they were haunted with so many frights on this occasion that they were in truth more uneasy than the persons whose case they lamented.

We had several visitors from Edenton, in the afternoon, that came with Mr. Gale, who had prudently left us at Currituck to scuffle through that dirty country by ourselves. These gentlemen, having good noses, had smelt out, at thirty miles' distance, the precious liquor with which the liberality of our good friend Mr. Meade had just before supplied us. That generous person had judged very right that we were now got out of the latitude of drink proper for men in affliction and therefore was so good as to send his cart loaden with all sorts of refreshments, for which the commissioners returned him their thanks and the chaplain his blessing.

21. The surveyors and their attendants began now in good earnest to be alarmed with apprehensions of famine, nor could they forbear looking with some sort of appetite upon a dog which had been the faithful companion of their travels. Their provisions were now near exhausted. They had this morning made the last distribution, that so each might husband his small pittance as he pleased. Now it was that the fresh-colored young man began to tremble every joint of him, having dreamt the night before that the Indians were about to barbecue him over live coals. The prospect of famine determined the people at last, with one consent, to abandon the line for the present, which

advanced but slowly, and make the best of their way to firm land. Accordingly they set off very early and, by the help of the compass which they carried along with them, steered a direct westerly course. They marched from morning till night and computed their journey to amount to about four miles, which was a great way, considering the difficulties of the ground. It was all along a cedar swamp, so dirty and perplexed that if they had not traveled for their lives they could not have reached so far. On their way they espied a turkey buzzard that flew prodigiously high to get above the noisome exhalations that ascend from that filthy place. This they were willing to understand as a good omen, according to the superstition of the ancients, who had great faith in the flight of vultures. However, after all this tedious journey they could yet discover no end of their toil, which made them very pensive, especially after they had eat the last morsel of their provisions. But to their unspeakable comfort, when all was hushed in the evening, they heard the cattle low and the dogs bark very distinctly, which, to men in that distress, was more delightful music than Faustina [19] or Farinelli [20] could have made.

In the meantime the commissioners could get no news of them from any of their visitors, who assembled from every point of the compass. But the good landlord had visitors of another kind while we were there, that is to say, some industrious masters of ships that lay in Nansemond River. These worthy commanders came to bespeak tobacco from these parts to make up their loadings, in contempt of the Virginia law which positively forbade their taking in any made in North Carolina. Nor was this restraint at all unreasonable, because they have no law in Carolina either to mend the quality or lessen the quantity of tobacco, or so much as to prevent the turning out of seconds, all which cases have been provided against by the laws of Virginia. Wherefore, there can be no reason why the inhabitants of that province should have the same advantage of shipping their tobacco in our parts when they will by no means submit to the same restrictions that we do.

22. Our patrol happened not to go far enough to the northward

---

[19] Faustina Bordoni (1693–1783), an Italian soprano.
[20] Carlo Broschi Farinelli (1705–1782), a famous *castrato*.

this morning; if they had, the people in the Dismal might have heard the report of their guns. For this reason they returned without any tidings, which threw us into a great though unnecessary perplexity. This was now the ninth day since they entered into that inhospitable swamp, and consequently we had reason to believe their provisions were quite spent. We knew they worked hard and therefore would eat heartily so long as they had wherewithal to recruit their spirits, not imagining the swamp so wide as they found it. Had we been able to guess where the line would come out, we would have sent men to meet them with a fresh supply; but as we could know nothing of that, and as we had neither compass nor surveyor to guide a messenger on such an errand, we were unwilling to expose him to no purpose; therefore, all we were able to do for them, in so great an extremity, was to recommend them to a merciful Providence.

However long we might think the time, yet we were cautious of showing our uneasiness for fear of mortifying our landlord. He had done his best for us, and therefore we were unwilling he should think us dissatisfied with our entertainment. In the midst of our concern, we were most agreeably surprised, just after dinner, with the news that the Dismalites were all safe. These blessed tidings were brought us by Mr. Swann, the Carolina surveyor, who came to us in a very tattered condition. After very short salutations, we got about him as if he had been a Hottentot and began to inquire into his adventures. He gave us a detail of their uncomfortable voyage through the Dismal and told us particularly they had pursued their journey early that morning, encouraged by the good omen of seeing the crows fly over their heads; that after an hour's march over very rotten ground they on a sudden began to find themselves among tall pines that grew in the water, which in many places was knee deep. This pine swamp, into which that of Corapeake drained itself, extended near a mile in breadth; and though it was exceedingly wet, yet was much harder at bottom than the rest of the swamp; that about ten in the morning they recovered firm land, which they embraced with as much pleasure as shipwrecked wretches do the shore.

After these honest adventurers had congratulated each other's deliverance, their first inquiry was for a good house where they might satisfy the importunity of their stomachs. Their good genius directed them to Mr. Brinkley's, who dwells a little to the southward of the line. This man began immediately to be very inquisitive, but they declared they had no spirits to answer questions till after dinner. "But pray, gentlemen," said he, "answer me one question at least: what shall we get for your dinner?" To which they replied, "No matter what, provided it be but enough." He kindly supplied their wants as soon as possible, and by the strength of that refreshment they made a shift to come to us in the evening, to tell their own story. They all looked very thin and as ragged as the Gibeonite ambassadors did in the days of yore.

Our surveyors told us they had measured ten miles in the Dismal and computed the distance they had marched since to amount to about five more, so they made the whole breadth to be fifteen miles in all.

23. It was very reasonable that the surveyors and the men who had been sharers in their fatigue should now have a little rest. They were all, except one, in good health and good heart, blessed be God! notwithstanding the dreadful hardships they had gone through. It was really a pleasure to see the cheerfulness wherewith they received the order to prepare to re-enter the Dismal on the Monday following in order to continue the line from the place where they had left off measuring, that so we might have the exact breadth of that dirty place. There were no more than two of them that could be persuaded to be relieved on this occasion or suffer the other men to share the credit of that bold undertaking; neither would these have suffered it had not one of them been very lame and the other much indisposed.

By the description the surveyors gave of the Dismal, we were convinced that nothing but the exceeding dry season we had been blessed with could have made the passing of it practicable. It is the source of no less than five several rivers which discharge themselves southward into Albemarle Sound and of two that run northerly into Virginia. From thence 'tis easy to imagine that the soil must be thoroughly soaked with water or else there must be plentiful stores of it under-ground to supply so many rivers, especially since there is no lake or any considerable body of that element to be seen on the surface. The rivers that head in it from Virginia are the south branch of Nanse-mond and the west branch of Elizabeth, and those from Carolina are Northwest River, North River, Pasquotank, Little River, and Per-quimans.

There is one remarkable part of the Dismal, lying to the south of the line, that has few or no trees growing on it but contains a large tract of tall reeds. These, being green all the year round and waving with every wind, have procured it the name of the Green Sea. We are not yet acquainted with the precise extent of the Dismal, the whole having never been surveyed; but it may be computed at a medium to be about thirty miles long and ten miles broad, though where the line crossed it, 'twas completely fifteen miles wide. But it seems to grow narrower toward the north, or at least does so in many places.

The exhalations that continually rise from this vast body of mire and nastiness infect the air for many miles round and render it very unwholesome for the bordering inhabitants. It makes them liable to agues, pleurisies, and many other distempers that kill abundance of people and make the rest look no better than ghosts. It would re-quire a great sum of money to drain it, but the public treasure could not be better bestowed than to preserve the lives of His Majesty's liege people and at the same time render so great a tract of swamp very profitable, besides the advantage of making a channel to trans-port by water carriage goods from Albemarle Sound into Nansemond and Elizabeth rivers in Virginia.

24. This being Sunday, we had a numerous congregation, which flocked to our quarters from all the adjacent country. The news that our surveyors were come out of the Dismal increased the number very much, because it would give them an opportunity of guessing, at least, whereabouts the line would cut, whereby they might form some judgment whether they belonged to Virginia or Carolina. Those who had taken up land within the disputed bounds were in great

pain lest it should be found to lie in Virginia; because this being done contrary to an express order of that government, the patentees had great reason to fear they should in that case have lost their land. But their apprehensions were now at an end when they understood that all the territory which had been controverted was like to be left in Carolina.

In the afternoon, those who were to re-enter the Dismal were furnished with the necessary provisions and ordered to repair the overnight to their landlord, Peter Brinkley's, that they might be ready to begin their business early on Monday morning. Mr. Irvin was excused from the fatigue in compliment to his lungs; but Mr. Mayo and Mr. Swann were robust enough to return upon that painful service, and, to do them justice, they went with great alacrity. The truth was, they now knew the worst of it and could guess pretty near at the time when they might hope to return to land again.

25. The air was chilled this morning with a smart northwest wind, which favored the Dismalites in their dirty march. They returned by the path they had made in coming out and with great industry arrived in the evening at the spot where the line had been discontinued. After so long and laborious a journey, they were glad to repose themselves on their couches of cypress bark, where their sleep was as sweet as it would have been on a bed of Finland down.

In the meantime, we who stayed behind had nothing to do but to make the best observations we could upon that part of the country. The soil of our landlord's plantation, though none of the best, seemed more fertile than any thereabouts, where the ground is near as sandy as the deserts of Africa and consequently barren. The road leading from thence to Edenton, being in distance about twenty-seven miles, lies upon a ridge called Sandy Ridge, which is so wretchedly poor that it will not bring potatoes. The pines in this part of the country are of a different species from those that grow in Virginia: their bearded leaves are much longer and their cones much larger. Each cell contains a seed of the size and figure of a black-eyed pea, which, shedding in November, is very good mast for hogs and fattens them in a short time. The smallest of these pines are full of cones which are eight or nine inches long, and each affords commonly sixty or seventy seeds. This kind of mast has the advantage of all other by being more constant and less liable to be nipped by the frost or eaten by the caterpillars.

The trees also abound more with turpentine and consequently yield more tar than either the yellow or the white pine and for the same reason make more durable timber for building. The inhabitants hereabouts pick up knots of lightwood in abundance, which they burn into tar and then carry it to Norfolk or Nansemond for a market. The tar made in this method is the less valuable because it is said to burn the cordage, though it is full as good for all other uses as that made in Sweden and Muscovy.

Surely there is no place in the world where the inhabitants live with less labor than in North Carolina. It approaches nearer to the description of Lubberland [21] than any other, by the great felicity of the climate, the easiness of raising provisions, and the slothfulness of the people. Indian corn is of so great increase that a little pains will subsist a very large family with bread, and then they may have meat without any pains at all, by the help of the low grounds and the great variety of mast that grows on the high land. The men, for their parts, just like the Indians, impose all the work upon the poor women. They make their wives rise out of their beds early in the morning, at the same time that they lie and snore till the sun has risen one-third of his course and dispersed all the unwholesome damps. Then, after stretching and yawning for half an hour, they light their pipes, and, under the protection of a cloud of smoke, venture out into the open air; though if it happen to be never so little cold they quickly return shivering into the chimney corner. When the weather is mild, they stand leaning with both their arms upon the cornfield fence and gravely consider whether they had best go and take a small heat at the hoe but generally find reasons to put it off till another time. Thus they loiter away their lives, like Solomon's sluggard, with their arms across, and at the winding up of the year scarcely have bread to eat.

[21] Cockaigne, a fabulous land of ease and plenty, subject of a thirteenth-century fabliau.

To speak the truth, 'tis a thorough aversion to labor that makes people file off to North Carolina, where plenty and a warm sun confirm them in their disposition to laziness for their whole lives.

26. Since we were like to be confined to this place till the people returned out of the Dismal, 'twas agreed that our chaplain might safely take a turn to Edenton to preach the Gospel to the infidels there and christen their children. He was accompanied thither by Mr. Little, one of the Carolina commissioners, who, to show his regard for the church, offered to treat him on the road with a fricassee of rum. They fried half a dozen rashers of very fat bacon in a pint of rum, both which being dished up together served the company at once both for meat and drink.

Most of the rum they get in this country comes from New England and is so bad and unwholesome that it is not improperly called "kill-devil." It is distilled there from foreign molasses, which, if skillfully managed, yields near gallon for gallon. Their molasses comes from the same country and has the name of "long sugar" in Carolina, I suppose from the ropiness of it, and serves all the purposes of sugar, both in their eating and drinking. When they entertain their friends bountifully, they fail not to set before them a capacious bowl of bombo, so called from the admiral of that name. This is a compound of rum and water in equal parts, made palatable with the said long sugar. As good humor begins to flow and the bowl to ebb they take care to replenish it with sheer rum, of which there always is a reserve under the table.

But such generous doings happen only when that balsam of life is plenty; for they have often such melancholy times that neither landgraves nor caciques can procure one drop for their wives when they lie in or are troubled with the colic or vapors. Very few in this country have the industry to plant orchards, which, in a dearth of rum, might supply them with much better liquor. The truth is, there is one inconvenience that easily discourages lazy people from making this improvement: very often, in autumn, when the apples begin to ripen, they are visited with numerous flights of parakeets,[22] that bite

[22] Spelled "paroquets" in the manuscript. Byrd refers to the Carolina parakeet, a bird now extinct.

all the fruit to pieces in a moment for the sake of the kernels. The havoc they make is sometimes so great that whole orchards are laid waste, in spite of all the noises that can be made or mawkins [23] that can be dressed up to fright 'em away. These ravenous birds visit North Carolina only during the warm season and so soon as the cold begins to come on retire back toward the sun. They rarely venture so far north as Virginia, except in a very hot summer, when they visit the most southern parts of it. They are very beautiful but, like some other pretty creatures, are apt to be loud and mischievous.

27. Betwixt this [plantation] [24] and Edenton there are many huckleberry slashes,[25] which afford a convenient harbor for wolves and foxes. The first of these wild beasts is not so large and fierce as they are in other countries more northerly. He will not attack a man in the keenest of his hunger but run away from him, as from an animal more mischievous than himself. The foxes are much bolder and will sometimes not only make a stand but likewise assault anyone that would balk them of their prey. The inhabitants hereabouts take the trouble to dig abundance of wolf pits, so deep and perpendicular that when a wolf is once tempted into them he can no more scramble out again than a husband who has taken the leap can scramble out of matrimony.

Most of the houses in this part of the country are log houses, covered with pine or cypress shingles, three feet long and one broad. They are hung upon lathes with pegs, and their doors, too, turn upon wooden hinges and have wooden locks to secure them, so that the building is finished without nails or other ironwork. They also set up their pales without any nails at all, and, indeed, more securely than those that are nailed. There are three rails mortised into the posts, the lowest of which serves as a sill, with a groove in the middle big enough to receive the end of the pales; the middle part of the pale rests against the inside of the next rail, and the top of it is brought forward to the outside of the uppermost. Such wreathing of the pales

[23] An obsolete form of "malkin," a scarecrow.
[24] Added from the manuscript of the "History" in the American Philosophical Society.
[25] Swamps.

in and out makes them stand firm and much harder to unfix than when nailed in the ordinary way.

Within three or four miles of Edenton the soil appears to be a little more fertile, though it is much cut with slashes, which seem all to have a tendency toward the Dismal. This town is situate on the north side of Albemarle Sound, which is there about five miles over. A dirty slash runs all along the back of it, which in the summer is a foul annoyance and furnishes abundance of that Carolina plague, mosquitoes. There may be forty or fifty houses, most of them small and built without expense. A citizen here is counted extravagant if he has ambition enough to aspire to a brick chimney. Justice herself is but indifferently lodged, the courthouse having much of the air of a common tobacco house. I believe this is the only metropolis in the Christian or Mahometan world where there is neither church, chapel, mosque, synagogue, or any other place of public worship of any sect or religion whatsoever. What little devotion there may happen to be is much more private than their vices. The people seem easy without a minister as long as they are exempted from paying him. Sometimes the Society for Propagating the Gospel has had the charity to send over missionaries to this country; but, unfortunately, the priest has been too lewd for the people, or, which oftener happens, they too lewd for the priest. For these reasons these reverend gentlemen have always left their flocks as arrant heathen as they found them. Thus much, however, may be said for the inhabitants of Edenton, that not a soul has the least taint of hypocrisy or superstition, acting very frankly and aboveboard in all their exercises.

Provisions here are extremely cheap and extremely good, so that people may live plentifully at a trifling expense. Nothing is dear but law, physic, and strong drink, which are all bad in their kind, and the last they get with so much difficulty that they are never guilty of the sin of suffering it to sour upon their hands. Their vanity generally lies not so much in having a handsome dining room as a handsome house of office: in this kind of structure they are really extravagant. They are rarely guilty of flattering or making any court to their governors but treat them with all the excesses of freedom and familiarity.

They are of opinion their rulers would be apt to grow insolent if they grew rich, and for that reason take care to keep them poorer and more dependent, if possible, than the saints in New England used to do their governors. They have very little coin, so they are forced to carry on their home traffic with paper money. This is the only cash that will tarry in the country, and for that reason the discount goes on increasing between that and real money and will do so to the end of the chapter.

28. Our time passed heavily in our quarters, where we were quite cloyed with the Carolina felicity of having nothing to do. It was really more insupportable than the greatest fatigue and made us even envy the drudgery of our friends in the Dismal. Besides, though the men we had with us were kept in exact discipline and behaved without reproach, yet our landlord began to be tired of them, fearing they would breed a famine in his family. Indeed, so many keen stomachs made great havoc amongst the beef and bacon which he had laid in for his summer provision, nor could he easily purchase more at that time of the year with the money we paid him, because people having no certain market seldom provide any more of these commodities than will barely supply their own occasions. Besides the weather was now grown too warm to lay in a fresh stock so late in the spring. These considerations abated somewhat of that cheerfulness with which he bid us welcome in the beginning and made him think the time quite as long as we did till the surveyors returned.

While we were thus all hands uneasy, we were comforted with the news that this afternoon the line was finished through the Dismal. The messenger told us it had been the hard work of three days to measure the length of only five miles and mark the trees as they passed along; and by the most exact survey they found the breadth of the Dismal in this place to be completely fifteen miles. How wide it may be in other parts, we can give no account, but believe it grows narrower toward the north; possibly toward Albemarle Sound it may be something broader, where so many rivers issue out of it. All we know for certain is that from the place where the line entered the Dismal to where it came out we found the road round that portion of it which belongs to Virginia to be about sixty-five miles. How great the distance may be from each of those points round that part that falls within the bounds of Carolina we had no certain information, though 'tis conjectured it cannot be so little as thirty miles. At which rate the whole circuit must be about an hundred. What a mass of mud and dirt is treasured up within this filthy circumference, and what a quantity of water must perpetually drain into it from the rising ground that surrounds it on every side! Without taking the exact level of the Dismal, we may be sure that it declines toward the places where the several rivers take their rise, in order to carrying off the constant supplies of water. Were it not for such discharges, the whole swamp would long since have been converted into a lake. On the other side this declension must be very gentle, else it would be laid perfectly dry by so many continual drains; whereas, on the contrary, the ground seems everywhere to be thoroughly drenched even in the driest season of the year. The surveyors concluded this day's work with running twenty-five chains up into the firm land, where they waited farther orders from the commissioners.

29. This day the surveyors proceeded with the line no more than one mile and fifteen chains, being interrupted by a mill swamp, through which they made no difficulty of wading in order to make their work more exact. Thus, like Norway mice,[26] these worthy gentlemen went right forward, without suffering themselves to be turned out of the way by any obstacle whatever. We are told by some travelers that those mice march in mighty armies, destroying all the fruits of the earth as they go along. But something peculiar to those obstinate little animals is that nothing stops them in their career, and if a house happen to stand in their way, disdaining to go an inch about, they crawl up one side of it and down the other, or if they meet with any river or other body of water they are so determined that they swim directly over it, without varying one point from their course for the sake of any safety or convenience. The surveyors were also hindered some time by setting up posts in the great road to show the bounds between the two colonies.

[26] Byrd describes the migrations of the lemming in periods of food scarcity.

Our chaplain returned to us in the evening from Edenton in company with the Carolina commissioners. He had preached there in the courthouse, for want of a consecrated place, and made no less than nineteen of Father Hennepin's Christians.[27]

By the permission of the Carolina commissioners, Mr. Swann was allowed to go home as soon as the survey of the Dismal was finished; he met with this indulgence for a reason that might very well have excused his coming at all: namely, that he was lately married. What remained of the drudgery for this season was left to Mr. Moseley, who had hitherto acted only in the capacity of a commissioner. They offered to employ Mr. Joseph Mayo as their surveyor in Mr. Swann's stead, but he thought it not proper to accept of it, because he had hitherto acted as a volunteer in behalf of Virginia and did not care to change sides, though it might have been to his advantage.

30. The line was advanced this day six miles and thirty-five chains, the woods being pretty clear and interrupted with no swamp or other wet ground. The land hereabouts had all the marks of poverty, being for the most part sandy and full of pines. This kind of ground, though unfit for ordinary tillage, will however bring cotton and potatoes in plenty, and consequently food and raiment to such as are easily contented and, like the wild Irish, find more pleasure in laziness than luxury. It also makes a shift to produce Indian corn, rather by the felicity of the climate than by the fertility of the soil. They who are more industrious than their neighbors may make what quantity of tar they please, though indeed they are not always sure of a market for it. The method of burning tar in Sweden and Muscovy succeeds not well in this warmer part of the world. It seems they kill the pine trees by barking them quite round at a certain height, which in those cold countries brings down the turpentine into the stump in a year's

[27] The Franciscan friar Louis Hennepin, who accompanied LaSalle on his western expedition in 1678, reported pessimistically on the prospect of converting the American Indians: "They will suffer themselves to be baptized ten times a Day for a Glass of Brandy, or a Pipe of Tobacco, and offer their children to be baptiz'd, but all without any Religious Motive" (quoted from *A New Discovery of a West Country in America*, edited by Reuben G. Thwaites [Chicago, 1903], II, 460). Hennepin's original narrative was entitled *Description de la Louisiane* (Paris, 1683); an English edition appeared in 1696.

time. But experience has taught us that in warm climates the turpentine will not so easily descend but is either fixed in the upper parts of the tree or fried out by the intense heat of the sun.

Care was taken to erect a post in every road that our line ran through, with Virginia carved on the north side of it and Carolina on the south, that the bounds might everywhere appear. In the evening the surveyors took up their quarters at the house of one Mr. Parker, who, by the advantage of a better spot of land than ordinary and a more industrious wife, lives comfortably and has a very neat plantation.

31. It rained a little this morning, but this, happening again upon a Sunday, did not interrupt our business. However the surveyors made no scruple of protracting and platting off their work upon that good day, because it was rather an amusement than a drudgery. Here the men feasted on the fat of the land and, believing the dirtiest part of their work was over, had a more than ordinary gaiety of heart. We christened two of our landlord's children, which might have remained infidels all their lives had not we carried Christianity home to his own door. The truth of it is, our neighbors of North Carolina are not so zealous as to go much out of their way to procure this benefit for their children; otherwise, being so near Virginia, they might without exceeding much trouble make a journey to the next clergyman upon so good an errand. And, indeed, should the neighboring ministers, once in two or three years, vouchsafe to take a turn among these gentiles to baptize them and their children, 'twould look a little apostolical, and they might hope to be requited for it hereafter, if that be not thought too long to tarry for their reward.

APRIL

1. The surveyors, getting now upon better ground quite disengaged from underwoods, pushed on the line almost twelve miles. They left Somerton Chapel near two miles to the northward, so that there was now no place of public worship left in the whole province of North Carolina.

The high land of North Carolina was barren and covered with a deep sand, and the low grounds were wet and boggy, insomuch that several of our horses were mired and gave us frequent opportunities to show our horsemanship.

The line cut William Speight's plantation in two, leaving little more than his dwelling house and orchard in Virginia. Sundry other plantations were split in the same unlucky manner, which made the owners accountable to both governments. Wherever we passed we constantly found the borderers laid it to heart if their land was taken into Virginia; they chose much rather to belong to Carolina, where they pay no tribute, either to God or to Caesar. Another reason was that the government there is so loose and the laws are so feebly executed that, like those in the neighborhood of Sidon formerly, everyone does just what seems good in his own eyes. If the Governor's hands have been weak in that province, under the authority of the Lords Proprietors, much weaker, then, were the hands of the magistrate, who, though he might have had virtue enough to endeavor to punish offenders, which very rarely happened, yet that virtue had been quite impotent for want of ability to put it in execution. Besides, there might have been some danger, perhaps, in venturing to be so rigorous, for fear of undergoing the fate of an honest justice in Currituck precinct. This bold magistrate, it seems, taking upon him to order a fellow to the stocks for being disorderly in his drink, was for his intemperate zeal carried thither himself and narrowly escaped being whipped by the rabble into the bargain.

This easy day's work carried the line to the banks of Somerton Creek, that runs out of Chowan River a little below the mouth of Nottoway.

2. In less than a mile from Somerton Creek the line was carried to Blackwater, which is the name of the upper part of Chowan, running some miles above the mouth of Nottoway. It must be observed that Chowan, after taking a compass round the most beautiful part of North Carolina, empties itself into Albemarle Sound a few miles above Edenton. The tide flows seven or eight miles higher than where the river changes its name and is navigable thus high for any small vessel. Our line intersected it exactly half a mile to the northward of the mouth of Nottoway. However, in obedience to His Majesty's command, we directed the surveyors to come down the river as far as the

mouth of Nottoway in order to continue our true-west line from thence. Thus we found the mouth of Nottoway to lie no more than half a minute farther to the northward than Mr. Lawson [28] had formerly done. That gentleman's observation, it seems, placed it in 36° 30′, and our working made it out to be 36° 30½′ — a very inconsiderable variance.

The surveyors crossed the river over against the middle of the mouth of Nottoway, where it was about eighty yards wide. From thence they run the line about half a mile through a dirty pocosin as far as an Indian field. Here we took up our lodging in a moist situation, having the pocosin above-mentioned on one side of us and a swamp on the other.

In this camp three of the Meherrin Indians made us a visit. They told us that the small remains of their nation had deserted their ancient town, situated near the mouth of the Meherrin River, for fear of the Catawbas, who had killed fourteen of their people the year before; and the few that survived that calamity had taken refuge amongst the English on the east side of Chowan. Though if the complaint of these Indians were true, they are hardly used by our Carolina friends. But they are the less to be pitied because they have ever been reputed the most false and treacherous to the English of all the Indians in the neighborhood.

Not far from the place where we lay, I observed a large oak which had been blown up by the roots, the body of which was shivered into perfect strings and was, in truth, the most violent effect of lightning I ever saw.

But the most curious instance of that dreadful meteor happened at York, where a man was killed near a pine tree in which the lightning made a hole before it struck the man and left an exact figure of the tree upon his breast, with all its branches, to the wonder of all that beheld it; in which I shall be more particular hereafter.

We made another trial of the variation in this place and found it

[28] John Lawson, Surveyor General of North Carolina, was one of the North Carolina commissioners who made an effort to determine the boundary line between Virginia and North Carolina in 1710. Lawson wrote a narrative first published in London in 1709, *A New Voyage to Carolina*, which contains valuable information about the physical terrain and the North Carolina Indians. Byrd reports Lawson's ultimate fate at the hands of the Indians, who felt he had cheated them, on p. 303.

some minutes less than we had done at Currituck Inlet; but so small a difference might easily happen through some defect in one or other of the observations, and therefore we altered not our compass for the matter.

3. By the advantage of clear woods the line was extended twelve miles and three-quarters, as far as the banks of Meherrin. Though the mouth of this river lie fifteen miles below the mouth of Nottoway, yet it winds so much to the northward that we came upon it after running this small distance.

During the first seven miles we observed the soil to be poor and sandy, but as we approached Meherrin it grew better, though there it was cut to pieces by sundry miry branches which discharge themselves into that river. Several of our horses plunged up to the saddle skirts and were not disengaged without difficulty.

The latter part of our day's work was pretty laborious because of the unevenness of the way and because the low ground of the river was full of cypress snags, as sharp and dangerous to our horses as so many *chevaux de frise*. We found the whole distance from the mouth of Nottoway to Meherrin River, where our line intersected it, thirteen miles and a quarter.

It was hardly possible to find a level large enough on the banks of the river whereupon to pitch our tent. But though the situation was, on that account, not very convenient for us, yet it was for our poor horses, by reason of the plenty of small reeds on which they fed voraciously. These reeds are green here all the year round and will keep cattle in tolerable good plight during the winter. But whenever the hogs come where they are they destroy them in a short time by plowing up their roots, of which, unluckily, they are very fond.

The river was in this place about as wide as the river Jordan, that is, forty yards, and would be navigable very high for flat-bottom boats and canoes, if it were not choked up with large trees brought down by every fresh. Though the banks were full twenty feet high from the surface of the water, yet we saw certain marks of their having been overflowed. These narrow rivers that run high up into the country are subject to frequent inundations, when the waters are rolled down with such violence as to carry all before them. The logs that are then floated are very fatal to the bridges built over these rivers, which can hardly be contrived strong enough to stand against so much weight and violence joined together.

The Isle of Wight County begins about three miles to the east of Meherrin River, being divided from that of Nansemond only by a line of marked trees.

4. The river was here hardly fordable, though the season had been very dry. The banks, too, were so steep that our horses were forced to climb like mules to get up them. Nevertheless we had the luck to recover the opposite shore without damage.

We halted for half an hour at Charles Anderson's, who lives on the western banks of the river, in order to christen one of his children. In the meantime, the surveyors extended the line two miles and thirty-nine chains,[29] in which small distance Meherrin River was so serpentine that they crossed it three times. Then we went on to Mr. Kinchen's, a man of figure and authority in North Carolina, who lives about a mile to the southward of the place where the surveyors left off. By the benefit of a little pains and good management, this worthy magistrate lives in much affluence. Amongst other instances of his industry, he had planted a good orchard, which is not common in that indolent climate; nor is it at all strange that such improvident people, who take no thought for the morrow, should save themselves the trouble to make improvements that will not pay them for several years to come. Though if they could trust futurity for anything, they certainly would for cider, which they are so fond of that they generally drink it before it has done working lest the fermentation might unluckily turn it sour.

It is an observation which rarely fails of being true, both in Virginia and Carolina, that those who take care to plant good orchards are in their general characters industrious people. This held good in our landlord, who had many houses built on this plantation and every one kept in decent repair. His wife, too, was tidy, his furniture clean, his pewter bright, and nothing seemed to be wanting to make his home comfortable.

Mr. Kinchen made us the compliment of his house, but because we

[29] The surveyor's chain measures four rods.

were willing to be as little troublesome as possible, we ordered the tent to be pitched in his orchard, where the blossoms of the apple trees contributed not a little to the sweetness of our lodging.

5. Because the spring was now pretty forward and the rattlesnakes began to crawl out of their winter quarters and might grow dangerous both to the men and their horses, it was determined to proceed no farther with the line till the fall. Besides, the uncommon fatigue the people had undergone for near six weeks together and the inclination they all had to visit their respective families made a recess highly reasonable.

The surveyors were employed great part of the day in forming a correct and elegant map of the line from Currituck Inlet to the place where they left off. On casting up the account in the most accurate manner, they found the whole distance we had run to amount to seventy-three miles and thirteen chains. Of the map they made two fair copies, which, agreeing exactly, were subscribed by the commissioners of both colonies, and one of them was delivered to those on the part of Virginia and the other to those on the part of North Carolina.

6. Thus we finished our spring campaign, and having taken leave of our Carolina friends and agreed to meet them again the tenth of September following at the same Mr. Kinchen's in order to continue the line, we crossed Meherrin River near a quarter of a mile from the house. About ten miles from that we halted at Mr. Kindred's plantation, where we christened two children.

It happened that some of Isle of Wight militia were exercising in the adjoining pasture, and there were females enough attending that martial appearance to form a more invincible corps. Ten miles farther we passed Nottoway River at Bolton's Ferry and took up our lodgings about three miles from thence at the house of Richard Parker, an honest planter whose labors were rewarded with plenty, which, in this country, is the constant portion of the industrious.

7. The next day being Sunday, we ordered notice to be sent to all the neighborhood that there would be a sermon at this place and an opportunity of christening their children. But the likelihood of rain

got the better of their devotion and, what perhaps might still be a stronger motive, of their curiosity. In the morning we dispatched a runner to the Nottoway town to let the Indians know we intended them a visit that evening, and our honest landlord was so kind as to be our pilot thither, being about four miles from his house. Accordingly, in the afternoon we marched in good order to the town, where the female scouts, stationed on an eminence for that purpose, had no sooner spied us but they gave notice of our approach to their fellow citizens by continual whoops and cries, which could not possibly have been more dismal at the sight of their most implacable enemies. This signal assembled all their great men, who received us in a body and conducted us into the fort.

This fort was a square piece of ground, enclosed with substantial puncheons or strong palisades about ten feet high and leaning a little outwards to make a scalade more difficult. Each side of the square might be about a hundred yards long, with loopholes at proper distances through which they may fire upon the enemy. Within this enclosure we found bark cabins sufficient to lodge all their people in case they should be obliged to retire thither. These cabins are no other but close arbors made of saplings, arched at the top and covered so well with bark as to be proof against all weather. The fire is made in the middle, according to the Hibernian fashion, the smoke whereof finds no other vent but at the door and so keeps the whole family warm, at the expense both of their eyes and complexion. The Indians have no standing furniture in their cabins but hurdles to repose their persons upon which they cover with mats or deerskins. We were conducted to the best apartments in the fort, which just before had been made ready for our reception and adorned with new mats that were very sweet and clean.

The young men had painted themselves in a hideous manner, not so much for ornament as terror. In that frightful equipage they entertained us with sundry war dances, wherein they endeavored to look as formidable as possible. The instrument they danced to was an Indian drum, that is, a large gourd with a skin braced taut[30] over the mouth

[30] The manuscript reads "tort," an erroneous variant form of "taut."

of it. The dancers all sang to this music, keeping exact time with their feet while their head and arms were screwed into a thousand menacing postures.

Upon this occasion the ladies had arrayed themselves in all their finery. They were wrapped in their red and blue matchcoats, thrown so negligently about them that their mahogany skins appeared in several parts, like the Lacedaemonian damsels of old. Their hair was braided with white and blue peak and hung gracefully in a large roll upon their shoulders.

This peak consists of small cylinders cut out of a conch shell, drilled through and strung like beads. It serves them both for money and jewels, the blue being of much greater value than the white for the same reason that Ethiopian mistresses in France are dearer than French, because they are more scarce. The women wear necklaces and bracelets of these precious materials when they have a mind to appear lovely. Though their complexions be a little sad-colored, yet their shapes are very straight and well proportioned. Their faces are seldom handsome, yet they have an air of innocence and bashfulness that with a little less dirt would not fail to make them desirable. Such charms might have had their full effect upon men who had been so long deprived of female conversation but that the whole winter's soil was so crusted on the skins of those dark angels that it required a very strong appetite to approach them. The bear's oil with which they anoint their persons all over makes their skins soft and at the same time protects them from every species of vermin that use to be troublesome to other uncleanly people.

We were unluckily so many that they could not well make us the compliment of bedfellows according to the Indian rules of hospitality, though a grave matron whispered one of the commissioners very civilly in the ear that if her daughter had been but one year older she should have been at his devotion. It is by no means a loss of reputation among the Indians for damsels that are single to have intrigues with the men; on the contrary, they account it an argument of superior merit to be liked by a great number of gallants. However, like the ladies that game,[31] they are a little mercenary in their amours and seldom bestow

[31] Engage in prostitution.

their favors out of stark love and kindness. But after these women have once appropriated their charms by marriage, they are from thenceforth faithful to their vows and will hardly ever be tempted by an agreeable gallant or be provoked by a brutal or even by a fumbling husband to go astray.

The little work that is done among the Indians is done by the poor women, while the men are quite idle or at most employed only in the gentlemanly diversions of hunting and fishing. In this, as well as in their wars, they now use nothing but firearms, which they purchase of the English for skins. Bows and arrows are grown into disuse, except only amongst their boys. Nor is it ill policy, but on the contrary very prudent, thus to furnish the Indians with firearms, because it makes them depend entirely upon the English, not only for their trade but even for their subsistence. Besides, they were really able to do more mischief while they made use of arrows, of which they would let silently fly several in a minute with wonderful dexterity, whereas now they hardly ever discharge their firelocks more than once, which they insidiously do from behind a tree and then retire as nimbly as the Dutch horse used to do now and then formerly in Flanders.

We put the Indians to no expense but only of a little corn for our horses, for which in gratitude we cheered their hearts with what rum we had left, which they love better than they do their wives and children. Though these Indians dwell among the English and see in what plenty a little industry enables them to live, yet they choose to continue in their stupid idleness and to suffer all the inconveniences of dirt, cold, and want rather than disturb their heads with care or defile their hands with labor.

The whole number of people belonging to the Nottoway town, if you include women and children, amount to about two hundred. These are the only Indians of any consequence now remaining within the limits of Virginia. The rest are either removed or dwindled to a very inconsiderable number, either by destroying one another or else by the smallpox and other diseases. Though nothing has been so fatal to them as their ungovernable passion for rum, with which, I am sorry to say it, they have been but too liberally supplied by the English that live near them.

And here I must lament the bad success Mr. Boyle's charity has hitherto had toward converting any of these poor heathens to Christianity.[32] Many children of our neighboring Indians have been brought up in the College of William and Mary. They have been taught to read and write and been carefully instructed in the principles of the Christian religion till they came to be men. Yet after they returned home, instead of civilizing and converting the rest, they have immediately relapsed into infidelity and barbarism themselves.

And some of them, too, have made the worst use of the knowledge they acquired among the English by employing it against their benefactors. Besides, as they unhappily forget all the good they learn and remember the ill, they are apt to be more vicious and disorderly than the rest of their countrymen.

I ought not to quit this subject without doing justice to the great prudence of Colonel Spotswood in this affair. That gentleman was Lieutenant Governor of Virginia when Carolina was engaged in a bloody war with the Indians. At that critical time it was thought expedient to keep a watchful eye upon our tributary savages, who we knew had nothing to keep them to their duty but their fears. Then it was that he demanded of each nation a competent number of their great men's children to be sent to the College, where they served as so many hostages for the good behavior of the rest and at the same time were themselves principled in the Christian religion. He also placed a schoolmaster among the Saponi Indians, at the salary of £50 per annum, to instruct their children. The person that undertook that charitable work was Mr. Charles Griffin, a man of a good family, who by the innocence of his life and the sweetness of his temper was perfectly well qualified for that pious undertaking. Besides, he had so much the secret of mixing pleasure with instruction that he had not a scholar who did not love him affectionately. Such talents must needs

---

[32] Robert Boyle, the English philosopher-scientist, left money in his will to be used for the propagation of Christianity among the heathen. James Blair used his influence with the trustees of Boyle's estate to have the College of William and Mary made the chief beneficiary of the money. Brafferton Hall, where Indians were to be schooled, was built in 1723 from this bequest; see Hugh Jones, *The Present State of Virginia*, edited by Richard L. Morton (Chapel Hill, 1956), pp. 185–186.

have been blest with a proportionable success, had he not been unluckily removed to the College, by which he left the good work he had begun unfinished. In short, all the pains he had taken among the infidels had no other effect but to make them something cleanlier than other Indians are.

The care Colonel Spotswood took to tincture the Indian children with Christianity produced the following epigram, which was not published during his administration for fear it might then have looked like flattery.

> Long has the furious priest assayed in vain,
> With sword and faggot, infidels to gain,
> But now the milder soldier wisely tries
> By gentler methods to unveil their eyes.
> Wonders apart, he knew 'twere vain t'engage
> The fixed preventions of misguided age.
> With fairer hopes he forms the Indian youth
> To early manners, probity, and truth.
> The lion's whelp thus, on the Libyan shore,
> Is tamed and gentled by the artful Moor,
> Not the grim sire, inured to blood before.

I am sorry I can't give a better account of the state of the poor Indians with respect to Christianity, although a great deal of pains has been and still continues to be taken with them. For my part, I must be of opinion, as I hinted before, that there is but one way of converting these poor infidels and reclaiming them from barbarity, and that is charitably to intermarry with them, according to the modern policy of the Most Christian King in Canada and Louisiana. Had the English done this at the first settlement of the colony, the infidelity of the Indians had been worn out at this day with their dark complexions, and the country had swarmed with people more than it does with insects. It was certainly an unreasonable nicety that prevented their entering into so good-natured an alliance. All nations of men have the same natural dignity, and we all know that very bright talents may be lodged under a very dark skin. The principal difference between one people and another proceeds only from the different opportunities of improvement. The Indians by no means want understanding and are in their figure tall and well proportioned. Even their copper-colored complexion would admit of blanching, if not in the first, at the farthest in the second, generation. I may safely venture to say, the Indian women would have made altogether as honest wives for the first planters as the damsels they used to purchase from aboard the ships. 'Tis strange, therefore, that any good Christian should have refused a wholesome, straight bedfellow, when he might have had so fair a portion with her as the merit of saving her soul.

8. We rested on our clean mats very comfortably, though alone, and the next morning went to the toilet of some of the Indian ladies, where, what with the charms of their persons and the smoke of their apartments, we were almost blinded. They offered to give us silk-grass baskets of their own making, which we modestly refused, knowing that an Indian present, like that of a nun, is a liberality put out to interest and a bribe placed to the greatest advantage. Our chaplain observed with concern that the ruffles of some of our fellow travelers were a little discolored with puccoon,[33] wherewith the good man had been told those ladies used to improve their invisible charms.

About ten o'clock we march[ed] out of town in good order, and the war captains saluted us with a volley of small arms. From thence we proceeded over Blackwater Bridge to Colonel Henry Harrison's, where we congratulated each other upon our return into Christendom.

Thus ended our progress for this season, which we may justly say was attended with all the success that could be expected. Besides the punctual performance of what was committed to us, we had the pleasure to bring back every one of our company in perfect health. And this we must acknowledge to be a singular blessing, considering the difficulties and dangers to which they had been exposed. We had reason to fear the many waters and sunken grounds through which we were obliged to wade might have thrown the men into sundry acute distempers; especially the Dismal, where the soil was so full of

[33] The colonists seemed to apply the term "puccoon," in any number of spellings, to red dye used by the Indians, whatever the source of the coloring. They did not always identify it as a particular plant. Sometimes the Virginia pokeberry or poke-weed seems to be meant by the word. Another plant, *Sanguinaria canadensis*, provided a root which was also used for red dye.

water and the air so full of damps that nothing but a Dutchman could live in them. Indeed, the foundation of all our success was the exceeding dry season. It rained during the whole journey but rarely, and then, as when Herod built his temple, only in the night or upon the Sabbath, when it was no hindrance at all to our progress.

PART THE SECOND

SEPTEMBER

The tenth of September being thought a little too soon for the commissioners to meet in order to proceed on the line on account of snakes, 'twas agreed to put it off to the twentieth of the same month, of which due notice was sent to the Carolina commissioners.

19. We, on the part of Virginia, that we might be sure to be punctual, arrived at Mr. Kinchen's, the place appointed, on the nineteenth, after a journey of three days in which nothing remarkable happened. We found three of the Carolina commissioners had taken possession of the house, having come thither by water from Edenton. By the great quantity of provisions these gentlemen brought and the few men they had to eat them, we were afraid they intended to carry the line to the South Sea. They had five hundred pounds of bacon and dried beef and five hundred pounds of biscuit, and not above three or four men. The misfortune was, they forgot to provide horses to carry their good things, or else trusted to the uncertainty of hiring them here, which, considering the place, was leaving too much to that jilt, Hazard.

On our part we had taken better care, being completely furnished with everything necessary for transporting our baggage and provisions. Indeed, we brought no other provisions out with us but a thousand pounds of bread and had faith enough to depend on Providence for our meat, being desirous to husband the public money as much as possible. We had no less than twenty men, besides the chaplain, the surveyors, and all the servants, to be subsisted upon this bread. However, that it might hold out the better, our men had been ordered to provide themselves at home with provision for ten days, in which time we judged we should get beyond the inhabitants, where forest game of all sorts was like to be plenty at that time of the year.

20. This being the day appointed for our rendezvous, great part of it was spent in the careful fixing our baggage and assembling our men, who were ordered to meet us here. We took care to examine their arms and made proof of the powder provided for the expedition. Our provision horses had been hindered by the rain from coming up exactly at the day; but this delay was the less disappointment by reason of the ten days' subsistence the men had been directed to provide for themselves. Mr. Moseley did not join us till the afternoon nor Mr. Swann till several days after.

Mr. Kinchen had unadvisedly sold the men a little brandy of his own making, which produced much disorder, causing some to be too choleric and others too loving; insomuch that a damsel who assisted in the kitchen had certainly suffered what the nuns call martyrdom had she not capitulated a little too soon. This outrage would have called for some severe discipline, had she not bashfully withdrawn herself early in the morning and so carried off the evidence.

21. We dispatched away the surveyors without loss of time, who, with all their diligence, could carry the line no farther than 3 miles and 176 poles, by reason the low ground was one entire thicket. In that distance they crossed Meherrin River the fourth time. In the meanwhile, the Virginia commissioners thought proper to conduct their baggage a farther way about for the convenience of a clearer road.

The Carolina gentlemen did at length, more by fortune than forecast, hire a clumsy vehicle, something like a cart, to transport their effects as far as Roanoke. This wretched machine, at first setting-out, met with a very rude shock that broke a case bottle of cherry brandy in so unlucky a manner that not one precious drop was saved. This melancholy beginning foreboded an unprosperous journey and too quick a return to the persons most immediately concerned.

In our way we crossed Fontaine Creek, which runs into Meherrin River, so called from the disaster of an unfortunate Indian trader who had formerly been drowned in it.[34] We took up our quarters on the plantation of John Hill, where we pitched our tent, with design to tarry till such time as the surveyors could work their way to us.

22. This being Sunday, we had an opportunity of resting from our labors. The expectation of such a novelty as a sermon in these parts brought together a numerous congregation. When the sermon was over, our chaplain did his part toward making eleven of them Christians.

Several of our men had intermitting fevers but were soon restored to their health again by proper remedies. Our chief medicine was dogwood bark, which we used, instead of that of Peru, with good success. Indeed, it was given in large quantity, but then, to make the patients amends, they swallowed much fewer doses.

In the afternoon our provision horses arrived safe in the camp. They had met with very heavy rains but, thank God, not a single biscuit received the least damage thereby. We were furnished by the neighbors with very lean cheese and very fat mutton, upon which occasion 'twill not be improper to draw one conclusion from the evidence of North Carolina, that sheep would thrive much better in the woods than in pasture land, provided a careful shepherd were employed to keep them from straying and, by the help of dogs, to protect them also from the wolves.

23. The surveyors came to us at night, though they had not brought the line so far as our camp, for which reason we thought it needless to go forward till they came up with us. They could run no more than four miles and five poles, because the ground was everywhere grown up with thick bushes. The soil here appeared to be very good, though much broken betwixt Fontaine Creek and Roanoke River. The line crossed Meherrin the fifth and last time; nor were our people sorry to part with a stream the meanders of which had given them so much trouble.

Our hunters brought us four wild turkeys, which at that season began to be fat and very delicious, especially the hens. These birds

[34] Possibly John Fontaine, who accompanied Alexander Spotswood on his expedition in 1716 to explore the Virginia hinterland.

seem to be of the bustard kind and fly heavily. Some of them are exceedingly large and weigh upwards of forty pounds; nay, some bold historians venture to say upwards of fifty. They run very fast, stretching forth their wings all the time, like the ostrich, by way of sails to quicken their speed. They roost commonly upon very high trees, standing near some river or creek, and are so stupefied at the sight of fire that, if you make a blaze in the night near the place where they roost, you may fire upon them several times successively before they will dare to fly away. Their spurs are so sharp and strong that the Indians used formerly to point their arrows with them, though now they point them with a sharp white stone. In the spring the turkey cocks begin to gobble, which is the language wherein they make love.

It rained very hard in the night with a violent storm of thunder and lightning, which obliged us to trench in our tent all round to carry off the water that fell upon it.

24. So soon as the men could dry their blankets we sent out the surveyors, who, now meeting with more favorable grounds, advanced the line seven miles and eighty-two poles. However, the commissioners did not think proper to decamp that day, believing they might easily overtake the surveyors the next. In the meantime, they sent out some of their most expert gunners, who brought in four more wild turkeys.

This part of the country being very proper for raising cattle and hogs, we observed the inhabitants lived in great plenty without killing themselves with labor. I found near our camp some plants of that kind of rattlesnake root called star grass. The leaves shoot out circularly and grow horizontally and near the ground. The root is in shape not unlike the rattle of that serpent and is a strong antidote against the bite of it. It is very bitter and where it meets with any poison works by violent sweats, but where it meets with none has no sensible operation but that of putting the spirits into a great hurry and so of promoting perspiration. The rattlesnake hath an utter antipathy to this plant, insomuch that if you smear your hands with the juice of it, you may handle the viper safely. Thus much I can say on my own experience: that once in July, when these snakes are in their greatest vigor, I besmeared a dog's nose with the powder of this root and made him trample on a large snake several times, which, however, was so far from biting him that it perfectly sickened at the dog's approach and turned its head from him with the utmost aversion.

Our chaplain, to show his zeal, made an excursion of six miles to christen two children, but without the least regard to the good cheer at these solemnities.

25. The surveyors, taking the advantage of clear woods, pushed on the line seven miles and forty poles. In the meantime the commissioners marched with the baggage about twelve miles and took up their quarters near the banks of the Beaver Pond (which is one branch of Fontaine Creek), just by the place where the surveyors were to finish their day's work. In our march one of the men killed a small rattlesnake, which had no more than two rattles. Those vipers remain in vigor generally till toward the end of September, or sometimes later if the weather continue a little warm. On this consideration we had provided three several sorts of rattlesnake root, made up into proper doses and ready for immediate use, in case any one of the men or their horses had been bitten. We crossed Fontaine Creek once more in our journey this day and found the grounds very rich, notwithstanding they were broken and stony. Near the place where we encamped, the county of Brunswick is divided from the Isle of Wight. These counties run quite on the back of Surry and Prince George and are laid out in very irregular figures. As a proof the land mended hereabouts, we found the plantations began to grow thicker by much than we had found them lower down.

26. We hurried away the surveyors without loss of time, who extended the line 10 miles and 160 poles, the grounds proving dry and free from underwoods. By the way the chain carriers killed two more rattlesnakes, which I own was a little ungrateful, because two or three of the men had strided over them without receiving any hurt, though one of these vipers had made bold to strike at one of the baggage horses as he went along, but by good luck his teeth only grazed on the hoof without doing him any damage. However, these accidents were, I think, so many arguments that we had very good

reason to defer our coming out till the twentieth of September. We observed abundance of St.-Andrew's-cross in all the woods we passed through, which is the common remedy used by the Indian traders to cure their horses when they are bitten by rattlesnakes. It grows on a straight stem about eighteen inches high and bears a yellow flower on the top that has an eye of black in the middle, with several pairs of narrow leaves shooting out at right angles from the stock over against one another. This antidote grows providentially all over the woods and upon all sorts of soil, that it may be everywhere at hand in case a disaster should happen, and may be had all the hot months while the snakes are dangerous.

About four o'clock in the afternoon we took up our quarters upon Cabin Branch, which also discharges itself into Fontaine Creek. On our way we observed several meadows clothed with very rank grass and branches full of tall reeds, in which cattle keep themselves fat good part of the winter. But hogs are as injurious to both as goats are said to be to vines, and for that reason it was not lawful to sacrifice them to Bacchus. We halted by the way to christen two children at a spring, where their mothers waylaid us for that good purpose.

27. It was ten of the clock before the surveyors got to work, because some of the horses had straggled a great distance from the camp. Nevertheless, meeting with practicable woods, they advanced the line 9 miles and 104 poles. We crossed over Pea Creek about four miles from our quarters and three miles farther Lizard Creek, both which empty their waters into Roanoke River. Between these two creeks a poor man waited for us with five children to be baptized, and we halted till the ceremony was ended. The land seemed to be very good, by the largeness of the trees, though very stony. We proceeded as far as Pigeon Roost Creek, which also runs into Roanoke, and there quartered.

We had not the pleasure of the company of any of the Carolina commissioners in this day's march except Mr. Moseley's, the rest tarrying behind to wait the coming up of their baggage cart, which they had now not seen nor heard (though the wheels made a dismal noise) for several days past. Indeed, it was a very difficult undertaking to conduct a cart through such pathless and perplexed woods, and no wonder if its motion was a little planetary. We would have paid them the compliment of waiting for them, could we have done it at any other expense but that of the public.

In the stony grounds we rode over we found great quantity of the true ipecacuanha, which in this part of the world is called Indian physic. This has several stalks growing up from the same root about a foot high, bearing a leaf resembling that of a strawberry. It is not so strong as that from Brazil but has the same happy effects if taken in somewhat a larger dose. It is an excellent vomit and generally cures intermitting fevers and bloody fluxes at once or twice taking. There is abundance of it in the upper part of the country, where it delights most in a stony soil intermixed with black mold.

28. Our surveyors got early to work, yet could forward the line but 6 miles and 121 poles because of the uneven grounds in the neighborhood of Roanoke, which they crossed in this day's work. In that place the river is forty-nine poles wide and rolls down a crystal stream of very sweet water, insomuch that when there comes to be a great monarch in this part of the world, he will cause all the water for his own table to be brought from Roanoke, as the great kings of Persia did theirs from the Nile and Choaspes, because the waters of those rivers were light and not apt to corrupt. The same humor prevails at this day in the kings of Denmark, who order all the East India ships of that nation to call at the Cape of Good Hope and take in a butt of water from a spring on the Table Hill and bring it to Copenhagen for Their Majesties' own drinking.

The great falls of Roanoke lie about twenty miles lower, to which a sloop of moderate burden may come up. There are, besides these, many smaller falls above, though none that entirely intercept the passage of the river, as the great ones do by a chain of rocks for eight miles together. The river forks about thirty-six miles higher, and both branches are pretty equal in breadth where they divide, though the southern, now called the Dan, runs up the farthest. That to the north runs away near northwest and is called the Staunton, and heads not far from the source of Appomattox River, while the Dan stretches away pretty near west and runs clear through the great mountains.

We did not follow the surveyors till toward noon, being detained in our camp to christen several more children. We were conducted a nearer way by a famous woodsman called Epaphroditus Bainton. This forester spends all his time in ranging the woods and is said to make great havoc among the deer and other inhabitants of the forest not much wilder than himself.

We proceeded to the canoe landing on Roanoke, where we passed the river with the baggage. But the horses were directed to a ford about a mile higher, called by the Indians Moniseep, which signifies in their jargon "shallow water." This is the ford where the Indian traders used to cross with their horses in their way to the Catawba nation. There are many rocks in the river thereabouts, on which grows a kind of water grass, which the wild geese are fond of and resort to it in great numbers.

We landed on the south side of Roanoke at a plantation of Colonel Mumford's, where by that gentleman's special directions we met with sundry refreshments. Here we pitched our tent, for the benefit of the prospect, upon an eminence that overlooked a broad piece of low ground, very rich, though liable to be overflowed.

By the way one of our men killed another rattlesnake with eleven rattles, having a large gray squirrel in his maw, the head of which was already digested while the body remained still entire. The way these snakes catch their prey is thus: they ogle the poor little animal till by force of the charm he falls down stupefied and senseless on the ground. In that condition the snake approaches and moistens first one ear and then the other with his spawl, and after that the other parts of the head to make all slippery. When that is done, he draws this member into his mouth and after it, by slow degrees, all the rest of the body.

29. This being Sunday, we had divine service and a sermon, at which several of the borderers assisted, and we concluded the duties of the day with christening five children. Our devotion being performed in the open field, like that of Mr. Whitefield's flocks, an unfortunate shower of rain had almost dispersed our congregation.

About four in the afternoon, the Carolina commissioners made a shift to come up with us, whom we had left at Pigeon Roost Creek the Friday before, waiting for their provisions. When their cart came up, they prudently discharged it and rather chose to hire two men to carry some part of their baggage. The rest they had been obliged to leave behind in the crotch of an old tree for want of proper conveniences to transport it any farther.

We found in the low ground several plants of the fern root, which is said to be much the strongest antidote yet discovered against the poison of the rattlesnake. The leaves of it resemble those of fern, from whence it obtained its name. Several stalks shoot from the same root, about six inches long, that lie mostly on the ground. It grows in a very rich soil, under the protection of some tall tree that shades it from the meridian beams of the sun. The root has a faint spicy taste and is preferred by the southern Indians to all other counterpoisons in this country. But there is another sort preferred by the northern Indians that they call Seneca rattlesnake root,[35] to which wonderful virtues are ascribed in the cure of pleurisies, fevers, rheumatisms, and dropsies, besides it being a powerful antidote against the venom of the rattlesnake.

In the evening the messenger we had sent to Christanna returned with five Saponi Indians.[36] We could not entirely rely on the dexterity of our own men, which induced us to send for some of the Indians. We agreed with two of the most expert of them upon reasonable terms to hunt for us the remaining part of our expedition. But one of them falling sick soon after, we were content to take only the other, whose hunting name was Bearskin. This Indian, either by his skill or good luck, supplied us plentifully all the way with meat, seldom discharging his piece in vain. By his assistance, therefore, we were able to keep our men to their business, without suffering them to straggle about the woods on pretense of furnishing us with necessary food.

30. It had rained all night and made everything so wet that our surveyors could not get to their work before noon. They could there-

[35] *Polygala senega.*

[36] Byrd has not mentioned this in the *History*; but see p. 101 of the *Secret History.*

fore measure no more than 4 miles and 220 poles, which, according to the best information we could get, was near as high as the uppermost inhabitant at that time.

We crossed the Indian trading path above-mentioned about a mile from our camp and a mile beyond that forded Hawtree Creek. The woods we passed through had all the tokens of sterility, except a small poisoned field on which grew no tree bigger than a slender sapling. The larger trees had been destroyed either by fire or caterpillar, which is often the case in the upland woods, and the places where such desolation happens are called poisoned fields. We took up our quarters upon a branch of Great Creek, where there was tolerable good grass for the poor horses. These poor animals, having now got beyond the latitude of corn, were obliged to shift as well as they could for themselves.

On our way the men roused a bear, which being the first we had seen since we came out, the poor beast had many pursuers. Several persons contended for the credit of killing him, though he was so poor he was not worth the powder. This was some disappointment to our woodsmen, who commonly prefer the flesh of bears to every kind of venison. There is something indeed peculiar to this animal, namely, that its fat is very firm and may be eaten plentifully without rising in the stomach. The paw (which when stripped of the hair looks like a human foot) is accounted a delicious morsel by all who are not shocked at the ungracious resemblance it bears to a human foot.

OCTOBER

1. There was a white frost this morning on the ground, occasioned by a northwest wind, which stood our friend in dispersing all aguish damps and making the air wholesome at the same time that it made it cold. Encouraged, therefore, by the weather, our surveyors got to work early and, by the benefit of clear woods and level ground, drove the line twelve miles and twelve poles.

At a small distance from our camp we crossed Great Creek and about seven miles farther Nutbush Creek, so called from the many hazel trees growing upon it. By good luck, many branches of these creeks were full of reeds, to the great comfort of our horses. Near five miles from thence we encamped on a branch that runs into Nutbush Creek, where those reeds flourished more than ordinary. The land we marched over was for the most part broken and stony and in some places covered over with thickets almost impenetrable.

At night the surveyors, taking advantage of a very clear sky, made a third trial of the variation and found it still something less than three degrees; so that it did not diminish by advancing toward the west or by approaching the mountains, nor yet by increasing our distance from the sea, but remained much the same we had found it at Currituck Inlet.

One of our Indians killed a large fawn, which was very welcome, though, like Hudibras' horse, it had hardly flesh enough to cover its bones.

In the low grounds the Carolina gentlemen showed us another plant, which they said was used in their country to cure the bite of the rattlesnake. It put forth several leaves in figure like a heart and was clouded so like the common Asarabacca that I conceived it to be of that family.

2. So soon as the horses could be found, we hurried away the surveyors, who advanced the line 9 miles and 254 poles. About three miles from the camp they crossed a large creek, which the Indians called Massamony, signifying in their language "Paint Creek," because of the great quantity of red ocher found in its banks. This in every fresh tinges the water, just as the same mineral did formerly, and to this day continues to tinge, the famous river Adonis in Phoenicia, by which there hangs a celebrated fable.

Three miles beyond that we passed another water with difficulty called Yapatsco or Beaver Creek. Those industrious animals had dammed up the water so high that we had much ado to get over. 'Tis hardly credible how much work of this kind they will do in the space of one night. They bite young saplings into proper lengths with their foreteeth, which are exceeding strong and sharp, and afterwards drag them to the place where they intend to stop the water. Then they know how to join timber and earth together with so much skill that their work is able to resist the most violent flood that can happen. In this they are qualified to instruct their betters, it being certain their dams will stand firm when the strongest that are made by men will be carried down the stream. We observed very broad, low grounds upon this creek, with a growth of large trees and all the other signs of fertility, but seemed subject to be everywhere overflowed in a fresh. The certain way to catch these sagacious animals is this: squeeze all the juice out of the large pride of the beaver and six drops out of the small pride. Powder the inward bark of sassafras and mix it with this juice; then bait therewith a steel trap and they will eagerly come to it and be taken.

About three miles and an half farther we came to the banks of another creek, called in the Saponi language Ohimpamony, signifying "Jumping Creek," from the frequent jumping of fish during the spring season.

Here we encamped, and by the time the horses were hobbled our hunters brought us no less than a brace and an half of deer, which made great plenty and consequently great content in our quarters. Some of our people had shot a great wildcat, which was that fatal moment making a comfortable meal upon a fox squirrel, and an ambitious sportsman of our company claimed the merit of killing this monster after it was dead. The wildcat is as big again as any household cat and much the fiercest inhabitant of the woods. Whenever it is disabled, it will tear its own flesh for madness. Although a panther will run away from a man, a wildcat will only make a surly retreat, now and then facing about if he be too closely pursued, and will even pursue in his turn if he observe the least sign of fear or even of caution in those that pretend to follow him. The flesh of this beast, as well as of the panther, is as white as veal and altogether as sweet and delicious.

3. We got to work early this morning and carried the line 8 miles and 160 poles. We forded several runs of excellent water and afterwards traversed a large level of high land, full of lofty walnut, poplar, and white oak trees, which are certain proofs of a fruitful soil. This level was near two miles in length and of an unknown breadth, quite

out of danger of being overflowed, which is a misfortune most of the low grounds are liable to in those parts. As we marched along, we saw many buffalo tracks and abundance of their dung very fresh but could not have the pleasure of seeing them. They either smelt us out, having that sense very quick, or else were alarmed at the noise that so many people must necessarily make in marching along. At the sight of a man they will snort and grunt, cock up their ridiculous short tails, and tear up the ground with a sort of timorous fury. These wild cattle hardly ever range alone but herd together like those that are tame. They are seldom seen so far north as forty degrees of latitude, delighting much in canes and reeds which grow generally more southerly.

We quartered on the banks of a creek that the inhabitants call Tewahominy or Tuskarooda [37] Creek, because one of that nation had been killed thereabouts and his body thrown into the creek.

Our people had the fortune to kill a brace of does, one of which we presented to the Carolina gentlemen, who were glad to partake of the bounty of Providence at the same time that they sneered at us for depending upon it.

4. We hurried away the surveyors about nine this morning, who extended the line 7 miles and 160 poles, notwithstanding the ground was exceedingly uneven. At the distance of five miles we forded a stream to which we gave the name of Bluewing Creek because of the great number of those fowls that then frequented it.[38] About two and a half miles beyond that, we came upon Sugartree Creek, so called from the many trees of that kind that grow upon it. By tapping this tree in the first warm weather in February, one may get from twenty to forty gallons of liquor, very sweet to the taste and agreeable to the stomach. This may be boiled into molasses first and afterwards into very good sugar, allowing about ten gallons of liquor to make a pound. There is no doubt, too, that a very fine spirit may be distilled from the molasses, at least as good as rum. The sugar tree delights only in rich ground, where it grows very tall, and by the softness and sponginess

[37] The manuscript gives variant spellings of this Indian name, now normalized to Tuscarora.
[38] The bluewinged teal.

of the wood should be a quick grower. Near this creek we discovered likewise several spice trees, the leaves of which are fragrant and the berries they bear are black when dry and of a hot taste, not much unlike pepper. The low grounds upon the creek are very wide, sometimes on one side, sometimes on the other, though most commonly upon the opposite shore the high land advances close to the bank, only on the north side of the line it spreads itself into a great breadth of rich low ground on both sides the creek for four miles together, as far as this stream runs into Hyco River, whereof I shall presently make mention. One of our men spied three buffaloes, but his piece being loaded only with goose shot, he was able to make no effectual impression on their thick hides; however, this disappointment was made up by a brace of bucks and as many wild turkeys killed by the rest of the company. Thus Providence was very bountiful to our endeavors, never disappointing those that faithfully rely upon it and pray heartily for their daily bread.

5. This day we met with such uneven grounds and thick underwoods that with all our industry we were able to advance the line but 4 miles and 312 poles. In this small distance it intersected a large stream four times, which our Indian at first mistook for the south branch of Roanoke River; but, discovering his error soon after, he assured us 'twas a river called Hycootomony, or Turkey Buzzard River, from the great number of those unsavory birds that roost on the tall trees growing near its banks.

Early in the afternoon, to our very great surprise, the commissioners of Carolina acquainted us with their resolution to return home. This declaration of theirs seemed the more abrupt because they had not been so kind as to prepare us by the least hint of their intention to desert us. We therefore let them understand they appeared to us to abandon the business they came about with too much precipitation, this being but the fifteenth day since we came out the last time. But although we were to be so unhappy as to lose the assistance of their great abilities, yet we, who were concerned for Virginia, determined, by the grace of God, not to do our work by halves but, all deserted as we were like to be, should think it our duty to push the line quite to the mountains; and if their government should refuse to be bound by so much of the line as was run without their commissioners, yet at least it would bind Virginia and stand as a direction how far His Majesty's lands extend to the southward. In short, these gentlemen were positive, and the most we could agree upon was to subscribe plats of our work as far as we had acted together; though at the same time we insisted these plats should be got ready by Monday noon at farthest, when we on the part of Virginia intended, if we were alive, to move forward without farther loss of time, the season being then too far advanced to admit of any unnecessary or complaisant delays.

6. We lay still this day, being Sunday, on the bank of Hyco River and had only prayers, our chaplain not having spirits enough to preach. The gentlemen of Carolina assisted not at our public devotions, because they were taken up all the morning in making a formidable protest against our proceeding on the line without them. When the divine service was over, the surveyors set about making the plats of so much of the line as we had run this last campaign. Our pious friends of Carolina assisted in this work with some seeming scruple, pretending it was a violation of the Sabbath, which we were the more surprised at because it happened to be the first qualm of conscience they had ever been troubled with during the whole journey. They had made no bones of staying from prayers to hammer out an unnecessary protest, though divine service was no sooner over but an unusual fit of godliness made them fancy that finishing the plats, which was now matter of necessity, was a profanation of the day. However, the expediency of losing no time, for us who thought it our duty to finish what we had undertaken, made such a labor pardonable.

In the afternoon, Mr. Fitzwilliam, one of the commissioners for Virginia, acquainted his colleagues it was his opinion that by His Majesty's order they could not proceed farther on the line but in conjunction with the commissioners of Carolina; for which reason he intended to retire the next morning with those gentlemen. This looked a little odd in our brother commissioner; though, in justice to him as well as to our Carolina friends, they stuck by us as long as our good liquor lasted and were so kind to us as to drink our good journey to the mountains in the last bottle we had left.

7. The duplicates of the plats could not be drawn fair this day

before noon, where they were countersigned by the commissioners of each government. Then those of Carolina delivered their protest, which was by this time licked into form and signed by them all. And we have been so just to them as to set it down at full length in the Appendix, that their reasons for leaving us may appear in their full strength. After having thus adjusted all our affairs with the Carolina commissioners and kindly supplied them with bread to carry them back, which they hardly deserved at our hands, we took leave both of them and our colleague, Mr. Fitzwilliam. This gentleman had still a stronger reason for hurrying him back to Williamsburg, which was that neither the General Court might lose an able judge nor himself a double salary, not despairing in the least but he should have the whole pay of commissioner into the bargain, though he did not half the work. This, to be sure, was relying more on the interest of his friends than on the justice of his cause; in which, however, he had the misfortune to miscarry when it came to be fairly considered.

It was two o'clock in the afternoon before these arduous affairs could be dispatched, and then, all forsaken as we were, we held on our course toward the west. But it was our misfortune to meet with so many thickets in this afternoon's work that we could advance no further than 2 miles and 260 poles. In this small distance we crossed the Hyco the fifth time and quartered near Buffalo Creek, so named from the frequent tokens we discovered of that American behemoth. Here the bushes were so intolerably thick that we were obliged to cover the bread bags with our deerskins, otherwise the joke of one of the Indians must have happened to us in good earnest: that in a few days we must cut up our house to make bags for the bread and so be forced to expose our backs in compliment to our bellies. We computed we had then biscuit enough left to last us, with good management, seven weeks longer; and this being our chief dependence, it imported us to be very careful both in the carriage and the distribution of it.

We had now no other drink but what Adam drank in Paradise, though to our comfort we found the water excellent, by the help of which we perceived our appetites to mend, our slumbers to sweeten, the stream of life to run cool and peaceably in our veins, and if ever we dreamt of women, they were kind.

Our men killed a very fat buck and several turkeys. These two kinds of meat boiled together, with the addition of a little rice or French barley, made excellent soup, and, what happens rarely in other good things, it never cloyed, no more than an engaging wife would do, by being a constant dish. Our Indian was very superstitious in this matter and told us, with a face full of concern, that if we continued to boil venison and turkey together we should for the future kill nothing, because the spirit that presided over the woods would drive all the game out of our sight. But we had the happiness to find this an idle superstition, and though his argument could not convince us, yet our repeated experience at last, with much ado, convinced him.

We observed abundance of coltsfoot and maidenhair in many places and nowhere a larger quantity than here. They are both excellent pectoral plants and seem to have greater virtues much in this part of the world than in more northern climates; and I believe it may pass for a rule in botanics that where any vegetable is planted by the hand of Nature it has more virtue than in places whereto it is transplanted by the curiosity of man.

8. Notwithstanding we hurried away the surveyors very early, yet the underwoods embarrassed them so much that they could with difficulty advance the line four miles and twenty poles. Our clothes suffered extremely by the bushes, and it was really as much as both our hands could do to preserve our eyes in our heads. Our poor horses, too, could hardly drag their loads through the saplings, which stood so close together that it was necessary for them to draw and carry at the same time. We quartered near a spring of very fine water, as soft as oil and as cold as ice, to make us amends for the want of wine. And our Indian knocked down a very fat doe, just time enough to hinder us from going supperless to bed.

The heavy baggage could not come up with us because of the excessive badness of the ways. This gave us no small uneasiness, but it went worse with the poor men that guarded it. They had nothing in the world with them but dry bread, nor durst they eat any of that for fear of inflaming their thirst in a place where they could find no water to quench it. This was, however, the better to be endured because it was the first fast anyone had kept during the whole journey, and then, thanks to the gracious guardian of the woods, there was no more than a single meal lost to a few of the company.

We were entertained this night with the yell of a whole family of wolves, in which we could distinguish the treble, tenor, and bass very clearly. These beasts of prey kept pretty much upon our track, being tempted by the garbage of the creatures we killed every day, for which we were serenaded with their shrill pipes almost every night. This beast is not so untamable as the panther, but the Indians know how to gentle their whelps and use them about their cabins instead of dogs.

9. The thickets were hereabouts so impenetrable that we were obliged, at first setting-off this morning, to order four pioneers to clear the way before the surveyors. But after about two miles of these rough woods, we had the pleasure to meet with open grounds, and not very uneven, by the help of which we were enabled to push the line about six miles. The baggage that lay short of our camp last night came up about noon, and the men made heavy complaints that they had been half-starved, like Tantalus in the midst of plenty, for the reason above-mentioned.

The soil we passed over this day was generally very good, being clothed with large trees of poplar, hickory, and oak. But another certain token of its fertility was that wild angelica grew plentifully upon it. The root of this plant, being very warm and aromatic, is coveted by woodsmen extremely as a dry dram, that is, when rum, that cordial for all distresses, is wanting.

Several deer came into our view as we marched along, but none into the pot, which made it necessary for us to sup on the fragments we had been so provident as to carry along with us. This, being but a temperate repast, made some of our hungry fellows call the place we lodged at that night Bread-and-Water Camp.

A great flock of cranes flew over our quarters, that were exceeding clamorous in their flight. They seem to steer their course toward the south (being birds of passage) in quest of warmer weather. They only took this country in their way, being as rarely met with in this part of the world as a highwayman or a beggar. These birds travel generally in flocks, and when they roost they place sentinels upon some of the highest trees, which constantly stand upon one leg to keep themselves waking. Nor are these birds the only animals that appoint scouts to keep the main body from being surprised. For the baboons, whenever they go upon any mischievous expedition, such as robbing an orchard, they place sentinels to look out toward every point of the compass and give notice of any danger. Then, ranking themselves in one file that reaches from the mountain where they harbor to the orchard they intend to rob, some of them toss the fruit from the trees to those that stand nearest; these throw them to the next, and so from one to tother till the fruit is all secured in a few minutes out of harm's way. In the meantime, if any of the scouts should be careless at their posts and suffer any surprise, they are torn to pieces without mercy. In case of danger, these sentinels set up a fearful cry, upon which the rest take the alarm and scour away to the mountains as fast as they can.

Our Indian killed nothing all day but a mountain partridge, which a little resembled the common partridge in the plumage but was near as large as a dunghill hen. These are very frequent toward the mountains, though we had the fortune to meet with very few. They are apt to be shy and consequently the noise of so great a number of people might easily scare them away from our sight. We found what we conceived to be good limestone in several places and a great quantity of blue slate.

10. The day began very fortunately by killing a fat doe and two brace of wild turkeys; so the plenty of the morning made amends for the short commons overnight. One of the new men we brought out with us the last time was unfortunately heard to wish himself at home and for that show of impatience was publicly reprimanded at the head of the men, who were all drawn up to witness his disgrace. He was asked how he came so soon to be tired of the company of so many

brave fellows and whether it was the danger or the fatigue of the journey that disheartened him? This public reproof from thenceforward put an effectual stop to all complaints, and not a man amongst us after that pretended so much as to wish himself in Paradise.

A small distance from our camp we crossed a pleasant stream of water called Cockade Creek, and something more than a mile from thence our line intersected the south branch of Roanoke River the first time, which we called the Dan. It was about two hundred yards wide where we forded it, and when we came over to the west side we found the banks lined with a forest of tall canes that grew more than a furlong in depth. So that it cost us abundance of time and labor to cut a passage through them wide enough for our baggage.

In the meantime, we had leisure to take a full view of this charming river. The stream, which was perfectly clear, ran down about two knots, or two miles, an hour when the water was at the lowest. The bottom was covered with a coarse gravel, spangled very thick with a shining substance that almost dazzled the eye, and the sand upon either shore sparkled with the same splendid particles. At first sight, the sunbeams, giving a yellow cast to these spangles, made us fancy them to be gold dust and consequently that all our fortunes were made. Such hopes as these were the less extravagant because several rivers lying much about the same latitude with this have formerly abounded with fragments of that tempting metal. Witness the Tagus in Portugal, the Heber[39] in Thrace, and the Pactolus in Lesser Asia; not to mention the rivers on the Gold Coast in Africa, which lie in a more southern climate. But we soon found ourselves mistaken, and our gold dust dwindled into small flakes of isinglass. However, though this did not make the river so rich as we could wish, yet it made it exceedingly beautiful.

We marched about two miles and a half beyond this river as far as Cane Creek, so called from a prodigious quantity of tall canes that fringed the banks of it. On the west side of this creek we marked out our quarters and were glad to find our horses fond of the canes, though they scoured them smartly at first and discolored their dung. This

[39] The Hebrus.

beautiful vegetable grows commonly from thirteen to sixteen feet high, and some of them as thick as a man's wrist. Though these appeared large to us, yet they are no more than spires of grass, if compared to those which some curious travelers tell us grow in the East Indies, one joint of which will make a brace of canoes if sawed in two in the middle. Ours continue green through all the seasons during the space of six years and the seventh shed their seed, wither away, and die. The spring following they begin to shoot again and reach their former stature the second or third year after. They grow so thick and their roots lace together so firmly that they are the best guard that can be of the riverbank, which would otherwise be washed away by the frequent inundations that happen in this part of the world. They would also serve excellently well to plant on the borders of fishponds and canals to secure their sides from falling in; though I fear they would not grow kindly in a cold country, being seldom seen here so northerly as thirty-eight degrees of latitude.

11. At the distance of four miles and sixty poles from the place where we encamped, we came upon the river Dan a second time, though it was not so wide in this place as where we crossed it first, being not above 150 yards over. The west shore continued to be covered with the canes above-mentioned but not to so great a breadth as before, and 'tis remarkable that these canes are much more frequent on the west side of the river than on the east, where they grow generally very scattering. It was still a beautiful stream, rolling down its limpid and murmuring waters among the rocks, which lay scattered here and there to make up the variety of the prospect.

It was about two miles from this river to the end of our day's work, which led us mostly over broken grounds and troublesome underwoods. Hereabout, from one of the highest hills we made the first discovery of the mountains on the northwest of our course. They seemed to lie off at a vast distance and looked like ranges of blue clouds rising one above another.

We encamped about two miles beyond the river, where we made good cheer upon a very fat buck that luckily fell in our way. The Indian likewise shot a wild turkey but confessed he would not bring it us lest we should continue to provoke the guardian of the forest by cooking the beasts of the field and the birds of the air together in one vessel. This instance of Indian superstition, I confess, is countenanced in some measure by the Levitical law, which forbade the mixing things of a different nature together in the same field or in the same garment, and why not, then, in the same kettle? But, after all, if the jumbling of two sorts of flesh together be a sin, how intolerable an offense must it be to make a Spanish olla, that is, a hotchpotch of every kind of thing that is eatable? And the good people of England would have a great deal to answer for for beating up so many different ingredients into a pudding.

12. We were so cruelly entangled with bushes and grapevines all day that we could advance the line no farther than five miles and twenty-eight poles. The vines grew very thick in these woods, twining lovingly round the trees almost everywhere, especially to the saplings. This makes it evident how natural both the soil and climate of this country are to vines, though I believe most to our own vines. The grapes we commonly met with were black, though there be two or three kinds of white grapes that grow wild. The black are very sweet but small, because the strength of the vine spends itself in wood, though without question a proper culture would make the same grapes both larger and sweeter. But, with all these disadvantages, I have drunk tolerable good wine pressed from them, though made without skill.[40] There is then good reason to believe it might admit of great improvement if rightly managed.

Our Indian killed a bear, two years old, that was feasting on these grapes. He was very fat, as they generally are in that season of the year. In the fall the flesh of this animal has a high relish different from

[40] The English colonists made continuing efforts to develop a wine industry. The first explorers of the American continent were impressed by the abundance of grapes, and from the time of Raleigh's expeditions until the end of the colonial period efforts were made to plant vineyards and produce wine. Byrd's brother-in-law, Robert Beverley, attempted to establish a vineyard, as did other Virginians, including Byrd himself. See William Strachey, *Historie of Travell into Virginia Britania*, edited by Louis B. Wright and Virginia Freund (London, 1953), pp. 121–122; for Beverley, Hugh Jones, *Present State of Virginia*, pp. 91, 140; *American Husbandry* (1775), edited by Harry J. Carman (New York, 1939), pp. 192–193, 194; and Louis B. Wright, *The Dream of Prosperity in Colonial America* (New York, 1965), *passim*.

that of other creatures, though inclining nearest to that of pork, or rather of wild boar. A true woodsman prefers this sort of meat to that of the fattest venison, not only for the *haut goût*, but also because the fat of it is well tasted and never rises in the stomach. Another proof of the goodness of this meat is that it is less apt to corrupt than any other we are acquainted with.

As agreeable as such rich diet was to the men, yet we who were not accustomed to it tasted it at first with some sort of squeamishness, that animal being of the dog kind, though a little use soon reconciled us to this American venison. And that its being of the dog kind might give us the less disgust, we had the example of that ancient and polite people, the Chinese, who reckon dog's flesh too good for any under the quality of a mandarin. This beast is in truth a very clean feeder, living, while the season lasts, upon acorns, chestnuts, and chinquapins, wild honey and wild grapes. They are naturally not carnivorous, unless hunger constrain them to it after the mast is all gone and the product of the woods quite exhausted. They are not provident enough to lay up any hoard like the squirrels, nor can they, after all, live very long upon licking their paws, as Sir John Mandeville and some travelers tell us, but are forced in the winter months to quit the mountains and visit the inhabitants. Their errand is then to surprise a poor hog at a pinch to keep them from starving. And to show that they are not flesh eaters by trade, they devour their prey very awkwardly. They don't kill it right out and feast upon its blood and entrails, like other ravenous beasts, but, having, after a fair pursuit, seized it with their paws, they begin first upon the rump and so devour one collop after another till they come to the vitals, the poor animal crying all the while for several minutes together. However, in so doing, Bruin acts a little imprudently, because the dismal outcry of the hog alarms the neighborhood, and 'tis odds but he pays the forfeit with his life before he can secure his retreat.

But bears soon grow weary of this unnatural diet, and about January, when there is nothing to be gotten in the woods, they retire into some cave or hollow tree, where they sleep away two or three months very comfortably. But then they quit their holes in March, when the fish begin to run up the rivers, on which they are forced to keep Lent till some fruit or berry comes in season. But bears are fondest of chestnuts, which grow plentifully toward the mountains, upon very large trees, where the soil happens to be rich. We were curious to know how it happened that many of the outward branches of those trees came to be broke off in that solitary place and were informed that the bears are so discreet as not to trust their unwieldy bodies on the smaller limbs of the tree that would not bear their weight, but after venturing as far as is safe, which they can judge to an inch, they bite off the end of the branch, which falling down, they are content to finish their repast upon the ground. In the same cautious manner they secure the acorns that grow on the weaker limbs of the oak. And it must be allowed that in these instances a bear carries instinct a great way and acts more reasonably than many of his betters, who indiscreetly venture upon frail projects that won't bear them.

13. This being Sunday, we rested from our fatigue and had leisure to reflect on the signal mercies of Providence.

The great plenty of meat wherewith Bearskin furnished us in these lonely woods made us once more shorten the men's allowance of bread from five to four pounds of biscuit a week. This was the more necessary because we knew not yet how long our business might require us to be out.

In the afternoon our hunters went forth and returned triumphantly with three brace of wild turkeys. They told us they could see the mountains distinctly from every eminence, though the atmosphere was so thick with smoke that they appeared at a greater distance than they really were.

In the evening we examined our friend Bearskin concerning the religion of his country, and he explained it to us without any of that reserve to which his nation is subject. He told us he believed there was one supreme god, who had several subaltern deities under him. And that this master god made the world a long time ago. That he told the sun, the moon, and stars their business in the beginning, which they, with good looking-after, have faithfully performed ever since. That the same power that made all things at first has taken care to keep them in the same method and motion ever since. He believed that God had formed many worlds before he formed this, but that those worlds either grew old and ruinous or were destroyed for the dishonesty of the inhabitants. That God is very just and very good, ever well pleased with those men who possess those godlike qualities. That he takes good people into his safe protection, makes them very rich, fills their bellies plentifully, preserves them from sickness and from being surprised or overcome by their enemies. But all such as tell lies and cheat those they have dealings with he never fails to punish with sickness, poverty, and hunger and, after all that, suffers them to be knocked on the head and scalped by those that fight against them.

He believed that after death both good and bad people are conducted by a strong guard into a great road, in which departed souls travel together for some time till at a certain distance this road forks into two paths, the one extremely level and the other stony and mountainous. Here the good are parted from the bad by a flash of lightning, the first being hurried away to the right, the other to the left. The right-hand road leads to a charming, warm country, where the spring is everlasting and every month is May; and as the year is always in its youth, so are the people, and particularly the women are bright as stars and never scold. That in this happy climate there are deer, turkeys, elks, and buffaloes innumerable, perpetually fat and gentle, while the trees are loaded with delicious fruit quite throughout the four seasons. That the soil brings forth corn spontaneously, without the curse of labor, and so very wholesome that none who have the happiness to eat of it are ever sick, grow old, or die. Near the entrance into this blessed land sits a venerable old man on a mat richly woven, who examines strictly all that are brought before him, and if they have behaved well, the guards are ordered to open the crystal gate and let them enter into the land of delight. The left-hand path is very rugged and uneven, leading to a dark and barren country where it is always winter. The ground is the whole year round covered with snow, and nothing is to be seen upon the trees but icicles. All the people are hungry yet have not a morsel of anything to eat except a bitter kind of potato, that gives them the dry gripes and fills their whole body with loathsome ulcers that stink and are insupportably painful. Here all the women are old and ugly, having claws like a panther with which they fly upon the men that slight their passion. For it seems these haggard old furies are intolerably fond and expect a vast deal of cherishing. They talk much and exceedingly shrill, giving exquisite pain to the drum of the ear, which in that place of the torment is so tender that every sharp note wounds it to the quick. At the end of this path sits a dreadful old woman on a monstrous toadstool, whose head is covered with rattlesnakes instead of tresses, with glaring white eyes that strike a terror unspeakable into all that behold her. This hag pronounces sentence of woe upon all the miserable wretches that hold up their hands at her tribunal. After this they are delivered over to huge turkey buzzards, like harpies, that fly away with them to the place above-mentioned. Here, after they have been tormented a certain number of years according to their several degrees of guilt, they are again driven back into this world to try if they will mend their manners and merit a place the next time in the regions of bliss.

This was the substance of Bearskin's religion and was as much to the purpose as could be expected from a mere state of nature, without one glimpse of revelation or philosophy. It contained, however, the three great articles of natural religion: the belief of a god, the moral distinction betwixt good and evil, and the expectation of rewards and punishments in another world. Indeed, the Indian notion of a future happiness is a little gross and sensual, like Mahomet's Paradise. But how can it be otherwise in a people that are contented with Nature as they find her and have no other lights but what they receive from purblind tradition?

14. There having been great signs of rain yesterday evening, we had taken our precautions in securing the bread and trenching in our tent. The men had also stretched their blankets upon poles, penthouse fashion, against the weather, so that nobody was taken unprepared. It began to fall heavily about three o'clock in the morning and held not up till near noon. Everything was so thoroughly soaked that we laid aside all thoughts of decamping that day.

This gave leisure to the most expert of our gunners to go and try their fortunes, and they succeeded so well that they returned about noon with three fat deer and four wild turkeys. Thus Providence took care of us, and however short the men might be in their bread, 'tis certain they had meat at full allowance. The cookery went on merrily all night long, to keep the damps from entering our pores; and, in truth, the impressions of the air are much more powerful upon empty stomachs. In such a glut of provisions, a true woodsman when he has nothing else to do, like our honest countrymen the Indians, keeps eating on, to avoid the imputation of idleness; though in a scarcity the Indian will fast with a much better grace than they. They can subsist several days upon a little rockahominy, which is parched Indian corn reduced to powder. This they moisten in the hollow of their hands with a little water, and 'tis hardly credible how small a quantity of it will support them. 'Tis true they grow a little lank upon it, but to make themselves feel full they gird up their loins very tight with a belt, taking up a hole every day. With this slender subsistence they are able to travel very long journeys; but then, to make themselves amends, when they do meet with better cheer they eat without ceasing till they have ravened themselves into another famine.

This was the first time we had ever been detained a whole day in our camp by the rain and therefore had reason to bear it with the more patience.

As I sat in the tent, I overheard a learned conversation between one of our men and the Indian. He ask[ed] the Englishman what it was that made that rumbling noise when it thundered. The man told him merrily that the god of the English was firing his great guns upon the god of the Indians, which made all that roaring in the clouds, and that the lightning was only the flash of those guns. The Indian, carrying on the humor, replied very gravely he believed that might be the case indeed, and that the rain which followed upon the thunder must be occasioned by the Indian god's being so scared he could not hold his water.

The few good husbands amongst us took some thought of their backs as well as their bellies and made use of this opportunity to put their habiliments in repair, which had suffered woefully by the bushes.

The horses got some rest by reason of the bad weather, but very little food, the chief of their forage being a little wild rosemary, which resembles the garden rosemary pretty much in figure but not at all in taste or smell. This plant grows in small tufts here and there on the barren land in these upper parts, and the horses liked it well, but the misfortune was, they could not get enough of it to fill their bellies.

15. After the clouds brake away in the morning, the people dried their blankets with all diligence. Nevertheless, it was noon before we were in condition to move forward and then were so puzzled with passing the river twice in a small distance that we could advance the line in all no farther than one single mile and three hundred poles. The first time we passed the Dan this day was 240 poles from the place where we lay, and the second time was one mile and seven poles beyond that. This was now the fourth time we forded that fine river, which still tended westerly, with many short and returning reaches.

The surveyors had much difficulty in getting over the river, finding it deeper than formerly. The breadth of it here did not exceed fifty yards. The banks were about twenty feet high from the water and beautifully beset with canes. Our baggage horses crossed not the river here at all but, fetching a compass, went round the bent of it. On our way we forded Sable Creek, so called from the dark color of the water, which happened, I suppose, by its being shaded on both sides with canes.

In the evening we quartered in a charming situation near the angle of the river, from whence our eyes were carried down both reaches, which kept a straight course for a great way together. This prospect was so beautiful that we were perpetually climbing up to a neighboring eminence that we might enjoy it in more perfection.

Now the weather grew cool, the wild geese began to direct their flight this way from Hudson's Bay and the lakes that lay northwest of us. They are very lean at their first coming but fatten soon upon a sort of grass that grows on the shores and rocks of this river. The Indians call this fowl "cohunks," from the hoarse note it has, and begin the year from the coming of the cohunks, which happens in the beginning of October. These wild geese are guarded from cold by a down that is exquisitely soft and fine, which makes them much more valuable for their feathers than for their flesh, which is dark and coarse.

The men chased a bear into the river, that got safe over, notwithstanding the continual fire from the shore upon him. He seemed to swim but heavily, considering it was for his life. Where the water is shallow 'tis no uncommon thing to see a bear sitting in the summertime on a heap of gravel in the middle of the river, not only to cool himself but likewise for the advantage of fishing, particularly for a small shellfish that is brought down with the stream. In the upper part of James River I have observed this several times, and wondered very much at first how so many heaps of small stones came to be piled up in the water, till at last we spied a bear sitting upon one of them, looking with great attention on the stream and raking up something with his paw, which I take to be the shellfish above-mentioned.

16. It was ten o'clock this morning before the horses could be found, having hid themselves among the canes, whereof there was great plenty just at hand. Not far from our camp we went over a brook whose banks were edged on both sides with these canes. But three miles farther we forded a larger stream, which we called Lowland Creek by reason of the great breadth of low grounds enclosed between that and the river.

The high land we traveled over was very good, and the low grounds promised the greatest fertility of any I had ever seen. At the end of 4 miles and 311 poles from where we lay, the line intersected the Dan the fifth time. We had day enough to carry it farther, but the surveyors could find no safe ford over the river. This obliged us to ride two miles up the river in quest of a ford, and by the way we traversed several small Indian fields, where we conjectured the Sauros had been used to plant corn, the town where they had lived lying seven or eight miles more southerly upon the eastern side of the river. These Indian fields produced a sweet kind of grass, almost knee-high, which was excellent forage for the horses. It must be observed, by the way, that Indian towns, like religious houses, are remarkable for a fruitful situation; for, being by nature not very industrious, they choose such a situation as will subsist them with the least labor.

The trees grew surprisingly large in this low ground, and amongst the rest we observed a tall kind of hickory, peculiar to the upper parts of the country. It is covered with a very rough bark and produces a nut with a thick shell that is easily broken. The kernel is not so rank as that of the common hickory but altogether as oily. And now I am upon the subject of these nuts, it may not be improper to remark that a very great benefit might be made of nut oil in this colony. The walnuts, the hickory nuts, and pignuts contain a vast deal of oil that might be pressed out in great abundance with proper machines. The trees grow very kindly [41] and may be easily propagated. They bear plenty of nuts every year that are now of no other use in the world but to feed hogs. 'Tis certain there is a large consumption of this oil in several of our manufactures, and in some parts of France, as well as in other countries, it is eaten instead of oil olive, being tolerably sweet and wholesome.

The Indian killed a fat buck, and the men brought in four bears and a brace of wild turkeys, so that this was truly a land of plenty both for man and beast.

17. We detached a party of men this morning early in search of a ford, who after all could find none that was safe; though, dangerous as it was, we determined to make use of it to avoid all farther delay. Accordingly we rode over a narrow ledge of rocks, some of which lay below the surface of the water and some above it. Those that lay under the water were as slippery as ice; and the current glided over them so swiftly that though it was only water it made us perfectly drunk. Yet we were all so fortunate as to get safe over to the west shore with no other damage than the sopping some of our bread by the flouncing of the horses. The tedious time spent in finding out this ford and in getting all the horses over it prevented our carrying the line more than 2 miles and 250 poles.

This was the last time we crossed the Dan with our line, which now began to run away more southerly with a very flush and plentiful stream, the description whereof must be left to future discoveries, though we are well assured by the Indians that it runs through the

---

[41] Naturally, spontaneously.

mountains. We conducted the baggage a roundabout way for the benefit of evener grounds, and this carried us over a broad level of exceeding rich land, full of large trees with vines married to them, if I may be allowed to speak so poetically.

We untreed a young cub in our march that made a brave stand against one of the best of our dogs. This and a fawn were all the game that came in our way.

In this day's journey, as in many others before, we saw beautiful marble of several colors, and particularly that of the purple kind with white streaks, and in some places we came across large pieces of pure alabaster.

We marked out our quarters on the banks of a purling stream, which we called Cascade Creek by reason of the multitude of waterfalls that are in it. But, different from all other falls that ever I met with, the rocks over which the water rolled were soft and would split easily into broad flakes, very proper for pavement; and some fragments of it seemed soft enough for hones and the grain fine enough.

Near our camp we found a prickly shrub rising about a foot from the ground, something like that which bears the barberry though much smaller. The leaves had a fresh, agreeable smell, and I am persuaded the ladies would be apt to fancy a tea made of them, provided they were told how far it came and at the same time were obliged to buy it very dear.[42]

About a mile to the southwest of our camp rose a regular mount that commanded a full prospect of the mountains and an extensive view of the flat country. But being, with respect to the high mountains, no more than a pimple, we called it by that name.

Presently, after sunset, we discovered a great light toward the west, too bright for a fire and more resembling the aurora borealis. This, all our woodsmen told us, it was a common appearance in the highlands and generally foreboded bad weather. Their explanation happened to be exactly true, for in the night we had a violent gale of wind, accompanied with smart hail that rattled frightfully amongst the trees, though it was not large enough to do us any harm.

[42] Byrd refers to the proverbial saying "Dear-bought and far-fetched are dainties for ladies."

18. We crossed Cascade Creek over a ledge of smooth rocks and then scuffled through a mighty thicket at least three miles long. The whole was one continued tract of rich high land, the woods whereof had been burnt not long before. It was then overgrown with saplings of oak, hickory, and locust, interlaced with grapevines. In this fine land, however, we met with no water, till at the end of three miles we luckily came upon a crystal stream which, like some lovers of conversation, discovered everything committed to its faithless bosom. Then we came upon a piece of rich low ground, covered with large trees, of the extent of half a mile, which made us fancy ourselves not far from the river; though after that we ascended gently to higher land, with no other trees growing upon it except butterwood, which is one species of white maple.

This, being a dead level without the least declivity to carry off the water, was moist in many places and produced abundance of grass. All our woodsmen call these flat grounds highland ponds and in their trading journeys are glad to halt at such places for several days together to recruit their jaded horses, especially in the winter months, when there is little or no grass to be found in other places. This highland pond extended above two miles, our palfreys snatching greedily at the tufts of grass as they went along.

After we got over this level, we descended some stony hills for about half a mile and then came upon a large branch of the river which we christened the Irvin, in honor of our learned professor. This river we forded with much difficulty and some danger, by reason of the hollow spaces betwixt the rocks, into which our horses plunged almost every step. The Irvin runs into the Dan about four miles to the southward of the line and seemed to roll down its waters from the north-northwest in a very full and limpid stream, and the murmur it made in tumbling over the rocks caused the situation to appear very romantic and had almost made some of the company poetical, though they drank nothing but water.

We encamped on a pleasant hill overlooking the river, which seemed to be deep everywhere except just where we forded. In the meantime, neither that chain of rocks nor any other that we could observe in this stream was so uninterrupted but that there were several breaks where a canoe, or even a moderate flat-bottomed boat, might shear clear. Nor have we reason to believe there are any other falls (except the great ones thirty miles below Moniseep Ford) that reach quite across so as to interrupt the navigation for small craft. And I have been informed that, even at those great falls, the blowing up a few rocks would open a passage at least for canoes, which certainly would be an unspeakable convenience to the inhabitants of all that beautiful part of the country.

The Indian killed a very fat doe and came across a bear, which had been put to death and was half devoured by a panther. The last of these brutes reigns absolute monarch of the woods and in the keenness of his hunger will venture to attack a bear; though then 'tis ever by surprise, as all beasts of the cat kind use to come upon their prey. Their play is to take the poor bears napping, they being very drowsy animals, and though they be exceedingly strong yet their strength is heavy, while the panthers are too nimble and cunning to trust themselves within their hug. As formidable as this beast is to his fellow brutes, he never hath the confidence to venture upon a man but retires from him with great respect, if there be a way open for his escape. However, it must be confessed his voice is a little contemptible for a monarch of the forest, being not a great deal louder nor more awful than the mewing of a household cat. Some authors who have given an account of the southern continent of America would make the world believe there are lions; but in all likelihood they were mistaken, imagining these panthers to be lions. What makes this probable is that the northern and southern parts of America being joined by the Isthmus of Darien, if there were lions in either they would find their way into the other, the latitudes of each being equally proper for that generous animal.

In South Carolina they call this beast a tiger, though improperly, and so they do in some parts of the Spanish West Indies. Some of their authors, a little more properly, compliment it with the name of a leopard. But none of these are the growth of America, that we know of.

The whole distance the surveyors advanced the line this day amounted to six miles and thirty poles, which was no small journey, considering the grounds we had traversed were exceedingly rough and uneven and in many places intolerably entangled with bushes.

All the hills we ascended were encumbered with stones, many of which seemed to contain a metallic substance, and the valleys we crossed were interrupted with miry branches. From the top of every hill we could discern distinctly, at a great distance to the northward, three or four ledges of mountains, rising one above another, and on the highest of all rose a single mountain, very much resembling a woman's breast.

19. About four miles beyond the river Irvin we forded Matrimony Creek, called so by an unfortunate married man because it was exceedingly noisy and impetuous. However, though the stream was clamorous, yet like those women who make themselves plainest heard, it was likewise perfectly clear and unsullied. Still half a mile farther we saw a small mountain about five miles to the northwest of us, which we called the Wart because it appeared no bigger than a wart in comparison of the great mountains which hid their haughty heads in the clouds.

We were not able to extend the line farther than 5 miles and 135 poles, notwithstanding we began our march early in the morning and did not encamp till it was almost dark. We made it the later by endeavoring to quarter in some convenient situation either for grass or canes. But night surprising us, we were obliged to lodge at last upon high and uneven ground, which was so overgrown with shrubs and saplings that we could hardly see ten yards around us. The most melancholy part of the story was that our horses had short commons. The poor creatures were now grown so weak that they staggered when we mounted them. Nor would our own fare have been at all more plentiful, had we not been so provident as to carry a load of meat along with us. Indeed, the woods were too thick to show us any sort of game but one wild turkey, which helped to enrich our soup. To make us amends, we found abundance of very sweet grapes, which, with the help of bread, might have furnished out a good Italian repast in the absence of more savory food.

The men's mouths watered at the sight of a prodigious flight of wild pigeons, which flew high over our heads to the southward.[43] The

[43] Many observers in early America commented on the numerous flights of passenger pigeons, which were easily killed by pot hunters and are now extinct.

flocks of these birds of passage are so amazingly great sometimes that they darken the sky, nor is it uncommon for them to light in such numbers in the larger limbs of mulberry trees and oaks as to break them down. In their travels they make vast havoc amongst the acorns and berries of all sorts that they waste whole forests in a short time and leave a famine behind them for most other creatures; and under some trees where they light, it is no strange thing to find the ground covered three inches thick with their dung. These wild pigeons commonly breed in the uninhabited parts of Canada and as the cold approaches assemble their armies and bend their course southerly, shifting their quarters, like many of the winged kind, according to the season. But the most remarkable thing in their flight, as we are told, is that they never have been observed to return to the northern countries the same way they came from thence but take another route, I suppose for their better subsistence. In these long flights they are very lean and their flesh is far from being white or tender, though good enough upon a march, when hunger is the sauce and makes it go down better than truffles and morels would do.

20. It was now Sunday, which we had like to have spent in fasting as well as prayer; for our men, taking no care for the morrow, like good Christians but bad travelers, had improvidently devoured all their meat for supper. They were ordered in the morning to drive up their horses, lest they should stray too far from the camp and be lost in case they were let alone all day. At their return they had the very great comfort to behold a monstrous fat bear, which the Indian had killed very seasonably for their breakfast. We thought it still necessary to make another reduction of our bread, from four to three pounds a week to every man, computing that we had still enough in that proportion to last us three weeks longer.

The atmosphere was so smoky all round us that the mountains were again grown invisible. This happened not from the haziness of the sky but from the firing of the woods by the Indians, for we were now near the route the northern savages take when they go out to war against the Catawbas and other southern nations. On their way, the fires they make in their camps are left burning, which, catching the dry leaves that lie near, soon put the adjacent woods into a flame. Some of our men in search of their horses discovered one of those Indian camps, where not long before they had been a-furring and dressing their skins.

And now I mention the northern Indians, it may not be improper to take notice of their implacable hatred to those of the south. Their wars are everlasting, without any peace, enmity being the only inheritance among them that descends from father to son, and either party will march a thousand miles to take their revenge upon such hereditary enemies. These long expeditions are commonly carried on in the following manner: some Indian remarkable for his prowess, that has raised himself to the reputation of a war captain, declares his intention of paying a visit to some southern nation; hereupon as many of the young fellows as have either a strong thirst of blood or glory list themselves under his command. With these volunteers he goes from one confederate town to another, listing all the rabble he can till he has gathered together a competent number for mischief. Their arms are a gun and tomahawk, and all the provisions they carry from home is a pouch of rockahominy. Thus provided and accoutered, they march toward the enemy's country, not in a body or by a certain path but straggling in small numbers for the greater convenience of hunting and passing along undiscovered. So soon as they approach the grounds on which the enemy is used to hunt, they never kindle any fire themselves for fear of being found out by the smoke, nor will they shoot at any kind of game, though they should be half famished, lest they might alarm their foes and put them upon their guard. Sometimes, indeed, while they are still at some distance, they roast either venison or bear till it is very dry and, then, having strung it on their belts, wear it round their middle, eating very sparingly of it because they know not when they shall meet with a fresh supply. But coming nearer, they begin to look all round the hemisphere to watch if any smoke ascends and listen continually for the report of guns, in order to make some happy discovery for their own advantage. 'Tis amazing to see their sagacity in discerning the track of a human foot, even amongst dry leaves, which to our shorter sight is quite undiscoverable. If by one or more of those signs they be able to find out the camp of any southern Indians, they squat down in some thicket and keep themselves hush and snug till it is dark; then, creeping up softly, they approach near enough to observe all the motions of the enemy. And about two o'clock in the morning, when they conceive them to be in a profound sleep, for they never keep watch and ward, pour in a volley upon them, each singling out his man. The moment they have discharged their pieces they rush in with their tomahawks and make sure work of all that are disabled. Sometime, when they find the enemy asleep round their little fire, they first pelt them with little stones to wake them, and when they get up, fire in upon them, being in that posture a better mark than when prostrate on the ground.

They that are killed of the enemy or disabled, they scalp: that is, they cut the skin all round the head just below the hair, and then, clapping their feet to the poor mortal's shoulders, pull the scalp off clean and carry it home in triumph, being as proud of those trophies as the Jews used to be of the foreskins of the Philistines. This way of scalping was practiced by the ancient Scythians, who used these hairy scalps as towels at home and trappings for their horses when they went abroad. They also made cups of their enemies' skulls, in which they drank prosperity to their country and confusion to all their foes.

The prisoners they happen to take alive in these expeditions generally pass their time very scurvily. They put them to all the tortures that ingenious malice and cruelty can invent. And (what shows the baseness of the Indian temper in perfection) they never fail to treat those with greatest inhumanity that have distinguished themselves most by their bravery, and if he be a war captain, they do him the honor to roast him alive and distribute a collop to all that had a share in stealing the victory. Though who can reproach the poor Indians for this, when Homer makes his celebrated hero, Achilles, drag the body of Hector at the tail of his chariot for having fought gallantly in defense of his country? Nor was Alexander the Great, with all his famed generosity, less inhuman to the brave Tyrians, two thousand of which he ordered to be crucified in cold blood for no other fault but for having defended their city most courageously against him during a siege of seven months. And what was still more brutal, he dragged —— alive at the tail of his chariot through all the streets, for defending the town with so much vigor.

They are very cunning in finding out new ways to torment their unhappy captives, though, like those of hell, their usual method is by fire. Sometimes they barbecue them over live coals, taking them off every now and then to prolong their misery; at other times they will stick sharp pieces of lightwood all over their bodies and, setting them on fire, let them burn down into the flesh to the very bone. And when they take a stout fellow that they believe able to endure a great deal, they will tear all the flesh off his bones with red-hot pincers. While these and suchlike barbarities are practicing, the victors are so far from being touched with tenderness and compassion that they dance and sing round these wretched mortals, showing all the marks of pleasure and jollity. And if such cruelties happen to be executed in their towns, they employ their children in tormenting the prisoners, in order to extinguish in them betimes all sentiments of humanity. In the meantime, while these poor wretches are under the anguish of all this inhuman treatment, they disdain so much as to groan, sigh, or show the least sign of dismay or concern so much as in their looks; on the contrary, they make it a point of honor all the time to soften their features and look as pleased as if they were in the actual enjoyment of some delight; and if they never sang before in their lives, they will be sure to be melodious on this sad and dismal occasion. So prodigious a degree of passive valor in the Indians is the more to be wondered at, because in all articles of danger they are apt to behave like cowards. And what is still more surprising, the very women discover on such occasions as great fortitude and contempt, both of pain and death, as the gallantest of their men can do.

21. The apprehensions we had of losing the horses in these copsewoods were too well founded, nor were the precautions we used yesterday of driving them up sufficient to prevent their straying away afterwards, notwithstanding they were securely hobbled. We therefore ordered the men out early this morning to look diligently for them, but it was late before any could be found. It seems they had

straggled in quest of forage, and, besides all that, the bushes grew thick enough to conceal them from being seen at the smallest distance. One of the people was so bewildered in search of his horse that he lost himself, being no great forester. However, because we were willing to save time, we left two of our most expert woodsmen behind to beat all the adjacent woods in quest of him.

In the meanwhile, the surveyors proceeded vigorously on their business, but were so perplexed with thickets at their first setting-off that their progress was much retarded. They were no sooner over that difficulty but they were obliged to encounter another. The rest of their day's work lay over very sharp hills, where the dry leaves were so slippery that there was hardly any hold for their feet. Such rubs as these prevented them from measuring more than 4 miles and 270 poles. Upon the sides of these hills the soil was rich, though full of stones, and the trees reasonably large.

The smoke continued still to veil the mountains from our sight, which made us long for rain or a brisk gale of wind to disperse it. Nor was the loss of this wild prospect all our concern, but we were apprehensive lest the woods should be burnt in the course of our line before us or happen to take fire behind us, either of which would effectually have starved the horses and made us all foot soldiers. But we were so happy, thank God, as to escape this misfortune in every part of our progress.

We were exceedingly uneasy about our lost man, knowing he had taken no provision of any kind; nor was it much advantage toward his support that he had taken his gun along with him, because he had rarely been guilty of putting anything to death. He had unluckily wandered from the camp several miles, and after steering sundry unsuccessful courses in order to return either to us or to the line, was at length so tired he could go no farther. In this distress he sat himself down under a tree to recruit his jaded spirits and at the same time indulge a few melancholy reflections. Famine was the first phantom that appeared to him and was the more frightful because he fancied himself not quite bear enough to subsist long upon licking his paws. In the meantime, the two persons we had sent after him hunted diligently great part of the day without coming upon his track. They fired their pieces toward every point of the compass but could perceive no firing in return. However, advancing a little farther, at last they made a lucky shot that our straggler had the good fortune to hear, and, he returning the salute, they soon found each other with no small satisfaction. But though they light of [44] the man, they could by no means light of his horse, and therefore he was obliged to be a foot soldier all the rest of the journey.

Our Indian shot a bear so prodigiously fat that there was no way to kill him but by firing in at his ear. The fore part of the skull of that animal, being guarded by a double bone, is hardly penetrable, and when it is very fat, a bullet aimed at his body is apt to lose its force before it reaches the vitals. This animal is of the dog kind, and our Indians, as well as woodsmen, are as fond of its flesh as the Chinese can be of that of the common hound.

22. Early in the morning we sent back two men to make farther search for the horse that was strayed away. We were unwilling the poor man should sustain such a damage as would eat out a large part of his pay or that the public should be at the expense of reimbursing him for it. These foresters hunted all over the neighboring woods and took as much pains as if the horse had been their own property, but all their diligence was to no purpose. The surveyors, in the meantime, being fearful of leaving these men too far behind, advanced the line no farther than 1 mile and 230 poles.

As we rode along we found no less than three bears and a fat doe, that our Indian, who went out before us, had thrown in our course, and we were very glad to pick them up. About a mile from the camp we crossed Miry Creek, so called because several of the horses were mired in its branches. About 230 poles beyond that, the line intersected another river that seemed to be a branch of the Irvin, to which we gave the name of the Mayo in compliment to the other of our surveyors. It was about fifty yards wide where we forded it, being just below a ledge of rocks which reached across the river and made a natural cascade. Our horses could hardly keep their feet over these

[44] Happened upon, came across.

slippery rocks, which gave some of their riders no small palpitation. This river forks about a quarter of a mile below the ford and has some scattering canes growing near the mouth of it.

We pitched our tent on the western banks of the Mayo, for the pleasure of being lulled to sleep by the cascade. Here our hunters had leisure to go out and try their fortunes, and returned loaded with spoil. They brought in no less than six bears, exceedingly fat, so that the frying pan had no rest all night. We had now the opportunity of trying the speed of these lumpish animals by a fair course it had with the nimblest of our surveyors. A cub of a year old will run very fast, because, being upon his growth, he is never encumbered with too much fat; but the old ones are more sluggish and unwieldy, especially when mast is plenty. Then their nimblest gait is only a heavy gallop, and their motion is still slower downhill, where they are obliged to sidle along very awkwardly to keep their lights from rising up into their throat. These beasts always endeavor to avoid a man, except they are wounded or happen to be engaged in the protection of their cubs. By the force of these instincts and that of self-preservation, they will now and then throw off all reverence for their Maker's image. For that reason, excess of hunger will provoke them to the same desperate attack for the support of their being. A memorable instance of the last case is said to have happened not long ago in New England, where a bear assaulted a man just by his own door, and rearing himself upon his haunches, offered to take him lovingly into his hug. But the man's wife, observing the danger her husband was in, had the courage to run behind the bear and thrust her two thumbs into his eyes. This made Bruin quit the man and turn short upon the woman to take his revenge, but she had the presence of mind to spring back with more than female agility, and so both their lives were preserved.

23. At the distance of sixty-two poles from where we lay, we crossed the south branch of what we took for the Irvin, nor was it without difficulty we got over, though it happened to be without damage. Great part of the way after that was mountainous, so that we were no sooner got down one hill but we were obliged to climb up another. Only for the last mile of our stage we encountered a locust

thicket, that was level but interlaced terribly with briers and grape-vines. We forded a large creek no less than five times, the banks of which were so steep that we were forced to cut them down with a hoe. We gave it the name of Crooked Creek because of its frequent meanders. The sides of it were planted with shrub canes extremely inviting to the horses, which were now quite jaded with clambering up so many precipices and tugging through so many dismal thickets; notwithstanding which we pushed the line this day four miles, sixty-nine poles.

The men were so unthrifty this morning as to bring but a small portion of their abundance along with them. This was the more unlucky because we could discover no sort of game the whole livelong day. Woodsmen are certainly good Christians in one respect at least, that they always leave the morrow to care for itself; though for that very reason they ought to pray more fervently for their daily bread than most of them remember to do.

The mountains were still concealed from our eyes by a cloud of smoke. As we went along we were alarmed at the sight of a great fire which showed itself to the northward. This made our small corps march in closer order than we used to do, lest perchance we might be waylaid by Indians. It made us look out sharp to see if we could discover any track or other token of these insidious foresters, but found none. In the meantime, we came often upon the track of bears, which can't without some skill be distinguished from that of human creatures made with naked feet. And, indeed, a young woodsman would be puzzled to find out the difference, which consists principally in a bear's paws being something smaller than a man's foot and in its leaving sometimes the mark of its claws in the impression made upon the ground.

The soil where the locust thicket grew was exceedingly rich, as it constantly is where that kind of tree is naturally and largely produced. But the desolation made there lately, either by fire or caterpillars, had been so general that we could not see a tree of any bigness standing within our prospect. And the reason why a fire makes such havoc in these lonely parts is this: the woods are not there burnt every year as they generally are amongst the inhabitants. But the dead leaves and trash of many years are heaped up together, which, being at length kindled by the Indians that happen to pass that way, furnish fuel for a conflagration that carries all before it.

There is a beautiful range of hills, as level as a terrace walk, that overlooks the valley through which Crooked Creek conveys its spiral stream. This terrace runs pretty near east and west about two miles south of the line and is almost parallel with it. The horses had been too much harassed to permit us to ride at all out of our way for the pleasure of any prospect or the gratification of any curiosity. This confined us to the narrow sphere of our business and is at the same time a just excuse for not animating our story with greater variety.

24. The surveyors went out the sooner this morning by reason the men lost very little time in cooking their breakfast. They had made but a spare meal overnight, leaving nothing but the hide of a bear for the morrow. Some of the keenest of them got up at midnight to cook that nice morsel after the Indian manner. They first singed the hair clean off, that none of it might stick in their throats; then they boiled the pelt into soup, which had a stratum of grease swimming upon it full half an inch thick. However, they commended this dish extremely; though I believe the praises they gave it were more owing to their good stomach than to their good taste.

The line was extended six miles and three hundred poles and in that distance crossed Crooked Creek at least eight times more. We were forced to scuffle through a thicket about two miles in breadth, planted with locusts and hickory saplings as close as they could stand together. Amongst these there was hardly a tree of tolerable growth within view. It was a dead plain of several miles extent and very fertile soil. Beyond that the woods were open for about three miles but mountainous. All the rest of our day's journey was pestered with bushes and grapevines, in the thickest of which we were obliged to take up our quarters near one of the branches of Crooked Creek.

This night it was the men's good fortune to fare very sumptuously. The Indian had killed two large bears, the fattest of which he had taken napping. One of the people, too, shot a raccoon, which is also of the dog kind and as big as a small fox, though its legs are shorter and when fat has a much higher relish than either mutton or kid. 'Tis naturally not carnivorous but very fond of Indian corn and persimmons. The fat of this animal is reckoned very good to assuage swellings and inflammations. Some old maids are at the trouble of breeding them up tame for the pleasure of seeing them play over as many humorous tricks as a monkey. It climbs up small trees, like a bear, by embracing the bodies of them.

Till this night we had accustomed ourselves to go to bed in our nightgowns, believing we should thereby be better secured from the cold, but upon trial found we lay much warmer by stripping to our shirts and spreading our gowns over us. A true woodsman, if he have no more than a single blanket, constantly pulls all off and, lying on one part of it, draws the other over him, believing it much more refreshing to lie so than in his clothes; and if he find himself not warm enough, shifts his lodging to leeward of the fire, in which situation the smoke will drive over him and effectually correct the cold dews that would otherwise descend upon his person, perhaps to his great damage.

25. The air clearing up this morning, we were again agreeably surprised with a full prospect of the mountains. They discovered themselves both to the north and south of us on either side, not distant above ten miles, according to our best computation. We could now see those to the north rise in four distinct ledges one above another, but those to the south formed only a single ledge and that broken and interrupted in many places, or rather they were only single mountains detached from each other. One of the southern mountains was so vastly high it seemed to hide its head in the clouds, and the west end of it terminated in a horrible precipice that we called the Despairing Lover's Leap. The next to it, toward the east, was lower except at one end, where it heaved itself up in the form of a vast stack of chimneys. The course of the northern mountains seemed to tend west-southwest and those to the southward very near west. We could descry other mountains ahead of us, exactly in the course of the line though at a much greater distance. In this point of view, the ledges on the right and left both seemed to close and form a natural amphi-

theater. Thus 'twas our fortune to be wedged in betwixt these two ranges of mountains, insomuch that if our line had run ten miles on either side it had butted before this day either upon one or the other, both of them now stretching away plainly to the eastward of us.

It had rained a little in the night, which dispersed the smoke and opened this romantic scene to us all at once, though it was again hid from our eyes as we moved forward by the rough woods we had the misfortune to be engaged with. The bushes were so thick for near four miles together that they tore the deerskins to pieces that guarded the bread bags. Though, as rough as the woods were, the soil was extremely good all the way, being washed down from the neighboring hills into the plain country. Notwithstanding all these difficulties, the surveyors drove on the line 4 miles and 205 poles.

In the meantime we were so unlucky as to meet with no sort of game the whole day, so that the men were obliged to make a frugal distribution of what little they left in the morning. We encamped upon a small rill, where the horses came off as temperately as their masters. They were by this time grown so thin by hard travel and spare feeding that henceforth, in pure compassion, we chose to perform the greater part of the journey on foot. And as our baggage was by this time grown much lighter, we divided it after the best manner so that every horse's load might be proportioned to the strength he had left. Though after all the prudent measures we could take, we perceived the hills began to rise upon us so fast in our front that it would be impossible for us to proceed much farther.

We saw very few squirrels in the upper parts, because the wildcats devour them unmercifully. Of these there are four kinds: the fox squirrel, the gray, the flying, and the ground squirrel. These last resemble a rat in everything but the tail and the black and russet streaks that run down the length of their little bodies.

26. We found our way grow still more mountainous, after extending the line three hundred poles farther. We came then to a rivulet that ran with a swift current toward the south. This we fancied to be another branch of the Irvin, though some of these men, who had been Indian traders, judged it rather to be the head of Deep River, that dis-

charges its stream into that of Pee Dee, but this seemed a wild conjecture. The hills beyond that river were exceedingly lofty and not to be attempted by our jaded palfreys, which could now hardly drag their legs after them upon level ground. Besides, the bread began to grow scanty and the winter season to advance apace upon us. We had likewise reason to apprehend the consequences of being intercepted by deep snows and the swelling of the many waters between us and home. The first of these misfortunes would starve all our horses and the other ourselves, by cutting off our retreat and obliging us to winter in those desolate woods. These considerations determined us to stop short here and push our adventures no farther. The last tree we marked was a red oak growing on the bank of the river; and to make the place more remarkable, we blazed all the trees around it.

We found the whole distance from Currituck Inlet to the rivulet where we left off to be, in a straight line, 240 miles and 230 poles. And from the place where the Carolina commissioners deserted us, 72 miles and 302 poles. This last part of the journey was generally very hilly, or else grown up with troublesome thickets and underwoods, all which our Carolina friends had the discretion to avoid. We encamped in a dirty valley near the rivulet above-mentioned for the advantage of the canes, and so sacrificed our own convenience to that of our horses. There was a small mountain half a mile to the northward of us, which we had the curiosity to climb up in the afternoon in order to enlarge our prospect. From thence we were able to discover where the two ledges of mountains closed, as near as we could guess about thirty miles to the west of us, and lamented that our present circumstances would not permit us to advance the line to that place, which the hand of Nature had made so very remarkable.

Not far from our quarters one of the men picked up a pair of elk's horns, not very large, and discovered the track of the elk that had shed them. It was rare to find any tokens of those animals so far to the south, because they keep commonly to the northward of thirty-seven degrees, as the buffaloes, for the most part, confine themselves to the southward of that latitude. The elk is full as big as a horse and of the deer kind. The stags only have horns and those exceedingly large and spreading. Their color is something lighter than that of the red deer and their flesh tougher. Their swiftest speed is a large trot, and in that motion they turn their horns back upon their necks and cock their noses aloft in the air. Nature has taught them this attitude to save their antlers from being entangled in the thickets, which they always retire to. They are very shy and have the sense of smelling so exquisite that they wind a man at a great distance. For this reason they are seldom seen but when the air is moist, in which case their smell is not so nice. They commonly herd together, and the Indians say if one of the drove happen by some wound to be disabled from making his escape, the rest will forsake their fears to defend their friend, which they will do with great obstinacy till they are killed upon the spot. Though, otherwise, they are so alarmed at the sight of a man that to avoid him they will sometimes throw themselves down very high precipices into the river.

A misadventure happened here which gave us no small perplexity. One of the commissioners was so unlucky as to bruise his foot against a stump, which brought on a formal fit of the gout. It must be owned there could not be a more unseasonable time, nor a more improper situation for anyone to be attacked by that cruel distemper. The joint was so inflamed that he could neither draw shoe or boot upon it, and to ride without either would have exposed him to so many rude knocks and bruises in those rough woods as to be intolerable even to a stoic. It was happy indeed that we were to rest here the next day, being Sunday, that there might be leisure for trying some speedy remedy. Accordingly, he was persuaded to bathe his foot in cold water in order to repel the humor and assuage the inflammation. This made it less painful and gave us hopes, too, of reducing the swelling in a short time.

Our men had the fortune to kill a brace of bears, a fat buck, and a wild turkey, all which paid them with interest for yesterday's abstinence. This constant and seasonable supply of our daily wants made us reflect thankfully on the bounty of Providence. And that we might not be unmindful of being all along fed by Heaven in this great and solitary wilderness, we agreed to wear in our hats the maosti, which is in Indian the beard of a wild turkey cock, and on our breasts the figure of that fowl with its wings extended and holding in its claws a scroll with this motto, *Vice coturnicum,* meaning that we had been supported by them in the wilderness in the room of quails.

27. This being Sunday, we were not wanting in our thanks to Heaven for the constant support and protection we had been favored with. Nor did our chaplain fail to put us in mind of our duty by a sermon proper for the occasion. We ordered a strict inquiry to be made into the quantity of bread we had left and found no more than would subsist us a fortnight at short allowance. We made a fair distribution of our whole stock and at the same time recommended to the men to manage this, their last stake, to the best advantage, not knowing how long they would be obliged to live upon it. We likewise directed them to keep a watchful eye upon their horses, that none of them might be missing the next morning to hinder our return.

There fell some rain before noon, which made our camp more a bog than it was before. This moist situation began to infect some of the men with fevers and some with fluxes, which however we soon removed with Peruvian bark and ipecacuanha.

In the afternoon we marched up again to the top of the hill to entertain our eyes a second time with the view of the mountains, but a perverse fog arose that hid them from our sight. In the evening we deliberated which way it might be most proper to return. We had at first intended to cross over at the foot of the mountains to the head of James River, that we might be able to describe that natural boundary so far. But, on second thoughts, we found many good reasons against that laudable design, such as the weakness of our horses, the scantiness of our bread, and the near approach of winter. We had cause to believe the way might be full of hills, and the farther we went toward the north, the more danger there would be of snow. Such considerations as these determined us at last to make the best of our way back upon the line, which was the straightest and consequently the shortest way to the inhabitants. We knew the worst of that course and were sure of a beaten path all the way, while we were totally ignorant what difficulties and dangers the other course might be attended with. So prudence got the better for once of curiosity, and the itch for new discoveries gave place to self-preservation.

Our inclination was the stronger to cross over according to the course of the mountains, that we might find out whether James River and Appomattox River head there or run quite through them. 'Tis certain that Potomac passes in a large stream through the main ledge and then divides itself into two considerable rivers. That which stretches away to the northward is called Cohungaroota [45] and that which flows to the southwest hath the name of Sharantow. The course of this last stream is near parallel to the Blue Ridge of mountains, at the distance only of about three or four miles. Though how far it may continue that course has not yet been sufficiently discovered, but some woodsmen pretend to say it runs as far as the source of Roanoke; nay, they are so very particular as to tell us that Roanoke, Sharantow, and another wide branch of Mississippi all head in one and the same mountain. What dependence there may be upon this conjectural geography I won't pretend to say, though 'tis certain that Sharantow keeps close to the mountains, as far as we are acquainted with its tendency. We are likewise assured that the south branch of James River, within less than twenty miles east of the main ledge, makes an elbow and runs due southwest, which is parallel with the mountains on this side. But how far it stretches that way before it returns is not yet certainly known, no more than where it takes its rise.

In the meantime, it is strange that our woodsmen have not had curiosity enough to inform themselves more exactly of these particulars, and it is stranger still that the government has never thought it worth the expense of making an accurate survey of the mountains, that we might be masters of that natural fortification before the French, who in some places have settlements not very distant from it. It therefore concerns His Majesty's service very nearly and the safety of his subjects in this part of the world to take possession of so im-

[45] The manuscript has the following passage added in the margin: "Which by a late survey has been found to extend above two hundred miles before it reaches its source, in a mountain from which Allegheny, one of the branches of the Mississippi, takes it rise, and runs southwest, as this river does southeast." Sharantow is an old name for Shenandoah.

portant a barrier in time, lest our good friends, the French, and the Indians through their means, prove a perpetual annoyance to these colonies. Another reason to invite us to secure this great ledge of mountains is the probability that very valuable mines may be discovered there. Nor would it be at all extravagant to hope for silver mines among the rest, because part of these mountains lie exactly in the same parallel, as well as upon the same continent, with New Mexico and the mines of St. Barb.[46]

28. We had given orders for the horses to be brought up early, but the likelihood of more rain prevented our being overhasty in decamping. Nor were we out in our conjectures, for about ten o'clock it began to fall very plentifully. Our commissioner's pain began now to abate as the swelling increased. He made an excellent figure for a mountaineer, with one boot of leather and the other of flannel. Thus accoutered he intended to mount, if the rain had not happened opportunely to prevent him. Though, in truth, it was hardly possible for him to ride with so slender a defense without exposing his foot to be bruised and tormented by the saplings that stood thick on either side of the path. It was therefore a most seasonable rain for him, as it gave more time for his distemper to abate.

Though it may be very difficult to find a certain cure for the gout, yet it is not improbable but some things may ease the pain and shorten the fits of it. And those medicines are most likely to do this that supple the parts and clear the passage through the narrow vessels that are the seat of this cruel disease. Nothing will do this more suddenly than rattlesnake's oil, which will even penetrate the pores of glass when warmed in the sun. It was unfortunate, therefore, that we had not taken out the fat of those snakes we had killed some time before, for the benefit of so useful an experiment as well as for the relief of our fellow traveler. But lately the Seneca rattlesnake root has been discovered in this country, which, being infused in wine and drank morning and evening, has in several instances had a very happy effect upon the gout, and enabled cripples to throw away their crutches and walk several miles, and, what is stranger still, it takes away the pain in half an hour.

[46] Santa Barbara, Chihuahua, Mexico.

Nor was the gout the only disease amongst us that was hard to cure. We had a man in our company who had too voracious a stomach for a woodsman. He eat as much as any other two, but all he swallowed stuck by him till it was carried off by a strong purge. Without this assistance, often repeated, his belly and bowels would swell to so enormous a bulk that he could hardly breathe, especially when he lay down, just as if he had had an asthma; though, notwithstanding this oddness of constitution, he was a very strong, lively fellow and used abundance of violent exercise, by which 'twas wonderful the peristaltic motion was not more vigorously promoted. We gave this poor man several purges, which only eased him for the present, and the next day he would grow as burly as ever. At last we gave him a moderate dose of ipecacuanha in broth made very salt, which turned all its operation downwards. This had so happy an effect that from that day forward to the end of our journey all his complaints ceased and the passages continued unobstructed.

The rain continued most of the day and some part of the night, which incommoded us much in our dirty camp and made the men think of nothing but eating, even at a time when nobody could stir out to make provision for it.

29. Though we were flattered in the morning with the usual tokens of a fair day, yet they all blew over, and it rained hard before we could make ready for our departure. This was still in favor of our podagrous friend, whose lameness was now grown better and the inflammation fallen. Nor did it seem to need above one day more to reduce it to its natural proportion and make it fit for the boot; and effectually the rain procured this benefit for him and gave him particular reason to believe his stars propitious.

Notwithstanding the falling weather, our hunters sallied out in the afternoon and drove the woods in a ring, which was thus performed: from the circumference of a large circle they all marched inward and drove the game toward the center. By this means they shot a brace of fat bears, which came very seasonably, because we had made clean work in the morning and were in danger of dining with St. Anthony, or His Grace Duke Humphrey.[47] But in this expedition the unhappy

[47] Humphrey, Duke of Gloucester. A statue in old St. Paul's Cathedral, erron-

man who had lost himself once before straggled again so far in pursuit of a deer that he was hurried a second time quite out of his knowledge; and, night coming on before he could recover the camp, he was obliged to lie down without any of the comforts of fire, food, or covering; nor would his fears suffer him to sleep very sound, because, to his great disturbance, the wolves howled all that night and panthers screamed most frightfully.

In the evening a brisk northwester swept all the clouds from the sky and exposed the mountains as well as the stars to our prospect. That which was the most lofty to the southward and which we called the Lover's Leap, some of our Indian traders fondly fancied was the Kiawan Mountain, which they had formerly seen from the country of the Cherokees. They were the more positive by reason of the prodigious precipice that remarkably distinguished the west end of it. We seemed however not to be far enough south for that, though 'tis not improbable but a few miles farther the course of our line might carry us to the most northerly towns of the Cherokees. What makes this the more credible is the northwest course that our traders take from the Catawbas for some hundred miles together, when they carry goods that roundabout way to the Cherokees.

It was a great pity that the want of bread and the weakness of our horses hindered us from making the discovery. Though the great service such an excursion might have been to the country would certainly have made the attempt not only pardonable but much to be commended. Our traders are now at the vast charge and fatigue of traveling above five hundred miles for the benefit of that traffic which hardly quits cost. Would it not then be worth the Assembly's while to be at some charge to find a shorter cut to carry on so profitable a trade, with more advantage and less hazard and trouble than they do at present? For I am persuaded it will not then be half the distance that our traders make it now nor half so far as Georgia lies from the northern clans of that nation. Such a discovery would certainly prove an un-

---

eously identified as that of the Duke, was a meeting place for needy gallants and rogues. A penniless gallant with nowhere to go for dinner was said to "dine with Duke Humphrey," meaning to go dinnerless.

speakable advantage to this colony by facilitating a trade with so considerable a nation of Indians, which have sixty-two towns and more than four thousand fighting men. Our traders at that rate would be able to undersell those sent from the other colonies so much that the Indians must have reason to deal with them preferably to all others. Of late the new colony of Georgia has made an act obliging us to go four hundred miles to take out a license to traffic with these Cherokees, though many of their towns lie out of their bounds and we had carried on this trade eighty years before that colony was thought of.

30. In the morning early the man who had gone astray the day before found his way to the camp by the sound of the bells that were upon the horses' necks.

At nine o'clock we began our march back toward the rising sun, for though we had finished the line yet we had not yet near finished our fatigue. We had, after all, two hundred good miles at least to our several habitations, and the horses were brought so low that we were obliged to travel on foot great part of the way, and that in our boots, too, to save our legs from being torn to pieces by the bushes and briers. Had we not done this, we must have left all our horses behind, which could now hardly drag their legs after them; and with all the favor we could show the poor animals we were forced to set seven of them free not far from the foot of the mountains.

Four men were dispatched early to clear the road, that our lame commissioner's leg might be in less danger of being bruised and that the baggage horses might travel with less difficulty and more expedition. As we passed along, by favor of a serene sky we had still from every eminence a perfect view of the mountains, as well to the north as to the south. We could not forbear now and then facing about to survey them, as if unwilling to part with a prospect which at the same time, like some rakes, was very wild and very agreeable. We encouraged the horses to exert the little strength they had and, being light, they made a shift to jog on about eleven miles.

We encamped on Crooked Creek near a thicket of canes. In the front of our camp rose a very beautiful hill that bounded our view at about a mile's distance, and all the intermediate space was covered with green canes. Though to our sorrow, firewood was scarce, which was now the harder upon us because a northwester blew very cold from the mountains.

The Indian killed a stately, fat buck, and we picked his bones as clean as a score of turkey buzzards could have done. By the advantage of a clear night, we made trial once more of the variation and found it much the same as formerly. This being His Majesty's birthday, we drank all the loyal healths in excellent water, not for the sake of the drink (like many of our fellow subjects), but purely for the sake of the toast. And because all public mirth should be a little noisy, we fired several volleys of canes, instead of guns, which gave a loud report. We threw them into the fire, where the air enclosed betwixt the joints of the canes, being expanded by the violent heat, burst its narrow bounds with a considerable explosion.

In the evening one of the men knocked down an opossum, which is a harmless little beast that will seldom go out of your way, and if you take hold of it will only grin and hardly ever bite. The flesh was well tasted and tender, approaching nearest to pig, which it also resembled in bigness. The color of its fur was a goose gray, with a swine's snout and a tail like a rat, but at least a foot long. By twisting this tail about the arm of a tree, it will hang with all its weight and swing to anything it wants to take hold of. It has five claws on the forefeet of equal length, but the hinder feet have only four claws and a sort of thumb standing off at a proper distance. Their feet, being thus formed, qualify them for climbing up trees to catch little birds, which they are very fond of. But the greatest particularity of this creature, and which distinguishes it from most others that we are acquainted with, is the false belly of the female, into which her young retreat in time of danger. She can draw the slit, which is the inlet into this pouch, so close that you must look narrowly to find it, especially if she happen to be a virgin. Within the false belly may be seen seven or eight teats, on which the young ones grow from their first formation till they are big enough to fall off like ripe fruit from a tree. This is so odd a method of generation that I should not have believed it without the testimony of mine own eyes. Besides, a knowing and credible person has assured me he has more than once observed the embryo opossums growing to the teat before they were completely shaped, and afterwards watched their daily growth till they were big enough for birth.[48] And all this he could the more easily pry into because the dam was so perfectly gentle and harmless that he could handle her just as he pleased.

I could hardly persuade myself to publish a thing so contrary to the course that nature takes in the production of other animals unless it were a matter commonly believed in all countries where that creature is produced and has been often observed by persons of undoubted credit and understanding. They say that the leather-winged bats produce their young in the same uncommon manner; and that young sharks at sea and young vipers ashore run down the throats of their dams when they are closely pursued.

[31.][49] The frequent crossing of Crooked Creek and mounting the steep banks of it gave the finishing stroke to the foundering our horses, and no less than two of them made a full stop here and would not advance a foot farther, either by fair means or foul. We had a dreamer of dreams amongst us who warned me in the morning to take care of myself or I should infallibly fall into the creek; I thanked him kindly and used what caution I could but was not able, it seems, to avoid my destiny, for my horse made a false step and laid me down at my full length in the water. This was enough to bring dreaming into credit, and I think it much for the honor of our expedition that it was graced not only with a priest but also with a prophet. We were so perplexed with this serpentine creek, as well as in passing the branches of the Irvin, which were swelled since we saw them before, that we could reach but five miles this whole day.

In the evening we pitched our tent near Miry Creek, though an uncomfortable place to lodge in, purely for the advantage of the canes. Our hunters killed a large doe and two bears, which made all other misfortunes easy. Certainly no Tartar ever loved horseflesh or Hottentot guts and garbage better than woodsmen do bear. The truth of it is, it may be proper food perhaps for such as work or ride it off, but, with

[48] Byrd seems to think that the embryos were formed in the pouch, whereas in fact the mother places the immature embryos there after natural birth.

[49] The date has been added from the Secret History.

our chaplain's leave, who loved it much, I think it not a very proper diet for saints, because 'tis apt to make them a little too rampant. And, now, for the good of mankind and for the better peopling an infant colony, which has no want but that of inhabitants, I will venture to publish a secret of importance which our Indian disclosed to me. I asked him the reason why few or none of his countrywomen were barren. To which curious question he answered, with a broad grin upon his face, they had an infallible secret for that. Upon my being importunate to know what the secret might be, he informed me that if any Indian woman did not prove with child at a decent time after marriage, the husband, to save his reputation with the women, forthwith entered into a bear diet for six weeks, which in that time makes him so vigorous that he grows exceedingly impertinent to his poor wife, and 'tis great odds but he makes her a mother in nine months. And thus much I am able to say besides for the reputation of the bear diet, that all the married men of our company were joyful fathers within forty weeks after they got home, and most of the single men had children sworn to them within the same time, our chaplain always excepted, who, with much ado, made a shift to cast out that importunate kind of devil by dint of fasting and prayer.

NOVEMBER

1. By the negligence of one of the men in not hobbling his horse, he straggled so far that he could not be found. This stopped us all the morning long; yet, because our time should not be entirely lost, we endeavored to observe the latitude at twelve o'clock. Though our observation was not perfect by reason the wind blew a little too fresh, however, by such a one as we could make, we found ourselves in 36° 20' only. Notwithstanding our being thus delayed and the unevenness of the ground over which we were obliged to walk (for most of us served now in the infantry), we traveled no less than six miles. Though as merciful as we were to our poor beasts, another of 'em tired by the way and was left behind for the wolves and panthers to feast upon.

As we marched along, we had the fortune to kill a brace of bucks, as many bears, and one wild turkey. But this was carrying our sport to wantonness, because we butchered more than we were able to transport. We ordered the deer to be quartered and divided among the horses for the lighter carriage and recommended the bears to our daily attendants, the turkey buzzards. We always chose to carry venison along with us rather than bear, not only because it was less cumbersome but likewise because the people could eat it without bread, which was now almost spent. Whereas the other, being richer food, lay too heavy upon the stomach unless it were lightened by something farinaceous.

This is what I thought proper to remark for the service of all those whose business or diversion shall oblige them to live any time in the woods. And because I am persuaded that very useful matters may be found out by searching this great wilderness, especially the upper parts of it about the mountains, I conceive it will help to engage able men in that good work if I recommend a wholesome kind of food of very small weight and very great nourishment, that will secure them from starving in case they should be so unlucky as to meet with no game. The chief discouragement at present from penetrating far into the woods is the trouble of carrying a load of provisions. I must own, famine is a frightful monster and for that reason to be guarded against as well as we can. But the common precautions against it are so burdensome that people cannot tarry long out and go far enough from home to make any effectual discovery. The portable provisions I would furnish our foresters withal are glue broth and rockahominy: one contains the essence of bread, the other of meat. The best way of making the glue broth is after the following method: take a leg of beef, veal, venison, or any other young meat, because old meat will not so easily jelly. Pare off all the fat, in which there is no nutriment, and of the lean make a very strong broth after the usual manner, by boiling the meat to rags till all the goodness be out. After skimming off what fat remains, pour the broth into a wide stewpan, well tinned, and let it simmer over a gentle, even fire till it come to a thick jelly. Then take it off and set it over boiling water, which is an evener heat and not so apt to burn the broth to the vessel. Over that let it evaporate, stirring it very often till it be reduced, when cold, into a solid substance like glue. Then cut it into small pieces, laying them single in the cold, that they may dry the sooner. When the pieces are perfectly dry, put them into a canister, and they will be good, if kept dry, a whole East India voyage. This glue is so strong that two or three drams, dissolved in boiling water with a little salt, will make half a pint of good broth, and if you should be faint with fasting or fatigue, let a small piece of this glue melt in your mouth and you will find yourself surprisingly refreshed.

One pound of this cookery would keep a man in good heart above a month and is not only nourishing but likewise very wholesome. Particularly it is good against fluxes, which woodsmen are very liable to, by lying too near the moist ground and guzzling too much cold water. But as it will be only used now and then, in times of scarcity when game is wanting, two pounds of it will be enough for a journey of six months.

But this broth will be still more heartening if you thicken every mess with half a spoonful of rockahominy, which is nothing but Indian corn parched without burning and reduced to powder. The fire drives out all the watery parts of the corn, leaving the strength of it behind, and this, being very dry, becomes much lighter for carriage and less liable to be spoilt by the moist air. Thus half a dozen pounds of this sprightly bread will sustain a man for as many months, provided he husband it well and always spare it when he meets with venison, which, as I said before, may be very safely eaten without any bread at all.

By what I have said, a man needs not encumber himself with more than eight or ten pounds of provisions, though he continue half a year in the woods. These and his gun will support him very well during that time, without the least danger of keeping one single fast. And though some of his days may be what the French call *jours maigres*, yet there will happen no more of those than will be necessary for his health and to carry off the excesses of the days of plenty, when our travelers will be apt to indulge their lawless appetites too much.

2. The heavens frowned this morning and threatened abundance of rain, but our zeal for returning made us defy the weather and de-

camp a little before noon. Yet we had not advanced two miles before a soaking shower made us glad to pitch our tent as fast as we could. We chose for that purpose a rising ground half a mile to the east of Matrimony Creek. This was the first and only time we were catched in the rain during the whole expedition. It used before to be so civil as to fall in the night after we were safe in our quarters and had trenched ourselves in, or else it came upon us on Sundays, when it was no interruption to our progress nor any inconvenience to our persons. We had, however, been so lucky in this particular before that we had abundant reason to take our present soaking patiently, and the misfortune was the less because we had taken our precautions to keep all our baggage and bedding perfectly dry.

This rain was enlivened with very loud thunder, which was echoed back by the hills in the neighborhood in a frightful manner. There is something in the woods that makes the sound of this meteor more awful and the violence of the lightning more visible. The trees are frequently shivered quite down to the root and sometimes perfectly twisted. But of all the effects of lightning that ever I heard of the most amazing happened in this country in the year 1736. In the summer of that year a surgeon of a ship, whose name was Davis, came ashore at York to visit a patient. He was no sooner got into the house but it began to rain with many terrible claps of thunder. When it was almost dark there came a dreadful flash of lightning, which struck the surgeon dead as he was walking about the room but hurt no other person, though several were near him. At the same time it made a large hole in the trunk of a pine tree which grew about ten feet from the window. But what was most surprising in this disaster was that on the breast of the unfortunate man that was killed was the figure of a pine tree, as exactly delineated as any limner in the world could draw it, nay, the resemblance went so far as to represent the color of the pine as well as the figure. The lightning must probably have passed through the tree first before it struck the man and by that means have printed the icon of it on his breast. But whatever may have been the cause, the effect was certain and can be attested by a cloud of witnesses who had the curiosity to go and see this wonderful phenomenon.

The worst of it was, we were forced to encamp in a barren place, where there was hardly a blade of grass to be seen; even the wild rosemary failed us here, which gave us but too just apprehensions that we should not only be obliged to trudge all the way home on foot but also to lug our baggage at our backs into the bargain. Thus we learnt by our own experience that horses are very improper animals to use in a long ramble into the woods, and the better they have been used to be fed, they are still the worse. Such will fall away a great deal faster and fail much sooner than those which are wont to be at their own keeping. Besides, horses that have been accustomed to a plain and champaign country will founder presently when they come to clamber up hills and batter their hoofs against continual rocks. We need Welsh runts and Highland Galloways to climb our mountains withal; they are used to precipices and will bite as close as Banstead Down sheep. But I should much rather recommend mules, if we had them, for these long and painful expeditions; though, till they can be bred, certainly asses are the fittest beasts of burden for the mountains. They are sure footed, patient under the heaviest fatigue, and will subsist upon moss or browsing on shrubs all the winter. One of them will carry the necessary luggage of four men without any difficulty and upon a pinch will take a quarter of bear or venison upon their backs into the bargain.

Thus, when the men are light and disengaged from everything but their guns, they may go the whole journey on foot with pleasure. And though my dear countrymen have so great a passion for riding that they will often walk two miles to catch a horse in order to ride one, yet, if they'll please to take my word for it, when they go into the woods upon discovery I would advise them by all means to march afoot, for they will then be delivered from the great care and concern for their horses which takes up too large a portion of their time. Overnight we are now at the trouble of hobbling them out and often of leading them a mile or two to a convenient place for forage, and then in the morning we are some hours in finding them again, because they are apt to stray a great way from the place where they were turned out. Now and then, too, they are lost for a whole day together and are frequently so weak and jaded that the company must lie still several days near some meadow or highland pond to recruit them.

All these delays retard their progress intolerably; whereas, if they had only a few asses they would abide close by the camp and find sufficient food everywhere, and in all seasons of the year. Men would then be able to travel safely over hills and dales, nor would the steepest mountain obstruct their progress. They might also search more narrowly for mines and other productions of nature, without being confined to level grounds in compliment to the jades they ride on. And one may foretell without the spirit of divination that so long as woodsmen continue to range on horseback we shall be strangers to our own country and few or no valuable discoveries will ever be made.

The French *coureurs de bois*, who have run from one end of the continent to the other, have performed it all on foot or else, in all probability, must have continued full as ignorant as we are. Our country has now been inhabited more than 130 years by the English, and still we hardly know anything of the Appalachian Mountains, that are nowhere above 250 miles from the sea. Whereas the French, who are later-comers, have ranged from Quebec southward as far as the mouth of Mississippi in the Bay of Mexico and to the west almost as far as California, which is either way above two thousand miles.

3. A northwest wind having cleared the sky, we were now tempted to travel on a Sunday for the first time, for want of more plentiful forage, though some of the more scrupulous amongst us were unwilling to do evil that good might come of it and make our cattle work a good part of the day in order to fill their bellies at night. However, the chaplain put on his casuistical face and offered to take the sin upon himself. We therefore consented to move a Sabbath Day's journey of three or four miles, it appearing to be a matter of some necessity.

On the way our unmerciful Indian killed no less than two brace of deer and a large bear. We only primed the deer, being unwilling to be encumbered with their whole carcasses. The rest we consigned to the wolves, which in return serenaded us great part of the night. They are very clamorous in their banquets, which we know is the way some other brutes have, in the extravagance of their jollity and sprightliness, of expressing their thanks to Providence.

We came to our old camp in sight of the river Irvin, whose stream was swelled now near four foot with the rain that fell the day before. This made it impracticable for us to ford it, nor could we guess when the water would fall enough to let us go over. This put our mathematical professor, who should have set a better example, into the vapors, fearing he should be obliged to take up his winter quarters in that doleful wilderness. But the rest were not infected with his want of faith but preserved a firmness of mind superior to such little adverse accidents. They trusted that the same good Providence which had most remarkably prospered them hitherto would continue its goodness and conduct them safe to the end of their journey.

However, we found plainly that traveling on the Sunday, contrary to our constant rule, had not thriven with us in the least. We were not gainers of any distance by it, because the river made us pay two days for violating one. Nevertheless, by making this reflection, I would not be thought so rigid an observer of the Sabbath as to allow of no work at all to be done or journeys to be taken upon it. I should not care to lie still and be knocked on the head, as the Jews were heretofore by Antiochus, because I believed it unlawful to stand upon my defense on this good day. Nor would I care, like a certain New England magistrate, to order a man to the whipping post for daring to ride for a midwife on the Lord's Day. On the contrary, I am for doing all acts of necessity, charity, and self-preservation upon a Sunday as well as other days of the week. But, as I think our present march could not strictly be justified by any of these rules, it was but just we should suffer a little for it.

I never could learn that the Indians set apart any day of the week or the year for the service of God. They pray, as philosophers eat, only when they have a stomach, without having any set time for it. Indeed these idle people have very little occasion for a Sabbath to refresh themselves after hard labor, because very few of them ever labor at all. Like the wild Irish, they had rather want than work and are all men of pleasure, to whom every day is a day of rest. Indeed, in their hunting they will take a little pains; but this being only a diversion, their spirits are rather raised than depressed by it and therefore need at most but a night's sleep to recruit them.

284

4. By some stakes we had driven into the river yesterday, we perceived the water began to fall but fell so slowly that we found we must have patience a day or two longer. And because we were unwilling to lie altogether idle, we sent back some of the men to bring up the two horses that tired the Saturday before. They were found near the place where we had left them, but seemed too sensible of their liberty to come to us. They were found standing indeed, but as motionless as the equestrian statue at Charing Cross.

We had great reason to apprehend more rain by the clouds that drove over our heads. The boldest amongst us were not without some pangs of uneasiness at so very sullen a prospect. However, God be praised, it all blew over in a few hours. If much rain had fallen, we resolved to make a raft and bind it together with grapevines to ferry ourselves and baggage over the river. Though in that case we expected the swiftness of the stream would have carried down our raft a long way before we could have tugged it to the opposite shore.

One of the young fellows we had sent to bring up the tired horses entertained us in the evening with a remarkable adventure he had met with that day. He had straggled, it seems, from his company in a mist and made a cub of a year old betake itself to a tree. While he was new-priming his piece with intent to fetch it down, the old gentlewoman appeared and, perceiving her heir apparent in distress, advanced open-mouthed to his relief. The man was so intent upon his game that she had approached very near him before he perceived her. But finding his danger, he faced about upon the enemy, which immediately reared upon her posteriors and put herself in battle array. The man, admiring at the bear's assurance, endeavored to fire upon her, but by the dampness of the priming his gun did not go off. He cocked it a second time and had the same misfortune. After missing fire twice, he had the folly to punch the beast with the muzzle of his piece; but Mother Bruin, being upon her guard, seized the weapon with her paws and by main strength wrenched it out of the fellow's hands. The man, being thus fairly disarmed, thought himself no longer a match for the enemy and therefore retreated as fast as his legs could carry him. The brute naturally grew bolder upon the flight of her adversary and pursued him with all her heavy speed. For some time it was doubtful whether fear made one run faster or fury the other. But after an even course of about fifty yards, the man had the mishap to stumble over a stump and fell down at his full length. He now would have sold his life a pennyworth; but the bear, apprehending there might be some trick in the fall, instantly halted and looked with much attention on her prostrate foe. In the meanwhile, the man had with great presence of mind resolved to make the bear believe he was dead by lying breathless on the ground, in hopes that the beast would be too generous to kill him over again. To carry on the farce, he acted the corpse for some time without daring to raise his head to see how near the monster was to him. But in about two minutes, to his unspeakable comfort, he was raised from the dead by the barking of a dog belonging to one of his companions, who came seasonably to his rescue and drove the bear from pursuing the man to take care of her cub, which she feared might now fall into a second distress.

5. We judged the waters were assuaged enough this morning to make the river fordable. Therefore about ten we tried the experiment, and everybody got over safe except one man, whose horse slipped from a rock as he forded over and threw him into the river. But, being able to swim, he was not carried down the stream very far before he recovered the north shore. At the distance of about six miles we passed Cascade Creek, and three miles farther we came upon the banks of the Dan, which we crossed with much difficulty, by reason the water was risen much higher than when we forded it before. Here the same unlucky person happened to be ducked a second time and was a second time saved by swimming. My own horse, too, plunged in such a manner that his head was more than once under water but with much ado recovered his feet, though he made so low an obeisance that the water ran fairly over my saddle.

We continued our march as far as Lowland Creek, where we took up our lodging for the benefit of the canes and winter grass that grew upon the rich grounds thereabouts. On our way thither we had the misfortune to drop another horse, though he carried nothing the whole day but his saddle. We showed the same favor to most of our horses, for fear, if we did not do it, we should in a little time be turned into

a Rock, as he forded over, and threw him into the River. But being able to swim, he was not carry'd down the Stream very far, before he recover'd the North Shoar.

At the Distance of about 6 miles we past Cascade Creek, and 3 Miles farther we came upon the Banks of the Dan, which we cross'd with much Difficulty, by reason the Water was risen much higher than when we forded it before.

Here the same Unlucky Person happen'd to be duck't a Second time, and was a Second time Sav'd by Swiming. My own Horse too plunged in such a Manner, that his Head was more than once under Water: but with much ado recover'd his Feet, tho' he made so low an Obeisance, that the water ran fairly over my Saddle.

We continued our march as far as Low-Land-Creek, where we took up our Lodging for the benefit of the Canes, and Winter Grass, that grew upon the rich Ground thereabouts. On our way thither we had the Misfortune to drop another Horse, tho' he carry'd nothing the whole Day but his Saddle. We Shew'd the same favour to most of our Horses, for fear, if we did not do it, we should in a little time be turn'd into Beasts of Burthen our selves.

Custom had now made travelling on foot so familiar, that we were able to walk ten Miles with Pleasure. This we could do in our Boots, notwithstanding our way lay over rough Woods, and uneven Ground.

Our learning to walk in heavy Boots was the same advantage to us, that learning to Dance High Dances in wooden Shoes, is to the French, it made us most exceeding nimble without them.

The Indians, who have no way of travelling but on the Hoof, make nothing of going 25 Miles a day, and carrying their little Necessaries at their backs, and sometimes a Stout Pack of Skins into the Bargain. And very often they laugh at the English, who can't Stir to a next Neighbour without a Horse, and say that 2 Legs are too much for such lazy people, who can't visit their next Neighbour without Six.

For their Parts, they were utter Strangers to all our Beasts of Burthen or Carriage, before the Slothfull Europeans came amongst them. They had no part of the American Continent, or in any of the Islands, either Horses or Asses, Camels, Dromedaries, or Elephants to ease the Legs of the Original Inhabitants, or to lighten their Labour.

Indeed in South America, and particularly in Chili, they have an usefull Animal call'd Paco. This Creature resembles a Sheep very much, only in the Length of the Neck, and figure of the Head it is more like a Camel. It is very near as high as an Ass, and the Indians there make use of it for carrying moderate Burthens.

The Fleece that grows upon it, is very Valuable for the fineness, length, and Glossiness of the Wool. It has one remarkable Singularity that the Hoofs of its fore feet have three Clefts, and those behind no more than one. The Flesh of this Animal is far

A Page from the Westover Manuscript of *The History of the Dividing Line*

(The pointer indicates a line with an insertion probably in Byrd's hand.)

beasts of burden ourselves. Custom had now made traveling on foot so familiar that we were able to walk ten miles with pleasure. This we could do in our boots, notwithstanding our way lay over rough woods and uneven grounds. Our learning to walk in heavy boots was the same advantage to us that learning to dance high dances in wooden shoes is to the French: it made us most exceeding nimble without them.

The Indians, who have no way of traveling but on the hoof, make nothing of going twenty-five miles a day and carrying their little necessaries at their backs, and sometimes a stout pack of skins into the bargain. And very often they laugh at the English, who can't stir to a next neighbor without a horse, and say that two legs are too much for such lazy people, who can't visit their next neighbor without six. For their parts, they were utter strangers to all our beasts of burden or carriage before the slothful Europeans came amongst them. They had on no part of the American continent, or in any of the islands, either horses or asses, camels, dromedaries, or elephants to ease the legs of the original inhabitants or to lighten their labor. Indeed, in South America, and particularly in Chile, they have a useful animal called "paco." This creature resembles a sheep pretty much, only in the length of the neck and figure of the head it is more like a camel. It is very near as high as the ass, and the Indians there make use of it for carrying moderate burdens. The fleece that grows upon it is very valuable for the fineness, length, and glossiness of the wool. It has one remarkable singularity, that the hoofs of its forefeet have three clefts and those behind no more than one. The flesh of this animal is something drier than our mutton but altogether as well tasted. When it is angry, it has no way of resenting its wrongs but by spitting in the face of those that provoke it, and if the spawl happen to light on the bare skin of any person, it first creates an itching and afterwards a scab, if no remedy be applied. The way to manage these pacos and make them tractable is to bore a hole in their ears, through which they put a rope and then guide them just as they please. In Chile they weave a beautiful kind of stuff with thread made of this creature's wool, which has a gloss superior to any camlet and is sold very dear in that country.

6. The difficulty of finding the horses among the tall canes made it late before we decamped. We traversed very hilly grounds but, to make amends, it was pretty clear of underwood. We avoided crossing the Dan twice by taking a compass round the bent of it. There was no passing by the angle of the river without halting a moment to entertain our eyes again with that charming prospect. When that pleasure was over, we proceeded to Sable Creek and encamped a little to the east of it. The river thereabouts had a charming effect, its banks being adorned with green canes sixteen feet high, which make a spring all the year as well as plenty of forage all the winter.

One of the men wounded an old buck that was gray with years and seemed by the reverend marks he bore upon him to confirm the current opinion of that animal's longevity. The smart of his wound made him not only turn upon the dogs but likewise pursue them to some distance with great fury. However he got away at last, though by the blood that issued from his wound he could not run far before he fell and without doubt made a comfortable repast for the wolves. However, the Indian had better fortune and supplied us with a fat doe and a young bear two years old. At that age they are in their prime and, if they be fat withal, are a morsel for a cardinal.

All the land we traveled over this day and the day before, that is to say, from the river Irvin to Sable Creek, is exceedingly rich, both on the Virginia side of the line and that of Carolina.[50] Besides whole forests of canes, that adorn the banks of the river and creeks thereabouts, the fertility of the soil throws out such a quantity of winter grass that horses and cattle might keep themselves in heart all the cold season without the help of any fodder. Nor have the low grounds only this advantage but likewise the higher land, and particularly that which we call the Highland Pond, which is two miles broad and of a length unknown.

I question not but there are thirty thousand acres at least, lying all

[50] Boyd comments: "Byrd is here describing the lands which he purchased from the North Carolina commissioners, who had secured them in payment for their services. Byrd called the region the Land of Eden. He inserted in the manuscript of *The Journey to the Land of Eden* a map of his purchases, which was published in Wynne's version and is here reproduced." See p. 413 of this edition.

together, as fertile as the lands were said to be about Babylon, which yielded, if Herodotus tells us right, an increase of no less than two or three hundred for one. But this hath the advantage of being a higher, and consequently a much healthier, situation than that. So that a colony of one thousand families might, with the help of moderate industry, pass their time very happily there. Besides grazing and tillage, which would abundantly compensate their labor, they might plant vineyards upon the hills, in which situation the richest wines are always produced. They might also propagate white mulberry trees, which thrive exceedingly in this climate, in order to the feeding of silkworms and making of raw silk. They might too produce hemp, flax, and cotton in what quantity they pleased, not only for their own use but likewise for sale. Then they might raise very plentifully orchards both of peaches and apples, which contribute as much as any fruit to the luxury of life. There is no soil or climate will yield better rice than this, which is a grain of prodigious increase and of very wholesome nourishment. In short, everything will grow plentifully here to supply either the wants or wantonness of man. Nor can I so much as wish that the more tender vegetables might grow there, such as orange, lemon, and olive trees, because then we should lose the much greater benefit of the brisk northwest winds, which purge the air and sweep away all the malignant fevers which hover over countries that are always warm. The soil would also want the advantages of frost and snow, which by their nitrous particles contribute not a little to its fertility. Besides, the inhabitants would be deprived of the variety and sweet vicissitude of the seasons, which is much more delightful than one dull and constant succession of warm weather diversified only by rain and sunshine.

There is also another convenience that happens to this country by cold weather: it destroys a great number of snakes and other venomous reptiles and troublesome insects, or at least lays them to sleep for several months, which otherwise would annoy us the whole year round and multiply beyond all enduring. Though oranges and lemons are desirable fruits and useful enough in many cases, yet when the want of them is supplied by others more useful we have no cause to complain. There is no climate that produces everything since the Deluge wrenched the poles of the world out of their place, nor is it fit it should be so, because it is the mutual supply one country receives from another which creates a mutual traffic and intercourse amongst men. And in truth, were it not for this correspondence in order to make up each other's wants, the wars betwixt bordering nations, like those of the Indians and other barbarous people, would be perpetual and irreconciliable.

As to olive trees, I know by experience they will never stand the sharpness of our winters; but their place may be supplied by the plant called sesamum, which yields an infinite quantity of large seed from whence a sweet oil is pressed that is very wholesome and in use amongst the people of Lesser Asia. Likewise it is used in Egypt, preferably to oil olive, being not so apt to make those that eat it constantly break out into scabs, as they do in many parts of Italy. This would grow very kindly here and has already been planted with good success in North Carolina by way of experiment.

7. After crossing the Dan, we made a march of eight miles over hills and dales as far as the next ford of that river. And now we were by practice become such very able footmen that we easily outwalked our horses and could have marched much farther, had it not been in pity to their weakness. Besides here was plenty of canes, which was reason enough to make us shorten our journey. Our gunners did great execution as they went along, killing no less than two brace of deer and as many wild turkeys.

Though practice will soon make a man of tolerable vigor an able footman, yet, as a help to bear fatigue, I used to chew a root of ginseng[51] as I walked along. This kept up my spirits and made me trip away as nimbly in my half-jack boots as younger men could do in their shoes. This plant is in high esteem in China, where it sells for its weight in silver. Indeed it does not grow there but in the mountains of Tartary, to which place the Emperor of China sends ten thousand men every year on purpose to gather it. But it grows so scatteringly there that even so

---

[51] Byrd was enthusiastic about ginseng for various ills and, like many others, regarded it as an aphrodisiac.

many hands can bring home no great quantity. Indeed, it is a vegetable of so many virtues that Providence has planted it very thin in every country that has the happiness to produce it. Nor, indeed, is mankind worthy of so great a blessing, since health and long life are commonly abused to ill purposes. This noble plant grows likewise at the Cape of Good Hope, where it is called "kanna" and is in wonderful esteem among the Hottentots. It grows also on the northern continent of America, near the mountains, but as sparingly as truth and public spirit. It answers exactly both to the figure and virtues of that which grows in Tartary, so that there can be no doubt of its being the same. Its virtues are that it gives an uncommon warmth and vigor to the blood and frisks the spirits beyond any other cordial. It cheers the heart even of a man that has a bad wife and makes him look down with great composure on the crosses of the world. It promotes insensible perspiration, dissolves all phlegmatic and viscous humors, that are apt to obstruct the narrow channels of the nerves. It helps the memory and would quicken even Helvetian dullness. 'Tis friendly to the lungs, much more than scolding itself. It comforts the stomach and strengthens the bowels, preventing all colics and fluxes. In one word, it will make a man live a great while, and very well while he does live. And what is more, it will even make old age amiable, by rendering it lively, cheerful, and good humored. However, 'tis of little use in the feats of love, as a great prince once found, who, hearing of its invigorating quality, sent as far as China for some of it, though his ladies could not boast of any advantage thereby.

We gave the Indian the skins of all the deer that he shot himself and the men the skins of what they killed. And every evening after the fires were made they stretched them very tight upon sticks and dried them. This, by a nocturnal fire, appeared at first a very odd spectacle, everything being dark and gloomy round about. After they are dried in this manner they may be folded up without damage till they come to be dressed according to art. The Indians dress them with deer's brains, and so do the English here by their example. For expedition's sake, they often stretch their skins over smoke in order to dry them, which makes them smell so disagreeably that a rat must have a good stomach to gnaw them in that condition; nay, it is said, while that perfume continues in a pair of leather breeches, the person that wears them will be in no danger of that villainous little insect the French call *morpion*.

And now I am upon the subject of insects, it may not be improper to mention some few remedies against those that are most vexatious in this climate. There are two sorts withoutdoors that are great nuisances: the ticks and the horseflies. The ticks are either deer ticks or those that annoy the cattle. The first kind are long and take a very strong gripe, being most in remote woods above the inhabitants. The other are round and more gently insinuate themselves into the flesh, being in all places where cattle are frequent. Both these sorts are apt to be troublesome during the warm season, but have such an aversion to pennyroyal that they will attack no part that is rubbed with the juice of that fragrant vegetable. And a strong decoction of this is likewise the most effectual remedy against seed ticks, which bury themselves in your legs when they are so small you can hardly discern them without a microscope.

The horseflies are not only a great grievance to horses but likewise to those that ride them. These little vixens confine themselves chiefly to the woods and are most in moist places. Though this insect be no bigger than an ordinary fly, it bites very smartly, darting its little proboscis into the skin the instant it lights upon it. These are offensive only in the hot months and in the daytime, when they are a great nuisance to travelers; insomuch that it is no wonder they were formerly made use for one of the plagues of Egypt. But dittany, which is to be had in the woods all the while those insects remain in vigor, is a sure defense against them. For this purpose, if you stick a bunch of it on the headstall of your bridle, they will be sure to keep a respectful distance.

Thus, in what part of the woods soever anything mischievous or troublesome is found, kind Providence is sure to provide a remedy. And 'tis probably one great reason why God was pleased to create these and many other vexatious animals, that men should exercise their wits and industry to guard themselves against them.

Bears' oil is used by the Indians as a general defense against every species of vermin. Among the rest, they say it keeps both bugs and mosquitoes from assaulting their persons, which would otherwise devour such uncleanly people. Yet bears' grease has no strong smell, as that plant had which the Egyptians formerly used against mosquitoes, resembling our palma Christi,[52] the juice of which smelt so disagreeably that the remedy was worse than the disease. Against mosquitoes in Egypt, the richer sort used to build lofty towers, with bedchambers in the tops of them, that they might rest undisturbed. 'Tis certain that these insects are no high fliers, because their wings are weak and their bodies so light that if they mount ever so little the wind blows them quite away from their course and they become an easy prey to the martins, East India bats, and other birds that fly about in continual quest of them.

8. As we had twice more to cross the Dan over two fords that lay no more than seven miles from each other, we judged the distance would not be much greater to go round the bent of it. Accordingly, we sent the Indian and two white men that way, who came up with us in the evening, after fetching a compass of about twelve miles. They told us that about a mile from our last camp they passed a creek fortified with steep cliffs, which therefore gained the name of Cliff Creek. Near three miles beyond that they forded a second creek, on the margin of which grew abundance of tall canes, and this was called Hix's Creek from one of the discoverers. Between these two creeks lies a level of exceeding rich land, full of large trees, and covered with black mold, as fruitful, if we believe them, as that which is yearly overflowed by the Nile.

We who marched the nearest way upon the line found the ground rising and falling between the two fords of the Dan, which almost broke our own winds and the hearts of our jaded palfreys. When we had passed the last ford, it was a sensible joy to find ourselves safe over all the waters that might cut off our retreat. And we had the greater reason to be thankful because so late in the year it was very unusual to find the rivers so fordable.

[52] The castor-oil plant.

We catched a large terrapin in the river, which is one kind of turtle. The flesh of it is wholesome and good for consumptive people. It lays a great number of eggs, not larger but rounder than those of pigeons. These are soft but withal so tough that 'tis difficult to break them, yet are very sweet and invigorating, so that some wives recommend them earnestly to their husbands. One of the men, by an overstrain, had unhappily got a running of the reins, for which I gave him every morning a little sweet gum dissolved in water, with good success. This gum distills from a large tree, called the sweet gum tree, very common in Virginia, and is as healing in its virtue as balm of Gilead or the balsams of Tolú and of Peru. It is likewise a most agreeable perfume, very little inferior to ambergris.

And now I have mentioned ambergris, I hope it will not be thought an unprofitable digression to give a faithful account how it is produced, in order to reconcile the various opinions concerning it. It is now certainly found to be the dung of the spermaceti whale, which is at first very black and unsavory. But after having been washed for some months in the sea and blanched in the sun, it comes at length to be of a gray color, and from a most offensive smell contracts the finest fragrancy in the world. Besides the fragrancy of this animal substance, 'tis a very rich and innocent cordial, which raises the spirits without stupefying them afterwards like opium or intoxicating them like wine. The animal spirits are amazingly refreshed by this cordial, without the danger of any ill consequence, and if husbands were now and then to dissolve a little of it in their broth, their consorts might be the better for it as well as themselves. In the Bahama Islands (where a great quantity is found by reason the spermaceti whales resort thither continually), it is used as an antidote against the venomous fish which abound thereabouts, wherewith the people are apt to poison themselves. We are not only obliged to that whale for this rich perfume but also for the spermaceti itself, which is the fat of that fish's head boiled and purged from all its impurities. What remains is of a balsamic and detersive quality, very friendly to the lungs and useful in many other cases.

The Indian had killed a fat doe in the compass he took round the elbow of the river but was contented to prime it only, by reason it was too far off to lug the whole carcass upon his back. This and a brace of wild turkeys which our men had shot made up all our bill of fare this evening but could only afford a philosophical meal to so many craving stomachs. The horses were now so lean that anything would gall those that carried the least burden; no wonder, then, if several of them had sore backs, especially now the pads of the saddles and packs were pressed flat with long and constant use. This would have been another misfortune, had we not been provided with an easy remedy for it. One of the commissioners, believing that such accidents might happen in a far journey, had furnished himself with plasters of strong glue spread pretty thick. We laid on these, after making them running hot, which, sticking fast, never fell off till the sore was perfectly healed. In the meantime, it defended the part so well that the saddle might bear upon it without danger of further injury.

9. We reckoned ourselves now pretty well out of the latitude of bears, to the great grief of most of the company. There was still mast enough left in the woods to keep the bears from drawing so near to the inhabitants. They like not the neighborhood of merciless man till famine compels them to it. They are all black in this part of the world, and so is their dung, but [it] will make linen white, being tolerable good soap, without any preparation but only drying. These bears are of a moderate size, whereas within the polar circles they are white and much larger. Those of the southern parts of Muscovy are of a russet color, but among the Samoyeds,[53] as well as in Greenland and Nova Zembla, they are as white as the snow they converse with and, by some accounts, are as large as a moderate ox. The excessive cold of that climate sets their appetites so sharp, that they will attack a man without ceremony and even climb up a ship's side to come at him. They range about and are very mischievous all the time the sun is above the horizon, which is something more than five months; but after the sun is set for the rest of the year they retire into holes or bury themselves under the snow and sleep away the dark season without any sustenance at all. 'Tis pity our beggars and pickpockets could not do the same.

[53] A Mongoloid tribe of Siberia.

Our journey this day was above twelve miles and more than half the way terribly hampered with bushes. We tired another horse, which we were obliged to leave two miles short of where we encamped, and indeed several others were upon the career almost every step. Now we wanted one of those celebrated musicians of antiquity who, they tell us, among many other wonders of their art, could play an air which by its animating briskness would make a jaded horse caper and curvet much better than any whip, spur, or even than swearing. Though I fear our poor beasts were so harassed that it would have been beyond the skill of Orpheus himself so much as to make them prick up their ears.

For proof of the marvelous power of music among the ancients, some historians say that one of those skillful masters took upon him to make the great Alexander start up from his seat and handle his javelin, whether he would or not, by the force of a sprightly tune which he knew how to play to him. The king ordered the man to bring his instruments, and then, fixing himself firmly in his chair and determining not to stir, he bade him strike up as soon as he pleased. The musician obeyed and presently roused the hero's spirits with such warlike notes that he was constrained, in spite of all his resolution, to spring up and fly to his javelin with great martial fury.

We can the easier credit these profane stories by what we find recorded in the oracles of truth, where we are told the wonders David performed by sweetly touching his harp. He made nothing of driving the evil spirit out of Saul, though a certain rabbi assures us he could not do so much by his wife, Michal, when she happened to be in her airs.

The greatest instance we have of the power of modern music is that which cures those who in Italy are bit by the little spider called the tarantula, the whole method of which is performed in the following manner: in Apulia 'tis a common misfortune for people to be bit by the tarantula, and most about Taranto and Gallipoli. This is a gray spider, not very large, with a narrow streak of white along the back. It is no wonder there are many of these villainous insects, because, by a ridiculous superstition, 'tis accounted great inhumanity to kill them. They believe, it seems, that if the spider come to a violent death, all those who had been bit by it will certainly have a return of their frenzy every year as long as they live. But if it die a natural death, the patient will have a chance to recover in two or three years.

The bite of the tarantula gives no more pain than the bite of a mosquito and makes little or no inflammation on the part, especially when the disaster happens in April or May; but its venom, increasing with the heat of the season, has more fatal consequences in July and August. The persons who are so unhappy as to be bitten in those warm months fall down on the place in a few minutes and lie senseless for a considerable time, and when they come to themselves feel horrible pains, are very sick at their stomachs, and in a short time break out into foul sores; but those who are bit in the milder months have much gentler symptoms. They are longer before the distemper shows itself, and then they have a small disorder in their senses, are a little sick, and perhaps have some moderate breakings-out.

However, in both cases the patient keeps upon the bed, not caring to stir till he is roused by a tune proper for his particular case. Therefore, as soon as the symptoms discover themselves, a tarantula doctor is sent for, who, after viewing carefully the condition of the person, first tries one tune and then another, till he is so fortunate as to hit the phrenetic turn of the patient. No sooner does this happen but he begins first to wag a finger, then a hand, and afterwards a foot, till at last he springs up and dances round the room with a surprising agility, rolling his eyes and looking wild the whole time. This dancing fit lasts commonly about twenty-five minutes, by which time he will be all in a lather. Then he sits down, falls a-laughing, and returns to his senses. So plentiful a perspiration discharges so much of the venom as will keep off the return of the distemper for a whole year. Then it will visit him again and must be removed in the same merry manner. But three dancing bouts will do the business, unless, peradventure, the spider, according to the vulgar notion, hath been put to a violent death.

The tunes played to expel this whimsical disorder are of the jig kind and exceed not fifteen in number. The Apulians are frequently dancing off the effects of this poison, and no remedy is more commonly applied to any other distemper elsewhere than those sprightly tunes are to the bite of the tarantula in that part of Italy.

It is remarkable that these spiders have a greater spite to the natives of the place than they have to strangers, and women are oftener bit than men. Though there may be a reason for the last, because women are more confined to the house, where these spiders keep, and their coats make them liable to attacks unseen, whereas the men can more easily discover and brush them off their legs. Nevertheless, both sexes are cured the same way and thereby show the wonderful effects of music.

Considering how far we had walked and, consequently, how hungry we were, we found but short commons when we came to our quarters. One brace of turkeys were all the game we could meet with, which almost needed a miracle to enable them to suffice so many voracious appetites. However, they just made a shift to keep famine, and consequently mutiny, out of the camp. At night we lodged upon the banks of Buffalo Creek, where none of us could complain of loss of rest for having eat too heavy and luxurious a supper.

10. In a dearth of provisions our chaplain pronounced it lawful to make bold with the Sabbath and send a party out a-hunting. They fired the dry leaves in a ring of five miles' circumference, which, burning inwards, drove all the game to the center, where they were easily killed. 'Tis really a pitiful sight to see the extreme distress the poor deer are in when they find themselves surrounded with this circle of fire; they weep and groan like a human creature, yet can't move the compassion of those hardhearted people who are about to murder them. This unmerciful sport is called fire-hunting and is much practiced by the Indians and frontier inhabitants, who sometimes, in the eagerness of their diversion, are punished for their cruelty and are hurt by one another when they shoot across at the deer which are in the middle.

What the Indians do now by a circle of fire the ancient Persians performed formerly by a circle of men; and the same is practiced at this day in Germany upon extraordinary occasions when any of the princes of the empire have a mind to make a general hunt, as they call it. At such times they order a vast number of people to surround a whole territory. Then, marching inwards in close order, they at last force all the wild beasts into a narrow compass, that the prince and his company may have the diversion of slaughtering as many as they please with their own hands. Our hunters massacred two brace of deer after this unfair way, of which they brought us one brace whole and only the primings of the rest.

So many were absent on this occasion that we who remained excused the chaplain from the trouble of spending his spirits by preaching to so thin a congregation.

One of the men, who had been an old Indian trader, brought me a stem of silk grass, which was about as big as my little finger. But, being so late in the year that the leaf was fallen off, I am not able to describe the plant. The Indians use it in all their little manufactures, twisting a thread of it that is prodigiously strong. Of this they make their baskets and the aprons which their women wear about their middles for decency's sake. These are long enough to wrap quite round them and reach down to their knees, with a fringe on the under part by way of ornament. They put on this modest covering with so much art that the most impertinent curiosity can't, in the negligentest of their motions or postures, make the least discovery. As this species of silk grass is much stronger than hemp, I make no doubt but sailcloth and cordage might be made of it with considerable improvement.

11. We had all been so refreshed by our day of rest that we decamped earlier than ordinary and passed the several fords of Hyco River. The woods were thick great part of this day's journey, so that we were forced to scuffle hard to advance seven miles, being equal in fatigue to double that distance of clear and open grounds. We took up our quarters upon Sugartree Creek, in the same camp we had lain when we came up, and happened to be entertained at supper with a rarity we had never had the fortune to meet with before during the whole expedition.

A little wide of this creek, one of the men had the luck to meet with a young buffalo of two years old. It was a bull which, notwithstanding he was no older, was as big as an ordinary ox. His legs were very thick and very short and his hoofs exceeding broad. His back rose into a kind of bunch a little above the shoulders, which I believe contributes not a little to that creature's enormous strength. His body is vastly deep from the shoulders to the brisket, sometimes six feet in those that are full grown. The portly figure of this animal is disgraced by a shabby little tail, not above twelve inches long. This he cocks up on end whenever he's in a passion and, instead of lowing or bellowing, grunts with no better grace than a hog. The hair growing on his head and neck is long and shagged and so soft that it will spin into thread not unlike mohair, which might be wove into a sort of camlet. Some people have stockings knit of it that would have served an Israelite during his forty years' march through the wilderness. Its horns are short and strong, of which the Indians make large spoons which they say will split and fall to pieces whenever poison is put into them. Its color is a dirty brown and its hide so thick that it is scarce penetrable. However, it makes very spongy sole leather by the ordinary method of tanning, though this fault might by good contrivance be mended.

As thick as this poor beast's hide was, a bullet made shift to enter it and fetch him down. It was found all alone, which seldom buffaloes are. They usually range about in herds like other cattle, and, though they differ something in figure, are certainly of the same species. There are two reasons for this opinion: the flesh of both has exactly the same taste and the mixed breed betwixt both, they say, will generate. All the difference I could perceive between the flesh of buffalo and common beef was that the flesh of the first was much yellower than that of the other and the lean something tougher. The men were so delighted with this new diet that the gridiron and frying pan had no more rest all night than a poor husband subject to curtain lectures.

Buffaloes may be easily tamed when they are taken young. The best way to catch them is to carry a milch mare into the woods and, when you find a cow and calf, to kill the cow and then, having catched the calf, to suckle it upon the mare. After once or twice sucking her, it will follow her home and become as gentle as another calf. If we could get into a breed of them, they might be made very useful, not only for the dairy, by giving an ocean of milk, but also for drawing vast and cumbersome weights by their prodigious strength. These, with the other advantages I mentioned before, would make this sort of cattle more profitable to the owner than any other we are acquainted with, though they would need a world of provender.

12. Before we marched this morning, every man took care to pack up some buffalo steaks in his wallet, besides what he crammed into his belly. When provisions were plenty, we always found it difficult to get out early, being too much embarrassed with a long-winded breakfast. However, by the strength of our beef, we made a shift to walk about twelve miles, crossing Bluewing and Tewahominy creeks. And because this last stream received its appellation from the disaster of a Tuscarora Indian, 'twill not be straggling much out of the way to say something of that particular nation.[54]

These Indians were heretofore very numerous and powerful, making, within time of memory, at least a thousand fighting men. Their habitation before the war with Carolina was on the north branch of Neuse River, commonly called Connecta Creek,[55] in a pleasant and fruitful country. But now the few that are left of that nation live on the north side of Moratuck, which is all that part of Roanoke below the great falls toward Albemarle Sound. Formerly there were seven towns of these savages, lying not far from each other, but now their number is greatly reduced. The trade they have had the misfortune to

[54] "The Tuscarora [of Iroquoian stock], who lived on the Roanoke and Tar-Pamlico Rivers until their migration northward, were an important people, though comparatively little is known about them . . . The seizure of more and more lands by the settlers led to resentment, and when the whites began to kidnap and enslave the Indians open warfare developed. In 1710 the Tuscarora sent a petition to the provisional government of Pennsylvania embodying their grievances. Eight proposals, each attested by a wampum belt, were framed to cover the relations between Indians and whites. These belts with their pitiful messages were finally sent to the Five Nations of the North. At the beginning of the first war between the Tuscarora and the whites the Indians had 15 towns and a fighting strength of 2,000. The war opened with the capture (September 1711) of Lawson and Baron de Graffenried. Lawson was put to death but de Graffenried was liberated. Five tribes then formed a compact to annihilate the whites, each operating in its own district . . . By 1714 the remnants of the Tuscarora migrated northward to take shelter with the Five Nations" (*North Carolina: A Guide to the Old North State* [Chapel Hill, 1944], pp. 26–27).
[55] This is now called Contentnea Creek, apparently a corruption of the name of Cotechney, a Tuscarora town in this area to which Lawson was taken by his captors in 1711.

drive with the English has furnished them constantly with rum, which they have used so immoderately that, what with the distempers and what with the quarrels it begat amongst them, it has proved a double destruction. But the greatest consumption of these savages happened by the war about twenty-five years ago, on account of some injustice the inhabitants of that province had done them about their lands. It was on that provocation they resented their wrongs a little too severely upon Mr. Lawson, who, under color of being Surveyor General, had encroached too much upon their territories, at which they were so enraged that they waylaid him and cut his throat from ear to ear but at the same time released the Baron de Graffenreid, whom they had seized for company, because it appeared plainly he had done them no wrong.

This blow was followed by some other bloody actions on the part of the Indians which brought on the war, wherein many of 'em were cut off and many were obliged to flee for refuge to the Senecas; so that now there remain so few that they are in danger of being quite exterminated by the Catawbas, their mortal enemies.

These Indians have a very odd tradition amongst them that many years ago their nation was grown so dishonest that no man could keep any of his goods or so much as his loving wife to himself; that, however, their god, being unwilling to root them out for their crimes, did them the honor to send a messenger from Heaven to instruct them and set them a perfect example of integrity and kind behavior toward one another. But this holy person, with all his eloquence and sanctity of life, was able to make very little reformation amongst them. Some few old men did listen a little to his wholesome advice, but all the young fellows were quite incorrigible. They not only neglected his precepts but derided and evil entreated his person. At last, taking upon him to reprove some young rakes of the Conechta [56] clan very sharply for their impiety, they were so provoked at the freedom of his rebukes that they tied him to a tree and shot him with arrows through the heart. But their god took instant vengeance on all who had a hand in that monstrous act by lightning from Heaven, and has ever since

[56] The same name as in "Conneccta Creek" on p. 302.

visited their nation with a continued train of calamities; nor will he ever leave off punishing and wasting their people till he shall have blotted every living soul of them out of the world.

Our hunters shot nothing this whole day but a straggling bear, which happened to fall by the hand of the very person who had been lately disarmed and put to flight, for which he declared war against the whole species.

13. We pursued our journey with all diligence and forded Ohimpamony Creek about noon, and from thence proceeded to Yapatsco, which we could not cross without difficulty. The beavers had dammed up the water much higher than we found it at our going-up, so that we were obliged to lay a bridge over a part that was shallower than the rest to facilitate our passage. Beavers have more of instinct, that half brother of reason, than any other animal, especially in matters of self-preservation. In their houses they always contrive a sally port, both toward the land and toward the water, that so they may escape by one if their retreat should happen to be cut off at the other. They perform all their works in the dead of night to avoid discovery and are kept diligently to it by the master beaver, which by his age or strength has gained to himself an authority over the rest. If any of the gang happen to be lazy or will not exert himself to the utmost in felling of trees or dragging them to the place where they are made use of, this superintendent will not fail to chastise him with the flat of the tail, wherewith he is able to give unmerciful strokes. They lie snug in their houses all day, unless some unneighborly miller chance to disturb their repose by demolishing their dams for supplying his mill with water. 'Tis rare to see one of them, and the Indians for that reason have hardly any way to take them but by laying snares near the place where they dam up the water. But the English hunters have found out a more effectual method, by using the following receipt: take the large pride of the beaver, squeeze all the juice out of it, then take the small pride and squeeze out about five or six drops; take the inside of sassafras bark, powder it, and mix it with the liquor, and place this bait conveniently for your steel trap.

The story of biting off their testicles to compound for their lives when they are pursued is a story taken upon trust by Pliny, like many others. Nor is it the beaver's testicles that carry the perfume, but they have a pair of glands just within the fundament as sweet as musk, that perfume their dung and communicate a strong scent to their testicles by being placed near them.

'Tis true several creatures have strange instincts for their preservation, as the Egyptian frog, we are told by Aelian, will carry a whole joint of a reed across its mouth, that it may not be swallowed by the ibis. And this long-necked fowl will give itself a clyster with its beak whenever it finds itself too costive or feverish. The dogs of that country lap the water of the Nile in a full trot, that they may not be snapped by the crocodiles.[57] Both beavers and wolves, we know, when one of their legs is catched in a steel trap, will bite it off, that they may escape with the rest.

The flesh of the beavers is tough and dry, all but the tail, which, like the parrot's tongue, was one of the farfetched rarities with which Heliogabalus used to furnish his luxurious table. The fur of these creatures is very valuable, especially in the more northern countries, where it is longer and finer. This the Dutch have lately contrived to mix with their wool and weave into a sort of drugget that is not only warm but wonderfully light and soft. They also make gloves and stockings of it that keep out the cold almost as well as the fur itself and don't look quite so savage.

There is a deal of rich low ground on Yapatsco Creek, but I believe liable to be overflowed in a fresh. However, it might be proper enough for rice, which receives but little injury from water. We encamped on the banks of Massamony Creek, after a journey of more than eleven

[57] Byrd probably used either the English translation of Claudius Aelianus by Abraham Fleming, printed in 1576 with the title *A Register of Histories*, or the 1665 English translation by Thomas Stanley titled *Claudius Aelianus His Various History*; in both of these editions the note about the frog appears as Chapter iii and that on the Nile dogs as chapter iv, which suggests that Byrd may have referred to the book itself when writing this section. Aelianus' frog uses the reed to protect itself from a snake. Byrd may have deliberately altered this to an ibis in order to be able to introduce the information about the ibis' method of maintaining metabolic regularity, a matter to which he gave great attention in his diary. The item (which Byrd could have found in Pliny) is included in the notes in the manuscript commonplace book in Byrd's hand recently acquired by the Virginia Historical Society.

miles. By the way we shot a fat doe and a wild turkey, which fed us all plentifully. And we have reason to say, by our own happy experience, that no man need to despair of his daily bread in the woods whose faith is but half so large as his stomach.

14. Being at length happily arrived within twenty miles of the uppermost inhabitants, we dispatched two men who had the ablest horses to go before and get a beef killed and some bread baked to refresh their fellow travelers upon their arrival. They had likewise orders to hire an express to carry a letter to the Governor giving an account that we were all returned in safety. This was the more necessary because we had been so long absent that many now began to fear we were by this time scalped and barbecued by the Indians.

We decamped with the rest of the people about ten o'clock and marched near twelve miles. In our way we crossed Nutbush Creek, and four miles farther we came upon a beautiful branch of Great Creek, where we took up our quarters. The tent was pitched on an eminence which overlooked a wide piece of low grounds, covered with reeds and watered by a crystal stream gliding through the middle of it. On the other side of this delightful valley, which was about half a mile wide, rose a hill that terminated the view and in the figure of a semicircle closed in upon the opposite side of the valley. This had a most agreeable effect upon the eye and wanted nothing but cattle grazing in the meadow and sheep and goats feeding on the hill to make it a complete rural landscape.

The Indian killed a fawn which, being upon its growth, was not fat but made some amends by being tender. He also shot an otter, but our people were now better fed than to eat such coarse food. The truth of it is, the flesh of this creature has a rank fishy taste and for that reason might be a proper regale for the Samoyeds, who drink the Czar of Muscovy's health and toast their mistresses in a bumper of train oil.[58] The Carthusians, to save their vow of eating no flesh, pronounce this amphibious animal to be a fish and feed upon it as such without wounding their consciences. The skin of the otter is very soft, and the Swedes make caps and socks of it, not only for warmth but also because

[58] Whale oil.

they fancy it strengthens the nerves and is good against all distempers of the brain. The otter is a great devourer of fish, which are its natural food, and whenever it betakes itself to a vegetable diet it is as some high-spirited wives obey their husbands, by pure necessity. They dive after their prey, though they can't continue long under water but thrust their noses up to the surface now and then for breath. They are great enemies to weirs set up in the rivers to catch fish, devouring or biting to pieces all they find there. Nor is it easy either to fright them from this kind of robbery, or to destroy them. The best way I could ever find was to float an old wheel just by the weir, and so soon as the otter has taken a large fish he will get upon the wheel to eat it more at his ease, which may give you an opportunity of firing upon him from the shore.

One of our people shot a large gray squirrel with a very bushy tail, a singular use of which our merry Indian discovered to us. He said whenever this little animal has occasion to cross a run of water, he launches a chip or piece of bark into the water on which he embarks and, holding up his tail to the wind, sails over very safely. If this be true, 'tis probable men learnt at first the use of sails from these ingenious little animals, as the Hottentots learnt the physical use of most of their plants from the baboons.

15. About three miles from our camp we passed Great Creek, and then, after traversing very barren grounds for five miles together, we crossed the trading path and soon after had the pleasure of reaching the uppermost inhabitant. This was a plantation belonging to Colonel Mumford, where our men almost burst themselves with potatoes and milk. Yet as great a curiosity as a house was to us foresters, yet still we chose to lie in the tent, as being much the cleanlier and sweeter lodging.

The trading path above-mentioned receives its name from being the route the traders take with their caravans when they go to traffic with the Catawbas and other southern Indians. The Catawbas live about 250 miles beyond Roanoke River, and yet our traders find their account in transporting goods from Virginia to trade with them at their own town. The common method of carrying on this Indian commerce is as follows: gentlemen send for goods proper for such a trade from England and then either venture them out at their own risk to the Indian towns or else credit some traders with them of substance and reputation, to be paid in skins at certain price agreed betwixt them. The goods for the Indian trade consist chiefly in guns, powder, shot, hatchets (which the Indians call tomahawks), kettles, red and blue planes,[59] Duffields,[60] Stroudwater blankets,[61] and some cutlery wares, brass rings, and other trinkets.

These wares are made up into packs and carried upon horses, each load being from 150 to 200 pounds, with which they are able to travel about twenty miles a day if forage happen to be plentiful. Formerly a hundred horses have been employed in one of these Indian caravans under the conduct of fifteen or sixteen persons only, but now the trade is much impaired, insomuch that they seldom go with half that number.

The course from Roanoke to the Catawbas is laid down nearest southwest and lies through a fine country that is watered by several beautiful rivers. Those of the greatest note are: first, Tar River, which is the upper part of Pamptico,[62] Flat River, Little River, and Eno River, all three branches of Neuse.

Between Eno and Saxapahaw rivers are the Haw old fields, which have the reputation of containing the most fertile high land in this part of the world, lying in a body of about fifty thousand acres. This Saxapahaw is the upper part of Cape Fear River, the falls of which lie many miles below the trading path. Some mountains overlook this rich spot of land, from whence all the soil washes down into the plain and is the cause of its exceeding fertility. Not far from thence the path crosses Aramanchy River,[63] a branch of Saxapahaw, and about forty

[59] I.e., plain cloth.

[60] Duffels, coarse woolen cloth, named for the town of the same name near Amsterdam.

[61] Coarse woolen blankets, named for Stroud, Gloucestershire, on the Thames and Severn canal.

[62] The old name for Pamlico River.

[63] Now Alamance Creek, in the county of the same name. The fact that most of the early settlers of the country were German led to the conjecture that the name originated from "Allemania." "Allemanni" is one of the spellings found in old records. But it is possible that this is simply a corruption of the original Indian name. An l-r interchange occurred in some Algonquian Indian dialects.

miles beyond that, Deep River, which is the north branch of Pee Dee. Then forty miles beyond that, the path intersects the Yadkin, which is there half a mile over and is supposed to be the south branch of the same Pee Dee.

The soil is exceedingly rich on both sides the Yadkin, abounding in rank grass and prodigious large trees, and for plenty of fish, fowl, and venison, is inferior to no part of the northern continent. There the traders commonly lie still for some days, to recruit their horses' flesh as well as to recover their own spirits. Six miles farther is Crane Creek, so named from its being the rendezvous of great armies of cranes, which wage a more cruel war at this day with the frogs and the fish than they used to do with the pygmies in the days of Homer.

About threescore miles more bring you to the first town of the Catawbas, called Nauvasa, situated on the banks of the Santee River. Besides this town, there are five others belonging to the same nation, lying all on the same stream within the distance of twenty miles. These Indians were all called formerly by the general name of the Usherees and were a very numerous and powerful people. But the frequent slaughters made upon them by the northern Indians and, what has been still more destructive by far, the intemperance and foul distempers introduced amongst them by the Carolina traders have now reduced their numbers to little more than four hundred fighting men, besides women and children. It is a charming place where they live, the air very wholesome, the soil fertile, and the winters are mild and serene.

In Santee River, as in several others of Carolina, a smaller kind of alligator is frequently seen, which perfumes the water with a musky smell. They seldom exceed eight feet in length in these parts, whereas near the equinoctial they come up to twelve or fourteen. And the heat of the climate don't only make them bigger but more fierce and voracious. They watch the cattle there when they come to drink and cool themselves in the river; and because they are not able to drag them into the deep water, they make up by stratagem what they want in force. They swallow great stones, the weight of which, being added to their strength, enables them to tug a moderate cow under water and, as soon as they have drowned her, discharge the stones out of their maw and then feast upon the carcass. However, as fierce and as strong as these monsters are, the Indians will surprise them napping as they float upon the surface, get astride upon their necks, then whip a short piece of wood like a truncheon into their jaws, and holding the ends with their two hands, hinder them from diving by keeping their mouths open; and when they are almost spent, they will make to the shore, where their riders knock them on the head and eat them.[64]

This amphibious animal is a smaller kind of crocodile, having the same shape exactly, only the crocodile of the Nile is twice as long, being when full grown from twenty to thirty feet. This enormous length is the more to be wondered at because the crocodile is hatched from an egg very little larger than that of a goose. It has a long head, which it can open very wide, with very sharp and strong teeth. Their eyes are small, their legs short, with claws upon their feet. Their tail makes half the length of their body, and the whole is guarded with hard impenetrable scales, except the belly, which is much softer and smoother. They keep much upon the land in the daytime but toward the evening retire into the water to avoid the cold dews of the night. They run pretty fast right forward but are very awkward and slow in turning by reason of their unwieldy length. It is an error that they have no tongue, without which they could hardly swallow their food; but in eating they move the upper jaw only, contrary to all other animals. The way of catching them in Egypt is with a strong hook fixed to the end of a chain and baited with a joint of pork, which they are very fond of. But a live hog is generally tied near, the cry of which allures them to the hook. This account of the crocodile will agree in most particulars with the alligator; only the bigness of the last cannot entitle it to the name of "leviathan," which Job gave formerly to the crocodile, and not to the whale as some interpreters would make us believe.

So soon as the Catawba Indians are informed of the approach of the Virginia caravans, they send a detachment of their warriors to bid them welcome and escort them safe to their town, where they are received with great marks of distinction. And their courtesies to the

[64] This method of capturing alligators is attributed by Pliny to a Nile people, who employed it with crocodiles (viii.38).

Virginia traders, I dare say, are very sincere, because they sell them better goods and better pennyworths than the traders of Carolina. They commonly reside among the Indians till they have bartered their goods away for skins, with which they load their horses and come back by the same path they went. There are generally some Carolina traders that constantly live among the Catawbas and pretend to exercise a dictatorial authority over them. These petty rulers don't only teach the honester savages all sorts of debauchery but are unfair in their dealings and use them with all kinds of oppression. Nor has their behavior been at all better to the rest of the Indian nations among whom they reside, by abusing their women and evil entreating their men; and, by the way, this was the true reason of the fatal war which the nations round about made upon Carolina in the year 1713.[65] Then it was that all the neighbor Indians, grown weary of the tyranny and injustice with which they had been abused for many years, resolved to endure their bondage no longer but entered into a general confederacy against their oppressors of Carolina. The Indians opened the war by knocking most of those little tyrants on the head that dwelt amongst them under pretense of regulating their commerce, and from thence carried their resentment so far as to endanger both North and South Carolina.

16. We gave orders that the horses should pass Roanoke River at Moniseep Ford, while most of the baggage was transported in a canoe. We landed at the plantation of Cornelius Keith, where I beheld the wretchedest scene of poverty I had ever met with in this happy part of the world. The man, his wife, and six small children lived in a pen like so many cattle, without any roof over their heads but that of Heaven. And this was their airy residence in the daytime; but then there was a fodder stack not far from this enclosure in which the whole family sheltered themselves anights and in bad weather. However, 'twas almost worth while to be as poor as this man was, to be as perfectly contented. All his wants proceeded from indolence and not from misfortune. He had good land, as well as good health and good limbs to

---

[65] After the Tuscaroras' massacre of the colonists in 1711 there were intermittent conflicts, culminating in a crushing defeat of the Tuscaroras in 1713.

work it and, besides, had a trade very useful to all the inhabitants round about. He could make and set up quernstones very well and had proper materials for that purpose just at hand if he could have taken the pains to fetch them. There are no other kind of mills in those remote parts, and, therefore, if the man would have worked at his trade, he might have lived very comfortably. The poor woman had a little more industry and spun cotton enough to make a thin covering for her own and her children's nakedness.

I am sorry to say it, but idleness is the general character of the men in the southern parts of this colony as well as in North Carolina. The air is so mild and the soil so fruitful that very little labor is required to fill their bellies, especially where the woods afford such plenty of game. These advantages discharge the men from the necessity of killing themselves with work, and then for the other article, of raiment, a very little of that will suffice in so temperate a climate. But so much as is absolutely necessary falls to the good women's share to provide. They all spin, weave, and knit, whereby they make a good shift to clothe the whole family; and to their credit be it recorded, many of them do it very completely and thereby reproach their husbands' laziness in the most inoffensive way, that is to say, by discovering a better spirit of industry in themselves.

From hence we moved forward to Colonel Mumford's other plantation, under the care of Miles Riley, where by that gentleman's directions we were again supplied with many good things. Here it was we discharged our worthy friend and fellow traveler, Mr. Bearskin, who had so plentifully supplied us with provisions during our long expedition. We rewarded him to his heart's content, so that he returned to his town loaden with riches and the reputation of having been a great discoverer.

17. This being Sunday, we were seasonably put in mind how much we were obliged to be thankful for our happy return to the inhabitants. Indeed, we had great reason to reflect with gratitude on the signal mercies we had received. First, that we had day by day been fed by the bountiful hand of Providence in the desolate wilderness, insomuch that if any of our people wanted one single meal during the

whole expedition, it was entirely owing to their own imprudent management. Secondly, that not one man of our whole company had any violent distemper or bad accident befall him, from one end of the line to the other. The very worst that happened was that one of them gave himself a smart cut on the pan of his knee with a tomahawk, which we had the good fortune to cure in a short time without the help of a surgeon. As for the misadventures of sticking in the mire and falling into rivers and creeks, they were rather subjects of mirth than complaint and served only to diversify our travels with a little farcical variety. And, lastly, that many uncommon incidents have concurred to prosper our undertaking. We had not only a dry spring before we went out, but the preceding winter, and even a year or two before, had been much drier than ordinary. This made not only the Dismal but likewise most of the sunken grounds near the seaside just hard enough to bear us, which otherwise had been quite unpassable. And the whole time we were upon the business, which was in all about sixteen weeks, we were never catched in the rain except once, nor was our progress interrupted by bad weather above three or four days at most.

Besides all this, we were surprised by no Indian enemy, but all of us brought our scalps back safe upon our heads. This cruel method of scalping of enemies is practiced by all the savages in America and perhaps is not the least proof of their original from the northern inhabitants of Asia. Among the ancient Scythians it was constantly used, who carried about these hairy scalps as trophies of victory. They served them too as towels at home and trappings for their horses abroad.[66] But these were not content with the skin of their enemies' heads but also made use of their skulls for cups to drink out of upon high festival days, and made greater ostentation of them than if they had been made of gold or the purest crystal.

Besides the duties of the day, we christened one of our men who had been bred a Quaker. The man desired this of his own mere motion, without being tampered with by the parson, who was willing everyone should go to Heaven his own way. But whether he did it by the conviction of his own reason or to get rid of some troublesome forms

[66] Byrd repeats himself; see p. 259.

313

and restraints to which the saints of that persuasion are subject, I can't positively say.

18. We proceeded over a level road twelve miles as far as George Hix's plantation on the south side Meherrin River, our course being for the most part northeast. By the way we hired a cart to transport our baggage, that we might the better befriend our jaded horses. Within two miles of our journey's end this day we met the express we had sent the Saturday before to give notice of our arrival. He had been almost as expeditious as [a] carrier pigeon, riding in two days no less than two hundred miles.

All the grandees of the Saponi nation did us the honor to repair hither to meet us, and our worthy friend and fellow traveler, Bearskin, appeared among the gravest of them in his robes of ceremony. Four young ladies of the first quality came with them, who had more the air of cleanliness than any copper-colored beauties I had ever seen; yet we resisted all their charms, notwithstanding the long fast we had kept from the sex and the bear diet we had been so long engaged in. Nor can I say the price they set upon their charms was at all exorbitant. A princess for a pair of red stockings can't, surely, be thought buying repentance much too dear.

The men had something great and venerable in their countenances, beyond the common mien of savages; and indeed they ever had the reputation of being the honestest as well as the bravest Indians we have ever been acquainted with. This people is now made up of the remnant of several other nations, of which the most considerable are the Saponis, the Occaneechis, and Stoukenhocks,[67] who, not finding themselves separately numerous enough for their defense, have agreed to unite into one body, and all of them now go under the name of the Saponis. Each of these was formerly a distinct nation, or rather a several clan or canton of the same nation, speaking the same language and using the same customs. But their perpetual wars against all other Indians in time reduced them so low as to make it necessary to join

[67] Another name for the Stegaraki, a Siouan tribe who were found by the early settlers on the Rappahannock. William Strachey called them the Stegaras and described them as at that time (1608–1609) "contributary" to the Manahoacs and confederates of the Monacans (*Historie of Travell*, p. 107).

their forces together. They dwelt formerly not far below the mountains, upon Yadkin River, about two hundred miles west and by south from the falls of Roanoke. But about twenty-five years ago they took refuge in Virginia, being no longer in condition to make head [68] not only against the northern Indians, who are their implacable enemies, but also against most of those to the south. All the nations round about, bearing in mind the havoc these Indians used formerly to make among their ancestors in the insolence of their power, did at length avenge it home [69] upon them and made them glad to apply to this government for protection. Colonel Spotswood, our then Lieutenant Governor, having a good opinion of their fidelity and courage, settled them at Christanna, ten miles north of Roanoke, upon the belief that they would be a good barrier on that side of the country against the incursion of all foreign Indians. And in earnest they would have served well enough for that purpose if the white people in the neighborhood had not debauched their morals and ruined their health with rum, which was the cause of many disorders and ended at last in a barbarous murder committed by one of these Indians when he was drunk, for which the poor wretch was executed when he was sober. It was matter of great concern to them, however, that one of their grandees should be put to so ignominious a death. All Indians have as great an aversion to hanging as the Muscovites, though perhaps not for the same cleanly reason, these last believing that the soul of one that dies in this manner, being forced to sally out of the body at the postern, must needs be defiled.

The Saponis took this execution so much to heart that they soon after quitted their settlement and removed in a body to the Catawbas. The daughter of the Totero [70] king went away with the Saponis, but, being the last of her nation and fearing she should not be treated according to her rank, poisoned herself, like an old Roman, with the root

[68] Make war.
[69] Completely.
[70] A variant form of Tutelo, originally applied by the Iroquois to all the Siouan tribes of Virginia. Byrd apparently refers, however, to a tribe that migrated from Salem, Virginia, to the junction of the Staunton and the Dan, later to the Yadkin, and in 1714 joined the Saponi and other tribes at Fort Christanna, only to move northward in 1722. They ultimately joined the League of the Iroquois.

of the trumpet plant. Her father died two years before, who was the most intrepid Indian we have been acquainted with. He had made himself terrible to all other Indians by his exploits and had escaped so many dangers that he was esteemed invulnerable. But at last he died of a pleurisy, the last man of his race and nation, leaving only that unhappy daughter behind him, who would not long survive him.

The most uncommon circumstance in this Indian visit was that they all come on horseback, which was certainly intended for a piece of state, because the distance was but three miles and 'tis likely they had walked afoot twice as far to catch their horses. The men rode more awkwardly than any Dutch sailor, and the ladies bestrode their palfreys *à la mode de France* but were so bashful about it that there was no persuading them to mount till they were quite out of our sight. The French women use to ride astraddle, not so much to make them sit firmer in the saddle as from the hopes the same thing might peradventure befall them that once happened to the nun of Orleans, who, escaping out of a nunnery, took post *en cavalier* and in ten miles' hard riding had the good fortune to have all the tokens of a man break out upon her. This piece of history ought to be the more credible because it leans upon much the same degree of proof as the tale of Bishop Burnet's two Italian nuns, who, according to His Lordship's account, underwent the same happy metamorphosis, probably by some other violent exercise.[71]

19. From hence we dispatched the cart with our baggage under a guard and crossed Meherrin River, which was not thirty yards wide in that place. By the help of fresh horses that had been sent us, we now began to mend our pace, which was also quickened by the strong inclinations we had to get home. In the distance of five miles we forded Meherrin Creek, which was very near as broad as the river. About eight miles farther we came to Sturgeon Creek, so called from the dexterity an Occaneechi Indian showed there in catching one of those royal fish, which was performed after the following manner: in the summertime 'tis no unusual thing for sturgeons to sleep on the sur-

[71] Gilbert Burnet, Bishop of Salisbury, *Some Letters Containing an Account of What Seemed Most Remarkable in Switzerland, Italy, etc.* (Rotterdam, 1686), pp. 246–247.

face of the water, and one of them, having wandered up into this creek in the spring, was floating in that drowsy condition. The Indian above-mentioned ran up to the neck into the creek a little below the place where he discovered the fish, expecting the stream would soon bring his game down to him. He judged the matter right, and as soon as it came within his reach, he whipped a running noose over his jowl. This waked the sturgeon, which, being strong in its own element, darted immediately under water and dragged the Indian after him. The man made it a point of honor to keep his hold, which he did to the apparent danger of being drowned. Sometimes both the Indian and the fish disappeared for a quarter of a minute and then rose at some distance from where they dived. At this rate they continued flouncing about, sometimes above and sometimes under water, for a considerable time, till at last the hero suffocated his adversary and haled his body ashore in triumph.

About six miles beyond that, we passed over Wiccoquoi Creek,[72] named so from the multitude of rocks over which the water tumbles in a fresh with a bellowing noise. Not far from where we went over is a rock much higher than the rest that strikes the eye with agreeable horror, and near it a very talkative echo that like a fluent helpmeet will return her goodman seven words for one and after all be sure to have the last. It speaks not only the language of men but also of birds and beasts, and often a single wild goose is cheated into the belief that some of his company are not far off by hearing his own cry multiplied; 'tis pleasant to see in what a flutter the poor bird is when he finds himself disappointed. On the banks of this creek are very broad, low grounds in many places and abundance of good high land, though a little subject to floods.

We had but two miles more to Captain Embry's, where we found the housekeeping much better than the house. Our bountiful landlady had set her oven and all her spits, pots, gridirons, and saucepans to work to diversify our entertainment, though after all it proved but a Mahometan feast, there being nothing to drink but water. The worst of it was we had unluckily outrid the baggage and for that reason were

[72] Waqua Creek. Various spellings of the name appear in the manuscript.

317

obliged to lodge very sociably in the same apartment with the family, where, reckoning women and children, we mustered in all no less than nine persons, who all pigged lovingly together.

20. In the morning Colonel Bolling, who had been surveying in the neighborhood, and Mr. Walker, who dwelt not far off, came to visit us; and the last of these worthy gentlemen, fearing that our drinking so much water might incline us to pleurisies, brought us a kind supply both of wine and cider. It was noon before we could disengage ourselves from the courtesies of this place, and then the two gentlemen above-mentioned were so good as to accompany us that day's journey, though they could by no means approve of our Lithuanian fashion of dismounting now and then in order to walk part of the way on foot.

We crossed Nottoway River not far from our landlord's house, where it seemed to be about twenty-five yards over. This river divides the county of Prince George from that of Brunswick. We had not gone eight miles farther before our eyes were blessed with the sight of Sapony Chapel, which was the first house of prayer we had seen for more than two calendar months. About three miles beyond that, we passed over Stony Creek, where one of those that guarded the baggage killed a polecat, upon which he made a comfortable repast. Those of his company were so squeamish they could not be persuaded at first to taste, as they said, of so unsavory an animal; but seeing the man smack his lips with more pleasure than usual, they ventured at last to be of his mess, and instead of finding the flesh rank and high tasted they owned it to be the sweetest morsel they had ever eat in their lives. The ill savor of this little beast lies altogether in its urine,[73] which nature had made so detestably ill scented on purpose to furnish a helpless creature with something to defend itself. For as some brutes have horns and hoofs, and others are armed with claws, teeth, and tusks for their defense; and as some spit a sort of poison at their adversaries, like the paco; and others dart quills at their pursuers, like the porcupine; and as some have no weapons to help themselves but their tongues, and others none but their tails; so the poor polecat's safety lies altogether in the irresistible stench of its water, insomuch that

[73] Byrd is mistaken in thinking that the skunk's offensive secretion is urine.

when it finds itself in danger from an enemy it moistens its bushy tail plentifully with this liquid ammunition and then, with great fury, sprinkles it like a shower of rain full into the eyes of its assailant, by which it gains time to make its escape. Nor is the polecat the only animal that defends itself by a stink. At the Cape of Good Hope is a little beast called a "stinker," as big as a fox and shaped like [a] ferret, which, being pursued, has no way to save himself but by farting and squittering, and then such a stench ensues that none of its pursuers can possibly stand it.

At the end of thirty good miles, we arrived in the evening at Colonel Bolling's, where first from a primitive course of life we began to relapse into luxury. This gentleman lives within hearing of the falls of Appomattox River, which are very noisy whenever a flood happens to roll a greater stream than ordinary over the rocks. The river is navigable for small craft as high as the falls and at some distance from thence fetches a compass and runs near parallel with James River almost as high as the mountains.

While the commissioners fared sumptuously here, the poor chaplain and two surveyors stopped ten miles short at a poor planter's house in pity to their horses, where they made a St. Anthony's meal, that is, they supped upon the pickings of what stuck in their teeth ever since breakfast. But to make them amends, the good man laid them in his own bed, where they all three nestled together in one cotton sheet and one of brown Osnaburgs, made still something browner by two months' copious perspiration.

21. But those worthy gentlemen were so alert in the morning after their light supper that they came up with us before breakfast and honestly paid their stomachs all they owed them.

We made no more than a Sabbath Day's journey from this to the next hospitable house, namely, that of our great benefactor, Colonel Mumford. We had already been much befriended by this gentleman, who, besides sending orders to his overseers at Roanoke to let us want for nothing, had in the beginning of our business been so kind as to recommend most of the men to us who were the faithful partners of our fatigue. Although in most other achievements those who command are apt to take all the honor to themselves of what perhaps was more owing to the vigor of those who were under them, yet I must be more just and allow these brave fellows their full share of credit for the service we performed and must declare that it was in a great measure owing to their spirit and indefatigable industry that we overcame many obstacles in the course of our line which till then had been esteemed insurmountable. Nor must I at the same time omit to do justice to the surveyors, and particularly to Mr. Mayo, who, besides an eminent degree of skill, encountered the same hardships and underwent the same fatigue that the forwardest of the men did, and that with as much cheerfulness as if pain had been his pleasure and difficulty his real diversion. Here we discharged the few men we had left, who were all as ragged as the Gibeonite ambassadors, though, at the same time, their rags were very honorable by the service they had so vigorously performed in making them so.

22. A little before noon we all took leave and dispersed to our several habitations, where we were so happy as to find all our families well. This crowned all our other blessings and made our journey as prosperous as it had been painful. Thus ended our second expedition, in which we extended the line within the shadow of the Cherokee mountains, where we were obliged to set up our pillars, like Hercules, and return home. We had now, upon the whole, been out about sixteen weeks, including going and returning, and had traveled at least six hundred miles, and no small part of that distance on foot. Below, toward the seaside, our course lay through marshes, swamps, and great waters; and above, over steep hills, craggy rocks, and thickets, hardly penetrable. Notwithstanding this variety of hardship, we may say without vanity that we faithfully obeyed the King's orders and performed the business effectually in which we had the honor to be employed. Nor can we by any means reproach ourselves of having put the Crown to any exorbitant expense in this difficult affair, the whole charge, from beginning to end, amounting to no more than £1,000.[74] But let no one concerned in this painful expedition complain of the

[74] As in the *Secret History*, the total of the disbursements enumerated is actually only £999.

scantiness of his pay so long as His Majesty has been graciously pleased to add to our reward the honor of his royal approbation and to declare, notwithstanding the desertion of the Carolina commissioners, that the line by us run shall hereafter stand as the true boundary betwixt the governments of Virginia and North Carolina.

APPENDIX

to the foregoing journal, containing the second charter to the proprietors of Carolina confirming and enlarging the first and also several other acts to which it refers. These are placed by themselves at the end of the book that they may not interrupt the thread of the story and the reader will be more at liberty whether he will please to read them or not, being something dry and unpleasant.

The second charter granted by King Charles II to the Proprietors of Carolina [75]

CHARLES, by the grace of God, etc.

Whereas, by our letters patent bearing date the four-and-twentieth day of March in the fifteenth year of our reign we were graciously pleased to grant unto our right trusty and right well-beloved cousin and counselor, Edward, Earl of Clarendon, our High Chancellor of England; our right trusty and right entirely beloved cousin and counselor, George, Duke of Albemarle, Master of our Horse; our right trusty and well-beloved William, now Earl of Craven; [76] our right trusty and well-beloved counselor, Anthony, Lord Ashley, Chancellor of our Exchequer; our right trusty and well-beloved counselor, Sir George Carteret, knight and baronet, Vice Chamberlain of our household; our right trusty and well-beloved Sir John Colleton, knight and baronet; and Sir William Berkeley, knight, all that province, territory, or tract of ground called Carolina, situate, lying, and being within our dominions of America, extending from the north end of the island called Luke Island, which lies in the southern Virginia seas and within six-and-thirty degrees of the northern latitude; and to the west as far as the South Seas; and so respectively as far as the river of Mathias, which bordereth upon the coast of Florida, and within one-and-thirty de-

[75] We have followed the example of previous editors in reprinting only the portion of the charter relevant to the controversy. For the complete document see *North Carolina Charters and Constitutions, 1578–1698*, edited by Mattie E. E. Parker (Raleigh, 1963), pp. 90–104. The transcription of the document as printed therein appears to have several misreadings.

[76] The manuscript inadvertently omits the name of John, Lord Berkeley, following that of the Earl of Craven.

grees of the northern latitude; and so west in a direct line as far as the South Seas aforesaid.

Now know ye that we, at the humble request of the said grantees in the aforesaid letters patent named, and as a further mark of our especial favor toward them, we are graciously pleased to enlarge our said grant unto them according to the bounds and limits hereafter specified; and in favor to the pious and noble purpose of the said Edward, Earl of Clarendon; George, Duke of Albemarle; William, Earl of Craven; John, Lord Berkeley; Anthony, Lord Ashley; Sir George Carteret, Sir John Colleton, and Sir William Berkeley, we do give and grant to them, their heirs and assigns, all that province, territory, or tract of ground situate, lying, and being within our dominions of America aforesaid, extending north and eastward as far as the north end of Currituck River or Inlet, upon a straight westerly line to Weyanoke Creek, which lies within or about the degrees of 36° 30′ northern latitude, and so west in a direct line as far as the South Seas; and south and westward as far as the degrees of twenty-nine inclusive northern latitude, and so west in a direct line as far as the South Seas; together with all and singular ports, harbors, bays, rivers, and inlets belonging unto the province or territory aforesaid. And also, all the soil, lands, fields, woods, mountains, firms, lakes, rivers, bays and inlets situate or being within the bounds or limits last before mentioned; with the fishing of all sorts of fish, whales, sturgeons, and all other royal fishes in the sea, bays, inlets, and rivers within the premises, and the fish therein taken; together with the royalty of the sea, upon the coast within the limits aforesaid. And, moreover, all veins, mines, and quarries, as well discovered as not discovered, of gold, silver, gems, and precious stones, and all other whatsoever, be it of stones, metals, or any other thing found or to be found within the province, territory, inlets, and limits aforesaid. . . .

At the Court of St. James, the first day of March, 1710.
Present, the Queen's Most Excellent Majesty in Council

Upon reading this day at the Board a representation from the Right Honorable the Lords Commissioners for Trade and Plantations, in the words following:

In pursuance of Your Majesty's pleasure, commissioners have been appointed on the part of Your Majesty's colony of Virginia, as likewise on the part of the province of Carolina, for the settling the bounds between those governments; and they have met several times for that purpose but have not agreed upon any one point thereof, by reason of the trifling delays of the Carolina commissioners and of the many difficulties by them raised in relation to the proper observations and survey they were to make. However, the commissioners for Virginia have delivered to Your Majesty's Lieutenant Governor of that colony an account of their proceedings, which account has been under the consideration of Your Majesty's Council of Virginia, and they have made a report thereon to the said Lieutenant Governor, who having lately transmitted unto us a copy of that report, we take leave humbly to lay the substance thereof before Your Majesty, which is as follows.

That the commissioners of Carolina are both of them persons engaged in interest to obstruct the settling the boundaries between that province and the colony of Virginia; for one of them has for several years been Surveyor General of Carolina, has acquired to himself great profit by surveying lands within the controverted bounds, and has taken up several tracts of land in his own name and sold the same to others, for which he stands still obliged [to] obtain patents from the government of Carolina. The other of them is at this time Surveyor General and hath the same prospect of advantage by making future surveys within the said bounds.

That the behavior of the Carolina commissioners has tended visibly to no other end than to protract and defeat the settling this affair; and particularly Mr. Moseley has used so many shifts and excuses to disappoint all conferences with the commissioners of Virginia as plainly show his aversion to proceed in a business that tends so manifestly to his disadvantage. His prevaricating on this occasion has been so undiscreet and so unguarded as to be discovered in the presence of the Lieutenant Governor of Virginia. He started so many objections to the powers granted to the commissioners of that colony, with design to render their conferences ineffectual, that his joint commissioner could hardly find an excuse for him. And when the Lieutenant Governor had with much ado prevailed with the said Mr. Moseley to appoint a time for meeting the commissioners of Virginia and for bringing the necessary instruments to take the latitude of the bounds in dispute, which instruments he owned were ready in Carolina, he not only failed to comply with his own appointment, but, after the commissioners of Virginia had made a journey to his house and had attended him to the places proper for observing the latitude, he would not take the trouble of carrying his own instrument but contented himself to find fault with the quadrant produced by the Virginia commissioners, though that instrument had been approved by the best mathematicians and is of universal use.

From all which it is evident how little hopes there are of settling the boundaries above-mentioned in concert with the present commissioners for Carolina.

That though the bounds of the Carolina charter are in express words limited to Weyanoke Creek, lying in or about 36° 30′ of northern latitude, yet the commissioners for Carolina have not by any of their evidences pretended to prove any such place as Weyanoke Creek, the amount of their evidence reaching no further than to prove which is Weyanoke River, and even that is contradicted by affidavits taken on the part of Virginia; by which affidavits it appears that before the date of the Carolina charter to this day the place they pretend to be Weyanoke River was, and is still, called Nottoway River. But supposing the same had been called Weyanoke River, it can be nothing to their purpose, there being a great difference between a river and a creek. Besides, in that country there are divers rivers and creeks of the same name, as Potomac River and Potomac Creek, Rappahannock River and Rappahannock Creek, and several others, though there are many miles' distance between the mouths of these rivers and the mouths of these creeks.

It is also observable that the witnesses on the part of Carolina are all very ignorant persons, and most of them of ill fame and reputation, on which account they had been forced to remove from Virginia to Carolina. Further, there appeared to be many contradictions in their testimonies, whereas, on the other hand, the witnesses to prove that the right to those lands is in the government of Virginia are persons of good credit, their knowledge of the lands in question is more ancient than any of the witnesses for Carolina and their evidence fully corroborated by the concurrent testimony of the tributary Indians. And that right is further confirmed by the observations lately taken of the latitude in those parts; by which 'tis plain that the creek proved to be Weyanoke Creek by the Virginia evidences and sometimes called Wiccacon answers best to the latitude described in the Carolina charter, for it lies in 36° 40′, which is ten minutes to the northward of the limits described in the Carolina grant, whereas Nottoway River lies exactly in the latitude of 37° and can by no construction be supposed to be the boundary described in their charter. So that upon the whole matter, if the commissioners of Carolina had no other view than to clear the just right of the Proprietors, such undeniable demonstrations would be sufficient to convince them; but the said commissioners give too much cause to suspect that they mix their own private interest with the claim of the Proprietors and for that reason endeavor to gain time in order to obtain grants for the land already taken up and also to secure the rest on this occasion; we take notice, that they proceed to survey the land in dispute, notwithstanding the assurance given by the government of Carolina to the contrary by their letter of the seventeenth of June, 1707, to the government of Virginia, by which letter they promised that no lands should be taken up within the controverted bounds till the same were settled.

Whereupon we humbly propose that the Lords Proprietors be acquainted with the foregoing complaint of the trifling delays of their commissioners, which delays, 'tis reasonable to believe, have proceeded from the self-interest of those commissioners, and that therefore Your Majesty's pleasure be signified to the said Lords Proprietors, that by the first opportunity they send orders to their Governor or commander in chief of Carolina for the time being to issue forth a new commission, to the purport of that lately issued, thereby constituting two other persons, not having any personal interest in or claim to any of the land lying within the boundaries, in the room of Edward Moseley and John Lawson. The Carolina commissioners to be appointed being strictly required to finish their survey and to make a return thereof in conjunction with the Virginia commissioners within six months, to be computed from the time that due notice shall be given by Your Majesty's Lieutenant Governor of Virginia to the Governor or commander in chief of Carolina of the time and place which Your Majesty's said Lieutenant Governor shall appoint for the first meeting of the commissioners on one part and the other. In order whereunto, we humbly offer that directions be sent to the said Lieutenant Governor to give such notice accordingly; and if, after notice so given, the Carolina commissioners shall refuse or neglect to join with those on the part of Virginia in making such survey, as likewise a return thereof within the time before mentioned, that then and in such case the commissioners on the part of Virginia be directed to draw up an account of the proper observations and survey, which they shall have made for ascertaining the bounds between Virginia and Carolina, and to deliver the same in writing under their hands and seals to the Lieutenant Governor and Council of Virginia, to the end the same may be laid before Your Majesty for Your Majesty's final determination therein, within, with regard to the settling of those boundaries; the Lords Proprietors having, by an instrument under their hands, submitted the same to Your Majesty's royal determination, which instrument, dated in March 1708, is lying in this office.

And lastly, we humbly propose that Your Majesty's further pleasure be signified to the said Lords Proprietors, and in like manner to the Lieutenant Governor of Virginia, that no grants be passed by either of those governments of any of the lands lying within the controverted bounds until such bounds shall be ascertained and settled as aforesaid, whereby it may appear whether those lands do of right belong to Your Majesty or to the Lords Proprietors of Carolina.

Her Majesty in Council, approving of the said representation, is pleased to order, as it is hereby ordered, that the Right Honorable the Lords Commissioners for Trade and Plantations do signify Her Majesty's pleasure herein to Her Majesty's Lieutenant Governor or commander in chief of Virginia for the time being, and to all persons to whom it may belong, as is proposed by Their Lordships in the said representation, and the Right Honorable the Lords Proprietors of Carolina are to do what on their part does appertain.

EDWARD SOUTHWELL

Proposals for determining the controversy relating to the bounds between the governments of Virginia and North Carolina, most humbly offered for His Majesty's royal approbation and for the consent of the Right Honorable the Lords Proprietors of Carolina

Forasmuch as the dispute between the said two governments about their true limits continues still, notwithstanding the several meetings of the commissioners and all the proceedings of many years past, in order to adjust that affair, and seeing no speedy determination is likely to ensue unless some medium be found out in which both parties may incline to acquiesce: wherefore both the underwritten governors, having met and considered the prejudice both to the King and the Lords Proprietors' interest by the continuance of this contest, and truly endeavoring a decision which they judge comes nearest the intention of royal charter granted to the Lords Proprietors, do, with the advice and consent of their respective councils, propose as follows.

That from the mouth of Currituck River or Inlet, and setting the compass on the north shore thereof, a due-west line be run and fairly marked, and if it happen to cut Chowan River, between the mouths of Nottoway River and Wiccacon Creek, then shall the same direct course be continued toward the mountains and be ever deemed the sole dividing line between Virginia and Carolina.

That if the said west line cuts Chowan River to the southward of Wiccacon Creek, then from point of intersection the bounds shall be allowed to continue up the middle of the said Chowan River to the middle of the entrance into the said Wiccacon Creek, and from thence a due-west line shall divide the said two governments.

That if a due-west line shall be found to pass through islands or to cut out small slips of land, which might much more conveniently be included in one province or the other by natural water bounds, in such cases the persons appointed for running the line shall have power to settle natural bounds, provided the commissioners of both sides agree thereto and that all such variations from the west line be particularly noted in the maps or plats which they shall return to be put upon the records of both governments. All which is humbly submitted by

CHARLES EDEN
A. SPOTSWOOD

Order of the King and Council upon the foregoing proposals, at the Court of St. James, the twenty-eighth day of March, 1729.[77] Present, the King's Most Excellent Majesty in Council

Whereas it has been represented to His Majesty at the Board that for adjusting the disputes which have subsisted for many years past between the colonies of Virginia and North Carolina concerning their true boundaries, the late governors of the said colonies did some time since agree upon certain proposals for regulating the said boundaries for the future, to which proposals the Lords Proprietors of Carolina have given their assent; and whereas the said proposals were this day presented to His Majesty as proper for his royal approbation,

His Majesty is thereupon pleased, with the advice of his Privy Council, to approve of the said proposals, a copy whereof is hereunto annexed, and to order, as it is hereby ordered, that the Governor or commander in chief of the colony of Virginia do settle the said boundaries in conjunction with the Governor of North Carolina agreeable to the said proposals.

EDWARD SOUTHWELL

The Lieutenant Governor of Virginia's commission in obedience to His Majesty's order

George the Second, by the grace of God of Great Britain, France, and Ireland King, Defender of the Faith, to our trusty and well-beloved William Byrd, Richard Fitzwilliam, and William Dandridge, Esqrs., members of our Council of the colony and dominion of Virginia, greeting:

Whereas our late royal father of blessed memory was graciously pleased, by order in his Privy Council bearing date the twenty-eighth day of March, 1727, to approve of certain proposals agreed upon by Alexander Spotswood, Esq., late Lieutenant Governor of Virginia, on the one part, and Charles Eden, Esq., late Governor of the province of North Carolina, for determining the controversy relating to the bounds between the said two

[77] A scribal error for "1727."

328

governments, and was farther pleased to direct and order that the said boundaries should be laid out and settled agreeable to the said proposals. Know ye, therefore, that reposing special trust and confidence in your ability and provident circumspection, [we] have assigned, constituted, and appointed, and by these presents do assign, constitute, and appoint you and every of you, jointly and severally, our commissioners for and on behalf of our colony and dominion of Virginia to meet the commissioners appointed or to be appointed on the part of the province of North Carolina, and in conjunction with them to cause a line or lines of division to be run and marked to divide the said two governments according to the proposals above-mentioned and the order of our late royal father, copies of both which you will herewith receive.

And we do farther give and grant unto you — and in case of the death or absence of any of you, such of you as shall be present — full power and authority to treat and agree with the said commissioners of the province of North Carolina on such rules and methods as you shall judge most expedient for the adjusting and finally determining all disputes or controversies which may arise touching any islands or other small slips of land which may happen to be intersected or cut off by the dividing line aforesaid and which may with more conveniency be included in the one province or the other by natural water bounds agreeable to the proposals afore-mentioned, and generally to do and perform all matters and things requisite for the final determination and settlement of the said boundaries according to the said proposals.

And to the end our service herein may not be disappointed through the refusal or delay of the commissioners for the province of North Carolina to act in conjunction with you in settling the boundaries aforesaid, we do hereby give and grant unto you, or such of you as shall be present at the time and place appointed for running the dividing line aforesaid, full power and authority to cause the said line to be run and marked out, conformable to the said proposals, having due regard to the doing equal justice to us and to the Lords Proprietors of Carolina, any refusal, disagreement, or opposition of the said commissioners of North Carolina notwithstanding. And in that case we do hereby require you to make a true report of your proceedings to our Lieutenant Governor or commander in chief of Virginia, in order to be laid before us for our approbation and final determination herein.

And in case any person or persons whatsoever shall presume to disturb, molest, or resist you, or any of the officers or persons by your direction, in running the said line and executing the powers herein given you, we do by these presents give and grant unto you, or such of you as shall be attending the service aforesaid, full power and authority by warrant under your or any of your hands and seals to order and command all and every the militia officers in our counties of Princess Anne, Norfolk, Nansemond, and Isle of Wight, or other the adjacent counties, together with the sheriff of each of the said counties, or either of them, to raise the militia and posse of the said several counties for the removing all force and opposition which shall or may be made to you in the due execution of this our commission; and we do hereby will and require as well the officers of the said militia as all other our officers and loving subjects within the said counties and all others whom it may concern, to be obedient, aiding, and assisting unto you in all and singular the premises.

And we do in like manner command and require you to cause fair maps and descriptions of the said dividing line and the remarkable places through which it shall pass to be made and returned to our Lieutenant Governor or commander in chief of our said colony for the time being, in order to be entered on record in the proper offices within our said colony. Provided that you do not, by color of this our commission, take upon you or determine any private man's property, in or to the lands which shall by the said dividing line be included within the limits of Virginia, nor of any other matter or thing that doth not relate immediately to the adjusting, settling, and final determination of the boundary aforesaid, conformable to the proposals hereinbefore mentioned and not otherwise. In witness whereof we have caused these presents to be made. Witness our trusty and well-beloved William Gooch, Esq., our Lieutenant Governor and commander in chief of our colony and dominion of Virginia, under the seal of our said colony, at Williamsburg, the fourteenth day of December, 1727, in the first year of our reign.

WILLIAM GOOCH

The Governor of North Carolina's commission in obedience to His Majesty's order

Sir Richard Everard, Baronet, Governor, Captain General, Admiral, and Commander in Chief of the said province, to Christopher Gale, Esq., Chief Justice; John Lovick, Esq., Secretary; Edward Moseley, Esq., Surveyor General; and William Little, Esq., Attorney General, greeting:

Whereas many disputes and differences have formerly been between the inhabitants of this province and those of His Majesty's colony of Virginia concerning the boundaries and limits between the said two governments, which having been duly considered by Charles Eden, Esq., late

Governor of this province, and Alexander Spotswood, Esq., late Governor of Virginia, they agreed to certain proposals for determining the said controversy and humbly offered the same for His Majesty's royal approbation and the consent of the true and absolute Lords Proprietors of Carolina. And His Majesty having been pleased to signify his royal approbation of those proposals (consented unto by the true and absolute Lords Proprietors of Carolina) and given directions for adjusting and settling the boundaries as near as may be to the said proposals,

I, therefore, reposing especial trust and confidence in you, the said Christopher Gale, John Lovick, Edward Moseley, and William Little, to be commissioners on the part of the true and absolute Lords Proprietors, and that you, in conjunction with such commissioners as shall be nominated for Virginia, use your utmost endeavors and take all necessary care in adjusting and settling the said boundaries by drawing such a distinct line or lines of division between the said two provinces as near as reasonable you can to the proposals made by the two former governors and the instructions herewith given you.

Given at the council chamber in Edenton, under my hand and the seal of the colony, the twenty-first day of February, anno Domini 1727, and in the first year of the reign of our sovereign lord, King George the Second.

RICHARD EVERARD

The protest of the Carolina commissioners against our proceeding on the line without them

We, the underwritten commissioners for the government of North Carolina, in conjunction with the commissioners on the part of Virginia, having run the line for the division of the two colonies from Currituck Inlet to the south branch of Roanoke River — being in the whole about 170 miles and near 50 miles without the inhabitants — being of opinion we had run the line as far as would be requisite for a long time, judged the carrying it farther would be a needless charge and trouble. And the grand debate which had so long subsisted between the two governments about Weyanoke River or Creek being settled at our former meeting in the spring, when we were ready on our parts to have gone with the line to the utmost inhabitants, which if it had been done, the line at any time after might have been continued at an easy expense by a surveyor on each side; and if at any time hereafter there should be occasion to carry the line on further than we have now run it — which, we think, will not be in an age or two — it may be done in the same easy manner without the great expense that now attends it. And, on a conference of all the commissioners, we have communicated our sentiments thereon and declared our opinion that we had gone as far as the service required and thought proper to proceed no farther; to which it was answered by the commissioners for Virginia that they should not regard what we did, but if we desisted, they would proceed without us. But we, conceiving by His Majesty's order in council they were directed to act in conjunction with the commissioners appointed for Carolina, and having accordingly run the line jointly so far and exchanged plans, thought they could not carry on the bounds singly but that their proceedings without us would be irregular and invalid and that it would be no boundary, and thought proper to enter our dissent thereto.

Wherefore, for the reasons aforesaid, in the name of His Excellency the Lord Palatine and the rest of the true and absolute Lords Proprietors of Carolina, we do hereby dissent and disallow of any farther proceeding with the bounds without our concurrence, and pursuant to our instructions do give this our dissent in writing.

EDWARD MOSELEY
WILLIAM LITTLE
C. GALE
J. LOVICK

October 7, 1728

The answer of the Virginia commissioners to the foregoing protest

Whereas on the seventh of October last a paper was delivered to us by the commissioners of North Carolina in the style of a protest against our carrying any farther without them the dividing line between the two governments, we, the underwritten commissioners on the part of Virginia, having maturely considered the reasons offered in the said protest why those gentlemen retired so soon from that service, beg leave to return the following answer:

They are pleased in the first place to allege by way of reason that having run the line near fifty miles beyond the inhabitants, it was sufficient for a long time, in their opinion for an age or two. To this we answer that by breaking off so soon they did but imperfectly obey His Majesty's order, assented to by the Lords Proprietors. The plain meaning of that order was to ascertain the bounds betwixt the two governments as far toward the mountains as we could, that neither the King's grants may hereafter encroach on the Lords Proprietors' nor theirs on the rights of His Majesty.

And though the distance toward the great mountains be not precisely determined, yet surely the west line should be carried as near them as may be, that both the King's lands and those of Their Lordships may be taken up the faster, and that His Majesty's subjects may as soon as possible extend themselves to that natural barrier. This they will certainly do in a few years, when they know distinctly in which government they may enter for the land, as they have already done in the more northern parts of Virginia. So that 'tis strange the Carolina commissioners should affirm that the distance only of fifty miles above the inhabitants would be sufficient to carry the line for an age or two, especially considering that two or three days before the date of their protest Mr. Mayo had entered with them for two thousand acres of land within five miles of the place where they left off. Besides, if we reflect on the richness of the soil in those parts and the convenience for stock, we may foretell, without the spirit of divination, that there will be many settlements higher than those gentlemen went in less than ten years, and perhaps in half that time.

Another reason mentioned in the protest for their retiring so soon from the service is that their going farther would be a needless charge and trouble. And they allege that the rest may be done by one surveyor on a side in an easy manner, whenever it shall be thought necessary.

To this we answer that frugality for the public is a rare virtue, but when the public service must suffer by it, it degenerates into a vice. And this will ever be the case when gentlemen execute the orders of their superiors by halves. But had the Carolina commissioners been sincerely frugal for their government, why did they carry out provisions sufficient to support them and their men for ten weeks when they intended not to tarry half that time? This they must own to be true, since they brought one thousand pounds of provisions along with them. Now, after so great an expense in their preparations, it had been no mighty addition to their charge had they endured the fatigue five or six weeks longer. It would at most have been no more than they must be at whenever they finish their work, even though they should fancy it proper to trust a matter of that consequence to the management of one surveyor. Such a one must have a number of men along with him, both for his assistance and defense, and those men must have provisions to support them.

These are all the reasons these gentlemen think fit to mention in their protest, though they had in truth a more powerful argument for retiring so abruptly, which, because they forgot, it will be neighborly to help them out. The provisions they intended to bring along with them, for want of horses to carry them, were partly dropped by the way, and what they could bring was husbanded so ill that after eighteen days (which was the whole time we had them in our company) they had no more left, by their own confession, than two pounds of biscuit for each man to carry them home. However, though this was an unanswerable reason for gentlemen for leaving the business unfinished, it was none at all for us, who had at that time bread sufficient for seven weeks longer. Therefore, lest their want of management might put a stop to His Majesty's service and frustrate his royal intentions, we judged it our duty to proceed without them and have extended the dividing line so far west as to leave the great mountains on each hand to the eastward of us. And this we have done with the same fidelity and exactness as if the gentlemen had continued with us. Our surveyors (whose integrity I am persuaded they will not call in question) continued to act under the same oath which they had done from the beginning. Yet, notwithstanding all this, if the government of North Carolina should not hold itself bound by that part of the line which we made without the assistance of its commissioners, yet we shall have this benefit in it at least: that His Majesty will know how far his lands reach toward the south, and consequently where his subjects may take it up, and how far they may be granted without injustice to the Lords Proprietors. To this we may also add that, having the authority of our commission to act without the commissioners of Carolina in case of their disagreement or refusal, we thought ourselves bound upon their retreat to finish the line without them, lest His Majesty's service might suffer by any honor [38] or neglect on their part.

WILLIAM DANDRIDGE

WILLIAM BYRD

[78] The sense of the word "honor" is not clear; perhaps the scribe wrote "honor" instead of "humor."

THE NAMES OF THE COMMISSIONERS TO DIRECT THE RUNNING OF THE
LINE BETWEEN VIRGINIA AND NORTH CAROLINA

William Byrd
Richard Fitzwilliam } Esquires, commissioners
William Dandridge   for Virginia

Christopher Gale
John Lovick } Esquires, commissioners
Edward Moseley   for Carolina
William Little

Alexander Irvin } Surveyors for Virginia
William Mayo

Edward Moseley } Surveyors for North Carolina
Samuel Swann

The Reverend Peter Fontaine, Chaplain

NAMES OF THE MEN EMPLOYED ON THE PART OF VIRGINIA TO RUN THE
LINE BETWEEN THAT COLONY AND NORTH CAROLINA

On the first expedition	On the second expedition
1. Peter Jones	Peter Jones
2. Thomas Jones	Thomas Jones
3. Thomas Short	Thomas Short
4. Robert Hix	Robert Hix
5. John Evans	John Evans
6. Stephen Evans	Stephen Evans
7. John Ellis	John Ellis
8. John Ellis, Jr.	John Ellis, Jr.
9. Thomas Wilson	Thomas Wilson
10. George Tilman	George Tilman
11. Charles Kimball	Charles Kimball
12. George Hamilton	George Hamilton
13. Robert Allen	Thomas Jones, Jr.
14. Thomas Jones, Jr.	James Petillo
15. James Petillo	Richard Smith
16. Richard Smith	Abraham Jones
17. John Rice	Edward Powell
	William Pool
	William Calvert
	James Whitlock
	Thomas Page

335

ACCOUNT OF THE EXPENSE OF RUNNING THE LINE BETWEEN VIRGINIA
AND NORTH CAROLINA

To the men's wages in current money	£277	10	0
To sundry disbursements for provisions, etc.	174	1	6
To paid the men for seven horses lost	44	0	0
	£495	11	6
The sum of £495 11s.6d. current money reduced at 15% to sterling amounts to	£430	8	10
To paid to Colonel Byrd	142	5	7
To paid to Colonel Dandridge	142	5	7
To paid Mr. Fitzwilliam	94	0	0
To paid the chaplain, Mr. Fontaine	20	0	0
To paid to Mr. William Mayo	75	0	0
To paid to Mr. Alexander Irvin	75	0	0
To paid for a tent and marquee	20	0	0
	£1000	0	0

This sum was discharged by a warrant out of His Majesty's quitrents from the lands in Virginia.

A PROGRESS TO THE MINES

IN THE YEAR 1732

*F*OR the pleasure of the good company of Mrs. Byrd and her little governor, my son, I went about halfway to the falls in the chariot. There we halted, not far from a purling stream, and upon the stump of a propagate oak picked the bones of a piece of roast beef. By the spirit which that gave me I was better able to part with the dear companions of my travels and to perform the rest of my journey on horseback by myself.

I reached Shacco's before two o'clock and crossed the river to the mills.[1] I had the grief to find them both stand as still for the want of water as a dead woman's tongue for want of breath. It had rained so little for many weeks above the falls, that the naiads had hardly water enough left to wash their faces. However, as we ought to turn all our misfortunes to the best advantage, I directed Mr. Booker, my first minister there, to make use of the lowness of the water for blowing up the rocks at the mouth of the canal. For that purpose I ordered iron drills to be made about two foot long, pointed with steel, chisel fashion, in order to make holes into which we put our cartridges of powder, containing each about three ounces. There wanted skill among my engineers to choose the best parts of the stone for boring, that we might blow to the most advantage. They made all their holes quite perpendicular, whereas they should have humored the grain of the stone for the more effectual execution. I ordered the points of the drills to be made chisel

[1] Byrd's father, William Byrd I, inherited land on both sides of the James near the falls from his uncle, Thomas Stegge, Jr. On the south side of the river was developed the Falls plantation. "Shacco's," on the north side, was established as a trading post and an outpost against Indian attack in the time of the first William Byrd. The name derives from an old creek name, probably a corruption of the name of an Indian tribe (either the Shakori or the Shackaconians). A public warehouse at this spot was provided for in a law enacted by the Virginia Assembly in 1730. It was here that Byrd laid out the town of Richmond in 1737; see p. 388. The name survives in Richmond in Shockoe Hill Cemetery and Shockoe Slip.

way, rather than the diamond, that they might need to be seldomer repaired, though in stone the diamond points would make the most dispatch. The water now flowed out of the river so slowly that the miller was obliged to pond it up in the canal by setting open the flood-gates at the mouth and shutting those close at the mill. By this contrivance he was able at any time to grind two or three bushels, either for his choice customers or for the use of my plantations.

Then I walked to the place where they broke the flax, which is wrought with much greater ease than the hemp and is much better for spinning. From thence I paid a visit to the weaver, who needed a little of Minerva's inspiration to make the most of a piece of fine cloth. Then I looked in upon my Caledonian spinster, who was mended more in her looks than in her humor. However, she promised much, though at the same time intended to perform little. She is too high-spirited for Mr. Booker, who hates to have his sweet temper ruffled and will rather suffer matters to go a little wrong sometimes than give his righteous spirit any uneasiness. He is very honest and would make an admirable overseer where servants will do as they are bid. But eye-servants, who want abundance of overlooking, are not so proper to be committed to his care.

I found myself out of order and for that reason retired early, yet with all this precaution had a gentle fever in the night, but toward morning Nature set open all her gates and drove it out in a plentiful perspiration.

19. The worst of this fever was that it put me to the necessity of taking another ounce of bark.[2] I moistened every dose with a little brandy and filled the glass up with water, which is the least nauseous way of taking this popish medicine and besides hinders it from purging.

After I had swallowed a few poached eggs, we rode down to the mouth of the canal and from thence crossed over to the broad rock island in a canoe. Our errand was to view some iron ore, which we dug up in two places. That on the surface seemed very spongy and poor, which gave us no great encouragement to search deeper, nor did the

[2] Peruvian (Cinchona) bark, which Byrd mentions on p. 225 of the *History*. There are numerous references in his diary to taking "bark." Byrd calls it "popish medicine" because it was also known as "Jesuit's bark."

quantity appear to be very great. However, for my greater satisfaction I ordered a hand to dig there for some time this winter.

We walked from one end of the island to the other, being about half a mile in length, and found the soil very good and too high for any flood less than that of Deucalion to do the least damage. There is a very wild prospect both upward and downward, the river being full of rocks over which the stream tumbled with a murmur loud enough to drown the notes of a scolding wife. This island would make an agreeable hermitage for any good Christian who had a mind to retire from the world.

Mr. Booker told me how Dr. Ireton had cured him once of a looseness which had been upon him two whole years. He ordered him a dose of rhubarb, with directions to take twenty-five drops of laudanum so soon as he had had two physical stools. Then he rested one day, and the next he ordered him another dose of the same quantity of laudanum to be taken, also after the second stool. When this was done, he finished the cure by giving him twenty drops of laudanum every night for five nights running. The doctor insisted upon the necessity of stopping the operation of the rhubarb before it worked quite off, that what remained behind might strengthen the bowels. I was punctual in swallowing my bark, and that I might use exercise upon it, rode to Prince's Folly and My Lord's islands,[3] where I saw very fine corn.

In the meantime, Vulcan came in order to make the drills for boring the rocks and gave me his parole he would, by the grace of God, attend the works till they were finished, which he performed as lamely as if he had been to labor for a dead horse and not for ready money.

I made a North Carolina dinner upon fresh pork, though we had a plate of green peas after it, by way of dessert, for the safety of our noses.[4] Then my first minister and I had some serious conversation about my affairs, and I find nothing disturbed his peaceable spirit so much as the misbehavior of the spinster above-mentioned. I told him I could not pity a man who had it always in his power to do himself and

[3] Possibly lands belonging to George Hamilton, Earl of Orkney, absentee Governor of Virginia at this time.

[4] See Byrd's reference in the *Secret History* (p. 60) to his belief that too heavy a diet of pork caused yaws, with consequent destruction of the nose.

her justice and would not. If she were a drunkard, a scold, a thief, or a slanderer, we had wholesome laws that would make her back smart for the diversion of her other members, and 'twas his fault he had not put those wholesome severities in execution. I retired in decent time to my own apartment and slept very comfortably upon my bark, forgetting all the little crosses arising from overseers and Negroes.

20. I continued the bark and then tossed down my poached eggs with as much ease as some good breeders slip children into the world. About nine I left the prudentest orders I could think of with my vizier and then crossed the river to Shacco's. I made a running visit to three of my quarters, where, besides finding all the people well, I had the pleasure to see better crops than usual both of corn and tobacco. I parted there with my intendant,[5] and pursued my journey to Mr. Randolph's at Tuckahoe[6] without meeting with any adventure by the way.

Here I found Mrs. Fleming, who was packing up her baggage with design to follow her husband the next day, who was gone to a new settlement in Goochland. Both he and she have been about seven years persuading themselves to remove to that retired part of the country, though they had the two strong arguments of health and interest for so doing. The widow smiled graciously upon me and entertained me very handsomely. Here I learnt all the tragical story of her daughter's humble marriage with her uncle's overseer. Besides the meanness of this mortal's aspect, the man has not one visible qualification except impudence to recommend him to a female's inclinations. But there is sometimes such a charm in that Hibernian endowment that frail woman can't withstand it, though it stand alone without any other recommendation. Had she run away with a gentleman or a pretty fellow there might have been some excuse for her, though he were of inferior fortune; but to stoop to a dirty plebeian without any kind of merit is the lowest prostitution. I found the family justly enraged at it, and though I had more good nature than to join in her condemnation, yet

[5] Supervisor.
[6] Tuckahoe, on the creek of the same name, was the plantation of Thomas Randolph, son of William Randolph, who founded the famous Virginia family.

I could devise no excuse for so senseless a prank as this young gentle-woman had played.

Here good drink was more scarce than good victuals, the family being reduced to the last bottle of wine, which was therefore husbanded very carefully. But the water was excellent. The heir of the family did not come home till late in the evening. He is a pretty young man but had the misfortune to become his own master too soon. This puts young fellows upon wrong pursuits before they have sense to judge rightly for themselves, though at the same time they have a strange conceit of their own sufficiency when they grow near twenty years old, especially if they happen to have a small smattering of learning. 'Tis then they fancy themselves wiser than all their tutors and governors, which makes them headstrong to all advice and above all reproof and admonition.

21. I was sorry in the morning to find myself stopped in my career by bad weather brought upon us by a northeast wind. This drives a world of raw, unkindly vapors upon us from Newfoundland, loaden with blights, coughs, and pleurisies. However, I complained not, lest I might be suspected to be tired of the good company, though Mrs. Fleming was not so much upon her guard but mutinied strongly at the rain that hindered her from pursuing her dear husband. I said what I could to comfort a gentlewoman under so sad a disappointment. I told her a husband that stayed so much at home as hers did could be no such violent rarity as for a woman to venture her precious health to go daggling through the rain after him or to be miserable if she happened to be prevented; that it was prudent for married people to fast sometimes from one another, that they might come together again with the better stomach; that the best things in this world, if constantly used, are apt to be cloying, which a little absence and abstinence would prevent. This was strange doctrine to a fond female who fancies people should love with as little reason after marriage as before.

In the afternoon Monsieur Marij,[7] the minister of the parish, came

---

[7] The Reverend James Marye, born a Roman Catholic in Rouen, who came to Virginia via England, where he had been ordained in the Protestant Episcopal Church and had married Letitia Maria Ann Staige. He was called to the parish of

to make me a visit. He had been a Romish priest but found reasons, either spiritual or temporal, to quit that gay religion. The fault of this new convert is that he looks for as much respect from his Protestant flock as is paid to the popish clergy, which our ill-bred Huguenots don't understand. Madam Marij had so much curiosity as to want to come too, but another horse was wanting, and she believed it would have too vulgar an air to ride behind her husband. This woman was of the true Exchange breed, full of discourse but void of discretion,[8] and married a parson with the idle hopes he might some time or other come to be His Grace of Canterbury. The gray mare is the better horse in that family, and the poor man submits to her wild vagaries for peace's sake. She has just enough of the fine lady to run in debt and be of no signification in her household. And the only thing that can prevent her from undoing her loving husband will be that nobody will trust them beyond the sixteen thousand,[9] which is soon run out in a Goochland store. The way of dealing there is for some small merchant or peddler to buy a Scots' pennyworth of goods and clap 150 per cent upon that. At this rate the parson can't be paid much more for his preaching than 'tis worth. No sooner was our visitor retired but the facetious widow was so kind as to let me into all this secret history, but was at the same time exceedingly sorry that the woman should be so indiscreet and the man so tame as to be governed by an unprofitable and fantastical wife.

22. We had another wet day, to try both Mrs. Fleming's patience and my good breeding. The northeast wind commonly sticks by us three or four days, filling the atmosphere with damps, injurious both to man and beast. The worst of it was we had no good liquor to warm

St. James' Northam in Goochland County. See Robert A. Brock, *Documents . . . Relating to the Huguenot Emigration to Virginia* (Baltimore, 1962), pp. 183–184.

[8] The Royal Exchange in London was a noted place to meet and gossip, in addition to being a place of business.

[9] Commissary Blair reported to the Bishop of London in a letter of February 10, 1724: "The livings are settled by law at 16,000 lbs. of tobacco per annum, besides glebes and perquisites; and this in the sweet scented parishes is better than £100 sterling; and all the rest about £80." The Virginia Assembly had fixed this salary in 1696 and it remained stationary until the Revolution. See Hugh Jones, *The Present State of Virginia*, edited by Richard L. Morton (Chapel Hill, 1956), p. 99 and pp. 230–231, n. 203.

our blood and fortify our spirits against so strong a malignity. However, I was cheerful under all these misfortunes and expressed no concern but a decent fear lest my long visit might be troublesome. Since I was like to have thus much leisure, I endeavored to find out what subject a dull married man could introduce that might best bring the widow to the use of her tongue. At length I discovered she was a notable quack and therefore paid that regard to her knowledge as to put some questions to her about the bad distemper that raged then in the country. I mean the bloody flux, that was brought us in the Negro ship consigned to Colonel Braxton.[10] She told me she made use of very simple remedies in that case, with very good success. She did the business either with hartshorn drink that had plantain leaves boiled in it, or else with a strong decoction of St.-Andrew's-cross in new milk instead of water. I agreed with her that those remedies might be very good but would be more effectual after a dose or two of Indian physic.

But for fear this conversation might be too grave for a widow, I turned the discourse and began to talk of plays, and, finding her taste lay most toward comedy, I offered my service to read one to her, which she kindly accepted. She produced the second part of *The Beggar's Opera*, which had diverted the town for forty nights successively and gained £4,000 to the author. This was not owing altogether to the wit or humor that sparkled in it but to some political reflections that seemed to hit the ministry. But the great advantage of the author was that his interest was solicited by the Duchess of Queensberry, which no man could refuse who had but half an eye in his head or half a guinea in his pocket.[11] Her Grace, like death, spared nobody but even took My Lord Selkirk in for two guineas, to repair which extravagance he lived upon Scots herrings two months afterwards. But the best story was she made a very smart officer in His Majesty's guards give her a guinea, who swearing at the same time 'twas all he had in the

---

[10] Probably George Braxton, Jr. His importation of Negro slaves is mentioned in Byrd's diary for 1739–1741 (*Another Secret Diary of William Byrd of Westover*, edited by Maud H. Woodfin and Marion Tinling [Richmond, Va., 1942], p. 22).

[11] Catherine Hyde Douglas, Duchess of Queensberry, and her husband were devoted patrons of John Gay, who actually died in the Duke's house in Burlington Gardens in 1732. *The Beggar's Opera*, first printed in 1728, had a fourth edition in the year Byrd wrote.

world, she sent him fifty for it the next day to reward his obedience. After having acquainted my company with the history of the play, I read three acts of it, and left Mrs. Fleming and Mr. Randolph to finish it, who read as well as most actors do at a rehearsal. Thus we killed the time and triumphed over the bad weather.

23. The clouds continued to drive from the northeast and to menace us with more rain. But as the lady resolved to venture through it I thought it a shame for me to venture to flinch. Therefore, after fortifying myself with two capacious dishes of coffee and making my compliments to the ladies, I mounted, and Mr. Randolph was so kind as to be my guide.

At the distance of about three miles, in a path as narrow as that which leads to Heaven but much more dirty, we reached the homely dwelling of the Reverend Mr. Marij. His land is much more barren than his wife and needs all Mr. Bradley's [12] skill in agriculture to make it bring corn. Thence we proceeded five miles farther to a mill of Mr. Randolph's, that is apt to stand still when there falls but little rain and to be carried away when there falls a great deal. Then we pursued a very blind path four miles farther, which puzzled my guide, who I suspect led me out of the way. At length we came into a great road, where he took leave, after giving me some very confused directions, and so left me to blunder out the rest of the journey by myself. I lost myself more than once but soon recovered the right way again. About three [?] miles after quitting my guide, I passed the south branch of Pamunkey River, near fifty yards over and full of stones.

After this I had eight miles to Mr. Chiswell's, [13] where I arrived about two o'clock and saved my dinner. I was very handsomely entertained, finding everything very clean and very good. I had not seen Mrs. Chiswell in twenty-four years, which, alas! had made great havoc with her pretty face and plowed very deep furrows in her fair skin. It was impossible to know her again, so much the flower was

[12] Richard Bradley, author of a number of works on agriculture, such as *New Improvements of Planting and Gardening* (1717), *The Gentleman and Gardener's Calendar* (1720), and *The County Housewife* (1727). Byrd's library contained several of Bradley's works.

[13] Charles Chiswell was clerk of the General Court, 1706. See p. 30 for Byrd's earlier acquaintance with Mrs. Chiswell.

faded. However, though she was grown an old woman, yet she was one of those absolute rarities, a very good old woman.

I found Mr. Chiswell a sensible, well-bred man and very frank in communicating his knowledge in the mystery of making iron, wherein he has had long experience. I told him I was come to spy the land and inform myself of the expense of carrying on an ironwork with effect; that I sought my instruction from him, who understood the whole mystery, having gained full experience in every part of it, only I was very sorry he had bought that experience so dear. He answered that he would with great sincerity let me into the little knowledge he had, and so we immediately entered upon the business.

He assured me the first step I was to take was to acquaint myself fully with the quantity and quality of my ore. For that reason I ought to keep a good pickax man at work a whole year to search if there be a sufficient quantity, without which it would be a very rash undertaking. That I should also have a skillful person to try the richness of the ore. Nor is it great advantage to have it exceeding rich, because then it will yield brittle iron, which is not valuable. But the way to have it tough is to mix poor ore and rich together, which makes the poorer sort extremely necessary for the production of the best iron. Then he showed me a sample of the richest ore they have in England, which yields a full moiety of iron. It was of a pale red color, smooth and greasy, and not exceedingly heavy; but it produced so brittle a metal that they were obliged to melt a poorer ore along with it.

He told me, after I was certain my ore was good and plentiful enough, my next inquiry ought to be how far it lies from a stream proper to build a furnace upon, and again what distance that furnace will be from water carriage; because the charge of carting a great way is very heavy and eats out a great part of the profit. That this was the misfortune of the mines of Fredericksville, where they were obliged to cart the ore a mile to the furnace, and after 'twas run into iron to carry that twenty-four miles over an uneven road to Rappahannock River, about a mile below Fredericksburg, to a plantation the company rented of Colonel Page.[14] If I were satisfied with the situation, I was in the

[14] Probably Colonel Mann Page, of Gloucester County, member of the Virginia Council from 1714 until his death in 1730.

next place to consider whether I had woodland enough near the furnace to supply it with charcoal, whereof it would require a prodigious quantity. That the properest wood for that purpose was that of oily kind, such as pine, walnut, hickory, oak, and in short all that yields cones, nuts, or acorns. That two miles square of wood would supply a moderate furnace, that so what you fell first may have time to grow up again to a proper bigness (which must be four inches over) by that time the rest is cut down.

He told me farther that 120 slaves, including women, were necessary to carry on all the business of an ironwork, and the more Virginians amongst them the better; though in that number he comprehended carters, colliers, and those that planted the corn. That if there should be much carting, it would require 1,600 barrels of corn yearly to support the people and the cattle employed; nor does even that quantity suffice at Fredericksville.

That if all these circumstances should happily concur, and you could procure honest colliers and firemen, which will be difficult to do, you may easily run eight hundred tons of sow iron [15] a year. The whole charge of freight, custom, commission, and other expenses in England, will not exceed 30s. a ton, and 'twill commonly sell for £6, and then the clear profit will amount to £4 10s. So that allowing the 10s. for accidents, you may reasonably expect a clear profit of £4, which being multiplied by eight hundred, will amount to £3,200 a year, to pay you for your land and Negroes. But then it behooved me to be fully informed of the whole matter myself, to prevent being imposed upon; and if any offered to put tricks upon me, to punish them as they deserve.

Thus ended our conversation for this day, and I retired to a very clean lodging in another house and took my bark, but was forced to take it in water, by reason a light-fingered damsel had ransacked my baggage and drank up my brandy. This unhappy girl, it seems, is a baronet's daughter; but her complexion, being red-haired, inclined her so much to lewdness that her father sent her, under the care of the virtuous Mr. Cheep, to seek her fortune on this side the globe.

[15] Iron cast in a mold larger than a pig.

24. My friend Mr. Chiswell made me reparation for the robbery of his servant by filling my bottle again with good brandy.

It being Sunday, I made a motion for going to church to see the growth of the parish, but unluckily the sermon happened to be at the chapel, which was too far off. I was unwilling to tire my friend with any farther discourse upon iron and therefore turned the conversation to other subjects. And talking of management, he let me into two secrets worth remembering. He said the quickest way in the world to stop the fermentation of any liquor was to keep a lighted match of brimstone under the cask for some time. This is useful in so warm a country as this, where cider is apt to work itself off both of its strength and sweetness. The other secret was to keep weevils out of wheat and other grain. You have nothing to do, said he, but to put a bag of pepper into every heap or cask, which those insects have such an antipathy to that they will not approach it. These receipts he gave me, not upon report, but upon his own repeated experience. He farther told me he had brewed as good ale of malt made of Indian corn as ever he tasted; all the objection was he could neither by art or standing ever bring it to be fine in the cask. The quantity of corn he employed in brewing a cask of forty gallons was two bushels and a half, which made it very strong and pleasant.

We had a haunch of venison for dinner, as fat and well-tasted as if it had come out of Richmond Park. In these upper parts of the country the deer are in better case than below, though I believe the buck which gave us so good a dinner had eat out his value in peas, which will make deer exceedingly fat.

In the afternoon I walked with my friend to his mill, which is half a mile from his house. It is built upon a rock very firmly, so that 'tis more apt to suffer by too little water (the run not being over plentiful) than too much. On the other side of this stream lie several of Colonel Jones's[16] plantations. The poor Negroes upon them are a kind of Adamites, very scantily supplied with clothes and other necessaries; nevertheless (which is a little incomprehensible), they continue in perfect health and none of them die except it be of age. However, they

[16] Colonel Thomas Jones, a member of the House of Burgesses.

are even with their master and make him but indifferent crops, so that he gets nothing by his injustice but the scandal of it.

And here I must make one remark, which I am a little unwilling to do for fear of encouraging of cruelty, that those Negroes which are kept the barest of clothes and bedding are commonly the freest from sickness. And this happens, I suppose, by their being all face and therefore better proof against the sudden changes of weather to which this climate is unhappily subject.

25. After saying some very civil things to Mrs. Chiswell for my handsome entertainment, I mounted my horse and Mr. Chiswell his phaeton, in order to go to the mines at Fredericksville. We could converse very little by the way, by reason of our different *voitures*. The road was very straight and level the whole journey, which was twenty-five miles, the last ten whereof I rode in the chair and my friend on my horse, to ease ourselves by that variety of motion.

About a mile before we got to Fredericksville we forded over the north branch of Pamunkey, about sixty yards over. Neither this nor the south branch run up near so high as the mountains but many miles below them spread out into a kind of morass, like Chickahominy. When we approached the mines there opened to our view a large space of cleared ground, whose wood had been cut down for coaling.

We arrived here about two o'clock, and Mr. Chiswell had been so provident as to bring a cold venison pasty with which we appeased our appetites without the impatience of waiting. When our tongues were at leisure for discourse, my friend told me there was one Mr. Harrison in England who is so universal a dealer in all sorts of iron that he could govern the market just as he pleased. That it was by his artful management that our iron from the plantations sold for less than that made in England, though it was generally reckoned much better. That ours would hardly fetch £6 a ton, when theirs fetched seven or eight, purely to serve that man's interest. Then he explained the several charges upon our sow iron after it was put on board the ships. That in the first place it paid 7s. 6d. a ton for freight, being just so much clear gain to the ships, which carry it as ballast or wedge it in among the hogsheads. When it gets home, it pays 3s. 9d. custom.

These articles together make no more than 11s. 3d., and yet the merchants, by their great skill in multiplying charges, swell the account up to near 30s. a ton by that time it gets out of their hands, and they are continually adding more and more, as they serve us in our accounts of tobacco.

He told me a strange thing about steel, that the making of the best remains at this day a profound secret in the breast of a very few and therefore is in danger of being lost, as the art of staining of glass and many others have been. He could only tell me they used beechwood in the making of it in Europe and burn it a considerable time in powder of charcoal; but the mystery lies in the liquor they quench it in.

After dinner we took a walk to the furnace, which is elegantly built of brick, though the hearth be of firestone. There we saw the founder, Mr. Derham, who is paid 4s. for every ton of sow iron that he runs, which is a shilling cheaper than the last workman had. This operator looked a little melancholy because he had nothing to do, the furnace having been cold ever since May for want of corn to support the cattle. This was, however, no neglect of Mr. Chiswell, because all the persons he had contracted with had basely disappointed him. But, having received a small supply, they intended to blow very soon. With that view they began to heat the furnace, which is six weeks before it comes to that intense heat required to run the metal in perfection. Nevertheless, they commonly begin to blow when the fire has been kindled a week or ten days.

Close by the furnace stood a very spacious house full of charcoal, holding at least four hundred loads, which will be burnt out in three months. The company has contracted with Mr. Harry Willis to fall the wood, and then maul it and cut it into pieces of four feet in length and bring it to the pits where it is to be coaled. All this he has undertaken to do for 2s. a cord, which must be four foot broad, four foot high, and eight foot long. Being thus carried to the pits, the collier has contracted to coal it for 5s. a load, consisting of 160 bushels. The fire in the furnace is blown by two mighty pair of bellows that cost £100 each, and these bellows are moved by a great wheel of twenty-six foot diameter. The wheel again is carried round by a small stream of water, conveyed about 350 yards overland in a trough, from a pond made by a wooden dam. But there is great want of water in a dry season, which makes the furnace often blow out, to the great prejudice of the works.

Having thus filled my head with all these particulars, we returned to the house, where, after talking of Colonel Spotswood and his stratagems to shake off his partners and secure all his mines to himself, I retired to a homely lodging which, like a homespun mistress, had been more tolerable if it had been sweet.

26. Over our tea, Mr. Chiswell told me the expense which the company had been already at amounted to near £12,000; but then the land, Negroes, and cattle were all included in that charge. However, the money began now to come in, they having run twelve hundred tons of iron, and all their heavy disbursements were over. Only they were still forced to buy great quantities of corn, because they had not strength of their own to make it. That they had not more than eighty Negroes, and few of those Virginia born. That they need forty Negroes more to carry on all the business with their own force. They have 15,000 acres of land, though little of it rich except in iron, and of that they have a great quantity.

Mr. Fitzwilliam took up the mine tract and had the address to draw in the Governor, Captain Pearse, Dr. Nicholas, and Mr. Chiswell to be jointly concerned with him, by which contrivance he first got a good price for the land and then, when he had been very little out of pocket, sold his share to Mr. Nelson for £500; and of these gentlemen the company at present consists. And Mr. Chiswell is the only person amongst them that knows anything of the matter, and has £100 a year for looking after the works, and richly deserves it.

After breaking our fast we took a walk to the principal mine, about a mile from the furnace, where they had sunk in some places about fifteen or twenty feet deep. The operator, Mr. Gordon, raised the ore, for which he was to have by contract 1s. 6d. per cartload of twenty-six hundredweight. This man was obliged to hire all the laborers he wanted for this work of the company, after the rate of 25s. a month, and for all that was able to clear £40 a year for himself.

We saw here several large heaps of ore of two sorts, one of rich, and the other spongy and poor, which they melted together to make the metal more tough. The way of raising the ore was by blowing it up, which operation I saw here from beginning to end. They first drilled a hole in the mine, either upright or sloping, as the grain of it required. This hole they cleansed with a rag fastened to the end of an iron with a worm at the end of it. Then they put in a cartridge of powder containing about three ounces and at the same time a reed full of fuse that reached to the powder. Then they rammed dry clay or soft stone very hard into the hole, and lastly they fired the fuse with a paper that had been dipped in a solution of saltpeter and dried, which, burning slow and sure, gave leisure to the engineer to retire to a proper distance before the explosion. This in the miner's language is called "making a blast," which will loosen several hundredweight of ore at once; and afterwards the laborers easily separate it with pickaxes and carry it away in baskets up to the heap.

At our return we saw near the furnace large heaps of mine with charcoal mixed with it, a stratum of each alternately, beginning first with a layer of charcoal at the bottom. To this they put fire, which in a little time spreads through the whole heap and calcines the ore, which afterwards easily crumbles into small pieces fit for the furnace. Then was likewise a mighty quantity of limestone brought from Bristol by way of ballast, at 2s. 6d. a ton, which they are at the trouble to cart hither from Rappahannock River, but contrive to do it when the carts return from carrying of iron. They put this into the furnace with the iron ore, in the proportion of one ton of stone to ten of ore, with design to absorb the sulphur out of the iron, which would otherwise make it brittle. And if that be the use of it, oyster shells would certainly do as well as limestone, being altogether as strong an alkali, if not stronger. Nor can their being taken out of salt water be any objection, because 'tis pretty certain the West India limestone, which is thrown up by the sea, is even better than that imported from Bristol. But the founders who never tried either of these will by no means be persuaded to go out of their way, though the reason of the thing be never so evident.

I observed the richer sort of mine, being of a dark color mixed with rust, was laid in a heap by itself, and so was the poor, which was of a liver or brick color. The sow iron is in the figure of a half round, about two feet and a half long, weighing sixty or seventy pounds, whereof three thousandweight make a cartload drawn by eight oxen, which are commonly shod to save their hoofs in those stony ways. When the furnace blows, it runs about twenty tons of iron a week. The founders find it very hot work to tend the furnace, especially in summer, and are obliged to spend no small part of their earnings in strong drink to recruit their spirits.

Besides the founder, the collier, and miner, who are paid in proportion to their work, the company have several other officers upon wages: a stocktaker, who weighs and measures everything, a clerk, who keeps an account of all receipts and disbursements; a smith to shoe their cattle and keep all their ironwork in repair; a wheelwright, cartwright, carpenter, and several carters. The wages of all these persons amount to £100 a year; so that including Mr. Chiswell's salary they disburse £200 per annum in standing wages. The provisions, too, are a heavy article, which their plantations don't yet produce in a sufficient quantity, though they are at the charge of a general overseer. But while corn is so short with them, there can be no great increase of stock of any kind.

27. Having now pretty well exhausted the subject of sow iron, I asked my friend some questions about bar iron. He told me we had as yet no forge erected in Virginia, though we had four furnaces. But there was a very good one set up at the head of the bay in Maryland, that made exceeding good work. He let me know that the duty in England upon bar iron was 24s. a ton, and that it sold there from £10 to £16 a ton. This would pay the charge of forging abundantly, but he doubted the parliament of England would soon forbid us that improvement, lest after that we should go farther and manufacture our bars into all sorts of ironware, as they already do in New England and Pennsylvania. Nay, he questioned whether we should be suffered to cast any iron, which they can do themselves at their furnaces.

Thus ended our conversation, and I thanked my friend for being so free in communicating everything to me. Then, after tipping a pistole to the clerk, to drink prosperity to the mines with all the workmen, I accepted the kind offer of going part of my journey in the phaeton.

I took my leave about ten and drove over a spacious level road ten miles to a bridge built over the river Po, which is one of the four branches of Mattaponi, about forty yards wide. Two miles beyond that we passed by a plantation, belonging to the company, of about five hundred acres, where they keep a great number of oxen to relieve those that have dragged their loaded carts thus far. Three miles farther we came to the Germanna road, where I quitted the chair and continued my journey on horseback. I rode eight miles together over a stony road, and had on either side continual poisoned fields, with nothing but saplings growing on them. Then I came into the main county road that leads from Fredericksburg to Germanna,[17] which last place I reached in ten miles more.

This famous town consists of Colonel Spotswood's enchanted castle on one side of the street and a baker's dozen of ruinous tenements on the other, where so many German families had dwelt some years ago, but are now removed ten miles higher, in the fork of Rappahannock, to land of their own. There had also been a chapel about a bowshot from the colonel's house, at the end of an avenue of cherry trees, but some pious people had lately burnt it down, with intent to get another built nearer to their own homes.

Here I arrived about three o'clock and found only Mrs. Spotswood at home, who received her old acquaintance with many a gracious smile. I was carried into a room elegantly set off with pier glasses, the largest of which came soon after to an odd misfortune. Amongst other favorite animals that cheered this lady's solitude, a brace of tame deer

[17] Governor Spotswood had secured the Council's approval in 1714 to settle a community of German miners at the falls of the Rappahannock as a barrier against the Indians. The German settlers did not remain satisfied and moved elsewhere. In 1720 the town became the seat of the newly formed Spotsylvania County, but in the year of Byrd's visit Fredericksburg replaced Germanna as the chief settlement of the county. Germanna was described in 1715 as containing "nine houses, built all in a line; and before every house, about twenty feet distant from it, they have small sheds built for their hogs and hens, so that the hog-sties and houses make a street"; quoted from Ann Maury, *Memoirs of a Huguenot Family* (New York, 1872), p. 269, by Leonidas Dodson in *Alexander Spotswood* (Philadelphia, 1932), p. 232.

ran familiarly about the house, and one of them came to stare at me as a stranger; but, unluckily spying his own figure in the glass, he made a spring over the tea table that stood under it and shattered the glass to pieces and, falling back upon the tea table, made a terrible fracas among the china. This exploit was so sudden, and accompanied with such noise, that it surprised me and perfectly frightened Mrs. Spotswood. But 'twas worth all the damage to show the moderation and good humor with which she bore this disaster.

In the evening the noble colonel came home from his mines, who saluted me very civilly, and Mrs. Spotswood's sister, Miss Theky,[18] who had been to meet him *en cavalier*, was so kind too as to bid me welcome. We talked over a legend of old stories, supped about nine, and then prattled with the ladies till 'twas time for a traveler to retire. In the meantime, I observed my old friend to be very uxorious and exceedingly fond of his children. This was so opposite to the maxims he used to preach up before he was married that I could not forbear rubbing up the memory of them. But he gave a very good-natured turn to his change of sentiments by alleging that whoever brings a poor gentlewoman into so solitary a place, from all her friends and acquaintance, would be ungrateful not to use her and all that belongs to her with all possible tenderness.

28. We all kept snug in our several apartments till nine, except Miss Theky, who was the housewife of the family. At that hour we met over a pot of coffee, which was not quite strong enough to give us the palsy.

After breakfast the Colonel and I left the ladies to their domestic affairs and took a turn in the garden, which has nothing beautiful but three terrace walks that fall in slopes one below another. I let him understand that besides the pleasure of paying him a visit I came to be instructed by so great a master in the mystery of making iron, wherein he had led the way and was the Tubal-cain of Virginia. He corrected me a little there by assuring me he was not only the first in

---

[18] Presumably a nickname for "Dorothea," the first name of Mrs. Spotswood's sister. Colonel Spotswood married Anne Butler Brayne of Westminster in 1724 and brought her to Virginia in 1730; see Dodson, *Alexander Spotswood*, p. 299.

this country but the first in North America who had erected a regular furnace. That they ran altogether upon bloomeries in New England and Pennsylvania till his example had made them attempt greater works.[19] But in this last colony, they have so few ships to carry their iron to Great Britain that they must be content to make it only for their own use, and must be obliged to manufacture it when they have done. That he hoped he had done the country very great service by setting so good an example. That the four furnaces now at work in Virginia circulated a great sum of money for provisions and all other necessaries in the adjacent counties. That they took off a great number of hands from planting tobacco and employed them in works that produced a large sum of money in England to the persons concerned, whereby the country is so much the richer. That they are besides a considerable advantage to Great Britain, because it lessens the quantity of bar iron imported from Spain, Holland, Sweden, Denmark, and Muscovy, which use to be no less than twenty thousand tons yearly, though at the same time no sow iron is imported thither from any country but only from the plantations. For most of this bar iron they do not only pay silver, but our friends in the Baltic are so nice they even expect to be paid all in crown pieces. On the contrary, all the iron they receive from the plantations, they pay for it in their own manufactures and send for it in their own shipping.

Then I inquired after his own mines, and hoped, as he was the first that engaged in this great undertaking, that he had brought them to the most perfection. He told me he had iron in several parts of his great tract of land, consisting of forty-five thousand acres. But that the mine he was at work upon was thirteen miles below Germanna. That his ore (which was very rich) he raised a mile from his furnace and was obliged to cart the iron, when it was made, fifteen miles to Massaponax, a plantation he had upon Rappahannock River; but that the road was exceeding good, gently declining all the way, and had no

[19] Dodson points out that Spotswood is mistaken, since blast furnaces and forges had been in operation in New England seventy years earlier (*Alexander Spotswood*, p. 296). William B. Weeden, *Economic and Social History of New England, 1620–1780* (Boston and New York, 1890), I, 177–178, describes iron working at Lynn and Braintree. Lynn began smelting, forging, and refining iron in 1643.

more than one hill to go up in the whole journey. For this reason his loaded carts went it in a day without difficulty.

He said it was true his works were of the oldest standing; but that his long absence in England, and the wretched management of Mr. Graeme,[20] whom he had entrusted with his affairs, had put him back very much. That, what with neglect and severity, above eighty of his slaves were lost while he was in England and most of his cattle starved. That his furnace stood still great part of the time, and all his plantations ran to ruin. That, indeed, he was rightly served for committing his affairs to the care of a mathematician, whose thoughts were always among the stars. That nevertheless, since his return he had applied himself to rectify his steward's mistakes and bring his business again into order. That now he had contrived to do everything with his own people, except raising the mine and running the iron, by which he had contracted his expense very much. Nay, he believed that by his directions he could bring sensible Negroes to perform those parts of the work tolerably well.

But at the same time he gave me to understand that his furnace had done no great feats lately, because he had been taken up in building an air furnace at Massaponax, which he had now brought to perfection and should be thereby able to furnish the whole country with all sorts of cast iron as cheap and as good as ever came from England. I told him he must do one thing more to have a full vent for those commodities: he must keep a *chaloupe*[21] running into all the rivers, to carry his wares home to people's own doors. And if he would do that I would set a good example and take off a whole ton of them.

Our conversation on this subject continued till dinner, which was both elegant and plentiful. The afternoon was devoted to the ladies, who showed me one of their most beautiful walks. They conducted me through a shady lane to the landing and by the way made me drink some very fine water that issued from a marble fountain and ran incessantly. Just behind it was a covered bench, where Miss Theky

---

[20] He had appointed John Graeme, his cousin, manager of his American estate in 1725 (Dodson, *Alexander Spotswood*, p. 298).

[21] The French form of the word anglicized to "shallop," a light open boat, used chiefly on rivers.

often sat and bewailed her virginity. Then we proceeded to the river, which is the south branch of Rappahannock, about fifty yards wide and so rapid that the ferryboat is drawn over by a chain and therefore called the Rapidan. At night we drank prosperity to all the Colonel's projects in a bowl of rack punch and then retired to our devotions.

29. Having employed about two hours in retirement, I sallied out at the first summons to breakfast, where our conversation with the ladies, like whip sillabub, was very pretty but had nothing in it. This it seems was Miss Theky's birthday, upon which I made her my compliments and wished she might live twice as long a married woman as she had lived a maid. I did not presume to pry into the secret of her age, nor was she forward to disclose it, for this humble reason, lest I should think her wisdom fell short of her years. She contrived to make this day of her birth a day of mourning, for, having nothing better at present to set her affections upon, she had a dog that was a great favorite. It happened that very morning the poor cur had done something very uncleanly upon the Colonel's bed, for which he was condemned to die. However, upon her entreaty, she got him a reprieve, but was so concerned that so much severity should be intended on her birthday that she was not to be comforted; and lest such another accident might oust the poor cur of his clergy,[22] she protested she would board out her dog at a neighbor's house, where she hoped he would be more kindly treated.

Then the Colonel and I took another turn in the garden to discourse farther on the subject of iron. He was very frank in communicating all his dear-bought experience to me and told me very civilly he would not only let me into the whole secret but would make a journey to James River and give me his faithful opinion of all my conveniences. For his part, he wished there were many more ironworks in the coun-

[22] Referring to the appeal to "benefit of clergy" by which offenders were enabled to escape the death penalty for a first offense of a capital nature. Originally designed to exempt members of the clergy from secular jurisdiction, the benefit was later extended to all who could prove their literacy by reading a passage that came to be called "neck verse." An act of Parliament in 1707 abolished the literacy test; but by this time most felonies were "non-clergyable." Benefit of clergy itself was abolished in 1827. See Theodore F. T. Plucknett, *A Concise History of the Common Law* (London, 1948), pp. 414–416.

try, provided the parties concerned would preserve a constant harmony among themselves and meet and consult frequently what might be for their common advantage. By this they might be better able to manage the workmen and reduce their wages to what was just and reasonable. After this frank speech he began to explain the whole charge of an ironwork. He said there ought at least to be an hundred Negroes employed in it, and those upon good land would make corn and raise provisions enough to support themselves and the cattle and do every other part of the business. That the furnace might be built for £700 and made ready to go to work, if I went the nearest way to do it, especially since, coming after so many, I might correct their errors and avoid their miscarriages. That if I had ore and wood enough and a convenient stream of water to set the furnace upon, having neither too much nor too little water, I might undertake the affair with a full assurance of success, provided the distance of carting be not too great, which is exceedingly burdensome. That there must be abundance of wheel carriages shod with iron and several teams of oxen provided to transport the wood that is to be coaled, and afterwards the coal and ore to the furnace, and last of all the sow iron to the nearest water carriage, and carry back limestone and other necessaries from thence to the works; and a sloop also would be useful to carry the iron on board the ships, the masters not being always in the humor to fetch it.

Then he enumerated the people that were to be hired, viz.: a founder, a mine-raiser, a collier, a stocktaker, a clerk, a smith, a carpenter, a wheelwright, and several carters. That these altogether will be a standing charge of about £500 a year. That the amount of freight, custom, commission, and other charges in England, comes to 27s. a ton. But that the merchants yearly find out means to inflame the account with new articles, as they do in those of tobacco. That, upon the whole matter, the expenses here and in England may be computed modestly at £3 a ton. And the rest that the iron sells for will be clear gain, to pay for the land and Negroes, which 'tis to be hoped will be £3 more for every ton that is sent over. As this account agreed pretty near with that which Mr. Chiswell had given me, I set it down (notwithstanding it may seem a repetition of the same thing) to prove that both these gentlemen were sincere in their representations.

We had a Michaelmas goose for dinner of Miss Theky's own raising, who was now good-natured enough to forget the jeopardy of her
dog. In the afternoon we walked in a meadow by the riverside, which
winds in the form of a horseshoe about Germanna, making it a peninsula containing about four hundred acres. Rappahannock forks a-
bout fourteen miles below this place, the northern branch being the
larger and consequently must be the river that bounds My Lord
Fairfax's grant of the Northern Neck.[23]

30. The sun rose clear this morning, and so did I, and finished all
my little affairs by breakfast. It was then resolved to wait on the ladies
on horseback, since the bright sun, the fine air, and the wholesome
exercise all invited us to it. We forded the river a little above the ferry
and rode six miles up the neck to a fine level piece of rich land, where
we found about twenty plants of ginseng, with the scarlet berries growing on the top of the middle stalk. The root of this is of wonderful
virtue in many cases, particularly to raise the spirits and promote perspiration, which makes it a specific in colds and coughs. The Colonel
complimented me with all we found in return for my telling him the
virtues of it. We were all pleased to find so much of this king of plants
so near the Colonel's habitation and growing, too, upon his own land,
but were, however, surprised to find it upon level ground, after we
had been told it grew only upon the north side of stony mountains.
I carried home this treasure with as much joy as if every root had been
a graft of the tree of life, and washed and dried it carefully.

This airing made us as hungry as so many hawks, so that, between
appetite and a very good dinner, 'twas difficult to eat like a philosopher.
In the afternoon the ladies walked me about amongst all their little
animals, with which they amuse themselves and furnish the table; the
worst of it is, they are so tender-hearted they shed a silent tear every
time any of them are killed.

At night the Colonel and I quitted the threadbare subject of iron

[23] The portion of Virginia bounded by the Rappahannock and Potomac Rivers.
The original charter of the land had been ambiguously phrased, and Lord Fairfax
claimed a wider extent of land than Virginians were willing to concede. Byrd was
one of the commissioners appointed to represent the King against Fairfax in a review of the matter in 1735. Fairfax ultimately won his case, the boundaries being
set at the southern branch of the Rappahannock and the northern branch of the
Potomac; see Richard L. Morton, *Colonial Virginia* (Chapel Hill, 1960), II, 546–547.

and changed the scene to politics. He told me the ministry[24] had receded from their demand upon New England to raise a standing salary for all succeeding governors, for fear some curious members of the House of Commons should inquire how the money was disposed of that had been raised in the other American colonies for the support of their governors. And particularly what becomes of the 4½ per cent paid in the sugar colonies for that purpose. That duty produces near £20,000 a year, but, being remitted into the Exchequer, not one of the West India governors is paid out of it; but they, like falcons, are let loose upon the people, who are complaisant enough to settle other revenues upon them, to the great impoverishing of those colonies.[25] In the meantime 'tis certain the money raised by the 4½ per cent molders away between the minister's fingers, nobody knows how, like the quitrents of Virginia. And 'tis for this reason that the instructions forbidding all governors to accept of any presents from their assemblies are dispensed with in the Sugar Islands, while 'tis strictly insisted upon everywhere else, where the assemblies were so wise as to keep their revenues among themselves. He said further that if the assembly in New England would stand buff,[26] he did not see how they could be forced to raise money against their will, for if they should direct it to be done by act of Parliament, which they have threatened to do (though it be against the right of Englishmen to be taxed but by their representatives), yet they would find it no easy matter to put such an act in execution.

Then the Colonel read me a lecture upon tar, affirming that it can't be made in this warm climate after the manner they make it in Sweden and Muscovy, by barking the tree two yards from the ground, whereby the turpentine descends all into the stump in a year's time, which is then split in pieces in order for the kiln. But here the sun fries out the turpentine in the branches of the tree, when the leaves

[24] The Board of Trade and Plantations.

[25] Virginians, like other colonists, habitually complained about the avarice of governors, who expected to recoup their fortunes from moneys which they might wring from the colonies; see *An Essay upon the Government of the English Plantations on the Continent of America* (1701), edited by Louis B. Wright (San Marino, Calif., 1945), *passim*.

[26] To stand firm; not to flinch.

are dried, and hinders it from descending. But, on the contrary, those who burn tar of lightwood in the common way and are careful about it, make as good as that which comes from the East Country,[27] nor will it burn the cordage more than that does.

Then we entered upon the subject of hemp, which the Colonel told me he never could raise here from foreign seed but at last sowed the seed of the wild hemp (which is very common in the upper parts of the country) and that came up very thick. That he sent about five hundred pounds of it to England, and that the Commissioners of the Navy, after a full trial of it, reported to the Lords of the Admiralty that it was equal in goodness to the best that comes from Riga. I told him if our hemp were never so good it would not be worth the making here, even though they should continue the bounty. And my reason was because labor is not more than twopence a day in the East Country where they produce hemp, and here we can't compute it at less than tenpence, which being five times as much as their labor, and considering besides that our freight is three times as dear as theirs, the price that will make them rich will ruin us, as I have found by woeful experience. Besides, if the King, who must have the refusal, buys our hemp, the Navy is so long in paying both the price and the bounty that we who live from hand to mouth cannot afford to wait so long for it. And then our good friends the merchants load it with so many charges that they run away with great part of the profit themselves, just like the bald eagle which, after the fishing hawk has been at great pains to catch a fish, powders down [28] and takes it from him.

Our conversation was interrupted by a summons to supper, for the ladies, to show their power, had by this time brought us tamely to go to bed with our bellies full, though we both at first declared positively against it. So very pliable a thing is frail man when women have the bending of him.

OCTOBER

1. Our ladies overslept themselves this morning, so that we did not break our fast till ten. We drank tea made of the leaves of ginseng,

[27] The Baltic area.
[28] Descends hastily.

which has the virtues of the root in a weaker degree and is not disagreeable.

So soon as we could force our inclinations to quit the ladies, we took a turn on the terrace walk and discoursed upon quite a new subject. The Colonel explained to me the difference betwixt the galleons and the flota, which very few people know. The galleons, it seems, are the ships which bring the treasure and other rich merchandise to Cartagena from Portobelo, to which place it is brought overland from Panama and Peru. And the flota is the squadron that brings the treasure, etc., from Mexico and New Spain, which make up at La Vera Cruz. Both these squadrons rendezvous at the Havana, from whence they shoot the Gulf of Florida in their return to Old Spain. That this important port of the Havana is very poorly fortified and worse garrisoned and provided, for which reason it may be easily taken. Besides, both the galleons and flota, being confined to sail through the gulf, might be intercepted by our stationing a squadron of men-of-war at the most convenient of the Bahama Islands. And that those islands are of vast consequence for that purpose. He told me also that the *azogue* ships are they that carry quicksilver to Portobelo and La Vera Cruz to refine the silver, and that in Spanish *azogue* signifies quicksilver.

Then my friend unriddled to me the great mystery why we have endured all the late insolences of the Spaniards so tamely. The *Asiento* Contract [29] and the liberty of sending a ship every year to the Spanish West Indies make it very necessary for the South Sea Company to have effects of great value in that part of the world. Now these, being always in the power of the Spaniards, make the directors of that company very fearful of a breach and consequently very generous in their offers to the ministry to prevent it. For fear these worthy gentlemen should suffer, the English squadron under Admiral Hosier lay idle at the bastimentos till the ship's bottoms were eat out by the worm and the officers and men, to the number of five thousand, died like rotten sheep, without being suffered, by the strictest orders, to strike one stroke, though they

[29] By the Treaty of Utrecht (1713), Great Britain received a 33-year monopoly of selling Negro slaves to the Spanish colonies and the right to send one ship annually to trade with the Spanish Indies; the concessions were to be managed by the South Sea Company.

might have taken both the flota and galleons and made themselves masters of the Havana into the bargain, if they had not been chained up from doing it. All this moderation our peaceable ministry showed even at a time when the Spaniards were furiously attacking Gibraltar and taking all the English ships they could, both in Europe and America, to the great and everlasting reproach of the British nation. That some of the ministry, being tired out with the clamors of the merchants, declared their opinion for war and while they entertained those sentiments they pitched upon him, Colonel Spotswood, to be Governor of Jamaica, that by his skill and experience in the art military they might be the better able to execute their design of taking the Havana. But the courage of these worthy patriots soon cooled and the arguments used by the South Sea directors persuaded them once again into more pacific measures. When the scheme was dropped, his government of Jamaica was dropped at the same time, and then General Hunter was judged fit enough to rule that island in time of peace.

After this the Colonel endeavored to convince me that he came fairly by his place of Postmaster General,[30] notwithstanding the report of some evil-disposed persons to the contrary. The case was this: Mr. Hamilton of New Jersey, who had formerly had that post, wrote to Colonel Spotswood in England to favor him with his interest to get it restored to him. But the Colonel, considering wisely that charity began at home, instead of getting the place for Hamilton, secured it for a better friend; though, as he tells the story, that gentleman was absolutely refused before he spoke the least good word for himself.

2. This being the day appointed for my departure from hence, I packed up my effects in good time; but the ladies, whose dear companies we were to have to the mines, were a little tedious in their equipment. However, we made a shift to get into the coach by ten o'clock; but little master,[31] who is under no government, would by all means

[30] Spotswood was appointed Deputy Postmaster General in 1730 for a term of ten years. By 1732 he had extended to Williamsburg a service which had formerly stopped at Philadelphia. Benjamin Franklin wrote that in 1737 "Colonel Spotswood, . . . being dissatisfied with the conduct of his deputy at Philadelphia respecting some negligence in rendering, and inexactitude of his accounts, took from him the commission and offered it to me" (Dodson, *Alexander Spotswood*, pp. 300–301).

[31] Spotswood had two sons, John (the elder) and Robert.

go on horseback. Before we set out I gave Mr. Russel [32] the trouble of distributing a pistole among the servants, of which I fancy the nurse had a pretty good share, being no small favorite.

We drove over a fine road to the mines, which lie thirteen measured miles from Germanna, each mile being marked distinctly upon the trees. The Colonel has a great deal of land in his mine tract exceedingly barren, and the growth of trees upon it is hardly big enough for coaling. However, the treasure underground makes amends and renders it worthy to be his lady's jointure.

We light[ed] at the mines, which are a mile nearer to Germanna than the furnace. They raise abundance of ore there, great part of which is very rich. We saw his engineer blow it up after the following manner. He drilled a hole about eighteen inches deep, humoring the situation of the mine. When he had dried it with a rag fastened to a worm, he charged it with a cartridge containing four ounces of powder, including the priming. Then he rammed the hole up with soft stone to the very mouth; after that he pierced through all with an iron called a primer, which is taper and ends in a sharp point. Into the hole the primer makes the priming is put, which he fired by a paper moistened with a solution of saltpeter. And this burns leisurely enough, it seems, to give time for the persons concerned to retreat out of harm's way. All the land hereabouts seems paved with iron ore; so that there seems to be enough to feed a furnace for many ages.

From hence we proceeded to the furnace, which is built of rough stone, having been the first of that kind erected in the country. It had not blown for several moons, the Colonel having taken off great part of his people to carry on his air furnace at Massaponax. Here the wheel that carried the bellows was no more than twenty feet [in] diameter but was an overshot wheel that went with little water. This was necessary here, because water is something scarce, notwithstanding 'tis sup-

---

[32] Possibly this should be Mrs. Russell (Katharine Russell), described "as the niece of Governor Spotswood, [who] presided over his household"; see *The Secret Diary of William Byrd of Westover, 1709–1712*, edited by Louis B. Wright and Marion Tinling (Richmond, Va., 1941), p. 206. However, there was some gossip about her relations with the Governor, which might have made her presence in the household uncomfortable when he brought home a bride, and Byrd calls Miss Theky the "housewife of the family" on p. 356.

plied by two streams, one of which is conveyed 1,900 feet through wooden pipes and the other sixty.

The name of the founder employed at present is one Godfrey of the kingdom of Ireland, whose wages are 3s.6d. per ton for all the iron he runs and his provisions. This man told me that the best wood for coaling is red oak. He complained that the Colonel starves his works out of whimsicalness and frugality, endeavoring to do everything with his own people, and at the same time taking them off upon every vagary that comes into his head. Here the coal carts discharge their load at folding doors, made at the bottom, which is sooner done and shatters the coal less. They carry no more than 110 bushels. The Colonel advised me by all means to have the coal made on the same side the river with the furnace, not only to avoid the charge of boating and bags, but likewise to avoid breaking of the coals and making them less fit for use.

Having picked the bones of a sirloin of beef, we took leave of the ladies and rode together about five miles, where the roads parted. The Colonel took that to Massaponax, which is fifteen miles from his furnace and very level, and I that to Fredericksburg, which can't be less than twenty. I was a little benighted and should not have seen my way, if the lightning, which flashed continually in my face, had not befriended me. I got about seven o'clock to Colonel Harry Willis', a little moistened with the rain; but a glass of good wine kept my pores open and prevented all rheums and defluxions for that time.

3. I was obliged to rise early here that I might not starve my landlord, whose constitution requires him to swallow a beefsteak before the sun blesses the world with its genial rays. However, he was so complaisant as to bear the gnawing of his stomach till eight o'clock for my sake. Colonel Waller, after a score of loud hems to clear his throat, broke his fast along with us.

When this necessary affair was dispatched, Colonel Willis walked me about his town of Fredericksburg. It is pleasantly situated on the south shore of Rappahannock River, about a mile below the falls. Sloops may come up and lie close to the wharf, within thirty yards of the public warehouses, which are built in the figure of a cross. Just by the wharf is a quarry of white stone that is very soft in the ground and hardens in the air, appearing to be as fair and fine-grained as that of Portland. Besides that, there are several other quarries in the river bank, within the limits of the town, sufficient to build a great city. The only edifice of stone yet built is the prison, the walls of which are strong enough to hold Jack Sheppard,[33] if he had been transported hither.

Though this be a commodious and beautiful situation for a town, with the advantages of a navigable river and wholesome air, yet the inhabitants are very few. Besides Colonel Willis, who is the top man of the place, there are only one merchant, a tailor, a smith, and an ordinary keeper; though I must not forget Mrs. Levistone,[34] who acts here in the double capacity of a doctress and coffee woman. And were this a populous city, she is qualified to exercise two other callings. 'Tis said the courthouse and the church are going to be built here, and then both religion and justice will help to enlarge the place.

Two miles from this place is a spring strongly impregnated with alum, and so is the earth all about it. This water does wonders for those that are afflicted with a dropsy. And on the other side the river, in King George County, twelve miles from hence, is another spring of strong steel water as good as that at Tunbridge Wells. Not far from this last spring are England's Iron Mines, called so from the chief manager of them, though the land belongs to Mr. Washington.[35] These mines are two miles from the furnace, and Mr. Washington raises the ore, and carts it thither for 20s. the ton of iron that it yields. The furnace is built on a run, which discharges its waters into Potomac. And when the iron is cast, they cart it about six miles to a landing on that river. Besides Mr. Washington and Mr. England, there are several

[33] A notorious highwayman of the 1720's, a onetime associate of Jonathan Wild. Sheppard made several spectacular escapes from custody, two from Newgate itself, before the authorities finally succeeded in hanging him. For a resumé of his colorful career see Patrick Pringle, *Stand and Deliver* (London, 1951), pp. 200–205.

[34] Mrs. Susanna Levingstone was the widow of the William Levingstone who operated a theater in Williamsburg in about 1717. See Robert H. Land, "The First Williamsburg Theatre," *William and Mary Quarterly*, 3rd Ser., 5:359–374 (July 1948). Byrd implies that she was capable of being a whore as well as an actress.

[35] Augustine Washington, father of George. Washington's iron foundry was operated during the Revolution by James Hunter and furnished the American forces with pots, pans, camp kettles, anchors, and bayonets.

other persons in England concerned in these works. Matters are very well managed there, and no expense is spared to make them profitable, which is not the case in the works I have already mentioned. Mr. England can neither write nor read, but without those helps is so well skilled in ironworks that he don't only carry on his furnace but has likewise the chief management of the works at Principia, at the head of the bay, where they have also erected a forge and make very good bar iron.

Colonel Willis had built a flue to try all sorts of ore in, which was contrived after the following manner. It was built of stone four foot square, with an iron grate fixed in the middle of it for the fire to lie upon. It was open at the bottom, to give a free passage to the air up to the grate. Above the grate was another opening that carried the smoke into a chimney. This makes a draft upward, and the fire, rarefying the air below, makes another draft underneath, which causes the fire to burn very fiercely and melt any ore in the crucibles that are set upon the fire. This was erected by a mason called Taylor, who told me he built the furnace at Fredericksville and came in for that purpose at 3s.6d. a day, to be paid him from the time he left his house in Gloucestershire to the time he returned thither again, unless he chose rather to remain in Virginia after he had done his work.

It happened to be court day here, but the rain hindered all but the most quarrelsome people from coming. The Colonel brought three of his brother justices to dine with us, namely, John Taliaferro,[36] Major Lightfoot,[37] and Captain Green, and in the evening Parson Kenner edified us with his company, who left this parish for a better without any regard to the poor souls he had half saved, of the flock he abandoned.

[36] Probably the son of the Robert "Talifer" from whose house near the falls of the Rappahannock John Lederer set out on his journey of exploration in 1670; see Clarence W. Alvord and Lee Bidgood, *The First Explorations of the Trans-Allegheny Regions* (Cleveland, 1912), p. 163. A well-known Virginia family descended from Robert Taliaferro, who arrived in Virginia in 1657 (*Dictionary of American Biography*, under William Booth Taliaferro). John Taliaferro traded with the Indians up the Rappahannock and to the southwest; see Hugh Jones, *Present State of Virginia*, p. 169, n. 42.

[37] One of the numerous relatives of Colonel Philip Lightfoot of Sandy Point, Charles City County, member of the Council and one of the richest men in Virginia.

4. The sun, rising very bright, invited me to leave this infant city; accordingly, about ten I took leave of my hospitable landlord and persuaded Parson Kenner to be my guide to Massaponax, lying five miles off, where I had agreed to meet Colonel Spotswood.

We arrived there about twelve and found it a very pleasant and commodious plantation. The Colonel received us with open arms and carried us directly to his air furnace, which is a very ingenious and profitable contrivance. The use of it is to melt his sow iron in order to cast it into sundry utensils, such as backs for chimneys, andirons, fenders, plates for hearths, pots, mortars, rollers for gardeners, skillets, boxes for cartwheels; and many other things, which, one with another, can be afforded at 20s. a ton and delivered at people's own homes, and, being cast from the sow iron, are much better than those which come from England, which are cast immediately from the ore for the most part.

Mr. Flowry is the artist that directed the building of this ingenious structure, which is contrived after this manner. There is an opening about a foot square for the fresh air to pass through from without. This leads up to an iron grate that holds about half a bushel of charcoal and is about six feet higher than the opening. When the fire is kindled, it rarefies the air in such a manner as to make a very strong draft from without. About two foot above the grate is a hole [that] leads into a kind of oven, the floor of which is laid shelving toward the mouth. In the middle of this oven, on one side, is another hole that leads into the funnel of a chimney, about forty feet high. The smoke mounts up this way, drawing the flame after it with so much force that in less than an hour it melts the sows of iron that are thrust toward the upper end of the oven. As the metal melts, it runs toward the mouth into a hollow place, out of which the potter lades it in iron ladles, in order to pour it into the several molds just by. The mouth of the oven is stopped close with a movable stone shutter, which he removes so soon as he perceives through the peepholes that the iron is melted. The inside of the oven is lined with soft bricks made of Sturbridge or Windsor clay, because no other will endure the intense heat of the fire. And over the floor of the oven they strew sand taken from the land and not from

370

the waterside. This sand will melt the second heat here, but that which they use in England will bear the fire four or five times. The potter is also obliged to plaster over his ladles with the same sand moistened, to save them from melting. Here are two of these air furnaces in one room, so that in case one wants repair the other may work, they being exactly of the same structure.

The chimneys and other outside work of this building are of free-stone, raised near a mile off on the Colonel's own land, and were built by his servant, whose name is Kerby, a very complete workman. This man disdains to do anything of rough work, even where neat is not required, lest anyone might say hereafter Kerby did it. The potter was so complaisant as to show me the whole process, for which I paid him and the other workmen my respects in the most agreeable way. There was a great deal of ingenuity in the framing of the molds wherein they cast the several utensils, but without breaking them to pieces I found there was no being let into that secret. The flakes of iron that fall at the mouth of the oven are called geets,[38] which are melted over again.

The Colonel told me in my ear that Mr. Robert Cary in England was concerned with him, both in this and his other ironworks, not only to help support the charge but also to make friends to the undertaking at home. His Honor has settled his cousin, Mr. Graeme, here as postmaster, with a salary of £60 a year to reward him for having ruined his estate while he was absent. Just by the air furnace stands a very substantial wharf, close to which any vessel may ride in safety.

After satisfying our eyes with all these sights, we satisfied our stomachs with a sirloin of beef, and then the parson and I took leave of the Colonel and left our blessing upon all his works. We took our way from thence to Major Woodford's[39] seven miles off, who lives upon a high hill that affords an extended prospect, on which account 'tis dignified with the name of Windsor. There we found Rachel Cocke, who stayed with her sister[40] some time, that she might not lose the use

---

[38] Jets.

[39] William Woodford, whose son William later led the American forces in the first defeat of the British troops on Virginia soil (at Great Bridge) during the Revolution; see *Dictionary of American Biography*.

[40] Major Woodford was married to Anne Cocke, daughter of Dr. William Cocke, secretary of the College of William and Mary.

of her tongue in this lonely place. We were received graciously and the evening was spent in talking and toping, and then the parson and I were conducted to the same apartment, the house being not yet finished.

5. The parson slept very peaceably and gave me no disturbance, so I rose fresh in the morning and did credit to the air by eating a hearty breakfast. Then Major Woodford carried me to the house where he cuts tobacco. He manufactures about sixty hogsheads yearly, for which he gets after the rate of 11d. a pound and pays himself liberally for his trouble. The tobacco he cuts is Long Green, which, according to its name, bears a very long leaf and consequently each plant is heavier than common sweet-scented[41] or Townsend tobacco. The worst of it is, the veins of the leaf are very large, so that it loses its weight a good deal by stemming. This kind of tobacco is much the fashion in these parts, and Jonathan Forward[42] (who has great interest here) gives a good price for it. This sort the Major cuts up and has a man that performs it very handily. The tobacco is stemmed clean in the first place and then laid straight in a box and pressed down hard by a press that goes with a nut. This box is shoved forward toward the knife by a

[41] This variety, more valuable than other tobacco, was comparatively scarce, perhaps because, as the Reverend Hugh Jones declared in his *Present State of Virginia*, it required "particular seed and management," or because it required light, sandy soil to thrive, as was declared by the Reverend John Clayton in 1688; see Jones, *Present State of Virginia*, pp. 197–198. According to the letter of Commissary Blair quoted earlier, a minister's living was worth £20 more per year in a "sweet scented" parish than in other parishes.

[42] Forward was a London merchant who was also active in the trade supplying convicts from Newgate Prison and the home counties for the labor market in Virginia and Maryland. Parliament had passed an act in 1717 "for the further preventing robbery, burglary, and other felonies, and for the more effectual transportation of felons," which conflicted with an act of the Virginia General Court forbidding the importation of convicts. As a result of the act of Parliament, the Virginia Assembly in May 1722 passed a law requiring masters of vessels to give bond not to let the convicts go on shore until they had been disposed of and to guarantee their good behavior for two months thereafter. They were also required to register with the county courts the name of each convict and the offense for which he was transported. Forward, who had made a contract with the Treasury in 1718 to be paid £3 apiece for Newgate felons and £5 for those from the counties, promptly appealed to the Privy Council, pointing out that the Virginia law made the transportation of convicts wholly impracticable, and on August 27, 1723, the Privy Council formally disallowed it. See Abbot E. Smith, *Colonists in Bondage: White Servitude and Convict Labor in America, 1607–1776* (Chapel Hill, 1947), pp. 110–111, 113, 120, and 363, n. 13; Morton, *Colonial Virginia*, II, 494–495.

screw, receiving its motion from a treadle that the engineer sets a-going with his foot. Each motion pushes the box the exact length which the tobacco ought to be of, according to the saffron, or oblong, cut, which it seems yields one penny in a pound more at London than the square cut, though at Bristol they are both of equal price. The man strikes down the knife once at every motion of the screw, so that his hand and foot keep exact pace with each other. After the tobacco is cut in this manner, 'tis sifted first through a sand riddle, and then through a dust riddle, till 'tis perfectly clean. Then 'tis put into a tight hogshead and pressed under the nut, till it weighs about a thousand neat. One man performs all the work after the tobacco is stemmed, so that the charge bears no proportion to the profit.

One considerable benefit from planting Long Green tobacco is that 'tis much hardier and less subject to fire than other sweet-scented, though it smells not altogether so fragrant.

I surprised Mrs. Woodford in her housewifery in the meat house, at which she blushed as if it had been a sin. We all walked about a mile in the woods, where I showed them several useful plants and explained the virtues of them. This exercise and the fine air we breathed in sharpened our appetites so much that we had no mercy on a rib of beef that came attended with several other good things at dinner.

In the afternoon we tempted all the family to go along with us to Major Ben Robinson's, who lives on a high hill called Moon's Mount, about five miles off. On the road we came to an eminence from whence we had a plain view of the mountains, which seemed to be no more than thirty miles from us in a straight line, though to go by the road it was near double that distance. The sun had just time to light us to our journey's end, and the Major received us with his usual good humor. He has a very industrious wife, who has kept him from sinking by the weight of gaming and idleness. But he is now reformed from those ruinous qualities and by the help of a clerk's place in a quarrelsome county will soon be able to clear his old scores.

We drank exceeding good cider here, the juice of the white apple, which made us talkative till ten o'clock, and then I was conducted to a bedchamber where there was neither chair nor table; however I slept sound and waked with strong tokens of health in the morning.

6. When I got up about sunrise I was surprised to find that a fog had covered this high hill; but there's a marsh on the other side the river that sends its filthy exhalation up to the clouds. On the borders of that morass lives Mr. Lomax,[43] a situation fit only for frogs and otters.

After fortifying myself with toast and cider and sweetening my lips with saluting the lady, I took leave and the two majors conducted me about four miles on my way as far as the church. After that, Ben Robinson ordered his East Indian to conduct me to Colonel Martin's. In about ten miles we reached Caroline [County] courthouse, where Colonel Armistead[44] and Colonel Will Beverley have each of 'em erected an ordinary well supplied with wine and other polite liquors for the worshipful bench. Besides these, there is a rum ordinary for persons of a more vulgar taste. Such liberal supplies of strong drink often make Justice nod and drop the scales out of her hands.

Eight miles beyond the ordinary I arrived at Colonel Martin's, who received me with more gravity than I expected. But, upon inquiry, his lady was sick, which had lengthened his face and gave him a very mournful air. I found him in his nightcap and banian,[45] which is his ordinary dress in that retired part of the country. Poorer land I never saw than what he lives upon, but the wholesomeness of the air and the goodness of the roads make some amends. In a clear day the mountains may be seen from hence, which is, in truth, the only rarity of the place.

At my first arrival, the Colonel saluted me with a glass of canary and soon after filled my belly with good mutton and cauliflowers. Two people were as indifferent company as a man and his wife, without a little inspiration from the bottle; and then we were forced to go as far as the kingdom of Ireland to help out our conversation. There, it seems,

---

[43] Possibly the Lunsford Lomax who acted as one of the commissioners representing the King in a settlement of the dispute concerned with the bounds of Lord Fairfax's estate in 1746 and who was one of the Virginia commissioners in a conference with the Ohio Indians on April 28, 1752, at Logstown, Pennsylvania (Morton, *Colonial Virginia*, II, 547, 615).

[44] Colonel Henry Armistead of Hesse, Gloucester County.

[45] A dressing gown, derived from a loose garment of that name worn in India.

the Colonel had an elder brother, a physician, who threatens him with an estate some time or other; though possibly it might come to him sooner if the succession depended on the death of one of his patients.

By eight o'clock at night we had no more to say, and I gaped wide as a signal for retiring, whereupon I was conducted to a clean lodging, where I would have been glad to exchange one of the beds for a chimney.

7. This morning Mrs. Martin was worse, so that there were no hopes of seeing how much she was altered. Nor was this all, but the indisposition of his consort made the Colonel intolerably grave and thoughtful. I prudently eat a meat breakfast, to give me spirits for a long journey and a long fast.

My landlord was so good as to send his servant along with me to guide me through all the turnings of a difficult way. In about four miles we crossed Mattaponi River at Norman's Ford and then slanted down to King William County road. We kept along that for about twelve miles, as far as the new brick church. After that I took a blind path that carried me to several of Colonel Jones's quarters, which border upon my own. The Colonel's overseers were all abroad, which made me fearful I should find mine as idle as them. But I was mistaken, for when I came to Gravel Hall, the first of my plantations in King William, I found William Snead (that looks after three of them) very honestly about his business. I had the pleasure to see my people all well and my business in good forwardness. I visited all the five quarters on that side, which spent so much of my time that I had no leisure to see any of those on the other side the river; though I discoursed Thomas Tinsley, one of the overseers, who informed me how matters went.

In the evening Tinsley conducted me to Mrs. Syme's house,[46] where I intended to take up my quarters. This lady, at first suspecting I was some lover, put on a gravity that becomes a weed, but so soon as she learnt who I was brightened up into an unusual cheerfulness and serenity. She was a portly, handsome dame, of the family of Esau, and

[46] This was Studley, home of John Syme. Mrs. Syme married John Henry after Syme's death and gave birth to Patrick Henry at Studley in 1736.

seemed not to pine too much for the death of her husband, who was of the family of the Saracens. He left a son by her who has all the strong features of his sire, not softened in the least by any of hers, so that the most malicious of her neighbors can't bring his legitimacy in question, not even the parson's wife, whose unruly tongue, they say, don't spare even the Reverend Doctor, her husband. This widow is a person of a lively and cheerful conversation, with much less reserve than most of her countrywomen. It becomes her very well and sets off her other agreeable qualities to advantage. We tossed off a bottle of honest port, which we relished with a broiled chicken. At nine I retired to my devotions and then slept so sound that fancy itself was stupefied, else I should have dreamt of my most obliging landlady.

8. I moistened my clay with a quart of milk and tea, which I found altogether as great a help to discourse as the juice of the grape. The courteous widow invited me to rest myself there that good day and go to the church with her, but I excused myself by telling her she would certainly spoil my devotion. Then she civilly entreated me to make her house my home whenever I visited my plantations, which made me bow low and thank her very kindly.

From thence I crossed over to Shacco's and took Thomas Tinsley for my guide, finding the distance about fifteen miles. I found everybody well at the Falls, blessed be God, though the bloody flux raged pretty much in the neighborhood. Mr. Booker had received a letter the day before from Mrs. Byrd giving an account of great desolation made in our neighborhood by the death of Mr. Lightfoot, Mrs. Soan, Captain Gerald, and Colonel Henry Harrison. Finding the flux had been so fatal, I desired Mr. Booker to make use of the following remedy, in case it should come amongst my people: to let them blood immediately about eight ounces; the next day to give them a dose of Indian physic, and to repeat the vomit again the day following, unless the symptoms abated. In the meantime, they should eat nothing but chicken broth and poached eggs and drink nothing but a quarter of a pint of milk boiled with a quart of water and medicated with a little mullein root or that of the prickly pear, to restore the mucus of the bowels and heal the excoriation. At the same time, I ordered him to communicate this method to all the poor neighbors, and especially to my overseers, with strict orders to use it on the first appearance of that distemper, because in that and all other sharp diseases delays are very dangerous.

I also instructed Mr. Booker in the way I had learnt of blowing up the rocks, which were now drilled pretty full of holes, and he promised to put it in execution. After discoursing seriously with the father about my affairs, I joked with the daughter in the evening and about eight retired to my castle and recollected all the follies of the day, the little I had learnt and the still less good I had done.

9. My long absence made me long for the domestic delights of my own family, for the smiles of an affectionate wife and the prattle of my innocent children. As soon as I sallied out of my castle, I understood that Colonel Carter's Sam was come, by his master's leave, to show my people to blow up the rocks in the canal. He pretended to great skill in that matter but performed very little, which, however, might be the effect of idleness rather than ignorance. He came upon one of my horses, which he tied to a tree at Shacco's, where the poor animal kept a fast of a night and a day. Though this fellow worked very little at the rocks, yet my man Argalus stole his trade and performed as well as he. For this good turn, I ordered Mr. Samuel half a pistole, all which he laid out with a New England man for rum and made my weaver and spinning woman, who has the happiness to be called his wife, exceedingly drunk. To punish the varlet for all these pranks, I ordered him to be banished from thence forever, under the penalty of being whipped home from constable to constable if he presumed to come again.

I left my memorandums with Mr. Booker of everything I ordered to be done and mounted my horse about ten, and in little more reached Bermuda Hundred and crossed over to Colonel Carter's.[47] He, like an industrious person, was gone to oversee his overseers at North Wales, but his lady was at home and kept me till suppertime before we went to dinner. As soon as I had done justice to my stomach, I made my honors to the good-humored little fairy and made the best of my

[47] Not Robert "King" Carter, who had died in August of this year, but his eldest son, John Carter, who had married Elizabeth Hill, heiress of Shirley on the James River.

way home, where I had the great satisfaction to find all that was dearest to me in good health, nor had any disaster happened in the family since I went away. Some of the neighbors had worm fevers, with all the symptoms of the bloody flux, but, blessed be God, their distempers gave way to proper remedies.

A JOURNEY TO THE LAND OF EDEN ANNO 1733

11. *H*AVING recommended my family to the protection of the Almighty, I crossed the river with two servants and four horses and rode to Colonel Mumford's. There I met my friend, Mr. Banister, who was to be the kind companion of my travels. I stayed dinner with the good Colonel, while Mr. Banister made the best of his way home, to get his equipage ready in order to join me the next day.

After dining plentifully and wishing all that was good to the household, I proceeded to Major Mumford's,[1] who had also appointed to go along with me. I was the more obliged to him because he made me the compliment to leave the arms of a pretty wife to lie on the cold ground for my sake. She seemed to chide me with her eyes for coming to take her bedfellow from her, now the cold weather came on, and to make my peace I was forced to promise to take abundance of care of him, in order to restore him safe and sound to her embraces.

12. After the Major had cleared his pipes in calling with much authority about him, he made a shift to truss up his baggage about nine o'clock. Near the same hour my old friend and fellow traveler, Peter Jones, came to us completely accoutered. Then we fortified ourselves with a beefsteak, kissed our landlady for good luck, and mounted about ten. The Major took one Robin Bolling with him, as squire of his body, as well as conductor of his baggage. Tom Short had promised to attend me but had married a wife and could not come.

We crossed Hatcher's Run, Gravelly Run, Stony Creek, and in the distance of about twenty miles reached Sapony Chapel, where Mr. Banister joined us. Thus agreeably reinforced, we proceeded ten miles further to Major Embry's, on the south side of Nottoway River. The

---

[1] James Mumford, major of militia of Prince George County; see *Another Secret Diary of William Byrd of Westover, 1739–1741*, edited by Maude H. Woodfin and Marion Tinling (Richmond, Va., 1942), p. 153.

Major was ill of a purging and vomiting, attended with a fever which had brought him low, but I prescribed him a gallon or two of chicken broth, which washed him as clean as a gun and quenched his fever. Here Major Mayo met us, well equipped for a march into the woods, bringing a surveyor's tent that would shelter a small troop. Young Tom Jones also repaired hither to make his excuse; but old Tom Jones, by the privilege of his age, neither came nor sent, so that we were not so strong as we intended, being disappointed of three of our ablest foresters.

The entertainment we met with was the less sumptuous by reason of our landlord's indisposition. On this occasion we were as little troublesome as possible, by sending part of our company to Richard Birch's, who lives just by the bridge over the river.

We sent for an old Indian called Shacco-Will,[2] living about seven miles off, who reckoned himself seventy-eight years old. This fellow pretended he could conduct us to a silver mine that lies either upon Eno River or a creek of it, not far from where the Tuscaroras once lived. But by some circumstances in his story, it seems to be rather a lead than a silver mine. However, such as it is, he promised to go and show it to me whenever I pleased. To comfort his heart I gave him a bottle of rum, with which he made himself very happy and all the family very miserable by the horrible noise he made all night.

13. Our landlord had great relief from my remedy and found himself easy this morning. On this account we took our departure with more satisfaction about nine and, having picked up our friends at Mr. Birch's, pursued our journey over Quoique[3] Creek and Sturgeon Run, as far as Brunswick courthouse, about twelve miles beyond Nottoway. By the way I sent a runner half a mile out of the road to Colonel Drury Stith's, who was so good as to come to us. We cheered our hearts

[2] The name may indicate that he was a member of the Shakori tribe, who lived with Eno tribes on the Eno River in 1701 and later united with the Catawbas. The surveyor John Lawson had an Indian guide named Eno Will, for whom the Eno River was named, but who was believed to be a Shakori; this may be the same man. See John R. Swanton, *The Indians of the Southeastern United States* (Washington D.C., 1946), p. 183; and *North Carolina: A Guide to the Old North State* (Chapel Hill, 1944), p. 482.

[3] Waqua; the same creek as that spelled "Wiccoquoi" in the *History* (p. 317) and "Queocky" later in this narrative (p. 410), where we have changed it to "Waqua."

with three bottles of pretty good Madeira, which made Drury talk very hopefully of his copper mine. We easily prevailed with him to let us have his company, upon condition we would take the mine in our way.

From thence we proceeded to Meherrin River, which lies eight miles beyond the courthouse, and in our way forded Great Creek. For fear of being belated, we called not at my quarter, where Don Pedro is overseer and lives in good repute amongst his neighbors. In compliment to the little Major we went out of our way to lie at a settlement of his upon Cox Creek, four miles short of Roanoke. Our fare here was pretty coarse, but Mr. Banister and I took possession of the bed, while the rest of the company lay in bulk upon the floor. This night the little Major made the first discovery of an impatient and peevish temper, equally unfit both for a traveler and a husband.

14. In the morning my friend Tom Wilson made me a visit and gave me his parole that he would meet us at Bluestone Castle.[4] We took horse about nine and in the distance of ten miles reached a quarter of Colonel Stith's, under the management of John Tomasin. This plantation lies on the west side of Stith's Creek, which was so full of water, by reason of a fresh in the river, that we could not ford it, but we and our baggage were paddled over in a canoe and our horses swam by our sides. After staying here an hour, with some of Diana's maids of honor, we crossed Miles Creek a small distance off, and at the end of eight miles were met by a tall, meager figure which I took at first for an apparition, but it proved to be Colonel Stith's miner. I concluded that the unwholesome vapors arising from the copper mine had made this operator such a skeleton, but upon inquiry understood it was sheer famine had brought him so low. He told us his stomach had not been blessed with one morsel of meat for more than three weeks, and that too he had been obliged to short allowance of bread, by reason corn was scarce and to be fetched from Tomasin's, which was ten long miles from the mine where he lived. However, in spite of this spare diet, the man was cheerful and uttered no complaint.

[4] At this time Byrd had a house on this site and refers to it as Bluestone Castle. He later built here a hunting lodge; he mentions marking out the site on p. 408.

Being conducted by him, we reached the mines about five o'clock and pitched our tents for the first time, there being yet no building erected but a log house to shelter the miner and his two Negroes. We examined the mine and found it dipped from east to west and showed but a slender vein, embodied in a hard rock of white spar. The shaft they had opened was about twelve feet deep and six over. I saw no more than one peck of good ore aboveground, and that promised to be very rich. The engineer seemed very sanguine and had not the least doubt but his employer's fortune was made. He made us the compliment of three blasts, and we filled his belly with good beef in return, which in his hungry circumstances was the most agreeable present we could make him.

15. It rained in the morning, which made us decamp later than we intended, but, the clouds clearing away about ten, we wished good luck to the mine and departed. We left Colonel Stith there to keep fast with his miner and directed our course through the woods to Butcher's Creek, which hath its name from an honest fellow that lives upon it. This place is about six miles from Colonel Stith's works and can also boast of a very fair show of copper ore. It is dug out of the side of a hill that rises gradually from the creek to the house. The good man was from home himself, but his wife, who was as old as one of the Sibyls, refreshed us with an ocean of milk. By the strength of that entertainment we proceeded to Mr. Mumford's quarter, about five miles off, where Joseph Colson is overseer. Here our thirsty companions raised their drooping spirits with a cheerful dram, and, having wet both eyes, we rode on seven miles farther to Bluestone Castle, five whereof were through my own land, that is to say, all above Sandy Creek.

My land there in all extends ten miles upon the river, and three charming islands, namely Sappony, Occaneechee, and Totero, run along the whole length of it. The lowest of these islands is three miles long, the next four, and the uppermost three, divided from each other by only a narrow strait. The soil is rich in all of them, the timber large, and a kind of pea, very grateful to cattle and horses, holds green all the winter. Roanoke River is divided by these islands; that part which runs on the north side is about eighty yards and that on the south more than one hundred. A large fresh will overflow the lower part of these islands but never covers all, so that the cattle may always recover a place of security. The middlemost island, called Occaneechee Island, has several fields in it where Occaneechi Indians formerly lived, and there are still some remains of the peach trees they planted. Here grow likewise excellent wild hops without any cultivation. My overseer, Harry Morris, did his utmost to entertain me and my company; the worst of it was, we were obliged all to be littered down in one room, in company with my landlady and four children, one of which was very sick and consequently very fretful.

16. This being Sunday, and the place where we were quite out of Christendom, very little devotion went forward. I thought it no harm to take a Sabbath Day's journey and rode with my overseer to a new entry I had made upon Bluestone Creek, about three miles from the castle, and found the land very fertile and convenient. It consists of low grounds and meadows on both sides the creek. After taking a view of this, we rode two miles farther to a stony place where there were some tokens of a copper mine, but not hopeful enough to lay me under any temptation. Then we returned to the company and found Tom Wilson was come according to his promise in order to proceed into the woods along with us. Joseph Colson likewise entered into pay, having cautiously made his bargain for a pistole. There were three Tuscarora Indians (which I understood had been kept on my plantation to hunt for Harry Morris) that with much ado were also persuaded to be of the party.

My landlady could not forbear discovering some broad signs of the fury by breaking out into insolent and passionate expressions against the poor Negroes. And if my presence could not awe her, I concluded she could be very outrageous when I was an hundred miles off. This inference I came afterwards to understand was but too true, for between the husband and the wife the Negroes had a hard time of it.

17. We set off about nine from Bluestone Castle and rode up the river six miles (one half of which distance was on my own land) as far as Major Mumford's quarter, where Master Hogen was tenant upon

halves. Here were no great marks of industry, the weeds being near as high as the corn. My islands run up within a little way of this place, which will expose them to the inroad of the Major's creatures. That called Totero Island lies too convenient not to receive damage that way, but we must guard against it as well as we can.

After the Major had convinced himself of the idleness of his tenant, he returned back to Bluestone, and Harry Morris and I went in quest of a copper mine which he had secured for me in the fork. For which purpose, about a quarter of a mile higher than Hogen's, we crossed a narrow branch of the river into a small island, not yet taken up and, after traversing that, forded a much wider branch into the fork of Roanoke River. Where we landed was near three miles higher up than the point of the fork. We first directed our course easterly toward that point, which was very sharp, and each branch of the river where it divided first seemed not to exceed eighty yards in breadth. The land was broken and barren off from the river till we came within half a mile of the point where the low ground began. The same sort of low ground ran up each branch of the river. That on the Staunton (being the northern branch) was but narrow, but that on the south, which is called the Dan, seemed to carry a width of at least half a mile. After discovering this place, for which I intended to enter, we rode up the midland five miles to view the mine, which in my opinion hardly answered the trouble of riding so far out of our way.

We returned downwards again about four miles and a mile from the point found a good ford over the north branch into the upper end of Totero Island. We crossed the river there and near the head of the island saw a large quantity of wild hops growing that smelt fragrantly and seemed to be in great perfection. At our first landing we were so hampered with brambles, vines, and poke bushes that our horses could hardly force their way through them. However, this difficulty held only about twenty-five yards at each end of the island, all the rest being very level and free from underwood.

We met with old fields where the Indians had formerly lived and the grass grew as high as a horse and his rider. In one of these fields were large duck ponds, very firm at the bottom, to which wild fowl resort in the winter. In the woody part of the island grows a vetch that is green all winter and a great support for horses and cattle, though 'tis to be feared the hogs will root it all up. There is a cave in this island in which the last Totero king, with only eight of his men, defended himself against a great host of northern Indians and at last obliged them to retire.

We forded the strait out of this into Occaneechee Island, which was full of large trees and rich land, and the south part of it is too high for any flood less than Noah's to drown it. We rode about two miles down this island (being half the length of it) where, finding ourselves opposite to Bluestone Castle, we passed the river in a canoe which had been ordered thither for that purpose and joined our friends, very much tired, not so much with the length of the journey as with the heat of the weather.

18. We lay by till the return of the messenger that we sent for the ammunition and other things left at the courthouse. Nor had the Indians yet joined us according to their promise, which made us begin to doubt of their veracity. I took a solitary walk to the first ford of Bluestone Creek, about a quarter of a mile from the house. This creek had its name from the color of the stones which paved the bottom of it and are so smooth that 'tis probable they will burn into lime. I took care to return to my company by dinnertime, that I might not trespass upon their stomachs.

In the afternoon I was paddled by the overseer and one of my servants up the creek but could proceed little farther than a mile because of the shoal water. All the way we perceived the bottom of the creek full of the blue stones above-mentioned, sufficient in quantity to build a large castle. At our return we went into the middle of the river and stood upon a large blue rock to angle, but without any success. We broke off a fragment of the rock and found it as heavy as so much lead.

Discouraged by our ill luck, we repaired to the company, who had procured some pieces of copper ore from Cargill's mine, which seemed full of metal. This mine lies about two miles higher than Major Mumford's plantation and has a better show than any yet discovered. There are so many appearances of copper in these parts that the inhabitants seem to be all mine-mad and neglect making of corn for their present necessities in hopes of growing very rich hereafter.

19. The heavens loured a little upon us in the morning, but, like a damsel ruffled by too bold an address, it soon cleared up again. Because I detested idleness, I caused my overseer to paddle me up the river as far as the strait that divides Occaneechee from Totero Island, which is about twenty yards wide. There runs a swift stream continually out of the south part of the river into the north and is in some places very deep. We crossed the south part to the opposite shore to view another entry I had made, beginning at Buffalo Creek, and running up the river to guard my islands and keep off bad neighbors on that side. The land seems good enough for corn along the river, but a quarter of a mile back 'tis broken and full of stones. After satisfying my curiosity, I returned the way that I came and shot the same strait back again and paddled down the river to the company.

When we got home, we laid the foundation of two large cities: one at Shacco's, to be called Richmond, and the other at the point of Appomattox River, to be named Petersburg. These Major Mayo offered to lay out into lots without fee or reward. The truth of it is, these two places, being the uppermost landing of James and Appomattox rivers, are naturally intended for marts where the traffic of the outer inhabitants must center. Thus we did not build castles only, but also cities in the air.

In the evening our ammunition arrived safe and the Indians came to us, resolved to make part of our company upon condition of their being supplied with powder and shot and having the skins of all the deer they killed to their own proper use.

20. Everything being ready for a march, we left Bluestone Castle about ten. My company consisted of four gentlemen (namely, Major Mayo, Major Mumford, Mr. Banister, and Mr. Jones) and five woodsmen, Thomas Wilson, Henry Morris, Joseph Colson, Robert Bolling, and Thomas Hooper, four Negroes and three Tuscarora Indians. With this small troop we proceeded up the river as far as Hogen's, above which, about a quarter of a mile, we forded into the little island and

from thence into the fork of the river. The water was risen so high that it ran into the top of my boots but without giving me any cold, although I rid in my wet stockings.

We landed three miles above the point of the fork and, after marching three miles farther, reached the tenement of Peter Mitchell, the highest inhabitant on Roanoke River. Two miles above that we forded a water, which we named Birch Creek, not far from the mouth, where it discharges itself into the Dan. From thence we rode through charming low grounds for six miles together to a larger stream, which we agreed to call Banister River. We were puzzled to find a ford, by reason the water was very high, but at lost got safe over about one and a half miles from the banks of the Dan. In our way we killed two very large rattlesnakes, one of fifteen and the other of twelve rattles. They were both fat, but nobody would be persuaded to carry them to our quarters, although they would have added much to the luxury of our supper.

We pitched our tents upon Banister River, where we feasted on a young buck which had the ill luck to cross our way. It rained great part of the night, with very loud thunder, which rumbled frightfully amongst the tall trees that surrounded us in that low ground, but, thank God, without any damage. Our Indians killed three deer but were so lazy they brought them not to the camp, pretending for their excuse that they were too lean.

21. The necessity of drying our baggage prevented us from marching till eleven o'clock. Then we proceeded through low grounds which were tolerably wide for three miles together, as far as a small creek, named by us Morris Creek. This tract of land I persuaded Mr. Banister to enter for, that he might not be a loser by the expedition. The low grounds held good a mile beyond the creek and then the high land came quite to the river and made our traveling more difficult.

All the way we went we perceived there had been tall canes lately growing on the bank of the river but were universally killed; and, inquiring into the reason of this destruction, we were told that the nature of those canes was to shed their seed but once in seven years and the succeeding winter to die and make room for young ones to grow up in their places. Thus much was certain, that four years before we saw canes grow and flourish in several places where they now lay dead and dry upon the ground.

The whole distance we traveled this day by computation was fifteen miles, and then the appearance of a black cloud, which threatened a gust, obliged us to take up our quarters. We had no sooner got our tents over our heads but it began to rain and thunder furiously, and one clap succeeded the lightning the same instant and made all tremble before it. But, blessed be God, it spent its fury upon a tall oak just by our camp.

Our Indians were so fearful of falling into the hands of the Catawbas that they durst not lose sight of us all day, so they killed nothing and we were forced to make a temperate supper upon bread and cheese. It was strange we met with no wild turkeys, this being the season in which great numbers of them used to be seen toward the mountains. They commonly perch on the high trees near the rivers and creeks. But this voyage, to our great misfortune, there were none to be found. So that we could not commit that abomination in the sight of all Indians of mixing the flesh of deer and turkeys in our broth.[5]

22. We were again obliged to dry our baggage, which had thoroughly soaked with the heavy rain that fell in the night. While we stayed for that, our hunters knocked down a brace of bucks, wherewith we made ourselves amends for our scanty supper the aforegoing night. All these matters being duly performed made it near noon before we sounded to horse.

We marched about two miles over fine low grounds to a most pleasant stream which we named the Medway, and by the way discovered a rich neck of high land that lay on the south side of the Dan and looked very tempting. Two miles beyond the Medway we forded another creek, which we called Maosti Creek. The whole distance between these two streams lay exceeding rich lands, and the same continued two miles higher. This body of low ground tempted me to enter

[5] This taboo may have been peculiar to the Saponi Indians. The only mention of it in Swanton, *Indians of the Southeastern United States*, is a citation of Byrd's being warned by the Saponis of the evil of mixing meat and fowl.

for it, to serve as a stage between my land at the fork and the Land of Eden.

The heavens looked so menacing that we resolved to take up our quarters two miles above Maosti Creek, where we entrenched ourselves on a rising ground. We had no sooner taken these precautions but it began to rain unmercifully and to put out our fire as fast as we could kindle it; nor was it only a hasty shower but continued with great impetuosity most part of the night. We preferred a dry fast to a wet feast, being unwilling to expose the people to the weather to gratify an unreasonable appetite. However it was some comfort in the midst of our abstinence to dream of the delicious breakfast we intended to make next morning upon a fat doe and two-year-old bear our hunters had killed the evening before. Notwithstanding all the care we could take, several of the men were dripping wet and, among the rest, Harry Morris dabbled so long in the rain that he was seized with a violent fit of an ague that shook him almost out of all his patience.

23. It was no loss of time to rest in our camp according to the duty of the day, because our baggage was so wet it needed a whole day to dry it. For this purpose we kindled four several fires in the absence of the sun, which vouchsafed us not one kind look the whole day. My servant had dropped his greatcoat yesterday, and two of the men were so good-natured as to ride back and look for it today, and were so lucky as to find it.

Our Indians, having no notion of the Sabbath, went out to hunt for something for dinner and brought a young doe back along with them. They laughed at the English for losing one day in seven, though the joke may be turned upon them for losing the whole seven, if idleness and doing nothing to the purpose may be called loss of time.

I looked out narrowly for ginseng, this being the season when it wears its scarlet fruit, but neither now nor any other time during the whole journey could I find one single plant of it. This made me conclude that it delighted not in quite so southerly a climate; and in truth I never heard of its growing on this side of thirty-eight degrees latitude. But to make amends we saw abundance of sugar trees in all these low grounds, which the whole summer long the woodpeckers tap for the sweet juice that flows out of them. Toward the evening a strong nor-wester was so kind as to sweep all the clouds away that had blackened our sky and moistened our skins for some time past.

24. The rest the Sabbath had given us made everybody alert this morning, so that we mounted before nine o'clock. This diligence happened to be the more necessary by reason the woods we encountered this day were exceedingly bushy and uneven.

At the distance of four miles we forded both branches of Forked Creek, which lay within one thousand paces from each other. My horse fell twice under me but, thank God, without any damage either to himself or his rider; and Major Mayo's baggage horse rolled down a steep hill and ground all his biscuit to rockahominy. My greatest disaster was that in mounting one of the precipices my steed made a short turn and gave my knee an unmerciful bang against a tree, and I felt the effects of it several days after. However, this was no interruption of our journey, but we went merrily on and two miles farther crossed Peter's Creek, and two miles after that Jones's Creek. Between these creeks was a good breadth of low grounds, with which Mr. Jones was tempted, though he shook his head at the distance.

A little above Jones's Creek we met with a pleasant situation where the herbage appeared more inviting than usual. The horses were so fond of it that we determined to camp there, although the sun had not near finished his course. This gave some of our company leisure to go out and search for the place where our line first crossed the Dan, and by good luck they found it within half a mile of the camp. But the place was so altered by the desolation which had happened to the canes (which had formerly fringed the banks of the river a full furlong deep) that we hardly knew it again. Pleased with this discovery, I forgot the pain in my knee, and the whole company eat their venison without any other sauce than keen appetite.

25. The weather now befriending us, we dispatched our little affairs in good time and marched in a body to the line. It was already grown very dim, by reason many of the marked trees were burnt or blown down. However, we made shift, after riding little more than half a mile, to find it and, having once found it, stuck as close to it as we could.

After a march of two miles we got upon Cane Creek, where we saw the same havoc amongst the old canes that we had observed in other places and a whole forest of young ones springing up in their stead. We pursued our journey over hills and dales till we arrived at the second ford of the Dan, which we passed with no other damage than sopping a little of our bread and shipping some water at the tops of our boots. The late rains, having been a little immoderate, had raised the water and made a current in the river.

We drove on four miles farther to a plentiful run of very clear water and quartered on a rising ground a bowshot from it. We had no sooner pitched the tents, but one of our woodsmen alarmed us with the news that he had followed the track of a great body of Indians to the place where they had lately encamped. That there he had found no less than ten huts, the poles whereof had green leaves still fresh upon them. That each of these huts had sheltered at least ten Indians, who by some infallible marks must have been northern Indians. That they must needs have taken their departure from thence no longer ago than the day before, having erected those huts to protect themselves from the late heavy rains.

These tidings I could perceive were a little shocking to some of the company, and, particularly, the little Major, whose tongue had never lain still, was taken speechless for sixteen hours. I put as good a countenance upon the matter as I could, assuring my fellow travelers that the northern Indians were at peace with us, and although one or two of them may now and then commit a robbery or a murder (as other rogues do), yet nationally and avowedly they would not venture to hurt us. And in case they were Catawbas, the danger would be as little from them, because they are too fond of our trade to lose it for the pleasure of shedding a little English blood. But supposing the worst, that they might break through all the rules of self-interest and attack us, yet we ought to stand bravely on our defense and sell our lives as dear as we could. That we should have no more fear of this occasion than just to make us more watchful and better provided to receive the enemy, if they had the spirit to venture upon us.

This reasoning of mine, though it could not remove the panic, yet it abated something of the palpitation and made us double our guard.

However, I found it took off the edge of most of our appetites for everything but the rum bottle, which was more in favor than ever because of its cordial quality. I hurt my other knee this afternoon, but not enough to spoil either my dancing[6] or my stomach.

26. We liked the place so little that we were glad to leave it this morning as soon as we could. For that reason we were all on horseback before nine and after riding four miles arrived at the mouth of Sable Creek. On the eastern bank of that creek, six paces from the mouth and just at the brink of the river Dan, stands a sugar tree, which is the beginning of my fine tract of land in Carolina called the Land of Eden. I caused the initial letters of my name to be cut on a large poplar and beech near my corner, for the more easy finding it another time. We then made a beginning of my survey, directing our course due south from the sugar tree above-mentioned. In a little way we perceived the creek forked and the western branch was wide enough to merit the name of a river. That to the east was much less, which we intersected with this course. We ran southerly a mile and found the land good all the way, only toward the end of it we saw the trees destroyed in such a manner that there were hardly any left to mark my bounds. Having finished this course, we encamped in a charming peninsula formed by the western branch of the creek. It contained about forty acres of very rich land, gradually descending to the creek, and is a delightful situation for the manor house.

My servant had fed so intemperately upon bear that it gave him a scouring, and that was followed by the piles, which made riding worse to him than purgatory. But, anointing with the fat of the same bear, he soon grew easy again.

27. We were stirring early from this enchanting place and ran eight miles of my back line, which tended south 84½ westerly. We found the land uneven but tolerably good, though very thin of trees, and those that were standing fit for little but fuel and fence rails. Some conflagration had effectually opened the country and made room for the air to circulate. We crossed both the branches of Lowland Creek and sundry other rills of fine water. From every eminence we dis-

[6] The calisthenics that Byrd habitually performed.

covered the mountains to the northwest of us, though they seemed to be a long way off. Here the air felt very refreshing and agreeable to the lungs, having no swamps or marshes to taint it. Nor was this the only good effect it had, but it likewise made us very hungry, so that we were forced to halt and pacify our appetites with a frugal repast out of our pockets, which we washed down with water from a purling stream just by.

My knees pained me very much, though I broke not the laws of traveling by uttering the least complaint. Measuring and marking spent so much of our time that we could advance no further than eight miles, and the chain carriers thought that a great way.

In the evening we took up our quarters in the low grounds of the river, which our scouts informed us was but three hundred yards ahead of us. This was no small surprise, because we had flattered ourselves that this back line would not have intersected the Dan at all; but we found ourselves mistaken and plainly perceived that it ran more southerly than we imagined and in all likelihood pierces the mountains where they form an amphitheater.

The venison here was lean; and the misfortune was we met no bear in so open a country to grease the way and make it slip down.

In the night our sentinel alarmed us with an idle suspicion that he heard the Indian whistle (which amongst them is a signal for attacking their enemies). This made everyone stand manfully to our arms in a moment, and I found nobody more undismayed in this surprise than Mr. Banister; but after we had put ourselves in battle array, we discovered this whistle to be nothing but the nocturnal note of a little harmless bird that inhabits those woods. We were glad to find the mistake and, commending the sentinel for his great vigilance, composed our noble spirits again to rest till the morning. However, some of the company dreamed of nothing but scalping all the rest of the night.

28. We snapped up our breakfast as fast as we could, that we might have the more leisure to pick our way over a very bad ford across the river, though, bad as it was, we all got safe on the other side. We were no sooner landed but we found ourselves like to encounter a very rough and almost impassable thicket. However, we scuffled through it

without any dismay or complaint. This was a copse of young saplings, consisting of oak, hickory, and sassafras, which are the growth of a fertile soil.

We gained no more than two miles in three hours in this perplexed place and after that had the pleasure to issue out into opener woods. The land was generally good, though pretty bare of timber, and particularly we traversed a rich level of at least two miles. Our whole day's journey amounted not quite to five miles, by reason we had been so hampered at our first setting-out. We were glad to take up our quarters early in a piece of fine low grounds lying about a mile north of the river. Thus we perceived the river edged away gently toward the south and never likely to come in the way of our course again. Nevertheless, the last time we saw it, it kept much the same breadth and depth that it had where it divided its waters from the Staunton and in all likelihood holds its own quite as high as the mountains.

29. In measuring a mile and a half farther we reached the lower ford of the Irvin, which branches from the Dan about two miles to the south-southeast of this place. This river was very near threescore yards over and in many places pretty deep. From thence in little more than a mile we came to the end of this course, being in length fifteen miles and eighty-eight poles. And so far the land held reasonably good; but when we came to run our northern course of three miles to the place where the country line intersects the same Irvin higher up, we passed over nothing but stony hills and barren grounds, clothed with little timber and refreshed with less water.

All my hopes were in the riches that might lie underground, there being many goodly tokens of mines. The stones which paved the river both by their weight and color promised abundance of metal; but whether it be silver, lead, or copper is beyond our skill to discern. We also discovered many shows of marble, of a white ground, with streaks of red and purple. So that 'tis possible the treasure in the bowels of the earth may make ample amends for the poverty of its surface.

We encamped on the bank of this river, a little below the dividing line and near the lower end of an island half a mile long, which, for the metallic appearances, we dignified with the name of Potosi.[7] In our

[7] The Bolivian city famous for its silver mines.

way to this place we treed a bear of so mighty a bulk that when we fetched her down she almost made an earthquake. But neither the shot nor the fall disabled her so much but she had like to have hugged one of our dogs to death in the violence of her embrace.

We exercised the discipline of the woods by tossing a very careless servant in a blanket for losing one of our axes.

30. This being Sunday, we were glad to rest from our labors; and, to help restore our vigor, several of us plunged into the river, notwithstanding it was a frosty morning. One of our Indians went in along with us and taught us their way of swimming. They strike not out both hands together but alternately one after another, whereby they are able to swim both farther and faster than we do.

Near the camp grew several large chestnut trees very full of chestnuts. Our men were too lazy to climb the trees for the sake of the fruit but, like the Indians, chose rather to cut them down, regardless of those that were to come after. Nor did they esteem such kind of work any breach of the Sabbath so long as it helped to fill their bellies.

One of the Indians shot a bear, which he lugged about half a mile for the good of the company. These gentiles have no distinction of days but make every day a Sabbath, except when they go out to war or a-hunting, and then they will undergo incredible fatigues. Of other work the men do none, thinking it below the dignity of their sex, but make the poor women do all the drudgery. They have a blind tradition amongst them that work was first laid upon mankind by the fault of a female, and therefore 'tis but just that sex should do the greatest part of it. This they plead in their excuse; but the true reason is that the weakest must always go to the wall, and superiority has from the beginning ungenerously imposed slavery on those who are not able to resist it.

OCTOBER

1. I plunged once more into the river Irvin this morning, for a small cold I had caught, and was entirely cured by it.

We ran the three-mile course from a white oak standing on my corner upon the western bank of the river and intersected the place where we ended the back line exactly, and fixed that corner at a hickory. We steered south from thence about a mile and then came upon the Dan, which thereabouts makes but narrow low grounds. We forded it about a mile and a half to the westward of the place where the Irvin runs into it. When we were over, we determined to ride down the river on that side and for three miles found the high land come close down to it, pretty barren and uneven.

But then on a sudden the scene changed, and we were surprised with an opening of large extent where the Sauro Indians once lived, who had been a considerable nation. But the frequent inroads of the Senecas annoyed them incessantly and obliged them to remove from this fine situation about thirty years ago. They then retired more southerly as far as Pee Dee River and incorporated with the Keyauwees, where a remnant of them is still surviving. It must have been a great misfortune to them to be obliged to abandon so beautiful a dwelling, where the air is wholesome and the soil equal in fertility to any in the world. The river is about eighty yards wide, always confined within its lofty banks and rolling down its waters, as sweet as milk and as clear as crystal. There runs a charming level of more than a mile square that will bring forth like the lands of Egypt, without being overflowed once a year. There is scarce a shrub in view to intercept your prospect but grass as high as a man on horseback. Toward the woods there is a gentle ascent till your sight is intercepted by an eminence that overlooks the whole landscape. This sweet place is bounded to the east by a fine stream called Sauro Creek, which, running out of the Dan and tending westerly, makes the whole a peninsula.

I could not quit this pleasant situation without regret but often faced about to take a parting look at it as far as I could see, and so indeed did all the rest of the company. But at last we left it quite out of sight and continued our course down the river till where it intersects my back line, which was about five miles below Sauro Town.

We took up our quarters at the same camp where we had a little before been alarmed with the supposed Indian whistle, which we could hardly get out of our heads. However, it did not spoil our rest but we dreamt all night of the delights of Tempe and the Elysian fields.

2. We awaked early from these innocent dreams and took our way

along my back line till we came to the corner of it. From thence we slanted to the country line and kept down that as far as the next fording place of the river, making in the whole eighteen miles. We breathed all the way in pure air, which seemed friendly to the lungs and circulated the blood and spirits very briskly. Happy will be the people destined for so wholesome a situation, where they may live to fullness of days and, which is much better still, with much content and gaiety of heart.

On every rising ground we faced about to take our leave of the mountains, which still showed their towering heads. The ground was uneven, rising into hills and sinking into valleys great part of the way, but the soil was good, abounding in most places with a greasy black mold. We took up our quarters on the western bank of the river where we had forded it at our coming up.

One of our men, Joseph Colson by name, a timorous, lazy fellow, had squandered away his bread and grew very uneasy when his own ravening had reduced him to short allowance. He was one of those drones who love to do little and eat much and are never in humor unless their bellies are full. According to this wrong turn of constitution, when he found he could no longer revel in plenty, he began to break the rules by complaining and threatening to desert. This had like to have brought him to the blanket, but his submission reprieved him.

Though bread grew a little scanty with us, we had venison in abundance, which a true woodsman can eat contentedly without any bread at all. But bears' flesh needs something of the farinaceous to make it pass easily off the stomach.

In the night we heard a dog bark at some distance, as we thought, when we saw all our own dogs lying about the fire. This was another alarm, but we soon discovered it to be a wolf, which will sometimes bark very like a dog but something shriller.

3. The fine season continuing, we made the most of it by leaving our quarters as soon as possible. We began to measure and mark the bounds of Major Mayo's land on the south of the country line. In order to do this, we marched round the bent of the river, but, he being obliged to make a traverse, we could reach no farther than four miles.

In the distance of about a mile from where we lay, we crossed Cliff Creek, which confined its stream within such high banks that it was difficult to find a passage over. We kept close to the river, and two miles farther came to Hix's Creek, where abundance of canes lay dry and prostrate on the ground, having suffered in the late septennial slaughter of that vegetable.

A mile after that we forded another stream, which we called Hatcher Creek, from two Indian traders of that name who used formerly to carry goods to the Sauro Indians. Near the banks of this creek I found a large beech tree with the following inscription cut upon the bark of it, "JH, HH, BB, lay here the 24th of May, 1673." It was not difficult to fill up these initials with the following names, Joseph Hatcher, Henry Hatcher, and Benjamin Bullington, three Indian traders, [who] had lodged near that place sixty years before in their way to the Sauro town. But the strangest part of the story was this, that these letters cut in the bark should remain perfectly legible so long. Nay, if no accident befalls the tree, which appears to be still in a flourishing condition, I doubt not but this piece of antiquity may be read many years hence. We may also learn from it that the beech is a very long-lived tree, of which there are many exceedingly large in these woods.

The Major took in a pretty deal of rich low ground into his survey, but unhappily left a greater quantity out, which proves the weakness of making entries by guess.

We found the Dan fordable hereabouts in most places. One of the Indians shot a wild goose that was very lousy, which nevertheless was good meat and proved those contemptible tasters to be no bad tasters.[8] However, for those stomachs that were so unhappy as to be squeamish, there was plenty of fat bear, we having killed two in this day's march.

4. I caused the men to use double diligence to assist Major Mayo in fixing the bounds of his land, because he had taken a great deal of pains about mine. We therefore mounted our horses as soon as we had swallowed our breakfast. Till that is duly performed, a woodsman makes a conscience of exposing himself to any fatigue. We proceeded

[8] I.e., proved that the contemptible lice themselves had a taste for good food.

then in this survey and made an end before night, though most of the company were of opinion the land was hardly worth the trouble. It seemed most of it before below the character the discoverers had given him of it.

We fixed his eastern corner on Cockade Creek and then continued our march over the hills and far away along the country line two miles farther. Nor had we stopped there unless a likelihood of rain had obliged us to encamp on an eminence where we were in no danger of being overflowed.

Peter Jones had a smart fit of an ague which shook him severely, though he bore it like a man; but the small Major [9] had a small fever and bore it like a child. He groaned as if he had been in labor and thought verily it would be his fate to die like a mutinous Israelite in the wilderness and be buried under a heap of stones.

The rain was so kind as to give us leisure to secure ourselves against it but came however time enough to interrupt our cookery, so that we supped as temperately as so many philosophers and kept ourselves snug within our tents. The worst part of the story was that the sentinel could hardly keep our fires from being extinguished by the heaviness of the shower.

5. Our invalids found themselves in traveling condition this morning and began to conceive hopes of returning home and dying in their own beds. We pursued our journey through uneven and perplexed woods and in the thickest of them had the fortune to knock down a young buffalo of two years old. Providence threw this vast animal in our way very seasonably just as our provisions began to fail us. And it was the more welcome, too, because it was change of diet, which of all varieties, next to that of bedfellows, is the most agreeable. We had lived upon venison and bear until our stomachs loathed them almost as much as the Hebrews of old did their quails.[10] Our butchers were so unhandy at their business that we grew very lank before we could get our dinner. But when it came, we found it equal in goodness to the best beef. They made it the longer because they kept sucking the

[9] Probably Major Mumford; see the comment on Major Mayo's disposition on p. 410 and the comment on Mumford on p. 383.
[10] Referring to Num. 11:20, 31–33.

water out of the guts, in imitation of the Catawba Indians, upon the belief that it is a great cordial, and will even make them drunk, or at least very gay.

We encamped upon Hyco River pretty high up and had much ado to get our house in order before a heavy shower descended upon us. I was in pain lest our sick men might suffer by the rain but might have spared myself the concern, because it had the effect of a cold bath upon them and drove away their distemper, or rather changed it into a canine appetite that devoured all before it. It rained smartly all night long, which made our situation on the low ground more fit for otters than men.

6. We had abundance of drying work this morning after the clouds broke away and showed the sun to the happy earth. It was impossible for us to strike the tents till the afternoon and then we took our departure and made an easy march of four miles to another branch of Hyco River, which we called Jesuit's Creek because it misled us.

We lugged as many of the dainty pieces of the buffalo along with us as our poor horses could carry, envying the wolves the pleasure of such luxurious diet. Our quarters were taken upon a delightful eminence that scornfully overlooked the creek and afforded us a dry habitation. We made our supper on the tongue and udder of the buffalo, which were so good that a cardinal legate might have made a comfortable meal upon them during the carnival. Nor was this all, but we had still a rarer morsel, the bunch rising up between the shoulders of this animal, which is very tender and very fat. The primings of a young doe, which one of the men brought to the camp, were slighted amidst these dainties, nor would even our servants be fobbed off with cates so common.

The low grounds of this creek are wide in many places and rich but seem to lie within reach of every inundation, and this is commonly the case with most low grounds that lie either on the rivers or the creeks that run into them. So great an inconvenience lessens their value very much and makes high land that is just tolerable of greater advantage to the owner. There he will be more likely to reap the fruits of his industry every year and not run the risk, after all his toil, to see the sweat of his brow carried down the stream and perhaps many of his cattle drowned into the bargain. Perhaps in times to come people may bank their low grounds as they do in Europe, to confine the water within its natural bounds to prevent these inconveniences.

7. The scarcity of bread, joined to the impatience of some of our company, laid us under a kind of necessity to hasten our return home. For that reason we thought we might be excused for making a Sabbath Day's journey of about five miles as far as our old camp upon Sugartree Creek. On our way we forded Buffalo Creek, which also empties its waters into Hyco River. The woods we rode through were open and the soil very promising, great part thereof being low grounds, full of tall and large trees. A she-bear had the ill luck to cross our way, which was large enough to afford us several luxurious meals. I paid for violating the Sabbath by losing a pair of gold buttons.

I pitched my tent on the very spot I had done when we ran the dividing line between Virginia and Carolina. The beech whose bark recorded the names of the Carolina commissioners was still standing, and we did them the justice to add to their names a sketch of their characters.

We got our house in order time enough to walk about and make some slight observations. There were sugar trees innumerable growing in the low grounds of this creek, from which it received its name. They were many of them as tall as large hickories with trunks from fifteen to twenty inches through. The woodpeckers, for the pleasure of the sweet juice which these trees yield, pierce the bark in many places and do great damage, though the trees live a great while under all these wounds. There grows an infinite quantity of maidenhair, which seems to delight most in rich ground. The sorrel tree is frequent there, whose leaves, brewed in beer, are good in dropsies, greensickness, and cachexies. We also saw in this place abundance of papaw trees, the wood whereof the Indians make very dry on purpose to rub fire out of it. Their method of doing it is this: they hold one of these dry sticks in each hand and by rubbing them hard and quick together rarefy the air in such a manner as to fetch fire in ten minutes. Whenever they offer any sacrifice to their god they look upon it as a profanation to make use of a fire already kindled but produce fresh virgin fire for that purpose by rubbing two of these sticks together that never had been used before on any occasion.

8. After fortifying ourself with a bear breakfast, Major Mayo took what help he thought necessary and began to survey the land with which the commissioners of Carolina had presented him upon this creek. After running the bounds, the Major was a little disappointed in the goodness of the land, but as it had cost him nothing it could be no bad pennyworth, as his upper tract really was.

While that business was carrying on, I took my old friend and fellow traveler Tom Wilson and went to view the land I had entered for upon this creek on the north of the country line. We rode down the stream about six miles, crossing it sundry times, and found very wide low grounds on both sides of it, only we observed wherever the low grounds were broad on one side of the creek they were narrow on the other. The high lands we were obliged to pass over were very good and in some places descended so gradually to the edge of the low grounds that they formed very agreeable prospects and pleasant situations for building. About four miles from the line, Sugartree Creek emptied itself into the Hyco, which with that addition swelled into a fine river. In this space we saw the most, and most promising, good land we had met with in all our travels.

In our way we shot a doe, but, she not falling immediately, we had lost our game had not the ravens by their croaking conducted us to the thicket where she fell. We plunged the carcass of the deer into the water, to secure it from these ominous birds till we returned, but an hour afterwards were surprised with the sight of a wolf which had been fishing for it and devoured one side.

We knocked down an ancient she-bear that had no flesh upon her bones, so we left it to the freebooters of the forest. In coming back to the camp we discovered a solitary bull buffalo, which boldly stood his ground, contrary to the custom of that shy animal. We spared his life, from a principle of never slaughtering an innocent creature to no purpose. However, we made ourselves some diversion by trying if he would face our dogs. He was so far from retreating at their approach that he ran at them with great fierceness, cocking up his ridiculous little tail and grunting like a hog. The dogs in the meantime only played about him, not venturing within reach of his horns, and by their nimbleness came off with a whole skin.

All these adventures we related at our return to the camp, and, what was more to the purpose, we carried to them the side of venison which the wolf had vouchsafed to leave us. After we had composed ourselves to rest, our horses ran up to our camp as fast as their hobbles would let them. This was to some of us a certain argument that Indians were near, whose scent the horses can no more endure than they can their figures; though it was more likely they had been scared by a panther or some other wild beast, the glaring of whose eyes are very terrifying to them in a dark night.

9. Major Mayo's survey being no more than half done, we were obliged to amuse ourselves another day in this place. And that the time might not be quite lost, we put our garments and baggage into good repair. I for my part never spent a day so well during the whole voyage. I had an impertinent tooth in my upper jaw that had been loose for some time and made me chew with great caution. Particularly I could not grind a biscuit but with much deliberation and presence of mind. Toothdrawers we had none amongst us, nor any of the instruments they make use of. However, invention supplied this want very happily, and I contrived to get rid of this troublesome companion by cutting a caper. I caused a twine to be fastened round the root of my tooth, about a fathom in length, and then tied the other end to the snag of a log that lay upon the ground in such a manner that I could just stand upright. Having adjusted my string in this manner, I bent my knees enough to enable me to spring vigorously off the ground as perpendicularly as I could. The force of the leap drew out the tooth with so much ease that I felt nothing of it, nor should have believed it was come away unless I had seen it dangling at the end of the string. An under tooth may be fetched out by standing off the ground and fastening your string at due distance above you. And, having so fixed your gear, jump off your standing, and the weight of your body, added to the force of the spring, will prize out your tooth with less pain than

any operator upon earth could draw it. This new way of toothdrawing, being so silently and deliberately performed, both surprised and delighted all that were present, who could not guess what I was going about. I immediately found the benefit of getting rid of this troublesome companion by eating my supper with more comfort than I had done during the whole expedition.

10. In the morning we made an end of our bread, and all the rest of our provision, so that now we began to travel pretty light. All the company were witnesses how good the land was upon Sugartree Creek, because we rode down it four miles till it fell into Hyco River. Then we directed our course over the high land, thinking to shorten our way to Tom Wilson's quarter. Nevertheless, it was our fortune to fall upon the Hyco again, and then kept within sight of it several miles together till we came near the mouth. Its banks were high and full of precipices on the east side, but it afforded some low grounds on the west. Within two miles of the mouth are good shows of copper mines, as Harry Morris told me, but we saw nothing of them. It runs into the Dan just below a large fall, but the chain of rocks don't reach quite cross the river to intercept the navigation. About a mile below lives Aaron Pinston, at a quarter belonging to Thomas Wilson, upon Tewahominy Creek. This man is the highest inhabitant on the south side of the Dan and yet reckons himself perfectly safe from danger. And if the bears, wolves, and panthers were as harmless as the Indians, his stock might be so too.

Tom Wilson offered to knock down a steer for us, but I would by no means accept of his generosity. However, we were glad of a few of his peas and potatoes and some rashers of his bacon, upon which we made good cheer. This plantation lies about a mile from the mouth of Tewahominy and about the same distance from the mouth of Hyco River and contains a good piece of land. The edifice was only a log house, affording a very free passage for the air through every part of it, nor was the cleanliness of it any temptation to lie out of our tents, so we encamped once more, for the last time, in the open field.

11. I tipped our landlady with what I imagined a full reward for the trouble we had given her and then mounted our horses, which

pricked up their ears after the two meals they had eaten of corn. In the distance of about a mile we reached the Dan, which we forded with some difficulty into the fork. The water was pretty high in the river and the current something rapid, nevertheless all the company got over safe, with only a little water in their boots. After traversing the fork, which was there at least two good miles across, we forded the Staunton into a little island and then the narrow branch of the same to the main-land.

We took Major Mumford's tenant in our way, where we moistened our throats with a little milk and then proceeded in good order to Bluestone Castle. My landlady received us with a grim sort of a wel-come, which I did not expect, since I brought her husband back in good health, though perhaps that might be the reason. 'Tis sure some-thing or other did tease her, and she was a female of too strong pas-sions to know how to dissemble. However, she was so civil as to get us a good dinner, which I was better pleased with because Colonel Cock [11] and Mr. Mumford came time enough to partake of it. The Colonel had been surveying land in these parts, and particularly that on which Mr. Stith's copper mine lies, as likewise a tract on which Cornelius Cargill has fine appearances. He had but a poor opinion of Mr. Stith's mine, foretelling it would be all labor in vain, but thought something better of Mr. Cargill's.

After dinner these gentlemen took their leaves, and at the same time I discharged two of my fellow travelers, Thomas Wilson and Joseph Colson, after having made their hearts merry and giving each of them a piece of gold to rub their eyes with.

We now returned to that evil custom of lying in a house, and an evil one it is, when ten or a dozen people are forced to pig together in a room, as we did, and were troubled with the squalling of peevish, dirty children into the bargain.

12. We ate our fill of potatoes and milk, which seems delicious fare to those who have made a campaign in the woods. I then took my first

---

[11] The name probably should be Cocke, as he was very likely a member of the Cocke family descended from Richard Cocke, who arrived in Virginia sometime before 1628.

minister, Harry Morris, up the hill, and marked out the place where Bluestone Castle was to stand and overlook the adjacent country. After that I put my friend in mind of many things he had done amiss, which he promised faithfully to reform. I was so much an infidel to his fair speeches (having been many times deceived by them) that I was forced to threaten him with my highest displeasure unless he mended his conduct very much. I also let him know that he was not only to correct his own errors but likewise those of his wife, since the power certainly belonged to him in virtue of his conjugal authority. He scratched his head at this last admonition, from whence I inferred that the gray mare was the better horse.

We gave our heavy baggage two hours' start, and about noon followed them and in twelve miles reached John Butcher's, calling by the way for Master Mumford, in order to take him along with us. Mr. Butcher received us kindly and we had a true Roanoke entertainment of pork upon pork, and pork again upon that. He told us he had been one of the first seated in that remote part of the country and in the beginning had been forced, like the great Nebuchadnezzar, to live a considerable time upon grass. This honest man set a mighty value on the mine he fancied he had in his pasture and showed us some of the ore, which he was made to believe was a gray copper and would certainly make his fortune. But there's a bad distemper rages in those parts that grows very epidemical. The people are all mine-mad and, neglecting to make corn, starve their families in hopes to live in great plenty hereafter. Mr. Stith was the first that was seized with the frenzy, and has spread the contagion far and near. As you ride along the woods, you see all the large stones knocked to pieces, nor can a poor marcasite rest quietly in its bed for these curious inquirers. Our conversation ran altogether upon this darling subject till the hour came for our lying in bulk together.

13. After breaking our fast with a sea of milk and potatoes, we took our leave, and I crossed my landlady's hand with a piece of money. She refused the offer at first but, like a true woman, accepted of it when it was put home to her. She told me the utmost she was able to do for me was a trifle in comparison of some favor I had formerly done her; but

what that favor was neither I could recollect nor did she think proper to explain. Though it threatened rain, we proceeded on our journey and jogged on in the new road for twenty miles, that is as far as it was cleared at that time, and found it would soon come to be a very good one after it was well grubbed.

About nine miles from John Butcher's, we crossed Allen's Creek, four miles above Mr. Stith's mine. Near the mouth of this creek is a good body of rich land, whereof Occaneechee Neck is a part. It was entered for many years ago by Colonel Harrison [12] and Colonel Allen but to this day is held without patent or improvement. And they say Mr. Bolling does the same with a thousand acres lying below John Butcher's.

After beating the new road for twenty miles, we struck off toward Meherrin, which we reached in eight miles farther and then came to the plantation of Joshua Nicholson, where Daniel Taylor lives for halves. There was a poor dirty house, with hardly anything in it but children that wallowed about like so many pigs. It is a common case in this part of the country that people live worst upon good land, and the more they are befriended by the soil and the climate the less they will do for themselves. This man was an instance of it, for though his plantation would make plentiful returns for a little industry, yet he, wanting that, wanted everything. The woman did all that was done in the family, and the few garments they had to cover their dirty hides were owing to her industry. We could have no supplies from such neighbors as these but depended on our own knapsacks, in which we had some remnants of cold fowls that we brought from Bluestone Castle. When my house was in order, the whole family came and admired it, as much as if it had been the Grand Vizier's tent in the Turkish army.

14. The Sabbath was now come round again, and although our horses would have been glad to take the benefit of it, yet we determined to make a Sunday's journey to Brunswick Church, which lay about eight miles off. Though our landlord could do little for us, nevertheless we did him all the good we were able by bleeding his sick Negro and giving him a dose of Indian physic. We got to church in decent time,

[12] Benjamin Harrison, owner of Berkeley, a plantation adjoining Westover.

and Mr. Betty, the parson of the parish, entertained us with a good honest sermon, but whether he bought it or borrowed it would have been uncivil in us to inquire. Be that as it will, he is a decent man, with a double chin that sits gracefully over his band, and his parish, especially the female part of it, like him well.

We were not crowded at church, though it was a new thing in that remote part of the country. What women happened to be there were very gim [13] and tidy in the work of their own hands, which made them look tempting in the eyes of us foresters.

When church was done we refreshed our teacher with a glass of wine and then, receiving his blessing, took horse and directed our course to Major Embry's. The distance thither was reputed fifteen miles but appeared less by the company of a nymph of those woods, whom innocence and wholesome flesh and blood made very alluring.

In our way we crossed Sturgeon Creek and Waqua Creek but at our journey's end were so unlucky as not to find either master or mistress at home. However, after two hours of hungry expectation, the good woman luckily found her way home and provided very hospitably for us. As for the Major, he had profited so much by my prescription as to make a journey to Williamsburg, which required pretty good health, the distance being a little short of one hundred miles.

15. After our bounteous landlady had cherished us with roast beef and chicken pie, we thankfully took leave. At the same time we separated from our good friend and fellow traveler, Major Mayo, who steered directly home. He is certainly a very useful, as well as an agreeable, companion in the woods, being ever cheerful and good-humored under all the little crosses, disasters, and disappointments of that rambling life.

As many of us as remained jogged on together to Sapony Chapel, where I thanked Major Mumford and Peter Jones for the trouble that they had taken in this long journey.

That ceremony being duly performed, I filed off with my honest friend Mr. Banister to his habitation on Hatcher Run, which lay about fourteen miles from the chapel above-mentioned. His good-humored

[13] Smart, spruce.

little wife was glad to see her runaway spouse returned in safety and treated us kindly. It was no small pleasure to me that my worthy friend found his family in good health and his affairs in good order. He came into this ramble so frankly that I should have been sorry if he had been a sufferer by it.

In the gaiety of our hearts we drank our bottle a little too freely, which had an unusual effect on persons so long accustomed to simple element. We were both of us raised out of our beds in the same manner and near the same time, which was a fair proof that people who breathe the same air and are engaged in the same way of living will be very apt to fall into the same indispositions. And this may explain why distempers sometimes go round a family, without any reason to believe they are infectious, according to the superstition of the vulgar.

16. After pouring down a basin of chocolate, I wished peace to that house and departed. As long as Mr. Banister had been absent from his family, he was yet so kind as to conduct me to Major Mumford's, and, which was more, his wife very obligingly consented to it. The Major seemed overjoyed at his being returned safe and sound from the perils of the woods, though his satisfaction had some check from the change his pretty wife had suffered in her complexion. The vermilion of her cheeks had given place a little to the saffron, by means of a small tincture of the yellow jaundice. I was sorry to see so fair a flower thus faded and recommended the best remedy I could think of.

After a refreshment of about an hour, we went on to Colonel Bolling's, who was so gracious as to send us an invitation. As much in haste as I was to return to my family, I spent an hour or two at that place, but could by no means be persuaded to stay dinner, nor could even Madam de Graffenried's [14] smiles on one side of her face shake my resolution.

From thence we proceeded to Colonel Mumford's, who seemed to have taken a new lease, were any dependence to be upon looks or any indulgence allowed to the wishes of his friends. An honester a man, a fairer trader, or a kinder friend, this country never produced: God

[14] Mrs. Barbara Graffenried, who taught dancing at Williamsburg; see *Another Secret Diary . . . 1739–1741*, p. 86.

send any of his sons may have the grace to take after him. We took a running repast with this good man and then, bidding adieu both to him and Mr. Banister, I mounted once more and obstinately pursued my journey home, though the clouds threatened and the heavens looked very louring. I had not passed the courthouse before it began to pour down like a spout upon me. Nevertheless, I pushed forward with vigor and got dripping wet before I could reach Merchant's Hope Point. My boat was there luckily waiting for me and wafted me safe over. And the joy of meeting my family in health made me in a moment forget all the fatigues of the journey, as much as if I had been huskanawed.[15] However, the good Providence that attended me and my whole company will, I hope, stick fast in my memory and make me everlastingly thankful.

[15] A ceremony of the Virginia Indians for preparing young men for mature manhood by means of solitary confinement and the use of narcotics. Byrd is thinking of Robert Beverley's description of the aftereffects of fasting and the use of intoxicating roots: "Upon this occasion it is pretended that these poor creatures drink so much of that water of Lethe that they perfectly lose the remembrance of all former things, even of their parents, their treasure, and their language"; *The History and Present State of Virginia*, edited by Louis B. Wright (Chapel Hill, 1947), p. 207.

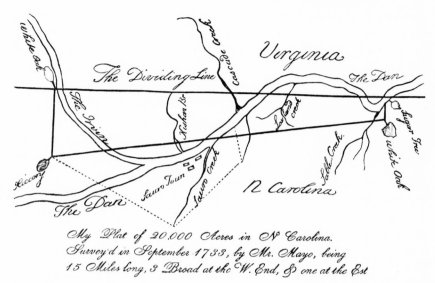

My Plat of 20,000 Acres in N? Carolina.
Survey'd in September 1733, by Mr. Mayo, being
15 Miles long, 3 Broad at the W. End, & one at the East

William Byrd's Map of his "Land of Eden," from the Westover Manuscripts
(*The lettering at the bottom is not in Byrd's hand.*)

A list of our company of all sorts

Myself	Thomas Wilson	Lawson
Major Mayo	Joseph Colson	3 Indians
Major Mumford	Harry Morris	3 Negroes
Mr. Banister	Robert Bolling	20 horses
Mr. Jones	Thomas Hooper	4 dogs

An account of the distances of places

	miles
From Westover to Colonel Mumford's	16
From Colonel Mumford's to Major Mumford's	6
From thence to Sapony Chapel	20
From thence to Major Embry's on Nottoway	10
From thence to Brunswick courthouse	15

From thence to Meherrin River	8
From thence to the ford on Roanoke	12
From thence to Colonel Stith's copper mine	20
From thence to Butcher's Creek	6
From thence to Bluestone Castle	12
From thence to the ford into the fork	7
From thence to Birch's Creek	5
From thence to Banister River	6
From thence to Morris Creek	3
From thence to the Medway	14
From thence to Maosti Creek	2
From hence to Forked Creek	6
From hence to Peter's Creek	2
From hence to Jones's Creek	2
From hence to the first ford over the Dan	1½
From hence to Cane Creek	2½
From hence to the second ford of the Dan	4½
From hence to the mouth of Sable Creek	8
From hence to the southeast corner of my land	1
From thence to the Dan on my back line	8
From thence to the Irvin on my back line	6
From thence to my southwest corner	1
From thence to my corner on the west of the Irvin	3
From thence to the Dan along my upper line	4½
From thence to the mouth of the Irvin	1½
From thence to Sauro Creek	2½
From thence to where my back line crosses the Dan	5
From thence to my southeast corner	8
From thence to Cliff Creek	10
From thence to Hix's Creek	2
From thence to Hatcher's Creek	1
From thence to Cockade Creek	5
From thence to the upper ford of Hyco River	7
From thence to Jesuit's Creek	4
From thence to where the line cuts Sugartree Creek	5
From thence to the mouth of Sugartree Creek	4
From thence to the mouth of Hyco River	7
From thence to Wilson's quarter on Tewahominy Creek	1
From thence to the Dan	1
From thence across the fork to the Staunton	2

From thence to Bluestone Castle	7
From thence to Sandy Creek	5
From thence to Mr. Mumford's plantation	2
From thence to Butcher's Creek	5
From thence to Allen's Creek	9
From thence to Joshua Nicholson's on Meherrin	18
From thence to Brunswick courthouse	8
From thence to Nottoway Bridge	14
From thence to Sapony Chapel	10
From thence to Mr. Banister's on Hatcher Run	12
From thence to Colonel Bolling's plantation	9
From thence to Colonel Mumford's plantation	5
From thence to Westover	16
	——
	184[16]

[16] The correct total of this column is 186.

APPENDIX

Notes on the Text and Provenance of the Byrd Manuscripts

By Kathleen L. Leonard

THE four major prose works of William Byrd II, *The History of the Dividing Line, The Secret History of the Line, A Journey to the Land of Eden,* and *A Progress to the Mines,* are here printed together for the first time. The present edition was encouraged by the Virginia Historical Society's recent purchase of the large Westover folio of miscellaneous Byrd manuscripts. This bound vellum folio, the sole text for *A Journey to the Land of Eden* and *A Progress to the Mines* and the primary source for *The History of the Dividing Line,* has been in the hands of Byrd descendants since his death, and the texts have not been subject to critical re-examination since Thomas Hicks Wynne edited the folio contents in 1866. Not included in the folio is the remaining work, *The Secret History of the Line.* It has been printed only once, by William K. Boyd in 1929, and exists in only one full-length manuscript, located in the library of the American Philosophical Society in Philadelphia. Also in the A.P.S. library is another manuscript version of Byrd's main work, *The History of the Dividing Line,* differing only slightly from the Virginia Historical Society Westover folio copy.

Although the two Byrd manuscripts in the A.P.S. library are in the same scribal hand and on the same octavo-size paper, they seem to have reached the A.P.S. library by different routes. Byrd's manuscript of *The History of the Dividing Line* appears to have been presented to the A.P.S. in 1815 (after the death of William Byrd III's widow, Mary Willing Byrd, in 1814) by Mrs. E. C. Izard of Philadelphia, a "granddaughter of the late deceased Colonel Byrd, son of the Commissioner and author." On July 14, 1815, the "Bird Journal" was referred to the A.P.S. Historical and Literary Committee, consisting of Peter S. DuPonceau, J. Correa de Serra, and Dr. Caspar Wistar, which reported on May 22, 1816:

The journal of the commissioners to fix the limits between Virginia and North Carolina from the library of the late Colonel Bird, is well worthy being published for the important and curious information that it affords, not only on the object of that operation, but more particularly on the state of civilisation of these states about the middle of last century.

The manuscript had several pages missing, however, and Peter Du-Ponceau immediately sought means of supplying the lacunae. With the support of Mrs. Izard he wrote to Benjamin Harrison of Berkeley, an executor of Byrd's estate, for assistance in locating the deficient parts of the "Manuscript Journal of the Commissioners appointed by Virginia, in the year 1728, to run the boundary line between that Province and North Carolina, ascribed to the father of the late Dr. Byrd . . ." He described the manuscript ("The Book had the form of a long receipt Book & was written across in a small neat hand") and inquired about other valuable historical papers in Byrd's possession as well. In his reply to Mrs. Izard of April 28, 1816, Mr. Harrison stated that although he had not been serving as actual executor of the Byrd estate he nevertheless had access to the papers. He generously offered to commence an investigation of them, "and such as have any reference to the great objects of the Society shall be forwarded to your literary friends by some safe conveyance."

DuPonceau also apparently consulted Thomas Jefferson early in 1816 but received no real assistance until a year later, when Jefferson wrote on January 26, 1817, that he had obtained from Mr. Harrison a manuscript of the journal of the dividing line and offered to supply the missing parts in DuPonceau's copy. Jefferson's letter reads:

I promised you in my letter of Jan. 22.16. to make enquiry on the subject of the MS. journal of the boundary between Virginia and North Carolina, run in 1728, of which you have a defective transcript. I have since been able to obtain the original for perusal, and now have it in my possession. I call it *original*, because it is that which has been preserved in the Westover family, having probably been copied fair by the Amanuensis of Dr. Byrd from his rough draught . . . This MS. wants pages 155 & 156. The 154th page ending with the words 'our landlord who,' and the 157th beginning with the words 'fortify'd ourselves with a meat breakfast.' You say that your copy wants the first 24 pages, and about a dozen more pages in the middle of the work. Let us concur then in making both compleat.

Jefferson's further description of the manuscript in his possession revealed, however, that it was not a copy of the *History* but rather an entirely different manuscript, the *Secret History*:

In one place the writer identifies himself with the person whom he calls Steddy, and from other passages it is sufficiently evident that

Meanwell	is	Fitzwilliam
Firebrand		Dandridge
Astrolabe		Irving
Orion		Mayo
Dr. Humdrum		non constet.

. . . The MS. is of 162 pages small 8vo., is entitled 'The secret history of the line,' begins with the words "The Governor and Council of Virginia in 1727 received' etc. and ends its narration with the words 'for which blessings may we all be sincerely thankful,' and then subjoins a list of the Commissioners and Surveyors under feigned names, the Virginia attendants by their real names, and a statement of expences and distances.

After DuPonceau and Jefferson discovered that the two manuscripts were not the same, Jefferson's offer to supply the missing segments in the A.P.S. copy was postponed until a later date when it might prove to be of value. Further correspondence indicates that on November 6, 1817, Jefferson instead deposited the *Secret History* manuscript in the A.P.S. collection. This was apparently done with full approval of Benjamin Harrison, who had written Jefferson in July 1817: "I shall approve entirely of any use which you may think proper to make of it, but would recommend its not being published immediately, as I have every reason to hope that I shall be able to obtain a copy of a MS on the same subject & by the same author, which is in the possession of Mr. Harrison of Brandon."

The third manuscript mentioned by Harrison turned out to be the Westover folio, which, according to the inscription on its flyleaf, had been given to "Mrs. Evelyn Taylor Harrison from her Affectionate mother Mary [Willing] Byrd. For Master George Evelyn Harrison of Brandon. Westover May the 12th 1809." By January 17, 1818, Benjamin Harrison had arranged to borrow the folio from its owner, George Evelyn Harrison of Brandon, for Jefferson's use in copying extracts, on the condition that it not be allowed out of his possession. Jefferson immediately notified DuPonceau of the situation and offered again "to extract from the folio what may be necessary to supply the lacunae" in either of his manuscripts. It appears likely that he also enclosed copies of a few sample sheets of the folio manuscript of the *History*, for DuPonceau replied on January 24, 1818, that he believed the folio in Jefferson's hands to be a copy of the *History*, which he preferred to publish:

There is no part in which the two MSS of the line in our possession are both alike defective; what is wanting in the one is supplied by the other as far as they respectively go; but I ought to observe that the MS which you have had the goodness to deposit with us is not so Satisfactory or so full as the other in what relates to the country, its natural history & the manners of its inhabitants, it contains more of the gossip, if I may so speak, of the Commissioners, & less of what Historians or posterity will look for. For this reason, it would be very satisfactory if the larger work [the longer work, the *History*], of which I presume the folio MS. in your hands is a copy, would be completed. The Committee have not the most distant idea of your taking the trouble to supply what is deficient; but it might, perhaps, so happen, that among your numerous Visitors, some young Gentleman might be found, a friend to the Literature of his Country, who for the honor of Virginia would be disposed to undertake the task. In any event, I shall take the liberty of stating the parts of our MS. that are wanting. as the events are related by their dates, the easiest way will be to refer to them.

Whereas the main body of DuPonceau's letter supports his opinion of the *History* as embodying the kind of historical knowledge valued by posterity, his tactful postscript includes some apt commentary on and appreciation of the qualities of the *Secret History*:

P.S. In the comparison I made of the two MSS. I did not mean to disparage the one which you had the goodness to deposit with us. It is highly valuable for the wit & humor with which it abounds, & the insight which it gives into the Characters of the influential men of the day; I only mean to say that the other contains more matter of topographical and general historical information.

Blank sheets the size of the A.P.S. volume were enclosed with DuPonceau's list of missing portions by date, page numbers, and catch phrases, and the supplements were returned by Jefferson on February 19, 1818. The three portions described as missing by DuPonceau almost exactly correspond to the three sections which appear in a different hand in the copy of the *History* now in the A.P.S. library.

1. From the beginning to the passage under the date of the 9th of March which has the words "Bush, which is a beautiful evergreen, & may be cut into any Shape." Our MS begins with the word "Bush." *

2. From the passage in the date 12th Oct: to another in Oct: 15th. The paragraph in Oct. 12 begins "But Bears are fond of Chestnuts" and proceeds a few lines to these words with which our MS ends, "But as far as is safe which they can judge to an inch, they bite off the." Here begins the hiatus in our MSS. Six pages from 122 to 129, which last page begins with the words "that is exquisitely soft & fine," which will be found near the end of a paragraph, under the date Oct. 15th.

3. Part of the dates 20th & 21st Oct. (two pages 139 & 140). Our date 20th Oct. ends with the words: "The Prisoners they happen to take alive in these Expedi-" & that of the 21st begins with "their first setting off, that their progress was much retarded" — which ends a paragraph.

Furthermore, these supplied portions are headed and concluded by catch phrases tying them conclusively to the main text, in still another hand, identified by the editor of the Jefferson papers, Dr. Julian Boyd, as Thomas Jefferson's. Jefferson presumably went over the work after it was copied

---

* The portion supplied by Jefferson actually extends from the beginning of the *History* to March 5 (instead of March 9). DuPonceau seems mistaken about the date his copy starts, for in another place he says it lacks the first twenty-four pages (putting it much closer to March 5 than 9), and Thomas Jefferson was unable to find the catch phrase DuPonceau gave for the March 9 entry.

and added these catch lines himself, for greater clarity and for DuPonceau's convenience.

The hiatus in the *Secret History* manuscript (pp. 155–156) mentioned by Jefferson in his letter to DuPonceau of January 26, 1817, was not so readily supplied. Until recently the A.P.S. copy was thought to be the only existing manuscript of the *Secret History*. Lately, two fragments have appeared: one in the Brock collection at the Huntington Library, including the portion of the journal from the beginning to March 11, and one in the Blathwayt papers at Colonial Williamsburg, covering the period from November 5 to the end of the journal on November 22 (four pages are missing, November 12–16). Both of these *Secret History* fragments are rough drafts containing corrections and interlineations; both are on the same size paper and in the same hand (possibly Byrd's). Fortunately, the two pages (155–156) missing in the A.P.S. manuscript, for the entries November 20–22, are found in the Blathwayt fragment and have been supplied in the present edition, footnoted accordingly.

Although the A.P.S. Historical and Literary Committee expressed interest in the publication of the Byrd journals in 1817–1818, nothing appears to have been done at that time. At some point, presumably for purposes of intended publication, a large sprawling hand marked the A.P.S. copy of the *History*, introducing elegancies of language and crossing out segments to be omitted. For example, the word "cultivate" was in one place substituted for "propagate" (fol. 52), the "Dunghill Hen" was changed to "common" hen (fol. 117), and the descriptive phrase "a single mountain very much resembling a Woman's Breast" (fol. 134) was shortened to "a single conical mountain." Entirely crossed out were the sections on the Indian women as potential bed partners (fols. 87, 92), the effect of bear diet on sexual potency (fols. 161–162), the story of the man who was directed out of the great Dismal Swamp by a louse he plucked from his collar (fols. 49–50), and the comparison of a skinned bear's paw to the human foot (fol. 105) — as well as other items of doubtful scientific accuracy or outdated significance. The delicate sensibility evidenced by this editor is reflected in a report of 1834 by an A.P.S. committee appointed to examine the manuscripts in the Society's library and to report whether any should be published in the second volume of the *Historical and Literary Transactions*:

Among the Mss. in the possession of the Society are two Volumes, containing the History of what took place on the drawing of the line between the Colonies of Virginia and North Carolina in 1728, written by one of the Commissioners from Virginia & communicated to us by Mr. Jefferson; an Extract from those Volumes, judiciously made, or a review of their Contents, might be of some interest; but your Committee are of opinion, that the style and manner in which they are written, forbid their publication as a whole, & that even Extracts or a review of them, tho' they might amuse elsewhere, would not be in their place in the transactions of our Society.

Consequently, not even the more factual *History* was printed in the A.P.S. *Transactions*. The only use of either manuscript by outside editors has been by William K. Boyd when he edited the first and only printing of the *Secret History*, solely from the A.P.S. text. Earlier Byrd editors appear to have been either unaware of the existence of the A.P.S. Byrd journals or unable to consult them. The five editions of *The History of the Dividing Line* prior to the present one have all relied exclusively on the Westover folio. Edmund Ruffin, editing the first publication of the *History* in 1841, stated that the Westover folio contained all the known Byrd works. Thomas Hicks Wynne re-examined the Westover folio and issued a more authentic edition in 1866; in his Introduction to this edition he mentioned the existence of both a "History" and a "Secret History" manuscript in the A.P.S. library but stated that he had not seen the items and suspected that they might even be original or rough drafts. In their editions of the *History* of 1901 and 1929 respectively, John Spencer Bassett and William K. Boyd seem to have followed the text of Wynne's edition; neither mentioned the A.P.S. copy, although Boyd used the A.P.S. manuscript as the source for his edition of the *Secret History* in the same volume. Mark Van Doren in his 1929 edition of the *History* admittedly reprinted Ruffin's text and does not mention the existence of an A.P.S. manuscript.

Although Jefferson and DuPonceau (and possibly later editors) assumed that the A.P.S. octavo copy of the *History* was identical with the Westover folio lent by Harrison, further examination of the manuscripts reveals several textual differences. Some of these are variations in wording, others are phrases existing in the Westover folio but lacking in the A.P.S. copy. Thus, a comparison of the opening sentences of the respective entries for March 14 reveals:

Westover folio	*A.P.S. octavo*
We quarter'd with our Friend and Fellow-Traveller William Wilkins, who had been our *faithfull* pilot to Coratuck . . . (fol. 22)	We quarter'd with our Friend and Fellow Traveller William Wilkins, who had been our Pilot to Coratuck . . . (fol. 47)

So with a passage in the April 7th entries, and the final sentence of the October 17th entries:

Within this Inclosure *We found Bark* Cabanes sufficient to lodge all their People . . . (fol. 43)	Within this Enclosure are Cabanes sufficient to lodge all their People . . . (fol. 85)

. . . in the Night we had a Violent Gale of Wind, accompany'd with Smart Hail, that rattled frightfully amongst the Trees, *tho' it was not large enough to do us any Harm* (fol. 69)

. . . in the Night we had a Violent Gale of Wind, accompany'd with smart Hail, that rattled frightfully amongst the Trees. (fol. 132)

Apart from a few obvious scribal errors, all of the variations in the two manuscripts seem to be the result of erasures and subsequent additions made in the Westover folio, in a darker ink and a different hand, one closely resembling samples of Byrd's own handwriting. While both the A.P.S. and Westover versions appear to be fair copies done by an amanuensis, it seems likely that Byrd himself at a later time may have returned to the Westover folio copy and made corrections in the text that were never entered in the A.P.S. copy. The corrections and additions, all apparently made in the interest of clarity and stylistic refinement, resemble in character the interlineations found on the rough-draft fragments of the *Secret History*, and the paleography of both manuscripts is similar. However, the A.P.S. copyist, in the case of the *Secret History* manuscript, has almost consistently incorporated into his copy of that work all of the interlineations noted on the obviously rough-draft fragments now in Colonial Williamsburg and the Huntington Library. Therefore, since it seems likely that the Westover folio is the final version of Byrd's *History*, the present editor has used that text as the standard for the *History* and has followed the A.P.S. text for the *Secret History*, supplying only the one hiatus from the Williamsburg fragment. As the Westover folio remains the only known source for the two smaller works, *A Progress to the Mines* and *A Journey to the Land of Eden*, the texts for this edition were, of course, transcribed from it.

INDEX

INDEX